Maternal Theory

Essential Readings

Maternal Theory

Essential Readings

Edited by

ANDREA O'REILLY

DEMETER

DEMETER PRESS
TORONTO, CANADA

Published by:
Demeter Press
726 Atkinson College, York University
4700 Keele Street
Toronto, Ontario M3J 1P3
Telephone: (416) 736-2100 x 60366
Email: arm@yorku.ca Web site: www.yorku.ca/arm

Printed and Bound in Canada

Cover Art: Fran Forman
"The Woman," photographic assemblage, 10.5" x 7", © Fran Forman, 2005.
Cover Design/Interior Design: Luciana Ricciutelli

National Library of Canada Cataloguing in Publication Data
Main entry under title:

Maternal theory : essential readings / edited by Andrea O'Reilly.

Includes bibliographical references.
ISBN 978-1-55014-482-6

1. Motherhood. 2. Feminist theory. 3. Motherhood—Philosophy.
I. O'Reilly, Andrea, 1961–

HQ759.M38 2007   306.874'3   C2007-902924-8

To Demeter Press' Other Mothers – Renée Knapp,
Luciana Ricciutelli, Sarah Trimble, Randy Chase, and Althea Prince –
for delivering this book with care and competence.
Should all authors be so fortunate.

Table of Contents

Introduction

ANDREA O'REILLY

MY FIRST BOOK PUBLICATION, the edited volume *Redefining Motherhood: Changing Identities and Patterns* opens with Adrienne Rich's oft-cited quote "We know more about the air we breath, the seas we travel, than about the nature and meaning of motherhood" (11).[1] By 1998, 20 years after the publication of Rich's ovarian work *Of Woman Born*, most academic disciplines, from anthropology to women' studies, were engaged in some form of motherhood research. And while scholarship on motherhood in some disciplines still struggled for legitimacy and centrality, there was the recognition that motherhood studies was emerging as a distinct field within the larger disciplines of feminist scholarship or Women's Studies.[2] Thus by 1998, when I published my first book on motherhood I could draw upon a canon of motherhood research that was not available to Rich two decades earlier. And while much research on motherhood still needed to be done, particularly in the area of marginalized and disadvantaged mothers, we could claim by 1998, to paraphrase Rich, an understanding of the nature and meaning of motherhood.

In the last ten years the topic of motherhood has developed from an emergent to an established field of scholarly inquiry. Indeed, today it would be unthinkable to cite Rich's quote on the dearth of maternal scholarship as I did a mere nine years ago. A cursory review of motherhood research reveals that hundreds of scholarly monographs, anthologies, and journal issues have been published on every imaginable motherhood theme. *The Journal of the Association for Research on Mothering* and Demeter Press alone have examined motherhood topics as diverse as sexuality, peace, religion, public policy, literature, work, popular culture, health, carework/caregiving, ethnicity, becoming a mother, young mothers, motherhood and feminism, mothers and sons, mothers and daughters, lesbian mothers, mothering in the African diaspora, Aboriginal mothering, queer parenting, third-wave mothering, adoption, mothering and blogging, and the motherhood movement.[3] Significantly, however, we cannot find among these many recent collections on motherhood a single anthology on theories of motherhood. The only book that could be considered an anthology of maternal theory is the important but very dated Joyce Trebilcot's 1983 collection *Mothering: Essays in Feminist Theory.*[4] It would seem that while research on motherhood is well represented in various collections, motherhood theory had yet to be anthologized. This absence of an anthology or Reader on maternal theory is particularly surprising given that maternal theory, like research on mothering, is now recognized as an established field within motherhood studies and feminist theory more generally. The aim of this book is to bring together for the first time the essential readings in maternal theory.

The *Oxford Canadian Dictionary* defines theory as "a supposition or system of ideas explaining something, especially one based on general principles independent of the particular things to be explained." The entry goes on to define theory as "the principles on which a subject of study is based." For the purposes of this collection, the writing in question must develop a supposition or system of ideas *independent* of the particular issue being discussed in order for it to be considered a theory. The chapter must, in other words, craft a concept, model, or idea that may be applicable to other motherhood texts or contexts. Thus, an article that studies a particular motherhood topic cannot, despite its otherwise merit, be considered theory unless it produces a motherhood concept. In limiting the selection of chapters to those that function as theory is not to suggest that research in and of itself is less important or deserving. Rather, this criterion is used for the simple reason that the focus and purpose of this anthology is to introduce readers to the central concepts, ideas, and models of maternal theory.[5]

The Reader is composed of the essential theoretical texts on mothers, mothering, and motherhood. More specifically, the chapters theorize motherhood from three perspectives: motherhood as experience/role, motherhood as institution/ideology, and motherhood as identity/subjectivity.[6] Most of the chapters in this collection are reprinted and are well-known to motherhood scholars. In selecting the chapters, I choose ones that have most influenced the development of maternal theory; writers whose motherhood concepts have shaped the way we think about motherhood. Such concepts include Adrienne Rich's distinction between motherhood versus mothering; Chodorow's "reproduction of mothering"; Sara Ruddick's "maternal thinking"; bell hooks' "homeplace"; Baba Copper's "radical mothering"; Patricia Hill Collins "other-mothering"; Marianne Hirsh's "mother/daughter plot"; Sharon Hays' "intensive mothering"; Susan Maushart's "mask of motherhood"; Ann Crittenden's "price of motherhood"; and Daphne de Marneffe's "maternal desire," to name but a few. Some of the chapters were written specifically for this collection. Ariel Gore (hip mothering), Chris Bobel (natural mothering), Patrizia Albanese (motherhood and nationalism), and I (feminist mothering) wrote new chapters for this anthology developed from previous publications. Kim Anderson was invited to write a chapter on Aboriginal mothering, and a piece on Chicana mothering by Larissa Mercado-López was reprinted from the forthcoming Demeter Press book, *Mothering in the Third Wave*. In some instances, there are two chapters by one author. A highlight of this Reader is its attention to diversity. African American, Chicana, Latina, Aboriginal motherhood theories are represented as are theories concerned with mothers and disabilities, single mothers, working class mothers, adoptive and young mothers. As well, the anthology covers a wide range of motherhood themes including such recent topics as motherhood and globalization and (trans)nationalism. Finally, the Reader draws from disciplines as diverse as Sociology, Philosophy, Psychoanalysis, Cultural Studies, History, English, Political Science, Queer Studies to name but a few. In all, the anthology covers a 31-year time period—1976-2007—includes 45 contributors and 50 chapters. The chapters are arranged chronologically.

The anthology was designed to work in a variety of formats. It can be used as the main course text for a general course on Maternal Theory, at both the Undergraduate or Graduate level. As well, the anthology would suit a unit on maternal theory in a Feminist Theory or in a Motherhood Studies course. As well, many thematic motherhood courses or units may be developed from this anthology. A course on maternal identity and subjectivity for a psychology or philosophy course could select from Nancy Chodorow, Mary O'Brien, Miriam Johnson, Mielle Chandler, Elaine Tuttle Hansen, Baba Copper, Jessica Benjamin, Julia Kristeva, Patricia Hill Collins, Carol Thomas, Drucilla Cornell, Patrice Di-Quinzio and Daphne de Marneffe. A unit or course on "Motherhood: History and Sociology" could use Sheri Thurer, Adrienne Rich, bell hooks, Ann Snitow, Valerie Walkerdine and Helen Lucey, Patricia Hill Collins, Sharon Hays, Ann Crittenden, Susan Douglas and Meredith Michaels, Shu-Ju Ada Cheng, Emily J. Noonan, Judith Warner, Molly Ladd-Taylor, Kim Anderson, Chris Bobel, and Patrizia Albanese. A "Mothering as Resistance" unit or course could draw from Larissa Mercado-López, Andrea O'Reilly, Kim Anderson, Jane Juffer, Katherine Arnup, Elena R. Gutiérrez, Ariel Gore, Ellen Lewis, bell hooks, Audre Lorde, and Sara Ruddick. Chapters for a unit on "Mothers and Sons/Daughters" would include Alice Walker, Audrey Lorde, Nancy Polikoff, Baba Cooper, Valerie Walkerdine and Helen Lucey, Patricia Hill Collins, Marianne Hirsh, Olga Silverstein and Beth Rashbaum. Elena Gutiérrez, Dorothy Roberts, Barbara Katz Rothman, and Mary O'Brien, among others could be used for a unit on "The Politics of Reproduction." Finally, many chapters, including Anderson, Cheng, Noonan, Hill-Collins, Arnup, Lorde, and hooks, would fit a Motherhood course on difference and diversity. Finally, in any of the above formats the anthology could be read alongside novels, films, and short stories for an English, Humanities, Film or Cultural Studies course on motherhood.

The anthology is much, much bigger than initially planned. We devised –and I may add budgeted for—an anthology of 25 chapters and approximately 300 pages in length. However, after reviewing the literature on motherhood and consulting with motherhood scholars I found myself with a list of approximately 40 "must-read" chapters on maternal theory. A review of this list revealed omissions in various motherhood perspectives and themes, most notably theory by Aboriginal, Chicana, Latina mothers, mothers with disabilities, and topics such as adoption, globalization, and (trans)nationalism. So I found myself locating and soliciting yet another ten chapters. And even this massive list did not represent all of the theorists that I thought should be in this collection.[7] Preparing this anthology I was reminded of my teenage self trying to select my favourite songs for a 90-

minute cassette I was taping. I could not cut my beloved songs then, nor could I edit my "must-read" list today. I simply could not make a Sophie's choice. So I found myself left with this mammoth text of maternal theory: truly, "an embarrassment of riches." However, remembering Rich's lament at the absence of maternal scholarship 30 years ago, I see such as abundance as most appropriate. That we have created such a vast and diverse tradition of maternal theory in a mere three decades is a huge achievement, a cause for celebration indeed!

Notes

[1]Edited with Sharon Abbey (Toronto: Second Story Press, 1998).

[2]From 1996-1999 as part of a research project, I met with professors across Canada and United States to discuss their experiences of teaching and researching the topic of motherhood in academe. Discussions with these women revealed that the topic of motherhood was frequently marginalized or trivialized in various academic disciplines. These maternal scholars recalled and recounted various instances where their motherhood research was viewed with suspicion, if not outright dismissal. Real academics don't do motherhood (either in research or in life); at least not ones who seek a "real" tenured job. In response to this, in 1998, I established the *Association for Research on Mothering* and in 1999, the *Journal of the Association for Research on Mothering.* ARM and its journal were formed to promote, showcase, and make visible maternal scholarship and to accord legitimacy to this academic field. Most importantly, ARM was established to provide a community for like-minded scholars who research and work in the area of motherhood. Scholarship, both at the university and community level, as we all know, is enriched by dialogue and debate, broadened through knowledge/ resources sharing and sustained by a sense of belonging. ARM's mandate is to simultaneously build a community of maternal scholars, academic and grassroots, and to promote maternal scholarship. ARM was formed in the in the hope of creating a maternal community that Sara Ruddick, among others, has argued is essential, in this instance, for the well-being of maternal scholarship. As Virginia Woolf recognized the need for women writers to have "a room of one's own," I believed that feminist scholars of motherhood, likewise, need an association to call our own. To this end, ARM and its journal were instituted. In 2005, as part of this larger initiative, ARM launched Demeter Press, the first feminist press on motherhood. For more information on ARM, *JARM*, and Demeter Press, please visit our website: www.yorku.ca/arm.

[3]Please see the ARM website for a full list of *JARM* and Demeter Press publications: www.yorku.ca/arm.

[4]One book does call itself a motherhood reader: *Mother Reader: Essential Writings on Motherhood* by Moyra Davey (New York: Seven Stories Press, 2001). While an important collection, this book is made up of stories, essays, and memoirs on motherhood, and therefore is not an anthology of maternal theory.

[5]Demeter Press plans to publish a reader on motherhood topics in the near fu-

ture. The aim of this planned collection is to introduce readers to the essential readings in key motherhood areas, such as work, health, representation, religion, sexuality and so forth.

[6]Consequently, theoretical works on pregnancy, childbirth, breastfeeding, or the maternal body were chosen for the anthology only if they related to the larger concept of motherhood as experience, institution/ideology, and identity/subjectivity. Mary O'Brien, Barbara Katz Rothman, and Dorothy Roberts would be examples of such chapters.

[7]Though I read and consulted widely to develop this anthology of "must-read' theorists, the selections are ultimately my own. No doubt, others would devise a different reading list.

Chapter 1

Introduction from *Of Woman Born*

ADRIENNE RICH

ALL HUMAN LIFE on the planet is born of woman. The one unifying, incontrovertible experience shared by all women and men is that months-long period we spent unfolding inside a woman's body. Because young humans remain dependent upon nurture for a much longer period than other mammals, and because of the division of labor long established in human groups, where women not only bear and suckle but are assigned almost total responsibility for children, most of us first know both love and disappointment, power and tenderness, in the person of a woman.

We carry the imprint of this experience for life, even into our dying. Yet there has been a strange lack of material to help us understand and use it. We know more about the air we breathe, the seas we travel, than about the nature and meaning of motherhood. In the division of labor according to gender, the makers and sayers of culture, the namers, have been the sons of the mothers. There is much to suggest that the male mind has always been haunted by the force of the idea of *dependence* on *a woman for life itself,* the son's constant effort to assimilate, compensate for, or deny the fact that he is "of woman born."

Women are also born of women. But we know little about the effect on culture of that fact, because women have not been makers and sayers of patriarchal culture. Woman's status as child-bearer has been made into a major fact of her life. Terms like "barren" or "childless" have been used to negate any further identity. The term "non-father" does not exist in any realm of social categories.

Because the fact of physical motherhood is so visible and dramatic, men recognized only after some time that they, too, had a part in generation. The meaning of "fatherhood" remains tangential, elusive. To "father" a child suggests above all to beget, to provide the sperm that fertilizes the ovum. To "mother" a child implies a continuing presence, lasting at least nine months, more often for years. Motherhood is earned, first through an intense physical and psychic rite of passage—pregnancy and childbirth—then through learning to nurture, which does not come by instinct.

A man may beget a child in passion or by rape, and then disappear; he need never see or consider child or mother again. Under such circumstances, the mother faces a range of painful, socially weighted choices: abortion, suicide, abandonment of the child, infanticide, the rearing of a child branded "illegitimate," usually in poverty, always outside the law. In some cultures she faces murder by her kinsmen. Whatever her choice, her body has undergone irreversible changes, her mind will never be the same, her future as a woman has been shaped by the event.

Most of us were raised by our mothers, or by women who for love, necessity, or money took the place of our biological mothers. Throughout history women have helped birth and nurture each others' children. Most women have been mothers in the sense of tenders and carers for the young, whether as sisters, aunts, nurses, teachers, foster-mothers, stepmothers. Tribal life, the village, the extended family, the female networks of some cultures, have included the very young, very old, unmarried, and infertile women in the process of "mothering." Even those of us whose fathers played an important part in our early childhood rarely remember them for their patient attendance when we were ill, their doing the humble tasks of feeding and cleaning us; we remember scenes, expeditions, punishments, special occasions. For most of us a woman provided the continuity and stability—but also the rejections and refusals of our early lives, and it is with a woman's hands, eyes, body, voice, that we associate our primal sensations, our earliest social experience.

Throughout this book I try to distinguish between two meanings of motherhood, one superimposed on the other: the *potential relationship* of any woman to her powers of reproduction and to children; and the *institution,* which aims at ensuring that that potential–and all women—shall remain under male control. This institution has been a keystone of the most diverse social and political systems. It has withheld over one-half the human species from the decisions affecting their lives; it exonerates men from fatherhood in any authentic sense; it creates the dangerous schism between "private" and "public" life; it calcifies human choices and potentialities. In the most fundamental and bewildering of contradictions, it has alienated women from our bodies by incarcerating us in them. At certain points in history, and in certain cultures, the idea of woman as mother has worked to endow all women with respect, even with awe, and to give women some say in the life of a people or a clan. But for most of what we know as the "mainstream" of recorded history, motherhood as institution has ghettoized and degraded female potentialities.

The power of the mother has two aspects: the biological potential or capacity to bear and nourish human life, and the magical power invested in women by men, whether in the form of Goddess-worship or the fear of being controlled and overwhelmed by women. We do not actually know much about what power may have meant in the hands of strong, prepatriarchal women. We do have guesses, longings, myths, fantasies, analogues. We know far more about how, under patriarchy, female possibility has been literally massacred on the site of motherhood. Most women in history have become mothers without choice, and an even greater number have lost their lives bringing life into the world.

Women are controlled by lashing us to our bodies. In an early and classic essay, Susan Griffin pointed out that "rape is a form of mass terrorism, for the victims of rape are chosen indiscriminately, but the propagandists for male supremacy broadcast that it is women who cause rape by being unchaste or in the wrong place at the wrong time—in essence, by behaving as though they were free.... The fear of rape keeps women off the streets at night. Keeps women at home. Keeps women passive and modest for fear that they be thought provocative." In a later development of Griffin's analysis, Susan Brownmiller suggests that enforced, indentured motherhood may originally have been the price paid by women to the men who became their "protectors" (and owners) against the casual violence of other men.[1] If rape has been terrorism, motherhood has been penal servitude. It *need not be.*

This book is not an attack on the family or on mothering, *except as defined and restricted under patriarchy.* Nor is it a call for a mass system of state-controlled childcare. Mass childcare in patriarchy has had but two purposes: to introduce large numbers of women into the labor force, in a developing economy or during a war, and to indoctrinate future citizens.[2] It has never been conceived as a means of releasing the energies of women into the mainstream of culture, or of changing the stereotypic gender-images of both women and men.

I told myself that I wanted to write a book on motherhood because it was a crucial, still relatively unexplored, area for feminist theory. But I did not choose this subject; it had long ago chosen me.

This book is rooted in my own past, tangled with parts of my life which stayed buried even while I dug away at the strata of early childhood, adolescence, separation from parents, my vocation as a poet; the geographies of marriage, spiritual divorce, and death, through which I entered the open ground of middle age. Every journey into the past is complicated by delusions, false memories, false naming of real events. But for a long time, I avoided this journey back into the years of pregnancy, childbearing, and the dependent lives of my children, because it meant going back into pain and anger that I would have preferred to think of as long since resolved and put away. I could not begin to think of writing a book on motherhood until I began to feel strong enough, and unambivalent enough in my love for my children, so that I could dare to return to a ground which seemed to me the most painful, incomprehensible, and ambiguous I had ever traveled, a ground hedged by taboos, mined with false-namings.

I did not understand this when I started to write the book.

I only knew that I had lived through something which was considered central to the lives of women, fulfilling even in its sorrows, a key to the meaning of life; and that I could remember little except anxiety, physical weariness, anger, self-blame, boredom, and division within myself: a division made more acute by the moments of passionate love, delight in my children's spirited bodies and minds, amazement at how they went on loving me in spite of my failures to love them wholly and selflessly.

It seemed to me impossible from the first to write a book of this kind without being often autobiographical, without often saying "I." Yet for many months I buried my head in historical research and analysis in order to delay or prepare the way for the plunge into areas of my own life that were painful and problematical, yet from the heart of which this book has come. I believe increasingly that only the willingness to share private and sometimes painful experience can enable women to create a collective description of the world which will be truly ours. On the other hand, I am keenly aware that any writer has a certain false and arbitrary power. It is *her* version, after all, that the reader is reading at this moment, while the accounts of others—including the dead—may go untold.

This is in some ways a vulnerable book. I have invaded various professional domains, broken various taboos. I have used the scholarship available to me where I found it suggestive, without pretending to make myself into a specialist. In so doing, the question, *But what was it like for women?* was always in my mind, and I soon began to sense a fundamental perceptual difficulty among male scholars (and some female ones) for which "sexism" is too facile a term. It is really an intellectual defect, which might be named "patrivincialism" or "patriochialism": the assumption that women are a subgroup, that "man's world" is the "real" world, that patriarchy is equivalent to culture and culture to patriarchy, that the "great" or "liberalizing" periods of history have been the same for women as for men, that generalizations about "man," "humankind," "children," "Blacks," "parents," "the working class" hold true for women, mothers, daughters, sisters, wet-nurses, infant girls, and can include them with no more than a glancing reference here and there, usually to some specialized function like breastfeeding. The new historians of "family and childhood," like the majority of theorists on child-rearing, pediatricians, psychiatrists, are male. In their work, the question of motherhood as an institution or as an idea in the heads of grown-up male children is raised only where "styles" of mothering are discussed and criticized. Female sources are rarely cited (yet these sources exist, as the feminist historians are showing); there are virtually no primary sources from women-as-mothers; and all this is presented as objective scholarship.

It is only recently that feminist scholars such as Gerda Lerner, Joan Kelly, and Carroll Smith-Rosenberg have begun to suggest that, in Lerner's words: "the key to understanding women's history is in accepting—painful though it may be that it is the history of the *majority* of mankind.... History, as written and perceived up to now, is the history of a minority, who may well turn out to be the 'subgroup'" (8, 13).

I write with a painful consciousness of my own western cultural perspective and that of most of the sources available to me: painful because it says so much about how female culture is fragmented by the male cultures, boundaries, groupings in which women live. However, at this point any broad study of female culture can be at best partial, and what any writer hopes—and knows—is that others like her, with different training, background, and tools, are putting together other parts of this immense half-buried mosaic in the shape of a woman's face.

Notes

[1]Reviewing Brownmiller's book, a feminist newsletter commented: "It would be

extreme and contentious ... to call mothers rape victims in general; probably only a small percentage are. But rape is the crime that can be committed because women are vulnerable in a special way; the opposite of 'vulnerable' is 'impregnable.' Pregnability, to coin a word, has been the basis of female identity, the limit of freedom, the futility of education, the denial of growth" ("Rape Has Many Forms").

[2]To these American capitalism is adding a third: the profit motive. Franchised, commercially operated child-care centers have become "big business." Many such centers are purely custodial; overcrowding limits physical and educational flexibility and freedom; the centers are staffed almost entirely by women, working for a minimum salary. Operated under giant corporations such as Singer, Time Inc., and General Electric, these profit-making preschools can be compared to commercial nursing homes in their exploitation of human needs and of the most vulnerable persons in the society (see Sassen, Arvin, and the Corporations and Child Care Research Project 21-23, 38-43).

References

Brownmiller, Susan. *Against Our Will: Men, Women and Rape.* New York: Simon and Schuster, 1975.

Griffin, Susan. "Rape: The All-American Crime." *Women: A Feminist Perspective.* Ed. Jo Freeman. Stanford, CA: Mayfield Publishing, 1975.

Lerner, Gerda, Joan Kelly, and Carroll Smith-Rosenberg. "Placing Women in History: Definitions and Challenges." *Feminist Studies* 3 (1-2) (Fall 1975).

"Rape Has Many Forms." *The Spokeswoman* 6 (5) (November 15,1975).

Sassen, Georgia, Cookie Arvin, and the Corporations and Child Care Research Project. "Corporate Child Care." *The Second Wave: A Magazine of the New Feminism* 3 (3).

Chapter 2

Anger and Tenderness

ADRIENNE RICH

> … To understand is always an ascending movement; that is why comprehension ought always to be concrete. (One is never got out of the cave, one comes out of it. —Simone Weil, *First and Last Notebooks*

ENTRY FROM MY journal, November 1960

My children cause me the most exquisite suffering of which I have any experience. It is the suffering of ambivalence: the murderous alternation between bitter resentment and raw-edged nerves, and blissful gratification and tenderness. Sometimes I seem to myself, in my feelings toward these tiny guiltless beings, a monster of selfishness and intolerance. Their voices wear away at my nerves, their constant needs, above all their need for simplicity and patience, fill me with despair at my own failures, despair too at my fate, which is to serve a function for which I was not fitted. And I am weak sometimes from held-in rage. There are times when I feel only death will free us from one another, when I envy the barren woman who has the luxury of her regrets but lives a life of privacy and freedom (see also Lerner 149-50).[1]

And yet at other times I am melted with the sense of their helpless, charming and quite irresistible beauty—their ability to go on loving and trusting—their staunchness and decency and unselfconsciousness. *I love them.* But it's in the enormity and inevitability of this love that the sufferings lie.

April 1961

A blissful love for my children engulfs me from time to time and seems almost to suffice—the aesthetic pleasure I have in these little, changing creatures, the sense of being loved, however dependently, the sense too that I'm not an utterly unnatural and shrewish mother—much though I am!

May 1965

To suffer with and for and against a child—maternally, egotistically, neurotically, sometimes with a sense of helplessness, sometimes with the illusion of learning wisdom—but always, everywhere, in body and soul, with that child—because that child is a piece of oneself.

To be caught up in waves of love and hate, jealousy even of the child's childhood; hope and fear for its maturity; longing to be free of responsibility, tied by every fibre of one's being.

That curious primitive reaction of protectiveness, the beast defending her cub, when anyone attacks or criticizes him. And yet no one more hard on him than I!

September 1965

Degradation of anger. Anger at a child. How shall I learn to absorb the violence and make explicit only the caring? Exhaustion of anger. Victory of will, too dearly bought—far too dearly!

March 1966

Perhaps one is a monster—an anti-woman-something driven and without recourse to the normal and appealing consolations of love, motherhood, joy in other....

Unexamined assumptions: First, that a "natural" mother is a person without further identity, one who can find her chief gratification in being all day with small children, living at a pace tuned to theirs; that the isolation of mothers and children together in the home must be taken for granted; that maternal love is, and should be, quite literally selfless; that children and mothers are the "causes" of each others' suffering. I was haunted by the stereotype of the mother whose love is "unconditional"; and by the visual and literary images of motherhood as a single-minded identity. If I knew parts of myself existed that would never cohere to those images, weren't those parts then abnormal, monstrous? And—as my eldest son, now aged twenty-one, remarked on reading the above passages: "You seemed to feel you ought to love us all the time. But there *is* no human relationship where you love the other person at every moment." Yes, I tried to explain to him, but women—above all, mothers—have been supposed to love that way.

From the 1950s and early 1960s, I remember a cycle. It began when I had picked up a book or began trying to write a letter, or even found myself on the telephone with someone toward whom my voice betrayed eagerness, a rush of sympathetic energy. The child (or children) might be absorbed in busyness, in his own dreamworld; but as soon as he felt me gliding into a world which did not include him, he would come to pull at my hand, ask for help, punch at the typewriter keys. And I would feel his wants at such a moment as fraudulent, as an attempt moreover to defraud me of living even for fifteen minutes as myself. My anger would rise; I would feel the futility of any attempt to salvage myself, and also the inequality between us: my needs always balanced against those of a child, and always losing. I could love so much better, I told myself, after even a quarter-hour of selfishness, of peace, of detachment from my children. A few minutes! But it was as if an invisible thread would pull taut between us and break, to the child's sense of inconsolable abandonment, if I moved—not even physically, but in spirit—into a realm beyond our tightly circumscribed life together. It was as if my placenta had begun to refuse him oxygen. Like so many women, I waited with impatience for the moment when their father would return from work, when for an hour or two at least the circle drawn around mother and children would grow looser, the intensity between us slacken, because there was another adult in the house.

I did not understand that this circle, this magnetic field in which we lived, was not a natural phenomenon.

Intellectually, I must have known it. But the emotion-charged, tradition-heavy form in which I found myself cast as the Mother seemed, then, as ineluctable as the tides. And, because of this form—this microcosm in which my children and I formed a tiny, private emotional cluster, and in which (in bad weather or when someone was ill) we sometimes passed days at a time without seeing another adult except for their father—there *was* authentic need underlying my child's invented claims upon me when I seemed to be wandering away from him. He was reassuring himself that warmth, tenderness, continuity, solidity were still there for him, in my person. My singularity, my uniqueness in the world as *his* mother—perhaps more dimly also as Woman—evoked a need vaster than any single human being could satisfy, except by loving continuously, unconditionally, from dawn to dark, and often in the middle of the night.

In a living room in 1975, I spent an evening with a group of women poets, some of whom had children. One had brought hers along, and they slept or played in adjoining rooms. We talked of poetry, and also of infanticide, of the case of a local woman, the mother of eight, who had been in severe depression since the birth of her third child, and who had recently murdered and decapitated her two youngest, on her suburban front lawn. Several women in the group, feeling a direct connection with her desperation, had signed a letter to the local newspaper protesting the way her act was perceived by the press and handled by the community mental health system. Every woman in that room who had children, every poet, could identify with her. We spoke of the wells of anger that her story cleft open in us. We spoke of our own moments of murderous anger at our children, because there was no one and nothing else on which to discharge anger. We spoke in the sometimes tentative, sometimes rising, sometimes bitterly witty, unrhetorical tones and language of women who had met together over our common work, poetry, and who found another common ground in an unacceptable, but undeniable anger. The words are being spoken now, are being written down; the taboos are being broken, the masks of motherhood are cracking through.

For centuries no one talked of these feelings. I became a mother in the family-centered, consumer-oriented, Freudian-American world of the 1950s. My husband spoke eagerly of the children we would have; my parents-in-law awaited the birth of their grandchild. I had no idea of what I wanted, what I could or could not choose. I only knew that to have a child was to assume adult womanhood to the full, to prove myself, to be "like other women."

To be "like other women" had been a problem for me. From the age of thirteen or fourteen, I had felt I was only acting the part of a feminine creature. At the age of sixteen my fingers were almost constantly ink-stained. The lipstick and high heels of the era were difficult-to-manage disguises. In 1945 I was writing poetry seriously, and had a fantasy of going to postwar Europe as a journalist, sleeping among the ruins in bombed cities, recording the rebirth of civilization after the fall of the Nazis. But also, like every other girl I knew, I spent hours trying to apply lipstick more adroitly, straightening the wandering seams of stockings, talking about "boys." There were two different compartments, already, to my life. But writing poetry, and my fantasies of travel and self-sufficiency, seemed more real to me; I felt that as an incipient "real woman" I was a fake. Particularly was I paralyzed when I encountered young children. I think I felt men could be—wished to be—conned into thinking I was truly "feminine"; a child, I suspected, could see through me like a shot. This sense of acting a part created a curious sense of guilt, even though it was a part demanded for survival.

I have a very clear, keen memory of myself the day after I was married: I was sweeping a floor. Probably the floor did not really need to be swept; probably I simply did not know what else to do with myself. But as I swept that floor I thought: "Now I am a woman. This is an age-old action, this is what women have always done." I felt I was bending to some ancient form, too ancient to question. *This is what women have always done.*

As soon as I was visibly and clearly pregnant, I felt, for the first time in my adolescent and adult life, not-guilty. The atmosphere of approval in which I was bathed—even by strangers on the street, it seemed—was like an aura I carried with me, in which doubts, fears, misgivings, met with absolute denial. *This is what women have always done.*

Two days before my first son was born, I broke out in a rash which was tentatively diagnosed as measles, and was admitted to a hospital for contagious diseases to await the onset of labor. I felt for the first time a great deal of conscious fear, and guilt toward my unborn child, for having "failed" him with my body in this way. In rooms near mine were patients with polio; no one was allowed to enter my room except in a hospital gown and mask. If during pregnancy I had felt in any vague command of my situation, I felt now totally dependent on my obstetrician, a huge, vigorous, paternal man, abounding with optimism and assurance, and given to pinching my cheek. I had gone through a healthy pregnancy, but as if tranquilized or sleep-walking. I had taken a sewing class in which I produced an unsightly and ill-cut maternity jacket which I never wore. I had made curtains for the baby's room, collected baby clothes, blotted out as much as possible the woman I had been a few months earlier. My second book of poems was in press, but I had stopped writing poetry, and read little except household magazines and books on childcare. I felt myself perceived by the world simply as a pregnant woman, and it seemed easier, less disturbing, to perceive myself so. After my child was born the "measles" were diagnosed as an allergic reaction to pregnancy.

Within two years, I was pregnant again, and writing in a notebook:

November 1956

Whether it's the extreme lassitude of early pregnancy or something more fundamental, I don't know; but of late I've felt, toward poetry—both reading and writing it—nothing but boredom and indifference. Especially toward my own and that of my immediate contemporaries. When I receive a letter soliciting mss., or someone alludes to my "career," I have a strong sense of wanting to deny all responsibility for and interest in that person who writes—or who wrote.

If there is going to be a real break in my writing life, this is as good a time for it as any. I have been dissatisfied with myself, my work, for a long time.

My husband was a sensitive, affectionate man who wanted children and who—unusual in the professional, academic world of the 1950s—was willing to "help." But it was clearly understood that this "help" was an act of generosity; that *his* work, *his* professional life, was the real work in the family; in fact, this was for years not even an issue between us. I understood that my struggles as a writer were a kind of luxury, a peculiarity of mine; my work brought in almost no money: it even cost money, when I hired a household helper to allow me a few hours a week to write. "Whatever I ask he tries to give me," I wrote in March 1958, "but always the initiative has to be mine." I experienced my depressions, bursts of anger, sense of entrapment, as burdens my husband was forced to bear because he loved me; I felt grateful to be loved in spite of bringing him those burdens.

But I was struggling to bring my life into focus. I had never really given up on poetry, nor on gaining some control over my existence. The life of a Cambridge tenement backyard swarming with children, the repetitious cycles of laundry, the night-wakings, the interrupted moments of peace or of engagement with ideas, the ludicrous dinner parties at which young wives, some with advanced degrees, all seriously and intelligently dedicated to their children's welfare and their husbands' careers, attempted to reproduce the amenities of Brahmin Boston, amid French recipes and the pretense of effortlessness—above all, the ultimate lack of seriousness with which women were regarded in that world—all of this defied analysis at that time, but I *knew* I had to remake my own life. I did not then understand that we—the women of that academic community ... as in so many middle-class communities of the period—were expected to fill both the part of the Victorian Lady of Leisure, the Angel in the House, and also of the Victorian cook, scullery maid, laundress, governess, and nurse. I only sensed that there were false distractions sucking at me, and I wanted desperately to strip my life down to what was essential.

June 1958

These months I've been all a tangle of irritations deepening to anger: bitterness, disillusion with society and with myself; beating out at the world, rejecting out of hand. What, if anything, has been positive? Perhaps the attempt to remake my life, to save it from mere drift and the passage of time....

The work that is before me is serious and difficult and not at all clear even as to plan. Discipline of mind and spirit, uniqueness of expression, ordering of daily existence, the most effective functioning of the human self—these are the chief things I wish to achieve. So far the only beginning I've been able to make is to waste less time. That is what some of the rejection has been all about.

By July of 1958 I was again pregnant. The new life of my third—and, as I determined, my last—child, was a kind of turning for me. I had learned that my body was not under my control; I had not intended to bear a third child. I knew now better than I had ever known what another pregnancy, another new infant, meant for my body and spirit. Yet, I did not think of having an abortion. In a sense, my third son was more actively chosen than either of his brothers; by the time I knew I was pregnant with him, I was not sleepwalking any more.

August 1958 (Vermont)
I write this as the early rays of the sun lights up our hillside and eastern windows. Rose with [the baby] at 5:30 A.M. and have fed him and breakfasted. This is one of the few mornings on which I haven't felt terrible mental depression and physical exhaustion.

...I have to acknowledge to myself that I would not have chosen to have more children, that I was beginning to look to a time, not too far off, when I should again be free, no longer so physically tired, pursuing a more or less intellectual and creative life.... The only way I can develop now is through much harder, more continuous, connected work than my present life makes possible. Another child means postponing this for some years longer—and years at my age are significant, not to be tossed lightly away.

And yet, somehow, something, call it Nature or that affirming fatalism of the human creature, makes me aware of the inevitable as already part of me, not to be contended against so much as brought to bear as an additional weapon against drift, stagnation and spiritual death. (For it is really death that I have been fearing—the crumbling to death of that scarcely—born physiognomy which my whole life has been a battle to give birth to—a recognizable, autonomous self, a creation in poetry and in life.)

If more effort has to be made then I will make it. If more despair has to be lived through, I think I can anticipate it correctly and live through it.

Meanwhile, in a curious and unanticipated way, we really do welcome the birth of our child.

There was, of course, an economic as well as a spiritual margin which allowed me to think of a third child's birth not as my own death-warrant but as an "additional weapon against death." My body, despite recurrent flares of arthritis, was a healthy one; I had good prenatal care; we were not living on the edge of malnutrition; I knew that all my children would be fed, clothed, breathe fresh air; in fact it did not occur to me that it could be otherwise. But, in another sense, beyond that physical margin, I knew I was fighting for my life through, against, and with the lives of my children, though very little else was clear to me. I had been trying to give birth to myself; and in some grim, dim way I was determined to use even pregnancy and parturition in that process.

Before my third child was born I decided to have no more children, to be sterilized. (Nothing is removed from a woman's body during this operation; ovulation and menstruation continue. Yet the language suggests a cutting—or burning—away of her essential womanhood, just as the old word "barren" suggests a woman eternally empty and lacking.) My husband, although he supported my decision, asked whether I was sure it would not leave me feeling "less feminine." In order to have the operation at all, I had to present a letter, counter-signed by my husband, assuring the committee of physicians who approved such operations that I had already produced three children, and stating my reasons for having no more. Since I had had rheumatoid arthritis for some years, I could give a reason acceptable to the male panel who sat on my case; my own judgment would not have been acceptable. When I awoke from the operation, twenty-four hours after my child's birth, a young nurse looked at my chart and remarked coldly: "Had yourself spayed, did you?"

The first great birth-control crusader, Margaret Sanger, remarks that of the hundreds of women who wrote to her pleading for contraceptive information in the early part of the twentieth century, all spoke of wanting the health and strength to be better mothers to the children they already had; or of wanting to be physically affectionate to their husbands without dread of conceiving. None was refusing motherhood altogether, or asking for an easy life. These women—mostly poor, many still in their teens, all with several children—simply felt they could no longer do "right" by their families, whom they expected to go on serving and rearing. Yet there always has been, and there remains, intense fear of the suggestion that women shall have the final say as to how our bodies are to be used. It is as if the suffering of the mother, the primary identification of woman *as* the mother, were so necessary to the emotional grounding of human society that the mitigation, or removal, of that suffering, that identification, must be fought at every level, including the level of refusing to question it at all.

"*Vous travaillez pour l'armee, madame?*" (You are working for the army?), a French-woman said to me early in the Vietnam war, on hearing I had three sons.

April 1965

Anger, weariness, demoralization. Sudden bouts of weeping. A sense of insufficiency to the moment and to eternity....

Paralyzed by the sense that there exists a mesh of relations, between e.g. my rejection and anger at [my eldest child], my sensual life, pacifism, sex (I mean in its broadest significance, not merely physical desire)—an interconnectedness which, if I could see it, make it valid, would give me back myself, make it possible to function lucidly and passionately—Yet I grope in and out among these dark webs.

I weep, and weep, and the sense of powerlessness spreads like a cancer through my being.

August 1965, 3:30 A.M.

> Necessity for a more unyielding discipline of my life.
> Recognize the uselessness of blind anger.
> Limit society.
> Use children's school hours better, for work & solitude.
> Refuse to be distracted from own style of life.
> Less waste.
> Be harder & harder on poems.

Once in a while someone used to ask me, "Don't you ever write poems about your children?" The male poets of my generation did write poems about their children—especially their daughters. For me, poetry was where I lived as no-one's mother, where I existed as myself.

The bad and the good moments are inseparable for me. I recall the times when, suckling each of my children, I saw his eyes open full to mine, and realized each of us was fastened to the other, not only by mouth and breast, but through our mutual gaze: the depth, calm, passion, of that dark blue, maturely focused look. I recall the physical pleasure of having my full breast suckled at a time when I had no other physical pleasure in the world except the guilt-ridden pleasure of addictive eating. I remember early the sense of conflict, of a battleground none of us had chosen, of being an observer who, like it or not, was also an actor in an endless contest of wills. This was what it meant to me to have three children under the age of seven. But I recall too each child's individual body, his slenderness, wiriness, softness, grace, the beauty of little boys who have not been taught that the male body must be rigid. I remember moments of peace when for some reason it was possible to go to the bathroom alone. I remember being uprooted from already meager sleep to answer a childish nightmare, pull up a blanket, warm a consoling bottle, lead a half-asleep child to the toilet. I remember going back to bed starkly awake, brittle with anger, knowing that my broken sleep would make next day a hell, that there would be more nightmares, more need for consolation, because out of my weariness I would rage at those children for no reason they could understand. I remember thinking I would never dream again (the unconscious of the young mother—where does it entrust its messages, when dream-sleep is denied her for years?)

For many years I shrank from looking back on the first decade of my children's lives. In snapshots of the period I *see* a smiling young woman, in maternity clothes or bent over a half-naked baby; gradually she stops smiling, wears a distant, half-melancholy look, as if she were listening for something. In time my sons grew older, I began changing my own life, we began to talk to each other as equals. Together we lived through my leaving the marriage, and through their father's suicide. We became survivors, four distinct people with strong bonds connecting us. Because I always tried to tell them the truth, because their every new independence meant new freedom for me, because we trusted each other even when we wanted different things, they became, at a fairly young age, self-reliant and open to the unfamiliar. Something told me that if they had survived my angers, my self-reproaches, and still trusted my love and each others', they were strong. Their lives have not been, will not be, easy; but their very existences seem a gift to me, their vitality, humor, intelligence, gentleness, love of life, their separate life-currents which here and there stream into my own. I don't know how we made it from their embattled childhood and my embattled motherhood into a mutual recognition of ourselves and each other. Probably that mutual recognition, overlaid by social and traditional circumstance, was always there, from the first gaze between the mother and the infant at the breast. But I do know that for years I believed I should never have been anyone's mother, that because I felt my own needs acutely and often expressed them violently, I was Kali, Medea, the sow that devours her farrow, the unwomanly woman in flight from womanhood, a Nietzschean monster. Even today, rereading old journals, remembering, I feel grief and anger; but their objects are no longer myself and my children. I feel grief at the waste of myself in those years, anger at the mutilation and manipulation of the relationship between mother and child, which is the great original source and experience of love.

On an early spring day in the 1970s, I meet a young woman friend on the street. She has a tiny infant against her breast, in a bright cotton sling; its face is pressed against her blouse, its tiny hand clutches a piece of the cloth. "How old is she?" I ask. "Just two weeks old," the mother tells me. I am amazed to feel in myself a passionate longing to have, once again, such a small, new being clasped against my body. The baby belongs there, curled, suspended asleep between her mother's breasts, as she belonged curled in the womb. The young mother—who already has a three-year-old—speaks of how quickly one forgets the pure pleasure of having this new creature, immaculate, perfect. And I walk away from her drenched with memory, with envy. Yet I know other things: that her life is far from simple; she is a mathematician who now has two children under the age of four; she is living even now in the rhythms of other lives—not only the regular cry of the infant but her three-year-old's needs, her husband's problems. In the building where I live, women are still raising children alone, living day in and day out within their individual family units, doing the laundry, herding the tricycles to the park, waiting for the husbands to come home. There is a baby-sitting pool and a children's playroom, young fathers push prams on weekends, but child-care is still the individual responsibility of the individual woman. I envy the sensuality of having an infant of two weeks curled against one's breast; I do not envy the turmoil of the elevator full of small children, babies howling in the laundromat, the apartment in winter where pent-up seven- and eight-year-olds have one adult to look to for their frustrations, reassurances, the grounding of their lives.

But, it will be said, this is the human condition, this interpenetration of pain and pleasure, frustration and fulfillment. I might have told myself the same thing, fifteen or eighteen years ago. But the patriarchal institution of motherhood is not the "human condition" any more than rape, prostitution, and slavery are. (Those who speak largely of the human condition are usually those most exempt from its oppressions—whether of sex, race, or servitude.)

Motherhood—unmentioned in the histories of conquest and serfdom, wars and treaties, exploration and imperialism—has a history, it has an ideology, it is more fundamental than tribalism or nationalism. My individual, seemingly private pains as a mother, the individual, seemingly private pains of the mothers around me and before me, whatever our class or color, the regulation of women's reproductive power by men in every totalitarian system and every socialist revolution, the legal and technical control by men of contraception, fertility, abortion, obstetrics, gynecology, and extrauterine reproductive experiments—all are essential to the patriarchal system, as is the negative or suspect status of women who are not mothers.

Throughout patriarchal mythology, dream-symbolism, theology, language, two ideas flow side by side: one, that the female body is impure, corrupt, the site of discharges, bleedings, dangerous to masculinity, a source of moral and physical contamination, "the devil's gateway." On the other hand, as mother the woman is beneficent, sacred, pure, asexual, nourishing; and the physical potential for motherhood-that same body with its bleedings and mysteries—is her single destiny and justification in life. These two ideas have become deeply internalized in women, even in the most independent of us, those who seem to lead the freest lives.

In order to maintain two such notions, each in its contradictory purity, the masculine imagination has had to divide women, to see us, and force us to see ourselves, as polarized into good or evil, fertile or barren, pure or impure. The asexual Victorian angel—wife and the Victorian prostitute were institutions created by this double thinking, which had nothing to do with women's actual sensuality and everything to do with the male's subjective experience of women. The political and economic expediency of this kind of thinking is most unashamedly and dramatically to be found where sexism and racism become one. The social historian A. W. Calhoun describes the encouragement of the rape of Black women by the sons of white planters, in a deliberate effort to produce more mulatto slaves, mulattos being considered more valuable. He quotes two mid-nineteenth century southern writers on the subject of women:

> "The heaviest part of the white racial burden in slavery was the African woman of strong sex instincts and devoid of a sexual conscience, at the white man's door, in the white man's dwelling."... "Under the institu-

tion of slavery, the attack against the integrity of white civilization was made by the insidious influence of the lascivious hybrid woman at the point of weakest resistance. In the uncompromising purity of the white mother and wife of the upper classes lay the one assurance of the future purity of the race."[2]

The motherhood created by rape is not only degraded; the raped woman is turned into the criminal, the *attacker*. But who brought the Black woman to the white man's door, whose absence of a sexual conscience produced the financially profitable mulatto children? Is it asked whether the "pure" white mother and wife was not also raped by the white planter, since she was assumed to be devoid of "strong sexual instinct?" In the American South, as elsewhere, it was economically necessary that children be produced; the mothers, Black and white, were a means to this end.

Neither the "pure" nor the "lascivious" woman, neither the so-called mistress nor the slave woman, neither the woman praised for reducing herself to a brood animal nor the woman scorned and penalized as an "old maid" or a "dyke," has had any real autonomy or selfhood to gain from this subversion of the female body (and hence of the female mind). Yet, because short-term advantages are often the only ones visible to the powerless, we, too, have played our parts in continuing this subversion.

Most of the literature of infant care and psychology has assumed that the process toward individuation is essentially the *child's* drama, played out against and with a parent or parents who are, for better or worse, givens. Nothing could have prepared me for the realization that I *was* a mother, one of those givens, when I knew I was still in a state of un-creation myself. That calm, sure, unambivalent woman who moved through the pages of the manuals I read seemed as unlike me as an astronaut. Nothing, to be sure, had prepared me for the intensity of relationship already existing between me and a creature I had carried in my body and now held in my arms and fed from my breasts. Throughout pregnancy and nursing, women are urged to relax, to mime the serenity of madonnas. No one mentions the psychic crisis of bearing a first child, the excitation of long-buried feelings about one's own mother, the sense of confused power and powerlessness, of being taken over on the one hand and of touching new physical and psychic potentialities on the other, a heightened sensibility which can be exhilarating, bewildering, and exhausting. No one mentions the strangeness of attraction—which can be as single-minded and overwhelming as the early days of a love affair—to a being so tiny, so dependent, so folded-in to itself—who is, and yet is not, part of oneself.

From the beginning the mother caring for her child is involved in a continually changing dialogue, crystallized in such moments as when, hearing her child's cry, she feels milk rush into her breasts; when, as the child first suckles, the uterus begins contracting and returning to its normal size, and when later, the child's mouth, caressing the nipple, creates waves of sensuality in the womb where it once lay; or when, smelling the breast even in sleep, the child starts to root and grope for the nipple.

The child gains her first sense of her own existence from the mother's responsive gestures and expressions. It's as if, in the mother's eyes, her smile, her stroking touch, the child first reads the message: *You are there!* And the mother, too, is discovering her own existence newly. She is connected with this other being, by the most mundane and the most invisible strands, in a way she can be connected with no one else except in the deep past of her infant connection with her own mother. And she, too, needs to struggle from that one-to-one intensity into new realization, or reaffirmation, of her being-un to-herself.

The act of suckling a child, like a sexual act, may be tense, physically painful, charged with cultural feelings of inadequacy and guilt; or, like a sexual act, it can be a physically delicious, elementally soothing experience, filled with a tender sensuality. But just as lovers have to break apart after sex and become separate individuals again, so the mother has to wean herself from the infant and the infant from herself. In psychologies of child-rearing the emphasis is placed on "letting the child go" for the child's sake. But the mother needs to let it go as much or more for her own.

Motherhood, in the sense of an intense, reciprocal relationship with a particular child, or children, is *one part* of female process; it is not an identity for all time. The housewife in her mid-forties may jokingly say, "I feel like someone out of a job." But in the eyes of society, once having been mothers, what are we, if not always mothers? The process of "letting-go"—though we are charged with blame if we do not—is an act of revolt against the grain of patriarchal culture. But it is not enough to let our children go; we need selves of our own to return to.

To have borne and reared a child is to have done that thing which patriarchy joins with physiology to render into the definition of femaleness. But also, it can mean the experiencing of one's own body and emotions in a powerful way. We experience not only physical, fleshly changes but the feeling of a change in character. We learn, often through painful self-discipline and self-cauterization, those qualities which are supposed to be "innate" in us: patience, self-sacrifice, the willingness to repeat endlessly the small, routine chores of socializing a human being. We are also, often to our amazement, flooded with feelings both of love and violence intenser and fiercer than any we had ever known. (A well-known pacifist, also a mother, said recently on a platform: "If anyone laid a hand on *my* child, I'd murder him").

These and similar experiences are not easily put aside. Small wonder that women gritting their teeth at the incessant demands of child-care still find it hard to ac-knowledge their children's growing independence of them; still feel they must be at home, on the *qui vive,* be that ear always tuned for the sound of emergency, of being needed. Children grow up, not in a smooth ascending curve, but jaggedly, their needs inconstant as weather. Cultural "norms" are marvelously powerless to decide, in a child of eight or ten, what gender s/he will assume on a given day, or how s/he will meet emergency, loneliness, pain, hunger. One is constantly made aware that a human existence is anything but linear, long before the labyrinth of puberty; because a human being of six is still a human being.

In a tribal or even a feudal culture a child of six would have serious obligations; ours have none. But also, the woman at home with children is not believed to be doing serious work; she is just supposed to be acting out of maternal instinct, doing chores a man would never take on, largely uncritical of the meaning of what she does. So child and mother alike are depreciated, because only grown men and women in the paid labor force are supposed to be "productive."

The power-relations between mother and child are often simply a reflection of power-relations in patriarchal society:

"You will do this because I know what is good for you" is difficult to distinguish from "You will do this because I can *make* you." Powerless women have always used mothering as a channel—narrow but deep—for their own human will to power, their need to return upon the world what it has visited on them. The child dragged by the arm across the room to be washed, the child cajoled, bullied, and bribed into taking "one more bite" of a detested food, is more than just a child which must be reared according to cultural traditions of "good mothering." S/he is a piece of reality, of the world, which can be acted on, even modified, by a woman restricted from acting on anything else except inert materials like dust and food.[3]

When I try to return to the body of the young woman of twenty-six, pregnant for the first time, who fled from the physical knowledge of her pregnancy and at the same time from her intellect and vocation, I realize that I was effectively alienated from my real body and my real spirit by the institution—not the fact of motherhood. This institution—the foundation of human society as we know it—allowed me only certain views, certain expectations, whether embodied in the booklet in my obstetrician's waiting room, the novels I had read, my mother-in-law's approval, my memories of my own mother, the Sistine Madonna or she of the Michelangelo *Pieta*, the floating notion that a woman pregnant is a woman calm in her fulfillment or, simply, a woman waiting. Women have always been seen as waiting: waiting to be asked, waiting for our menses, in fear lest they do or do not come, waiting for men to come home from wars, or from work, waiting for children to grow up, or for the birth of a new child, or for menopause.

In my own pregnancy I dealt with this waiting, this female fate, by denying every active, powerful aspect of myself. I became dissociated both from my immediate, present, bodily experience and from my reading, thinking, writing life. Like a traveler in an airport where her plane is several hours delayed, who leafs through magazines she would never ordinarily read, surveys shops whose contents do not interest her, I committed myself to an outward serenity and a profound inner boredom. If boredom is simply a mask for anxiety, then I had learned, as a woman, to be supremely bored rather than to examine the anxiety underlying my Sistine tranquility. My body, finally truthful, paid me back in the end: I was allergic to pregnancy.

I have come to believe, as will be clear throughout this book, that female biology—the diffuse, intense sensuality radiating out from clitoris, breasts, uterus, vagina; the lunar cycles of menstruation; the gestation and fruition of life which can take place in the female body—has far more radical implications than we have yet come to appreciate. Patriarchal thought has limited female biology to its own narrow specifications. The feminist vision has recoiled from female biology for these reasons; it will, I believe, come to view our physicality as a resource, rather than a destiny. In order to live a fully human life we require not only *control* of our bodies (though control is a prerequisite); we must touch the unity and resonance of our physicality, our bond with the natural order, the corporeal ground of our intelligence.

The ancient, continuing envy, awe, and dread of the male for the female capacity to create life has repeatedly taken the form of hatred for every other female aspect of creativity. Not only have women been told to stick to motherhood, but we have been told that our intellectual or aesthetic creations were inappropriate, inconsequential, or scandalous, an attempt to become "like men," or to escape from the "real" tasks of adult womanhood: marriage and childbearing. To "think like a man" has been both praise and prison for women trying to escape the body-trap. No wonder that many intellectual and creative women have insisted that they were "human beings" first and women only incidentally, have minimized their physicality and their bonds with other women. The body has been made so problematic for women that it has often seemed easier to shrug it off and travel as a disembodied spirit.

But this reaction against the body is now coming into synthesis with new inquiries into the actual—as opposed to the culturally warped—power inherent in female biology, however we choose to use it, and by no means limited to the maternal function.

My own story, which is woven throughout this book, is only one story. What I carried away in the end was a determination to heal—insofar as an individual woman can, and as much as possible with other women—the separation between mind and body; never again to lose myself both psychically and physically in that way. Slowly I came to understand the paradox contained in "my" experience of motherhood; that, although different from many other women's experiences it was not unique; and that only in shedding the illusion of my uniqueness could I hope, as a woman, to have any authentic life at all.

The "Sacred Calling"

One of the letters quoted in Margaret Sanger's *Motherhood in Bondage* (1928) comes from a woman seeking birth-control advice so that she can have intercourse with her husband without fear, and thus carry out her duties both as mother and wife: "I am not passionate," she writes, "but try to treat the sexual embrace the way I should, be natural and play the part, for you know, it's so different a life from what all girls expect" (234). The history of institutionalized motherhood and of institutionalized heterosexual relations (in this case, marriage), converge in these words from an ordinary woman of half a century ago, who sought only to fulfill the requirements of both institutions, "be natural and play the part" —that impossible contradiction demanded of women. What strategy handed from ashamed mother to daughter, what fear of losing love, home, desirability as a woman, taught her—taught us all—to fake orgasm? "What all girls expect"—is that, was it for her, more than what the institution had promised her in the form of romance, of transcendent experience? Had she some knowledge of her own needs, for tenderness, perhaps, for being touched in certain ways, for being treated as more than a body for sex and procreation? What gave her the courage to write to Margaret Sanger, to try to get some modest control over the use of her body—the needs of her existing children? Her husband's demands? The dim, simmering voice of self? We may assume all three. For generations of women have asserted their courage existence—a new relationship to the universe. Sexuality, politics, intelligence, power, motherhood, work, community, intimacy will develop new meanings; thinking itself will be transformed.

This is where we have to begin.

Notes

[1] The term "barren woman" was easy for me to use, unexamined, fifteen years ago. As should be clear throughout this book, it seems to me now a term both tendentious and meaningless, based on a view of women that sees motherhood as our only positive definition.

[2] See also Lerner 149-150 ff.

[3] 1986: the work of the Swiss psychotherapist Alice Miller has made me reflect further on the material in this chapter and in Chapters IX and X. Miller (1981) identifies the "hidden cruelty" in child-rearing as the repetition of "poisonous pedagogy" inflicted by the parents of the generation before and as providing the soil in which obedience to authoritarianism and fascism take root. She notes that "there is one taboo that has withstood all the recent efforts at demystification: the idealization of mother love" (4). Her work traces the damages of that idealization (of both parents, but especially the mother) upon children forbidden to name or protest their suffering, who side with their parents against themselves. Miller (1983) notes, "I cannot listen to my child with empathy if I am inwardly preoccupied with being a good mother; I cannot be open to what she is telling me" (258). Miller explores the sources of what has been defined as *child abuse*—i.e., physical violation and sadistic punishment—but she is equally concerned with the "gentle violence" of child-rearing, including that of "anti-authoritarian" or "alternative" prescriptions, based on the denial and suppression of the child's own vitality and feelings. Miller does not consider the predominance of women as primary care-givers, the investment of authoritarian or fascist systems in perpetuating male control of women's sexuality and reproductivity, or the structural *differences* between father-as-parent and mother-as-parent. She does acknowledge

that in America, women especially "have discovered the power of their knowledge. They do not shrink from pointing out the poisonous nature of false information, even though it has been well-concealed for millennia behind sacrosanct and well-meaning labels" (1983: xii).

References

Calhoun, Arthur W. A. *Social History of the American Family from Colonial Times to the Present.* Cleveland: 1917.

Lerner, Gerda. *Black Women in White America: A Documentary History.* New York: Vintage, 1973.

Miller, Alice. *The Drama of the Gifted Child: How Narcissistic Parents Form and Deform the Emotional Lives of Their Talented Children.* New York: Harper and Row, 1981.

Miller, Alice. *For Your Own Good: Hidden Cruelty in Childrearing and the Roots of Violence.* New York: Farrar, Straus and Giroux, 1983.

Sanger, Margaret. *Motherhood in Bondage.* New York: Maxwell Reprint, 1956.

Chapter 3

Early Psychological Development

Psychoanalysis and the Sociology of Gender

NANCY CHODOROW

> I once said: "There is no such thing as an infant," meaning, of course,
> that whenever one finds an infant one finds maternal care, and without
> maternal care there would be no infant. (Winnicott 1960)

THE REPRODUCTION OF mothering begins from the earliest mother-infant relationship in the earliest period of infantile development. This early relationship is basic in three ways. Most important, the basic psychological stance for parenting is founded during this period. Second, people come out of it with the memory of a unique intimacy which they want to recreate. Finally, people's experience of their early relationship to their mother provides a foundation for expectations of women as mothers.

Psychoanalysts have long stressed the importance of the infant's early relationship to its caretaker or caretakers. They argue that the infant's mental as well as physical survival depends on this social environment and relationship. In Western industrial society, biological or adoptive mothers have tended to have nearly exclusive care for infants.[1] In Western society, also, households have tended to be nuclear, in that there is usually only one married couple with children in any household (and thus only one mother with young children), even though in large numbers of households until recently there were also grown children and non-family members like boarders, lodgers, and servants (Gordon 1973; B. Laslett 1973; P. Laslett 1972). Caretaking typically has been synonymous with single mothering. The earliest relationship has been a relationship to a *mother,* and the mother-infant bond has been intense and relatively exclusive. Early development, then, consists in the building of a social and emotional relationship between mother and infant, both in the world and within the infantile psyche.

Total Dependence and the Narcissistic Relation to Reality

A human newborn is not guided by instinct, nor does it yet have any of those adaptive ego capacities which enable older humans to act instrumentally.[2] The infant, "separated from the maternal body too early" (Balint 1965, 82) is totally dependent on parental care until it can develop adaptive capacities. Parenting during this period must therefore include acting, in Margaret Mahler's term, as an infant's "external ego" (Mahler 1968, 16), serving to both mediate and provide its total environment.

The maturation of adaptive ego capacities that can take over from the parent, however, requires the development of an integrated ego, which controls and organizes these functions and behavior.[3] This maturation, although following innate biological potentialities, requires a particular kind of parental care from the time of the infant's birth, and varies according to the extent to which this care is consistent and free from arbitrariness. Anna Freud (1962) suggests that analysts have often attributed inadequate ego capacities to constitutional failing, when these are in fact the result of this early care: "At this early time of life the actions of the mother and her libidinal cathexis and involvement with the child exert a selective growth of some, and hold back, or fail to stimulate and libidinize, the growth of other potentialities. This determines certain basic trends in the child concerning his motility, the earliness or lateness of his verbalization, etc." (241).

The quality of care also conditions the growth of the self and the infant's basic emotional self-image (sense of goodness or badness, alrightness or wrongness). The absence of overwhelming anxiety and the presence of continuity—of holding, feeding, and a relatively consistent pattern of interaction—enable the infant to develop what Benedek (1949, 1959) calls "confidence" and Erik Erikson (1950) "basic trust," constituting, reflexively, a core beginning of self or identity.

The infant's development is totally dependent on parental care, on the fit between its needs and wants and the care its caretaker provides. Fundamental aspects of the person's sense of self develop through this earliest relationship. Michael Balint (1968) claims that his or her earliest experience produces a basic stance in the individual "whose influence extends widely, probably over the whole psychobiological structure of the individual, involving in varying degrees both his mind and his body" (22). When there is some major discrepancy in the early phases between needs and (material and psychological) care,[4] including attention and affection, the person develops a "basic fault," an all-pervasive sense, sustained by enormous anxiety, that something is not right, is lacking in her or him. This sense, which may be covered over by later development and defenses, informs the person's fundamental nature and may be partly irreversible. The area of the basic fault is not conscious or easily talked about (and hence analyzed), because it originates in a preverbal period before the infant is self-consciously social.

Dependence, then, is central to infancy and central to the coming into being of the person. Fairbairn (1952) calls the early period "infantile dependence," and describes most infantile psychological activity as a reaction to this feeling of helplessness. As long as the infant cannot get along without its mother—because she acts as external ego, provides holding and nourishment, and is in fact not experienced by the infant as a separate person at all—it will employ techniques which attempt to prevent or deny its mother's departure or separateness. Orality and the oral attitude of incorporation (the fantasy of taking in the mother or her breast) as a primary infantile mode, for instance, is not an inevitable extrapolation from nursing. It is one defensive technique for retaining primary identification (a sense of oneness) when this is being eroded—when the mother is beginning to be experienced as a separate person. Or, for instance, the infant's internalization of aspects of its relationship to its mother which are experienced as bad often results in splitting off and repression of that part of the ego involved in this bad relationship. This internalization avoids reacting to these bad aspects in the outside world and possibly driving the infant's mother away. Separateness during this early period threatens not only anxiety at possible loss, but the infant's very sense of existence.

The development away from "absolute dependence" (the infant's original state) through relationship to its caretakers is, according to Winnicott (1960), the same thing as the "coming into being" of the infant as a self (588). The "ego support which maternal care provides" (590) protects the infant and gives the illusion that the infantile ego is stable and powerful when in fact it is weak. This protection of the infant is necessary for the development of a "true self" or "central self." Threats to the development of a self are a "major anxiety" of the early period (in fact, the "very nature of psychotic anxiety") (590). An infant who experiences this anxiety develops instead a "false self" based on reactions to intrusion.

The distinction between a "true" and "false" self here, although one of degree, is important. Winnicott's "true self" is the ability to experience oneself as an effective emotional and interpersonal agent. By contrast, a person who develops a "false self" develops reactively: "A false self emerges on the pattern of conformity or adaptation to, or else rebellion against, the unsatisfactory environment. Its aim is survival in minimum discomfort, not full vigorous spontaneous creative selfhood. The result is either tame goodness or criminality" (Guntrip 104).[5]

Physiology and psyche are thus indistinguishable in the newborn. The very continued existence and development of both depends on parental care. Winnicott's and Fairbairn's perceptions are supported by studies of institutionalized children provided with the apparent physical requirements for growth but not provided with emotional relationships (Bowlby 1951; Spitz 1965). These children may grow up without ego capacities sufficient to establish relationships, may not develop basic motor and verbal skills, may be psychotic, and, in extreme cases, die.

The care that is provided in any society is not randomly assigned or performed. When individual women—mothers—provide parenting, total dependence is on the mother. It is aspects of the relationship to *her* that are internalized defensively; it is *her* care that must be consistent and reliable; it is *her* absence that produces anxiety. The infant's earliest experience and development is in the context of, and proceeds out of, an interpersonal relationship to its mother.

This relationship, however, is not symmetrical. Mother and child participate in it in radically different ways, though they may be equally involved. At birth, the infant is not only totally dependent but does not differentiate itself cognitively from its environment. It does not differentiate between subject/self and object/other. This means that it does not differentiate the gratifications of its needs and wants. The infant experiences itself as merged or continuous with the world generally, and with its mother or caretakers in particular. Its demands and expectations (not expressed as conscious wants but unconscious and preverbal) flow from this feeling of merging. Analysts call this aspect of the earliest period of life primary identification, aptly emphasizing the infant's object cathexis of someone it does not yet differentiate from its self. Freud (1923) claims that primary identification is "not in the first instance the consequence or outcome of an object cathexis; it is a direct and immediate identification and takes place earlier than any object cathexis" (31).

In this period the infant is cognitively narcissistic; its experience of self is an experience of everything else in its world: "What is 'not-I' is libidinally and cognitively perceived as part of 'I'" (Parens 108). Originally, the infant's lack of reality principle—its narcissistic relation to reality—is total. Mahler (1968) emphasizes this totality, and calls the first few weeks of life the period of "normal autism,"[6] "a stage of *absolute* primary narcissism, which is marked by the infant's lack of awareness of a mothering agent" (10). From this state of undifferentiation—between the "I" and the "not-I," and between inside and outside—the infant first begins to differentiate the quality of experience ("pleasurable and good" from "painful and bad"). From this develops a "dim awareness" of the object helping to produce this experience.

After this, the infant reaches a "symbiotic" stage of "mother-child dual unity," a stage reaching its height during the fourth or fifth month, and lasting approximately through the infant's first year.

During this stage, the infant oscillates between perceptions of its mother as separate and as not separate. For the most part, in spite of cognitive perception of separateness, it experiences itself as within a common boundary and fused, physically and psychologically, with its mother. Accordingly, it does not experience gratifications and protections as coming from her.

Thus the infant's cognitive narcissistic relation to objects has conventionally "narcissistic" consequences. Mahler, following Freud (1914), who pointed to the baby's seeming self-sufficiency and lack of attention to the world by referring to "'His majesty the baby,'" refers to "infantile omnipotence." This omnipotence, she suggests, stems from the sense of the mother's continual presence and hence power in relation to the world for the child. The mother functions, and is experienced, as the child's "external ego." The child maintains this sense of omnipotence by projecting any unpleasurable sensation or perception, of whatever origin, beyond the boundary of its symbiotic unity with its mother. The child behaves as if it were still a unit with its mother; it does not yet knowingly initiate protection, care, or contact.

Alice Balint (1939) describes this situation in more forceful terms. The infant's behavior, she says, is functionally egoistic, in that it ignores the interests of the mother: "We come nearest to it with the conception of egoism. It is in fact an *archaic, egoistic* way of loving, originally directed exclusively to the mother; its main characteristic is the complete lack of reality sense in regard to the interests [both libidinal and ego-interests] of the love-object" (95). However, this behavior is not egoistic in our adult sense—conscious ignoring of its mother's interests. It is, rather, "naive egoism," an unintended consequence of the infant's lack of reality sense and perception of its mother as separate.

Thus the early period of total dependence is dual (Angel 1972). The infant is totally dependent. When separateness is not a threat, and the mother is feeling totally dependable, total dependence transforms itself into an unproblematic feeling on the part of the infant that this is of course how things should be. Yet the infant is not aware of the other as separate, so experiences dependence only when such separation comes to its attention, through frustration, for instance, or the mother's departure. At this point, it is not only helplessness and object loss which threaten, but also loss of (incipient) self—disintegration.

Primary Love

The infant can be emotionally related to an object, even as its self and object representations are merged. Cognitive narcissism does not entail the infant's loving only itself. Several theorists, best represented by Michael and Alice Balint and John Bowlby, have pointed to an emotional cathexis highly charged by its embeddedness in total dependence and in the infant's experience of fusion with its mother and unreflective expectation of everything from her. They argue for a primary and fundamental sociality in the infant.[7] They imply, further, that the infant experiences this primary sociality in our society in relation to its mother. Their theory, like those of other object-relations theorists, has been developed in opposition to an alternate psychoanalytic position derived from Freud and followed by ego psychologists. This Freudian position hypothesizes primary narcissism and primary autoerotism on the part of the infant, and it holds that the earliest object-relation derives from the infant's need for food.

Freud (1914) asserts that the infant originally cathects both itself *and* its caretaker: "The human being has originally two sexual objects: himself and the woman who tends him—and in doing so we are postulating a primary narcissism in everyone" (88). The most straightforward reading of this claim is that the infant's libidinal cathexes are shared among all important objects including its incipient self, that "a primary narcissism" is not the same thing as "total primary narcissism." The libido directed toward itself would be the forerunner of later necessary self-esteem and self-love.

However, Freud, in his other writings, and his ego psychology followers have instead taken the position that the infant originally has no cathexis of its environment or of others, but concentrates all its libido on its self (or on its predifferentiated psyche). The infant is generally libidinally narcissistic; hence, the hypothesis of primary narcissism. (Freud and others occasionally speak instead of primary autoerotism, since narcissism in the true sense—libido turned toward the ego—is possible only after an ego has developed.) This Freudian position also holds that the infant seeks only the release of tension from physiologically based drives—operates according to the "pleasure principle." The source of this gratification, whether it is self-induced (burping, elimination) or from a caretaker, is irrelevant to the infant. Accordingly, the child is first drawn from its primary libidinally narcissistic stage because of its need for food. Freud suggests that the infant's ego (self-preservative) instincts direct it to the source of nurturance—the mother's breast—and then to the mother. Thus, in this formulation (in the same essay where he speaks of *two* original sexual objects), the original relation to the mother is for self-preservation and a libidinal attachment develops out of this. The child comes to cathect the mother only because she nourishes and cares for it.[8]

From this theory Freud (1914) derives the notion of an "anaclitic" or "attachment"-type object-relationship—literally "leaning-on." In this case, sexual instincts "lean on" (or depend on) self-preservative instincts.[9] The attachment here is not that of child to mother, but of sexual instincts to ego instincts. More generally, people who choose an "anaclitic object," or love in an anaclitic manner, choose an object modeled on the mother, more broadly as an opposite to the self. Those who choose a "narcissistic" object, or who love narcissistically, choose someone modeled on the self. Freud does not note the contradiction here. He considers anaclitic love—loving someone like the mother—as "complete object love," but expects women to take men for sexual objects.

Michael Balint (1965, 1968) and Alice Balint, in contrast to Freud and the ego psychologists, have developed a theory of primary love which explains the early cathexis as the (still nonverbal) infant experiences it. According to them, the infant, even while not differentiating itself from its environment or among the objects in its environment, brings from its antenatal state a strong cathexis of this environment. This generalized cathexis very quickly becomes focused on those primary people, or that person, who have been particularly salient in providing gratification and a holding relationship. These people are the objects of primary love, which is object-directed and libidinal, and which exists in rudimentary form from birth.

The hypothesis of primary love holds that infants have a primary need for human contact for itself. Attempts to fulfill this need play a fundamental role in any person's development and eventual psychic makeup. Balint and Fairbairn support this position from logical argument and clinical finding: All extreme narcissism can be explained as a withdrawal from object relations; psychotics are defended against object relationships and not returned to an earlier state; infants need holding and contact from a person who is emotionally there, not simply food and cleaning; how and by whom a want is fulfilled is as important to all their patients as that it is fulfilled.

Alice and Michael Balint (1937) propose that primary love is observable only in its breach. If satisfied, it brings forth a quiet sense of well-being and perfect tranquility in the infant. If not satisfied, it calls forth vehement demands—crying and a violent display of energy. This form of love is totalistic and characterized by naive egoism. The infant's ultimate aim is to "*be loved and satisfied, without being under any obligation to give anything in return*" (82).[10]

Michael Balint suggests that the character of primary love accounts for both Freud's conception that the infant is originally passive and Klein's that it is driven primarily by innate aggressive drives. Freud did not notice that the tranquillity he noted had a cause, that it resulted from satisfied primary object love. Klein did not notice the tranquillity itself, because such tranquillity is not noticeable in the way that crying and screaming are.

Bowlby (1969) argues the same position from his research on the development of attachment behavior in infants and from the evidence of ethnology. This evidence, he claims, supports the hypothesis that animals show many responses which are from the first comparatively independent of physiological requirements and which promote social interaction between species members.[11] Bowlby argues for a "primary object clinging" theory: "There is in infants an in-built propensity to be in touch with and to cling to a human being. In this sense there is a 'need' for an object independent of food which is as primary as the 'need' for food and warmth" (222).

I am persuaded by Bowlby's evidence and by Alice and Michael Balint's and Fairbairn's clinical arguments (and by my own informal observations). Freud and many other psychoanalysts incorrectly based their theory of psychological origin on a physiological foundation. This error stemmed from not noticing that much touching and clinging happens in the routine case during feeding, and from observing that the social relations of feeding are important, and that orality and the oral mode can become a focus of severe conflict and a symbol for the whole experience of infancy.[12]

Another psychoanalytic claim apparently at odds with Alice and Michael Balint's account derives from the traditional psychoanalytic tendency to understand object-relations as deriving from specific libidinal modes and zones. Benedek, Fairbairn, and to a certain extent Freud and Klein stress the infant's oral relationship to the mother and her breast.[13] Benedek (1956), for example, suggests that the early mother-infant symbiosis is "oral" and "alimentary" (but that it also concerns more generalized issues of giving and succoring on the part of the mother). Fairbairn (1941) claims that in addition to primary identification, infantile dependence consists in an oral-incorporative libidinal attitude. Following Klein he revises Freudian theory to suggest that all neurotic patterns—formerly thought to derive from the stages of development of the component instincts—are at bottom "techniques" for dealing with conflicts in object-relations modeled on early oral conflicts and deriving from the way that objects have been internalized during the oral stage.

Fairbairn in this context does not free analytic theory from libidinal determinism. He simply offers the statement that between infancy and a "mature" object-relationship (which includes a genital and giving libidinal attitude), all object-relationships, both internal and external, are primarily based on the oral incorporative, "taking" mode (concerned with taking and giving, emptying and filling). Infantile dependence here is the same thing as oral dependence, although it is not simply the need for food, but rather the need for relationship to the orally providing mother which is at issue. Fairbairn's grounding in Kleinian theory here is apparent, and probably accounts for his zonal emphasis, in spite of his denial of zonal determinism.[14]

Alice (1939) and Michael Balint argue that their observations of primary love, and their analytic finding that all forms of narcissism have their root in originally disturbed object-relations, replace the hypothesis of primary narcissism and go beyond the subsumption of the primary relationship under the need for food and oral contact: "The oral tendency to incorporate appeared as only one special form of expression of this kind of love which could be present in a more or less clearly marked form. The conception of narcissism did not do justice to the fact that this kind of love was always firmly directed towards an object; the concept of passive object-love (the wish to be loved) was least satisfactory, especially because of the essentially active quality of this kind of love (95).

It is possible to bring clinical and observational support to either position in these debates. To my mind the support for the object relations position is stronger. However, each position reflects a fundamentally different conception of human nature—whether human connection and sociality or human isolation and self-centeredness are more in need of psychological and social explanation. Each affects arguments about the basis for human selfishness and human cooperation. For our immediate purposes, these positions imply different starting points from which to describe human development.

The Beginnings of Self and the Growth of Object Love

Neither the primary narcissism position nor that of primary orality is typically advanced in an extreme form, however. For Freud, primary narcissism gives way to some object relation in the normal course of development. And for those who stress the primacy of orality or the need for food, the relation to the mother eventually broadens to include nonoral components and an emotional, nonphysiological component. All psychoanalysts agree with Alice Balint (1939) that, finally, the infant's active libidinal and emotional "love for the mother" comes to be uniquely important in its own right.

During the early months, the child comes gradually to perceive the mother as separate and as "not-me." This occurs both through physiological maturation and through repeated experiences of the mother's departure. At the same time, it begins to distinguish aspects of maternal care and interaction with its mother, and to be "able to wait for and confidently expect satisfaction" (Mahler 1968: 12). This beginning perception of its mother as separate, in conjunction with the infant's inner experience of continuity in the midst of changing instances and events, forms the basis for its experience of a self.

Thus a person's self, or identity, has a twofold origin and twofold orientation, both of which derive from its early relational experiences. One origin is an inner physical experience of body integrity and a more internal "*core* of the self." This core derives from the infant's inner sensations and emotions, and remains the "central, the crystallization point of the 'feeling of self,' around which a 'sense of identity' will become established" (Mahler 1968, 11). Its development is not inevitable, but depends on the provision of a continuity of experience. As Winnicott (1960) puts it, the "inherited potential which is experiencing a continuity of being, and acquiring in its own way and at its own speed a personal psychic reality and a personal body scheme" (590) comes to constitute the infant as a person.[15]

The second origin of the self is through demarcation from the object world. Both ego boundaries (a sense of personal psychological division from the rest of the world) and a bounded body ego (a sense of the permanence of physical separateness and of the predictable boundedness of the body) emerge through this process. The development of the self is relational. Winnicott (1958) suggests that a good relationship between infant and caretaker allows the infant to develop a sense of separate self—a self whose existence does not depend on the presence of another—at the same time as it develops a sense of basic relatedness.

Along with the growth of the self and of differentiation from the mother goes the lessening of dependence. At first, the infant is absolutely dependent and, because it does not experience itself as separate, has no way of knowing about maternal care and can do nothing about it. It "is only in a position to gain profit or to suffer disturbance" (Winnicott 1960, 589). As absolute dependence lessens, the infant becomes aware of its need for particular aspects of maternal care and relationship, and can relate them to personal impulse. Gradually thereafter, the infant no longer experiences this environment entirely as acting upon it. It develops capacities that enable it to influence and not simply react to the environment.

The mother is no longer interchangeable with any other provider of care once absolute dependence is mitigated. The developing self of the infant comes to cathect its particular mother, with all the intensity and absoluteness of primary love and infantile dependence. While it has attained perceptual and cognitive recognition of the separateness and permanence of objects, it does not yet have an emotional certainty of the mother's permanent being, nor the emotional certainty of being an individuated whole self.[16] Separation from her during this period, then, brings anxiety that she will not return, and with it a fundamental threat to the infant's still precarious sense of self. Felt dependence increases as real dependence declines.

Unfortunately (from the point of view of the naively egoistic infant) its mother has (and always has had) things to do and interests which take her away from it. Even those analysts who argue that the emotional-libidinal mutuality, or complementarity, in the mother-infant relationship derives from an instinctual bond between them, recognize that there is an asymmetry in this mutuality. As Benedek (1959) puts it, "The infant's need for the mother is absolute, while the mother's for the infant is relative. Accordingly, the participation of primary drives in the symbiotic state has different 'meanings' for mother and child" (390).

Alice Balint (1939) discusses the implications for the child of the fact that "maternal love is the *almost* perfect counterpart to love for the mother" (390). According to her, the child experiences from early in life an "instinctual rejection by the mother," which disturbs its naive egoism. This disturbance requires it to face the essential difference between love for the mother and mother-love: Its mother is unique and irreplaceable, whereas it is replaceable—by another infant, by other people, and by other activities.

The reality principle, then, intrudes on an emotional level as well as on the cognitive level. The child comes to recognize that its mother is a separate being with separate interests and activities. The reality principle is in the first instance this separateness: "It is at this point that the rule of the reality sense starts in the emotional life of man" (A. Balint 103). The fact that the infant still needs maternal love is of course crucial. One possible solution—turning the naive egoism to hatred in retaliation for the mother's "rejection"—would simply preserve the same (lack of reality-based) attachment and perpetuate the infant's feeling of vulnerability (A. Balint 1939). This is the reaction that Fairbairn (1952) describes: The infant does not simply reject early bad objects but internalizes them in order to both hate and control them. They are internalized, Fairbairn says, because they seem indispensable, and then repressed because they seem intolerable.

This change in its situation is not wholly to the infant's disadvantage. From the point of view of adult life, and from the point of view of that side of the infant that wants independence, total merging and dependence are not so desirable. Merging brings the threat of loss of self or of being devoured as well as the benefit of omnipotence. Discomfort and the loss of merging result both in the further development of the infantile ego and in the growth of a different kind of object love.

As I have indicated, the infant achieves a differentiation of self only insofar as its expectations of primary love are frustrated. If the infant were not frustrated, it would not begin to perceive the other as separate. Frustration and ambivalence generate anxiety. Freud (1926) first argued that anxiety triggers the development of ego capacities which can deal with and help to ward off anxiety. Thus, anxiety spurs the development of ego capacities as well as the creation of ego boundaries.[17]

For my purposes, what is important is that much of this anxiety, conflict, and ambivalence is not generated endogenously through infantile development, but is an infantile reaction to disruptions and discomforts in its relation with its mother. Once again, this primary object-relation has fundamental consequences for infantile experience. For instance, as a defense against ambivalence toward its mother and feelings of helplessness, the infant may split its perception of her and internalize only the negative aspect of their relationship. Or, it may internalize the whole relationship and split and repress only its negative aspect.

Early defenses lead to psychic structure formation. Internalization and repression of negatively experienced aspects of relationships often lead to a splitting off of those aspects of the self that participate in and are committed to these relationships. They are one major early ploy which structures the ego and its object-relationships. They help to demarcate that which will be experienced as external from that which will be experienced as internal. They help to constitute and organize the internal in ways which, once repressed, continue well beyond the period in which they were experienced as necessary.[18] Another defense emerging from frustration which structures the ego is the development of identifications. The child moves from primary identification to identification with aspects of its mother as a differentiated person, as one who frustrates or (seemingly) aggresses. Or it takes over controls previously exercised from without in order to prevent such control.

An important element in the child's introduction to "reality" is its mother's involvement with other people—with its father and possibly with siblings.[19] These people are especially important in the development of a sense of self and in the child's identifications. The sense of boundary, for instance, develops not only in relation to the mother, but also through comparison with others. Father and siblings—or other important people in the caretaker's life who are perceived as coming between caretaker and infant, but do not do primary caretaking themselves—are in some ways more easily differentiated from the self, because the infant's first association with them involves envy and a perception of self in opposition.

In a nuclear family, a father plays a central role in differentiation for the child. Because he is so involved with the child's mother, his role in the child's later defensive identifications—identification with his power or closeness to the child's mother, for instance—is also crucial. The ego develops partly as a system of defenses against such early experiences.

The child uses its father not only in its differentiation of self. The father also enables more firm differentiation of objects. The infant, as it struggles out of primary identification, is less able to compare itself and its mother, than to compare mother and father, or mother and other important people she relates to. This comparison indicates the mother's boundedness and existence as a separate person. The comparison also reveals the mother's special qualities—finding out that the whole world does not provide care increases her uniqueness in the child's eyes.

Father and other people are important as major constituting elements of the "reality principle" and as people enabling differentiation of self and differentiation among objects. Yet it is the relation to the mother, if she is primary caretaker, which provides the continuity and core of self, and it is primarily the relation to her which must be worked out and transformed during the child's earliest years. This is because the development of a libidinal relationship to the father and oppositional identifications with him are well in advance of his becoming an internal object. The construction of a mental image of him and internalization of aspects of relationship to him lag well behind those of the mother. Therefore, the relation to the father does not become as early involved in the internal organization of psychic structure and the development of fundamental representations of self (Abelin 1971).

The infant's object-relationships, in addition to the nature of its self, change with its growing recognition of its mother's separateness. The infant uses its developing physical and mental capacities to adapt to her interests and her modes of behavior and thus attempts to retain connection to her.

John Bowlby (1969) describes one major form this reaction takes in his account of attachment. Attachment behavior is behavior directed toward binding the mother to the child, especially through the maintenance of physical closeness to her. Children preoccupied with attachment are concerned to keep near their mother and demand a large amount of body contact. Attachment behavior, which begins to develop around six months and reaches its peak around a year to eighteen months, requires experienced separateness, and the ability to perceive and differentiate objects. It is directed toward and grows in relation to a particular person or persons who have provided the most intensive and strong relationship to the infant.

In a conventional nuclear family, the primary attachment figure is almost always the mother, but Bowlby and others are careful to distinguish attachment from dependence. A child is dependent on whoever is providing care at any moment, whereas attachment develops in response to the quality of interaction, and not to having primary physiological needs met. Attachment develops in relation to a particular person who is often, but does not need to be, the child's primary caretaker. This person is the child's primary affectional object, however, and interacts in some intense and strong way with it.

Children may develop attachments to more than one person, to the degree that they have played an important emotional part in the child's life. Thus, kibbutz children are more "attached" to their natural parents than to their nurses, who provide most of their care but do not interact as intensively or exclusively with any single child. Children whose mothers are available all day but are not responsive or sociable with them may become more "attached" to their fathers, who are not frequently available but interact intensively and strongly with these infants when they are around. Moreover, children may be equally attached to mother and father in comparison with strangers (Schaffer and Emerson 1964; H.R. Schaffer 1971; Kotelchuck 1972).[20]

Learning to crawl and walk allows the child progressively to control proximity. To separate and return physically to its mother permits it to gain feelings of independence through mastery of its environment and greater equality in relationship.

Emotionally, the child's primary love for its mother, characterized by naive egoism, must usually give way to a different kind of love, which recognizes her as a separate person with separate interests. This attachment to the mother, and the growing ability to take her interests into account, is a prototype for later attachment to other objects experienced as separate. For many analysts, this is the most important aspect of relational development.[21]

This change on the part of the infant is gradual. The infant's experience is a cycle of fusion, separation, and re-fusion with its mother. It progressively differentiates itself through maturation of its perceptual and cognitive capacities and through the variety of its experiences of relationship.[22] Boundaries grow weak and strong, are sometimes between whole self and whole mother (or other object), sometimes include parts of the mother within the self boundaries or exclude parts of the self as outside. Qualities of the mother are introjected and become part of the self-image and qualities of the self are projected outward. Along with these shifts go equally varied emotional changes, as the child goes from contented oneness, fulfilled primary love, and feelings of trust and omnipotence to feelings of help-lessness and ambivalence at the mother's power and her control of satisfactions and proximity; from assertions of separateness, rejection, and distancing of the mother to despair at her distance and fleeing to the mother's arms.

By the end of the first few years, a sense of identity and wholeness, a sense of self in relationship, has emerged. Many of the vicissitudes of these shifts have resolved themselves or disappeared. Others have become permanent elements of the psyche.

A Note on Exclusive Mothering

My account here concerns the person who provides primary care in a particular family structure at a particular time, and not, inevitably, the mother.[23] It is impor-tant to stress this point, because psychoanalytic theory (and accounts influenced by it) assumes an inevitable and necessary *single* mother-infant relationship. Such an assumption implies major limits to changing the social organization of gender. The reason for this psychoanalytic assumption is that psychoanalytic writers, who focus on primary relationships themselves, by and large do not analyze, or even notice, these relationships in the context of a particular historical period and particular social arrangements. They tend rather to reify arrangements that in our society ensure that women who are at least social, and usually biological, mothers do provide almost exclusive care.

Because the mother-infant relationship is so largely nonlinguistic, and because caretaking does include some minimal physiological and psychological require-ments, it is easy to assume exclusive parenting by the biological mother. And it is easy to accept such a position, to see this relationship as a less socially constructed relationship than other relationships we engage in or study. There has, moreover, been confusion concerning whose interests exclusive mothering serves. As I argue here, the psychoanalytic theory of the mother-infant relationship confounds an implicit claim for the inevitability and necessity of exclusive mothering by the biological mother with an argument for the necessity of constancy of care and a certain quality of care by *someone* or some few *persons*.

A certain constancy and quality of care are most certainly necessary to achieve basic requirements of being a person (the ability to relate, protection against psychosis, and so on). Psychoanalysts, though, assume and even argue that any dilution of primary care militates against basic ego development (Bowlby 1951; Mahler 1968; Spitz 1965). This claim results partly from the kinds of situations of multiple parenting and maternal deprivation that psychoanalysts have chosen to discuss.[24] They have studied infants who have suddenly lost their mother after becoming attached to her; infants in situations when any early change in the parenting person has gone along with great family turmoil and crisis (a maternal death, or sudden breakdown or hospitalization); infants in understaffed foundling homes, war nurseries, and child-care centers for the children of women prisoners; and infants in institutions where there was no attempt to provide constancy of care in any infant's life. The psychoanalytic claim for the necessity of primary care is made in spite of the fact that an astonishing proportion of clinical cases reported by psychoanalysts mention that a nurse cared for the person under discussion in childhood, without noting this as abnormal, as controverting evidence, as an exception to the rule, or as worthy of investigation.[25]

The psychoanalytic claim is also made in spite of the fact that those few studies which do compare children who have been singly and multiply parented, provided other factors are kept constant, do not support their conclusions. Bowlby (1969) recognizes in his recent work that household structure makes a difference in the number and nature of attachment figures. He even suggests that attachment may be more secure and intense in an infant who has a few attachment figures rather than only one (367). Bettye Caldwell (1963) reports only slight differences among infants and among mother-infant relationships in cases of rearing by a single mother and cases where the "caretaking role was shared with another female" (663). In a later study (1970), she reports no differences in child-mother and mother-child attachment between infants who spent time in day-care centers and those cared for at home exclusively by their mothers. She points out, moreover, that good day care—several adults and several children together—may be closer to the historical and cross-cultural norm for child-rearing than that which we have come to think natural.[26]

Child psychiatrist Michael Rutter (1972) and psychologist Rudolph Schaffer (1977) both summarize studies which evaluate variations in parenting. When one major mothering person shares her duties with a small but stable number of mother-surrogates (when she goes out to work, for instance),[27] when there is shared responsibility for infants with a high degree of continuity (as in the Israeli kibbutzim),[28] when societies have extended households and share child care (Mead 1954, 1962), there is no evidence that children suffer from such arrangements. Where children do suffer is in multiple parenting situations associated with sudden separation from their primary caretaker, major family crisis or disruption in their life, inadequate interaction with those caretakers they do have, or with so many caretakers that the child cannot form a growing and ongoing bond with a small number of people. In fact, these are the settings in which the psychoanalytic argument was formed. Schaffer (1977) affirms, "There is, we must conclude, nothing to indicate any biological need for an exclusive primary bond; nothing to suggest that mothering cannot be shared by several people" (100).[29]

There does not seem to be evidence to demonstrate that exclusive mothering is necessarily better for infants. However, such mothering is "good for society." Exclusive and intensive mothering, as it has been practiced in Western society, does seem to have produced more achievement-oriented men and people with psychologically monogamic tendencies. This form of parenting, along with other reductions in the role of kinship and size of household, also contributes to the interchangeability and mobility of families.[30] It has facilitated several other tendencies in the modern family such as nuclearization and isolation of the household, and the belief that the polity, or the society, has no responsibility for young children.

Another problem with the psychoanalytic account's false universality is its assumption that the type of exclusive care mothers in this society give is, like the fact of exclusivity, natural and inevitable. The account thus reifies the quality of care as well as the gender and number of people who provide it. Psychoanalysts do not often notice[31] the extensive differences within single mothering that are possible. Infants may be carried on the hip, back, or chest, in a loose sling which molds to the mother's body or directly against her body, or they may be swaddled, left in a cradle board, or left in a crib except for brief nursing periods. They may sleep alone, with their mother, or with their mother and father. They may be weaned at six months, when they can just begin to experience the cognitive difference between themselves and the outside world, or at two, three, or five, when they can walk and talk. These differences obviously have effects, which, again, have not been treated sufficiently in the psychoanalytic literature.[32] The typical Western industrial arrangement, in which infants are left in cribs except for brief periods of time when they are held and nursed, and in which they are weaned during the first year, provides relatively little contact with caretakers in the world societal spectrum. In a comparative framework, it is not the extreme constancy of care which psychoanalysts assume.

These objections do not invalidate the psychoanalytic account, but they show how to read it. And they indicate its real subject: a socially and historically specific mother-child relationship of a particular intensity and exclusivity and a particular infantile development that this relationship produces. Psychoanalysis does not describe those parenting arrangements that have to be for infants to become people. The account is certainly adequate and accurate for the situation it describes and interprets. It should not be read, however, as prescription or inevitable destiny. An account of the early mother-infant relationship in contemporary Western society reveals the overwhelming importance of the mother in everyone's psychological development, in their sense of self, and in their basic relational stance. It reveals that becoming a person is the same thing as becoming a person in relationship and in social context.

Notes

[1]In some classes during an earlier period, mothers may have shared or turned over this care to a nurse; in others, they may have been aided by a female relative. Recently, with the increase of labor force participation of mothers with very young children, they are probably aided during some hours by individual or group day-care arrangements.

[2]In what follows, my account assumes proper biological maturation. We are physiological creatures, and the development of any psychological stance, any capacity for intention, interpretation of meaning, communication—that is, any

nonreflex behavior—requires the maturation of the physiological capacity which enables it.

[3]My usage here follows Sylvia Brody and Sidney Axelrad (1970). They say, "'Ego apparatuses' seems to us an unwieldy term because it suggests ... that the ego is composed of a group of functions or that the functions are part of an ego equipment, whereas it is more precise and economical to say that the ego controls the functions. It also appears to us simpler to think of organic *structures* that allow for the maturation of behavior, and ego *functions* that serve to organize small units of behavior. ... The term *apparatus* often dulls necessary distinctions between what is organic, what is behavioral, and what is functional" (9).

[4]I will use care and caretaker to refer to the whole primary relationship, and specify when I mean it to refer to the taking care of body needs. A primary relationship does not necessarily develop with anyone who sees to these needs, as we will see. Since I am trying to distinguish between quality of care and interaction and who provides it, I do not want always to use "mothering." Other terms which analysts use—attachment figure, mothering figure—seem too specific. What I mean is relating—one, or interacting one.

[5]R. D. Laing (1959) has worked extensively with this distinction in his early studies, as has Sullivan (1953) in his work on the self-system. As many critics of ego psychology have pointed out, Hartmann (1939), in extolling the adaptive ego, and Anna Freud (1936), Edith Jacobson (1964), and others, in claiming that defenses are the basis of ego formation, verge on making a necessary virtue out of what object-relations theorists (Laing, Guntrip, Fairbairn, Winnicott) and nonpsychoanalytic critics of the contemporary family consider a product of specific modes of child care and family organization.

[6]Psychoanalysts first studied the earliest period of development through adult psychotics—through the "narcissistic neuroses"—and their language concerning this period often retains the imprint of these origins. Mahler (1968) has developed her account of normal development from her work with psychotic children. Her use of the label autism derives from her observation of "a most striking inability, on the part of the psychotic child, even to see the human object in the outside world, let alone to interact with him as with a separate human entity" (3). She speaks of the normal infant's "state of primitive hallucinatory disorientation" (7-8).

[7]See, in addition to Michael Balint's (1935, 1937, 1968) extended refutation of Freud's hypothesis of primary narcissism, Fairbairn's (1952, 1954) account of autoeroticism, and his more general arguments that people seek object-connection for itself and use libidinal channels as a vehicle toward this goal, as well as Winnicott's (1965) analysis of the importance of basic relatedness in the facilitating environment. See, for summary comparisons of the positions of object-relations theory and ego psychology on the earliest state of the infant, John Bowlby (1969, appendix); and Mary Salter Ainsworth (1969).

[8]Freud's position, and that followed, according to Bowlby (1969), by Anna Freud, Spitz, and to some extent by Klein, is what Bowlby usefully characterizes as a "secondary drive theory" about the nature of the child's original tie to

the mother: "In so far as a baby becomes interested in and attached to a human figure, especially mother, this is the result of the mother's meeting the baby's physiological needs and the baby's learning in due course that she is the source of his gratification" (222).

[9]See editor's footnote to Freud, "On Narcissism" (1914), *Standard Edition of the Completed Psychological Works* (hereafter SE), Vol. 14, p. 87.

[10]Here, as in much of the theory of the primary relationship, the imputation of such advanced causative and relational thinking to the newborn is not demonstrated. Balint is trying to render in words a behavioral manifestation and nonverbal (to use Fairbairn's term) "libidinal attitude" in the infant.

[11]Harlow's (1959) famous finding that the infant monkeys prefer artificial mothers made of warm soft terrycloth, but without a bottle, to wire mothers with a bottle, is a good example of this.

[12]As Jacobson (1964) puts it, "The memory traces left by any kind of libidinal stimulation and gratification in the past are apt to cluster around this primitive, first, visual mother-image.... The images of the orally gratified or deprived self will tend to absorb the engrams of all kinds of physical and emotional stimuli, satisfactions or derivations experienced in any area of the whole self" (35-36).

[13]Bowlby (1969) characterizes the theories of Benedek and Fairbairn as "primary object seeking" theories (222) in that they hold that there is an inbuilt propensity to relate to the human breast for its own sake and not only as a channel for milk, and that relationship to the mother comes when the infant learns that the mother is related to (or comes with) her breast.

[14]For Klein also, the early period is defined in terms of the oral relation to the mother's breast and the handling of innate sadistic and aggressive impulses toward it. Klein describes the primary psychological modes of relating also in oral terms—of projection and introjection, of taking and giving, of greed.

[15]For an analysis of the twofold development of the self which emphasizes the development of a body self, or body ego, see Phyllis Greenacre (1958).

[16]What Mahler (1968) calls "libidinal object constancy."

[17]Anna Freud (1936) and Brody and Axelrad (1970) have made this insight the basis for major analyses of these processes. Bypassing Hartmann's (1939) analysis of the development of autonomous ego functions, they argue that the ego as a control apparatus (Brody and Axelrad) and as the seat of character defenses (Anna Freud) is entirely a product of conflict and ambivalence, and of attempts to deal with anxiety. As Brody and Axelrad put it, "The emergence of the affect of anxiety and the beginning of ego formation take place in conjunction with one another, and ... the two events flow out of a joint process" (8).

[18]Fairbairn is the major theorist of these processes. See also Parens (1971). For an interesting clinical account, see Herman Roiphe and Eleanor Galenson (1973).

[19]For further discussion of the role of the father and other rivals in individuation, see Jacobson (1964); Mitchell (1974); and Ernest L. Abelin (1971).

[20]These findings are crucial for those of us who think there are enormous benefits to be gained by everyone—men, women, children—if men and women parent

equally and who support researchers arguing for the developmental importance of attachment and the constancy of object relations.

[21]They use a variety of concepts to describe the same transition. For Winnicott (1960), the transition is "from a relationship to a subjectively conceived object to an object objectively perceived" (589). For Fairbairn (1952), it is a shift from "infantile dependence," characterized by a taking attitude, to 'mature dependence," characterized by giving or by mutual cooperation in which the object is seen as a separate person with her or his own interests. For Jacobson (1964), the infant develops "true object relationships"—relationships based on a sense of totality of self in relation to totality of separate other. For Alice Balint (1939), the infant must replace egoistic love with "altruistic love"—a "social-reality-based form of love" which takes into account the mother's (or later loved object's) interests. She suggests that "archaic love without reality sense is the form of love of the id," and that "the social-reality-based form of love represents the manner of loving of the ego" (107).

[22]My account here derives mainly from Jacobson (1964), The *Self and the Object World.*

[23]Whether or not, as I have argued, women have hitherto always been primary caretakers, and whether or not this was once (close to) necessary for species survival.

[24]Rose Coser reminded me of this (personal communication).

[25]The only exception I have found is a study by Cambor (1969), who reports a clinical case demonstrating the effect on superego formation of dual parenting by a rejecting, white biological mother and a nurturant black nurse.

[26]Although I am obviously more sympathetic to this position than to the traditional psychoanalytic one, I think it only fair to point out that it, like the other, is probably a historical product. Bowlby (1969), Spitz (1965), and others who argued for the importance of the mother were reacting to a variety of makeshift arrangements that had not given children sufficient emotional care during the war and against traditional practices in many child-care institutions. At the same time, I think, they were probably also riding the tide of the feminine mystique and the attempt to return Rosie the Riveter to her home. Currently the economy needs women in the paid labor force, and the women's movement has raised questions about parenting. In this context, today's researchers find that the quality of care is what is important, not that it be provided by a biological mother. Psychoanalysis shifts from emphasizing the breast (which only a biological mother can provide) to the total holding and caring relationship (which can be provided by anyone with appropriate emotional capacities).

[27]Yudkin and Holme (1963) cited in Rutter, (61), and Schaffer (105).

[28]Irvine (1966) and Miller (1969), cited in Rutter (62).

[29]See also for an equivalent conclusion, Rutter (125).

[30]Whose usefulness Parsons (1942, 1943) and Goode (1963) have described.

[31]With the exception of periodic generalization about primitive society and longer nursing periods.

[32]An exception here is Muensterberger (1969), whose discussion, though marred by Western ethnocentrism, nevertheless makes a persuasive case that psychoanalytic theory derives from dealing with a specific developmental situation. See also George W. Goethals (1974) for further cross-cultural comparison of the effects of these differences, as well as Margaret Mead (1954) and John W. M. Whiting (1971).

References

Abelin, Ernest L. "The Role of the Father in the Separation-Individuation Phase." *Separation-Individuation: Essays in Honor of Margaret S. Mahler.* Eds. John B. McDevitt and Calvin F. Settlage. New York: International Universities Press, 1971. 229-252.

Ainsworth, Mary Salter. "Object Relations, Dependency, and Attachment: A Theoretical Review of the Infant-Mother Relationship." *Child Development.* 40.4 (1969): 969-1025.

Angel, Klaus. "The Role of the Internal Object and External Object in Object Relationships, Separation Anxiety, Object Constancy, and Symbiosis." *International Journal of Psycho-Analysis.* 53 (1972): 541-546.

Balint, Alice. "Love for the Mother and Mother-Love." 1939. *Primary Love and Psycho-Analytic Technique.* Ed. Michael Balint. New York: Liveright Publishing, 1965. 91-108.

Balint, Michael. "Early Developmental States of the Ego, Primary Object-Love." 1937. *Primary Love and Psychoanalytic Technique.* New York: Liveright Publishing, 1965. 74-90.

Balint, Michael. *Primary Love and Psychoanalytic Technique.* New York: Liveright Publishing, 1965.

Balint, Michael. *The Basic Fault: Therapeutic Aspects of Regression.* London: Tavistock Publications, 1968.

Benedek, Therese. "Psychosomatic Implications of the Primary Unit, Mother-Child." *American Journal of Orthopsychiatry.* 19.4 (1949): 642-654.

Benedek, Therese. "Psychobiological Aspects of Mothering." *American Journal of Orthopsychiatry* 26 (1956): 272-278.

Benedek, Therese. "Parenthood as a Developmental Phase: A Contribution to the Libido Theory." *Journal of the American Psychoanalytic Association* 7 (3) (1959): 389-417.

Bowlby, John. *Maternal Care and Mental Health.* 1951. New York: Schocken Books, 1966.

Bowlby, John. *Attachment and Loss. Volume I: Attachment.* 1969. London: Penguin Books, 1971.

Brody, Sylvia and Sidney Axelrad. *Anxiety and Ego Formation in Infancy.* New York: International Universities Press, 1970.

Caldwell, Bettye, Leonard Hersher, Earl L. Lipton, *et al.* "Mother-Infant Interaction in Monomatric and Polymatric Families." *American Journal of Orthopsychiatry.* 33 (1963): 653-664.

Caldwell, Bettye, Charlene Wright, Alice Honig and Jordan Tannenbaum. "Infant Day Care and Attachment." *American Journal of Orthopsychiatry* 40 (3) (1970): 397-412.

Cambor, C. Glenn. "Preoedipal Factors in Superego Development: The Influence of Multiple Mothers." *Psychoanalytic Quarterly* 38.1 (1969): 81-96.

Erikson, Erik. *Childhood and Society*. New York: W.W. Norton, 1950.

Fairbairn, W. R. D. "A Revised Psychopathology of the Psychoses and Psychoneuroses." 1941. *An Object Relations Theory of the Personality*. New York: Basic Books, 1952. 28-58.

Fairbairn, W. R. D. *An Object-Relations Theory of the Personality*. New York: Basic Books, 1952.

Fairbairn, W. R. D. "Observations of the Nature of Hysterical States." *British Journal of Medical Psychology* 27 (3) (1954): 105-125.

Freud, Anna. *The Ego and the Mechanisms of Defense*. 1936. New York: International Universities Press, 1966.

Freud, Anna. "Contribution to Discussion, 'The Theory of the Parent-Infant Relationship.'" *International Journal of Psycho-Analysis* 43 (1962): 240-242.

Freud, Sigmund. 1914. "On Narcissism: An Introduction." *Standard Edition of the Completed Psychological Works*. Vol. 14. London: Hogarth Press and Institute of Psycho-Analysis. 69-102.

Freud, Sigmund. 1923. "The Ego and the Id." *Standard Edition of the Completed Psychological Works* Vol. 19. 3-59.

Freud, Sigmund. 1926. "Inhibitions, Symptoms and Anxiety." *Standard Edition of the Completed Psychological Works*. Vol. 20. 77-174.

Goethals, George W. "Mother-Infant Attachment and Premarital Behavior: The Contact Hypothesis." Unpublished paper delivered, Grand Rounds, Harvard Medical School, Department of Psychology. 1974.

Goode, William J. *World Revolution and Family Patterns*. New York: Free Press, 1963.

Gordon, Michael, ed. *The American Family in Social-Historical Perspective*. New York: St. Martin's Press, 1973.

Greenacre, Phyllis. "Early Physical Determinants in the Development of the Sense of Identity." *Journal of the American Psychoanalytic Association* 6 (4) (1958): 612-627.

Guntrip, Harry. *Psychoanalytic Theory, Therapy, and the Self*. New York: Basic Books, 1971.

Harlow, H.F. and R.R. Zimmerman. "Affectional Responses in the Infant Monkey." *Science* 130 (1959): 421-432.

Hartmann, Heinz. *Ego Psychology and the Problem of Adaptation*. 1939. New York: International Universities Press, 1958.

Jacobson, Edith. *The Self and the Object World*. New York: International Universities Press, 1964.

Kotelchuck, Milton. "The Nature of the Child's Tie to His Father." Diss. Harvard University, 1972.

Laing, R.D. *The Divided Self.* London: Penguin Books, 1959.

Laslett, Barbara. "The Family as a Public and Private Institution: An Historical Perspective." *Journal of Marriage and the Family* 35 (1973): 480-492.

Laslett, Peter. *Household and Family in Past Time.* Cambridge: Cambridge University Press, 1972.

Mahler, Margaret S. *On Human Symbiosis and the Vicissitudes of Individuation. Volume I: Infantile Psychosis.* New York: International Universities Press, 1968.

Mead, Margaret. "Some Theoretical Considerations on the Problem of Mother-Child Separation." *American Journal of Orthopsychiatry* 24 (1954): 471-483.

Mead, Margaret. "A Cultural Anthropologist's Approach to Maternal Deprivation." 1962. *Maternal Care and Mental Health/Deprivation of Maternal Care.* New York: Schocken Books, 1966. 237-254.

Mitchell, Juliet. *Psychoanalysis and Feminism.* New York: Pantheon Books, 1974.

Muensterberger, Warner. "Psyche and Environment: Sociocultural Variations in Separation and Individuation." *Psychoanalytic Quarterly.* 38 (1969): 191-216.

Parens, Henri. "A Contribution of Separation-Individuation to the Development of Psychic Structure." *Separation-Individuation: Essays in Honor of Margaret S. Mahler.* Eds. John B. McDevitt and Calvin F. Settlage. New York: International Universities Press, 1971. 100-112.

Parsons, Talcott. "Age and Sex in the Social Structure of the United States." 1942. *Essays in Sociological Theory.* New York: Free Press, 1964.

Parsons, Talcott. "The Kinship System of the Contemporary United States." 1943. *Essays in Sociological Theory.* New York: Free Press, 1964.

Roiphe, Herman and Eleanor Galenson. "Object Loss and Early Sexual Development." *Psychoanalytic Quarterly* 42 (1973): 73-90.

Rutter, Michael. *Maternal Deprivation Reassessed.* Baltimore: Penguin Books, 1972.

Schaffer, H. R. *The Growth of Sociability.* Baltimore: Penguin Books, 1971.

Schaffer, H. R. *Mothering.* Cambridge: Harvard University Press, 1977.

Schaffer, H. Rudolph and Peggy E. Emerson. "The Development of Social Attachments in Infancy." *Monographs of the Society for Research in Child Development* 29 (3) (1964).

Spitz, Rene. *The First Year of Life: A Psychoanalytic Study of Normal and Deviant Object Relations.* New York: International Universities Press, 1965.

Sullivan, Harry Stack. *The Interpersonal Theory of Psychiatry.* New York: W. W. Norton, 1953.

Whiting, John W. M. "Causes and Consequences of the Amount of Body Contact between Mother and Infant." Paper presented to the American Anthropological Association Meetings, New York, 1971.

Winnicott, D. W. "The Capacity to Be Alone." 1958. *The Maturational Processes and the Facilitating Environment.* New York: International Universities Press, 1965. 29-36.

Winnicott, D. W. "The Theory of the Parent-Infant Relationship." *International Journal of Psycho-Analysis*. 41 (1960): 585-595.

Winnicott, D. W. *The Maturational Processes and the Facilitating Environment*. New York: International Universities Press, 1965

Chapter 4

The Dialectics of Reproduction

MARY O'BRIEN

WHEN WE ASK questions about the suppression of women and its causes, the answers which are given usually relate the social condition of women to female reproductive function. The trap in this correlation is, of course, that it suggests that male dominance is in some sense "natural," as natural as motherhood. Biological reproduction, the argument goes, is a natural process with which human reason can only deal from the standpoint of natural science. If we want clearer understanding of the process, we should turn to biology, anatomy and physiology or, increasingly, to the problematic wonders of genetics. What these sciences show us is that mammalian reproduction is but one class of animal reproduction. Anything specifically human in the process apparently must await the appearance of the product of the process, the child, as a separate but dependent creature. The actual business of fertilization, parturition and birth, the anatomy and physiology of reproduction, we are told does not differ significantly between human females and, say, baboons. The sexual instinct, naturally strong and irresistible as it is, ensures that the species will continue, and women are in an understandable sense the handmaidens of biological continuity. To be sure, this non-differentiation between the human and other animals is superseded in terms of human inventiveness with regard to the social relations which are developed to deal with the questions of the helplessness of the newborn, the socialization and education of the child and the sexual relations of men and women. The human family in all its varied forms is quite different from the animal pack, herd or whatever. The family is a historical development with its roots in a natural necessity. The necessity itself is invariant, and women's place in the social relations of reproduction is therefore circumscribed by her childbearing function. While this view has been a staple of masculine thought, it has also been shared by important feminist writers, including Simone de Beauvoir and Shulamith Firestone.[1] Feminist versions retain the premise of the argument but alter the conclusion. Traditional wisdom says: Women are naturally trapped in the childbearing function. Women therefore cannot participate in social life on equal terms with men. In place of this, a new syllogism is coined: Women are naturally trapped in the childbearing function. Therefore the liberation of women depends on their being freed from this trap.

Perhaps it is not the conclusion which is wrong, but the premise. What does it mean to be trapped in a natural function? Clearly, reproduction has been regarded as quite different from other natural functions which, on the surface, seem to be equally imbued with necessity; eating, sexuality and dying, for example, share with birth the status of biological necessities. Yet it has never been suggested that these topics can be understood only in terms of natural science. They have all become the subject matters of rather impressive bodies of philosophical thought; in fact, we have great modern theoretical systems firmly based upon just these biological necessities. Dialectical materialism takes as its fundamental postulate the need to eat: Marx has transformed this very simple fact of biological necessity into the breeding ground of a theoretical system of enormous vitality and explanatory utility, in which productive labour remakes our consciousness, our needs and our world. The simple sex act has been transformed by the clinical genius of Freud into a theoretical *a priori* of a system in which libido shapes our consciousness and our world. Death has haunted the male philosophical imagination since Man the Thinker first glimmered into action, and in our own time has become the stark reality which preoccupies existentialism, an untidy and passionately pessimistic body of thought in which lonely and heroic man attempts to defy the absurdity of the void which houses his consciousness and his world. The inevitability and necessity of these biological events has quite clearly not exempted them from historical force and theoretical significance.

We have no comparable philosophies of birth. Birth was at one time important in a symbolic way to theological visions, mostly with a view to depreciating women's part, and rendering it passive and even virginal, while paternity took on divine trappings. Reproductive process is not a process which male-stream thought finds either ontologically or epistemologically interesting on the biological level. The human family is philosophically interesting, but its biological base is simply given.

Women cannot be so dense nor so perverse. This male theoretical attitude towards birth is neither natural, accidental nor conspiratorial. It has a material base, and that base lies in the philosophically neglected and generically differentiated process of human reproduction itself. The general thesis which is to be proffered here is that reproductive process is not only the material base of the historical forms of the social relations of reproduction, but that it is also a dialectical process, which changes historically. There are a couple of essential preconditions which need to be posited before a dialectical, historical and material analysis of reproductive process can make sound theoretical sense. The first of these arises from the claim that the process changes historically. This contentious proposition rests upon the neglected consideration that human reproduction is inseparable from human consciousness. This seems self-evident, but the strong historical tendency which we have just discussed to see reproduction as 'pure' biological process carries the implication that reproduction is all body and without mind; irrational or at least prerational. The presupposition of an inseparability of experienced process and human consciousness of process is central to the theory of the dialectics of reproduction to be developed here. This unity of event and consciousness of event is the base of the attribution of historicity to reproductive process: it will be argued that the first and significant historical change in the process was not a biological mutation of some kind, but a transformation in male reproductive consciousness, which was triggered by the historical discovery of physiological paternity. The second and much more recent change in reproductive praxis is brought about by technology. Technology, we may note, has been the historical process which has accelerated changes in modes of production, but contraceptive technology is qualitatively different from all other technologies. Its impact on the economic realm is not especially striking, except that the profits are obscenely large and little interest is shown in utilizing them for the development of a safer and better technology. Yet this technology, even in its imperfect form, brings about a fundamental historical change of the kind which Hegel called a world historical event. This is not simply because of the effects on demographic patterns and family relations, which are already obvious. Beneath these changes and, indeed, essential to the growth of the women's movement, is a change in the underlying dialectics of reproductive consciousness. The freedom for women to choose parenthood is a historical development as significant as the discovery of physiological paternity. Both create a transformation in human consciousness of human relations with the natural world which must, as it were, be re-negotiated or, to use the language of dialectical analysis, be mediated.

It is precisely because of this world historical event that we are able now to begin to look at the process of reproduction in a different way. Women have been in a similar position to that which Karl Marx diagnosed as that of utopian socialists in the early nineteenth century.[2] Marx and Engels described the activities of these earlier prophets as the work of those who sensed that something was fundamentally out of kilter in the society in which they lived, and who saw that the progressive promise of human control over the natural and social environment was being sadly eroded by the brutality of industrial production and the exploitation of the working class. Unable to articulate the grounds of this process in correct theoretical terms, utopians advocated a total destruction and rebuilding of society, a breaking up of all values and a rejection of all conventional morality. This would bring about the arrival of a world which they had spun in the humane and indignant web of their own outraged sensibilities. Utopians were so innocent of the true nature of class struggle that they even called on the ruling class for help in destroying itself.

The failure to develop a correct theoretical understanding of their own historical situation did not emerge from defective understanding or a paucity of intellectual gifts on the part of the utopian socialists, Marx and Engels argue. The pace of history does not flag while the process of history waits for a good idea to come along and give it a push. Ideas are, as Marx famously argued, the product of history, and history is not the product of ideas. In the lived lives of early socialists, the development of the capitalist mode of production and the forms of class struggle which it was creating were still at a primitive stage. It could be seen that there were indeed antagonistic classes, but the significance of class struggle in human history could not be understood until the struggle itself had been developed and uncovered in the clear opposition of bourgeoisie and proletariat. This required a high level of generality in the capitalist mode of production and a critique of the developed theory and ideology of political economy, the bourgeois mode of production and the bourgeois philosophy. Only then could a new and higher form of social theory even begin to be developed. Marx was never a foolishly modest man, and he considered that his own theoretical activity was a significant stage in this development, but he recognized his own historical specificity in a clear-headed way which his more orthodox and ahistorical followers would do well to cultivate. What we now call Marxism was the theoretical interpretation of a set of particular historical conditions in relation to a universal process of history, the history of class struggle. Until this struggle reached an advanced stage of polarity, which development depended in turn upon a particular stage of technological and ideological sophistication and a simplification of class division, the substructure of historical process remained obscure.

This short analysis of utopian socialism in the "Communist Manifesto" (Marx 1969) is a very useful one. It provides a method for analysing the subsequent impact of technology on the social relations of reproduction, an event quite obscure to Marx in his own epoch. We are presently emerging from a stage of feminist utopianism, which calls for the destruction of the world of male supremacy, and even sometimes expects the ruling sex to assist in its own funeral rites. Like the stage of utopian socialism, this feminist utopianism is an important stage, for it publicizes injustice and pinpoints problems. However, the social relations of reproduction are now increasingly displaying evidence of transformation, evidence which permits a clearer understanding of the historical forces at work. This understanding will come from women who, as the dehumanized people of this dialectical struggle, are at the same time the progressive social force in the restructuring of the social relations in question. Yet women cannot accomplish this historical mission without a clear theoretical understanding of the dimensions of the task and of the processes at work, and it is clear that the struggle in process cannot be subsumed in class struggle. We cannot analyse reproduction from the standpoint of any existing theory. The theories themselves are products of male-stream thought, and are among the objects to be explained, but embedded somewhere in the theory and practice of male supremacy are the seeds of its growth and inevitable decay. What we must therefore do is turn to the fundamental biological process in which reproductive relations are grounded and subject it to analysis from a female perspective. This cannot be done in terms of a critique of political economy, nor in terms of the canons of psychoanalysis, existentialism or any other fine flowering branch of male-stream thought. As we have observed, there is no philosophy of birth, and yet it is of birth that we must theorize. What this means is that we must not only develop a theory, but develop a *feminist perspective* and a *method of enquiry* from which such a theory can emerge.

Of these rather daunting tasks, the methodological one turns out to be the least difficult. Here we can borrow from intellectual tradition, not because dialectical analysis is groovier and ideologically more congenial than other modes of theorizing, but because reproductive process is dialectical, material and historical. Clearly, an analysis which claims to be historical, material and dialectical owes a great deal to Marx, and in fact the strategy of analysing reproductive process—"as such," as some philosophers would say—is inspired by Marx's analysis of "pure" productive labour in *Capital* (1867: I,3,VII, i). "Pure" here means abstracted from the social context. This is done for purposes of theoretical clarity, for of course neither production nor reproduction can appear in isolation from their social and historical context. What is attempted is not simply an adaptation of Marx's analysis, but an immanent critique of that analysis. Put in the simplest way, we may claim to retain what is of value in Marx's analysis while using his own method to transcend and revise his own theoretical model. This sense of the history of thought as a dialectical process is more commonly associated with the work of Hegel than with Marx's materialism, and we shall also borrow from Hegel, whose insight into the dialectical structure of reproductive process was the major stimulus to this analysis. In one sense, this is a Hegelian/Marxist analysis, but no claim at all is made on the authority of these luminous thinkers, nor any apology to their orthodox disciples. This is a feminist analysis, and the two gentlemen in question were immersed in the tradition of male-stream thought, Hegel in particular being an unrepentant and often bitter misogynist. None the less, the debt to both of these men is acknowledged without reservation, while we proceed quite buoyantly and without embarrassment to ignore, with a calculated naiveté, the major propositions of their respective systems, concentrating on the social relations of reproduction which both seriously misunderstood.

It was Hegel, the objective idealist, and not Marx, the materialist, who noticed that the process of reproduction was dialectically structured.[3] The further consideration that it is also capable of significant transformation in historical terms, however, eluded the highly refined historical understanding of the old wizard of dialectics. The effect of this combination of perspicacity and opacity in Hegel's own work was an odd one, for Hegel placed vital aspects of reproductive relations outside of history proper, history being understood to start only when the human rational faculty had clearly separated the human world from the rest of the animal world in the development of self-consciousness and historical consciousness. For Hegel, the patriarchy was not a historical institution but a "prehistorical," natural arrangement.[4] Likewise, the restriction of women to activities related to the care of individual lives in the limited area of family and domestic life was also prehistorical. Hegel was irritated by the fact that women, because they are defective in the exercise of reason, don't always appear to appreciate the limitations of their organic and ancestral preoccupations. For Hegel, the household was the arena of death.[5] He understood, of course, that the forms of family do change historically, and indeed saw the process by which the self-sufficiency of the family in both economic and moral terms was progressively eroded as a significant part of historical dialectics. In his bourgeois understanding of paterfamilias, which was a strong factor in Hegel's own self-understanding, he was a little nostalgic about this. As the plotter of the progress of reason in history, however, he recognized the inevitability of the contraction of the family over time, for reason's most complete appearance in history was realized for Hegel in the modern state. The contraction of the family and the expansion of civil society, political rule and inventive economics were the inevitable manifestations of the rationalization of human affairs.

The family in Hegel's scheme gives us a clearer idea of dialectical process. Though each particular family dies out, the universal family form is never abolished; it is transcended and transformed while it is at the same time preserved. Nothing is ever lost in Hegel's view of history, yet nothing is static either. The family remains for the very good reason that it is necessary, but less necessary, because less rational, than other wholly man-made institutions, such as the economic, legal and religious institutions in which reason systematically hitches a ride from the abstract realm of metaphysics to the concrete realities of collective human life. The necessity embodied in the family can never transcend its natural component, which is the biological need of each life. Thus, the reproduction of the race is a dead core in the dynamics of human history, inert, intransigent and often downright irritating. The mute genealogical continuity of the genderically differentiated human race is quite different from the continuity of the history which man creatively struggles to make for himself. None the less, the family does have one characteristic which transcends the merely organic, and this has to do with its ethical aspect. The family is, as it were, ethical by compulsion, an ethics quite different from that, for example, by which men learn the rational and noble morality of going to war, to kill and be killed in the imperative conservation of the society which they have made in unwitting compliance with cunning reason. The ethical essence of the family lies in the dependence of infants, which makes the first demand on people to think of the welfare of another rather than only on personal survival. It is because of this demand that women can add to their limited rational capacity a limited moral understanding. Women care for their children, just as they keep green the memory of ancestors. The family is the sole source and appropriate realm of female ethical being.[6] Female morality, like women themselves, remains particular, and relates only to the individuals in the family, concentrating on biological life. It is because female morality is essentially biological that Hegel sees the perfect moral male/female relationship as that of brother and sister, and Antigone appears in his work as history's only heroine. Women cannot understand the necessity to rise above the consideration of individual survival to the "higher" appreciation of the community and its more sophisticated and rational ethics. Male morality, on the other hand, transcends particularity to become the ethics of universal man and the socio-historical realities in which this universally is expressed. Boys grow up under the eye of a particular male parent, who counteracts the limitations of maternal particularity until such time as the male child can transcend this patriarchal domination, and proceed to take his place in the larger male-dominant society which meets the young man's need to become, among other things, a patriarch himself.

Of the two needs, biological and ethical, which guarantee the survival of some form of family in history, the ethical function is clearly superior to the reproductive function, for it has a moral and human component added to the merely organic workings of biology. Male supremacy is therefore ethical and rational rather than biological, for men have this capacity to struggle for universality, to disregard particular life in the affirmation of a more rational whole. Male supremacy is therefore necessary to historical development; it is a historical constant.

We are not concerned to demonstrate in detail Hegel's male chauvinism, nor are we dismissing "the system" in a couple of pages.[7] What is unique and significant is Hegel's recognition that the process of reproduction is formally structured in a dialectical way. In fact, reproductive process, like the history of the family, serves to clarify a little further our understanding of dialectics. As a young man, Hegel was much concerned with the relation of sexuality to self-consciousness, and with the question of how this relation comes to be realized in the institution of the family. Sexual desire, which young Hegel (1948) decorously refers to as "love," is a problematic affair, for it appears at first sight to destroy one's sense of self in a very thorough way. The lover is swept pell-mell into a unity with another which negates his sense of individuality and annuls his consciousness of self: "the individual cannot bear to think of himself in this nullity ... nothing carries the root of its own being in itself ... true union consists only between living things which are alike in power" (303-304).

When Hegel claims that self-consciousness "cannot bear" negation and separation from itself, or, to put this another way, that human consciousness resists alienation and negation of the self, he is making a claim about the structure of consciousness which is vital to the theory of reproductive consciousness developed here. Hegel sees this lack of distinction as emerging from an identity of power in the lovers, as each contributes a seed. This is an elementary instance of the synthesis of oppositions. The uniting seeds of the lovers, young Hegel says, constitute a unity which annuls the distinction between the particular seed of each individual donor. As donors of seed, therefore, male and female are alike in power. Yet this power is problematic: not only does the new and unified seed annul the distinction between the separate seeds, but the individuals themselves, in the grip of sexual passion, suffer a loss of self-distinction. Sexuality annuls the distinction between the lover as human lover and the lover as mere physical organism. Lovers are stripped first of their identity, which is submerged in the other, and secondly of their general humanity. The seed itself cannot unify these separations, because, at this stage, it is still only what Hegel (1948) calls an "undifferentiated unity" (307). Yet it has the potential for the restoration of a new and restored unity in that it is "a seed of immortality, of the eternal and self-generating race" (305). The process of reproduction is therefore a process of "unity, separated opposites, reunion" (307), for the child breaks free from the original unity to constitute a new potential self-consciousness which affirms the continuity of the species.

It is, I think, important to struggle with Hegel's difficult analysis for a number

of reasons. The first of these applies to many of the philosophical fathers of patriarchy whose views of reproduction and the family we shall be analysing. This
is not simply an academic exercise. What underlies these notions is not simply
prejudice, but clues as to the lived experience which informs male reproductive
consciousness. The process by which this experience is transformed into an ideology of male supremacy is crucial to our analysis of reproductive consciousness.
The feminist critique of male-stream thought in general must, however, proceed
from something more dynamic than mere standpoint; it must have a theory and
a method. Hegel is extraordinarily illuminating in that he gives us not only large
hints as to what to look for, but a great deal of help in knowing how to go about
our search in a systematic and methodical way. Most great thinkers have aspired
in some sense to give an account of the whole of human experience, or at least
to define the limits of holistic possibility. Hegel is particularly ambitious in his
passionate pursuit of absolute knowledge. Yet any account of human experience
which has been taken seriously has had to deal with ancient and vexed questions
relating to the contradictions within human experience of individuality and
sociability and, in many instances, the extension of this problem to questions
about the origins of individual and social reality and the forms of individual and
social consciousness. Clearly, there is enormous historical variation in the way
in which these kinds of questions are asked and answered, yet there is a guiding
thread of assumptions of male superiority emerging from the process of history,
whether perceived as evolutionary, spiritual, factual or romantic, whether unilinear, cyclical or dialectical. In Hegel's work, and, as we shall see, in the work
of Marx too, there exists side by side a powerful statement of important human
realities, and a powerful and immanent mode of critique of the limitations built
into the work in question.

Thus we may accept Hegel's insight that the process of reproduction is dialectically structured. We also accept the proposition that human consciousness resists
alienation. We can then proceed to show that Hegel's analysis of the process is,
in important respects, simply wrong.

Let us take the important questions separately, and apply the perspective of
female reproductive consciousness to the male reproductive experience instead
of the other way round. First of all, there are questions relating to the "unity" of
the seeds and the nature of the successive separations which Hegel posits. Second,
there is a problem with the notion of the child "breaking free" into the world.
Third, there are unresolved ambiguities in Hegel's notion of the relation of the
continuity of the race, which I shall call "genetic continuity," and the actual
course of human history.

In terms of the separation and reunification by which human reproduction
proceeds, Hegel's errors stem from his failure to give proper consideration to the
generic differentiation in consciousness of reproductive process, and to a misrepresentation—and whether this is deliberate or merely misguided is really not
very important—to a misrepresentation of what actually happens. The "unity"
which Hegel posits, the unity of the previously differentiated seeds, is an abstract

unity. Hegel would not be upset by this charge, because for Hegel that which is biological and uncoloured by reason is by definition abstract. Nature, pre-rational old lady that she is, is, in historical terms, both impotent and abstract. However it is not by virtue of the nature of Nature that Hegel posits the unity of the male and female seeds as abstract. It is because, from the male perspective, the unity of the seeds is actually an abstract affair. Hegel simply fails to recognize that it is not as lover that man is negated, and that it is not in terms of sexuality that he is annulled. Man is negated not as lover but as *parent*, and this negation rests squarely on the alienation of the male seed in the copulative act. The unity of the seeds is quite objective, not abstract at all, but it is a unity and development which is experientially present in an immediate way only to female reproductive consciousness. It is hard to grasp, given the immense and visible parcel in which man-made history has packaged the idea of paternity, that paternity is in fact an abstract idea. It rests very specifically on theory, not unified immediately with practice. Paternity is the conceptualization of a cause and effect relationship, the relationship between copulation and childbirth, and even the idea of paternity must await the development of a certain level of human intellectual development before it can be discovered. Hegel appears to have been at least uneasy about his too facile analysis of the unities and oppositions within the dialectics of re-production. His original manuscript states that the child is the embodied unity of the separated parents. Later, he added the words, "The child is the parents themselves," but then scored them out and let the original formulation stand ("On Love"). He may have seen that the too total identification of child with parents rather spoilt the argument for the creation of a new tool of reason in the world which would develop autonomously, but be differentiated generically by something other than mere anatomy. We shall never know. What we do know is that Hegel did see the need to objectify paternity, to make particular fatherhood real rather than abstract, to transform the child as the product only of man in general, which *some man* has fathered, to a living and less ambiguous unity with one particular man which makes sense of patriarchy. The reality he actually chooses to transform the spirituality of sexual love to the reality of the lived marriage is not, finally, the child who is the transcendent but uncertain carrier of the paternal seed, but the more reliable bourgeois standby of family property.[8] To be sure, the child cannot embody the unity of the parents for ever, for it must grow and in turn become a parent and create a new family. Property passes from generation to generation, it is a principle of genetic continuity rendered in a tangible way. Yet, from a feminist standpoint, Hegel does rather seem to have abandoned, or "transcended," biological continuity on inadequate grounds. Why, we may ask, is this "embodied unity," represented by the child, not sufficiently concrete to realize the relationship of love between the man and the woman in the ordinary world? The answer, which Hegel does not clarify, is that the alienation of the seed cannot be cancelled in the act of love, but is a much more complex affair. "Between the conception and the creation," T. S. Eliot writes, "Falls the shadow." Male-stream thought has not analysed its shadows, perhaps, with sufficient rigour.

Clearly, the alienation of the seed is a masculine experience, but there is a female form of alienation, too. The male alienates the individual seed in copulation, but the woman alienates the unified and transformed form of the originally opposing seeds in the act of giving birth.

This leads us to the second difficulty with Hegel's analysis, the assertion that the child "breaks free" from impotent biology to arrive in the world clothed in dependence and the potential, if he is male, to partake of the universality of man. This notion of children falling from eternity into time, and from infinity into space, by virtue of some dynamic essence donated by the male seed is one of the most venerable of chauvinist chestnuts. From Aristotle's attribution of soul to the sperm to the melancholy "thrownness" which precipitates the Heideggerian existent into the world, children evidently arrive without any theoretically important assistance from their mothers, so that the mediative nature of labour and the formation of female reproductive consciousness remain unanalysed. In fact, of course, children are the products of labour. It is particularly interesting to find Hegel totally neglecting this consideration. It was Hegel, after all, who offered the profound and brilliant insight that labour is an active force in the mediation of man and the natural world, a mediation in which the labourer and the world are transformed in significant ways.[9] In labouring, man in a real sense creates a world of his own and a history for himself and his species. As far as this labour is productive labour, or the creative labours of the legislators, philosophers, theologians and poets, it is not in fact exclusively male activity, though it is mostly male activity which finds its way into the written records and ideologies of male supremacy. Hegel not only neglects women's participation in productive labour, but does not even recognize reproductive labour as a category of labour in general, requiring analysis and understanding. He evidently does not consider that reproductive labour has the creative and mediative powers which he finds even in slave labour. Hegel held the remarkable view that the only thing comparable to work in the reproductive process is copulation, for it is in "love" that the race is reproduced (1979: 429-31).[10] Historically, of course, the idea of copulation as work is one with which women have had, bitterly, to learn to live; but in prostitution it is the body which is the commodity. For Hegel, the product of the "work" of copulation is the child, and the real work, reproductive labour, finds no place in the analysis.

There is more here than mere neglect. Reproductive labour has a function which transcends the production of the infant, and is significant in understanding the generic differentiation of reproductive consciousness. The birth of the child is women's alienation of that unity to which men have no experiential access, but women's alienation from their seed is *mediated in labour*. Women do not, like men, have to take further action to annul their alienation from the race, for their labour confirms their integration. Not only does this fact differentiate male and female reproductive consciousness, it differentiates male and female temporal consciousness. The philosophers of history have shown little interest in this opposition of temporal modes of being, which is, after all, rather significant in any understanding of historical process. Female temporal consciousness is continuous, whereas male temporal consciousness is discontinuous. A central problem, and one to which we shall come back again and again, is the problem of continuity. History, even where it is perceived dialectically as struggle and change and eternal restlessness, is continuous, yet Hegel feels able to make the extraordinary claim in his later work that history has been completed. Hegel believed that his own achievement in comprehending the unity of reason and history had somehow signalled this completion of history. Despite this claim, however, history is indubitably a continuous process.

The nature of this continuity is for Hegel a complex relation of two opposing things: ideas on the one hand, and man's historical creations on the other, including the creation and control of property. Property is not recognized by Hegel as a symbol of continuity which men need and women do not, but simply as an instance of reason at work. Hegel was annoyed at the Romans for permitting women to hold property, for this sullied the purity of women's true work in the world, which has to do with individual survival and the mindless continuity of the generations. What all this means is that the family has among its functions the care for biological and emotional life via the activities of women, on the one hand; on the other hand, it protects the family's material wealth via the proprietorial activities of men. This latter task of conserving property cannot be done, however, by the family alone, and the scope of family responsibility is continually contracted. Property needs a civil society to make the laws of inheritance and proprietorship binding on all patriarchs. Men are forced out of the family situation into community, co-operation and friction with other men, for if the only relationship to an object which is possible is the relationship of control, there is clearly room for a lot of masculine struggle over property.

Hegel does not retreat to myths of primitive contracts to explain how this struggle is regulated. He transcends the limitations of contract theory by attempting to unify reason with history, rather than simply imposing reason on a not obviously rational reality. Here, he advances significantly from the limitations of the notion of process as progress which had been popular in the Enlightenment. Yet despite this, the elaboration of principles of continuity divorced from genetic continuity is important to Hegel, as it is to male-stream thought in general. Men have always sought principles of continuity outside of natural continuity. Historically there have been all kinds of such principles, some of which have attempted to subsume both biological continuity and political society, such as hereditary monarchy and primogeniture. There have been theories of continuity which have nothing to do with human reality at all, but cleave to a notion of eternity expressed in contemplative or religious terms. Politics has been a prime candidate as a principle of continuity in male historical praxis in the western tradition, ever since Plato and Aristotle defined the political community as the stabilizer of human relations. The political community is here when we are born and remains when we die. Certainly, it may change its spots once in a while, but the perceived need for stability over time and for regulation of both property relations and the social relations of reproduction all require a political-legal context which mere genetic continuity evidently could not provide.

Hegel's great achievement is to attempt to spell out the actual relation between opposing ideal and real aspects of continuity. History is continuity. The questions which interest us relate to men's need for principles of continuity, ideologies of continuity, and why they translate these principles into social realities which are shot through with the oppression of men by men and rest foursquarely on the greater and "naturally" justified oppression of women. Marxist class analysis offers a realistic account of the first of these, but says nothing about the second. We must ask again: What is *wrong* with genetic continuity as a necessary material base of history? Hegel gives hints that he knows the answer, but these are expressed in such recondite and abstract terms that it is difficult to be sure. For the answer is really not obscure. The fact is that men make principles of continuity because they are separated from genetic continuity with the alienation of the male seed. Genetic continuity constitutes one pole of the substructure of necessity which is the material condition of human history. Unlike the other pole—the necessity to produce—the reproductive pole resists male participation and control.

Hegel's view of reproduction is very valuable to a feminist analysis, though it is hardly the easiest way into the ramifications by which male-stream thought has elaborated the ideological justification of male supremacy. Yet even in this very preliminary and limited engagement with Hegel, a number of considerations emerge. Perhaps we should try to review them in an orderly way. First, we have from Hegel the discovery that the process of reproduction is structured in a dialectical way, though Hegel's insight does not stretch to the proposition that the process changes historically. This is because, for Hegel, all historical change is made real by reason, but he does not see rationality operating within merely organic process, and he does not discuss the real-life problems created for men by their alienation from genetic continuity. Second, we have from Hegel the beginnings of a method, the method of dialectical analysis, which shows promise of usefulness to feminist critique provided that its masculine limitations and internal contradictions can be transcended. Third, we have begun this process of immanent critique of Hegel by identifying, in a still crude way, realities of reproductive process which will bear further examination. Finally, we note that some of the problems which are emerging are related in a significant way to philosophical problems which are much older than Hegel, and which his system, so magnificently ambitious, cannot finally resolve. We have tentatively identified these as problems of alienation, of separation of man from nature and from continuous time. To make a bold preliminary generalization, they are problems of the *dualism* which is the persistent motif of male philosophy. Under this general category, we find a whole series of oppositions which haunt the male philosophical imagination: mind and body, subject and object, past and present, spirit and matter, individual and social, and so forth. Hegel was confident that his philosophical system could mediate these ancient antagonisms, and we are not especially concerned here with the quarrels which have emerged in discussions of whether or not he succeeded. What we must note is that the one dualism which Hegel himself finally failed to mediate successfully was the opposition of male and female.[11] We are entitled to wonder if the two are connected, if the masculine reproductive consciousness is not a possible basis for the dualistic preoccupation of male-stream thought.

The limitations of Hegel's vision also emerge from the fact that, despite his insistence on the objective reality of history, he cannot ultimately transcend the idealist tradition. This, of course, is the nitty-gritty of Marx's immanent critique of the Hegelian dialectics. Yet Marx's own insistence on a materialist interpretation of history does not produce a materialist view of the social relations of reproduction. Uncharacteristically, Marx applies to the history and prospects of women a different idealist abstraction, and one very popular in current social science. The condition of women becomes for Marx merely a *quantitative* indicator of how well men are progressing in their struggle towards a truly human history. This notion he takes from Proudhon, whose other quantitative fallacies he treats with vigorous and quite mordant blasts of criticism. We shall be discussing the significance and limitations of Marx's work for a feminist philosophy in a later chapter. Here, we are still concerned with questions of theory and method. It is disappointing to Marxist feminists that Marx's materialist viewpoint produces a less sophisticated understanding of reproduction than that which Hegel offers. None the less, this analysis of reproductive process accepts Marx's view of a dialectical logic of necessity grounded in material process as essentially correct. What is argued is that necessity has two poles, two appetites, two processes with which to deal. Marx tells us that human consciousness develops dialectically because it reflects the primordial experience of people in their productive existence in the world, and the *process* of labour is dialectically structured. The labour process is a dialectical process (Marx 1867: Vol. I, Pt. III, Ch. VII, Section I). This is true, but it is also true that reproductive process is formally dialectical, and it is argued that at a very primordial level the operation of these two processes determines the mode of operation of human consciousness. Yet the poles themselves are in an opposition to one another, an opposition whose mediation cannot be left to the workings of subjective consciousness, but must be worked out in terms of real live people living a conscious life in a world which they continuously transform. At a very practical level, there can be real and often devastating tension between the level of subsistence and the numbers of mouths to feed. This situation is the root of Malthusian pessimism, against which Marx argues the possibility of rational regulation of productivity. The possibility of rational control of reproductivity was not an idea which either Malthus or Marx could seriously entertain. Today, of course we can, although the notion is still new enough to present a utopian face. None the less, even the possibility of rational and harmonizing human control of both poles of necessity is a pretty mind-blowing affair. However long and difficult the route to such a state of affairs may be, it cannot be dismissed as mere romance.

The opposition of production and reproduction is not, in any case, a merely quantitative calculation, but has more complex ramifications. Productive labour is common to all people, for all individuals can produce, even though all are not identically productive. Productive labour is in this sense a universal. Antagonisms between producers are created historically by the division of labour, in which the universality of labour is obscured by the opposition between those who labour and those who do not. Marx does not think that what he calls the "natural," genderic division of labour gives rise to this kind of opposition. This is because he does not perceive the possibility of a change in the process of reproduction, which is assumed to be wholly biological and indifferent to conscious comprehension of its workings. Reproductive relations do change historically, in Marx's view, but only as reflections of a change in productive relations. The fact that as material process, biological reproduction necessarily also sets up an opposition between those who labour reproductively (women) and those who do not (men), does not command Marx's attention. None the less, the alienation of the male seed does in fact set up a series of real oppositions in social terms. Standing opposed to each other are:

1) The man and the child, who may or may not be his;
2) The woman who labours to bring forth her child and the man who does not labour;
3) The man who is separated from biological continuity, and the women whose integration with natural process and genetic time is affirmed in reproductive labour;
4) Following from 1, individual man and all other possible potencies, men in general.

Maternal reproductive consciousness is a unity of consciousness and involuntary labour which is, of course, quite different from the unity of head and hand which makes productive labour creative and permits a multiplication and diversification of products, but maternal labour does confirm for women the conception of the child as *her* child. Fathers do not labour and do not have this certainty; paternity is a unity of thought (specifically the knowledge of the relation between sexuality and childbirth) and action. The action in which men commonly annul the alienation of their seed is that action which is described here as the "appropriation of the child."

In his analysis of the dialectics of labour process, Marx offered his useful and celebrated parable of the architect and the bee: "what distinguishes the worst architect from the best of bees is this, that the architect raises his structure in his imagination" (1867: 198). What the architect is clearly doing is objectifying a concept, making real that which is currently still ideal. He is also, incidentally, drawing attention to the status of ideas in Marx's work which he does not often make quite so explicit, and which so many of his putative disciples have chosen to ignore. The architect is, himself, a historical "product," but he is not merely a predetermined actor in a predetermined social drama. He functions by unifying the work of head and hand, though doubtless a few bricklayers will be needed before the structure opens its doors. These men too, however, will know what they are doing. Marx's metaphor helps us to understand something of the distinction between productive labour, which is the process he is describing, and reproductive process, about which he has nothing to say. The processes are similar in form, though quite different in content. In its "pure" form, as described by Marx, productive labour is the act of an individual. To comprehend a self and a world and a task to be done, to work out the way to do it, to act upon this determination, to make something and know that one has made it, to "reproduce" oneself daily by means of the labour process; all of this is the unity of thinking and doing, the fundamental praxis of production which is embedded in socio-historical modes of production. Reproduction is quite different. What has generally been argued or implied is that biological reproduction differs in that it is not an act of rational will. No one denies a motherly imagination, which foresees the child in a variety of ways. Women have their visions of the child to be born; visions, perhaps, of its beauty and its intellectual brilliance, its sex and its moral worth. The vision may also be less idyllic. In Scotland, there is an old phrase still used by women who are asked the usual question about whether they want a boy or a girl. "As long as it's like the world" is the traditional answer, which reflects the dread of deformity or mental incapacity. Maternal imagination may also be fraught with anxiety about another mouth to feed, another dependence to bear. In other words, female reproductive consciousness knows that a child will be born, knows what a child is, and speculates in general terms about this child's potential. Yet mother and architect are quite different. The woman cannot realize her visions, cannot make them come true, by virtue of the reproductive labour in which she involuntarily engages, if at all. Unlike the architect, her will does not influence the shape of her product. Unlike the bee, she knows that her product, like herself, will have a history. Like the architect, she knows what she is doing; like the bee, she cannot help what she is doing.

These differentiations are real, but they are not so important as the formal similarities in the two processes. Both processes are dialectical, and the modes of understanding which grasp them are dialectically structured. Our friend Hegel went to tremendous and often obscure lengths to demonstrate that the structure of human consciousness itself, and the process of thinking, are dialectically structured. This is because mind and world are in some sense opposed, that the thinking subject stands apart from the object of perception and of thought. Hegel argues that the gap between the self and world is mediated by an objectified ideal unity of reason and action, while Marx argues for a lived, experiential unity of action and theory. The structure of consciousness is in any case dialectical because it reflects upon a being in the world which is dialectically structured. We want to extend and reinforce the theory that human consciousness is dialectical by arguing that the most primordial of human experiences are dialectically structured, but that there are two of them, the reproduction of the self and the reproduction of the race, which stand in opposition to one another.

Let us think back from the need to produce to the hunger which produced the need, and consider the process of digestion, and how it is experienced. This particular process is not usually used in an exemplary way, for as a "product," human excrement is not regarded as a higher stage of anything, nor as a suitable object of philosophy. The honourable exception is Freud. In his theories of infant development, Freud assumed the presence of alimentary and sexual hungers in all subjects, but the great fuss over his theories of polymorphous infantile sexuality and the emotional satisfactions of defecation has obscured an important truth. From our own digestive processes, we are conscious of a basic structure of process, our own participation in the opposition of externality and internality, and of the unification and transformation of objects.

People did not perish from the earth, however, as they sat in mute contemplation of their stool, and human history has surged somehow from scatology to eschatology. All that is argued here is that human consciousness apprehends the living body primordially as a medium of the opposition of internality and externality, of mediation, of negation and of qualitative transformation. Negation is rather a fancy word for the disappearance of an apple into the alimentary tract, but none the less that is what happens to the apple. It is negated and transformed. When Marx argues that production and consumption are inseparable, he is enunciating not an economic dogma but an epistemological truth. Human consciousness *is* structured dialectically because the most basic human experiences are structured dialectically. In his analysis of labour process, however, Marx analyses the product of production and simply neglects the product of consumption. For Marx, the product of consumption is not the excretory product of mere digestion; the product of consumption is the *reproduction* of the life of the individual. We all understand in a common-sense and relatively uncritical way this relation of life and livelihood, of "making a living," which is what Marx means by the reproductive aspect of producing. At an immediate level, however, we also understand the dialectical structure of our biological functions, but Marx does not analyse these. Whether this was a question of delicacy or not we cannot say; iconoclast though he was, Marx never freed himself entirely from the fetters of Victorian notions of respectability. Probably too, Marx, like Hegel, perceived organic functions as resistant to the operations of the free and rational human will, and therefore not true instances of human praxis. Marx and Hegel are not interested in immediate experience, but in mediated experience, though they did not consider the mediations involved in paternity. Further, though digestive metabolism is, as it were, experienced dialectics in a formal sense, it is not the creation of value, and Marx's definition of labour is that labour is the production of value. Freud, on the other hand, insists that the product of metabolism is a value for infants. Neither of them argues that a child itself is a value produced by reproductive labour.

The value created by productive labour is for Marx twofold. There is, of course, the value of the product, but there is also the value of sociability. Marx's abstract formulation of the labour process never loses sight of the social nature of labour. The need to produce sets up definable sets of social relations. This is, of course, historically true, but is not true in the pure case. If we were able to abstract any individual from the social world and dump her into the natural world, the possibility of personal survival would not automatically disappear; the individual could, like all those legendary castaways on desert islands, survive in a biological sense, could "reproduce" her organism. Likewise, if we visualize primeval man ranging in the fecund forest, his personal survival by his own efforts is not impossible. In the most primordial and abstract sense, "reproduction" in Marx's sense—the daily reproduction of oneself—is *not necessarily social.* It becomes social historically. Reproduction in the biological sense, however, is necessarily social from any perspective, practical or abstract. The arch wisdom of the baby congratulation card is correct: One plus one equals three. This has not, of course, stopped men making myths of self-regenerating creatures. Yet the more common male arguments as to the essential sociability of mankind are rarely grounded in the essential integrative sociability of reproductive process.[12] Men are awarded some "essence" of sociability by idealist philosophers, usually related to human nature theories or God's will. Marx's materialism grounds sociability in the historical development of productive relations. A feminist philosophy of birth must ground sociability and the ethics of integration where they belong: in the essentially social process of reproduction.

Freud, after his impressive insight into the relation of the structure of individual consciousness and alimentary dialectics, turns his attention less successfully to the question of the childhood of the race (182-207). He wants to argue that psychic structure is a response to both individual and collective experience, and he looks rather yearningly on the romantic notion of some kind of subconscious ancestral memory. Freud's primitive man is, as it were, an adult child and, being romantic, he not only disregards productive activity, but has no reproductive consciousness either.[13] He is concerned with his sexuality, a sexuality related to reproduction only in a regressive way: this man is preoccupied with his parents and his brothers, the existing kin, and thinks not one whit of his own progeny. The significance of male/female opposition is seen by Freud to rest on sexual antagonisms between men, rather than in reproductive relations. The truth is, of course, that reproductive activity is generically differentiated, while sexuality as such is not. Sexuality, like digestion, is a biological universal. Men and women are sexual creatures, and libido is not the prerogative of the male. Freud's error in separating primitive sexuality from reproductive process is magnificent in scale, and is only possible because it has an objective base: the process of reproduction does impose a temporal gap between sexuality and parturition for men, and it also separates men from all stages of the process except copulation. It is thus from the standpoint of separated sexuality rather than integrated birth that Freud launches humanity on to the guilty tides of history. He offers us a group of primitive brothers eager to appropriate their mother as sex-object, the apparent absence of other women being not actual and historical but psychological and Oedipal. Female sexuality remains insignificant in this creation drama, as does reproduction. The brothers are constrained to kill one source of life, their father, while the mother lives on.

With a sensitivity remarkable under the circumstances, the brothers are ashamed of their lust and their patricide. Freud even suggests that out of this sense of guilt they not only renounced the sexual favours which their patricide was intended to ensure, but also bestowed upon their mother, presumably as compensation, the "mother right discovered by Bachofen" (Freud 186). This was a temporary aberration, however. Once they had sublimated their guilt, men assumed their natural position of superiority and sexual entrepreneurship.

Freud's creation myth is wrong because he posits a primordial opposition in sexuality—passive woman versus active man—while he neglects the real generic oppositions in reproductive process. He offers us a sexual myth which is myth precisely because it separates sexuality from reproduction. It is, however, a persuasive myth in the masculine mind, because the process of reproduction actually does separate *male* sexuality from reproduction, in the alienation of the male seed. Freud's myth, like all masculine creation myths, defies the dialectical significance of the uncertainty of paternity.

Marx, on the other hand, finds at the dawn of human history a happy primitive man, guiltlessly and satisfyingly discovering his unity with people and nature in productive activity, and, in the dialectical process of need⇨ labour⇨production ⇨consumption, changing the world, himself and his social relations. This man appears to be untroubled by sexual yearnings: his problem is his species continuity. Marx's man is related to his forefathers, not biologically, but in terms of his status as heir to the tools of his ancestors. How is this affirmed? Because, says Marx, the simplest observation of the instruments of production, of tools, shows the labour of past ages (1867: 199). Perhaps so: but past ages are not then apprehended in action but in passive observation, and it is difficult to see how these artifacts advertise their human content immediately. Women do not apprehend the reality of past ages in a meditation on the probable history of a hammer, but in the mediation of real labour. This fact is not discussed by Marx. What he wants to do is to show that human continuity is a continuity of labour, the labour of ancestors congealed in the means of reproduction. This is important, for it abolishes the notion that the appropriation of the means of production can ever be understood as a fair and rational exchange, for there can be no rational commerce with the dead. Marx needs a continuity which is both material and historical, and his single productive individual is integrated in productive activity with a universal class of heirs and successors for whom the presence of ancestors is made manifest in tools. Living children cannot be recognized as the guarantors of the reality of the dead within this framework, for there is no dead productive labour power congealed in their living persons. The fact that there is reproductive labour power congealed in every living or dead person presumably does not count. Marx is not wrong about these tools as evidence of past generations: the question that feminist consciousness asks relates to the one-sidedness of the analysis.

The task of reconciling the contributions of Marx and Freud to human understanding is a major intellectual problem of our times, and one which many feminists see as crucial. Freud tells us a great deal about the repressive conditions of the bourgeois form of family; Marx extends our knowledge of the problem of oppression in general. None the less, the theories as they are handed down to us are both one-sided. Freud is insensitive to the importance of both production and reproduction, leaning heavily upon an autonomously determinant libido. Marx conflates production and reproduction, analyses productive labour only, and thus reduces the awareness of species continuity to an economist construction.

Hegel, Marx and Freud contribute to understanding of reproductive process in both negative and positive ways. Negatively, the question is largely one of omission. Hegel does not grasp the sense in which paternity is in fact an idea, precisely because he does not see that man is negated, not as lover, but as parent. This is the nullity which men clearly "cannot bear," and history demonstrates the lengths to which men have gone to ameliorate the uncertainty of paternity, both conceptually and institutionally. Marx, prodigious though his humanity indubitably is, analyses "value" in a way which has nothing to say about the human value which inheres in the "product" of reproductive labour, the value of the individual therefore tends to disappear in the collectivity of class. Freud becomes a little confused in his attempts to draw a parallel between the infancy of the individual and the infancy of the race. Having shrewdly perceived the importance of both of the biologically immediate experiences of digestion and sexuality for the infant, he analyses the childhood of the race only in terms of sexuality, not considering that adults must somewhere and at some time have comprehended both digestive and reproductive process as *discovery*. The discovery of reproductive dialectics is likely to have been historically later, in that it is neither individual nor immediate, and cannot be understood as dialectical process without the discovery of the causal relation of impregnation and birth. This requires an advanced stage of the development of human mental capacity.

The failure to take reproduction seriously in theoretical terms is not a failure only of these three particular men. Later on, we shall look at the way in which other thinkers, including some feminist ones, have tended to regard reproductive process as something prior and irrelevant to the more interesting questions of the history of the family, the ethics of parenthood or the processes of child development, to name but a few aspects of the social relations of reproduction which have been treated in serious and scholarly ways. The general neglect of reproductive process is itself a historical phenomenon of great interest. It is simply not good enough to dismiss people like Hegel, Marx, Freud and their philosophical predecessors as male supremacists whose vision was distorted by mere prejudice. As we have argued, it is only at a certain stage of development that the significance of the process of reproduction, as the grounds of specific sets of social relations, can be grasped in a theoretical way. Thus, the omissions in the work of these and other social thinkers challenge us to enquire into their roots. The development of a sophisticated technology of contraception, which transforms reproductive process, changes the historical situation in a way which demands such an enquiry from a specifically feminist perspective. This, of course, was something which male-stream thought could not and cannot do, so that the inevitability of male supremacy barely and only rarely bothered even to justify itself, and even less often turned a critical perspective on its reproductive consciousness. The few male critics of male supremacy, of whom Marx is one and John Stuart Mill another, were not able to mount their critiques on solid theoretical grounds. Marx and Engels are trapped in economic history. Mill falls back on the twin notions of superior male physical strength and defective masculine moral sense to explain and condemn the oppression of women.

Our feminist perspective is a material perspective, in that it attempts to root this long oppression in material biological process, rather than in mute, brute biology. For this reason, we have begun with some discussion of the nature and form of process as such, and have argued that the process of human understanding is indeed, as Hegel and Marx argued, dialectical. We have further argued that the dialectical structure of forms of consciousness is rooted in the dialectical structure of the primordial biological experience of our lived bodies, in that both digestive process and reproductive process are dialectically structures: they are instances of separation, unification and transformation. Likewise, the necessary human processes which these fundamental needs entail—which are the act of producing, in the case of the provision of sustenance, and the birth and care of infants, in the case of reproduction—are also dialectically structured. This dialectical form is carried into the social relations which emerge from the primal processes, social relations constituted by human praxis. The dialectics of productive experience and productive relations have been analysed and comprehended in an enlightening theoretical way in the work of Hegel and Marx. Reproductive dialectics and reproductive consciousness have not been subjected to such rigorous treatment. The dialectical model is useful for this purpose, but it must undergo considerable modification. Reproductive experience is not differentiated by the division of labour and subsequent social class formations, which is the historical form of development of production. Reproductive experience is differentiated at its most fundamental level in terms of gender: the opposition in question is the male/female opposition. This relation also becomes historically one of dominance and subordination, a relation which has developed for itself a lived reality, a powerful ideology and a determinable psychology. Male supremacy is not wholly material, wholly ideal or wholly psychological, but has aspects of all of these. This we saw even in our brief discussion of Hegel the idealist, Marx the materialist and Freud the psychoanalyst. What we must now do is to gather these partial gleanings and the immanent critique which has begun to develop into a more systematic expression. If, as is claimed, the biological process of reproduction and the human reproductive consciousness which emerge from it are dialectically structured, we must attempt a dialectical analysis of that process. As it has also been argued that the process changes historically, then we must also state which historical form of the process is under consideration. What follows is a consideration of that form of reproductive process which falls between the discovery of physiological paternity and the development of mass contraceptive technology, which is, of course, the form which has prevailed throughout most of recorded history.

The Dialectics of Reproduction

As a young student midwife, I learned about the stages of gestation and the stages of labour. This was a description of a unilinear process, starting at conception and finishing with the satisfactory establishment of lactation. In Canada, as in the United States, there are no midwives, and obstetrics is a branch of nursing, a development against which British midwives fought hard and unsuccessfully in the nineteenth century.[14] However, the texts available in obstetrical nursing still conform to the descriptive unilinear format.[15] They do not discuss questions of reproductive consciousness. We find discussions of the empirical signs by which pregnancy can be detected. There will usually be a chapter on the psychological stresses of pregnancy, and a chapter on the social aspects of childcare, and social support services available to mothers. There may even be a couple of sentences about fathers, but there will be no discussion at all of the formal problematic of paternity, nor of the significance of patriarchy.[16] We may even find some theoretical work, theories of technique and physiological theory, but a theory of birth as such and the language of traditional philosophy will not intrude upon these practical treatises. Hegel's observation that the unity of the male and female seeds is at the same time the negation of the particularity of each seed would seem like a hopelessly obscure way of expressing a quite straightforward natural mechanism. Finally, the crucial differentiations in male and female reproductive experience are not particularly significant in terms of descriptive anatomy and physiology. What happens in textbooks, in fact, is much closer formally to what happens in male reproductive experience, despite the fact that the texts are indubitably dealing with an actual female experience and the books referred to here are intended for the predominantly female group of student nurses. What we find is that the whole process of reproduction is separated in an arbitrary way from the historical, experiential reality of generic relationships, of species continuity and of the social relations of reproduction. It becomes abstract process, just as paternity is essentially abstract process. This is not surprising. Modern obstetrics, as opposed to ancient midwifery, has been a male enterprise.[17] Men have brought to obstetrics the sense of their own alienated parental experience of reproduction, and have translated this into the forms and languages of an "objective" science. Thus, the process appears as a neat unilinear affair going on in women's bodies in a rather mechanistic way. We do not claim that this is wrong or useless: we claim that it is not enough. We learn nothing from descriptive obstetrics which can further our knowledge of the dialectics of reproductive experience and reproductive consciousness, and we learn very little of the social relations of reproduction. We have therefore to identify the significant aspects of reproductive process in a way which can deal with the ambivalences gleaned from our preliminary meditation on masculine thought, as well as the inadequacies of the naturalistic descriptive approach to reproductive process.

Immediately, we have a problem with vocabulary. Physiological description moves from well-marked stage to well-marked stage in a unilinear time sequence:

ovulation, conception, pregnancy, labour. We shall have to use a different language of process for a dialectical analysis. It is proposed that we start by referring to the identifiable and important points in reproductive process as "moments." Marx says sarcastically that this terminology has little value except to make things clear to the Germans, which is a crack at Hegelians (Marx and Engels, *The German Ideology* 18). However, the word is useful if its usage is explicated carefully. The moments in question are not ticks on a clock, nor are they moments in the idealist sense of abstracted instants in the flow of subjective consciousness. What we want to catch is the sense of determining, active factors which operate in a related way at both the biological and conceptual levels. We also want to capture the sense of a non-isolated *event in time,* a happening which unifies the sense of the two words "momentous" and "momentary." The moments in question have nothing at all to do with stop-watches, X-rays or microscopes. The terminology is intended to evade both empirical inertia and biological determinism. This cannot be done without semantic juggling, but it cannot be rendered intelligible without language either. We can start by making a simple taxonomy of reproductive moments, but we must go on to elaborate the way in which they differ from "stages" of reproductive process, the ways in which they interact; and we must also develop a theoretical framework for the analysis of the social relations which, it is claimed, constitute a historical superstructure in which the contradictions within and between these moments are worked out.

First, then, a simple statement of the moments of reproductive process:

> The moment of menstruation
> The moment of ovulation
> The moment of copulation
> The moment of alienation
> The moment of conception
> The moment of gestation
> The moment of labour
> The moment of birth
> The moment of appropriation
> The moment of nurture.

Immediately, we see that there are important differences in these moments. Most, for example, are involuntary: appropriation and nurture are the only completely voluntary moments. Copulation is a halfway house: it has a strong instinctual component, but a great deal of human effort has been invested historically in demonstrating that it can or at least ought to be controlled by the human will. Alienation and appropriation are male moments: copulation and nurture are genderically shared moments; all of the others are women's moments. Yet these latter are differentiated too. Ovulation and conception are not tangible moments; they are not only involuntary, but are not immediately apprehended by consciousness. We therefore have quite a complex process going on, in terms of several factors quite outside the realm of simple biology. When we speak of voluntary and involuntary moments, we have entered the realm of the human will. When we speak of copulation and nurture, we speak of social relations. When we speak of appropriation, we speak of a relationship of dominance and control. Clearly, there is much more to reproduction than meets a narrow physiological eye.

However, not all of these moments are of equal interest to our analysis. Menstruation, for example, might be called a negative moment: it signifies its importance to reproductive process by not happening. Further, it shares with many of these moments a great big burden of accumulated symbolism and sheer superstition. Later on in our discussion we shall look at some of the bizarre ideological currents which have been introduced into the bloody flux of femininity, which seems to have fairly consistently frightened men out of their wits. Scientific understanding of the menstrual cycle was relatively late in developing, and Aristotle's deductions about the role of menstruation in reproduction are marvelous instances of the strength and weakness of formal logic; impeccably structured, they are quite untrue.[18] Aristotle appears to have believed that, as the blood disappeared with pregnancy, it must be needed for the manufacture of the child, and one can admire the ingenuity of that speculation. It may well have been commonly held in antiquity, and is perhaps part of the linguistic development which understands kin as "blood" relations. Aristotle's further deduction that women contribute nothing to the child but this arrested menstrual flow has more to do with ideological patriarchy than it has to do with logical speculation, but this idea that women contribute only "material" to babies while men contribute spirit or soul or some other human "essence" must have struck chords in the masculine imagination, for it lingered for centuries. It is worth noting here to reinforce the contention that men do indeed attempt to resist the alienation of their seed, in this instance by claiming superior procreative potential for a sanctified sperm. Against this contention, it might be argued, quite persuasively, that men are quite indifferent to the uncertainty of paternity and, indeed, have very often been reluctant husbands who might well prefer to exploit that uncertainty to evade the responsibilities which male history has decreed for paternity. There can be no doubt that this sort of evasion has happened in particular cases, but far more powerful has been men's collective and concentrated attention to the problem of male separation from reproduction, both in their development of human institutions and in their articulation of ideologies of male supremacy. To suggest that men in general are indifferent to paternity is to make nonsense of centuries of strenuous masculine activity to negate the uncertainty of fatherhood, activity of which the institution of marriage is only the most obvious example.

The fact that menstruation seems to have inspired men to derogatory efforts in myth, magic and mania, despite the involuntary and wholly female nature of menstruation, is probably at least partly due to the visibility of menstruation. Such moments of reproduction as ovulation and conception are also involuntary, but being neither visible nor understood for a very long stretch of history, they have not excited quite such extravagant symbolism. As early as classical times, the notion of conception had already passed from any notion of unification, if such a notion ever did exist, to the notion of the domination of the male seed. This clearly has significant aspects for the understanding of the nature of man's perception of his role in copulation, and is part of the structure of what became known as male *potency*. However, we cannot simply say that men "naturally" understood copulation not only as pleasurable, but as an exercise in domination and perhaps even priestly or political duty.[19] Pleasurability is an immediate property of copulation, whereas dominance and superiority are not. The notion of potency requires historical development; it is a complex concept, which goes far beyond the mere capacity to impregnate. Potency is a masculine triumph over men's natural alienation from the process of reproduction, a triumph to whose dimensions and historical manifestations we shall have to return. Potency is the name men have given to their historically wrought success in mediating experienced contradictions in their reproductive consciousness.

The involuntary mechanics, then, of ovulation and conception remain abstract in terms of male reproductive consciousness, while masculine science and speculation orders their structure according to masculine needs. The gestation period is also involuntary, although it has always been possible to terminate pregnancy with varying degrees of feminine suffering, up to and including the deaths of mothers, children or both. Pregnancy is clearly significant in terms of women's understanding of their reproductive capacity. It also has visible manifestations, a fact which can bring pride or shame to women in societies where patriarchal values prevail. The most rigorous feminist theorizing must swerve away from the path of detached analysis when it contemplates the anguish in which millions of women through the ages have concealed and terminated pregnancy. This is one reason why we must develop different modes of understanding and expression of female experience. Objectivity is a fraud if it rejects sisterhood as wishful sentiment, or spurns the understanding of the unifying reality of transhistorical female suffering as romantic subjectivity. The point is important not only humanistically but theoretically. The female reproductive consciousness whose historical reality we are attempting to establish is a universal consciousness, common to all women. We are not at all engaged in a psychology of pregnancy, or in the subjective experience of one man who parts with his seed and one woman whose femininity involuntary creates and gives birth to one or more children. Pregnancy is the positive pole, as it were, of the negative pole of menstruation. These are the visible and communally understood signs of female potency, of the unity of potential and actual. All women carry the consciousness of this unity, just as all women carry the notion of suffering and labour and decisions to be made. Women do not need to bear children to know themselves as women, for women's reproductive consciousness is culturally transmitted. It is a tribute to the indelibility of male-stream thought that we should have to make this point. Man knows himself as some kind of universal being with all kinds of shades of power and promises of immortality which particular men do not and cannot demonstrate. Man as universal may indeed be rational and noble and creative, but in the particular man these qualities are quite often as invisible as ovulation or conception. It is precisely this capacity to posit himself as universal, to assert a brotherhood of man, which has permitted men to make the history of man. The historical isolation of women from each other, the whole language of female internality and privacy, the exclusion of women from the creation of a political community: all of these have obscured the cultural cohesiveness of femininity and the universality of maternal consciousness. Menstruation and pregnancy have been at times "decorously" shrouded, at other times bravely waved as the flag of the potent male. Breasts have been sometimes flaunted, sometimes flattened, understood as sensual tit-bits rather than as purposeful instruments of nurture. All the while, men have fashioned their world with a multiplicity of phallic symbols which even Freud could not catalogue exhaustively.

These involuntary, feminine moments of reproductive experience are symbolically important in the development of female universality, so that we do not simply ignore them in our elaboration of the dialectics of reproduction. They represent, as it were, "pure" opposition between male and female, an abstract and formal opposition which cannot be resolved. They are the biological manifestations of the material oppositions of female and male which must be worked out in a sociohistorical way by real, live men and women. Menstruation, ovulation and pregnancy represent the integrative potency of all women, which may terrify men, but the history of male supremacy is a great deal more than male psychological response to ignorance, terror and envy of the womb. The history of male supremacy is the history of the real domination of women, and to understand man's power to proclaim the triumph and universality of his potency over her organic and particular potency we must move on to the analysis of the more complex moments of reproductive process. We shall have to deal in a rather artificial sequence with the four moments which our taxonomy has isolated from each other, but which are in fact related in a dynamic and dialectical way. These are the moments of alienation, appropriation, nurture and labour. This alteration of sequence is deliberate. Alienation and appropriation are the male pole of a process to which female labour stands as the opposite: this is an opposition of separation and integration, but that abstract statement needs to be explained, and will be. Nurture, the sharing of responsibility for dependent infants between men and women, is the synthesis of the male/female opposition in social terms, which in turn creates a new opposition, the opposition of public and private life. This, too, is an abstract formulation to which we must give human and historical content. Perhaps we can come to grips with these complex moments of reproduction if we examine them separately, and then analyse their relationships.

Much has already been said about the alienation of the male seed in the act of ejaculation. Perhaps we should make it clear once more that we are not speaking here about some kind of psychological process, a sense of loss or something like that. Alienation is not a neurosis, but a technical term describing separation and the consciousness of negativity. We have criticized Freud for his reduction of reproductive consciousness to anxiety neurosis, but we do not, of course, deny that there are important psychological dimensions to reproductive experience. Our interest, though, which we have derived from Hegel in a way which neither he nor his followers would like very much, is in a more fundamental view of the nature of human consciousness and the form of process of that consciousness. Consciousness, we have argued, resists alienation, the separation of the thinking subject from the world and from experience of the world and the negation of the self. It is in this sense that we speak of the alienation of the seed. Men experience themselves as alienated from reproductive process, and the questions we have to ask are these: What exactly are men alienated from? What do men do about it?

Fortunately, we do not have simply to guess at the answers. They are written in the history of patriarchy and in the philosophies developed by male-stream thought. We shall be looking at some of this evidence presently, but here let us state possible answers in a way which catches the fundamental dialectical sense of separation and opposition.

First, we note that men's (or women's) discovery of physiological paternity is the discovery *at the same time* of men's inclusion in and exclusion from natural reproductive process. This opposition of inclusion and exclusion must be mediated by praxis.

Second, men's discovery of physiological paternity is the discovery of freedom. Men are free in both the senses of freedom which liberal thought has developed: there are positive and negative aspects of paternal freedom, freedom *from* and freedom *to*. Men are aware of parenthood but free from reproductive labour. They are also free to choose paternity, or, as they have liked to put it, to "acknowledge" the child as theirs. Yet, to borrow a famous phrase from Rousseau, men are "forced to be free." This is a further contradiction, for, of course, to be forced to be free is to render that freedom problematic.

Third, men are separated by the alienation of the seed from continuity over time. There is no tangible, experiential link between generations, no mediation of the time gap as women experience in the act of reproductive labour. Men are isolated in their individual historicity, the dimensions of their own lifespan. The notion of man as a historical creature has been a very important component of male philosophical activity since Giambattista Vico first articulated the theory that history constitutes what men can "hope to know" (quoted in Gardner 14), for men have created history. The notion of man as a historical being is also, of course, a fundamental postulate of both Hegel's and Marx's social theory, to say nothing of Heidegger's powerful ontological assertion that Being *is* Time. Yet man's relationship to history, to continuity over time, is fundamentally problematic. At the primordial level of genetic continuity, of the continuity of the species, men are separated from natural continuity. Male reproductive consciousness is a consciousness of discontinuity. Underlying the doctrine that man makes history is the undiscussed reality of why he must. The alienation of his seed separates him from natural genetic continuity, which he therefore knows only as idea. To give this idea substance, man needs praxis, a way of unifying what he knows as real with an actual worldly reality. Men must therefore make, and have made, artificial modes of continuity.

The significance of the alienation of the male seed, then, lies in resultant forms of male reproductive consciousness. This is a consciousness of contradiction, a series of oppositions which must be *mediated.* Men are separated from nature, from the race and from the continuity of the race over time. This brings us to the second question: What do men do about it? More properly, perhaps, the question should be framed in the past tense and in a collective way: What has man done about it?

Over against the alienation of the seed we find posed, in the first instance, the moment of appropriation of the child, the almost universal mode of paternal mediation. Paternity is a universal phenomenon, though, unlike maternity, it takes versatile forms, as the anthropologists have shown us.[20] The appropriation of the child defies the uncertainty of paternity, yet it cannot do so in biological terms. It must do so in social and ideological terms. Unlike maternity, which is fundamentally social in so far as it involves at the very least the dyad of mother and child, paternity becomes social historically. The appropriation of the child cannot be made without the co-operation of other men. This is, in the first instance, because of the true "universality" of paternity: some man, any man, has fathered this child. The assertion of one man's right to a particular child has to include some means of excluding all possible fathers from this relationship. There are several possible ways of doing this, which include:

1) Relations of trust between men and women;
2) Relations of trust between men;
3) The limitation of physical access to women;
4) The definition of paternity in a non-biological way: e.g. as related to the social role of husband.

Historically, all of these can be found in developed relations of reproduction, but two factors militate against the first. One is the strength of the sexual impulse in both men and women: trust and lust make uneasy bedfellows, and there is little evidence to support a view that humans are "naturally" monogamous. In the second place, the relation of men and women within reproductive relations is a relation of the free and the unfree, the non-labourer and the labourer. Relations between men have an objectively causal base: they are relations of those who are forced to be free, a *brotherhood* of free appropriators. At the same time, they are rivals, and the guaranteeing of paternity forces cooperative agreements between men in relation to access to "their" women.

Paternity, then, is not a natural relationship to a child, but a right to a child. "Right," of course, is a political concept, which makes no sense in anything other than a socio-legal-political context. The assertion of right demands a social support system predicated on forced cooperation between men forced to be free. It is the historical movement to provide this support system which transforms the individual uncertainties of paternity into the triumphant universality of patriarchy.

This is also the point at which the notion of potency expands far beyond a merely sexual connotation. The creation of a patriarchate is, in every sense of the phrase, a triumph over nature. The notion of man as nature's master is often regarded a product of the modern age and the development of science. This is too limited a view. Men did not suddenly discover in the sixteenth century that they might make a historical project out of the mastery of nature. They have understood their separation from nature and their need to mediate this separation ever since that moment in dark prehistory when the idea of paternity took hold in the human mind. Patriarchy is the power to transcend natural realities with historical, man-made realities. This is the potency principle in its primordial form. It simply is not an accidental fact that politics has been generally understood as an exercise in power. We cannot say categorically that paternity was the first historical development of the concept of right. We cannot say categorically that man's discovery of the problematic freedom embedded in his reproductive experience was his first notion of the concept of freedom. We cannot say categorically that the discovery of the ability to rearrange nature's more problematic strictures was man's first taste of potency and power. What we can say is that, if these things are true, then the history of patriarchy makes a great deal more sense than it otherwise can. Men have resolved their separation from nature in a new integration which at the same time conserves their "natural" freedom. This has been a very tricky business, for at its heart there remains the reality of alienation and exclusion which is the soft core of the potency principle.

The question of a right to appropriate children does not exist in an inert theoretical vacuum, nor is it without its own tensions. It is the translation of this right to real social relations and the internal stresses inherent in reproductive process which both relate and divide male and female reproductive consciousness. This complexity leads us directly to consideration of the moments of nurture and of parturitive labour.

As a political concept, and as a major concern of political theory, right has usually been posited as one side of a coin of which the other side is the doctrine of responsibility. This relationship is by no means so consistent in terms of actual experience, for the assertion of right without responsibility is the hallmark of naked power, a phenomenon not entirely unknown in human history. The old question of the relation of right and responsibility has always exercised liberal theorists, who have historically sweated over the fine distinctions between liberty and license, to say nothing of the tangled problems of the dichotomy of responsibility and free will. Despite these difficulties, "right" by itself remains an abstract concept which has to be given a manifest presence in the world, an appearance which is recognizable. This can be done in symbolic terms, and has been done in this way, from the trappings of monarchy and the X on the ballot to the certificates which proclaim the right of obstetricians to exclusive access to women's reproductive anatomy, or the rights of husbands to the exclusive sexual use of women's bodies and the right to the title of father of a particular woman's children. The symbols, though, are not in themselves enough, nor can the important development of real property right say all that can be said about rights. Rights must be related to actual social relations between people, and it is in these social relations that the question of responsibility arises. The appropriation of an infant is the appropriation of a helpless creature. This does not necessarily mean that women must turn to men for help. Quite apart from nature's own provision of nutrition for the child, there is nothing to stop women turning to other women where they need assistance, and historically they have always done so in varying degrees. Paternal responsibility grows out of the fact that appropriation of the child requires a community of actively cooperating men, and the creation of social institutions to buttress the abstract notion of right.

Man the procreator, by virtue of his need to mediate his alienation from procreation, is essentially man the creator. What he has created are the institutional forms of the social relations of reproduction, forms which mediate the contradictions in male reproductive consciousness. Obviously, the most persistent and successful form is marriage, with all its variations. Yet marriage in itself is not an adequate expression of the right to appropriation. We must recall that the need to co-operate with other men in the creation of the conditions of appropriation is at the same time a relationship with rival potencies. The appropriation of the child symbolizes the rights of the father, but does little to reduce the uncertainty of paternity in experiential terms. The exclusive right to a particular woman is therefore buttressed by the physical separation of that woman from other men. In creating the right to the appropriation of children, men created that social space which political theorists have called the private realm. Whether mud hut or extended household, the private realm is a necessary condition of the affirmation of particular paternity, while the public realm is the space where men fore-gather to make the laws and ideologies which shape and justify patriarchy.

This separation of women from the larger social and natural world separates them from other men, most women, the means of expanding production and the developed political realm. It is an enforced separation, a condition and a result of the potency principle in action. It is as lord of the private realm that man gives substance to the right of paternal appropriation as a proprietary right. The need to appropriate children is specifically human, and men's participation in nurture emerges from the exercise of proprietary right. This is not simply because men partake in nurture; so do many male animals. The difference is that in one sense, with his knowledge of his separation from reproductive process, man sees his participation in nurture as voluntary. All wolves, for example, assist in nurture; some men assist in nurture. Further, and unlike papa wolf, men can assist in nurture indirectly. They can enslave or buy the labour power of others to assist in the task of rearing children. What men and wolves do share is *recognition*.[21] They both have status as providers, but to the wolf in his pack accrues neither the addition to status of political right nor moral righteousness, for he is doing what he must necessarily do. Men, on the other hand, have choices. To be sure, these choices come to be circumscribed in customary and legal ways, and the claim of a *right* to the child has in most societies entailed obligations towards the child, most particularly in societies and social classes where the separation of public and private is most effective. This developed pattern of right and obligation confirms paternity as both a political and a moral phenomenon. The "good father" is admired on ethical grounds, and rewarded with domestic power and, in many societies, with political citizenship. The "good mother" is merely natural, though family law provides safeguards to ensure that she stays so. Yet male participation in nurture also has symbolic social significance: it confirms a right to the child and a recognition of paternity which in fact rest on shaky biological foundations.

None of these considerations should be construed as implying some kind of rejection of any notion of affection, warmth and love between people and children. The family has frequently been defined as the realm of affective life, and it would be perverse to deny this. To be sure, affective life includes powerful emotions which are hardly loving, and both dramatists and psychoanalysts, for example, have found tragedy as well as romance and comedy in the endless generic accommodations of men and women in intimate relation with one another. Millions of men have loved their children, just as the unfeeling mother is not exactly an unknown phenomenon. These are the relations of *particular* families, and they vary in different societies. What this analysis is doing, in a still abstract way, is attempting to show the *general* relationship between the biological substructure and the social superstructure of reproductive relations, and to begin to indicate the real historical development of mediations of the contradictions in reproductive process. This includes the need men have to gain recognition of themselves as parents. The combined historical development of the right of men to appropriate children and the separation of social life into private and public realms are the significant means of mediation which men have adopted to this end. The forms that these mediations have taken are matters for empirical enquiry.

"Appropriation" has become a pejorative word, especially on the left of the political spectrum. Here, in the sense in which we have thus far used it, it simply means the assertion of a proprietorial right to a child which nature has omitted to provide for male parents. Given the historical attempts to combine this right with some level of responsibility for nurture of the infant, it does not seem in any logical way to entail the suppression of women. This suppression, it has been suggested, is tied to the need to ameliorate the ambiguity of paternity by the creation of a private realm, and the distrust of other men which complicates the necessary co-operation of patriarchs. Even then, there is still no irresistible process of domination involved in this development. There is no obvious or inherent reason, for example, why the work performed in the private realm should not have equal or even superior status to work performed in the public realm. We have noted that male reproductive consciousness has developed the notion of potency, but the ideological aspects of the potency principle itself have to stand over against the real potency of women whose labour actually reproduces the race. Further, we have argued that appropriation is the appropriation of a helpless infant, but that infant does not stay helpless; the edifice of patriarchy could not be built on the temporary helplessness of the very young. We thus must examine this act of appropriation a little more closely, and in doing so we must move from the generically shared moment of nurture to the female moment of reproductive labour.

The male appropriation of the child is more than the transformation of the infant to a rather troublesome piece of individual property. Embedded in the child is the alienated reproductive labour of the mother. Men claim more than the child; they claim ownership of the woman's reproductive labour power in a sense recognizably similar to, but by no means analogous with, the sense in which capitalists appropriate the surplus labour power of wage labourers.[22] Men are naturally alienated from their children; women are willfully alienated by men from their own reproductive labour power.

Yet what does it mean to say that reproductive labour power is alienated and appropriated? It means, among other things, that the dialectical structure of reproductive consciousness is reaffirmed in the social relations of reproduction, and thus in female reproductive consciousness. At the biological level, reproductive labour is a synthesizing and mediating act. It confirms women's unity with nature experientially, and guarantees that the child is hers. Labour is inseparable from reproductive process in its biological involuntariness, but it is also integrative. It is a mediation between mother and nature and mother and child; but it is also a *temporal* mediation between the cyclical time of nature and unilinear genetic time. Woman's reproductive consciousness is a consciousness that the child is hers, but also a consciousness that she herself was born of a woman's labour, that labour confirms genetic coherence and species continuity. Male reproductive consciousness is splintered and discontinuous, and cannot be mediated within reproductive process. Female reproductive consciousness is continuous and integrative, for it is mediated within reproductive process. The fact that this integration has been labeled as "passivity" by male-stream thought is part of the ideology of male supremacy. It is now hopelessly outdated, for the introduction of freedom of choice in a potentially universal way by the development of contraceptive technology means that women must create their mediations with procreative necessities.

Reproductive labour, like all human labour, creates value. What sort of value can this be said to be? Historically, instances can be found of the attribution to children of use value and exchange value, but this value inheres in the potential of the child. It is in its own potentiality as a labourer, an object of sexual gratification or as a reproducer of extra children that the child can have and has had a market value. This value is a socio-historically developed value which is not the product of reproductive labour, nor is it necessarily the value which men appropriate. Paternity is not theft. Further, the child has a human value simply by virtue of being human, of growing and maturing in all the wonder of nature's most stunning performance. For this, the child is not appropriated: it is loved. This is the value of the child's distinct personality, and is not the product of reproductive labour. It represents the unity and eventual separation of both parents and their child which Hegel talked about, and is considerably enhanced by relations of mutual trust.

The value which is produced by reproductive labour might be called "synthetic" value.[23] It represents the unity of sentient beings with natural process and the integrity of the continuity of the race. These are what men lose in the alienation of the seed, and, in a very real sense, nature is unjust to men. She includes and excludes at the same moment. It is an injustice, however, which male praxis might reasonably be said to have overcorrected.

The fact that synthetic value is the product of reproductive labour power means that the appropriation without labour of the child is, at the same time, the appropriation of the mother's labour power, embodied as synthetic value in the child. It is in a very real sense the appropriation of both a product of labour and of its "means of production," the woman and her reproductive labour power. Women are not privatized solely to guard them from other potencies. They are privatized because their own reproductive labour power must be appropriated along with the child in whom it is embedded.

The complexity of male participation in reproductive process is such that it has presented challenges to men which it has not presented to women. Historically developed paternity represents a real triumph over the ambiguities of nature. It is achieved by masculine praxis, a unity of knowledge and activity integrated in an act of will, and objectifying the idea of paternity in the social reality of patriarchy. Men understand themselves as sharing a power over nature, a potency to give to their dualistic reproductive experience a unity which defies nature's injustice while it treasures her gift of freedom. In vulgar terms, fatherhood is a paradigm case of the possibility of getting something for nothing. The social forms which emerge from this complex series of mediations are therefore governed by what we have called the potency principle. They are relations of labourer and non-labourer, of appropriated and appropriator, of dualism and integration, of artificial potency and actual potency, of continuous time consciousness and discontinuous time consciousness, of female and of male. Yet the potency principal remains profoundly problematic, in constant need of revving up and redefining, of symbolizing and justifying. A huge and oppressive structure of law and custom and ideology is erected by the brotherhood of Man to affirm and protect their potency, and it is a structure which must be actively maintained, because at the heart of male potency lies the intransigent reality of estrangement and uncertainty.

The question of temporality, which has cropped up steadily in this analysis, deserves some further comment. The appropriation of the child and its synthetic value plugs men in, as it were, both to the cycle of nature which is completed in the birth of the child, and to the unilinear continuity of species time, which is a properly "material" base of human history. All of women's reproductive moments except the ones she shares with men—copulation and nurture—are cyclical moments. Copulation and nurture are linear but episodic. Gestation does not automatically follow copulation, and the operations of sex-drive are unpredictable. There are thus three time modes involved in reproductive process: cyclical time, unilinear time and irregular episodicity. There are additional important considerations which emerge from this situation, which we can now elaborate in tidier form.

Female sexual receptivity differs from that of all other animals: women are immune to the cyclical compulsions of oestrus, and their sexual receptiveness, like that of men, is episodic. No other animals have this motivation to keep a sexual partner constantly at hand, but it should be noticed that this is not an exclusively male motivation, but applies equally to men and women. As one area of natural generic equality, this may well be a significant factor in the transformed social relations of reproduction which must emerge in the Age of Contraception. Liberated from the twin threats of unwanted pregnancy and the lumpen sensualist, women now share with men not only sexual needs, but the potentiality of shared sexuality and chosen parenthood.

Additionally, the differentiation of male and female time consciousness is a fact which male-stream thought has not sufficiently noticed, and which feminist scholarship must explore. The differentiation of natural time and historical time has been performed often enough, but the generic differentiation has not. Female time, we have noted, is continuous, while male time is discontinuous.[24] The discontinuity in male time consciousness partakes of a now familiar ambivalence: it frees men to some extent from the contingency of natural cyclical time, but deprives them of experienced generational continuity. Historically, men have clearly felt compelled to create principles of continuity, principles which operate in the public realm under male control and are limited only by men's creative imagination.

The problem of continuity over time has developed in western societies as a political problem, a quest for an "order" of procession which transcends individual life spans in some self-regenerating way. Principles of continuity appeal either to cyclical time, and appear in all organic theories of the state, to an idealized form of continuity, such as the notion of eternity, which are a component of theocratic formulations, or to a practical instance of stable continuity, such as an economic order or a hereditary monarchy. The notion of history as a principle of continuity is a modern one, but time, separated from its biological roots, appears as a philosophical problem, which it undoubtedly is. However, thought about time is distorted where it neglects the generic differentiations in human time consciousness.

Finally, the time lapse between copulation and parturition exacerbates the uncertainty of paternity, and may well be a factor in man's conception of time as an enemy, to say nothing of the hardiness of the fear of the stranger which is a staple of the history of male domination. The idea of time as an enemy no doubt has connections with the fact of mortality, but it has roots in natality too. The shadow of lapsed time is the separation of men from the destiny of their seed. Paternity is, in a real sense, an alienated experience in abstract time: for men, physiology is fate.

This preliminary, and still very crude, analysis of the dialectics of reproduction is intended to be suggestive and heuristic, and by no means definitive and complete. The ultimate aim is to develop a feminist theory of historical process which can transcend the unsatisfactory reductionism which has bedeviled male-stream thought. The most interesting and promising socio-historical theory, it has been suggested, is that developed by Marx, and some further criticism of the limitations and strengths of Marx's model are offered in a later chapter. What we have been doing so far is attempting to develop a conceptual apparatus with which to ask our questions from a feminist perspective. Just as men have put nature to the question, women must now put male historical praxis to the question. This is not because women have suddenly decided not to put up with all this nonsense any more. The institutions of patriarchy are vulnerable because the Age of Contraception has changed the *process* of reproduction, and the social relations of reproduction must therefore undergo transformation.

Prior to the Age of Contraception, the most recent world historical change in the substructure of material necessities which determine the course of history took place in the productive rather than the reproductive mode. This was, of course, the development of capitalism. That event produced a new science, the "dismal" science of political economy, developed by the revolutionary class of that struggle, the bourgeoisie. The changes wrought by the possibilities inherent in the mind-blowing capacity for rational human control of reproduction will no doubt also produce a new science. There are signs that this is happening: the development of feminist theory and feminist practice is still at a rudimentary level, but not so rudimentary that it is not recognizable as an irreversible historical force. However, we may have to be patient for a while before an Eve Smith joins Adam in the annals of intellectual history. The new mode of reproduction radically transforms the social relations of reproduction, and in this historical movement women constitute the progressive social force. This fact will take quite a bit of getting used to.

Here, we do not claim to have discovered the new and still nameless science which can provide the theoretical component of feminist praxis. Our perspective is a limited one, growing out of the discipline of political theory, and growing furthermore in a still partial and idiosyncratic way which will no doubt infuriate many political theorists. Yet the shadow of a theory is beginning to emerge. There is no need to develop a new vocabulary. The notions of power, of continuity and stability over time, of the opposition of individual and collective interest, of the separation of the public and private realm, of the organic state, of freedom and responsibility, of dialectical process, of the brotherhood of man: none of these notions are foreign to traditional political thought. The suggestion that these concepts are related to reproductive process is not new either, as I hope to show in subsequent discussions. What is new is the standpoint of analysis; the standpoint of women.

There is one further conceptual notion which will be examined in some detail, a concept which has not yet been utilized, but which in a sense summarizes the series of contradictions and the essential dualism of male reproductive experience which I have attempted to analyse. It relates to perhaps the oldest and most persistent problematic that has jiggled the ruminations of political philosophers, which is the human nature question. It is no longer quite so fashionable to argue for a fixed human nature, and such arguments as do persist have taken a woeful fall from heavenly Edens to those steamy jungles where sociobiologists discover their own smiles on the faces of tigers and fruit flies. No attempt will be made here to argue a theory of fixed human nature. What is interesting is that such arguments have never proved adequate: from early days, male-stream thought has toyed with the notion that man, in fact, has two natures. The nature of these two natures has been the subject of endless debate. It went on in the Athenian polis, and the notion of "second nature" is embedded in ordinary language: it is "second nature" to stop at a red light, to love children, to pursue survival, and so forth. In philosophical terms, the Greek view that man is divided, between his first (biological) nature and his second (cultural) nature has remained a tenable proposition. What has never been clear is whether or not women have a second nature. Probably not: women, by virtue, of their reproductive function, are "closer" to nature, and by virtue of their passivity have never bothered to develop a second nature.

This is an important theme. The difference between man's first and second natures is that he makes his own second nature historically. Included in that historical view of himself is his sense of superiority over women, even though the sociobiologists are now defensively arguing that he is actually also superior by virtue of his first (animal) nature. Our analysis of the dialectics of reproduction suggests a more concrete foundation for man's felt need for two natures: they emerge from his real separation from the natural world and from species continuity. This is a hypothesis which is probably worth testing, for it is related to the persistent dualism of male modes of understanding, to which I have already referred. The testing of such a radical hypothesis will require a great deal of philosophical effort, and no claim is made to have "proved" it here. Yet in a world in which the need for reintegration with nature is becoming more and more apparent, it may well be an urgent task, and one for which integrated female consciousness is preeminently suited.

Notes

[1] These views are discussed in detail in Chapter 2 of *The Politics of Reproduction* (O'Brien 1981).

[2] See Karl Marx and Frederick Engels. "Manifesto of the Communist Party," in *Selected Works* (1969) pp. 134-6.

[3] Hegel struggled with the problem of reproduction in his early work. The significant passage here is the fragment "On Love" in his *Early Theological Writings* (1948: 303-4). I have also been fortunate in having access to the manuscript of an unpublished translation of the *System der Siulichkeit* by T. M. Knox and H. S. Harris. I am grateful to Professor Harris for his permission to quote from this work and to read in manuscript his invaluable "Introductory essay to Hegel's *The System of Ethical Life.*"

[4] "Prehistorical" is used in the sense in which Hegel used the word "anthropological," a sense now misleading. For Hegel, "anthropological" means the preconscious, pre-rational, therefore prehistorical, forms of human spirit.

[5]For Hegel's conception of death rather than birth as the "lord and master" of family life, see his *The Phenomenology of Mind* (1967: 471-2).

[6]This is a recurrent theme in Hegel's work, given its most austere expression in the *Philosophy of Right* (1967).

[7]A feminist critique of the Hegelian system might well be an exciting task. For our limited purpose here, we make no claims to a critique of the system: we have not, for example, dealt with the long discussion of reproduction in *The Philosophy of Nature*. For a more detailed but still tentative discussion of Hegel, see O'Brien (1977).

[8]"Since possession and property make up an important part of men's lives, even lovers cannot refrain from reflection on this aspect of their relations" (Hegel 1948).

[9]Hegel already sees the significance of productive labour in the 1804 lectures (1979: 437, 438). The more developed treatment of the status of labour as mediator with, and transformer of, the world comes in the famous parable of lordship and bondage in *The Phenomenology* (Hegel 1967: B.IV.A).

[10]See also Harris, "Introductory Essay" (34-5).

[11]Ultimately, male/female relations become essentially spiritual: "Just as the individual divine man [the historical Christ] has an implied father and only an actual mother, in like manner the universal divine man, the spiritual communion, has as its father its own proper action and knowledge, while its mother is eternal Love, which it merely feels, but does not behold in its consciousness as an actual immediate object (Hegel 1967: 784).

[12]For a discussion of the need to conserve the past as a condition of the humanity of a proletarian solidarity, see Lenhardt (133-54).

[13]It is thus not surprising that Freud tells us that, in his account of the evolution from primal horde to totemic society, he is "at a loss to indicate the place of the great maternal deities who perhaps everywhere preceded the paternal deities" (192).

[14]For a recent description of this battle, see Donnison.

[15]Josephine Iorio divides the process into antepartal, intrapartal and postpartal stages.

[16]See M. Edward Davis and Reva Rubin, eds., *Dr. Lee's Obstetrics for Nurses* (18th edition, 1966), which not only gives short shift to fathers, but even manages to plug some male-supremacist assumptions: "[woman's] sexual life in general is more intense and plays a greater role in her existence" (30). Obviously, there is room for romantic poetry in textbooks. Davis and Rubin give one third of a column to fathers, under the rather forbidding rubric of "sperm transport" (46). Perhaps the nineteenth edition will be better, for this is a "classic" work.

[17]The current movement to restore even limited midwifery in the United States carries these overtones. Dr. George A. Slater deplores the poor showing of the USA in infant mortality statistics (24.8 in the USA, 14.12 in Sweden) (3). He calls for a new professional category, and "we must think how to train *him*" (10) and "what kind of job would *he* do?" (11) [*my italics*].

[18]See Aristotle, especially II.737a.25 and I.724b, 725a, 725b. For a discussion on Aristotle's reproductive biology and its generic prejudice, see Cherniss (269-88).

[19]See Plato's *Symposium* (s. 192a).

[20]My colleague, Dr. Dorothy Smith, has properly cautioned me against the assertion that patriarchy, as opposed to paternity, is a universal phenomenon. Most familiar of the studies of non-patriarchal societies is, of course, Margaret Mead's affectionate portrait of the Arapesh in *Sex and Temperament in Three Primitive Societies*. What does seem to be the case is that what are known as "great civilizations" are patriarchal (Mogul, Inca, Greek, Roman and so forth). Patriarchy is associated fairly consistently with class differentiation, imperialism and some form of racism, and may therefore have been, in the Marxist sense, historically necessary. The difficulty with historically necessary movements is inertia and an incapacity to recognize the end of their usefulness. This is the reason why human history is always the history of struggle.

[21]The selection of wolves in this analogy is prompted by Farley Mowatt's sensitive but anthropomorphic observations in *Never Cry Wolf*.

[22]The Marxist notion of surplus value as the value appropriated cannot readily be adapted to reproductive labour. Surpluses in terms of reproductive product have quite often tended to be eliminated rather than appropriated. In very early societies, this appears to have been done without regard for gender, though in developed patriarchal societies girls appear to have been considered more dispensable, and the myths of these societies are concerned to demonstrate the perfidy of destroying male children: Isaac, Romulus, Remus and Oedipus are among the more noted victors over child sacrifice and exposure. There are no reliable statistics relating to child exposure in Greece, but there are many references to child destruction, practical or ritual, in ancient writings. Both Jane Harrison and Philip Slater argue that infanticide was an important component in the fantasy "life of the ancients." See Philip E. Slater's *The Glory of Hera* (214-16) and Jane Ellen Harrison's *Prolegomena to the Study of Greek Religion* (482-8). Harrison quotes Plutarch, Clement and Arnobius in support of the contention that infanticide was practised well into the fifth century. It is a contentious and grey area, floating uneasily between economic, religious and psychoanalytic interpretations.

[23]This is a term which Marx scorned in its usage in relation to productive activity (1847: 43-50).

[24]For a discussion of Claude Levi-Strauss's misunderstanding of this point, see chapter 3 of *The Politics of Reproduction* (O'Brien 1981).

References

Aristotle. "De Generatione Animalium." Trans. Arthur Platt. *The Works of Aristotle*. Eds. J. A. Smith and W. D. Ross. Oxford: The Clarendon Press, 1912.

Beauvoir, Simone de. *The Second Sex*. Trans. H. M. Parshley. New York: Bantam Books, 1953.

Cherniss, Harold. *Aristotle's Criticism of Pre-Socratic Philosophy*. 1935. New York: Octagon Books, 1971.

Davis, M. Edward and Reva Rubins, Eds. *Dr. Lee's Obstetrics for Nurses*, 18th Edition. Philadelphia and London: W.B. Sanders, 1966.

Donnison, Jean. *Midwives and Medical Men*. London: Heinemann Educational Books, 1977.

Firestone, Shulamith. *The Dialectic of Sex: The Case for Feminist Revolution*. New York: Bantam Books, 1971.

Freud, Sigmund. *Totem and Taboo*. 1913. Trans. A. A. Brill. New York: Vintage Books, 1918 [1913].

Gardner, Patrick, Ed. *Theories of History*. Chicago: Free Press, 1959.

Harris, H. S. "Introductory Essay to Hegel's *The System of Ethical Life*." *The System of Ethical Life* (Hegel's 1802-03 Lectures) Trans. T. M. Knox and H. S. Harris. Albany: SUNY Press, 1979.

Harrison, Jane E. *Prolegomena to the Study of Greek Religion*. New York: Meridian Books, 1957.

Hegel, G. W. F. *Early Theological Writings*. 1802. Ed. and Trans. T.M. Knox. University of Chicago Press, 1948.

Hegel, G. W. F. *The Phenomenology of Mind*. 1807. Trans. J.B. Baillie. New York and Evanston: Harper Torchbooks, 1967.

Hegel, G. W. F. *The Philosophy of Right*. 1821. Trans. T.M. Knox. London, Oxford and New York: Oxford University Press, 1967.

Hegel, G. W. F. *The System of Ethical Life*. (Hegel's 1802-03 Lectures.) Trans. T. M. Knox and H.S. Harris. Albany: SUNY Press, 1979.

Iorio, Josephine. *Principles of Obstetrics and Gynecology for Nurses*. St. Louis: C.V. Mosby, 1971.

Knox, T. M. and H. S. Harris. *System der Siulichkeit*.

Lenhardt, Christian. "Anamnestic solidarity: the proletariat and its manes." *Telos*. 25 (Fall 1975). 133-54.

Levi-Strauss, Claude. *Totemism*. Boston: Beacon Press, 1963.

Marx, Karl. *Capital*. Vol. I. 1867. Trans. Samuel Moore and Edward Aveling. New York: Modern Library, 1906.

Marx, Karl. *The Poverty of Philosophy*. 1847. New York: International Publishers, 1963.

Marx, Karl. "Manifesto of the Communist Party." *Selected Works*. Moscow: Progress Publishers, 1969.

Marx, Karl and Frederick Engels. *The German Ideology*. (Completed but not published, 1846.) Ed. R. Pascal. New York: International Publishers, 1947.

Mead, Margaret. *Sex and Temperament in Three Primitive Societies*. 1935. New York: William Morrow, 1963.

Mowatt, Farley. *Never Cry Wolf*. Toronto: McClelland and Stewart, 1963.

O'Brien, Mary. "Man, Physiology and Fate: Hegel." *GROW* 13 (1977). Toronto: Ontario Institute for Studies in Education (OISE).

O'Brien, Mary. *The Politics of Reproduction*. 1981. Boston: Routledge and Kegan

Paul, 1983.

Plato. *Symposium*. Trans. Benjamin Jowett. New York: Library of Liberal Arts, 1956.

Slater, George A. "The Problem." *The Midwife in the United States: A Macy Conference*. New York: Josiah Macy, Jr. Foundation, 1968.

Slater, Philip E. *The Glory of Hera*. Boston: Beacon Press, 1971.

Chapter 5

In Search of Our Mothers' Gardens

ALICE WALKER

I described her own nature and temperament. Told how they needed a larger life for their expression.... I pointed out that in lieu of proper channels, her emotions had overflowed into paths that dissipated them. I talked, beautifully I thought, about an art that would be born, an art that would open the way for women the likes of her. I asked her to hope, and build up an inner life against the coming of that day, I sang, with a strange quiver in my voice, a promise song.

—*Jean Toomer, "Avey," CANE*

The poet speaking to a prostitute who falls asleep while he's talking—

WHEN THE POET Jean Toomer walked through the South in the early twenties, he discovered a curious thing: black women whose spirituality was so intense, so deep, so *unconscious,* that they were themselves unaware of the richness they held. They stumbled blindly through their lives: creatures so abused and mutilated in body, so dimmed and confused by pain, that they considered themselves unworthy even of hope. In the selfless abstractions their bodies became to the men who used them, they became more than "sexual objects," more even than mere women: they became "Saints." Instead of being perceived as whole persons, their bodies became shrines: what was thought to be their minds became temples suitable for worship. These crazy Saints stared out at the world, wildly, like lunatics—or quietly, like suicides; and the "God" that was in their gaze was as mute as a great stone.

Who were these Saints? These crazy, loony, pitiful women?

Some of them, without a doubt, were our mothers and grandmothers.

In the still heat of the post-Reconstruction South, this is how they seemed to Jean Toomer: exquisite butterflies trapped in an evil honey, toiling away their lives in an era, a century, that did not acknowledge them, except as "the *mule* of the world." They dreamed dreams that no one knew—not even themselves, in any coherent fashion—and saw visions no one could understand. They wandered or sat about the countryside crooning lullabies to ghosts, and drawing the mother of Christ in charcoal on courthouse walls.

They forced their minds to desert their bodies and their striving spirits sought to rise, like frail whirlwinds from the hard red clay. And when those frail whirlwinds fell, in scattered particles, upon the ground, no one mourned. Instead, men lit candles to celebrate the emptiness that remained, as people do who enter a beautiful but vacant space to resurrect a God.

Our mothers and grandmothers, some of them: moving to music not yet written. And they waited.

They waited for a day when the unknown thing that was in them would be made known; but guessed, somehow in their darkness, that on the day of their revelation they would be long dead. Therefore to Toomer they walked, and even ran, in slow motion. For they were going nowhere immediate, and the future was not yet within their grasp. And men took our mothers and grandmothers, "but got no pleasure from it." So complex was their passion and their calm.

> To Toomer, they lay vacant and fallow as autumn fields, with harvest time never in sight: and he saw them enter loveless marriages, without joy; and become prostitutes, without resistance; and become mothers of children, without fulfillment.

For these grandmothers and mothers of ours were not Saints, but Artists; driven to a numb and bleeding madness by the springs of creativity in them for which there was no release. They were Creators, who lived lives of spiritual waste, because they were so rich in spirituality—which is the basis of Art—that the strain of enduring their unused and unwanted talent drove them insane. Throwing away this spirituality was their pathetic attempt to lighten the soul to a weight their work-worn, sexually abused bodies could bear.

> What did it mean for a black woman to be an artist in our grandmothers' time? In out great-grandmothers' day? It is a question with an answer cruel enough to stop the blood.

Did you have a genius of a great-great-grandmother who died under some ignorant and depraved white overseer's lash? Or was she required to bake biscuits for a lazy backwater tramp, when she cried out in her soul to paint watercolors of sunsets, or the rain falling on the green and peaceful pasturelands? Or was her body broken and forced to bear children (who were more often than not sold away from her)—eight, ten, fifteen, twenty children—when her one joy was the thought of modeling heroic figures of rebellion, in stone or clay?

How was the creativity of the black woman kept alive, year after year and century after century, when for most of the years black people have been in America, it was a punishable crime for a black person to read or write? And the freedom to paint, to sculpt, to expand the mind with action did not exist. Consider, if you can bear to imagine it, what might have been the result if singing, too, had been forbidden by law. Listen to the voices of Bessie Smith, Billie Holiday, Nina

Simone, Roberta Flack, and Aretha Franklin, among others, and imagine those voices muzzled for life. Then you may begin to comprehend the lives of our "crazy," "Sainted" mothers and grandmothers. The agony of the lives of women who might have been Poets, Novelists, Essayists, and Short-Story Writers (over a period of centuries), who died with their real gifts stifled within them.

And, if this were the end of the story, we would have cause to cry out in my paraphrase of Okot p'Bitek's great poem:

> O, my clanswomen Let us all cry together!
> Come,
> Let us mourn the death of our mother,
> The death of a Queen
> The ash that was produced by a great fire!
> O, this homestead is utterly dead
> Close the gates
> With *lacari* thorns,
> For our mother
> The creator of the Stool is lost! And all the young women
> Have perished in the wilderness!

But this is not the end of the story, for all the young women—our mothers and grandmothers, *ourselves*—have not perished in the wilderness. And if we ask ourselves why, and search for and find the answer, we will know beyond all efforts to erase it from our minds, just exactly who, and of what, we black American women are.

One example, perhaps the most pathetic, most misunderstood one, can provide a backdrop for our mothers' work: Phillis Wheatley, a slave in the 1700s.

Virginia Woolf, in her book *A Room of One's Own,* wrote that in order for a woman to write fiction she must have two things, certainly: a room of her own (with key and lock) and enough money to support herself.

What then are we to make of Phillis Wheatley, a slave, who owned not even herself? This sickly, frail black girl who required a servant of her own at times—her health was so precarious—and who, had she been white, would have been easily considered the intellectual superior of all the women and most of the men in the society of her day.

Virginia Woolf wrote further, speaking of course not of our Phillis, that "any woman born with a great gift in the sixteenth century [insert "eighteenth century," insert "black woman," insert "born or made a slave"] would certainly have gone crazed, shot herself, or ended her days in some lonely cottage outside the village, half witch, half wizard [insert "Saint"], feared and mocked at. For it needs little skill and psychology to be sure that a highly gifted girl who had tried to use her gift for poetry would have been so thwarted and hindered by contrary instincts [add "chains, guns, the lash, the ownership of one's body by someone else, submission to an alien religion"], that she must have lost her health and sanity to a certainty."

The key words, as they relate to Phillis, are "contrary instincts." For when we read the poetry of Phillis Wheatley—as when we read the novels of Nella Larsen or the oddly false-sounding autobiography of that freest of all black women writers, Zora Hurston—evidence of "contrary instincts" is everywhere. Her loyalties were completely divided, as was, without question, her mind.

But how could this be otherwise? Captured at seven, a slave of wealthy, doting whites who instilled in her the "savagery" of the Africa they "rescued" her from ... one wonders if she was even able to remember her homeland as she had known it, or as it really was.

Yet, because she did try to use her gift for poetry in a world that made her a slave, she was "so thwarted and hindered by . . . contrary instincts, that she ... lost her health .... "In the last years of her brief life, burdened not only with the need to express her gift but also with a penniless, friendless "freedom" and several small children for whom she was forced to do strenuous work to feed, she lost her health, certainly. Suffering from malnutrition and neglect and who knows what mental agonies, Phillis Wheatley died.

So torn by "contrary instincts" was black, kidnapped, enslaved Phillis that her description of "the Goddess"—as she poetically called the Liberty she did not have—is ironically, cruelly humorous. And, in fact, has held Phillis up to ridicule for more than a century. It is usually read prior to hanging Phillis's memory as that of a fool. She wrote:

> The Goddess comes, she moves divinely fair,
> Olive and laurel binds her *golden* hair.
> Wherever shines this native of the skies,
> Unnumber'd charms and recent graces rise. [my emphasis]

It is obvious that Phillis, the slave, combed the "Goddess's" hair every morning; prior, perhaps, to bringing in the milk, or fixing her mistress's lunch. She took her imagery from the one thing she saw elevated above all others.

With the benefit of hindsight we ask, "How could she?"

But at last, Phillis, we understand. No more snickering when your stiff, struggling, ambivalent lines are forced on us. We know now that you were not an idiot or a traitor; only a sickly little black girl, snatched from your home and country and made a slave; a woman who still struggled to sing the song that was your gift, although in a land of barbarians who praised you for your bewildered tongue. It is not so much what you sang, as that you kept alive, in so many of our ancestors, *the notion of song.*

Black women are called, in the folklore that so aptly identifies one's status in society, "the *mule* of the world," because we have been handed the burdens that everyone else—*everyone* else refused to carry. We have also been called "Matriarchs," "Superwomen," and "Mean and Evil Bitches." Not to mention "Castraters" and "Sapphire's Mama." When we have pleaded for understanding, our character has been distorted; when we have asked for simple caring, we have been handed empty inspirational appellations, then stuck in the farthest corner. When we have asked for love, we have been given children. In short, even our plainer gifts, our labors of fidelity and love, have been knocked down our throats. To be an artist and a black woman, even today, lowers our status in many respects, rather than raises it: and yet, artists we will be.

Therefore we must fearlessly pull out of ourselves and look at and identify with our lives the living creativity some of our great-grandmothers were not allowed to know. I stress *some* of them because it is well known that the majority of our great-grandmothers knew, even without "knowing" it, the reality of their spirituality, even if they didn't recognize it beyond what happened in the singing at church—and they never had any intention of giving it up.

How they did it—those millions of black women who were not Phillis Wheatley, or Lucy Terry or Frances Harper or Zora Hurston or Nella Larsen or Bessie Smith; or Elizabeth Catlett, or Katherine Dunham, either—brings me to the title of this essay, "In Search of Our Mothers' Gardens," which is a personal account that is yet shared, in its theme and its meaning, by all of us. I found, while thinking about the far-reaching world of the creative black woman, that often the truest answer to a question that really matters can be found very close.

In the late 1920s my mother ran away from home to marry my father. Marriage, if not running away, was expected of seventeen-year-old girls. By the time she was twenty, she had two children and was pregnant with a third. Five children later, I was born. And this is how I came to know my mother: she seemed a large, soft, loving-eyed woman who was rarely impatient in our home. Her quick, violent temper was on view only a few times a year, when she battled with the white landlord who had the misfortune to suggest to her that her children did not need to go to school.

She made all the clothes we wore, even my brothers' overalls. She made all the towels and sheets we used. She spent the summers canning vegetables and fruits. She spent the winter evenings making quilts enough to cover all our beds.

During the "working" day, she labored beside—not behind—my father in the fields. Her day began before sun-up, and did not end until late at night. There was never a moment for her to sit down, undisturbed, to unravel her own private thoughts; never a time free from interruption—by work or the noisy inquiries of her many children. And yet, it is to my mother—and all our mothers who were not famous—that I went in search of the secret of what has fed that muzzled and often mutilated, but vibrant, creative spirit that the black woman has inherited, and that pops out in wild and unlikely places to this day.

But when, you will ask, did my overworked mother have time to know or care about feeding the creative spirit?

The answer is so simple that many of us have spent years discovering it. We have constantly looked high, when we should have looked high—and low.

For example: in the Smithsonian Institution in Washington, D.C., there hangs a quilt unlike any other in the world. In fanciful, inspired, and yet simple and identifiable figures, it portrays the story of the Crucifixion. It is considered rare, beyond price. Though it follows no known pattern of quilt-making, and though it is made of bits and pieces of worthless rags, it is obviously the work of a person of powerful imagination and deep spiritual feeling. Below this quilt I saw a note that says it was made by "an anonymous Black woman in Alabama, a hundred years ago."

If we could locate this "anonymous" black woman from Alabama, she would turn out to be one of our grandmothers: an artist who left her mark in the only materials she could afford, and in the only medium her position in society allowed her to use.

As Virginia Woolf wrote further, in *A Room of One's Own*:

> Yet genius of a sort must have existed among women as it must have existed among the working class. [Change this to "slaves" and "the wives and daughters of sharecroppers."] Now and again an Emily Brontë or a Robert Burns [change this to "a Zora Hurston or a Richard Wright"] blazes out and proves its presence. But certainly it never got itself on to paper. When, however, one reads of a witch being ducked, of a woman possessed by devils [or "Sainthood"], of a wise woman selling herbs [our root workers], or even a very remarkable man who had a mother, then I think we are on the track of a lost novelist, a suppressed poet, of some mute and inglorious Jane Austen .... Indeed, I would venture to guess that Anon, who wrote so many poems—without signing them, was often a woman....

And so our mothers and grandmothers have, more often than not anonymously, handed on the creative spark, the seed of the flower they themselves never hoped to see: or like a sealed letter they could not plainly read.

And so it is, certainly, with my own mother. Unlike "Ma" Rainey's songs, which retained their creator's name even while blasting forth from Bessie Smith's mouth, no song or poem will hear my mother's name. Yet so many of the stories that I write, that we all write, are my mother's stories. Only recently did I fully realize this: that through years of listening to my mother's stories of her life, I have absorbed not only the stories themselves, but something of the manner in which she spoke, something of the urgency that involves the knowledge that her stories—like her life—must be recorded. It is probably for this reason that so much of what I have written is about characters whose counterparts in real life are so much older than I am.

But the telling of these stories, which came from my mother's lips as naturally as breathing, was not the only way my mother showed herself as an artist. For stories, too, were subject to being distracted, to dying without conclusion. Dinners must be started, and cotton must be gathered before the big rains. The artist that was and is my mother showed itself to me only after many years. This is what I finally noticed:

Like Mem, a character in *The Third Life of Grange Copeland,* my mother adorned with flowers whatever shabby house we were forced to live in. And not just your typical straggly country stand of zinnias, either. She planted ambitious gardens —and still does—with over 50 different varieties of plants that bloom profusely from early March until late November. Before she left home for the fields, she watered her flowers, chopped up the grass, and laid out new beds. When she returned from the fields she might divide clumps of bulbs, dig a cold pit, uproot and replant roses, or prune branches from her taller bushes or trees—until night came and it was too dark to see.

Whatever she planted grew as if by magic, and her fame as a grower of flowers spread over three counties. Because of her creativity with her flowers, even my memories of poverty are seen through a screen of blooms—sunflowers, petunias, roses, dahlias, forsythia, spirea, delphiniums, verbena ... and on and on.

And I remember people coming to my mother's yard to be given cuttings from her flowers; I hear again the praise showered on her because whatever rocky soil she landed on, she turned into a garden. A garden so brilliant with colors, so original in its design, so magnificent with life and creativity, that to this day people drive by our house in Georgia—perfect strangers and imperfect strangers—and ask to stand or walk among my mother's art.

I notice that it is only when my mother is working in her flowers that she is radiant, almost to the point of being invisible—except as Creator: hand and eye. She is involved in work her soul must have. Ordering the universe in the image of her personal conception of Beauty.

Her face, as she prepares the Art that is her gift, is a legacy of respect she leaves to me, for all that illuminates and cherishes life. She has handed down respect for the possibilities—and the will to grasp them.

> For her, so hindered and intruded upon in so many ways, being an artist
> has still been a daily part of her life. This ability to hold on, even in very
> simple ways, is work black women have done for a very long time.

This poem is not enough, but it is something, for the woman who literally covered the holes in our walls with sunflowers:

> They were women then
> My mama's generation
> Husky of voice-Stout of Step
> With fists as well as
> Hands
> How they battered down Doors
> And ironed
> Starched white
> Shirts
> How they led

Armies
Headragged Generals
Across mined
Fields
Booby-trapped
Kitchens
To discover books
Desks
A place for us
How they knew what we
Must know
Without knowing a page
Of it
Themselves.

Guided by my heritage of a love of beauty and a respect for strength—in search of my mother's garden, I found my own.

And perhaps in Africa over two hundred years ago, there was just such a mother; perhaps she painted vivid and daring decorations in oranges and yellows and greens on the walls of her hut; perhaps she sang—in a voice like Roberta Flack's—*sweetly* over the compounds of her village; perhaps she wove the most stunning mats or told the most ingenious stories of all the village storytellers. Perhaps she was herself a poet—though only her daughter's name is signed to the poems that we know.

Perhaps Phillis Wheatley's mother was also an artist. Perhaps in more than Phillis Wheatley's biological life is her mother's signature made clear.

References

Woolf, Virginia. *A Room of One's Own.* Orlando, FL: Harcourt, 2005.

Chapter 6

Maternal Thinking

SARA RUDDICK

WE ARE FAMILIAR with Victorian renditions of Ideal Maternal Love. My own favorite, like so many of these poems, was written by a son.

> There was a young man loved a maid
> Who taunted him, "Are you afraid,"
> She asked, "to bring me today
> Your mother's head upon a tray?"
>
> He went and slew his mother dead,
> Tore from her breast her heart so red,
> Then towards his lady love he raced,
> But tripped and fell in all his haste.
>
> As the heart rolled on the ground
> It gave forth a plaintive sound.
> And it spoke, in accents mild:
> "Did you hurt yourself, my child?"[1]

Though many of the story's wishes and fantasies are familiar, there is an unfamiliar twist to the poem. The maid asked for the mother's head, the son brought her heart. The maid feared and respected thoughts; the son believed only feelings are powerful. Again we are not surprised. The passions of maternity are so sudden, intense, and confusing that we often remain ignorant of the perspective, the *thought* that has developed from mothering. Lacking pride, we have failed to deepen or articulate that thought. This is a paper about the head of the mother.

I speak about a mother's *thought*—the intellectual capacities she develops, the judgments she makes, the metaphysical attitudes she assumes, the values she affirms. A mother engages in a discipline. That is, she asks certain questions rather than others; she establishes criteria for the truth, adequacy, and relevance of proposed answers; and she cares about the findings she makes and can act on. Like any discipline, hers has *characteristic* errors, temptations, and goals. The discipline of maternal thought consists in establishing criteria for determining failure and success, in setting the priorities, and in identifying the virtues and liabilities the criteria presume. To describe the capacities, judgments, metaphysical attitudes, and values of maternal thought does not presume maternal achievement. It is to describe a *conception* of achievement, the end to which maternal efforts are directed, conceptions and ends that are different from dominant public ones.[2]

In stating my claims about maternal thinking, I use a vocabulary developed in formulating theories about the general nature of thought (Habermas; Kessler and McKenna; Winch; Wittgenstein, 1953, 1956, 1967, 1969). According to these theories, *all* thought arises out of social practice. In their practices, people respond to a reality that appears to them as given, as presenting certain *demands*. The response to demands is shaped by *interests* that are generally interests in preserving, reproducing, directing, and understanding individual and group life.

These four interests are general in the sense that they arise out of the conditions of humans-in-nature and characterize us as a species. In addition, particular practices are characterized by specific interests in meeting the demands that some reality imposes on its participants. Religious, scientific, historical, mathematical, or any other thinking constitutes a disciplined response to a reality that appears to be "given." Socially organized thinkers name, elaborate, and test the particular realities to which they respond.

Maternal practice responds to the historical reality of a biological child in a particular social world. The agents of maternal practice, acting in response to the demands of their children, acquire a conceptual scheme—a vocabulary and logic of connections—through which they order and express the facts and values of their practice. In judgments and self-reflection, they refine and concretize this scheme. Intellectual activities are distinguishable but not separable from disciplines of feeling. There is a unity of reflection, judgment, and emotion. This unity I call "maternal thinking." Although I will not digress to argue the point here, it is important that maternal thinking is no more interest-governed, no more emotional, and no more relative to a particular reality (the growing child) than the thinking that arises from scientific, religious, or any other practice.

The demands of children and the interests in meeting those demands are always and only expressed by people in particular cultures and classes of their culture, living in specific geographical, technological, and historical settings. Some features of the mothering experience are invariant and nearly unchangeable; others, though changeable, are nearly universal.[3] It is therefore possible to identify interests that seem to govern maternal practice throughout the species. Yet it is impossible even to begin to specify these interests without importing features specific to the class, ethnic group, and particular sex-gender system in which the interests are realized. In this essay I draw upon my knowledge of the institutions of motherhood in middle-class, white, Protestant, capitalist, patriarchal America, for these have expressed themselves in the heterosexual nuclear family in which I mother and was mothered. Although I have tried to compensate for the limits of my particular social and sexual history, I principally depend on others to correct my interpretations and translate across cultures.[4]

Interests Governing Maternal Practice

Children "demand" their lives be preserved and their growth fostered. Their social group "demands" that growth be shaped in a way acceptable to the next generation. Maternal practice is governed by (at least) three interests in satisfying these demands for preservation, growth, and acceptability. Preservation is the most invariant and primary of the three. Because a caretaking mother typically bears her own children, preservation begins when conception is recognized and accepted. Although the form of preservation depends on widely variant beliefs about the fragility and care of the fetus, women have always had a lore in which they recorded their concerns for the baby they "carried." Once born, a child is physically vulnerable for many years. Even when she lives with the father of her child or other female adults, even when she has money to purchase or finds available supportive health and welfare services, a mother typically considers herself, and is considered by others, to be responsible for the maintenance of the life of her child.

Interest in fostering the physical, emotional, and intellectual growth of her child soon supplements a mother's interest in its preservation. The human child is typically capable of complicated emotional and intellectual development; the human adult is radically different in kind from the child it once was. A woman who mothers may be aided or assaulted by the help and advice of fathers, teachers, doctors, moralists, therapists, and others who have an interest in fostering and shaping the growth of her child. Although rarely given primary credit, a mother typically holds herself, and is held by others, responsible for the *malfunction* of the growth process. From early on, certainly by the middle years of childhood, a mother is governed by a third interest: she must shape natural growth in such a way that her child becomes the sort of adult that she can appreciate and others can accept. Mothers will vary enormously, individually and socially, in the traits and lives they will appreciate in their children. Nevertheless, a mother typically takes as the criterion of her success the production of a young adult acceptable to her group.

The three interests in preservation, growth, and acceptability of the child govern maternal practices in general. Not all mothers are, as individuals, governed by these interests, however. Some mothers are incapable of interested participation in the practices of mothering because of emotional, intellectual, or physical disability. Severe poverty may make interested maternal practice and therefore maternal thinking nearly impossible. Then, of course, mothers engage in practices other than, and often conflicting with, mothering. Some mothers, aware of the derogation and confinement of women in maternal practice, may be disaffected. In short, actual mothers have the same relation to maternal practice as actual scientists have to scientific practice, or actual believers have to religious practices.

As mothers, they are governed by the interests of their respective practices. But the style, skill, commitment, and integrity with which they engage in these practices differ widely from individual to individual.

Interests in the preservation, growth, and acceptability of the child are frequently and unavoidably in conflict. A mother who watches a child eagerly push a friend aside as she or he climbs a tree is torn between preserving the child from danger, encouraging the child's physical skills and courage, and shaping a child according to moral restraints, which might, for example, inhibit the child's joy in competitive climbing. Although some mothers deny or are insensitive to the conflict, and others are clear about which interest should take precedence, mothers typically know that they cannot secure each interest, they know that goods conflict, and they know that unqualified success in realizing interests is an illusion. This unavoidable conflict of basic interests is one objective basis for the maternal humility I will shortly describe.

The Interest in Preserving the Life of the Child

A mother, acting in the interest of preserving and maintaining life, is in a peculiar relation to "nature." As childbearer, she often takes herself, and is taken by others, to be an especially "natural" member of her culture. As child tender, she must respect nature's limits and court its favor with foresightful actions that range from immunizations, to caps on household poisons, to magical imprecation, warnings, and prayers. "Nature" with its unpredictable varieties of dirt and disease is her enemy as much as her ally. Her children are natural creatures, often unable to understand or abet her efforts to protect them. Because they frequently find her necessary direction constraining, a mother can experience her children's own liveliness as another enemy of the life she is preserving.

No wonder, then, that as she engages in preservation, a mother is liable to the temptations of fearfulness and excessive control. If she is alone with and responsible for two or more young children, then control of herself, her children, and her physical environment is her only option, however rigid or excessive she appears to outsiders. Though necessarily controlling their acts, *reflecting* mothers themselves identify rigid or excessive control as the likely defects of the virtues they are required to practice. The identification of liability as such, with its implication of the will to overcome, characterizes this aspect of maternal thought. The epithet "controlling mother" is often unsympathetic, even matriphobic. On the other hand, it may, in line with the insights of maternal thought, remind us of what maternal thinking *counts as* failure.

To a mother, "life" may well seem "terrible, hostile, and quick to pounce on you if you give it a chance" (Woolf 92). In response, she develops a metaphysical attitude toward "Being as such," an attitude I call "holding," an attitude governed by the priority of keeping over acquiring, of conserving the fragile, of maintaining whatever is at hand and necessary to the child's life. It is an attitude elicited by the work of "world-*protection*, world-*preservation*, world-*repair*... the invisible weaving of a frayed and threadbare family life" (Rich, "Conditions" xvi, italics mine).

The priority of holding over acquiring distinguishes maternal thinking from scientific thinking and from the instrumentalism of technocracy. To be sure, under the pressures of consumerism, holding may become frantic accumulating and storing. More seriously, a parent may feel compelled to preserve her *own* children, whatever befalls other children. The more competitive and hierarchical the society, the more thwarted a mother's individual, autonomous pursuits, the more likely that preservation will become egocentric, frantic, and cruel. Mothers recognize these dangers and fight them.

Holding, preserving mothers have distinctive ways of seeing and being in the world that are worth considering. For example, faced with the fragility of the lives it seeks to preserve, maternal thinking recognizes humility and resilient cheerfulness as virtues of its practice. In so doing it takes issue with popular moralities of assertiveness and much contemporary moral theory. [5]

Humility is a metaphysical attitude one takes toward a world beyond one's control. One might conceive of the world as governed by necessity and change (as I do) or by supernatural forces that cannot be comprehended. In either case, humility implies a profound sense of the limits of one's actions and of the unpredictability of the consequences of one's work. As the philosopher Iris Murdoch puts it: "Every natural thing, including one's own mind, is subject to chance.... One might say that chance is a subdivision of death....We cannot dominate the world" (99). Humility that emerges from maternal practices accepts not only the facts of damage and death, but also the facts of the independent and uncontrollable, developing and increasingly separate existences of the lives it seeks to preserve. "Humility is not a peculiar habit of self-effacement, rather like having an inaudible voice, it is selfless respect for reality and one of the most difficult and central of virtues" (Murdoch 95).

If, in the face of danger, disappointment, and unpredictability, mothers are liable to melancholy, they are also aware that a kind, resilient good humor is a virtue. This good humor must not be confused with the cheery denial that is both a liability and, unfortunately, a characteristic of maternal practice. Mothers are tempted to denial simply by the insupportable difficulty of passionately loving a fragile creature in a physically threatening, socially violent, pervasively uncaring and competitive world. Defensive denial is exacerbated as it is officially encouraged, when we must defend against perceptions of our own subordination. Our cheery denials are cruel to our children and demoralizing to ourselves.

Clear-sighted cheerfulness is the virtue of which denial is the degenerative form. It is clear-sighted cheerfulness that Spinoza must have had in mind when he said: "Cheerfulness is always a good thing and never excessive"; it "increases and assists the power of action" (*Ethics* Book 3, proposition 42, demonstration).[6] Denying cheeriness drains intellectual energy and befuddles the will; the cheerfulness honored in maternal thought increases and assists the power of maternal action.

In a daily way, cheerfulness is a matter-of-fact willingness to continue, to give birth and to accept having given birth, to welcome life despite its conditions. Resilient good humor is a style of mothering "in the deepest sense of 'style' in which to discover the right style is to discover what you are really trying to do" (Williams 11).

Because in the dominant society "humility" and "cheerfulness" name virtues of subordinates, and because these virtues have in fact developed in conditions of subordination, it is difficult to credit them and easy to confuse them with the self-effacement and cheery denial that are their degenerative forms. Again and again, in attempting to articulate maternal thought, language is sicklied o'er by the pale cast of sentimentality and thought itself takes on a greeting-card quality. Yet literature shows us many mothers who in their "holding" actions value the humility and resilient good humor I have described. One can meet such mothers, recognize their thought, any day one learns to listen. One can appreciate the effects of their disciplined perseverance in the unnecessarily beautiful artifacts of the culture they created. "I made my quilt to keep my family warm. I made it beautiful so my heart would not break."[7]

The Interest in Fostering the Child's Growth

Mothers must not only preserve fragile life. They must also foster growth and welcome change. If the "being" preserved seems always to be endangered, undone, slipping away, the "being" that changes is always developing, building, purposively moving away. The "holding," preserving mother must, in response to change, be simultaneously a changing mother. Her conceptual scheme in terms of which she makes sense of herself, her child, and their common world will be more the Aristotelian biologist's than the Platonic mathematician's. Innovation takes precedence over permanence, disclosure and responsiveness over clarity and certainty. The idea of "objective reality" itself "undergoes important modification when it is to be understood, not in relation to the world described by science, but in relation to the progressing life of a person" (Murdoch 26).

Women are said to value open over closed structure, to eschew the clear-cut and unambiguous, to refuse a sharp division between inner and outer or self and other. They also are said to depend on and prize the private inner lives of the mind.[8] If these facets of the "female mind" are elicited by maternal practices, they may well be interwoven responses to the changeability of a growing child. A child is itself an "open structure" whose acts are irregular, unpredictable, often mysterious. A mother, in order to understand her child, must assume the existence of a conscious continuing person whose acts make sense in terms of perceptions and responses to a meaning-filled world. She knows that her child's fantasies and thoughts are connected not only to the child's power to act, but often are the only basis for her understanding of the child and for the child's self-understanding.

A mother, in short, is committed to two philosophical positions: she is a mentalist rather than a behaviorist, and she assumes the priority of personhood over action.

Moreover, if her "mentalism" is to enable her to understand and love, she must be realistic about the psyche whose growth she fosters. All psyches are moved by fear, lust, anger, pride, and defenses against them; by what Simone Weil (1951) called "natural movements of the soul" and likened to laws of physical gravity (see "Gravity and Grace"). This is not to deny that the soul is also blessed by "grace," "light," and erotic hungering for goodness.[9] Mothers cannot take grace for granted, however, nor can they force or deny the less flattering aggrandizing and consolatory operations of childhood psychic life.

Her realistic appreciation of a person's continuous mental life allows a mother to expect change, to change with change. As psychologist Jean Baker Miller puts it: "In a very immediate and day to day way women *live* for change" (54). Change requires a kind of learning in which what one learns cannot be applied exactly, often not even by analogy, to a new situation. If science agrees to take as real the reliable results of *repeatable* experiments,[10] its learning will be different in kind from maternal learning. Miller is hopeful that if we attend to maternal practices, we can develop new ways of studying learning that are appropriate to the changing natures of all people and communities, for it is not only children who change, grow, and need help in growing; those who care for children must also change in response to changing reality. And we all might grow—as opposed to aging—if we could learn how. For everyone's benefit, "women must now face the task of putting their vast unrecognized experience with change into a new and broader level of operation" (Miller 56).

Miller writes of achievement, of women who have learned to change and re-spond to change. But she admits: "Tragically in our society, Women are prevented from fully enjoying these pleasures [of growth] themselves by being made to feel that fostering them in others is the only valid role for all women and by the loneliness, drudgery and isolated non-cooperative household setting in which they work" (40).

In delineating maternal thought, I do not claim that mothers realize, in them-selves, the capacities and virtues we learn to value as we care for others. Rather, mothers develop *conceptions* of abilities and virtues, according to which they measure themselves and interpret their actions. It is no great sorrow that some mothers never acquire humility, resilient good humor, realism, respect for persons, and responsiveness to growth—that all of us fail often in many ways. What is a great sorrow is to find the task itself misdescribed, sentimentalized, and devalued.

The Interest in Shaping an Acceptable Child

The third demand that governs maternal practice is the demand, at once social and personal, that the child's growth be shaped in a manner that makes life acceptable. "Acceptability" is defined in terms of the values of the mother's social group—what-ever of its values she has internalized as her own plus values of group members whom she feels she must please or is fearful of displeasing. Society demands that a mother produce an adult acceptable to the next generation. Mothers, roughly half of society, have an interest in meeting that demand. They are also governed by a more stringent form of acceptability. They want the child they produce to be a person whom they themselves, and those closest to them, can appreciate. The demand of appreciability gives an urgency—sometimes exhilarating, sometimes anguishing—to maternal practice.

The task of producing an appreciable child gives a mother a unique opportunity to explore, create, and insist on her own values; to train her children for strength and virtue; and ultimately to develop openness and reciprocity in regard to her child's most threatening differences from her, namely, moral ones. As a mother thinks upon the appreciability of her child, her maternal work becomes a self-conscious, reflective expression of a disciplined conscience.

In response to the demand of acceptability, maternal thinking becomes contradictory—that is, it betrays its own interest in the growth of children. Almost everywhere, the practices of mothering take place in societies in which women of all classes are less powerful than men of their class to determine the conditions under which their children grow. Throughout history, most women have mothered in conditions of military and social violence and often of extreme poverty. They have been governed by men, and increasingly by managers and experts of both sexes, whose policies mothers neither shape nor control. Out of maternal powerlessness, in response to a society whose values it does not determine, maternal thinking has often and largely opted for inauthenticity and the "good" of others.

By "inauthenticity" I designate a double willingness—first, a willingness to *travailler pour l'armee*[11] to accept the uses to which others put one's children; and second, a willingness to remain blind to the implications of those uses for the actual lives of women and children. Maternal thought embodies inauthenticity by taking on the values of the dominant culture. Like the "holding" of preservation, "inauthenticity" is a mostly nonconscious response to Being as Such. Only this attitude is not a caretaker's response to the natural exigencies of child tending, but a subordinate's reaction to a social reality essentially characterized by the domination and subordination of persons. Inauthenticity constructs and then assumes a world in which one's own values do not count. It is allied to fatalism and to some religious thought—some versions of Christianity, for example. As inauthenticity is lived out in maternal practice, it gives rise to the values of obedience and "being good"; that is, to fulfill the values of the dominant culture is taken as an achievement. Obedience is related to humility in the face of the limits of one's powers. But unlike humility, which respects indifferent nature, the incomprehensible supernatural, and human fallibility, obedience respects the actual control and preferences of dominant people.

Individual mothers, living out maternal thought, take on the values of the subcultures to which they belong and the men with whom they are allied. Because some groups and many men are vibrantly moral, these values are not necessarily inadequate. Nevertheless, even moral groups and men almost always accept the relative subordination of women, whatever other ideals of equality and autonomy they may hold. A "good" mother may well be praised for colluding in her own subordination, with destructive consequences to herself and her children. Moreover, most groups and men impose at least some values that are psychologically and physically damaging to children. Yet, to be "good," a mother may be expected to endorse these inimical values. She is the person principally responsible for training her children in the ways and desires of obedience. This may mean training her daughters for powerlessness, her sons for war, and both for crippling work in dehumanizing factories, businesses, and professions. It may mean training both daughters and sons for defensive or arrogant power over others in sexual, economic, or political life. A mother who trains either for powerlessness or abusive power over others betrays the life she has preserved, whose growth she has fostered. She denies her children even the possibility of being strong and good.

The strain of colluding in one's own powerlessness, coupled with the frequent and much greater strain of betraying the children one has tended, would be insupportable if conscious. A mother under strain may internalize as her own some values that are clearly inimical to her children. She has, after all, usually been rewarded for such protective albeit destructive internalization. In addition, she may blind herself to the implications of her obedience, a blindness excused and exacerbated by the cheeriness of denial. For precariously but deeply protected mothers, feminist accounts of power relations and their cost call into question the worthiness of maternal work and the genuineness of maternal love. It is understandable that such women fight insight as others fight bodily assault, revealing in their struggles a commitment to their own sufferings that may look "neurotic" but is in fact, given their options, realistic.

When I described maternal thought arising out of the interests in growth and preservation, I was not speaking of the actual achievement of mothers, but of a conception of achievement. Similarly, in describing the thought arising out of the interest in acceptability, I am not speaking of actual mothers' adherence to dominant values, but of a conception of their relations to those values in which obedience and "being good" is considered an achievement. Many individual mothers "fail," that is, they insist on their own values and will not remain blind to the implications of dominant values for the lives of their children. Moreover, given the damaging effects of prevailing sexual arrangements and social hierarchies on maternal lives, it is clearly outrageous to blame mothers for their (our) obedience.

Obedience is largely a function of social powerlessness. Maternal work is done according to the Law of the Symbolic Father and under His Watchful Eye, as well as, typically, according to the desires, even whims, of the father's house. "This is my Father's world/Oh let me ne'er forget/that though the wrong be oft so strong,/He is the ruler yet." In these conditions of work, inauthentic obedience to dominant patriarchal values is as plausible a maternal response as respect for the results of experiment is in scientific work.

As I have said, the work of mothering can become a rewarding, disciplined expression of conscience. In order for this opportunity to be realized, either collectively or by individual mothers, maternal thought will have to be transformed by feminist consciousness.

> Coming to have a feminist consciousness is the experience of coming to know the truth about oneself and one's society.... The very *meaning* of what the feminist apprehends is illuminated by the light of what ought to be.... The feminist apprehends certain features of social reality *as* intolerable, as to be rejected in behalf of a transforming project for the future. ... Social reality is revealed as deceptive.... What is really happening is quite different from what appears to be happening. (Bartky 33, 25, 28, 29)

Feminist consciousness will first transform inauthentic obedience into wariness, uncertain reflection, and at times, anguished confusion. The feminist becomes "marked by the experience of moral ambiguity" as she learns new ways of living without betraying her women's past, without denying her obligations to others. "She no longer knows what sort of person she ought to be, and therefore, she does not know what she ought to do. One moral paradigm is called into question by the laborious and often obscure emergence of another" (Bartky 31).[12]

Out of confusion will arise new voices, recognized not so much by the content of the truths they enunciate as by the honesty and courage of enunciation. They will be at once familiar and original, these voices arising out of maternal practice, affirming its own criteria of acceptability, insisting that the dominant values are unacceptable and need not be accepted.

The Capacity for Attentive Love

Finally, I would like to discuss a capacity—attention—and a virtue—love—that are central to the conception of achievement that maternal thought as a whole articulates. This capacity and virtue, when realized, invigorate preservation and enable growth. Attention and love again and again undermine a mother's inauthentic obedience as she perceives and endorses a child's experience though society finds it intolerable. The identification of the capacity of attention and the virtue of love is at once the foundation and the corrective of maternal thought.

The notion of "attention" is central to the philosophy of Simone Weil and is developed, along with the related notion of "love," by Iris Murdoch, who was profoundly influenced by Weil. Attention and love are fundamental to the construction of "objective reality" understood "in relation to the progressing life of a person," a "reality which is revealed to the patient eye of love" (Murdoch 40). Attention is an *intellectual* capacity connected even by definition with love, a special "knowledge of the individual" (Murdoch 28). "The name of this intense, pure, disinterested, gratuitous, generous attention is love" (Weil 1977: 333). Weil thinks that the capacity for attention is a "miracle." Murdoch ties it more closely to familiar achievement: "The task of attention goes on all the time and at apparently empty and everyday moments we are 'looking,' making those little peering efforts of imagination which have such important cumulative results" (Murdoch 43).

For Weil and Murdoch, the enemy of attention is what they call "fantasy," defined not as rich imaginative play, which does have a central role in maternal thinking, but as the "proliferation of blinding self-centered aims and images" (Murdoch 67). Fantasy, according to their original conception, is intellectual and imaginative activity in the service of consolation, domination, anxiety, and aggrandizement. It is reverie designed to protect the psyche from pain, self-induced blindness designed to protect it from insight. Fantasy, so defined, works in the service of inauthenticity. "The difficulty is to keep the attention fixed on the real situation" (Murdoch 91)—or, as I would say, on the real children. Attention to real children, children seen by the "patient eye of love, ... teaches us how real things [real children] can be looked at and loved without being seized and used, without being appropriated into the greedy organism of the self" (Murdoch 65).

Much in maternal practices works against attentive love: intensity of identification, vicarious living through a child, daily wear of maternal work, harassment and indignities of an indifferent social order, and the clamor of children themselves. Although attention is elicited by the very reality it reveals—the reality of a growing person—it is a discipline that requires effort and self-training. The love of children is not only the most intense of attachments, but it is also a detachment, a giving up, a letting go. To love a child without seizing or using it, to see the child's reality with the patient, loving eye of attention—such loving and attending might well describe the separation of mother and child from the mother's point of view. Of course, many mothers fail much of the time in attentive love and loving attention. Many mothers also train themselves in the looking, self-restraining, and empathy that is loving attention. They can be heard doing so in any playground or coffee klatch.

I am not saying that mothers, individually or collectively, are (or are not) especially wonderful people. My point is that out of maternal practices distinctive ways of conceptualizing, ordering, and valuing arise. We *think* differently about what it *means* and what it takes to be "wonderful," to be a person, to be real.

Murdoch and Weil, neither mothers themselves nor especially concerned with mothers, are clear about the absolute value of attentive love and the reality it reveals. Weil writes:

> In the first legend of the Grail, it is said that the Grail ... belongs to the first comer who asks the guardian of the vessel, a king three-quarters paralyzed by the most painful wound, "What are you going through?"
> The love of our neighbor in all its fullness simply means being able to say to him: "What are you going through?" ...Only he who is capable of attention can do this. (1952: 115)

I do not claim absolute value, but only that attentive love, the training to ask

"What are you going through?" is central to maternal practices. If I am right about its place in maternal thought, and if Weil and Murdoch are right about its absolute value, the self-conscious inclusion of maternal thought in the dominant culture will be of general intellectual and moral benefit.

Some Social and Political Implications

I have described a "thought" arising out of maternal practices organized by the interests of preservation, growth, and acceptability. Although in some respects the thought is "contradictory" (i.e., it betrays its own values and must be transformed by feminist consciousness), the thought as a whole, with its fulcrum and correction in attentive love, is worthy of being expressed and respected. This thought has emerged out of maternal practices that are oppressive to women and children. I believe that it has emerged largely in response to the relatively invariable requirements of children and despite oppressive circumstances. As in all women's thought, some worthy aspects of maternal thought may arise out of identification with the powerless and excluded. Nevertheless, oppression is largely responsible for the defects rather than the strengths of maternal thought, as in the obedient goodness to which mothers find themselves "naturally" subscribing. When the oppressiveness of gender arrangements is combined with the oppression of race, poverty, or the multiple injuries of class, it is a miracle that maternal thought can arise at all. On the other hand, that it does indeed arise, miraculously, is clear both from literature (Alice Walker, Tillie Olsen, Maya Angelou, Agnes Smedley, Lucille Clifton, Louisa May Alcott, Audre Lorde, Marilyn French, Grace Paley, and countless others) and from daily experience. Maternal thought *identifies* priorities, attitudes, and virtues; it *conceives* of achievement. The more oppressive the institutions of motherhood, the greater the pain and struggle in living out the worthy and transforming the damaging aspects of thought.

Maternal thinking is only one aspect of "womanly" thinking.[13] In articulating and respecting the maternal, I do not underwrite the still current, false, and pernicious identification of womanhood with biological or adoptive mothering of particular children in families. For me, "maternal" is a social category. Although maternal thinking arises out of actual child-caring practices, biological parenting is neither necessary nor sufficient. Many women and some men express maternal thinking in various kinds of working and caring with others. And some biological mothers, especially in misogynistic societies, take a fearful, defensive distance from their own mothering and the maternal lives of any women.

Maternal thought does, I believe, exist for all women in a radically different way than for men. It is because we are *daughters,* nurtured and trained by women, that we early receive maternal love with special attention to its implications for our bodies, our passions, and our ambitions. We are alert to the values and costs of maternal practices whether we are determined to engage in them or avoid them.

It is now argued that the most revolutionary change we can make in the institution of motherhood is to include men equally in every aspect of childcare. When men and women live together with children, it seems not only fair but deeply moral that they share in every aspect of childcare. To prevent or excuse men from maternal practice is to encourage them to separate public action from private affection, the privilege of parenthood from its cares. Moreover, even when men are absent from the nursery, their dominance in every other public and private room shapes a child's earliest conceptions of power. To familiarize children with "natural" domination at their earliest age in a context of primitive love, assertion, and sexual passion is to prepare them to find equally "natural" and exhaustive the division between exploiter and exploited that pervades the larger world. Although daughter and son alike may internalize "natural" domination, neither typically can live with it easily. Identifying with and imitating exploiters, we are overcome with self-hate; aligning ourselves with the exploited, we are fearful and manipulative. Again and again, family power dramas are repeated in psychic, interpersonal, and professional dramas, while they are institutionalized in economic, political, and international life. Radically recasting the power-gender roles in those dramas just might revolutionize social conscience.[14]

Assimilating men into childcare both inside and outside the home would also be conducive to serious social reform. Responsible, equal childcaring would require men to relinquish power and their own favorable position in the division between intellectual/professional and service labor as that division expresses itself domestically. Loss of preferred status at home might make socially privileged men more suspicious of unnecessary divisions of labor and damaging hierarchies in the public world. Moreover, if men were emotionally and practically committed to childcare, they would reform the work world in parents' interests. Once no one "else" was minding the child, good day-care centers with flexible hours would be established to which parents could trust their children from infancy on. These day-care centers, like the workweek itself, would be managed flexibly in response to human needs as well as to the demands of productivity, with an eye to growth rather than measurable profit. Such moral reforms of economic life would probably begin with professions and managers servicing themselves. Even in nonsocialist countries, however, their benefits could be unpredictably extensive.

I would not argue that the assimilation of men into childcare is the primary social goal for mothers. Rather, we must work to bring a *transformed* maternal thought in the public realm, to make the preservation and growth of *all* children a work of public conscience and legislation. This will not be easy. Mothers are no less corrupted than anyone else by concerns of status and class. Often our misguided efforts on behalf of the success and purity of our children frighten them and everyone else around them. As we increase and enjoy our public effectiveness, we will have less reason to live vicariously through our children. We may then begin to learn to sustain a creative tension between our inevitable and fierce desire to foster our own children and the less compulsive desire that all children grow and flourish.

Nonetheless, it would be foolish to believe that mothers, just because they are mothers, can transcend class interest and implement principles of justice. All feminists must join in articulating a theory of justice shaped by and incorporating maternal thinking. Moreover, the generalization of attentive love to *all* children requires politics. The most enlightened thought is not enough.

Closer to home again, we must refashion our domestic life in the hope that the personal will in fact betoken the political. We must begin by resisting the temptation to construe "home" simplemindedly, as a matter of justice between mothers and fathers. Single parents, lesbian mothers, and coparenting women remind us that many ways to provide children with examples of caring do not incorporate sexual inequalities of power and privilege. Those of us who live with the fathers of our children will eagerly welcome shared parenthood—for overwhelming practical as well as ideological reasons. But in our eagerness, we must not forget that as long as a mother is not effective publicly and self-respecting privately, male presence can be harmful as well as beneficial. It does a woman no good to have the power of the Symbolic Father brought right into the nursery, often despite the deep, affectionate egalitarianism of an individual man. It takes a strong mother and father to resist temptations to domination and subordination for which they have been trained and are socially rewarded. And whatever the hard-won equality and mutual respect an individual couple may achieve, as long as a mother—even if she is no more parent than father—is derogated and subordinate outside the home, children will feel angry, confused, and "wildly unmothered" (Rich 1976: 225).

Despite these reservations, I look forward to the day when men are willing and able to share equally and actively in transformed maternal practices. When that day comes, will we still identify some thought as maternal rather than merely parental? Might we echo the cry of some feminists—there shall be no more "women"—with our own—there shall be no more "mothers," only people engaging in childcare? To keep matters clear I would put the point differently. On that day there will be no more "fathers," no more people of either sex who have power over their children's lives and moral authority in their children's world, though they do not do the work of attentive love. There will be mothers of both sexes who live out a transformed maternal thought in communities that share parental care—practically, emotionally, economically, and socially. Such communities will have learned from their mothers how to value children's lives.

I began circulating an early draft of this paper in the fall of 1978. Since then, the constructive criticism and warm response of readers has led me to believe that this draft is truly a collective endeavor. I would like especially to thank Sandra Bartky, Gail Bragg, Bell Chevigny, Nancy Chodorow, Margaret Comstock, Mary Felstiner, Berenice Fisher, Marilyn Frye, Susan Harding, Evelyn Fox Keller, Jane Lilienfeld, Jane Marcus, Adrienne Rich, Amelie Rorty, William Ruddick, Barrie Thorne, Marilyn Blatt Young, readers for Feminist Studies, *and Rayna Rapp.*

A longer version of this essay appeared in Feminist Studies *6 (2) (Summer 1980).* © *1980 by Feminist Studies, Inc. Reprinted by permission of the publisher and the author. The present version appeared in* Rethinking the Family, *edited by Barrie Thorne with Marilyn Yalom (New York: Longman, 1982).*

Notes

[1] From J. Echegaray, "Severed Heart," quoted in Bernard, *The Future of Motherhood* (4).

[2] Nothing I say about maternal thought suggests that the women who engage in it cannot engage in other intellectual discourse. A maternal thinker may also be an experimental psychologist, a poet, a mathematician, an architect, a physicist. I believe that because most thinkers have been men, most disciplines are partly shaped by "male" concepts, values, styles, and strategies. Unless we have identified "male" and "female" aspects of thought, however, the claim of gender bias is an empty one. I do not doubt that disciplines are also shaped by transgender interests, values, and concepts, which women, whether or not they engage in maternal practices, may fully share. To the extent that the disciplines are shaped by "male" thought, mothers and other women may feel alienated by the practices and thinking of their own discipline. Correlatively, when thinkers are as apt to be women as men, thought itself may change. On these and related points see Evelyn Keller (1978).

[3] Examples of the invariant and *nearly* unchangeable include long gestation inside the mother's body; prolonged infant and childhood dependence; physical fragility of infancy; radical qualitative and quantitative change ("growth") in emotional and intellectual capacities from infancy to adulthood; long development and psychological complexity of human sexual desire, of memory and other cognitive capacities, and of "object relations." Features that are *nearly* universal and certainly changeable include the identification of childbearing and childcaring, the consequent delegation of childcare to biological mothers and other women, and the relative subordination of women in any social class to men of that class.

[4] To see the universal in particulars, to assimilate differences and extend kinship, is a legacy of the ecumenical Protestantism in which I was raised. I am well aware that even nonviolent, well-meaning Protestant assimilations can be obtuse and cruel for others. Therefore I am dependent on others, morally as well as intellectually, for the statement of differences, the assessment of their effects on every aspect of maternal lives, and finally for radical correction as well as for expansion of any general theory I would offer. I do not *believe*, however, that the thinking I describe is limited only to "privileged white women," as one reader put it. I first came to the notion of "maternal thinking" and the virtues of maternal practices through personal exchange with Tillie Olsen and then through reading her fiction. Similarly, I believe that "Man Child: A Black Lesbian Feminist's Response" by Audre Lorde (1979), is an excellent example of what I call maternal thinking transformed by feminist consciousness. My "assimilation" of Olsen's and Lorde's work in no way

denies differences that separate us nor the biases those differences may introduce into my account. These are only two of many examples of writers in different social circumstances who express what I take to be "maternal thinking."

[5]For the comparison, see Iris Murdoch, *The Sovereignty of Good* (1971). Popular moralities as well as contemporary moral theory tend to emphasize decision, assertion, happiness, authenticity, and justification by principle.

[6]See also Proposition 40, Note, and Proposition 45, both in Book 3 of *Ethics*.

[7]The words are those of a Texas farmwoman who quilted as she huddled with her family in a shelter as, above them, a tornado destroyed their home. The story was told to me by Miriam Schapiro.

[8]These are differences often attributed to women both by themselves and by psychologists. For a critical review of the literature, see Eleanor Maccoby and Carol Jacklin, *The Psychology of Sex Differences* (1974). For a plausible account of women's valuing of inner life, see Patricia Meyer Spacks, *The Female Imagination* (1975). Maccoby and Jacklin are critical both of the findings I mentioned and of the adequacy of the psychological experiments they survey for testing or discovering these differences. I make little use of psychology, more of literature, in thinking about the cognitive sex differences I discuss. Psychologists are not, as far as I know, talking about women who have empathically identified with and assimilated maternal practices, either by engaging in them or by identifying with their own or other mothers. It would be hard to identify such a subgroup of women without circularity. But even if one could make the identification, tests would have to be devised that measure not achievement but conception of achievement. Mothers, to take one example, may well prize the inner life, but they have so little time for it or are so self-protectively defended against their own insights that they gradually lose the capacity for inner life. Or again, a mother may not maintain sharp boundaries between herself and her child or between her child's "outer" action and inner life. She *must* maintain some boundaries, however. We value what we are in danger of losing (e.g., inner life); we identify virtues because we recognize temptations to vice (e.g., openness because we are tempted to rigid control); we refuse what we fear giving way to (e.g., either pathological symbiotic identification *or* an unworkable division between our own and our children's interests). It is difficult to imagine tests sophisticated and sensitive enough to measure such conceptions, priorities, and values. I have found psychoanalytic theory the most useful of psychologies and Nancy Chodorow's *The Reproduction of Mothering* (1978) the most helpful in applying psychoanalytic theory to maternal practices.

[9]See "Gravity and Grace" and other essays in *Gravity and Grace* (Weil 1951); both the language and concepts are indebted to Plato.

[10]As Habermas argues in *Knowledge and Human Interests* (1971).

[11]I am indebted to Adrienne Rich's *Of Woman Born* (1976), especially chapter 8, both for this phrase and for the working out of the idea of inauthenticity. My debt to this book as a whole is pervasive.

[12]On the riskiness of authenticity, the courage it requires of women, see also Miller, *Toward a New Psychology of Women*, chapter 9.

[13]Among other possible aspects of women's thought are those that might arise from our sexual lives, from our "home-making," from the special conflict women feel between allegiance, on the one hand, to women and their world and, on the other hand, to all people of their kin and culture. Any identifiable aspect of women's thought will be interrelated to all the others. Since women almost everywhere are relatively powerless in relation to men of their class, all aspects of women's thought will be affected by powerlessness. Whether we are discussing the thought arising from women's bodily, sexual, maternal, homemaking, linguistic, or any other experience, we are faced with a confluence of powerlessness and the "womanly," whatever that might be.

[14]These points have been made by many feminists, most provocatively and thoroughly by Dorothy Dinnerstein in *The Mermaid and the Minotaur* (1976).

References

Bartky, Sandra Lee. "Toward a Phenomenology of Feminist Consciousness." *Feminism and Philosophy*. Eds. Mary Vetterling-Braggin, Frederick A. Elliston and Jane English. Totowa: Littlefield, Adams, 1977. 22-37.

Bernard, Jessie. *The Future of Motherhood*. New York: Dial, 1974.

Chodorow, Nancy. *The Reproduction of Mothering*. Berkeley: University of California Press, 1978.

Dinnerstein, Dorothy. *The Mermaid and the Minotaur*. New York: Harper and Row, 1976.

Habermas, Jurgen. *Knowledge and Human Interests*. Boston: Beacon Press, 1971.

Keller, Evelyn. "Gender and Science." *Psychoanalysis and Contemporary Thought* 3 (1978): 409-53.

Kessler, Suzanne and Wendy McKenna. *Gender*. New York: John Wiley and Sons, 1978.

Lorde, Audre. "Man Child: A Black Lesbian Feminist's Response." *Conditions* 4 (1979): 30-36.

Maccoby, Eleanor and Carol Jacklin. *The Psychology of Sex Differences*. Stanford: Stanford University Press, 1974.

Miller, Jean Baker. *Toward a New Psychology for Women*. Boston: Beacon Press, 1973.

Murdoch, Iris. *The Sovereignty of Good*. New York: Shocken Books, 1971.

Rich, Adrienne. "Conditions for Work: The Common World of Women." *Working It Out*. Eds. Sara Ruddick and Pamela Daniels. New York: Pantheon, 1977.

Rich, Adrienne. *Of Woman Born*. New York: W.W. Norton, 1976.

Spacks, Patricia Meyer. *The Female Imagination*. New York: Alfred A. Knopf, 1975.

Weil, Simone. *Collected Essays*. Trans. Richard Rees. London: Oxford University Press, 1962.

Weil, Simone. *Gravity and Grace*. London: Routledge and Kegan Paul, 1951.

Weil, Simone. *Simone Weil Reader*. Ed. George A. Panichas. New York: McKay, 1977.

Weil, Simone. *Waiting for God*. New York: G. Putnam's, 1952.

Williams, Bernard. *Morality*. New York: Harper Torchbooks, 1972.

Winch, Peter. "Understanding a Primitive Society." *Ethics and Action*. London: Routledge and Kegan Paul, 1972.

Wittgenstein, Ludwig. *On Certainty*. Oxford: Basil Blackwell, 1969.

Wittgenstein, Ludwig. *Philosophical Investigations*. Oxford: Basil Blackwell, 1953.

Wittgenstein, Ludwig. *Remarks on the Foundations of Mathematics*. Oxford: Basil Blackwell, 1956.

Wittgenstein, Ludwig. *Zettel*. Oxford: Basil Blackwell, 1967.

Woolf, Virginia. *To the Lighthouse*. New York: Harcourt, Brace and World, 1927.

Chapter 7

Preservative Love and Military Destruction
Some Reflections on Mothering and Peace

SARA RUDDICK

IN 1979, DR. HELEN CALDICOTT called women to nonviolent battle.

> A Women's Party for Survival is being organized throughout the U.S. and women all over the world are mobilizing for disarmament ... Women have tremendous power. As mothers we must make sure the world is safe for our babies.... Look at the changing seasons ... Look at our growing children. Look at one child, one baby.... I have three children. And I'm a doctor who treats children.... I live with dying children. I live with grieving parents. I understand the value of every human life.... We have only a short time to turn the destructive powers around. A short time. I appeal especially to the women to do this work because we understand the genesis of life. Our bodies are built to nurture life. We have wombs, we have breasts, we have menstrual periods to remind us that we can produce life! We also have a voice in the affairs of the world and are becoming more influential every day. I beg of you: do what you can today.[1]

Three claims are embodied in this call: (a) Women have distinctive interests in and capacities for peacemaking; (b) these interests and capacities are connected with maternity; and (c) although women's peacemaking has hitherto been confined to maternal life, we have "more influence every day" in making the *world* safe for our children.

These claims are plausible and alluring. Men and women alike tend to believe women are peaceful and to notice and reward peacefulness in women and girls. Surveys confirm these beliefs by showing women voters as more anti-militarist than men and predominant among followers of pacifists. Women who organize themselves in peace groups often draw upon images of maternity to explain their commitment and urge it on others. And many men who are dramatically linked with peace reveal a strong identification with their mothers and sometimes themselves come to speak in a recognizably maternal voice. Gandhi, Wilfred Owen, Andre Trocmé, and Randall Jarrell are all examples, in different ways, of maternal men. We can understand why it has been tempting to imagine a world governed by maternal peacefulness. Now that peaceful women are inspirited by feminist assertion, it seems possible for maternal vision to acquire "tremendous power."

Although plausible and alluring, Dr. Caldicott's claims are also dubious and dangerous. Women, perhaps especially mothers, have played their assigned roles in a militarized world. On the sidelines of battle, women have been applauders and suppliers; plunder at the end of the day; home at the end of the war; mourners who let the fighting go on. Mothers have sacrificed their sons to the most vile as well as the most just of causes. When officers deem it appropriate for women to fight—to defend a besieged city, to take up arms when men have fallen—women fight no less fiercely than men. Women have always been expected to fight defensively in protection of their children and homes. Increasingly, women ask to be in the front lines of combat, "carrying the fight to the enemy" with the fiercest weapons their armies possess.

Women historically have played a dominant role in pacifist movements. Because of their courage and effectiveness as pacifists in a society where women had little voice, these women publicized a pacifism that was self-consciously maternal. But while women pacifists struggled against war and male dominance, other women prepared for war (see, especially, Steinson; Elshtain). Both militarists and pacifists have justified their choices in maternal terms. Some mothers wanted their sons freed forever from the threat of war; others wanted them to fight with the best guns and ships their state could produce. "Earlier I buttered bread for him, now I paint grenades and think."[2]

Even if we could believe in the peacefulness of mothers, it is not clear that we would want to. If feminism has empowered women, it has often done so by attacking the identification of women with maternity. Conversely, emphasizing the maternity of women has proved an effective strategy of male supremacists. Dr. Caldicott herself, in her celebration of female bodies, slips into a romanticism that is both silly and dangerous. To confine mothers in domestic work and nurturant bodies, and then to praise them for peacefulness, disparages both the woman and the virtue she is said to possess. Mothers rightly resent a sentimentality which obscures the complex power and real, limited abilities of maternal work. Men and women doubt the effectiveness of a virtue acquired in conditions of powerlessness and confined to the home.

Hopes and doubts about traditional female work and virtues are part of a dialog in which feminists are now engaged, a dialog many of us carry on in our heads. As I write in America, in the winter of 1982, the dangers of connecting being female with being a mother seem stark. Once again, women are being forced and are forcing each other into accepting unchosen maternity and into leading powerless, if idealized, maternal lives. Yet at the same time, we are living in a militarized state, armed with insanely destructive and self-destructive weapons, plagued by violences not only against individuals and nations, but against classes and races. "Enemies" abound, self-righteous hatred seems a virtue, murder is legitimate. In these circumstances, any resource of peacefulness should be made politically effective.

Despite the risk and because of the dangers we find ourselves in, I stop the dialog in my head and respond to Dr. Caldicott's call. I believe mothers do have a tradition of peacefulness that can be strengthened and mobilized for the public good. Attending to this female virtue seems justified by the horrors of military and domestic violence. Moreover, on reflection, feminist politics and maternal peacefulness are not at odds. Indeed, I argue later that if domestic pacifism is to become a public good, it must be transformed by feminism. It is true that appeals to womanly maternity have a reactionary sound, if not effect. But finally the dangers of reaction seem outweighed by the possibility that mothers and other women have a distinctive contribution to make to the cause of peace.

Were I a leader and persuader, I would attempt to rally mothers and other women to a mother-identified politics of protest. What I will do here, instead, is to explore some of the connections that justify such a politics: connections between mothers and other women, between maternal thinking and pacifism, between maternal pacifism and feminism. Briefly my claim is this: the conventional and symbolic association between women and peace has a real basis in maternal practice. Out of maternal practice a distinctive kind of thinking arises that is incompatible with military strategy but consonant with pacifist commitment to non-violence. The peacefulness of mothers, however, is not now a reliable source for peace. In order for motherly peacefulness to be publicly significant, maternal practice must respect and extend its pacifism. For this to happen, maternal thinking would have to be transformed by a feminist politics.

The Very Idea of Maternal Thinking

In an earlier paper, I tried to show that distinctive ways of thinking arise out of the work mothers do (see Ruddick). In their practices, people respond to a reality they experience as *given,* as presenting certain "demands." Their "interest" in meeting these demands seems equally *given,* a requirement of reason, and therefore a particular kind of psychological motivation.

Maternal practice is governed by "interests" in satisfying "demands" for the preservation, growth, and acceptability of children. In saying that maternal practice is governed by these interests, I am not implying that individual mothers are enthusiastically dedicated to these aims. Actual mothers have the same kind of relation to maternal practices as scientists have to scientific practice, as believers have to religious practice. An individual scientist may hate her work, wish she were writing poetry or swimming in the Caribbean, fabricate her "evidence" (by, for example, painting spots on her laboratory animals), and write up her experiments with half an eye while watching "General Hospital." Nonetheless, in scientific practice the very idea of truth is dependent upon replication by experiment, a logical dependence unaffected by the attitudes of the individual experimenter. To engage in the practice is, *inter alia,* to accept the connection between truth and experimental replication (see Habermas). Similarly, a mother may, on most days, hate her work or even her children. She may ignore or assault them, adore or despair of them. The style, skill, and enthusiasm with which mothers engage in their practice vary enormously. Nonetheless, achievement, in maternal work, is defined by the aims of preserving, fostering, and shaping the growth of a child; insofar as one engages in maternal practice, one accepts these aims as one's own.

Despite differences between mothers, I believe that a distinctive kind of thinking arises when one attempts to understand, control, and communicate the strategies and aims of maternal practice. That is, there is a commonality of childhood life and maternal experience which allows us to speak of the demands of *human* children and of interests in meeting them. But every common feature of childhood development and maternal experience is also subject to social as well as individual variation. The very definition of "childhood," the meaning of "dependence," opportunities for sexual and intellectual development, recognition of complexity, and of course ideas of acceptability are culturally and historically determined. The technological, medical, and material resources available to a woman vary from culture to culture and between classes of a culture. At different times, a child's life is more or less fragile, a child's growth may be a fairly natural process or a struggle to survive. Although the concept of maternal thinking depends upon similarity, to describe that thinking requires recognizing differences that shape every aspect of a mother's day and life.

The particularity, the cultural relativity of maternal thinking is not a defect to be overcome. It is good that we cannot talk meaningfully about "*the* maternal," outside of the technological, historical, geographical, and political contexts in which women mother. We will not, to paraphrase Simone de Beauvoir, be able to float in the universal. Any generalization about maternal thinking must be embodied and exhibited in particular mother-child relations. This requirement has both epistemological and political consequences. For example, fiction, memoirs, and oral history become the primary source material of maternal thought. The silences of mothers can be deafening; no theory, philosophic or statistical, can teach us what mothers would say if they themselves respected and expressed their ordering of our allegedly common world. Moreover, when we look at maternal practice through the lens of shared maternal interest we see the centrality and the devastating effects of poverty or war or racial oppression on mothers' lives. To be a "good enough mother" in a society that does not value your child's life or self-respect transforms the everyday unromantic work of mothering into a heroic task.

Whether one is struck by similarity or differences between people seems partly a matter of temperament and training. The ecumenical Protestantism in which I was raised, and the study of philosophy which followed, taught me to look for a *human* condition underlying social and individual variation. A tendency to universalize, underestimating differences one cannot or will not see, can be personally cruel as well as politically arrogant and dangerous. The very idea of maternal thinking reflects personal and social biases; the application of that notion to a philosophy of conflict accentuates them. It is notorious that definitions of violence and techniques of reconciliation differ markedly in different social groups. I allow that the basis for pacifism I here ascribe to "maternal" thinking may exist only in certain groups with which I am familiar. I necessarily depend upon others of different training and social identity to compensate for the limits of my particular history, to correct my interpretations and expand my vision. Blindness to the differences that truly separate us and to the suffering they cause is, after all, a primary cause of war. It is also true, I believe, that peace in a nuclear age depends upon our learning to understand ourselves as members of a species precariously inhabiting together a particular planet.

My claim that aspects of maternal practice are shared throughout the species should not be confused with a different claim that there are essential ineradicable differences between male and female parents. In a degenderized society, where political and economic power as well as every aspect of childcare are shared between men and women, it is difficult to predict what differences our bodies and distinctive histories would make. We cannot preclude the possibility that some aspects of maternal thinking derive from the infant's, and perhaps from the mother's, biological constitution and experience. In less technologically developed societies the connection between maternal bodies and mothering is made visible in repeated pregnancies and public nursing. Even so, the biological moments of a mother's life make up only a small part of the caretaking her children receive. Almost all grown women menstruate, many bear children, many of these nurse them. I do not believe, however, as Dr. Caldicott seems to, that distinctive peacefulness arises from these ovarian adventures. A love affair with our own bleeding, gestating, birthing, lactating bodies only diverts attention from the daily work women do. I do not deny the intense, if ambivalent, pleasures women get from their own and each others' sexual, nurturing bodies. But these pleasures provide at best an inspiration and metaphor for peacefulness. The real basis of female pacifism lies in the complicated social activity of preservative love.

Mothers and Other Women

Not all women are mothers, nor is maternal thinking the whole of women's thought. Equally important, maternal thinking is not the whole of a *mother's* thought any more than maternity is the whole of a mother's life. Although maternal thinking arises out of the care of actual children, not only mothers are maternal thinkers. Many women express maternal thinking in various kinds of caring for others. Moreover, some men now acquire maternal thinking, and many more could. Nevertheless, in our society, now, their ways of acquisition are necessarily different from ours. It is because we are *daughters* that we early receive maternal love with special attention to its implications for our bodies, passions, and ambitions.

In a society where primary parents are still likely to be mothers and other women, and where so many women eventually become mothers, it is impossible to separate practically or conceptually the maternal from the womanly. Consider, for example, women's alleged greater capacity for empathy arising from a less sharply delineated sense of self, which is a consequence of the special intensity and character of mother-daughter relations (see, especially, Chodorow 1978; Gilligan). The young girl acquires a capacity for empathy from her mother(s) whom she gradually learns is more or less the same kind of creature she is, an "identity" the mother herself appreciates and conveys. When the young empathic girl becomes a mother, empathy is both elicited and developed in the care of children. (Remember that mothers are typically very young women, their adult psyches are strongly shaped by the maternal practices they engage in.) In the course of maternal caring, empathy becomes a mode of apprehension and caring which I have called "attentive love." The daughter learns this attentiveness from the mother as the mother herself is developing it. Attentiveness is appropriate to maternal care, and (in part) makes possible a maternal competence, which makes possible identification with a mother. Other aspects of maternal thought, such as the cheerfulness, holding, and philosophy of conflict that I will mention later have similar roles. Often, in the literature, attention to the quality and intensity of mother-daughter relations scants their content. When a daughter "identifies" with a mother, the mother does not represent contentless female being, but a distinctive way of caring and knowing. The daughter is a kind of apprentice, learning a work and a way of thinking about it. These "lessons" may shape her intellectual and emotional life even if she comes to hate the work, the thought or, for that matter, the mother.

To put my point generally, female nature both explains and is explained by maternal thinking. Alleged sex differences shape maternal thought. On the other hand, the appropriateness of the sex characteristics to maternal work partly explains their existence and adult development. In the growing feminist literature on sex differences I have found widespread agreement in judgments that are expressed in different disciplinary contexts and languages. Almost always, I have been able to relate these independent findings to maternal thought doubly, both as *explicans* and *explicandum*.

Mothers and Virtue

When I first started writing about motherliness, it was important to me to stress that mothers *think*, that a maternal perspective is not only a matter of feeling or of virtue. I underlined the fact that I was not claiming that mothers are especially wonderful people, nor that maternal practices are noted for their achievements. Rather, I was saying that mothers had a distinctive sense of what it meant to be "wonderful," to be a "person"; that they had distinctive *conceptions* of achievement worth considering. Partly because of my increasing commitment to mothers as a class, a passion which seeped through the lines of my paper, I left unclear the relation of maternal thinking to maternal virtue.

The confusion has important political consequences. If, as some believe, mothers are, just as mothers, especially *good*, then one political strategy is to increase the power of mothers in the interests of the public good. But the story is more complicated. In some cases, maternal thinking does name virtues, that is, it identifies certain strengths appropriate to the work of preservation and growth and acceptability. This is to say not that mothers *have* the virtue, but that they *recognize* it. Moreover, maternal thinkers in recognizing a virtue do not pick out a trait mothers should acquire, but instead identify a struggle they experience. Let me give two examples.

While preserving the physical and psychic life of a child in an indifferent world, a mother identifies a kind of resilient good humor as a virtue, a clear-sighted cheerfulness, which, in Spinoza's words, "increases and assists the power of action." Yet cheerfulness always threatens to break down into cheery denial, its degenerative form. We so wish the world were better for our children—and ourselves—that we deny its true character and power to hurt. If I were to express the moral theory of maternal thinking in simple form, I would say something like this: resilient good humor is necessary to preservation and growth. Yet equally necessary is a realistic perception of the natural and social threats that mothers, and eventually children, must counter. Just because cheerfulness is such a good, the smiles of our children are so comforting, and the natural and social order so indifferent or hostile, cheery denial is always a temptation. We must expect an ongoing struggle, then, to maintain cheerfulness in the face of many reasons for despair, while refusing the dangerous tranquility of cheery denial.

Another example. At the center of maternal thinking is a capacity which, following Simone Weil, I have termed attention, and which is defined interdependently with love (Ruddick). Attention is "a special kind of knowledge of the individual"; it is an ability to ask "what are you going through" and an ability to hear the answer. Continuously, attention calls for a radical kind of self-denial. "The soul empties itself of all its contents in order to receive into itself the being it is looking at, just as he is, in all his truth" (Murdoch 28, 65, 91, passim; Weil 1977a, 1977b). But such self-denial, necessary at moments, is not identical with attentive love. On the contrary, attentive love calls for a realistic self-preservation on the part of the mother, a mother-self that can be seen and identified by the child who is itself learning attentive love. Again, to put the point very simply, maternal thinking might be construed as saying: attentive love is a mode of apprehension inseparable from care, through which mothers know as they love, and create as they respect, their children. In developing the discipline of attention, however, one must be constantly wary that moments of radical self-denial—which are necessary—do not become the perverted aim of attention rather than its occasional expression. Self-denial is always tempting, especially in societies where adults and children reward mothers for their *failures* in self-preservation. But the attentiveness that aids growth, and which, if children learn it, will enable *them* to love attentively while remaining the assertive creatures whose growth we foster, is an attention that respects both self and other (Chodorow 1979; Gilligan; Miller). Pervasive, chronic self-denial leads to a mother's spiritual impoverishment and to her projecting denied needs onto others. It encourages tyranny in the children, especially in the sons who can reject it as a mode of *their* being, and it rewards the misogyny of the world. Maternal thinking identifies attentive love as the fulcrum, the foundation of maternal practice; at the same time it identifies chronic self-denial in its many forms as the characteristic temptation of mothers and the besetting vice of maternal work. In naming the virtue and its degenerative form, it points to a struggle.

I have been discussing virtues and their degenerative forms which maternal thinking has appropriately identified, thereby naming a struggle and imposing a discipline on the practice. I believe that there are also instances in which maternal thinking has misidentified virtue, i.e., where the thinking itself is in need of transformation. I have argued that this is the case with much of the thinking arising out of the demand of a social group that children be raised in an *acceptable* way. In response to the demand of acceptability maternal thinking becomes contradictory—that is, betrays its own interests in the preservation and growth of children. It does so by misidentifying inauthenticity as a necessary mode of apprehension and obedience to the good of others as a virtue. Inauthenticity is one of the many forms of maternal self-denial, an inability to take one's self as authority, to trust one's own perceptions of children's needs and capacities.

Finally, in maternal thinking a central tension is created between the fierce desire to foster one's own children and the commitment to the well-being of all children. The more individualistic, hierarchical, and competitive the social system, the more likely that a mother will see the good of her child and her group's children as *opposed* to the good of children of another mother or another "kind." However, I do not foresee that in *any* society mothers will typically and wholeheartedly endorse the common good of children when it conflicts with their own children's interests. Maternal practice assumes a legitimate special concern for the children one has engendered and passionately loves as well as for the families (of various forms) in which they live. Any attempt to deny this special form of self-interest will only lead to hypocritical false consciousness or rigid, totalistic loyalties. Mothers can, I believe, come to realize that the good of their own children is entwined with the good of all children, that in a world divided between exploiter and exploited no children can be both good and strong, that in a world at war all children are endangered. We can as mothers learn to sustain a conflicted but creative tension between personal loyalties and impersonal moral concerns. The conflict between the demands of one's own and the demand of the whole, however, will not disappear. This maternal conflict can bring a sense of realism and moral humility to political struggle; it also suggests real limits to the effectiveness of maternal thinking in political life.

In sum, then, many aspects of maternal thinking embody a metaphysical and moral perspective that anyone might profitably consider. But the relation of maternal thinking to virtue is at best complex. Some aspect of the contradictoriness of maternal thinking will be ameliorated by a feminist consciousness that works against various forms of self-denial. In a less hierarchical society, disciplined imagination and moral reflection could reveal the interconnectedness of children's interests with the causes of peace, ecological sanity, and distributive justice. But mothers know better than to expect perfection of themselves. In the best of non-patriarchal, socialist worlds, maternal practice will involve conflict; "maternal thinking" will describe a moral activity rather than a virtue achieved.

Maternal Practice and Pacifist Commitment

Maternal virtue cannot translate directly into public good. Nonetheless, there may be goods that mothers have both conceptualized and realized in distinctive ways. One such good is peacefulness. By "peacefulness" I mean a commitment to avoid battle whenever possible. to fight necessary battles nonviolently, and to take, as the aim of battle, reconciliation between opponents and restoration of connection and community. I will call this the "pacifist commitment." Its most prominent controversial feature is the renunciation of violence even in causes whose justice is undisputed. By "violence" I mean strategies or weapons which are intended to *damage* an opponent, or which can reasonably be expected to do so. By "damage" I mean at least physical or psychological harm for which there is no compensatory benefit to the person damaged and which is, or is likely to be, indefinitely lasting.[3] Military strategy is opposed to pacifist commitment in that it accepts violence to achieve causes deemed good or advantageous and values victory over reconciliation.[4]

In what sense do mothers share with pacifists a rejection of military strategy arising from the renunciation of violence and commitment to reconciliation? Most obviously, maternal preservative love is incompatible with military destruction. Most important, maternal practice gives rise to a theory of conflict similar to that of pacifists, especially to Gandhian *satyagraha*. There is also a war-like cognitive style and an erotics of destruction. I believe that maternal sexuality and cognition contrast with these and are therefore potentially anti-militarist. I will consider in turn each of the four pacifist elements of maternal practice and thinking: preservative love, a philosophy of conflict, cognition, and sexuality.

Preservative Love and Military Strategy

Maternal practice is governed by the primary demand that a child's life and health be preserved. From an early age, a mother trains her children, shapes their growth in a way that is acceptable to adults and, one hopes, good for the child. The child's physical, psychological, and moral well-being are all fragile, are all the object of preservative love. By "preservative love" I do not mean a feeling. Mothers' feelings toward their children vary from hour to hour, year to year. A single day can encompass fury, infatuation, boredom, and simple dislike without being in any way atypical. Preservative love is an *activity* of caring or treasuring creatures whose well-being is at risk.

In response to the demand that she preserve her child in an indifferent and often hostile world, a mother develops an attitude to human and nonhuman nature that I call "holding." This attitude is characterized by the priority given to keeping over acquiring, to reconciling difference, to conserving the fragile, to maintaining the minimal harmony and material conditions necessary to a child's life. Preservative love defines and rewards certain virtues like the clear-sighted cheerfulness I mentioned earlier, just because they enable a mother to hold and maintain the lives of others in an unpredictable world.[5]

It seems obvious, even without resorting to war memoirs and analyses, that military endeavors endanger what a mother seeks to preserve. Quite aside from endangering her children's bodies, military action tends to undermine their capacities for pleasure and work as well as their moral sensibilities. War is terrifying, numbing, morally erosive. Treasuring lives, holding them and the materiel that sustains them, seems directly opposed to the conquest of battlefields, the destruction of wills, bodies, landscapes and artifacts, expected of soldiers.

Nonetheless, good officers are supposed to preserve the lives of their soldiers and to maintain at least the modicum of psychological strength required for fighting. It used to be that soldiers of all ranks were pledged to spare the lives of civilians—though now we no longer expect the pledge, let alone the honoring of it. Officers differ as individuals. Many (I hope) are "maternal" men, determined to avoid "unnecessary" damage to their own—and enemy?—people. Moreover, armies differ nationally and. within a nation, historically, in the kinds and degrees of destructiveness they will encompass.[6]

Soldiers themselves are often said to delight in the destruction battles encourage. Yet many individual soldiers are also said to develop a kind of preservative love suitable for the battlefield. Partly reacting to the destruction around them, they develop a "maternal concern" for themselves, bits of nature, stray animals, fellow fighters, and the wounded enemy. Such concern is the special province of the medic but also necessary for the common soldier. "When soldiers lose this need to preserve and become impersonal killers, they are truly figures of terror" (Gray 86). Anyone who doubts that maternal thinking can be expressed on the battlefield and preservative love survive there should read the poetry of Wilfred Owen.

Nonetheless, military strategy, in its very aims, puts at risk not only the bodies but the "hearts and minds" a mother has cared for. And this is to put the point mildly. Twentieth-century technology has only accentuated and made visible what battle reports across the centuries have told us. The "waste" of people by military strategies goes well beyond the requirements of victory. Victory itself is defined in such a way as to be compatible with immense psychological and physical damage to the victorious as well as the defeated. Moreover, war itself undermines whatever responsibility armies or particular officers initially undertake in order to limit their own destructiveness.

> Hatred, bitterness and fear—all of which increase throughout the period of hostility—produce tremendous temptations to set aside the self-denying ordinances (which limit one's own destructiveness).... Each war traces a path of moral descent.... This is a fearful descent. But it can

scarcely be described as astonishing in view of its inevitability. For the pressures of war are such that it is as predictable as anything in human life. (Horsburgh)

On the one side, we have maternal practice whose end is defined by the demand to preserve what is both treasured and at risk. On the other we have military practice which puts at risk those same treasured lives in the name of "victory" or other abstract causes. "Holding," treasuring whatever can maintain or lighten lives, attitudes or preservative love emerge in an unmysterious way as one meets the demands of childcare. These same attitudes can emerge for soldiers as a reaction against the destruction their work involves. Preservative love is an intelligible response to maternal work; on the battlefield it is truly marvelous.

Preservative love is almost too sharply opposed to military strategy. We are apt to sentimentalize both, sanctifying mothers, demonizing soldiers. I repeat, I am not speaking of good or bad, loving or destroying individuals, but of the practices in which individuals engage. Moreover, the sharp opposition of maternity and militarism raises a question of its own. Why *have* mothers played their parts in military scripts, allowing, even encouraging the sacrifice of their sons? This question may be all the more acute as we appreciate still other, less obvious pacifist tendencies in maternal practice.

Pacifism and Maternal Practice

The pacifist renounces those strategies which the militarist accepts—strategies which, at the very least put at risk, at the worst set out to destroy, the lives which mothers preserve. Pacifist renunciation seems closely linked to preservative love, especially for those religious and (occasionally) secular pacifists who make the "sanctity of life" a basis for their commitment. Preservative love, however, does not play the defining role in pacifist theory that it does in maternal thinking. Pacifism is *defined* by its theory of conflict, with its two components of reconciliation and nonviolent resistance. Explicit beliefs about the preservation of life may, but also may not, underlie the theory. Maternal practice, on the other hand, takes as its defining aim, first, the preservation of life and then maintenance of conditions in which psychological and moral growth take place. Mothers would be happy if conflict were so rare that no theory of conflict were necessary. In fact, conflict is a part of maternal daily life. A mother finds herself embattled with her children, with an outside world at odds with her or their interests, with a man or other adults in her home, with her children's enemies. She is spectator and arbiter of her children's battles with each other and their companions. It is not surprising, then, that maternal thinking has articulated a theory of conflict consonant with the aims of maternal practice. This theory in several ways is congruent with pacifism.

Both in their homes and outside them, mothers typically experience themselves as powerless. They cannot control the vagaries of fate, visited upon them most painfully in the form of accidents and disease that befall their children and people their children depend upon. They are powerless as mothers, unable to determine the wills, friendships, and ambitions of their children. They are usually powerless socially—objects rather than agents of wars, economic plans, and political policies. Most mothers are directly dependent upon the good favor of individual men and publicly effective people—teachers, doctors, welfare workers, dentists, park supervisors, clinic directors, restaurant keepers, movie house owners, selective service administrators, and all those others who decide under what conditions children will be provided with services from the "outside" world.

Like other powerless combatants, mothers often resort to nonviolent strategies because they have no weapons to damage—neither guns, nor legal effectiveness, nor economic clout. Mothers know that officials—teachers, welfare workers, landlords, doctors, and the like-can retaliate against their children as well as against themselves at the hint of maternal violence, perhaps even of anger. Instead of force, then, mothers engage in nonviolent techniques: prayer, persuasion, appeasement, self-suffering, psychological manipulation, negotiation, and bribery. Each of these techniques has its place in public nonviolent coercion.

A striking fact about mothers is that they remain peaceful in situations in which they are powerful, namely in battles with their own and other children. Dorothy Dinnerstein has written eloquently about the power of mothers perceived from the infant-child's point of view. A mother is our first audience, jailor, trainer, protector—a being upon whose favor we depend for our happiness, even survival. The more isolated she is, the greater her power is, since it is shared among other adults and a wider caretaking community. We have learned that at least in our society, we are intensely ambivalent about our early pleasurable and fearful dependency on mothers and other women.

Little has been written about this same maternal power from a mother's point of view. A young, typically powerless woman confronts her children. Hassled if not harassed by the officials of an outside world and, usually, by her own employers, she is nonetheless powerful, the more so precisely the more alone she is. Such a young woman finds herself embattled with weak creatures whose wills are unpredictable and resistant, whose bodies she could quite literally destroy, whose psyches are at her mercy. I can think of no other situation in which someone with the resentments of social powerlessness, under enormous pressures of time and anger, faces a recalcitrant but helpless combatant with so much restraint. It is clear that violence—techniques of struggle that *damage*—is by definition inimical to the interests of maternal work. Indeed, maternal thinking would count as violent just those actions which deliberately or predictably risk the child's life, health, psychological strength, or moral well-being. It is also clear that physical and psychological violence is a temptation of maternal practice and a fairly common occurrence. What is remarkable is that in a daily way mothers make so much peace instead of fighting, and then, when peace fails, conduct so many battles without resorting to violence.

I do not claim that maternal pacifist commitment is a product of deliberation or virtue. There are heavy social penalties for maternal violence, even for the appearance of violence. Moreover, there is a sense in which non-violence comes naturally to many mothers. Young women who have internalized maternal thinking take as their own the demands of preservation, growth, and acceptability from which a commitment to non-violence follows. Renunciation of certain techniques of struggle may come too early, bringing in its wake cheery denial, passivity, inauthenticity, and obedience—forms of *self* renunciation which are the defining vices of maternal practice. I do not want to trumpet a virtue but to point to a fact: that non-violence is a constitutive principle of maternal thinking, and that mothers honor it not in the breach, but in their daily practice, despite objective temptations to violence.

In addition to her own battles a mother must prevent or resolve battles among her children and between her children and their friends. Here too, peace-making is both complex and in a mother's interest. Siblings themselves present a study in relative strength and weakness. A mother working for the growth of each of her children must restrain the powerful, training them in kinds of renunciation, while at the same time preventing the powerless from premature acquiescence or excessive reliance on techniques of manipulation and "self-suffering." Her own favoritism, varieties of inattention, or acceptance of conventional sexual stereotypes often interfere with a mother's task. Again, however, the demands of the practice are clear: a mother must prevent her children from deliberately or predictably using or accepting techniques of struggle that damage.

Battles between her children and their companions present a similar challenge to a mother. Most of her children's "enemies" will be members of her neighborhood and school community, often indeed children of her close friends. Whatever her own intense partisan feelings, a mother will typically be held responsible for the damage her children cause as well as for damage she lets them suffer. Among both siblings and friends peace-making is in a mother's interest. It is also in her interest to let some battles occur so that children may learn to fight back and defend themselves in nondamaging ways. A mother's role as judge, arbiter, and instructor in non-violence (including nonviolent tussling and sparring) gives her an opportunity for reflection, often shared with other mothers and adults she lives with. In moments of reflection she tests and refines a pacifist theory of conflict.

Toward one group of combatants, however, a mother is not reliably non-violent, namely the families and children of her own "enemies." Class, racial, neighborhood, and personal divisions may be played out through children. Indeed, group violence may provide a mother with a rare opportunity for expressing the anger she has abjured. Political or religious allegiance, misguided desire for purity and order, the sheer lust to see one's *children* privileged, all may fuel a violence otherwise too crude to tolerate. The repulsive, contorted faces of white mothers shouting at black children seeking to enter schoolrooms may haunt most women. But they are faces of maternal practice and represent a temptation to which mothers are liable—self-righteous violence against the outsider. Militarists who wish to mobilize mothers in the national interest find this same fearful self-righteousness a resource for violent patriotism.

Maternal theories of conflict are often restricted in scope to those near and alike and are therefore politically weak and morally flawed. I will return later to the imperfections of maternal thinking. Now, however, I would like to compare the pacifist and maternal theories of conflict, each of which, I believe has something to learn from the other.

Maternal and Pacifist Theories of Conflict

Central to both pacifist theory and maternal thinking is the subordination of ends to means. This subordination is most apparent in the renunciation of violence even if—and where—violence seems the only means to achieve a desired end. This way of putting the point is somewhat misleading. For both pacifism and maternal practice the desirability of a goal is not separable from its being achieved non-violently. However much an outcome may appear identical with an original goal—a child asleep, a sibling left alone—if the methods have physically damaged a child, the "end" is not achieved. One continually redefines and responds to goals in ways that preclude violent means of achieving them. Gandhi made this point when he defined "Truth" interdependently with "God"—and therefore "good"—and then said:

> Without Ahimsa (non-violence) it is not possible to seek and find Truth. Ahimsa and Truth are so intertwined that it is practically impossible to disentangle and separate them. They are like two sides of a coin, or rather of a smooth, unstamped, metallic disc. Who can say which is the obverse, and which is the reverse (Gandhi 43)?[7]

Yet Gandhi continues, "Ahimsa is the means; Truth is the end." Ends are central to a practice, never more than when they are contested. Without ends, participants could neither understand or direct their daily struggles, nor place their limited goals within a larger context. Pacifist theory gives an account of ends, which is tacitly assumed in maternal practice. This account allows ends to be firmly held while at the same time subordinate to means. One of its features is the narrowing of specific, immediate ends to a point where they are quite precise: a particular wage settlement or law repealed: a particular homework lesson finished or household task accomplished. These narrow ends are then subject to negotiation and compromise. (Although legend describes him as an idealistic saint, Gandhi was appropriately criticized in his lifetime because of his willingness to compromise.) The task of parent or pacifist activist is to determine some end which both parties can accept. Acceptance is, to be sure, largely a response to nonviolent coercion. But pride is preserved on both sides in the interests of reconciliation.

Narrowly specified immediate, negotiable ends are related to general goals, such as "home rules," or a "viable, independent adult." These general ends are subject to discussion and redefinition. They can be postponed without being relinquished. One appeals to them to make sense both of the narrower goal and the way it is negotiated. While these discussions about general goals among comrades and mothers are important to clarity and morale, conflict is focused on the specific and negotiable.

Gandhi insisted that both larger and narrower goals be defined in terms of what he called "human needs"—which included for him dignity and autonomy as well as material well-being. The demand to relate ends to needs in fact works as permission to compromise and relativize. One asks of one's opponents what they, and our common community, need now in order to continue to work for the larger ends we have set ourselves. Mothers, of course, assume a common interest between themselves, other members of their household, and children's well-being. Pacifists must create a common humanity where (often) the clear evil of opponents seems to preclude it. The opposition is not as sharp as it first looks. We are increasingly coming to see that children, parents, and other household members have distinctive, often conflicting needs. Conversely, in a nuclear age, finding common humanity among opponents has become a condition of survival, turning the heroic, creative vision of a King or Gandhi into a required belief.

Even the desire to seek a common humanity depends, as does non-violence itself, upon transforming enemies into opponents for whose well-being one is concerned. Although this transformation is sometimes described as the requirement to "love" one's enemy, words like "respect," "concern," and "consideration" seem more appropriate.

> We should be happy [Jesus] did not say "like your enemies." It is almost impossible to like some people. "Like" is a sentimental and affectionate word…. We must develop and maintain the capacity to forgive…. We must recognize that the evil deed of the enemy-neighbor—the thing that hurts—never quite expresses all he is…. We must not seek to defeat or humiliate the enemy (King).

> … to act on the assumption that all men's lives are of value, that there is something about any man to be loved, whether one can feel love for him or not. (Deming)

The reasons pacifists give for "loving" the enemy are various, combining practical with moral, selfish with altruistic, considerations. They *must* give reasons. Mothers, by contrast, though they do not like their children all of the time, are expected to love them. They needn't justify their refusal to harm the beings whose growth is in their care. Pacifist commitment is a conscious and surprising choice; maternal non-violence is a presupposition of maternal practice and often unquestioned. Despite differences in origin and justification there are striking similarities between pacifist and maternal conceptions of the "enemy."

Both mothers and pacifists, for example, believe that forcing opponents to change their "evil" ways is an act of love, because it is good for the opponents. Mothers believe this most obviously about their own children, but also about many of their children's enemies. Both tend to believe that hatred "scars the soul" (King), injuring both hater and hated. Both believe that it is wrong to accept injustice or aggression passively, wrong for the sufferer and harmful to the aggressor. "Personal defense" is a part of pacifist as well as maternal practice; finding nonviolent means of proud resistance is an urgent task of both maternal and pacifist strategists. And again, both mothers and pacifists believe that non-violence *works* not only to preserve community but also to change the opponent.

> It is precisely solicitude for his person in combination with a stubborn interference with his actions that can give us a very special degree of control.... We put upon him two pressures—the pressure of our defiance of him and the pressure of our respect for his life—and it happens that in combination these two pressures are effective. (Deming)

We expect a mother to control a child by non-violence; we are skeptical that the pacifist even tries to do so. Nonetheless, Deming's description of pacifist action could serve to describe a mother's action as well. Moreover, when mothers are locked in combat with adolescents or young adults whose actions frighten, disappoint, or enrage them, even maternal love for the "enemy" can seem astounding. Yet mothers take risks, accepting their children's words and claims, trusting in their futures when no objective observer would, hoping when despair seems the saner council, displaying their belief in the permanent possibility of reconciliation. I am not saying that this always happens, that many mothers don't go through long nights of rejecting, hating, giving up on their children. But the risking, trusting, and hoping so central to a pacifist's relation to an enemy seems predictable in maternal practice.

I hope I have made the case for similarities between pacifist theory and maternal thinking. I believe that both pacifist and maternal thinkers could learn from their differences, especially if they were conscious of their kinship. A clear instance of similarity and beneficial difference emerges if we consider "self-suffering," a central feature of both Gandhian Satyagraha and maternal practice. Both mothers and pacifists use their own suffering to force their opponents to change. Self-sufferers appeal to the conscience of their opponents and, where conscience is unavailable, to reputation in the eyes of others. An opponent may feel guilty, ashamed, or simply inconvenienced by the long-suffering innocent endurance of an adversary. However, neither mothers nor Satyagrahi are morally easy or politically confident about the moral emotions they induce. Mothers, I believe, have a clearer sense of the temptations and limits of self-suffering. This is largely because of the different circumstances in which their non-violent acts are called for. Whereas pacifists turn what might rightly be seen as a holy war into a conflict between humans, mothers must never allow what is only human conflict to become unduly moralized.

The limits of self-suffering illustrate the general limitation of moralism in maternal practice. Conscientiousness is a slowly developing, unpredictable capacity.

Children must not see themselves as "bad," since shame and guilt can lead to anger, indifference, or uncontrollable inhibition. Although a mother will resort to techniques of self-suffering in order to affect her child's behavior, she (usually) knows that a child will not be, and cannot afford to be, too long or deeply affected by maternal tears. Nor can she restrain bigger, stronger children by a moralism that turns conscience against its possessor; nor can she allow younger, smaller children to rely excessively on the power of their suffering to influence age mates or adults.

Mothers themselves would suffer from the use of moralism. Violence is a temptation and frequent occurrence of maternal practice. Mothers do, for example, see their children, and let them see themselves, as "bad"; mothers hate and they hit; they moralize and despair. Hence, if they are committed to nonviolence they must learn to blame themselves without self-hate and to forgive themselves compassionately. Maternal thinking recognizes the inevitability of "failure" and identifies moral humility as a virtue. Yet guilty self-hate (on bad days, or years) and competitive self-righteousness (in the good times) are liabilities. Both stem from an inability to acknowledge the strains and complexities of maternal life.

Violence and non-violence take many forms. What can be expected to damage, what actually damages, varies from family to family, from culture to culture. Mothers know this and avoid rigid definitions of violence or quick, judgmental identifications of the violent. Nor are they likely to escalate requirements for nonviolence, to include thoughts and feelings as well as action, or to count as violent an action which only hurts or offends. Gandhi's exhortations to his satyagrahi would sound strange to maternal ears.

> Not to hurt any living thing is no doubt a part of ahimsa [non-violence]. But it is its least expression. The principle of ahimsa is hurt by every evil thought, by undue haste, by lying, by hatred, by wishing ill to anybody. Ahimsa really means that you may not offend anybody, you may not harbor an uncharitable thought even in connection with one who may consider himself to be your enemy. (Bondurant 24-25)[8]

Mothers who adopted the Gandhian ideal would be in for sleepless nights. In contrast to Gandhi, they ask just which hurts, hastes, and lyings are truly damaging. They want to distinguish between the hating thought and the hateful action, since they must accept themselves as well as the complicated, unpretty psychic lives of their children.

In short, when pacifism and maternal thinking are joined, mothers can bring to the meeting realism, distrust of moralism, a sense of the limitations of self-suffering, and an awareness of the dangers of masochism and moral heroism. Rather than sharp division, the meeting could produce a shift in emphasis: from what one is willing to suffer, to what one is determined to enjoy and preserve. Though I will not argue the case here, I believe such a shift is necessary if pacifism is to become practical, widely accepted, and truly loving.

It is equally true that mothers have much to learn from the meeting. Knowledge of pacifist history and theories would make mothers aware of the pacifist bases of practices they take for granted. This would, perhaps, increase mothers' self-respect. Aware of their own kind of pacifism, mothers could extend their philosophy of conflict to enemies of their "kind," neighborhood, class or nation. Nevertheless, the natural pacifism of maternity, natural because it arises from the demands of work, feels unnatural, like vulnerable weakness in the larger world. Even humanist mothers of goodwill toward all people would have to *learn* the political significance of domestic pacifism. I maintain, first, that a basis for this lesson already exists in the maternal philosophy of conflict and, second, that mothers will be not only pupils, but teachers as well.

Thinking Warfully

I am convinced that a certain style of thinking—a tendency and ability to abstract—is connected to warfare. "Abstraction" refers to a cluster of interrelated dispositions to simplify, dissociate, generalize, and sharply define. Its opposite, which I will call "concreteness," respects complexity, connection, particularity, and ambiguity. Neither abstraction nor concreteness is good or bad in itself. Most intellectual activities require ability to abstract and in some, mathematics for example, ability and pleasure in abstraction are central. Nonetheless, I believe an inclination to think abstractly helps to explain why so many of us undertake or support violent enterprises.

There is no a priori reason why men should think more abstractly than women. I hope that in time women will take as much pleasure in their mathematical powers as men. There are, however, fairly well substantiated claims that in our society women have a cognitive style distinctly less abstract than men's.[9] I would like provisionally to accept this claim of gender difference in order to make three separate points about the possible connections between maternity, abstraction, and war.

First, if we assume that women do have a concrete cognitive style, this characteristic can be partly explained as an intelligible response to maternal work. Concreteness can be seen as a mix of interwoven responses to a growing, changing child. Neither a child nor a mother responding to her can sharply distinguish reality from fantasy, body from mind, or the child herself from the people she lives among. A mother attends to a particular child and understands her as best she can on a given day, tolerating both the ambiguity of the child's actions and the tentativeness of her own interpretations. She will eschew generalization, not only because children are very particular beings to whom she attends, but also because they confound prediction. A mother will express her knowledge in a personal voice, respecting the complexity of the children she studies and the human, social situation in which they learn.[10] In short, her thinking will be "holistic," "field-dependent," "open-ended," not because of any innate sex differences, but because that is the kind of thinking her work calls for.

Second, abstraction and concreteness have consequences for morality and therefore yield differences in men's and women's moral lives. Separating moral and human significance from other aspects of a plan or action is an aspect of abstraction. It is often said that men are more apt to engage in this sort of moral dissociation than women. Certainly, it is impossible to separate sharply moral from other aspects of maternal work or, usually of child behavior. Along with pervasiveness of morality goes a distinctive female moral voice (Gilligan). Women are said to be less concerned with claiming rights, more with sharing responsibilities. They do not value independence and autonomy over connection and the restraints of caring, but rather assume that the conflict between rightful self-assertion and responsible interdependence is at the heart of moral life. "Aware of the danger of an ethics abstracted from life," the development of women's moral judgment "appears to proceed from an initial concern with survival (first of herself, then of her own) to a focus on goodness, and finally to a principled understanding of non-violence as the most adequate guide to the just resolution of moral conflicts" (Gilligan 515).

Concreteness and its moral consequences seem an unmysterious development in mothers and daughters (or sons), who learn from them a cognitive style, but evidence about the distribution of abstraction or concreteness between men and women is inconclusive. What seems to me much clearer is that abstraction and the morality to which it is conducive are warlike. Willing warriors are loyal to abstract causes and abstract states. They are encouraged to develop an "abstract hatred for the enemy" that will allow them to kill.[11] They invent weapons and pray for victories whose victims most of them would not be willing to imagine. The Physicians for Social Responsibility, who tell us what we would suffer in a nuclear holocaust, are in a long tradition of pacifist poets and writers.[12] Now, however, abstraction seems to have gripped the imagination itself. People cannot see the battles they contemplate fighting nor speak in any detail of the causes which drive them to arm themselves.

We may be able to fight only if war remains an abstract idea; we may forgive ourselves for fighting only because we can resort to the idea of a "just war" to legitimize our violence. In distinguishing between permitted and forbidden acts of war, just-war theories actually give us the conceptual tools to justify any war. They do so partly by inventing a language that encourages us to turn away from the details of suffering, to see instead the just causes and conventional rules of war. Good is distinguished from evil, soldier from civilian, war from peace. States are real entities with clear boundaries in which one's pride is invested. Autonomy, a distinct way of life, collective ownerships and identities, take precedence over the particularities of individual and community well-being. Although a civilizing presence when compared to amoral militarism, just-war theory is an exercise in abstraction.[13]

Abstract hatred and loyalties play their part in maternal militarism, too. A woman is apt to acquire men's loyalties and hate with vehemence the enemies they fight. Just as it is easier for many warriors to kill from a distance, so also it is easier to hate from well behind the lines. Often a woman finds the loss of "her" men and boys so painful that she must brutalize an image of the killer to explain his act. Moreover, her inability to separate morality from politics, combined with her long tradition of non-violence, may lead a woman to assume that a great evil is required to match the violence her "good" men perpetrate. Yet women often declare themselves disloyal to states and other abstract entities and causes. ("As a woman I have no country. As a woman I want no country. My country is the whole world" [Woolf]).[14] Even now women seem especially susceptible to an imaginative grasp of the pain and hope of all fighters, and of the dailiness of the lives fighting destroys.[15] When women no longer take refuge in supportive, mourning activities, or when we no longer fight vicariously but assume responsibility for the fighting done in our name, then the "female imagination" elicited by maternal practice may apprehend the horrors of violence in all their specificity.

For warriors and for mothers, for all people, fear has a complicated significance in war and the preparation for war. Fear of our enemies gives us reason for arming, later for firing. But effective fear both creates and depends upon an abstract idea of "enemy." When we see that we are shooting at conscripts, who are young, often poor, boys, when we look at the homes where the bombs fall, pity and realism tend to crowd out fear. On the other hand, in a nuclear age, if we look closely at the destruction we contemplate, we become truly terrified. In this instance, abstraction blankets fear; close attention may terrify us into disarmament.

Fear is, then, a force for war when it creates and can depend upon abstraction; but it is also a force for peace when it is an emotional response to the apprehension of weapons' horror. Mothers are often said to be fearful creatures, which is not surprising since their children are fragile, willful beings. Fearful people feel the need of arms, and mothers are no exception. But if fear is informed by maternal concreteness, it will give way to compassion in war and to terror at its prospect. In either case, a maternal cognitive style becomes an instrument of peace.

Concreteness seems a condition of nonviolent battle. Nonviolent combatants are more apt to consider their opponents, to understand the pain their coercion causes, and of course the suffering which they themselves choose to bear. Some weapons and some opponents may be abstract—for example, an economic boycott at a distance. But if the struggle is committed to avoiding psychological as well as physical damage, the fighters or their leaders must retain some grasp of the lives they are affecting.[16] Although pacifists—like all of us—will *tend* to conceive opponents in the abstract in terms of their hated or feared group characteristics, nonviolent "love" for the "enemy" is a built-in corrective for the abstract moralism to which all fighters are liable.

Even pacifism is not immune from abstraction. In particular, the renunciation of violence may itself become abstract. If pacifists demand (as our draft boards require) that a person abjure violence in every place, at every time, or that s/he take as opponents those who choose differently, then pacifism too is asking for abstract commitment. This may show that abstraction has its place in peace as in war; I myself think it shows that pacifists should learn from maternal practice to attend to the battle at hand. But the question is a difficult one. Many people refuse to rule out in advance the violence that might be necessary to protect oneself or one's loved ones from immediate danger. But except in the case of a single, instantaneous response to physical attack, violence requires of good people denial and abstraction for the sake of conscience. Abstraction, once induced, then works in the interests of further violence, violence having a tendency to escalate (or so Gandhi and others thought when they demanded a general and simple renunciation of violence). When mothers become self-conscious pacifists, it will be interesting to see whether pacifism itself will change.

Eros and Destruction

Popular legend has it that the lust for battle and sexual desire are closely akin. Gandhi was sufficiently convinced of the connection between sex and violence that he urged celibacy on his followers except for rare procreative acts. On the other hand, many believe that sex and destruction are enemies, that if we would only make love we would not make war. Maternal sexuality figures ambiguously in these popular beliefs. Some pacifists and militarists who connect sex with violence believe mothers are the friends of peace, partly because they are (wrongly thought to be) asexual; nonmaternal women, by contrast, whether as adorers of the soldier-hero or submissive objects of his love, fuel the pleasure of destroyers. But to those who urge love as an alternative to war, asexual "puritanical" maternity is an obstacle to the deployment of eros in the service of peace. Each of these beliefs catches a part of the complex connections between maternity, sex, and violence. I myself believe that there is a kind of opposition between military and maternal sexuality, one that pacifists could but have not exploited. On the other hand, given the present institutions of motherhood and sexuality in America, maternal sexuality tends to be a force for war rather than peace. These hunches (they are not yet more than that) I will explore briefly.

Battlefield love and sexual fantasies arise in a misogynistic military society that exploits rigid, dichotomous definitions of "male" and "female." Indeed, it seems that soldiers are deliberately trained in a masculinist ideology that endorses blatant contempt for women. Many marching chants include degrading references to anything feminine. Sexist terms for women and their bodily parts (the two often taken to be the same) are common in military discipline as well as in play. Given the prevailing gender ideology, it is not surprising that the sexuality ascribed to soldiers on the battlefield is not only distinctly male but also narcissistic, assaultive (if not actually rapist) and predatory, indifferent to women if not actually violent toward them. Whatever destructive and abusive tendencies men may have controlled in civilian life are not only permitted but encouraged in war.

Moreover, not only is sexuality misogynistic and destructive, but worse, destruction is eroticized. Many battlefield accounts report the obvious sexual pleasure some men take in killing and in various other abusive acts—to women certainly, but also to men, especially racially different men, and even children. Officers often encourage this lust, for no abstraction or moral conviction can insure the battle spirit that will ensure easy killing.[17]

Destruction, heterosexual fantasy, and heterosexual acts take place within a military society that, at least in our society, is officially and blatantly homophobic. The all-male military experience would seem to provide considerable opportunity for exploring homoerotic pleasures unavailable in civilian life. Certainly the ecstatic bonding between men responsible for many acts of courage or outrageous cruelty has its strong erotic components. And surely some homosexual love flourishes in the battlefield. But explicit homophobia and masculinism preclude for many the homosexual experiences that could recall the pleasures of connection, could make the body adored and treasured. Friendship between men has been called the "true enemy of battle," for it encourages a love of self—one's own and one's friend's—which destroys the destroyer's pleasure (Gray). Were such love sexualized, battle might stop. On the other hand, Plato felt that an army of homosexual lovers would be invincible. They would fight for love and for honor in each others' eyes, and their courage would know no moderation. Certainly, our own ecstatic male bonders seem akin to Plato's ideal soldiers.

I myself am not sure of anything about soldiers' sexual lives let alone sexual fantasies. Often the individual soldier seems anything but excitedly battle-like. Cold, frightened, exhausted, numb, confused, and eager to get home, he seems neither sexually excited nor sexually (as opposed to maternally) desirable. I believe that many soldiers sometimes take an orgasmic pleasure in acts of destruction and cruelty, that many more routinely abuse women as a matter of battle right. How many? And how central are these erotic destroyers and destructive lovers to the military enterprise? I don't know.

Some soldiers, of course, have romantic attachments to their sweethearts at home or those they meet behind the lines and love passionately, poignantly, and tenderly in the midst of danger. Moreover, soldiers engage in one kind of love that is attributed to women (at least it is specifically feared and punished in women): love between a woman and a soldier she considers her enemy. Who is this woman? Who is the sweetheart? How does female sexuality fit into the military picture?

There is some reason to believe that women are less apt than men to eroticize combat, more apt to eroticize reconciliation. "Sleeping with the enemy" arises, I suppose, as often from poverty and fear as from any passion. Yet men may be correct to suspect in women a sexuality that is in the service of connection rather than separation, a "making-up" rather than an undoing. When women do eroticize combat, they may be more apt to eroticize submission than conquest. If women do tend to eroticize reconciliation and, in combat, submission, then female libidinal energy will not inspire in women the lust for battle. The sweetheart, however, may reward, or at least condone, that lust in men. Her purer love is able to redeem the soldier from the destructive sexuality and eroticized destruction which he undergoes, as it were, carried "outside of himself." Were the women at home to find a fighting soldier disgusting, his pleasure in fighting might be significantly diminished.

I have been talking about possible *female* sexual fantasies and sexual roles. Female sexuality includes, for some women who are mothers or are otherwise intensely involved in maternal work, a maternal sexuality that is a quieter, less obviously sexual aspect of the whole erotic life. Maternal sexuality is not, of course, separable from the entire adult sexual life in which it is embedded. Although some mothers insist on separating maternal from sexual love, even those women bring to their relation with children their own variant of "female" sexual fantasies, whatever these may be. I cannot explore here the fascinating connections between adult sexuality and maternal love. Rather, I want to focus on a narrower maternal sexuality with interesting connections to military gender ideology and the erotics of destruction.

By *maternal sexuality* I mean the diffuse eroticism that arises from and is shaped by caring for children. This sexuality has at least two aspects, one deriving from the infant-mother, then child-mother, relation, the other deriving from the independent eroticism of the maturing child. Much has been written about maternal sexuality from the child's point of view. Dorothy Dinnerstein has evocatively described our longing for the pleasure of mother love with its diffuse sensuality, guiltless materiality, and total merging. We know that we resentfully abandon our first mother-loves and both long for and fear a return to them. Nonetheless, little has been written about this phenomenon from the point of view of a mother who is herself a grown-up infant with the ambivalent longings that Dinnerstein describes.

Mothers witness, to some extent direct, and are frequently an object of the infant-child's primitive, pan-erotic desires. Mothers enjoy, control, or deny their own erotic responses to their children. Later a mother watches with mixed feelings as a child develops a sexuality nearly independent of her. Contrary to legend, many mothers recognize that their children's independent sexuality is a condition of their autonomous, pleasurable adulthood. Yet this same sexuality is an important phase in a mother's "losing" her children to adulthood and in her recalling her own unresolved earlier sexual conflicts. Moreover, in our society, especially for girls, sexuality is frequently a source of folly, pain, and danger to her children which a mother is helpless to control. This watching, separating, fearing, and vicariously enjoying is part of a mother's life in a society which most often denies and exploits her own sexuality, leaves her little control over her own sexual-reproductive life, and little power except over small children. It is not surprising that explicable tendencies to fearfulness and suppression are magnified. Even now, many mothers take the adolescence of their children as an occasion to reflect upon and reaffirm the good of sexual pleasure and autonomy.

It may be true, however, that in our society maternal sexuality is as conducive to battle as to peace. The sexual morality explicitly urged on mothers is one of denial and repression. Unrecognized desires can enhance the lure of the soldier, find vicarious expression in battlefield lust, or be transmogrified by projection into the body of an enemy attacker. Moreover, denial and repression can take on a life of their own, psychically impoverishing the mother and estranging the child. I believe, however, that a mother freed from excesses of denial and repression could encourage an eroticism inimical to the military in at least two ways. She could welcome the surprisingly various erotic pleasures and fluid gender identities she witnesses and experiences with her children. Second, and at the same time, she could control in herself and in her children battlelike sexual impulses.

Mothers have a special opportunity to welcome infant-child erotic life. This involves protecting, even cherishing, disordered, sensual, bodily being; it requires tolerating surprising, intense desires in one's self and one's child; it means playing with new and expansive gender identities rather than fearfully controlling them. Welcoming and acknowledging eroticism where it begins is a first step in what Dorothy Dinnerstein has called the "mobilization of eros." A mother at ease with the complexities of eroticism could welcome in young adults genuine diversity in sexual expression and choices. Sexual freedom and the pleasure it allows are at odds with a rigid, dichotomous gender ideology, with monolithic military control of sexual variety and with the simple, predatory sexuality of battle.

On the other hand, a kind of sexual permissiveness dear to libertarians (and to me) will remain at odds with maternal practices in the freest societies. The vulnerability of an infant, the necessity of adolescent independence, the inappropriateness of genital or other explicit sexual acts with children all make maternal self-control necessary, not just some puritan fantasy. Recognizing the complexities of eroticism, mothers can also respect its power. A mother will insist upon "moralizing" sexual-aggressive life. Many sexual impulses, if acted upon, could only exploit or hurt her children. For example, the alluring helplessness of a child who is also stubborn and disobedient could be a powerful stimulus to sadistic excitement both for a mother and an older sibling. But sadism, however understandable, is not permitted. Children are not "consenting adults." For good reasons, a mother must often control in herself and discourage in her children the sexualization of conquest, cruelty, destruction, and domination, the very same impulses that are encouraged and sexualized in battle. In general, the simultaneous acceptance of disorderly, pleasureful eroticism, combined with the moralization of specific sexual-aggressive impulses, could put maternal sexuality distinctly at odds with military mores.

Military Mothers and Feminist Politics: A Concluding Note

I hope I have shown that there is some basis for the claim that mothers have distinctive interests in and capacities for reconciliation and nonviolent battle. Maternal preservative love is at odds with military destruction but requires a philosophy of conflict with many similarities to pacifism. The cognitive style that arises from maternal practice and articulates its thinking is opposed to war-like abstraction. If there is a female sexuality, it may well be opposed to the sexuality encouraged in battle. Ideal maternal sexuality encourages a self-respecting, disorderly eroticism inimical to military control. Moreover, mothers control in themselves and their children the very impulses that militarists exploit.

Yet, as we know, mothers are militarists. Some mothers, those we (pacifists) like to remember first, fight in defense of their homeland or in civil revolutionary struggles to bring justice to their children. Self-defense and armed revolutionary justice can seem a direct expression of preservative love, as long as we allow the use of violence in any cause. Thus, these cases, although crucial for developing a realistic, humane commitment to non-violence, do not seriously undermine the case for a pacifist basis of maternal practice. But self-defense and revolutionary struggle often acquire erotic destructiveness, abstract hatreds, and chimerical victories so characteristic of war. Moreover, women in increasing numbers are insisting on the right to fight—to bomb, spray nerve gas, release torpedoes—and their reasons for fighting seem no more moral, no less moralized, rationalized, and abstract, than men's. Or, more accurately, since I know little about these women, even if female warriorhood is now less easily violent than men's, there is no reason to believe that such a difference would survive military training, changed social relations, and a new conception of female strength.

Pacifism certainly does not flow from women's nature. Even if it arises understandably from maternal practice, it will have to be articulated and honored if it is to become a basis for organizing women in the interests of peace. But, for this to occur, maternal pacifism would have to become publicly pacifist. I do not believe that the militancy of mothers is incompatible with the maternal pacifism I have described. But if maternal peacefulness is to become a force for peace, maternal practice itself must be transformed.

The principal agent of transformation is, I believe, feminist politics. By "feminist politics" I mean the commitment to eliminate all restrictions of power, pleasure, and mastery arising from biological sex or social constructions of gender, so that women will have as much (and as little) control as men over their individual and collective lives. This is both a restrictive and inclusive definition of feminism. It is inclusive because it allows people to be feminists who are statists or anarchists, capitalists or socialists, men or women. It focuses on a single intellectual and emotional source of feminism, a sense of injustice to women and a determination to rectify it. It is restrictive because it ignores the many other social ideals feminists hold. Most feminists, (and I too) believe that a commitment to justice for all women entails a commitment to economic and racial justice for all people. Many feminists (and I too) believe that feminism leads to anti-militarism both on economic and moral grounds. For the purposes of this paper, however, I leave the wider implications of feminism to one side. Feminists, in my sense, committed to women's equality with men, can be (and unfortunately have been) racist, exploitative, hierarchical, and militarist. Nonetheless, I believe this restricted feminism will be a transformative agent in rendering maternal peacefulness publicly effective. Maternal militarism arises in part from womens' confinement and powerlessness.[18] It also arises from human, broadly social, and maternal conditions. Feminism is not the only force for maternal peacefulness, nor is it a sufficient one. But by undermining a number of interdependent motives for militarism, it can free women to articulate for themselves a publicly effective pacifism. Let me give some examples.

For women confined in domestic life, war offers real education, new training and job experience, economic power, travel, and a sense of communal life. It is no wonder then that they welcome its occurrence. "Consciously she desire(s) our splendid empire; unconsciously she desire(s) our war" (Woolf 39). Freedom and effectiveness would do much to reduce this desire. Mothers' need for order, frustrated by the unpredictability of the world, finds a relief in military discipline. When women and men share both the burdens of parenthood and the pleasures of mastery, mothers will have new opportunities and energies for satisfying their need for control and order. In war, unacknowledged violent impulses find a legitimate expression, vicariously safe. Feminism breaks down the split between male and female, attributing to both sexes capacities for rage as well as gentleness. It insists on human—not sexual—responsibility for public actions. It grants to women the authority of conscience, with all its discomforts. Mothers beginning to see the world through feminist eyes would find it difficult to enjoy *vicarious* battle pleasures and angers, and impossible to maintain a split-off innocence.

Even women who are now true peace lovers, who dread war's horrors and value the texture of the lives it destroys, can come to endorse the war policies of their government. Women, a powerless group, may be especially fearful of alleged aggression. In the face of real or imagined threats, weapons can be wonderful, especially if carried by others, while to let one's "own men" remain unarmed can seem the epitome of vulnerability. And perhaps most important, even peace-loving women, especially if undereducated and economically dependent, allow men, both the leaders and those at home, to judge for them the reality of a danger and the best method of meeting it. "The mother of her race, with all her fine emotions of sheltering care, comes through dependence to the opinions of the fighting male" (Blatch 169).

Feminism, by increasing women's power, independence, and authority, undermines all these sources of militarism. Perhaps its effect would be most profound in changing maternal sexuality into a moral, welcoming eroticism opposed to the military. Even the most restricted feminism takes as one of its central aims understanding and overcoming homophobia. For only women undaunted by charges of lesbianism and unafraid of their own homoerotic desires will be able to sustain an identity with women and rid themselves of female self-hatred. Mothers aware and unafraid of their homosexual as well as heterosexual desires should be better able to tolerate the surprising complexity of their own and their children's eroticism. Feminist analysis of sexuality breaks down the distinction between socially constructed and biologically compelling desire, between "normal" and "deviant" sexual practices. It reveals the power politics of sexuality and asks everyone to be responsible for the choices and character of their sexual lives. Some women will still be liable to the psychosexual desire to serve and adore an armed endangered male. But any sexual desire is less compelling and more subject to reflection, if most sexual desires can seem normally natural and socially variable.

No amount of feminist change is sufficient to eliminate tendencies toward or trust in violence. Parents of both sexes will always have to deal with the mess and chanciness of mortal life, varieties of desire that make sex destructive or destruction erotic, unmanageable fears of those who hate, of the hateful who are armed. Nor is feminist politics always the surest way to combat motherly militarism. At this time in America, for example, I believe that the full employment of young people in minimally dignified work would do more to undermine maternal support for the All Volunteer Forces than any feminist reform. But feminism, I believe, undermines most deeply and lastingly a variety of interdependent motives mothers have for trusting in violence and in the states which organize and perpetrate it.

No one cay say what, if anything, will enable our species to renounce weapons that damage and to learn nonviolent methods of getting what we need and protecting what we love. Our nightmare fears and moral visions reveal the same truth: we must learn to live together nonviolently or perish as a species, as peoples, as the individuals we are and care for. I know that "peace" is not a single condition but means very different things to oppressor and oppressed, to privileged and impoverished. Yet pacifist renunciation seems to be a necessity—eventually for everyone, right now for any people whose armies possess nuclear or even highly destructive conventional weapons.

In my hopeful moments, it seems to me that women who insist simultaneously on newly defined independent female strength and on traditional feminine nurturance comprise an original peace brigade—erotic, courageous, protective, and sane. The origins of war and peacefulness are obscure. Yet it is certain that some of the roots of violence are embedded in our sexuality and gender arrangements, while important roots of protectiveness and connection are embedded in our memories and visions of maternal care. It seems, then, not unreasonable to expect new possibilities of peace when a feminist transformation of gender and sexuality is joined with an ancient preservative love.

I am grateful to Carol Ascher, Evelyn Keller, William Ruddick, and Marilyn Young for careful, critical readings of an earlier draft of this paper.

Notes

[1]Dr. Helen Caldicott, quoted in the War Resisters League Calendar, 1981.
[2]A Nazi mother cited in Rupp.
[3]Throughout, I will present the basic concepts of pacifism oversimply. Although I myself am increasingly pacifist and certainly believe that non-violence is required of any nuclear power, I am not, in this essay, attempting to convince the reader or assuming her agreement. Nor am I doing justice to the intricacies and complexity of pacifist theory, which would require a paper in itself.
[4]Whether or not there is a military strategy which all warring nations and groups fall into as violence escalates is a controversial question. I am inclined to think that, despite variation, there is a "law of violence" to which the best intended

fighters fall prey. But I do not argue this point—which is one that divides pacifists and just-war theorists—here.

[5]The phrase "preservative love" comes from Blatch. By "preservative love" I mean the activity of caring for children, governed by the three interests in preservation, growth, and acceptability. For more on this activity and the thinking that arises from it, see my "Maternal Thinking."

[6]I have drawn my very limited knowledge of the military from several battle memoirs and, more important, from analyses of battle and just-war theory, I recommend particularly Kegan; Danto; Horsburgh; Walzer; Fussell; Kaunda. By far the most useful book on war has been J. Glenn Gray, *The Warriors*. I have cited nothing from Gray that was not corroborated in at least two other analyses or memoirs.

[7]Also quoted in Bondurant.

[8]Many of the points I make here are similar to those made by Erikson.

[9]For a critical review of the literature, see Maccoby and Jacklin who are critical of the beliefs I report here. For a discussion of my use of "evidence" see my "Maternal Thinking." See also the evidence summarized in Lewis; Spack. See also the research reported by Rose on the work of psychologist David McClelland (101). The preliminary reports of Belenky, Clinchy, Goldberger and Tarule on their project "Education for Women's Development" seem to me strongly to support these claims. Belief in women's relative concreteness is widespread; it is supported by the work of numerous women writers of fiction and (especially feminist) art critics and literary critics of women's work. Chodorow (1978, 1979) and Gilligan make theoretical sense of the difference, if it exists, as does Keller in her various writings on women and science (1978, forthcoming). Miller has undertaken to describe and honor women's special interests and capacities while insisting on the possibility and necessity of change. I consider her work to be the clearest predecessor of my own.

[10]Belenky, *et al.*, "Education for Women's Development." (May be obtained from Nancy Goldberger, Simon's Rock of Bard College, Great Barrington, MA 02130.)

[11]See Gray (passim); Horsburgh (especially chapter 1).

[12]For example, Mark Twain's "War Prayer" and several poems of Wilfred Owen. It is now becoming commonplace to speak of the abstraction required of those who plan for or contemplate nuclear war. Nonetheless, I continue to find truly shocking the way in which men and women deny and distort the activities in which they are engaged, concealing the human significance of those activities in clichés suitable, if at all, for former conventional wars in which some died and some survived, or, more often, concealing the true nature of their projects in the language of high-tech weapons research. My (few) personal conversations with Pentagon officials and military advisors entirely support the now-common claim that planners do not think of lives—of the bodies or psyches they are putting at risk—but of numbers, "victories," "enemies" and the like. One short illustration of the inclination to abstract by one who formerly engaged in it is by Nash.

[13]Walzer is the best (and an excellent) presentation of just-war theory. Kaunda both attacks the theory and expresses a moving and coherent version of it. Danto defends the theory but gives a provocative rendition of it that seems to require non-violence of any country possessing and therefore likely to use (see Horsburgh; Walzer) high-tech conventional, let alone nuclear, weapons.

[14]Woolf's words—and this particular statement—have obviously appealed to countless women who now make use of them. Other feminist writing also expresses anti-state sentiments of feminists.

[15]For a wonderful example of the struggle between concreteness and ferocious abstraction as a young girl tries to understand war and its killing, see Leffland.

[16]In discussing nonviolent action it is important to distinguish damage—serious and indefinitely lasting, often irreparable harm—from temporary psychological or physical pain, which may be a necessary adjunct to change, and/or which has compensatory benefits.

[17]See Gray, O'Brien, and Marlowe for three quite different accounts of misogyny, masculinism, and sexuality in the military. My remarks here do not seem controversial (although they sound as if they should be). On the other hand, many believe that military misogyny and predatory sexuality are not *necessarily* adjuncts of war, and even that certain armies (e.g., the army of Israel) may now be free of them.

[18]Restrictive feminism is nonetheless radical. To confront, analyze, and work against the subordination of women requires rethinking and changing our sexual, domestic, intellectual—and eventually even fantasy—lives. I use this restrictive definition of feminism for three reasons. First, by being inclusive, it allows feminists of quite different persuasions to talk (and listen?) to each other. Second, it acknowledges the dangers many feminists (and I too) feel when women begin to celebrate the maternal. A restrictive definition of feminism at least allows and supplies words for the plausible charge that projects like mine are *anti*-feminist. I want to maintain tension and keep the dialogues going, including those within our ranks and within our own heads. Finally, I believe that this restrictive feminism leads quickly to a focus on the very issues of authority, cheery denial, inauthenticity, homophobia, and repressive sexuality that are central both to the failures of maternal thinking and the militarism of mothers.

References

Belenky, Mary, Blythe Clinchy, Nancy Goldberger and Jill Tarule. "Education for Women's Development." (May be obtained from Nancy Goldberger, Simon's Rock of Bard College, Great Barrington, MA 02130).

Blatch, Harriet Stanton. *A Woman's Point of View: Some Roads to Peace.* New York: The Woman's Press, 1920.

Bondurant, Joan V. *Conquest of Violence: The Gandhian Philosophy of Conflict.* Berkeley: University of California Press, 1971.

Chodorow, Nancy. "Feminism and Difference: Gender, Relation and Difference in Psychoanalytic Perspective." *Socialist Review* (July-August 1979).

Chodorow, Nancy. *The Reproduction of Mothering.* Berkeley: University of California Press, 1978.

Danto, Arthur. "On Moral Codes and Modern War." *Social Research* (Spring 1978).

Deming, Barbara. *Revolution and Equilibrium.* New York: A. J. Muste Memorial Institute Essay Series, 1981.

Dinnerstein, Dorothy. *The Mermaid and the Minotaur.* New York: Harper and Row, 1976.

Elshtain, Jean Bethke. "Women as Mirror and Other: Towards a Theory of Women, War and Feminism." Unpublished manuscript.

Erikson, Erik. *Oandhl's Truth.* New York: W.W. Norton, 1969.

Fussell, Paul. *The Great War and Modern Memory.* New York: Oxford University Press, 1975.

Gandhi, M. K. *Non-Violent Resistance.* New York: Schocken Books, 1961. Gray, J. Glenn *The Warriors.* New York: Harper Torchbook, 1959.

Gilligan, Carol. *In a Different Voice: Psychological Theory and Women's Development.* Cambridge, Mass.: Harvard University Press, 1982.

Habermas, Jurgen. *Knowledge and Human Interests.* Boston: Beacon Press, 1971.

Horsburgh, H. J. N. *Non-Violence and Aggression.* London: Oxford University Press, 1978.

Kaunda, Kenneth. *The Riddle of Violence.* New York: Harper and Row, 1980.

Kegan, John. *The Face of Battle.* New York: Viking, 1976.

Keller, Evelyn Fox. *He, She, and Id in Scientific Discourse.* New York: Longman, forthcoming.

Keller, Evelyn Fox. "Gender and Science." *Psychoanalysis and Contemporary Thought.* New York: International Universities Press, 1978.

King, Martin Luther. "Loving Your Enemies." Speech delivered Christmas, 1957, at Montgomery, Alabama.

Leffland, Ella *Rumours of Peace.* New York: Popular Library, 1980.

Lewis, Helen Block. *Shame and Guilt In Neurosis.* New York: International Universities Press, 1971.

Maccoby, Eleanor and Carol Jacklin. *The Psychology of Sex Differences.* Stanford: Stanford University Press, 1974.

Marlowe, David. "The Manning of the Force and the Structure of Battle; A VF, Draft, Men, Women." *Conscripts and Volunteers: Military Requirements, Social Justice, and the All-Volunteer Force.* Ed. Robert K. Fullinwider. Totowa, NJ: Rowman and Allanheld, 1983.

Miller, Jean Baker. *Toward a New Psychology of Women.* Boston: Beacon Press, 1976.

Murdoch, Iris. *The Sovereignty of Good.* New York: Schocken, 1971.

Nash, Henry T. "The Bureaucratization of Homicide." *Protest and Survive.* Ed. B. P. Thompson. New York: Monthly Review Press, 1981.

O'Brien, Tim. *If I Die in a Combat Zone.* New York: Dell, 1979.

Plato. *The Symposium.*

Rose, Phyllis. *Woman of Letters: A Biography of Virginia Woolf.* London: Oxford University Press, 1978.

Ruddick, Sara. "Maternal Thinking." *Feminist Studies* 6 (2) (Summer): 342-67.

Rupp, Leila J. *Mobilizing Women for War.* Princeton: Princeton University Press, 1978.

Spack, Patricia Meyers. *The Female Imagination.* New York: Alfred A. Knopf, 1972.

Steinson, Barbara J. "'The Mother Half of Humanity': American Women in the Peace and Preparedness Movements in World War I." *Women, War and Revolution.* Eds. Carol R. Berkin and Clara M. Lovett. New York: Holmes and Meier, 1980.

Walzer, Michael. *Just and Unjust Wars.* New York: Basic Books, 1977.

Weil, Simone. "Human Personality." *Simone Weil Reader.* Ed. George A. Panichas. New York: McKay, 1977a.

Weil, Simone. "Reflections on the Right Use of School Studies with an Eye Toward the Love of God." *Simone Weil Reader.* Ed. George A. Panichas. New York: McKay, 1977b.

Virginia Woolf. *Three Guineas.* New York: Harcourt, Brace and World, 1936.

Chapter 8

Revolutionary Parenting

BELL HOOKS

During the early stages of contemporary women's liberation movement, feminist analyses of motherhood reflected the race and class biases of participants. Some white middle class, college-educated women argued that motherhood was a serious obstacle to women's liberation, a trap confining women to the home, keeping them tied to cleaning, cooking, and childcare. Others simply identified motherhood and childrearing as the locus of women's oppression. Had black women voiced their views on motherhood, it would not have been named a serious obstacle to our freedom as women. Racism, availability of jobs, lack of skills or education and a number of other issues would have been at the top of the list—but not motherhood. Black women would not have said motherhood prevented us from entering the world of paid work because we have always worked. From slavery to the present day black women in the U.S. have worked outside the home, in the fields, in the factories, in the laundries, in the homes of others. That work gave meager financial compensation and often interfered with or prevented effective parenting. Historically, black women have identified work in the context of family as humanizing labor, work that affirms their identity as women, as human beings showing love and care, the very gestures of humanity white supremacist ideology claimed black people were incapable of expressing. In contrast to labor done in a caring environment inside the home, labor outside the home was most often seen as stressful, degrading, and dehumanizing.

These views on motherhood and work outside the home contrasted sharply with those expressed by white women's liberationists. Many black women were saying, "we want to have more time to share with family, we want to leave the world of alienated work." Many white women's liberationists were saying "we are tired of the isolation of the home, tired of relating only to children and husband, tired of being emotionally and economically dependent; we want to be liberated to enter the world of work." (These voices were not those of working class white women who were, like black women workers, tired of alienated labor.) The women's liberationists who wanted to enter the work force did not see this world as a world of alienated work. They do now. In the last twenty years of feminist movement many middle class white women have entered the wage earning work force and have found that working within a social context where sexism is still the norm, where there is unnecessary competition promoting envy, distrust, antagonism, and malice between individuals, makes work stressful, frustrating, and often totally unsatisfying. Concurrently, many women who like and enjoy the wage work they do feel that it takes too much of their time, leaving little space for other satisfying pursuits. While work may help women gain a degree of financial independence or even financial self-sufficiency, for most women it has not adequately fulfilled human needs. As a consequence women's search for fulfilling labor done in an environment of care has led to re-emphasizing the importance of family and the positive aspects of motherhood. Additionally, the fact that many active feminists are in their mid- to late-30s, facing the biological clock, has focused collective attention on motherhood. This renewed attention has led many women active in the feminist movement who were interested in childrearing to choose to bear children.

Although early feminists demanded respect and acknowledgment for housework and childcare, they did not attribute enough significance and value to female parenting, to motherhood. It is a gesture that should have been made at the onset of feminist movement. Early feminist attacks on motherhood alienated masses of women from the movement, especially poor and/or non-white women, who find parenting one of the few interpersonal relationships where they are affirmed and appreciated. Unfortunately, recent positive feminist focus on motherhood draws heavily on sexist stereotypes. Motherhood is as romanticized by some feminist activists as it was by the nineteenth century men and women who extolled the virtues of the "cult of domesticity." The one significant difference in their approach is that motherhood is no longer viewed as taking place primarily within the framework of heterosexual marriage or even heterosexual relationships. More than ever before, women who are not attached to males, who may be heterosexual or lesbian, are choosing to bear children. In spite of the difficulties of single parenting (especially economic) in this society, the focus is on "joys of motherhood," the special intimacy, closeness, and bonding purported to characterize the mother/child relationship. Books like Phyllis Chesler's *With Child: A Diary of Motherhood* rhapsodizes over the pleasures and joys of childbirth and childcare. Publication of more scholarly and serious works like Jessie Bernard's *The Future of Motherhood,* Elisabeth Badinter's *Mother Love,* Nancy Friday's *My Mother/My Self,* and Nancy Chodorow's *The Reproduction of Mothering* reflect growing concern with motherhood.

This resurgence of interest in motherhood has positive and negative implications for the feminist movement. On the positive side there is a continual need for study and research of female parenting, which this interest promotes and encourages. In the foreword to *Of Woman Born*, Adrienne Rich states that she felt it was important to write a book on motherhood because it is "a crucial, still relatively unexplored area for feminist theory." It is also positive that women who choose to bear children need no longer fear that this choice excludes them from recognition by feminist movement, although it may still exclude them from active participation. On the negative side, romanticizing motherhood, employing the same terminology that is used by sexists to suggest that women are inherently life-affirming nurturers, feminist activists reinforce central tenets of male supremacist ideology. They imply that motherhood is a woman's truest vocation; that women who do not mother, whose lives may be focused more exclusively on a career, creative work, or political work are missing out, are doomed to live emotionally unfulfilled lives. While they do not openly attack or denigrate women who do not bear children, they (like the society as a whole) suggest that it is more important than women's other labor and more rewarding. They could simply state that it is important and rewarding. Significantly, this perspective is often voiced by many of the white bourgeois women with successful careers who are now choosing to bear children. They seem to be saying to masses of women that careers or work can never be as important, as satisfying, as bearing children.

This is an especially dangerous line of thinking, coming at a time when teenage women who have not realized a number of goals, are bearing children in large numbers rather than postponing parenting; when masses of women are being told by the government that they are destroying family life by not assuming sexist-defined roles. Through mass media and other communication systems, women are currently inundated with material encouraging them to bear children. Newspapers carry headline stories with titles like "motherhood is making a comeback"; women's magazines are flooded with articles on the new motherhood; fashion magazines have special features on designer clothing for the pregnant woman; television talk shows do special features on career women who are now choosing to raise children. Coming at a time when women with children are more likely to live in poverty, when the number of homeless, parentless children increases by the thousands daily, when women continue to assume sole responsibility for parenting, such propaganda undermines and threatens feminist movement.

To some extent, the romanticization of motherhood by bourgeois white women is an attempt to repair the damage done by past feminist critiques and give women who mother the respect they deserve. It should be noted that even the most outrageous of these criticisms did not compare with sexism as a source of exploitation and humiliation for mothers. Female parenting is significant and valuable work which must be recognized as such by everyone in society, including feminist activists. It should receive deserved recognition, praise, and celebration within a feminist context where there is renewed effort to re-think the nature of motherhood, to make motherhood neither a compulsory experience for women nor an exploitative or oppressive one, to make female parenting good effective parenting whether it is done exclusively by women or in conjunction with men.

In a recent article, "Bringing Up Baby," Mary Ellen Schoonmaker stressed the often made point that men do not share equally in parenting:

> Since the early days of ambivalence toward motherhood, the overall goal of the women's movement has been a quest for equality—to take the oppression out of mothering, to join "mothering" to "parenting,"

and for those who choose to have children to share parenting with men and with society in general. Looking back over the past twenty years, it seems as if these goals have been among the hardest for the women's movement to reach.

If men did equally share in parenting, it would mean trading places with women part of the time. Many men have found it easier to share power with women on the job than they have in the home. Even though millions of mothers with infants and toddlers now work outside the home, many women still do the bulk of the housework. (13)

Men will not share equally in parenting until they are taught, ideally from childhood on, that fatherhood has the same meaning and significance as motherhood. As long as women or society as a whole see the mother/child relationship as unique and special because the female carries the child in her body and gives birth, or makes this biological experience synonymous with women having a closer, more significant bond to children than the male parent, responsibility for childcare and childrearing will continue to be primarily women's work. Even the childless woman is considered more suited to raise children than the male parent because she is seen as an inherently caring nurturer. The biological experience of pregnancy and childbirth, whether painful or joyful, should not be equated with the idea that women's parenting is necessarily superior to men's.

Dictionary definitions of the word "father" relate its meaning to accepting responsibility, with no mention of words like tenderness and affection, yet these words are used to define what the word mother means. By placing sole responsibility for nurturing onto women, that is to say for satisfying the emotional and material needs of children, society reinforces the notion that to mother is more important than to father. Structured into the definitions and the very usage of the terms father and mother is the sense that these two words refer to two distinctly different experiences. Women and men must define the work of fathering and mothering in the same way if males and females are to accept equal responsibility in parenting.

Even feminist theorists who have emphasized the need for men to share equally in childrearing are reluctant to cease attaching special value to mothering. This illustrates feminists' willingness to glorify the physiological experience of motherhood as well as unwillingness to concede motherhood as an arena of social life in which women can exert power and control.

Women and society as a whole often consider the father who does equal parenting unique and special rather than as representative of what should be the norm. Such a man may even be seen as assuming a "maternal" role. Describing men who parent in her book *Mother Love*, Elisabeth Badinter comments:

Under the pressure exerted by women, the new father mothers equally and in the traditional mother's image. He creeps in, like another mother, between the mother and the child, who experiences almost indiscriminately as intimate a contact with the father as with the mother. We have only to notice the increasingly numerous photographs in magazines showing fathers pressing newborns against their bare chests. Their faces reflect a completely motherly tenderness that shocks no one. After centuries of the father's authority or absence, it seems that a new concept has come into existence—father love, the exact equivalent of mother love. While it is obvious that women who parent would necessarily be the models men would strive to emulate, (since women have been doing effective parenting for many more years) these men are becoming parents, effective fathers. They are not becoming mothers. (324)

Another example of this tendency occurs at the end of Sara Ruddick's essay "Maternal Thinking." She envisions a time in which men will share equally in childrearing and writes:

On that day there will be no more "fathers," no more people of either sex who have power over their children's lives and moral authority in their children's worlds, though they do the work of attentive love. There will be mothers of both sexes who live out a transformed maternal thought in communities that share parental-care practically, emotionally, economically, and socially. Such communities will have learned from their mothers how to value children's lives. (91)

In this paragraph, as in the entire essay, Ruddick romanticizes the idea of the "maternal" and places emphasis on men becoming maternal, a vision which seems shortsighted. Because the word "maternal" is associated with the behavior of women, men will not identify with it even though they may be behaving in ways that have traditionally been seen as "feminine." Wishful thinking will not alter the concept of the maternal in our society. Rather than changing it, the word paternal should share the same meaning. Telling a boy acting out the role of caring parent with his dolls that he is being maternal will not change the idea that women are better suited to parenting; it will reinforce it. Saying to a boy that he is behaving like a good father (in the way that girls are told that they are good mothers when they show attention and care to dolls) would teach him a vision of effective parenting, of fatherhood, that is the same as motherhood.

Seeing men who do effective parenting as "maternal" reinforces the stereotypical sexist notion that women are inherently better suited to parent, that men who parent in the same way as women are imitating the real thing rather than acting as a parent should act. There should be a concept of effective parenting that makes no distinction between maternal and paternal care. The model of effective parenting that includes the kind of attentive love Ruddick describes has been applied only to women and has prevented fathers from learning how to parent. They are allowed to conceive of the father's role solely in terms of exercising authority and providing for material needs. They are taught to think of it as a role secondary to the mother's. Until males are taught how to parent using the same model of effective parenting that has been taught to women, they will not participate equally in childcare. They will even feel that they should not participate because they have been taught to think they are inadequate or ineffective childrearers.

Men are socialized to avoid assuming responsibility for childrearing and that avoidance is supported by women who believe that motherhood is a sphere of power they would lose if men participated equally in parenting. Many of these women do not wish to share parenting equally with men. In feminist circles it is often forgotten that masses of women in the United States still believe that men cannot parent effectively and should not even attempt to parent. Until these women understand that men should and can do primary parenting, they will not expect the men in their lives to share equally in childrearing. Even when they do, it is unlikely that men will respond with enthusiasm. People need to know the negative impact that male non-participation in childrearing has on family relationships and child development.

Feminist efforts to point out to men what they lose when they do not participate in parenting tend to be directed at the bourgeois classes. Little is done to discuss non-sexist parenting or male parenting with poor and working class women and men. In fact, the kind of maternal care Ruddick evokes in her essay, with its tremendous emphasis on attention given children by parents, especially mothers, is a form of parental care that is difficult for many working class parents to offer when they return home from work tired and exhausted. It is increasingly difficult for women and men in families struggling to survive economically to give special attention to parenting. Their struggle contrasts sharply with the family structure of bourgeois. Their white women and men who are likely to be better informed about the positive effects of male participation in parenting, who have more time to parent, and who are not perpetually anxious about their material well being. It is also difficult for women who parent alone to juggle the demands of work and childrearing.

Feminist theorists point to the problems that arise when parenting is done exclusively by an individual or solely by women: female parenting gives children few role models of male parenting; perpetuates the idea that parenting is a woman's vocation; and reinforces male domination and fear of women. Society, however, is not concerned. This information has little impact at a time when men, more than ever before, avoid responsibility for childrearing and when women are parenting less because they work more but are parenting more often alone. These facts raise two issues that must be of central concern for future feminist movement: the right of children to effective childcare by parents and other childrearers; the restructuring of society so that women do not exclusively provide that care.

Eliminating sexism is the solution to the problem of men participating unequally or not at all in childcare. Therefore more women and men must recognize the need to support and participate in feminist movement. Masses of women continue to believe that they should be primarily responsible for childcare—this point cannot be over emphasized. Feminist efforts to help women unlearn this socialization could lead to greater demands on their part for men to participate equally in parenting. Making and distributing brochures in women's health centers and in other public places that would emphasize the importance of males and females sharing equally in parenting is one way to make more people aware of this need. Seminars on parenting that emphasize non-sexist parenting and joint parenting by women and men in local communities is another way more people could learn about the subject. Before women become pregnant, they need to understand the significance of men sharing equally in parenting. Some women in relationships with men who may be considering bearing children do not do so because male partners make it known that they will not assume responsibility for parenting. These women feel their decision not to bear children with men who refuse to share parenting is a political statement reinforcing the importance of equal participation in parenting and the need to end male dominance of women. We need to hear more from these women about the choices they have made. There are also women who bear children in relationships with men who know beforehand that the man will not participate equally in parenting. It is important for future studies of female parenting to understand their choices.

Women need to know that it is important to discuss childcare with men before children are conceived or born. There are women and men who have made either legal contracts or simply written agreements that spell out each individual's responsibility. Some women have found that men verbally support the idea of shared parenting before a child is conceived or born and then do not follow through. Written agreements can help clarify the situation by requiring each individual to discuss what they feel about parental care, who should be responsible, etc. Most women and men do not discuss the nature of childrearing before children are born because it is simply assumed that women will be caretakers.

Despite the importance of men sharing equally in parenting, large numbers of women have no relationship to the man with whom they have conceived a child. In some cases, this is a reflection of the man's lack of concern about parenting or the woman's choice. Some women do not feel it is important for their children to experience caring, nurturing parenting from males. In black communities, it is not unusual for a single female parent to rely on male relatives and friends to help with childrearing. As more heterosexual and lesbian women choose to bear children with no firm ties to male parents, there will exist a greater need for community-based childcare that would bring children into contact with male childrearers so they will not grow to maturity thinking women are the only group who do or should do childrearing. The childrearer does not have to be a parent. Childrearers in our culture are teachers, librarians, etc. and even though these are occupations which have been dominated by women, this is changing. In these contexts, a child could experience male childrearing. Some female parents who raise their children without the mutual care of fathers feel their own positions are undermined when they meet occasionally with male parents who may provide a good time but be totally unengaged in day-to-day parenting. They sometimes have to cope with children valuing the male parent more because he is male (and sexist ideology teaches them that his attentions are more valuable than female care). These women need to know that teaching their children non-sexist values could help them appreciate female parenting and could eradicate favoritism based solely on sexist standards.

Because women are doing most of the parenting, the need for tax-funded public childcare centers with equal numbers of non-sexist male and female workers continues to be a pressing feminist issue. Such centers would relieve individual women of the sole responsibility for childrearing as well as help promote awareness of the necessity for male participation in childraising. Yet this is an issue that has yet to be pushed by masses of people. Future feminist organizing (especially in the interests of building mass-based feminist movement) could use this issue as a platform. Feminist activists have always seen public childcare as one solution to the problem of women being the primary childrearers. Commenting on the need for childcare centers in her article "Bringing Up Baby," Mary Ellen Schoonmaker writes:

> As for childcare outside the home, the seemingly simple concept envisioned by the women's movement of accessible, reliable, quality day care has proven largely elusive. While private, often overpriced sources of day care have risen to meet middle class needs, the inadequacy of public day care remains an outrage. The Children's Defense Fund, a child advocacy and lobbying group in Washington, D.C., reports that perhaps six to seven million children, including preschoolers, may be left at home alone while their parents work because they can't afford day care.... (13)

Most childcare centers, catering either to the needs of the working classes or the bourgeoisie, are not non-sexist. Yet until children begin to learn at a very early age that it is not important to make role distinctions based on sex, they will continue to grow to maturity thinking that women should be the primary childrearers.

Many people oppose the idea of tax-funded public childcare because they see it as an attempt by women to avoid parenting. They need to know that the extent to which the isolated parenting that women do in this society is not the best way to raise children or treat women who mother. Elizabeth Janeway makes this point in her most recent book *Cross Sections,* emphasizing that the idea of an individual having sole responsibility for childrearing is the most unusual pattern of parenting in the world, one that has proved to be unsuccessful because it isolates children and parents from society:

> ... How extreme that family isolation can be today is indicated by these instances listed in a study undertaken for the Massachusetts Advisory Council on Education.... This group found:
>
> 1. Isolation of wage earners from spouses and children, caused by the

wage earners' absorption into the world of work.

2. The complementary isolation of young children from the occupational world of parents and other adults.

3. The general isolation of young children from persons of different ages, both adults and other children.

4. The residential isolation of families from persons of different social, ethnic, religious, and racial backgrounds.

5. The isolation of family members from kin and neighbors.

Such isolation means that the role of the family as the agent for socializing children is inadequately fulfilled at present whether or not mothers are at work outside the home. Children are now growing up without the benefit of a variety of adult role models of both sexes and in ignorance of the world of paid work. Returning women to a life centered in home and family would not solve the fundamental loss of connection between family and community. The effort by the women's movement to see that centers for childcare are provided by society is not an attempt to hand over to others the duties of motherhood but to enlist community aid to supplement the proper obligations of parents, as was often the practice in the past. (66-67)

Ideally, small, community-based, public childcare centers would be the best way to overcome this isolation. When parents must drive long distances to take children to day care, dependency on parents is increased and not lessened. Community-based public childcare centers would give small children great control over their lives.

Childcare is a responsibility that can be shared with other childrearers, with people who do not live with children. This form of parenting is revolutionary in this society because it takes place in opposition to the idea that parents, especially mothers, should be the only childrearers. Many people raised in black communities experienced this type of community-based childcare. Black women who had to leave the home and work to help provide for families could not afford to send children to day care centers and such centers did not always exist. They relied on people in their communities to help. Even in families where the mother stayed home, she could also rely on people in the community to help. She did not need to go with her children every time they walked to the playground to watch them because they would be watched by a number of people living near the playground. People who did not have children often took responsibility for sharing in childrearing. In my own family, there were seven children and when we were growing up it was not possible for our parents to watch us all the time or even give that extra special individual attention children sometimes desire. Those needs were often met by neighbors and people in the community.

This kind of shared responsibility for childcare can happen in small community settings where people know and trust one another. It cannot happen in those settings if parents regard children as their "property," their "possession." Many parents do not want their children to develop caring relationships with others, not even relatives. If there were community-based day care centers, there would be a much greater likelihood that children would develop ongoing friendships and caring relationships with adult people rather than their parents. These types of relationships are not formed in day care centers where one teacher takes care of a large number of students, where one never sees teachers in any context other than school. Any individual who has been raised in an environment of communal childcare knows that this happens only if parents can accept other adults assuming parental type care for their children. While it creates a situation where children must respect a number of caretakers, it also gives children resources to rely on if their emotional, intellectual, and material needs are not met solely by parents. Often in black communities where shared childrearing happens, elderly women and men participate. Today many children have no contact with the elderly. Another hazard of single parenting or even nuclear family parenting that is avoided when there is community-based childraising is the tendency of parents to over-invest emotion in their children. This is a problem for many people who choose to have children after years of thinking they would not. They may make children into "love objects" and have no interest in teaching them to relate to a wide variety of people. This is as much a problem for feminist women and men who are raising children as it is for other parents.

Initially, women's liberationists felt that the need for population control coupled with awareness of this society's consumption of much of the world's resources, were political reasons not to bear children. These reasons have not changed even though they are now ignored or dismissed. Yet if there were less emphasis on having one's "own" children and more emphasis on having children who are already living and in need of childcare, there would be large groups of responsible women and men to share in the process of childrearing. Lucia Valeska supported this position in an essay published in a 1975 issue of *Quest* "If All Else Fails, I'm Still a Mother":

> To have our own biological children today is personally and politically irresponsible. If you have health, strength, energy, and financial assets to give to children, then do so. Who, then will have children? If the childfree raise existing children, more people than ever will "have" children. The line between biological and non-biological mothers will begin to disappear. Are we in danger of depleting the population? Are you kidding? (62)

Right now in your community there are hundreds of thousands of children and mothers who desperately need individual and community support.

Some people who choose not to bear children make an effort to participate in childrearing. Yet, like many parents, most people without children assume they should be uninterested in child are until they have their "own" children. People without children who try to participate in childrearing must confront the suspicions and resistance of people who do not understand their interest, who assume that all people without children do not like them. People are especially wary of individuals who wish to help in childrearing if they do not ask for pay for their services. At a time in my life when my companion and I were working hard to participate in childrearing we had children stay with us in our home for short periods of time to give the parent, usually a single mother, a break and to have children in our lives. If we explained the principle behind our actions, people were usually surprised and supportive but wary. I think they were wary because our actions were unusual. The difficulties we faced have led us to accept a life in which we have less interaction with children than we would like, the case for most people who do not have children. This isolation from children has motivated many feminists to bear children.

Before there can be shared responsibility for childrearing that relieves women of the sole responsibility for primary childcare, women and men must revolutionize their consciousness. They must be willing to accept that parenting in isolation (irrespective of the sex of the parent) is not the most effective way to raise children or be happy as parents. Since women do most of the parenting in this society and it does not appear that this situation will alter in the coming years, there has to be renewed feminist organizing around the issue of childcare. The point is not to stigmatize single parents, but to emphasize the need for collective parenting. Women all over the United States must rally together to demand that tax money spent on the arms race and other militaristic goals be spent on improving the quality of parenting and childcare in this society. Feminist theorists who emphasize the hazards of single parenting, who outline the need for men to share equally in parenting, often live in families where the male parent is present. This leads them to ignore the fact that this type of parenting is not an option for many women (even though it may be the best social framework in which to raise children). That social framework could be made available in community-based public day care centers with men and women sharing equal responsibility for childcare. More than ever before, there is a great need for women and men to organize around the issue of childcare to ensure that all children will be raised in the best possible social frameworks; to ensure that women will not be the sole, or primary, childrearers.

References

Badinter, Elisabeth. *Mother Love: Myth and Reality.* New York: Macmillan, 1981.

Bernard, Jessie. *The Future of Motherhood.* New York: Dial, 1974.

Chesler, Phyllis. *With Child: A Diary of Motherhood.* 1979. New York: Four Walls Eight Windows, 1998.

Chodorow, Nancy. *The Reproduction of Mothering.* Berkeley: University of California Press, 1978.

Friday, Nancy. *My Mother/My Self: The Daughter's Search for Identity.* New York: Delacorte Press, 1977.

Janeway, Elizabeth. *Cross Sections From a Decade of Change.* New York: W. Morrow, 1982.

Rich, Adrienne. *Of Woman Born.* New York: W. W. Norton, 1976.

Ruddick, Sarah. *Maternal Thinking: Toward a Politics of Peace.* Boston: Beacon Press, 1995.

Schoonmaker, Mary Ellen. "Bringing Up Baby." *These Times* September 7, 1983. 12-13, 22.

Valeska, Lucia. "If All Else Fails, I'm Still a Mother." *Quest* 1 (3) (Winter 1975): 52-63.

Chapter 9

Man Child

A Black Lesbian Feminist's Response

AUDRE LORDE

THIS ARTICLE IS NOT a theoretical discussion of Lesbian Mothers and their Sons, nor a how-to article. It is an attempt to scrutinize and share some pieces of that common history belonging to my son and to me. I have two children: a fifteen-and-a-half-year-old daughter Beth, and a fourteen-year-old son Jonathan. This is the way it was/is with me and Jonathan, and I leave the theory to another time and person. This is one woman's telling.

I have no golden message about the raising of sons for other lesbian mothers, no secret to transpose your questions into certain light. I have my own ways of rewording those same questions, hoping we will all come to speak those questions and pieces of our lives we need to share. We are women making contact within ourselves and with each other across the restrictions of a printed page, bent upon the use of our own/one another's knowledges.

The truest direction comes from inside. I give the most strength to my children by being willing to look within myself, and by being honest with them about what I find there, without expecting a response beyond their years. In this way they begin to learn to look beyond their own fears.

All our children are outriders for a queendom not yet assured. My adolescent son's growing sexuality is a conscious dynamic between Jonathan and me. It would be presumptuous of me to discuss Jonathan's sexuality here, except to state my belief that whomever he chooses to explore this area with, his choices will be non-oppressive, joyful, and deeply felt from within, places of growth.

One of the difficulties in writing this piece has been temporal; this is the summer when Jonathan is becoming a man, physically. And our sons must become men—such men as we hope our daughters, born and unborn, will be pleased to live among. Our sons will not grow into women. Their way is more difficult than that of our daughters, for they must move away from us, without us. Hopefully, our sons have what they have learned from us, and a howness to forge it into their own image.

Our daughters have us, for measure or rebellion or outline or dream; but the sons of lesbians have to make their own definitions of self as men. This is both power and vulnerability. The sons of lesbians have the advantage of our blueprints for survival, but they must take what we know and transpose it into their own maleness. May the goddess be kind to my son, Jonathan.

Recently I have met young Black men about whom I am pleased to say that their future and their visions, as well as their concerns within the present, intersect more closely with Jonathan's than do my own. I have shared vision with these men as well as temporal strategies for our survivals and I appreciate the spaces in which we could sit down together. Some of these men I met at the First Annual Conference of Third World Lesbians and Gays held in Washington D.C. in October, 1979. I have met others in different places and do not know how they identify themselves sexually. Some of these men are raising families alone. Some have adopted sons. They are Black men who dream and who act and who own their feelings, questioning. It is heartening to know our sons do not step out alone.

When Jonathan makes me angriest, I always say he is bringing out the testosterone in me. What I mean is that he is representing some piece of myself as a woman that I am reluctant to acknowledge or explore. For instance, what does "acting like a man" mean? For me, what I reject? For Jonathan, what he is trying to redefine?

Raising Black children—female and male—in the mouth of a racist, sexist, suicidal dragon is perilous and chancy. If they cannot love and resist at the same time, they will probably not survive. And in order to survive they must let go. This is what mothers teach—love, survival—that is, self-definition and letting go. For each of these, the ability to feel strongly and to recognize those feelings is central: how to feel love, how to neither discount fear nor be overwhelmed by it, how to enjoy feeling deeply.

I wish to raise a Black man who will not be destroyed by, nor settle for, those corruptions called *power* by the white fathers who mean his destruction as surely as they mean mine. I wish to raise a Black man who will recognize that the legitimate objects of his hostility are not women, but the particulars of a structure that programs him to fear and despise women as well as his own Black self.

For me, this task begins with teaching my son that I do not exist to do his feeling for him.

Men who are afraid to feel must keep women around to do their feeling for them while dismissing us for the same supposedly "inferior" capacity to feel deeply. But in this way also, men deny themselves their own essential humanity, becoming trapped in dependency and fear.

As a Black woman committed to a liveable future, and as a mother loving and raising a boy who will become a man, I must examine all my possibilities of being within such a destructive system.

Jonathan was three-and-one-half when Frances, my lover, and I met; he was seven when we all began to live together permanently. From the start, Frances' and my insistence that there be no secrets in our household about the fact that we were lesbians has been the source of problems and strengths for both children. In the beginning, this insistence grew out of the knowledge, on both our parts, that whatever was hidden out of fear could always be used either against the children or ourselves—one imperfect but useful argument for honesty. The knowledge of fear can help make us free.

> for the embattled
> there is no place
> *that cannot be*
> *home*
> *nor is.*[1]

For survival, Black children in America must be raised to be warriors. For survival, they must also be raised to recognize the enemy's many faces. Black children of lesbian couples have an advantage because they learn, very early, that oppression comes in many different forms, none of which have anything to do with their own worth.

To help give me perspective, I remember that for years, in the name-calling at school, boys shouted at Jonathan not—"your mother's a lesbian"—but rather—"your mother's a nigger."

When Jonathan was eight years old and in the third grade we moved, and he went to a new school where his life was hellish as a new boy on the block. He did not like to play rough games. He did not like to fight. He did not like to stone dogs. And all this marked him early on as an easy target.

When he came in crying one afternoon, I heard from Beth how the corner bullies were making Johnathan wipe their shoes on the way home whenever Beth wasn't there to fight them off. And when I heard that the ringleader was a little boy in Jonathan's class his own size, an interesting and very disturbing thing happened to me.

My fury at my own long-ago impotence, and my present pain at his suffering, made me start to forget all that I knew about violence and fear, and blaming the victim, I started to hiss at the weeping child. "The next time you come in here crying…" and I suddenly caught myself in horror.

This is the way we allow the destruction of our sons to begin—in the name of protection and to ease our own pain. *My* son get beaten up? I was about to demand that he buy that first lesson in the corruption of power, that might makes right. I could hear myself beginning to perpetuate the age-old distortions about what strength and bravery really are.

And no, Jonathan didn't have to fight if he didn't want to, but somehow he did have to feel better about not fighting. An old horror rolled over me of being the fat kid who ran away, terrified of getting her glasses broken.

About that time a very wise woman said to me, "Have you ever told Jonathan that once you used to be afraid, too?"

The idea seemed far-out to me at the time, but the next time he came in crying and sweaty from having run away again, I could see that he felt shamed at having failed me, or some image he and I had created in his head of mother/woman. This image of woman being able to handle it all was bolstered by the fact that he lived in a household with three strong women, his lesbian parents and his forthright older sister. At home, for Jonathan, power was clearly female.

And because our society teaches us to think in an either/or mode—kill or be killed, dominate or be dominated—this meant that he must either surpass or be lacking. I could see the implications of this line of thought. Consider the two western classic myth/models of mother/son relationships: Jocasta/Oedipus, the son who fucks his mother, and Clytemnestra/Orestes, the son who kills his mother.

It all felt connected to me.

I sat down on the hallway steps and took Jonathan on my lap and wiped his tears. "Did I ever tell you about how I used to be afraid when I was your age?"

I will never forget the look on that little boy's face as I told him the tale of my glasses and my after-school fights. It was a look of relief and total disbelief, all rolled into one.

It is as hard for our children to believe that we are not omnipotent as it is for us to know it, as parents. But that knowledge is necessary as the first step in the reassessment of power as something other than might, age, privilege, or the lack of fear. It is an important step for a boy, whose societal destruction begins when he is forced to believe that he can only be strong if he doesn't feel, or if he wins.

I thought about all this one year later when Beth and Jonathan, ten and nine, were asked by an interviewer how they thought they had been affected by being children of a feminist.

Jonathan said that he didn't think there was too much in feminism for boys, although it certainly was good to be able to cry if he felt like it and not to have to play football if he didn't want to. I think of this sometimes now when I see him practicing for his Brown Belt in Tae Kwon Do.

The strongest lesson I can teach my son is the same lesson I teach my daughter: how to be who he wishes to be for himself. And the best way I can do this is to be who I am and hope that he will learn from this not how to be me, which is not possible, but how to be himself. And this means how to move to that voice from within himself, rather than to those raucous, persuasive, or threatening voices from outside, pressuring him to be what the world wants him to be.

And that is hard enough.

Jonathan is learning to find within himself some of the different faces of courage and strength, whatever he chooses to call them. Two years ago, when Jonathan was twelve and in the seventh grade, one of his friends at school who had been to the house persisted in calling Frances "the maid." When Jonathan corrected him, the boy then referred to her as "the cleaning woman." Finally Jonathan said, simply, "Frances is not the cleaning woman, she's my mother's lover." Interestingly enough, it is the teachers at this school who still have not recovered from his openness.

Frances and I were considering attending a lesbian/feminist conference this summer, when we were notified that no boys over ten were allowed. This presented logistic as well as philosophical problems for us, and we sent the following letter:

Sisters:
Ten years as an interracial lesbian couple has taught us both the dangers of an oversimplified approach to the nature and solutions of any oppression, as well as the danger inherent in an incomplete vision.

Our thirteen-year-old son represents as much hope for our future world as does our fifteen-year-old daughter, and we are not willing to abandon him to the killing streets of New York City while we journey west to help form a Lesbian-Feminist vision of the future world in which we can all survive and flourish. I hope we can continue this dialogue in the near future, as I feel it is important to our vision and our survival.

The question of separatism is by no means simple. I am thankful that one of my children is male, since that helps to keep me honest. Every line I write shrieks there are no easy solutions.

I grew up in largely female environments, and I know how crucial that has been to my own development. I feel the want and need often for the society of women, exclusively. I recognize that our own spaces are essential for developing and recharging.

As a Black woman, I find it necessary to withdraw into all Black groups at times for exactly the same reasons—differences in stages of development and differences in levels of interaction. Frequently, when speaking with men and white women, I am reminded of how difficult and time-consuming it is to have to reinvent the pencil every time you want to send a message.

But this does not mean that my responsibility for my son's education stops at age ten, any more than it does for my daughter's. However, for each of them, that responsibility does grow less and less as they become more woman and man.

Both Beth and Jonathan need to know what they can share and what they cannot, how they are joined and how they are not. And Frances and I, as grown women and lesbians coming more and more into our power, need to relearn the experience that difference does not have to be threatening.

When I envision the future, I think of the world I crave for my daughters and my sons. It is thinking for survival of the species—thinking for life.

Most likely there will always be women who move with women, women who live with men, men who choose men. I work for a time when women with women, women with men, men with men, all share the work of a world that does not barter bread or self for obedience, nor beauty, nor love. And in that world we will raise our children free to choose how best to fulfill themselves. For we are jointly responsible for the care and raising of the young, since *that* they be raised is a function, ultimately, of the species.

Within that tripartite pattern of relating/existence, the raising of the young will be the joint responsibility of all adults who choose to be associated with children. Obviously, the children raised within each of these three relationships will be different, lending a special savor to that eternal inquiry into how best can we live our lives.

Jonathan was three-and-a-half when Frances and I met. He is now fourteen years old. I feel the living perspective that having lesbian parents has brought to Jonathan is a valuable addition to his human sensitivity.

Jonathan has had the advantage of growing up within a nonsexist relationship, one in which this society's pseudo-natural assumptions of ruler/ruled are being challenged. And this is not only because Frances and I are lesbians, for unfortunately there are some lesbians who are still locked into patriarchal patterns of unequal power relationships.

These assumptions of power relationships are being questioned because Frances and I, often painfully and with varying degrees of success, attempt to evaluate and measure over and over again our feelings concerning power, our own and others'. And we explore with care those areas concerning how it is used and expressed between us and between us and the children, openly and otherwise. A good part of our biweekly family meetings are devoted to this exploration.

As parents, Frances and I have given Jonathan our love, our openness, and our dreams to help form his visions. Most importantly, as the son of lesbians, he has had an invaluable model not only of a relationship—but of relating.

Jonathan is fourteen now. In talking over this paper with him and asking his permission to share some pieces of his life, I asked Jonathan what he felt were the strongest negative and the strongest positive aspects for him in having grown up with lesbian parents.

He said the strongest benefit he felt he had gained was that he knew a lot more about people than most other kids his age that he knew, and that he did not have a lot of the hang-ups that some other boys did about men and women.

And the most negative aspect he felt, Jonathan said, was the ridicule he got from some kids with straight parents.

"You mean, from your peers?" I said.

"Oh no," he answered promptly. "My peers know better. I mean other kids."

This article was first published in Conditions: Four *(1979).*

Notes

[1]From "School Note," in *The Black Unicorn* (W.W. Norton and Company, New York, 1978), p. 55.

Chapter 10

Stabat Mater

JULIA KRISTEVA

The Paradox: Mother or Primary Narcissism

IF IT IS NOT POSSIBLE to say of a *woman* what she *is* (without running the risk of abolishing her difference), would it perhaps be different concerning the *mother,* since that is the only function of the "other sex" to which we can definitely attribute existence? And yet, there too, we are caught in a paradox. First, we live in a civilization where the *consecrated* (religious or secular) representation of femininity is absorbed by motherhood. If, however, one looks at it more closely, this motherhood is the *fantasy* that is nurtured by the adult, man or woman, of a lost territory; what is more, it involves less an idealized archaic mother than the idealization of the *relationship* that binds us to her, one that cannot be localized—an idealization of primary narcissism. Now, when feminism demands a new representation of femininity, it seems to identify motherhood with that idealized misconception and, because it rejects the image and its misuse, feminism circumvents the real experience that fantasy overshadows. The result? A negation or rejection of motherhood by some avant-garde feminist groups. Or else, an acceptance—conscious or not—of its traditional representations by the great mass of people, women and men.

FLASH—instant of time or of dream without time; inordinately swollen atoms of a bond, a vision, a shiver, a yet formless, unnamable embryo. Epiphanies. Photos of what is not yet visible and that language necessarily skims over from afar, allusively. Words that are always too distant too abstract for this underground swarming of seconds, folding in unimaginable spaces. Writing them Christianity is doubtless the most refined symbolic construct in which femininity to the extent that it transpires through it—and it does so incessantly—is focused on *Maternality.*[1] Let us call "maternal" the ambivalent principle that is bound to the species, on the one hand, and on the other stems from an identity catastrophe that causes the Name to topple over into the unnamable that

down is an ordeal of
discourse, like love. What is
loving, for a woman, the same
thing as writing. Laugh. Impossible.
Flash on the unable,
Weaving of abstractions to be
torn, Let a body venture
at last out of its shelter,
take a chance with meaning
under a veil of words.
WORD FLESH.
From one to the other, Eternally
up visions, metaphors of the invisible.

one imagines as femininity,
nonlanguage or body. Thus
Christ, the Son of man, when
all is said and done, is "human"
only through his mother—as
if Christly of Christian humanism
could only be a maternalism (this is,
besides, what some secularizing
trends within its orbit do
not cease claiming in their
esotericism). And yet, the
humanity of the Virgin mother
is not always obvious, and we

shall see how, in her being cleared of sin, for instance, Mary distinguishes herself from mankind. But at the same time the most intense revelation of God, which occurs in mysticism, is given only to a person who assumes himself as "maternal?" Augustine, Bernard of Clairvaux, Meister Eckhart, to mention but a few; played the part of the Father's virgin spouses, or even, like Bernard, received drops of virginal milk directly on their lips. Freedom with respect to the maternal territory then becomes the pedestal upon which love of God is erected. As a consequence, mystics, those "happy Schrebers" (Sollers) throw a bizarre light on the psychotic sore of modernity: it appears as the incapability of contemporary codes to tame the maternal, that is, primary narcissism. Uncommon and "literary," their present-day counterparts are always somewhat oriental, if not tragical—Henry Miller, who says he is pregnant; Artaud, who sees himself as "his daughters" or "his mother." It is the orthodox constituent of Christianity, through John Chrysostom's golden mouth, among others, that sanctioned the transitional function of the Maternal by calling the Virgin a "bond;" a "medium;" or an "interval;" thus opening the door to more or less heretical identifications with the Holy Ghost.

This resorption of femininity within the Maternal is specific to many civilizations, but Christianity, in its own fashion, brings it to its peak. Could it be that such a reduction represents no more than a masculine appropriation of the Maternal, which, in line with our hypothesis, is only a fantasy masking primary narcissism? Or else, might one detect in it, in other respects, the workings of enigmatic sublimation? These are perhaps the workings of masculine sublimation, a sublimation just the same, if it be true that for Freud picturing Da Vinci, and even for Da Vinci himself, the taming of that economy (of the Maternal or of primary narcissism) is a requirement for artistic, literary, or painterly accomplishment?

Within that perspective, however, there are two questions, among others, that remain unanswered. What is there, in the portrayal of the Maternal in general and particularly in its Christian, virginal, one, that reduces social anguish and gratifies a male being; what is there that also satisfies a woman so that a commonality of the sexes is set up, beyond and in spite of their glaring incompatibility and permanent warfare? Moreover, is there something in that Maternal notion that ignores what a woman might say or want. As a result, when women speak out today it is in matters of conception and motherhood that their annoyance is basically centered. Beyond social and political demands, this takes the well-known "discontents" of our civilization to a level where Freud would not follow—the discontents of the species.

A Triumph of the Unconscious in Monotheism

It would seem that the "virgin" attribute for Mary is a translation error, the translator having substituted for the Semitic term that indicates the sociolegal status of a young unmarried woman the Greek word *parthenos,* which on the other hand specifies a physiological and psychological condition: virginity. One might read into this the Indo-European fascination (which Dumezil analyzed)[2] with the virgin daughter as guardian of paternal power; one might also detect an ambivalent conspiracy, through excessive spiritualization, of the mother-goddess and the underlying matriarchy with which Greek culture and Jewish monotheism kept struggling. The fact remains that western Christianity has organized that "translation error;" projected its own fantasies into it, and produced one of the most powerful imaginary constructs known in the history of civilizations.

The story of the virginal cult in Christianity amounts in fact to the imposition of pagan-rooted beliefs in, and often against, dogmas of the official Church. It is true that the Gospels already posit Mary's existence. But they suggest only very discreetly the immaculate conception of Christ's mother, they say nothing concerning Mary's own background and speak of her only seldom at the side of her son or during crucifixion. Thus Matthew 1:20 ("… the angel of the Lord appeared to him in a dream and said, 'Joseph, son of David, do not be afraid to take Mary home as your wife, because she has conceived what is in her by the Holy Spirit'"), and Luke 1:34 ("Mary said to the angel, 'But how can this come about since I do not know man?'") opened a door, a narrow opening for all that, but one that would soon widen thanks to apocryphal additions, on impregnation without sexuality; according to this notion a woman, preserved from masculine intervention, conceives alone with a "third party," a nonperson, the Spirit. In the rare instances when the Mother of Jesus appears in the Gospels, she is informed that filial relationship rests not with the flesh but with the name or, in other words, that any possible matrilinearism is to be repudiated and the symbolic link alone is to last. We thus have Luke 2:48-49 ("… his mother said to him, 'My child, why have you done this to us? See how worried your father and I have been, looking for you: 'Why were you looking for me?" he replied. 'Did you not know that I must be busy with my father's affairs?'"), and also John 2:3-5 ("…the mother of Jesus said to him, 'They have no wine.' Jesus said, 'Woman, why turn to me?[3] My hour has not come yet?") and 19:26-27 ("Seeing his mother and the disciple he loved standing near her, Jesus said to his mother, 'Woman, this is your son?' Then to the disciple he said, 'This is your mother.' And from that moment the disciple made a place for her in his home.")

Starting from this programmatic material, rather skimpy nevertheless, a compelling imaginary construct proliferated in essentially three directions. In the· first place, there was the matter of drawing a parallel between Mother and Son by expanding the theme of the "Immaculate Conception," inventing a biography of Mary similar to that of Jesus, and, by depriving her of sin to deprive her of death. Mary leaves by way of Dormition or Assumption. Next, she needed letters patent of nobility, a power that, even though exercised in the beyond, is nonetheless political, since Mary was to be proclaimed queen, given the attributes and paraphernalia of royalty and, in parallel fashion, declared Mother of the divine institution on earth, the Church. Finally, the relationship with Mary and from Mary was to be revealed as the prototype of a love relationship and followed two fundamental aspects of western love: courtly love and child love, thus fitting the entire range that goes from sublimation to asceticism and masochism.

Neither Sex Nor Death

Mary's life, devised on the model of the life of Jesus, seems to be the fruit of apocryphal literature. The story of her own miraculous conception, called "Immaculate Conception" by Ann and Joachim, after a long, barren marriage, together with her biography as a pious maiden, show up in· apocryphal sources as early as the end of the first century. Their entirety may be found in the *Secret Book of James* and also in one of the pseudoepigrapha, the Gospel according to the Hebrews (which inspired Giotto's frescoes, for instance). Those "facts" were quoted by Clement of Alexandria and Origen but not officially accepted; even though· the Eastern Church tolerated them readily, they were translated into Latin only in the sixteenth century. Yet the West was not long before glorifying the life of Mary on its own but always under orthodox guidance. The first Latin poem, "Maria," on the birth of Mary, was written by the nun Hrotswith von Gandersheim (who died before 1002), a playwright and poet.

Fourth-century asceticism, developed by the Fathers of the Church, was grafted on that apocryphal shoot in order to bring out and rationalize the immaculate conception postulate. The demonstration was based on a simple logical relation: the intertwining of sexuality and death. Since they are mutually implicated with each other, one cannot avoid the one without fleeing the other. This asceticism, applicable to both sexes, was vigorously expressed by John Chrysostom (*On Virginity:* "For where there is death there is also sexual copulation, and where there is no death there is no sexual copulation either"); even though he was attacked by Augustine and Aquinas, he nonetheless fueled Christian doctrine. Thus, Augustine condemned "concupiscence" *(epithumia)* and posited that Mary's virginity is in fact only a logical precondition of Christ's chastity. The Orthodox Church, heir no doubt to a matriarchy that was more intense in eastern European societies, emphasized Mary's virginity more boldly. Mary was contrasted with Eve, life with death (Jerome, *Letter* 22) "Death came through Eve but life came through Mary";

Irenaeus, "Through Mary the snake becomes a dove and we are freed from the chains of death"). People even got involved in tortuous arguments in order to demonstrate that Mary remained a virgin after childbirth (thus the second Constantinople council, in 381, under Arianistic influence, emphasized the Virgin's role in comparison to official dogma and asserted Mary's perpetual virginity; the 451 council called her *Aeiparthenos—ever* virgin). Once this was established, Mary, instead of being referred to as Mother of man or Mother of Christ, would be proclaimed Mother of God: *Theotokos.* Nestorius, patriarch of Constantinople, refused to go along; Nestorianism, however, for all practical purposes died with the patriarch's own death in 451, and the path that would lead to Mary's deification was then clear.

Head reclining, nape
finally relaxed, skin, blood,
nerves warmed up, luminous
flow: stream of hair made of
ebony, of nectar, smooth
darkness through her fingers,
gleaming honey under
the wings of bees, sparkling
strands burning bright...
silk, mercury, ductile copper:
frozen light warmed under
fingers. Mane of beast-
squirrel, horse, and the happiness
of a faceless head,
Narcissus-like touching
without eyes, sight dissolving in
muscles, hair, deep, smooth,
peaceful colors. Mamma:
anamnesis.

Taut eardrum, tearing
sound out of muted silence.
Wind among grasses, a
seagull's faraway call, echoes of
waves, auto horns, voices, or
nothing? Or his own tears,
my newborn, spasm of
syncopated void. I no longer
hear anything, but the
eardrum keeps transmitting this
resonant vertigo to my skull,
the hair. My body is no
longer mine, it doubles up,

Very soon, within the complex relationship between Christ and his Mother where relations of God to mankind, man to woman, son to mother, etc., are hatched, the problematics of *time* similar to that of cause loomed up. If Mary preceded Christ and he originated in her if only from the standpoint of his humanity, should not the conception of Mary herself have been immaculate? For, if that were not the case, how could a being conceived in sin and harboring it in herself produce a God? Some apocryphal writers had not hesitated, without too much caution, to suggest such an absence of sin in Mary's conception, but the Fathers of the Church were, more careful. Bernard of Clairvaux is reluctant to extol the conception of Mary by Anne, and thus he tries to check the homologation of Mary with Christ. But it fell upon Duns Scotus to change the hesitation over the promotion of a mother goddess within Christianity into a logical suffers, bleeds, catches cold, puts its teeth in, slobbers, coughs, is covered with pimples, and it laughs. And yet, when its own joy, my child's, returns, its smile washes only my eyes. But the pain, its pain—it comes from inside, never remains apart, other, it inflames me at once, without a second's respite. As if that was what I had given birth to and, not willing to part from me, insisted on coming back, dwelled in me permanently. One does not give birth in pain, one gives birth to pain: the child represents it and henceforth it settles in, it is continuous. Obviously you may close your eyes, cover up your ears, teach courses, run errands, tidy up the house, think about objects, subjects. But a mother is always branded by pain, she yields to it. "And a sword will pierce your own soul too…"

Dream without glow, without sound, dream of brawn. Dark twisting, pain in the back, the arms, the thighs—pincers turned into fibers, infernos bursting veins, stones breaking bones: grinders of volumes, expanses, spaces, lines, points. All those words, now, ever visible things to register the roar of a silence that hurts all over. As if a geometry ghost could suffer when collapsing

problem, thus saving them both, the Great Mother as well as logic. He viewed Mary's birth as a *praeredemptio,* as a matter of congruency: if it be true that Christ alone saves us through his redemption on the cross, the Virgin who bore him can but be preserved from sin in "recursive" fashion, from the time of her own conception up to that redemption.

For or against, with dogma or logical shrewdness, the battle around the Virgin intensified between Jesuits and Dominicans, but the Counter-Reformation, as is well known, finally ended the resistance: henceforth, Catholics venerated Mary in herself. The Society of Jesus succeeded in completing a process of popular pressure distilled by patristic asceticism, and in reducing, with neither explicit hostility nor brutal rejection, the share of the Maternal (in the sense given above) useful to a certain balance between the two sexes. Curiously and necessarily, when that balance began to be seriously threatened in the nineteenth century, the Catholic Church—more dialectical and subtle here than the Protestants who were already spawning the first suffragettes—raised the Immaculate Conception to dogma status in 1854. It is often suggested that the

in a noiseless tumult… Yet
the eye picked up nothing,
the ear remained deaf. But
everything swarmed, and
crumbled, and twisted, and
broke—the grinding continued…
Then, slowly, a shadowy
shape gathered, became
detached, darkened, stood
out: seen from what must be
the true place of my head, it
was the right side of my pelvis.
Just bony, sleek, yellow,
misshapen, a piece of my
body jutting out unnaturally,
asymmetrically, but slit: severed
scaly surface, revealing
under this disproportionate
pointed limb the fibers of a
marrow… Frozen placenta,
live limb of a skeleton,
monstrous graft of life on myself,
a living dead. Life…
death… undecidable. During
delivery it went to the left
with the afterbirth… My
removed marrow, which
nevertheless acts as a graft,
which wounds but increases
me. Paradox: deprivation
and benefit of childbirth. But
calm finally hovers over pain,
over the terror of this dried
branch that comes back to
life, cut off, wounded,
deprived of its sparkling bark.
The calm of another life, the
life of that other who wends
his way while I remain
henceforth like a framework.
Still life. There is him,
however, his own flesh, which
was mine yesterday. Death,
then, how could I yield to it?

blossoming of feminism in
Protestant countries is due,
among other things, to the
greater initiative allowed
women on the social and
ritual plane. One might wonder
if, in addition, such a flowering
is not the result of a *lack*
in the Protestant religious
structure with respect to the
Maternal, which, on the contrary,
was elaborated within
Catholicism with a refinement
which the Jesuits gave the
final touch, and which still
makes Catholicism very
difficult to analyze.
The fulfillment, under the
name of Mary, of a totality
made of woman and God is
finally accomplished through
the avoidance of death. The
Virgin Mary experiences a
fate more radiant than her
son's: she undergoes no
calvary, she has no tomb, she
doesn't die and hence has no
need to rise from the dead.
Mary doesn't die but, as if to
echo oriental beliefs, Taoists
among others, according to
which human bodies pass
from one place to another in
an eternal flow that constitutes
a carbon copy of the
maternal receptacle—she is
transported.
Her transition is more passive
in the Eastern Church: it
is a Dormition *(Koimesis)* during
which, according to a
number of iconographic
representations, Mary can be
seen changed into a little girl

in the arms of her son who henceforth becomes her father; she thus reverses her role as Mother into a Daughter's role for the greater pleasure of those who enjoy Freud's "Theme of the Three Caskets."

Indeed, *mother* of her son and his *daughter* as well, Mary is also, and besides, his *wife:* she therefore actualizes the threefold metamorphosis of a woman in the tightest parenthood structure. From 1135 on, transposing the *Song of Songs,* Bernard of Clairvaux glorifies Mary in her role of beloved and wife. But Catherine of Alexandria (said to have been martyred in 307) already pictured herself as receiving the wedding ring from Christ, with the Virgin's help, while Catherine of Siena (1347-80) goes through a mystical wedding with him. Is it the impact of Mary's function as Christ's beloved and wife that is responsible for the blossoming out of the Marian cult in the West after Bernard and thanks to the Cistercians? "*Vergine Madre, figlia del tuo Figlio,*" Dante exclaims, thus probably best condensing the gathering of the three feminine functions (daughter-wife-mother) within a totality where they vanish as specific corporealities while retaining their psychological functions. Their bond makes up the basis of unchanging and timeless spirituality; "the set time limit of an eternal design" *(Termine fisso d'eterno consiglio),* as Dante masterfully points out in his *Divine Comedy.*

The transition is more active in the West, with Mary rising body and soul toward the other world in an *Assumption.* That feast, honored in Byzantium as early as the fourth century, reaches Gaul in the seventh under the influence of the Eastern Church; but the earliest Western visions of the Virgin's assumption, women's visions (particularly that of Elizabeth von Schonau who in 1164) date only from the twelfth century. For the Vatican, the Assumption became dogma only in 1950. What death anguish was it intended to soothe after the conclusion of the deadliest of wars?

Image of Power

On the side of "power," *Maria Regina* appears in imagery as early as the sixth century in the church of Santa Maria Antiqua in Rome. Interestingly enough, it is she, woman and mother, who is called upon to represent supreme earthly power. Christ is king but neither he nor his father are pictured wearing crowns, diadems, costly paraphernalia, and other external signs of abundant material goods. That opulent infringement to Christian idealism is centered on the Virgin Mother. Later, when she assumed the title of *Our Lady,* this would also be an analogy to the earthly power of the noble feudal lady of medieval courts. Mary's function as guardian of power, later checked when the Church became wary of it, nevertheless persisted in popular and pictorial representation, witness Piero della Francesca's impressive painting, *Madonna della Misericordia,* which was disavowed by Catholic authorities at the time. And yet, not only did the papacy revere more and more the Christly mother as the Vatican's power over cities and municipalities was strengthened, it also openly identified its own institution with" the Virgin Mary was officially proclaimed Queen by Pius XII in 1954 and *Mater Ecclesiae* in 1964.

Eia Mater, Fons Amoris!

Fundamental aspects of Western love finally converged on Mary. In a first step, it indeed appears that the Marian cult homologizing Mary with Jesus and carrying asceticism to the extreme was opposed to courtly love for the noble lady, which, while representing social transgression, was not at all a physical or moral sin. And yet, at the very dawn of a "courtliness" that was still very carnal, Mary and the Lady shared one common trait: they are the focal point of men's desires and aspirations. Moreover, because they were unique and thus excluded all other women, both the Lady and the Virgin embodied an absolute authority the more attractive as it appeared removed from paternal sternness. This feminine power must have been experienced as denied power, more pleasant to seize because it was both archaic and secondary, a kind of substitute for effective power in the family and the city but no less authoritarian, the underhand double of explicit phallic power. As early as the thirteenth century, thanks to the implantation of ascetic Christianity and especially, as early as 1328, to the promulgation of Salic laws, which excluded daughters from the inheritance and thus made the loved one very vulnerable and colored one's love for her with all the hues of the impossible, the Marian and courtly streams came together. Around the time of Blanche of Castile (who died in 1252), the Virgin explicitly became the focus of courtly love, thus gathering the attributes of the desired woman and of the holy mother in a totality as accomplished as it was inaccessible. Enough to make any woman suffer, any man dream. One finds indeed in a *Miracle de Notre Dame* the story of a young man who abandons his fiancee for the Virgin: the latter came to him in a dream and reproached him for having left her for an "earthly woman?"

Nevertheless, besides that ideal totality that no individual woman could possibly embody, the Virgin also became the

Scent of milk, dewed greenery, acid and clear, recall of wind, air, seaweed (as if a body lived without waste): it slides under the skin, does not remain in the mouth or nose but fondles the veins, detaches skin from bones, inflates me like an ozone balloon, and I hover with feet firmly planted on the ground in order to carry, him, sure, stable, ineradicable while he dances in my neck, flutters with my hair, seeks a smooth shoulder on the right, on the left, slips on

fulcrum of the humanization of the West in general and of love in particular. It is again about the thirteenth century with Francis of Assisi, that, this tendency takes shape with the representation of Mary as poor, modest, and humble-madonna of humility, at the same time as a devoted, fond mother. The famous nativity of Pierodella Francesca in London, in which Simone de Beauvoir too hastily saw a feminine defeat because the mother kneeled, before her barely born son, in fact,

the breast, swingles, silver
vivid blossom of my belly,
and finally flies away on my
navel in his dream carried by
my hands. My son.

Nights of wakefulness,
scattered sleep, sweetness of
the child, warm mercury in
my arms, cajolery, affection,
defenseless body, his or
mine, sheltered, protected. A
wave swells again, when he
goes to sleep, under my
skin-tummy, thighs, legs:
sleep of the muscles, not of
the brain, sleep of the flesh.
The wakeful tongue quietly
remembers another withdrawal,
mine: a blossoming
heaviness in the middle of
the bed, of a hollow, of the
sea... Recovered childhood,
dreamed peace restored, in
sparks, flash of cells, instants
of laughter, smiles in the
blackness of dreams, at
night, opaque joy that roots
me in her bed, my mother's,
and projects him, a son, a
butterfly soaking up dew
from her hand, there, nearby,
in the night. Alone: she, I,
and he.

He returns from the
depths of the nose, the vocal
chords, the lungs, the ears,
pierces their smothering
stopping sickness swab, and
awakens in his eyes. Gentleness
of the sleeping face, contours
of pinkish jade—
forehead, eyebrows, nostrils,

consolidates the new "cult" of
humanistic sensitivity. It replaces
the high spirituality that
assimilated the Virgin to Christ
with an earthly conception of
a wholly human mother. As a
source for the most popularized
pious images, such maternal
humility comes closer
to "lived" feminine experience
than the earlier representations
did. Beyond this, however,
it is true that it integrates
a certain feminine masochism
but also displays its counterpart
in gratification and
jouissance. The truth of it is
that the lowered head of the
mother before her son is
accompanied by the immeasurable
pride of the one who
knows she is also his wife and
daughter. She knows she is
destined to that eternity (of
the spirit or of the species), of
which every mother is
unconsciously aware, and with
regard to which maternal
devotion or even sacrifice is
but an insignificant price to
pay. A price that is borne all
the more easily since,
contrasted with the love that
binds a mother to her son, all
other "human relationships"
burst like blatant shams. The
Franciscan representation of
the Mother conveys many
essential aspects of maternal
psychology, thus leading up to
an influx of common people
to the churches and also a
tremendous increase in the
Marian cult—witness, the building

cheeks, parted features of the
mouth, delicate, hard,
pointed chin. Without fold
or shadow, neither being nor
unborn, neither, present nor
absent, but real, real inaccessible
innocence, engaging
weight, and seraphic lightness.
A child? —An angel, a
glow on an Italian painting,
impassive, peaceful dream—
dragnet of Mediterranean
fishermen. And then, the
mother-of-pearl bead
awakens: quicksilver. Shiver of
the eyelashes, imperceptible
twitch of the eyebrows, quivering
skin, anxious reflections,
seeking, knowing,
casting their knowledge
aside in the face of my non-
knowledge: fleeting irony of
childhood gentleness that
awakens to meaning, surpasses
it, goes past it, causes
me to soar in music, in dance.
Impossible refinement, subtle
rape of inherited genes:
before what has been learned
comes to pelt him, harden
him, ripen him. Hard,
mischievous gentleness of the
first ailment overcome,
innocent wisdom of the first
ordeal undergone, yet hopeful
blame on account of the
suffering I put you through,
by calling for you, desiring,
creating. Gentleness, wisdom
blame: your face is already
human, sickness has
caused you to join our species,
you speak without
words but your throat no

of many churches dedicated to
her ("Notre Dame"). Such a
humanization of Christianity
through the cult of the
mother also led to an interest
in the humanity of the father
man: the celebration of
"family life" showed Joseph to
advantage as early as the
fifteenth century.

What Body?

We are entitled only to the ear
of the virginal body, the tears,
and the breast. With the female
sexual organ changed
into an innocent shell, holder
of sound, there arises a possible.
tendency to eroticize hearing,
voice, or even understanding.
By the same token,
however, sexuality is brought
down to the level of innuendo.
Feminine sexual experience
is thus rooted in the
universality of sound, since
wit is distributed *equally*
among all men, all women. A
woman will only have the
choice to live her life either
hyperabstractly ("immediately
universal," Hegel said) in order
thus to earn divine grace
and homologation with
symbolic order; or merely
different, other, fallen ("immediately
particular:" Hegel said).
But she will not be able to
accede to the complexity of
being divided, of heterogeneity,
of the catastrophic—fold

longer gurgles—it harkens
with me to the silence of
your born meaning that
draws my tears toward a
smile.

The lover gone, forgetfulness
comes, but the pleasure
of the sexes remains, and
there is nothing lacking. No
representation, sensation, or
recall. Inferno of vice. Later,
forgetfulness returns but this
time as a fall—leaden—grey,
dull, opaque. Forgetfulness:
blinding, smothering foam,
but on the quiet. Like the fog
that devours the park, wolfs
down the branches, erases
the green, rusty ground, and
mists up my eyes.
Absence, inferno, forgetfulness.
Rhythm of our loves.
A hunger remains, in place
of the heart. A spasm that
spreads, runs through the
blood vessels to the tips of
the breasts, to the tips of the
fingers. It throbs, pierces the
void, erases it, and gradually
settles in. My heart: a
tremendous pounding wound.
A thirst.
Anguished, guilty. Freud's
Vaterkomplex on the Acropolis?
The impossibility of
being without repeated
legitimation (without books
man, family). Impossibility—
depressing possibility—
of "transgression."
Either repression in which
I hands the Other what I
want from others.

of "being" ("never singular,"
Hegel said).
Under a full, blue gown, the
maternal, virginal body
allowed only the breast to show,
while the face, with the stiffness
of Byzantine icons
gradually softened, was covered
with tears. Milk and tears
became the privileged signs of
the *Mater Dolorosa* who invaded
the West beginning
with the eleventh century,
reaching the peak of its influx
in the fourteenth. But it never
ceased to fill the Marian visions
of those, men or women
(often children), who were
racked by the anguish of a
maternal frustration. Even
though orality—threshold of
infantile regression—is
displayed in the area of the
breast, while the spasm at the
slipping away of eroticism is
translated into tears, this
should not conceal what milk
and tears have in common
they are the metaphors of
nonspeech, of a "semiotics"
that linguistic communication
does not account for. The
Mother and her attributes,
evoking sorrowful humanity,
thus become representatives
of a "return of the repressed"
in monotheism. They reestablish
what is nonverbal and
show up as the receptacle of a
signifying disposition that is
closer to so-called primary
processes. Without them the
complexity of the Holy Ghost
would have been mutilated.

Or this squalling of the void, open wound in my heart, which allows me to be only in purgatory I yearn for the Law. And since it is not made for me alone, I venture to desire outside the law. Then narcissism awakened— narcissism that wants to be sex—roams, astonished. In sensual rapture I am distraught Nothing reassures for only the law sets anything down. Who calls such a suffering jouissance? It is the pleasure of the damned.

On the other hand, as they return by way of the Virgin Mother, they find their outlet in the arts—painting and music—of which the Virgin necessarily becomes both patron saint and privileged object. The function of this "Virginal Maternal" may thus be seen taking shape in the Western symbolic economy. Starting with the high Christly sublimation for which it yearns and occasionally exceeds, and extending to the extralinguistic regions of the unnamable; the Virgin Mother occupied the tremendous territory on this and that side of the parenthesis of language. She adds to the Christian trinity and to the Word that delineates their coherence the heterogeneity they salvage.

The ordering of the maternal libido reached its apotheosis when centered in the theme of death. The *Mater Dolorosa* knows no masculine body save that of her dead son, and her only pathos (which contrasts with the somewhat vacant, gentle serenity of the nursing Madonnas) is her shedding tears over a corpse. Since resurrection there is, and, as Mother of God, she must know this, nothing justifies Mary's outburst of pain at the foot of the cross, unless it be the desire to experience within her own body the death of a human being, which her feminine fate of being the source of life spares her. Could it be that the love, as puzzling as is ancient, of mourners for corpses relates to the same longing of a woman whom nothing fulfills—the longing to experience the wholly masculine pain of a man who expires at every moment on account of *jouissance* due to obsession with his own death? And yet, Marian pain is in no way connected with tragic outburst: joy and even a kind of triumph follow upon tears, as if the conviction that death does not exist were an irrational but unshakable maternal certainty, on which the principle of resurrection had to rest. The brilliant illustration of the wrenching between desire for the masculine corpse and negation of death, a wrenching whose paranoid logic cannot be overlooked, is masterfully presented by the famous *Stabat Mater.* It is likely that all beliefs in resurrections, are rooted in mythologies marked by the strong

Belief in the mother is rooted in fear, fascinated with a weakness—the weakness of language. If language

dominance of a mother goddess Christianity, it is true, finds its calling in the displacement of that bio-maternal

is powerless to locate myself
for and state myself to the
other, I assume—I want to
believe—that there is someone who makes up for that
weakness. Someone, of either
sex, *before* the id speaks,
before language, who might
make me be by means of border,
separations, vertigos.
In asserting that "in the
beginning was the Word,"
Christians must have found
such a postulate sufficiently
hard to believe and, for
whatever it was worth, they
added its compensation, its
permanent lining: the maternal
receptacle, purified as it
might be by the virginal
fantasy. Archaic maternal love
would be an incorporation of
my suffering that is unfailing,
unlike what often happens
with the lacunary
network of signs. In that
sense, any belief, anguished
by definition, is upheld by
the fascinated fear of language's
impotence. Every
God, even including the God
of the Word, relies on a
mother Goddess. Christianity
is perhaps also the last of
the religions to have
displayed in broad daylight the
bipolar structure of belief:
on the one hand, the difficult
experience of the Word—a
passion; on the other, the
reassuring wrapping in the
proverbial mirage of the
mother—a love. For that
reason, it seems to me that there

determinism, through the
postulate that immortality is
mainly that of the name of the
Father. But it does not succeed
in imposing *its* symbolic
evolution without relying on
the feminine representation of
an immortal biology. Mary
defying death is the theme
that has been conveyed to us
by the numerous variations of
the *Stabat Mater;* which, in the
text attributed to Jacopone da
Todi, enthralls us today
through the music of Palestrina,
Pergolesi, Haydn, and
Rossini.
Let us listen to the baroque
style of the young Pergolesi
(1710-36), who was dying of
tuberculosis when he wrote
his immortal *Stabat Mater.*
His musical inventiveness,
which, through Haydn, later
reverberated in the work of
Mozart, probably constitutes
his one and only claim to
immortality. But when this cry
burst forth, referring to Mary
facing her son's death, *"Eia
Mater, fons amoris!"* ("Hail"
mother, source of love!")—
was it merely a remnant of the
period? Man overcomes the
unthinkable of death by
postulating maternal love in its
place—in the place and stead
of death and thought. This
love, of which divine love is
merely a not always convincing
derivation, psychologically
is perhaps a recall, on the
near side of early identifications,
of the primal shelter

is only one way to go
through the religion of the
Word, or its counterpart, the
more or less discreet cult of
the Mother; it is the "artists'"
way, those who make
up for the vertigo of language
weakness with the
oversaturation of sign systems.
By this token, all art is
a kind of counter reformation,
an accepted baroqueness.
For is it not true that if
the Jesuits finally did persuade
the official Church to
accept the cult of the Virgin,
following the puritanical
wave of the Reformation,
that dogma was in fact no
more than a pretext, and its
efficacy lay elsewhere. It did
not become the opposite of
the cult of the mother but its
inversion through expenditure
in the wealth of signs
that constitutes the baroque.
The latter renders belief in
the Mother useless by overwhelming the symbolic
weakness where she takes refuge,
withdrawn from history,
with an overabundance
of discourse.
The immeasurable, unconfinable
maternal body.
First there is the separation,
previous to pregnancy,
but which pregnancy brings
to light and imposes without
remedy.
On the one hand—the
pelvis: center of gravity,
unchanging
ground, solid

that insured the survival of
the newborn. Such a love is in
fact, logically speaking, a
surge of anguish at the very
moment when the identity of
thought and living body collapses
The possibilities of
communication having been
swept away, only the subtle
gamut of sound, touch, and
visual traces, older than language
and newly worked out,
are preserved as an ultimate
shield against death. It is only
"normal" for a maternal
representation to set itself up at
the place of this subdued
anguish called love. No one
escapes it. Except perhaps the
saint, the mystic, or the writer
who, through the power of
language, nevertheless
succeeds in doing no better than
to take apart the fiction of the
mother as mainstay of love,
and to identify with love itself
and what he is in fact—a *fire
of tongues)* an exit from
representation. Might not modern
art then be, for the few
who are attached to it, the
implementation of that maternal
 love—a veil over death, in
death's very site and with full
knowledge of the facts? A
sublimated celebration of
incest …

Alone of her Sex

Freud collected, among other
objects of art and archeology,
countless statuettes representing
mother goddesses. And

pedestal, heaviness and
weight to which the thighs
adhere, with no promise of
agility on that score. On the
other—the torso, arms, neck,
head, face, calves, feet: un-
bounded liveliness, rhythm
and mask, which furiously
attempt to compensate for
the immutability of the central
tree. We live on that border,
crossroads beings,
crucified beings. A woman is
neither nomadic nor a male
body that considers itself
earthly only in erotic passion.
A mother is a continuous
separation, a division of the
very flesh. And consequently
a division of language—and
it has always been so.
Then there is this other
abyss that opens up between
the body and what had been
its inside: there is the abyss
between the mother and the
child. What connection is
there between myself, or
even more unassumingly
between my body and this
internal graft and fold, which
once the umbilical cord has
been severed, is an inaccessible
other? My body and...
him. No connection. Nothing
to do with it. And this,
as early as the first gestures,
cries, steps, long before *its*
personality has become
my opponent. The child,
whether *he* or *she* irremediably
another. To say that
there are no sexual relationships constitutes a skimpy

yet his interest in them comes
to light only indiscreet fashion
in his work. It shows up
when Freud examines artistic
creation and homosexuality in
connection with Leonardo da
Vinci and deciphers there the
ascendancy of an archaic
mother, seen therefore from
the standpoint of her effects
on man and particularly on
this strange function of his
sometimes to change
languages. Moreover, when
Freud analyzes the advent and
transformations of monotheism
he emphasizes that
Christianity comes closer to
pagan myths by integrating,
through and against Judaic rigor,
a preconscious acknowledgment
of a maternal
feminine. And yet, among the
patients analyzed by Freud,
one seeks in vain for mothers
and their problems. One
might be led to think that
motherhood was a solution to
neurosis and, by its very nature,
ruled out psychoanalysis
as a possible other solution.
Or might psychoanalysis, at
this point, make way for religion?
In simplified fashion,
the only thing Freud tells us
concerning motherhood is
that the desire for a child is a
transformation of either penis
envy or anal drive, and this
allows her to discover the
neurotic equation child-penis-
feces. We are thus enlightened
concerning an essential aspect
of male phantasmatics with

assertion when confronting the flash that bedazzles me when I confront the abyss between what was mine and is henceforth but irreparably alien. Trying to think through that abyss: staggering vertigo. Identity holds up. A mother's identity is maintained only through the well-known closure of consciousness within the indolence of habit, when a woman protects herself from the borderline that severs her body and expatriates it from her child. Lucidity, on the contrary, would restore her as cut in half, alien to its other—and a ground favorable to delirium. But also and for that very reason, motherhood destines us to a demented jouissance that is answered, by chance, by the nursling's laughter in the sunny waters of the ocean. What connection is there between it and myself? No connection, except for that overflowing laughter where one senses the collapse of some ringing, subtle, fluid identity or other, softly buoyed by the waves.

Concerning that stage of my childhood, scented, warm, and soft to the touch, I have only a spatial memory. No time at all. Fragrance of honey, roundness of forms, silk and velvet under my fingers, on my cheeks. Mummy. Almost no sight—a shadow

respect to childbirth, and female male phantasmatics as well, to the extent that it embraces, in large part and in its hysterical labyrinths, the male one. The fact remains, as far as the complexities and pitfalls of maternal experience are involved, that Freud offers only a massive *nothing*, which for those who might care to analyze it, is punctuated with this or that remark on the part of Freud's mother, proving to him in the kitchen that his own body is anything but immortal and will crumble away like dough; or the sour photograph of Marthe. Freud, the wife, a whole mute story.... There thus remained for his followers an entire continent to explore, a black one indeed, where Jung was the first to rush in, getting all his esoteric fingers burnt, but not without calling attention to some sore points of the imagination with regard to motherhood, points that are still analytical rationality.[4] There might doubtless be a way to approach the dark area that motherhood constitutes for a woman; one needs to listen, more carefully than ever, to what mothers are saying today through their economic difficulties and, beyond the guilt that a too existentialist feminism handed down, through their discomforts, insomnias, joys, angers, desires, pains, and pleasures ... One

that darkens, soaks me up, or
vanishes amid flashes.
Almost no voice in her placid
presence. Except, perhaps,
and more belatedly, the echo
of quarrels: her exasperation,
her being fed up, her hatred.
Never straightforward, always
held back, as if, although
the unmanageable
child deserved it, the daughter
could not accept the
mother's hatred—it was not
meant for her. A hatred
without recipient or rather
whose recipient was no "I"
and which, perturbed by
such a lack of recipience, was
toned down into irony or
collapsed into remorse before
reaching its destination
With others, this maternal;
aversion may be worked up
to a spasm that is held like
a delayed orgasm. Women
doubtless reproduce among
themselves, the strange gamut
of forgotten body relationships with their mothers.
Complicity in the unspoken,
connivance of the inexpressible,
of a wink, a tone of
a gesture, a. tinge, a
scent. We are in it, set free of
our identification papers and
names, on an ocean of
preciseness, a computerization
of the unnamable. No
communication between individuals
but connections between
atoms, molecules, wisps,
words, droplets of sentences.
The community of women is
a community of dolphins.

might, in similar fashion, try
better to understand the
incredible construct of the
Maternal that the
West elaborated by means of
the Virgin, and of which I have
just mentioned a few episodes
in a never-ending history.
What is it then in this maternal
representation that,
alone of her sex, goes against
both of the two sexes,[5] and
was able to attract women's
wishes for identification as well
as the very precise interposition
of those who assumed
to keep watch over the
symbolic and social order?
Let me suggest, by way of
hypothesis, that the virginal
maternal is a way (not among
the less effective ones) of dealing
with feminine paranoia.
—The Virgin assumes her
feminine denial of the other
sex (of man) but overcomes
him by setting up a third
person: *I* do not conceive with
you but with *Him*. The result
is an immaculate conception
(therefore with neither man
nor sex), conception of a God
with whose existence a
woman has indeed something
to do, on condition that she
acknowledge being subjected
to it.
—The Virgin assumes the
paranoid lust for power by
changing a woman into a
Queen in heaven and a
Mother of the earthly institutions
(of the Church). But
she succeeds in stifling that

Conversely, when the other woman posits herself as such, that is, as singular and inevitably in opposition, "I" am startled, so much that "I" no longer know what is going on. There are then two paths left open to the rejection that bespeaks the recognition of the other woman as such. Either, not wanting to experience her, I ignore her and, "alone of my sex," I turn my back on her in friendly fashion. It is a hatred that, lacking a recipient worthy enough of its power changes to unconcerned complacency. Or else, outraged by her own stubbornness, by that other's belief that she is singular, I unrelentingly let go at her claim to address me and find respite only in the eternal return of power strokes, bursts of hatred— blind and dull but obstinate I do not see her as herself but beyond her I aim at the claim to singularity, the unacceptable ambition to be something other than a child or a fold in the plasma that constitutes us, an echo of the cosmos that unifies us. What an inconceivable ambition it is to aspire to singularity, it is not natural, hence it is in-human; the mania smitten with Oneness ("There is only One woman") can only im-pugn it by condemning it as "masculine"...Within this strange feminine see-saw megalomania by putting it on its knees before the child-god.

—The Virgin obstructs the desire for murder or devouring by means of a strong oral cathexis (the breast), valorization of pain (the sob), and incitement to replace the sexed body with the ear of understanding.

—The Virgin assumes the paranoid fantasy of being excluded from time and death through the very flattering representation of Dormition or Assumption.

—The Virgin especially agrees with the repudiation of the other woman (which doubtless amounts basically to a repudiation of the woman's mother) by suggesting the image of a woman as unique: alone among mothers, alone among humans since she is without sin. But the acknowledgment of a longing for uniqueness is immediately checked by the postulate according to which uniqueness is attained only through an exacerbated maso-chism: a concrete woman, worthy of the feminine ideal embodied by the Virgin as an inaccessible goal, could only be a nun, a martyr, or, if she is married, one who leads a life that would remove her from that "earthly" condition and dedicate her to the highest sublimation alien to her body. A bonus, however: the promised jouissance.

that makes "me" swing from the unnamable community of women over to the war of individual singularities, it is unsettling to say "I." The languages of the great formerly matriarchal civilizations must avoid, do avoid, personal pronouns: they leave to the context the burden of distinguishing protagonists and take refuge in tones to recover an underwater, transverbal communication between bodies. It is a music from which so-called oriental civility tears away suddenly through violence, murder, blood baths. A woman's discourse, would that be it? Did not Christianity attempt, among other things, to freeze that see-saw? To stop it, tear women away from its rhythm, settle them permanently in the spirit? Too permanently...

A skillful balance of concessions and constraints involving feminine paranoia, the representation of virgin motherhood appears to crown the efforts of a society to reconcile the social remnants of matrilinearism and the unconscious needs of primary narcissism on the one hand, and on the other the requirements of a new society based on exchange and before long on increased production, which require the contribution of the superego and rely on the symbolic paternal agency. While that clever balanced architecture today appears to be crumbling, one is led to ask the following: what are the aspects of the feminine psyche for which that representation of motherhood does not provide a solution or else provides one that is felt as too coercive by twentieth-century women?

The unspoken doubtless weighs first on the maternal body: as no signifier can uplift it without leaving a remainder, for the signifier is always meaning, communication, or structure, whereas a woman as mother would be, instead, a strange fold that changes culture into nature, the speaking into biology. Although it concerns every woman's body, the heterogeneity that cannot be subsumed in the signifier nevertheless explodes violently with pregnancy (the threshold of culture and nature) and the child's arrival (which extracts woman out of her oneness and gives her the possibility—but not the certainty—of reaching out to the other, the ethical). Those particularities of the maternal body compose woman into a being of folds, a catastrophe of being that the dialectics of the trinity and its supplements would be unable to subsume.

Silence weighs heavily nonetheless on the corporeal and psychological suffering of childbirth and especially the self-sacrifice involved in becoming anonymous in order to pass on the social norm, which one might repudiate for one's own sake but within which *one must* include the child in order to educate it along the chain of generations. A suffering lined with jubilation—ambivalence of masochism—on account of which a woman, rather refractory to perversion, in fact allows herself a coded, fundamental, perverse behavior, ultimate guarantee of society, without which society will not reproduce and will not maintain a constancy of standardized household. Feminine perversion does reside in the parceling or the Don Juan-like multiplying of objects of desire; it is at once legalized, if not rendered paranoid, through the agency of masochism: all sexual "dissoluteness" will be accepted and hence become insignificant, provided a child seals up such outpourings. Feminine perversion [père-version] is coiled up in the desire for law as desire for reproduction and continuity, it promotes feminine masochism to the rank of structure stabilizer (against its deviations); by assuring the mother that she may thus enter into an order that is above humans, it gives her her reward of pleasure. Such coded perversion, such close combat between maternal masochism and the law have been utilized by totalitarian powers of all times to bring women to their side, and, of course, they succeed easily. And yet, it is not enough to "declaim against" the reactionary role of mothers in the service of "male dominating power." One would need to examine to what extent that role corresponds to the biosymbolic latencies of motherhood and, on that basis, to try and understand, since the myth of the Virgin does not subsume them, or no longer does, how their surge lays women open to the most fearsome manipulations, not to mention blinding, or pure and, simple rejection by progressive activists who refuse to take a close look.

Among things left out of the virginal myth there is the war between mother and daughter, a war masterfully but too quickly settled by promoting Mary as universal and particular, but never singular—as "alone of her sex." The relation to the other woman has presented our culture, in massive fashion during the past century, with the necessity to reformulate its representations of love and hatred—inherited from Plato's *Symposium,* the troubadours, or Our Lady. On that level, too, motherhood opens out a vista: a woman seldom (although not necessarily) experiences her passion (love and hatred) for another woman without having taken her own mother's place—without having herself become a mother, and especially without slowly learning to differentiate between same beings—as being face to face with her daughter forces her to do.

Finally, repudiation of the other sex (the masculine) no longer seems possible under the aegis of the third person, hypostatized in the child as go-between: "neither me, nor you, but him, the child, the third person, the nonperson, God, which I still am in the final analysis...." Since there is repudiation, and if the feminine being that struggles within it is to remain there, it henceforth calls for, not the deification of the third party, but countercathexes in strong values, in strong *equivalents of power.* Feminine psychosis today is sustained and absorbed through passion for politics, science, art..... The variant that accompanies motherhood might be analyzed perhaps more readily than the others from the standpoint of the rejection of the other sex

The love of God and for God resides in a gap: the broken space made explicit by sin on the one side, the that it comprises. To allow what? Surely not some understanding or other on the part of "sexual partners" within

beyond on the other. Discontinuity, lack, and arbitrariness: topography of the sign, of the symbolic relation that posits my otherness as impossible. Love, here, is only for the impossible. For a mother, on the other hand, strangely so, the other as arbitrary (the child) is taken for granted. As far as she is concerned—impossible, that is just the way it is: it is reduced to the implacacable. The other is inevitable, she seems to say, turn it into a God if you wish, it is nevertheless natural, for such an other has come out of myself, which is yet not myself but a flow of unending germinations, an eternal cosmos. The other goes much without saying and without my saying that, at the limit, it does not exist for itself. The "just the same" of motherly peace of mind, more persistent than philosophical doubt, gnaws, on account of its basic disbelief, at the symbolic's allmightiness. It bypasses perverse negation ("I know, but just the same") and constitutes the basis of the social bond in its generality, in the sense of "resembling others and eventually the species." Such an attitude is frightening when one imagines that it can crush everything the other (the child) has that is specifically irreducible: rooted in that disposition of

the pre-established harmony of primal androgyny. Rather, to lead to an acknowledgment of what is irreducible, of the irreconcilable interest of both sexes in asserting their differences in the quest of each one— and of women, after all—for an appropriate fulfillment. These, then, are a few among others concerning a motherhood that today remains, after the Virgin, without a discourse. They suggest, all in all, the need of an ethics for this "second" sex, which, as one asserts it, is reawakening.

Nothing, however, suggests that a feminine ethics is possible, and Spinoza excluded women from his (along with children and the insane). Now, if a contemporary ethics is no longer seen as being the same as morality; if ethics amounts to not. avoiding the embarrassing and problematics of the law but giving it flesh, language, and jouissance—in that case its re-formulation demands the contribution of women. Of women who harbor the desire to reproduce (to have stability). Of women who are available so that our speaking species, which knows it is mortal, might withstand death. Of mothers. For an heretical ethics separated from morality, an *herethics* is perhaps no more than that which in life makes bonds, motherly love, besides, we find the leaden strap it can become, smothering any different individuality. But it is there, too, that the speaking being finds a refuge when his/her symbolic shell cracks and a crest emerges where speech causes biology to show through: I am thinking of the time of illness, of sexual-intellectual-physical passion, of death....

thoughts, and therefore the thought of death, bearable: herethics is undeath *[a-mort]* love ... *Eia mater, fons amoris* ...So let us again listen to the *Stabat Mater*; and the music, all the music ... it swallows up the goddesses and removes their necessity.

Notes

[1]Between the lines of this section one should be able to detect the presence of Marina Warner, *Alone of All Her Sex: The Myth and Cult of the Virgin Mary* (New York: Knopf, 1976) and Ilse Barande, *Le Maternel singulier* (Paris: Aubier-Montaigne, 1977), which underlay my reflections.

[2]Georges Dumezil, *La Religion romaine archaïque* (Paris: Payot, 1974).

[3][The French version quoted by Kristeva ("Woman, what is there in common between you and me?") is even stronger than the King James' translation, "Woman, what have I to do with thee?"]

[4]Jung thus noted the "hierogamous" relationship between Mary and Christ as well as the over-protection given the Virgin with respect to original sin, which places her on the margin of mankind; finally, he insisted very much on the Vatican's adop¬tion of the Assumption as dogma, seeing it as one of the considerable merits of Catholicism as opposed to Protestantism (C. J. Jung, *Answer to Job*, Princeton: Princeton University Press, 1969).

[5]As Caelius Sedulius wrote, "She ... had no peer/ Either in our first mother or in all women! Who were to come. But alone of all her sex! She pleased the Lord" ("Paschalis Carminis," Book II, 11. 68ff. of Opera Omnia, Vienna, 1885). Epigraph to Marina Warner, *Alone of All Her Sex.*

Chapter 11

The Radical Potential in Lesbian Mothering of Daughters

BABA COPPER

RADICAL MOTHERHOOD. Surely it is a measure of woman's defeat that this phrase has a self-contradictory ring. The practice of motherhood embodies legitimate power—the power of early childhood socialization and a lifelong position of influence on one's children. Each different culture-the sand mold in which every individual is cast—is transmitted by women. The process, if not the goals, of this fundamental source of social cohesion rests uncontested in the hands of women. All that potential, and yet mothers almost always function, and expect to function, in continual denial of their own self-interest.

Within the context of female-to-female training in motherhood lies yet another potential—that of strong, women-come-first female bonding. The mother who teaches her daughter how to mother could be an alchemist of culture, vaporizing woman-hating traditions into the gold of feminist change. Yet mothers do not use their power to commit their daughters to resistance to patriarchal conformity. The very women who insist that radical feminists should live their politics question the *political* potential of motherhood. Many lesbians continue to view motherhood as locked in tradition—an institution that, even with antisexist reforms, can be of service only to the patriarchy. How can we understand the connection between being a lesbian mother and radical mothering—motherhood that involves conscious detachment from much of the programming women carry out, generation to generation, in the service of patriarchy.

I am a lesbian mother to a lesbian daughter. I have moved from traditional to radical feminist lesbian midstream in my mothering process. My two married daughters reflect the "success" of the patriarchal mothering I did within a nuclear family; traditional socialization that more or less mirrored those values and practices my mother used with me. But my midlife switch has allowed me, as an old lesbian, to explore—in practice as well as theory—active resistance to the ideology and institutions of heteromotherhood. I am extending and politicizing my mothering. I am making a connection between my radicalism and the lesbianism of my daughter.

Recently I sought out other mother/daughter dyads who are both lesbians. In carrying out this search, I discerned a suppressed anxiety surrounding the whole subject, resulting, I suspect, from the "congenital disease" theory of homosexuality promulgated by psychiatrists, and reinforced by the Gay Rights we-are-just-like-everybody-else defense against homophobia. The relationship my daughter and I share often appears invisible, even to our friends and lovers who see it as apolitical—a personal anomaly, threateningly different. Perhaps lesbians have not yet identified either the goals or the "rules" of heteropatriarchal mothering with sufficient clarity to be able to change them.

Why is there strong support among women for the separation between mothers and adult daughters? Why should they not remain close, expanding their ways of being together into adult-to-adult intimacy that provides mutual support and growth? Surely the separation of the daughter from the mother is not an appropriate expectation to guide the behavior of two lesbians?

A tight mother/adult daughter bonding may be the ultimate patriarchal no-no. Therapists reinforce the definition of female maturity as a woman who has separated from, not bonded with her mother. There are the oft-repeated mother-in-law jokes which pressure married women to discard their mother as ally. Although loving relationships between traditional mothers and their heterosexual daughters are not unknown, most daughters value the distances that their lives have generated away from their mothers. Here is a rule of heteromothering worth breaking.

My lesbian daughter and I are exploring the mined territory of mother/adult daughter bonding. We do so without honor in the lesbian community. She suffers the indignity of derogatory comments from her peers, such as being told to "grow up" when she expresses yearning for my presence. I face the assumptions that my motherhood somehow defines my life, instead of being a small but important part of it.

Yet she and I, as well as other lesbian mothers/lesbian daughters I have questioned, express a high level of satisfaction and pride about the relationship we share. I know that without her support, I could not be nearly as courageous or willful in my pursuit of the mysteries of my aging identity. A realistic response to these postmenopausal days demands that I be militant about my age, and vocal about the prejudice that surrounds it. What if all four of my children were heterosexual! Could my unconventional life choices survive another son-in-law sitting in judgment on his dangerous mother-in-law as he badgers his wife, my daughter, to deny the validity of my feminism or my lesbianism? As one of my married daughters explained to me, "He is doing the best he can, under the circumstances."

If my lesbian daughter gives me magical permission to explore oldwomanhood, I supply her with a supportive continuity of trust and intimacy as she navigates the years of changing partners and careers that often characterize the late twenties. We continue to struggle with the residual power imbalances that linger from our mother/child past. In practical terms, our bonding has translated into some financial interdependency, occasional shared living situations (including two-and-one-half hectic years in a lesbian separatist rural community), traveling together to foreign countries, at least weekly exchanges of the details of our lives. We are, I believe, truly intimates "for keeps."

I do not want to imply that lesbian mother/lesbian daughter relationships are easy. One of my lesbian mother respondents described her relationship with her two lesbian daughters as "passionate, fraught, exciting, compelling." New demands are put upon mother/daughter relations by the heightened awareness of erotic energy between women that lesbians cultivate. The mother may fear that she and her daughter will find themselves being lovers with the same woman, since often they both circulate socially in a relatively small lesbian community. The daughter, tending to ignore the handicap of ageism that diminishes her mother in the sexual marketplace, may feel intimidated in an imagined sexual competition with her. I know one daughter in a very close mother/daughter dyad who came out at sixteen with her mother's lover of that time. Another mother said to me with great feeling, "There is something oppressive about my lover's need to like my daughter and my daughter's need to like my lover." Insecurity in mothers, in daughters, or in lovers, breeds tensions between them. The assumptions of accessibility that play back and forth between lesbian mothers and lesbian daughters may be extremely threatening to lovers.

On the other hand, the daughter of a lesbian may have a great advantage over her heterosisters by being able to learn from loving woman-to-woman interactions as she grows up. Not many daughters learn the "hows" of this liberating knowledge from traditional nuclear families. In my own case, it was only when I broke out of the selflessness of marriage that I was able to demand an *exchange* of nurturing from those around me, including my children. Now, only the daughter who saw me loved by women is able to give as well as take nurturance. Knowing how to nurture the nurturer is the best path out of dependency and the ugly feelings that often accompany feeling dependent. Being validated as equal nurturer by one's mother can be a key factor in female self-esteem.

My own experience, and my learnings from other lesbian mother/lesbian daughter dyads, indicate that something different is happening between lesbians that merits attention. To extend and deepen the mother/daughter bond into adulthood did not seem a radical act to me, until I encountered the degree of opposition and misinterpretation that it evoked in other lesbians. I had assumed we were a threat to men, not to women-loving-women. Now I believe lesbians are fully as prejudiced toward mothers—any mothers—as any other segment of the population. The sooner lesbians detach from the heteromythology that clusters around motherhood, the better.

Although many mothers, hetero and lesbian, diligently study whatever expertise they can find on mothering as their bellies swell, probably half of what they do, once the hectic dance of mothering begins, are repetitions of the mothering they learned at a nonverbal level from their own mothers. Teaching little girls to cater to male supremacy—to serve and submit—have been the basic lessons of female survival. Any woman who is herself adequately socialized by male standards, transmits some of this. Built into these unconscious patterns of communication between mother and daughter is content that lesbians will want to raise to a conscious level and judge with modern, politicized eyes.

Lesbians cannot look for satisfactory guidance from heterofeminists who write books about raising antisexist boys and liberated girls. These children are expected to be high achievers in a man's world without questioning the assumptions underpinning that goal. There is also a great deal of lyrical psychobabble by heterofeminists about the redemption of the human psyche possible through male mothering of infants. Theory needs some basis in evidence. No one has been denying fathers the joys of parenting. Some men have been successful fathers. But for every well-fathered child, there are a million who were conceived irresponsibly or abandoned or raped or physically terrorized or emotionally denied by their fathers. The true circumstances of women and children in the heterofamily are not reflected in the heterofeminist party line, which seems to say: if mothers will encourage little girls to have a demanding career and choose a feminist man who will help her with the babies, then all will be equal between the sexes in the next generation. Unfortunately, the intention that lies behind most decisions to have a baby is the desire to prove the permanency and value of a romantic attachment (half of which end in divorce). The reality that underlies this mythic intention is the disastrous institution of traditional motherhood, in which female children are taught to love everyone but themselves.

There are issues important to lesbian mothers that heterofeminists do not address. First and foremost, we must acknowledge that the mothering of daughters is of primary importance to us. If women come first, then daughters come first. The next step in disengaging motherhood from male definitions is to identify the mother/daughter dyad as *the* evolutionary crucible of society. Any abuse by the adult males of the former family—daughter rape, or battery, or harsh labor exploitation—may diminish female autonomy in that family tree for generations. The mother teaches the next generation of mothers how to mother—how to transmit much of the societal information which humans share at an unconscious level.

What are the hidden agendas built into heteromotherhood that are destructive to females, both daughters and mothers? Is it possible, at this particular herstorical juncture, to successfully enable both boys and girls within the same early behavioral environment? Are there psychological chains between the generations of women, analogous to those created by alcohol or sexual abuse, that pass the damage from mother to daughter—damage done in the name of female survival or being a loving mother or a good wife; damage done during the times of the Burnings, or in concentration or refugee camps, or during other mass atrocities suffered by women; damage done century after century, so that acceptance of those ways became the norm? Radical lesbian analysis of these kinds of questions can help lesbian mothers to: 1) avoid falling into the traps of "naturalness" built around the assumptions, rules, and myths of heteromothering; 2) devise active resistance to the repeated betrayals by mothers of daughters, and daughters of mothers; and 3) identify the inherent and unique benefits of lesbian mothering.

Lesbian mothers are, almost without exception, themselves products of heteromothering. Lesbians raise their children within patriarchy, just like other women. However, the lesbian can make choices in relation to the degree of assimilation of her daughter into patriarchy, choices not possible to the heteromother, if she is willing to raise to a conscious level some of the unconscious roots of female subordination.

All mammals teach appropriate responses of submission to their young. Within the context of the heterosexual tradition from which she sprang, the lesbian mother has learned to communicate to both her boy and girl children her understanding of the current cultural parameters of male entitlement—e.g. the cluster of expectations which surround being a man in a man's world. Since this is never a static body of information—there are infinite variations on male entitlement operative from one family structure to the next, one religion to the next, one ethnic or national group to the next—the child is raised to meet the expectations of the mother. By ten years of age, a daughter has always needed to know the limitations upon her identity that is the other side of the coin of male entitlement. Daughters of sixteen must be prepared to find opportunity and fulfillment within an elaborate system never clearly articulated by anyone. Male entitlement is created by assumptions, mythologized to be natural, justified, universal.

Obviously, the mother is not the only source of this information flow. However, she is the one most strongly motivated to communicate successful manipulation of this hidden system to her daughters, since she herself learned it from her mother *as the key to female survival.* Depending on which culture one looks at, maternal collusion in male entitlement takes various forms: preferring the birth of a son, female infanticide, selective neglect of girl babies which impairs their development, grossly unequal educational opportunities or attention, the sale or exchange of daughters in marriage. Does anyone know how many generations it will take without these practices to erase their psychological scars?

There is no counterpart system of female entitlement—only the obvious sex-segregated labor and sex-differentiated customs that all cultures have. In order to keep patriarchy functioning as a self-sustaining heterosystem, daughters must be taught to mistrust females and to attend/depend on males. Mothers teach daughters, even at a preverbal level, that their instinct of self-preservation is best served by the *absence* of female bonding, the *absence* of female-to-female entitlement. Mothers must also imprint their daughters with allegiance to patriarchal aesthetics. By example, mothers train their daughters to fear female aging, to find continual fault with their own bodies, to believe they must cash in on natural beauty or youth. Teaching daughters to be "attractive" and "successful" has been the innocuous justification for some of the most pernicious betrayals of daughters by mothers: foot-binding; physical weakness and mental shallowness; cosmetic surgery and dieting; sexual ignorance; child brides, child prostitution, and child pornography; genital mutilation. Teaching daughters to succeed in the lifelong struggle to assimilate into a manmade hierarchy of female worth has always been a trap.

This subtle process and its woman-hating content is buried in the often harried day-to-day interactions between a mother and her daughters. Radical mothering means involving children in disloyalty to the culture the mother is expected to transmit at the expense of woman-bonding and female empowerment. Excavating the heteromyths buried in the transmitted information of daughter-rearing is the most important work of the lesbian radical mother. These heteromyths embody the unconscious informational chains between the generations of women that lesbians have the potential to break, if they will consciously accept the task.

The fact of lesbian existence as radical lesbians in patriarchy gives their mothering some clear advantages. For instance, lesbian mothers for the most part eschew that bedrock heteromyth which says a child needs a resident father in order to grow up whole. Lesbian mothering can enhance the development of female autonomy and self-love. Lesbian mothers may also have more motivation to imagine what might constitute positive female rights and role expectations for our daughters.

There are also aspects of lesbian radicalism that need to be adapted for lesbian mothers, such as separatism. Few lesbians live or work in a male-free world. Of necessity, even a separatist's daughter will someday have men in her life: how can she best be prepared for this eventuality? First, radical mothers need a new definition of lesbian separatism that takes into account the vulnerability of the children in our community. We cannot afford to pretend that the statistics of incest, rape, battery, and addiction to female-degrading pornography do not apply to the men we all know. I would like to suggest the following: Each adult woman needs to make her own determination as to which males she will allow into her life, as well as the degree of access these males will have to her home and person. However, no woman should assume that the males *she* trusts can be trusted by any other female, including female children, or that another woman should trust them because she does. The presence of males in the life of her female child demands that a radical mother not only live by this maxim, but that she does so openly, with the full and early knowledge of her female child.

If this seems extreme, then the mother should ask, *How much harm does one incident of sexual abuse cause to the trust the child is building toward her world in general, and men in particular?* If it were a serious but avoidable communicable disease that crippled one female out of five, would it be an "acceptable risk?" How does the female child raised in a heterosexual household learn to cede space, body integrity, or verbal prerogative to males, even before she is five years old? It seems clear that the daughter of a lesbian who has the opportunity to watch women exchange power, attention, and trust—preferably between as many different kinds of women as possible—will learn new ways of being a woman in the world.

Another heteromyth that needs radical defusing is the notion that lesbian mothers must maintain neutrality in relation to the future sexual preference of their daughters. *Sexual preference* is not the issue. The reality underlying the myth is one we all know: female heterosexuality cannot be called a choice when it is compulsory in all cultures, everywhere. But we are lesbian, and it is a fundamental expression of self-love to want our daughters to grow up reflecting our woman-identified choices. Although many heteromothers have tried to force their daughters out of lesbianism, it is hard to imagine a lesbian mother who would deny choice to her daughter.

Radical mothering must also encompass many of the same struggles that conscientious heteromothers face. As all politically committed mothers have discovered, it is not enough to verbalize antiracist, antiageist, antilooksist sentiments to our children. In addition to talk, we must communicate by modeling the behavior we expect in them. This necessitates viewing one's lifestyle not as an extension of who-I-am but of who-I-want-them-to-learn-to-be. No mother succeeds in always being how she wants her children to be, but the radical mother structures her lifestyle so that her child has ample opportunity to see her trying. Lesbians do not hesitate to choose for our daughters when it comes to the prevention of childhood diseases, but we balk at inoculating them against assimilation into heterofemininity—into the addictive satisfactions of female normalcy.

We need to make some dramatic changes in the information usually shared with daughters. Daughters have been deprived *by their mothers* of knowledge of their orgasmic potential and the various ways of satisfying it, detailed knowledge of both the history and the current oppression of women world- wide, information about matrifocal civilizations and woman-defined women of the past, and revelations about their mothers' lives and sexuality. This suppression of information is a learned pattern of behavior passed from mother to daughter that teaches mistrust between women. Honor between women starts with honesty and with the determination to empower each other. Our children are the daughters of women who love women over men. Daughters of lesbians, like freedom fighters everywhere, need to be enlisted in infancy, and protected against heterofemininity by words and actions—not for the mother's sake nor for the movement's sake-but for their own psychological well-being.

With my lesbian daughter, I have never asked that perennial lament of motherhood, "Where did I go wrong?" although she and I joke a lot about both her strengths and her weaknesses being my fault. All mothers make a terrible investment in their children. All mothers are brainwashed to believe they are totally responsible for the results. I recognize I have not diminished that heteromyth by the questions I have raised about the goals of lesbian mothering. Nor have I addressed the issues of comothering or group mothering, both of which represent new and important variations on heteromothering that lesbians are exploring. Uninvestigated allegiances and assumptions clutter the actions of all women who mother. Many of them are pivotal to self-hatred and the absence of female bonding. My own experience, and that of the other lesbian mothers I have interviewed, has encouraged me to think that lesbian motherhood has a unique role to play in these areas.

Lesbians are political women, whether or not our politics are radical, or even at an aware level. What all lesbians need is a woman-identified world, in which female self-love is the norm, not the exception. Part of the lesbian image has been to contrast the woman-who-asserts-her-self, the Amazon, as the opposite of the-woman-who-sacrifices-her-self, the Mother. This, like so many binary concepts, is a false division of the possibilities, intended to divide women. True, most lesbians probably will not reproduce or mother, but the lesbian community will continue to include lots of mothers, comothers, and children. True, even the most radical lesbian mothering will include considerable altruism. But it is also true that lesbian mothering embodies a remarkable chance to redesign woman's primary biologically-based role in the service of woman-chosen goals.

Chapter 12

Lesbians Choosing Children
The Personal is Political Revisited

NANCY D. POLIKOFF

FIVE YEARS PASSED from the time i decided i wanted to have a child until i adopted my daughter. During those years I had dozens, maybe hundreds, of conversations about having a child—as a lesbian—with friends, acquaintances, and men who were possible fathers. I watched close lesbian friends have children: one got pregnant in a one-night stand, one adopted after many miscarriages, one got married to a man. I joined a group of lesbians considering motherhood which now, more than two years later, has seven children and one on the way.

There were several dominant themes in those discussions: how to get pregnant; whether to have an involved father and, if so, how involved; how to deal with family and work. Looking back, I am struck by the extent to which virtually all of these discussions had as their basic premise the *personal* nature of the issues and concomitant decisions involved. For example, I do not believe that anyone ever pushed me to examine, from a feminist perspective, my adherence to a belief in a known and involved father. For a movement that was built on the premise that the personal is political, there was, and there continues to be, surprisingly little political analysis of our choices to have children and all the decisions that flow from that choice.

There is a difference between doing political analysis and making judgments. As I have begun to raise these issues in my immediate circle of friends, I have met resistance from those who believe these decisions are so personal that no one else can or should say that there is a "correct" answer. Such a response misses the point. Our choices have political implications; they are made in a political context. If we are to build a stronger movement for radical social change and pass down to our children a sense of what is possible, a vision of a world less dominated by patriarchy and other oppression, and a desire to continue to struggle, we have to understand the political dimensions of all of our apparently personal choices.

This is not a new idea. Consider the "choice" to be heterosexual or lesbian. The feminist movement has produced volumes on the subject of the politics of sexual orientation. At its core is an awareness that the issues are not purely personal because the world does not make heterosexuality and lesbianism equally available and attractive options, and because there are social, economic, and political consequences of one's sexual orientation.

In the same way it is essential that the discussions of choices surrounding lesbian motherhood include the political context and ramifications of each of our decisions. This will, of course, produce divisions between us. It is easier not to ask each other the hard questions, and not to see the differences. We mothers need a lot of help and support in our work of raising children, and other mothers are our easiest and most logical allies. It is hard to jeopardize that support by raising difficult political issues. I am convinced, however, that the failure to address these issues is destructive to the goals of building a strong women's movement and ending all oppression.

Being a mother in this society is in fact no more a free choice than being a heterosexual. The cultural pressure is enormous, the propaganda overwhelming. Women who never have children are considered empty ("barren"), selfish, peculiar. Until they reach their mid-thirties or so, others will tell them they will change their minds; that it's just a stage; that, as soon as other aspects of their lives are established, they will want children. As the "biological clock" ticks, women without children are told they will be sorry, sorry, sorry.

Turn the pages of popular magazines. You will find successful career women extolling motherhood, saying they never realized how little meaning their lives had before their children were born.

Listen to the rhetoric about abortion. Politicians talk only about rape and incest victims; feminists talk about married women with several children already who can't afford more, or about teen-agers too young to be expected to bear the responsibilities of motherhood. Who is talking about women who don't ever want to be mothers? No one.

Examine the burgeoning industry of reproductive technology. There is now always something else that can be done to facilitate pregnancy. One more dangerous drug. One more invasive surgical procedure. The time. The money. The energy. The obsession. Literally years out of a woman's life devoted to producing a biological child. Where is the room to say *no*, to say *enough?* Where is the room not to try?

Are lesbians immune to a culture of compulsory motherhood? Of course not. We were girls before we were aware lesbians, and we were raised by families that expected us to become mothers. We read the same books and saw the same movies as our heterosexual sisters. And today we live in the same world, one which purports to value motherhood above anything else a woman can do.[1] We rarely ask each other why we want children, and when we do, we are satisfied with personal answers. (Mine was that I liked kids and looked forward to a relationship with an adult child which would be as positive as my relationship with my father.) My own introspection has forced me to recognize that I wanted a child in part because I wanted to be "normal," because I wanted to have more in common with other women, and because I didn't want a life that seemed so clearly on the fringe of society. I also wanted a relationship I could depend upon, a product that would survive my death, and a focus for my life at a time when organized political activism seemed either too amorphous or too rigidly sectarian for me.

It is rare to hear a lesbian say she wants a child because she wants to put her politics into practice, and childrearing is one way to do that. I am not sure I have ever heard a lesbian say she wanted a child because she wanted to make a public statement that there was another model for childrearing, and that it was better than the traditional model. The practice of lesbian childrearing as an avenue for political action and change is not a prominent part of lesbian discussions about whether to have children.

Many lesbians feel defensive about their decision to have children. Motherhood alters a women's lifestyle drastically, and nonmother friends are not always anxious to adapt. It is easy to feel, as a mother, that old friends no longer understand your needs.

But how do those lesbians who don't want children feel? In a culture that values childbearing and childrearing as much as ours does, there is no easy way to talk about not wanting children or about valuing other activities more. Rarely does anyone challenge making a baby the focus of one's life and one's reason for doing or not doing just about everything. Women without children who question this prioritizing are dismissed as not understanding what it means to be a mother. What does this mean for the full-time political activist who can no longer get enough help sending out mailings? For the feminist candidate with fewer campaign workers? For lesbians who are not mothers but who have pressing responsibilities and get little sleep—like the lesbian photographer recording days and nights of political demonstrations; or the legal worker in the middle of a political trial, staying up all night preparing for the next day? Who nurtures them? Who sympathizes with their fatigue? Not their parents, not their coworkers at straight jobs, and, too often, not their lesbian friends. No wonder they are hostile, or at least skeptical.

These thoughts have not led me to conclude that lesbians should remain childless. They have, however, led me to believe that a lesbian who chooses motherhood has a concomitant obligation to defend the right of others not to have children, and especially to support those women who make feminism their full-time work. No one else will say that their choices are as valuable as ours. No one else will say that it's strong, positive and self-affirming not to have children, that it's more than just "all right." What's more, our decisions to have children will be used to reinforce the isolation of lesbians without children from mainstream society. We who are raising children are in the best position to make it clear that we fully support a decision not to have children.

I am also concerned about the impact of lesbians choosing motherhood on another group of lesbians—those who had children within marriage and voluntarily gave up custody of them. Although many lesbians have lost custody of their children against their wishes, others have decided not to assume primary responsibility for the ongoing care of their children. For those who have turned away from the day-to-day work of mothering as part of a process of embracing a lesbian lifestyle, the choice of motherhood by significant numbers of lesbians must at least appear puzzling and may seem to be an implicit judgment. All of society views women who give up custody of their children with suspicion, disapproval, and disbelief. If we who have children as lesbians do not explicitly support our sisters who have decided to stop the daily tasks of raising their children, we become part of their oppression and contribute to divisiveness in our community.

In practical terms, this translates into a need for lesbians who choose motherhood to affirm in all relevant public forums—conferences, meetings, publications—the decisions of other lesbians not to mother or to withdraw from being mothers.

It is important to analyze why we want children because the reasons reflect larger truths about our community. For some, having a child signals a retreat from the political to the personal, from the public to the private. Why? And why now? On a more intimate level, lesbian couples may be having children to keep their relationships together, or to avoid confronting issues within their relationships, such as no longer making love. What are the ramifications of deflecting attention from the root issues of our relationships or from the crucial task of building a more positive vision of lesbian sexuality?

Although some of the reasons lesbians are having children stem from aspects of their personal, intimate lives, others seem to be more connected to the current climate of options for political work. For me, the one or two-year period before I adopted was characterized by political inaction, almost lethargy. I thought, I read, but I didn't do much because there was no focused political action which seemed to have any likelihood of meaningful success. During a time of increasing political repression, with the mainstream moving farther and farther to the right, it is hard to feel that any radical political work will be effective. The sense of isolation overwhelmed and immobilized me. I felt in my gut that my involvement in political action would make no difference, so I saw raising a child as a concrete, creative, focused activity.

Naturally, I now wonder how many other lesbians look to motherhood to get them out of this rut. To the extent that motherhood drains the available pool of lesbians engaging in ongoing political work, its long-term significance is overwhelming. Additionally, these motivations are bound to aggravate the tensions between non-mothers and mothers, as mothers take on society's most acceptable excuse for not doing anything in the public sphere.

Certainly, childrearing itself is subject to political analysis and can be guided by positive political principles. But childrearing probably should not become the total focus of one's political energy anymore than other important, intimate endeavors, such as coming out to parents and working on homophobia. There is a lot of work to do. And all of us who don't do it must ask ourselves why, must try to understand the nature of these times, and must struggle to find a way for more people to resume the larger fights. Mothers cannot let themselves off the hook. I am afraid also that this particular motivation to have children has an impact on childrearing practices, allowing less clarity, understanding, and questioning about the political ramifications of our childrearing choices. If this is true, then having a child becomes not a way to focus political activity but a way to avoid it.

The other motivation to have a child I felt, which I believe is common and needs to be more fully discussed, is the desire to be more normal and have more in common with most women. Political isolation and personal isolation are related. It is easy to get tired of political work which appears to have minimal impact. We are all worn down by the personal traumas we experienced with lovers and friends that shattered our naive beliefs in building one large lesbian community. Once I was no longer energized by the feeling of being different, I began to seek ways of fitting in. Having a baby because of this motivation is the same kind of defeat as returning to heterosexuality. It is testimony to the power of the most repressive parts of our society. And it is a larger defeat as well, as it makes the road harder for all those who continue to resist society's prescribed roles for women.

A realignment according to motherhood or childfreeness means that a lesbian mother believes she has more in common with a heterosexual, usually married, mother than with a lesbian who has no children. I have seen lesbians whose social lives have come to revolve around families, usually straight, with other children close in age to their own. I have seen child-care plans made with heterosexual families of unknown politics because it was the most convenient arrangement. As the mother of a two-year old, I understand the difficulties of arranging child care. But I also believe the perception that one's interest as a mother supercedes one's interest as a lesbian is politically devastating. I am especially troubled when alliances with straight mothers do not include explicit openness about being lesbian.

Few lesbians are always out. With various coworkers, colleagues, customers, clients, family members, etc., we may choose to say little about our personal lives so that our lesbianism remains hidden, or at least unspoken. Having a child, however, is a principal indicator of heterosexuality. To most of the world, a mother is by definition a heterosexual, and one who embraces the social norm. I have never felt that lesbians should always come out in all situations; survival sometimes demands otherwise. But to not come out as a lesbian mother is to assume a public position of heterosexuality.

I have done it myself. I have chatted with colleagues about disciplining and birthday parties; I have told potential employers about the connections between my child-care arrangements and my work commitments; I have been able to make small talk with just about anyone on the universal subject of our children. Every time I do it, I separate myself from my lesbian sisters. Unless I also identify myself as a lesbian, which is sometimes impractical and sometimes unwise, I put myself in an implicitly heterosexual woman's place and accept it as natural. On a larger scale, this makes it harder for lesbians to come out and is not neutral but incredibly destructive to building a lesbian and feminist movement.

Interestingly enough, even when someone knows I am a lesbian my motherhood makes me seem more normal. It is amazingly easy for people to put difficult information in the back of their minds. The ability to talk about preschool programs as two mothers virtually eclipses my differences from married woman, unless I say I am specifically looking for a program that will foster my daughter's pride in being part of a lesbian family, which I do not always do. My experience is that straight women clearly feel that my choice to have a child *balances* my choice to be a lesbian and makes me more normal, easier to understand, woman, less of a challenge to their lives.

When I have put out this analysis to other lesbian mothers or mothers-to-be, I have been challenged by some who say that having a child forces them out of the closet, thereby making them *less* normal, especially when two women raise a child coequally and the child calls them both *mommy*. There is certainly truth to this, although I believe it is limited to situations involving equal co-mothering. The *family unit* will not appear normal anywhere it functions as a unit, with schoolteachers, storekeepers, or family members. But the individual mother, and even the non-legally recognized mother, will be more normal in her life as an individual. And she will have many times in her life when she will be put to the test of explicitly disclosing her lesbianism or accepting the presumption of heterosexuality that makes the "deviant" choices of lesbianism and childfreeness less possible for others.

It might well be asked why I inquire so intently into the reasons lesbians have children, as though we need better, or even different, reasons than our heterosexual sisters have. After all, our right to have children can be seen, almost on a civil rights level, as a right to the same opportunities that heterosexuals have. It is especially tempting to take this approach in the face of recent moves in Massachusetts and New Hampshire to bar lesbians and gay men from foster parenting and adoption.

Certainly it is critical to assert and defend our right to have and care for children. Those who would deny us this right are profoundly anti-gay and anti-lesbian, and this manifestation of homophobia, like all others, must be vigorously opposed. But while we fight for the ability to make the same choices as our heterosexual sisters, we must nonetheless critique those very choices.

Many lesbians have taken this precise posture with respect to the legal ability to get married. While most would agree that as long as marriage is available to heterosexuals it should also be available to lesbians, many lesbians have profoundly questioned the institution of marriage, have expressed reservations about our ability to transform that institution even if we were allowed access to it, and have concluded that they would not marry even if legally permitted to do so.

I find this a compelling analogy to childbearing and childrearing. Motherhood is an institution.[2] It functions as an integral part of patriarchal society to maintain and promote patriarchy. Our lesbianism does not negate or transform the institution of motherhood. Motherhood, like marriage, is too loaded with this patriarchal history and function to be an entirely different phenomenon just because lesbians are doing it. If we fail to ask ourselves the kinds of questions I have raised here, and many more, we essentially embrace not only the personal experience of mothering but the institution of motherhood as well.

The great challenge of lesbians choosing motherhood and the possibilities opened by it lie precisely in asking questions, a lot of questions, a lot of hard questions. This article has principally addressed the issues of choosing whether to have a child. In future articles, I would like to go farther and examine how we have our children and how we raise them. The dialogue we can have about these questions, the answers we come up with, and the process of developing those answers are a great gift which we have to offer to our community and to our children.

Notes

[1]There have been, of course, historical periods when motherhood has not been encouraged because economics dictated the need for use of women as a "reserve labor force." This is often associated with a nation being at war. At the moment, dominant economic ideology (as opposed to reality, which mandates the employment of women for the survival of many families) dictates just the opposite, that high unemployment rates are at least in part a function of the number of women in the labor market. Furthermore, it is beyond the scope of this article to examine the different pressures upon women and girls of different races and classes to become mothers. It is unquestionable that differences in status and options in the larger society impact upon the circumstances under which women become mothers.

[2]Adrienne Rich's *Of Woman Born* is probably still the most eloquent analysis of motherhood as an institution.

Chapter 13

Women's Mothering and Male Misogyny

MIRIAM M. JOHNSON

DURING THE 1970s, feminists using psychoanalytic theory considered women's mothering to be highly problematic. In this chapter I trace the vicissitudes of the hypothesis that women's mothering—that is, being the primary caretakers of children—lies behind male misogyny and male dominance itself.[1] The hypothesis derives from psychoanalytic theory and its extensions and has been discovered and rediscovered, worked over and overworked in various ways by feminists, including myself, since the early days of psychoanalysis. But only in the 1970s was it called upon to bear the burden of explaining the entire system of male dominance. This argument that blames male misogyny on women's mothering has an important element of truth in it, but in my view, it does not hold the key to a viable solution to systems of male dominance; moreover, the argument has become an impediment to seeing the positive aspects of women's mothering, or better, of a maternal stance.

Feminists who use psychoanalytic theory in conjunction with an analysis of social structure suggest that male misogyny is far from superficial and cannot be easily eradicated. Psychoanalytic explanations focus on the generation of motivation that is nonrational and operates outside conscious awareness. These motivational explanations offer an alternative to simplistic "role theory" explanations of male dominance that suggest that to do away with male dominance, all we need to do is to redefine roles or eliminate gender-based role differentiation. Similarly, these explanations at the motivational level seem preferable to those nonpsychoanalytic "psychological" analyses that suggest that male dominance can be eradicated by getting rid of outmoded stereotypes. There is nothing wrong with advocating role and stereotype change, but attempts to effect real change (as opposed to a change in the forms male misogyny takes) may fail unless we recognize unconscious motivational tendencies and their underlying dynamics.

Moreover, psychoanalytic theory offers an alternative to simplistic biological explanations that attempt to account for male dominance by recourse to some presumably immutable genetic or hormonal differences between men and women. Psychoanalytic theory used in conjunction with an analysis of social structure appealed to feminists precisely because it could explain the persistence and seeming intractability of certain attitudes without recourse to biological factors. The structural fact the theorists under consideration use is that women, not men, tend to be responsible for early child care. In later chapters I will be increasingly critical of some important elements in psychoanalytic interpretations of gender, but my concern now is with how psychoanalysis can help explain the generation of sexist motivation in men and women.

Two major themes in psychoanalytic accounts of male personality development relate to the early primacy of women in the lives of male children. One is the idea that infants and children of both genders, but especially males, feel fear and envy toward the mother and develop defenses against these feelings; the other theme is the problems males encounter in establishing a secure sense of masculine gender identity. The first tendency emphasizes infantile dependency needs and the "primary process" thinking in which the mother appears overwhelmingly powerful; the second emphasizes the idea that identity develops from a process of separating the self from the mother, including boys' learning that they are a different gender from mother. Both these strands of gynecentric (i. e., mother-centered) psychoanalytic theory have been used to explain why men are motivated to denigrate and dominate women, whereas women feel few or no comparable motives toward men.

I begin by showing how the earlier themes fit into feminist explanations of male dominance, while also pointing out the limitations of such analyses.[2] I then discuss the work of Evelyn Fox Keller and Jessica Benjamin, who relate males' special problems with separation from the mother to their greater tendency to emphasize difference, hierarchy, and domination in their thinking. Keller's and Benjamin's analyses, which derive from combining psychoanalytic hypotheses with a "critical theory" perspective, differ from earlier analyses and need to be examined separately. ("Critical theory" is the name adopted in the United States by the Frankfurt School of Marxism, which emphasizes cultural and psychological factors.) I find problems with the specific psychoanalytic account Keller and Benjamin use, but the direction they take in emphasizing women's lesser concern with preserving gender difference and lesser tendency to control through domination is progressive. It also fits in with my interest in how fathers, not mothers, are the main focus of the more narrowly "sexual" aspects of gender differentiation.

The Fear and Envy Hypothesis

The fear and envy hypothesis is almost as old as psychoanalysis itself. The early names most associated with the hypothesis are Ernest Jones, Melanie Klein, and Karen Horney. Although their accounts differ substantially, they all have a common thread of opposition to what Jones labels Freud's "phallocentric" views. Each stresses the significance of the preoedipal period and the mother rather than of the oedipal period and the father; all see the penis envy in girls, which Freud took for granted as being primary, as being in fact a secondary response. Although male dominance itself is not problematic for these theorists, their ideas nevertheless can be used to shed light on the motives behind male dominance.

Jones tried to be an arbiter in what came to be called the Freud-Jones controversy, which represents the conflict between phallocentric and gynecentric approaches (Mitchell 120). Jones draws heavily on the views of both Klein and Horney, both of whom take as their starting point the helplessness of the infant, that is, the infant's almost total physical and emotional dependence on an adult. Klein (1932) emphasizes the infant's sadistic aggressive responses to this dependency coupled with anxiety engendered by a fear of the mother's reprisal for aggression. According to Klein, the boy compensates for his feelings of "hate, anxiety, envy and inferiority that spring from his feminine phase by reinforcing his pride in the possession of a penis" (338).[3]

Horney (1967), by contrast, links men's general fear of women to the boy's fear of being rebuffed by the all-important mother and the subsequent loss of self-esteem. This fear of deflation by a woman on whom he was dependent then becomes the prime motivating factor in men's compulsion to prove themselves and their manhood and to seek to possess many women or to attempt to "diminish the self-respect of the woman" (145-46).

Horney (1974) suggests that, in addition to fear, there is in men a strong element of envy and even awe of women's capacity for motherhood. Surely, she says, there must have been a time in the psychic development of boys and girls when neither sex was convinced that women were inferior. She backs this up by describing how in analyzing men "one receives a most surprising impression of the intensity of this envy of pregnancy, childbirth, motherhood as well as the breasts and the act of suckling" (176-77). Boys, she suggests, defend themselves against this envy by asserting the phallocentric idea that motherhood is in reality a burden and that what women basically want is not a child, but a penis. In Horney's view, Freud's phallocentric idea represents a masculine defense against womb envy.

Margaret Mead, who was influenced considerably in the 1940s by psychoanalytic thinking, has also argued that men envy women's procreative powers. Rather than using clinical experience, she uses the myths that abound in various cultures, including our own, to bolster her interpretations. According to Mead, in the areas of New Guinea she studied, "It is men who spend their ceremonial lives pretending that it was they who had borne the children, that they can 'make men'" (97). Mead also describes how men in New Guinea tell stories about how their mythical man-making powers were invented by a woman and stolen from her by men. Mead attributes men and women's according higher value to what men do than to what women do (that is, what men do is considered an achievement) to a perception of males' psychological need to compensate for their lack of procreative powers.

Dorothy Dinnerstein's *The Mermaid and the Minotaur* offers the most sustained account to date that attributes male dominance directly to infantile fear and envy of mothers.[4] Dinnerstein states explicitly that she is concerned not with personal male misogyny but with the entire system of male dominance. This system, she says, is created not by men alone but rather is based on a conspiracy by both men and women. This conspiracy consists of substituting male dominance for the far more threatening dominance that mothers held over us as male and female infants.

Although it is not always clear what Dinnerstein thinks the crucial mechanisms are that intervene between male dominance and early child care by women, her central theme is that the power we as infants ascribe to mothers creates a need in us for a more bounded authority. Formal authority is always vested in males because male authority appears to be a refuge from the primitive and seemingly unlimited despotism of the mother as perceived by the infant. Dinnerstein follows Melanie Klein in explaining men's fear and contempt for women and argues that in the child's mind, since the mother does not always meet the infant's needs, she is perceived as "capricious" and "sometimes actively malevolent" (Dinnerstein 95). But there is also the child's ambivalence, made up of destructive rage when disappointed as well as abounding gratitude when satiated. This ambivalence is then projected onto women in general. Dinnerstein sees men's sexual possessiveness as an attempt to "own" women's life-giving powers, and sex-segregated institutions as being created by men in order to defend themselves from "the temptation to give way to ferocious voracious dependence" on women (67).

In Dinnerstein's analysis, women take on characteristics as unlovely as those she attributes to men. Whereas men may express their vindictive feelings against the mother directly in "arrogance toward everything female," women express those feelings "directly in distrust and disrespect toward other women, and indirectly by offering ourselves up to male vindictiveness" (174). Women have supported men in their evil deeds against Mother Nature because of their own infantile rage, but women then use their powerlessness to absolve themselves from blame and take some pleasure in blaming men. Now, Dinnerstein says, women have come to hate men as much as men have always hated women.

According to Dinnerstein, male dominance must be ended, not so much because it oppresses women as because masculine "achievements" threaten to destroy the world. Dinnerstein sees us as having created a "megamachine" (Lewis Mumford's term) bent on destroying the earth and the vitality of human life. Her main interest, in fact, is to criticize the enterprises in which men are engaged and to which women are acquiescing. In so doing, she breaks with Simone de Beauvoir, whom she generally holds in high esteem. Dinnerstein dislikes de Beauvoir's uncritical acceptance of masculine ways of thinking—for taking "the male world-making enterprise at face value" and for believing that freedom for women can be had by "a simple entering into man's realm" (24).

It is true that Dinnerstein blames women's mothering for the ills of the world, but at the same time she defines what those ills are from a maternal, caring, preserving perspective. But in spite of Dinnerstein's own maternal values (one wonders where she got them), the women in the horror show Dinnerstein depicts are not thinking like mothers; they are thinking like dependent *wives* and girlfriends, supporting men in their madness. Her final message is that women can stop providing support for men's life-threatening enterprises. This is the reading I prefer to give Dinnerstein, but the message that comes across more strongly is that women's mothering, by causing men and women to reject the overwhelmingness of their early experience with female power, is to blame for all this.

Dinnerstein's book is written not from the point of view of an adult mother doing the best she can under the circumstances, but from the perspective of an infant who expects nothing short of perfection.[5] She communicates to the reader through the language of "primary process thinking," that is, thinking in which only infantile needs matter. She does this well, presumably in hopes that we will recognize this thinking in ourselves and also the infant in ourselves. Dinnerstein is saying that infants blame mothers when the world is not right, but she becomes so totally caught up in her own apocalyptic vision that she never stops taking the point of view she attributes to infants.

Dinnerstein does not argue that women do not mother well; rather, she argues that infants are not rational and only gradually learn to take the point of view of the mother instead of looking at the world from the standpoint of their own voracious needs. She sets up the problem as infantile thinking but prescribes that the realistic solution is for fathers to mother. After her description of what men are like (because of their infantile thinking), however, one is inclined to agree with Pauline Bart, who exclaimed in a review of Dinnerstein's book, "I wouldn't even buy a used car from people like that! What kind of generation would they produce?" Moreover, Dinnerstein does not explain how an infant might be persuaded to disperse its apparently unlimited needs and resentments equally between a male and a female parent and thereby presumably cease to be misogynist.

It seems to me that the basic problem here is not so much women's mothering but the nonrational, "unprocessed," or primary process thinking that continues to influence the adult's responses in certain triggering situations. A more effective solution to this kind of thinking than equal parenting would be for all of us to grow up and for women to take the lead in helping us do so. That is, we all need to recognize the nonrational elements in our thinking, the elements that make us expect perfection from mothers and fear abandonment and humiliation by them. Here, of course, I mean not one's own real mother but rather women perceived as mothers. Growing up would mean learning to take others' needs and perspectives into account besides our own and thus putting one's self into a wider perspective. Most of us do grow up, more or less, and women are in a better position than men to take the lead in insisting that men and women take others into account as mothers do, rather than continuing to take the point of view of the egocentric child. Perhaps this is implied in Dinnerstein's idea of equal parenting, but it does not come through.

The devaluation of women (by both men and women) is not an inevitable reaction formation to women's prominence in early child care. It is a choice, helped along by the male dominance institutionalized in political and economic structures and supported in male peer groups. I am convinced that all of us harbor irrational ideas and expectations focused on women because women are so prominent in our early life and that these ideas feed into male rage and male misogyny. Feminists with an awareness of the psychoanalytic tradition naturally focused on these ideas as an explanation of the roots of male misogyny, and these ideas suggest that the roots run very deep. Male fear and envy of mothers cannot stand alone, however, as the explanation of male dominance even on a psychological level, in part because it ignores the positive consequences that being mothered has for both men and women.

The Tenuous Masculine Identity Hypothesis

Generally, the theorists concerned with the various consequences of a boy's making an initial "feminine identification" have been social scientists who have been influenced by psychoanalytic ideas. Social learning theorists have often readily assumed that because mothers are far more available and primary in the lives of young children than fathers, children of both sexes initially make a "feminine identification." From this perspective, growing up for males means shifting from a feminine identification to a masculine one. Psychoanalysts and social learning theorists alike have assumed that it is important for the son to have a "good" relationship with his father in order to be helped "to identify" with him or to learn by observing him and thus to become "masculine" or to learn "masculinity." Few of these accounts specify what is meant by identification and sometimes the term is used simply as a synonym for modeling or copying the parent of the same gender.

In the 1950s, worry about a boy's problematic identification gave rise to the concept of "compulsive masculinity." For example, Walter Miller (1958) argued that lower-class boys who grew up in predominantly female homes that lacked "a consistently present male figure with whom to identify" were likely to become compulsively concerned with toughness and masculinity as a reaction formation against the femininity surrounding them. Miller claimed that father-deprived males were likely to commit delinquent acts to prove their masculinity to the gang (270). In a similar vein, Rohrer and Edmonson studied a group of black males in New Orleans and argued that the black male joined a gang in a "search for masculinity he cannot find at home." These gangs in turn come to see "the common enemy not as a class, nor even as a sex, but as the 'feminine principle' in society" (162-63).

Whereas most of the studies in this country on compulsive masculinity were on the "lower class" and particularly blacks, Talcott Parsons (1954) applied the idea to middle-class children. He pointed out that in highly industrialized societies the place of work is separated from the place of residence and fathers leave home to work. In the middle class this work is time-consuming and often incomprehensible to a child. Thus there is a kind of "father absence" in the middle class that causes children to interact chiefly with their mothers and other women. Women, not men, become the rule givers and represent the demand to "be good." This situation tends to produce what Parsons called "the bad boy pattern" and the "tenderness taboo," whereby males in attempting to be masculine without a clear masculine model express masculinity in largely negative ways by being "bad" and "tough." In trying not to be feminine, the boy unconsciously identifies "goodness" with femininity, and being a "bad boy" becomes a positive goal. Leslie Fiedler (1968) has described this "bad boy pattern" as a pervasive theme in U. S. fiction. From Mark Twain's stories to Ken Kesey's *One Flew Over the Cuckoo's Nest* are numerous sagas in which men (or boys) seek to escape a world that they perceive to be dominated by female morality.

The idea of boys making an initial "feminine identification" was also used by anthropologists in the 1950s in interpreting other behavior patterns found in a given society. These anthropologists reported that societies in which fathers were absent or virtually absent during a boy's infancy were more likely than others to have compensating rituals later on that symbolically broke the mother-son bond and affirmed the boy's masculinity (Whiting *et al.*; Burton and Whiting). In a different but related vein, an analysis of forty-eight societies reported that the frequency of crime in these societies was associated with situations in which the opportunity for the young boy to form an identification with his father was limited (Bacon *et al.*). More recently, Beatrice Whiting reported that in her and her associates' study of children from six different cultures there was greater adult violence in the two societies where infants saw their fathers infrequently. She specifically assumed the "status envy" hypothesis that young children would identify with the person who seems most important to them, the person who is seen as controlling the resources that they want. In the earliest years when this person is almost exclusively the mother, boys would be expected to make a feminine identification. Whiting then used the idea of compulsive masculinity to explain the violence that erupted in later years when the boys had to break this feminine identification.

Whiting points out that in the six cultures study described above and in the studies by other anthropologists, the phenomenon of sex-identity conflict occurs only when a great deal of gender segregation and male dominance exists in the adult society. This finding suggests that in more egalitarian societies, where femininity is not so devalued, one of the motives for males' compulsive resistance to femininity (both within and outside themselves) is lost.

At the time it was published, the research I have been describing was used to bolster the argument that fathers were vital to the well-being of children. It played into a persistent worry about father absence and the fear that males would be made "effeminate" by their mothers. Fathers were needed, it was claimed, to show boys what masculinity was and to prevent them from being made into sissies by their mothers or from overdoing masculinity as a defense against feminization.

The idea of "compulsive masculinity," or exaggerated masculinity, became something of a bridge to a feminist use of the idea that maleness was a less secure identity than femaleness and that this insecure identity provided a motive for male misogyny. Ruth Hartley moved in this direction in 1959. Writing at a time when male dominance was seldom subjected to criticism, she noted that males generally learn what they must *not* be in order to be masculine, before they learn what they can be. Because adult males are rarely closely involved with boys, many boys define masculinity as simply "not being feminine." Hartley argued that males compensate themselves for the pains involved in breaking away from the world of women by viewing females in very negative ways. The eight- to eleven-year-old boys she studied described adult women as weak, afraid, easily tired, in need of help, squeamish, inadequate in emergencies, making an undue fuss over things, not very intelligent, and demanding and jealous of their husbands! (Significantly, this description is clearly more congruous with definitions of women as wives than of women as mothers.) Boys, at least middle-class white boys in the United States, seem to force themselves into masculinity to avoid being such a pitiful specimen as a stereotypical wife. Hartley's article was reprinted in a widely used text on the "male sex role" that popularized the idea that one of the cornerstones of "masculinity" was its "antifeminine" element—whatever else one does, at all costs, do not be like a female (David and Brannon).

In 1974, in "Family Structure and Feminine Personality," Chodorow stated the above premise from a more psychoanalytic perspective and took its implications much further, suggesting that the male tendency to define masculinity as "that which is not feminine or involved with women ... explains the psychological dynamics of the universal social and cultural devaluation and subordination of women." The boy denies his attachment and deep personal identification with his mother "by repressing whatever he takes to be feminine inside himself, and, importantly, by denigrating and devaluing whatever he considers to be feminine in the outside world." Beyond this, Chodorow suggests that as a member of society, "he also appropriates to himself and defines as superior particular social activities and cultural spheres—possibly, in fact, 'society' ... and 'culture' ... themselves" (50). Thus Chodorow uses the search for masculinity as an explanation for the male view that society and culture are male products.[6] In 1979, Jean Stockard and I suggested that the greater rewards and power of masculinity act as an inducement to boys to break with femaleness. Women, in contrast, do not have a psychological need for "greater glory" as an inducement to be mothers.

Nowadays when feminists and, increasingly, modern psychologists speak of masculine gender identity, they usually do not mean the degree of masculinity as measured by ordinary psychological tests or the degree of conformity to a stereotyped "male role." Since the early 1970s, the idea of gender identity has referred not to the extent to which one is masculine, feminine, or even androgynous but rather to the simple emotional, cognitive, and bodily grounded conviction of being male or female and to being able to take this conviction for granted as a comfortable and desirable reality (Money and Ehrhardt). The tenuous gender identity hypothesis then claims that this secure sense of gender is considerably less problematic for women than it is for men.

Robert Stoller's studies of transsexuals provide empirical support for the tenuous masculine identity hypothesis at this deeper level. On the basis of his research, Stoller concludes that masculinity is not a "core-gender identity" for males in the same way that femininity is for females. Rather, masculinity is achieved by males only after they have separated themselves from the "femininity" of the mother.

Stoller thinks that female transsexualism has quite different origins than transsexualism in males. He considers female transsexuals to be a type of either homosexuals or transvestites. Their "femininity" goes much deeper; psychically (but not physically) they *are* women. Stoller sees this phenomenon as the result of a too-close and too-gratifying mother-infant "symbiosis." This symbiosis occurs before the child has enough of an ego structure to actually "identify with" the mother. It is something even more primitive. It is "*being the same as* mother, which would be the destruction of masculinity" (353).

Stoller's most significant argument is that every male must overcome and resist the excessive merging with the mother that happens with the transsexual. As Stoller sees it, every male infant experiences some degree of oneness with the mother; transsexuals are simply those at the far end of a continuum. Thus Stoller considers males making a feminine identification not a "defense" of one sort or another but rather the primary state. This view takes the idea of the primacy of the feminine in its maternal aspects in the male ego farther than most other psychoanalysts have done. Stoller's emphasis on the fundamentality of the maternal identification and his association of it with femininity implies that masculinity represents a deviation from femininity in its maternal aspects. Stoller does not relate his idea of primitive symbiosis with the mother to male misogyny, much less to male dominance. He also sees a sharp difference between his theory and the fear and envy hypothesis; his emphasis on idyllic symbiosis causes him to deny that there is early ambivalence and conflict in the mother-child relationship. Chodorow uses Stoller's work to bolster the argument that if fathers also mothered, it would not eliminate gender identity altogether but it would help the child feel that he is a male and that males can nurture too, and that it is not necessary to denigrate women to convince oneself that one really is a male.

Linking the Two Hypotheses in Gynecentric Thought

The fear and envy hypothesis and the tenuous masculine identity hypothesis are quite different from a psychoanalytic standpoint and seem to rest on different assumptions about the nature of the earliest infant-mother relationship. They may be viewed as essentially compatible, however, if they are seen as representing differing phases of the mother-infant relationship. Stoller is probably correct in assuming that the overriding emotion in the earliest mother-child relationship is love. Yet it is also possible to imagine how something akin to both fear and envy might accompany the infant's developing capacities for autonomy. As Melanie Klein suggests, infants fear that this person on whom they are so dependent might turn against them, and, as Horney suggests, they envy her capacities. Those who stress the fear and envy hypothesis, then, seem essentially to be saying that men's motive to segregate and dominate women comes not so much from the necessity to break their identification with the mother but rather from a fear of the consequences of their dependency on a woman whose powers they do not possess.

These same hypotheses can be couched in language more compatible with developmental theory and more relevant to development beyond earliest infancy. The tenuous gender identity hypothesis holds that since male figures tend to be conspicuously absent in early childhood, the boy, in trying to compensate for his lack of clarity about what it means to be masculine, is constrained to devalue and degrade female-typed activities and to stress the superiority of males over females and of male roles over female roles. The fear and envy hypothesis (which is likely to strike cognitively oriented developmentalists and role theorists as embarrassing and exaggerated) can be translated to refer to boys' efforts to cope with their recognition of relative powerlessness and the concomitant recognition that dependency is disparaged in males. Thus, in a sense, males are motivated to dominate females as a means of coping with their dependency needs.

Males, then, face both their dependency and their lack of clear gender identity as they move toward greater autonomy. Girls also experience the dangers of dependency and often struggle with their own mothers to escape it, but girls do not have to form a gender identity different from that of the mother. Males, however, continue throughout their lives to be threatened in different ways and on different levels with an identity problem and with a fear of dependency that is linked to it. The institutional arrangements embodying male dominance and the cultural justification of male dominance serve males well in coping with these threats by assuring them of their gender's superiority. Moreover, institutionalized male dominance gives even greater significance to not being female and in the end exacerbates rather than quells male identity and dependency problems (Whiting 1965).

Pleck's Critique

Joseph Pleck, in his book *The Myth of Masculinity*, extensively criticizes the kinds of hypotheses and research I have been describing relating mainly to the tenuous gender identity hypothesis. Basically, he argues that empirical support for the hypotheses embodied in what he calls the Masculine Sex Role Identity (MSRI) paradigm is lacking and that from a political standpoint the paradigm has been used to discredit mothers and poor or black males (in the absent-father studies) and to justify traditional male role expectations. In a brief statement toward the end of his book, Pleck exempts Dinnerstein's work and at least part of Chodorow's work from his critique (156-57). He also speaks favorably of Stoller's ideas concerning transsexuals. Pleck says all of the work he has exempted has been misinterpreted by the general public, however, as supporting the importance of clear-cut sex roles; actually, the implication of these works is that a secure sense of self as male or female may make it easier rather than harder to play nontraditional roles. This is quite correct. Pleck has a general bias against psychodynamic hypotheses, and even against developmental hypotheses, however, and this bias limits his later analysis.[7]

In essence Pleck would have us substitute a normative explanation for problems associated with men for a psychodynamic one. As an alternative to the Masculine Sex Role Identity paradigm, Pleck proposes a Sex Role Strain (SRS) paradigm. This paradigm maintains that it is difficult, if not impossible, for anyone to live up to the normative male role and that this places undue strain on men and women. This strain, Pleck believes, can account for male aggressiveness. Although I have no particular quarrel with the rather bland propositions in Pleck's alternative paradigm, I believe it focuses attention away from the gut-level emotional issues involved in gender attitudes and away from male dominance itself. Pleck asks rhetorically, "Are psychodynamic theories to account for men's attitudes toward women necessary?" My answer is yes, because the emotions that males and females have about themselves and each other are deeply felt and cannot be adequately accounted for by biology or role theory alone. Feminists who use psychoanalytic theory suggest that male dominance is far from superficial, because it gets built into our deepest feelings and understandings about what being masculine or feminine means. Moreover, Pleck's "critique of the male role" approach to gender relations minimizes the pervasiveness of male dominance, male privilege, and male power.

Equal Parenting as Solution?

Nancy Chodorow and Dorothy Dinnerstein argue that the remedy for the male motive to dominate women, which they see as being set in motion by the social assignment of mothering to women, is equal parenting by fathers and mothers. Neither of them suggests that women should not mother but rather that fathers should mother too. One gets the feeling, however, that the solution they propose is a rather distant prospect even in their own minds, and one that they feel cannot bear too-close scrutiny. Chodorow clearly understands that other aspects of social organization will have to change if fathers are to be able to mother, but she does not deal with this in any detail. Then too, these authors completely ignore the many obvious practical problems with precisely what is meant by an "equal division."

Many critics, including Chodorow herself, have pointed out that it is difficult to see why, in terms of her own analysis, men would ever be motivated to mother. According to the analysis, men are presumably made hostile to female activities by virtue of being dominated by a female, so why would they take on this female activity? In addition to the problem of getting men to mother in the first place, there is the danger (suggested by phallocentric versions of psychoanalytic theory that I will discuss later) that men will father in such a way as to reproduce patri-archy instead of gender equality.

The equal parenting "solution" would also strengthen the heterosexual couple relationship by making mothering a joint activity. Certainly lesbian coparents and heterosexual single mothers would hardly be served by this solution, which would work against any kind of female bonding, sexual or otherwise, and further empha-size the male-dominated couple relationship. A more effective way of reducing male resentments of women may be to diffuse mothering in this society not equally between a mother and a father but between mothers and other caretakers, male and female, with mothers retaining primary responsibility. This in fact seems to be the direction in which this society and other industrialized Western societies are moving in their childcare arrangements.

Difference and Dominance

I agree with those who say the most significant psychological difference between the thought tendencies of men and women is that men tend to emphasize and focus on gender difference more than women. That is, men seem to have a greater psychological investment in seeing and emphasizing gender difference than women do (Chodorow 1979: 13-14). My own work on fathers has long been concerned with this phenomenon (Johnson 1975). The difference as men see it is likely to be expressed in terms of hierarchy—strong-weak, dominant-submissive, independent-dependent, subject-object, penetrator-penetrated, and so forth. The tendency can easily lead men (and women) to define relational virtues, such as openness to the perspectives and needs of others, as "weakness" (Tooley).

Both Evelyn Fox Keller and Jessica Benjamin relate the male emphasis on preserving a rigid distinction between self and other to a need to objectify and control the other, in short, to dominate the other. Their accounts bear some resemblance to those I reviewed above, especially that of Dinnerstein, that at-tempt to explain the devaluation of women and male dominance as a system by the fact that women mother. Keller's and Benjamin's focus, however, is less on male attitudes toward women as a group than on general masculine ways of thinking, which have come to characterize Western science and Western eroticism. Keller and Benjamin are both essentially critics of capitalist culture, but in their criticism they link the "critical theory" of the Frankfurt School of Marxism, with its focus on domination, to masculinity by making domination a male propensity. In a sense they turn that school's "critique of domination" into a "critique of masculinity." As Hester Eisenstein points out, the critique of Western culture that connects it with men and their orientations became a basis for woman-centered analysis that sees "maleness and masculinity as a deformation of the human, and a source of ultimate danger to the continuity of life" (101). Keller's and Benjamin's analyses differ considerably from one another both in terms of the substantive problems they address and in terms of the implications for action that they suggest. Specifically, Keller (1978, 1982, 1985) is concerned with domination in Western science and Benjamin (1980) is primarily concerned with "erotic domination."

Both Benjamin and Keller rely on a complex account of the infantile roots of the more typically masculine impulse toward domination. Following the work of the object relations theorist D. W. Winnicott, they propose that in making the transition from "symbiotic union" with the mother to a recognition of the autonomy of self and others, the infant develops unconscious ideation to the effect that the subject (the self) has actually destroyed the object (the other person) in the process of becoming separate. To believe the other has been destroyed is highly anxiety-producing because if the object does not exist, how is the subject to maintain any relatedness? The child is thus not only afraid of having destroyed the other in becoming a self but also afraid of losing its own self if the other survives. The child then seeks to defend against both possibilities by seeking mastery over the other. At a later point, in the oedipal stage, this innocent mastery (in which presumably both genders partake) can become converted into mastery over and against the other. This latter mastery for various reasons (including the assumptions that males must not be females and must "disidentify" from the mother) becomes associated with masculinity at both the individual and the cultural level.

Also, in contrast to Dinnerstein and Chodorow, neither Benjamin nor Keller focuses on equal parenting as a primary solution to male dominance, probably because they see masculine ways of thinking as highly problematic. Benjamin (1981), especially, is concerned about the oedipal, authoritarian father, whom both see as enforcing gender polarity and representing authority (209).

Science and Domination

Keller (1978) suggests that the cultural identification of science and objectivity with masculinity is connected to the developmental process of separating self from mother. The boy, who must not only become a separate self but also a separate gender from the mother, is likely to defend himself both from "reengulfment" by the mother and from femaleness by assuming a more objective and distanced stance. The culture helps the process by associating both objectivity and masculinity with science, by making scientific thinking a model for all thinking, and by defining as "scientific" only that which is objective and distanced. Thus science itself has become genderized and has lost much in the process.

But Western science is not only objective and distanced; it also places great emphasis on power and control. Keller (1982) suggests that the impulse to dominate is a natural concomitant of "defensive separateness" (596). The impulse feeds into and is fed by the cultural construct of masculinity in which, for example, nature is seen as the mother who must be conquered and subdued. Keller is concerned not with reiterating this familiar connection and its variants but with purveying an alternative view of science. According to Keller, science is not intrinsically dominating; but it may also involve "conversing with," rather than controlling, nature and becoming part of the system under consideration rather than viewing the system from above.

Keller (1982) illustrates this with Barbara McClintock's work on DNA, which long went unrecognized, in part because her vision was difficult to grasp if one used a control model of science. McClintock challenged the prevailing view that "the DNA encodes and transmits all instructions for the unfolding of a living cell" with "a view of the DNA in delicate interaction with the cellular environment" so that "the program encoded by the DNA is itself subject to change. No longer is a master control to be found in a single component of the cell; rather control resides in the complex interactions of the entire system" (601). Keller does not claim that only women approach science in this manner. Rather, her argument is that this method of approach can and has been chosen and needs more emphasis. The value of consciousness is that we are able to make choices as individuals and as scientists. Both women and men seek competence, mastery, and rational understanding. Science is a human endeavor. The contribution feminism can make is to "refine that effort" and to show that domination and control are not necessarily intrinsic to science.

Love and Domination

Jessica Benjamin (1980) uses the sadomasochistic, master-slave relationship described in Pauline Reage's *The Story of O* as her prototype of erotic domination, or what she calls "rational violence." She contends that the fantasy involved flows underneath "all sexual imagery" and "normal" adult love relationships and sees this fantasy as being ultimately caused by what she calls "false differentiation." In such differentiation, the solution to the fear of aloneness brought about by separation becomes one of preserving the other individual not as a separate being (which would be true differentiation) but by controlling and dominating the other person and denying him or her autonomy. This domination contains the threat of violence against the other and thereby becomes associated with male identity. But the violence must be "rational" for the strategy to succeed. In rational violence the perpetrator controls the victim in such a way as to obtain "recognition" from the victim while at the same time negating the victim's autonomy. In *The Story of O*, the female, O, is constantly recognizing her torturer-lover by her statements of "consent," and he is constantly negating her and testing her boundaries with more and more humiliating requests to which she must consciously and explicitly acquiesce.

It is less clear from Benjamin's account what the masochistic victim, O, gets out of her humiliation. Presumably, she gets recognition and avoids being alone, because she is needed by her lover in the sense that he needs her submission and her need for him. Benjamin also suggests that O identifies with her lover's rational control and thus protects herself from her own loss of control, which is equated with loss of self. In the last analysis, the explanation for 0 goes back to the differing positions of males and females in the infantile situation. "The male posture, whether assumed by all men or not, prepares for the role of master. The male is disposed to objectify the other, to instrumentalize and calculate his relation to her in order to deny his dependency. The female posture disposes the woman to accept objectification and control in order to flee separation. He asserts individual selfhood while she relinquishes it" (167).

In rational violence, the victim matters to the violator; in nonrational violence, the victim's responses do not matter to the violator. In both cases, the violator is very likely to be male. Benjamin's final statement argues against a politics that "tries to sanitize or rationalize the erotic, fantastic components of human life," because "it will not defeat domination but only play into it" (171). Benjamin says that Andrea Dworkin mistakes *The Story of 0* for an affirmation of female degradation (n.4, 171). It is hard not to take the novel this way, however. The acquiescence of the woman in the story and her appreciation of the male's "rational control" fits nicely into the convenient male belief that women are in reality masochists and want to be dominated. As a book that sells this idea, I believe *The Story of O* is pornographic and as such should be resisted. This is not to say that domination will end if we ban its description, but certainly it seems useful to point out the sense in which it is degrading to women. I do not say this to counter Benjamin's general argument, but I wish that "cool culturalists" such as Benjamin could find a place in their analyses to condemn the uses to which fantasy may be put.

Benjamin goes on to argue that erotic domination is closely connected to male domination in the culture as a whole. Here she means not direct male dominance over females but rather the cultural hegemony of the male stance; thus our culture is an "instrumental culture" of rational calculation in which nurturance becomes privatized and the maternal world dwindles.[8]

Keller and Benjamin as Culture Critics

Keller's and Benjamin's analyses are valuable in showing how dominant cultural trends are related to masculinity on a variety of levels; however, we must guard against overgeneralizing about the defects of modern culture. In this respect I found Keller's analysis exemplary and Benjamin's analysis problematic. Whereas Keller makes rationality a human propensity par excellence, Benjamin tends to see rationality, instrumentalism, and individualism as "bad." But the orientations she criticizes are the very ones that fueled the women's movement in the 1960s and 1970s. Women who had been restricted to the domains of wife and mother wanted to participate in the rational, instrumental world of work outside the home. In my view the feminist critique of modern culture needs to recognize the positive benefits that have accrued to women from the degree of integration and assimilation we have achieved in the society that we are now in a position to criticize.

In facing the question of change, Keller drops her analysis of infantile dilemmas and says we can change because consciousness makes choice possible. Benjamin (1981) tries to stay within the limits set by the underlying assumptions of her analysis and becomes pessimistic. In terms of the particular psychoanalytic premises she uses, the alternative to the development she describes is remaining "merged" with the mother and therefore being a nonself, or all of the world, that is, undifferentiated. In her terms, rational individualism is "a defense against helplessness and the ambivalence of differentiation." If we give that up, we would have to resort to "more primitive defenses (pathological narcissism) or to considering the possibility of a more terrifying state than we have yet been able to endure" (220). Fortunately, this terrible state of being a nonself may be more a male fantasy and fear in an individualistic world than an infantile state. At times Benjamin seems to understand that this fear of "merging" is more characteristic of males' ideation, but because of her use of a theory that assumes an initial total lack of differentiation, she seems to get caught up in it herself and become stymied by her own theory.

One cannot help suspecting that Keller's and Benjamin's speculations about infantile fantasies are adult projections onto infants of adult preoccupations with the typically Western cultural issues of freedom versus nurturance, autonomy versus belonging and (within the culture of the Frankfurt School) recognition versus negation. In my view Keller's and Benjamin's writings should be taken as insightful cultural analyses, but ones that remain at the cultural level. Even when Benjamin discusses fathers and the Oedipus complex, she is discussing the symbolic interpretation adults give to fathers, not necessarily the meaning that fathers have for children themselves at various stages of their development.

Infantile Ideation and Psychoanalysis

The issues discussed in this chapter, and perhaps especially Keller's and Benjamin's reliance on Winnicott's theories, are all relevant to a long-standing debate concerning the nature of infantile thought processes. Many psychoanalysts have been critical of a tendency among some of their colleagues to project adult ideation onto children. Emanuel Peterfreund (1978) has called this tendency "the adultomorphization of infancy" and suggests that those who study infants, especially those with a strong biological orientation, find little evidence to corroborate the speculations.[9] To say that psychoanalytic approaches can provide a useful framework for thinking about development is not the same as giving equal weight to every psychoanalytic idea that comes along in this highly speculative field. It is one thing to believe that deeply held emotional reactions are formed early and quite another to buy into an elaborate theory concerning infantile ideation that would be virtually impossible to verify empirically.

While some psychoanalytic theorists, such as Margaret Mahler, posit an initial stage of autism, others, such as Winnicott and Robert Stoller, posit, albeit in different ways, a primary state of symbiosis or nondifferentiation between infant and mother. In this latter state, it is assumed that the infant is merged or fused with the mother and does not differentiate self from mother.

Daniel Stern (1985), who is both a developmental psychologist and a psychoanalyst, contends that there is little reason to believe that a symbiotic state ever exists for the child. On the basis of detailed observations of infant-caretaker interactions as well as his analytic experience with adults, Stern maintains that there never is any confusion between self and other, no merger, no symbiosis in the mind of the infant (10). Stern suggests that fantasies about "merging" are possible only after the development of a capacity to symbolize. He does not reject psychoanalytic accounts, however, but implies that explanations such as Winnicott's could not apply until a later phase of development beyond infancy has been reached, that is, until after the acquisition of language (11).

Stern also suggests that issues such as autonomy versus dependence (or perhaps interdependence, in my terms) should be thought of as occurring not at one developmental stage or another but rather in different forms at various stages. Freud and Erikson placed the emergence of autonomy at the anal phase and related it to toilet training. Spitz located it at around fifteen months, when children begin to say no. Mahler thought the critical period for autonomy was learning to walk. Stern suggests that the development of autonomy can be seen in very young infants as they learn to control visual engagements with the caretaker. I believe Stern is correct to say that there is no decisive event; dilemmas related to autonomy occur and reoccur and are transformed at various stages in the development of the sense of self (22).

Stern places the self as structure and process in the center of developmental theory, and thus new senses of the self become the organizing principles of developmental stages. Stern sees this as a four-stage process beginning with an emergent sense of self as a physical entity. The second stage is a sense of a "core" self, which includes a sense of self and other as not only separate physical entities but separate entities of action, affect, and continuity. In the third stage the infant begins to become aware of the intentions and affects that guide behavior. This stage represents a quantum leap from the previous stage because it opens up the possibility of intersubjectivity, that is, communication in which we can understand the subjective states of others and communicate our subjective states to them. In Parsons's terms this would be the stage in which the infant learns that physical acts of care "mean" that the mother "cares about" the infant. During this period there might well be a pervasive sense of well-being, of being-at-one with the other, but Stern would not call this a primary state of symbiosis, because the infant is always an active participant.

Finally there is a sense of verbal self on which the capacity to be self-reflective depends. This sense is what G. H. Mead described as "the reflexive self," the capacity to take oneself as an object, to represent the self and the other to the self. This capacity to symbolize to oneself that which one wants to communicate to the other is the key to the phenomenon of intersubjectivity.

Stern's ideas about developmental stages of the self fit well with other developmental and sociological perspectives that view the self as being formed in and through social interaction.[10] The sense of self develops simultaneously with the sense of other. There is much we do not know about the specifics of the process at different levels of understanding and maturity. The points for now are that gender differentiation is involved with more general processes of self-definition and that parsimony is advisable in describing this process in terms of infant ideation. Both the fear and envy hypotheses and the tenuous masculine identity hypotheses can have validity without "adultomorphizing" infant ideation.

Although Stern does not mention gender differentiation in his description of the stages of self-awareness, one might argue that the sense of self, or conceptions about the self in relation to others, may vary as a consequence of the social definition of self as male or female. Does one *see* the self as separate from others and defending the boundaries of the self while still preserving contact by controlling others, or does one see the self and others as separate but interdependent and without the necessity for control?[11]

Summary and Discussion

The idea that men are more likely to think in terms of difference than women and to see the nature of gender difference in terms of superiority-inferiority could be the critical insight to bring together feminists who deemphasize gender difference with those who focus on and analyze the nature of the difference from a feminist perspective. Feminists who deemphasize gender difference are actually "woman-centered" in the sense that they see that an important virtue of women is that they are less likely to emphasize difference than men. Feminists who emphasize difference accept this larger truth that gender difference should not be as salient as it now is in male-female interaction but nevertheless want to examine the nature of the difference in order to create a woman-centered definition. In short, the insight that one key difference is that men emphasize difference can help integrate diverse positions with feminism.

In this chapter I give my own interpretation of the work of Dorothy Dinnerstein and some earlier work of Nancy Chodorow in connection with the hypothesis that women's early monopoly on child care accounts for male misogyny and male dominance itself. The arguments concerning the production of misogynist attitudes are as old as psychoanalysis, but generalizing these arguments to systems of male dominance is new. I interpret the fear and envy hypotheses as stressing how infantile dependency needs contribute to the primitive perception that women have great power to produce total bliss or total devastation. The more recent hypotheses concerning tenuous masculine identity stress boys' difficulties in "disidentifying" with the femaleness of mothers in order to identify as a male. Psychoanalytic explanations are useful because they take the unconscious and nonrational into account and thus can explain the relative intractability of certain attitudes without claiming that these attitudes are biologically rooted and cannot be changed.

Evelyn Fox Keller and Jessica Benjamin are less concerned with using psycho-analytic ideas to explain male dominance as a system than with using them to explain the development of the attitude of domination itself. This fits in with critical theorists' concern with domination and attaches it to masculine propensities. Both Benjamin and Keller soft-pedal equal parenting as a viable cure for the infantile dilemmas they envision. This down playing probably results from their fear that males would carry their dominating tendencies into mothering and reproduce the very system we seek to destroy. I share this fear and will develop the reasons for it in the chapters to follow.

The implications of all of these analyses at a psychological level is that we all need to become aware of the nonrational and unconscious bases of our behavior in order to "grow up." In one way or another all of the authors discussed imply that instead of sweeping male misogyny and propensities for domination under the table, we need to examine them not only to see that they run deep but also to hold them up to the light of criticism. I agree. Moreover, men and women are capable of taking thought and changing their own consciousness. It can happen, but it is important not just to give up old ways of seeing but to invent new ones, not out of whole cloth, but out of women's own intuitions. The new emphasis on interdependence amid self in relationship seems headed in the right direction. This emphasis keeps the issue from being that of autonomy versus dependence, self-assertion versus passivity, domination versus submission, and so forth.

Consciousness also depends on and creates social structural arrangements. At another level all of the analyses I have been discussing are limited to the psychological consequences of women's being responsible for early child care. If analysis goes no further than the mother-child relationship, we are left with the impression that women's mothering is the problem. This is hardly the case.

Notes

[1] For other summaries and critiques, see the articles in part 2 of Trebilcot's edited volume, *Mothering*. See also Gottlieb, "Mothering and the Reproduction of Power."

[2] Although Chodorow uses the argument relating male dominance to women's mothering in *Reproduction of Mothering* (1978), it is not the central theme of her book. The hypothesis was, however, an important theme in Chodorow's earlier work, and she developed a slightly different version of it in "Feminism and Difference" (1979).

[3] See also Melanie Klein's "Early Stages of Oedipus Conflict."

[4] Before Dinnerstein's book, the best popular work that clearly attempted to relate human institutional arrangements, including the exclusion of women from male affairs, to men's fear and envy of women was *The Dangerous Sex* by H. R. Hays, first published in 1964. Hays argues that social institutions in societies from the most primitive to the most modern have been designed to defend men against

their fears of women by circumscribing, regulating, and containing women. He ends with a plea not for equal parenting but for men to abandon their magical approach to women, to accept their existential anguish, and to realize that the menace of the female lies within themselves (283).

[5]In their article, "Fantasy of the Perfect Mother," Chodorow and Contratto contend that many feminists display primary process thinking with regard to mothers. Feminists have tended to talk either about the malevolence of mothers or they have overidealized motherhood. In either case, "the fantasy of the perfect mother" underlies these responses.

[6]Chodorow's earlier article, "Being and Doing" (1971), discusses male misogyny more from the standpoint of the fear and envy hypothesis than from the tenuous gender identity standpoint.

[7]For a more detailed discussion and critique of Pleck, see my review in *American Journal of Sociology* 88 (1983).

[8]Benjamin suggests that mothers may be making differentiation harder for their children because their lack of autonomous roles outside of the family gives them little else in which to invest except their children. Mothers' lack of autonomous roles may make it difficult for mothers to tolerate and encourage their children's differentiation. Benjamin's idea has been developed slightly differently by Philipson in "Narcissism and Mothering" (1982). She argues that the narcissistic personality of today is a result of the situation in which women mothered in the 1950s. These mothers were so frustrated by their isolation and the heavy expectations placed on them that they were unable to be sensitive to the child's need for autonomy and could not empathize with the child, but responded instead to the child in terms of their own needs. How women's isolation in the home might have affected the quality of their mothering is a complex issue and one that must be kept analytically separate from that of how the mother is perceived by the child. Benjamin's brief remarks tend to confuse the two.

[9]See also Greenberg and S. Mitchell, *Object Relations in Psychoanalytic Theory* and Horner, "Psychic Life of the Young Infant."

[10]For a discussion of various developmental approaches to the emergence of self during infancy, see Harter, "Developmental Perspectives on the Self System."

[11]Chodorow discusses some of these issues in "Feminism and Difference" (1979).

References

Bacon, Margaret K., Irvin L. Child, and Herbert Barry III. "A Cross-Cultural Study of Correlates of Crime." *Journal of Abnormal and Social Psychology* 66 (1963): 291-300.

Bart, Pauline. "The Mermaid and the Minotaur: A Fishy Story That's Part Bull." *Contemporary Psychology* 22 (1977): 834-835.

Benjamin, Jessica. "The Bonds of Love: Rational Violence and Erotic Domination." *Feminist Studies* 6 (1980): 144-174.

Benjamin, Jessica. "The Oedipal Riddle." *The Problem of Authority in America.* Eds. John P. Diggins and Mark E. Kann. Philadelphia: Temple University Press, 1981.

Burton, Roger V., and John W. M. Whiting. "The Absent Father and Cross-sex Identity." *Merrill-Palmer Quarterly* 7 (1961): 85-95.

Chodorow, Nancy. "Being and Doing: A Cross-Cultural Examination of the Socialization of Males and Females." *Woman in Sexist Society: Studies in Power and Powerlessness.* Eds. Vivian Gornick and Barbara K. Moran. New York: Basic Books, 1971. 259-291.

Chodorow, Nancy. "Family Structure and Feminine Personality." *Woman, Culture and Society.* Eds. Michelle Rosaldo and Louise Lamphere. Stanford: Stanford University Press, 1974. 43-66.

Chodorow, Nancy. *The Reproduction of Mothering.* Berkeley and Los Angeles: University of California Press, 1978.

Chodorow, Nancy. "Feminism and Difference: Gender, Relation, and Difference in Psychoanalytic Perspective." *Socialist Review* 46 (1979): 51-69.

Chodorow, Nancy, and Susan Contratto. "The Fantasy of the Perfect Mother." *Rethinking the Family.* Eds. Barrie Thorne with Marilyn Yalom. New York: Longman, 1982.

David, Deborah, and Robert Brannon, eds. *The Forty-Nine Percent Majority: The Male Sex Role.* Reading, MA: Addison-Wesley, 1976.

Dinnerstein, Dorothy. *The Mermaid and the Minotaur: Sexual Arrangements and Human Malaise.* New York: Harper and Row, 1976.

Eisenstein, Hester. *Contemporary Feminist Thought.* Boston: G.K. Hall, 1983.

Fiedler, Leslie. *The Return of the Vanishing American.* New York: Stein and Day, 1968.

Gottlieb, Roger. "Mothering and the Reproduction of Power: Chodorow, Dinnerstein, and Social Theory." *Socialist Review* 14 (1984): 93-119.

Greenberg, Jay R., and Stephen A. Mitchell. *Object Relations in Psychoanalytic Theory.* Cambridge: Harvard University Press, 1983.

Harter, Susan. "Developmental Perspectives on the Self System." *Socialization, Personality, and Social Development.* Ed. E. Mavis Hetherington. Vol. 4 of *Handbook of Child Psychology.* Ed. Paul Mussen. New York: John Wiley, 1983.

Hartley, Ruth. "Sex-role Pressures and the Socialization of the Male Child." *Psychological Reports* 5 (1959): 457-468.

Hays, H.R. *The Dangerous Sex: The Myth of Feminine Evil.* 1964. New York: Pocket Books, 1972.

Horner, Thomas M. "The Psychic Life of the Young Infant: Review and Critique of the Psychoanalytic Concepts of Symbiosis and Infantile Omnipotence." *American Journal of Orthopsychiatry* 55 (1985): 324-343.

Horney, Karen. "The Flight From Womanhood: The Masculinity Complex in Women as Viewed by Men and by Women." 1926. *Women and Analysis.* Ed. Jean Strouse. New York: Grossman, 1974. 171-186.

Horney, Karen. "The Dread of Women." In her *Feminine Psychology.* Ed. Harold

Kelman. New York: W.W. Norton, 1967. 133-146.

Johnson, Miriam. "Fathers, Mothers and Sex Typing." *Sociological Inquiry* 45 (1975): 15-26.

Johnson, Miriam. Rev. of *The Myth of Masculinity*, by Joseph Pleck. *American Journal of Sociology* 88 (1983): 1336-1338.

Keller, Evelyn Fox. "Gender and Science." *Psychoanalysis and Contemporary Thought* 1 (1978): 409-433.

Keller, Evelyn Fox. "Feminism and Science." *Signs* 7 (1982): 589-602.

Keller, Evelyn Fox. *Reflections on Gender and Science*. New Haven: Yale University Press, 1985.

Klein, Melanie. "Early Stages of the Oedipus Conflict." *International Journal of Psycho-Analysis* (1928): 167-180.

Klein, Melanie. *The Psychoanalysis of Children*. 1932. New York: Grove, 1960.

Mead, Margaret. "On Freud's View of Female Psychology." *Women and Analysis*. Ed. Jean Strouse. New York: Grossman, 1974.

Miller, Walter D. "Lower Class Culture as a Generating Milieu of Gang Delinquency." 1958. *The Sociology of Crime and Delinquency*. Eds. Marvin E. Wolfgang, Leonard Savitz, and Norman Johnston. New York: John Wiley, 1962.

Mitchell, Juliet. *Psychoanalysis and Feminism*. New York: Vintage, 1974.

Money, John, and Anke A. Ehrhardt. *Man and Woman, Boy and Girl*. Baltimore: Johns Hopkins University Press, 1972.

Parsons, Talcott. "Certain Primary Sources and Patterns of Aggression in the Social Structure of the Western World." *Essays in Sociological Theory*. Glencoe, IL: Free Press, 1954. 298-322.

Peterfreund, Emanuel. "Some Critical Comments on Psycho-analytic Conceptualizations of Infancy." *International Journal of Psycho-Analysis* 59 (1978): 427-441.

Philipson, Ilene. "Narcissism and Mothering: The 1950s Reconsidered." *Women's Studies International Forum* 5 (1982): 29-40.

Pleck, Joseph. *The Myth of Masculinity*. Cambridge: MIT Press, 1981.

Rohrer, John H., and Munro Edmonson. *The Eighth Generation*. New York: Harper, 1960.

Stern, Daniel. *The Interpersonal World of the Infant: A View from Psychoanalysis and Developmental Psychology*. New York: Basic Books, 1985.

Stockard, Jean, and Miriam M. Johnson. "The Social Origins of Male Dominance." *Sex Roles* 5 (1979): 199-218.

Stoller, Robert J. "Facts and Fancies: An Examination of Freud's Concept of Bisexuality." *Women and Analysis*. Ed. Jean Strouse. New York: Grossman, 1974.

Tooley, Kay. "Johnny, I Hardly Knew Ye." *American Journal of Orthopsychiatry* 47 (1977): 184-191.

Trebilcot, Joyce, ed. *Mothering: Essays in Feminist Theory*. Totowa, NJ: Rowman and Allanheld, 1983.

Whiting, Beatrice B. "Sex Identity Conflict and Physical Violence: A Comparative Study." *American Anthropologist* 67.6, part 2 (1965): 123-140.

Whiting, John W. M., Richard Kluckhohn, and Albert Anthony. "The Function of Male Initiation Rites at Puberty." *Readings in Social Psychology*. Eds. Eleanor E. Maccoby, T.M. Newcomb, and E.L. Hartley. New York: Holt, Rinehart and Winston, 1958.

Chapter 14

It's Only Natural

VALERIE WALKERDINE AND HELEN LUCEY

HERE ARE TWO ordinary girls, Dawn and Amanda. They are four years old and at home with their mothers. Their mothers are ordinary too, and yet they are quite different and apart from each other. Neither pair has met or knows of the other, nor are they likely to, but within these pages they have been brought together, and not for the first time, to have their lives and themselves compared (see Tizard and Hughes). Here are some extracts of their conversations:

Amanda and her mother are having lunch together.

C: Is ours a sloping roof?
M: Mmm, we've got two sloping roofs, and they sort of meet in the middle.
C: Why have we?
M: Oh, it's just the way our house is built. Most people have sloping roofs, so that the rain can run off them. Otherwise, if you have a flat roof, the rain would sit in the middle of the roof and make a big puddle, and then it would start coming through.
C: Our school has a flat roof, you know.
M: Yes, it does actually, doesn't it?
C: And the rain sits there and goes through.
M: Well, it doesn't go through. It's probably built with drains so that the water runs away. You have big blocks of flats with rather flat sort of roofs, but houses at the time this house was built usually had sloping roofs.
C: Does Rosie [friend] have a sloping roof?
M: Mmm. Rosie's house is very like ours. In countries where they have a lot of snow, they have even more sloping roofs. So that when they've got a lot of snow, the snow can just fall off.
C: Whereas, if you had a flat roof, what would it do? Would it just have a drain?
M: No, then it would sit on the roof, and when it melted it would make a big puddle.

Dawn, her small sister and her mother are also having lunch. The two girls are drinking juice.

> C: I got the wrong straw. (She has a white cup and yellow straw, while her sister has a yellow cup and white straw.)
> M: Huh?
> C: I got the wrong straw.
> M: Why's that?
> C: That side that colour, that. (points to cups.)
> M: What colour's that then? (Pointing to Dawn's cup.)
> C: That one?
> M: What colour is it then?
> C: Red.
> M: White.
> C: White.
> M: What colour's Sue's [sister] then?
> C: Blue.
> M: Your dress is blue. (Dawn then takes Sue's white straw to match her white cup.)
> M: Give her back her straw before she hits you. (M gives the white straw back to Sue.)
> C: That must be mine. (pointing to white straw.)
> M: Well, go without then.
> C: I want that one. (The argument continues.)

Two different families, you may say, but the difference is as devastating as the idea that one mother is imperfect because she does not get her wash as white as the next. In using the wrong detergent, she is neglecting her children, being a bad mother. As in advertising, the mothers in these two examples are compared and one of them wins the accolade: one of them washes whiter. The game is called "Find the Sensitive Mother," and it is a game beloved of psychologists and educators alike. Which mother do you think is sensitive and why do you think that this question is being asked?

Tizard and Hughes view Amanda and her mother's discussion about sloping roofs as "a remarkable attempt by a child not yet four to explore an abstract topic." This she does successfully, though she cannot do it alone. The pivot of her success is her mother, for it is she who responds to the girl's curiosity, her thirst for knowledge, by guiding, being explicit in her explanations and gradually building the basis for understanding the complexity of the concept. Contrast this to the "failure" of Dawn and her mother's exchange where neither achieves being understood or understanding. No sense here of direction, resolution, the meeting of needs.

[Dawn] was unable to express the concept in terms which her mother would understand, such as "I should have the white straw to go with my white cup." This difficulty was compounded by her mother's insensitivity or lack of patience. Mutual understanding was never achieved, and the conflict continued to escalate. (147)

The reason for seeking out the sensitive mother is a genuine concern for the educational prospects of young children. Tizard and Hughes's study attempts to understand and intervene in the educational opportunities and performance of working- and middle-class girls, but in order to address these issues, like many studies before it, it addresses the preparation made in the home for performance in school.[1] The mother is to precede the teacher: she is to prepare the child. Her effectiveness in performing this task is judged in terms of her sensitivity to the child's needs.

On one level this argument seems obvious. Children have needs, and therefore mothering turns out to be an essential function. What we want to demonstrate is that things are not that clear-cut. Indeed, these arguments are ones that feminists too have balked at, and often, shared parenting has been put forward as a way of attempting to take the burden of child care from women's shoulders.[2] And yet, implicitly the argument remains: children have needs and mothering is neces- sary as *a function* to meet them. The crucial importance of "mothering" frees it from biology, from gender. For while it is not coincidental that the ideal mother embodies all the characteristics of nurturant femininity, and while the bonds between this universal, ungendered "mother" just happen to be made virtually unbreakable by the "love bond" between the baby and the woman who gave birth to her, the notion nevertheless stands that, in prin- ciple, "anyone can mother," but that "mothering" *must* be done by someone. We want to demonstrate that current ideas about children as having needs to be met by a mother are not universal, timeless laws, but were developed in specific historical and political conditions, which make mothering a function that is central to the way our modem state educational and social welfare practices operate.[3]

What characteristics are taken to define a sensitive mother? Firstly, while the mother is being sensitive to the child's needs, she is not doing any housework. She has to be available and ready to meet demands, and those household tasks which she undertakes have to become pedagogic tasks. A feature of the sensi- tive mother then is that her domestic life is centered around her children and not around her housework. The boundaries between this work the children's play have to be blurred and so it comes as no surprise that any household task can transform itself into the basis of domestic pedagogy.

Why should we concern ourselves with these issues? In the course of this book we will argue that modem mothering has become one of the central aspects of the regulation of women. Yet, many debates about the socialisation and education of girls and women end up implicitly or explicitly blaming mothers for the fate of their daughters (i.e., Friday; Arcana; Eichenbaum and Orbach). This leaves women in a guilty impasse. In pursuing their own "needs," are they damaging their children by not meeting theirs? Should they or should they not have children? Where lies liberation? Most of this work, feminist or not, takes as a matter of incontrovertible fact that there is a certain account of child development, a certain account of mothering, which is natural and inevitable. We do not believe that there are any simple matters of fact in this case at all.

The Incontrovertible Proof of Mothering

In the Introduction we stated some of our anger, our feeling of a desperate need to engage in the possibility of a feminist politics that can take on the specificity of class. The story which we wish to unravel and explore here is one in which scientific proof about mothering has been so bound up with an account of the raising of working- and middle-class children that it is impossible to separate one from the other.

Over many years, a body of work condemning working-class child-rearing practices had grown up,[4] but now Tizard and Hughes, through their study, were seeking an alternative explanation of what had previously been seen as "alien" and "unnatural" practices. A diversion from much of the literature, the book bravely put forward a thesis of language development drawing on the work and ideas of the sociolinguist, Labov, who tried to revalue working-class childrearing practices as different rather than deficient. Although this kind of work was very important in criticizing the concept of deprivation, the concepts of "difference" and "deficiency" are not the only ways of understanding working-class childrearing practices. The idea of "difference" frees us from one trap only to ensnare us in another, and that trap is to remove any idea of exploitation and oppression, to end up with a liberal pluralism of difference. Tizard and Hughes offered an explanation of what they saw as "equal but different," seeking to normalize working-class practices and to defend them as not deprived. Although they produced an account based on empirical observation and on the interpretation of evidence, there are no hard facts in this matter. They asked certain questions about mothering, they collected evidence and used it within an already existing framework. This linked the education of working-class children to mothering and childrearing practices, leading on to the possibility of regulating mothering, so as to pave the way for educational success. These questions are neither neutral, nor are they the product of bad people or bad science. They are, however, caught up in a politics of liberal democracy which we question here.

Central to our argument is that the story of girls and mothers has tended to validate middle-class practices and pathologize working-class ones; others have tried to suggest that all women's lives are similar and that class should be subsumed under the category of gender (see, for example, Millett). We do not share this view. Working-class and middle-class women's and girls' lives are different, although not in the sense that one is normal and the other pathological, one oppressed and the other not. They are both the object of regulation and oppression, but differently. We want to bring back that difference. It often pits woman against woman, but ignoring those differences will get us ultimately nowhere.

What is a sensitive mother?

The kinds of tasks which are supposed to aid the intellectual development of young children, and on the basis of which well-known psychologists have constructed their accounts of that development, are almost all routine domestic tasks transformed into a pedagogy: a pedagogy that the mother can engage in when she is, for instance, making the family meal. Laying the table can teach one-to-one correspondence,[5] peeling vegetables can become an exercise in sorting. In the following examples from a pre-school mathematics scheme this becomes clear:

In the summer, washday may happen out of doors, and can stimulate lots of talk and valuable experience as children add soap to the water, wash the clothes (taking care that the water doesn't flood over the sides of the bowl), wring the clothes and peg them out on a line (Schools Council 15).

Charlotte's mother is a sensitive mother. She tirelessly answers Charlotte's unrelenting questions and makes her home, her everyday life, an assault course of developmental tasks. This she achieves by constantly engaging her daughter in essentially domestic work which she herself cannot escape from. Some "are routine tasks, like helping Mum put the shopping away, while others involve making things. Each becomes an opportunity for learning, growth and the monitoring of that growth. Charlotte mixes up a pudding and then puts coloured, decorative balls on the top. Her mother, as teacher, "tests" Charlotte on colour and number concepts:

M: How many colours are there?
C: That many.
M: Come on, how many?
C: One, two, three, four ... four!
Even "insensitive" (Tizard and Hughes) mothers get it right sometimes. Dawn watches her mother decorate her birthday cake with candles:
M: Four.
C: One.
M: Mmm.
C: Two. That one's got nothing on. (The candle holder has sunk into the icing.)
(---)
C: One, two, three, four.

On one level you might say that finding the principles of intellectual development in the routine activities of women's domestic labour is demonstrating that such activities or experiences are everywhere. But we could ask a deeper question, that is, why is domestic labour transformed into the very basis of children's cognitive development and what is the relationship between this and the idea that the sensitive mother is necessary to meet the child's intellectual and emotional needs?

The second feature of the sensitive mother is the way she regulates her children. Essentially there should be no overt regulation; regulation should go underground: no power battles, no insensitive sanctions as these would interfere with the child's illusion that she is the source of her wishes, that she has "free will." As the psychologists John and Elizabeth Newson remark:

> Some conflict between parent and child is inevitable: it arises because parents require children to do things, and this interferes with the child's autonomy as a person, with wishes and feelings of his own. In disciplinary conflicts, by definition, we have a situation where certain individuals exercise their rights as people of superior status (in age, power and presumed wisdom) to determine what younger and less experienced people, of inferior status, may or may not do. If the child complies willingly of course (even if his willingness has been engineered by offering him the illusion of choice) his self-esteem can be kept intact: but whenever he is forced into an unwilling compliance by threat of sanctions, whether these be pain inflicted or approval withdrawn, he will inevitably suffer in some degree feelings of powerlessness and humiliation. (331-2)

The mother, like Sally's mother below, who makes her power visible must be understood as abnormal and pathological. Sally shuts the connecting door between the dining-room and the living-room, even though her mother had previously told her to leave it open:

> M: Sally, open that door! Sally, open that door now! (M gets up and opens the door.) Close that door again and I'll give you a smack.

The sensitive mother therefore hides the fear, the spectre of authoritarianism, or rebellion which ensue if the child realizes herself to be powerless. This powerlessness must be hidden from her at all costs. At risk is not only what is counted in terms of the development of the child, but also the smooth-running society peopled by those who do not believe they are powerless, who believe they have some control. The sensitive mother therefore avoids conflict. She turns resistance and even violence from her children into "feelings" that make themselves and others unhappy and she rationalizes it so that it has no force. This is exactly what Julie's mother below does. Julie, jealous of her baby sister, shouts at the baby, who then cries.

> M: Oh, don't, love, don't be horrible to her.
> C: I'm not. Aaaahhhh!
> M: C'mon, you wouldn't like someone shouting at you if you were sad, now stop it!

Why do the Newsons, quoted above, think that disciplinary conflict is so harmful? They put together the possibility of autonomy, wishes and feelings which belong to the child. The adult has rights to discipline children, yet disciplining is considered potentially harmful, because feelings of powerlessness and humiliation will result, if the disciplining is not achieved by creating an illusion of choice where the child thinks that it is the agent of its own free will. The discourse of rights suggests a liberal analysis, but we are taken powerfully into libertarianism, where what is at stake is the production of a mode of disciplining free from overt authoritarianism: Newson and Newson do not go as far as to state that children must not be disciplined at all, but they suggest the creation of an illusion of the child as the originator of its actions. The autonomous child is the empowered child, the child potentially ready to take its place in a democracy. But wait, something is wrong here. The choice is an illusion, an elaborate charade.

There is a very common analysis, one that gained ascendancy in the late 1960s, which held authoritarianism to be the very basis of oppression, particularly of totalitarianism.[6] Libertarian theories depended upon an analysis of personal oppression as the stifling norms of coercion. Democracy was seen to be a sham, because hidden chains bound people together in oppressive personal and social relations. Equality was to be achieved through a politics of personal liberation, which stressed the removal of the "bourgeois family" and personal growth. Utilizing theories especially drawn from the Frankfurt school, such as the work of Herbert Marcuse,[7] other work began to be developed which documented the stifling nature of "the family" as a bourgeois institution.[8] Therapy and consciousness change became political weapons and the sons and daughters of the bourgeoisie tried to find new ways of relating to each other. Traditional working-class struggles were no longer placed centre-stage because now a politics of liberation included a personal politics which criticized middle-class lifestyles. A pleasurable and free sexuality was emphasized. This was, as many women have documented, to free men from the confines of the commitment and trap of bourgeois marriage; women were exhorted to be free and gain pleasure in their bodies, but male sexuality was celebrated more than anything else.[9] Women began to feel that this liberation gave little to them as they were left at home while male members of collective households expressed their own liberation by not attending to any domestic or child-care tasks. The children of the bourgeoisie also began to "drop out," they systematically disdained the careers mapped out for them and went off to the country in an attempt to escape the power and coercion of the System to make them take their place in society.

These were important attempts at revolt and a critique. They opened up a space for the possibility of middle-class women's liberation, and the exploration of sexuality and of the domain of the private, the domestic, as political issues, outside the scope of traditional working-class politics. In this context also a new Left politics began to be developed, one which was influenced by the sixties generation of middle-class children and their new questions. It stressed the politics of feminism, of anti-racist struggles, of cultural issues. All these have been very important. However, the concept of "bourgeois" came to be rather over-generalized, as in the idea of "the family" as "bourgeois." This meant that the working class were seen as a worse version of what the middle classes were struggling against. But, along with them something else happened. The white working class got dumped by the Left. They came to be seen, utilizing the new theories, as failing to support the demands for liberation because they were reactionary, conservative and authoritarian, not because these demands simply seemed quite extraordinary to working-class people.

It is for this reason, among many, that we want to talk about the dual and different regulation of the proletariat and the bourgeoisie. We are arguing that the issues and conditions of the lives of the two groups are different, and therefore subject them to different modes of regulation in the bourgeois—of manners, stiff upper lips, stifling correctness and continuation of privilege and tradition—order. Thus it was the position of the regulative bourgeoisie that the students rebelled against in 1968. They demanded a politics of personal liberation because the chains that bound them were not ones which chained them to the factory floor, but to bourgeois morality. They felt stifled and oppressed, but what could be the basis of their oppression? Unfortunately the theories that they chose to support their claims were theories of liberation from authority and a kind of power which presented a threat to democracy. This led to the idea that liberation depended upon the removal of authority, and personal equality on people being free from demands. It became an extreme form of liberalism, which stressed the path to individual liberation in the politics of the personal and tended to ignore the possibility of collective action. If it was the System which oppressed then one had to find a way of living outside that system.[10] Such a view could only be held by people who had the wealth and position to make this possible. It was thus quite out of step and sympathy with working-class demands.[11] It must have seemed like a bourgeoisie demanding its personal liberation at the expense of the workers.

One of the main preoccupations of the work of what became known as the Frankfurt school was to document and explain the rise of fascism as a mass phenomenon. Extensive use was made of aspects of psychoanalytic theory, especially the idea of repression. Following the psychoanalyst Wilhelm Reich (1975, 1983), others argued that fascism depended upon an authoritarianism which related to the patriarchal authority of the father in the nuclear family and a set of family relations stressing power through position and hierarchy. Liberation thus depended on the removal of repression and the authoritarian family form which produced it. To save democracy and promote equality children had to be brought up and educated free from repression. This led to the view that the children of the working class were in even more danger than those of the bourgeoisie. There was a spirit of missionary zeal to save children from their authoritarian families, which stripped from them the few coping strategies they had to deal with and protect themselves against the brutal routines of their daily lives. Liberal capitalism and liberalism joined forces in campaigns to liberalize the workplace. In education children were to be set free, in factories workers, like managers, were sent on the heady path towards self-actualization.[12] Not surprisingly, manual workers roundly rejected such humanism, pointing out that theirs was not the kind of work which led easily to the delights of self-actualization.

Liberalism and libertarianism got hopelessly mixed up, and in the process working-class families were watched and monitored as never before. Bourgeois liberal culture, the culture of being laid back, opting out, became the new road to liberation. Working-class people were to be saved from themselves. None of this did anything for women or for their labour, except cement the strong distinction between the normal and the pathological family. The answer which was sought came time and again to centre on the regulation of practices of the mothering of small children. There followed the idea that there was a kind of human nature or essence which lay underneath the trappings of the social world. If we could know what human needs were then the sensitive mother could meet these needs, and children would not be brought up in the stranglehold of authoritarianism.

Although there seem to be very good reasons to assume that mothering is indeed an important function to ensure democracy, an analysis is possible that sees it as upholding a fiction of autonomy. For the Newsons, successful parenting rests on creating an illusion of autonomy so convincing that the child actually believes itself to be free. We believe that this fiction, the illusion of autonomy, is central to the travesty of the word "freedom" embodied in a political system that has to have everyone imagining they are free the better to regulate them. In locating the problem of democracy in the home it is the mother who has to come to the rescue and the working-class mother who has to be watched above all others.

In the rest of the book we take apart several interlinking fictions. Science claims to tell the truth about natural mothering, but it is founded upon a set of fantasies and fears of what is to be found in the working class. Psychology has been centre-stage in providing the props to the production of these "truths." They leave mothers feeling that they have to "meet needs," leave them feeling guilty for their inadequacy. We suggest that this guilt is bought at a high price. The mother has to underpin the fragile illusion of democracy, for this fiction of equality is propped up by her oppression. We want to question the very idea of "meeting needs" and argue that it is not the best way to understand the relation of mothers to children.

A libertarian analysis of mother-child relations stresses "freedom" for the child. Freedom from repression so that the child can be free to discover individuality and autonomy, free to learn self-regulation—the only luggage needed on the conflict-free path to democracy. But the picture of harmony is a fantasy, one which ignores and denies the possibility of resistance and power. The child may learn to live with and exercise her autonomy, but to do this she must first regulate the mother. An examination of conflict and resistance might tell us much more about mother-daughter relations than any analysis of "harmony" can. Is there democracy in the kitchen? Is the kitchen the place where play and freedom and mother-love produce autonomous children, empowered and rational? The concepts of autonomy and empowerment are central to many analyses but we want to question their basis, suggesting that they may help to oppress rather than liberate women as mothers. Those mothers, almost exclusively working class, who separate work and play, who insist their daughters play by themselves and who insist also on getting the housework done, those mothers are insensitive, pathological. Their practices must be open to correction and scrutiny because they are abnormal. Some of these working-class families are poor, they live in cramped and unsatisfactory conditions, while some of the middle-class families seem wealthy in comparison. A few can employ cleaners and au pairs, the very jobs which some of the working-class women must do to keep the extra money coming in. But what do these differences mean? Are working-class mothers indeed pathological? How are class and cultural differences turned into perverse and unnatural practices?

Ours is not an argument which suggests that what is wrong with the working class is that we simply do not have the right conditions to allow us to behave properly. Rather, we are suggesting that the working class is constantly produced and reproduced as necessary, different, disgusting, Other—constantly told they are different in an order which ultimately depends upon their acceptance of oppression, exploitation and inequality as normal.

But it might be argued that mothering is a very pleasurable activity and we are making it sound totally oppressive. We certainly agree that such pleasure is crucial and yet we would also argue, following others (Donzelot), that such pleasure is also produced and regulated—correct and incorrect, normal and abnormal—and cannot be seen as given. However, our purpose here is rather different. It is to point out the great investment in the "naturalization" of "mother-love" and its place as a mode of regulation, examining the "serious burdens of love" (Riley), because certain assumptions about mothering and specifically about the mothering of daughters have serious implications for the lives of all women and for feminism. For so long accounts seem to have concentrated on motherhood either as a state of love, a meeting of, or failing to meet, needs, or as a myth (Badinter). We examine the effects in practice of ideas about female sexuality and mothering as they affect the day-to-day lives of two groups of mothers and daughters.

When we think about the idea of mothering, we are immediately drawn to the incontrovertible fact of biology: of women bearing children. Only in science fiction, in novels like those by Ursula Le Guin or Marge Piercy, is that biology altered to produce equality. In that case, are we at the mercy of our wombs, is anatomy our destiny? We are not going to challenge that, but we will be attempting to show in *Democracy and the Kitchen* that the line between scientific accounts and science-fictional narratives may be a lot finer than is usually thought. For many years now women have challenged the definition of ourselves presented through institutions, practices and theories dominated by men. We have argued that science was male "control over nature." We have offered theories of female power, matriarchy, nurturance, sensitivity. We have challenged scientific proof which claimed we were not as good as men. In many ways, over many years then, women have sought to challenge and resist those definitions. But biology returns to haunt us. Women mother because we give birth. We want to show how science has produced accounts of mothering which not only claim it to be natural, but state it as true. We are not out to "disprove" these accounts so much as to show how and why they were produced and what effects they have on women and girls now, and therefore to challenge their validity. The purpose of this is to demonstrate a way beyond a certain set of problems in the existing accounts—ideas about women's work, the role of the family, the needs of children. The story we want to construct is a narrative about power and regulation, fact and fiction. To tell it we will need to explain some theoretical concepts and examine how they differ from ones that have been used before. Our aim is not to be exhaustive, to back up and substantiate all our points, but to suggest how we might go about examining the issues we are raising. In other words, we want to explore what it might mean to tell a different story.

Why do we use the term "story?" We are arguing that scientific accounts are not true in any simple sense. Not that we are saying they are false, but rather, that scientists do not work in academic ivory towers, constructing unbiased, objective accounts, but work in and respond to particular historical and social conditions and concerns. The concerns we will spend most time exploring in *Democracy and the Kitchen* are those of the creation and maintenance of what we will call bourgeois liberal democracy. This is the democracy of rights, of individualism, related to the rise of science, of capitalism, of the bourgeoisie. In this we want to oppose a simple idea of science as truth, and ideology as distortion, by claiming that scientific accounts are narratives in their own way and that the distinction between science and ideology is unhelpful, but also that they have particular effects in practice when it comes to regulating the lives of women.

Although the scientist in this regulation is presented in the position of the unproblematic purveyor of truth, we want also to ask what lurks behind the apparatus of regulation. Behind the assurance of rationality of the scientist lurks a set of fears of the observed, fears of the dark uprisings that threaten the safety of the bourgeois order. Experiment and observation attempt to predict and control through the modern magic of numbers, of data, timed seconds, moments. The rise of the bourgeois order was premised on the possibility of scientific government, with its own particular forms of control and regulation through science.

Notes

[1]As we pointed out in the introduction to *Democracy and the Kitchen,* there is a whole tradition of work which does this. However, from the 1970s the mother was targeted specifically by psycholinguists and developmental psychologists who battled over whether or not the mother was capable of providing an adequate preparatory environment, or indeed was better at the job than any nursery or school.

[2]See for example arguments in Lynne Segal's *What Is to Be Done About the Family?*

[3]We are not going to argue, following Elizabeth Badinter, that the idea of the maternal instinct is a myth. Rather we want to examine how the idea that children have needs to be met by natural "Mothering" came to have a currency in, and be the bedrock of, arguments for bourgeois democracy.

[4]See, for example, the arguments surrounding deprivation in Rutter.

[5]One-to-one correspondence is a concept which comes from the work of the developmentalist Jean Piaget, whose work has become deeply embedded in modem approaches to early education and child development.

[6]See Adorno and later work such as Laing.

[7]See particularly Marcuse (1964, 1969).

[8]See Segal for a review.

[9]This is documented by, for example, in Campbell.

[10]For a critique of the idea of the System, see Henriques *et al.*

[11]To the workers in Paris in 1968, the students' demands that they join their struggle must have seemed like "much wants more" (see introduction to *Democracy and the Kitchen*). Students, the sons and daughters of the middle and upper classes, already had so much privilege. It might have seemed more appropriate to the workers if the students had supported increased entry for the sons and daughters of the workers to the kind of privilege that it now seemed the bourgeoisie was not content with.

[12]This is documented in Hollway.

References

Adorno, T. *et al. The Authoritarian Personality.* New York: Norton, 1982.

Arcana, J. *Our Mother's Daughter.* London: Women's Press, 1981.

Badinter, E. *The Myth of Motherhood: An Historical View of the Maternal Instinct.* London: Souvenir Press, 1981.

Campbell, B. "Feminist Sexual Politics." *Feminist Review* 5 (1980): l-18.

Donzelot, J. *The Policing of Families.* London: Hutchinson, 1980.

Eichenbaum, L. and S. Orbach. *Outside In. Inside Out.* Harmondsworth: Penguin 1982.

Friday, N. *My Mother/Myself.* London: Fontana, 1979.

Henriques, *et al. Changing The Subject: Psychology, Social Regulation and Subjectivity.* London: Methuen, 1984.

Hollway, W. *History of Industrial Psychology: A Reader.* Forthcoming.

Labov, W. "The Logic of Non-standard English." *The Study of Non-Standard English.* Urbana, IL: National Council of Teachers of English, 1978.

Laing, R. D. *The Politics of the Family and Other Essays.* London: Tavistock, 1971.

Le Guin, Ursula. *The Left Hand of Darkness.* New York: Ace Books, 1973.

Marcuse, H. *One-Dimensional Man: Studies in the Ideology of Advanced Industrial Society.* London: Routledge and Kegan Paul, 1964.

Marcuse, H. *An Essay on Liberation.* London: A. Lane, 1969.

Millett, K. *Sexual Politics.* New York: Doubleday, 1969.

Newson, J. and Newson, E., *Seven Years Old in the Home Environment,* London: Allen and Unwin, 1976.

Piercy, Marge, *Woman on the Edge of Time.* London: The Women's Press, 1973.

Reich, W. *The Mass Psychology of Fascism.* Harmondsworth: Penguin, 1975.

Reich, W. *Children of the Future: on the Prevention of Sexual Pathology.* New York: Farrar, Straus, Giroux, 1983.

Riley, D. "The Serious Burden of Love," *What Is to be Done About the Family?* Ed. L. Segal. Harmondsworth: Penguin, 1983.

Rutter, M. *Maternal Deprivation Reassessed.* Harmondsworth: Penguin, 1972.

Schools Council. *Early Mathematical Experiences: General Guide.* 1978.

Segal, L., ed. *What Is to Be Done About the Family?* Harmondsworth: Penguin, 1983.

Tizard, R, and M. Hughes. *Young Children Learning.* London: Fontana, 1984.

Chapter 15

Unspeakable Plots

MARIANNE HIRSCH

> Long afterward, Oedipus, old and blinded, walked the roads. He smelled
> a familiar smell. It was the Sphinx. Oedipus said, "1 want to ask you
> one question. Why didn't I recognize my mother?"
> "You gave the wrong answer," said the Sphinx.
> "But that was what made everything possible," said Oedipus. "No,"
> she said. "When I asked, What walks on four legs in the morning, two
> at noon and three in the evening, you answered, Man. You didn't say
> anything about woman."
> "When you say Man," said Oedipus, "you include women too. Every-
> one knows that."
> She said, "That's what you think."
>
> —Muriel Rukeyser, "Myth"

Why Didn't I Recognize My Mother?
(Or, Why Didn't My Mother Recognize Me?)
(Or, Why Didn't I Recognize My Child?)

MURIEL RUKEYSER'S 1968 revision of the Oedipus story anticipates more
recent feminist questions and reflections about women's relations to men's
plots. Rukeyser's poem "Myth" provides the Oedipus story—the classic and
paradigmatic story of individual development in Western civilization—with
a different female-centered ending. Unequivocally female, in possession of a
voice and a plot, a subjectivity of her own, and a sense of irony, Rukeyser's
Sphinx refuses to be included in the universal heading "Man." She poses the
question of sexual difference and asserts the particularity of women. Whereas
Sophocles erases the figure of the Sphinx from his play, subsuming her questions
within Oedipus's own questioning of his origins, Rukeyser has her speak out
for women and, thereby, for herself.[1] Re-writing a classic plot motivated by the
mechanisms of masculine desire, she begins to answer the question posed by Teresa
de Lauretis in *Alice Doesn't:* "What became of the Sphinx after the encounter with
Oedipus on his way to Thebes? …No one knows offhand and, what is more, it

seldom occurs to anyone to ask.... Medusa and the Sphinx, like other ancient monsters, have survived inscribed ... in someone else's story, not their own; so they are figures or markers of positions—places and topoi—through which the hero and his story move to their destination and to accomplish meaning" (109).

Both Rukeyser and de Lauretis have chosen the Oedipus story as the story through which to explore the relationship between plot and gender. By focusing on the Sphinx—the figure who is entirely absent from Sophocles's play and from Freud's developmental paradigm—both revise the conventional plot structure, in which men are central and women function as objects or obstacles. But what happened to Jocasta, the "other woman" in the tale? Virtually silent in Sophocles' play and present only as object of desire and exchange in Freud's theory, Jocasta is virtually ignored in feminist revisions as well. In de Lauretis's account she appears only in a parenthesis, to signal a parallel between the ending of her plot and the supposed ending of the Sphinx's: "The questions we might ask are obvious. Why did the Sphinx kill herself (like Jocasta)?" (110). Although there are two female plots inscribed and silenced in the Oedipus story, de Lauretis is curious only about one. Both she and Rukeyser are attracted by the enigmatic, powerful, monstrous, and terrifying Sphinx; both omit the powerless, maternal, emotional, and virtually silent Jocasta. So that, while Rukeyser's Oedipus wonders why he did not recognize his mother, no one asks why—in spite of clearcut indications ranging from oracular predictions to swollen feet—his mother did not recognize him. Even Helene Cixous, who devotes an opera to the story of Oedipus and Jocasta, casts Jocasta as the lover and clearly not as the mother of Oedipus. No one imagines a Jocasta who wonders why she did not recognize her child.

This book foregrounds the "other woman," the mother, in relation to the "other child," the daughter. The myths we read and take to be basic determine our vision of how individual subjects are formed in relation to familial structures. Freud's optic was determined by the story he took to be central, the story of Oedipus. Other mythologies, the stories of Iphigenia, Electra, and Clytemnestra, of Demeter and Persephone, or of Antigone, for example, suggest alternate economies which may shape different plot patterns. They revolve around mothers and daughters as well as around brothers, sisters, and fathers. Even here, however, as we turn from the story of mother and son to the stories of mothers and daughters, Jocasta's silence is not radically reversed.

This book takes as its point of departure the intersection of familial structures and structures of plotting, attempting to place at the center of inquiry mothers and daughters, the female figures neglected by psychoanalytic theories and submerged in traditional plot structures. It concentrates on novels by nineteenth- and twentieth-century women writers from the Western European and the North American traditions, reading them with psychoanalytic theories of subject-formation in the context of the narrative conventions of realism, modernism, and post-modernism. Thus its aim is to reframe the familial structures basic to traditional narrative, *and* the narrative structures basic to traditional conceptions of family, from the perspectives of the feminine and, more controversially, the maternal.

By way of introducing the territory to be mapped in the course of this book, two stories will serve as paradigms—Jocasta's missing story in the Oedipus narrative, and a very recent black feminist re-vision of that story in Toni Morrison's *Beloved*. In one, we find a silenced mother who remains the object of the child's process of subject-formation and the ground on which the conflict between father and son is played out. In the other, a mother emerges who attempts to speak for herself even while she knows that her story is unspeakable—"not a story to pass on."

What earns the Sphinx, the non-maternal woman, privilege over Jocasta, the mother? Why do even feminist analyses fail to grant Jocasta as mother a voice and a plot? An earlier poem of Rukeyser's, "Private Life of the Sphinx,"[2] suggests the advantages, for a feminist perspective, of distinguishing between these two female positions. In that poem, the Sphinx is actually conflated with Jocasta and presented as maternal:

> Simply because of a question, my life is implicated:
> my flesh and answer fly between chaos and their need....
> My questions are my body. And among this glowing, this sure,
> this fact, this mooncolored breast, I make memorial.

Sharing Jocasta's powerlessness, this Sphinx clearly has a maternal and bodily identity. She questions not Oedipus, who never appears in the text, but herself, her own legendary status as Mother and Poet in the story of Man. Compelled to respond to man's "need" and "babble of demand," this earlier Sphinx *embodies* Truth and "set[s][her] life among the questioning." Resisting the power projected onto her and the misconceptions circulating about her, she conveys the personal bodily cost of the terrible knowledge she possesses about life and death. She dreams of a listener, of someone who will understand the meaning of her name and who will listen to her song. Whereas the later, non-maternal, extra-bodily Sphinx of "Myth" can challenge Oedipus's self-confident answer "Man," the earlier maternal Sphinx is resigned to accept it: "the answer must be 'Man.'" While the later Sphinx can devastate her opponent with one ironic comment, the earlier figure agonizes about being known and recognized for herself. We can understand Rukeyser's eagerness to revise her own revision in the 1960s, to eliminate the Sphinx's vulnerability, and to claim power and equality for women. Yet her shift away from the maternal and bodily identity of women in "Myth" is symptomatic of the moves of North American and European feminist writing and theorizing in the 1970s and 80s. This feminist tradition can succeed in inscribing the female into the male plot only by further silencing one aspect of women's experience and identity—the maternal.

In wondering why the Sphinx is more interesting, more worthy of having her story rewritten than Jocasta, in asking where the story of Jocasta is in the story of Oedipus, I am asking not only where the stories of women are in men's plots, but where the stories of mothers are in the plots of sons and daughters. I am asking that we try to imagine those stories. What can we say about Jocasta? In *Oedipus Rex* she appears only to attempt to discourage Oedipus from his questionings; yet she barely succeeds in delaying the terrible revelation. About herself she merely says: "Have I not suffered enough?" (Sophocles 1. 1059). After announcing her eternal silence—"O lost and damned! This is my last and only word to you/ For ever!" (11.1070-72)—she kills herself.

From sources beyond the Sophoclean trilogy, we do find the antecedents to this moment: Laius's homosexual rape, his marriage to Jocasta, and his refusal to sleep with her after the oracular decree. We find her ruse—getting him drunk to conceive Oedipus (see Licht). We do not discover her feelings about handing her child over to die, except in Oedipus's own exclamation: "The child she bore!" (1. 1178). Beyond this Jocasta is represented by silence, negation, damnation, suicide. The story of her desire, the account of her guilt, the rationale for her complicity with a brutal husband, the materiality of the body which gave birth to a child she could not keep and which then conceived with that child other children—this story cannot be filled in because we have no framework within which to do it *from her perspective*. She remains, in Oedipus's words, "That wife, no wife of mine—that soil/where I was sown and where I reap my harvest" (11. 1258-59).

Harold Stewart asks why Oedipus survives although he committed two outrages, while Jocasta has to die for committing only one (see also Devereux; Goodhart; Vernant; Chase; Erlich; Swan; Kahn). Jocasta, he speculates, actually engineered the destruction of Laius as a revenge for his homosexuality. I would argue that such a reading cannot be valid, given that Jocasta's motives and desires are not only absent from the text, but also absent from the very framework upon which Sophocles' and Freud's texts are built.[3]

Inasmuch as Cixous grants a voice to Jocasta in *Le Nom d'Oedipe: Chant du corps interdit*, it is the voice of Oedipus's lover and wife, the voice of the woman whose body is the home of man, but who herself experiences that home as lover and not as mother. Cixous tells the story of two lovers tragically separated by their fate and their past—a tragedy which leads Jocasta to kill herself. Significantly, some of Jocasta's speeches echo her sparse dialogue, her call for silence and ignorance in *Oedipus Rex*: "Forget the world/ Forget the city/ Stay here…. Do not search for it/ Do not go out. Stay here" (14, 26; my translation). Clearly, to know Jocasta's maternal story, we would have to rewrite completely the story of Oedipus and of the child's development: we would have to *begin* with the mother, not the son or the father. If masculine plotting is to be rethought from the perspective of the feminine, such rethinking needs to include Jocasta as well as the Sphinx, Jocasta the mother as well as Jocasta the wife and lover, and to reject the distinction, upheld even in recent feminist writing, between maternal and non-maternal women. For such a reframing, we have to go beyond classic texts to the work of women writers, who, as Rukeyser's poem demonstrates, have revised those texts, and to feminist revisions of psychoanalytic paradigms. But, as Cixous's play demonstrates, we also need to evaluate the process of revision and to determine whether and to what extent a mere repetition and reproduction of classic conceptions can indeed be transcended.

Alternate women-centered mythologies—the story of Demeter and Persephone, for example—are available to women writers, such as Toni Morrison, who wish to re-write the story of mother-child relations from maternal perspectives and, in particular, from the perspective of the mothers of daughters (see "Hymn to Demeter").[4]

The differences are telling. Unlike the Oedipus story, Demeter and Persephone's tale is told from the perspective of a bereaved Demeter, searching for her daughter, mourning her departure, and effecting her return through her own divine power. A breech caused by rape and death is undone by the mother's power to fulfill a mutual desire for connection. The compromise solution achieved by Demeter is that Persephone will spend three quarters of the year with her and one quarter with her husband in the underworld. Loss itself provides the occasion for the story's inception. In this case, the story of mother and daughter depends on Hades, the male figure whose intervention constitutes the disruption which prompts the narrative. It is only when Hades abducts Persephone that mother and daughter enter time: Demeter becomes an old woman as Persephone reaches maturity. Simultaneously, seasonal growth and agriculture begin for humans. Loss is presented as inevitable, part of the natural sequence of growth, but, since time is cyclical, mother-daughter reunion forms a natural part of the cycle. In ancient times, the mysteries at Eleusis celebrated this mother-daughter connection as the union of light and darkness, life and death, death and rebirth (see Jung and Kerenyi; Kerenyi; Arthur).[5] The hymn itself, however, grants legitimacy to the mother's feelings of bereavement, anger, and wild desire, even as it insists on the inevitability and the necessity of separation. Its cyclicality offers an alternative to oedipal narratives structured according to principles of linear repetition. The "Hymn to Demeter" thus both inscribes the story of mother and daughter within patriarchal reality and allows it to mark a feminine difference. Hades occasions both the separation and a narrative which will repair the breech.

Toni Morrison's Sethe, the maternal protagonist of her 1987 novel, *Beloved,* is neither the silent Jocasta nor the powerful Demeter. Like the Oedipus story, however, Morrison's novel is about the murdered child, a daughter, returning from the other side to question the mother, and, like the story of Demeter and Persephone, it is about a temporary, perhaps a cyclical, reunion between mother and daughter. Yet Morrison's novel, unlike the Oedipus story, *begins* with the mother, and allows *her* to *tell* her tale, to attempt to explain her incomprehensible act.

Like the "Hymn," the mother-daughter story in Morrison's *Beloved* depends on male intervention to occasion the narrative. Returning after an eighteen-year absence, Paul D. disrupts the uneasy household in which Sethe, the mother, and Denver, the daughter, coexist with the ghost of Sethe's murdered baby daughter. His presence makes it possible for Sethe to tell the story of motherhood under slavery, a story by which she has been obsessed for the eighteen years following her escape.

Familial structures in this novel are profoundly distorted by the institution of slavery. The action begins in 1871 in Cincinnati, and returns, through flashbacks, to the Mississippi slave plantation ironically called "Sweet Home." Sethe herself spoke to her own mother only once, and, when she saw her hanged one morning, was not allowed to check for the mark by means of which she might have been able to recognize her definitively as her mother. Sethe is permanently separated from her husband Halle and separates herself from her own children when she sends them ahead to freedom. In a slave economy in which even one's own body is not one's property, the white masters can rob Sethe of everything, including her mother's milk. It is no surprise, then, that the inhabitants of 124 Bluestone Road do not constitute a nuclear family that might fit Freudian paradigms. Morrison underscores this incongruity when she insists on the 124 (the novel's first words): triangles are repeatedly broken up as a *fourth* term either supplements or replaces the third. Sethe, her daughter Denver, and the grandmother Baby Suggs are joined by the ghost; after the grandmother's death, Sethe, Denver, and the ghost are joined by Paul D.; and, after the ghost is chased off, Sethe, Denver, and Paul D., whose shadows on the road do form a triangle, are quickly joined by the ghostly Beloved who thoroughly disrupts any possible nuclear configuration.

In Morrison's novel, the economy of slavery circumscribes not only the process of individuation and subject-formation, but also heightens and intensifies the experience of motherhood—of connection and separation. It raises questions about what it means to have a self and to give that self away. It raises questions about what *family* means and about the ways in which nuclear configurations (dominant in the master culture) prevail as points of reference even in economies in which they are thoroughly distorted and disrupted. If mothers cannot "own" their children or even themselves, they experience separation and loss all the more intensely.

Largely female, Sethe's family is determined by the dynamics of the relationships among the women: the husband Halle never makes it to freedom and the two boys leave before the novel begins. The passionate interaction is between the mother and the two daughters, one of whom is killed while the other survives, and between the sisters, one of whom drank the other's blood with her mother's milk. The intensity of the women's passion becomes so stifling as to threaten paralysis. At such moments, Paul D. comes in to make the story move along, but, until the last scene, he is consistently excluded from the power of their interconnection.

Sethe's murder of her as yet unnamed baby girl (whose milk had already been taken by the white masters at "Sweet Home" and who, along with her three siblings, was about to be returned into slavery), and Sethe's own attempts to explain it—to Paul D., to herself, to Denver, and to Beloved—are at the core of the novel. "The truth was simple," Sethe insists. "I took and put my babies where they'd be safe." Sethe's own insistence that "she had done right because it came from true love" (251) and other characters' judgments of her mother-love as "too thick" or "wrong" suggest the moral complexity of the act, and demand that we examine our notion of mother-love, along with the value of life and self-possession.[6] The novel contains more than judgment: it contains the stories that precede and follow judgment, the stories that form and surround the relationship of mother and daughter during slavery and in post-abolition times. It contains stories both of maternal sorrow, guilt, and pain and of maternal joy and pleasure. As long as she can continue telling her stories and explaining her actions, the relationship continues: "It was as though Sethe didn't really want forgiveness given; she wanted it refused. And Beloved helped her out" (252).

But, just as for Demeter and Persephone, separation and loss are inevitable; Beloved must return to the dark side from which she came. The doubly bereaved Sethe, nursed back to life by the other daughter Denver, is ultimately comforted by Paul D. who "wants to put his story next to hers" (273). In response to her self-effacing "She was my best thing," he insists: "You your best thing, Sethe. You are." Holding her fingers, he enables Sethe to see herself as a subject, as a mother and a subject both. Her own subjectivity had been nurtured for a brief moment only (between her escape to freedom and the murder which was meant to preserve that freedom) and then abandoned by the shocked and disappointed mother-in-law, Baby Suggs. Now, holding Paul D.'s fingers, Sethe tentatively says "Me? Me?" Allowing a maternal voice and subjectivity to emerge, she questions, at least for a moment, the hierarchy of motherhood over selfhood on which her life had rested until that moment. The novel both explains and challenges that hierarchy.

Sethe's story, like Jocasta's (and like the story of slavery itself) is, as Morrison insists, "not a story to pass on," yet this novel does allow the mother to speak for herself, to speak her own name and the daughter's, to speak, after eighteen years, her unspeakable crime to her daughter. It allows Beloved to return, like Persephone, so that mother and daughter can speak to each other. And, it allows Sethe both to recognize Beloved as her child and to begin to recognize herself as "Me? Me?"

My book, *The Mother/Daughter Plot: Narrative, Psychoanalysis, Feminism*, traces the transformations, within narrative conventions, psychoanalytic theories, and feminist thinking, which enable the silent Jocasta gradually to give way to the vocal Sethe. Through the voices of daughters, speaking for their mothers, through the voices of mothers speaking for themselves and their daughters, and, eventually perhaps, through the voices of mothers and daughters speaking to each other, oedipal frameworks are modified by other psychological and narrative economies. Thus the plots of mothers and daughters do not remain unspeakable.

Mothers, Daughters, and Narrative

The Mother/Daughter Plot: Narrative, Psychoanalysis, Feminism is about Woman and about women, about the constructions of femininity in discourses of motherhood and daughterhood. In it I explore those discourses within the contexts of patriarchy as it "exists concretely, in social relations, and [as] it works precisely through the various discursive and representational structures that allow us to recognize it" (de Lauretis 165). In particular, I am interested in the texts of women writers who write within this Euro-American patriarchal context of discourse and representation and, more specifically, within a sex-gender system which, during much of the period *The Mother/Daughter Plot* covers, identifies writing as masculine and insists on the incompatibility of creativity and procreativity. These women write within literary conventions that define the feminine only in relation to the masculine, as object or obstacle. Female plots, as many feminist critics have demonstrated, act out the frustrations engendered by these limited possibilities and attempt to subvert the constraint of dominant patterns by means of various "emancipatory strategies"[7]—the revision of endings, beginnings, patterns of progression. This process of resistance, revision, and emancipation in the work of women writers is, as Nancy K. Miller has argued, a *feminist* act defining a *feminist* poetics and it needs to be identified as such.[8] In Miller's terms, then, the writers I study here are not only women writers marked biographically, by their biology and psychology, but *feminist* writers who define themselves by their dissenting relation to dominant tradition. Although I find Miller's definition of strategies of dissent extremely helpful, I prefer, in this book, to reserve the term *feminist* for an aesthetics connected to the feminist movement of active social resistance in the 1970s and '80s. For the earlier writers I discuss I use the less explicit terms *women's* or *female,* but would include in those terms the self-consciousness and resistance Miller identifies as feminist.[9] Because the writers I study are, for the most part, canonical and not forgotten women writers, they can illustrate the multiple and conflicting identifications engendered by women writers' place in hegemonic tradition—their predicaments of marginality and aspirations to centrality.[10] Yet that choice also erases other forms of difference—class, for example, certain racial differences, and generic differences, such as autobiography or popular fiction.

That choice is motivated by the fact that the novel is the optimal genre in which to study the interplay between hegemonic and dissenting voices. In recent years, narratologists have analyzed the novel's polyvocality, revealing the conflicting discourses that make possible, within the structures of the novel, the interrogation of dominant cultural codes and assumptions. Thus, the novel is at once, as Rachel Blau DuPlessis finds, "the place where ideology is coiled" (x) and the place where it can be called into question. I use the term ideology in the Althusserian sense of "the system of representations by which we imagine the world as it is" (Althusser 1977: 233; see also Althusser 1971; Belsey).

Especially in the nineteenth century the plot of heterosexual romance and marriage structures the novels of women writers, even if its conventional sequence is variously subverted.[11] By concentrating on the relationship between mothers and daughters, I interrogate and reframe these plot patterns in particular ways, discovering not only certain ideologies of maternity embedded within them, but also narrative patterns which call the more conventional constructions of the love plot into question. I have decided to use Freud's notion of a "Familienroman"—a "family romance"—as a controlling figure in these analyses.[12] In Freud's terms, the family romance is an imaginary interrogation of origins, an interrogation which embeds the engenderment of narrative within the experience of family. Through fantasy, the developing individual liberates himself from the constraints of family by imagining himself to be an orphan or a bastard and his "real" parents to be more noble than the "foster" family in which he is growing up. The essence of the Freudian family romance is the imaginative act of replacing the parent (for boys clearly the father) with another, superior figure.

In using the term family romance, I retain Freudian definitions as reference points but reframe them to be more broadly applicable. My aim is to focus at once on the discursive and imaginative role that the family plays in our narratives and the particular shape and nature of familial structures in particular narratives and social contexts. The family romance describes the experience of familial structures as discursive: the family romance is the story we tell ourselves about the social and psychological reality of the family in which we find ourselves and about the patterns of desire that motivate the interaction among its members. The family romance thus combines and reveals as indistinguishable the psychological subjective experience of family and the process of narrative. As Julia Kristeva says: "Narrative is, in sum, the most elaborate kind of attempt, on the part of the speaking subject, after syntactic competence, to situate his or her self among his or her desires and their taboos, that is at the interior of the oedipal triangle" (165). The family romance is a structure of fantasy—the imaginary construction of plots according to principles of wish fulfilment. The notion of family romance can thus accommodate the discrepancies between *social reality* and *fantasy construction,* which are basic to the experience and the institution of family.

Although Freud defines a particular shape of the family romance as universal, I find biases, both androcentric and ethnocentric, in his definition. I argue that patterns of family romance can and do vary, for male and female writers, during different periods and for different cultural traditions.[13] *The Mother/Daughter Plot* traces some of the variations family romances have undergone in a number of nineteenth and twentieth-century texts. Yet, even the variations I have found follow certain circumscribed patterns. By replaying classic mythic paradigms which serve as their models (Electra, Antigone, and Demeter), and which I discuss in some detail in *The Mother/Daughter Plot's* Prelude, these alternate plot patterns go beyond Oedipus, yet show that variations of the family romance in the Western European and North American novel are, in many ways, still classic ones. If the Freudian family romance reflects not only psychologically valid patterns but also, as I argue, the patterns of nineteenth- and twentieth-century fictional plots, then female and feminist family romances necessarily situate themselves in a revisionary relationship to the Freudian pattern, with the fictional heroine often having to occupy both the position of subject and that of object in the narrative. Revisions reframe the basic paradigm to include the stories of daughters and eventually also the stories of mothers, but, ultimately, they do not entirely reframe the basic conception of family as static structure, of the relationship of familial patterns and narrative patterns, of triangles as fundamental figures in familial interaction. This book explores, then, both the potentials and the limitations of certain psychoanalytic terms and concepts for a feminist analysis of women's writing and the persistent adherence of women's plots to the terms identified in classical mythology and psychoanalytic theory.[14]

By using the notion of family romance, I treat both motherhood and daughterhood as *story*—as narrative representation of social and subjective reality and of literary convention. I would argue that in conventional nineteenth-century plots of the European and American tradition the fantasy that controls the female family romance is the desire for the heroine's singularity based on a disidentification from the fate of other women, especially mothers. In modernist plots, this wish is supplemented by the heroines' artistic ambitions and the desire for distinction which now, however, needs to include affiliations with both male and female models. In post-modernist plots, other fantasies of a more multiple relational identity emerge, including the stories of mothers who by definition are entangled in relations which define and circumscribe all further desire. All of these variations, however, are based on the heroines' refusal of conventional heterosexual romance and marriage plots and, furthermore, on their disidentification from conventional constructions of femininity. Mothers—the ones who are not singular, who did succumb to convention inasmuch as they are mothers—thereby become the targets of this process of disidentification and the primary negative models for the daughter. At the same time, however, mothers and other women increasingly appear in these novels as alternate objects of desire, suggesting other possible subjective economies based in women's relationships. Eventually, mothers begin to appear as subjects.

The notion of family romance, extrapolated from Freudian definitions and extended beyond them, can account for the ambivalences and duplicities contained in the fantasy of difference and singularity, the pull toward complicity, and the difficulties of dissent. It accounts for the process of "becoming-woman," of en-genderment, which is intimately tied to the process of transmission and the relationship to previous and subsequent generations of women. It traces both the story of women's "consent to" and dissent from "femininity" [de Lauretis], and the process of what Althusser has called "interpellation"[15] and the process of conscious resistance against it. And, as subsequent chapters in *The Mother/Daughter Plot* will demonstrate, the structure of family romance, with its conjunction of desire and narrative, is operative both in fictional and in theoretical writings, including, of course, my own book.

I realize that my own relationship to psychoanalytic terms and concepts, and to certain familial patterns and fantasies, is an ambivalent one. Although I question the flexibility of psychoanalytic frameworks, I do so, for the most part, from within them, keenly aware of their compelling usefulness for feminist analysis of femininity as culturally constructed and internalized by individual female subjects. This section's [in *The Mother/Daughter Plot*] very subtitle, for example—"Mothers, Daughters, and Narrative"—repeats the triangular structure of the nuclear family, with narrative occupying the place of the paternal. *The Mother/Daughter Plot's* structure is also tripartite. At the same time, the book longs for other economies and other figures. It longs for a space in which maternal subjectivities could be articulated and for the means of politicizing the psychological and the familial; both of these goals conflict with some basic psychoanalytic assumptions. I believe that the tension introduced by this ambivalence motivates the book's dynamic progression in ways that are both conscious and unconscious. The strategy of reading theoretical texts as fictions and of reading theoretical fictions along with literary ones, moreover, has the effect of allowing them to illuminate each other so that they can reveal deeper cultural desires in given historical moments.

It is essential for feminists to be aware of the pervasiveness of familial metaphors and of the family as vantage point in our culture and in its analytic methodologies. Whether feminist theorizing should go beyond the family to other relational models is a question of crucial importance. I am well aware that *The Mother/Daughter Plot* remains firmly rooted within familial ideologies. I believe that before the familial can be transcended or left behind, all positions within the family must be probed from all directions, including that of mothers and daughters. Yet, the fundamental question that underlies these individual analyses is whether it is possible to arrive at a genuine critique of psychoanalytic assumptions and of familial ideologies from a vantage point which, of necessity, shares even some of these assumptions.

In *The Mother/Daughter Plot* these questions are posed in relation to maternal discourse. I believe that a thorough transformation of basic conceptual paradigms from a feminist perspective needs to include all women, mothers as well as daughters. Yet I find that while psychoanalytic feminism can add the female child to the male, allowing women to speak as daughters, it has difficulty accounting for the experience and the voice of the adult woman who is a mother. Like all psychoanalyses it is so profoundly child-centered that it has difficulty, even more generally, theorizing, beyond childhood, the experience of adulthood. But, so long as the figure of the mother is excluded from theory *psychoanalytic feminism* cannot become a *feminist psychoanalysis.*

Because of its concentration on mothers as well as on women and daughters, my argument offers a particular vantage point within the current debate among feminists about the female subject and the meaning of femininity.[16] First, by distinguishing between female positions—childless woman and mother, mother and daughter—it challenges the notion of woman as a singular, unified, transparent category. The multiplicity of "women" is nowhere more obvious than for the figure of the mother, who is always both mother and daughter. Her representation is controlled by her object status, but her discourse, when it is voiced, moves her from object to subject. But, as long as she speaks as mother, she must always remain the object in her child's process of subject-formation; she is never fully a subject. Second, the figure of mother is determined by her body more intensely than the figure of woman. By taking on the notion of essentialism so directly   maternity, inasmuch as it is represented as biological, poses the question of the body as pointedly as is possible—*The Mother/Daughter Plot* is able to look again at what feminists have hidden from view in both assertions and rejections of essentialism. It is easy to grant that neither sex nor gender can be invoked as fixed or unproblematic categories. It is more difficult to assert that reproduction provides a radical arena of *difference* and more than merely biological difference—and that it thereby challenges a positional, destabilized view of sex and gender more than perhaps anything else. The perspective of the maternal makes it difficult simply to reject the notion of biology and forces us to engage both the meaning of the body and the risks of what has been characterized as essentialist. This is equally true for adoptive mothers whose bodies, I would argue, are equally engaged in the process of mothering although they have not given birth to children. Third, the focus on mothers and daughters redefines the notion of difference. Difference here is not merely gender difference. It encompasses the (maternal) difference within the feminine and the multiple differences within the maternal, the differences among women, the individual woman's difference from Woman and even from other women, and the difference of maternal plots and stories from conventional romance plots. *What is a mother?* and *what is maternal?* are questions that underlie every page of this book without ever being answered directly. In fact, I generally prefer the adjectival term "maternal" because it signals that there is no transparent meaning of the concept. In the chapters that follow, moreover, I take neither the notion of "experience" nor that of "identity" as given, but find that the focus on the maternal makes it imperative to use and to attempt to theorize both.

These questions of definition—of motherhood, experience, and identity in rela-tion to sex and gender—have acquired particular urgency throughout the time of my work on in *The Mother/Daughter Plot*, and especially recently, in connection to the feminist debates over reproductive technologies. I believe that feminists need to clarify their positions on motherhood, particularly at a moment when science and the legal system are themselves engaged in a process of charting the definitions and rights of children, fathers, and mothers. The Baby M case, for example, has forced feminists to scrutinize their most fundamental assumptions as they confront impossible decisions: between Mary Beth Whitehead, the birth mother (or the surrogate, the natural, the contract mother, depending on which position one takes) and Elizabeth Stern, the wife of the biological father (the adop-tive mother, or the surrogate mother); between the rights of biological mothers and of biological fathers; between the "best interests" of children, or the "best interests" of mothers. The questions raised by this one case represent the most basic clash between biology and law, essentialism and constructivism. And as we begin to take into account the economic conditions of the Sterns and Whitehead, and of the lawyers who benefit from the legal confusions concerning the definition of maternity, we confront the variables of income level and class as they impinge on conceptual systems and social realities (see Chesler). As feminists try to decide about more complex technologies, such as in vitro fertilization, other variables intrude and other forms of oppression and appropriation become possible—poor and third world women renting their wombs to rich, first world women, for example. What does the term *mother,* what does the term *father* mean in this context? And how do these terms relate to bodies which are being transformed through technology, to laws which displace those bodies, to experiences displaced by these laws? Although it is unlikely that feminists will reach a comfortable consensus on these issues, it is crucial that we understand the terms of the argument, and to do so we must scrutinize motherhood from personal, subjective, legal, psychological, biological, economic, historical, and technological vantage points.

After a discussion of mythic "Origins and Paradigms" in the *The Mother/Daughter Plot's* Prelude, I start my analysis with the work of nineteenth-century women writers because I believe that motherhood as a concept is historically determined in ways that are parallel to the notion of childhood. As Ann Dally argues: "There have always been mothers, but motherhood was invented" (17; see also Badinter; Ehrenreich and English; Aries; O'Brien; Maroney). She cites 1597 as the first entry for "motherhood" in the *Oxford English Dictionary,* and then only as fact rather than ideology. The ideology of motherhood as the ideal of femininity coincides with the institutionalization of childhood during the eighteenth and nineteenth centuries. As representations of the child's vulnerability and need for nurturing and protection became more prominent, motherhood became an "instinct," a "natural" role and form of human connection, as well as a practice. As the private sphere was isolated from the public under industrial capitalism, and as women became identified with and enclosed within the private sphere, motherhood elevated middle-class and upper-class women into a position of increased personal status, if decreased social power. In a largely technological and impersonal public world, motherhood came to represent, as Elisabeth Badinter puts it, "a repository of society's idealism" (180); it became the force of conservation of traditional values. The focus of this ideology of the maternal, however, was not the *mother* but the *child,* that delicate and vulnerable organic being who required complete devotion and attention. Theories of child development and education, from Rousseau's work on, contain conflicting notions of the child's "best interests"—on the one hand, the "natural" mother-child connection, on the other, professional, often male-devised, educational strategies. In either case, however, the maternal role was figured in ways that are ultimately debilitating to women—equally so to those women who could afford to try to live up to the social ideal of maternity and to those who because of economic necessity could not. The mother became either the object of idealization and nostalgia or that which had to be rejected and surpassed in favor of allegiance to a morally and intellectually superior male world.

Notes

[1] See Susan Gubar's discussion of the poem in her article, "Mother, Maiden and the Marriage of Death: Women Writers and an Ancient Myth." See also DuPlessis (130).

[2] In Muriel Rukeyser's *The Green Wave.* I am grateful to Kate Daniels for bringing

this poem to my attention.

[3]See Erlich: "Whatever the reason, the 'oedipal mother' in Freud's early works is a static figure, a Jocasta who unknowingly plays out her destiny while Laius springs back to life" (284).

[4]To read the works of Afro-American writers within the contexts of a tradition shaped by the texts of Greek mythology is indeed to make very large claims for the influence of this tradition. I discuss this methodological problem in *The Mother/Daughter Plot*'s Prelude. Yet, I am convinced that in *Beloved* Morrison uses Oedipus and Demeter as intertexts which serve to confront a Western notion of family with the realities of a slave economy which served both to support and to distort that notion. Other intertexts come to mind, as well—the separation of Iphigenia and Clytemnestra, or the closeness of Ruth and Naomi which parallels the connection between Sethe and her mother-in-law, Baby Suggs.

[5]Helene Foley has been an invaluable resource in relation to all my discussions of classical texts.

[6]Carol Gilligan argues that women tend to construct moral dilemmas more contextually than men do.

[7]The term is Patricia Yaeger's in *Honey-Mad Women: Emancipatory Strategies in Women's Fiction*.

[8]The strategies Miller labels as feminist are: the self-consciousness about women's identity both as cultural fiction and as a process of social construction; the claim for the heroine's singularity; the contestation of available plots of female development and their revision; and the figuration of the existence of other subjective economies (see Miller 8). Elaine Showalter uses the terms *female, feminine,* and *feminist* to mark a historical progression. See also DuPlessis for a definition closer to Miller's: "These writers are 'feminist' because they construct a variety of oppositional strategies to the depiction of gender institution in narrative" (34).

[9]Following the constraints of the English language, I use the term *female* throughout this book and I connect it to cultural construction and not just to biology; I reserve the term *feminine* for more conventional notions of *femininity,* however.

[10]This is what Sandra Gilbert and Susan Gubar have called the "complex female affiliation complex." See "'Forward into the Past': The Female Affiliation Complex," in *No Man's Land: The Place of the Woman Writer in the Twentieth Century*.

[11]For an analysis of this dominant plot, see Boone.

[12]See "Family Romances" *The Standard Edition of the Complete Works of Sigmund Freud*. I discuss this essay in detail in Chapter 1 of *The Mother/Daughter Plot*.

[13]For a different feminist reading of the novel as family romance, see van Boheemen. Van Boheemen argues against the possibility of female or feminist transformations of family romance patterns, asserting that "the novel is the instrument of patriarchy, giving presence to its predominance in the act of utterance" (33).

[14]Deleuze and Guattari identify and criticize the "imperialism of Oedipus," arguing that the familial triangle has reached the status of the dominant signifying structure in Western thinking. Their far-reaching critique of familial ideologies is not, however, based on a gender analysis.

[15]Althusser says that "the individual is *interpellated as a (free) subject in order that he shall ... (freely) accept his subjection,*" in *Lenin and Philosophy* (169, emphasis in original).

[16]For a concise introduction to that debate, see the discussion between Nancy K. Miller and Peggy Kamuf in *Diacritics* 12 (Summer 1982): 42-53.

References

Althusser, Louis. *For Marx.* Trans. Ben Brewster. London: New Left Books, 1977.

Althusser, Louis. "Ideology and Ideological State Apparatuses (Notes toward an Investigation)." *Lenin and Philosophy and Other Essays* Trans. Ben Brewster. London: New Left Books, 1971.

Aries, Phillippe. *Centuries of Childhood.* London: Cape, 1962.

Arthur, Marylin. "Politics and Pomegranates: An Interpretation of the Homeric Hymn to Demeter." *Arethusa* 10 (1977): 7-47.

Badinter, Elisabeth. *Mother Love: Myth and Reality.* New York: Macmillan, 1981.

Belsey, Catherine "Constructing the Subject: Deconstructing the Text." *Feminist Criticism and Social Change.* Eds. Judith Newton and Deborah Rosenfelt. New York: Methuen, 1985.

Boone, Joseph Allen. *Tradition Counter Tradition: Love and the Form of Fiction.* Chicago: University of Chicago Press, 1987.

Chase, Cynthia. "Oedipal Textuality: Reading Freud's Reading of Oedipus." *Decomposing Figures.* Baltimore: Johns Hopkins University Press, 1986.

Chesler, Phyllis. *Sacred Bond.* New York: Times Books, 1988.

Cixous, Helene. *Le Nom d'Oedipe: Chant du corps interdit.* Paris: des femmes, 1978. Music by Andre Boucourechliev.

Dally, Ann. *Inventing Motherhood: The Consequences of an Ideal.* New York: Schocken, 1983.

de Lauretis, Teresa. *Alice Doesn't: Feminism, Semiotics, Cinema.* Bloomington: Indiana University Press, 1984.

Deleuze, Gilles and Felix Guattari. *Anti-Oedipus: Capitalism and Schizophrenia.* Trans. Robert Hurley, Mark Seem, and Helen R. Lane. Minneapolis: University of Minnesota Press, 1983.

Devereux, George. "Why Oedipus Killed Laius." *International Journal of Psychoanalysis* 34 (1951): 132-141.

DuPlessis, Rachel Blau. *Writing beyond the Ending: Narrative Strategies of Twentieth-Century Women Writers.* Bloomington: Indiana University Press, 1985.

Ehrenreich, Barbara and Deirdre English. *For Her Own Good: 150 Years of the Experts' Advice to Women.* Garden City, NY: Anchor, 1978.

Erlich, Iza. "What Happened to Jocasta?" *Bulletin of the Menninger Clinic* 41(May 1977): 280-284.

Freud, Sigmund. Family Romances" ("Der Familienroman der Neurotiker"). 1908. *The Standard Edition of the Complete Works of Sigmund Freud.* Vol. 9. Ed. and trans. James Strachey. London: Hogarth Press, 1953. 237-241.

Gilbert, Sandra and Susan Gubar. *No Man's Land: The Place of the Woman Writer in the Twentieth Century.* New Haven: Yale University Press, 1988.

Gilligan, Carol. *In a Different Voice: Psychological Theory and Women's Development.* Cambridge: Harvard University Press, 1982.

Goodhart, Sandor. "Oedipus and Laius's Many Murderers." *Diacritics* 8 (Spring 1978): 55-71.

Gubar, Susan. "Mother, Maiden and the Marriage of Death: Women Writers and an Ancient Myth." *Women's Studies: An Interdisciplinary Journal* 6 (1979): 301-315.

"Hymn to Demeter." *The Homeric Hymns.* Trans. and ed. Apostolos N. Athanassakis. Baltimore: Johns Hopkins University Press, 1976.

Jung, C. G. and C. Kerenyi. *Essays on a Science of Mythology: The Myths of the Divine Child and the Divine Maiden.* New York: Harper Torchbooks, 1963.

Kahn, Coppelia. "The Hand that Rocks the Cradle: Recent Gender Theories and their Implications." *The (M)Other Tongue: Essays in Feminist Psychoanalytic Interpretation.* Eds. Shirley Nelson Garner, Claire Kahane, and Madelon Sprengnether. Ithaca: Cornell University Press, 1985.

Kerenyi, C. *Eleusis: Archetypal Image of Mother and Daughter.* New York: Schocken, 1977.

Kristeva, Julia. *Powers of Horror: An Essay on Abjection.* Trans. Léon Roudiez. New York: Columbia University Press, 1982.

Licht, Hans. *Sexual Life in Ancient Greece.* London: Routledge and Kegan Paul, 1932.

Maroney, Heather Jon. "Embracing Motherhood: New Feminist Theory." *The Politics of Diversity.* Eds. Roberta Hamilton and Michele Barrett. London: Verso, 1986.

Miller, Nancy K. *Subject to Change: Reading Feminist Writing.* New York: Columbia University Press, 1988.

Morrison, Toni. *Beloved.* New York: Alfred A. Knopf, 1987.

O'Brien, Mary. *The Politics of Reproduction.* London: Routledge and Kegan Paul, 1981.

Rukeyser, Muriel. *The Green Wave.* New York: Doubleday, 1948.

Showalter, Elaine. *A Literature of Their Own: British Women Novelists from Bronte to Lessing.* Princeton: Princeton University Press, 1977.

Sophocles, *Oedipus Rex.* Trans. E. F. Watling. New York: Penguin Books, 1947.

Stewart, Harold. "Jocasta's Crimes." *International Journal of Psychoanalysis* 4 (1961): 424-430.

Swan, Jim. "Mater and Nannie: Freud's Two Mothers and the Discovery of the Oedipus Complex." *American Imago* 31 (1974): 1-64.

van Boheemen, Christine. *The Novel as Family Romance: Language, Gender and Authority from Fielding to Joyce.* Ithaca: Cornell University Press, 1987.

Vernant, Jean-Pierre. "Ambiguity and Reversal: On the Enigmatic Structure of *Oedipus Rex.*" *New Literary History* 9 (1978): 475-501.

Yaeger, Patricia. *Honey-Mad Women: Emancipatory Strategies in Women's Fiction.* New York: Columbia University Press, 1987.

Chapter 16

Prelude

Origins and Paradigms

MARIANNE HIRSCH

With some additions or subtractions, our imaginary still functions according to the patterns established through Greek mythologies and tragedies.   —Luce Irigaray

It was for Greece you gave me birth, not for yourself alone.
        —Euripides

Our family is in fact constituted by and in the general movement of History, but is experienced, on the other hand, as an absolute in the depths and opaqueness of childhood.
        —Jean-Paul Sartre

"WHEN FREUD DESCRIBES and theorizes … in *Totem and Taboo,* the murder of the father as the foundation of the primitive horde," says Luce Irigaray, "he forgets a more archaic murder, that of the woman-mother, necessitated by the establishment of a certain order in the city" (1981: 15, *my translation*).[1] For Irigaray, this mythic matricide, represented by the murder of Clytemnestra in Greek mythology, is the founding moment of civilization under paternal law. This moment is still timely today, she insists, for "mythology has not changed" (17).

It is significant that Freud chose Oedipus as the privileged paradigmatic representation of individual maturation in the context of familial structures as the paradigm for his family romance. The Oedipus story is the story of the *son's* relation to father and mother, male and female origin. To find the story of the *daughter* and the *mother,* alternative mythologies—female counterparts to Oedipus—with equal power and resonance, with equal presence in the work of modern writers, can indeed be discussed. And they do suggest alternate patterns of development, as well as alternate narrative patterns. Electra and Antigone, for example, function as particularly vital models for nineteenth-century representations of female development and female heroism. In the modernist period, the story of Demeter and Persephone enables the outlines of a different female family romance. And the figures of Jocasta, Clytemnestra, and Demeter suggest some reasons for the absence of a maternal subjectivity in contemporary feminist fiction. They begin to clarify the complicated shapes of a feminist family romance that moves only with difficulty from a daughterly to a maternal focus.

The classical paradigms I discuss briefly in this Prelude belong firmly to the tradition of Western patriarchy. To place them in such a prominent place in relation to fictions written by women writers many hundreds of years later, in cultures structured both similarly and differently from the ones that produced them, might seem to grant them too great an influence. It might seem, moreover, to predetermine the outcome of my exploration into feminocentric plot patterns, just as Freud might be said to have predetermined his theory by highlighting Oedipus. Yet I find not only that certain limited familial and narrative patterns do tend to predominate and to continue to inform modern writing, but also that they help to explain how, on the one hand, female difference is inscribed and attempted, and how, on the other, it can easily be subverted by a repetition of the same. The following discussion of classical texts, then, is both my recognition of their hegemonic power, their delimiting force, and my tribute to their explanatory potential. At the same time, these classic myths are seriously insufficient as paradigms for female and feminist plotting, especially as far as post-modernist fiction is concerned. As the book progresses, for example, I find a greater focus on women's relations to one another, on the relations of mothers, daughters, sisters, and friends, and much less emphasis on fathers, brothers, and husbands. Whereas the classical texts I analyze can illuminate some aspects of those female relationships, they are totally irrelevant to others. As I discuss the works of Afro-American women writers, in particular, the classical frameworks become more problematic. The familial structures which emerge from African traditions and from slave economies and which develop in the contexts of urban and rural poverty in the United States create different inflections in the plots of writers such as Toni Morrison and Alice Walker.[2] Yet, surprisingly, classic Western structures still serve as frames of reference even here, if only to be modified, reconstructed, and transformed; Morrison's play with oedipal triangles in *Beloved* is a good example of the power of classical paradigms. My intention is to let this discussion of origins stand here as a pre-text, a pre-figuration of *The Mother/Daughter Plot's* argument, a moment to return to and to depart from in the search for a female/feminist textuality that struggles toward and begins to define difference. Having it here, at the beginning, permits me to confront in a very direct way the problematic nature of "the classics" and "the tradition" in relation to a group of women writers who stand both inside and outside it, who both collude with it and contest it to various degrees.

Two classical Greek paradigms, the story of Clytemnestra and Electra and the story of Antigone, can help to define the parameters of the Victorian heroine's female family romance. Both are stories of daughters and fathers, sisters and brothers. Whereas Electra underwrites paternal law, Antigone rebels against the personal consequences of paternal and patriarchal identification and seems to uphold an alternative value structure. On closer analysis, however, it becomes obvious that both of these family romance models are based on maternal and sisterly repression and that Electra and Antigone represent not opposing but structurally quite similar options. And both had particular resonance during the Victorian period, offering models of female heroism at a moment of restricted social and economic opportunity and of severely limited legal rights for women.

For Luce Irigaray, the murder of Clytemnestra is the mythic representation of the mother's exclusion from culture and the symbolic order. Clytemnestra, Irigaray suggests, must be killed because she is not the virgin mother who had become a cultural ideal: she is passionate and sexual, she is guilty of having murdered her husband, and, worst of all, she is politically active and aware. In Aeschylus's *Oresteia,* the son who kills her is acquitted. With Athena's help Apollo denies the mother's procreative role: "The mother is not the true parent of the child / which is called hers. She is a nurse who tends the growth / of young seed planted by its true parent, the male.[3] Although Orestes, the son, actually commits matricide, and although he does so by the command of another son, Apollo, whose oracle Orestes has no choice but to obey, the passion and energy behind both the murder and the judgment belong to daughters, Electra and Athena. Both identify with and uphold a paternal law; both are, as Clytemnestra asserts in Euripides' *Electra* "daughters of the father." In fact, Electra, becomes heroic by conceiving and participating in an unspeakable crime—matricide.[4]

Whereas Athena, daughter of a divine father, exemplifies both the power that can come to the daughter from paternal identification—wisdom and victory in war, and the price—virginity and childlessness—Electra, the human father's daughter, suffers instead the ambiguities that come with paternal allegiance.[5] Electra's participation in her mother's murder is motivated not by an oracular decree but by an intense personal hatred of Clytemnestra and by an undying loyalty to Agamemnon. As Virginia Woolf suggests, "Clytemnestra and Electra are mother and daughter and therefore should have some sympathy, though perhaps sympathy gone wrong breeds the fiercest hate. E. is the type of woman who upholds the family above everything; the father. She has more veneration for tradition than the sons of the house; feels herself born of the father's side and not of the mother's" (5). In Sophocles' *Electra,* especially, the scenes between mother and daughter highlight their lack of sympathy. Electra accuses Clytemnestra of sexual betrayal, of hunger for power manifested in her marriage to a weaker man, and of non-maternal behavior toward herself and Orestes. She presents herself as everything her mother is not: she is a virgin, she is maternal to her brother, even while remaining submissive to him. Yet this polarity and this antagonism cannot disguise the profound similarity between mother and daughter, the strength of character and the rebelliousness they share. Equally similar are the conflicts they initially face—between *oikos* and *polis,* between familial values and allegiances to the state. As Woolf suggested, however, filial piety and official loyalty are indistinguishable in Electra's allegiance to her dead father. The need for loyalty to Clytemnestra has been eliminated: the agent of death, she is no longer maternal; as ruler of Athens and wife to Aegistus, she no longer represents the private. The two sides of Electra's dilemma have been subsumed into one: Agamemnon and Orestes have absorbed her divided loyalties erasing the influence of her mother and sister in the process.

Electra's lack of sympathy for the mother's choices and values emerges most clearly in relation to Clytemnestra's justification for the murder of her husband, i.e., vengeance for his sacrificial killing of her oldest daughter, Iphigenia. Electra, like Iphigenia herself, accepts this murder as necessary for the state, identifying completely with her father's discourse. In failing to understand her mother's outrage, and in justifying her sister's murder, Electra underwrites paternal law and male supremacy, as well as female antagonism, competition, and powerlessness. In planning the murder of her mother, in refusing to bond with her more conventional sister Chrysothemis, Electra eliminates the possibility for women to challenge the paternal order and perpetuates a sexual division of labor by which she can act only through her brother.

Electra may plot, but it is Orestes who commits the murder. He stands trial, is acquitted, and goes on to found a new public order. In both Sophocles' and Euripides' plays, Electra is featured on stage as her brother commits the murder off-stage. The emotion is hers; the action, his. In order to live her choice of paternal allegiance, Electra needs her brother to complement her intention, to carry out her plan, and to fulfill the emotional needs that result from her repudiation of mother and sister. Condemned to virginity, Electra needs Orestes to function in the roles of both lover and child; only with him can she act out the familial implications of the female posture she has adopted. Thus her fraternal love isolates her, excluding her from the possibility of becoming a mother and from any possible continuity.[6] Irigaray suggests that while the son/brother is saved from his madness, the daughter/sister is destined to remain mad (17). Although Euripides offers Electra a future in the marriage to Pilades, this different ending fails to present an alternative to what Irigaray calls Electra's "madness."

Euripides' *Electra* does contain a subtext of mother-daughter sympathy, a brief moment of caring and understanding between them and a moment of regret on Electra's part: "Weep greatly for me, my brother, I am guilty./ A girl flaming in hurt I marched against/the mother who bore me..." (ll. 1183-85). Unlike Sophocles' Electra, Euripides' perceives the tragedy of her separation from her mother; as she kneels to cover her mother's dead body, she exclaims: "Behold! I wrap her close in the robe,/ the one I loved and could not love" (ll. 1230-31). Yet Pilades is Orestes' friend and, by marrying him, Electra further strengthens her alliance with her brother and her separation from sister and mother.

In her reading of the *Oresteia,* Mary O'Brien has argued that Aeschylus negates femininity in the motherlessness of Athena, in the transformation of Clytemnestra into an agent of death rather than life, and in the banishment of the Furies. Thus he can prove that male supremacy, that male control of law and property are both factual and just. Denying the maternal, she claims, enables man to circumvent the danger posed by the uncertainty of paternity and to found a "second-nature bond"—a new political fraternity "predicated on the equality of death and a high and rational ethics of giving one's life for one's polity." It is this bond which Athena upholds, which Clytemnestra threatens, and which Electra envies (O'Brien 150-58).[7] Through Orestes and fraternal allegiance, Sophocles and Euripides allow Electra to gain access to this powerful political arena, if only indirectly and vicariously. Electra's choices—maternal repression and fraternal alliance—produce a female narrative that remains deeply embedded in and intertwined with a dominant and oppressive male plot. Here the father and brother, equivalent figures, subsume what initially appeared to be conflicting choices and values, and female heroism precludes any continuing bonding among women.

Irigaray sees Antigone as the woman whose absolute rebellion threatens the paternal order of the state, even if that rebellion results in her ostracism and death. For nineteenth-century writers, especially Hegel and Eliot, the play's conflict, which they read as a conflict between right and right, made Antigone the most tragic of tragic heroes: "Here lies the dramatic collision: the impulse of sisterly piety which allies itself with reverence for the Gods, clashes with the duties of citizenship; two principles, both having their validity, are at war with each other" (Eliot 263-64; see also Joseph; Steiner). According to Eliot, the struggle between Antigone and Creon amounts to a cosmic disorder, which leaves not only her culture but also Eliot's own in a permanent moral crisis, incapable of distinguishing between right and wrong. It is "that struggle between elemental tendencies and established laws by which the outer life of man is gradually and painfully being brought into harmony with his inward needs. Until this harmony is perfected, we shall never be able to attain a great right without also doing a wrong" (264). It is important to note, however, that this nineteenth-century reading offers an unorthodox interpretation of Sophocles' play in which Antigone's act of loyalty to her brother is upheld even by Haemon, her rejected husband-to-be. Irigaray's reading, for example, constitutes a serious critique of Eliot's and Hegel's formulations: she finds that the particular way they state the conflict in itself exacerbates Antigone's dilemma. Having her actions reduced to *either* loyalty to the family *or* obedience to the state locks her into a vascillation between two institutions which are, in fact, irredeemably patriarchal and from which the only escape is the execution/suicide she eventually chooses. Hegel's formulation inadvertently clarifies this—Antigone's ethical decision to bury Polyneices makes her into a sister, a woman who acknowledges her highest duty to the irreplaceable brother. Her desire for him is pure, free, and submissive, Hegel insists (see Hegel). The coincidence of the father and brother in the figure of Oedipus only underscores the closed system—the institutions of family and state—within which Antigone operates.

Unlike Electra, Antigone has no mother: her mother Jocasta killed herself after realizing that her husband was actually the son she had given away to be killed years before. Like Electra, Antigone rejects her more compliant and feminine sister Ismene. Unlike Electra, however, Antigone faces a choice: her brother and a seeming rejection of an autocratic patriarchal order, or her husband, the son of Creon, and an allegiance to the state. Antigone—daughter and sister of Oedipus whose exile she shares in *Oedipus at Colonus*, daughter and granddaughter of Jocasta—gives higher priority to her fraternal bond and to ancient burial laws. Her act amounts to a refusal of an exogamous marriage which could liberate her from the incestuous relationships within the family to which she remains undyingly loyal. In rejecting the laws of Creon's paternal state (Creon is the maternal uncle and thus the patriarch in the tale), and in affirming her familial/ maternal bond, Antigone will not be an object of exchange. She will not open herself to the guilt of Jocasta, that is, to bear children and risk further incest. Like Electra and unlike her mother, Antigone remains a virgin. Her loyalty is with the past, with what Creon contemptuously calls "woman's law" (l.524), with the brother she calls her "mother's son." "O but I would not have done the forbidden thing/ For any husband or for any son,/ For why? I could have had another husband/ And by him other sons, if one were lost;/ But father and mother lost, where would I get/ Another brother?" (Sophocles ll. 905-910).[8] Antigone's assertion of loyalty to Polyneices in *Antigone* follows her perfect fidelity to Oedipus in *Oedipus at Colonus*. Yet in what sense is this brother and this familial system truly an alternative to Creon's state?

Unlike Electra's action, Antigone's action in the play seems to present a serious challenge to the patriarchal state, an affirmation of past, familial, and private values over future and public ones, as well as a different narrative for women. It looks like an assertion of a female value system that stresses loyalty, fidelity, relationship over the expediencies demanded by Creon's politics.[9] Yet, as defiant as it might appear, and even though the play validates her choice, asserting that burial rites should not be legislated by the state, Antigone's bond with her brother does not pose an ultimate threat to a patriarchal order. That challenge can come only from the end of her tale, from the moment of her death, which motivates a succession of other suicides and spells the end of Creon's family. In reframing Antigone's conflict, in taking her position outside of the city walls to a place of what she chooses to see as potential female power, Irigaray wants to open the possibility of a new ethics among women, both vertically between mother and daughter, and horizontally among sisters, an ethics which for Antigone herself remains as unrealizable as it did for Electra (Irigaray 1984:113-15).

Electra and Antigone outline the bind in which the realist heroines I discuss in Chapters 1 and 2 are caught; as opposite as their choices may seem, both remain locked into two patriarchal institutions and separated from their female kin as long as they are alive. The plot patterns of Victorian heroines range between the parameters set by these two mythic figures, both daughters of fathers and sisters of brothers. Family loyalty in female family romances is motivated by the attempt to imagine a different plot for the heroine, outside of an economy in which women cannot be more than objects of exchange. This attempt leads Victorian heroines to enact either the matricide of Electra in support of patriarchal power, or the refusal and challenge of Antigone, still based on maternal repression. Women writers' attempts to imagine lives for their heroines which will be different from their mothers' make it imperative that mothers be silent or absent in their texts, that they remain in the prehistory of plot, fixed both as objects of desire and as examples not to be emulated. Like Clytemnestra or Jocasta, the mothers of Victorian fiction are profoundly compromised, whether they are submissive victims of the paternal system or rebellious challengers of it. Only fraternal bonds can promise to substitute for maternal support and to protect from paternal authority. Yet they too ultimately fail to live up to the promise of an alternative to women's position as object of exchange among men. Allegiance to fathers/brothers has the advantage of protecting heroines both from marriage and from maternity; the quasi-incestuous bonds that tend to take the place of romantic love and marriage cannot result in pregnancy and childbirth. But as they ally themselves with fathers and brothers, rather than mothers and sisters, nineteenth-century heroines remain isolated-from female companionship, from previous and subsequent generations of women. And because their "brothers" sometimes turn into the patriarchs from whom they were supposed to offer a refuge, the heroines' fate actually ends up, in some ways at least, duplicating that of their mothers. This, in fact, constitutes the nineteenth-century's repetition of classical plots of tragic heroism. In attempting to construct/imagine a different plot and a different economy, nineteenth-century women writers still duplicate the traditional story of what Teresa de Lauretis has called "women's consent to femininity." They thereby ally themselves with the "fathers" and "brothers" in their own literary tradition.

The emblematic example of the Demeter myth can serve to illustrate the complicated intersections of gender and plot exemplified in modernist fiction. This much earlier text, the Homeric "Hymn to Demeter," is indeed a mother-daughter narrative, not only the story of intense mother-daughter attachment and separation, but also the story of both the mother's and the daughter's reactions and responses. Its motifs—the pre-existence of timeless bliss vaguely identified with a matriarchal past, the descent to the underworld and the conflation of marriage and death, the connection of femininity with fertility and procreativity, the idealization of maternal power, the resolution of plot in cyclicity—carry a particular resonance for modernist writers. They connect to the images of Freudian psychoanalysis, such as the pre-oedipal, and to the anthropological and archaeological research of matriarchy theorists of the 1920s.

This unique mother-daughter narrative exists, however, only as a function of male intervention. Thus in the "Hymn to Demeter," a description of Persephone playing among the flowers precedes the actual inception of plot. The narrative and temporality itself only begin with Hades' intrusion and rape, with the abduction of the daughter from the mother. This initial distance illustrates quite clearly a particular dynamic of plotting prevalent for female as well as male writers, and present also in women's modernism. Peter Brooks outlines it as follows: "plot starts (or must give the illusion of starting) from the moment at which story, or 'life' is stimulated from quiescence into a state of narratability, into a tension, a kind of irritation, which demands narration" (103). The hymn seems to corroborate this insight: narrative demands some form of breech, some space of anxiety and desire into which to inscribe itself. The perpetuation of infantile plenitude, the blissful play among the flowers, it seems to suggest, cannot offer a model for plot. The story of mother and daughter comes into being only through the intervention of the father/husband who, here, does not occasion an irreparable separation but offers the occasion for narrative itself.

Yet, the progression of the plot and the cyclic solution that mother and daughter work out together in response to the patriarchal reality in which they live resolves this plot in a way that is quite unique. Demeter tries to regain what she has lost, to repair the breech, both by living out several different powerless human plots and by asserting her divine power over humans, by denying them grain and by causing irreparable destruction and the end of plot. Neither of these opposing strategies succeeds. The compromise solution, however, differs significantly from the linear, repetitive, and ultimately self-defeating plot structures exemplified by the stories of Electra and Antigone. This mother-daughter narrative is resolved through continued *opposition, interruption,* and *contradiction.* As we follow Persephone's return to her mother for one part of the year and her repeated descent to marriage and the underworld for the rest, we have to revise our very notion of resolution. At the end of the story, Persephone is both alive and dead, both young and old, both above and below the earth. She lives both symbiotically united to her mother and ineluctably distant from her. Her allegiance is split between mother and husband, her posture is dual. The repeated cycle relies neither on murder nor on reconciliation, but on continued opposition—what in psychoanalytic terms might be called "bi-sexual oscillation"—to sustain and perpetuate it. The pomegranate seed Persephone eats signals her allegiance to her husband, while the ritual and seasonal celebration of her reunion with Demeter signifies her continuing attachment to her mother, an attachment which turns into identification in those representations in which Persephone is no longer the maiden but herself the mother of Triptolemus.

The story of Demeter and Persephone does not simply reverse heterosexual plots of disconnection in favor of a model of female connection. More complicated affiliative patterns are revealed here, patterns which describe the affiliative intricacies of female modernism. Still, Demeter's plot which progresses through *contradiction* offers an alternative to the limiting repetitions and deathly closures of Electra and Antigone.

The "Hymn to Demeter" does grant voice and legitimacy not only to the daughter's but also to the mother's story. Nowhere, for example, does the poem question Demeter's right to be angry. Zeus's compromise and the Eleusinian mysteries which celebrate the cyclic reunion of mother and daughter do recognize the needs of the mother as well as those of the child. In the hymn, sung to the mother-goddess, the poet identifies with the mother, he recognizes and legitimates her anger and its expression, as long as it can be properly channeled, contained, and ritually resolved. Still, maternal anger, maternal responses to the process of mother-child separation, to the loss of a child, are represented as terribly threatening in this story. Any discussion of maternal subjectivity—the subject of Part 3 of *The Mother/Daugher Plot*—has to take into account the pervasive cultural fears contained in the powerful and angry figures of Demeter and Clytemnestra. The threatening figure of the angry mother dominates even feminist writing about the maternal and creates particular conflicts for maternal self-representation, especially within the context of a feminist moment which values female consensus, eschews female difference, and is suspicious of women's power. As I argue in Part 3 of *The Mother/Daugher Plot*, 1970s and early 1980s European and United States feminisms relate precisely in this manner to maternal subjectivity. A brief look at mythic representations of maternal power and maternal anger can set the stage for my later analysis of the peculiar distance between feminist discourse and maternal discourse.

Allowing us to see how Western culture imagines and represents the maternal, Clytemnestra and Demeter might serve as adult female counterparts to the Oedipal narrative—the story of maternal attachment and separation. The story of Clytemnestra, even more than that of the at least partially powerful Demeter, illustrates how Western culture represents the mother's position in a familial and social configuration in which women carry children in their bodies, give birth to them, and then relinquish them to a world in which they themselves are powerless to determine the course of their children's development. Separation between mothers and children is provoked by murder, abandonment, and betrayal and Clytemnestra's angry response offers an emblem of how culture deals with maternal rage. For, if the anger of Menelaus and, by extension, of Agamemnon (based on male rivalry over woman and on male bonding, its underside), stands at the origin of the war with Troy that initiates the legitimate battle of culture, and if the deathly anger of Orestes and Electra is exonerated by Apollo and Athena as a legitimate expression of filial loyalty to the father, then Clytemnestra's anger remains at the edge of legitimacy and of representation. As the Furies, the fearsome subterranean representatives of maternal rage, are transformed into a new Athenian law upholding paternal right, the mother is supplanted and the father comes to control the laws of justice and discourse.

Euripides' *Iphigenia in Aulis* begins with Agamemnon's conflict between love for his daughter and loyalty to his brother, to the state, and to the gods who demand Iphigenia's sacrifice. When the scene shifts to Clytemnestra, her manner of constructing her husband's moral dilemma gains our fullest sympathies. She is the mother who protects her child from the father's brutality and deceit. The child's loss is presented as a fate that cannot be evaded, but nonetheless it deeply wounds the deprived and abandoned mother. The bond between mother and child is subordinated to another order which has political primacy, but which is both emotionally and morally questionable. The mother herself is abandoned and betrayed by both husband and child: "Suppose, now, you're with the army,/ leaving me at home,/ And the slow months drag on, and you're still there at *Troy*, / What thoughts do you imagine will occupy my heart,/ When every chair I see will be empty of her,! Her bedroom empty; and I sit alone in *tears*/ Mourning for her, day in, day out? ... / In the gods' name, my husband, don't force me to *be*/ A disloyal wife to you; nor be disloyal yourself" (ll. 1171-83).

Whereas Aeschylus's Iphigenia is gagged and "struggling for voice" (l. 241), Euripides admits us to her moving dialogue with her mother, in which the submissive daughter comes to see her own death as necessary and attempts to pacify the protective angry mother. Subordinating her own life to the good of Greece, Iphigenia embraces the father's logic and abandons the maternal value structure which raises life above death, private above public worth. She makes the shift to the father that is so central to Freud's vision of female maturity, even though that shift signals her death. "And indeed I have no right to cling to life so passionately,/ Since it was for Greece you gave me birth, not for yourself alone" (ll. 1384-85). The grieving mother is told to suppress her anger by the daughter who speaks in her father's name: "Mother, listen now to me! Anger against your husband is beside the point" (ll. 136-9). When Clytemnestra asks at parting "Is there some wish I could fulfill for you at home?" Iphigenia answers, "Yes. Do not hate Agamemnon. He is mine, and yours" (ll. 1450-51), again validating the father's values over the mother's.

Maternal anger in this play can be briefly expressed, only to be redefined and revalued by the daughter whose last wish is to silence her mother's grief at her death and at their separation: "What do you mean? Must I not grieve for your lost life? / No grief at all; and no grave shall be heaped for me" (ll. 1440-41). Although it cannot eliminate Clytemnestra's threatening anger, the play's ambiguous ending justifies Iphigenia's position: the daughter is saved from death by the gods and "survives," but she is forever separate from and unknown to her mother and other humans.

Iphigenia's position is, of course, confirmed in all of the later plays where Clytemnestra's anger, leading to adultery, violence, ambition, and murder confirms the worst unconscious fears of maternal omnipotence and destructiveness. Here, Clytemnestra's violent anger at Agamemnon appears self-serving and unnatural. In the conflict between paternal and maternal right, as Aeschylus presents it in the *Oresteia*, Agamemnon who performs the unnatural act of killing his daughter is vindicated, because he does so in the service of the state; but Clytemnestra's holding on to her child is presented as motivated by self-interest. That Agamemnon's violence and ambition should be more acceptable than Clytemnestra's says a great deal about gender distinction and about the distinction between paternal and maternal power. The perversion of Clytemnestra's maternity demonstrates the perceived dangers of maternal anger. Despite her repeated expressions of concern over the fate of her son Orestes, despite her reminder of the sacrifice of Iphigenia as the cause of her violent murder of Agamemnon, Clytemnestra continues to be seen as an "unnatural mother" who has abandoned all maternal activity and responsibility. In Aeschylus's *Oresteia,* in Sophocles' and Euripides' Electra plays, the anger that Clytemnestra experiences over the sacrifice of Iphigenia gets lost and perverted as a different range of ambitions take over in her. The physical sign of her maternity—the breast she bares to Orestes to show him the bodily tie that binds them—is also the place where he thrusts the knife that kills her. Maternal anger at separation and betrayal takes on deathly proportions; it must be domesticated or eradicated if the structure of civilization is to be maintained.[10]

Both Clytemnestra and Electra point to the incompatibility of maternity (the only legitimate form of adult womanhood in the culture) and action, of maternity and the expression of anger. And because their anger is not legitimatized, they also become incapable of experiencing love. The active, angry rebellious woman cannot be a mother; the mother can be neither active nor rebellious.

The Furies cult in Aeschylus's *The Eumenides* further demonstrates the altogether fearsome and dangerous character of maternal anger: the Furies have the power to leave "manhood unmanned," to "rain pestilence on our soil, corroding every seed/ Till the whole land is sterile desert" (ll. 797-99). Although superseded by Athena's new law, the Furies survive, giving lasting recognition, if not legitimation, to the maternal. Yet at the end of the play, as all sing together in a communal celebration, the Furies are placated and domesticated, robbed of their power, transformed into Friendly Goddesses and despatched to an underground home.

Iphigenia, Electra, Orestes—Clytemnestra's children—share in the fearful fantasy of maternal omnipotence, a fantasy which leads them to conspire in silencing maternal anger, and thus in erasing all other aspects of maternal subjectivity, including maternal love. The representation of Demeter as the powerful goddess who is capable of destroying the earth, the representation of Clytemnestra as the vengeful wife who can kill her husband and punish her children, these representations suggest how, as a culture, we imagine the mother's part in the child's development. In the context of a patriarchal culture in which mothers have little control over their children's paths to maturity, in a culture where children betray their mothers and abandon them, or are forcibly abducted, and where husbands act as enemies, maternal anger is depicted as powerful and threatening. Such figurations necessarily shape maternal representations and self-representations even within feminism. They explain why, even in post-modern feminist fiction, maternal stories are mediated and suppressed, especially if they involve anger. The last two chapters of this book outline these processes of mediation and chart the course of a maternal representation which seems still to be shaped by a cultural imaginary that participates in and underwrites unconscious fears of the maternal. Anger and fear insure that maternal plots will remain unspeakable; post-modern feminist narrative continues to be shaped by mythic taboos.

Underlying the discussion of maternal subjectivity in feminist fiction and theory is the crucial question of the discursive power of the mythic representations discussed in this Prelude. At the same time, this discussion is only partial: the novels discussed in *The Mother/Daugher Plot* outline a range of female relationships and narrative storylines that go beyond the paradigms charted here. Although anger does remain an object of fear as well as one of the primary markers of maternal subjectivity—a subjectivity that is in the process of being erased as it makes room for the emerging subjectivity of the child—the texts of post-modernist feminist fiction do present a greater spectrum of maternal experiences. They go beyond the narrow confines of a privatized maternal anger, suggesting possibilities of integrating anger with love and nurturance. Yet even here, in the absence of fathers, brothers, and husbands, some of the plots of mothers and daughters, especially the permutations of maternal subjectivities, remain fractured and self-contradictory—unspeakable. Yet the unspeakable itself acquires a different significance in texts that combine, without subsuming, the personal with the political.

Notes

[1] Reprinted in a revised edition in *Sexes et parentés* (Paris: Minuit, 1988). All subsequent references are to the earlier edition.

[2] For an illuminating analysis of the varieties of family structures in a black working-class community, see Stack.

[3] See *The Eumenides* (ll. 657-659) in Aeschylus, *The Oresteian Trilogy* (169). I shall also refer to Sophocles' *Electra* in *Electra and Other Plays* and Euripides' *Electra* in *Euripides V*.

[4] In a paper delivered at the conference on "The First Decade: Ten Years of Co-education at Dartmouth," Christian Wolff suggests how Sophocles resolves this paradox by radically privatizing Electra's heroism. Sophocles' play, Wolff suggests, is successful to the extent that it suppresses its matricide as a public issue (how else could Electra be praised for her filial piety?), depoliticizes Electra's heroism, and closes off any reference to future consequences of the murder, either for Electra or Orestes.

[5] See the analysis of Electra's paternal allegiance in Kristeva (31-32).

[6] Christina Sorum argues that Electra persists in an "unseasonable childhood with neither husband nor child" (209).

[7] O'Brien rightly points out that, in *The Oresteia*, Clytemnestra's divine parentage is never mentioned; she is, after all, the daughter of Zeus as much as Athena is, but because of her rebelliousness she must be ostracized.

[8] Sophocles, *Antigone*, in *The Theban Plays* (ll. 905-910). See also Irigaray's discussion of Antigone in *Speculum of the Other Woman* and Feral in "Antigone or the Irony of the Tribe." For a critique of these feminist readings, see du Bois.

[9] In an analysis of patterns of brother-sister incest, Elizabeth Abel suggests that for the sister, incest is most often motivated by political concerns, while for the brother, the motivation tends to be erotic.

[10] See Simon for some fascinating reflections on familial plots in classical and modem tragedy.

References

Abel, Elizabeth. "The Sister's Choice: Antigone, Incest and Fiction by Women." Paper presented at the 1982 Convention of the Modern Language Association.

Aeschylus. *The Oresteian Trilogy*. Trans. Philip Vellacott. London: Penguin Books, 1959.

Brooks, Peter. "Reading for the Plot: Design and Intention." *Narrative*. New York: Alfred A. Knopf, 1984.

de Lauretis, Teresa. *Alice Doesn't: Feminism, Semiotics, Cinema.* Bloomington: Indiana University Press, 1984.

du Bois, Page. "Antigone and the Feminist Critic." *Genre* 19 (4) (Winter 1986): 371-382.

Eliot, George. *Essays of George Eliot.* Ed. Thomas Pinney. New York: Columbia University Press, 1963.

Euripides. *Euripides V.* Ed. David Grene and Richmond Lattimore. Trans. Emily Townsend Vermeule. Chicago: University of Chicago Press, 1959.

Euripides. *Orestes and Other Plays.* Trans. Philip Vellacott. London: Penguin Books, 1980.

Feral, Josette. "Antigone or the Irony of the Tribe." *Diacritics* (September 1978): 2-14.

Hegel, G. W. F. *The Phenomenology of Mind.* Trans. J. B. Baillie. Rev. 2nd ed. London: Allen and Unwin, 1949. 456-506.

"Hymn to Demeter." *The Homeric Hymn.* Trans. and ed. Apostolos N. Athanassakis. Baltimore: Johns Hopkins University Press, 1976.

Irigaray, Luce. *Le corps-à-corps avec la mere.* Montreal: Les éditions de la pleine lune, 1981.

Irigaray, Luce. *Ethique de la différance sexuelle.* Paris: Minuit, 1984.

Irigaray, Luce. *Speculum of the Other Woman.* Trans. Gillian C. Gill. Ithaca: Corncll University Press, 1985.

Joseph, Gerhard. "The *Antigone* as Cultural Touchstone: Matthew Arnold, Hegel, George Eliot, Virginia Woolf and Margaret Drabble." *PMLA* 96 (l) (January 1981): 22-35.

Kristeva, Julia. *About Chinese Women.* Trans. Anita Barrows. New York: Urizen Books, 1977.

Loewenberg, Bert J. and Ruth Bogin, eds. *Black Women in Nineteenth-Century American Life.* University Park: Pennsylvania State University Press, 1976.

O'Brien, Mary. *The Politics of Reproduction.* London: Routledge and Kegan Paul, 1981.

Simon, Bennett. "Tragic Drama and the Family: The Killing of Children and the Killing of Storytelling." *Discourse in Psychoanalysis and Literature.* Ed. Shlomith Rimmon-Kenan. London: Methuen, 1987.

Sophocles. *Electra and Other Plays.* Trans. E. F. Watling. New York: Penguin, 1953.

Sophocles. *The Theban Plays.* Trans. E. F. Watling. London: Penguin Books, 1980.

Sorum, Christina. "The Family in Sophocles's *Antigone* and *Electra.*" *The Classical World* 75 (4) (1982).

Stack, Carol B. *All Our Kin: Strategies for Survival in a Black Community.* New York: Harper and Row, 1974.

Steiner, George. *Antigones.* Oxford: Oxford University Press, 1984.

Woolf, Virginia. *A Writer's Diary.* New York: Harcourt Brace Jovanovich, 1954.

Chapter 17

Homeplace

A Site of Resistance

BELL HOOKS

WHEN I WAS a young girl the journey across town to my grandmother's house was one of the most intriguing experiences. Mama did not like to stay there long. She did not care for all that loud talk, the talk that was usually about the old days, the way life happened then—who married whom, how and when somebody died, but also how we lived and survived as black people, how the white folks treated us. I remember this journey not just because of the stories I would hear. It was a movement away from the segregated blackness of our community into a poor white neighborhood. I remember the fear, being scared to walk to Baba's (our grandmother's house) because we would have to pass that terrifying whiteness—those white faces on the porches staring us down with hate. Even when empty or vacant, those porches seemed to say "danger," "you do not belong here," "you are not safe."

Oh! that feeling of safety, of arrival, of homecoming when we finally reached the edges of her yard, when we could see the soot black face of our grandfather, Daddy Gus, sitting in his chair on the porch, smell his cigar, and rest on his lap. Such a contrast, that feeling of arrival, of homecoming, this sweetness and the bitterness of that journey, that constant reminder of white power and control.

I speak of this journey as leading to my grandmother's house, even though our grandfather lived there too. In our young minds houses belonged to women, were their special domain, not as property, but as places where all that truly mattered in life took place—the warmth and comfort of shelter, the feeding of our bodies, the nurturing of our souls. There we learned dignity, integrity of being; there we learned to have faith. The folks who made this life possible, who were our primary guides and teachers, were black women.

Their lives were not easy. Their lives were hard. They were black women who for the most part worked outside the home serving white folks, cleaning their houses, washing their clothes, tending their children—black women who worked in the fields or in the streets, whatever they could do to make ends meet, whatever was necessary. Then they returned to their homes to make life happen there. This tension between service outside one's home, family, and kin network, service provided to white folks which took time and energy, and the effort of black women to conserve enough of themselves to provide service (care and nurturance) within their own families and communities is one of the many factors that has historically distinguished the lot of black women in patriarchal white supremacist society from that of black men. Contemporary black struggle must honor this history of service just as it must critique the sexist definition of service as women's "natural" role.

Since sexism delegates to females the task of creating and sustaining a home environment, it has been primarily the responsibility of black women to construct domestic households as spaces of care and nurturance in the face of the brutal harsh reality of racist oppression, of sexist domination. Historically, African-American people believed that the construction of a homeplace, however fragile and tenuous (the slave hut, the wooden shack), had a radical political dimension. Despite the brutal reality of racial apartheid, of domination, one's homeplace was the one site where one could freely confront the issue of humanization, where one could resist. Black women resisted by making homes where all black people could strive to be subjects, not objects, where we could be affirmed in our minds and hearts despite poverty, hardship, and deprivation, where we could restore to ourselves the dignity denied us on the outside in the public world.

This task of making homeplace was not simply a matter of black women providing service; it was about the construction of a safe place where black people could affirm one another and by so doing heal many of the wounds inflicted by racist domination. We could not learn to love or respect ourselves in the culture of white supremacy, on the outside; it was there on the inside, in that "homeplace," most often created and kept by black women, that we had the opportunity to grow and develop, to nurture our spirits. This task of making a homeplace, of making home a community of resistance, has been shared by black women globally, especially black women in white supremacist societies.

I shall never forget the sense of shared history, of common anguish, I felt when first reading about the plight of black women domestic servants in South Africa, black women laboring in white homes. Their stories evoked vivid memories of our African-American past. I remember that one of the black women giving testimony complained that after traveling in the wee hours of the morning to the white folks' house, after working there all day, giving her time and energy, she had "none left for her own." I knew this story. I had read it in the slave narratives of African-American women who, like Sojourner Truth, could say, "When I cried out with a mother's grief none but Jesus heard" (qtd. in Loewenberg and Bogin 235). I knew this story. I had grown to womanhood hearing about black women who nurtured and cared for white families when they longed to have time and energy to give to their own.

I want to remember these black women today. The act of remembrance is a conscious gesture honoring their struggle, their effort to keep something for their own. I want us to respect and understand that this effort has been and continues to be a radically subversive political gesture. For those who dominate and oppress us benefit most when we have nothing to give our own, when they have so taken from us our dignity, our humanness that we have nothing left, no "homeplace" where we can recover ourselves. I want us to remember these black women today, both past and present. Even as I speak there are black women in the midst of racial apartheid in South Africa, struggling to provide something for their own. "We ... know how our sisters suffer" (qtd. in the petition for the repeal of the pass laws, August 9, 1956). I want us to honor them, not because they suffer but because they continue to struggle in the midst of suffering, because they continue to resist. I want to speak about the importance of homeplace in the midst of oppression and domination, of homeplace as a site of resistance and liberation struggle. Writing about "resistance," particularly resistance to the Vietnam war, Vietnamese Buddhist monk Thich Nhat Hahn says:

> ...resistance, at root, must mean more than resistance against war. It is a resistance against all kinds of things that are like war.... So perhaps, resistance means opposition to being invaded, occupied, assaulted and destroyed by the system. The purpose of resistance, here, is to seek the healing of yourself in order to be able to see clearly.... I think that communities of resistance should be places where people can return to themselves more easily, where the conditions are such that they can heal themselves and recover their wholeness.

Historically, black women have resisted white supremacist domination by working to establish homeplace. It does not matter that sexism assigned them this role. It is more important that they took this conventional role and expanded it to include caring for one another, for children, for black men, in ways that elevated our spirits, that kept us from despair, that taught some of us to be revolutionaries able to struggle for freedom. In his famous 1845 slave narrative, Frederick Douglass tells the story of his birth, of his enslaved black mother who was hired out a considerable distance from his place of residence. Describing their relationship, he writes:

> I never saw my mother, to know her as such more than four or five times in my life; and each of these times was very short in duration, and at night. She was hired by Mr. Stewart, who lived about twelve miles from my house. She made her journeys to see me in the night, traveling the whole distance on foot, after the performance of her day's work. She was a field hand, and a whipping is the penalty of not being in the field at sunrise.... I do not recollect of ever seeing my mother by the light of day. She was with me in the night. She would lie down with me and get me to sleep, but long before I waked she was gone.

After sharing this information, Douglass later says that he never enjoyed a mother's "soothing presence, her tender and watchful care" so that he received the "tidings of her death with much the same emotions I should have probably felt at the death of a stranger." Douglass surely intended to impress upon the consciousness of white readers the cruelty of that system of racial domination which separated black families, black mothers from their children. Yet he does so by devaluing black womanhood, by not even registering the quality of care that made his black mother travel those twelve miles to hold him in her arms. In the midst of a brutal racist system, which did not value black life, she valued the life of her child enough to resist that system, to come to him in the night, just to hold him.

Now I cannot agree with Douglass that he never knew a mother's care. I want to suggest that this mother, who dared to hold him in the night, gave him at birth a sense of value that provided a groundwork, however fragile, for the person he later became. If anyone doubts the power and significance of this maternal gesture, they would do well to read psychoanalyst Alice Miller's book, *The Untouched Key: Tracing Childhood Trauma in Creativity and Destructiveness.* Holding him in her arms, Douglass' mother provided, if only for a short time, a space where this black child was not the subject of dehumanizing scorn and devaluation but was the recipient of a quality of care that should have enabled the adult Douglass to look back and reflect on the political choices of this black mother who resisted slave codes, risking her life, to care for her son. I want to suggest that devaluation of the role his mother played in his life is a dangerous oversight. Though Douglass is only one example, we are currently in danger of forgetting the powerful role black women have played in constructing for us homeplaces that are the site for resistance. This forgetfulness undermines our solidarity and the future of black liberation struggle.

Douglass's work is important, for he is historically identified as sympathetic to the struggle for women's rights. All too often his critique of male domination, such as it was, did not include recognition of the particular circumstances of black women in relation to black men and families. To me one of the most important chapters in my first book, *Ain't I A Woman: Black Women and Feminism,* is one that calls attention to "Continued Devaluation of Black Womanhood." Overall devaluation of the role black women have played in constructing for us home places that are the site for resistance undermines our efforts to resist racism and the colonizing mentality which promotes internalized self-hatred. Sexist thinking about the nature of domesticity has determined the way black women's experience in the home is perceived. In African-American culture there is a long tradition of "mother worship." Black autobiographies, fiction, and poetry praise the virtues of the self-sacrificing black mother. Unfortunately, though positively motivated, black mother worship extols the virtues of self-sacrifice while simultaneously implying that such a gesture is not reflective of choice and will, rather the perfect embodiment of a woman's "natural" role. The assumption then is that the black woman who works hard to be a responsible caretaker is only doing what she should be doing. Failure to recognize the realm of choice, and the remarkable re-visioning of both woman's role and the idea of "home" that black women consciously exercised in practice, obscures the political commitment to racial uplift, to eradicating racism, which was the philosophical core of dedication to community and home.

Though black women did not self-consciously articulate in written discourse the theoretical principles of decolonization, this does not detract from the importance of their actions. They understood intellectually and intuitively the meaning of homeplace in the midst of an oppressive and dominating social reality, of home-place as site of resistance and liberation struggle. I know of what I speak. I would not be writing this essay if my mother, Rosa Bell, daughter to Sarah Oldham, granddaughter to bell hooks, had not created homeplace in just this liberatory way, despite the contradictions of poverty and sexism.

In our family, I remember the immense anxiety we felt as children when mama would leave our house, our segregated community, to work as a maid in the homes of white folks. I believe that she sensed our fear, our concern that she might not return to us safe, that we could not find her (even though she always left phone numbers, they did not ease our worry). When she returned home after working long hours, she did not complain. She made an effort to rejoice with us that her work was done, that she was home, making it seem as though there was nothing about the experience of working as a maid in a white household, in that space of Otherness, which stripped her of dignity and personal power.

Looking back as an adult woman, I think of the effort it must have taken for her to transcend her own tiredness (and who knows what assaults or wounds to her spirit had to be put aside so that she could give something to her own). Given the contemporary notions of "good parenting" this may seem like a small gesture, yet in many post-slavery black families, it was a gesture parents were often too weary, too beaten down to make. Those of us who were fortunate enough to receive such care understood its value. Politically, our young mother, Rosa Bell, did not allow the white supremacist culture of domination to completely shape and control her psyche and her familial relationships. Working to create a homeplace that affirmed our beings, our blackness, our love for one another was necessary resistance. We learned degrees of critical consciousness from her. Our lives were not without contradictions, so it is not my intent to create a ro-manticized portrait. Yet any attempts to critically assess the role of black women in liberation struggle must examine the way political concern about the impact of racism shaped black women's thinking, their sense of home, and their modes of parenting.

An effective means of white subjugation of black people globally has been the perpetual construction of economic and social structures that deprive many folks of the means to make homeplace. Remembering this should enable us to understand the political value of black women's resistance in the home. It should provide a framework where we can discuss the development of black female political consciousness, acknowledging the political importance of resistance ef-fort that took place in homes. It is no accident that the South African apartheid regime systematically attacks and destroys black efforts to construct homeplace, however tenuous, that small private reality where black women and men can renew their spirits and recover themselves. It is no accident that this homeplace, as fragile and as transitional as it may be, a makeshift shed, a small bit of earth where one rests, is always subject to violation and destruction. For when a people no longer have the space to construct homeplace, we cannot build a meaningful community of resistance.

Throughout our history, African-Americans have recognized the subversive value of homeplace, of having access to private space where we do not directly encounter white racist aggression. Whatever the shape and direction of black liberation struggle (civil rights reform or black power movement), domestic space has been a crucial site for organizing, for forming political solidarity. Homeplace has been a site of resistance. Its structure was defined less by whether or not black women and men were conforming to sexist behavior norms and more by our struggle to uplift ourselves as a people, our struggle to resist racist domination and oppression.

That liberatory struggle has been seriously undermined by contemporary efforts to change that subversive homeplace into a site of patriarchal domination of black women by black men, where we abuse one another for not conforming to sexist norms. This shift in perspective, where homeplace is not viewed as a political site, has had negative impact on the construction of black female identity and political consciousness. Masses of black women, many of whom were not formally educated, had in the past been able to play a vital role in black liberation struggle. In the contemporary situation, as the paradigms for domesticity in black life mirrored white bourgeois norms (where home is conceptualized as politically neutral space), black people began to overlook and devalue the importance of black female labor in teaching critical consciousness in domestic space. Many black women, irrespective of class status, have responded to this crisis of meaning by imitating leisure-class sexist notions of women's role, focusing their lives on meaningless compulsive consumerism.

Identifying this syndrome as "the crisis of black womanhood" in her essay, "Considering Feminism as a Model for Social Change," Sheila Radford-Hill points to the mid-sixties as that historical moment when the primacy of black woman's role in liberation struggle began to be questioned as a threat to black manhood and was deemed unimportant. Radford-Hill asserts:

> Without the power to influence the purpose and the direction of our collective experience, without the power to influence our culture from within, we are increasingly immobilized, unable to integrate self and role identities, unable to resist the cultural imperialism of the dominant culture which assures our continued oppression by destroying us from within. Thus, the crisis manifests itself as social dysfunction in the black community-as genocide, fratricide, homicide, and suicide. It is also manifested by the abdication of personal responsibility by black women for themselves and for each other ... The crisis of black womanhood is a form of cultural aggression: a form of exploitation so vicious,

so insidious that it is currently destroying an entire generation of black women and their families.

This contemporary crisis of black womanhood might have been avoided had black women collectively sustained attempts to develop the latent feminism expressed by their willingness to work equally alongside black men in black liberation struggle. Contemporary equation of black liberation struggle with the subordination of black women has damaged collective black solidarity. It has served the interests of white supremacy to promote the assumption that the wounds of racist domination would be less severe were black women conforming to sexist role patterns.

We are daily witnessing the disintegration of African-American family life that is grounded in a recognition of the political value of constructing homeplace as a site of resistance; black people daily perpetuate sexist norms that threaten our survival as a people. We can no longer act as though sexism in black communities does not threaten our solidarity; any force which estranges and alienates us from one another serves the interests of racist domination.

Black women and men must create a revolutionary vision of black liberation that has a feminist dimension, one which is formed in consideration of our specific needs and concerns. Drawing on past legacies, contemporary black women can begin to reconceptualize ideas of homeplace, once again consider-ing the primacy of domesticity as a site for subversion and resistance. When we renew our concern with homeplace, we can address political issues that most affect our daily lives. Calling attention to the skills and resources of black women who may have begun to feel that they have no meaningful contribu-tion to make, women who mayor may not be formally educated but who have essential wisdom to share, who have practical experience that is the breeding ground for all useful theory, we may begin to bond with one another in ways that renew our solidarity.

When black women renew our political commitment to homeplace, we can address the needs and concerns of young black women who are groping for struc-tures of meaning that will further their growth, young women who are struggling for self-definition. Together, black women can renew our commitment to black liberation struggle, sharing insights and awareness, sharing feminist thinking and feminist vision, building solidarity.

With this foundation, we can regain lost perspective, give life new meaning. We can make homeplace that space where we return for renewal and self-recovery, where we can heal our wounds and become whole.

References

Douglass, Frederick. *Narrative of the Life of Frederick Douglass.* Cambridge, MA: Belknap Press, 1960.

Hahn, Thich Nhat. *The Raft is Not the Shore.* Boston: Beacon Press, 1975.

hooks, bell. *Ain't I A Woman: Black Women and Feminism.* Boston: South End Press, 1981.

Miller, Alice. *The Untouched Key: Tracing Childhood Trauma in Creativity and Destructiveness.* New York: Doubleday, 1990.

Radford-Hill, Sheila. "Considering Feminism as a Model for Social Change." *Feminist Studies, Critical Studies.* Ed. Teresa de Lauretis. Bloomington: Indiana University Press, 1986.

Chapter 18

The Meaning of Motherhood in Black Culture and Mother-Daughter Relationships

PATRICIA HILL COLLINS

"What did your mother teach you about men?" is a question I often ask students in my courses on African-American women. "Go to school first and get a good education—don't get too serious too young," "Make sure you look around and that you can take care of yourself before you settle down," and "Don't trust them, want more for yourself than just a man," are typical responses from Black women. My students share stories of how their mothers encouraged them to cultivate satisfying relationships with Black men while anticipating disappointments, to desire marriage while planning viable alternatives, to become mothers only when fully prepared to do so. But, above all, they stress their mothers' insistence on being self-reliant and resourceful.

These daughters, of various ages and from diverse social class backgrounds, family structures and geographic regions, had somehow received strikingly similar messages about Black womanhood. Even though their mothers employed diverse teaching strategies, these Black daughters had all been exposed to common themes about the meaning of womanhood in Black culture.[1]

This essay explores the relationship between the meaning of motherhood in African-American culture and Black mother-daughter relationships by addressing three primary questions. First, how have competing perspectives about motherhood intersected to produce a distinctly Afrocentric ideology of motherhood? Second, what are the enduring themes that characterize this Afrocentric ideology of motherhood? Finally, what effect might this Afrocentric ideology of motherhood have on Black mother-daughter relationships?

Competing Perspectives on Motherhood
The Dominant Perspective: Eurocentric Views or White Motherhood

The cult of true womanhood, with its emphasis on motherhood as woman's highest calling, has long held a special place in the gender symbolism of White Americans. From this perspective, women's activities should be confined to the care of children, the nurturing of a husband, and the maintenance of the household. By managing this separate domestic sphere, women gain social influence through their roles as mothers, transmitters of culture, and parents for the next generation.[2]

While substantial numbers of White women have benefited from the protections of White patriarchy provided by the dominant ideology, White women themselves have recently challenged its tenets. On one pole lies a cluster of women, the traditionalists, who aim to retain the centrality of motherhood in women's lives. For traditionalists, differentiating between the experience of motherhood, which for them has been quite satisfying, and motherhood as an institution central in reproducing gender inequality, has proved difficult. The other pole is occupied by women who advocate dismantling motherhood as an institution. They suggest that compulsory motherhood be outlawed and that the experience of motherhood can only be satisfying if women can also choose not to be mothers. Arrayed between these dichotomous positions are women who argue for an expanded, but not necessarily different, role for women—women can be mothers as long as they are not *just* mothers.[3]

Three themes implicit in White perspectives on motherhood are particularly problematic for Black women and others outside of this debate. First, the assumption that mothering occurs within the confines of a private, nuclear family household where the mother has almost total responsibility for child-rearing is less applicable to Black families. While the ideal of the cult of true womanhood has been held up to Black women for emulation, racial oppression has denied Black families sufficient resources to support private, nuclear family households. Second, strict sex-role segregation, with separate male and female spheres of influence within the family, has been less commonly found in African-American families than in White middle-class ones. Finally, the assumption that motherhood and economic dependency on men are linked and that to be a "good" mother one must stay at home, making motherhood a full-time "occupation," is similarly uncharacteristic of African-American families (Mullings; Dill; Carby).[4]

Even though selected groups of White women are challenging the cult of true womanhood and its accompanying definition of motherhood, the dominant ideology remains powerful. As long as these approaches remain prominent in scholarly and popular discourse, Eurocentric views of White motherhood will continue to affect Black women's lives.

Eurocentric Views of Black Motherhood

Eurocentric perspectives on Black motherhood revolve around two interdependent images that together define Black women's roles in White and in African-American families. The first image is that of the Mammy, the faithful, devoted domestic servant. Like one of the family, Mammy conscientiously "mothers" her White children, caring for them and loving them as if they were her own. Mammy is the ideal Black mother for she recognizes her place. She is paid next to nothing and yet cheerfully accepts her inferior status. But when she enters her own home, this same Mammy is transformed into the second image, the too-strong matriarch who raises weak sons and "unnaturally superior" daughters.[5] When she protests, she is labeled aggressive and unfeminine, yet if she remains silent, she is rendered invisible.

The task of debunking Mammy by analyzing Black women's roles as exploited domestic workers and challenging the matriarchy thesis by demonstrating that Black women do not wield disproportionate power in African-American families has long preoccupied African-American scholars.[6] But an equally telling critique concerns uncovering the functions of these images and their role in explaining Black women's subordination in systems of race, class, and gender oppression. As Mae King points out, White definitions of Black motherhood foster the dominant group's exploitation of Black women by blaming Black women for their characteristic reactions to their own subordination. For example, while the stay-at-home mother has been held up to all women as the ideal, African-American women have been compelled to work outside the home, typically in a very narrow range of occupations. Even though Black women were forced to become domestic servants and be strong figures in Black households, labeling them Mammys and matriarchs denigrates Black women. Without a countervailing Afrocentric ideology of motherhood, White perspectives on both White and African-American motherhood place Black women in a no-win situation. Adhering to these standards brings the danger of the lowered self-esteem of internalized oppression, one that, if passed on from mother to daughter, provides a powerful mechanism for controlling African-American communities.

African Perspectives on Motherhood

One concept that has been constant throughout the history of African societies is the centrality of motherhood in religions, philosophies, and social institutions. As Barbara Christian points out, "There is no doubt that motherhood is for most African people symbolic of creativity and continuity" (214).

Cross-cultural research on motherhood in African societies appears to support Christian's claim (see Oppong 1983; Sudarkasa 1981a; Tanner). West African sociologist Christine Oppong (1982) suggests that the Western notion of equating household with family be abandoned because it obscures women's family roles in African cultures. While the archetypal White, middle-class nuclear family conceptualizes family life as being divided into two oppositional spheres—the "male" sphere of economic providing and the "female" sphere of affective nurturing—this type of rigid sex role segregation was not part of the West African tradition. Mothering was not a privatized nurturing "occupation" reserved for biological mothers, and the economic support of children was not the exclusive responsibility of men. Instead, for African women, emotional care for children and providing for their physical survival were interwoven as interdependent, complementary dimensions of motherhood.

In spite of variations among societies, a strong case has been made that West

African women occupy influential roles in African family networks.[7] First, since they are not dependent on males for economic support and provide much of their own and their children's economic support, women are structurally central to families (Sudarkasa 1981a). Second, the image of the mother is one that is culturally elaborated and valued across diverse West African societies. Continuing the lineage is essential in West African philosophies, and motherhood is similarly valued (Mbiti). Finally, while the biological mother-child bond is valued, childcare was a collective responsibility, a situation fostering cooperative, age-stratified, woman-centered "mothering" networks.

Recent research by Africanists suggests that much more of this African heritage was retained among African-Americans than had previously been thought. The retention of West African culture as a culture of resistance offered enslaved Africans and exploited African-Americans alternative ideologies to those advanced by dominant groups. Central to these reinterpretations of African-American institutions and culture is a reconceptualization of Black family life and the role of women in Black family networks (Sudarkasa 1981b; White). West African perspectives may have been combined with the changing political and economic situations framing African-American communities to produce certain enduring themes characterizing an Afrocentric ideology of motherhood.

Enduring Themes of an Afrocentric Ideology of Motherhood

An Afrocentric ideology of motherhood must reconcile the competing worldviews of these three conflicting perspectives of motherhood. An ongoing tension exists between efforts to mold the institution of Black motherhood for the benefit of the dominant group and efforts by Black women to define and value their own experiences with motherhood. This tension leads to a continuum of responses. For those women who either aspire to the cult of true womanhood without having the resources to support such a lifestyle, or who believe the stereotypical analyses of themselves as dominating matriarchs, motherhood can be oppressive. But the experience of motherhood can provide Black women with a base of self-actualization, status in the Black community, and a reason for social activism. These alleged contradictions can exist side by side in African-American communities, families, and even within individual women.

Embedded in these changing relationships are four enduring themes that I contend characterize an Afrocentric ideology of motherhood. Just as the issues facing enslaved African mothers were quite different from those currently facing poor Black women in inner cities, for any given historical moment the actual institutional forms that these themes take depend on the severity of oppression and Black women's resources for resistance.

Bloodmothers, Othermothers, and Women-Centered Networks

In African-American communities, the boundaries distinguishing biological mothers of children from other women who care for children are often fluid and changing. Biological mothers or bloodmothers are expected to care for their children. But African and African-American communities have also recognized that vesting one person with full responsibility for mothering a child may not be wise or possible. As a result, "othermothers," women who assist bloodmothers by sharing mothering responsibilities, traditionally have been central to the institution of Black motherhood.[8]

The centrality of women in African-American extended families is well known (see Tanner; see also, McCray; Martin and Martin; Aschenbrenner, Stack). Organized, resilient, women-centered networks of blood mothers and othermothers are key to this centrality. Grandmothers, sisters, aunts, or cousins acted as othermothers by taking on childcare responsibilities for each other's children. When needed, temporary childcare arrangements turned into long-term care or informal adoption (Martin and Martin; Young).

In African-American communities, these women-centered networks of community-based childcare often extend beyond the boundaries of biologically related extended families to support "fictive kin" (Stack). Civil rights activist Ella Baker describes how informal adoption by other-mothers functioned in the Southern, rural community of her childhood:

> My aunt who had thirteen children of her own raised
> three more. She had become a midwife, and a child was
> born who was covered with sores. Nobody was particularly
> wanting the child, so she took the child and raised
> him ... and another mother decided she didn't want to
> be bothered with two children. So my aunt took one
> and raised him ... they were part of the family. (qtd. in Cantarow 59)

Even when relationships were not between kin or fictive kin, African-American community norms were such that neighbors cared for each other's children. In the following passage, Sara Brooks, a Southern domestic worker, describes the importance of the community-based childcare that a neighbor offered her daughter. In doing so, she also shows how the African-American cultural value placed on cooperative childcare found institutional support in the adverse conditions under which so many Black women mothered:

> She kept Vivian and she didn't charge me nothin either. You see, people
> used to look after each other, but now it's not that way. I reckon it's
> because we all was poor, and I guess they put theirself in the place of
> the person that they was helpin. (qtd. in Simonsen 181)

Othermothers were key not only in supporting children but also in supporting bloodmothers who, for whatever reason, were ill-prepared or had little desire to care for their children. Given the pressures from the larger political economy, the emphasis placed on community-based childcare and the respect given to othermothers who assume the responsibilities of childcare have served a critical function in African-American communities. Children orphaned by sale or death of their parents under slavery, children conceived through rape, children of young mothers, children born into extreme poverty, or children who for other reasons have been rejected by their bloodmothers have all been supported by othermothers who, like Ella Baker's aunt, took in additional children, even when they had enough of their own.

Providing as Part of Mothering

The work done by African-American women in providing the economic resources essential to Black family well-being affects motherhood in a contradictory fashion. On the one hand, African-American women have long integrated their activities as economic providers into their mothering relationships. In contrast to the cult of true womanhood, in which work is defined as being in opposition to and incompatible with motherhood, work for Black women has been an important and valued dimension of Afrocentric definitions of Black motherhood. On the other hand, African-American women's experiences as mothers under oppression were such that the type and purpose of work Black women were forced to do had. a great impact on the type of mothering relationships bloodmothers and othermothers had with Black children.

While slavery both disrupted West African family patterns and exposed enslaved Africans to the gender ideologies and practices of slaveowners, it simultaneously made it impossible, had they wanted to do so, for enslaved Africans to implement slaveowner's ideologies. Thus, the separate spheres of providing as a male domain and affective nurturing as a female domain did not develop within African-American families (White; Dill; Mullings 1986b). Providing for Black children's physical survival and attending to their affective, emotional needs continued as interdependent dimensions of an Afrocentric ideology of motherhood. However, by changing the conditions under which Black women worked and the purpose of the work itself, slavery introduced the problem of how best to continue traditional Afrocentric values under oppressive conditions. Institutions of community-based childcare, informal adoption, greater reliance on othermothers, all emerge as adaptations to the exigencies of combining exploitative work with nurturing children.

In spite of the change in political status brought on by emancipation, the majority of African-American women remained exploited agricultural workers. However, their placement in Southern political economies allowed them to combine childcare with field labour. Sara Brooks describes how strong the links between providing and caring for others were for her:

> When I was about nine I was nursin my sister Sally—I'm about seven or eight years older than Sally. And when I would put her to sleep, instead of me goin somewhere and sit down and play, I'd get my little old hoe

and get out there and work right in the field around the house. (qtd. in Simonsen 86)

Black women's shift from Southern agriculture to domestic work in Southern and Northern towns and cities represented a change in the type of work done, but not in the meaning of work to women and their families. Whether they wanted to or not, the majority of African-American women had to work and could not afford the luxury of motherhood as a noneconomically productive, female "occupation."

Community Othermothers and Social Activism

Black women's experiences as othermothers have provided a foundation for Black women's social activism. Black women's feelings of responsibility for nurturing the children in their own extended family networks have stimulated a more generalized ethic of care where Black women feel accountable to all the Black community's children.

This notion of Black women as community othermothers for all Black children traditionally allowed Black women to treat biologically unrelated children as if they were members of their own families. For example, sociologist Karen Fields describes how her grandmother, Mamie Garvin Fields, draws on her power as a community othermother when dealing with unfamiliar children.

> She will say to a child on the street who looks up to no good, picking out a name at random, "Aren't you Miz Pinckney's boy?" in that same reproving tone. If the reply is, "No, ma'am, my mother is Miz Gadsden," whatever threat there was dissipates. (Fields and Fields xvii)

The use of family language in referring to members of the Black community also illustrates this dimension of Black motherhood. For example, Mamie Garvin Fields describes how she became active in surveying the poor housing conditions of Black people in Charleston.

> I was one of the volunteers they got to make a survey of the places where we were paying extortious rents for indescribable property. I said "we," although it wasn't Bob and me. We had our own home, and so did many of the Federated Women. Yet we still felt like it really was "we" living in those terrible places, and it was up to us to do something about them. (Fields and Fields 195)

To take another example, while describing her increasingly successful efforts to teach a boy who had given other teachers problems, my daughter's kindergarten teacher stated, "You know how it can be—the majority of children in the learning disabled classes are *our children*. I know he didn't belong there, so I volunteered to take him." In these statements, both women invoke the language of family to describe the ties that bind them as Black women to their responsibilities to other members of the Black community as family.

Sociologist Cheryl Gilkes suggests that community othermother relationships are sometimes behind Black women's decisions to become community activists (1980; 1983). Gilkes notes that many of the Black women community activists in her study became involved in community organizing in response to the needs of their own children and of those in their communities. The following comment is typical of how many of the Black women in Gilkes' study relate to Black children: "There were a lot of summer programs springing up for kids, but they were exclusive ... and I found that most of *our kids* (emphasis mine) were excluded" (Gilkes 1980: 219). For many women, what began as the daily expression of their obligations as community othermothers, as was the case for the kindergarten teacher, developed into full-fledged roles as community leaders.

Motherhood as a Symbol of Power

Motherhood, whether bloodmother, othermother, or community othermother, can be invoked by Black women as a symbol of power. A substantial portion of Black women's status in African-American communities stems not only from their roles as mothers in their own families but from their contributions as community othermothers to Black community development as well.

The specific contributions Black women make in nurturing Black community development form the basis of community-based power. Community othermothers work on behalf of the Black community by trying, in the words of late nineteenth century Black feminists, to "uplift the race," so that vulnerable members of the community would be able to attain the self-reliance and independence so desperately needed for Black community development under oppressive conditions. This is the type of power many African-Americans have in mind when they describe the "strong, Black women" they see around them in traditional African-American communities.

When older Black women invoke this community othermother status, its results can be quite striking. Karen Fields recounts an incident described to her by her grandmother illustrating how women can exert power as community othermothers:

> One night ... as Grandmother sat crocheting alone at about two in the morning, a young man walked into the living room carrying the portable TV from upstairs. She said, "Who are you looking for this time of night?" As Grandmother [described] the incident to me over the phone, I could hear a tone of voice that I know well. It said, "Nice boys don't do that." So I imagine the burglar heard his own mother or grandmother at that moment. He joined in the familial game just created: "Well, he told me that I could borrow it." "*Who* told you?" "John." "Urh umh, no John

lives here. You got the wrong house." (Fields and Fields xvi)

After this dialogue, the teenager turned around, went back upstairs and returned the television.

In local Black communities, specific Black women are widely recognized as powerful figures, primarily because of their contributions to the community's well-being through their roles as community othermothers. Sociologist Charles Johnson describes the behavior of an elderly Black woman at a church service in rural Alabama of the 1930s. Even though she was not on the program, the woman stood up to speak. The master of ceremonies rang for her to sit down but she refused to do so claiming "I am the mother of this church, and I will say what I please." The master of ceremonies later explained to the congregation, "Brothers, I know you all honour Sister Moore. Course our time is short but she has acted as a mother to me…. Any time old folks get up I give way to them" (Johnson 173).

Implication for Black Mother-Daughter Relationships

In her discussion of the sex-role socialization of Black girls, Pamela Reid identifies two complementary approaches in understanding Black mother-daughter relationships. The first, psychoanalytic theory, examines the role of parents in the establishment of personality and social behavior. This theory argues that the development of feminine behavior results from girls' identification with adult female role models. This approach emphasizes how an Afrocentric ideology of motherhood is actualized through Black mothers' activities as role models.

The second approach, social learning theory, suggests that the rewards and punishments attached to girls' childhood experiences are central in shaping women's sex-role behavior. The kinds of behaviors that Black mothers reward and punish in their daughters are seen as key in the socialization process. This approach examines specific experiences that Black girls have while growing up that encourage them to absorb an Afrocentric ideology of motherhood.

African-American Mothers as Role Models

Feminist psychoanalytic theorists suggest that sex-role socialization process is different for boys and girls. While boys learn maleness by rejecting femaleness via separating themselves from their mothers, girls establish feminine identities by embracing the femaleness of their mothers. Girls identify with their mothers, a sense of connection that is incorporated into the female personality. However, this mother-identification is problematic because, under patriarchy, men are more highly valued than women. Thus, while daughters identify with their mothers, they also reject them, since in patriarchal families, identifying with adult women as mothers means identifying with persons deemed inferior.[9]

While Black girls learn by identifying with their mothers, the specific female role with which Black girls identify may be quite different than that modeled by middle-class White mothers. The presence of working mothers, extended family othermothers, and powerful community othermothers offers a range of role models that challenge the tenets of the cult of true womanhood.

Moreover, since Black mothers have a distinctive relationship to White patriarchy, they may be less likely to socialize their daughters into their pro-scribed role as subordinates. Rather, a key part of Black girls' socialization involves "incorporating the critical posture that allows Black women to cope with contradictions. For example, Black girls have long had to learn how to do domestic work while rejecting definitions of themselves as Mammies. At the same time they've had to take on strong roles in Black extended families without internalizing images of themselves as matriarchs.

In raising their daughters, Black mothers face a troubling dilemma. To ensure their daughters' physical survival, they must teach their daughters to fit into systems of oppression. For example, as a young girl in Mississippi, Black activ-ist Ann Moody questioned why she was paid so little for the domestic work she began at age nine, why Black women domestics were sexually harassed by their White male employers, and why Whites had so much more than Blacks. But her mother refused to answer her questions and actually became angry whenever Ann Moody stepped out of her "place" (Moody). Black daughters are raised to expect to work, to strive for an education so that they can support themselves, and to anticipate carrying heavy responsibilities in their families and communities because these skills are essential for their own survival as well as for the survival of those for whom they will eventually be responsible (Ladner; Myers). And yet mothers know that if daughters fit too well into the limited opportunities offered Black women, they become willing participants in their own subordination. Mothers may have ensured their daughters' physi-cal survival at the high cost of their emotional destruction.

On the other hand, Black daughters who offer serious challenges to op-pressive situations may not physically survive. When Ann Moody became involved in civil rights activities, her mother first begged her not to participate and then told her not to come home because she feared the Whites in Moody's hometown would kill her. In spite of the dangers, many Black mothers routinely encourage their daughters to develop skills to confront oppressive conditions. Thus, learning that they will work, that education is a vehicle for advancement, can also be seen as ways of preparing Black girls to resist oppression through a variety of mothering roles. The issue is to build emotional strength, but not at the cost of physical survival.

This delicate balance between conformity and resistance is described by his-torian Elsa Barkley Brown as the "need to socialize me one way and at the same time to give me all the tools I needed to be something else."[10] Black daughters must learn how to survive in interlocking structures of race, class, and gender oppression while rejecting and transcending those very same structures. To develop these skills in their daughters, mothers demonstrate varying combinations of behaviors devoted to ensuring their daughters' survival—such as providing them with basic necessities and ensuring their protection in dangerous environments—to helping their daughters go farther than mothers themselves were allowed to go.

The presence of othermothers in Black extended families and the modeling symbolized by community othermothers offer powerful support for the task of teaching girls to resist White perceptions of Black womanhood while appearing to conform to them. In contrast to the isolation of middle-class White mother / daughter dyads, Black women-centered extended family networks foster an early identification with a much wider range of models of Black womanhood, which can lead to a greater sense of empowerment in young Black girls.

Social Learning Theory and Black Mothering Behavior

Understanding this goal of balancing the needs of ensuring their daughters' physical survival with the vision of encouraging them to transcend the boundaries confronting them sheds some light on some of the apparent contradictions in Black mother-daughter relationships. Black mothers are often described as strong disciplinarians and overly protective parents; yet these same women manage to raise daughters who are self-reliant and assertive (Joseph; Myers). Professor Gloria Wade-Gayles offers an explanation for this apparent contradiction by suggesting that Black mothers "do not socialize their daughters to be passive or irrational. Quite the contrary, they socialize their daughters to be independent, strong and self-confident. Black mothers are suffocatingly protective and domineering precisely because they are determined to mold their daughters into whole and self-actualizing persons in a society that devalues Black women" (12).

Black mothers emphasize protection either by trying to shield their daughters as long as possible from the penalties attached to their race, class, and gender or by teaching them how to protect themselves in such situations. Black women's autobiographies and fiction can be read as texts revealing the multiple strategies Black mothers employ in preparing their daughters for the demands of being Black women in oppressive conditions. For example, in discussing the mother-daughter relationship in Paule Marshall's *Brown Girl, Brownstones,* Rosalie Troester catalogues some of these strategies and the impact they may have on relationships themselves:

> Black mothers, particularly those with strong ties to their community, sometimes build high banks around their young daughters, isolating them from the dangers of the larger world until they are old and strong enough to function as autonomous women. Often these dikes are religious, but sometimes they are built with education, family, or the restrictions of a close-knit and homogeneous community ... this isolation causes the currents between Black mothers and daughters to run deep and the relationship to be fraught with an emotional intensity often missing

from the lives of women with more freedom. (13)

Black women's efforts to provide for their children also may affect the emotional intensity of Black mother-daughter relationships. As Gloria Wade-Gayles points out, "Mothers in Black women's fiction are strong and devoted ... but ... they are rarely affectionate (10). For far too many Black mothers, the demands of providing for children are so demanding that affection often must wait until the basic needs of physical survival are satisfied.

Black daughters raised by mothers grappling with hostile environments have to confront their feelings about the difference between the idealized versions of maternal love extant in popular culture and the strict, assertive mothers so central to their lives (Joseph). For daughters, growing up means developing a better understanding that offering physical care and protection is an act of maternal love. Ann Moody describes her growing awareness of the personal cost her mother paid as a single mother of three children employed as a domestic worker. Watching her mother sleep after the birth of another child, Moody remembers:

> For a long time I stood there looking at her. I didn't want to wake her up. I wanted to enjoy and preserve that calm, peaceful look on her face, I wanted to think she would always be that happy.... Adline and Junior were too young to feel the things I felt and know the things I knew about Mama. They couldn't remember when she and Daddy separated. They had never heard her cry at night as I had or worked and helped as I had done when we were starving. (57)

Renita Weems's account of coming to grips with maternal desertion provides another example of a daughter's efforts to understand her mother's behavior. In the following passage, Weems struggles with the difference between the stereotypical image of the super strong Black mother and her own alcoholic mother, who decided to leave her children:

> My mother loved us. I must believe that. She worked all day in a department store bakery to buy shoes and school tablets, came home to curse out neighbors who wrongly accused her children of any impropriety (which in an apartment complex usually meant stealing), and kept her house cleaner than most sober women. (26)

Weems concludes that her mother loved her because she provided for her to the best of her ability.

Othermothers often play central roles in defusing the emotional intensity of relationships between bloodmothers and their daughters and in helping daughters understand the Afrocentric ideology of motherhood. Weems describes the women teachers, neighbors, friends, and othermothers that she turned to for help in negotiating a difficult mother/daughter relationship.

These women, she notes, "did not have the onus of providing for me, and so had the luxury of talking to me" (Weems 27).

June Jordan offers one of the most eloquent analyses of a daughter's realization of the high personal cost Black women have paid as bloodmothers and othermothers in working to provide an economic and emotional foundation for Black children. In the following passage, Jordan captures the feelings that my Black women students struggled to put into words:

> As a child I noticed the sadness of my mother as she sat alone in the kitchen at night.... Her woman's work never won permanent victories of any kind. It never enlarged the universe of her imagination or her power to influence what happened beyond the front door of our house. Her woman's work never tickled her to laugh or shout or dance. But she did raise me to respect her way of offering love and to believe that hard work is often the irreducible factor for survival, not something to avoid. Her woman's work produced a reliable home base where I could pursue the privileges of books and music. Her woman's work invented the potential for a completely different kind of work for us, the next generation of Black women: huge, rewarding hard work demanded by the huge, new ambitions that her perfect confidence in us engendered. (145)

Jordan's words not only capture the essence of the Afrocentric ideology of motherhood so central to the well-being of countless numbers of Black women. They simultaneously point the way into the future, one where Black women face the challenge of continuing the mothering traditions painstakingly nurtured by prior generations of African-American women.

Notes

[1] The definition of culture used in this essay is taken from Mullings. According to Mullings, culture is composed of "the symbols and values that create the ideological frame of reference through which people attempt to deal with the circumstances in which they find themselves" (1986a: 13).

[2] For analyses of the relationship of the cult of true womanhood to Black women, see Mullings (1986b); Dill; Carby (esp. chapter 2).

[3] Contrast, for example, the traditionalist analysis of Fraiberg to that of Allen. See also Rich. For an overview of how traditionalists and feminists have shaped the public policy debate on abortion, see Luker.

[4] Feminist scholarship is also challenging Western notions of the family. See Thorne and Yalom.

[5] Since Black women are no longer heavily concentrated in private domestic service, the Mammy image may be fading. In contrast, the matriarch image, popularized in Moynihan, is reemerging in public debates about the feminization of poverty and the urban underclass. See Zinn.

[6]For an alternative analysis of the Mammy image, see Rollins. Classic responses to the matriarchy thesis include Hill; Billingsley; Ladner. For a recent analysis, see Burnham.

[7]The key distinction here is that, unlike the matriarchy thesis, women play central roles in families and this centrality is seen as legitimate. In spite of this centrality, it is important not to idealize African women's family roles. For an analysis by a Black African feminist, see Thiam.

[8]The terms used in this section appear in Troester.

[9]For works in the feminist psychoanalytic tradition, see Chodorow (1974, 1978); Flax.

[10]This essay appeared in the "Black Women's Studies" issue of *SAGE: A Scholarly Journal on Black Women* 6 (1): 4-11.

References

Allen, Jeffner. "Motherhood: The Annihilation of Women." *Mothering: Essays in Feminist Theory.* Ed. Joyce Trebilcot. Totawa, NJ: Rowan & Allanheld, 1983.

Aschenbrenner, Joyce. *Lifelines, Black Families in Chicago.* Prospect Heights, IL: Waveland, 1975.

Billingsley, Andrew. *Black Families in White America.* Englewood Cliffs, NJ: Prentice-Hall, 1968.

Brown, Elsa Barkley. "Hearing Our Mothers' Lives." Paper presented at fifteenth anniversary of African-American and African Studies at Emory College, Atlanta, 1986.

Burnham, Linda. "Has Poverty Been Feminized in Black America?" *Black Scholar* 16 (1985): 15-24.

Cantarow, Ellen. *Moving the Mountain: Women Working for Social Change.* Old Westbury, NY: Feminist Press, 1980.

Carby, Hazel. *Reconstructing Womanhood: The Emergence of the Afro-American Woman Novelist.* New York: Oxford University Press, 1987.

Chodorow, Nancy. "Family Structure and Feminine Personality." *Woman, Culture, and Society.* Eds. Michelle Zimbalist Rosaldo and Louise Lamphere. Stanford: Stanford University Press, 1974.

Chodorow, Nancy. *The Reproduction of Mothering.* Berkeley, CA: University of California, 1978.

Christian, Barbara. "An Angle of Seeing: Motherhood in Buchi Emecheta's *Joys of Motherhood* and Alice Walker's *Meridian.*" *Black Feminist Criticism.* Ed. Barbara Christian. New York: Pergamon, 1985.

Dill, Bonnie Thornton. "Our Mothers' Grief: Racial Ethnic Women and the Maintenance of Families.," Research Paper 4, Center for Research on Women. Memphis, TN: Memphis State University, 1986.

Fields, Mamie Garvin and Karen Fields. *Lemon Swamp and Other Places, A Carolina Memoir.* New York: Free Press, 1983.

Flax, Jane. "The Conflict Between Nurturance and Autonomy in Mother-Daughter

Relationships and Within Feminism." *Feminist Studies* 4 (1978): 171-89.

Fraiberg, Selma. *Every Child's Birthright: In Defense of Mothering*. New York: Basic Books, 1977.

Gilkes, Cheryl. "'Holding Back the Ocean with a Broom': Black Women and Community Work." *The Black Woman*. Ed. LaFrances Rogers-Rose. Beverly Hills, CA: Sage, 1980. 217-31.

Gilkes, Cheryl. "Going Up for the Oppressed: The Career Mobility of Black Women Community Workers." *Journal of Social Issues* 39 (1983):115-39.

Hill, Robert. *The Strengths of Black Families*. New York: Urban League, 1972.

Johnson, Charles. *Shadow of the Plantation*. 1979. Chicago: University of Chicago Press, 1934.

Jordan, June. *On Call, Political Essays*. Boston: South End Press, 1985.

Joseph, Gloria. "Black Mothers and Daughters: Their Roles and Functions in American Society." *Common Differences*. Eds. Gloria Joseph and Jill Lewis. Garden City, NY: Anchor, 1981. 75-126.

King, Mae. "The Politics of Sexual Stereotypes." *Black Scholar* 4 (1973):12-23.

Ladner, Joyce. *Tomorrow's Tomorrow*. Garden City, NY: Doubleday, 1971.

Luker, Kristin. *Abortion and the Politics of Motherhood*. Berkeley, CA: University of California, 1984.

Martin, Elmer and Joanne Mitchell Martin. *The Black Extended Family*. Chicago: University of Chicago Press, 1978.

Mbiti, John. *African Religions and Philosophies*. New York: Anchor, 1969.

McCray, Carrie Allen. "The Black Woman and Family Roles." *The Black Woman*. Ed. LaFrances Rogers-Rose. Beverly Hills, CA: Sage, 1980. 67-78.

Moody, Ann. *Coming of Age in Mississippi*. New York: Dell, 1968.

Moynihan, Daniel Patrick. *The Negro Family: The Case for National Action*. Washington, D.C.: U.S. Government Printing Office, 1965.

Mullings, Leith. "Anthropological Perspectives on the Euro-American Family." *American Journal of Social Psychiatry* 6 (1986a): 11-16.

Mullings, Leith. "Uneven Development: Class, Race and Gender in the United States Before 1900." *Women's Work, Development and the Division of Labor by Gender*. Eds. Eleanor Leacock and Helen Safa. South Hadley, MA: Bergin & Garvey, 1986b. 41-57.

Myers, Lena Wright. *Black Women: Do They Cope Better?* Englewood Cliffs, NJ: Prentice-Hall, 1980.

Oppong, Christine. "Family Structure and Women's Reproductive and Productive Roles: Some Conceptual and Methodological Issues." *Women's Roles and Population Trends in the Third World*. Eds. Richard Anker, Myra Buvinic, and Nadia Youssef. London: Croom Helm, 1982. 133-50.

Oppong, Christine ed. *Female and Male in West Africa*. London: Allen & Unwin, 1983.

Reid, Pamela. "Socialization of Black Female Children." *Women: A Developmental Perspective*. Eds. Phyllis Berman and Estelle Ramey. Washington, DC: National Institutes of Health, 1983.

Rich, Adrienne. *Of Woman Born: Motherhood as Experience and Institution*. New York: Norton, 1976.

Rollins, Judith. *Between Women: Domestics and Their Employers*. Philadelphia: Temple University, 1985.

Simonsen, Thordis ed., *You May Plow Here, The Narrative of Sara Brooks*. New York: Touchstone, 1986.

Stack, Carol B. *All Our Kin*. New York: Harper & Row, 1974.

Sudarkasa, Niara. "Female Employment and Family Organization in West Africa." *The Black Woman Cross-Culturally*. Ed. Filomina Chiamo Steady. Cambridge, MA: Schenkman, 1981a. 49-54.

Sudarkasa, Niara. "Interpreting the African Heritage in Afro-American Family Organization." *Black Families*. Ed. Harriette Pipes McAdoo. Beverly Hills, CA: Sage, 1981b. pp. 37-53.

Tanner, Nancy. "Matrifocality in Indonesia and Africa and Among Black Americans." *Woman, Culture, and Society*. Eds. Michelle Rosaldo and Louise Lamphere. Stanford, CA: Stanford University Press, 1974. 129-56.

Thiam, Awa. *Black Sisters, Speak Out: Feminism and Oppression in Black Africa*. London: Pluto, 1978.

Thorne, Barrie and Marilyn Yalom, eds., *Rethinking the Family*. New York: Longman, 1982.

Troester's Rosalie Riegle. "Turbulence and Tenderness: Mothers, Daughters, and 'Othermothers' in Paule Marshall's *Brown Girl, Brownstones*." *SAGE: A Scholarly Journal on Black Women* 1 (Fall 1984): 13-16.

Wade-Gayles, Gloria. "The Truths of Our Mothers' Lives: Mother-Daughter Relationships in Black Women's Fiction." *SAGE: A Scholarly Journal on Black Women* 1 (Fall 1984): 8-12.

Weems, Renita. "'Hush. Mama's Gotta Go Bye Bye': A Personal Narrative." *SAGE: A Scholarly Journal on Black Women* 1 (Fall 1984): 25-28.

White, Deborah Gray. *Ar'n't I a Woman? Female Slaves in the Plantation South*. New York: W.W. Norton, 1985.

Young, Virginia. "Family and Childhood in a Southern Negro Community." *American Anthropologist* 72 (1970): 269-88.

Zinn, Maxine Baca, "Minority Families in Crisis: The Public Discussion." Research Paper 6, Center for Research on Women. Memphis, TN: Memphis State University, 1987.

Chapter 19

Feminism and Motherhood

An American Reading

ANN SNITOW

I'VE JUST EMERGED from a bout of reading, a wide eclectic sampling of what this wave of U.S. feminism has had to say about motherhood. My conclusions are tentative, and there's another study that I've learned arises directly out of this one—a study of how feminists have *mis*read our own texts on this subject. My reading came as the end point of a year and a half of infertility treatments and, although I see now how heavy that experience lies on my own readings, perhaps my misreadings, I've also come to see that *anyone* doing this work is likely to worry about where to stand. I want to criticize the pervasive pronatalism that has so shaped my recent experience—a pronatalism not only in the culture at large but also inside feminism—but this desire inevitably raises the question: who is allowed to criticize pronatalism, to question the desire for children? The mothers might feel it disingenuous to take on this task; they have their children after all. And the childless are bound to feel that their critique is a species of sour grapes. Certainly, women like me who have tried so hard to have babies late might well feel sheepish and hypocritical about mounting a heavy critique of pronatalism. Will the lesbian community speak up with unembarrassed enthusiasm for the child-free life? Not now. Far more typical at the moment is the recent book *Politics of the Heart: A Lesbian Parenting Anthology.* (Although I find there Nancy D. Polikoff's question to the community: 'Who is talking about the women who don't ever want to be mothers?' Her answer: "No one") (Pollack and Vaughn 1987). In one of the best collections of essays about the decision to mother I've found, *Why Children?*, the editors say they searched for mothers unhappy with motherhood and they found them, but they could not get these mothers to write (Dowrick and Grundberg 1981). The dissatisfied mothers feared hurting their children if they admitted how little they had liked mothering. And what about the mothers who had children against their will? Are they in a position to complain? Not really, once again: it will hurt the children to know they were unwanted. Besides, women have made an art of turning these defeats into triumphs; women have made a richer world out of their necessities. And so the children rarely hear a forthright critique of how women come to mother in a patriarchy although, of course, they usually know all about it at one level or another, and guilt is left to fill in the holes of the story.

Women with children and women without them have been bristling at each other for years over the question of authenticity. The fight over the Equal Rights Amendment was a national example of this kind of warfare, but even inside feminism there's no particularly friendly entry point for this discussion. Which speaker has the necessary experience, hence the authority, to speak? Mothers can say they've seen both sides, can make judgements about what motherhood is like. Initiates, they are the ones who can measure the true dimensions of the choice. It's harder to imagine what the non-mothers can tell about their condition. One rises each morning to children—and often, of course, all through the night—but does one rise to the counter-condition—Ah, another day without children? The two conditions are not precisely parallel. And each one has its own narrative taboos.

What I want to argue is that feminism set out to break *both* taboos—those surrounding the experiences of the mothers and of the non-mothers, but for reasons I find both inside our movement and even more in the American society in which that movement unfolded, in the long run we were better able to attend to mothers' voices (or at least to *begin* on that project) than we were able to imagine a full and deeply meaningful life without motherhood, without children. Finally, in the defensive Reagan years, feminist ambivalence and guilt about blaming mothers, and our ambivalence about becoming mothers ourselves, toned down and tuned out a more elusive discussion of what choice might mean if there were really two imaginable lives for women—with and without children.

Building a supportive culture for both the mothers and the non-mothers is a crucial feminist task, but in the rising national babble of pronatalism in the 1980s, listening to the mothers was a project subtly susceptible to co-optation. Meanwhile, although I certainly felt that feminism was my shield at the infertility clinic, and that the often desperate women I met there were relatively lucky to be experiencing this loss of a baby now, when feminism is in the air, when middle-class married women work, when the birth rate is 1.9 children per woman, not the 3.7 of 1956, none the less feminist culture didn't seem to be producing alluring images or thinkable identities for the childless. What feminist idea about independence of work or political life seemed bracing enough to counter the yearning miasma of the infertility clinic? Could one turn to the feminist critique of the new reproductive technologies? Middle class and well informed, the women in infertility support groups (set up by the national organisation, *Resolve)* had already intimated most of the useful social and medical feminist analysis in books like Andrea Eagan's, Barbara Katz Rothman's, Gina Correa's and Barbara Stanworth's. Certainly, we all knew we were test animals (for example, record-keeping was the major undertaking at the clinic I attended), but this knowledge of the down-sides of medicalization had little bearing on the questions of our desire and need. Where was the feminist critique of our motivation? Why were we such eager consumers of twice-daily injections of pergonal and mood-altering progesteron?

In 1970, feminism would have been quite hostile to these extreme undertakings, but that can't help anyone now. Indeed, it may well be that that earlier reaction to the pressure to mother was so historically specific that it can have no direct descendants. Young women now can be angry about the threat to abortion without feeling the terrible claustrophobia about the future my generation felt as children of the 1950s. All the same, historical shifts like these cannot fully explain the current flaccidity of the critique of motherhood in feminism. Surely we can't claim that young women have made peace with mothers, or that mothers now have social services or more help, so where has the rage gone? Why does the pronatalism of our period flourish with so little argument from us, the feminists?

To answer questions like these, I've begun to construct a time-line of feminism on motherhood. (This research is very much in progress and I hope readers will suggest titles, key moments, significant shifts as they also experienced them). Here are the main features of the line as it has emerged so far.

Although the record is complex, and although my generalizations are often contradicted by important exceptions, I see three distinct periods along the time-line. First, 1963 (Friedan, of course) to about 1974—the period of what I call the "demon texts," for which we have been apologizing ever since. Second, 1975 to 1979, the period in which feminism tried to take on the issue of motherhood seriously, to criticize the institution, explore the actual experience, theorize the social and psychological implications. In this period, feminists began on the project of breaking the first of the two taboos I mentioned earlier—the taboo on mothers' own descriptions of the fascination and joy of mothering (even in a patriarchy) and also the pain, isolation, boredom, murderousness.

By 1979, in a massive shift in the politics of the whole country, some feminist work shifts, too, from discussing motherhood to discussing families. Feminism continues to anatomize motherhood, but the movement is on the defensive. Certain once-desired changes recede as imaginable possibilities. In this period, feminists speak of "different voices" and "single mothers by choice"; the feminist hope of breaking the iron bond between mother and child seems gone, except in rhetorical flourishes, perhaps gone for good in this wave.

I'm going to try—briefly—to substantiate this periodization, but first a reminder: precision about generations is particularly important in a discussion of motherhood. In Paula Giddings' fine phrase, "when and where I enter" matters. Each one has her own point of entry on this line.

None the less, the line has its own power to impose similar conditions, pressures, meanings on women of different ages, races, classes. The particular piece of feminist intellectual history I'm exploring here follows quite closely the trajectory of the baby-boom generation, what demographers call the mouse in the python, a large bulge traveling down the decades.

As Atina Grossmann has pointed out, this bulging generation is very powerful and continues to set its own rules. Its late child-bearing has made an upward blip on the generally descending graph of births per thousand. Its experiences disproportionately influence the social atmosphere. When it has babies, the stores are flooded with baby food. The culture this group creates, including the culture of feminism, shapes the era I'm describing here. For the young, the next bit of the line remains a mystery. Current debates about the real meaning of black teenage pregnancy and the low rate of marriage and fertility among college students give hints of how women may now be experimenting with the placement of children in their life cycles. It's a cheerful thought that many readers of this journal will have experiences that don't correspond to this outline.

Period 1: 1963 to About 1975

1963 is the year of *The Feminine Mystique*. The inadequacies of that book are well known. For example, in *From Margin to Center* (1984), bell hooks flips Friedan's story of the home-bound misery of the suburban housewife: for black women of the same period, paid work (which Friedan recommends for middle-class women) was usually drudgery, alienated work; work in the home seemed far more satisfying. Many have criticized Friedan's classism, racism, homophobia, her false universals. But Friedan herself has ignored all this and criticized *The Feminine Mystique* on different grounds altogether. In *The Second Stage* (1981), Friedan blames her earlier book for being antifamily, for trying to pry women away from children, and for overemphasizing women as autonomous individuals. In fact, *The Feminine Mystique* is rather mild on these points; it says nothing most feminists wouldn't agree to today about the need for women to have some stake in the world beyond their homes.

The Feminine Mystique is the first of my demon texts, by which I mean books demonized, apologized for, endlessly quoted out of context, to prove that the feminism of the early seventies was, in Friedan's words of recantation, "strangely blind." She excoriates her earlier self for thinking too much about "women alone, or women against men," but not enough about "the family." In retrospect, it's an amazing thing that books in the early seventies dared to speak of "women alone, or women against men." It was, plain and simple, a breakthrough. Yet we've been apologizing for these books and often misreading them as demon texts ever since.

The most famous demon text is Shulamith Firestone's *The Dialectic of Sex: The Case for Feminist Revolution* (1970). This book is usually the starting point for discussions of how feminism has been "strangely blind" about motherhood. Certainly, there are few of its sentences that Firestone would leave unmodified if she were writing with the same intent today. Her undertheorized enthusiasm for cybernetics, her self-hating disgust at the pregnant body ("Pregnancy is barbaric"), her picture of the female body as a prison from which a benign, nonpatriarchal science might release us have all dated. Her call for an end to childhood—although more interesting, I think, than scoffers have been prepared to grant—doesn't resonate with any experience of children at all. Finally, though, it's her tone we can't identify with, the '60s atmosphere of free-wheeling, shameless speculation. Part of the demonizing of this text arises out of a misreading of genre. *The Dialectic of Sex* is an example of utopian writing. (Some of this atmosphere has now been reclaimed—at least for academic feminism—in such work as Donna Haraway's (1985) "Manifesto for Cyborgs.")

Besides this tendency by feminists as well as nonfeminists to misread the tone and genre of *The Dialectic of Sex,* everyone colludes in calling it a mother-hating book. Search the pages; you won't find the evidence. I find instead:

> At the present time, for a woman to come out openly against motherhood on principle is physically dangerous. She can get away with it only if she adds that she is neurotic, abnormal, childhating and therefore "unfit" ... This is hardly a free atmosphere of inquiry. Until the taboo is lifted, until the decision not to have children or not to have them "naturally" is at least as legitimate as traditional childbearing, women are as good as forced into their female roles. (199-200)

In other words, Firestone's work is reactive and rhetorical. The point is always "smash patriarchy," not mothers.

Of course, there are real demon texts inside feminism, callow works like a few of the essays in the collection *Pronatalism: The Myth of Mom and Apple Pie* (Peck and Senderowitz 1974), which reject childbearing in favour of having unsoiled white rugs and the extra cash to buy them. There's also some panic during this period about the new term then, the "population explosion." An ecology influenced by feminism has reinterpreted this material for us since, but some of the early essays talk as if once again it's up to women to populate the world properly, this time by abstaining from a killing overproduction of children.

But, inside feminism, such moments are rare. Instead I found extreme rhetoric meant to break the inexorable tie between mothers and children. For example, Lucia Valeska in "If all else fails, I'm still a mother" (1975): "All women who are able to plot their destinies with the relative mobility of the childfree should be encouraged to take on at least one existing child ... to have our own bio-logical children today is personally and politically irresponsible" (82-3). In the demonizing mode it's easy to hear this as a party line with biological mothers as self-indulgent backsliders. I hear in it, too, an effort to imagine a responsibility to kids which is not biological. The early texts are trying to pull away from the known and, like all utopian thinking, they can sound thin, absurd, undigested. But mother-hating? No.

The real demon texts I've found in my first period are works of social science outside feminism like the Moynihan report of 1965 on the so-called "tangled pathology" of the black family. Mother really *is* named as the problem there, and the cure? More power for fathers! Black feminists often have to wrestle with this text when they set out to write about the motherhood experience. Ambivalence about the culture of black mothering is hard to express in the same universe where one has also to find ways to contradict the Moynihan report.

Finally, in my search for early feminist mother-hating what I found was—most-ly—an absence. In the major anthologies like *Sisterhood is Powerful* (1970), *Women in a Sexist Society* (1971) and *Liberation Now!* (1971) there are hardly any articles on any aspect of mothering. Nothing strange, really, about this blindness. The mouse had only just started down the python; most of the writers were young.

The exceptions, such as several articles in Leslie Tanner's *Voices from Women's Liberation* (1970), offer a programme that is unexceptionable even today—for example, Vicki Pollard's "Producing Society's Babies" or the much reprinted "On Day Care" by Louise Gross and Phyllis MacEwan. This second piece argues mildly that women shouldn't just want day care because it will liberate *them,* but also because day care is good for kids, too.

The revisions between the *Our Bodies, Ourselves* which was a newsprint booklet in 1971 and the glossy tome *Ourselves and Our Children* of 1978 reveals, I think, the hidden dynamics of our alienation from that earlier time. Under the section "Pregnancy," the early version says such things as: "We, as women, grow up in a society that subtly leads us to believe that we will find our ultimate fulfillment by living out our reproductive function and at the same time discourages us from trying to express ourselves in the world of work" (73). Only after pages and pages of reassurance that "we as women can be whole human beings without having children" (74) does the 1971 text finally ask, "What are the positive reasons for having children?" (76). The feminism of 1970 established a harsh self-questioning about a motherhood which formerly had been taken for granted.

But soon, very soon, this pre-emptory and radical questioning was misread as an attack on housewives. This has been as effective an instance of divide-and-conquer as I know. By the late seventies, both the mothers and the nonmothers were on the defensive. What a triumph of backlash, with internal dynamics which have been fully explored by Faye Ginsburg (1989) and others, feminists seeking to understand the special bitterness among women in our era.

The rewriting of the material on whether or not to have a child, in the *Ourselves and Our Children* of 1978, carries me into my second period, 1976 to 1980.

Period 2: 1976-1979

The 1978 text couldn't be more different from the earlier version of *Our Bodies, Ourselves.* It acknowledges that "until quite recently" having a baby wasn't really considered a decision, but then goes on to assume that all that has changed, ending with this gee-whiz sentence: "Now almost five percent of the population has declared its intentions to remain child-free" (17).

This is a liberal text, celebrating variety without much concern for uneven consequences. Both people who have decided to have children and people who have decided against are quoted at some length; but the effect is false symmetry, with no dialectic tension. The proliferation of people's reasons here is useful and instructive, an effort to get at difference, but the structural result is an aimless pluralism, a series of life-style questions, no polities.

But if in my description of *Ourselves and Our Children* I'm using the word liberal pejoratively, this my second period is also liberal in the best sense of the word: a time of freer speech, wider inquiry, a refusal of orthodoxy, an embrace of the practical reality. In these years the feminist work of exploring motherhood took off, and books central to feminist thinking in this wave were written, both about the daily experience of being a mother and about motherhood's most far-reaching implications.

1976 alone saw the publication of Adrienne Rich's *Of Woman Born,* Dorothy Dinnerstein's *The Mermaid and the Minotaur,* Jane Lazarre's *The Mother Knot,* and Linda Gordon's *Woman's Body, Woman's Right.* Also in that year, French feminism began to be a power in American feminist academic thinking. *Signs* published Hélène Cixous's "The Laugh of the Medusa" which included these immediately controversial words: "There is always within [woman] at least a little of that good mothers milk. She writes in white ink." Mysteries and provocations—which introduced a flood!

My Mother/Myself (1977), Nancy Friday's book, popularized the motherhood discussions in feminism, though it has often been criticized as essentially a daughter's book. Julia Kristeva split the page of *Tel Quel* down the middle in that year in "Love's heretical ethics"; she was digging for the semiotic, the mother language of the body before speech. And 1978: Nancy Chodorow's *The Reproduction of Mothering* and Michele Wallace's *Black Macho and the Myth of the Super-Woman.* These books were events. The intellectual work of feminism has its renaissance in these years. Not only does this period give rise to important work but also to fructifying debate.

Rachel DuPlessis introduced the brilliant special issue of *Feminist Studies* on motherhood in 1978 with an encomium to Rich's *Of Woman Born.* She honoured what Rich was trying to do—to pry mothering away from the patriarchal insti-tution, *motherhood.* But then, DuPlessis went on to worry that Rich might be over-reacting, overprivileging the body. DuPlessis wrote, "If, by the process of touching physicality, Rich wants to find that essence beyond conflict, the place where all women necessarily meet, the essence of woman, pure blood, I cannot follow there. Discussions like these inaugurate our continuing debates about es-sentialism, the body and social construction."

DuPlessis says she won't discuss practical politics, but she does ask the larger political question that nags throughout the period but is rarely addressed: which construction of motherhood is productive for feminist work? If we take Dinner-stein at her word, we're trying to get men to be mothers. If we follow Rich, our energies move towards building a female culture capable of the support not only of women but also of their children. Neither author would put these implications so baldly, without shading. Yet these texts create rival political auras and feminist theory is still far from sorting out the implications for activism of this great period of groundbreaking work.

It's important to add that, right in the middle of this period, in 1977, the first Hyde Amendment was passed; we lost Medicaid abortion. Abortion—the primal scene of this wave, won, to our amazement, in 1973, was only affordable for all classes for *four years* before this barely established right began slipping away again.

While feminist thinkers were elaborating on the themes of motherhood, that other question—whether or not mothering is to remain a female universal—was slipping, slipping away. Feminist work of this period largely ignores the subject of my second taboo, the viability of the choice not to mother. Meanwhile the New Right was mounting a massive offensive against all efforts to separate women and mothering.

Period 3: 1980-1990

My second period ends—and my third begins—with the important threshold article by Sara Ruddick in 1980, "Maternal thinking." This piece pushed the work of the late seventies to some logical conclusions. Ruddick took seriously the question of what women actually *do* when they mother. She developed a rich description of what she called "maternal practice" and "maternal thinking." A whole separate study deserves to be made of how this much-reprinted article has been read, reread, misread, appropriated into a variety of arguments. Ruddick herself says that the implications for feminism of her splendid anatomy of mothering are unclear. Is motherhood really a separable practice? Are its special features capable of translation into women's public power? Does motherhood have the universality Ruddick's work implies? Does the different voices argument (also developed by Carol Gilligan in 1982) lead to a vigorous feminist politics?

This is not even the beginning of a proper discussion of Ruddick but, for my purposes here, it's important to point out that Ruddick herself says that her book is not really about what feminism should say or do about mothering. Rather, it provides one of the best descriptions feminism has of *why* women are so deeply committed to the mothering experience, even under very oppressive conditions. Ruddick's work is a song to motherhood—multiphonic, without sugar—but still a song. "Maternal thinking" is the fullest response since Adrienne Rich to the call to end my first taboo, the taboo on speaking the life of the mother.

It leaves my other taboo untouched, but this might well have seemed benign neglect in any other year but 1980. It was not part of Ruddick's intention to publish her work in the same year Reagan was elected, yet the meeting of the twain is, I think, part of this small history of feminism on motherhood.

Ruddick argues—with much reason—that hers is a specifically anti-Reagan text: it includes men as mothers; it includes lesbians as mothers; it demands public support for women's work. But it is extremely difficult to do an end-run around Reaganism by a mere proliferation of family forms. The left tried it; feminism tried it; everyone failed. (I'm thinking of Michael Lerner's Friends of Families organizing between about 1979 and 1982. I'm thinking of NOW's National Assembly on the Future of the Family in November of 1979. I'm thinking of Betty Friedan's retreat in *The Second Stage* of 1981). As Barbara Ehrenreich and others pointed out, the word "family" was a grave in which the more autonomous word "women" got buried. The problem with defining any cohabiting group as family and leaving it at that was the disappearance of any discussion of power within that group. Arlie Hochschild's *The Second Shift* (1989) reaffirms what we already intimate from experience: women, not families, continue to do almost all domestic work.

My time-line for the eighties is a record of frustration, retrenchment, defeat and sorrow. Out of the Baby M case in 1986-7 in which a so-called surrogate mother battled for and lost custody of the child she had carried but contracted away before birth, comes Phyllis Chesler's *Sacred Bond* (1988), the very title unthinkable a decade earlier. Certainly, things weren't going our way, and the studies to prove it poured out. In 1986 and 1987 we get Chesler on the injustice of child-custody laws, including feminist-initiated reforms, and Lenore Weitzman's frightening figures about what happens to women after no-fault divorce.

1986: my peak year for backlash at least partially internalized by feminism, gives us Sue Miller's novel *The Good Mother* and Sylvia Ann Hewlett's *A Lesser Life*. *A Lesser life* concerns itself with the horrendous struggles of working mothers, that is of most mothers now. Hewlett, once a self-defined feminist, is now against the ERA and sees nothing but liberal blarney in legal-equality models. In this particularly mean season, in which mothers do everything without social supports, Hewlett wants protection. She simply can't imagine social support for childrearing except as special programmes for women, whom she assumes will be the main ones responsible for children forevermore. Hewlett blames feminism for not making demands on the state. Of course we *did* make them. Our failure to win is a complex, historical event Hewlett oversimplifies. Further, one might argue that Hewlett's assumption, that women will inevitably do most of the childrearing, is broadly shared by the men in power, too, and that this attitude itself is one reason it is hard to coerce the state to do the work.

There are exceptions to backlash thinking on the eighties time-line, of course, although several turned out to be books and articles published elsewhere (I find my line doesn't work outside the U.S.). Kathleen Gerson's *Hard Choices: How Women Decide About Work, Careers and Motherhood* (1985) tried to get at how profoundly women's lives are being changed by work. Sacred bond or not, women are simply spending less of their lives on mothering, more and more on a variety of other things. This book was among the very few I found that tried to address my second taboo, to take seriously the idea that women may well come to see mothering as one element in life, not its defining core. However raggedly, the women Gerson interviewed are already living out basically new story lines, making piecemeal changes over which feminism must struggle to preside.

Also during this period have come the great books on abortion: Rosalind Petchesky's *Abortion and Women's Choice* and Kristen Luker's *Abortion and the Politics of Motherhood* in 1984 and Faye Ginsburg's *Contested Lives* in 1989. But on the political front it's been some time since feminists demanding abortion have put front and centre the idea that one good use to which one might put this right is to choose not to have kids *at all*. Chastised in the Reagan years, pro-choice strategists—understandably—have emphasized the right to wait, the right to space one's children, the right to have each child wanted. They feared invoking any image that could be read as a female withdrawal from the role of nurturer.

Broad societal events like the steady rise of divorce and women's increasing workplace participation collide with women's failure to get day care, child support, fair enough custody laws, changes in the structure of a work day and a typical work life, and finally any reliable, ongoing support from men. Our discouragement is, in my view, the subtext of most of what we have written about motherhood in the past decade. I think women are heartbroken. Never has the baby been so delicious. We are—in this period of reaction—elaborating, extending, reinstitutionalizing this relation for ourselves. Mary Gordon writes in *The New York Times* book review (1985): "It is impossible for me to believe that anything I write could have a fraction of the importance of the child growing inside me." A feminist theorist tells me she is more proud of her new baby than of all her books.

I don't mean to criticize these deep sentiments but to situate them.

They are freely expressed now; in 1970, feminist mothers, like all mothers, were briefly on the defensive, and ecstatic descriptions of mothering were themselves taboo. But now, since 1980, that brief past, with whatever its excesses or limitations, feels long gone. Even the still acceptable project of elaborating the culture of motherhood tends now to leave out the down part of the mother's story—her oppression, fury, regrets. One can't speak blithely of wanting an abortion anymore nor sceptically about the importance of motherhood. In the 1980s we have apologized again and again for ever having uttered what we now often name a callow, classist, immature or narcissistic word against mothering. Instead, we have praised the heroism of women raising children alone, or poor, usually both. We have embraced nurturance as an ethic, sometimes wishing that men would share this ethic without much hoping they will, and we have soldiered on, caring for the kids (in the U.S., more first children were born in 1988 than in any year on record), and continued to do 84 percent of the housework. Complaints now have a way of sounding monstrous, even perhaps to our own ears. For here the children are, and if we're angry, in backlash times like these it's easy for feminism's opponents to insist that anger at oppression is really anger at children or at mothers. The New Right has been brilliant at encouraging this slippage, making women feel that being angry at the present state of mothering will poison the well of life. Guilt complicates feminist rage—and slows down feminist activism. There is the mother's guilt towards her children, and the nonmother's guilt that she has evaded this mass sisterhood now elaborated for us all as full of joy and pain, blood and passion, that she has evaded the central life dramas of intimacy and separation described so well in feminist writing about motherhood.

So, in conclusion, what? I hope it's clear that it's no part of my argument to say women shouldn't want children. This would be to trivialize the complexity of wishes, to call mothering a sort of false consciousness—a belittling suggestion. Women have incorporated a great deal into their mothering, but one question for feminism should surely be: Do we want this presently capacious identity, mother, to expand or to contract? How special do we want mothering to be? In other words, what does feminism gain by the privileging of motherhood? My reading makes more obvious than ever that feminists completely disagree on this point—or rather that there are many feminisms, different particularly on this point. And here's another viper's nest: do feminists want men to become mothers, too, that is, to have primary childcare responsibilities?

Again, the feminist work on this point veers wildly, is murky.

Women disagree about what we should want—also about what we can get—from men. bell hooks thinks we're afraid to let men know how really mad we are, afraid to finally confront them. That may be one reason we falter, but there are others: women ask, for example, "Can men really nurture?" And behind that doubt, or that insult, hides our knowledge of what psychological power mothers have. Why give that up, we may well ask? I suspect that in addition, in our period, women are eager to establish that we don't really need men. This wave of feminism was a great outburst of indignation and it's important to us to feel that men are no longer necessary, particularly since lots of men are gone before the baby is two. In so far as patriarchy means the protective law of the father, patriarchy's over.

I find a great cynicism among us about ever getting men's help, or the state's. Because we have won so few tangible victories, women tend to adopt a sort of Mother Courage stance now—long suffering, almost sometimes a parody of being tireless.

But it occurs to me that, finally, this picture I'm painting is much too bleak. One can ask other questions that hint at a more volatile situation altogether. The low spirits of recent movement history are an irony. Actually, we are living in a moment in which women's identities are extremely labile and expanding. How do we feminists greet and interpret the fact that women are voting with their feet, marrying later, using contraception and abortion and having fewer children? Do we look forward to some golden age when parental leave, childcare and flexitime will have helped women so much that the birth-rate will rise again? Such a thought seems buried in the current feminist piety about abortion, that we want not only the right to abort but also the right to have children, etc. A worthy thought, but one that has not yet been fully examined. Are we to consider the lowered birth-rate merely one more proof that women are so over-worked they're ready to drop, or might there be some opportunities for feminism buried in these broad demographic changes?

Under what banner are we going to fly our demands for mothers? I like best the gender-neutral constructions of this cohort of the brilliant feminist lawyers. Yet, as they would be first to point out, gender-neutral demands—for parenting leaves, disability, gender-blind custody, have their short-term price. We give up something, a special privilege wound up in the culture-laden word "mother" which we will not instantly regain in the form of freedom and power. We're talking about a slow process of change when we talk about motherhood; we're talking about social divisions which are still fundamental. Giving up the exclusivity of motherhood is bound to feel to many like loss. Deirdre English called this "the fear that feminism will free men first." Men will have the power of the world *and* the nurturant experience, the centrality to their children. Only a fool gives up something present for something intangible and speculative, Jack and the Beanstalk exchanging the cow for a couple of beans. But even if we can't yet imagine our passage from here to there, from control over motherhood to shared, socialized parenthood, couldn't we talk about it, structure demands? An epigram keeps forming in my mind: "Just because you can't have something doesn't mean you don't want it or shouldn't fight for it."

Let me end with a cautionary analogy: In the nineteenth century, feminism's *idée fixe* was the vote. We won it, but it was hard to make it mean something larger than mere voting, to make it into a source of public authority for women. In our wave, the *idée fixe* has been abortion. If we're lucky, and if we work very hard, we may win it. But just like with the vote, there will be much resistance to letting the right to abortion expand to its larger potential meaning. We seem—this time around—to really want abortion. And this right carries within it the seed of new identities for women.

Postscript

On 30 April 1991, I made a visit, kindly arranged by Hester Eisenstein, to the State University of New York at Buffalo, where a wonderful group addressed the question of the time-line.

The younger women in the room reported that they were under acute pressure to have children—and soon. We older ones felt consternation: what form does the pressure take? "Medical. The media, doctors, other women all tell us that if we don't have children, we're opening ourselves to all kinds of diseases like endometriosis and uterine cancer."

Dispirited about the current atmosphere, we compared this threat with the nineteenth century idea that if women went to college, their uteruses would shrivel up as their brains developed. At the same time, we noted for the record the problem with the counter-claim sometimes made by feminism that all medical limits set in a patriarchy are merely corrupt, that without patriarchy we could control our bodies. This misleading promise led some to assume late babies were no problem at all, and contributed to the very atmosphere which has brought so many women to put faith in erratic and experimental technologies which promise this elusive control.

In yet another turn of the argument, we worried that some recent feminist critiques of birth technology ignore advances on which we've come usefully to rely. Claire Kahane went so far as to wonder if some sectors of the ecology movement, by romanticizing "the natural," had added to the pressures the younger women in the room were feeling to do "the natural" thing.

We moved on to men: are men trying to break in upon the mother-child dyad with the new birth technologies, or with law suits against women who smoke, drink or take crack while pregnant? If the mother is the enemy of the foetus, the state becomes the paternal rescuer. These thoughts led us to question just how paranoid we wanted to be: male appropriations are legion and female scepticism is justly epidemic, but how, then, to leave the path open for men to make a more progressive move towards joining women and children?

Certainly, men still fade out of most motherhood discussions. For example, several reported that their college alumni magazines were flooded in the mid-1980s with reports from career women who didn't want to go to work anymore, who wanted to stay home with their kids. This was the new "choice" of the middle class. What made this potentially rich option for variety and change ominous besides its unrepentant class-bound character was the utter lack of this "choice" for men. The "Mommy track" as it was called in the US was a revised work trajectory which would include time for children. Revolutionary if it were a rethinking of work for everyone, this corporate plan became a symbol of the continuing divide between male and female life-stories—with motherhood the signpost at the crossroads.

Thank you to the feminists of Buffalo.

In other responses, several women have questioned my observation that the U.S. time-line of feminism on motherhood won't work for other countries. Marti Scheel writes that in the case she knows, West Germany, the line works if one starts three to five years later, as the baby boom was delayed there. Of course, I'd like to know what other readers outside the U.S. think.

Greetings from New York.

Time-Line: Feminism on Motherhood

Compiled by Ann Snitow and Carolyn Morell.

Key: All items are feminist or feminist-related unless marked*. Items marked* are relevant articles and events.

1963
Friedan, Betty. *The Feminine Mystique*. New York: W. W. Norton and Co.

1964
Rossi, Alice. "Transition to Parenthood." *Journal of Marriage and the Family* 1 (30).

1965
*Moynihan, Daniel Patrick. "The Negro Family: The Case for National Action."

1969
Willis, Eden. "Whatever Happened to Women? Nothing, That's the Trouble." *Mademoiselle* (September).

1970

Firestone, Shulamith. *The Dialectic of Sex.* New York: William Morrow.

Pollard, Vicki. "Producing Society's Babies." *Women: A Journal of Liberation* (Fall).

Tanner, Leslie, ed. *Voices From Women's Liberation.* New York: Signet.

1971

Boston Women's Health Course Collective. *Our Bodies, Ourselves.* Boston: New England Free Press.

Peck, Eden. The Baby Trap. New York: Pinnacle Books.

Comprehensive Child Development Act. Passed by Congress, vetoed by Richard Nixon (Child care funds).

1973

Radl, Shirley. *Mother's Day is Over.* New York: Charterhouse.

Gilder, George. *Sexual Suicide.* New York: Quadrangle Books.

Roe v. Wade. The Supreme Court guarantees the abortion right.

1974

Peck, Ellen and Judith Senderowitz. *Pronatalism: The Myth of Mom and Apple Pie.* New York: Thomas Y. Crowell.

Bernard, Jessie. *The Future of Motherhood.* New York: The Dial Press.

Mitchell, Juliet. *Psychoanalysis and Feminism: Freud, Reich, Laing, and Women.* New York: Pantheon Books.

1975

Hammer, Signe. *Daughters and Mothers, Mothers and Daughters.* New York: Quadrangle Books.

Valeska, Lucia. "If All Else Fails, I'm Still a Mother." *Quest* 1 (3) (Winter).

1976

Chodorow, Nancy and Susan Contratto. "The fantasy of the perfect mother." *Social Problems* 23.2.

Cixous, Hélène. "The Laugh of the Medusa." *Signs* 1 (4) (Summer): 875-93.

Dinnerstein, Dorothy. *The Mermaid and the Minotaur: Sexual Arrangements* and Human Malaise. New York: Harper and Row.

Gordon, Linda. *Woman's Body, Woman's Right: Birth Control in America.* Grossman Publishers.

Lazarre, Jane. *The Mother Knot.* New York: McGraw-Hill.

Rich, Adrienne. *Of Woman Born: Motherhood as Experience and Institution.* New York: W. W. Norton.

Russo, N. F. "The Motherhood Mandate." *Journal of Social Issues* 32.3.

1977

Friday, Nancy. *My Mother/Myself: The Daughter's Search for Identity.* New York:

Delacorte Press.

Klepfisz, Irena. "Women without children/women without families/women alone." Reprinted in *Dreams of an Insomniac: Jewish Feminist Essays, Speeches, and Diatribes*. Eight Mountain Press (1990).

Joffe, Carole. *Friendly Intruders: Childcare Professionals and Family Life*. Berkeley: University of California Press.

Kristeva, Julia. "Love's Heretical Ethics." *Tel Quel* 74 (Winter): 39-49.

Rossi, Alice. "A Biosocial Perspective on Parenting." *Daedelus* 106 (3).

*Hyde Amendment. No Medicaid abortions, end of abortions for poor women.

*Lasch, Christopher. *Haven in a Heartless World*. New York: Basic Books.

1978

Chodorow, Nancy. *The Reproduction of Mothering: Psychoanalysis and The Sociology of Gender*. Berkeley: University of California Press.

Boston Women's Health Book Collective. *Ourselves and Our Children: A Book by and for Parents*. New York: Random House.

Feminist Studies. Special Issue. "Toward a Feminist Theory of Motherhood." 4 (2) (June).

Hoffner, Elaine. *Mothering: The Emotional Experience of Motherhood after Freud and Feminism*. New York: Doubleday Inc.

Wallace, Michele. *Black Macho and the Myth of the Super-Woman*. New York: The Dial Press.

1979

Arcana, Judith. *Our Mother's Daughters*. Berkeley: Shameless Hussy Press.

CARASA (Committee for Abortion Rights and Against Sterilization Abuse). *Women Under Attack: Abortion, Sterilization Abuse and Reproductive Freedom*. New York.

Chesler, Phyllis. *With Child: A Diary of Motherhood*. New York: Thomas Y. Crowell.

Feminist Studies. Special Issue. "Workers, Reproductive Hazards and the Politics of Protection." 5 (Summer).

Friedan, Betty. "Feminism Takes a New Turn." *The New York Times* 26 August.

Lorde, Audre. "Man Child: A Black Lesbian Feminist's Response." *Conditions* 4.

Willis, Eden. "The Family: Love it or Leave it." *The Village Voice* 24 (38) (17 September): 1, 29-35.

Lerner, Michael. "Friends of Families." Organizing drive, California, c. 1979-82.

NOW. "National Assembly on the Future of the Family" conference. New York Hilton Hotel, 19 November.

"The Scholar and the Feminist VI: The Future of Difference." Conference, Barnard College, New York 29 April.

1980

Badinter, Elizabeth. *Mother Love: Myth and Reality*. New York: Macmillan.

Ehrensaft, Diane. "When Men and Women Mother." *Socialist Review* 49 10 (4) (Summer).

Eisenstein, Beater and Alice Jardine, eds. *The Future of Difference.* Boston: G. K Hall and Co.

Marks, Elaine and Isabelle De Courtivron, eds. *New French Feminisms, An Anthology.* Amherst: University of Massachusetts Press.

Oakley, Ann. *Becoming a Mother.* New York: Schocken Books; *Women Confused: Toward a Sociology of Childbirth.* New York: Schocken Books.

Ruddick, Sara. "Maternal Thinking." *Feminist Studies* 6 (2) (Summer): 342-67.

Weisskopf, Susan Contratto. "Maternal Sexuality and Asexual Motherhood." *Signs* 5 (4) (Summer).

1981

Bridenthal, Renate, Joan Kelly, Amy Swerdlow, and Phyllis Vine, eds. *Household and Kin: Families in Flux.* New York: The Feminist Press.

Brown, Carol. "Mothers, Fathers, and Children: From Private to Public Patriarchy." Reprinted in *Women and Revolution.* Ed. Lydia Sargent. Boston: South End Press.

Dowrick, Stephanie and Sibyl Grundberg. *Why Children?* New York: Harcourt Brace Jovanovich.

Friedan, Betty. *The Second Stage.* New York: Simon and Schuster.

Hirsch, M. "Mothers and Daughters: A Review." *Signs* 7 (1).

Lorber, J., R. L. Coser, A. S. Rossi, and N. Chodorow. "On *The Reproduction of Mothering:* A Methodological Debate." *Signs* 7 (1).

O'Brien, Mary. *The Politics of Reproduction.* New York: Routledge.

The Family Protection Act proposed.

1982

Barrett, Michele and Mary McIntosh. *The Anti-Social Family.* London: Verso.

Gilbert, Lucy and Paula Webster. *Bound by Love: The Sweet Trap of Daughterhood.* Boston: Beacon Press.

Gilligan, Carol. *In a Different Voice: Psychological Theory and Women's Development.* Cambridge and London: Harvard University Press.

Lerner, L. "Reproduction of Mothering: An Appraisal." *The Psychoanalytic Review* 51 (1).

Rothman, Barbara Katz. *In Labor: Women and Power in the Birth Place.* New York: W. W.Norton.

Thorne, Barrie and Marilyn Yalom. *Rethinking the Family: Some Feminist Questions.* New York and London: Longman.

*ERA defeated.

1983

Dally, Ann. *Inventing Motherhood: The Consequences of an Ideal.* New York: Shocken Books.

Daniels, Pamela and Kathy Weingarten. *Sooner or Later.* New York: W.W. Norton.

Diamond, Irene, ed. *Families, Politics and Public Policy: A Feminist Dialogue On the State.* New York: Longman.

Folbre, Nancy. "Of Patriarchy Born: The Political Economy of Fertility Decisions." *Feminist Studies* 9 (2) (Summer).

Porter, Nancy. Rev. of "Mothering: Essays in Feminist Theory." *Women's Studies Quarterly* 7 (Winter).

Riley, Denise. *War in the Nursery: Theories of the Child and the Mother.* London: Virago.

1984

Alpert, J. L., M. Gerson, and M. S. Richardson. "Mothering: The View From Psychological Research." *Signs* 9 (3).

Arditti, Rita, Renate Duelli Klein, and Shelley Minden. *Test-Tube Women: What Future for Motherhood?* London: Pandora Press.

Boston Women's Health Book Collective. *The New Our Bodies, Ourselves: A Book by and for Women.* New York: Touchstone/Simon and Schuster.

Delphy, Christine. *Close to Home: A Materialist Analysis of Women's Oppression.* Amherst: University of Massachusetts.

Gerson Mary-Joan. "Feminism and the Wish for a Child." *Sex Role* 7 (September).

Giddings, Paula. *When and Where I Enter: The Impact of Black Women on Race and Sex in America.* New York: William Morrow.

Greer, Germaine. *Sex and Destiny: The Politics of Human Fertility.* New York: Harper and Row.

hooks, bell. "Revolutionary Parenting." Reprinted in *From Margin to Center.* Boston: South End Press.

Luker, Kristen. *Abortion and the Politics of Motherhood.* Berkeley and London: University of California Press.

Petchesky, Rosalind. *Abortion and Women's Choice: The State, Sexuality, and Reproductive Freedom.* New York: Longman.

Rapp, Rayna. "The Ethics of Choice: After My Amniocentesis, Mike and I Faced the Toughest Decision of our Lives." *Ms.* (April).

Sevenhuijsen, Selma and Petra Devries. "The Women's Movement and Motherhood." Reprinted in A *Creative Tension: Key Issues of Socialist Feminism: An International Perspective from Activist Dutch Women*, 9-25. Boston: South End Press.

Simons, Margaret A. "Motherhood, Feminism, and Identity." *Women's Studies International Forum* 7 (5): 349-59.

Trebilcott, Joyce, ed. *Mothering: Essays in Feminist Theory.* Totowa: Rowman and Allanheld.

1985

Corea, Gena. *The Mother Machine: Reproductive Technologies from Artificial In-*

semination to Artificial Wombs. New York: Harper and Row.

Folbre, Nancy. "The Pauperization of Motherhood: Patriarchy and Public Policy in the United States." *Review of Radical Political Economics* 16 (4) (Winter).

Gerson, Kathleen. *Hard Choices: How Women Decide About Work, Career, and Motherhood*. Berkeley and London: University of California Press.

Gittins, Diana. *The Family in Question*. London and New York: Macmillan.

Haraway, Donna. "A Manifesto for Cyborgs: Science, Technology, and Socialist Feminism in the 1980s." *Socialist Review* 80.

Pies, Cheri. *Considering Parenthood*. San Francisco: Spinsters Book Co.

Renvoize, Jean. *Going Solo: Single Mothers by Choice*. Boston: Routledge and Kegan Paul.

Sschulenberg, Joy. *Gay Parenting: A Complete Guide for Gay Men and Lesbians with Children*. New York: Anchor Press/Doubleday.

Weitzman, Lenore J. *The Divorce Revolution: The Unexpected Social and Economic Consequences for Women and Children in America*. New York: Free Press.

Zelizer, Viviana. *Pricing the Priceless Child: The Changing Social Value of Children*. New York: Basic Books.

1986

Allen, Jeffner. "Motherhood: The Annihilation of Women." In *Lesbian Philosophy: Explorations*. Palo Alto: Institute of Lesbian Studies.

Atwood, Margaret. *The Handmaid's Tale*. Boston: Houghton Mifflin Co.

Barrett, Michele and Roberta Hamilton. *The Politics of Diversity: Feminism, Marxism, and Nationalism*. London: Verso.

Chesler, Phyliss. *Mothers on Trial: The Battle for Children and Custody*. Seattle: Seal Press.

Gerson, Kathleen. "Emerging Social Divisions Among Women: Implications for Welfare State Politics." *Politics and Society* 15.2: 213-24.

Heron, Liz. "Motherhood ... To Have or Have Not?" In *Changes of Heart: Reflections on Women's Independence*. Boston: Pandora Press, 177-218.

Hewlett, Sylvia Ann. *A Lesser Life: The Myth of Women's Liberation in America*. New York: William Morrow.

Hypatia. Special Issue. "Motherhood and Sexuality" 1 (2) (Fall).

Kantrowitz, Barbara. "Three's a Crowd." *Newsweek* 1 September: 68-76.

Mairs, Nancy. "On Being Raised by a Daughter." *Plaintext*. University of Arizona.

Miller, Sue. *The Good Mother*. New York: Harper and Row.

Ms. Special Issue. "When to Have Your Baby." December.

Omolade, Barbara. "It's a Family Affair: The Real Lives of Black Single Mothers." *Village Voice* 16 July.

Rothman, Barbara Katz. *The Tentative Pregnancy: Prenatal Diagnosis and the Future of Motherhood*. New York: Viking.

*McBroom, Patricia A. *The Third Sex: The New Professional Woman*. New York: William Morrow.

*New York Times Magazine. "The American Wife." 26 October.

1987

Ehrensaft, Diane. *Parenting Together*. New York: Free Press.

Genevie, Louis E. and Eva Margolies. *The Motherhood Report: How Women Feel About Being Mothers*. New York: Macmillan.

Gleve, Katherine. "Rethinking Feminist Attitudes Towards Motherhood." *Feminist Review* 25 (Spring).

Martin, Emily. *The Woman in the Body: A Cultural Analysis of Reproduction*. Boston: Beacon Press.

Petchesky, Rosalind. "Fetal Images." *Feminist Studies* 13.2.

Pollack, Sandra and Jeanne Vaughan, eds. *Politics of the Heart: A Lesbian Parenting Anthology*. Ithaca: Firebrand Books.

Pruett, Kyle. *The Nurturing Father: Journeys Toward the Complete Man*. New York: Warner Books.

Rosenfelt, Deborah and Judith Stacey. "Second Thoughts on the Second Wave." *Feminist Studies* 13.2.

Segal, Lynne. *Is the Future Female? Troubled Thoughts on Contemporary Feminism*. New York: Peter Bedrick Books.

Segal, Lynne. "Back to the Nursery." *New Statesman*. 1 February.

Sojourner. Special Issue. "Motherhood is Political: The Ideal vs the Real."

Spallone, Patricia and Lynn Steinberg. *Made to Order: The Myth of Reproductive and Genetic Progress*. New York: Pergamon Press.

Stanworth, Michelle, ed. *Reproductive Technologies: Gender, Motherhood and Medicine*. Minneapolis: University of Minnesota Press.

* *Time Magazine*. "Here come the dinks." 20 April: 75.

*Wattenberg, Ben J. "The Birth Dearth" Pharos Books.

*The Baby M Case in the news.

1988

Aguero, Kathi and Marea Gordetit. "Mothering and Writing: A Conversation." *Women's Review of Books*. July.

Benjamin, Jessica. *The Bonds of Love: Psychoanalysis, Feminism, and the Problem of Domination*. New York: Pantheon Books.

CARASA (Committee for Abortion Rights and Against Sterilization Abuse). *Women Under Attack: Victories, Backlash, and the Fight for Reproductive Freedom*. Ed. Susan E. Davis. Boston: South End Press, Pamphlet No.7 (The Athene Series).

Chesler, Phyllis. *Sacred Bond: The Legacy of Baby M*. New York: Times Books.

Eisenstein, Zillah R. *The Female Body and the Law*. Berkeley and London: University of California Press.

Epstein, Cynthia Fuchs. *Deceptive Distinctions: Sex, Gender, and the Social Order*. Boston: Yale University Press.

Grabucher, Marianne. *There's a Good Girl: Gender Stereotyping in the First Three*

Years of Life: A Diary. Trans. Wendy Philipson. London: The Women's Press Ltd.

Herman, Ellen. "Desperately Seeking Motherhood." *Zeta* (March).

Quindlen, Anna. "Mother's Choice." *Ms*. February.

Weideger, Paula. "Womb Worship." *Ms*. February.

Weinberg, Joanna. "Shared Dreams: A Left Perspective on Disability Rights and Reproductive Rights." *Women with Disabilities*. Eds. Adrienne Asch and Michelle Fine. Temple.

*Family Support Act (Workfare).

1989

Douglas, Susan J. "Otherhood." *These Times*. September. 12-13.

Edwards, Harriet. *How Could You? Mothers Without Custody of Their Children*. The Crossing Press.

Ferguson, Ann. *Blood at the Root: Motherhood, Sexuality, and Male Dominance*. London: Pandora Press.

Gerson, Deborah. "Infertility and the Construction of Desperation." *Socialist Review* 19 (3) (July/September).

Ginsburg, Faye D. *Contested Lives: The Abortion Debate in an American Community*. Berkeley and London: University of California Press.

Hirsch, Marianne. *The Mother-Daughter Plot: Narrative, Psychoanalysis, and Feminism*. Indiana University Press.

Hochschild, Arlie. *The Second Shift*. London and New York: Viking Penguin.

Hypatia. Special Issue. "Ethics and Reproduction." 4.3 (Fall).

Olivier, Christiane. *Jocasta's Children: The Imprint of the Mother*. New York: Routledge.

Rothman, Barbara Katz. *Recreating Motherhood: Ideology and Technology in a Patriarchal Society*. New York: W. W. Norton.

Ruddick, Sara. *Maternal Thinking: Towards a Politics of Peace*. Boston: Beacon.

Sevenhuljsen, S. and Carol Smart, eds. *Child Custody and the Politics of Gender*. New York: Routledge.

1990

Arnup, Katherine, Andree Levesque, and Ruth Roach Pierson. *Delivering Motherhood: Maternal Ideologies and Practices in the 19th and 20th Centuries*. New York: Routledge.

Chamberlayne, Prue. "The Mother's Manifesto and Disputes over 'Mutterlichkeit.'" *Feminist Review* 35 (Summer): 9-23.

Cole, Ellen and Jane Price Knowles, eds. *Woman-Defined Motherhood*. Binghamton: Harrington Park Press.

Ehrensaft, Diane. "Feminists fight (for) fathers." *Socialist Review* 4: 57-80.

Finger, Ann. *Past Due: A Story of Disability, Pregnancy, and Birth*. Seattle: Seal Press.

Gordon, Tuula. *Feminist Mothers*. New York: New York University Press.

Kaminer, Wendy. A *Fearful Freedom: Women's Flight from Equality*. Addison-Wesley.

Morell, Carolyn MacKelcan. "Unwomanly conduct: the challenges of intentional childlessness." Dissertation, Bryn Mawr.

O'Barr, Jean, *et al*., eds. *Ties that Bind: Essays on Mothering and Patriarchy*. Chicago and London: University of Chicago Press.

Rapping, Elayne. "The Future of Motherhood: Some Unfashionably Visionary Thoughts." In *Women, Class, and the Feminist Imagination*. Eds. Karen V. Hanson and llene J. Philipson. Temple.

Sandellowski, Margarete. "Fault lines: Infertility and Imperiled Sisterhood." *Feminist Studies* 16 (1) (Spring): 33-51.

White, Evelyn C., ed. *The Black Women's Health Book: Speaking for Ourselves*. Seattle: Seal Press.

Wilt, Judith. *Abortion, Choice, and Contemporary Fiction: The Armageddon of the Maternal Instinct*. Chicago and London: University of Chicago Press.

Chapter 20

Shifting the Center

Race, Class, and Feminist Theorizing About Motherhood

PATRICIA HILL COLLINS

I dread to see my children grow, I know not their fate. Where the white boy has every opportunity and protection, mine will have few opportunities and no protection. It does not matter how good or wise my children may be, they are colored.
    —Anonymous African-American mother in 1904
(cited in Lerner 158)

FOR NATIVE AMERICAN, African-American, Hispanic, and Asian-American women, motherhood cannot be analyzed in isolation from its context. Motherhood occurs in specific historical situations framed by interlocking structures of race, class, and gender, where the sons and daughters of white mothers have "every opportunity and protection," and the "colored" daughters and sons of racial ethnic mothers "know not their fate." Racial domination and economic exploitation profoundly shape the mothering context, not only for racial ethnic women in the United States, but for all women.[1]

Despite the significance of race and class, feminist theorizing routinely minimizes their importance. In this sense, feminist theorizing about motherhood has not been immune to the decontextualization of Western social thought overall.[2] While many dimensions of motherhood's context are ignored, the exclusion of race and/or class from feminist theorizing generally (Spelman), and from feminist theorizing about motherhood specifically, merit special attention.[3]

Much feminist theorizing about motherhood assumes that male domination in the political economy and the household is the driving force in-family life, and that understanding the struggle for individual autonomy in the face of such domination is central to understanding motherhood (Eisenstein).[4] Several guiding principles frame such analyses. First, such theories posit a dichotomous split between the public sphere of economic and political discourse and the private sphere of family and household responsibilities. This juxtaposition of a public, political economy to a private, noneconomic and apolitical, domestic household allows work and family to be seen as separate institutions. Second, reserving the public sphere for men as a "male" domain leaves the private domestic sphere as a "female" domain. Gender roles become tied to the dichotomous constructions of these two basic societal institutions—men work and women take care of families. Third, the public/private dichotomy separating the family/household from the paid labor market shapes sex-segregated gender roles within the private sphere of the family. The archetypal white, middle-class nuclear family divides family life into two oppositional spheres—the "male" sphere of economic providing and the "female" sphere of affective nurturing, mainly mothering. This normative family household ideally consists of a working father who earns enough to allow his spouse and dependent children to withdraw from the paid labor force. Due in large part to their superior earning power, men as workers and fathers exert power over women in the labor market and in families. Finally, the struggle for individual autonomy in the face of a controlling, oppressive, "public" society, or the father as patriarch, comprises the main human enterprise.[5] Successful adult males achieve this autonomy. Women, children, and less successful males, namely those who are working-class or from racial ethnic groups, are seen as dependent persons, as less autonomous, and therefore as fitting objects for elite male domination. Within the nuclear family, this struggle for autonomy takes the form of increasing opposition to the mother, the individual responsible for socializing children by these guiding principles (Chodorow; Flax).

Placing the experiences of women of color in the center of feminist theorizing about motherhood demonstrates how emphasizing the issue of father as patriarch in a decontextualized nuclear family distorts the experiences of women in alternative family structures with quite different political economies. While male domination certainly has been an important theme for racial ethnic women in the United States, gender inequality has long worked in tandem with racial domination and economic exploitation. Since work and family have rarely functioned as dichotomous spheres for women of color, examining racial ethnic women's experiences reveals how these two spheres actually are interwoven (Glenn 1985; Dill; Collins).

For women of color, the subjective experience of mothering/motherhood is inextricably linked to the sociocultural concern of racial ethnic communities—one does not exist without the other. Whether because of the labor exploitation of African-American women under slavery and its ensuing tenant farm system, the political conquest of Native American women during European acquisition of land, or exclusionary immigration policies applied to Asian-Americans and Hispanics, women of color have performed motherwork that challenges social constructions of work and family as separate spheres, of male and female gender roles as similarly dichotomized, and of the search for autonomy as the guiding human quest. "Women's reproductive labor—that is, feeding, clothing, and psychologically supporting the male wage earner and nurturing and socializing the next generation—is seen as work on behalf of the family as a whole, rather than as work benefiting men in particular," observes Asian-American sociologist Evelyn Nakano Glenn (1986: 192). The locus of conflict lies outside the household, as women and their families engage in collective-effort to create and maintain family life in the face of forces that undermine family integrity. But this "reproductive labor" or "motherwork" goes beyond ensuring the survival of one's own biological children or those of one's family. This type of motherwork recognizes that individual survival, empowerment, and identity require group survival empowerment, and identity.

In describing her relationship with her "Grandmother," Marilou Awiakta, a Native American poet and feminist theorist, captures the essence of motherwork.

> Putting my arms around the Grandmother, I lay my head on her shoulder. Through touch we exchange sorrow, despair that anything really changes.

Awiakta senses the power of the Grandmother and of the motherwork that mothers and grandmothers do.

> "But from the presence of her arms I also feel the stern, beautiful power that flows from all the Grandmothers, as it flows from our mountains themselves. It says, "Dry your tears. Get up. Do for yourselves or do without. Work for the day to come." (127)

Awiakta's passage places women and motherwork squarely in the center of what are typically seen as disjunctures, the place between human and nature, between private and public, between oppression and liberation. I use the term "motherwork" to soften the existing dichotomies in feminist theorizing about motherhood that posit rigid distinctions between private and public, family and work, the individual and the collective, identity as individual autonomy and identity growing from the collective self-determination of one's group. Racial ethnic women's mothering and work experiences occur at the boundaries demarking these dualities. "Work for the day to come," is motherwork, whether it is on behalf of one's own biological children, or for the children of one's own racial ethnic community, or to preserve the earth for those children who are yet unborn. The space that this motherwork occupies promises to shift our thinking about motherhood itself.

Shifting the Center: Women of Color and Motherwork

What themes might emerge if issues of race and class generally, and understanding of racial ethnic women's motherwork specifically, became central to feminist theorizing about motherhood? Centering feminist theorizing on the concerns of white, middle-class women leads to two problematic assumptions. The first is that a relative degree of economic security exists for mothers and their children. The second is that all women enjoy the racial privilege that allows them to see themselves primarily as individuals in search of personal autonomy, instead of members of racial ethnic groups struggling for power. It is these assumptions that allow feminist theorists to concentrate on themes such as the connections among mothering, aggression, and death, the effects of maternal isolation on mother-child relationships within nuclear family households, maternal sexuality, relationships among family members, all-powerful mothers as conduits for gender oppression, and the possibilities of an idealized motherhood freed from patriarchy (Chodorow and Contratto; Eisenstein).

While these issues merit investigation, centering feminist theorizing about motherhood in the ideas and experiences of African-American, Native American, Hispanic, and Asian-American women might yield markedly different themes (Andersen; Brown). This stance is to be distinguished from one that merely adds racial ethnic women's experiences to preexisting feminist theories, without considering how these experiences challenge those theories (Spelman). Involving much more than simply the consulting of existing social science sources, the placing of ideas and experiences of women of color in the center of analysis requires invoking a different epistemology. We must distinguish between what has been said about subordinated groups in the dominant discourse, and what such groups might say about themselves if given the opportunity. Personal narratives, autobiographical statements, poetry, fiction, and other personalized statements have all been used by women of color to express self-defined standpoints on mothering and motherhood. Such knowledge reflects the authentic standpoint of subordinated groups. Therefore, placing these sources in the center and supplementing them with statistics, historical material, and other knowledge produced to justify the interests of ruling elites should create new themes and angles of vision (Smith).[6]

Specifying the contours of racial ethnic women's motherwork promises to paint the way toward richer feminist theorizing about motherhood. Themes of survival, power, and identity form the bedrock and reveal how racial ethnic women in the United States encounter and fashion motherwork. That is to understand the importance of working for the physical survival of children and community, the dialectical nature of power and powerlessness in structuring mothering patterns, and the significance of self-definition in constructing individual and collective racial identity is to grasp the three care themes characterizing the experiences of Native American, African-American, Hispanic and Asian-American women. It is also to suggest how feminist theorizing about motherhood might be shifted if different voices became central in feminist discourse.

Motherwork and Physical Survival

When we are not physically starving we have the luxury to realize psychic and emotional starvation. (Moraga 29)

Physical survival is assumed for children who are white and middle-class. The choice to thus examine their psychic and emotional well-being and that of their mothers appears rational. The children of women of color, many of whom are "physically starving," have no such choices however. Racial ethnic children's lives have long been held in low regard: African-American children face an infant mortality rate twice that for white infants; and approximately one-third of Hispanic children and one-half of African-American children who survive infancy live in poverty. In addition racial ethnic children often live in harsh urban environments where drugs, crime, industrial pollutants, and violence threaten their survival. Children in rural environments often fare no better. Winona LaDuke, far example, reports that Native Americans on reservations often must use contaminated water. And on the Pine Ridge Sioux Reservation in 1979, thirty-eight percent of all pregnancies resulted in miscarriages before the fifth month, or in excessive hemorrhaging. Approximately 65 percent of all children born suffered breathing problems caused by underdeveloped lungs and jaundice (63).

Struggles to foster the survival of Native American, Hispanic, Asian-American, and African-American families and communities by ensuring the survival of children comprise a fundamental dimension of racial ethnic women's motherwork. African-American women's fiction contains numerous stories of mothers fighting for the physical survival both of their own biological children and of those of the larger Black community.[7]

"Don't care how much death it is in the land, I got to make preparations for my baby to live!" proclaims Mariah Upshur, the African-American heroine of Sara Wright's 1986 novel *This Child's Gonna Live* (143). Like Mariah Upshur, the harsh climates which confront racial ethnic children require that their mothers "make preparations for their babies to live" as a central feature of their motherwork.

Yet, like all deep cultural themes, the theme of motherwork for physical survival contains contradictory elements. On the one hand, racial ethnic women's motherwork for individual and community survival has been essential. Without women's motherwork, communities would not survive, and by definition, women of color themselves would not survive. On the other hand, this work often extracts a high cost for large numbers of women. There is loss of individual autonomy and there is submersion of individual growth for the benefit of the group. While this dimension of motherwork remains essential, the question of women doing more than their fair share of such work for individual and community development merits open debate.

The histories of family-based labor have been shaped by racial ethnic women's motherwork for survival and the types of mothering relationships that ensued. African-American, Asian-American, Native American and Hispanic women have all worked and contributed to family economic well-being (Glenn 1985; Dill). Much of their experiences with motherwork, in fact, stem from the work they performed as children. The commodification of children of color, starting with the enslavement of African children who were legally "owned" as property, to the subsequent treatment of children as units of labor in agricultural work, family businesses, and industry, has been a major theme shaping motherhood for women of color. Beginning in slavery and continuing into the post- World War II period, Black children were put to work at young ages in the fields of Southern agriculture. Sara Brooks began full-time work in the fields at the age of eleven, and remembers, "we never was lazy cause we used to really work. We used to work like men. Oh, fight sometime, fuss sometime, but worked on" (Collins 54).

Black and Hispanic children in contemporary migrant farm families make similar contributions to their family's economy. "I musta been almost eight when I started following the crops," remembers Jessie de la Cruz, a Mexican-American mother with six grown children. "Every winter, up north. I was on the end of the row of prunes, taking care of my younger brother and sister. They would help me fill up the cans and put 'em in a box while the rest of the family was picking the whole row" (de la Cruz 168). Asian-American children spend long hours working in family businesses, child labor practices that have earned Asian Americans the dubious distinction of being "model minorities." More recently, the family-based labor of undocumented racial ethnic immigrants, often mother-child units doing piecework for the garment industry, recalls the sweatshop conditions confronting turn-of-the-century European immigrants.

A certain degree of maternal isolation from members of the dominant group characterizes the preceding mother-child units. For women of color working along with their children, such isolation is more appropriately seen as reflecting a placement in racially and class stratified labor systems than as a result of a patriarchal system. The unit may be isolated, but the work performed by the mother-child unit closely ties the mothering experiences to wider political and economic issues. Children, too, learn to see their work and that of their mother's not as isolated from wider society, but as essential to their family's survival. Moreover, in the case of family agricultural labor or family businesses, women and children work alongside men, often performing the same work. If isolation occurs, the family, not the mother-child unit, is the focus of such isolation.

Children working in close proximity to their mothers receive distinctive types of mothering. Asian-American children working in urban family businesses, for example, report long days filled almost exclusively with work and school. In contrast, the sons and daughters of African-American sharecroppers and migrant farm children of all backgrounds have less access to educational opportunities. "I think the longest time I went to school was two months in one place," remembers Jessie de la Cruz. "I attended, I think, about forty-five schools. When my parents or my brothers didn't find work, we wouldn't attend school because we weren't sure of staying there. So I missed a lot of school (de la Cruz 167-8)." It was only in the 1950s in fact, that Southern school districts stopped the practice of closing segregated Black schools during certain times of the year so that Black children could work.

Work that separated women of color from their children also framed the mothering relationship. Until the 1960s, large numbers of African-American, Hispanic, and Asian-American women worked in domestic service. Even though women worked longer hours to ensure their children's physical survival, that same work ironically denied mothers access to their children. Different institutional arrangements emerged in these mothers' respective communities, to resolve the tension between maternal separation due to employment and the needs of dependent children. The extended family structure in African-American communities endured as a flexible institution that mitigated some of the effects of maternal separation. Grandmothers are highly revered in Black communities, often because grandmothers function as primary caretakers of their daughters' and daughter-in-laws' children (Collins). In contrast, exclusionary immigration policies that mitigated against intergenerational family units in the United States led Chinese-American and Japanese-American families to make other arrangements (Dill).

Some mothers are clearly defeated by the demands for incessant labor they must perform to ensure their children's survival. The magnitude of their motherwork overwhelms them. But others, even while appearing to be defeated, manage to pass on the meaning of motherwork for survival to their children. African-American feminist June Jordan remembers her perceptions of her mother's work:

> As a child I noticed the sadness of my mother as she sat alone in the kitchen at night…. Her woman's work never won permanent victories of any kind. It never enlarged the universe of her imagination or her power to influence what happened beyond the front door of our house. Her woman's work never tickled her to laugh or shout or dance. (Jordan 105)

But Jordan also sees her mother's work as being essential to individual and community survival.

> She did raise me to respect her way of offering love and to believe that hard work is often the irreducible factor for survival, not something to avoid. Her woman's work produced a reliable home base where I could pursue the privileges of books and music. Her woman's work invented the potential for a completely new kind of work for us, the next generation of Black women: huge, rewarding hard work demanded by the huge, different ambitions that her perfect confidence in us engendered. (Jordan 105)

Motherwork and Power

Jessie de la Cruz, a Mexican-American migrant farm worker, experienced firsthand the struggle for empowerment facing racial ethnic women whose daily motherwork centers on issues of survival.

> How can I write down how I felt when I was a little child and my grandmother used to cry with us 'cause she didn't have enough food to give us? Because my brother was going barefooted and he was cryin' because he wasn't used to going without shoes? How can I describe that? I can't describe when my little girl died because I didn't have money for a doctor. And never had any teaching on caring for sick babies. Living out in labor camps. How can I describe that? (de la Cruz 177)

A dialectical relationship exists between efforts of racial orders to mold the institution of motherhood to serve the interests of elites, in this case, racial elites, and efforts on the part of subordinated groups to retain power over motherhood so that it serves the legitimate needs of their communities (Collins). African-American, Asian-American, Hispanic, and Native American women have long been preoccupied with patterns of maternal power and powerlessness because their mothering experiences have been profoundly affected by this dialectical process. But instead of emphasizing maternal power in dealing with father as patriarch (Chodorow; Rich), or with male dominance in general (Ferguson 1989), women of color are concerned with their power and powerlessness within an array of social institutions that frame their lives.

Racial ethnic women's struggles for maternal empowerment have resolved around three main themes. First is the struggle for control over their own bodies in order to preserve choice over whether to become mothers at all. The ambiguous politics of caring for unplanned children has long shaped African-American women's motherwork. For example, the widespread institutionalized rape of Black women by white men, both during slavery and in the segregated South, created countless biracial children who had to be absorbed into African-American families and communities (Davis). The range of skin colors and hair textures in contemporary African-American communities bears mute testament to the powerlessness of African-American women in controlling this dimension of motherhood.

For many women of color, choosing to become a mother challenges institutional policies that encourage white, middle-class women to reproduce, and discourage and even penalize low-income racial ethnic women from doing so (Davis). Rita Silk-Nauni, an incarcerated Native American woman, writes of the difficulties she encountered in trying to have additional children. She loved her son so much that she only left him to go to work. "I tried having more after him and couldn't," she laments.

> "I went to a specialist and he thought I had been fixed when I had my son. He said I would have to have surgery in order to give birth again. The surgery was so expensive but I thought I could make a way even if I had to work 24 hours a day. Now that I'm here, I know I'll never have that chance." (Brant 94)

Like Silk-Nauni, Puerto Rican and African-American women have long had to struggle with issues of sterilization abuse (Davis). More recent efforts to manipulate the fertility of women dependent on public assistance speaks to the continued salience of this issue.

A second dimension of racial ethnic women's struggles for maternal empowerment concerns the process of keeping the children that are wanted, whether they were planned for or not. For mothers like Jessie de la Cruz whose "little girl died" because she "didn't have money for a doctor," maternal separation from one's children becomes a much more salient issue than maternal isolation with one's children within an allegedly private nuclear family. Physical and/or psychological separation of mothers and children, designed to disempower individuals, forms the basis of a systematic effort to disempower racial ethnic communities.

For both Native American and African-American mothers, situations of conquest introduced this dimension of the struggle for maternal empowerment. In her fictional account of a Native American mother's loss of her children in 1890, Brant explores the pain of maternal separation.

> It has been two days since they came and took the children away. My body is greatly chilled. All our blankets have been used to bring me warmth. The women keep the fire blazing. The men sit. They talk among themselves. We are frightened by this sudden child-stealing. We signed papers, the agent said. This gave them rights to take our babies. It is good for them, the agent said. It will make them civilized. (101)

A legacy of conquest has meant that Native American mothers on "reservations" confront intrusive government institutions such as the Bureau of Indian Affairs in deciding the fate of their children. For example, the long-standing policy of removing Native American children from their homes and housing them in reservation boarding schools can be seen as efforts to disempower Native American mothers. For African-American women, slavery was a situation where owners controlled numerous dimensions of their children's lives. Black children could be sold at will, whipped, or even killed, all without any recourse by their mothers. In such a situation, getting to keep one's children and raise them accordingly fosters empowerment.

A third dimension of racial ethnic women's struggles for empowerment concerns the pervasive efforts by the dominant group to control the children's minds. In her short story, "A Long Memory," Beth Brant juxtaposes the loss felt by a Native American mother in 1890 whose son and daughter had been forcibly removed by white officials, to the loss that she felt in 1978 upon losing her daughter in a custody hearing. "Why do they want our babies?" queries the turn-of-the-century mother. "They want our power. They take our children to remove the inside of them. Our power" (Brant 1988: 105). This mother recognizes that the future of the Native American way of life lies in retaining the power to define that worldview through the education of children. By forbidding children to speak their native languages, and in other ways encouraging children to assimilate into Anglo culture, external agencies challenge the power of mothers to raise their children as they see fit.

Schools controlled by the dominant group comprise one important location where this dimension of the struggle for maternal empowerment occurs. In contrast to the white, middle-class children, whose educational experiences affirm their mothers' middle-class values, culture, and authority, the educational experiences of African-American, Hispanic, Asian-American and Native American children typically denigrate their mothers' perspective. For example, the struggles over bilingual education in Hispanic communities are about much more than retaining Spanish as a second language. Speaking the language of one's childhood is a way of retaining the entire culture and honoring the mother teaching that culture (Moraga; Anzaldua).

Jenny Yamoto describes the stress of continuing to negotiate with schools regarding her Black-Japanese sons.

> I've noticed that depending on which parent, Black mom or Asian dad, goes to school open house, my oldest son's behavior is interpreted as disruptive and irreverent, or assertive and clever.... I resent their behavior being defined and even expected on the basis of racial biases their teachers may struggle with or hold.... I don't have the time or energy to constantly change and challenge their teacher's and friends' misperceptions. I only go after them when the children really seem to be seriously threatened. (Yamoto 24)

In confronting each of these three dimensions of their struggles for empowerment, racial ethnic women are not powerless in the face of racial and class oppression. Being grounded in a strong, dynamic, indigenous culture can be central in these women's social constructions of motherhood. Depending on their access to traditional culture, they invoke alternative sources of power.[8]

"Equality per se, may have a different meaning for Indian women and Indian people," suggests Kate Shanley. "That difference begins with personal and tribal sovereignty—the right to be legally recognized as people empowered to determine our own destinies" (214). Personal sovereignty involves the struggle to promote the survival of a social structure whose organizational principles represent notions of family and motherhood different from those of the mainstream. "The nuclear family has little relevance to Indian women," observes Shanley. "In fact, in many ways, mainstream feminists now are striving to redefine family and community in a way that Indian women have long known" (214).

African-American mothers can draw upon an Afrocentric tradition where motherhood of varying types, whether bloodmother, othermother, or community othermother, can be invoked as a symbol of power. Many Black women receive respect and recognition within their local communities for innovative and practical approaches not only to mothering their own "blood" children, but also to being othermothers to the children in their extended family networks, and those in the community overall. Black women's involvement in fostering Black community development forms the basis of this community-based power. In local African-American communities, community othermothers can become identified as powerful figures through their work in furthering the community's well-being (Collins).

Despite policies of dominant institutions that place racial ethnic mothers in positions where they appear less powerful to their children, mothers and children empower themselves by understanding each other's position and relying on each other's strengths. In many cases, children, especially daughters, bond with their mothers instead of railing against them as symbols of patriarchal power. Cherrie Moraga describes the impact that her mother had on her. Because she was repeatedly removed from school in order to work, by prevailing standards Moraga's mother would be considered largely illiterate. But she was also a fine storyteller, and found ways to empower herself within dominant institutions. "I would go with my mother to fill out job applications for her, or write checks for her at the supermarket," Moraga recounts.

> We would have the scenario all worked out ahead of time. My mother would sign the check before we'd get to the store. Then, as we'd approach the checkstand, she would say—within earshot of the cashier—"oh, honey, you go 'head and make out the check," as if she couldn't be bothered with such an insignificant detail. (28)

Like Cherrie Moraga and her mother, racial ethnic women's motherwork involves collaborating to empower mothers and children within structures that oppress.

Motherwork and Identity

> Please help me find out who I am. My mother was Indian, but we were taken from her and put in foster homes. They were white and didn't want to tell us about our mother. I have a name and maybe a place of birth. Do you think you can help me? (Brant 9)

Like this excerpt from a letter to the editor, the theme of lost racial ethnic identity and the struggle to maintain a sense of self and community pervade many of the stories, poetry and narratives in Beth Brant's volume, *A Gathering of Spirit*. Carol Lee Sanchez offers another view of the impact of the loss of self. "Radicals look at reservation Indians and get very upset about their poverty conditions," observes Sanchez.

> But poverty to us is not the same thing as poverty is to you. Our poverty is that we can't be who we are. We can't hunt or fish or grow our food because our basic resources and the right to use them in traditional ways are denied us. (Brant 165)

Racial ethnic women's motherwork reflects the tensions inherent in trying to foster a meaningful racial identity in children within a society that denigrates people of color. The racial privilege enjoyed by white, middle-class women makes unnecessary this complicated dimension of the mothering tradition of women of color. While white children can be prepared to fight racial oppression, their survival does not depend on gaining these skills. Their racial identity is validated by their schools, the media, and other social institutions. White children are socialized into their rightful place in systems of racial privilege. Racial ethnic women have no such guarantees for their children; their children must first be taught to survive in systems that oppress them. Moreover, this survival must not come at the expense of self-esteem. Thus, a dialectical relationship exists between systems of racial oppression designed to strip subordinated groups of personal identity and a sense of collective peoplehood, and the cultures of resistance extant in various racial ethnic groups that resist the oppression. For women of color, motherwork for identity occurs at this critical juncture (Collins).

"Through our mothers, the culture gave us mixed messages," observes Mexican-American poet Gloria Anzaldua. "Which was it to be—strong, or submissive, rebellious or conforming?" (1987: 18). Thus women of color's motherwork requires reconciling contradictory needs concerning identity. Preparing children to cope with and survive within systems of racial oppression is extremely difficult because the pressures for children of racial ethnic groups to assimilate are pervasive. In order to compel women of color to participate in their children's assimilation, dominant institutions promulgate ideologies that belittle people of color. Negative controlling images infuse the worlds of male and female children of color (Tajima; Collins; Green). Native American girls are encouraged to see themselves as "Pocahontases" or "squaws"; Asian-American girls as "geisha girls" or "Suzy Wongs"; Hispanic girls as "Madonnas" or "hot-blooded whores"; and African-American girls as "mammies," "matriarchs" and "prostitutes." Girls of all groups are told that their lives cannot be complete without a male partner, and that their educational and career aspirations must always be subordinated to their family obligations.

This push toward assimilation is part of a larger effort to socialize racial ethnic children into their proper, subordinate places in systems of racial and class oppression. Since children of color can never be white, however, assimilation by becoming white is impossible despite the pressures. Thus, a second dimension of the mothering tradition involves equipping children with skills to confront this contradiction and to challenge systems of racial oppression. Girls who become women believing that they are only capable of being maids and prostitutes cannot contribute to racial ethnic women's motherwork.

Mothers make varying choices in negotiating the complicated relationship of preparing children to fit into, yet resist, systems of racial domination. Some mothers remain powerless in the face of external forces that foster their children's assimilation and subsequent alienation from their families and communities. Through fiction, Native American author Beth Brant again explores the grief felt by a mother whose children had been taken away to live among whites. A letter arrives giving news of her missing children.

> This letter is from two strangers with the names Martha and Daniel. They say they are learning civilized ways. Daniel works in the fields, growing food for the school. Martha is being taught to sew aprons. She will be going to live with the schoolmaster's wife. She will be a live-in

girl. What is live-in girl? I shake my head. The words sound the same to me. I am afraid of Martha and Daniel. These strangers who know my name. (Brant 102-103)

Other mothers become unwitting conduits of the dominant ideology. Gloria Anzaldua (16) asks:

How many time have I heard mothers and mothers-in-law tell their sons to beat their wives for not obeying them, for being *hociconas* (big mouths), for being *callajeras* (going to visit and gossip with neighbours), for expecting their husbands to help with the rearing of children and the housework, for wanting to be something other than housewives?

Some mothers encourage their children to fit in, for reasons of survival. "My mother, nursed in the folds of a town that once christened its black babies Lee, after Robert E., and Jackson, after Stonewall, raised me on a dangerous generation's old belief," remembers African-American author Marita Golden.

Because of my dark brown complexion, she warned me against wearing browns or yellow and reds ... and every summer I was admonished not to play in the sun "cause you gonna have to get a light husband anyway, for the sake of your children." (24)

To Cherrie Moraga's mother,

On a basic economic level, being Chicana meant being "less." It was through my mother's desire to protect her children from poverty and illiteracy we became "anglocized"; the more effectively we could pass in the white world, the better guaranteed our future. (28).

Despite their mothers' good intentions, the costs to children taught to submit to racist and sexist ideologies can be high. Raven, a Native American woman, looks back on her childhood:

I've been raised in white man's world and was forbade more or less to converse with Indian people. As my mother wanted me to be educated and live a good life, free from poverty. I lived a life of loneliness. Today I am desperate to know my people. (Brant 221)

To avoid poverty, Raven's mother did what she thought best, but ultimately, Raven experienced the poverty of not being able to be who she was.

Still other mothers transmit sophisticated skills to their children, enabling them to appear to be submissive while at the same time to be able to challenge inequality. Willi Coleman's mother used a Saturday-night hair-combing ritual to impart a Black women's standpoint to her daughters:

> Except for special occasions mama came home from work early on Sat-
> urdays. She spent six days a week mopping, waxing and dusting other
> women's houses and keeping out of reach of other women's husbands.
> Saturday nights were reserved for "taking care of them girls" hair and the
> telling of stories. Some of which included a recitation of what she had
> endured and how she had triumphed over "folks that were lower than
> dirt" and "no-good snakes in the grass." She combed, patted, twisted
> and talked, saying things which would have embarrassed or shamed her
> at other times. (34)

Historian Elsa Barkley Brown captures this delicate balance that racial ethnic
mothers negotiate. Brown points out that her mother's behavior demonstrated
the "need to teach me to live my life one way and, at the same time, to provide
all the tools I would need to live it quite differently" (929).

For women of color, the struggle to maintain an independent racial identity
has taken many forms: All reveal varying solutions to the dialectical relationship
between institutions that would deny their children their humanity and institutions that would affirm their children's right to exist as self-defined people. Like
Willi Coleman's mother, African-American women draw upon a long-standing
Afrocentric feminist worldview, emphasizing the importance of self-definition,
self-reliance, and the necessity of demanding respect from others (Terborg-Penn;
Collins).

Racial ethnic cultures, themselves, do not always help to support women's self-
definition. Poet and essayist Gloria Anzaldua, for example, challenges many of the
ideas in Hispanic cultures concerning women. "Though I'll defend my race and
culture when they are attacked by non-*mexicanos*.... I abhor some of my culture's
ways, how it cripples its women, *como burras,* our strengths used against us" (21).
Anzaldua offers a trenchant analysis of the ways in which the Spanish conquest
of Native Americans fragmented women's identity and produced three symbolic
"mothers." *La Virgen de Guadalupe,* perhaps the single most potent religious,
political and cultural image of the Chicano people, represents the virgin mother
who cares for and nurtures an oppressed people. *La Chingada (Malinche)* represents the raped mother, all but abandoned. A combination of the other two, *La
Llorona* symbolizes the mother who seeks her lost children. "Ambiguity surrounds
the symbols of these three "Our Mothers," claims Anzaldua.

> In part, the true identity of all three has been *subverted—Guadalupe,* to
> make us docile and enduring, *la Chingada,* to make us ashamed of our
> Indian side, and *la Llorona* to make us a long-suffering people. (31)

For Anzaldua, the Spanish conquest, which brought racism and economic
subordination to Indian people, and created a new mixed-race Hispanic people,

simultaneously devalued women:

> No, I do not buy all the myths of the tribe into which I was born. I can
> understand why the more tinged with Anglo blood, the more adamantly
> my colored and colorless sisters glorify their colored culture's values—to
> offset the extreme devaluation of it by the white culture. It's a legitimate
> reaction. But I will not glorify those aspects of my culture which have
> injured me and which have injured me in the name of protecting me.
> (Anzaldua 1987: 22)

Hispanic mothers face the complicated task of shepherding their children
through the racism extant in dominant society, and the reactions to that racism
framing cultural beliefs internal to Hispanic communities.

Many Asian American mothers stress conformity and fitting in as a way to
challenge the system. "Our parents are painted as hard workers who were socially
uncomfortable and had difficulty expressing even the smallest opinion," observes
Japanese-American Kesaya Noda, in her autobiographical essay "Growing Up Asian
in America" (246). Noda questioned this seeming capitulation on the part of her
parents: "'Why did you go into those camps,' I raged at my parents, frightened
by my own inner silence and timidity. 'Why didn't you do anything to resist?'"
But Noda later discovers a compelling explanation as to why Asian-Americans
are so often portrayed as conformist:

> I had not been able to imagine before what it must have felt like to be
> an American-to know absolutely that one is an American-and yet to
> have almost everyone else deny it. Not only deny it, but challenge that
> identity with machine guns and troops of white American soldiers. In
> those circumstances it was difficult to say, "I'm a Japanese-American."
> " American" had to do. (247)

Native American women can draw upon a tradition of motherhood and woman's
power inherent in Native American cultures (Allen; Awiakta). In such philosophies,
"water, land, and life are basic to the natural order," claims Winona LaDuke.

> All else has been created by the use and misuse of technology. It is only
> natural that in our respective struggles for survival, the native peoples are
> waging a way to protect the land, the water, and life, while the consumer
> culture strives to protect its technological lifeblood. (65)

Marilou Awiakta offers a powerful summary of the symbolic meaning of motherhood in Native American cultures. "I feel the Grandmother's power. She sings
of harmony, not dominance," offers Awiakta. "And her song rises from a culture
that repeats the wise balance of nature: the gender capable of bearing life is not
separated from the power to sustain it" (126). A culture that sees the connected-

ness between the earth and human survival, and sees motherhood as symbolic of the earth itself, holds motherhood as an institution in high regard.

Concluding Remarks

Survival, power and identity shape motherhood for all women. But these themes remain muted when the mothering experiences of women of color are marginalized in feminist theorizing. Feminist theorizing about motherhood reflects a lack of attention to the connection between ideas and the contexts in which they emerge. While such decontextualization aims to generate universal "theories" of human behavior, in actuality, it routinely distorts, and omits huge categories of human experience.

Placing racial ethnic women's motherwork in the center of analysis recontextualizes motherhood. While the significance of race and class in shaping the context in which motherhood occurs remains virtually invisible when white, middle-class women's mothering experiences assume prominence, the effects of race and class on motherhood stand out in stark relief when women of color are accorded theoretical primacy. Highlighting racial ethnic mothers' struggles concerning their children's right to exist focuses attention on the importance of survival. Exploring the dialectical nature of racial ethnic women's empowerment in structures of racial domination and economic exploitation demonstrates the need to broaden the definition of maternal power. Emphasizing how the quest for self-definition is mediated by membership in different racial and social class groups reveals how the issues of identity are crucial to all motherwork.

Existing feminist theories of motherhood have emerged in specific intellectual and political contexts. By assuming that social theory will be applicable regardless of social context, feminist scholars fail to realize that they themselves are rooted in specific locations, and that the specific contexts in which they are located provide the thought-models of how they interpret the world. While subsequent theories appear to be universal and objective, they actually are partial perspectives reflecting the white, middle-class context in which their creators live. Large segments of experience, specifically those of women who are not white and middle-class, have been excluded (Spelman).

Feminist theories of motherhood are thus valid as partial perspectives, but cannot be seen as *theories* of motherhood generalizable to all women. The resulting patterns of partiality inherent in existing theories, such as, for example, the emphasis placed on all-powerful mothers as conduits for gender oppression, reflect feminist theorists' positions in structures of power. These theorists are themselves participants in a system of privilege that rewards them for not seeing race and class privilege as being important.

Theorizing about motherhood will not be helped by supplanting one group's theory with that of another; for example, by claiming that women of color's experiences are more valid than those of white, middle-class women. Varying placement in systems of privilege, whether race, class, sexuality, or age, generates divergent experiences with motherhood; therefore, examination of motherhood and mother-as-subject from multiple perspectives should uncover rich textures of difference. Shifting the center to accommodate this diversity promises to re-contextualize motherhood and point us toward feminist theorizing that embraces difference as an essential part of commonality.

Notes

[1] In this essay, I use the terms "racial ethnic women" and "women of color" interchangeably. Grounded in the experiences of groups who have been the targets of racism, the term "racial ethnic" implies more solidarity with men involved in struggles against racism. In contrast, the term "women of color" emerges from a feminist background where racial ethnic women committed to feminist struggle aimed to distinguish their history and issues from those of middle-class, white women. Neither term captures the complexity of African-American, Native American, Asian-American and Hispanic women's experiences.

[2] Positivist social science exemplifies this type of decontextualization. In order to create scientific descriptions of reality, positivist researchers aim to produce ostensibly objective generalizations. But because researchers have widely differing values, experiences, and emotions, genuine science is thought to be unattainable unless all human characteristics except rationality are eliminated from the research process. By following strict methodological rules, scientists aim to distance themselves from the values, vested interests, and emotions generated by their class, race, sex, or unique situation. By decontextualizing themselves, they allegedly become detached observers and manipulators of nature. Moreover, this researcher decontextualization is paralleled by comparable efforts to remove objects of study from their contexts (Jaggar).

[3] Dominant theories are characterized by this decontextualization. Boyd's helpful survey of literature on the mother-daughter relationship reveals that while much work has been done on motherhood generally, and on the mother-daughter relationship, very little of it tests feminist theories of motherhood. Boyd lists two prevailing theories, psychoanalytic theory and social learning theory, that she claims form the bulk of feminist theorizing. Both of these approaches minimize the importance of race and class in the context of motherhood. Boyd ignores Marxist-feminist theorizing about motherhood, mainly because very little of this work is concerned with the mother-daughter relationship. But Marxist-feminist analyses of motherhood provide another example of how decontextualization frames feminist theories of motherhood. See, for example, Ann Ferguson's *Blood at the Root: Motherhood, Sexuality, and Male Dominance*, an ambitious attempt to develop a universal theory of motherhood that is linked to the social construction of sexuality and male dominance. Ferguson's work stems from a feminist tradition that explores the relationship between motherhood and sexuality by either bemoaning their putative incompatibility or romanticizing maternal sexuality.

[4] Psychoanalytic feminist theorizing about motherhood, such as Nancy Chodorow's

groundbreaking work, *The Reproduction of Mothering*, exemplifies how decontextualization of race and/or class can weaken what is otherwise strong feminist theorizing. Although I realize that other feminist approaches to motherhood exist, see Eisenstein's summary for example, I have chosen to stress psychoanalytic feminist theory because the work of Chodorow and others has been highly influential in framing the predominant themes in feminist discourse.

[5]The thesis of the atomized individual that underlies Western psychology is rooted in a much larger Western construct concerning the relation of the individual to the community (Hartsock). Theories of motherhood based on the assumption of the atomized human proceed to use this definition of individual as the unit of analysis, and then construct theory from this base. From this grow assumptions based on the premise that the major process to examine is one between freely choosing rational individuals engaging in bargains (Hartsock).

[6]The narrative tradition in the writings of women of color addresses this effort to recover the history of mothers. Works from African-American women's autobiographical tradition, such as Ann Moody's *Coming of Age in Mississippi,* Maya Angelou's *I Know Why the Caged Bird Sings,* Linda Brent's *Narrative in the Life of a Slave Girl,* and Marita Golden's *The Heart of a Woman* contain the authentic voices of Black women centered on experiences of motherhood. Works from African-American women's fiction include Sarah Wright's *This Child's Gonna Live,* Alice Walker's *Meridian,* and Toni Morrison's *Sula* and *Beloved.* Asian-American women's fiction, such as Amy Tan's *The Joy Luck Club* and Maxine Kingston's *Woman Warrior,* and autobiographies such as Jean Wakatsuki Houston's *Farewell to Manzanar* offer a parallel source of authentic voice. Connie Young Yu entitles her article on the history of Asian-American women "The World of Our Grandmothers," and proceeds to recreate Asian-American history with her grandmother as a central figure. Cherrie Moraga writes a letter to her mother as a way of coming to terms with the contradictions in her racial identity as a Chicana. In *Borderlands/La Frontera,* Gloria Anzaldua weaves autobiography, poetry and philosophy together in her exploration of women and mothering.

[7]Notable examples include Lutie Johnson's unsuccessful attempt to rescue her son from the harmful effects of an urban environment in Ann Petry's *The Street;* and Meridian's work on behalf of the children of a small Southern town after she chooses to relinquish her own child, in Alice Walker's *Meridian.*

[8]Noticeably absent from feminist theories of motherhood is a comprehensive theory of power and explanation of how power relations shape theories. Firmly rooted in an exchange-based marketplace, with its accompanying assumptions of rational economic decision-making and white, male control of the marketplace, this model of community stresses the rights of individuals, including feminist theorists, to make decisions in their own self-interests, regardless of the impact on larger society. Composed of a collection of unequal individuals who compete for greater shares of money as the medium of exchange, this model of community legitimizes relations of domination either by denying they exist or by treating them as inevitable but unimportant (Hartsock).

References

Allen, Paula Gunn. *The Sacred Hoop: Recovering the Feminine in American Indian Traditions.* Boston: Beacon, 1986.

Andersen, Margaret. "Moving Our Minds: Studying Women of Color and Reconstructing Sociology." *Teaching Sociology* 16 (2) (1988): 123-132.

Anzaldua, Gloria. *Borderlands/La Frontera: The New Mestiza.* San Francisco: Spinsters, 1987.

Awiakta, Marilou. "Amazons in Appalchia." *A Gathering of Spirit.* Ed. Beth Brant. Ithaca, NY: Firebrand, 1988. 125-130.

Boyd, Carol J. "Mothers and Daughters: A Discussion of Theory and Research." *Journal of Marriage and the Family* 51 (1988): 291-301.

Brant, Beth, ed. *A Gathering of Spirit: A Collection by North American Indian Women.* Ithaca, NY: Firebrand, 1988.

Brown, Elsa Barkley. "African-American Women's Quilting: A Framework for Conceptualizing and Teaching African-American Women's History." *Signs* 14 (4) (1989): 921-929.

Chodorow, Nancy. *The Reproduction of Mothering.* Berkeley, CA: University of California Press, 1978.

Chodorow, Nancy and Susan Contratto. "The Fantasy of the Perfect Mother." *Rethinking the Family: Some Feminist Questions.* Eds. Barrie Thorne and Marilyn Yalom. New York: Longman, 1982: 54-75.

Coleman, Willi. "Closets and Keepsakes." *Sage: A Scholarly Journal on Black Women* 4 (2) (1987): 34-35.

Collins, Patricia Hill. *Black Feminist Thought: Knowledge, Consciousness and the Politics of Empowerment.* New York: Unwin Hyman/Routledge, 1990.

de la Cruz, Jessie. "Interview." *American Dreams: Lost and Found.* Ed. Studs Terkel. New York: Ballantine, 1980.

Davis, Angela Y. *Women, Race, and Class.* New York: Random House, 1981.

Dill, Bonnie Thornton. "Our Mothers' Grief: Racial Ethnic Women and the Maintenance of Families." *Journal of Family History* 13 (4) (1988): 415-431.

Eisenstein, Hester. *Contemporary Feminist Thought.* Boston: G. K. Hall, 1983.

Ferguson, Ann. *Blood at the Root: Motherhood, Sexuality, and Male Dominance.* New York: Unwin Hyman/Routledge, 1989.

Flax, Jane. "The Conflict between Nurturance and Autonomy in Mother-Daughter Relationships and within Feminism." *Feminist Studies* 4 (2) (1978):171-189.

Glenn, Evelyn Nakano. "Racial Ethnic Women's Labor: The Intersection of Race, Gender and Class Oppression." *Review of Radical Political Economics* 17 (3) (1985): 86-108.

Glenn, Evelyn Nakano. *Issei, Nisei, War Bride: Three Generations of Japanese American Women in Domestic Service.* Philadelphia: Temple University Press, 1986.

Golden, Marita. *Migrations of the Heart.* Garden City: Anchor Press, 1983.

Green, Rayna. 1990. "The Pocahontas Perplex: The Image of Indian Women in American Culture." Ellen Carol DuBois and Vicki Ruiz, eds., *Unequal Sisters.*

New York: Routledge, pp. 15-21.

Hartsock, Nancy. *Money, Sex and Power.* Boston: Northeastern University Press, 1983.

Jaggar, Alison M. *Feminist Politics and Human Nature.* Totowa, NJ: Rowman and Allanheld, 1983.

Jordan, June. *On Call.* Boston: South End Press, 1985.

LaDuke, Winona. "They Always Come Back." *A Gathering of Spirit.* Ed. Beth Brant. Ithaca, NY: Firebrand, 1988. 62-67.

Lerner, Gerda. *Black Women in White America.* New York: Pantheon, 1972.

Moraga, Cherrie. "La Guera." *This Bridge Called My Back: Writings By Radical Women of Color.* Eds. Cherrie Moraga and Gloria Anzaldua. Watertown, MA: Persephone Press, 1979. 27-34.

Noda, Kesaya E. "Growing Up Asian in America." *Making Waves: An Anthology of Writings By and About Asian American Women.* Eds. Asian Women United of California. Boston: Beacon, 1989. 243-50.

Rich, Adrienne. *Of Woman Born: Motherhood as Institution and Experience.* 1976. New York: W. W. Norton, 1986.

Shanley, Kate. "Thoughts on Indian Feminism." *A Gathering of Spirit.* Ed. Beth Brant. Ithaca, NY: Firebrand, 1988. 213-215.

Smith, Dorothy E. *The Conceptual Practices of Power: A Feminist Sociology of Knowledge.* Boston: Northeastern University Press, 1990.

Spelman, Elizabeth V. *Inessential Woman: Problems of Exclusion in Feminist Thought.* Boston: Beacon Press, 1988.

Tajima, Renee E. "Lotus Blossoms Don't Bleed: Images of Asian Women." *Making Waves: An Anthology of Writings By and About Asian American Women.* Eds. Asian Women United of California. Boston: Beacon, 1989. 308-317.

Terborg-Penn, Rosalyn. "Black Women in Resistance: A Cross-Cultural Perspective." *Resistance: Studies in African, Caribbean and Afro-American History.* Ed. Gary Y. Okhiro. Amherst University of Massachusetts Press, 1986. 188-209.

Wright, Sarah. *This Child's Gonna Live.* Old Westbury, NY: Feminist Press, 1986.

Yamoto, Jenny. "Mixed Bloods, Half Breeds, Mongrels, Hybrids...." *Changing Our Power: An Introduction to Women's Studies* Eds. Jo Whitehorse Cochran, Donna Langston and Carolyn Woodward. Dubuque: Kendall/Hunt, 1988. 22-24.

Yu, Connie Young. "The World of Our Grandmothers." *Making Waves: An Anthology of Writings By and About Asian American Women.* Eds. Asian Women United of California. Boston: Beacon, 1989. 33-41.

Chapter 21

The Myths of Motherhood

SHARI L. THURER

As a psychologist I cannot recall ever treating a mother who did not harbor shameful secrets about how her behavior or feelings damaged her children. Mothers do not take easy pride in their competence. Popular mother culture implies that our children are exquisitely delicate creatures, hugely vulnerable to our idiosyncrasies and deficits, who require relentless psychological attunement and approval. A sentimentalized image of the perfect mother casts a long, guilt-inducing shadow over real mothers' lives. Actual days on Planet Earth include few if any perfect moments, perfect children, perfectly cared for. Watching a three-year-old dress in agonizing slow motion, or a ten-year-old gorge herself on junk food and then despair of her appearance and blame us, provokes powerful emotions in us that do not cohere with our notion of the maternal. We have become highly judgmental about the practice of mothering, and especially about ourselves as mothers. Parental performance anxiety reigns.

Did parents always feel this way? Did those staid nineteenth-century people blankly staring out from the family album experience such self-doubt? What about all those Madonnas in Renaissance paintings? Were children of the seventeenth century more neurotic than children of today because their empathic needs were not met? Were children always so precious? If so, how did my great-grandmother ever bear the loss of three children? Did women want children when delivery may have meant their own death? Did fathers love children when they had to share already meager food supplies? What is good mothering? Am I a good mother? Was Medea? The old woman who lived in a shoe? Donna Reed? Aunt Jemima? Is Murphy Brown? How important is mothering, anyway?

This is not a "how to mother" book. I wish it were. I wish there could be such a guide, a compendium of foolproof techniques for raising a happy child. As a mother, I desperately want to do whatever it takes to do it right. But as a social scientist, I know that the ideal parent does not exist. There are no easy answers, no magical solutions, no absolutes. Good mothering is *not* a formulaic procedure, despite the assurances of all those books on the shelves of your local bookstore.

The current ideology of good mothering is not only spurious, it is oblivious of a mother's desires, limitations, and context, and when things go wrong, she tends to get blamed. This has resulted in a level of confusion and self-consciousness among mothers that their predecessors never knew. There is a glaring need to restore to mother her own presence, to understand that she is a person, not merely an object for her child, to recognize her subjectivity.

The briefest glance at history will dispel any notion that there is but one correct way to mother. Your grandmother may have bottle-fed your father on a rigid schedule and started his toilet training when he was the tender age of three months, practices generally regarded as ridiculous today. Yet he managed to grow up. Youngsters tend to survive their parents' bungled efforts on their behalf. By examining the patchwork of changing expectations for mothers—in psychology, child-rearing manuals, cultural history, the arts, anthropology, and religion—I will show that many of our cherished ideals of parental excellence are about as useless and ephemeral as daily doses of castor oil. Such an analysis has the potential to free mothers from arbitrary, culturally imposed restraints. Mothers may stop worrying about how they stack up against some capricious, external standard. The nervousness parents feel about their adequacy will dissipate when decent people are encouraged to mother in their own decent way.

Today, we all want to be the mom in the baby food advertisements. (You know her: the mother who is always loving, selfless, tranquil; the one who finds passionate fulfillment in every detail of child rearing.) It's only natural. The vulnerability of children makes us want fervently to be our best selves, to embody tender nurturance and sweet concern. Besides, how our children turn out has become the final judgment on our lives. Even Queen Elizabeth's image has been tarnished by the marital failures of her children. The rising generation has the power of rendering history's verdict on us (Sommerville, 1982, 1990). This is a daunting prospect. We want to do a good job. One false move and our precious bundle of joy will turn into an ax-murderer. But as we do more, we seem less sure of ourselves and of what we ought to do for our children. If we enroll our children in day care, we may deprive them of personalized parental attention; if we isolate them in the home, they may not become socialized. We wonder whether we are hurrying our children or, worse, not providing sufficient stimulation. We obsess about creativity, values, lead poisoning, violence on television, responsible diapers, and, of course, about spending "quality" time together. And these are only some of our *overt* concerns.

Beneath them lurk greater fears, for even as we experience a fierce attachment to our children there is the suspicion that we are not cut out for this. We are too impatient; we are haunted by the cultural ideal: the mommy whose love for children is unconditional. In spite of our having grown up with our own mothers—or, some might argue, because of it—we cling to the romantic version of mother, a chilling reminder of our own inadequacy.

But to suggest that mothers are made miserable by mothering is egregiously inaccurate. Bearing and caretaking a child tapped feelings in me that I did not know existed ... manic highs, extravagant joy, monumental wonder, syrupy tenderness. In a cold and ruthless world, the relation between mother and child may be the most genuine, natural, spontaneous, and exquisite love there is. A baby answers the existential questions. The mere smell and texture of the baby's clothes and skin will evoke a Proustian reverie in most persons who have mothered. When a woman nurtures an infant, she creates someone who loves her passionately and exclusively, who needs her more than any adult does or will. And a mother is socially rewarded for her work by the shared pleasures and confirmation of other mothers, often by the gratitude and pride of grandparents, and by the intense appreciative love of her mate. When a child flourishes, most mothers enjoy a sense of well-being (Ruddick).

But not every child flourishes all the time. Even the luckiest may become ill, lonely, mean, selfish, sloppy, lazy. And the mother may succumb to occupational maladies—possessiveness, parochialism, fearfulness, lack of interest, self-righteousness, and a rage for order that frightens even her. Sometimes she takes out her frustrations on the child, who is often by no means the cause. A mother can infuriate her offspring and disappoint herself (Ruddick).

If the truth be known, many of us are, at times, less than fascinated by the endless chores of socializing a little human being, of living at a pace established by the child, of the relentlessness of it all. Maternal altruism is difficult to sustain. While our children fill us with cosmic joy, while we would defend them with the fierceness of a lioness protecting her cubs, they also provoke in us at times such anger and frustration that we hardly recognize the fury as our own. If motherhood is the dreamy relationship it is often billed as, then those flashes of hostility must be unnatural, traitorous, destructive of all that is normal, good, and decent. The resulting self-doubt is not much talked about. Mothers may joke about it, but they do not talk about it seriously. It is a cultural conspiracy of silence.

Even the daughters of the *Feminine Mystique* generation—those 1950s' housewives who finally admitted that life behind the Electrolux was itself a vacuum—shy away from acknowledging their ambivalence. While women today are freer than their mothers to complain about domestic chores, on the maternity front they are as silent as ever; it is the last stronghold of Friedan's "problem that has no name." Our society simply refuses to know about a mother's experience—how being yoked to a little one all day transforms her. To confess to being in conflict about mothering is tantamount to being a bad person; it violates a taboo; and, worse, it feels like a betrayal of one's child. In an age that regards mothers' negative feelings, even subconscious ones, as potentially toxic to their children, it has become mandatory to enjoy mothering (Ehrenreich and English chap. 7).

So we work at enjoying it. We try hard to improve our attitude, to bury unacceptable feelings, or at least to disguise them, even to ourselves—all of which is pointless. This turbulent inner war is not only unwinnable; it will, ironically, make casualties of those we are fighting to save. Children know very well when they have irritated us; they see right through our bluff. Covering up conflicts does not resolve them; indeed, it allows them to fester and grow larger. Besides, it sends out bad signals to our children: that anger is shameful (why else hide it?); that they should deny their own hostilities (that's what mommy does); that to think of violence, even subconsciously, is to commit it; that negative feelings cancel out positive ones, as if emotions were like arithmetic.

Truth in mothering is a far better policy. After all, criticism of the role of mother is not the same thing as disapproval of children or lack of love for a particular child.

Motherhood—the way we perform mothering—is culturally derived. Each society has its own mythology, complete with rituals, beliefs, expectations, norms, and symbols. Our received models of motherhood are not necessarily better or worse than many others. The way to mother is not writ in the stars, the primordial soup, the collective unconscious, nor in our genes. Our predecessors followed a pattern very different from our own, and our descendants may hew to one that is no less different (Demos 64). Our particular idea of what constitutes a good mother is only that, an idea, not an eternal verity. The good mother is reinvented as each age or society defines her anew, in its own terms, according to its own mythology.

As with most myths, the current Western version is so pervasive that, like air, it is unnoticeable. Yet it influences our domestic arrangements, what we think is best for our children, how we want them to be raised, and whom we hold accountable. Because we are inevitably caught up in our own cultural vortex, we fail to question our most basic suppositions. Today we assume, for example, that little children should be free to explore. Forget that for two thousand years infants were swaddled and managed to grow up without dire consequences. We now assume that a good mother should dutifully drag around her child's "security blanket." Never mind that granny regards it as unhygienic and would have summarily thrown it out. Her children managed to survive the loss, just as ours survive the germs.

But the current standards for good mothering are so formidable, self-denying, elusive, changeable, and contradictory that they are unattainable. Our contemporary myth heaps upon the mother so many duties and expectations that to take it seriously would be hazardous to her mental health.

Today, mother love has achieved the status of a moral imperative. Our current myth holds that the well-being of our children depends almost entirely on the quality of their upbringing (read *mother*, since it is she who usually has primary responsibility for raising children). An intense, prolonged loving bond between mother and child is essential. Though many believe that the mother need not be the biological mother or even female, it is considered fundamental that children have the continuous and exclusive presence of at least one devoted adult, and that anything separating' children from their loving caretaker is psychologically damaging.

Mother love is powerful stuff. Even the least sentimental among us regards parental affection as a child's birthright, average and expectable, a signifier of harmony. A mother's kisses and hugs provide the building blocks to a future of mental health, but—and this is important—only when they are adequately bestowed on a child during its infancy and early years. Later, mother must gradually relinquish her intense attachment. As her child grows up, she must accept obsolescence with grace. The myth tells us that timing is everything. If the dispensation of mother love is stingy, excessive, or ill-timed, harm to the child is irreversible. There are no second chances (Clarke and Clarke ix). The precise dose of a mother's love, punctually delivered, is the central factor in the well-being of the next generation, that is, the future.

With this in mind, common sense has given way to an obsession with the mother-child relationship. Yet even a cursory examination reveals this preoccupation to be a linear way of thinking. At worst, it makes a scapegoat of mom; even at best, it leads to an over-emphasis on what she does, at the expense of a broader understanding of child development. It obscures the importance of family dynamics, of the social environment, life events, and the character and inner psychodynamics of the child.

The all-importance of mother love has been fueled by a giant collective wish for perfect mothering. It is bolstered by a religion that gave us the Virgin Mary, nursery tales that supplied us with fairy godmothers, and a psychology that failed to question many cultural assumptions. It is supported by a history that forgot the benign effect of centuries of wet-nursing, an anthropology that romanticized the child-rearing practices of "primitive" cultures like the Trobriand Islanders and Samoans, and by post-Freudian psychoanalytic thought implying that a mother's moods could cause mental illness in her children. Added to this are modern literary classics like D. H. Lawrence's *Sons and Lovers* and Philip Roth's *Portnoy's Complaint,* plus decades of popular movies like *Now, Voyager; Psycho;* and *Mommie Dearest,* all of which are alarming tales about maternally induced psychic paralysis.

It is no wonder that mother is terrified by her own power. Yet, even as mother is all-powerful, she ceases to exist. She exists bodily, of course, but her needs as a person become null and void. On delivering a child, a woman becomes a factotum, a life-support system. Her personal desires either evaporate or metamorphose so that they are identical with those of her infant. Once she attains motherhood, a woman must hand in her point of view. Midcentury psychoanalytic thinking assumed that motherhood is essentially the child's drama, with mom in a supporting role. The popular French version of psychoanalysis of Jacques Lacan and even feminist revisionist psychoanalysis colluded in her obliteration, as have our "dead white male" literary canon, religion, and, to a certain extent, feminism, until very recently. No one spoke with a mother's voice. Apparently, it never occurred to anyone that Portnoy's mother might have a complaint of her own.

Even baby experts acquired the cultural amnesia for the personhood of mothers, thereby biting the hands that feed them, for mothers are their target audience. During the first half of the twentieth century, child-rearing manuals—which, in actuality, are mother-rearing tracts—dramatically increased demands on the mother. In the beginning of the century, advice books offered a vast sympathy for mother and were filled with practical short-cuts. But by midcentury, most notably with Dr. Benjamin Spock's *Baby and Child Care*—the all-time best-selling book in American history after the Bible—the sympathy was switched to the child. Mother's role was greatly complicated: she had to serve as a constant comforting presence, to consider the child's every need, to create a stimulating environment exactly suited to each developmental stage, and to tolerate any regression and deflect all conflict (Weiss).

Now, for example, the mother not only had to offer her child vitamin-rich food, but had to "enjoy him [sic]," "don't be afraid of him," and to remember that "feeding is learning" (Spock). Spock's book imposed a psychic workday on top of the physical workday, presuming a two-parent family, where the mother has nothing to do but care for one child. The role is not only more time-consuming than before; it is highly ambiguous. Exactly how does mom proceed to "enjoy" the baby who is spitting out food, mashing it into every crevice in reach, and throwing it in her face? While child-care specialists intend to reassure mothers, in fact they often foster a nagging sense of bewilderment, wrongdoing, and guilt. In effect, "they have invented a motherhood that excluded the experience of the mother (Weiss).

The prevailing mythology does concede that some mothers have to work outside the home, but it classifies such an endeavor as a necessary evil. The really good mother is a full-time mother. One senses a stubborn feeling in the land that stay-at-home mothers will redeem family values and restore morality to our citizenry. There was an almost audible sigh of relief when the wholesome, family-centered Barbara Bush replaced the too-thin, too-fashion-conscious Nancy Reagan as First Lady. Mrs. Bush projected motherliness; Mrs. Reagan projected narcissism. Her brittle image suggested that she had never been maternally preoccupied, a fact corroborated by her daughter. The jury is still out with regard to Hillary Rodham Clinton, the first First Lady who has made no pretense about her professional ambitions.

The public does not warm to mothers who are otherwise engaged, especially when they don't have to be. We grudgingly accept it when a woman "has" to work, meaning that her family's survival depends on her income. It is when a woman chooses to pursue a career that a shadow is cast over her motherliness. After all, what kind of mother could leave a shiny new baby unless her bottom line depended on it? Maternal devotion, it seems, is contingent on economics. The 1992 film *The Hand That Rocks the Cradle* was a parable of what happens to a bourgeois mother who hires a nanny: she must be punished.

Nobody believes in the efficacy of Mary Poppins anymore.

It was the hiring of an illegal alien as a nanny ("Nannygate") that cost Zoe Baird the post of attorney general, for which she had been nominated by President Clinton. Yet it is hardly a secret that there is virtually no pool of legally acceptable candidates for domestic work. The extent to which child care is degraded as gainful employment in this country betrays the real value of mothers' work, despite the idealization of the stay-at-home mom (Cowan 126). The Baird ordeal begs a lot of questions on the wide front of the gender wars, but it can't have escaped anyone's notice that this woman, this highly paid successful career woman, lost her opportunity to become a member of the cabinet on a maternal technicality, a technicality that had never been invoked to derail the candidacy of a man. The fiasco showed how raw, divisive, and unprocessed are people's ideas about mothers and work.

The truth is that working mothers are doing what mothers have always done. Throughout most of human history, mothers have devoted more time to other duties than to child care and have delegated aspects of child rearing to others, except for a brief period after the Second World War (Coontz 215). Fleeting as it was, this period was ossified in a number of TV sitcoms (a new rage in the 1950s), like *The Adventures of Ozzie & Harriet*, and *Leave It to Beaver*, so that even now we think of those mid-century family arrangements as good and right, and the way things were since time immemorial. But the 1950s was a decade unique in American history, and the breadwinner-housewife form of family was short-lived (Davis). As for the decade itself, it was never the familial paradise it was cracked up to be, even in white, middle-class suburbia, where outward domestic cheer often masked a good deal of quiet desperation, especially among women.

This is not to say that full-time, stay-at-home mothers were uniformly miserable; most mothers at the time preferred domestic to outside work. But keep in mind that their options were largely pink-collar. At least 1950s' culture accorded its full-time mothers unconditional positive regard. Today such mothers experience a jumble of mixed messages. The stay-at-home mothers I know dread the question, "And what do *you* do?" They know full well that adults who keep close company with children all day long, though applauded in some circles, raise eyebrows in others. Child rearing, inherently a splendid experience for many, is not a source of money, status, or power in society or even in the family. If it were, more men would probably choose to rear children (Polatnick).

Consider the plight of Snow White's stepmother. She has a story, too, but we have not had a chance to hear it. Until just twenty years ago, no one spoke with a maternal voice. No one wrote about the experience of mothering. We have a literary tradition in which a mother existed only in relation to her children she was trivialized or idealized or disparaged—and was never allotted a point of view. Mothers didn't star in their own dramas.

"Snow White" is a daughter's story. From beginning to end, the girl orients the perspective of the narrative. It is she who must flee from the murderous intentions of a jealous mother figure. The daughter is an angel; the mother, a witch. But if we were to look at the situation from the vantage of the stepmother, could we blame her for her desperation? In a kingdom where a woman's reflection in a mirror determines her access to power, why would the stepmother warm to a woman younger and more beautiful than she? Female bonding is extraordinarily difficult in patriarchy (Gilbert and Gubar 1979, 1984: 38; Barzilai). What were the stepmother's options? Indeed, what will Snow White's be, once she marries the prince, has babies of her own, and proceeds to age? She will face the same dilemma that terrified her stepmother. This tale, like most Western fiction and poetry, offers mother no viable option. She can die like her good biological mother or defend her position like her bad stepmother. Self-annihilation or odiousness: those are her alternatives.

Consider, too, the plight of Hamlet's mother. Hamlet cannot forgive his widowed mother for marrying too hastily and too happily (in Hamlet's view) his father's brother after his father's murder. But is his mother's conduct inexcusable (Heilbrun 15)? Why should she be denied a new lease on life simply because her "lust" is shameful to her son? A mother's sexuality is usually threatening to her nuclear family: that is the human condition. But how long should a son's discomfort determine the moral culpability of a mother's behavior? Sex and motherhood have not mixed well since the demise of the goddess religions, when men began to split women into madonnas or whores in every sphere. Presumably a good mother extinguishes her libido with conception or else expels it along with her placenta in childbirth. The extent of the anxiety aroused by the convergence of sexuality and maternity may be seen in the outraged reaction to a stunning photograph of the very pregnant and very naked actress Demi Moore on the cover of *Vanity Pair* in August 1991. The idea of subjecting a maternal figure to an erotic gaze was just too transgressive for many people, and the editors were forced to conceal Moore's protruding abdomen by a white paper wrapper in some cities.

The adulterous mother Mrs. Robinson, played by Anne Bancroft in the film *The Graduate,* remains a character we love to hate. She has impressive forebears. Passionate mothers take center stage in *The Scarlet Letter, Anna Karenina, Madame Bovary,* and *The Awakening,* novels that are among the greatest of the nineteenth century. Though initially sympathetic toward their heroines, the authors were all severely punitive to them in the end. The implication is that had these mothers been less sensual, more self-denying and conventionally maternal, they would have escaped their fate. But the conclusion (maybe even the goal) was punishment or, worse, self-punishment: Hester Prynne could not give up the scarlet embroidered A on her breast as penance for her adultery; the others committed suicide. The situation of amorous mothers may not be much better today. In her recent novel *The Good Mother,* Sue Miller pits a mother's maternity against her sexuality; she ends up losing both.

Psychological theories, especially those which have trickled down to a general audience, also have not been kind to mothers. If a mother is too involved with her children, whatever that means, she is considered overprotective, stifling, or intrusive. If she is not sufficiently involved with her children, whatever that means, she is rejecting, cold, and narcissistic. Some psychotherapists are so sure that bad mothering is the cause of all later idiosyncrasies that they tend to discover it in every patient they treat. For almost every "victim" of paternal incest, a mother is accused of collusion; for every person with an eating disorder, there is, presumably, an emotionally hungry mother behind the scenes emotionally starving her child. One therapist wrote recently that in the dozen years she worked in an outpatient psychiatric service at a major Harvard teaching hospital, she could not remember ever having heard a clinician suggest that a patient had a really good mother (Smith 32).

Taking cues from the experts, the media reflexively look at mothers when assigning blame. A recent *New York Times* story on cannibalistic mass murderer Jeffrey Dahmer is a case in point. The article prominently featured a head shot of Dahmer (Barron and Tabor), next to which was an equally large head shot of his mother. I suppose that the juxtaposition gratified the public's presumed interest in the manner of creature that produced such a monster. But why would the public be curious about Dahmer's mother if it did not already, on some level, somehow, insinuate her into his crimes?

All of this is not to deny, of course, that mothering does have an enormous impact on child development, or that many mothers do fail their children. Nor, by defending mothers, do I mean to condemn fathers. (Indeed, fathers are getting their share of censure these days for sexual abuse, violence, alcoholism, for being "deadbeat" or just plain absent.) In my psychotherapy practice, I have come across parents of unconscionable vileness; grotesque mothers, hideous fathers. It is just that the indictment of parents (usually mothers) in the psychological literature has been so automatic, so nasty, so massive, so undifferentiated, and so oblivious of the limits of a mother's power that it precludes a sensible assessment of any clinical situation (Smith 1990: 32). A sympathetic evaluation of the social context of the mother is virtually ignored in nearly all accounts of parenting. Yet poverty, sexism, racism, or war can undo any mother's best efforts. Mothering is largely socially created and, sometimes, politically remediable. And the power of a child's own psychodynamics should not be underestimated.

But in the current mother mythology, children are seen as eminently perfectible. There are no bad children, only bad parents. What is at issue here is the old nature-nurture controversy about the determinants of child behavior, now heavily weighted in favor of nurture. Just why this view has taken hold probably has to do with its inherent optimism and impartiality. It resonates in these multicultural times; it is hopeful, egalitarian, pragmatic, and it seems to offer endless possibilities for transforming a child, if only mom were to do the right thing. Never mind genes, class, adversity. Biological differences (a factor that makes people nervous) do not matter. No one believes in the "bad seed" anymore. All children are redeemable. If there is parental will, there is a way.

This wishful idea, that there is a way, keeps parents permanently on the hook. Parenting is a precarious business. Do it wrong, suggest the advice columns and child-care manuals, and your child will be warped. But, as we shall see, child-care experts disagree on the "right" way. To be sure, now that the extended family is no longer around, parents probably can't do without baby-care manuals of some sort, if only to tell them about teething and whooping cough. But what Drs. Spock and Brazelton and others convey is merely kindly, humane folklore, not incontrovertible fact. Their advice is based not so much on scientific comparisons of child rearing as on their experience with babies, on child-development theories still in flux, on studies of discrete child behaviors that do not lend themselves to broad child-rearing generalizations, along with a big dollop of their personal philosophies. What they offer is informed opinion, not child-raising absolutes. To quote the wise old Native American in the film *Little Big Man*, "Sometimes the magic works ... sometimes it doesn't."

It goes without saying today that every child is precious. We put so much emphasis on the individual child that it is widely held we should produce a child only if we have a reasonable prospect of giving it the prolonged and intensive loving care we believe it needs (Dally 1983: 19). Our society has become unabashedly pronatal. People are going gaga over parenthood, especially in older, educated, baby boomer circles, where the consumers and tastemakers wield an influence far exceeding their numbers. A rash of movies in the 1980s portrayed procreation as redemptive, even for men— *Baby Boom; Three Men and a Baby; Mr. Mom; Look Who's Talking; She's Having a Baby;* and *For Keeps.*

Never has a baby been so delicious. Capitalizing on this sentiment, hospital administrators boost business by romanticizing their maternity services with gourmet postpartum dinners and private Jacuzzis. Advertisers' from the Gap to IBM to Tyson Chicken and Calvin Klein fragrances have turned to photographs of babies to sell their products. Giving birth turns out to improve the popularity ratings of female television newscasters. Children have become fashion accessories in women's magazines. Politicians and British royalty need only demonstrate affection for their offspring to add warmth and likability to their image. Motherhood is utterly sentimentalized.

What we have today is a myth of motherhood that defies common sense. Never before have the stakes of motherhood been so high—the very mental health of the children. Yet never before has the task been so difficult, so labor intensive, subtle, and unclear. At the very moment when women have been socialized into wanting more than a diaper in one hand and a dust rag in the other, they are obliged to subordinate their personal objectives by an ideology that insists that unless they do, they will damage their children for life. Media images of happy, fulfilled mothers, and the onslaught of advice from experts, have only added to mothers' feelings of inadequacy, guilt, and anxiety. Mothers today cling to an ideal that can never be reached but somehow cannot be discarded.

I recall treating a young mother whose care of her gravely ill child was nothing short of heroic. She told me of nearly two years of terror during which she stayed up night after night to monitor her child's breathing, performed nursing procedures of frightening complexity and delicacy, and fought medical bureaucracies to obtain the best care for her child. She was labeled a "nuisance" by hospital staff and "overly intrusive" by a therapist, though, in fact, she insisted on a hospitalization for her child which turned out to save the girl's life.

Months after her child was well, the mother developed severe agoraphobia, which was why she was seeing me. This bravest of young women was now afraid to leave her home. Her panic turned out to be self-punishment for ambivalent feelings, now breaking through, about her little girl and the traumatic course of events. While her child was acutely ill, my patient had functioned on automatic pilot; but now that her youngster was out of danger, she found herself dreaming of murdering her. It was all so irrational: her little girl was the most precious thing in the world to her. In her mind, a good mother would never wish to harm her child, whose sickness had not been the child's fault. What this mother came to recognize was that her resentment toward her child was understandable in light of the hell she had been through when caring for her and that despite her suppressed rage, she had functioned wonderfully. Coming to accept her own ambivalence helped her shed the crippling agoraphobia. Unfortunately many women never gain that insight, and live forever in the shadow of an impossible maternal ideal.

My aim in writing this book is to make mothers' internal lives acceptable to them, to undo some of the *angst* among mothers (and mothering persons) at large. I do not mean to quell the guilty conscience of the mean-spirited mother, or the frivolous or neglectful or self-centered mother (who, in my view, needs treatment and some sort of social intervention), but to calm the jangled nerves of your garden-variety mother, the one who is neither villain nor saint. I want to soothe the mind of a mother who mostly loves her children, who worships them at times and is repelled at others, who appreciates their beauty and intricacies, but is still tempted to lead her life outside and beyond them (to paraphrase Tillie Olsen). I want to free this mother from an uncritical dependency on an ideology of good mothering that is ephemeral, of doubtful value, unsympathetic to caretakers, arbitrary, and, literally, man-made.

Our current ideal of the mother is, like all ideals, culture-bound, historically specific, and hopelessly tied to fashion. And, of course, fashions change. As we shall see, the diverse roles that women play in raising their children are not linked to timeless truths, but to more mundane things, like subsistence strategies, population pressures, biology, technology, weather patterns, and speculations about women's nature.

Children may not have been precious when they competed with their parents for limited food and resources or were evidence of their mothers' "immoral" behavior. Remember that well into the nineteenth century many children arrived unbidden (there was little access to reliable birth control). Many inadvertently caused their mothers' death in delivery; often they themselves died before their fifth year. Infanticide seems to have been a part of Western European life until the late nineteenth century, when women finally gained some measure of control over their reproductive capacity (Anderson and Zinsser Vol. 2: 247). Usually the killing of infants is related to desperate poverty and illegitimacy—themselves related—but sometimes the cause is not at all clear. In both Classical Athens and Renaissance Italy, for example, parents may have abandoned babies, mostly girls, for motives far more frivolous than economic desperation. Misogyny, perhaps (Boswell 418; Klapisch-Zuber 1357; Golden; French cited in Grant 1988, 1989: 1357)?

Even when child-rearing practices spring from parents' best intentions, they may seem questionable to another generation. What was considered ideal at the end of the last century—devices to prevent masturbation, cold baths, the participation of children in elaborate mourning rituals—may be considered insensitive or even abusive in this one. How history will choose to interpret modern mothers' mandate to bond instantly, flash flashcards, shake the ubiquitous clear rattle, exude round-the-clock empathy, breast-feed again (after decades of bottle-feeding), is anyone's guess.

One of the great curiosities of maternal history that *The Myths of Motherhood* explores is wet-nursing. Michelangelo, Juliet, Scarlett O'Hara, and Winston Churchill all had wet nurses. This was not an obscure enterprise; it involved most infants born in certain European cities at various times (Badinter x; Sussman 20). Such a practice, if benign (and we have no evidence one way or the other), seems to contradict some of the most cherished beliefs about mother love and attachment held by today's psychologists, child experts, and, indeed, almost everyone.

Just as the practice of mothering has veered widely with the mores of different epochs, so has the status of mothers. From the beginning of time, woman was an awesome being; she seemed to swell and spew forth a child by her own law. Perhaps in those early days, twenty-five hundred years before the birth of Christ and other male gods, the idea of woman as mother endowed all women with respect. But as men realized their contribution to procreation and seized control, organizing much of what we know as mainstream history, the mother has been dehumanized, that is, either wildly idealized (with mothers becoming prisoners of their own symbolic inflation) or degraded (with mothers viewed as brood mares). In men's imaginations, the mother was the selfless nurturer or the wicked stepmother. Since the onset of male domination, mothers' sexuality has been split off from her maternity, and her bodily processes—menstruation, childbirth, lactation—have been deemed indecent. It was only during 1993, for instance, that the state of Florida guaranteed women the right to breastfeed in public.

The Myths of Motherhood traces the evolution of maternal personae from prehistory to present day. In the last half century alone we have witnessed vast diversity in parenting ideals; good mothering has abruptly shifted from training and control to permissiveness and empathy. And on the psychoanalytic front, an upheaval of such dimension has occurred that psychoanalysts, who previously had ignored mothers, now find themselves scrupulously scrutinizing mothers' behaviors during the first few weeks of an infant's life. The watchwords vary—attachment, mirroring, attunement, empathy, bonding, unconditional positive regard—but the required maternal *modus operandi* remains the same—altruistic love. "The ideal mother," wrote the psychoanalyst Alice Balint, "has no interests of her own."

In retrospect, I realize I began practicing psychotherapy and had a baby at precisely the time when psychological theories were least charitable to mothers. I worked outside the home when experts had not yet given mothers approval for doing so. The women's movement urged me to maximize my potential, but the dominant culture called me selfish for doing so. I tried to be a good mother and a good worker just when the prevailing wisdom insisted that those were mutually exclusive enterprises. I was confused. And it seems to me, more than a decade later, that mothers are even more conflicted and guilt-ridden.

In a time when society values the fulfillment of women as persons, we have an ethos of maternity that denies them that very thing. Just when some of us have been teased into believing that we have vocational options; just when we assumed we could share the burden of child raising; just when we have been driven by economic necessity to work outside the home and to jury-rig a childcare plan, we have a mythology that insists, with rising shrillness, on perfection in childcare. No caretaking arrangement can be that perfect. Nor, for that matter, can any full-time mom. Clearly the myth of motherhood deserves a hard reckoning, and that is what I have aimed for.

References

Anderson, Bonnie, and Judith Zinsser. *A History of Their Own: Women in Europe from Prehistory to the Present.* Vols. 1 and 2. New York: Harper and Row, 1988.

Badinter, Elizabeth. *Mother Love: Myth and Reality: Motherhood in Modern History.* Trans. Roger de Gravis. New York: Macmillan, 1980.

Balint, Alice. "Love for the Mother and Mother-Love." *International Journal of Psychoanalysis* 30 (1949): 251-259.

Barron, James, and Mary Tabor. "17 Killed and Life is Searched for Clue." *New York Times* August 4, 1991: 1, 30.

Barzilai, Shuli. "Reading 'Snow White': The Mother's Story." Signs 15.3 (Spring 1990).

Boswell, John. *The Kindness of Strangers: The Abandonment of Children in Western Europe from Late Antiquity to the Renaissance.* New York: Pantheon, 1988.

Clarke, Ann, and A. D. B. Clark, eds. *Early Experience: Myth and Evidence.* New York: Free Press, 1976.

Coontz, Stephanie. *The Way We Never Were: American Families and the Nostalgia Trap.* New York: Basic Books, 1992.

Cowan, Ruth Schwartz. *More Work for Mother: The Ironies of Household Technology from the Open Hearth to the Microwave*. New York: Basic Books, 1983.

Dally, Ann. *Inventing Motherhood: The Consequences of an Ideal*. New York: Schocken, 1983.

Davis, Kingsley. "Wives and Work: A Theory of the Sex-role Revolution and Its Consequences." *Feminism, Children, and the New Families*. Eds. Sanford M. Dornbusch and Myra H. Strober. New York: Guilford Press, 1988.

Demos, John P. "Images of the Family Then and Now." *Past, Present, and Personal: The Family and the Life Course in American History*. New York: Oxford, 1986. PAGES?

Ehrenreich, Barbara, and Deirdre English. *For Her Own Good: 150 Years of the Experts' Advice to Women*. New York: Doubleday Anchor, 1979.

French, Valerie. "Birth Control, Childbirth, and Early Childhood." *Civilization of the Ancient Mediterranean*. Vol. I. Eds. Michael Grant and Rachel Kitzinger. New York: Scribner's, 1988, 1989. 1355-1362.

Gilbert, Sandra, and Susan Gubar. *The Madwoman in the Attic*. New Haven: Yale University Press, 1979, 1984.

Golden, Mark. "Demography and the Exposure of Girls at Athens." *Phoenix* 35 (4) (1981): 316-331.

Heilbrun, Carolyn. *Hamlet's Mother and Other Women*. New York: Columbia University Press, 1990.

Klapisch-Zuber, Christiane. *Women, Family and Ritual in Renaissance Italy*. Chicago: University of Chicago Press, 1985.

Polatnick, M. Rivkal. "Why Men Don't Rear Children: A Power Analysis." *Mothering: Essays in Feminist Theory*. Ed. Joyce Trebilcot. Lanham, MD: Rowman and Littlefield, 1983. 21-41.

Ruddick, Sara. *Maternal Thinking: Toward a Politics of Peace*. Boston: Beacon Press, 1989.

Smith, Janna M. "Mothers: Tired of Taking the Rap." *New York Times Magazine* June 10, 1990. 32-38.

Sommerville, C. John. *The Rise and Fall of Childhood*. New York: Vintage, 1982, 1990.

Spock, Benjamin. *The Pocket Book of Baby and Child Care*. 1954. New York: Pocket Book, 1976.

Sussman, George. *Selling Mother's Milk: The Wet-Nursing Business in France 1715-1914*. Urbana: University of Illinois Press, 1982.

Weiss, Nancy Pottishman. "Mother, the Invention of Necessity: Dr. Benjamin Spock's Baby and Child Care." *American Quarterly* 29 (1977).

Chapter 22

Leaving Home

The Young Man's Rite of Passage

OLGA SILVERSTEIN AND BETH RASHBAUM

"Grown-up" ... should have some meaning for a boy other than "gone away."   —Barbara Ehrenreich

THE SEPARATION FOR which we begin training our sons at birth begins to loom large in the high school years. For some it can seem a veritable abyss, threatening to distance them from all love, comfort, security. Hence the indefinable, unassuageable nostalgia of the adolescent male. It is J. D. Salinger's *Catcher in the Rye* that best communicates what for most boys goes unspoken. At seventeen, Holden Caulfield looks back on childhood visits to the Museum of Natural History, explaining that what was great about that museum was that you could always count on everything in it to stay the same. No matter how many times you went back, you could always see the same Eskimo catching the same two fish, the same birds flying south on the same migration. What we hear in Holden's evocative description is the longing of a boy on the verge of what seem like overwhelming transitions—the longing to freeze time, to stave off the inevitability of movement, change, and loss. He wants certain unspecified "things," which we can readily guess at, to be preserved, just as surely as the creatures in the museum's glass cases are.

Ultimately, *The Catcher in the Rye* is about loss; indeed, the very last words in the book are about how much he misses everybody. Holden differs from his peers in his ability, and willingness, to express feelings of loss. But from birth on, most boys in Western society are on a trajectory intended to culminate in leavetaking—and loss. This is not the same as the leave-taking girls do. Boys and girls alike are expected to leave the parental home and eventually to make marriages and families of their own, of course. Only boys, however, are expected to make the kind of final break implicit in our belief that "A son's a son 'til he gets him a wife, a daughter's a daughter the rest of her life." Nowhere is this more true than in the U.S. and Great Britain, where it has become part of the cultural heritage.

Journey from the Motherland[1]

As a nation made up largely of immigrants and of citizens whose ancestors were immigrants, the United States has been marked in its very soul by the experiences of those millions who set off from faraway lands to make a new life here. The pattern was for the men, who were usually in their teens or twenties, to come first; once settled, they would send for their wives and children, if any, and sometimes their siblings and parents as well. England's hundreds of years as a colonizer of lands thousands of miles away have had a similarly profound effect on its men, who were (and are) trained in the self-reliance that enabled them to run the British Empire by being sent off to the harsh rigors of boarding school at a tender age. Indeed, since we were once a British colony ourselves, our national character is twice marked by expectations of displacement, exile, and loss.

Whether they left their homelands to escape persecution or to seek their fortunes, whether it was duty, fear, ambition, patriotism, or a sense of high adventure that drove them, the men who had this experience all understood that it was the mark of a man to be able to set forth alone on a great journey, to push on to new frontiers. The cost—the pain of separating from loved ones—was simply the price that had to be paid.

Women, I suspect, paid this price much less stoically. One of my earliest memories, dating from when I was seven, was of being on a boat in Hamburg harbor with my mother, my two brothers, and my sister. As desperate tears streamed down her face, my mother waved goodbye to her parents on shore. My father had preceded us to this country by seven years, and now that he had finally sent for us, she faced the certain knowledge that in joining him she was leaving her parents forever. Overwhelmed by the emotions of the moment, I, too, began to cry, only to be shushed by my mother: "Stop your crying," she said bitterly. "*You* have nothing to cry about. You're not leaving your mother." She never saw her parents again.

Though few people who now live in the United States or Europe will ever have to say such farewells—the farewells even of recent immigrants are in the past, not in the future—the way we raise our sons suggests we are preparing them for precisely that fate. It's not just Robert Bly calling for the "clean break from the mother" (19), or Sam Keen declaring, "To grow from man-child into man ... he must take leave of WOMAN and wander for a long time in the wild and sweet world of men" (16). No, there is nearly universal consensus that a boy must go out on his own, and that he must do it at the culturally mandated age, which is eighteen. Ready or not, he is to make his exit—to college, to the army, to marriage, to full-time employment. Otherwise, he is not a man.

The belief is so ingrained a part of our culture that we forget how arbitrary it is. In many other countries, including much of Europe, young men may choose to continue living with their parents until they marry, without any diminution of their manhood. Who better to speak to this issue than Italian-born soap star Antonio Sabato, profiled in *People* (15 February, 1993) as *General Hospital's* "newest throb," who lives with his parents in Los Angeles and claims to enjoy it: "I could be 30, and if I'm not married, I would still live at home," he says, perhaps a tad defiantly, out of recognition of how counter this is to the values of his new home.

"It doesn't make you a man to live on your own. That's an American thing" (54). In Spain, many a mother would be insulted if her son moved out before getting married, no matter how long he remains single.

The fact that most eighteen-year-olds in this country are not able to support themselves and will be reliant on parental help for many years to come; that in an era of decreasing wages and rising unemployment, 54 percent of eighteen-to twenty-four-year-olds were living in their parents' home in 1992[2]; that the many college and graduate school students who do live away from home are often the least independent in that they rely the most on financial support from their parents; that more men than women are living with their parents[3]—none of this seems to have made much of a dent in our collective psyche. Reality has not intruded on our expectations. We still expect a leave-taking, even if financial dependence renders it largely symbolic.

Perhaps because it is only symbolic, we seem to entertain ever higher expectations about the psychological component of the separation—hence the readiness to heed the call for the "clean break from the mother." Though their message may seem new, Bly and Keen and other men's movement gurus are simply reflecting the time-honored assumption that emotional ties to Mother's "apron strings"—as we call them—will get in a boy's way, will prevent him from developing suitably manly qualities of independence and self-reliance. Thus, the grief that mothers (and some fathers) feel over a young man's turning away from them is exceeded only by their concern if he doesn't.

In most families, it's sometime during the high school years that the psychological preparations for the "clean break" begin in earnest (if not always in full consciousness). Both parents and child have to be made ready.

The Self-Fulfilling Prophecy

When Irene and her son, Zeke, came in to see me, having been referred by a school counselor who was concerned about Zeke's rapidly falling grades during the past year, both seemed more upset by the recent deterioration of their formerly close relationship than by the decline in his academic performance. But it was Zeke, an unusually articulate, expressive boy, who redirected our discussion away from school and toward what was really on his mind: "I just kind of think that my Mom and I are having a really hard time recently," he said, as I questioned him about what he thought the problem was. "We used to have a really neat relationship, and that changed this year. Now we're always at odds with each other."

"That's true, but I don't want it to be that way," Irene said plaintively. "Zeke's fifteen now. In three more years he'll be gone, and this is not what I want him to remember. But these days I just seem to get angry and crabby a lot and to take it all out on him. Everything will be fine, and then some little thing will set me off and I'll be really pissy."

Gone, I thought. *He hasn't even begun his sophomore year in high school, but in his mother's eyes he's almost out the door. She's already thinking about how he'll "remember" her, as though memory will be all that's left to them after he "leaves."* Was her anger a way of jump-starting what she saw as the inevitable process of separation? I asked her to describe to me what she meant when she said "everything will be fine."

"It feels like when I say something, he understands and responds, and when he says something, I understand and respond. There is an even flow of communication."

"And at those times you're feeling comfortable and at ease with each other?" I asked, looking to Zeke for confirmation.

"Yeah."

"So who gets worried first that things are going too well?"—in response to which both of them looked blankly at me. This was a question I knew would take them by surprise. But I wanted to plant the idea that these sudden bad moods of Irene's might be serving a purpose.

"Well, let me rephrase that: Who's usually the one to break the even flow of communication?"

"Me," Irene said, thoughtfully, "but I don't know why."

Changing the subject, I asked about the family history, which was recounted during the course of that session and the next. When Zeke was only two, Irene divorced his father and moved to New York, leaving her ex-husband, Lloyd, and all the rest of her family behind in Oregon. There had been hard times in those early years, even some time spent on welfare while Irene went back to school, but eventually she earned her law degree and now had an excellent if underpaid job as a public defender. Though Lloyd was supposed to provide a modest amount of child support, he paid erratically, if at all. Zeke's contact with his father was limited to two weeks in Oregon every summer. Their relationship had been amicable in years past—in Zeke's words, Lloyd is "really, really nice"—but his last visit to his father, who had remarried a few years earlier, had apparently had some bad aftereffects.

"I think it was a catalyst," Irene told me, choosing her words carefully. "It kind of allowed something to surface that may have had an impact on what's been going on with Zeke's schoolwork this year."

Not long before he made his annual visit, Zeke had learned that Lloyd's always irregular payments had dwindled to nothing. The check he kept saying was in the mail never arrived. Once he got to Oregon, Zeke looked at his father with new eyes, and didn't much like what he saw. What had previously appeared to be gentleness now looked like passivity, and his easygoing nature like submissiveness, beneath which Zeke thought he could detect a silent but ineffectual anger. "Pretty much anything my stepmother wants, he does," Zeke said with contempt. Indeed, he seemed to Zeke to be at the beck and call of everyone in his environment—his new wife, his stepchildren, the people he worked for, and Zeke himself.

Irene felt Zeke's poor performance in school that year had something to do with his disappointment in his father. "I'm never going to be like him," he had declared shortly after returning home from the visit. "I'm going to make up my own mind about things and nobody is going to tell me what to do."

Zeke's attitude toward Lloyd dovetailed only too neatly with Irene's; both of them now became wary of any signs of resemblance between father and son. For Irene this concern translated into a determination that Zeke become someone completely different from his laid-back father. She began to wonder if she'd made Zeke too dependent on her—as though closeness meant dependence—and to worry incessantly about whether he'd do okay on his own, though he was still more than three years away from college age. Her way of dealing with these anxieties about his capacity for independence was to pressure him about his grades and to insist that he take on more responsibilities around the house. At the same time, her newly volatile temper got in the way of the easy give-and-take that had characterized their relationship until then.

For his part, Zeke began to resent not just his mother's new pushiness, but also her sudden irritability and irrationality, which he of course did not recognize as an unconscious distancing mechanism. Zeke balked, and soon his grades were lower than they had ever been, his contribution to housekeeping duties nil. As he explained to me: "I'll be going along doing real well and then she gets down on me for some little thing and I say to myself, 'What's the use?' So I don't do anything."

It seemed to me that these two had gotten locked into an escalating cycle of response and counterresponse: Zeke doing a passive-aggressive routine on his mother out of his newfound determination not to be "submissive," not to take orders from anyone; Irene growing ever more distressed at his resistance, which she saw as endangering his future. The "be-independent-do-what-I-say injunction" she had given him that fall was backfiring, and the passive aggression with which he countered it seemed to be generalizing to other areas of his life.

In our next session I decided to test my hunch about Zeke's behavior by exploring his attitude about school. "Do you find that you do better in subjects taught by teachers you like?" I asked.

"Mm-hmmm."

"And could you tell me what kind of teacher you don't like?"

"You know," he said, "the ones who try to force things out of a student, as though we're in a prison and they have the key and if we don't do what they say they'll punish us."

"So what's your usual response to that?"

"I get mad."

"And?"

"And—nothing. I don't feel like doing what they say. Maybe I'll do it, but I'll be late, or I won't finish it or something."

"That's just like your dad," Irene said, a flush of anger visible on her face. "Whenever things didn't go his way, he just ceased to function, didn't keep his commitments, walked away from his responsibilities."

"No way! That's not at all what I'm doing," Zeke retorted. "I just don't like to be bossed around."

I interrupted. "It sounds to me as though you're doing a little standstill number.

On your teachers at school, and on your mother at home. Is that how you get to feel that you're not being submissive? That you have some control?"

"I guess …."

"Well," I said, knowing my words would upset him, "that's a very male way of fighting. More like Dad's than Mom's, I would guess, since what you both tell me is that your mom has a bad temper, while your dad avoids conflict. And that's how some men express their anger—indirectly, not directly." Zeke was clearly uncomfortable with this comparison, but he was listening, so I went on. "There are really two ways you can express anger against a teacher who you think is being unreasonable. One is to do what you're doing—to do the opposite of whatever it is she wants you to do. But since you always have to be doing the opposite, that locks you into a certain kind of behavior just as much as if you did what she said; it doesn't give you any real freedom. The other way would be to say, 'You can't make me fail no matter how difficult you're being. You have no control over my performance.'"

During the rest of the session we talked some about Zeke's dreams for his future. Since he was interested in law school as a route to a possible political career, he agreed that it would be in his best interest to improve his grades.

The following session began on a tense note. Mother and son both looked grim. Irene announced, "We're pissed at each other now."

"Who got mad at whom first?" I asked.

Irene and Zeke, simultaneously: "He did." "She did."

His mother had been late again, Zeke explained, and since she'd been late to every session, he finally said something to her about it. But he had only been "a little bit mad," he said, whereas she "went ballistic" the minute he criticized her.

"I guess I did overreact," Irene conceded. "Does that happen often?"

"Often enough."

"If you blow up at Zeke whenever he expresses any criticism, even a legitimate criticism such as the one he made today, you leave him without any outlet for his own anger, and I think that may contribute to the passive-aggressive number he does."

Looking very unhappy, Irene said quietly, "I know, I know, I'm sure you're right. It's just I get so scared of his anger. So I get angry first and then he gets that hurt puppy-dog look on his face and I worry myself sick over him."

"Why? What are you worried about with him? He seems pretty together to me."

"I worry that he'll be unhappy."

"And? Is that the worst?"

"That's definitely the worst. But the second worst, which isn't far off, is that after he leaves home he'll never want to see me again. It's like I only have three more years to fix things between us and then he'll be gone."

We were back to the idea of Zeke's leaving, which seemed to haunt Irene. "I don't know where you got that notion," I began.

Irene: "That it ends at eighteen?"

"Yes.... Do you have the same notion," I asked Zeke, "that at eighteen you're going to disappear out of your mother's life? That you'll be finished with each other?"

"I didn't used to. But I'm starting to feel like maybe that is going to happen. Like maybe she'll treat me—not badly, exactly, but as an outsider."

Irene, puzzled, and trying to make light of it: "Like I'd pretend not to know you if I passed you on the street?"

"No, but like you'd not really do any more parenting."

Every once in a while the unadorned truth gets spoken. An extraordinarily bright, verbal, perceptive boy, Zeke expressed his fear, and helped his mother to express hers, about what both saw as the monster in the box: their impending separation. By bringing the monster into the light, they were able to tame it. Over the course of our next few sessions, both came to see that they need not ever be "finished" with each other. They were free to reject the conventional wisdom that boys cannot have as deep and enduring a connection to their parents as girls do.

It had taken three different but overlapping and synergistic sets of responses to turn an open, bright young boy into a passive-aggressive, refusenik teenager: (1) Irene's anxiety about their separation. The anticipatory distancing she then effected was her way of minimizing the pain of that loss three years hence, and of trying to toughen him up so he could function alone. (2) Zeke's reassessment of his father's behavior, which made him determined not to be similarly "submissive"—a particularly unacceptable quality in males. (3) Irene's fear of Zeke's open expression of any anger, which left him with few alternatives. He could not fight openly with his mother because, as he put it, "she always gets madder than me," and because he was reluctant to hurt her.

Had they not come into therapy, these two were set on a course that would have made all their fears about separation a self-fulfilling prophecy. Irene's angry outbursts, unconsciously motivated and thus puzzling even to her, would have served their dual function—to end their previous closeness so that neither of them would feel the pain of their eventual separation, and to drive Zeke as far away as he could get, both geographically (no doubt to a college or job on the opposite coast) and emotionally.

By expecting our sons to cut off from us, we make sure that they do. And there is surely no more commonplace a form of male cutoff than the passive aggression Zeke used with Irene. Millions of girlfriends, wives, and ex-wives will attest to that.

Stigmatizing the Stay-at-Home

Reinforcing our cultural heritage as a nation of immigrants, and more influential by far than the men's movement gurus, is the mental health establishment. With its notion of appropriate stages through which we all (ideally) pass, it has given new weight to the idea that the young man must put his parents behind him. Erik Erikson believes that's the only way of achieving a satisfactory resolution of the adolescent identity crisis. Similarly, psychiatrist Daniel Levinson (1978) sees the necessity of "numerous separations, losses and transformations" (73) during this "early adult transition" (60) on the road to "Becoming One's Own Man." As Carol Gilligan says, summing up the work of developmental psychologists like these: "Development itself [has] come to be identified with separation."[4]

Conversely, failure to achieve the goal of "greater psychological distance from the family" (Levinson 73), especially if it results in the boy's failure to leave home, is viewed as a form of pathology. True to the spirit of this Lone Ranger developmental ethos, family therapist Jay Haley published a book that was highly influential in the field. *Leaving Home: The Therapy of Disturbed Young People*, was written for the express purpose of giving fellow therapists practical techniques to help families through the difficult "leaving home transition." Most of the "disturbed young people" in this book were males, and they were so severely disturbed—drug addicts, recovering suicide attempters, schizophrenics—that they had been institutionalized, then released into their parents' care. With all the focus on facilitating a departure, too little consideration is given to the possibility that getting sick, or getting into serious trouble, may be a young man's only means of being able to come home again, and perhaps a sign that he needs to *be* home.

Unfortunately, the mental health field has managed to convince us that there is something wrong with any boy who is not ready to "leave the nest" on schedule. But human development is vastly more complex and variable than that of the birds who inspired this metaphor.

College Bound—Or Bust

Underlying the vague uneasiness we may feel about Bly's "soft men," Keen's "WOMAN"-driven men, and the psychologists' borderline mental cases is our very real fear that the boy who does not leave home at the proper time is going to be a failure in life. That was the not-so-subtle subtext of one of our most popular and endearing coming-of-age films, 1973's *American Graffiti*. Four boys spend a long summer night cruising the streets of a town in Southern California looking for action, sex, love, and the meaning of life. Two of them are about to go off together to a fancy college in the East—the very next day, as it happens; the third is a sweetly humpy hot-rodder who works in an auto repair shop; the fourth is a nerdy loser type who hangs out with the other three.

Curtis, one of the college-bound, is having second thoughts about leaving home. He has a variety of rationales for not leaving, which we hear him trying out on each of the many people who ask him about his plans during the course of that long night: "I'm not sure I'm the competitive type either," he confides to a teacher who has just recounted his own failure to stick it out at an East Coast college. "Why should I leave home to find a home?" is a line he has apparently used a lot, since various characters in the movie quote it to each other. And then there's "I don't know what the big hurry is. Maybe I should stick around here and go to the junior college until I figure out what I want out of life," and so forth. Whether Curtis is frightened of the challenges that he'll have to face in college, sad at the prospect of missing his parents, sorry to leave his hometown, apprehensive about life in the East, or what, we are never told. To plumb a young man's fears would perhaps be too great a violation of all our unspoken taboos. We don't want to know why he's reluctant to leave. In lieu of any specifics, there is a free-floating sense of anxiety about the future. Curtis's parents, also taboo, are never seen, or mentioned, until the end of the film, when we see him saying goodbye to them at the airport, after he has found the courage to make his off screen decision to go.

At the fadeout of the farewell scene, each young man's yearbook picture appears on screen with a brief summation of his destiny: the hot-rodder and the nerd are both killed within a couple of years, the first by a drunk driver, the second in Vietnam; Steve, who had looked forward confidently to college and tried throughout the film to talk Curtis into joining him there, decides at the last minute to stay home to be with his heartbroken, possessive girlfriend (the ties that bind!), and ends up selling insurance in Modesto, California.

Curtis is a writer living in Canada—a man who has gone far in every way. The moral is clear: Cut those ties and soar.

And so we have generations of men looking and longing for their lost connections, angry, isolated, and sometimes even dangerous. Most don't do anything dramatic, however. They simply become simultaneously needier and more remote on their journeys to success.

Michael on His Own

The summer after our son, Michael, graduated from high school was a hard one. He was eighteen, headed for the college of his choice in the fall, and, after several summers of working at typical teenage jobs (cashier in a burger joint, ice-cream-truck driver, etc.), he finally had a "real job" as an assistant in a research laboratory. We were very proud of him. With his high school diploma, his grown-up job, his admission to a first-rate university, and a girlfriend, he was clearly a finished person. Thus whatever distance had developed between us seemed appropriate.

We had rented a cottage at the beach where the girls and I were to spend two months that summer. Michael and his father, our two working men, were to join us for weekends. Fred came out every weekend, Michael hardly ever, and then only with his girlfriend.

I remember thinking there was something wrong with this, thinking that I should be home with Michael, since he would be leaving so soon. But I always put my unease down to my own problem with letting go, and reassured myself that a summer spent alone with his father was the best possible preparation for the new phase of life he was now entering.

Anyway, Michael didn't seem very happy when he was with us, so I didn't push it. He was always withdrawn and quiet, and I interpreted his behavior as impatience with family life, eagerness to be gone. That he might have been lonely, or even angry at my having left him that summer, never occurred to me, certainly not then. I missed him terribly, but I had read my Philip Wylie as well as a great deal of Freud and I was determined not be an intrusive, controlling, emasculating mother. Thus I never questioned him about his behavior, which I thought was a kind of psychological leavetaking that would serve him well when it came time to make his actual departure. Why didn't I realize that it was I who had left, taking with me his two sisters?

At the end of the summer Fred and I drove Michael to Boston to school. I remember that trip vividly: the men both very quiet, me chatting nervously away, trying to reassure all of us that this was an exciting and happy event. By the middle of the trip I had run out of chatter. Nobody spoke much from then on. When we finally arrived, we said hurried and strained goodbyes. Fred and I drove back home in sad silence.

Recently, Michael wrote and asked me if I had been aware of how lonely and unhappy he was in his first few years at college. No, I wasn't. My fantasy was that he was having a wonderful time, enjoying intellectual and social opportunities his father and I never had. His grades were excellent, he made new friends whom he brought home during the holidays, he seemed to me to be having just the kind of college life I had pictured in my mind's eye. Being so successful, surely he must be happy—so I would have reasoned, had I ever even thought to wonder. The remoteness, the coolness, and the long silences that continued to characterize his behavior whenever he was with his family I continued to rationalize as the attitude appropriate to a newly independent young man with his own, now separate, life. I wouldn't have dreamed of questioning him about it.

Even if I had had any inkling of his unhappiness, I would probably have been reluctant to try to discuss it with him, again out of the conviction that "mother hovering" would be harmful. A momentary blip in his developmental progress is how I would have described the problem to myself, something he had to simply hang tough to get past; surely talking wouldn't be of much use—might even be counterproductive, by blowing a small thing out of proportion.

Now I would do things very differently. Years of experience in the consulting room have taught me that the closed-off look I see on so many male faces is not boredom or indifference, nor a developmental inevitability, but is often, rather, a way of concealing pain. I think now I could see past the remoteness, past all the external signs of successful adjustment—the good grades, the new friends, the upbeat notes home—and dare to ask my male child about his feelings.

"You look unhappy. Is something wrong?" I might begin. If we didn't have the habit of talking about feelings (as Michael and I certainly did not at that time), he would probably respond by putting me off—either politely ("Everything's fine, Mom") or not ("Mind your own business"). But I would persist, if only in expressing my own feelings: "Seeing you looking this way upsets me, so I need to know what's going on with you. Maybe you don't want to share all the details, but please at least give me a general idea of what's wrong. I think it might help you to talk to me, and I know it would help me." After that, it's up to him. I would want him to feel welcomed into my confidence, not invaded by my insistence on knowing about his life.

Sometimes this sort of approach works, sometimes it doesn't. It almost doesn't matter whether the boy talks. He has the right not to, and the mother has the right to say what she feels. More, I think mothers have an obligation, that it would be the grossest neglect of their children for them to remain silent out of some mistaken notion of appropriate boundaries. All children, male *and* female, need to know that someone is concerned about them, ready to hear them out, sympathetically and nonjudgmentally, on the basic assumption that they are entitled to their feelings, whatever they are. And make no mistake: the message will get through, even if it goes unacknowledged.

There's a poignant little scene in Robb Forman Dew's novel *Fortunate Lives* where a mother tells her Harvard-bound son, who has been growing ever more distant from his family in that last summer at home, that they're going to miss him when he's gone. By this juncture in the narrative we've seen numerous instances of Dinah trying to negotiate a proper balance between intrusiveness and caring, and we know how fearful she is of overstepping the line with David. Since this is a kid who once snapped at her, in response to her question about what he wanted for dinner that night, "I don't know why you need to know *everything* about my life!" (28), she has good reason to be apprehensive. In fact, David is withdrawing from everyone that summer, not just his family but his friends and his girlfriend, Christie, who is the only one who seems to have any insight into the defensive nature of that withdrawal. In a moment of rage she calls him on it: "You're getting ready, aren't you, not to care about anybody? Won't that make your life easy? Won't you be *free?* You can just go away with your great, fucking *brilliance*, and your … *superiority*.…" (55). To which there is no satisfactory reply from David, because he can't allow himself to understand what's happening to him.

Nor is there much of a response to his mother's impulsive little gesture of affection, which is met first with silence, then by a flip, hurtful remark about empty-nest syndrome. Taken aback by his cruelty to her, Dinah doesn't realize how very much David needed to hear her words. This will become clear only in the final pages. But at that moment he is unable to respond in kind, to tell her that he'll miss her too, for "he was far too endangered to say such a thing. She had no way of knowing that he was full of alarm on his own behalf. He had no practice at leaving behind every familiar thing in his life" (230).

Fearful of rejections and dismissals such as the one David leveled at his mother, most parents opt for silence. Often they justify it with the rationale that they don't wish to be intrusive. But there's a difference between intrusiveness and caring. "Are you doing your homework? Are you sleeping with your girlfriend? Are you eating properly?"—questions like those are intrusive. They're accusations, not questions, statements that say, implicitly, "I'm worried you're not living up to par." They're not appropriate to a college-age son. "Are you unhappy?" however, is both appropriate and to my mind necessary if there are visible signs of trouble, for many a boy that age is indeed feeling "endangered." He should know there is someone he can turn to for help at those times.

Having asked the question, I would be prepared not just for stonewalling—the usual response—but for the possibility, however remote, that I might get a real answer: "Yes, I'm miserable. I'm dying of homesickness. I want to quit school." I hope that I would then have the courage not to panic, but to suggest, "Well, if you're that unhappy, perhaps you should come home for a semester. Let's talk about it." In fact it's unlikely that a boy would take his parents up on such an offer, because the cultural stigma against it is too great. But the knowledge that he could come home should he choose to, that his parents would not think it a disgrace, or a sign of severe mental problems, if he did, would help to get him through a difficult time.

Too often, however, our boys feel there's no way out. Perhaps that's one reason for the high rate of emotional breakdowns and suicides among young men—more than five times the number of suicides in their female counterparts.[5]

Ethan at Home

Sometimes a boy faced with the obligatory leave-taking is as clear as a bell about what he wants, but chances are his parents don't want to hear him. That was the case with Ethan, a seventeen-year-old boy in his last year at a good private school. He had procrastinated all year long about filling out his college applications, unswayed by endless amounts of parental persuasion, bribes, threats, and nagging, until in a fit of desperation his mother had filled them out herself. Now he had only to sign them, and even that he had declined to do. In fact, when she presented them to him for his signature he went to bed, turned his face to the wall, and refused to speak to either of his parents, or to leave his room, from that moment forward. All he would say was he didn't feel well. Hence Edith and Neal's distraught arrival in my office several days later—alone. "I'm afraid he just doesn't want to grow up," Neal said. "He's almost eighteen and still acts like an irresponsible kid." But in fact, until this year, he had done well in school, and except for his present inexplicable behavior, was "a good kid."

After ascertaining that Ethan seemed to be in no immediate danger, for he was eating the meals Edith brought to him on a tray, talking on the phone to friends, and getting a normal amount of sleep, I made the following suggestion: "Tell Ethan that it seems obvious to me that he is not ready to go away to school, but that I don't understand why he has chosen such an odd way to say no to his parents."

"Do you think that's what he's doing?" they asked.

"I don't know. I can only guess, without seeing him. So tell him I would like to help him find a better way of saying no, and that if he wants to he can call me. Give him my number, but don't say any more about it. Just casually leave my card by his bed."

I was counting on what I knew about seventeen- and eighteen year-old men. There's no permission in our culture for them to postpone the leaving-home rite of passage. To say, "I'm not ready to go" is virtually an impossibility. For a young man who is determined not to leave, the alternatives are covert maneuvers, such as the procrastination Ethan had been successfully deploying for many months, or sickness, the one he was deploying now (or really drastic actions like suicide attempts). "What sickness do you think he might have?" I had asked Edith and Neal, who were torn between their natural desire that their son should be healthy and their reluctance to accept the possibility that his taking to his bed had nothing to do with a physical ailment: "Mono?" one of them ventured, tentatively.

The message I asked Ethan's parents to give him was intended to reassure him that I was not necessarily going to become their ally in trying to pry him loose. Edith was willing to give it a try, but Neal was dubious: "I think it's just another way of indulging him," he said. "Maybe I should tell him to get out and get going. Sometimes you have to throw a kid out."

"Would it be so terrible if he spent a little more time at home?" I asked. "If maybe he worked for a year or two, grew up some?"

A hardworking man who had scrimped and saved to give his son the college education he never had, Neal was fearful that that scenario would be the end of college for Ethan. When we yearn to see our children enjoy our own thwarted dreams, it is a double disappointment when they refuse. He agreed, however, to give Ethan some space in which to make a decision.

A week later they were back in my office in a panic, again without Ethan. "We did what you suggested," Edith recounted. "That is, I did. Neal won't have anything to do with it, or with Ethan for that matter. When I told Ethan what you said about his not being ready to leave home and the rest of it, he said, 'I don't need help to say no. No, no, no, no! I am not going to college!' So what do we do now?"

"What do you want to do?"

"Well, we can't just throw him out, can we? But that's what Neal wants to do," Edith said, appealing to me for support.

"No, of course not," I obliged. "Why would you?"

Neal felt that tossing his son out on his ear was the only way to make a man of him, but I suggested that having reached his own decision about such an important matter, Ethan had already taken a big step toward growing up, which needed to be respected. The only thing remaining to be done was to negotiate an arrangement that would honor everyone's needs—Ethan's need to remain at home for some additional time, and Neal's and Edith's need to see that he didn't lapse into the kind of future Neal foresaw for him: "I know what he plans to do," Neal told me. "Lie around the house all day and have his mother wait on him hand and foot when she gets home from work." I agreed this was not acceptable. Therefore, Ethan was to be told that he must show up in my office, with his parents, at 5:00 P.M. on Friday of the following week, for discussions that would lead to a satisfactory settlement.

He did. He was sullen and sulky, but he was there. Neal was silent and angry. Edith twittered around trying to make everyone comfortable. I began by addressing Ethan: "You surprised your parents by making such a big decision by yourself. That took courage."

Ethan allowed that indeed it did, given how hard it was to say no to his father. That was the beginning of six sessions' worth of discussion, three with all three members of the family, two with Ethan alone, and one with Edith and Neal alone, at the end of which they had devised the following plan: Ethan would finish his senior year of high school as well as he could, trying to make up for his increasingly lax academic performance of the preceding months. He would also take his SATs over, since he had done poorly the first time. All this was with the understanding that he was not planning on going to college but was willing to please his father by keeping his options open. The postgraduation part of the plan, which surprised me very much but seemed acceptable to all three of them, was for Ethan to remain at home and earn his room and board, plus $50 a week in spending money, by doing the household cooking, cleaning, and marketing.

Since Edith was a very nurturing mother who liked to do all those things for her boy, and both parents were protective of what they saw as Ethan's shaky masculinity, I had my doubts about a plan that called for him to take on such a "feminine" role. But Ethan convinced me and his parents alike that these were skills he felt he would need before he could go out on his own. The plan worked very well for six months, with Edith even learning to enjoy the experience of coming home after work to a clean house and a freshly cooked meal.

At the end of six months, however, she called to say she had lost her houseboy. He was now paying room and board and working on a construction site. "Hard work," she reported him as saying, "but it beats housework." We both laughed. Six months later she called with another progress report. Ethan had decided he was interested in engineering and had applied to the local college, which he could attend while continuing to live at home. She was thrilled.

"How about Neal?" I asked.

"He's pleased but he doesn't understand why Ethan doesn't want a college life."

"That was his fantasy," I reassured her. "Ethan obviously has his own."

Throughout the time I had contact with his family I was committed to honoring Ethan's choices, and thus to helping him achieve genuine autonomy, which is the only kind of "manhood," or maturity, that matters. Unlike Ethan, however, few boys get to make a choice. Whether eased out, kicked out, escorted triumphantly to college, or bade a hero's farewell on the way to training camp, they go, often before they're ready, as soon as it becomes economically viable for them to do so.

An Alternative Rite of Passage

College is the preferred middle-class way of separating from home. But if college is not an option, for whatever reason, there are other routes, other ways of establishing manhood. Sometimes, unfortunately, they involve getting into trouble—or "getting a girl in trouble."

From Son to Father

One day I hailed a taxi in front of the Ackerman Institute for Family Therapy. The driver, one of the old-fashioned New York cabbies, immediately launched into conversation.

"You a therapist, lady?"

"Ummm," I replied noncommittally, hoping this was not an invitation to a free therapy session on what I had looked forward to as a quiet ride downtown.

Without missing a beat, however, he went on. "I've got six kids, God bless 'em. They're pretty good kids too. Three went to Brooklyn College, two got good jobs right out of high school. It's Nickie, my youngest, I'm worried about. Nick is nineteen, almost twenty." He glanced back to see if I was listening. I nodded very slightly. "But I don't understand kids these days." Long pause, during which he waited for some sign from me.

Undeterred by the silence, he went on: "Anyway, the kid wants to get married. It seems his girlfriend is pregnant. His mother is heartbroken. What do you think? You're an expert. Should the kid have to marry the girl because he got her pregnant?"

There I was, trapped. But before I could even say anything he continued. "It's funny, because of all the kids, Nick has always been the toughest. We used to call him Nickie the Bull." He laughed. "You never saw such a tough kid. You know, every day, a bloody nose, a black eye. And every week a new girl. Always screwing around, you know."

"Now he knocks up this chick and all of a sudden he thinks he should do the right thing and marry her. My wife—she's crying all the time. Nickie's her baby. She does everything for him. Everything. Waits on him hand and foot. Always has. So I always say to her, 'Next thing you know you'll be washing his ass' (you should pardon the expression). Anyway, what would you do?"

I mumbled something noncommittal in the back seat, while getting my money out in preparation for a quick getaway.

He continued: "I tell her it's okay. He'll settle down. It'll make a man of him. She babies him too much, you know."

I paid my fare, giving the poor man too big a tip, never saying a word. As I exited he was shaking his head resignedly. "Women...."

In a family that grades masculinity by the number of battles a boy fights with his peers and the number of conquests he makes in the bedroom, it's certainly no surprise that he would oblige with the requisite amount of swaggering in adolescence. When it's the youngest boy in the family, the "baby," who may have inadmissible yearnings to maintain his privileged position with his mother, the swaggering may be even more extreme, as a means of assuaging his painful anxiety about whether he's truly manly. Thus he will have a very well developed masculine self on the outside, masking frightening feelings of dependency on the inside. The result: a strong need to prove himself. And what better way of showing he's a man than by getting a girl pregnant, doing the "right thing" by marrying her, and thus negotiating the separation from mother—without ever having to be on his own? He may not get all that he's bargaining for, however (and his wife almost certainly won't).

To a boy in Nickie's situation, marriage probably represents delivery on the Oedipal deal: that if he makes a suitably manly identification, he will someday have a wife (read "mommy") of his very own. To his girlfriend it must seem the chance to get a husband for herself and a father for her unborn child. Instead she's likely to have two babies on her hands. In fact, her husband may be the more demanding of the two, since boys in families that place a high value on masculinity often get shortchanged of the emotional nurturing they need, and thus keep on demanding it forever after. In Nickie's case it might seem as if he had "too much mother," not too little. However, what some would call a close relationship between mother and son, citing Nickie's father's words—"she babies him," "she does everything for him"—sounds more like dependence than intimacy to me. Nonetheless, that kind of caretaking will be what Nickie has learned to recognize as love, and what he will expect from his wife. When the effort to take care of house, husband, and children begins to overwhelm her and she can no longer deliver on that expectation, then their battles will begin.

A Hole in the World

Sometimes "not enough mother" means none at all. A very dear friend and neighbor of mine died young, leaving four children behind—including six-year-old Daniel, who had been the apple of her eye, and three younger ones. Deeply affected by the loss of his mother, Daniel had become a troubled, difficult child by the time his father remarried, and he was never well accepted by his stepmother. I fell out of touch with the family soon after the remarriage, then moved several times, and was thus astonished some years later to answer my doorbell and find Daniel standing outside. At eighteen, he had left home and by some mysterious process found his way directly to me.

Though I doubt Daniel was even aware of his longing for his mother, it was surely his memory of my connection to her that made him seek me out at that terribly vulnerable moment in his life. I was as close as he could come to her. Nothing, however, could redeem his loss. As Richard Rhodes says in his memoir, which begins with the death of his mother when he was thirteen months old: "At the beginning of my life the world acquired a hole. That's what I knew, that there was a hole in the world. For me there still is" (15). And there was surely such a hole for Daniel too.

I often remember Daniel and the sad afternoon we spent together when I think about young men leaving home. Like him, many of those who must go out on their own for the first time at that age will find themselves reliving the early loss of their mother, though they almost certainly won't understand that that is what they are feeling. In most cases, of course, their mothers did not die when they were little, but they did distance themselves in the culturally mandated fashion, and that too is a loss, as we are only beginning to understand.[6] As products of the same culture, the boys would not only have accepted but encouraged this distancing, often without any conscious sense, or memory, of loss. But old griefs have a way of resurfacing when familiar supports disappear, as happens when a child leaves home. Then the illusion of connectedness is gone, and he realizes he's really on his own. The realization can be devastating, especially if the connection was tenuous to begin with. If he is also facing the possibility of new losses, he may find life all but insupportable.

Ashton at the End of the Earth

Ashton was one of the most charming, likable young men I ever met. A sophomore at a prestigious Ivy League university, he had the kind of good looks one rarely sees outside of the movies, a fine and subtle mind, and a thoroughly engaging way about him. He came to see me during his Christmas vacation, at the suggestion of his girlfriend, to whom he had confessed feelings of unreality and sadness.

"I don't understand why I should feel this way," he said by way of introduction. "I've got a great life." And by his account, he did. He went to a great school, was known as a "great guy," had a relationship with a terrific girl, who was his first serious love, and had no monetary worries whatsoever.

"What's wrong with me? I sit in class and it's like I'm not there. I'm just watching someone who looks like me sitting there. And I feel like crying a lot," he added, so softly I could barely hear him.

"And do you?"

"No."

"Why not?" At which he looked at me as though I'd lost my mind. "What do you do to keep from crying?" I persisted.

"I run. Sometimes I run two, three times a day. Sometimes I get up at night and I run."

"And that helps?"

"It helps while I'm running. Sometimes I have this fantasy I'll start running and I'll run and I'll run until I reach the end of the earth and I'll keep on running, right off the edge."

Now I began to be seriously worried about this young man. The incidence of suicide in male students during the college years is very high, particularly in the more competitive schools such as the one he attended, and Ashton struck me as a prime candidate.

Then we talked some more, about his fear of losing his girlfriend, who was supposed to have come home with him for the Christmas holidays but had decided at the last minute to go to her own parents', saying she needed more "space." "So she's in Maine with Mummy and Daddy and Santa Claus," he reported in the flip manner he used to deflect any expression of concern or sympathy. "She's got space and I'm spacing out."

At that point I became even more worried, for I knew that in young men the loss of a first love can reactivate the pain of earlier losses, which is why young men tend to be much more devastated by the pain of first love than women are. As I was about to learn, Ashton's early losses had been very early indeed, and all but total.

"Who else have you told about your feelings?" I asked, hoping that he had some network of support to fall back on if he and his girlfriend broke up.

"You."

"What about your parents?"

"What good would that do? I can hear it now. 'Dad, I think I'm flipping out.' 'Flipping out?' [Imitating his father's deep voice.] 'You know I hate slang. Speak up, boy. You need more money?'"

"Your mother?"

"Ah, yes, my mother. Let me see. 'Mother, I think I'm going crazy.' 'No you're not, darling. You just need to relax. Why don't you fly down and spend a few days at the house in Palm Beach?'"

"That's it?"

"That's it. End of conversation. Back to running."

Ashton was the youngest of four brothers in a socially prominent New England family. As the youngest by some eight years, however, he had been very much on his own, while the other three constituted what he called a "secret society" to which he had no access. Nor did he have much access to his parents, for, as "Mumsie" once explained in an excess of candor, he had been a midlife "surprise," and his father, having barely tolerated his wife's attentions to the first three, ran out of patience with the birth of the fourth. "I just couldn't disappoint him any longer," she told Ashton, so he would understand why she had given in to her husband's demand that she keep him company on his quite extensive business travels, thus essentially abandoning her son. And he did understand: "I'm a very understanding type," he told me in his wry way.

Ashton was left with a nursemaid (later a housekeeper) and a driver, until at the age of fifteen he begged to be sent to boarding school, thinking that there he might find the companionship he lacked at home. His father agreed with alacrity, for the usual reason: he thought it would make a man of the boy. But "it felt like another secret society, and I didn't know the password. I never felt like I belonged there either."

Deeply alarmed by now, I asked Ashton to bring his parents in the next day, which was his last day before returning to school. He only laughed.

"Don't laugh," I said. "This is important. You can tell them anything you want. Tell them simply that you're in trouble."

"I'm in trouble, all right. But it is my trouble and I'll handle it by myself."

I backed off, out of fear that, in a panic, Ashton would indeed run off the edge of the world—commit suicide—and out of a desire to respect the huge investment he had made, indeed had had to make, in notions of individualism and personal responsibility. But I insisted he come see me at 8:00 A.M. the next day, making an elaborate point of the fact that I was squeezing him into a very overcrowded schedule, and telling him how much I hated getting up early. That way I felt confident that the good-guy, responsible persona he had cultivated would see to it that he show up. In the meantime, I made phone calls to colleagues in the town where he went to school, looking for a suitable therapist to pick up where I was leaving off. When he arrived the next day, I gave him the name of the therapist I had found for him and asked his permission to call his parents to tell them about our plan. Perhaps because my sense of urgency was a challenge to his habitual flipness, he agreed, with surprising docility, to both of my suggestions. His parents, when I called, were exactly as he had described them.

A few weeks later I received the customary thanks-for-the-referral letter from his therapist, so I knew he had followed through. Two years later I saw an announcement of his wedding (to the woman he had wanted to marry all along) in *The New York Times.* So all seems to have worked out well.

A hole as big as the one in Ashton's life, however, has a way of never filling up, and of looming even larger in the middle years, the age of the so-called "male menopause." Young men like Ashton, who go out into the world without ever having mastered the losses from their early years, are the ones who have to be watched carefully when they reach midlife, lest they put a bullet to their heads.

Reparation and Reparenting Time

When a boy leaves home before he is ready, without having gotten what he needed, he may appear to the world to be someone who has grown up, but he is always going to have an inner sense of sadness and deprivation. For most, fortunately, the emptiness will not be as profound as it was for Ashton; his family was extreme in its distancing. For virtually all, however, there is going to be some feeling of loss, which will be different in both kind and degree from what girls feel, because of the different demands we make on boys. Sometimes that loss can be mediated in later life. Therapy is one way of doing it, especially if the man is willing to take the emotional risk of bringing his parents into the process and trying to repair the relationship. Even if they're dead, the very fact of his being willing to take on the task of re-examining his relationship with them can be healing.

Every once in a while, however, a man may get the opportunity to go home and get reparented. The trick is to see that as a blessing, not a curse—a hard thing to do in this culture.

Home Again

When Alison called in a panic, I remembered her and her husband, Barry, as a young couple whom I had last seen about seven years before, when they were in their early twenties. At that time Barry had been reluctant to take on the responsibilities of marriage, feeling that he first needed to prove himself professionally in order to demonstrate to Alison's highly successful father that he was worthy of her. Since Alison thought he was plenty worthy already and was eager to get married, the task of therapy had been to get Barry to see that he was marrying Alison, not her father—a task in which we all succeeded. Now they were married and the parents of a five-year-old daughter, Alison explained on the phone, but the troubles on Wall Street had hit home. Barry, like many another hotshot trader who had gloried in the bull market of the eighties, had lost his job a year ago and was now utterly demoralized. Alison feared for their marriage.

The immediate dilemma that was facing them, Barry explained when they came in a few days later, was where to live. Their lease was almost up, which was just as well, since they couldn't afford their apartment on Alison's salary alone. Barry's widowed mother had invited them to live with her and offered to take care of daughter Jennifer during the day, while Alison worked and Barry looked for work. Alison's parents had extended a similar invitation, though with her father still working and her mother busy on the golf course and the charity circuit, there would need to be some kind of after-school arrangements made for Jennifer. Alison longed to return to the comfort of her parents' big suburban house, while Barry wanted to go home to his mother, even though she lived in a small two-bedroom apartment.

Still fighting that old battle with Alison's father—or, more accurately, with himself and with his own father, a manual laborer of very modest means whom he regarded as a failure—Barry couldn't bear the shame of accepting "charity" from his well-to-do in-laws. "Alison actually expects me to live under her father's roof. To face him at the dinner table every night. But I can't do it. I'll live on the street first. She can take Jennifer and go home."

To Alison it was the same old story. "You see how stubborn he is," she said. "You helped us before. Now help us again so Barry will see that this is just his foolish pride."

Certainly that was part of the story. For Barry as for most men in this culture (if not all), his sense of himself as a man is tied in with his ability to compete, and the geography of his world is bound by the twin poles of failure and success. During the last several decades, when most bright, hardworking, ambitious young men of Barry's color and class could be assured some measure of success, this way of looking at the world was viable. Thus, it's no surprise that many of them have found it excruciating to have to adjust to the economic realities of the nineties.

Compounding the sense of failure Barry had over the loss of his job was the humiliation of accepting help from a man who had once thought him not good enough for his daughter, even though those feelings had long since changed. With all that he was facing, Barry was in no frame of mind to be able to understand that Alison, too, had needs, and that after a very difficult year she was now looking forward to going home and having her parents take care of her for a while.

After helping Alison and Barry to listen to each other, I told them, "You each have feelings that are valid. That's why you're having such a hard time making this decision. Go home and talk about it together. You'll come up with a solution as long as you recognize the validity of both sets of needs, and the possibility that, being different, those needs may bring you into conflict at the moment."

A week later they returned with the following plan: Barry and Jennifer would go to Barry's mother's, for a period not to exceed six months, while Alison went to her parents' for what she referred to as "rest and relaxation." At the end of six months, if Barry still didn't have a job, they would re-evaluate their situation.

When they first proposed this idea, I was concerned, because of what I remembered about the issues that had come up for Barry during the therapy seven years before. Specifically, I was worried that Alison's willingness to leave him and go back to her father's house might make Barry feel threatened, reawakening old feelings of abandonment from the year he turned sixteen. That was the year his father became an invalid after a serious construction-site accident, and his mother had had to all but turn her back on her children in order to care for her dying husband. From then until he and Alison began going together, several years after each had graduated from college, Barry had been, by his own description, a lonely, often driven man, working hard to put himself and his younger sister through undergraduate school, then studying for an MBA at night while holding a full-time job. But the same sad family history that made me apprehensive for Barry also suggested to me that now might be a good chance for him to get some of the reparenting he seemed to need, an opportunity for some reparation time with the mother who had been forced by circumstance to neglect her son.

Two months later Alison called me: Barry had a new job. Her parents, eager to see the young couple back on their feet, had offered to make the down payment on a house that Barry and Alison would carry from then on—an offer that Barry had agreed to accept. They were about to move in, and were very excited about getting back together. Having used their hard times as an unexpected opportunity to get what each of them needed, they—and their marriage—were much the better for it. Now that they had both touched home base, they were more than ready to resume their adult life together.

"Only Connect!"[7]

It's very rare for a man to get the chance to repair old losses as Barry did. Instead, he must deny the regressive longings that all of us feel, to varying degrees, at occasional junctures of our lives. The leaving-home juncture is obviously a critical one, when children of both sexes are likely to feel such longings, particularly for their mothers, who are generally the source of their first and most intense emotional connection. But eighteen-year-old boys are expected to have outgrown their need for Mother.

If we accept eighteen as the automatic, arbitrary age for separtion, we create a lot of frightened kids. If we push them out before they're ready, they may grab at various kinds of pseudo-adulthood—joining the army, making instant marriages, or simply going out, quite miserably, on their own. Alternatively, they may find dramatic ways of returning, like illness, nervous breakdowns, suicide attempts.

The intense form of male bonding that occurs in fraternal organizations is another possible way of overcoming the emptiness and loneliness that young men feel when they leave home. Anthropologist Peggy Reeves Sanday quotes one typical college student's comments to that effect: "When I left home I was both glad and scared to be independent of my parents.... Although I was noisily proclaiming and celebrating my new life as a free agent, I needed a family substitute, a tight social situation where I could count on emotional support. The fraternity provided me that support" (138).[8]

Often, alas, the brotherhood of men means hostility to women—hence the subject of Sanday's book, *Fraternity Gang Rape.* Much of the attraction of the brotherhood, which is evident in the elaborate initiation rituals required of each pledge, is the way in which it enables these young, vulnerable, unsure males to be "reborn" into the fraternity of men and thus "cleansed" of any dependence on Mother. Needless to say, such dependence will feel particularly shameful and troubling at this age. Hence the need of the brothers to "use their rituals, other brothers, and women to gain control over infantile desires" (Sanday 179).

Emotional invincibility is what they are seeking, and "the inner, despised female" (Sanday 157) is the obstacle to that goal. The phenomenon of gang rape, which a number of researchers now feel is an increasingly common practice in fraternities and other exclusively male enclaves, represents an extreme response to the insecurity—and resulting misogyny—of men's lives. Obviously, it is not standard practice among men, and as such is outside the scope of this book. But I think the psychological needs that fuel it *are* standard.

A more commonplace means of responding to the unassuaged, unacknowledged need for Mother is to replace her, with a new mommy (a wife). When I watch any of the movies or television shows depicting young people in their late teens and their twenties, that's what all the young men seem to be doing—trying desperately, by way of their frantic coupling, decoupling, and recoupling, to find Mother again. Everything about these shows is related to connection, as though nothing else matters—in which case perhaps we should recognize that the way we raise our boys results in feelings of loss that may never be overcome.

Look, for example, at *1996, Melrose Place, Singles, St. Elmo's Fire,* and *Bodies, Rest and Motion*—a representative sampling of the recent "twenty-something" media output. One episode after another of the sitcoms depicts lonely young men yearning for love, trying to fill an emptiness of which they (and the writers who created them) are no doubt unaware. As for the movies—*New York Times* film reviewer Caryn James said about this genre, "'Mommy!' might be the unspoken rallying cry behind the slew of films about people in their 20s and early 30s" (11). Indeed, the opening pan of *Singles* comes to rest on graffiti proclaiming "Mother Love." Did the filmmakers know what they were doing? Who can say? But whether consciously or unconsciously, they are expressing something powerful about the culture they live in. The final scene depicts the entire city of Seattle as an elaborate communications grid on which people strive ceaselessly to make connections. Between opening and finale, we watch a charming array of anxious, discombobulated young people as they go through their elaborate singles contortions. Ultimately, however, it's always the males who appear needier.

Ultimately, it's always the males who *are* needier. We raise them to be heroes, and the prevailing cultural mythology is that these valiant adventurers succumb to marriage only because of the wiles of the women lucky and skillful enough to capture them. The truth is very different.

Notes

[1] "Motherland" is Sam Keen's phrase (21).

[2] Statistics are from U.S. Census Bureau report, cited in *San Francisco Chronicle* article by Ramon G. McLeod, February 12, 1993.

[3] Jane Bryant Quinn, *Newsweek,* April 5, 1993, citing Census Bureau statistics showing that about sixteen percent of twenty-five- to thirty-four-year-old males lived at home, versus about nine percent of females, in 1992.

[4] Carol Gilligan, Jean Baker Miller, Nancy Chodorow, and a number of other researchers and writers in the field are challenging developmental theories that undervalue relatedness. In earlier writings the goal was to re-evaluate women's experience, to show that it is different but not inferior; now there are somewhat tentative attempts to challenge traditional accounts of the male developmental model as well, to suggest that it's neither healthy nor inevitable. As authors Judith V. Jordan, Alexandra G. Kaplan, Jean Baker Miller, Irene P. Stiver, and Janet L. Surrey say in the introduction to *Women's Growth in Connection: Writings from the Stone Center*: "We are just beginning to think about the use of this perspective to better understand men; we know that the shift we are suggesting from a psychology of 'The Self' to one emphasizing relationships does not apply to women's psychology only" (7). (See also chapter 4, "Empathy and Self Boundaries" by Judith V. Jordan, for an overview and challenge to the developmental theories emphasizing separation.) A similar point is made in Terri Apter's book, *Altered Loves: Mothers and Daughters During Adolescence*, which I think is representative of a growing number of books for a more general audience. Though it focuses mainly on challenging the conventional view that adolescent daughters must reject their mothers as part of their developmental process, it alludes often, if only parenthetically, to the possibility that the separation model need not necessarily apply to men either. Since I believe there is a potential for care and nurturing that is not only untapped in the male but actively squelched, I consider the reassessment promoted by such authors a great step forward.

[5] Among 15- to 24-year-olds, the male suicide rate is 22.2 per 100,000, the female rate 4.2 per 100,000—or less than one-fifth that of the boys. Statistical abstract of the United States, 1990, from the National Center for Health Statistics.

[6] Though the men's movement has spawned a revival of the notion that what's wrong with men today is "too much mother," there is beginning to be a recognition on the part of at least a few male members of the mental health community that in fact there is very often too little, and that this is a loss. Stephen J. Bergman, whose paper entitled "Men's Psychological Development" was cited in chapter 4 of my *The Courage to Raise Good Men*, is one of these men. William S. Pollack,

president of the Massachusetts Psychological Association and staff member at both McLean Hospital and Harvard Medical School, is another. He is quoted in Anita Diamant's March 14,1993, *Boston Globe Sunday Magazine* article, "What's the Matter With Men?" on the subject of the boy's early loss of closeness to the mother and the pain he must feel as a result. See also "No Man Is an Island: Reframing Masculinity," the paper Pollack presented to the August 1992 Centennial Meeting of the American Psychological Association in Washington, D.C.; and his book, *In a Time of Fallen Heroes: The Re-creation of Masculinity* (1993), coauthored with R. William Betcher.

[7]From E. M. Forster, *Howards End* (195).

[8]From Peggy Reeves Sanday's *Fraternity Gang Rape*, see chapters "The Initiation Ritual: A Model for Life" and "The Law of the Brothers" for an analysis of the meaning of fraternities in the lives of young men.

References

American Graffiti. 1973. Dir. George Lucas. VHS. 1978.

Apter, Terri. *Altered Loves: Mothers and Daughters During Adolescence*. New York: Ballantine Books, 1991.

Bergman, Stephen J. "Men's Psychological Development: A Relational Perspective." *Wellesley Centers for Women* 48 (1991): Wellesley College.

Bly, Robert. *Iron John: A Book About Men*. Reading, Mass.: Addison-Wesley, 1990.

Dew, Robb Forman. *Fortunate Lives*. New York: Harper Perennial, 1993.

Diamant, Anita. "What's the Matter with Men?" *Boston Globe Sunday Magazine*. 14 March 1993.

Ehrenreich, Barbara. *The Hearts of Men: American Dreams and the Flight from Commitment*. New York: Anchor Press, 1983.

Forster, E. M. *Howard's End*. 1910. New York: Vintage, 1989.

Gilligan, Carol. *In a Different Voice: Psychological Theory and Women's Development*. Cambridge: Harvard University Press, 1982.

Haley, Jay. *Leaving Home: The Therapy of Disturbed Young People*. New York: McGraw-Hill, 1980.

James, Caryn. "'Mommy!'..." *New York Times*. 18 April 1993: 11.

Jordan, Judith V. et al. "Introduction." *Women's Growth in Connection: Writings from the Stone Center*. New York: The Guilford Press, 1991.

Jordan, Judith V. "Empathy and Self Boundaries." *Women's Growth in Connection: Writings from the Stone Center*. New York: The Guilford Press, 1991.

Keen, Sam. *Fire in the Belly: On Being a Man*. New York: Bantam Books, 1991.

Levinson, Daniel J. et al. *The Seasons of a Man's Life*. New York: Alfred A. Knopf, 1978.

McLeod, Ramon G. *San Francisco Chronicle*. 12 February 1993.

People Magazine. February 15, 1993.

Pollack, William S. "No Man is an Island: Reframing Masculinity." Paper presented to the Centennial Meeting of the American Psychological Association, Washington, D.C. August, 1992.

Pollack, William S. and R. William Betcher. *In a Time of Fallen Heroes: The Re-creation of Masculinity*. New York: Atheneum, 1993.

Quinn, Jane Bryant. *Newsweek*. April 5, 1993.

Rhodes, Richard. *A Hole in the World*. New York: Touchstone, 1991.

Salinger, J.D. *Catcher in the Rye*. 1951. New York: Bantam Books, 1969.

Sanday, Peggy Reeves. *Fraternity Gang Rape*. New York: New York University Press, 1990.

Chapter 23

Negotiating Lesbian Motherhood
The Dialectics of Resistance and Accommodation

ELLEN LEWIN

WHEN I FIRST began to assemble resources for a study of lesbian mothers in 1976, very few people were aware of the existence of such a category, and if they were, they usually saw it as an oxymoron.[1] Lesbian mothers occasionally gained the attention of the general public when they were involved in custody cases that received publicity, but such notoriety was infrequent and typically fleeting. In fact, aside from those who had lesbian mothers in their social circles, even the wider lesbian population was aware of lesbian mothers mainly in connection with custody cases. In the early collections of articles on lesbian issues that emerged from the lesbian feminist movement, lesbian mothers were almost never mentioned except in connection with their vulnerability to custody litigation (see, for example, Vida). Mothers in these cases either lost custody of their children, or won custody only under highly compromised conditions, sometimes with the stipulation that the child have no contact with the mother's partner (Hitchens; Lewin 1981; Rivera).

Well-known custody cases in the 1970s demonstrated the likelihood that lesbian mothers would face considerable discrimination in court. The Mary Jo Risher case, in which a mother lost custody of her younger son after her teenaged son testified against her, was perhaps the best documented of these, particularly after the story was dramatized as a made-for-TV movie (Gibson). And the case of Sandy and Madeleine, two mothers who became lovers and subsequently had custody challenged by both ex-husbands, was extensively publicized in the lesbian community with the circulation of a film called "Sandy and Madeleine's Family." The case demonstrated that lesbian mothers' custody could be challenged repeatedly, even after a favorable ruling in court, at least until the children achieved majority. The film, originally produced for use in court, emphasized the strong religious values of the mothers, their involvement in wholesome activities with both sets of children, and the warmth and nurturance of the family environment they provided (Farrell, Hill and Bruce).

All these images of lesbian mothers were defensive. When lesbian mothers found themselves in court, they necessarily had to convince the judge (and in the Risher case, the jury) that they were as good at being mothers as any other women, that they were, in fact, *good* in the sense of possessing the moral attributes of altruism and nurturance that are culturally demanded of mothers in North American cultures. In these formulations, mothers are assumed to be *naturally* equipped to place their children's interests ahead of their own, to be selfless in a way that precludes or overshadows their own sexuality;[2] such assumptions are at the heart of twentieth-century presumptions of maternal suitability for custody (Hunter and Polikoff; Lewin 1981). When mothers are lesbians, however, the courts, reflecting popular views of homosexuality as "unnatural," tend to view them as morally flawed, and thus as unfit parents. Their task in dealing with the legal system, therefore, is to demonstrate that they possess the "natural" attributes expected of mothers, and are thus worthy of receiving custody of their children. Maternal virtue, therefore, shifts from being a quality inherent to women to being a behavior one must actively demonstrate in order to pursue a claim to custody (Lewin 1990).

While many lesbian mothers understood that the way to keep custody of their children was to show that they were "as good as" heterosexual mothers, they firmly believed that they would eventually be shown to be superior parents who were bringing new, nonsexist families into being. They viewed the two-parent, heterosexual, nuclear family as the arena in which the patriarchy inscribed gender expectations onto both women and men. If the power dynamics of that family form were largely responsible for the continuing devalued status of women, and for a variety of abusive practices, then a domestic arrangement based on presumably nongendered relations between two "equal" women partners would constitute a first step toward the better sort of world feminists dreamed of. Jeanne Vaughn, the coeditor of *Politics of the Heart: A Lesbian Parenting Anthology,* put it this way:

> We have an opportunity for radical social change beginning in our homes, change that requires rethinking our views of family, of kinship, of work, of social organization. We need to develop some specifically lesbian-feminist theories of family. How would/did/could we mother our children without the institution of compulsory heterosexuality? (26)

The image many lesbian mothers conjured up was utopian, resembling the broad outlines of Charlotte Perkins Gilman's *Herland,* a fictional society of women in which motherhood and caring were elevated to the center of the inhabitants' lives. Without the need to serve and please powerful males, without the degradations of daily experience in a patriarchal society, Gilman's image suggests, women might be free to express their true, nurturant natures. They would reveal abilities unlikely to emerge in male-dominated society, and would focus on creative, constructive projects rather than on frivolities such as fancy dress and (hetero) sexuality.

The popular images of mothers and families that dominated the lesbian community in the 1970s, then, focused on the ways in which being a mother and having a family could constitute a form of resistance to traditional, and thereby patriarchal, family forms. In particular, success at motherhood (as measured by how well one's child turned out) would demonstrate that children did not need the structure of a heterosexual family, and, most significantly, the regular contribution of a father, to develop normally. The achievement of lesbian mothers would both counteract the notion that lesbianism and motherhood are inherently contradictory and, in fact, redefine and desexualize what it means to be a lesbian.

At the same time, however, the complexities of living as a mother required lesbian mothers to reinstate the dichotomy of natural/unnatural and mother/nonmother that their redefinition of lesbianism sought to subvert. Negotiating the daily issues of being a mother and meeting obligations to one's children brought them into conflict both with the dominant heterosexist society and with lesbians who had not chosen motherhood.

Feminist Views of Resistance

When many of us took up a feminist agenda in our scholarship, directing our attention to documenting the experience of women from their point of view, it seemed that we had no choice but to concentrate on describing a depressing history of victimization and oppression. As we examined the social and cultural lives of women, not only in familiar terrain, but also outside Western traditions, we found over and over again that women were confined to secondary social status, relegated to devalued cultural roles, and often brutalized and demeaned in their daily lives. The evidence of despair poured in, bolstered at every turn by the grim discoveries we continued to make about our own society and our own lives.[3]

In many instances, the best it seemed that we could offer to help remedy this situation was to produce astute, woman-centered descriptions of the conditions under which women's lives were lived, paired with analyses geared toward change. In many instances, feminist scholars directed their energies toward the documentation of women's point of view, focusing on ways to dissolve the hegemony of male-centered assumptions about the organization of social life and women's place in it. In anthropology, such work often proposed alternative views of traditionally patriarchal institutions (see, for example, Goodale; Weiner; Wolf). But in other instances, feminist interpretations came to center on resistance, looking at how even clearly oppressed women might take action on their own behalf, either by directly sabotaging the instruments of male dominance, or by constituting their consciousness in a way that undermined their subordination.[4]

Feminist scholars have most commonly applied the concept of resistance to studies of women in the work force. Bonnie Thornton Dill's research on Black women household workers, for example, focuses on the way they manage their relationships with employers to enhance their own self-respect. She documents how these workers organized "strategies for gaining mastery over work that was socially defined as demeaning and ... actively resisted the depersonalization of household work " (Dill 33).

Along similar lines, Aihwa Ong, writing about women factory workers in Malaysia, shows how labor practices introduced by capitalism lead to the reconstruction of meanings of gender and sexuality. In response to proletarianization, Malay women organize cultural responses to their changing status, most markedly in the form of episodes of spirit possession. "Spirit attacks," Ong tells us, "were indirect retaliations against coercion and demands for justice in personal terms within the industrial milieu" (220).

Notions of resistance have also informed studies of women outside the workplace. Emily Martin, for example, has contrasted women's ideas about their bodies and the ideology of mainstream medicine, describing instances in which women resist medical assumptions at variance with their own experience. She sees working-class women as most able to reject scientific metaphors of women's bodies, particularly those that focus on production and failed production, perhaps because "they have less to gain from productive labor in the society" (110). Self-consciousness and verbal protest are taken as evidence of resistance in Martin's analysis, as are instances of sabotage or outright refusal to cooperate with medical instructions.

Louise Lamphere's study of immigrant factory workers in New England also looks carefully at resistance, but frames it as one of several strategies women can mount to cope with employers' efforts to control their lives. She views women "as active strategists, weighing possibilities and devising means to realize goals, and not as passive acceptors of their situations" (29-30). Lamphere cautions, however, against viewing all of women's actions on their own behalf as resistance. Rather, she emphasizes the importance of distinguishing between "strategies of resistance" and "strategies of accommodation," pointing out that some strategies may best be seen as adjustments that allow women to cope with their place in the labor market by diffusing employers' control of the workplace. Such strategies ought not to be viewed, Lamphere says, as resistance only, since they may not be based in purposeful opposition to the employer, and since they may only result in continuing exploitation of the workers, and, as such, constitute a kind of consent to existing relations of domination (30).

Taking a different approach, Judith Butler has proposed that scholars reconsider their dependence on the concept of gender, arguing that gender, as a dualistic formulation, rests on the same asymmetry that feminists seek to overturn. She urges the adoption of strategies that would "disrupt the oppositional binary itself" (27), and suggests that calling into question the "continuity and coherence" of gender identities, sabotaging the "intelligibility" of gender, would undermine the "regulatory aims" of gender as a cultural system (17). Butler's claim seems to be that lesbianism, or other sexual stances at odds with normative heterosexuality, could constitute a kind of resistance to the very existence of gender. She locates gender continuities within the domain of sexuality, viewing "intelligible" genders "… as those which in some sense institute and maintain relations of coherence and continuity among sex, gender, sexual practice, and desire" (17). The decisions one takes with regard to one's identity, then, and in particular, the extent to which they may be said to destabilize conventional expectations and representations, may constitute resistance not only to specific forms of oppression, but to the oppressive effects of gender as an ideological straitjacket.

All of these approaches to resistance reveal a commitment to render women as active subjects. While these scholars are reluctant to blame women for their subordination, neither are they willing to cast them as hapless victims of actions wholly beyond their control. Women are thus seen as capable of framing strategies for enhancing their situations, whether the battleground be material—as when women's resistance improves their working conditions—or symbolic—as when refusal to conform to common conventions of gender may be interpreted as constituting sabotage of the larger system.

This concern with subjectivity and agency raises significant questions for the study of women who seem to defy gender limitations in any aspect of their lives. Just as Butler has suggested that incongruent sexuality might be viewed as resistance, one might ask whether other "disorders" of sexuality and gender could also be viewed in this light. The question becomes particularly pressing when women themselves explain their behavior as subversive. We must then ask whether apparently conscious refusals by lesbian mothers, or any other group of women, to accept the strictures of gender are best understood as instances of resistance.

Lesbian Mothers and Resistance to Heterosexism

By the time I was well into my research, at the end of the 1970s, the custody problems that had concerned me at the outset were no longer the only issues facing lesbian mothers. Pregnant women were starting to appear at lesbian social gatherings, at political meetings and concerts, sometimes alone and sometimes in the company of their lovers. These women were not, for the most part, new to lesbian life; most had never been married, and child custody fears did not figure prominently for them. They certainly had not become pregnant by accident. While some of the mothers and mothers-to-be had had romantic interludes with men, more explained how they had "made themselves pregnant" by arranging a sexual situation with a man, or by using some form of "insemination."[5]

The emphasis in these women's accounts of their experiences was on how they had to overcome their earlier fears that being lesbian would preclude motherhood. Lesbians reported that they had often thought of themselves as not being suitable mothers, having internalized images of homosexuals as self-serving, immature, or otherwise not capable of the kind of altruism basic to maternal performance.

Sarah Klein,[6] 23, a lesbian who lives with her one-year-old daughter and her lover, explained the conflict as she perceived it:

> I've always wanted to have a child. In terms of being real tied up with being gay, it was one of the reasons that for a long time I was hesitant to call myself a lesbian. I thought that automatically assumed you had nothing to do with children.... I felt, well, if you don't *say* you're a lesbian, you can still work with children, you can still have a kid, you can have relationships with men. But once I put this label on myself, [it would] all [be] over.

By having a child, Sarah repudiated the boundaries she had once associated with being a lesbian; she has claimed what she sees as her right to be a mother.

But other lesbians' accounts indicate that not all perceive themselves as having had a lifelong desire for motherhood. Among those who claim not to remember wanting children when they were younger was Kathy Lindstrom. She had a child by insemination when she was in her early 30s, but says that she never considered the possibility until a few years earlier. She could only explain her behavior as arising from some sort of "hormonal change:" "It just kind of came over me. It wasn't really conscious at first. It was just a need."

Kathy's understanding of her desire to be a mother as something "hormonal," that is, natural, suggests an implicit assertion that this is something so deep and so essentially part of her that nothing, including her lesbianism, can undermine it. Her account indicates that she refuses to allow the associations others have with her status as a lesbian to interfere with her own perception of herself and her needs.

Other lesbian mothers view their urge to have a child as stemming from a desire to settle down, to achieve adulthood, and to counteract forces toward instability in their lives. Ruth Zimmerman, who had a five-year-old son from a relationship with a man she selected as a "good" father, had ended the relationship soon after she became pregnant.

> I definitely felt like I was marking time, waiting for something. I wasn't raised to be a career woman. I was raised to feel like I was grown up and finished growing up and living a regular normal life when I was married and had kids. And I knew that the married part wasn't going to happen. I feel like I've known that for a long time.

Like Kathy, Ruth defined her progress as a human being, and as a woman, in terms that are strikingly conventional and recall traditional feminine socialization. While clearly accepting motherhood as a marker of adulthood and "living a normal life," Ruth tried to overcome the equally conventional limits placed on lesbians in order to have her child.

The notion that having a child signifies adulthood, the acceptance of social responsibility, and demonstrates that one has "settled down" appears in the accounts of many lesbian mothers. Most often, lesbian mothers speak of their lives before motherhood as empty and aimless, and see the birth of their children as having centered them emotionally. They frequently cite new interests in education, nutrition, and health, and reconciliations with family members with whom they had not been on good terms, as evidence of their new maturity. As Louise Green, a young lesbian mother who describes herself as a former hippie, explains: "I think [having my daughter] has turned my life into this really good thing."

Louise describes herself as living a marginal, disorganized existence until she finally decided that she would have a child. She did not consider using mainstream medicine to get pregnant, assuming that such resources would never be available to her, both for financial reasons and because she would be viewed with hostility by medical professionals. Instead, she went about asking men she met whether they would like to be sperm donors; she finally located a willing prospect and obtained a sperm sample from him. Louise never told this man her real name, and once she had conceived she left the area, concerned that he could somehow pose a threat to her relationship with her child.

Louise's account focuses on conception and birth as "spiritual transitions" to a higher and better existence. She became pregnant on her first attempt, which she explained as evidence that mystical forces "meant" for this to happen. She wanted very much to have a home delivery, but after a protracted and complicated labor, she was transferred to a hospital, where she finally gave birth with the aid of multiple technological interventions. Despite this interference with the kind of spiritual environment she had hoped to give birth in, Louise describes the entire experience in mystical terms.

> It was about the best thing I ever experienced. I was totally amazed. The labor was like I had died…. I had just died. The minute she came out, I was born again. It was like we'd just been born together.

Louise did not allow either her counterculture life-style or her status as a lesbian to interfere with the spiritual agenda she felt destined to complete. She says the mystical process she underwent in becoming a mother has permitted her to become more fully herself, to explore aspects of her being that would have remained hidden if she allowed lesbianism alone to define who she is.

> [After] I had [my daughter] I felt it was okay to do these things I've been wanting to do real bad. One of them is to paint my toenails red. I haven't done it yet, but I'm going to do it. I felt really okay about wearing perfume and I just got a permanent in my hair…. I feel like I'm robbing myself of some of the things I want to do by trying to fit this lesbian code. I feel like by my having this child, it has already thrown me out in the sidelines.

Louise has used the process of becoming a mother to construct her identity in a way that includes being a lesbian but also draws from other sources. She sees her need to do this as essential and intended, and has moved along her path with the assurance that she is realizing her destiny.

Not all lesbians become mothers as easily as Louise. On a purely practical level, of course, the obstacles to a lesbian becoming pregnant can be formidable. Even if she knows a man who is interested in such a venture, she might not contemplate a heterosexual liaison with enthusiasm and might be equally reluctant to ask him to donate sperm. Mainstream medicine may not seem like an option either, because of financial considerations, or because of fears that doctors will be unwilling to inseminate a lesbian or even a single woman—a realistic concern, of course.

Once one has defined oneself as a lesbian, the barriers to becoming a mother are so significant, in fact, that many of the formerly married lesbian mothers I interviewed explained that they had gone through with marriages (sometimes of long duration) because this seemed the only way to realize their dream of being mothers and being normal in the eyes of their families and communities.

Harriet Newman, an artist who lives with her two daughters in a rural area north of San Francisco, fell in love with another woman during her first year in college. Her parents discovered the affair and forced her to leave school and to see a psychiatrist. The experience convinced her that it would be safer "to be a regular person in the world." When she met a gay man who also wanted to live more conventionally, they married, and almost immediately had their two children. "The main thing that made us decide to get married was that we very much wanted to part of the mainstream of life, instead of on the edges. We wanted to be substantial ... part of the common experience."

For lesbians who become mothers through insemination or some other method,[7] then, conscious resistance to rigid formulations of "the lesbian" seems to be central to their intentions. Unwilling to deny their identity as lesbians, they also demand the right to define what that identity constitutes. The intrinsic benefits of motherhood—the opportunity to experience birth and child development—are experiences they do not want to forego. In particular, once the relatively simple technology of donor insemination became widely known, and given the haphazard controls exerted over access to sperm donations, lesbians have come to understand that they can, indeed, be mothers. Access to motherhood thus comes to be viewed as a "civil right" not dissimilar to equal opportunity in the job market, or other rights lesbians and gay men now demand with increasing insistence.

In some instances, women explained that their age made having a child imperative. Laura Bergeron, who had two sons from a relationship prior to coming out, decided to find a donor for a third child when she entered her late 30s.

> I really did want to have a girl, and I was getting older.... I was feeling that I didn't really want to have children past the appropriate childbearing age. I had been doing too much reading about retardation and mongoloids and everything else ... so I put some ads [for donors] in the paper.

Annabel Jessop voices similar concerns, explaining that she decided to use artificial insemination to become pregnant even though she would have preferred being settled in a long-term relationship before embarking on motherhood.

> I decided that I wanted to have a kid, and that because I'm in my 30s my time was limited. I look at it as a life choice. There's only so many things you can do in your life, and this is one of the things I wanted to do, and it was time to do it. Waiting wasn't going to do any good. Professionally, I was together, I was as stable as I was every going to be

financially, I had a little put away, and there was just no reason not to do it now.

Becoming a mother is central to being able to claim to an identity as a "good" woman, drawn from one's association with children. Mothers describe childhood as a time of innocence and discovery, and a mother can gain spiritual benefits through her contribution to a child's development. One lesbian mother explained:

> You get to have a lot of input in another human being's very formative years. That's real special to have that privilege of doing that, and you get to see them growing and developing and it's sort of like you put in the fertile soil and ... hopefully what will happen is that they grow and blossom and become wonderful.... I think it's definitely the most important thing that people do ... to build the next generation.

As Louise Green's narrative indicated, lesbians often characterize their transformation into mothers as a spiritual journey, an experience that gives them access to special knowledge and that makes them worthier than they otherwise could have been. Regina Carter, whose daughter is six, put it this way:

> My kid has given me more knowledge than any other experience in my life. She's taught me more than all the teachings I've ever learned as far as education, and I mean that as far as academic education, spiritual education. Taught me things that no other person, place or thing could possibly teach me. And those are, you know, those things are without words.

Similarly, Bonnie Peters echoed these views when she told me that being a mother connected her with sources of honesty and worthiness.

> I've become more at peace with me [since having my daughter]. She's given me added strength; she's made me—it's like looking in the mirror in many ways; she's made me see myself for who I am. She's definitely given me self-worth. I've become, I think, a more honest person.

Motherhood, then, can draw a woman closer to basic truths, sensitizing her to the feelings of others and discovering a degree of altruism they had not perceived in themselves prior to having a child. It may provide the opportunity for a woman to make clear her involvement with a kind of authenticity, a naturalness, that brings her closer to profound, but ineffable, truths.

Managing Lesbian Motherhood

While the accounts given by some lesbian mothers suggest that they have resisted the cultural opposition between "mother" and "lesbian" and demanded the right to be both, the ongoing management of being a lesbian mother may depend on separating these two statuses, thus intensifying their dichotomization. Lesbian mothers frequently speak of these two dimensions of their identities as competing or interfering with each other; conflicts with lesbians who are not mothers sometimes further solidify these divisions.

Tanya Petroff, who lives with her seven-year-old daughter in an East Bay city, speaks evocatively of how being a mother overshadows her identity as a lesbian.

> The mothering thing, the thing about being a mother seems to be more important to me than my sexual orientation…. I've had [lesbians] tell me that I had chosen a privileged position in having a child and if it was going to be difficult for me then it was too goddam bad.

For Tanya, the conflict is most acute when she is developing a new relationship with another woman. She must then make clear that she views herself and her daughter as an indivisible social unit that takes precedence over other attachments. "I'm definitely part of a package deal. I come with my daughter and people who can't relate to both of us are not people I want to relate to for very long."

What this means in terms of other relationships is that Tanya sees other mothers, regardless of whether they are gay or straight, as the people with whom she has the most in common. Since relocating to the Bay Area from a town in the Midwest, Tanya has tended to minimize her contact with what she calls the "lesbian community" in favor of socializing with other mothers. She feels that she is better able to resist pressures to raise her daughter to be a "little amazon," an expectation she believes common to lesbians who are not mothers. Beyond this, Tanya feels that there are simply too many practical obstacles to meaningful friendships with women who are not mothers. Living alone and having a demanding job mean that Tanya has to plan ahead to arrange childcare. People who don't have children are no help with this; she accounts for this by explaining that they are "single," meaning that they have no children. There is such a deep gulf between mothers and nonmothers, in her view, that there is simply no meaningful basis for understanding trust.

> There is a difference between people who have children and people who don't have children. People who don't have children, to my way of thinking, are very selfish…. They needn't consider anyone other than themselves. They can do exactly what they want to do at any given time. And though I admire that, it's not possible for me to do that and I guess for that reason most of my friends are single mothers, because it's hard for me to coordinate my needs and my time with someone who's in a completely different head set. "Why can't you get a sitter for the kid?"—that kind of thing…. I just prefer being with people who have some sense of what it's like to be me, and I understand where they are too.

Tanya's belief that she can only find truly supportive friends among those whose situations closely mirror her own with respect to single motherhood grows not only out of her very real need for material assistance, but also from the importance she places on having friends who affirm or validate her identity. The most essential aspect of her identity, by this account, is that of being a mother. It supersedes her sexual orientation, her ethnicity, her job.

For some lesbian mothers, difficult experiences with lovers parallel disappointments with the wider lesbian community. Leslie Addison, who lives alone with her twelve-year-old daughter, describes a long series of conflicts with lesbian community groups over support for mothers. While she can easily explain the failure of these women to be conscious about mothers as stemming from their being "single," she has had a harder time dealing with lovers and prospective lovers who do not understand or are unwilling to accommodate her needs as a mother. Shortly after her divorce, she began her first relationship with a woman with the expectation that a woman lover would naturally help her with her child, and be eager to participate in their family activities. Leslie found instead that her lover was reluctant to spend more than minimal amounts of time with her daughter, never offering to help with child care or domestic responsibilities. Ironically, when she was straight, she says that she could always get a boyfriend to baby-sit for her; as a lesbian, she finds that women usually refuse to do childcare.

> That wasn't quite what I expected. I expected there would be more sharing between women of the child. But I found it's really not, because another woman has a role identity crisis. She can't be the mother, because you're already the mother. She can't be the father, because she's not the father, whereas the men sort of played that role. It was easier for them to fall into it. They could just play daddy, I could play momma, and everybody'd be happy.

The stark separation between "mother" and "lesbian" as elements of identity may be even more sharply drawn for women concerned with maintaining secrecy about their sexual orientation. In these instances, daily life is segregated into time when they are "mothers" and time when they are "lesbians," creating constant concern about information management and boundary maintenance. While some mothers who voice these concerns are motivated by fears about custody, others seem to be more worried by what they understand to be broad community standards. Segregation may seem the best way to protect children from being stigmatized, but in addition, lesbian mothers know that motherhood itself tends to preclude their being suspected of homosexuality. As one mother explained, "Of course, I have the mask. I have a child. I'm accepted [as heterosexual] because I have a child and that kind of protection."

Laura Bergeron, who had three children outside of marriage, is not only secretive about her lesbianism in her relations with the wider community, but she has not allowed her children to find out that she is a lesbian. Her lover, a married woman, is unwilling to do anything that might disrupt current arrangements, and Laura explains that her lover's situation is the major reason for her secrecy. But she is also concerned that the father of her two sons might try to get custody if he know about her sexual orientation, despite the fact that he only agreed to help her get pregnant with the stipulation that he would never have any formal obligations to their children. And she fears that her civil service job would somehow be compromised as well were her sexual orientation known.

> There's just no way that we could ever be anything but heavily closeted. We have a lot of women's activities that go on here, but we don't mix the worlds.... That's why my children can't know.... I've set up my life so that it doesn't include my children.

Laura has made complicated arrangements for supervising her children before and after school and, in order to spend more time with her lover, has installed an intercom between the two houses that enables her to monitor her kids' activities. Meeting both her children's and her lover's needs means that she has little time for herself, and she sees most of her time with her children as mechanical. While she describes motherhood as separate from her "life," it is clear that managing the division between the two worlds creates a problem in organizing her identity.

For some women who maintain strict separation between their identities as mothers and as lesbians, the threat of custody litigation is more than an abstract fear. Theresa Baldocchi, whose son is nine years old, survived a protracted custody trial at the time she divorced her former husband, John. Her legal expenses and liability for debts incurred by John during their marriage left her virtually bankrupt, and it has taken years for her to solidify her financial situation. Teresa was not a lesbian at the time of the divorce, but John made allegations that she was. Now that she has come out, she is convinced that she must carefully separate her life as a mother and as a lesbian, lest her former husband decide to institute another custody case against her. Despite the fact that John has an extensive history of psychiatric hospitalization, and that she is a successful professional, she is sure that her chances of winning in such a trial would be slim.

> Now that I'm gay, I'd lose. There's just no way in the world I would win, after having had my fitness questioned when I was Lady Madonna, let alone now.

Theresa has decided that living in a middle-class suburban area and arranging her home in an impeccably conventional fashion help shield her from suspicion of being anything other than a typical "mom." The Bay Bridge, which she must cross each day between her home and San Francisco, where she works and socializes with her lesbian friends, symbolizes her strategy. She feels that each trip involves a palpable transition, as she prepares herself to meet the requirements of her destination—home or San Francisco. Most crucial for her strategy is not telling her son that she is a lesbian, since she feels it would be inappropriate to expect him to maintain her secret.

If Theresa was concerned only with managing information about her homosexuality, she would probably avoid seeing her former husband, and thus be able to relax, at least, at home. But Theresa firmly believes that being a good mother demands that she take every opportunity to maximize her son's contact with John, a model father in her eyes. Because John is not regularly employed, he has offered to take care of their son each day while Theresa is at work. This arrangement has meant both that Theresa does not have to obtain paid child care during these hours, and that her son has daily contact with his father. It also means that she has virtually no privacy. She must control the kinds of friends who visit her, and must make sure that nothing that might reveal her sexual orientation can be found in her home. Most poignantly, she must limit her lover's access to her home for fear that her presence would somehow make the situation transparent. She consigns her most reliable potential source of support to the background, leaving herself isolated and anxious much of the time.

In other instances, lesbian mothers may separate the two aspects of their lives in order to maintain fragile relationships with their families. Rita Garcia, who lives in San Francisco with her eight-year-old son and her lover, Jill Hacker, has made arrangements with her family that she believes can be sustained only if she avoids mention of her partner and their relationship. She comes from a large and close Mexican-American family. When they first learned that she was a lesbian, shortly after her divorce, they were so angry, and so convinced that she was no longer a fit parent, that they briefly considered supporting her husband's claim for custody. Once the case finally came to trial, however, Rita's husband abandoned his interest in custody. The family learned, during these proceedings, that he had abused her on numerous occasions, once beating her so severely that she had to go to the hospital. They withdrew their support from her husband, but also refused to communicate with Rita.

Rita did not see her parents at all for over a year. When Rita's grandmother had surgery and demanded to see her favorite granddaughter, the family relented, and Rita became a central figure in the grandmother's nursing care. The crisis allowed her to be reintegrated into the family, and she began once again to be her mother's closest confidante. This rapprochement, however, was founded on an unspoken agreement that Rita not mention her lover or anything about her home life.

The situation had stabilized, with Rita spending a great deal of time with her parents. Her son attends a Catholic school in her parents' neighborhood, so she drops him off there each day on her way to work. Rita's mother makes him breakfast every morning, and after school he returns to his grandparents' house to play and do his homework. Before Rita picks him up in the evening, he usually eats dinner as well, which allows Rita to work overtime at her job. Whenever Rita and Jill have plans in the evening, he spends the night with his grandparents. Besides this kind of practical support, Rita depends on her father for help with her car and for advice about financial matters. She is close to her sister, and often exchanges overnight baby-sitting with her.

But Rita never mentions her lover to her family, and her parents have established a strict policy of never visiting her home. Jill is never invited to family events, spending Christmas and Thanksgiving with her own family. While her parents know that she is a lesbian, Rita has decided not to tell her son, reasoning that it might be difficult for him to manage his relations with his grandparents if he had to be secretive about this topic. Separating her identity as a lesbian from her identity as a mother is consistent with her notion of being a good mother. Her son's welfare is enhanced by his ties to his grandparents, and Rita is able to provide better for him with the assistance they provide. Anything that might undermine that relationship would have the effect of harming her child, and that would make her a bad mother, undeserving, should the issue come up again, of being the custodial parent.

Other mothers explain the separation of motherhood from other dimensions of their lives, and the centrality of being a mother, to framing their identities more practically, citing the weighty and unrelenting obligations faced by parents. Peggy Lawrence, who lives with her lover, Sue Alexander, her ten-year-old daughter, and Sue's two sons spoke at length about the effects of being a mother on her personal freedom. Being a mother means that she must be concerned about continuity and stability in ways that constrain her spontaneity, and earning money must be a priority no matter how oppressive her work. Peggy and Sue live in a neighborhood close to their children's school, and have chosen to live in San Francisco because they think their children will encounter less discrimination here as the children of lesbians than in the Midwest, where they would prefer to live. Peggy explains what being a mother means to her:

> Being a mother, to me—being a mother is more consuming than any other way that I could possibly imagine identifying myself ... any other way that I identify myself is an identification of some part of my being a mother. I am a lesbian mother, I am a working mother—"mother" hardly ever modifies any other thing. Mother is always the primary—it's always some kind of mother, but it's never a mother-anything. Mother is—mother, for mothers, is always the thing that is more consuming.

But others understand motherhood to mean the uniquely intense feelings that exist between mother and child. Lisa Stark, who describes the weightiness of single parenthood as almost unbearable, has come to see her children as the reason she can continue to struggle with her obligations, paradoxically the explanation for both her suffering and her very survival.

> I've ... never had to live for myself. The only reason I get up in the morning is to get them off to school. For me to trot off to work in order to earn the money to support them. I don't know what I'd do if

I didn't have them. They're everything I've got.... I love them so much that it really is painful.

Having a child or being a mother may be said to create and reinforce meaningful ties with the world, and to make struggle worthwhile. While being a lesbian mother can be difficult, and may make a woman's life complicated and stressful, children offer significant intrinsic rewards most importantly, a way to experience feelings of special intimacy, and to be connected to higher-order, spiritual values. Motherhood allows lesbians to be more like other women, at least with respect to the most defining feminine role expectation, but segregating these two dimensions of the self becomes the most efficient way to manage practical obligations, and intensifies the dichotomization of "lesbian" and "mother."

Lesbian Motherhood: Resistance or Accommodation?

The goals motherhood allows lesbians to enhance are, of course, no different from those heterosexual women describe for themselves. Being a mother, in particular, becoming a mother, is perceived as a transformative experience, an accomplishment that puts other achievements in their proper perspective. It is also construed as an individual achievement, something a woman can "do" to make herself a mother, that is, to transform herself into an altruistic, spiritually-aware human being. In a culture that elevates what has been characterized as "mythic individualism" as a central value, individuals idealize autonomy, self-reliance, and the notion that one must "find oneself" and "make something" of oneself (Bellah 65).

Clearly, the meaning of one's life for most Americans is to become one's own person, almost to give birth to oneself. (Bellah 82)

Women in America have particular difficulty living up to this cultural ideal. Individualistic and assertive behaviors valued in men are discouraged in women. Dependency, particularly through marriage, is represented as a specifically feminine sort of success. I have discussed elsewhere the remarkable congruences I observed in accounts both lesbian and heterosexual women offered of their divorces, and the similarities between these stories and lesbians' coming-out narratives (Lewin 1993). These narratives are constructed around themes of agency, independence, and individuality, and celebrate women's ability to define their own lives, to decide how to represent their identities, and to achieve adulthood and autonomy. Despite the fact that both divorce and coming out as a lesbian are popularly understood to be problematic, and, indeed, have historically been defined as stigmatized statuses, women represent them as odysseys of self-discovery leading to more authentic formulations of the self.

Accounts of becoming a mother, in similar fashion, focus on the power of the individual to construct herself as a mother, to negotiate the formation of her self and to bring something good into her life. For lesbians, particularly for lesbians who decided to become mothers once their identification as lesbians was firm, the process of becoming a mother demands agency. At the same time, to the extent that wanting to be a mother is perceived as a *natural* desire, one unmediated by culture or politics, then becoming a mother permits a lesbian to move into a more natural or normal status than she would otherwise achieve. In this sense, becoming a mother represents a sort of conformity with conventional gender expectations. At the same time, to the extent that becoming a mother means overcoming the equation of homosexuality with *unnaturalness,* then this transformation allows the lesbian mother to resist gendered constructions of sexuality. This act of resistance is paradoxically achieved through compliance with conventional expectations for women, so it may also be construed as a gesture of accommodation.

Placing motherhood at the center of one's identity often involves, as we have seen, simultaneously placing other aspects of the self, most notably lesbianism, at the margins. Demanding the right to be a mother suggests a repudiation of gender conventions that define "mother" and "lesbian" as inherently incompatible identities, the former natural and intrinsic to women, organized around altruism, the latter unnatural, and organized around self-indulgence. But living as a mother means making other choices, and these choices reinscribe the opposition between "mother" and "lesbian." Subversion of orderly gender expectations is hypothetical, at best, in the lives of many lesbian mothers, at the same time that knowledge of their existence can only be imagined by the wider public as a rebellion of the most fundamental sort.

The model I would suggest based on the accounts presented here is that lesbian mothers are neither resisters nor accommodators—or perhaps that they are both. A more accurate way of framing their narratives is that they are strategists, using the cultural resources offered by motherhood to achieve a particular set of goals. That these are the goals framed by past experience in a heterosexist and perhaps patriarchal society, and that these resources are culturally constrained and shaped by the exigencies of gender, does not simplify the analysis. While such women are often conscious resisters, others gladly organize their experience as a reconciliation with what they view as traditional values. At the same time that some outsiders may see their behavior as transgressive (and thereby label them resisters or subversives), others perceive lesbian motherhood (along with other indications of compliance with conventional behaviors, such as gay/lesbian marriage) as evidence that lesbians (and other "deviants") can be domesticated and tamed (Lewin 1993).[8]

The search for cultures of resistance continues to be a vital dimension of the feminist academic enterprise. At the same time that we cannot limit our analyses of women's lives to accounts of victimization, we cannot be complacent when we discover evidence of resistance and subversion. Either interpretation may fail to reveal the complex ways in which resistance and accommodation, subversion and compliance, are interwoven and interdependent, not distinct orientations, but mutually reinforcing aspects of a single strategy. Lesbian mothers are, in some sense, both lesbians and mothers, but they shape identity and renegotiate its meanings at every turn, reinventing themselves as they make their way in a difficult world.

Notes

[1] This paper draws on research conducted with the support of National Institute of Mental Health Grant MH-30890 and a grant from the Rockefeller Foundation Gender Roles Program. A more extensive treatment of this material appears in Lewin (1993).

[2] Not only lesbians, but heterosexual mothers whose sexual activity comes to the attention of the authorities, may be vulnerable in cases where their custody is challenged (see Polikoff).

[3] A number of works that have chronicled the second wave of feminism in the United States have noted that the treatment of agency and victimization has been a central issue in the framing of feminist theory. See, for example, Echols; Eisenstein; Jaggar. Central issues giving rise to these theories, particularly the essentialist stances taken by adherents of cultural feminism, were those of violence and abuse-rape, incest, battering, and the like.

[4] Lila Abu-Lughod has reviewed the diverse forms an emphasis on resistance has taken in anthropology and in other disciplines. Abu-Lughod urges us not to romanticize resistance, but to use its appearance "to teach us about the complex interworkings of historically changing structures of power." Some scholars, notably James Scott, have suggested that interest in resistance has blossomed as scholars on the left have been forced to confront the failure of socialist revolutions.

[5] Although artificial insemination is often included among the "new" reproductive technologies such as *in vitro* fertilization, embryo transfer, and sex predetermination, there is actually nothing particularly new about the procedure. Originally developed for use in animal husbandry, artificial insemination by donor (AID) conceptions are estimated as accounting for thousands of births in the United States each year (see Curie-Cohen, Luttrell, and Shapiro). The procedure itself introduces sperm into the vagina with a needle-less syringe at a time calculated to coincide with the woman's ovulation. Once methods for freezing sperm were perfected in 1949, the possibility of expanded use presented itself (both for animals and for humans), as sperm banks and various sorts of matching services came into existence (Corea 36). At present, there is only minimal government regulation of artificial insemination or of sperm banks. Sperm banks and access to medically supervised insemination are controlled almost exclusively by physicians, who act as gatekeepers in terms of who may have access to frozen sperm. This means both that medical screening of donors is far from consistent or reliable, and that physicians tend to use their personal values to determine who should have access to these services (Lasker and Borg). Since frozen sperm can be expensive, unmarried women, as well as low-income patients may not have the same access to insemination as affluent couples (Curie-Cohen, Luttrell, and Shapiro; McGuire and Alexander; Strong and Schinfeld).

Despite these obstacles, the low-tech nature of artificial insemination and the possibility of mobilizing alternatives to physician-controlled sperm banks have meant that women, in fact, can easily retain control of the procedure. Women whose physicians may be unwilling to inseminate—whether they be single, low-income, or lesbian—can use their informal networks to carry out insemination outside conventional medical settings (Achilles; Hornstein; Lewin 1985). In the late 1970s, this process was generally called "artificial insemination." Within a few years, however, mothers began to use alternate language, labelling the procedure either "donor insemination" or simply "insemination" in an effort to downplay the implication that there was anything intrinsically "unnatural" about getting pregnant in this way.

[6]Names and some other details have been changed to preserve the anonymity of women whom I interviewed. For a detailed account of the methods used in this research, see Lewin (1993).

[7]Adoption, though difficult, was another approach used by lesbians who wished to become mothers. Because of the large number of two-parent families who wish to adopt, and the small number of healthy newborn babies available for adoption, single women (and men) are rarely considered prime candidates as adoptive parents. Their chances are, of course, even slighter if they are known to be lesbian or gay. Adoption is more in reach of these prospective parents if they can arrange a private adoption or if they are willing to adopt an older, disabled, abused, or minority/mixed-race child-those considered less desirable. See editors of the *Harvard Law Review* "Sexual Orientation and the Law."

[8]See also Lewin (forthcoming) for a discussion of how the popular media has accommodated images of lesbian families and poses them in opposition to still-abnormal childless lesbians.

References

Abu-Lughod, Lila. "The Romance of Resistance: Tracing Transformations of Power Through Bedouin Women." *American Ethnologist* 17 (1) (February 1990): 41-55.

Achilles, Rona. "Donor Insemination: The Future of a Public Secret." *The Future of Human Reproduction*. Ed. Christine Overall. Toronto: The Women's Press, 1989. 105-119.

Bellah, Robert *et al. Habits of the Heart: Individualism and Commitment in American Life*. Berkeley: University of California Press, 1985.

Butler, Judith. *Gender Trouble: Feminism and the Subversion of Identity*. New York: Routledge, 1990.

Corea, Gena. *The Mother Machine: Reproductive Technologies from Artificial Insemination to Artificial Wombs*. New York: Harper and Row, 1985.

Curie-Cohen, Martin, Lesleigh Luttrell, and Sander Shapiro. "Current Practice of Artificial Insemination by Donor in the United States." *New England Journal of Medicine* 300 (11) (1979): 585-590.

Dill, Bonnie Thornton. "Domestic Service and the Construction of Personal Dignity." *Women and the Politics of Empowerment.* Eds. Ann Bookman and Sandra Morgen. Philadelphia: Temple University Press, 1988.

Echols, Alice. *Daring to be Bad: Radical Feminism in America, 1967-1975.* Minneapolis: University of Minnesota Press, 1989.

Eisenstein, Hester. *Contemporary Feminist Thought.* Boston: G. K. Hall, 1983.

Farrell, Sherrie, John Gordon Hill, and Peter M. Bruce. "Sandy and Madeleine's Family." (Film) San Francisco: Multi Media Resource Center, 1973.

Gibson, Clifford Guy. *By Her Own Admission: A Lesbian Mother's Fight to Keep Her Son.* Garden City, NY: Doubleday, 1977.

Gilman, Charlotte Perkins. *Herland.* 1915. New York: Pantheon Books, 1979.

Goodale, Jane. *Tiwi Wives: A Study of the Women of Melville Island, North Australia.* Seattle: University of Washington Press, 1971.

Harvard Law Review. "Sexual Orientation and the Law." Cambridge, MA: Harvard University Press, 1989.

Hitchens, Donna. "Social Attitudes, Legal Standards, and Personal Trauma in Child Custody Cases." *Journal of Homosexuality* 5 (1979): 89-95.

Hornstein, Francie. Children by Donor Insemination: A New Choice for Lesbians." *Test-Tube Women: What Future for Motherhood?* Eds. Rita Arditti, Renate Duelli Klein, and Shelley Minden. London: Pandora Press, 1984. 373-381.

Hunter, Nan and Nancy D. Polikoff. "Custody Rights of Lesbian Mothers: Legal Theory and Litigation Strategy," *Buffalo Law Review* 25 (1976): 691-733.

Jaggar, Alison M. *Feminist Politics and Human Nature.* Totowa, NJ: Rowman and Allanheld, 1983.

Lamphere, Louise. *From Working Daughters to Working Mothers: Immigrant Women in a New England Industrial Community.* Ithaca, N.Y.: Cornell University Press, 1987.

Lasker, Judith N. and Susan Borg. *In Search of Parenthood: Coping with Infertility and High-Tech Conception.* Boston: Beacon Press, 1987.

Lewin, Ellen. "On the Outside· Looking In: The Politics of Lesbian Motherhood." *Conceiving the New World Order: Local/Global Intersections in the Politics of Reproduction.* Eds. Faye Ginsburg and Rayna Rapp. Berkeley: University of California Press, forthcoming.

Lewin, Ellen. *Lesbian Mothers: Accounts of Gender in American Culture.* Ithaca, NY: Cornell University Press, 1993.

Lewin, Ellen. "Claims to Motherhood: Custody Disputes and Maternal Strategies." *Uncertain Terms: Negotiating Gender in American Culture.* Eds. Faye Ginsburg and Anna Lowenhaupt Tsing. Boston: Beacon Press, 1990. 199-214.

Lewin, Ellen. "By Design: Reproductive Strategies and the Meaning of Motherhood." *The Sexual Politics of Reproduction.* Ed. Hilary Homans. London: Gower, 1985. 123-138.

Lewin, Ellen. "Lesbianism and Motherhood: Implications for Child Custody." *Human Organization* 40 (1) (1981): 6-14.

Martin, Emily. *The Woman in the Body: A Cultural Analysis of Reproduction.*

Boston: Beacon Press, 1987.

McGuire, Maureen and Nancy Alexander. "Artificial Insemination of Single Women." *Fertility and Sterility* 43 (1985): 182-184.

Ong, Aihwa. *Spirits of Resistance and Capitalist Discipline: Factory Women in Malaysia.* Albany: State University of New York Press, 1987.

Polikoff, Nancy D. "Gender and Child Custody Determinations: Exploding the Myths." *Families, Politics, and Public Policy: A Feminist Dialogue on Women and the State.* Ed. Irene Diamond. New York: Longman, 1983. 183-202.

Rivera, Rhonda R. "Our Strait-Laced Judges: The Legal Position of Homosexual Persons in the United States." *Hastings Law Journal* 30 (1979): 799-055.

Scott, James. *Weapons of the Weak: Everyday Forms of Peasant Resistance.* New Haven: Yale University Press, 1985.

Strong, Carson and Jay Schinfeld. "The Single Woman and Artificial Insemination by Donor." *Journal of Reproductive Medicine* 29 (1984): 293-299.

Vaughn, Jeanne. "A Question of Survival." *Politics of the Heart: A Lesbian Parenting Anthology.* Eds. Sandra J. Pollack and Jeanne Vaughn. Ithaca, NY: Firebrand Books, 1987.

Vida, Ginny ed. *Our Right to Love: A Lesbian Resource Book.* Englewood Cliffs, NJ: Prentice-Hall, 1978.

Weiner, Annette B. *Women of Value, Men of Renown: New Perspectives in Trobriand Exchange.* Austin: University of Texas Press, 1976.

Wolf, Margery. *Women and the Family in Rural Taiwan.* Stanford: Stanford University Press, 1972.

Chapter 24

Beyond Mothers and Fathers

Ideology in a Patriarchal Society

BARBARA KATZ ROTHMAN

SOMETHING HAS GONE seriously awry in our cultural understanding of motherhood in America. We find ourselves surrounded by contradictions that would give George Orwell pause: the return of the midwife, and the rise of the cesarean section; cigarette ads, clearly aimed at young women, carrying a warning that smoking harms fetuses; the infant formula companies distributing sample packages of formula for new mothers, labeled "In support of your decision to breast feed." An angry Black social worker says of a grieving white woman whose Black foster child was taken away after three years: "She had no right to love that child. It was just a *job.*" Much the same is said of a pregnant woman who is not the "mother" of the fetus in her belly, because it was contracted to be there. Childbearing at forty is chic, at fifty is the new frontier, at eighteen is pathetic. Murphy Brown is supposed to be the epitome of something.

To understand it, to explain it, we need to step back and try to disentangle the contradictions. When we do, we find ourselves unweaving the strands of a fabric, understanding the pattern as we work it backwards to the underlying threads. American motherhood now rests on three, deeply rooted ideologies that shape what we see and what we experience, three central threads of motherhood: an ideology of patriarchy; an ideology of technology; and an ideology of capitalism. As these three come together, with all of their multiplicity of meaning, they give us the shape, and the discordance, of our experience—the fabric of motherhood.

As used in this chapter, ideology is the way a group looks at the world, the way it organizes its thinking about the world. An ideology can let us see things, but it can also blind us, close our eyes to our own lived reality, our own experiences, our own bodies. The ideologies of patriarchy, technology, and capitalism gives us our vision of motherhood while they block our view, give us a language for some things while they silence us for others.

The ideology of patriarchy is perhaps the easiest to understand of the three ideologies that shape motherhood. More than half the world has another reality called women's reality to contradict it. But women's reality is not the dominant ideology, and women's view of the world is overruled by men's view. Motherhood in a patriarchal society is what mothers and babies signify to men. For women this can mean too many pregnancies or too few; "trying again" for a son; covering up male infertility with donor insemination treated as the deepest darkest secret; having some of our children called "illegitimate"; not having access to abortions we do want; being pressured into abortions we may not want. The ideology of capitalism, that goods are produced for profit, is also something clear to us; we know that some societies avoid the profit motive, and that most societies feel there should be *some* limits to how much of life should be viewed as a commodity. It may seem farfetched to apply this ideology to motherhood and to children. But the family has always been an economic unit as well as a social and psychological unit. What is new, perhaps, is the shift from children as workers to children as commodities, accompanying the change in the family from its role as a unit of production to its new role as a unit of consumption.[1] Finally, the ideology of technology shapes motherhood. No longer an event shaped by religion and family, having a baby has become part of the high-tech medical world. But as an ideology, a way of thinking, technology is harder to pin down, so pervasive has it become in Western society. The ideology of technology encourages us to see ourselves as objects, to see people as made up of machines and part of larger machines. It is this mechanization that connects the ideology of patriarchy with capitalism, to create a worldview.

This chapter addresses each of these ideologies as separate ways of thinking; then, most importantly, it turns to the ways they weave together to create a pattern, a fabric, both a curtain and a cage.

The Ideology of Patriarchy

The term "patriarchy" is often used loosely as a synonym for "sexism," or to refer to any social system where men rule. The term technically means "rule of fathers," but in its current practical usage it more often refers to any system of male superiority and female inferiority. But male dominance and patriarchal rule are not quite the same thing, and when the subject is motherhood, the difference is important.

Patriarchal kinship is the core of what is meant by patriarchy: the idea that paternity is the central social relationship. A very clear statement of patriarchal kinship is found in the *Book of Genesis*, in the "begats." Each man, from Adam onward, is described as having "begat a son in his likeness, after his image." After the birth of this firstborn son, the men are described as having lived so many years and having begat sons and daughters. The text then turns to that firstborn son, and in turn his firstborn son after him. Women appear as the "daughters of men who bore them offspring." In a patriarchal kinship system, children are born to men, out of women. That is, women, in this system, bear the children of men.

While all societies appear to be male dominated to some degree, not all societies are patriarchal. In some, the line of descent is not from father to son, but along the lines of the women. These are called "matrilineal" societies: it is a shared mother that makes for a shared lineage or family group. Men still rule in these groups, but they do not rule as fathers. They rule the women and children who are related to them through their mother's line. Women in such a system are not a vulnerability, but a source of connection. As anthropologist Glenn Petersen says, in a matrilineal system "women, rather than infiltrating and subverting patrilinies, are acknowledged to produce and reproduce the body of society itself" (141). People are not men's children coming through the bodies of women, but the children of women.

In a patriarchal system, in contrast, the essential concept is the "seed," the part of men that grows into the children of their likeness within the bodies of women. Such a system is inevitably male dominated, but it is a particular kind of male domination. Men control women as daughters, much as they control their sons, but they also control women as the mothers of men's children. It is women's motherhood that men must control to maintain patriarchy. In a patriarchy, because what is valued is the relationship of a man to his sons, women are a vulnerability that men have: to beget these sons, men must pass their seed through the body of a woman.

In a patriarchal system, when people talk about blood ties, they are talking about a genetic tie, a connection by seed. In a mother-based system, the blood tie is the mingled blood of mothers and their children: children grow out of the blood of their mothers, of their bodies and being. The shared bond of kinship comes through mothers. The maternal tie is based on the growing of children. The patriarchal tie is based on genetics, the act of impregnating.

Each of these ways of thinking leads to different ideas about what a person is. In a mother-based system, a person is what mothers grow—people are made of the care and nurturance that bring a baby forth into the world, and turn the baby into a member of the society. In a patriarchal system, a person is what grows out of men's seed. The essence of the person, what the person really is, is there in the seed when it is planted in the mother. Early scientists in Western society were so deeply committed to the patriarchal concept that it influenced what they saw. One of the first uses of the microscope was to look at semen and see the little person, the homunculus, curled up inside the sperm. And in 1987 the director of a California sperm bank distributed T-shirts with a drawing of sperm swimming on a blue background accompanied by the words "Future People." Out of the patriarchal focus on the seed as the source of being, on the male production of children from men's seed, has grown our current, usually far more sophisticated thinking about procreation.

Modern procreative technology has been forced to go beyond the sperm as seed, however. "Daddy plants a seed in Mommy" won't work any more; modern science has had to confront the *egg* as seed also. Scientific thinking cannot possibly hold on to old notions of women as nurturers of men's seeds. The doctor who has spent time "harvesting" eggs from women's bodies for *in vitro* fertilization fully understands the significance of women's seed. But that does not mean we no longer continue to think of the seed as the essence of being. It is not the end of the belief that the seeds, the genes, are everything, that they are all that really matters in the making of a baby, that they are what *real* kinship is based on.

The old patriarchal kinship system had a clear place for women: they were the nurturers of men's seeds, the soil in which seeds grew, the daughters who bore men's offspring. When forced to acknowledge that a woman's genetic contribution is equal to a man's, Western patriarchy was in trouble. *But the central concept of patriarchy, the importance of the seed, was retained by extending the concept to women.* Valuing the seed of women extends to them some of the privileges of patriarchy. That is, when the significance of women's seed is acknowledged in their relationship with their children, women, too, have paternity rights in their children. In this modified system, based on the older ideology of patriarchy, women, too, can be seen to own their children, just like men do. Unlike what happens in a mother-based system, however, this relationship between women and their children is not based on motherhood *per se,* not on the unique nurturance, the long months of pregnancy, the intimate connections with the baby as it grows and moves inside her body, passes through her genitals, and sucks at her breasts. Instead, women are said to own their babies, have "rights" to them, just as men do: based on their seed. This does not end patriarchy, and it does not end the domination of the children of women by men. Instead, by maintaining the centrality of the seed, the ideology maintains the rights of men in their children, even as it recognizes something approaching equal rights of women in their children. Since men's control over women and the children of women is no longer based simply on men's (no longer) unique seed, men's economic superiority and other privileges of a male-dominated social system become increasingly important. Children are, based on the seed, presumptively "half his, half hers"—and might as well have grown in the backyard. Women do not gain their rights to their children in this society as *mothers,* but as father equivalents, equivalent sources of seed.

The ideology of patriarchal society thus goes much deeper than male dominance. It means far more than just having men in charge, or men making more decisions than women do. The ideology of patriarchy is a basic worldview, and in a patriarchal system that view permeates all of our thinking. In our society, the ideology of patriarchy provides us with an understanding not only of the relations between women and men, but also of the relations between mothers and their children.

In a patriarchal society, men use women to have their children. A man can use this woman or that woman to have *his* children. He can hire this woman or that woman to substitute for one or another aspect (biological, social, or psychological) of the mothering his child needs. From the view of the man, his seed is irreplaceable; the mothering, the nurturance, is substitutable.

And from the woman's point of view? We can use this man's sperm or that one's to have our children. With this or that man as father, our bellies will swell, life will stir, milk will flow. We may prefer one man's seed to another, just as a man may prefer one woman's nurturance to another for his child, but they are substitutable, they are interchangeable. For a man, what makes the child *his* is his seed. For women, what makes the child ours is the nurturance, the work of our bodies. Wherever the sperm came from, it is in our bodies that our babies grow, and it is our physical presence and nurturance that make our babies ours. But is that inevitable? Did not some women substitute other women's bodies when they hired wet nurses? Don't some women substitute other women's arms, other women's touch, when they hire housekeepers and baby-sitters and day-care workers? And now the new procreative technology lets us cut our seeds loose from our bodies, and plant them in other women's bodies. The seed, the egg, of one woman can be brought to term in the body of another.

We have a technology that takes Susan's egg and puts it in Mary's body. And so we ask, *who* is the mother? Who is the surrogate? Is Mary substituting for Susan's body, growing Susan's baby for Susan? Or is Susan's egg substituting for Mary's, growing into Mary's baby in Mary's body? Our answer depends on where we stand when we ask the question.

When we accept the patriarchal valuing of the seed, there is no doubt the real mother, like the real father, is the genetic parent. When we can contract for pregnancy at the present rate often thousand dollars, we can choose which women to substitute for us in the pregnancy. The brokers have books of pictures of women for potential parents to choose from, to take this woman or that woman to carry the pregnancy, to nurture the seed.

But for which women are these substitutes available? Who can afford to hire substitutes for the various parts of mothering? The situation today is exactly what it has been historically: women of privilege, wealthy or fairly wealthy women, hiring the services of poor, or fairly poor, women. Upper-class women can have some of the privileges of patriarchy. Upper-class women can buy some of the privileges of their paternity, using the bodies of poorer women to "bear them offspring." And upper-class women can, as they so often have, be bought off with these privileges, and accept men's worldview as their own. And so we have women, right along with men, saying that what makes a child one's own is the seed, the genetic tie, the "blood." And the blood they mean is not the real blood of pregnancy and birth, not the blood of the pulsing cord, the bloody show, the blood of birth, but the metaphorical blood of the genetic tie.

This is the ultimate meaning of patriarchy for mothers: seeds are precious; mothers are fungible.

The Ideology of Technology

In technological society we apply ideas about machines to people, asking them to be more efficient, productive, rational and controlled. We treat our bodies as machines, hooking them up to other machines, monitoring and managing bodily functions. When a doctor manages a woman's labor, controlling her body with drugs and even surgery, it is to make her labor more efficient, predictable, rational. And so it is when mothers and fathers push their babies into a schedule, so that feeding the baby meshes into the nine-to-five day. Books like *Toilet Training in One Day* show us how to "train" our children efficiently. When we think of our *relationships* with our children as a job to be done well, we are invoking the ideology of technology.

To do these parenting tasks efficiently, we divide them up into their component parts, organize them, systematize them, rationalize, *budget* our time, *order* our day, *program* our lives. All of this rationalizing, reducing, dividing, systematizing, organizing, in the name of efficiency, however, does harm to the human spirit. Clearly, not everything is best viewed as a resource.

The most obvious application of the technological ideology to motherhood has occurred in the medicalization of pregnancy and of childbirth. From the medical management of pregnancy, with its new, quality-control technology of prenatal diagnosis, through the rigidly monitored control of women's labor, the focus is on the "mechanics" of production, and not the social transformation of motherhood. It is as if biology were beyond culture, beyond ideology. The "mechanism" of contraception, the "mechanics" of labor, the "programming" of genetic development—these things are often seen as simple biological givens with which we must cope. But remember, that is the nature of ideology: the constructs look like common sense, the ideas are obvious, the descriptions are simply how things are, "naturally."

In our society, when we look at what we know, what our taken-for-granted reality about physical motherhood is, we are looking at medical ideology, a particular type of mechanical thinking, of technological ideology. Medical ideology is deeply rooted in the mind-body dualism expressed by Descartes: the body is a machine, the structure and operation of which falls within the province of human knowledge, as distinguished from the mind.

In the management of childbirth we see the ideology of technology played out, in all its inhumane absurdity. Pregnant women become workers in an unskilled assembly line, conceptualized as machines, containers holding precious, genetic material. What is it like to be the laborer in such a factory? Sheila Kitzinger, the extraordinary childbirth educator writes:

> Grateful as most women are for all this care and awed by the advanced technology, it is not difficult to understand how a woman can feel that she is merely a container for a fetus, the development and safe delivery of which is under the control of obstetric personnel and machinery, and that her body is an inconvenient barrier to easy access and the probing of all those rubber gloved fingers and the gleaming equipment, and even-ridiculous, but we are talking about feelings—that if she were not around the pregnancy could progress with more efficiency. (74)

It is not only the body that we treat as mechanical, but the social order as well. Rather than seeing society as an organic, deeply interconnected whole, technological ideology encourages us to see society as a collection of parts. Liberal philosophy, the intellectual underpinning of the American Revolution and American government, is the articulation of the technological ideology in the social order.

Carolyn Merchant's work *The Death of Nature* traces the development of a mechanical order in Western society to replace the organism of earlier times. She argues that whereas in the time of the Renaissance the earth was perceived as "alive and considered to be a beneficent, receptive, nurturing female" (28), by the seventeenth century the worldview had changed, and the machine became the metaphor. "As the unifying model for science and society, the machine has permeated and reconstructed human consciousness so totally that today we scarcely question its validity. Nature, society, and the human body are composed of interchangeable atomized parts that can be repaired or replaced from the outside." This "removal of animistic, organic assumptions about the cosmos constituted the death of nature-the most far-reaching effect of the scientific revolution" (Merchant 185).

The rise of mechanism, as Merchant calls technological ideology, laid the foundation for a new social order in which the relationship between mind and body, person and society was to be reevaluated. "A new concept of the self as a rational master of the passions housed in a machine-like body began to replace the concept of the self as an integral part of a close-knit harmony of organic parts united to the cosmos and society" (214).

The difficulty in reconciling the image of people as "atomized parts" with our very real desire for community, for interconnectedness between people, remains one of the ongoing problems of liberal society. This was addressed in *Habits of the Heart,* a book about the conflicts American society has structured between individualism and commitment. The authors describe modernity as a "culture of separation" (Bellah, Madsden, Sullivan, Swidler and Tipton 277). America as a world in which "it became clear that every social obligation was vulnerable, every tie between individuals fragile" (Bellah *et al.* 276).

And against this, we have motherhood, the physical embodiment of connectedness. We have in every pregnant woman the living proof that individuals do not enter the world as autonomous, atomistic, isolated beings, but begin socially, begin connected. And we have in every pregnant woman a walking contradiction to the segmentation of our lives: pregnancy does not permit it. In pregnancy the private self, the sexual, familial self, announces itself wherever we go. Motherhood is the embodied challenge to liberal philosophy, and that, I fear, is why a society founded on and committed to liberal philosophical principles cannot deal well with motherhood.

When the authors of the American Constitution declared "All men are created equal," they were drawing on this philosophical tradition of the Enlightenment. What made that statement reasonable was that the equality they spoke of was of the mind, of the rational being. Certainly some men were weak and some strong, some rich and some poor—but all shared the human essence, the rational mind. The extension of such "equality" to Blacks and to women is based on the claim that these groups, too, share the essence of humanity, the rational mind—housed, in the "accident of birth," in the body of the Black, the body of the woman. And it is that same belief that underlies the endless stream of movies and stories about the computer or robot, the machine, that learns to think and to feel, and so becomes essentially human—and ultimately tragic.

If we believe, then, as this liberal philosophic tradition holds, that what is especially valuable about human beings is the capacity for rationality, then the ordering, rationalizing, and purposeful efficiency of technology will be seen as good. But hand in hand with the valuing of rationality is a "theoretical disdain for the significance of the body," and a disdain for physical work in preference for "mental" work. The latter, dividing the physical from the mental work, and then using machines and people interchangeably to do the menial physical work, is the essence of technological organization.

In American society, blue-collar work is less valued than is managerial work. The white collar is a status symbol for having risen above the work of the body. The repair people who work on office copiers come in dressed as managers—white shirt and jacket, carrying a briefcase. To do the work, the briefcase unfolds to a tool bag, and the white shirt-sleeves get rolled up, but dressing in washable work clothes and carrying a tool bag, however much more practical, would be demeaning. Physical labor, the work of the hands and the bodies, is of low status.

This division of labor is a particular problem for women as mothers: mothers *do* the physical work of the body, we *do* the "menial" work of body maintenance. Thus women become identified with the physical, the body, and men with the higher, the rational. The distinction between menial physical labor and highly valued rationality goes a long way toward explaining the utter disdain with which a laboring woman may be strapped down and ignored or even insulted, while the doctor who "manages" her labor—reading her chart and ordering others to carry out his decisions—is held in such high esteem. Or similarly, why the woman who produces perfect nourishment from her body is seen as cowlike, animalistic in a negative way, while the pediatrician who "prescribes" a "formula" deserves such respect—and high pay.

The mind-body dualism has consequences at the macro level as well: viewing the body as a machine encourages us to see it as a resource to be used. If the mind and rationality are held as "above" the body, it becomes relatively easy to see the body as a resource for the use of the mind, and specifically, women's reproductive bodies as "societal" resources. So if the factories or the armies need fodder, women's bodies are the resources from which the young are produced. And if there are too many mouths to feed then the bodies are to be idle, like factories closed until inventories are reduced.

Here we have the ubiquitous problem of reconciling individual freedom and social order. In China, an increasingly technological society without the liberal tradition, the solution is simple: the needs of the society determine the rights of the individual, and the "one-child" policy is enacted. In the United States, such a policy would not be tolerated. And yet the birth rate does fluctuate with social need. In all kinds of ways people do what society needs them to do, and do so seemingly out of choice. What can we make of the choices of women to be used by the social order?

Because of their respect for the individual judgment of rational people, in principle "liberals are committed to the belief that individuals are fulfilled when they are doing what they have decided freely to do, however unpleasant, degrading or wrong this may appear to someone else" (Jaggar 186). The hook here is the notion of *freely chosen*. Thus, "informed consent" becomes a crucial American legal concept: if one consents or agrees to something *rationally*, then one accepts the consequences. But liberal thinking, with its emphasis' on rationality, does not seem equipped to understand the more subtle forms of coercion and persuasion, whether psychological or economic, so the "choices" people make out of their poverty or need, choices individuals may experience as being coerced, liberals tend to see as being freely chosen. To take a simple example: advertising campaigns that are shown to be highly effective in getting a targeted population to start smoking, such as those campaigns aimed at young women, are legal—as long as the ads include the information that cigarette smoking may be hazardous to your health.

The liberal position on prostitution is an even better example of how these ideas about mind-body dualism and individual choice come together:

> Liberals do not conceive one's body to be an essential part of oneself, so there seems to be no reason why one's sexual services may not just as well be sold as one's other abilities. Indeed, the propriety of selling one's intellectual capacities might be more problematic, on liberal grounds, than the sale of one's sexual services. (Jaggar 174)

The liberal vision of a better world does not inherently preclude people experiencing their bodies as salable commodities.

The extension is easily made from sexual prostitution to what some call "reproductive prostitution," the hiring of "surrogate" mothers. Here is what John Robertson, a liberal legal scholar, has to say about that:

> Baby selling laws prohibit fees for adoption in order to protect the child from unfit parents and the mother from exploitation and coercion. But these concerns do not apply to surrogate gestators who freely choose this reproductive role before pregnancy occurs, uninfluenced by the stigma of illegitimacy or the financial burdens of single parenthood. An acceptable system of paid surrogacy must assure that the surrogate is fully informed, has independent legal counsel, and has made a deliberative choice. There is also no fear that surrogates will be drawn primarily from poorer groups, who will serve the rich with their bodies as well as their housekeeping and childbearing services. Indeed, money is likely to be a prime motive to the decisions of women to serve as surrogates, but other factors are reported to play a role. It is not apparent that only

poor women will select that occupation, much less that the operation of a labor market in this area is more unjust than labor markets in other areas. (1022)

Surrogacy is then an "occupation" and a "reproductive role," freely chosen. The only protections needed are to make sure that the surrogate is operating "rationally"—informed, with counsel, making a deliberative choice. The patent absurdity of claiming fairness because wealthy, well-educated women have the same rights to be surrogates and poor women have the rights, although not at all the means, to hire surrogates slides by.

In sum liberal philosophy is an articulation of the values of technological society, with its basic themes of order, predictability, rationality, control, rationalization of life, the systematizing and control of things and people as things, the reduction of all to component parts, and ultimately the vision of everything including our very selves, as resources.

The Ideology of Capitalism

From the standpoint of the ideology of technology, we have seen that motherhood is perceived as work, and children as a product produced by the labor of mothering. Mother's work and mother's bodies are resources out of which babies are made. From the standpoint of the market, however, not all work is equally valuable, and not all products are equally valued. In other words there is not a direct relationship between the value of the worker and the value of the product.

What is essential to capitalism is the accumulation and investment of capital, of wealth, by people who are in a position to control others. Under capitalism, workers do not own or control the products of their own labor. This means we are no longer talking about mothers and babies at all we are talking about laborers and their products. Babies, at least healthy white babies, are very precious products these days. Mothers, rather like South African diamond miners, are the cheap, expendable, not-too-trustworthy labor necessary to product the precious products.[2] This is where it is all heading; the commodification of children and the proletarianization of motherhood. This is the end result of the evolution of these three ideological perspectives. This is what ties together the patriarchal and technological ideologies with the recreation of motherhood.

Because capitalism is complex, both as system and as ideology, here I will focus on only one essential aspect—the extension of ownership or property relations. There is a great deal of modern social criticism that claims the ways in which ownership has been extended is at best inappropriate, and too often morally wrong. For example, ecologists argue that it is inappropriate to think we can own the land, the waters: the earth, they claim—significantly—is our *mother*, not our property. The actual word *property* gets used relatively infrequently in discussions of human relations. More often the term is *rights*. Janet Farrell Smith says: "A right can be interpreted as an entitlement to do or have something, to exclude others from doing or having something or as an enforceable claim (202). What happens, then, when we start thinking of motherhood itself in terms of property? There are two directions in which property rights have extended that are directly relevant to motherhood: rights of ownership of one's own body, and rights to one's own child.

The way an ideology works is to focus our attention in certain ways, to give us a point of view, a perspective—often expressed in language as metaphor. People do not necessarily talk of or even actively think of their bodies or their children as *property* in the sense of real estate. As Smith points out, "In applying a property model to parenting, it is important to remember that a parent may not literally assert that a child is a piece of property, but may work on assumptions analogous to those which one makes in connection with property" (201).

Within the American system, intelligent feminist use of the individualist ethos has been invaluable in assuring women's rights in procreation. Once women themselves are recognized as full citizens, then individual women must be accorded the same rights of bodily autonomy and integrity that men have. For women, that means sexual and procreative autonomy. Because it is her body, she cannot be raped. Because it is her body, she cannot be forced to bear pregnancies she does not want. Because it is her body, she cannot be forced to abort pregnancies she does not want.

This does not mean that women are not forced by circumstance into these very situations and eventualities. It only means that the society will not use the official power of the state to force her. Women are in fact prevented from having abortions they might want by family pressure, by economic circumstances, by religious and social pressures. And women are forced into having abortions they might not want to have because of poverty, because of lack of services for children and mothers, because of lack of services for disabled children and adults. By offering amniocentesis to identify fetuses who would have disabilities, and by cutting back on services for disabled children and their families, we effectively force women to have selective abortions.

Because of our current battles over the right to abortion, Americans tend to think of the state as "permitting" women to have abortions, as if the drive for continuing pregnancies came from the state, and the drive for abortions from women. In fact, the legal protection works also to permit women not to have abortions. When women's ownership rights over their bodies are lost, the rights to have and the rights *not* to have abortions are likewise lost. Such was the case in Nazi Germany, where some abortions were indeed forced, but it is equally true that women lost the right to have the abortions they themselves chose, the abortions they as individual women felt they needed.

In American society, when we bring it back to the simple legal questions—who can force an abortion or forcibly prevent one—we wisely retreat to safety, calling forth our most sacred value. It's *her* body. We invoke a higher power, the power of ownership.

This then is the way that women have been able to combine dominant

American liberal philosophy with capitalist ideology to our benefit. We've made use of the mind-body dualism, to allow a view of the body as owned, like a shelter which houses the more important mind. If one claims rationality for women—the essential liberal claim for all people—then simple fairness gives women the same rights of bodily ownership that men have, and the very high value of ownership, of property rights, is then turned to the advantage of women, who can claim exclusive rights to our own bodies. In the name of ownership, women have demanded access to contraception, sterilization, and abortion. And given the prevailing liberal philosophy, we've gotten those rights to control our fertility—although given the capitalist class system, we have fared less well with access to the necessary means.

While the "owned-body" principle has worked for women in avoiding mother-hood, it is less clear how it can be made to work to empower women as mothers. Our bodies may be ours, but given the ideology of patriarchy, the bodies of mothers are not highly valued. The bodies are just the space in which genetic material matures into babies. In a patriarchal system, even if women own their bodies, it may not give them any real control in pregnancy. Women may simply be seen to own the space in which the fetuses are housed. This is the argument on which attempts to control women's behavior during pregnancy are based: owning her own body is not enough to assure her civil liberties if her body is believed to contain the property of someone else, somebody else's baby.

Of course, if women's bodies are understood to be the space in which sperm and egg grow to be a baby, and women are understood to be the owners of that space, then the acceptance of "surrogacy" follows logically, almost inevitably. The woman can rent out space in her body just as she can rent out the spare back bedroom. And she will have no more ownership rights over the inhabitants of that space in her body than over the boarder in her home. Whether she chooses to "rent" or not, the state can claim rights of passage through her body in the interests of the "citizens" within.

Reweaving the Fabric

From these ideologies of patriarchy, technology, and capitalism we get the supportive fabric for the strange patterns we see emerging. In varying combinations, with sometimes one thread dominating, and sometimes another, these patterns explain things as disparate as genetic testing, including prenatal diagnosis for selective abortion; micro and macro level eugenics programs; reproductive technologies that commodify and commercialize babies and pregnancy, including breast milk substitutes, "gestational surrogacy," electronic fetal monitoring, and eight-thousand-dollars-a-cycle *in vitro* fertilization; minimum wage for child care; the "mommy track"; the simultaneous commercialization and politicization of abortion; and-well, you get the picture.

Over the years many of us have railed against each of these emerging patterns. We have made Luddite-sounding noises about routine ultrasound, overly medicalized births, the false promises and dangerous drugs of infertility treatments; we have tilted at the windmills of "surrogacy," and of "affordable" child care. But our real concerns must go deeper. Our question must be: How best to create a supportive fabric for intimate human relations, including that most intimate of human relations that is motherhood, that is not blinded by the limitations of the ideologies of patriarchy, technology, and capitalism, and that is truly feminist in all its complexity.

The simplest and least threatening version of feminism is to ask for what is seen in North America as simple *fairness*. Even lots of Americans who would never, ever think of themselves as actually being feminists nonetheless expect fairness for women. Demands for fairness are generally based on insistence that prevailing liberal ideals be applied to women: ideals like equal pay for equal work. Since we are living in a society founded on liberal principles, it is liberal feminism that comes closest to mainstream values, and consequently often sounds like the very voice of reason, especially when juxtaposed with the more "strident" feminist positions.

Liberal feminism has its roots deep in American culture, with the feminists we have always had with us, as far back as Abigail Adams, who requested that the framers of the Constitution "remember the ladies." The liberal feminists, in asking that the ladies be remembered, are not so much offering a critique of American life and values as they are seeking full access. As Alison Jaggar writes:

> Liberal philosophy emerged with the growth of capitalism. It raised demands for democracy and political liberties that often expressed deeply held moral convictions about the inherent equality of men.... Consistently over the centuries, feminists have demanded that the prevailing liberal ideals should also be applied to women. (27)

Liberal feminism works best to defend women's rights to be like men, to enter into men's worlds; to work at men's jobs for men's pay, to have the rights and privileges of men. But what of our rights to be *women?*

The liberal argument, the fairness argument, the equal rights argument, these all begin to break down when we look at women who are, or are becoming, mothers. A woman lawyer is exactly the same as a man lawyer. A woman cop is just the same as a man cop. And a pregnant woman is just the same as ... well, as, uh, ... It's like disability, right? Or like serving in the army? Pregnancy is just exactly like pregnancy. There is nothing else quite like it. That statement is not glorification or mystification. It is a statement of fact. Having a baby grow in your belly is not like anything else one can do. It is unique.

The question is: how can uniqueness be made to fit into an equality model? Strangely enough, albeit for different reasons, both patriarchal ideology and liberal feminist thinking have come to the same conclusion about what to do with the problem of the uniqueness of pregnancy—devalue it; discount it so deeply that its uniqueness just doesn't matter. In strongly patriarchal systems, as described earlier, the genetic tie for men is the most important parental tie: women grow men's children, what Caroline Whitbeck calls "flower pot theory of pregnancy" (1-2). Men have the seeds and women are the flower pots. Liberal feminists, seeking equality and recognition of women's rationality and rights, claim equality of parenthood between men and women. Women too have seed, they argue, and men too can nurture children. Men cannot nurture with their bodies, not with their blood or their milk as women do—but that is just menial, body work. What matters is that both parents have seeds. Children are "half hers, half his." Instead of a flower pot, the woman is seen as an equal contributor of seed—and the baby might just as well have grown in the backyard. It is, after all, only women's bodily experience that is different from men's.

Liberal feminism does not challenge the mind-body dualism posited by and embedded in liberal philosophy, and so falters on the same grounds as discussed earlier. It has no place for the inherent physicality of gestation and lactation, and no respect for the "menial" work of body maintenance, the *mothering* work of early childhood.

Equal rights sounds good, and in many ways it is a fine goal, and one that has yet to be achieved for any of these groups: radical minorities, old people, women, disabled people. But a focus on "rights" ignores *needs*. Special attempts to get help based on need is called "reverse discrimination." Women as mothers are especially hard hit by this narrow equal rights approach. For one thing, those individuals who are not yet rational—our babies and children—need an awful lot of care and attention, and that falls to our lot. Liberal thinking, including liberal feminism, is a bit shy on what to do with the children—and the other deeply needy people. Even achieving a liberal goal of including men as child-tenders does not solve the problem: it remains individualized, privatized.

The second way that women as mothers are particularly hard hit by the "equality" approach of liberalism is that our specific needs as mothers are not taken into account. The liberal argument for formal equality has simply no place for the special needs of any group, including mothers. The *reductio ad absurdum* of formal equality for mothers, as Jaggar points out, is the 1976 Supreme Court decision in the case of *Gilbert v. General Electric Company* (Jaggar 42). The case was brought by the women employees, claiming sex discrimination because the disability benefits package at GE excluded pregnancy-related disabilities. The Supreme Court, in what Meredith Gould has called the "pregnant person school of thought," ruled that it was not sex discrimination. One physical condition had been removed from coverage, that's all. The discrimination, if such it was, was against *pregnant persons,* not against *women.*

For those people (and they may be the most traditional of conservatives or the most radical of feminists) who want to see women—our bodies, ourselves, our sexuality, or motherhood—treated with respect, liberal feminism fails. Clearly, while feminists are good and strong critics of patriarchal society, they do not fight the ideologies of technology or capitalism. The ideologies of patriarchy, technology, and capitalism support each other, prop each other up, but they are not the same thing. And so fighting one does not destroy the others.

It is the nature of this complex worldview, constructed of interlocking ideologies, that we cannot see through it clearly. And so we fear to pick at the fabric, fear to pull at the individual loose threads for fear of falling into some abyss. If we challenge any piece of the system, other pieces block our way. When we challenge technological ideology, people hear the sound of the baby being chucked out with the bathwater, fear and return of the angel of death hovering at every birth, fear unchecked fertility and untreatable infertility, women captured and held hostage to some mad biology. When we challenge ownership models of bodily integrity, we hear the enormous fear of someone else claiming ownership. So deep the ownership model lies that the only askable question seems to be: *whose* property? When we challenge patriarchal models of genetic-based parenthood, we hear the fears of women of privilege who have gained for themselves some of the privileges of patriarchy—often at the expense of other women, particularly women of color.

What if we genuinely valued that work that is motherhood? What if we valued intimacy and nurturance, and human relationships, not just as means toward some end, but in themselves? Would such a valuing privilege women as mothers—but simultaneously lock out nonmothering women and all men? I genuinely do not think so. Such a valuing would open up, and not close down, acts of nurturance and caring, free up, and not constrain, the gender boundaries of intimacy we now face. It would expand, and not restrict, the very definition of mothering.

Mothering is an activity, a project. Sara Ruddick has described "maternal thought," the intellectual work of mothering, the attitudes, the values—in essence, the *discipline* of mothering. That motherhood is a discipline does not mean that all who engage in it achieve its goals—not any more than all scientists live up to the demands of the discipline of science, or achieve its goals. But motherhood, Ruddick reminds us, is not just a physical or emotional relationship—it is *also* an intellectual activity. It is this unity of reflection, judgment, and emotion that she calls "maternal thinking."

Looking at motherhood this way, as a discipline, a way of thinking, a response to the needs and demands that exist outside of the mother, shifts our focus from who the mother is to what she is doing. Who she is, who she feels herself to be, is deeply gender based: she is a woman, a mother. What she is *doing* is not gender based: the similarities in behavior of mothers has more to do with the similarities in their situations, in the demands they face from their children and from their societies, than it has to do with the similarities in the women. And so the person engaged in this discipline of motherhood need not be a mother, need not be a woman, to engage in these activities, this way of thought and practice that is mothering.

The social relationship of parenting, of nurturing, and of caring needs a social base, not a genetic one. Through their pregnancies, women begin to establish that base. Through their relationships with women, and then with children, men too can establish that base. Pregnancy is one of the ways that we begin a social relationship with a child, but obviously not the only one.

If women are not to drop from exhaustion and lose all pleasure in life, someone is going to have to help with the kids. If women are sharing their lives, and sharing their children, with someone, then that is the obvious person to share the work of child care. For some it is a lesbian partner, for some it is one's own mother, and for many of us it is our husband. It is not by virtue of their paternity, their genetic ties to children, that men have an obligation to rear and to nurture them, but by virtue of their social relationship. If someone, man or woman, is going to be the life partner, the mate, of a woman who mothers, then that person must share the child care. And in turn it is by sharing the care and rearing of the children that the partner comes to have a place in the life of the child. We have to move beyond a paternity standard to a standard of nurturance.

Mothers also need men who can mother because we *ourselves* need that mothering—women are tired of mothering the whole world. Mothering, like everything else in life, is best learned by doing. Mothering women have taught many of us the skills of listening to what is said and to what is not said. In mothering we hone our empathic abilities, learn to understand the vulnerability in others without profiting from it. The experience of mothering teaches people how to be more emotionally and intellectually nurturant, how to take care of each other. It is not the only way we learn that lesson, but it is hard to mother and not learn it.

Mothering teaches us physical nurturance. Having nurtured the literally unself-conscious child, we are more competent, more confident providing other kinds of intimate, physical care. I remember my own awkwardness providing "nursing" care to my mother during an illness of hers in my adolescence. I compare that with the competence with which I can now, after mothering, provide such care. And I particularly remember my husband's awkwardness providing such care to me before our first child, and the skill and ease with which he does it now. Nursing me through my first labor, he was infinitely well-meaning. Nursing me through my second, he knew what he was doing. He had been nurturing for seven years of nursing earaches, bellyaches, changing diapers, calming night terrors, holding pans for vomit, taking out splinters, washing bloody wounds. He had grown accustomed to the sheer physicality of the body, the sights and sounds and smells. More essentially, what I showed him in my pain and my fear was not foreign—he saw the baby, the child in me, not the one I was birthing, but the one I myself am, and he nursed it. Now *that* is a man to enter old age with.

If men are not providing this kind of care, learning these skills, with their children, they're not going to be much help with their elderly fathers, or with their own sick wives. When women do all the mothering, it's not just the child care the men are being excused from—it's all of the intimate care women end up providing for children, for men, and for each other.

And finally, men should join women in mothering because it is the only way to avoid recreating the gender and class system and still live together. We can pool our resources, join together in infinite varieties of social arrangements to rear our children, but we must not recreate endlessly the separate worlds of power and of care. We must not do this in any of its guises: not as separate public and private worlds, not as separate worlds of men and of women. It is morally wrong to have children raised by one group for another group, whether it is Mrs. John Smith raising John Smith Jr. in her husband's image, slave nurses raising their masters, or hired caregivers raising the children of dual-career couples.

Caring people can and do raise whole and healthy children, and they do it across lines of gender, class, and race. It is not that the children are "subhuman," but that we ask them to turn away from humanity, away from care, and toward power. We do that whenever we separate the world into the kinds of people who take care of children and the kinds of people who rule the world.

In this I share a vision with Sara Ruddick. With her, I look forward to a day when:

> there will be no more "fathers," no more people of either sex who have power over their children's lives and moral authority in their children's world, though they do not do the work of attentive love. There will be mothers of both sexes who live out a transformed maternal thought in communities that share parental care—practically, emotionally, economically and socially. Such communities will have learned from their mothers how to value children's lives. (227)

And in so doing we will learn to value all of our lives-and that is still what I think the women's movement is about.

Notes

[1]For a fuller discussion of the changing economic value of children, see Zelizar.
[2]I want to express my appreciation to the Texas midwife who found it so hard to understand how babies could be valued and mothers not-reminding me again why I so deeply value midwives; and to the other Texas midwife in the audience who gave us the example of the South African diamond miners.

References

Bellah, Robert N., Richard Madsden, William M. Sullivan, Ann Swidler, and Steven M. Tipton. *Habits of the Heart: Individualism and Commitment in American Life*. Berkeley CA: University of California Press, 1985.

Meredith Gould, "Reproducing Gender: The Sociology of Constitutional Adjudication." Unpublished doctoral dissertation, New York University, 1980.

Jaggar, Alison M. *Feminist Politics and Human Nature*. Totowa NJ: Roman and Allenheld 1983.

Kitzinger, Sheila. *Women as Mothers: How They See Themselves in Different Cultures*. New York: Vintage Books, 1978.

Merchant, Carolyn. *The Death of Nature: Women, Ecology and the Scientific Revolu-*

tion. San Francisco: Harper and Row, 1980.

Petersen, Glenn. "Ponepean Matriliny: Production, Exchange and the Ties that Bind." *American Ethnologist* 9 (1) (1982): 129-144.

Robertson, John. "Embryos, Families and Procreative Liberty: The Legal Structure of the New Reproduction." *Southern California Law Review* 59 (5) (July 1986): 939-1041.

Ruddick, Sara, "Maternal Thinking." *Mothering: Essays in Feminist Theory*. Ed. Joyce Treblicot. Totowa NJ: Rowman and Allenheld, 1983. 213-230.

Smith, Janet Farrell. "Parenting and Property." *Mothering: Essays in Feminist Theory*. Ed. Joyce Treblicot. Totowa NJ: Rowman and Allenheld, 1983. 199-212.

Whitbeck, Caroline. "Theories of Sex Difference." *The Philosophical Forum* 5 (1) (Fall 1973): 54-80.

Zelizar, Viviana A. *Pricing the Priceless Child*. New York: Basic Books, 1985.

Chapter 25

Why Can't a Mother Be More Like a Businessman?

SHARON HAYS

The Trouble With Rachel

RACHEL IS A SUCCESSFUL professional woman with a demanding, well-paying job, a marriage she considers egalitarian, and a two-year-old daughter.[1] She told me the following story with measured rage. When her daughter was so ill as to be hospitalized, Rachel felt compelled to stay at her bedside "every second." The child's life was not in danger, Rachel explained, but she needed her mother's love and reassurance. Rachel's boss, on the other hand, needed Rachel for an important assignment and simply could not understand why Rachel had to be at the hospital all the time. Although Rachel's boss is a woman and therefore, Rachel implied, should have been sensitive to this situation, she is also a childless woman. Lacking empathy for Rachel's position, her boss was, as Rachel put it, "resentful and angry." Still Rachel refused to leave the hospital room. Her daughter was sick; she needed her mother—no one else would do.

It is clear to Rachel that her child is far more important than any work assignment, and she believes that everyone *should* understand that. People like her boss are simply ignorant and selfish, she tells me: "They have no conception at all of what it means to raise children; they just don't understand." To Rachel, the point of view of her boss is wholly unreasonable; the requirements of appropriate child rearing are self-evident, sacred, and untouchable.

But her boss's point of view might also be described as a sensible and rational one. Didn't Rachel understand that this assignment had to be completed right away? Couldn't Rachel's husband, sister, or mother stay with the child? Surely there were nurses as well. Or, even more cynically, this workplace manager might have inquired, "Is the child worth the cost?" Given that the child is neither a productive family member nor one bringing money into the household, from a certain point of view it would appear unclear what Rachel had to gain by maintaining her bedside vigil. Weren't the returns on Rachel's job much more tangible? And didn't she risk losing the next possible promotion by failing to follow through on her professional responsibilities? Certainly any self-respecting businessman would know better than to spend so much of *his* time comforting a sick child.

Rachel's unsympathetic portrait of her boss, and my cynical extension of it, may or may not be accurate, but the self-interested, calculating, cold-hearted behavior attributed to her is not that far-fetched. Though her attitude may seem strange with reference to children and family life, in the larger world her attitude does not seem strange at all: not only does it correspond to a scholarly portrait of a "rational actor," it also matches a commonly held view of human behavior in general.[2] According to this widely shared logic, any rational individual would seek to maximize her own interests (particularly her interests in material gain) without regard to the interests of others. Rachel's boss, then, would naturally attempt to manage her employees in the most efficient and profitable manner, since her own salary and career advancement depend upon it. And since Rachel is also dearly committed to pursuing a career, she does seem to be acting irrationally by devoting herself to her child at the expense of her paid work. From a hard-nosed outsider's point of view, Rachel appears morally and emotionally over-invested in her daughter and, without major changes, it seems that she will be facing the "mommy-track," her career permanently sidetracked by her commitment to mothering (Schwartz). Given the higher status and greater material gain associated with career success, why does she choose to dedicate herself to a notion of appropriate child rearing that seems to put the child's needs above her own?

The contradiction Rachel faces between her commitment to her work and her commitment to her child is not just an individual problem; it is part of a larger cultural contradiction. In C. Wright Mills's terms, what Rachel experiences as the "personal troubles of milieu" are in fact closely connected to the "public issues of social structure" (8). Rachel experiences these troubles, in part, because she is one of many mothers now in the paid labor force who must meet the dual demands of paid work and child care. More important, Rachel experiences these troubles because she shares with others a particular *perception* of those demands, one that is linked to contradictory cultural images of mothers who selflessly nurture their children and businessmen who selfishly compete in the paid labor force. To put it another way, Rachel's understanding of the logic of child rearing is connected to the cultural conception of women's private sphere in the home, and her boss's understanding of the logic of paid work is connected to the cultural conception of men's public sphere in the larger world. As an individual, Rachel is pulled between these two spheres.

The cultural contradiction between home and world has a long history, while the personal contradiction Rachel confronts as a mother and a career woman is a relatively recent historical phenomenon. Over the past two hundred years, Western society has been juggling the contradictory logics of appropriate behavior at home and appropriate behavior in the outside world. This tension, however, has been partially managed by attempts to maintain a clear ideological and practical separation between life at home and life in the outside world, with women responsible for one sphere and men responsible for the other.[3] In accordance with this, the public ideology of appropriate child rearing has urged mothers to stay at home with their children, thereby ostensibly maintaining consistency in women's nurturing and selfless behavior. But in reality the wall between home and world has always been structurally unstable and insufficiently high, and over the past fifty years the integrity of its construction has been increasingly threatened by the ever-greater number of women who have climbed over it to participate in the paid labor force.

The paradoxical nature of the situation this creates comes out most clearly against the contrast of the 1950s, the era of suburban life, domestic bliss, the "feminine mystique," Dr. Spock, and "momism." At a time when there were far fewer mothers of young children in the paid labor force than there are now, and when more American families than ever before were able to realize the middle-class family ideal, mothers' intense emotional attachment and moral commitment to their children seemed less contradictory. Today, however, when well over half of all mothers are in the paid labor force, when the image of a career woman is that of a competitive go-getter, and when the image of the family is one of disintegrating values and relationships, one would expect a de-emphasis on the ideology of child rearing as labor-intensive, emotionally absorbing women's work.

Since 1950, the number of employed women with young children has more than quadrupled: 58 percent of mothers with children under six years of age worked in the paid labor force in 1993 as compared to 12 percent in 1950.[4] While no social consensus has been reached regarding the desirability of women with young children working outside the home, there has been a general acceptance of this trend (Greenberger and O'Neil; Weiner). In this social context, white, middle-class women in particular have become more and more committed to pursuing careers.[5] Many of these women are entering the paid labor force not just reluctantly, or out of necessity, but because they *want* to. And when they choose a career over a job, they make a long-term commitment to a path that does not allow them to come and go at will but instead requires ongoing dedication to life in the world outside the home.

Under these conditions one might expect that women would fully assimilate the logic of the marketplace, that the barrier between home and world would completely crumble, and that the rational calculation of self-interest would lead all of us to perceive child rearing as a fairly simple task. Yet the commitment to emotionally demanding, financially draining, labor-consuming child rearing seems to be thriving. Like many other women faced with this burdensome contradiction, Rachel does not choose to give up one commitment for the other; she juggles both. For Rachel, appropriate childrearing is not an ideology but a given, a matter of what is natural and necessary—there is simply no question of ignoring the child's multifaceted needs.

However, this form of mothering is neither self-evidently natural nor, in any absolute sense, necessary; it is a social construction. Child-rearing ideologies vary widely, both historically and cross-culturally. In other times and places, simpler, less time- and energy-consuming methods have been considered appropriate, and the child's mother has not always and everywhere been the primary caregiver. The idea that correct child rearing requires not only large quantities of money but also professional-level skills and copious amounts of physical, moral, mental, and emotional energy on the part of the individual mother is a relatively recent historical phenomenon. Why, then, does Rachel persist in her commitment to intensive mothering?

Arlie Hochschild provides another version of this question in her book on two-career families, *The Second Shift*. She asks: Why has the cultural revolution that matches women's economic revolution stalled? When rapid industrialization took men out of the home and placed them in the factory, shop, or office, a corresponding ideological revolution encouraged women (middle-class white women, especially) to *want* to tend the home and care for the children. Hochschild argues that we now need a new ideological revolution encouraging men to want to cook, clean, and nurture children, and encouraging employers and the state to want to provide for child care, job sharing, and parental leave.

But what Hochschild suggests—that we shift the focus from intensive mothering to intensive *parenting*—is only a partial solution to the contradiction between the demands of home and work, and one that does not begin to address the larger cultural contradictions. If men and women shared the burden that Rachel now bears primarily, the larger social paradox would continue to haunt both of them and would grow even stronger for men. Given the power of the ideology of the marketplace, a more logical (and cynical) solution would be an ideological revolution that makes tending home and children a purely commercial, rationalized enterprise, one in which neither mother nor father need be highly involved. Why don't we convince ourselves that children need neither a quantity of time nor "quality time" with their mothers *or* their fathers?

After all, from a cold and calculating point of view, the ideology of intensive mothering seems to contradict the interests of almost everyone. Paid working women[6] might like to avoid the extra work on the "second shift," stay-at-home mothers might enjoy a bit more free time, capitalists surely want all of their paid laborers' energy and attention, and husbands might prefer the career promotions of a woman who dedicates herself to bringing home the bacon. Such propositions are not so outlandish when we think about how powerful utility-maximizing assumptions are in modern society. If I were a Martian who had just landed in the United States, I might notice that the primary activity of the society seemed to be the instrumentally rational pursuit of self-interested material gain in a situation of limited resources. Most of the humans appear to be engaged in attempts to buy low and sell high, calculating the best possible gain and systematically pursuing it in the most efficient manner, individualistically competing with others for available resources all the while. Nurturing, moral mothers, constantly attentive to the needs and desires of another who has little tangible to offer them in return, seem quite out of place.

Of course human infants require a certain amount of physical care. Cultures around the globe and throughout time seem to have taken into account that children are not prepared to enter the adult world until at least age six or seven (Rogoff *et al.* 6; Weisner and Gallimore). But modern American mothers do much more than simply feed, change, and shelter the child until age six. It is that "more" with which I am here concerned.

Why do many professional-class employed women seem to find it necessary to take the kids to swimming and judo and dancing and tumbling classes, not to mention orthodontists and psychiatrists and attention-deficit specialists? Why is the human bonding that accompanies breast-feeding considered so important that elaborate contraptions are now manufactured to allow children to suckle on mothers who cannot produce milk? Why are there aerobics courses for babies, training sessions in infant massage, sibling-preparedness workshops, and designer fashions for two-year-olds? Why must a "good" mother be careful to "negotiate" with her child, refraining from demands for obedience to an absolute set of rules? Why must she avoid spanking a disobedient child and instead feel the need to explain, in detail, the issues at hand? Why does she consider it important to be consciously and constantly attentive to the child's wishes? Why does she find it necessary to apologize to the child if she somehow deviates from the code of appropriate mothering? Why is it important to have all possible information on the latest child-rearing techniques? Why must she assure herself that prospective child-care providers are well-versed in psychological and cognitive development? Surely all these activities consume massive amounts of time and energy. Why would a woman who has the opportunity to gain so much more from focusing on her professional responsibilities choose to believe in the need for these intensive methods?

Intensive Mothering

Rachel is, without a doubt, a dedicated mother. Although she considers herself a feminist and has a fine, well-paying career with much room for advancement, a career that would be understood as meaningful and enriching by any standard, and one that consistently demands a good deal of her time and intellectual energy, she remains committed to what I call intensive mothering. She has juggled her schedule and cut back her hours so she can spend the maximum amount of time with her daughter, Kristin. And Rachel is very careful to choose the correct "alternate mothers" to care for Kristin while she is at work. Kristin now attends a preschool three mornings a week where cognitive and physical development is stressed but not, Rachel explains, at the expense of playtime. For the remaining hours that Rachel is at work, Kristin is cared for at home by highly qualified, credentialed, female childcare providers.

Rachel is active in La Leche League and for twelve months breast-fed Kristin on demand (against the advice of her pediatrician and friends). She also participates in a mothers' play group, made up of professional-class women who first met at an exercise class in which mothers and their babies jointly worked to strengthen their physiques. These women now collectively take their same-aged children on regular outings.

Rachel reads to Kristin daily. She takes her to ballet class and swimming lessons weekly. Every Thursday (the one weekday that Rachel is not working for pay) is designated "Kristin's day": Rachel works until midnight once a week in order to make this special day possible. And this day is just for Kristin: all activities are centered around Kristin and Kristin's desires.

Rachel's self-conscious commitment to intensive child rearing also appears in her belief that there is no such thing as a bad child: "If you love your child, your child is good. If a child acts badly, it's probably the parents who are to blame." It is crucial to avoid corruption of the child's goodness and the child's innocence, and parental love is the primary ingredient for the maintenance of these virtues. Appropriate parental love, Rachel reminds me repeatedly, includes the conviction that a mother should be, as Rachel is, ready to "kill and die" for her child.

Rachel has "smacked" Kristin only once. It was a particularly bad day, she explains, and Kristin was terribly fussy and demanding. Rachel hit her "once on the butt" when her behavior became too much to bear. However, she emphasizes, "I know I didn't hit her hard because I was *so* in control." Control is important to Rachel since every action of mothering is understood to have potentially damaging consequences. And Rachel is clearly sorry she hit her child. The incident required numerous subsequent discussions with the two-year-old: "We talked about it a lot afterwards," she continues, "you know, how mommy lost it, she was stressed. And I've never done it since."[7]

Rachel tells me that her husband is just as concerned with Kristin's happiness and development as she is. They regularly discuss the stages Kristin is going through, he reads and plays with Kristin frequently, and, in Rachel's account, he shares equally in housekeeping and child-rearing tasks. He is, Rachel says, "protective and possessive" of Kristin. But the person Rachel most often talks to about child rearing is a female friend, and it is Rachel, not her husband, who takes Kristin to her lessons, chooses her caregivers, participates in the play group, and cuts back on her paid work hours to make time for "Kristin's day." Further, Rachel stresses that, "the money from my salary goes to vacations and things for the house and Kristin's education and that sort of stuff." In Rachel's rendition, then, a mother's salary (not a father's) pays for the enhancement of family life and the requirements of socially appropriate child rearing.

Rachel's love for her home and her child is so powerful that it frequently spills over into her paid working life. At the office, she tells me, "our desks are shrines to our children and our marriages." Nonetheless, Rachel strives to retain a clear sense of the distinction between home and work: "I try to separate the two as much as I can. They're two different worlds." She continues: "My home is my private life, my child, my soul-mate. My nurturing side is there." Life on the job is public, cold, and uncaring; one needs to bring pictures and mementos from home as reminders of the warm and nurturing private side of life.

Does Rachel consider her child more important than her career? Absolutely.

> I think human beings all have the desire just to bring another human being into the world, and raise another human being that's ours. To see

a part of ourselves live on.... I think that we all have that desire. Most of us do. And that desire is more enriching [than a career] for most people, to share our lives with another human being.

Rachel's ideas of appropriate child rearing can be understood as a combination of three elements—all of them interfering with her commitment to her job, and all of them in contradiction to the ideology of the workplace and the dominant ethos of modern society.

First, in Rachel's image of appropriate child rearing it is critical that she, as the *mother*, be the central caregiver. It is Rachel who must be at her child's bedside throughout the hospital stay; her husband is not even mentioned in this context. It is Rachel who must make room for Kristin's day. And it is Rachel who is ultimately responsible for Kristin's development. Men, apparently, cannot be relied upon to provide the same level of care. There is an underlying assumption that the child absolutely requires consistent nurture by a single primary caretaker and that the mother is the best person for the job. When the mother is unavailable, it is other women who should serve as temporary substitutes.

Second, the logic that applies to appropriate child rearing, for Rachel, includes lavishing copious amounts of time, energy, and material resources on the child. A mother must put her child's needs above her own. A mother must recognize and conscientiously respond to all the child's needs and desires, and to every stage of the child's emotional and intellectual development. This means that a mother must acquire detailed knowledge of what the experts consider proper child development, and then spend a good deal of time and money attempting to foster it. Rachel understands that this is an emotionally taxing job as well, since the essential foundation for proper child development is love and affection. In sum, the methods of appropriate child rearing are construed as *child-centered, expert-guided, emotionally absorbing, labor-intensive,* and *financially expensive.*

Finally, Rachel believes that a comparison of her paid work and her childrearing activities is ludicrous. Not only is the child clearly more important, but a completely different logic applies to child rearing than to paid work. While Rachel's daughter may be a net financial drain, she is emotionally and morally outside the scope of market valuation: she is, in Zelizer's phrase, a "priceless child." Innocent and pure, children have a special value; they therefore deserve special treatment.

It is this fully elaborated, logically cohesive combination of beliefs that I call the ideology of intensive mothering. Although Rachel is a unique individual and her status as a white, middle-class career woman places her in a particular social category, I will show that this constellation of beliefs is held in common by many American mothers today. These ideas are certainly not followed in practice by every mother, but they are, implicitly or explicitly, understood as the *proper* approach to the raising of a child by the majority of mothers. In other words, the ideology of intensive mothering is, I maintain, the dominant ideology of socially appropriate child rearing in the contemporary United States.

The Cultural Contradictions

From the point of view of Rachel's boss and any self-respecting businessman—that is, from the point of view of self-interested, profit-maximizing utility—women's commitment to intensive mothering seems mysterious. While some might argue that the competitive, self-interested, efficiency-minded, and materialistically-oriented logic of Rachel's boss is likewise mysterious to Rachel and other mothers, the fact is that the two ideologies do not hold equal status in today's society. For instance, many Americans would assume that it is human nature to be self-interested; almost none would claim that it is human nature to give priority to the needs and desires of others. The logic of Rachel's boss is thus far more powerful, and Rachel and other mothers are fully aware of this. On the other hand, some might argue that the two logics are benignly complementary when they are clearly separated and functioning smoothly in distinct contexts. In these terms, Rachel's emphasis on intensive child rearing makes sense in the context of her life at home or the context of a hospital room where her sick daughter lies, whereas her boss's logic makes sense in the context of a busy office and an important work assignment that is not yet completed. But this analysis neglects the unequal status of the two logics, ignores the fact that these logics cannot always be neatly compartmentalized and, most crucially, implicitly denies the fact that these are *opposing* logics.[8] In fact, Rachel and other paid working mothers are faced with the power of both logics simultaneously and are forced to make choices between them. In today's society, then, the strength and persistence of the ideology of intensive mothering seems mysterious for two related reasons—the first from the standpoint of paid working mothers, the second in terms of certain important trends in society as a whole.

Practically speaking, mothers who work in the paid labor force seem to be acting irrationally when they dedicate so much time and energy to child rearing, because this strategy is physically and emotionally draining—wearing them down with added demands on the second shift. At the same time, they face the contradiction of engaging in the self-interested pursuit of financial gain at work while simultaneously pumping vast resources into the appropriate rearing of their children. Many women find their take-home pay nearly wiped out by the costs of day care; others, like Rachel, regard their salaries as the means of ensuring their children's education and happiness. In those societies where children offer some return on this investment—serving, for instance, as the providers of social security in their parents' old age—this outlay of time, energy, and capital might make more sense. But in this society most children are, in fact, a net financial loss (Huber and Spitze).

Furthermore, an employed woman faces the possibility of losing out on job promotions, endangering her current position, and decreasing her material returns because of all those days spent at home comforting sick children, all those hours spent arranging for daycare, dental appointments, birthday parties, shopping for new shoes and toys, and all those mornings when she arrives with less than her whole "body and soul" to dedicate to the job. Additionally, there is the strain of maintaining the two roles that these women experience as they attempt to be cool-headed and competitive at work but warm-hearted and nurturing at home. Finally, for those women with careers (rather than simply jobs), we know that professional success offers far more status in American society than success as a mother. Why pursue the latter at the expense of the former?

These practical contradictions faced by individual mothers are all related to a larger contradiction in society as a whole. The strength of the ideology of intensive, nurturing, moral motherhood is in tension with what many have identified as the central trends in modern Western culture. The classical sociological literature portrays our society as one that values the efficient, impersonal, competitive pursuit of self-interested gain above all else. For Max Weber, the impersonality and efficiency of the modern West are constituted by the rationalization of social life. For Marx and Engels, the competitive pursuit of private gain is the result of the extension and intensification of capitalist market relations. And for Ferdinand Tonnies, both impersonal and competitive relations are a part of the larger historical shift from the gemeinschaft system of beliefs and relationships, grounded in custom, tradition, and particularistic ties of mutual obligation and commitment, to the gesellschaft system, grounded in commodification, bureaucratization, and impersonal ties of competitive exchange and contract.[9]

These classical social theorists believed that the ethos of rationalized market society would eventually penetrate every sphere of social life.[10] But for a long time it seemed that some spheres remained immune. Throughout the nineteenth and much of the twentieth century, the family, in particular, seemed to be organized around a different set of ideas and practices. Of late, however, a number of prominent scholars have argued that *all* spheres of life, including the family (and, by implication, the mothering that goes on within it), are now penetrated by the utilitarian pursuit of personal profit that has long dominated the larger society.

For Heilbroner, this invasion of rationalized market relations takes the form of the "implosion of capitalism," as the norms and practices of the capitalist marketplace find their way into areas of life where they had not been before. For Bellah *et al.*, this invasion is evident in the growing prominence of the language of "utilitarian individualism," as all of social life is increasingly perceived and discussed as if it were merely a collection of individuals who calculate the most efficient means of maximizing their power and material advantage. Polanyi would concur, emphasizing the historically unprecedented nature of societies such as ours where "the motive of gain becomes a justification for action and behavior in everyday life" (30). And Sahlins echoes these analyses in his treatment of the ubiquitous nature of the ideology of "practical reason" in Western capitalist societies: when the market economy becomes the primary producer of cultural logic, he argues, all human behavior, in all spheres of life, comes to be pictured as that of *homo economicus*.

Many feminists seem to agree, as they portray the contemporary family as one in which members calculate the efficiency of various family strategies and compete among themselves for power and material resources (e.g., Allen; Bentson; Blumberg; Gordon; Hartmann 1981a, 1981b; Peterson; Polatnick; Rapp. Ross and Bridenthal). At the same time, other scholars emphasize the participation of the modern centralized state in this invasion: the bureaucratically organized, impersonal state, they say, continues to usurp and control more and more aspects of what were once private family matters (e.g., Bane; Donzelot; Foucault; Lasch; Rothman). What all these analyses have in common is a vision of self-interested individuals struggling for power and profit, in the family as elsewhere.

In concrete terms, this means that the family is invaded not only by public schools, the courts, social service workers, gardeners, housekeepers, day-care providers, lawyers, doctors, televisions, frozen dinners, pizza delivery, manufactured clothing, and disposable diapers, but also, and more critically, by the *ideology* behind such institutions, persons, and products. They bring with them, in whole or in part, the language and logic of impersonal, competitive, contractual, commodified, efficient, profit-maximizing, self-interested relations. Family members, theoretically, are not the least bit immune to this ideology—in their homes, as everywhere else, they are, more and more, simply looking out for themselves.[11] Women's "abandonment" of the home to seek more lucrative employment might alternately be interpreted as a result or a cause of this invasion.

Given the invasive logic of the larger society, one would expect mothers to consistently act like good capitalists or bureaucrats, consciously calculating the most efficient means of raising children—that which would offer them the highest personal returns based on the least amount of effort. This, after all, would not only make their lives easier but should, theoretically, constitute the most socially valued and socially appropriate method.

In determining the most efficient and least costly means of raising children, it would appear that mothers have a wealth of alternative ideologies to choose from. Western history and the practices of other cultures provide examples of child-rearing methods that are far less demanding than Rachel's, and just as well accomplished by a variety of persons other than parents.[12] Furthermore, there are contemporary ideas that might serve the needs of employed mothers and society as well. As Rachel's boss might suggest, more independence for the child could help to develop her character, and more weekly chores rather than ballet lessons might better prepare her for adulthood.[13] The examples modern mothers offer of "bad" parents are also indicative of the forms that simpler parenting might take. There are women, mothers told me in dismay, who leave their kids in day care from six in the morning until seven at night and hire someone else to pick them up at the end of the day. There are people who think children should be seen and not heard. Even worse, there are parents who regularly (and carelessly) spank their children when they are disobedient. There are parents who wear earplugs through the night to avoid being disturbed by their young babies. And I was told the story of a mother who, faced with a fussy child suffering from colic, first strapped him into a car seat and then placed him in a closet. These are surely efficient methods of dealing with children, so why do many mothers consider them not only socially inappropriate but downright evil and unconscionable?

The ideology and practices of appropriate child rearing are socially constructed. Logically speaking, shouldn't the present ideal of intensive mothering be reconstructed to fall more reasonably in line with the needs of paid working mothers and the ideology and practices of society as a whole? In the case of child rearing, at least, the implosion of capitalism and the invasion of gesellschaft relations are apparently incomplete.

Cynical Questions

For Rachel and many other mothers I have talked to, questioning the logic of intensive mothering is the cynical response of selfish, ignorant, and insensitive persons. Women who stay at home with their children rather than work for pay might attribute this response to those professional working men and women who disdainfully inquire, "You're *just* a housewife? How do you fill your time?" Rachel and other employed mothers might recognize it as the response of certain types of men and childless career women who ask, "Why do you *bother* so much about your kids when there's more important work to be done?" But for many mothers, children are clearly more important. They deserve and require far more than minimal physical care.

As a sociologist, I here join the selfish, ignorant, and insensitive. Cynical questions are crucial to cultural sociology. That is, it is important for sociologists to critically examine aspects of the culture of everyday life that are so sacred, so deeply held, so taken for granted as to remain generally unquestioned and regularly treated as common sense. Such ideas and practices often point to something crucial in social life. Notions of appropriate mothering fall into this category.

To make problematic that which is sacred is to understand it as neither natural nor given but as a socially constructed reality.[14] Understanding the socially constructed nature of ideas and practices must begin with the recognition that there are alternative ideologies available, no matter how much these may grate against our deepest sense of what is right and natural. To say that ideas and practices are social constructs does not mean, however, that they are therefore either infinitely malleable or somehow unworthy. Neither the ideology represented by Rachel nor that represented by her boss is more or less "correct" in any absolute sense, nor is either of these ideologies superficial and transitory. The point is that neither is natural, inevitable, or *inherently* more rational, worthy, or valuable. Further exploration is necessary to understand why these ideas rather than others have come to be socially chosen and socially valued. With reference to naturalized ideas like the ideology of intensive mothering, an exploration of their social roots becomes all the more necessary, precisely because its social grounding is so deeply hidden.[15]

There may be many interesting arguments regarding the natural or biological bases of intensive mothering, arguments that trace, for instance, a mother's commitment to her child to the fact that she produces estrogen and milk.[16] But there are layers upon layers of socially constructed elaboration and reinforcement of this "natural" base. Although women do get pregnant and lactate, and may even experience some animal-like instinct to protect and feed and thereby preserve their offspring, this makes up a only a minuscule portion of what is understood as socially appropriate mothering. Mothers all over the world get pregnant and produce estrogen and milk, yet ideas of appropriate child rearing vary widely. It is the socially constructed *meaning* of pregnancy and lactation that is important; it is the ideas and practices attached to childbirth and child rearing that constitute the culture of socially appropriate mothering.

Many American mothers (and fathers) would argue that their child-rearing ideas and practices flow from the love they "naturally" feel for their children. And it is true that one can find fairly consistent evidence that parents have always and everywhere experienced a strong emotional response to their young. But that emotional response has not always and everywhere been understood as "love," and it has led to widely varied practices in the history of American society and in cultures around the globe. The ideology of intensive mothering is a very specific and highly elaborate set of ideas that goes well beyond any simple emotional response to children. The beliefs and practices that follow from a mother's feelings toward her child, in other words, are no more natural or inevitable than those that follow from a mother's lactation.

The same logic can be applied to notions of the "natural" requirements of children. There seems to be no question that children need not only physical sustenance but also some level of emotional and cognitive nourishment in order to thrive. Studies have made clear, however, that the requirements of children do not "naturally" lead parents to approach child rearing in any particular way (e.g., Kagan; Mead; Rogoff *et al.*; Scheper-Hughes 1987, 1992). And, beyond these minimal requirements, the methods of child rearing that will *best* serve the needs of children are also ambiguous. Although some would argue that current methods of child rearing are the right methods or the most effective methods for preparing children for contemporary society, others would disagree. Given this, I will simply bracket claims to the correctness of the methods proposed by the ideology of intensive mothering and focus my attention on understanding why they are considered correct (and natural) by so many.

Deeply entrenched as it is, the ideology of intensive mothering that Rachel represents, just like the ideology of the marketplace that her boss represents, has not gone wholly unquestioned. As Berger points out, once cultural ideals that have been taken for granted are contested, they become ideologies. Such ideologies then become matters of public debate, each side attempting to make a claim to truth and righteousness. Their status as "common sense" is lost. The arguments of Rachel and her boss, however, are almost never deployed explicitly and systematically. Rarely is self-seeking completely championed; rarely is nurturing motherhood completely debunked; and just as rarely is it suggested that the whole of society would operate more effectively if it followed the logic of Rachel's child rearing. Rather, the argument between Rachel and her boss tends to take the form of debates over the participation of women in the labor force, the fate of "family values," the proper responsibilities of fathers, and the effects of day care. It seems that few would dare to question intensive child rearing in a straightforward manner, just as few would absolutely oppose the logic of efficiency and self-interest. Nonetheless, ambivalence and tension are apparent, and the cultural ideal of appropriate mothering is potentially called into question. It is therefore no longer a cultural given, it is instead an ideology.

To examine such an ideology within the tradition of the sociology of knowledge means to critically analyze its context, carriers, and content. What are the social contexts in which these ideas arise and persist? If ideologies are the result of a historical conversation in which each generation shares ideas and argues with members of future, former, and present generations, then it makes sense to examine the similarities and differences in the worlds in which those generations reside—in terms of both the framework of relations between groups and the ideas and practices that are accepted as appropriate.[18] Who, exactly, are the primary proponents of these ideas, and what is their position in the social hierarchy? Since some people will likely be more attached to certain ideas than other people will, information on the gender, class, race, education, religion, and other social characteristics of the carriers of ideas allows us to speculate on why these particular persons might find these particular ideas attractive and important. Finally, it is crucial to examine the content of the ideology: its logic, its component parts, and the meaning it holds for its carriers. Ideologies, in other words, must also be taken seriously on their own terms.

The purpose of such an analysis, then, is not to debunk ideologies as "mere" strategies used by their carriers in struggles for material and status advantage, nor to dismiss them as "mere" reflections of some absolute set of structural requirements in a given context. Rather, the point is to fully explore the content and logic of such ideologies, to place them in their context, and to locate their carriers as a method of understanding why certain ideas come to achieve salience over others, in certain contexts, among certain groups of people.[19] In these terms, while neither the ideology of Rachel nor that of her boss can be taken at face value, it would be equally inappropriate to see either as simply "mistakes" in need of correction; the logic of both sets of ideas speaks to crucial aspects of social life.

Rachel's Story and Beyond

Perhaps the context of social change caused by the entrance of large numbers of middle-class mothers into the paid labor force and the invasion of the family by the ideas and practices of impersonal, competitive, self-interested gain has created a space in which the cultural ideal of motherhood becomes a debatable ideology. As a carrier, Rachel might be understood as attempting to deny the social tension, while her boss may be attempting to define a new road ahead. Both tend to use their ideas as weapons—Rachel claims her boss is ignorant and insensitive, her boss views Rachel as simply irrational. Sociologically speaking, both are equally naive: Rachel assumes her ideas speak to the "natural" propensities of mothers and requirements of children; her boss assumes that an instrumentally rational approach should "naturally" take precedence. Rachel appears sentimental; her boss appears blindly selfish. Yet both Rachel and her boss continue to cling to the content of their contradictory ideologies, treating them not only as a means of legitimating what they actually do but also as important guides for what they *should* do.

Rachel emphasizes nurturing qualities and a sense of personal obligation to others. Her boss emphasizes utilitarian concerns and a calculating cost-benefit analysis of individual advantage. Rachel's story exemplifies the sacred status of motherhood. Her boss's response represents the potential breakdown of that status. Both arguments are historically constructed ideologies that include a whole set of assumptions about human nature and the appropriate framework for social life. That the two contradictory ideologies coexist in contemporary society highlights the tensions that have developed between the demands of work life and the demands of family life, between the historically constructed images of warm, nurturing mothers on the one side and cold, competitive career women on the other, between the call for a revival of "family values" and the call for greater workplace efficiency, and between the impersonal pursuit of self-interested gain in the context of a competitive market system and the empathic pursuit of nurturing personal relations in the context of a system of mutual obligations and commitments. These two ideologies are expressions of what are, arguably, the two central cultural frameworks in contemporary Western society. And the opposition between these two ideologies highlights not only the paradoxical nature of contemporary ideas about child rearing and motherhood but also a central recurring tension in society as a whole.

It is these tensions that I intend to explore by analyzing the historical context of changes in ideas about child rearing and the family, the different carriers of child-rearing ideologies, both past and present, and the content of the ideology of appropriate mothering as it is represented in popular child-rearing manuals and as it is expressed by mothers themselves.

Although I feel very close and much indebted to a number of modern-day mothers, through much of *The Cultural Contradictions of Motherhood* I take a distanced and apparently cold-hearted stance toward the ideology of socially appropriate child rearing that many of them hold dear. But I do so only because this is the best way I know to pry the ideology loose from its naturalized and sentimentalized moorings. It is not my intention to degrade or dismiss current notions of appropriate child rearing, to imply that mothers are somehow suffering from "false consciousness," or to suggest that we should (or could) simply dispense with the ideology of intensive mothering as if it were a bad joke. I am convinced that ideas of appropriate child rearing follow from sincerely felt responses, that they are rational and reasonable in this social context, and that they are an indication of deeply entrenched and deeply experienced, socially generated needs, interests, and concerns. At the same time, however, I want to avoid the unreflective valorization of intensive motherhood. The purpose of this book, in other words, is not to endorse or attack current methods of child rearing but to uncover the logic of the ideology of intensive mothering, clarify its historical emergence, demonstrate its persistence, and speculate on the reasons it remains so powerful.

There are a number of potential explanations for the power and persistence of the ideology of intensive mothering. Many have argued that modern ideas of appropriate child rearing are the result of progress in knowledge regarding children's needs that follows from natural parental love. Others claim that present-day paid working mothers are increasingly calculating their self-interest and setting aside notions of intensive child rearing as they focus their attention on career advancement. Still others emphasize the ways in which unequal power in society accounts for what contemporary mothers say and do.

Each of these arguments provides important clues. But, taken alone, they are insufficient for making sense of the complex reality that underlies the ideology of intensive mothering. Certainly, there is no question that women love their children and that there is, in fact, more information available on children and child rearing than there once was. But the specific ideas and practices that follow from this love and information are neither self-evident nor based in nature; they are a socially constructed reality. And there is no question that mothers are engaged in what may be perceived as self-interested utilitarian attempts to retain or achieve middle-class status for their children and themselves, to cast their position either as participants in the paid workforce or as stay-at-home mothers in a favorable light relative to their counterparts, and to organize their lives in manageable and efficient ways. But there is little indication that most mothers are choosing to ignore their children when more lucrative options present themselves. Further, there is no question that women's relative lack of power largely explains their role as the primary caregivers for children. It accounts for the fact that stay-at-home mothers are burdened with a socially devalued and potentially isolating position at home, while employed women are saddled with a "second shift" of domestic chores and child-rearing duties and are hindered in their attempts at career advancement. These forms of subordinating women ultimately benefit not only men but also capitalism and the modern state. Nonetheless, there is something more in what these women do and say.

While the contemporary ideal of intensive mothering involves the subordination of women, it also involves their *opposition* to the logic that subordinates them. As I will show, the historical construction of intensive mothering demonstrates that its early blooming was directly connected to the ideological separation of public and private spheres, a separation according to which the values of intimate and family life stood as an explicit rejection of the values of economic and political life. The arguments of best-selling contemporary childrearing advisers and, more importantly, the words of present-day mothers make it clear that this remains a powerful and deeply evocative distinction. The relationship between mother and child continues to symbolize, realistically or not, opposition to social relations based on the competitive pursuit of individual gain in a system of impersonal contractual relations. In pursuing a moral concern to establish lasting human connection grounded in unremunerated obligations and commitments, modern-day mothers, to varying degrees, participate in this implicit rejection of the ethos of rationalized market society.

The argument between Rachel and her boss, then, is symptomatic of a larger struggle in modern society. Although this struggle was not initiated by present-day mothers, they have become some of the primary persons who must cope with the problems it engenders. Given its deeply rooted nature, it is also certain that this conflict will not be won or lost in battles waged by individual mothers. In the final analysis, the argument between Rachel and her boss is indicative of a fundamental and irreducible ambivalence about a society based solely on the competitive pursuit of self-interest. Motherhood, I argue, is one of the central terrains on which this ambivalence is played out.

Notes

[1] This story is from one of 38 in-depth interviews I conducted with mothers of two- to four-year-old children. For a discussion of my methodology, see the preface of *The Cultural Contradictions of Motherhood*.

[2] The "rational actor" model implies a curious but nonetheless prevalent definition of rationality. Superficially, the logic operates this way: all individuals behave in such a way as to maximize their self-interests in a system of scarce resources. This means that they will systematically calculate their "comparative advantage" and choose the path that offers the greatest rewards at the lowest expense. The logical implication is that a rational person will treat other people in a purely instrumental fashion—as mere resources or obstacles in the universal struggle to maximize personal gain. If individuals don't act this way, it is implied, they are simply stupid or irrational. See Elster on the importance of rational action in social life; Becker for an analysis of the family using the logic of rational action; Coleman for a treatment of child rearing that employs the rational actor model; Folbre and Hartmann, Mansbridge, and Risman and Feree for various relevant responses to the use of this model.

[3] Although the ideological separation of home and world was powerful throughout this period, the practical separation of these two spheres has always been difficult (if not impossible) to achieve for poor and working-class women who have long participated simultaneously in the public world of paid work and the private sphere of domesticity (see chapter 2, "From Rods to Reasoning: The Historical Construction of Intensive Mothering," in *The Cultural Contradictions of Motherhood*; Weiner).

[4] More specifically, in the United States in 1950, 11.9 percent of women with children under six years of age were employed; in 1960, 18.6 percent; in 1970, 30.3 percent; in 1979, 43.2 percent; in 1988, 56.1 percent; and in 1993, 58.3 percent (U.S. Bureau of the Census 1994; U.S. Department of Labor 1980). Among married mothers with children under three, for instance, 66.6 percent held paying jobs for all or part of the year in 1992 (Hayghe and Bianchi). Over

half of mothers with children less than one year old, and nearly three-quarters of women with children aged six to sixteen, are now working for pay (U.S. Bureau of the Census 1992; U.S. Department of Labor 1991).

[5]I recognize that there are important differences among women and mothers along class, racial, and ethnic lines (not to mention age, marital status, and number of children). I will address those issues in later chapters. Throughout much of this introduction, however, I refer either to professional-class career women (for reasons that will become apparent) or to women and mothers in general, focusing on the socially constructed similarities among them.

[6]Although the phrase "paid working woman" may at times seem cumbersome, throughout this book I intentionally avoid using the more common expression "working woman" to refer to women who work outside the home. The common usage implies that women who are not working for pay do not actually work. Yet we know that most women who stay at home are engaged in housework, and that mothers who stay at home are also working to care for their children. I do not want to implicitly deny or devalue the unpaid work of these women and therefore consistently refer to women who work for pay as paid working women or employed women.

[7]Rachel's belief that bad children are purely the result of bad parenting coexists, curiously, with her sense that much of a child's personality is in the child's genes. After telling me the story of the swat to the butt and reminding me she "never" does this, she also let me know that Kristin was particularly disturbed by it since "she has gentle genes in her and she doesn't think it's right to hit." Although Kristin's gentleness and her belief that violence is not right could easily be interpreted as a result of Rachel's teachings, Rachel nonetheless attributes it to Kristin's nature. As will become clear, such attributions often imply the nature of females.

[8]The idea that these are simply two complementary logics that operate in two different contexts is most fully elaborated by Parsons and Bales. Men, they argue, are appropriately "instrumental" in the workplace, while women are appropriately "affective" in the home. And this, they say, is a "functional" solution to the different requirements of the two different spheres. But, as I have suggested, in a society where "affective" women regularly venture out into the "instrumental" workplace, the tension and opposition between the "functional" requirements of the two spheres is brought into striking relief.

[9]The portrait of gesellschaft relations corresponds to the rational actor model mentioned earlier. However, while classical social theorists understand this as a relatively recent historical phenomenon originating in the early period of industrialization, rational actor theorists believe that their model applies universally, to all people, at all times, in all places.

[10]Marx and Engels, in a famous passage from the *Manifesto of the Communist Party*, make this point quite eloquently: "The bourgeoisie, wherever it has got the upper hand, has put an end to all feudal, patriarchal, idyllic relations ... and has left remaining no other nexus between man and man than naked self-interest, than callous 'cash payment.' It has drowned the most heavenly ecstacies of

religious fervour, of chivalrous enthusiasm, of philistine sentimentalism, in the icy water of egotistical calculation .... The bourgeoisie has torn away from the family its sentimental veil, and has reduced the family relation to a mere money relation" (475-76).

[11]We see this, for instance, in spouses who keep separate checking accounts and make prenuptial agreements, and in children who sue their parents on the basis of emotional distress.

[12]The history of Western child rearing is discussed in depth in chapter 2 of *The Cultural Contradictions of Motherhood*.

[13]See Moore; Sennett; and Stone for more sophisticated versions of this argument. Sennett contends that the child-centered family inappropriately shields its children, leaving them ill prepared for the harsh reality of life beyond the front porch. Moore believes that specialized child-rearing institutions are far better equipped to provide proper socialization than are idiosyncratic parents—whose "obligation to give affection as a duty to a particular set of persons on account of the accident of birth ... is a true relic of barbarism" (163). Stone argues that authoritarian child rearing would be much more effective for disciplining a reliable labor force.

[14]Social constructions are not the work of isolated individuals, nor are they static. Our understanding of the social world is constructed through interaction between persons over time, as part of a historical process through which our culture is adjusted, transformed, and re-created on an ongoing basis (see, e.g., Bellah *et al.*; Berger and Luckmann; Giddens; Mehan 1989, 1983; Mehan and Wood 1). But culture is not only the product of human interaction; it also produces certain forms of interaction and actually makes possible human interaction as we know it. Socially constructed ideas enable us to think and act at the same time that they limit the range of what is thinkable and doable (Durkheim).

The social construction of culture regularly involves unequal power relations. Some people have more power to "name" and institutionalize culture than others. This, however, does not mean that "the ruling ideas [are] ... the ideas of the ruling class" (Marx and Engels 489). The ruling class is not always interested and does not have *that* much power. Less powerful people not only have the ability to interpret and resist the ideas of those who rule; they also have the power to create their own subcultures and to transform the larger culture as a whole (e.g., Gordon; Hebdige; Piess; Radway; Sewell; Willis).

For some interesting empirical studies that explicitly use the language of social construction, see Garfinkel (on the social construction of "woman"; Mehan, Hetweck, and Meihls on the social construction of "handicapped students"; Gusfield on the social construction of the "drinking-driving problem"; Corse on the social construction of national literary canons; and DeNora on the social construction of Beethoven's "genius."

[15]Although much of *The Cultural Contradictions of Motherhood* is dedicated to uncovering and elaborating the socially constructed ideology to which Rachel subscribes, I want to make it clear that the logic to which Rachel's boss subscribes, the logic of rationalized market societies, is also a socially constructed one. Much

of classical and contemporary social theorizing is dedicated to making this point (e.g., Polanyi; Sahlins; Weber). The ideology of intensive mothering, however, has received far less attention.

[16]See Rossi for a feminist version of this argument; and Popenoe for a more recent "family values" version.

[17]Many have argued that contemporary notions of appropriate child rearing are far from recommending what is best for our children or our society (e.g., Aries; Berger 1981a, 1981b; Berger and Berger; Donzelot; Foucault; Kagan; Laing 1972; Lasch; Moore; Plumb; Sennett; Slater 1976; Stone). Others have pointed out that Americans' culturally prescribed image of "good mothering" also tends to contain both an ethnocentric bias and a white, middle-class bias (e.g., Glenn et al.; Kagan; Scheper-Hughes 1992).

[18]Here I understand historical context in terms of social structure. The definition of social structure I use includes both social relations (the generally hierarchical systems of social positions, including class, race, ethnicity, gender, occupation, age, etc.) and culture (systems of meaning, including language, symbolic objects and representations, formal and informal rituals, conscious ideologies, and common sense). See Hays.

[19]My use of content, carriers, and context as the defining features of ideologies follows from an interpretation of Geertz's (193-233) outline of the three central theoretical conceptions of ideology. My analysis is also greatly influenced by Mannheim's (1971, 1985) classic works in the sociology of knowledge.

References

Allen, Jeffner. "Motherhood: The Annihilation of Women." *Mothering: Essays in Feminist Theory.* Ed. Joyce Trebilcot. Savage, Md.: Rowman and Littlefield, 1983. 315-30.

Aries, Phillipe. *Centuries of Childhood: A Social History of Family Life.* Translated by Robert Baldick. New York: Vintage, 1962.

Bane, Mary Jo. *Here to Stay: American Families in the Twentieth Century.* New York: Basic Books, 1976.

Becker, Gary S. *A Treatise on the Family.* Cambridge: Harvard University Press, 1981.

Beekman, Daniel. *The Mechanical Baby: A Popular History of the Theory and Practice of Child Raising.* Westport, CT.: Lawrence Hill. 1977.

Bellah, Robert, Richard Madsen, William M. Sullivan, Ann Swidler, and Steven M. Tipton. *Habits of the Heart: Individualism and Commitment in American Life.* Berkeley: University of California Press, 1985.

Bentson, Margaret. "The Political Economy of Women's Liberation." *Feminist Frameworks: Alternative Theoretical Accounts of the Relations between Women and Men.* Eds. Alison M. Jaggar and Paula S. Rothenberg. New York: McGraw-Hill, 1984. 239-47.

Berger, Bennett. *Survival of a Counterculture.* Berkeley: University of California

Press, 1981a.

Berger, Bennett. "Liberating Child Sexuality: Commune Experiences." *Children and Sex*. Eds. Larry L. Constantine and Floyd M. Martinson. Boston: Little, Brown, 1981b. 247-54.

Berger, Bennett. "Structure and Choice in the Sociology of Culture." *Theory and Society* 20 (1) (1991): 1-19.

Berger, Brigitte, and Peter Berger. *The War over the Family: Capturing the Middle Ground*. Garden City, NY: Anchor, 1983.

Berger, Peter, and Thomas Luckmann. *The Social Construction of Reality*. New York: Doubleday, 1966.

Blumberg, Rae Lesser, ed. *Gender, Family, and Economy: The Triple Overlap*. Newbury Park, CA: Sage, 1991.

Coleman, James S. "The Rational Reconstruction of Society." *American Sociological Review* 58 (1993): 1-15.

Corse, Sarah M. *Nationalism and Literature: The Politics of Culture in Canada and the United States*. Cambridge: Cambridge University Press, 1996.

DeNora, Tia. *Beethoven and the Construction of Genius: Musical Politics in Vienna, 1792-1803*. Berkeley: University of California Press, 1995.

Donzelot, Jacques. *The Policing of Families*. New York: Pantheon, 1979.

Durkheim, Emile. *Montesquieu and Rousseau: Forerunners of Sociology*. Ann Arbor: University of Michigan Press, 1965.

Elster, Jon. *Nuts and Bolts for the Social Sciences*. Cambridge: Cambridge University Press, 1989.

Folbre, Nancy, and Heidi Hartmann. "The Rhetoric of Self-Interest: Ideology and Gender in Economic Theory." *The Consequences of Economic Rhetoric*. Eds. Arjo Klamer, Donald N. McCloskey, and Robert M. Solow. Cambridge: Cambridge University Press, 1988. 184-203.

Foucault, Michel. *The History of Sexuality. Vol. I: An Introduction*. New York: Vintage, 1978.

Fraiberg, Selma. *Every Child's Birthright: In Defense of Mothering*. New York: Basic, 1977.

Garfinkel, Harold. *Studies in Ethnomethodology*. Englewood Cliffs, NJ: Prentice-Hall, 1967.

Geertz, Clifford. *The Interpretation of Cultures*. New York: Basic, 1973.

Giddens, Anthony. *Capitalism and Modern Social Theory. An Analysis of the Writings of Marx, Durkheim and Max Weber*. Cambridge : Cambridge University Press, 1971.

Glenn, Evelyn Nakano, Grace Chang, and Linda Rennie Forcey. *Mothering: Ideology, Experience, and Agency*. New York: Routledge, 1994.

Gordon, Linda. *Heroes of Their Own Lives: The Politics and History of Family Violence*. New York: Penguin, 1988.

Greenberger, Ellen, and Robin O'Neil. "Parents' Concerns about Their Child's Development: Implications for Fathers' and Mothers' Well-Being and Attitudes Toward Work." *Journal of Marriage and the Family* 52 (1990): 621-35.

Gusfield, Joseph. *The Culture of Public Problems: Drinking-Driving and the Symbolic Order*. Chicago: University of Chicago Press, 1981.

Hartmann, Heidi. "The Unhappy Marriage of Marxism and Feminism: Towards a More Progressive Union." *Women and Revolution: A Discussion of the Unhappy Marriage of Marxism and Feminism*. Ed. Lydia Sargent. Boston: South End Press, 1981a. 1-41.

Hartmann, Heidi. (1981b) "The Family as the Locus of Gender, Class, and Political Struggle: The Example of Housework." *Signs* 6 (3) (1981b): 366-94.

Hayghe, Howard V., and Suzanne M. Bianchi. "Married Mothers' Work Patterns: The Job-Family Compromise." *Monthly Labor Review* 117 (6) (1994): 24-30.

Hays, Sharon. "Structure and Agency and the Sticky Problem of Culture." *Sociological Theory* 12 (1) (1994): 57-72.

Hebdige, Dick. *Subculture: The Meaning of Style*. London: Methuen, 1979.

Heilbroner, Robert. "The Coming Meltdown of Traditional Capitalism." *Ethics and International Affairs* 2 (1988): 63-77.

Hochschild, Arlie, with Anne Machung. *The Second Shift: Working Parents and the Revolution at Home*. New York: Viking, 1989.

Huber, Joan, and Glenna Spitze. "Trends in Family Sociology." *Handbook of Sociology*. Ed. Neil J. Smelser. London: Sage, 1988. 425-48.

Kagan, Jerome. "The Psychological Requirements of Human Development." *Family in Transition*. Ed. Arlene S. Skolnick and Jerome H. Skolnick. 5th ed. Boston: Little, Brown, 1986. 373-83.

Lasch, Christopher. *Haven in a Heartless World*. New York: Basic, 1977.

Mannheim, Karl. "Conservative Thought." *From Karl Mannheim*. Ed. Kurt H. Wolff. New York: Oxford University Press, 1971. 132-222.

Mannheim, Karl. *Ideology and Utopia*. San Diego: Harcourt Brace Jovanovich, 1985.

Mansbridge, Jane J., ed. *Beyond Self-Interest*. Chicago: University of Chicago Press, 1990.

Marx, Karl, and Friedrich Engels. *The Marx-Engels Reader*. 1848. Edited by Robert C. Tucker. 2nd ed. New York: Norton, 1978.

Mead, Margaret. "A Cultural Anthropologist's Approach to Maternal Deprivation." *Deprivation of Maternal Care: A Reassessment of Its Effects*. Eds. Mary D. Ainsworth, R. B. Andry, Robert G. Harlow, S. Lebovici, Margaret Mead, Dane G. Prugh, and Barbara Wootton. Geneva: World Health Organization, 1962. 45-62.

Mehan, Hugh. "The Role of Language and the Language of Role." *Language and Society* 12 (3) (1983):1-39.

Mehan, Hugh. "Oracular Reasoning in a Psychiatric Setting." *Conflict Talk*. Ed. A. D. Grimshaw. Cambridge: Cambridge University Press, 1989. 160-77.

Mehan, Hugh, Alma Hetweck, and J. Lee Meihls. *Handicapping the Handicapped: Decision Making in Students' Careers*. Stanford: Stanford University Press, 1985.

Mehan, Hugh, and H. Wood. *The Reality of Ethnomethodology.* New York: Wiley-Interscience, 1975.

Mills, C. Wright. *The Sociological Imagination.* New York: Oxford University Press, 1959.

Moore, Barrington, Jr. *Political Power and Social Theory: Six Studies.* Cambridge: Harvard University Press, 1958.

Parsons, Talcott, and Robert F. Bales. *Family, Socialization and Interaction Process.* New York: Free Press, 1955.

Peterson, Susan Rae. "Against 'Parenting.'" *Mothering: Essays in Feminist Theory.* Ed. Joyce Trebilcot. Savage, Md.: Rowman and Littlefield, 1983. 62-69.

Piess, Kathy. *Cheap Amusements.* Philadelphia: Temple University Press, 1986.

Plumb, J. H. "The New World of Children." *The Birth of a Consumer Society: The Commercialization of Eighteenth-Century England.* Eds. Neil McKendrick, John Brewer, and J. H. Plumb. Bloomington: Indiana University Press, 1982. 285-315.

Polanyi, Karl. *The Great Transformation.* Boston: Beacon, 1944.

Polatnick, M. "Why Men Don't Rear Children: A Power Analysis." *Mothering: Essays in Feminist Theory.* Ed. Joyce Trebilcot. Savage, MD: Rowman and Littlefield, 1983. 21-40.

Popenoe, David. "Parental Androgyny." *Society* 30 (6) (1993): 6 11.

Radway, Janice. *Reading the Romance: Women, Patriarchy, and Popular Literature.* Chapel Hill: University of North Carolina Press, 1984.

Rapp, Rayna, Ellen Ross, and Renate Bridenthal. "Examining Family History." *Feminist Studies* 5 (1) (1979): 174-200.

Risman, Barbara, and Myra Marx Feree. "Making Gender Visible." *American Sociological Review* 60 (5) (1995): 775-82.

Rogoff, Barbara, Martha Julia Sellers, Sergio Pirrotta, Nathan Fox, and Sheldon H. White. "Age of Assignment of Roles and Responsibilities to Children: A Cross-Cultural Survey." *Rethinking Childhood: Perspectives on Development and Society.* Eds. Arlene Skolnick. Boston: Little, Brown, 1976. 249-68.

Rossi, Alice. "A Biosocial Perspective on Parenting." *Daedalus* 106 (2) (1977): 1-31.

Rothman, Barbara Katz. *Recreating Motherhood: Ideology and Technology in a Patriarchal Society.* New York: Norton, 1989.

Sahlins, Marshall. *Culture and Practical Reason.* Chicago: University of Chicago Press, 1976.

Scheper-Hughes, Nancy, ed. *Child Survival: Anthropological Perspectives on the Treatment and Maltreatment of Children.* Boston: D. Reidel, 1987.

Scheper-Hughes, Nancy. *Death without Weeping: The Violence of Everyday Life in Brazil.* Berkeley: University of California Press, 1992.

Schwartz, F. "Management Women and the New Facts of Life." *Harvard Business Review* 67 (1) (1989): 65-77.

Sennett, Richard. *Families against the City: Middle Class Homes of Industrial Chicago, 1872-1890.* Cambridge: Harvard University Press, 1970.

Sewell, William, Jr. "Ideologies and Social Revolutions: Reflections on the French Case." *Journal of Modern History* 57 (1) (1985):57-85.

Stone, Lawrence. *The Family, Sex and Marriage in England, 1500-1800.* New York: Harper and Row, 1977.

Tonnies, Ferdinand. *Community and Society (Gemeinschaft und Gesellschaft).* Ed. and Trans. Charles P. Loomis. East Lansign: Michigan State University Press, 1957.

U.S. Bureau of the Census. *Statistical Abstract of the United States.* Washington, D.c.: Government Printing Office, 1992.

U.S. Bureau of the Census. *Statistical Abstract of the United States.* Washington, D.C.: Government Printing Office, 1994.

U.S. Department of Labor. *Perspectives on Working Women: A Databook.* Bulletin 2080. Washington, D.C.: Government Printing Office, 1980.

U.S. Department of Labor. *Working Women: A Chartbook.* Bulletin 2385. Washington, D.C.: Government Printing Office, 1991.

Weber, Max. *The Protestant Ethic and the Spirit of Capitalism.* New York: Scribner, 1958.

Weiner, Lynn Y. *From Working Girl to Working Mother: The Female Labor Force in the United States, 1820-1980.* Chapel Hill: University of North Carolina Press, 1985.

Weisner, Thomas, and Ronald Gallimore. "My Brother's Keeper: Child and Sibling Caretaking." *Current Anthropology* 18 (1977):169-89.

Willis, Paul E. *Learning to Labor: How Working Class Kids Get Working Class Jobs.* New York: Columbia University Press, 1977.

Zelizer, Viviana A. *Pricing the Priceless Child.* New York: Basic, 1985.

Chapter 26

A Sketch in Progress

Introducing the Mother without Child

ELAINE TUTTLE HANSEN

Mother?

ONCE UPON A time, maternity seemed to be a biological fact fixed both literally and symbolically within the private, affective sphere. Now we debate the meaning and practice of motherhood and mothering in many public spaces. A survey of newspapers, bookstores, and academic conference programs yields catchy titles, all ending in question marks:

"Whose Child is This?" *Mothers without Custody: How Could a Mother* Do *Such a Thing?* "Will the Real Mother Please Stand Up?" What is said by and about mothers—full-time mothers, surrogate mothers, teenage mothers, adoptive mothers, mothers who live in poverty, mothers with briefcases—is increasingly complicated and divisive. Language is stretched to describe the bewildering fragmentation of a time in which one child may have a genetic mother, a gestational mother, and a custodial mother, each of whom is a different person.[1]

Although it seems clear that new, unprecedented pressures have recently called into question the meaning of *mother,* this assumption nonetheless simplifies the history of the term. Motherhood has meant many different things in the past, just as it means (and will no doubt continue to mean) different things in different cultures and subcultures today. Looking no further back than the late nineteenth century and no farther afield than England, we see that *mother* was already a slippery word with a complicated history. Like characters in *Desert of the Heart,* Jane Rule's novel about language and motherhood, I often find myself reaching for the dictionary and arguing about the implications that lie just beneath the surface of the lexicographer's formal efforts to capture meaning. As always, that monument of late-nineteenth-century industry and scholarship, the *Oxford English Dictionary (OED),* affords a complex and fascinating perspective on the historical semantics of *mother* in which the present crisis—both discursive and practical—is embedded.

The *OED* defined *mother* around 1908, under the editorship of Henry Bradley.[2] The first sense of *mother sb.I* grounds the concept in what until recently could hardly be seen as anything but its natural meaning, denoting a gendered, bodily, and relational identity: "a female parent, a woman who has given birth to a child." The second sense expands the referential field to "things more or less personified": "with reference either to a metaphorical giving birth, to the protecting care exercised by a mother, or to the affectionate reverence due to a mother." This second definition reminds us that long before surrogacy as we know it, the word *mother* was frequently extended from its essential link with childbearing women. But this metaphorical usage is still grounded either in the process of giving birth, at least symbolically, or in mothers' presumed function ("protecting") and status ("reverence due") in English-speaking culture. The third sense reconnects *mother* to a gendered identity: "a woman who exercises control like that of a mother, or who is looked up to as a mother." Like the second sense, this one disengages the word from any necessary connection to actual childbirth but firmly reattaches it to femaleness and again confirms that motherhood is a matter of a particular, clearly understood function "control" over whatever is mothered—and high status ("looked up to"). In contrast to the insistence on the defining obviousness of the elevated position of the mother in senses two and three, a fourth and last sense indicates that *mother* can be "a term of address for an elderly woman of the lower class." The citations that support this sense reveal that from at least the fourteenth to the nineteenth centuries in England, *mother* sometimes connoted the opposite of what it was normally supposed to mean: not high status, but a devaluation in two critical measures of a woman's worth—age and class.

Bradley and his staff also found an even more devalued sense of the word *mother,* one so fundamentally at odds with their educated, middle-class, late-Victorian understanding that they classified it as another lexical item altogether: *mother Sh.2,* meaning "dregs, scum." According to the *OED,* this *mother* was associated with alchemy and used especially in the sixteenth century to refer to the scum of oils and subsequently to the dregs of fermenting liquids. An extensive note preceding the definition explains that etymologists have long puzzled over this usage. Some have argued that the term is actually derived from Dutch *madder,* meaning mud or mire; the *OED* editor insists that there is no evidence for this view, however, and that *mother sb.2* is really an application of *sb.1.* Throwing up lexicographic hands at a debasement of the word *mother* that an English gentleman and scholar would be hard-pressed to comprehend, the editor concludes his lengthy discussion by noting that, "the transition of sense is difficult to explain."[3]

Today we might be less surprised by this semantic phenomenon. In the wake of extensive late-twentieth-century feminist debates about the nature, function, and status of motherhood, it is no longer hard to offer reasons why the concept of *mother,* so idealized by the dominant middle-class rhetoric of the recent past, can also carry this barely concealed trace of derogation, disgust, and dirtiness. If there is consensus to be found in these debates, it is that conventional sentiments about motherhood inadequately describe and serve to mystify the actual circumstances of most women who mother, even as they may also sublimate the fear and resentment of men who cannot be mothers, or of the always unsatisfied inner child. It is commonly recognized, in some circles at least, that the position of the mother in our culture and our language is riddled with its history of psychic and social contradictions. Motherhood offers women a site of both power and oppression, self-esteem and self-sacrifice, reverence and debasement.

At the same time, it is striking that other problematic and charged aspects of the concept of *mother* reflected in the *OED's* definition are at best made visible rather than explained or resolved by the diversity of recent feminist thought. For instance, the slippery and imprecisely overlapping equation of mothering and childbirth, or mothering and women, has been taxed but not exhausted by feminist debates about essentialism and exclusion. Many influential theorists still either root their arguments in a maternal (gestating, delivering, or lactating) body or insist that childbirth cannot simply be ignored as a gender-specific and probably gender-constructing experience. Others wish to see mothering as a more metaphorical act, a social position, available to any and all who choose to do maternal work, but this argument has been no less troublesome. Not only does it leave open to dispute the question of whether men can mother, but it continues to link feminine powers and capacities to child care and family roles, no matter how socially fashioned the position of mother is understood to be. So, too, the divides between women over their relationship to metaphorical mothering as well as biological mothering remain real and vexed, such as those between women who choose to mother and women who do not (or cannot), or between women who adopt and women who give birth.

What is taken for granted, both in the *OED's* definition and in many recent feminist struggles to interrogate and revise nineteenth-century notions of motherhood, is the *relational* aspect of the concept *mother*. Implicitly, in the *OED* and all subsequent formal definitions I have found, *mother* in the primary sense of the word is someone, maybe a woman or maybe not, who gives birth *to* a child or seeks protection and control *of* a child or is affectionately reverenced and looked up to *by* a child. The force of those prepositions is felt in feminist arguments as well. According to Sara Ruddick (1989), an innovative and influential feminist philosopher who has sought to redefine and revalue mothering, "to be a 'mother' is to take upon oneself the responsibility of child care, making its work a regular and substantial pan of one's working life"; "the concept of 'mother' depends on that of 'child'" (17, 22).[4] By throwing *mother* into quotation marks, feminist thinking challenges us to re-construe our assumptions about maternity in many ways, but Ruddick's formulation, like most others, reiterates the fundamental relationship to the "child" (a position that may be interrogated as well, but seldom is).

Certainly, we cannot and should not ignore the relational component of motherhood. Yet this component merits and rewards closer scrutiny. Both *mother* and *child* are problematic terms to conceptualize, not least of all because they are relational words, marking partial, quasi-temporary identities. This semantic feature reflects precisely the experiential and political problems that beset us as mothers, as children, and as citizens.

I begin here with questions of lexicography and semantics because definitions often usefully describe and focus attention on complicated problems. As I go on to discuss the importance of listening carefully to the stories we tell about mothers, this premise underlies my arguments: language is a conventional system and what we say always bears the burden of where we have been, what we have done, and what we believe. At the same time, language can function in a prescriptive as well as descriptive way; as others have argued, women have been harmed by cultural, legal, medical, and psychological discourses about motherhood. My purpose in this study, then, is not be to replace the old definitions of motherhood with a new one, but to turn attention to what I take to be the most inadequately explored aspect of *mother* as concept and identity: its relational features. This project needs to be situated, first, in the context that perhaps most deeply informs my thinking, the prolific and still growing feminist critique of motherhood that has evolved over the past three decades.

The Feminist Critique of Motherhood

Often, although not always, the story of feminists thinking about motherhood since the early 1960s is told as a drama in three acts: repudiation, recuperation, and, in the latest and most difficult stage to conceptualize, an emerging critique of recuperation that coexists with ongoing efforts to deploy recuperative strategies.[5] This story usually begins with key first-act figures like Simone de Beauvoir, Shulamith Firestone, Kate Millett, and Betty Friedan, early second-wave feminists who point out a strong link between women's oppression and women's naturalized position as mothers. In retrospect, as others have noted, the arguments of these early feminists may seem more subtle and ambivalent than they have often been taken to be. However, the assumption that feminists reject motherhood is so ingrained as early as 1971 that in an anthology of writing from the women's liberation movement published in that year, essays on "family" are prefaced with this disclaimer: "We are not against love, against men and women living together, against having children. What we are against is the role women play once they become wives and mothers" (Babcox and Belkin 106).

In the second act, many feminists seek to reclaim and reinterpret motherhood and revalue difference, although their efforts are almost always coupled with indictments of the negative aspects of "the role women play" as mother. (Some have suggested that this renewed feminist interest in motherhood can be understood as a return of the repressed, a consequence of the fact that many women were encouraged to "deny" or "defer" their maternal desires by the strength of the early critique.[6] This work begins in the mid-seventies and takes a wide variety of forms, in the hands of feminists as different as Adrienne Rich, Nancy Chodorow, Dorothy Dinnerstein, and Sara Ruddick in America; Mary O'Brien and Juliet Mitchell in England; and Luce Irigaray, Helene Cixous, and Julia Kristeva in France. In the third and as yet incomplete act, critiques and negotiations as well as applications, extensions, and defenses of this work begin to appear in the mid-'80s and continue into the present.[7] Although some of these critiques tend to reinforce the notion of a historical shift from early feminist attack to subsequent feminist celebration, others point out that the story is, as I have already indicated, less straightforward. Several of these more recent critiques attempt to revive and integrate as well as complicate earlier insights into the oppressive aspects of motherhood. There is also a growing sense of impasse. Feminists have demanded and gained new attention for the previously ignored problems of motherhood, but they have not arrived at consensus about how to redefine the concept or adjust the system. Many (but by no means all) women wish to refuse motherhood on the old terms without abandoning either the heavy responsibilities or the intense pleasures of bearing and raising children. The fear that no one will take care of our children if we don't makes it difficult to go forward, even as it seems impossible to go willingly back.[8]

Ann Snitow's (1992) recent efforts to overview and historicize the second-wave feminist debate about motherhood strongly emphasize this frustrating sense of impasse.[9] Snitow divides the last 30 years or so into periods a little different from the ones I have suggested above. Her first period, 1963-1974, includes the publication of what she calls the "demon texts" of writers like Friedan and Firestone, which are (often falsely, she says) associated with the repudiation of motherhood and, as we have seen, have been apologized for by subsequent feminists. The second period, 1976-1979, is for Snitow the great age of ground breaking feminist work on motherhood, including works by Rich, Dinnerstein, Kristeva, and Chodorow. The third and still current period, starting about 1980 with the "threshold" work of Ruddick, is one of "reaction" and failure to advance the original critique of pronatalism. In this last, comparatively long period, Snitow finds chiefly disarray and division, and she decries the "flaccidity" of the feminist critique. Feminism started out hoping to demolish both pronatalism and its dark underside, maternal devaluation. However, divided and conquered by the eighties backlash, the movement has been less able to achieve the former goal. "Indeed," Snitow speculates, "it may well be that earlier reaction to the pressure to mother was so historically specific that it can have no direct descendants" (1992: 34).[10]

Although I can easily understand her sense that thinking about motherhood has reached a kind of impasse, my initial response to Snitow's argument was that it overstated the case against the current critique. But as chance would have it, a few days after rereading a version of her work published in 1992 in *Feminist Review,* I picked up a copy of the first 1994 issue of *Feminist Studies.* Much to the prospective delight of someone with my interests, the table of contents on the back cover groups seven of the essays, stories, poems, and reviews in a box entitled "Scenarios of the Maternal." Inside, the preface further entices, promising the postmodern thinking about mothers that I am eager to find and engage in: "This recent intellectual and creative strand-skeptical, sophisticated, deconstructing, often playful and impious about maternal verities, is visible in a variety of forms in, articles included in this issue" ("Preface" 3). But disappointment quickly set in as I began to read through the volume. Each of the first three essays I mention is a worthwhile contribution to scholarship in its own right, but mothers and the maternal are oddly invisible, and these essays pay little attention to standing and difficult questions about motherhood or the feminist critique thereof.[11]

Iris Marion Young's characteristically thoughtful discussion of pregnant drug addicts, "Punishment, Treatment, Empowerment: Three Approaches to Policy for Pregnant Addicts," focuses on the failures of present treatment policies rather than explicitly suggesting how an addicted mother-to-be in theory or practice might challenge our "maternal verities." Young observes that the rage she thinks is revealed in punitive approaches to pregnant addicts reflects identification with the infant's perspective and the scapegoating of mothers, and implicitly her call for treatment that "empowers" the addict to participate more actively in her own recovery is suggestive. But Young does not elaborate on how this treatment would work or consider questions that her other writings about pregnancy and motherhood might give rise to. Can pregnant women be either "treated" or "empowered" in the same way that non-pregnant women can be? What might or should consciousness-raising (part of the recommended treatment) among pregnant addicts or mothers who are drug users reveal about maternal consciousness? Is there such a thing? Does it differ from and contribute to feminist consciousness? And—a key question for my own project here—if, as Young posits, most drug treatment programs teach women to "earn" their children by being "good," thereby reproducing "structures of privilege," does that mean that better, more effective programs would teach women to be "bad" mothers? What would this mean, for the women and for their children? What are the models of mothering that dissolve or open up "structures of privilege"?

In contrast to Young's piece, Judith Kegan Gardiner's equally interesting essay, "Empathic Ways of Reading: Narcissism, Cultural Politics, and Russ's *Female Man,*" has virtually nothing to say about actual mothers, mothers-to-be, or cultural biases about motherhood. The words *mother* and *maternal* or variants and synonyms thereof are not used in the essay, and the only reason I can imagine that it might be included under the rubric "Scenarios of the Maternal" is that empathy is so frequently associated with "maternal" ways of knowing and thinking. But Gardiner herself does not make such an association. In fact, she might be indirectly pressing a counterclaim when she says in passing, without further elaboration or evidence, that empathy is "a capacity developed through early relations between *parent* and child" (emphasis added) and when she later notes that empathy cannot be claimed by women as "natural" (91, 105).

The third scholarly article, Stacy Alaimo's "Cyborg and Ecofeminist Interventions: Challenges for an Environmental Feminism," criticizes both ecofeminism (presumably associated with motherhood, although this point is not directly made, by its use of the metaphor "Mother Earth") and aspects of Donna Haraway's "cyborg" metaphor, particularly as the latter tends to "bolster a destructive technophilia" (133). Alaimo calls instead for an alliance of "women" and "nature" as agents rather than passive victims. In asking whether this is possible—"Can we construct female alliances with nature that don't mystify nature or pose women as essentially victims or mothers?"—Alaimo may be implying that she wishes to detach women from motherhood. Depending on the stress we put on the word "essentially," she may also be equating mothers with victimization and passivity

(149). But, as in Gardiner's essay, we can only speculate about where the author stands on issues such as the particular problems that actual mothers encounter when they seek to be agents or readers, or the extent to which women might have to change the nature of maternal (or is it "parental"?) work if they became agents in alliance with "nature."

Unlike these three theoretical critiques, Molly Hite's piece, entitled "Mother Underground (Fiction)," turns the focus sharply back onto an actual mother (or at least a fictional version of one; the story reads like autobiography, but the parentheses in the title indicate otherwise). It is described by the preface as "another illustration of the new wave of feminist probing of motherhood—and daughterhood," showing how the daughter is turning in middle age from hate and self-blame to analysis. But it is not clear to me whether this story probes "old verities" or repeats them; it remains rooted in the daughter's point of view and ends on a note of retreat from the problems of mother-daughter relations. The memoir is sparked by the middle-aged daughter's new problem, now that she herself has a child: how to deal with her mother's childrearing advice. This concern leads quickly back to a familiar tale of the bright adolescent girl's struggles with her bright, frustrated, and eventually mad mother. The, speaker says, in closing, "I want to be forgotten"; she hopes that she can become "a generic daughter," able to talk to her mother and "able to receive advice as if it came from nobody's mother in particular" (Hite 66). The desire to pull back from the relationship in its particulars, to view herself and her mother generically, to forget and be forgotten, could be read as an effort to move beyond the mother-blaming that this story to my mind closely resembles. It also suggests, however, something very like the kind of distancing from—if not avoiding of—the outstanding concerns of the feminist critique of motherhood that we see in the scholarly essays, and such forgetting is a time-honored and dangerous strategy.

Undoubtedly, I thought after finishing the volume, it is unfair to measure these articles against a standard that they never intended to meet. My wish that the authors speak more directly to the way they enter into the feminist critique of motherhood and (re)define the terms *mother* and *maternal* might require retracing old arguments and repeating truisms. The authors may hesitate to say much for fear of saying nothing new—a fear that surely haunts anyone who thinks of speaking about motherhood in the late nineties. As it stands, however, the volume seems to confirm Snitow's sense that the feminist critique of motherhood is becoming more "flaccid" and frustrating rather than more rigorous and effective. But on second thought, something more potentially positive and useful also struck me about this sample collection of what is promoted as the cutting edge of feminist thinking. Despite the varying degrees of aloofness from the unresolved material and theoretical problems of mothers and motherhood in several of these pieces, all of them move tacitly toward taking into the feminist account—rather than just blaming or accepting—either "bad" mothers (pregnant addicts; the bizarre patriarchal mother in Molly Hite's story) or what we might call "metaphorical," nontraditional, nonbiological, maybe even nongendered mothers (readers who read empathically; cyborgs and agents as opposed to Mother Earth and victims).

Framed this way, these essays may not only express a self-protective, if not yet transformative, distance from empirical and historical mothers, but also look toward what scholars have just begun to call for: discussion of the borders of motherhood and the women who really live there, neither fully inside nor fully outside some recognizable "family" unit, and often exiles from their children. After overviewing the ways in which the critiques of essentialism and exclusion problematize feminist approaches to motherhood, Patrice DiQuinzio concludes a recent essay with this recommendation: "Further analysis of mothering would benefit from a focus on nontraditional instances of mothering—for example, lesbian mothering or the mothering of women without custody of children" (12). Jane Price Knowles makes a comparable suggestion in the introduction to her anthology, *Motherhood: A Feminist Perspective:* "The challenge of mothering seems to be not how to be 'good enough,' but to dare to believe in our goodness enough to also be 'bad enough'" (6-7). Janice Doane and Devon Hodges similarly note that "the role of the bad mother is, in fact, empowering" (28).

In this study, I demonstrate that if we turn to fiction written in the last three decades—an arena Snitow omits from her purview[12]—we discover the kind of rigorous, daring, and potentially empowering focus that scholars like Snitow, DiQuinzio, and Knowles call for. It is to be found, as DiQuinzio and others might not be surprised to learn, in a number of novels and stories that center on the "mother without child," a rubric that includes nontraditional mothers and "bad" mothers, including lesbians and slave mothers; women who have abortions and miscarriages; women who refuse to bear children, or whose children are stolen from them; and mothers who are, as we shall see, sometimes criminals, murderers, prisoners, suicides, time travelers, tricksters, or ghosts.

In bringing this fictional picture of not conventionally good enough mothers to the fore, we will find it helpful to understand that the multifaceted story of feminist thinking about motherhood is still emerging. Although the broad overviews that periodize the last three decades are accurate and useful in some respects, they may also represent what Biddy Martin, writing about lesbian identities, speaks of as "the too common homogenization of a more complicated past" (103). Martin points to the value, instead, of the kind of work Judith Butler attempts: "to redescribe those possibilities that *already* exist, but which exist within cultural domains designated as culturally unintelligible and impossible" (148-9). One such domain that demands and rewards further description is that of the mother without child in the kind of contemporary stories I call to attention here.

Feminist Literary Criticism and Motherhood

Feminist literary critics, especially those who draw on psychoanalytic theories, have been taking part in the more generalized feminist critique of motherhood as institution and experience for many years. One early and enduring question, particularly for American literary scholars, has been the question of whether mothers can write, or whether writers can be mothers. The theoretical obstacles—especially the position of the mother in dominant theories of language, as highlighted by French feminist thought—as well as the practical constraints on a mother's time, energy, and creative powers have repeatedly been considered. Some have seen a movement across the historical terrain of novel writing in particular that anticipates the pattern of second-wave feminism: from repudiation of the mother, in various ways, by both nineteenth- and early-twentieth-century women writers, towards efforts in the most recent fiction to recuperate her voice or write "as" a mother.[13] A related sub-theme of feminist criticism has been the position of the feminist critic as daughter, anxiously trying to sort out her relations to her (literary) foremothers and suffering, like most feminist daughters, from deeply unresolved feelings about mothers and motherhood (see, for example, Davis). In both literary critical and metacritical studies, it is thus possible to note the same pervasive, multifaceted ambivalence about motherhood that we see in feminist studies at large.

An important book focusing attention on the literary ramifications of this ambivalence, with particular interest in nineteenth-century women writers, is Margaret Homans's *Bearing the Word*.[14] Homans at once presupposes and reevaluates a Lacanian theory of language, in which both the speaking and writing subject and the signifier are constituted as masculine, and she argues that this theory has been understandably debilitating for women writers. As many theorists agree, entering the symbolic order is especially difficult if not impossible for the feminine subject, who is associated with the literal or nonsymbolic. As Homans sees it, nineteenth-century women novelists were forced at one and the same time to see themselves as mothers, fulfilling or failing to fulfill the true destiny of the proper woman, and yet in writing to betray the mother, circumventing the maternal (as in *Frankenstein)* or representing the mother as a passive transmitter of the Father's seed or word (as in works by George Eliot and Mrs. Gaskell). Women's very power as mother, given the possibilities for egotism and selfishness, had to be denied by norms of Victorian motherhood.

Marianne Hirsch's *Mother/Daughter Plot* presumes, with Homans, both the historical and strategic absence of the mother's perspective and the theoretical difficulty of representing this paradoxical perspective, or writing "as" a mother. Hirsch locates a major source of this problem in the conventional plots of western literature and the discursive myths of psychoanalysis (hence the missing or silent mother in Greek tragedy, upon which psychoanalytic theories often draw). Writing post-Bakhtin, Hirsch defines the novel as a genre open to dialogue between dominant and subversive voices, but she suggests that it has only recently become a genre in which the mother's voice could be heard. Nineteenth-century plots, on the contrary, are controlled by the family romance and depend on the heroine's "disidentification from the fate of other women, especially mothers" (10); and so mothers are missing, voiceless, or devalued in novels by writers such as Jane Austen, Mary Shelley, George Sand, the Brontes, George Eliot, and Kate Chopin. Hirsch adds, "The conventions of realism, resting on structures of consent and containment, shut out various forms of indeterminacy, instability, and social fragmentation" (14). The situation changes to some extent in modernist plots, which are "supplemented," according to Hirsch, by the heroine's artistic ambitions and desire for affiliation with other women, so that "for women writers contradiction and oscillation, rather than repetition, bind the modernist plot" (15). Finally, in what Hirsch calls "postmodern" plots, "more multiple relational identities emerge," although the mother remains the one "who did succumb to convention," a negative model from which the daughter must detach herself (10). In texts Hirsch considers by Margaret Atwood, Marguerite Duras, and Christa Wolf, although the mothers are prominent, the perspective remains "daughterly." Only in the most recent fiction especially, in Hirsch's view, in Toni Morrison's *Beloved,* do "mothers begin to appear as subjects" (11).

Other recent critics consider the impact of dominant myths of phallogocentrism on later women writers. In her study of H.D. and Jean Rhys, *The Unspeakable Mother,* Deborah Kelly Kloepfer supports the view that earlier in this century women writers tended to assume the role of daughters, not mothers. Modernist-women writers have also engaged the interest of feminist critics concerned with narratology, some of whom find more departure from the dominant psychoanalytic and discursive models than Homans, Hirsch, or Kloepfer may. Rachel DuPlessis sees twentieth-century women writers as revising maternal myths in order to express "the peculiarities of the female quest" (61), although, still in keeping with views expressed by Homans and others, she finds that women writers like Virginia Woolf, RD., and Alice Walker look back to the preoedipal. Susan Winnett suggests, however, that the traditional female experience of birth and breast-feeding has forced women "to think forward rather than backward"; we need to stop reading "in drag" in order to see that narratives for women work differently than theories based on male erotic experience have understood. Ellen G. Friedman also argues that the female modernists, like their male counterparts, yearn for the "unrepresentable." But whereas males see it buried in the past (hence the search for the father), women see it as "the not yet presented," so that their narratives look forward.

Another way in which motherhood has recently entered into literary studies from psychoanalysis is through the notion of the play space or potential space, taken primarily from object relations theory. Following key lines of French feminist thought, Claire Kahane has argued that this space is analogous to the discursive space the woman writer might occupy and that since "poetic discourse [is] dominated by the semiotic," it is the ideal vehicle for a maternal voice that questions "fixed structures of gender" in postmodernist discourse.[15] In *Subversive Intent,* Susan Rubin Suleiman (1990) shares this view of the importance of the play space and wonders at the absence of figures of the playing or laughing mother in contemporary women's experimental writing. Instead, she finds that many recent women's texts are like those of the male surrealists, who "repudiate the mother" even as they appropriate her place in their battle with the father (161). As an instance of this, Suleiman cites Jeanette Winterson's *Oranges Are Not the Only*

Fruit, where she reads the mother figure as "an instrument of patriarchy" whom the lesbian daughter-writer must abandon and deny (1990: 165). The positive figure of the mother in writers like Cixous and Irigaray could be seen as a reaction to this patriarchal mother, but she remains a myth and tends to lead to writing in the lyric mode, rather than in the humorous and narrative mode that Suleiman believes would be more subversive.

However, in a recent study of Alice Munro's *Mothers and Other Clowns,* Magdalene Redekop finds evidence of subversive "play and parody" in stories about a certain kind of humorous mother figure. The source of comedy in Munro's magic realism, Redekop argues, is what she calls the "mock mother," a type that includes numerous surrogates: "stepmothers, foster mothers, adoptive mothers, child mothers, nurses, old maids mothering their parents, lovers mothering each other, husbands mothering wives, wives mothering husbands, sisters mothering each other, and numerous women and men behaving in ways that could be described as maternal." Finding in Munro's writing a female version of Freud's "fort-da" game, Redekop argues that the toy in this case is a doll, a mother in masquerade, and that the intent of the game is to subvert traditional definitions of motherhood: "Dancing in front of the erasure, the conspicuous mock-maternal figures do not affirm something inexpressible or sacred.... The entertainments of her [Munro's] mock mothers enable us to walk 'disrespectfully' around our idealized images of maternity" (8-10).

The "mock mother" is clearly analogous to the figure of the mother without child; as Redekop notes, in Munro's stories as in the novels I have assembled here, *"Where are the children?"* is the question that triggers the collapse of the composition," a collapse that must precede revision and reconstitution.[16] However, with rare exceptions (notably the work of Fay Weldon), the novels I consider are not comic, and the mothers in them often cannot play, laugh, or make other people laugh.[17] This may be in part because theories that link "play" with "autonomous subjectivity" and "total freedom" (as Suleiman characterizes the theoretical insights of Freud and Winnicott) are often constructed from the infant's point of view, not that of the person who mothers. If "play" is a "non-purposive state," it might indeed be incompatible with maternal work and maternal thinking, which, as revalued by theories like Ruddick's, have to be understood as highly goal-directed behaviors. Moreover, as we shall see, these serious, often tragic stories may undercut the premise that (maternal) subjectivity itself can be so readily equated with autonomy and freedom. They also represent another way in which to imagine non patriarchal motherhood, a mother in a subversive, "culturally unintelligible and impossible" position.

Beyond the Patriarchal Mother

Feminists and feminist literary critics have in general assumed that if and when mothers could speak and write, in contradistinction to their earlier sivlence, they would tell us a new and different story. Some would add that only by telling new stories about their lives can women escape the traditional plots that confine them to the roles of wives and mothers. It is not yet obvious, however, that we have heard either a new or more accurate maternal narrative. In an important sense, many recent stories by or about mothers offer a mirror image of old stories: whereas for centuries the myths and literature of western culture assumed and arguably depended on the absence of the mother, many of our contemporary stories—and particularly the ones I am interested in here assume and arguably depend on the absence of the child. My goal is to explore what this means. As Sara Ruddick (1983) has noted, "Some of the most reflective maternal thinkers have been moved to think deeply about motherhood precisely because mothering does not come easily to them" (5). In this study, I consider a number of stories about women to whom motherhood does not come easily, or in easily recognizable ways, if indeed it comes at all. In all of these stories of the mother without child, the relational aspect of motherhood is disrupted or thwarted and thus thrown into relief.

This figure of the mother without child usefully derives from and elucidates a broad spectrum of experience, ranging from the literal circumstances of a woman who loses or relinquishes custody of a biological child to the psychological condition of a woman who miscarries or never becomes pregnant. One difficulty I faced early on in this project was deciding how to limit the field, how to decide which stories to consider. The more I looked, the more instances I found of what I was looking for. In what follows, I explain why I think the widespread appearance of the mother without child in fiction today is overdetermined and how we might begin to account for that overdetermination. But at the outset, it may be helpful to specify more precisely what kind of stories, what kind of female characters the rubric "mother without child" will comprise.

I have borrowed this rubric from Jane Rule's *Desert of the Heart,* a novel that is the principal subject of the next chapter and also the earliest of the works I include here (thereby constituting a *terminus a quo* for the relative notion of "contemporary fiction" in the present instance). In Rule's novel, "Mother without Child" is the title of a sketch in progress. With multiple ironies, it also describes the two main characters, who occupy one extreme of that broad spectrum: they are lesbians who, voluntarily in one case and involuntarily in the other, have no biological children but are perceived to have a fraught relationship to motherhood and to behave in ways that sometimes resist and are at other times conventionally associated with maternal practice. In chapters 3, 4, and 5 of *Mother Without Child: Contemporary Fiction and the Crisis of Motherhood,* I trace the figure of the mother without child through a series of biological mothers in novels by the better known American authors Toni Morrison, Alice Walker, Louise Erdrich and Michael Dorris, Marge Piercy, and Margaret Atwood, whose plots entail the loss of a child or children. The fictional circumstances that disrupt or endanger the mother-child relationship are usually traumatic but highly various. The mothers in these narratives murder their own children, send them away temporarily or give them up for adoption, abandon them, or lose them to an oppressive state. The lines between voluntary and involuntary loss are often, but not always, blurred, as are perceptions about motives. In several of these stories, women arguably act out of fierce maternal love, although in some cases their intentions are misunderstood, and in others those intentions remain unknown, unclear, or unspoken. Finally, in the last chapter of *Mother Without Child: Contemporary Fiction and the Crisis of Motherhood*, I turn to several novels by the British writer Fay Weldon in which the recurring figure of the mother without child includes not only women traumatically separated from the children they have borne but also instances elsewhere on the spectrum: a woman whose child is stillborn, a woman who murders another woman's infant with severe birth defects, a mother-to-be, a mother whose child is threatened by American presidential politics, and a childless woman who discovers, in her sixties, that she has four clones, thirty years younger but otherwise identical to herself.

These instances of the mother without child by no means exhaust the supply of contemporary stories that could qualify for inclusion under this rubric and that might confirm, extend, or possibly contradict the conclusions I draw. I suspect that most readers, like most colleagues and friends to whom I have described my work over the past few years, will immediately think of characters and stories that I could or should have added or chosen instead. This reaction testifies not only to the limits of anyone study and the misjudgments I may have made in deciding what to use but also to the fact that the scope of my concern here is large and still growing and that much remains to be charted. The issues raised in these novels are prominent and pervasive, and the contemporary story of the mother without child, called to attention, demands future considerations.

Primary among my principles of selection was the importance of considering texts that come from more than one of the subcultures comprising that loose collective we think of as first-world contemporary fiction in English. (Quite apparently, the inclusion of some of the "subcultures" I treat also calls into question any notion of a static, monolithic first world.) Although motherhood is often spoken of in terms of culturally homogenizing and universalizing ideals and standards, stories of the mother without child individually and collectively refuse to let us forget that experiences of motherhood depart from the theories that would inform them, and they also insist on embedding mothers in specific historical communities and groups. Looking at somewhat different communities and groups throws into relief the ways in which explicit norms and tacit assumptions about motherhood are compromised by varieties of material circumstances, especially in periods of rapid social and technological change and cultural clashes.[18]

I should say at the outset what will soon be apparent and possibly frustrating to readers of this study: I propose no single meaning to these narratives of thwarted motherhood. These novels and stories raise a variety of questions and represent a variety of takes on that most complicated, confounding aspect of motherhood, its relational nature. Wherever we find examples of the mother without child, meaning has to be constructed locally, specifically, in particular contexts. At the same time, I aim to posit some vital common ground. The number and range of instances that can be aptly described by this rubric, despite their differences, argue for treating them as speaking together, although not always in one voice, to concerns that cut across divisions and differences.

Given both material circumstances and the rise of the feminist critique of motherhood, the appearance of so many fictional stories about women distanced in one way or another from their actual or potential children might appear over-determined and predictable, and it might seem that we don't need to look very hard to understand the phenomenon: women are writing about loss because they are losing their children, literally and figuratively. I by no means wish to gloss over this concern. To paraphrase one of the characters in Rule's *Desert of the Heart,* the relational aspect of motherhood, so long taken *for* granted, may no longer *be* granted. Even the biological connection, once a solid starting place for thinking about motherhood, has recently been attenuated by the most scientifically advanced conceptive technologies. As many feminist critiques of medicine and technology have argued, this is in fact not an entirely new development; mothers and midwives have been increasingly disconnected from childbirth over the course of the last hundred years (or more).[19] Some of the latest, more dramatic medical advances have seemed to put new measures of control over procreation into many western women's hands. But what can be viewed as an unprecedented opportunity for women can also be perceived as a threat to born and unborn children. Anxiety over how best to use (or limit) the control women have or want manifests itself most visibly, perhaps, in the abortion wars. Others, meanwhile, have pointed out how uncertain and ephemeral the benefits of reproductive technology may be.[20] For some women, anxiety verges on panic when the relentless progress of technology used for conceptive purposes threatens to reappropriate power for the medical profession and at the same time further fragments and controls the experience of motherhood. The ambiguities of medical and technological developments are reflected in the tension between the simultaneously emerging discourses of fetal rights and women's rights. Despite their opposing political stances, both move-ments tend to call into question the ideal of mother *with* child.

For increasingly greater numbers of women worries about either fetal rights or women's rights are a luxury; the urgent issues are how a mother can survive and take care of her living children's most basic needs. Poverty puts pressure on the middle-class norms of maternal-child relations, and unthinkable numbers of children and their increasingly isolated, unsupported mothers are visibly at risk in ways that are heartbreaking and resistant to solution. Apologists for "family values" often ignore the actualities of maternal work, and hence they too say stand between the (biological) mother and any means of meeting the needs of an actual child. As the editors of a special issue of *Signs* on "Mothering and Patriarchy" have observed, "Sentimentalized tropes of idealized mothering—endlessly loving, serenely healing, emotionally rewarding—have no counterpart in a political and social reality where the labor of caring is devalued, unsupported, and unseen, and where mothers are more likely to be endlessly burdened, anxious, and blamed. Biological motherhood, as a discrete and exemplary feminine event, is elevated, providing of course it occurs within the prescribed cultural scenario" (see O'Barr,

Pope and Wyer 14). Novels by and about lesbians, African Americans, and Native Americans show with particular clarity that the mother without child has historically been the brutal norm rather than the tragic exception. As previously underrepresented voices struggle to speak, and as we look more carefully for places in which they have already spoken, it should come as no surprise that we repeatedly hear sad stories about rupture and loss.

It might alternatively be argued that second-wave feminism itself is chiefly responsible, in one way or another, for the rise of stories about mothers who give up or lose their children.[21] Most obviously, in its critique of motherhood as a site of female oppression, feminism, like birth control, seems to threaten to take women away from the children they bear, or ought to bear. More subtly, perhaps, these stories might be read as the work of the feminist-as-daughter, unable to forgive her own patriarchal mother—either for abandoning the daughter, or for failing to let her go—and barely able to imagine herself as a feminist mother or to represent anything but the anguish of motherhood that threatens from all sides. It has been suggested that feminists may devise distancing strategies to avoid confronting their ambivalence about mothering (Davis 513).In Ruddick's view, something like this may be going on, and the resultant distance between feminist mother and child explains the limits of feminist critique: "Partly because they wrote as daughters, feminist writing about mothers wrote very little about the children mothers think and speak about" (1994: 30).[22]

Given such ominous circumstances, it might seem inevitable and tragic that we find so many stories about the mother without child, all serving to reflect or critique the ways in which the mother-child bond is (and perhaps for some should be) currently loosened and endangered, if not severed. Why do the novels I consider need further analysis, then? Though I would not wish to deny that these stories express anxieties about a multifaceted, sometimes tragic reality, they offer more than reflection and critique. These narratives can be read in ways that do not forget or transcend but rather remember and look within the sense of loss and impasse. In doing so they insist that we reconsider our assumptions about what motherhood is "really" like, that we resist fundamental theories and practices that would oppress mothers and divide women, and even that we pause before assuming that "the" maternal voice or an autonomous maternal subject can or should be sought.

These stories address several general, often overlapping issues. Both conservative and radical definitions of *mother* oversimplify in assuming that the "mother's" position or identity depends on the presence of the child to whom the maternal figure gives birth, nurturance, protection, and so on. Common experiences alone tell us that there is something left out if we fail to take account of the many moments at which a person might act as, feel like, or be considered a mother in the absence of a child. Before a baby is born, a woman is often thought of or thinks of herself as a mother; whether or not she ever gives birth, both traditional pronatalist and some feminist assumptions define every woman as a potential mother. When a child grows up and stops requiring maternal protection, takes responsibility for caring for himself or herself, or fails to offer affectionate reverence, that child still has a mother, and that mother may still identify herself (or himself) as such. When a mother loses or gives up custody of a child, or gives up hope that a child will live and so stops doing the work required to keep that child alive, or even acts to take back the life she has given in order to protect the child from suffering or to defend some other principle, that person may still be or wish to be considered a mother. In any of these instances where the child is absent, where the relation is, for good or for bad, temporarily or permanently, voluntarily or involuntarily broken off, what does motherhood consist of, what does a "mother" feel like? Does a woman without a child simply become (at last or again) a subject, an autonomous self, free from the claims and contradictions of motherhood? Or does she suffer a tragic, irreparable trauma? The story of the mother without child addresses these questions and thereby brings us closer to that frequently stated goal of feminist study: seeing maternal points of view more fully, hearing maternal voices more clearly and variously, understanding maternal subjectivity more deeply and complexly.

At another level of abstraction, the figure of the mother without child expresses the complexity of maternal consciousness by literalizing aspects of the unconscious. American feminism of the 1970s and early 1980s has been critiqued for ignoring the unconscious and positing a "one dimensional," unitary female self.[23] Stories of the mother without child confront without flinching the often-ignored hate, the fantasies of aggression, the desire even to kill her child that is allegedly repressed by conventional accounts of maternity (including feminist accounts). This dimension of maternal experience is brought out in Elsa First's recent discussion of Winnicott's belief that "hate," for both mothers and psychoanalysts, is a necessary element of "self-respect." As First says, Winnicott argues that the mother must acknowledge her hatred if the child is to come to terms with its own aggression and that "maternal resilience" depends on the mother's ability to "play" with her aggression, to recognize the "constructive energy" of anger. The fiction of the mother without child functions in some circumstances as a way of exorcising fear and guilt and even "playing" with aggression, although the stories may not look "playful" in any recognizably light-hearted sense.

Alternatively, if we are trying to take into account the "unconscious" of mothering, the motif of the mother without child speaks to the perception of recent psychoanalytic approaches that stress the constitutive division of maternity, the mother as "site of an originary, constitutive splitting" (Jacobus 147; see also Suleiman 1988).[24] Along similar lines, we might consider that the intersubjectivity of mother and child is, from the moment of birth, always and properly tentative and temporary as much as it is fiercely connected and interdependent. In her revisionary reading of Freud, Madelon Sprengnether has argued that the separation of mother and child, again considered at the level of the unconscious, should be seen as fundamental in human development in a positive way: "Mother's 'desire' leads her away from her infant, and her absence in turn elicits the child's creativity" (234). This can be put in less abstract terms: an important part of being a good mother by today's popular standards, as experts and mothers will attest, is knowing when and how to let go. If the mother's work entails preparing the child, from the moment of birth, for independence from caretakers, and thus paradoxically engaging in a relationship whose ultimate goal is greater disengagement, distance, or even dissolution, the story of the mother without child may figure instead of repressing this paradox.

Yet another tightly connected concern involves the perception that the child has come first and overshadowed the mother in the most influential theories. As many have noted, Freud's is an infantile theory of human development; since Freud, it has been difficult if not impossible to express anything but the child's point of view of the maternal object, which later becomes the adult's. As Knowles puts it, it is hard to see the "reality" of mothers' feelings, including their ambivalence, their desire, or even their dislike of bearing and caring for children, in "a world full of adults whose inner children feel impoverished, who still yearn for the good mothering of their fantasies" (6-7).[25] Children really do need to come first, at many points, and it is hard in practice as in theory not to identify emotionally and rhetorically with their needs. If we do so, however, we may continue to ignore the other half of the relationship. The story of the mother without child frees us, experimentally and provisionally, to focus on the mother, and in doing so to see her as a multifaceted and changeful subject. If narrative theories move away from the preoedipal mother-child bond as the source and site of literary activity, this move may find its narrative form in these stories.

Finally, in order to understand and attend to the emergence at this point in time of a new significance to the fictional figure of the mother without child, we need to set these narratives in relief against the old stories, the available plots and standing myths about mothers who lose their children or are threatened with such loss. My primary interest is *stories* about mothers without children, and stories need to be accounted for not only at the level of how they may represent, reflect, and resist current psychic and social realities or theories, but also in terms of how they engage available narrative patterns, in this case entering into and arguably revising a diachronic tradition of fictionally represented motherhood.

In western culture, stories about the mother without child are not new. Abandonment and separation are common themes, although the point of view from which these stories have been told has been the point of view of the child, broadly speaking, rather than the mother. Most of these stories, perhaps concomitantly, have not sought or served to scrutinize the implications of the relational status of maternal identity, to dislodge conventional, naturalizing assumptions, or to help us see or see with the mother. In fact, quite the opposite is true: the loss or threatened loss of the other member of the dyad, the child, has often been used to define and stabilize a particularly disabling meaning of *mother* rather than to open motherhood up to analysis, to acknowledge let alone express the perspective of a woman who mothers, or to tell the particulars of her experience.

A foundational example of this old story is the biblical tale of King Solomon and two women who both claim to be the mother of the same child. The women are identified as harlots or prostitutes who live alone together with their babies; the story begins when one of them brings the other to Solomon's court to claim that in the middle of the night the other woman accidentally smothered her own child and then switched the babies, taking the living child for her own. Relatively early in his kingship, Solomon uses this case to prove his sagacity, determining who the true mother is by putting (or pretending to put) in imminent danger the life of a child that they both claim. His strategy, indeed, anticipates what I suggest is going on in today's fictional explorations of motherhood: to find out "the truth" about "mother," he creates the fiction that her worst fears for her child are about to be realized. The constitutional paradox or double bind for the "real" mother here is as clear, at least to a feminist reading, as the cleverness of the King's ploy: to claim a child and prove her identity as a lawful mother, to demonstrate the capacity to protect that child as a good mother naturally should, a woman must go so far as to give a child up—that is, to stop being a mother. This is a familiar plot. Women are pitted against each other in a competition for the scarce commodity that proves their fertility and, indirectly, their heterosexual activity and availability. The "good" mother is positioned so that she stands in opposition to a quintessentially "bad" mother, a woman so dangerous that she causes the death of her own child and is willing to see a child murdered rather than give up the irrational struggle for possession. The "good" woman and mother can speak only to erase her authority, to renounce possession, to disown her desire; a mother is someone who sacrifices something she has and wants, or is willing to do so, for the good of another. As we all might have learned from the case of Baby M and Mary Beth Whitehead, to want a child too much—so much that one breaks the law—is still to prove that one isn't really a fit mother, that one can't subordinate one's own needs for the child to the best interests of the child. The good mother understands the limits of her love and power and polices the dangers of maternal excess.

In thinking about Solomon's wisdom in this context and going back to the Old Testament to look again at how, exactly, the story was formulated, I noted something that struck me for the first time as peculiar: from the biblical narrative, it is impossible to tell which of the two nameless women—woman A, the one who brought the case to Solomon in the first place and accused her housemate of child stealing, or B, the one who was so accused—turned out to be the "real" mother, the one whose child was alive (or, in my reading, the one who was willing to sacrifice her own relationship to the child in order to save that child and identify herself). It would seem to be an odd omission of detail, but it is in fact consistent with the understanding that this story, like so many, obscures rather than represents anything about either woman's particular character or practical circumstances. The point is patriarchal wisdom in its starkest, purest form, founded on the construction of self-sacrificial motherhood and control over women whose maternity could otherwise manifest independent sexual and reproductive activity. Tellingly, these are "harlots" living alone, outside the marital bond, on the borders of the law.[26] The point is not to represent maternal subjectivity or maternal experience, and certainly not to explore female desire or agency.

If we focus on these latter-day concerns, we see what we already know about patriarchal wisdom: Solomon, its representative, is not interested in the truth or in the feelings and needs of the women in question. We might also wonder whether he is as wise as he seems, or whether he has been duped. Solomon misses or is unconcerned with the fact that both women are victims. One of them has already lost her infant, and if the mother of the dead child is in fact B, the woman who stands accused of child stealing, then her crime may be understood, if not excused, as a sign of her grief, perhaps even her denial and delusion. Or suppose that woman A is not telling the truth, that she is actually the one whose child died in the night, who then thinks up the clever idea of bringing woman B and B's still living baby to court, falsely claiming that B has stolen that baby. In this case, we might still want to see A as deranged with grief, but her stratagem would suggest that she has become canny, not irrational, in the face of loss. In either event, it seems altogether possible that Solomon (or the teller of the story, who equates the self-sacrificial woman with the mother of the living child) could be outsmarted in another way. How do we know that the mother who gets the child isn't just the better performer, the quicker witted one who understands what words to say in order to prove motherhood? Perhaps the "real" mother of the child is like Lear's truthful daughter, Cordelia, sure that her love is more ponderous than her tongue. Or perhaps she suffers from postpartum depression and, in a moment of great stress, standing before the King, almost welcomes the solution his sword pretends to offer.

We can, it seems, be sure of only one thing: the "patriarchal mother"—a term used by feminist critics to disparage a mother who is complicit with the system that devalues motherhood and oppresses women—wins the case and gets to keep the child. This, again, is the point of the story.[27] But how might feminist retellings of the Solomon story alter this point? In such revisions, maternal identity as formed in patriarchal contexts might still be tested by the loss or threatened loss of the child; but in that testing new definitions and alternative plots might emerge. In the process, the woman who refuses to perform like a mother might well be the heroine, the one who resists patriarchal law and so ends up losing her child. Indeed, all of the stories of the mother without child that I consider here do just this. They call into question the implications, for women, of Solomon's long-standing wisdom, with its troubling presupposition that, as one Old Testament scholar puts it, "the presence of a love that knows not the demands of ego, of possessiveness, or even of justice reveals motherhood."[28]

Other familiar stories about the voluntary or involuntary loss of a child reiterate the patriarchal definitions of motherhood fundamental to Solomon's wisdom. In Greek myth, mothers often have real power, but typically that power is horrifying and may be turned against a child or children by a vengeful mother such as Medea or Procne or Althea. Somewhat less frequently, a powerful mother is turned into a victim by the loss of a child, as in the story of Demeter. In several eighteenth- and nineteenth-century novels, mothers who abandon their children are invariably portrayed as rogues (like Moll Flanders or Emma Bovary) or victims (perhaps the most pathetic of whom is Isabel Vane in *East Lynne)*; in both categories, they often suffer terrible punishments.[29] Recent stories use the loss of a child to represent threatening social change and then reconsolidate a conventional definition of the good mother (as in Miller's *The Good Mother).*[30] Or the story of lost children is used to suggest different definitions of mother, but ones that bring us no closer to a particular woman's point of view. For example, in a recent discussion of maternal identity with an ostensibly far different notion of motherhood in mind, one that aims to de-essentialize the concept of the "mother" and lay claim to "parental" status for fathers, Thomas Laqueur demonstrates his wisdom in a way oddly analogous to Solomon's method. Laqueur suggests that since "facts" (such as whose body bore the child) can no longer prove parenthood, emotions can. To show that "mothering" today is or should be gender-neutral and that fathers do as much emotional work as mothers (or in some cases more), Laqueur cites two instances in which the loss or threatened loss of a child proves parental (or paternal) identity: Gladstone's moving account' of sitting for days by the bedside of his dying daughter, and Laqueur's own sadness when his wife miscarried (and was less upset, according to him, than he as the prospective father was).[31]

Such stories about mothers—or in this last instance, fathers—whose relational identity is at once disrupted and confirmed by loss of the child, interesting and affecting as they may be, do not seriously challenge normative, categorical definitions of *mother*, although they may, read from the point of view of feminist critique, expose their faultlines and constructedness. Nor do these familiar stories help us to learn more about the possibilities or implications of a maternal subject somehow distinct from or independent of a relation to a child. They confirm that there is no concept of *mother* unless, as Ruddick says, there is a concept of *child.* The longevity of the Solomon plot also confirms how commanding stories may be, how much they may serve to mold and interpret experience in particular ways.

In the new stories that I consider, the loss or absence of a child may or may not still be presented as tragic or heartrending, and it may or may not literalize a fundamental aspect of human psychology, a "liberatory" political agenda, or a set of deplorable historical circumstances. The important difference, however, is this: these fictional women who are mothers (actual or, in some cases, potential) and their conventional maternal capacities, including their relational, nurturant, and protective abilities, are not utterly devalued or destroyed by the loss of the child, although they may be more or less damaged and are *always changed* in some way. And so the story, insofar as we know it, does not serve to confirm or disprove a fixed and fundamentally conventional *or* unconventional maternal (or parental) identity, be it one that is unified around bonding and self-sacrifice or divided between self and child, pre symbolic and symbolic positions, and so on. On the contrary, it leads toward demystification, denaturalization, and reevaluation of the norms and needs of motherhood. It insists that the position of the mother without child is not only a traumatic present reality but also a logical impossibility, a taboo, and therefore a site of instability that facilitates thinking about motherhood and women beyond official logic and conventional possibility. It exemplifies precisely what Butler calls "subversion within the terms of the law" (93), representing the woman who, unlike the patriarchal mother, is "a mother and outside the father's law at the same time" (Suleiman 1990: 166).

The law, in assuming that a mother bears, takes care of, and is revered by a child, at once presupposes and oversimplifies the meaning of the relational aspect of motherhood. Most (but not all) of the female characters in the stories I consider have hoped consciously or unconsciously at some point in their lives to follow this law, but for various reasons they are unable to do so or choose not to do so. In the old stories, a mother is known to the law only by her willingness to sacrifice everything, even her relation to the child; in them, the mother without child can only be either a criminal who breaks the law or a victim of circumstances or evil forces. In the new stories, as we shall see, she can subvert these categories of criminal or victim, bad or good mother, by not fitting comfortably into either or by occupying both at the same time.[32] Emerging in the last three decades in conjunction with both the material crises of contemporary maternal practice and the feminist critique of motherhood, the fictional death, threatened death, or absence of a child thereby serves as the instigation to different ways of hearing, knowing, and being mothers.

Notes

[1] This fragmentation is noted by Bassin, Honey, and Kaplan: "The quest for the symbolic control of the term *mother* powerfully illustrates how language defines and constructs reality. Is she the egg that holds the genetic code, the womb that sustains and nurtures, or the person who practices maternal work?" (19).

[2] I cite from *The Compact Edition of the Oxford English Dictionary,* s.v. "mother." For the historical introduction, see pp. viii-x.

[3] Other, newer dictionaries add to the definition in ways that merit more discussion than is relevant here. The development of what the *American Heritage Dictionary* calls "vulgar slang," whereby *mother* refers to "something considered extraordinary, as in disagreeableness, size, or intensity" (e.g., the mother of all wars), is particularly worth further feminist exploration. Notably, the *American Heritage* and other dictionaries follow the *OED's* lead in offering a second lexical entry, *mother* 2, to refer to "a stringy slime composed of yeast cells and bacteria that forms on the surface of fermenting liquids."

[4] It would be tedious to cite all the definitions that stress this relational identity, but it is widespread, not particular in any way to Ruddick's work. To note just one more example, see Evelyn Nakano Glenn, quoting Alison M. Jaggar: "As a working definition, I propose looking at mothering as a historically and culturally variable relationship ' in which one individual nurtures and cares for another'" (qtd. in Glenn 3).

[5] For overviews that are helpful see Chodorow and Contratto; Eisenstein (chapters 7-9); Simons. Simons, among others, argues that the gap between feminist repudia-

tion and recuperation of motherhood is less "absolute" than it is sometimes said to be, and she discusses the possibility of a more "integrative feminist resolution" of this opposition.

[6]This point is made in Deborah Rosenfelt and Judith Stacey's review essay, "Second Thoughts on the Second Wave": "The reaction to the fifties' cloying cult of motherhood freed millions of women like us to consider motherhood a choice rather than an unavoidable obligation, but it may also have encouraged many to deny, or to defer dangerously long, our own desires for domesticity and maternity. One of the ironic effects of this history is the current obsession with maternity and children that seems to pervade aging feminist circles, a romanticization that occasionally rivals that of the fifties" (351).

[7]Interesting critiques of various types of eighties recuperation are found in works such as Parveen Adams; Drucilla Cornell (especially chapter 1); Patrice DiQuinzio; Janice Doane and Devon Hedges; Ann Ferguson; Jane Gallop; Sarah Hoagland; Nancy Scheper-Hughes; Donna Stanton.

[8]Several feminist critics have made this observation. In the words of Terri Apter, with reference to new feminist arguments in the eighties about why women should mother: "Where do they leave us? There is no going back, no prodigal's return to the kitchen, no fond farewell to the outside world. Yet how can we go forward in a working world created for man, but with a mother's responsibility?" (xi). Or as Susan Rubin Suleiman (1988) says in "On Maternal Splitting: A Propos of Mary Gordon's *Men and Angels*": "Can we choose or discard at will our most deep-seated fantasies and self-representations? Do we dare, in a time of increasing social conservatism and/or disintegrating family life, to give up our sense of an absolutely privileged relationship with our children?" (1). These are also the questions asked by all of the novels that I look at here.

[9]For a briefer version, see Snitow (1991; see also Snitow 1990). The notion of "impasse" has been current in feminist thinking about motherhood since the late '70s; for example, Barbara Ehrenreich and Deirdre English argued that feminism had already reached a theoretical impasse in this regard as early as 1978, in *For Her Own Good: 50 Years of Experts' Advice to Women*. But I speak here of the more recent articulation of this impasse, which responds specifically to the various modes of '80s recuperation of motherhood. I take Snitow as a particularly persuasive voice in this regard, but there are others making equally interesting cases for the failures of feminism to carry through on its original insights. Frequently these are also arguments that seek to justify childlessness as an ethical choice in the wake of eighties backlash. See, for example, Carolyn M. Morell: "The strong public feminist voice of the early 1970s, arguing that women could have good lives without motherhood, is barely a whisper today. A maternal revivalism has occurred over the past two decades within feminism as well as in the dominant culture" (xvi).

[10]In *Reproducing the Womb: Images of Childbirth in Science, Feminist Theory, and Literature*, Alice Adams implies agreement with Snitow when she argues that although the "essentialism" of early feminists may have been misguided, "the visions

contained in the '70s-era utopias … still represent some of the most advanced thinking [about mothering] produced in second-wave feminism" (177).

[11]My focus here is only on the original prose contributions. The two poems included in this section, by Joan Cusack Handler and Susan Ticky, are easier to understand as belonging under the rubric of "maternal scenarios," and the same may be said of Cora Kaplan's "Fictions of Feminism: Figuring the Maternal," a review essay. Kaplan takes on what she sees as "a dangerous overinvestment in idealized fictions of maternal and sororal relations" in two books published in 1989, but because of the five-year time lag, this well-thought-out critique doesn't seem particularly new and is not meant to explore alternative feminist ways of thinking about motherhood in any detail.

[12]Snitow makes a brief reference to Sue Miller's *The Good Mother.*

[13]In "Why Novels Make Bad Mothers," Jessamyn Jackson argues that whereas the novel in its earliest forms in English was associated with prominent female authors, the status of women writers and the redefinition of the novel as "a preserve of masculine authority" can be precisely located in the second decade of the nineteenth century.

[14]For an interesting critique of Homans, see Davis (18-20).

[15]For a brief discussion of how metaphor also serves to create a "transitional space" as an alternative to the play space that the mother fails to create in *Beloved* and *Sula,* see Vickroy.

[16]Cited from Alice Munro, *The Progress of Love* (emphasis added).

[17]For a good exploration of the mother's inability to play games and tell jokes, see Tillie Olsen's story, "Tell Me a Riddle."

[18]Since my goal was depth and specificity of analysis rather than coverage, I have not included all of the fictional subcultures (such as Asian American or Latina) where I think the figure of the mother without child is also being explored, and I have chosen only one author to represent the postwar encounter of pronatalism and feminism outside North America, in England.

[19]See, for example, McClaren for discussion of the loss of women's control over reproduction from the sixteenth century on.

[20]A few examples of the many books and essays debating this concern include Hubbard; Whiteford and Poland; Stanworth; *Science as Culture*; Homans; Rodin and Collins.

[21]As I noted earlier, some, like Rosenfelt and Stacey in "Second Thoughts on the Second Wave," have argued that "the current obsession" with motherhood is an effect of the earlier repudiation, which caused women to deny maternal instincts. If this is so, then certainly stories about lost children could be explained as a manifestation of that denial, a projection of the sense of loss. Rosenfelt makes this point explicitly in another essay when she speaks of the "sense of terrible loss" she finds in what she identifies as the "post-feminist" novel: "Though often they grieve explicitly for the loss of a child, I am convinced that the less tangible loss they mourn is the certainty of the feminist dream, the myth of progress toward liberation surely attainable within the immediate future" (287). Nancy Miller, in

an interesting footnote, speaks of the "double truth of liberation and deferral" (46) that marks the experience of motherhood for many feminists, including herself. Compare my argument in the epilogue of *Mother Without Child: Contemporary Fiction and the Crisis of Motherhood.* that the figure of the mother without child represents a "double strategy," expressing the need both to resist pronatalism and to revalue maternal experience.

[22] Here Ruddick also insists, again, that "maternal concepts can be reflective of mothers, and a help to them, only if they are anchored in thinking about children."

[23] For examples of such criticism, see Bower; and the introduction to Bassin, Honey, and Kaplan (1-25).

[24] For yet another suggestive discussion of the unconscious and motherhood that takes a very different tack, see Ireland,. Ireland's argument is too complex to summarize here, but notably she contends, as I would, that the current uncertainty about what motherhood means serves to open up what she calls "a psychic 'space' wherein additional signifiers of female identity may emerge into culture" (135). Childless women in particular, Ireland proposes, are "an apt metaphor of our postmodern times" and "the decentered or divided nature of the self" (142); as "other women," holding" a third position" in the gender system and representing the paradox of absence, they also call needed attention to "the undervalued presence of the unconscious" (145-6).

[25] This point has been made by many others. For one formulation, see Garner, Kahane, and Sprengnether: "Psychoanalysis, whether it posits in the beginning maternal presence or absence, has yet to develop a story of the mother as other than the object of the infant's desire" (25). See also Suleiman's essay "Writing and Motherhood" (1985: 356); and Gallop.

[26] In a chapter that includes a brief discussion of 1 Kings 3: 16-28, Danna Fewell and David M. Gunn discuss the use of the metaphor of "whoring" for religious apostasy and point out an irony: "female prostitutes as a class constitute a serious challenge to the patriarchal control of women's bodies"; although prostitutes serve men's needs, they also represent "the possibility of a woman controlling her own sexuality, her own body" (170). This is an issue that Fay Weldon addresses extensively in *Praxis,* a novel I consider in the final chapter of *Mother Without Child: Contemporary Fiction and the Crisis of Motherhood.* For another discussion of the Hebrew term *zona* ("prostitute") and the movement from a characteristic associated specifically with women, "whoring," to a metaphor for the bad behavior of Israel, see Bird. For this and other references to the Solomon story in religious studies, I am indebted to Anne McGuire. For recent contributions to the discussion among legal feminists about the topic of motherhood, see Fineman and Karpin; and Fineman.

[27] One of the most fully developed treatments of the patriarchal mother is in Nicole Brossard's *These Our Mothers*; see my discussion of this argument in *Mother Without Child: Contemporary Fiction and the Crisis of Motherhood.* For another brief discussion, see Suleiman (1990: 163 ff).

[28] Not all feminist readings of the Solomon story would see it my way. This quota-

tion is in fact taken from Phyllis Trible's pioneering feminist analysis of the Old Testament story, in which Trible more or less accepts the model of motherhood that I have critiqued here. Trible assumes that A was both the woman whose child was alive and the woman who brought the case to court and that the other woman, the bad mother B, is "the agent of both death and deceit" in this tale. The king is credited with exposing the fact that both women are locked in a power struggle as long as each claims possession of the fruits of her womb; only when compassion motivates the real mother to sacrifice justice for life does the possibility of "transcendent love which brings truth and life" appear (31-3).

[29]For a brief overview of *East Lynne* and other novels that punish the mother who abandons her children, see Rosie Jackson's *Mothers Who Leave* (50-7). It is difficult to find instances of more subtle literary treatments of the mother who abandons her child, but one interesting text that merits further feminist discussion is Oscar Wilde's *Lady Windermere's Fan.*

[30]As Ann Kaplan suggests, "liberatory discourses" about issues like single motherhood, female sexuality, and custody of children may exist "in complex relation" to something she calls "a renewed sentimentalizing of motherhood," and Sue Miller's *The Good Mother* is a case in point of such sentimentality. As Kaplan also points out, "mothering is presented as a woman's only satisfying activity. Anna is destroyed when she loses primary custody of her child" (262). For a discussion of Hollywood treatments of mothers who give up their children, such as *Kramer versus Kramer,* see Jackson (1994: 65-76).

[31]See also Ruddick's response to Laqueur' essay in the same volume (Hirsch and Fox 222-33).

[32]For a usefully comparable argument that lesbians should practice an "elemental resistance to being either included or excluded" in the category of the family, with particular reference to legal practice and theory, see Robson.

References

Adams, Alice. *Reproducing the Womb: Images of Childbirth in Science, Feminist Theory, and Literature.* Ithaca: Cornell University Press, 1994.

Adams, Parveen. "Mothering." *The Woman in Question.* Eds. Parveen Adams and Elizabeth Cowie. Cambridge, MA: MIT Press, 1990. 15-27.

Alaimo, Stacy. "Cyborg and Ecofeminist Interventions: Challenges for an Environmental Feminism." *Feminist Studies* 20 (1) (Spring 1994): 133-152.

Apter, Terri. *Why Women Don't Have Wives: Professional Success and Motherhood.* New York: Schocken Books, 1985.

Babcox, Deborah and Madeline Belkin, comps. *Liberation Now! Writings from the Women's Liberation Movement.* New York: Dell, 1971.

Bassin, Donna, Margaret Honey, and Meryle Mahler Kaplan, eds. *Representations of Motherhood.* New Haven: Yale University Press, 1994.

Bird, Phyllis. "'To Play the Harlot': An Inquiry into an Old Testament Metaphor." *Gender and Difference in Ancient Israel.* Ed. Peggy L. Day. Minneapolis: Fortress

Press, 1989. 75-94.

Bower, Lisa C. "'Mother' in Law: Conceptions of Mother and the Maternal in Feminism and Feminist Legal Theory." *Differences* 3 (1) (1991): 20-38.

Brossard, Nicole. *These Our Mothers.* Toronto: Coach House Press, 1984.

Butler, Judith. *Gender Trouble: Feminism and the Subversion of Identity.* New York: Routledge, 1990.

Chodorow, Nancy and Susan Contratto. "The Fantasy of the Perfect Mother." *Rethinking the Family.* Eds. Barrie Thorne and Marilyn Yalom. New York: Longman, 1982. 54-73.

Cornell, Drucilla. *Beyond Accommodation: Ethical Feminism, Deconstruction, and the Law.* New York: Routledge, 1991.

Davis, Deanna L. "Feminist Critics and Literary Mothers: Daughters Reading Elizabeth Gaskell." *Signs* 17 (3) (1992): 507-32.

DiQuinzio, Patrice. "Exclusion and Essentialism in Feminist Theory: The Problem of Mothering." *Hypatia* 8 (3) (Summer 1993): 1-20.

Doane, Janice and Devon Hodges. *From Klein to Kristeva: Psychoanalytic Feminism and the Search for the "Good Enough" Mother.* Ann Arbor: University of Michigan Press, 1992.

DuPlessis, Rachel. *Writing beyond the Ending: Narrative Strategies of Twentieth-Century Women Writers.* Bloomington: Indiana University Press, 1985.

Ehrenreich, Barbara and Deirdre English. *For Her Own Good: 50 Years of Experts' Advice to Women.* New York: Doubleday, 1978.

Eisenstein, Hester. *Contemporary Feminist Thought.* Boston: G. K. Hall, 1983.

Ferguson, Ann. *Blood at the Root: Motherhood, Sexuality, and Male Dominance.* London: Pandora Press, 1989.

Fewell, Danna and David M. Gunn. *Gender, Power, and Promise: The Subject of the Bible's First Story.* Nashville: Abington, 1993.

Fineman, Martha. *The Neutered Mother, the Sexual Family, and Other Twentieth Century Tragedies.* New York: Routledge, 1995.

Fineman, Martha and Isabel Karpin, eds. *Mother in Law: Feminist Theory and the Legal Regulation of Motherhood.* New York: Columbia University Press, 1995.

First, Elsa. "Mothering, Hate, and Winnicott." *Representations of Motherhood.* Eds. Donna Bassin, Margaret Honey, and Meryle Mahler Kaplan. New Haven: Yale University Press, 1994. 147-61.

Friedman, Ellen G. "Where are the Missing Contents? (Post)Modernism, Gender, and the Canon." *PMLA* 108 (3) (1993): 240-52.

Gallop, Jane. "Reading the Mother Tongue: Psychoanalytic Feminist Criticism." *Critical Inquiry* 13 (Winter 1987): 314-29.

Gardiner, Judith Kegan. "Empathic Ways of Reading: Narcissism, Cultural Politics, and Russ's *Female Man.*" *Feminist Studies* 20 (1) (Spring 1994): 87-111.

Garner, Shirley Nelson, Claire Kahane, and Madelon Sprengnether, eds. "Preface." *The (M)Other Tongue: Essays in Feminist Psychoanalytic Interpretation.* Ithaca: Cornell 1985.

Glenn, Evelyn Nakano. "Social Constructions of Mothering: A Thematic Overview." *Mothering: Ideology, Experience, and Agency.* Eds. Evelyn Nakano Glenn, Grace Chang, and Linda Rennie Forcey. New York: Routledge, 1994.

Hirsch, Marianne. *The Mother/Daughter Plot: Narrative, Psychoanalysis, Feminism.* Bloomington: Indiana University Press, 1989.

Hirsch, Marianne, and Evelyn Fox, eds. *Conflicts in Feminism.* New York: Routledge, 1990. 205-21.

Hite, Molly. "Mother Underground (Fiction)." *Feminist Studies* 20 (1) (Spring 1994): 58-66.

Hoagland, Sarah. "Some Thoughts about 'Caring.'" *Feminist Ethics.* Ed. Claudia Card. Lawrence: University Press of Kansas, 1991. 245-61.

Homans, Hilary, ed. *The Sexual Politics of Reproduction.* Aldershot: Gower Publishing, 1985.

Homans, Margaret. *Bearing the Word: Language and Female Experience in Nineteenth-Century Women's Writing.* Chicago: University of Chicago Press, 1986.

Hubbard, Ruth. *The Politics of Women's Biology.* New Brunswick: Rutgers University Press, 1990.

Ireland, Mardy. *Reconceiving Woman: Separating Motherhood from Female Identity.* New York: Guilford Press, 1993.

Jackson, Jessamyn. "Why Novels Make Bad Mothers." *Novel* 27 (2) (Winter 1994): 161-73.

Jackson, Rosie. *Mothers Who Leave.* London: Pandora, 1994.

Jacobus, Mary. "Dora and the Pregnant Madonna." *Reading Woman: Essays in Feminist Criticism.* Ed. Mary Jacobus. New York: Columbia University Press, 1986.

Jaggar, Alison M. *Feminist Politics and Human Nature.* Totowa, NJ: Rowman and Allanheld, 1983.

Kahane, Claire. "Questioning the Maternal Voice." *Genders* 3 (1988): 82-91.

Kaplan, Ann. "Sex, Work, and Motherhood: Maternal Subjectivity in Recent Visual Culture." *Representations of Motherhood.* Eds. Donna Bassin, Margaret Honey, and Meryle Mahler Kaplan. New Haven: Yale University Press, 1994. 256-271.

Kaplan, Cora. "Fictions of Feminism: Figuring the Maternal." *Feminist Studies* 20 (1) (Spring 1994): 153-67

Kloepfer, Deborah Kelly. *The Unspeakable Mother.* Ithaca: Cornell University Press, 1989.

Knowles, Jane Price. "Introduction." *Motherhood: A Feminist Perspective.* Ed. Jane Price Knowles and Ellen Cole. New York: The Haworth Press, 1990. 1-7.

Laqueur, Thomas. "The Facts of Fatherhood." *Conflicts in Feminism.* Eds. Marianne Hirsch and Evelyn Fox. New York: Routledge, 1990. 205-21.

Martin, Biddy. "Lesbian Practice and Changing Lesbian Identities." *Destabilizing Theory: Contemporary Feminist Debates.* Eds. Michele Barrett and Anne Phillips. Stanford: Stanford University Press, 1992. 93-119.

McClaren, Angus. *Reproductive Rituals.* New York: Methuen, 1984.

Miller, Nancy. "Decades." *Changing Subjects: The Making of Feminist Literary*

Criticism. Ed. Gayle Greene and Coppelia Kahn. London: Routledge, 1993.

Miller, Sue. *The Good Mother.* New York: Harper and Row, 1986.

Morell, Carolyn M. *Unwomanly Conduct: The Challenges of Intentional Childlessness.* New York: Routledge, 1994.

Munro, Alice. *The Progress of Love.* Toronto: McClelland and Stewart, 1986.

O'Barr, Jean F. Deborah Pope, and Mary Wyer, eds. "Introduction." *Ties That Bind: Essays on Mothering and Patriarchy.* Chicago: University of Chicago Press, 1990.

Olsen, Tillie. *Tell Me a Riddle.* Ed. Deborah Silverton Rosenfelt. New Brunswick, NJ: Rutgers University Press, 1995.

"Preface." *Feminist Studies* 20 (1) (Spring 1994): 3-6.

Redekop, Magdalene. *Mothers and Other Clowns: The Stories of Alice Munro.* New York: Routledge, 1992,

Robson, Ruthann. "Resisting the Family: Repositioning Lesbians in Legal Theory." *Signs* 19 (4) (Summer 1994): 975-96.

Rodin, Judith and Aila Collins, eds. *Women and New Reproductive Technologies: Medical, Psychosocial, Legal, and Ethical Dilemmas.* Hillsdale: Lawrence Erlbaum Associates, 1991.

Rosenfelt, Deborah. "Feminism, 'Postfeminism,' and Contemporary Women's Fiction." *Traditions and the Talents of Women.* Ed. Florence Howe. Urbana: University of Illinois Press, 1991.

Rosenfelt, Deborah and Judith Stacey. "Second Thoughts on the Second Wave." *Feminist Studies* 13 (2) (Summer 1987): 341-361.

Ruddick, Sara. "Thinking about Mothering and Putting Maternal Thinking to Use." *Women's Studies Quarterly* 11 (4) (Winter 1983): 4-7.

Ruddick, Sara. *Maternal Thinking: Toward a Politics of Peace.* New York: Ballantine Books, 1989.

Ruddick, Sara. "Thinking Mothers/Conceiving Birth." *Representations of Motherhood.* Eds. Donna Bassin, Margaret Honey, and Meryle Mahler Kaplan. New Haven: Yale University Press, 1994. 29-45.

Rule, Jane. *Desert of the Heart.* Vancouver: Talon Books, 1977.

Scheper-Hughes, Nancy. *Death Without Weeping: The Violence of Everyday Life in Brazil.* Berkeley: University of California Press, 1992.

Science as Culture 3, part 4, (17) (1993).

Simons, Margaret A. "Motherhood, Feminism, and Identity." *Hypatia Reborn: Essays in Feminism Philosophy.* Eds. Azizah Y. Al-Hibri and Margaret Simons. Bloomington: Indiana University Press, 1990. 156-74.

Sprengnether, Madelon. *The Spectral Mother: Freud, Feminism, and Psychoanalysis.* Ithaca: Cornell University Press, 1990.

Snitow, Ann. "Motherhood—Reclaiming the Demon Texts." *Ms.* (May/June 1991): 34-7.

Snitow, Ann. "Feminism and Motherhood: An American Reading." *Feminist Review* 40 (Spring 1992): 32-51.

Snitow, Ann. "A Gender Diary." *Conflicts in Feminism.* Eds. Marianne Hirsch and Evelyn Fox. New York: Routledge, 1990. 9-43.

Stanton, Donna. "Difference on Trial: A Critique of the Maternal Metaphor in Cixous, Irigaray, and Kristeva." *The Poetics of Gender.* Ed. Nancy K. Miller. New York: Columbia University Press, 1986. 157-82.

Stanworth, Michelle, ed. *Reproductive Technologies: Gender, Motherhood, and Medicine.* Minneapolis: University of Minnesota Press, 1987.

Suleiman, Susan Rubin. "Writing and Motherhood." *The (M)Other Tongue: Essays in Feminist Psychoanalytic Interpretation.* Eds. Shirley Nelson Garner, Claire Kahane, and Madelon Sprengnether. Ithaca: Cornell 1985. 352-377.

Suleiman, Susan Rubin. "On Maternal Splitting: A Propos of Mary Gordon's *Men and Angels.*" *Signs* 14 (1) (Autumn 1988): 25-41.

Suleiman, Susan Rubin. *Subversive Intent: Gender, Politics, and the Avant-Garde.* Cambridge: Harvard University Press, 1990.

Trible, Phyllis. *God and the Rhetoric of Sexuality.* Philadelphia: Fortress Press, 1978.

Vickroy, Laurie. "The Force Outside the Force Inside: Mother-Love and Regenerative Spaces in *Sula* and *Beloved.*" *Obsidian II* 8 (2) (Fall/Winter 1993): 28-45.

Weldon, Fay. *Praxis.* New York: Summit Books, 1978.

Whiteford, Linda M. and Marilyn L. Poland, eds. *New Approaches to Human Reproduction.* Boulder: Westview Press, 1989.

Wilde, Oscar. *Lady Windermere's Fan: A Play About a Good Woman.* 6th ed. London: Methuen and Co. 1911.

Winnett, Susan. "Coming Unstrung: Women, Men, Narrative, and Principles of Pleasure." *PMLA* 105 (3) (May 1990): 505-18.

Young, Iris Marion. "Punishment, Treatment, Empowerment: Three Approaches to Policy for Pregnant Addicts." *Feminist Studies* 20 (1) (Spring 1994): 32-57.

Chapter 27

Faking Motherhood

The Mask Revealed

SUSAN MAUSHART

Oh Mother, was it tender to tell me nothing of what was to come and what it meant about marriage, motherhood, death? Tender not to whisper to me even once about resistance or escape, about honor and freedom?
　　　　　　　　　　　　　　　　　　　　　　—Phyllis Chesler

ALL MASKS ARE props for pretending. They can be tragic or comic, serenely composed or agape with horror. Yet every mask, regardless of the content of its expression, projects uniformity, predictability, stasis. Which is why, of all the many kinds of masks in the world, there is no mask of ambivalence or of metamorphosis. Masks portray emotion inert and unmixed in a trade off of range for impact.

At the same time—and for the very same reasons—we need our masks. Or at least we need some of them, some of the time. For all human beings, but perhaps especially so for those inhabiting complex urban environments, social masks are an indispensable accessory in our emotional wardrobe. Indeed, a person incapable of masking her "true" feelings is often (and quite rightly) regarded as immature, sick, or both. To a very considerable degree, what we call self-control depends on our ability to "mask," to deny and repress what we experience, to misrepresent it, even to ourselves.

Although he is deeply misunderstood on this point, it was Freud who pointed out the multiple dividends such repression can pay. Our facility with masks, he argued, has made possible the very infrastructure of our collective lives, which he called "civilization." It is difficult to dispute the point. The capacity for emotional make-believe, for pretense, for the construction of situationally appropriate masks, is perhaps our most enduring evolutionary advantage. It is also our greatest curse. The critical distance, it seems to me, lies between self-control and self-delusion.

The mask of motherhood refers to a repertoire of socially constructed representations that have crossed that line. What I am calling the mask of motherhood is in fact an assemblage of fronts—mostly brave, serene, and all-knowing—that we use to disguise the chaos and complexity of our lived experience. Like all social masks, the mask of motherhood is an invaluable means for organizing and domesticating the more rapacious aspects of the realities we confront. Yet the personal and political price we pay for this control has far exceeded the value of its social dividends.

The mask of motherhood is what keeps women silent about what they feel and suspicious of what they know. It divides mother from daughter, sister from sister, friend from friend. It creates an abrupt and tragic chasm between adults who have children and adults who don't. It distorts the distance between childhood and adulthood, cutting ever deeper gaps between the generations. It pits male parents against female, amplifying the disjuncture between the verbs "to mother" and "to father." Above all, the mask of motherhood, by minimizing the enormity of women's work in the world, nourishes and sustains the profound ignorance that confuses humanity with mankind.

We see the mask of motherhood in:

- the values of a culture that glorifies the ideal of motherhood but takes for granted the work of motherhood, and ignores the experience of motherhood
- media images of Supermom, complete with briefcase, "serious" hair, and a pair of designer-clad preschoolers scampering happily to help with the dishes
- the secret worry of the new mother that "I just wasn't cut out for this"—and the gnawing fear that it shows
- books that describe labor contractions as "forceful urges"
- the apologetic tones of the embarrassed mother who murmurs over the screams of her toddler's tantrum, "She's not normally like this…."
- breastfeeding propaganda that portrays bottle feeding as a form of child abuse
- women's magazines that promise "Great Sex after Baby!"
- childcare manuals that imply that "easy" babies are made, not born, and that an infant's digestive tract is somehow linked by fiber-optic cable to his mother's state of mind
- the grim one-upmanship of play-group moms comparing relative rates of vegetable consumption and verbal development
- the tolerance of women for the selective deafness of fathers at 3:00am, especially in the belief that "a man needs his sleep" so he can "go to work in the morning"
- debates about child care that pass judgment on "what's best for the child" as if a child's needs were separable from those of its mother, father, and siblings
- the smugness of the mother-at-home who looks with disdain on her sisters in the workforce
- the smugness of the mother in the workforce who looks with disdain on her sisters-at-home.

I was recently asked to speak to a group of undergraduate sociology students about my research into the meaning of contemporary motherhood. I started by dividing the group into two teams: parents and non-parents. I asked them to sit on opposite sides of the lecture hall, leaving a gap of empty seats in the middle. "Do you believe there is a 'great divide' separating parents from non-parents in our society?" I asked. "That people who have children are fundamentally different from people who don't have children?"

I asked the non-parents to comment first. "Of course not," explained one young woman. "Having a child doesn't change who you are as a person." Her fellow teammates nodded in agreement, despite the stifled groans and giggles from the other side of the room. I called for a vote and found the vast majority of non-parents rejected the notion of a great divide.

I addressed the same question to the parent group. Or I should say, I tried to. Before the words were out of my mouth, people were fairly shouting their responses: "Absolutely!" "You better believe it!" "YES!" Most of the people on this team happened to be women, and they proved by far the most vocal contingent. "Let me tell you something," one fortyish woman began, "Not only is there a great divide between those who have kids and those who don't, but there's a conspiracy about keeping the whole thing a secret." Another added, "Yeah, and by the time you figure it out, it's too late!" With this, the parenting team exploded in laughter.

The non-parents were slightly nonplussed. And who could blame them? What the parent group had to say sounded positively sinister, yet there they were, cackling away gleefully and starting to trade wisecracks. Within a few more moments, they were beginning to sound like a group of old army buddies reminiscing about life in the trenches. I didn't even bother taking a vote. The consensus was clear, and it was total.

To me, this scene was forceful illustration of two truths about contemporary parenting. The first is that yes, Virginia, there does seem to be a great divide between parents and non-parents in our society: becoming a parent does change you in significant and irreversible ways into a different person. And the second is that admitting as much publicly means breaking one of our society's most enduring taboos. To tell the truth (or some of the truths) about motherhood to non-mothers, we seem to feel, would be a bit like debunking Santa Claus on the front page of the *New York Times*. There's no disputing the facts, but you'd have to be a pretty bad sport to go around advertising them, wouldn't you? What's more, the odds are good that the naïve audience for whom such revelations would be "news" might never believe them anyway.

For the uninitiated, the realities of parenthood and especially motherhood are kept carefully shrouded in silence, disinformation, and outright lies. The conspiracy of silence is real, and it's documentable. That much is clear. What is much less clear is what purpose the conspiracy serves, and why the vast majority of women participate in it.

What I am calling the mask of motherhood is the outward and visible sign of this silent conspiracy—the public face of motherhood that conceals from the world and from ourselves the momentousness of our common undertaking. The mask of motherhood is what mutes our rage into murmurs and softens our sorrow into resignation. The mask of motherhood is the semblance of serenity and control that enables women's work to pass unnoticed in the larger drama of human life. Above all, the mask keeps us quiet about what we know, to the point that we forget that we know anything at all … or anything worth the telling.

At the same time, the mask of motherhood is a useful coping mechanism. Yet the danger—and it is one to which women are particularly prone—is that the make-believe can become so convincing that we fool even ourselves. When the coping mechanism becomes a way of life, we divest ourselves of authenticity and integrity. We diminish our knowledge, our power, our spirit as women. Ultimately, we no longer *make* a life—we *fake* a life.

Psychologist Harriet Goldhor Lerner believes that "pretending is so closely associated with femininity that it is, quite simply, what the culture teaches women to do" (14). Yet women themselves are clearly co-conspirators in perpetuating the grand illusions of femininity, and the mask of motherhood is no exception. The mask is a disguise of our own choosing, a form of personal armor that, as Lerner points out, ensures the viability of the self as well as our relationships. Pretending, in other words, is a form of self-protection. From this point of view, the mask of motherhood is like a camouflage, rendering our experience safely indistinguishable in a hostile environment. As Lerner writes, "Pretending reflects deep prohibitions, real and imagined, against a more direct and forthright assertion of self" (14).

For the present generation of women, the mask of motherhood is among the most deeply repressed and destructive of all female deceptions. Today, women confess guiltily—or gleefully—to faking orgasms. Yet how many of us will admit, or are even aware, that we are faking motherhood? As Lerner points out, when we fake orgasm, we deceive another. But when we fake motherhood, we betray our deepest selves.

The mask of motherhood not only mutes our voices. It also muffles our ears. Journalist Nina Barrett relates the experience of a young mother whose marriage is coming adrift in the wild wake of early parenthood. "In some of the mother's groups I've joined, I've brought this up in a roundabout sort of way," she confesses.

> But people don't seem to want to talk about it. I've heard other women make references to similar problems. It seems like they're almost bursting to talk about it, but they're embarrassed. Like it's somehow their fault. Or maybe they shouldn't be feeling these things…. (Barrett 142)

The mask of motherhood keeps women from speaking clearly what they know, and from hearing truths too threatening to face. That for every woman who "blooms" in pregnancy there's another who develops root rot. That childbirth—however transcendent or revelatory it may or may not be—still hurts like hell. That the persistent cry of a newborn can make your husband's snoring sound like a sonata. That your child's physical demands will diminish at only a fraction of the rate at which her emotional ones will multiply and intensify. That getting the knack of combining motherhood with career is like getting the knack of brain surgery: nice work if you can get it, but 99.9 percent of us never will. That having a "joint project" called a baby drives most couples farther apart, reducing intimacy as it reinforces gender-role stereotypes.

It's not as if we enjoy the dishonest. It's more that we seem to need it. It is scary enough to face the fact that you yourself are faking it. But the possibility that everyone else may be faking it too is downright terrifying.

The gap between image and reality, between what we show and what we feel, has resulted in a peculiar cultural schizophrenia about motherhood. Canadian sociologist Amy Rossiter argues that our public discourse on the subject of motherhood tells us simultaneously "everything" and "nothing" that we need to know (177). On the one hand, today's mothers are virtually flooded with "information." On subjects ranging from pregnancy to childbirth to toilet training and preparation for preschool—in virtually every mass medium from books, magazines, and pamphlets to hotlines, videos and web sites—we have an unprecedented number of facts at our fingertips. Yet getting a grip on them seems to get harder and harder. It was Cervantes who remarked that "facts are the enemy of truth." For all the information we have amassed on "how to do it," we remain more clueless and insecure about what we are doing and why we are doing it than perhaps any previous generation.

Anthropologist Sheila Kitzinger has pointed out that the media bombard mothers with advice on health care, self-care, and the maintenance of relationships: how to look good, feel good, and be assertive; how to "keep the romance in her relationship with her man, cook gourmet food and produce candlelit dinners, and at the same time be a perfect mother" (7). Women's magazines, child-care manuals, and parenting classes dispense "tips" on every aspect of mothering from toilet training to postnatal depression. "But the image of motherhood that is presented is a false one," Kitzinger concludes. "A woman who catches sight of herself in the mirror"—as it were, unmasked—"sees a very different picture. And the message is clear: she is a failure" (8).

Quite simply, what we see of motherhood is not what we get. As a result, the conviction that we are not measuring up becomes almost inevitable. Women's magazines, with their relentless emphasis on "personal development," "success," and "achievement," depict a version of motherhood as glossy as any pin-up—and about as representative.

A generation ago, Betty Friedan described what happened when one such magazine invited readers to respond to the topic "Why Young Mothers at Home Feel Trapped." When the editors had finished digging their way out from under the twenty thousand responses, they wondered if they might have touched a nerve (Friedan 59). Twenty-five years later, there is a new generation of young mothers, and many of them are not "at home" at all, at least not exclusively. Yet for many women the perception of entrapment remains, along with the sense that life is somehow living them instead of vice versa. The fit between our images of motherhood and the realities we confront is more uncomfortable than ever.

Basically, we have swapped our old set of stereotypes for a new and improved set. In traversing the distance between June Cleaver and Murphy Brown, we've come a long way, baby, without making any appreciable progress at all. Today's media no longer glorify the housewife. Instead, the spotlight has shifted to the celebrity Supermom, She-who-has-it-all. The headlines tell us "Celebrities' Lives Change Completely After They Give Birth." Kathleen Turner volunteers for library duty at her child's school. Meg Ryan takes her kids along on shoots. Julie Walters's newly delivered daughter smelled so "divine" that she "wanted to lick her all over" (*The West Australian*, 17 May 1996). With such tales of metamorphosis to sustain us, it's no wonder we're starving to death. Such images are the maternal equivalents of Playboy bunnies, nicely proportioned lives with soft curves in all the right places. Trouble is, they bear about as much relation to reality as a backlit, airbrushed cleavage does to a set of lactating glands with cracked nipples.

Meanwhile, as Susan Sarandon breastfeeds her daughter during an important interview, researchers in the United Kingdom are working on a slightly different angle. They find that fully half of all mothers with kids under five years old experience symptoms of intense emotional distress on a regular or continual basis; that women are five times more likely to be diagnosed as mentally ill in the year after their first child's birth than at any other time in their lives (Knowles and Cole 4-5). As one mom who has never starred in anything told researcher and parenthood educator Margaret Gibson, "Every mother does not cope. It is a myth that she does. It is a big lie. Not every mother copes, but few are brave enough to admit it" (30).

Research suggests that in our society motherhood can be and often is dangerous to our mental health. If fully half the population of young mothers is having trouble "coping," but almost no one will say so publicly, whose lie is it anyway?

"The most common question I am asked by women with young children is, 'why didn't someone tell me that it was going to be like this?'" writes the editor of one recent study of contemporary mothering (Knowles and Cole 3). In another study (Oakley 1979), new mothers were asked "Is looking after the baby anything like you thought it would be?" Only nine percent said "yes." One among the remaining 91 percent commented, "It's really like living in a different world" (263). Amy Rossiter, who conducted an intensive study into the transition to motherhood, found the major categories to emerge from her interview data were "Shock," "Being unprepared," "Panic," "Anxiety," "Not knowing," and "Feeling out of control" (168).

Yet we are unprepared for mothering in less obvious ways too. It's not just that we don't anticipate the horrors and the hard work. Perhaps more than anything, we fail to anticipate the depth and breadth of the mothering experience, its sheer transformative power in a woman's life. In her classic reflection on the myths and meanings of motherhood, *Of Woman Born,* Adrienne Rich evokes this sense of the emotional complexity and richness of new motherhood that no one mentions:

That calm, sure, unambivalent woman who moved through the pages of the manuals I read seemed as unlike me as an astronaut.... No one mentions the psychic crisis of bearing a first child, the excitation of long-buried feelings about one's own mother, the sense of confused power and powerlessness, of being taken over on the one hand and of touching new physical and psychic potentialities on the other...." (35-36)

Child-care specialist Penelope Leach writes, "Bringing up children is probably the most difficult life task people undertake, yet society offers less preparation for it than for any other.... Who would embark on breeding horses or rearing dogs in such ignorance?" (241).

While reading this research, I found myself thinking back to a conversation I'd had with my older sister some thirteen years ago. It was a few weeks after the birth of her first child. In hindsight I realize that Gregory was a classic "high needs" baby: irritable, alert, and colicky. At the time I was aware only that he was cute and cried a lot. I could see that Karen was spending what seemed to me an inordinate amount of time in her darkened bedroom. She was trying to concentrate on breastfeeding, she explained. (What was there to concentrate on, I wondered? Could putting a nipple into a little mouth really take so much time and thought?)

I recalled asking later, in a playful sort of way, "Well, tell me about motherhood. What's it really like, anyway?" I was taken aback by the intensity of her response. She looked away from the baby (and that in itself was a rare occurrence), and stared straight into my eyes. "I'm going to tell you this now, and I want you to remember it," she began. "Everyone lies. Do you hear me? Everyone lies about what it's like to have a baby. Don't listen to them. Just watch me, and remember."

I had no idea what a gift she was giving me. I was in graduate school then, just embarking on a career. I didn't even have a boyfriend, let alone an agenda for family planning. But because she was my big sister, I took it on trust. I did watch her closely in those years. In fact, I had very little choice. Because, after Gregory's birth, I found it almost impossible to have a conversation with her. Her body was there, of course, but her mind? Her attention? Her ability to focus? To empathize? To get "outside herself?" These seemed to have vanished. And with each of two succeeding children things only got worse.

"Maybe she should go back to work," I used to think. "Her mind has gone completely to dust." I was aware that she was intensely (and, to my mind, ridiculously) focused on her children. But it was only after my own mind had gone to dust, several years later, that I was able to fathom why and to give some structure to those observations she had forced on me during her years of exile in Motherland.

"Hang in there," she says to me now—now that I am the one juggling three small children and the vestiges of my former self. "The end is almost in sight. And by the time you get there, you'll wonder how on earth you ever coped at all. Instead of berating yourself for the times you've snapped, you'll stand in awe that whole days went by when you didn't snap. And by the time that happens, none of it will really matter any more." Other women who have traveled even further down the road of parenthood assure me (somewhat sadly) that "It all goes so fast. And before you know it, they're gone." Just when you've finally figured out what you're doing, in other words, it's all over.

The thought of each of us laboriously reinventing the wheel of motherhood is disturbing enough. But the prospect of having nowhere to travel with it is even worse. Feminist critic Phyllis Chesler believes that in our society "pregnancy and childbirth are savage tests of your ability to survive the wilderness alone. And to keep quiet about what you've seen. Whether you're accepted back depends on your ability to learn without any confirmation that you've undergone a rite of passage....You must keep quiet and pretend to return to life as usual" (133).

In her book, *Motherself*, Kathryn Rabuzzi describes motherhood as a "heroic quest" for women, a journey into selfhood and ultimate meaning that cries out to be chronicled, celebrated, and, above all, shared. She writes, "If a society existed in which the way of the mother were the norm, tales of mothers would predominate the way tales of heroes do in cultures throughout the world" (63). Yet the way of the mother *is* the norm, and that's the infuriating part. This heroic journey, this steepest of learning curves, this drama of birth and rebirth –whatever fine metaphors we choose to dress it up in, the processes entailed in mothering children lie at the very cores of what it is to be human. The fact that it needs saying at all is quite remarkable. And enormously revealing. Like a superior athlete or (to use a more appropriate metaphor) a gifted actor, we make it all look so easy. So that instead of being seen as something we do, the work of mothering is something we are: the dancer become the dance. Yet with every pirouette we execute, we feel heavier, clumsier, more contorted. The effort it takes to appear effortless is enormous.

The urgent task of reconciling the realities of motherhood with the ideals of feminism attracted little enthusiasm among the movement's "first wave" thinkers, possibly because most were still too close to the mask to see it. One who wasn't was the young Shulamith Firestone, whose radical manifesto *The Dialectic of Sex* advocated the complete abolition of motherhood in social terms and, ultimately (for Firestone had high hopes for cloning technology), in the biological sense. It was a particularly bad case of throwing the baby out with the bath water. Understandably, few were willing to go quite this far. At the same time, Firestone grasped a nettle that few others could even discern through the thicket: that the issues surrounding the "unequal distribution" of responsibilities for reproduction and care of the young lie at the center of human sexual politics, that without redressing this particular imbalance in the division of human labor, feminism could provide only stopgap solutions—which is precisely what it has done.

Until very, very recently, this fatal flaw in the feminist vision remained successfully concealed—or perhaps "masked" is a better word—in our public discourse. Increasingly, thanks to the work of contemporary researchers such as Arlie Hochschild *(The Second Shift, The Time Bind)*; Sharon Hays *(The Cultural Contradictions of Motherhood)*; Martha Fineman *(The Neutered Mother, The Sexual*

Family and other Twentieth Century Tragedies); Maureen Freely *(What About Us? The Mothers Feminism Forgot)* and others, our mothering consciousness is rising almost as fast as our expectations. Almost, but not quite.

It remains extraordinary to me that so many of us continue to experience motherhood as so much more, yet so much less, than we were led to expect. During the last trimester of my first pregnancy, I found myself staring in wonderment at total strangers. At crowds passing in the street. "All of these people were born!" I marveled, as if I had never before quite grasped the facts of life. "All of these people had mothers!" I would repeat it to myself slowly and with deliberation, as if translating from code.

For reasons that should be obvious, it was not an epiphany I chose to broadcast. I could picture myself trying to convey my "insight": "Listen everybody! You all were carried in a woman's body! A woman gave birth to each and every one of you? Isn't that incredible?" It was a revelation that was self-evident to the point of utter banality. At the same time, I was dimly aware then (and am acutely aware now) that the implications of these basic biological facts are profoundly, unutterably significant.

So why are they so fiendishly difficult to discern? How can a woman with a working brain advance to the third decade of her life before the thought occurs to her? When I first began to think seriously and in depth about the implications of motherhood as a central human concern rather than as a peripheral life option, the silences became quite deafening. I began to be aware not so much of barking up the wrong tree but of barking up a tree that the other dogs kept insisting was a broomstick.

As author Sarah Dowse has suggested, the task of unmasking motherhood requires nothing less than a "new imagination—a knitting together of body and mind." She confesses. "When I was younger I imagined that childbirth was incidental, almost irrelevant to the achievements of the intellect, to industry, commerce, or politics." Now a grandmother, Dowse insists that mothering, as the ultimate act of human achievement, needs to be seen as the foreground for such endeavors: "a central, revelatory event" (120).

Other recent writers on the subject of motherhood agree. Yet the suspicion remains that the "new imagination" that dares to move motherhood from the periphery to the center may be sheer self-indulgence—a form of gender parochialism or a peculiarly feminine hubris. The temptation of self-censorship remains almost irresistible. Debra Adelaide has observed how often the urge to speak publicly about motherhood ("the most compelling experience of one's life") is suppressed. "The messages one receives say: Don't write about this. It's self-indulgent. Boring. Of limited interest"—even to mothers themselves (2-3). I know exactly what Adelaide means. One prospective publisher of this book, herself a mother, claimed to be personally interested in the topic but had severe doubts about whether anyone else would. "Mothers want to read about their babies, not themselves," she explained apologetically.

This sense that a discussion of motherhood is either immodest or somehow peripheral and irrelevant reflects the feelings of deep unworthiness that women ascribe to their work, a belief that what we do or fail to do doesn't really matter that much anyway. "My mother nearly died during each of her pregnancies," writes author Fiona Place. "But this, like so many details, I only found out by accident. I was dumbfounded. 'Why haven't you told me?' I asked her. 'I never considered it that important,' she replied" (44).

Women's experiences as mothers, writes Sarah Dowse, "continue to be locked out of history" (120). At one level, it is easy to see why. So few ever remark on the centrality of motherhood to the project of being human, because they simply cannot "see" it. It is a precondition of human existence, like air, water, food. For all human beings, motherhood begins as the invisible environment in which we grow and, to greater or lesser degrees, develop. "We don't know who discovered water," the critic Marshall McLuhan used to say, "but it wasn't a fish." It is no wonder we have not yet fully "discovered" motherhood. More than any other field of human endeavor, motherhood is the water in which all of us swim.

Yet this truth is not the whole truth. If it were, the notion of a "conspiracy of silence" would be easy to discount. Fish do not, after all, conspire to keep themselves in ignorance. But human beings do so conspire—both male human beings and female human beings, though for quite different reasons. Let's examine some of these reasons.

One of my favorite nuggets of wisdom is scrawled in a dank, dark subterranean passageway in the bowels of New York's prestigious Union Theological Seminary. It reads, "If men could get pregnant, abortion would be a sacrament." And so, too, using precisely the same logic, would childbirth and the rearing of children. One hugely important reason that scholarship, philosophy, and virtually every other form of public discourse have been so astonishingly silent on the subject of motherhood is simply that men do not experience it. And what we call public discourse is a forum for what men know.

Discounting the last millisecond of human history, human beings have dwelt almost exclusively in what feminists call "the patriarchy," what our grandmothers called "a man's world." Leaving aside for a moment the fascinating theories, both evolutionary and otherwise, that attempt to account for this state of affairs—and leaving aside also the indignation we might feel about it all—the fact remains that, on the "to do" list for advancing human knowledge, the experience of women has yet to rate an entry.

Instead (and quite naturally, given its authorship) the list concentrates on things that men do. This is why "history" is about wars and battles; why literature is so singularly concerned with love and death (and the variety of means by which they may be "conquered"); why philosophy is dominated by abstraction and deduction; and why science has produced atomic energy but struggles with biodegradable diapers. I'm being simplistic, of course. But then again, it's a simple notion.

Where motherhood has been the subject of serious, sustained inquiry, it has been seen almost invariably as a cause, not an effect. This tendency is particularly marked in the field of psychology, where researchers have historically been more interested in apprehending mothers than in comprehending them.

As psychologist Paula Caplan (1989) and many others have pointed out, "mother-blaming" is the bread and butter of traditional psychotherapy. Another piece of inspired graffiti illustrates the point: "My mother made me a homosexual." (Response: "If I give her the yarn, will she make me one too?"). The idea that, whatever we become—particularly if it's something socially unacceptable—"mother made us" is deeply ingrained in our collective cultural unconscious. It is no wonder that, as psychiatrist Ann Dally has observed, motherhood is so often approached as a minefield of psychological risk. "It is difficult," Dally writes, "because mothers know that they will have to devote most of themselves, and their time and energy, to it for many years, and that however diligently they do this they will be blamed for whatever goes wrong" (20). We are fascinated with criminal mothers and criminals' mothers, and the mother of the serial killer invariably rates a page-one interview. The mother of the Nobel laureate, on the other hand, remains (like everyone else's mother) discreetly offstage.

Psychological investigation into motherhood, until the past two decades, has concentrated almost exclusively on the impact (usually negative) of mothers on children. To the extent that it has been studied at all, motherhood has been cast in a supporting role in the higher drama of child development. The revolutionary notion that the effect of children on women might be equally worthy of study was identified as a "paradigm shift" as late as 1990 (O'Barr *et al.*).

Again, from one point of view, it is easy to see why. Male researchers have not perceived motherhood as a "primary experience" for the simple reason that men do not mother. Men get mothered. Consequently, motherhood has usually been examined as something that happens to people, and almost never as something that people do.

It's a bit like the way my six-year-old feels about her teacher—and the way, I venture to say, nearly all six-year-olds feel about their teachers. We saw Mrs. Cunningham get into her car one day, and Anna was astounded. "That's Mrs. Cunningham!" she shouted. "Getting into a ... car! Where is she going?"

It is not that children see their teachers as unimportant, or disempowered. Far from it. They see them as enormously powerful. But at the same time, the notion that a first grade teacher might have a life outside the classroom, or—even more shocking—might have emotions, needs, or desires within it, is almost literally unthinkable.

Does Mrs. Cunningham have an interior life? For that matter, does she have an exterior one? (Or does she, in fact, sleep right there in the classroom, under her desk?) Is she, in short, any more than the sum of her impressive individual effects on 26 semi-literate six-year-olds? These questions are easy to answer from a grown-up's perspective. But for a child they are not only unanswerable; they are inconceivable.

Male investigators have tended to regard mothers in much the same way as children regard their teachers. Those to whom mothering is done will inevitably frame the experience in the passive, rather than the active, voice (for example, "He was raised by his mother"). So that, in the psychological literature, motherhood is interesting to the extent that it is a "cause" of something beyond itself (of deviance, for example, or adjustment). But the imaginative leap required to see it as an "effect" in its own right, has been rarely, if ever, taken. Studies examining the impact of children on mothers are about as common as research into the effect of lung cancer on smoking.

There is no doubt that we see the world not as it is, but as we are, whether we are six or sixty, male or female. When we couple this brute fact with the equally brute fact that most of the world's recorded "observers" have been male, we can explain a great deal about how the mask of motherhood has been created. But the problem of perception, enormous as it is, is only the first obstacle to understanding. The limits of one's perceptual field might be described as a kind of "structural ignorance." Thus, men are necessarily structurally ignorant of women's experience, just as women are structurally ignorant of men's. The second great barrier to understanding, after ignorance, is fear.

Motherhood is fearsome because it is so intensely powerful, entailing acts of creation before which all other human endeavor withers into shadow. In the creation stakes, motherhood is the big league, and everything else—art, science, technology—is a farm team. Is it really any wonder that (as the evidence suggests) at some subconscious level all men are terrified, awestruck, and deeply envious of the gender-specific miracle of creation? This "womb envy" is apparent in the male initiation rites of traditional societies, which typically center on a symbolic mimicking of the childbirth experience. Our society has found its own ways, equally dramatic, to even up the score between the reproductive haves and have-nots.

Some observers have argued that the social contract called patriarchy rests on a trade-off in which the control by men of the "means of production" (of social and economic power) compensates for female control of the "means of reproduction." While impossible to verify or refute empirically, for me the theory makes intuitive sense. It is this trade-off that ensures that the hand that rocks the cradle does not rule the world, or at least not absolutely or for long. From this point of view, the familiar formulations of gender-specific spheres of endeavor—the domestic versus the economic; the heart versus the head; nature versus culture—reflect more than a division of labor. They reflect a primary division of power.

The second factor in our culture's intense fear of motherhood concerns our perceptions of maternal omnipotence: the sense that babies and young children have that mother is the source of all life and (as the flip side of the coin) that her absence, or the withdrawal of her love, threatens them with annihilation and death. This fear is experienced by males and females alike; indeed, it may be a key reason why women have so willingly aided and abetted the conspiracy of silence.

It was Freud who opened up the Pandora's box called motherlove. But the man who brought us the concept of penis envy was ill-equipped to understand the precise dynamics of such love. (We're talking about a person who seriously believed that, given a choice between the capacity to wee with precision into a milk bottle and the ability to conceive and bear new life, most of us would opt instantly for the former.) He did perceive that the terror of maternal power affected males and females quite differently. But it was left to psychoanalyst Nancy Chodorow to grasp the psychological imperatives underlying the creation of gender.

Chodorow argued that for males, who are structurally prohibited from competing with maternal power on its own terms, normal psychological development involves making a decisive flight from all things feminine, and seeking incorporation in an alternative power structure that specifically excludes female participation. Women, on the other hand, are able to resolve the problem more directly. We do not need to flee from mother in order to escape her power. We need only become her—to "reproduce" maternal power through identification and re-enactment of the mothering role.

We are not necessarily comfortable about this; indeed, in our own society, matraphobia—the fear of turning into one's mother—is rampant. The residue of contempt and distrust of female power felt by women themselves remains palpable. Nevertheless, we tend to become what in our mothers we beheld, and sooner or later most of us succeed to the throne of motherhood. Our brothers meanwhile—like second sons sent forcibly to the colonies—must establish alternative dominions.

Analyses of the power of motherlove end up in the same place as analyses of the power of reproduction: with the conclusion that our entire social organization is a highly elaborated attempt to "get even" by culture for the biases of nature. It's exactly the same division of spoils as in the traditional divorce settlement, as a lawyer friend recently explained it to me: "The wife gets the kids, and the husband gets everything else." What we have learned to call the patriarchy is the same notion writ large—a trade-off between biological power and social control.

And therein lies the first of many strange paradoxes of human motherhood: that mothering is the most powerful of all biological capacities, and among the most disempowering of all social experiences.

It's been a nasty piece of work, this business of redressing the biological power imbalance. At the same time as men have labored to develop separate but parallel competencies, they have transformed their subliminal rage against "maternal omnipotence" into contempt for women. Instead of avowing their awe (and thereby acknowledging their dependence), men resist engulfment by belittling what women know and deriding what women do.

It doesn't take much imagination to see why males would feel they have something to fear in relation to female reproductive power. It seems somehow natural (if perverse) for men to minimize motherhood, whether as a creative act or as a form of dignified human labor. But why would women themselves do so? And make no mistake—women *do* do so. If the mask of motherhood is a conspiracy of silence, women are card-carrying co-conspirators. Why?

The multiple reasons why women betray women, and thereby themselves, are complex. One thing is clear: their intricate tangles are woven into the very warp and weft of our social fabric. Among other things, this means that there is no simple cause and effect relationship that will explain the puzzling tenacity with which women cling to the mask of motherhood. An examination of patriarchy as a social structure is indispensable to analysis of this. At the same time, it is important to avoid the intellectual passive-aggression that piously proclaims "the patriarchy made me do it."

An irony that is all too easy to forget is that the majority of this patriarchy is female. Consequently, whenever we assign blame to patriarchy, we implicitly hold ourselves responsible too. Although it is true to say that the mask of motherhood has been forged on the anvil of patriarchy, it is no man-made delusion. Women have made the mask of motherhood, and women have worn it. And so, too, must we wear the responsibility, along with the conviction that what we have made, we can unmake.

As feminist theorist Dorothy Dinnerstein (1976) argues, feelings of misogyny are as strongly embedded in the female psyche as in the male because of our common experience of helpless dependency on a mother perceived as infinitely powerful. Only by empowering fathers to assume the real work of "mothering," she contends, will the hateful hegemony of female power be mitigated.

In the meantime, we can't quite bring ourselves to trash our entire sex. At the same time, there is a distinct sense in which we feel about being female the same way Groucho Marx felt about high society: that we don't want to belong to any club that would have us as a member. Consequently, we enact our ambivalence stealthily and through silence, in our deep distrust and disrespect towards other women.

Critic Phyllis Chesler agrees that, in this sense, women are their own worst enemies. As she puts it, we have "learned at a very early age to dismiss the words of our mothers and to listen to our fathers" (92). I thought of this during a recent interview, as I listened to a self-possessed young mother confide, "Most of Mom's ideas about childcare are old wives' tales. If I have a question, I'd rather ask my doctor." There is no doubt that, under patriarchy, what Chesler calls "the power and wisdom of old women" has been debased into what most of the rest of the population calls "old wives' tales." What has less often been remarked upon is the frequency with which the old wives themselves—and the young ones bringing up the rear—have proved willing accomplices in this treachery.

As we have observed already, the mutual fear and distrust that women feel for one another is a key element in the retention of the mask of motherhood, and in the disempowering of women generally. Another possible reason why, according to Paula Caplan, is that "competition is forbidden to women, at least in straight-forward terms" (99). Our natural, even instinctual, drives for achievement and success have been diverted into uncomfortably narrow channels. Until quite recently, most of these channels centered on home and family—making mother-hood a woman's central "career path," her primary means of self-expression, and her deepest source of self-worth. It's no wonder women have hedged it about with secrecy and silence, with disinformation and downright lies.

As Caplan puts it, "Because of the limitations on what women can do, the mother's success or failure accomplishing this task takes on immense importance

... she and others measure her personal worth by how well she has accomplished it" (16). Even worse, a woman's sense of personal worth as a successful mother is often enhanced by the perceived failures of others. This can culminate in the pathetic "one-upwomanship" all too frequently encountered among mothers—a phenomenon which seems as prevalent among today's high-achieving Supermoms as it was in the stay-at-home generation that spawned them.

Personally, I have known women with multiple higher degrees who took direct, personal credit for their child's early teething (or walking or reading or whatever), and who obviously derived a deep sense of gratification from the process of drawing odious comparisons with those whose children developed at a different rate. ("No teeth yet? Oh, what a pity! But don't worry, they're sure to come sooner or later.") The implicit assumption that precocity in relation to teeth, or sitting up, or verbal development is somehow an index of a child's intellectual or moral superiority is bad enough. But that these "accomplishments" should be read as signs of the mother's superiority is downright perverse. Yet, wittingly or no, it is a trap into which most new mothers continue to tumble headlong. So that, instead of an honest sharing of the experiences of mothering, women indulge in a fearsome kind of maternal grandstanding which has less to do with sharing their concerns than with showcasing their triumphs.

As one participant in a recent study explained, "I find a lot of my girlfriends and the girls I listen to at playgroup and so on, talk about how their kids go to bed at seven and they eat broccoli" (Brown et al. 162). It's no wonder so many women are turned off the notion of a mother's group. An informant from Australia, a biologist in her early thirties and the mother of a much-cherished baby girl, was so repulsed by the prospect of playing Comparative Babies that she refused to visit her local child health clinic (a free screening and advice service). "The first time we went, I saw a knot of mothers and babies in the playground next to the clinic," Caroline explained. "I made sure I crossed the road quickly so I wouldn't have to pass them."

Although Caroline's reaction was an extreme one, the expectation that other women constitute potential rivals, rather than prospective pals, is probably more widespread among mothers than most of us would like to admit. For all our skill and experience as nurturers, we seem constitutionally unable—or unwilling—to provide effective nurturance to one another. Not at all coincidentally, we are equally inept when it comes to nurturing ourselves.

Paula Caplan argues that, as little girls in our society grow into the role of nurturer, they internalize the lesson that, for them, the wish to be nurtured is "inappropriate" (30). By extension, the needs of other females for nurture will come to be regarded with suspicion also.

Caplan's observation is that these dynamics come into play in all female-female relationships, creating structural barriers between women on all kinds of levels. Perhaps this is why, as Kathryn Rabuzzi says, "the feelings of most women for each other in contemporary Western cultures are remote ... Rather than learning to love other women, we more typically learn to fear and distrust each other.

Instead of mirroring ourselves positively, other women therefore more often reflect what is least desirable in ourselves" (188). When it comes to relationships between women in the active phase of their mothering lives, these barriers seem to loom particularly large, creating even more than the usual distance of doubt and distrust.

The reason, I suspect, has much to do with the "nurture shock" most women experience (and almost no woman anticipates) in the transition to new motherhood. There is no doubt that, whatever other changes new motherhood may entail, the neediness of the helpless newborn presents a woman with the ultimate test of her fitness to nurture. Even for the "best," most settled baby, the new mother must confront the realities of being on 24-hour-a-day call; of long periods without proper rest; of the physically gruelling routines of frequent feedings, diaper changes, bathing and washing; of worry over wind, constipation, and other digestive woes; of pain and frustration in the establishment of a breastfeeding routine.

In this virtual frenzy of caring, many women have reported feeling as if they have ceased to function, or even to exist, as people in their own right. To this extent, coping with nurture shock is perhaps the ultimate expression of selflessness. At the same time, to exist without a clear sense of self—however temporarily—means living dangerously. Nurture shock renders women emotionally vulnerable, as their lives become quite literally unbalanced. The sense that the demands of nurture shock are outrageously unfair (by one's former standards of reckoning) is probably widely felt, but rarely expressed. But even more unsettling is the dawning awareness that one's old sense of "justice" has suddenly become a relic, a quaint, vestigial notion rendered abruptly irrelevant by the cutting of a cord. For me, this first epiphany of new motherhood came within a few hours of my first child's birth. I was fortunate in having a "good" birth: drug-free, without complications or interventions. Perhaps partly because of this, I experienced an instant bonding with my daughter, a great, euphoric gush of maternal love of an intensity that I had never imagined possible. In addition to all this was the sheer relief of finding myself gloriously un-pregnant. (Within minutes after the birth, I danced into the shower, laughing gleefully at the flaccid, floppy remains of my tummy.)

Nevertheless, even the "easiest" birth is the end product of the hardest work of which a human body is capable—in this case, a period of active labor lasting about eight hours. Anna had been born at a civilized 7:30 pm. By midnight, I was not only ready for sleep; I desperately needed it. I glanced adoringly at my baby sleeping peacefully in her little plexiglass crib, and closed my eyes. And opened them. Anna was crying.

Ah! She must be hungry again, I thought. I offered the breast, which she accepted greedily. A few minutes later, her eyes closed (just as the La Leche League book said they would), and I gently placed her back in the crib. She opened her eyes wide in what looked to me a lot like terror. And then she screamed. Of course, I picked her up straight away. I tried feeding her again, burping her, rocking her. All the while, she was quiet and happy (just as Penelope Leach had promised). And every time I tried putting her in that damned plexiglass cell, she screamed as if scalded.

By the time an hour had passed in this fashion, and then two hours, my weariness had turned to exhaustion. I found myself wondering guiltily whether a midwife might not want to "pop in" (their favorite phrase) and take Anna to the nursery. But surely this would defeat the whole point of rooming in, I reminded myself sternly. And yet … I was so tired. So tired. I had never been more tired in my life. I had never needed sleep more than I did at that moment—not in my whole life. Even more to the point, I had never deserved sleep as much as I felt I deserved it that night.

Yet, against all this familiar assertion of needs and rights, of history and justice and entitlement, there was counter-posed a strange and stubborn reality: a baby who continued to cry heedlessly, and piteously, in spite of it all. My guilty and barely conscious acknowledgment that this was truly unfair was followed swiftly by the shock of acceptance that justice would simply have to be jettisoned, perhaps indefinitely.

"Of course," I think now (and so will any other mother with a child older than about eight hours). Of course. And how naïve ever to have thought otherwise. That first night was the merest of trial runs for the unprecedented selflessness—the emptying of self—that new motherhood demands. Seven years and three children later, I have come to see the "injustice" with far greater clarity. On the one hand, there is the unmaskable truth that the price of parenthood is almost incalculably high, when reckoned against the adult autonomy once taken for granted. On the other, there is the gift of growth and discovery that comes from breaking those old boundaries of selfhood. The glimpses of the biblical truth that, in order to find life, you must lose it. That in "forgetting" herself, a woman may begin to discover at last who she is.

I know all this now. But at the same time, I wonder about the necessity of the "shock" part of nurture shock in the initiation to first motherhood. So many women have suggested that it is impossible to prepare anyone for this first, full-on plunge into parenthood, and that it is therefore useless even to try. Although I agree to an extent with the first part, I find myself more and more suspicious about the second. It all sounds too much like the old arguments given for keeping women in the dark about childbirth—that you can't know what it's like until you experience it, that no preparation is possible, that it is an experience to be endured, then, mercifully, forgotten. In the case of childbirth preparation, it's easy to see how such attitudes were self-perpetuating, keeping a woman's hard-won knowledge a churlishly guarded secret even from her own daughters, her own sisters.

Of course, no preparation for childbirth will actually equip a woman completely for her time of trial. The intensity, the texture, the timing of the experience—even if it were not so highly variable and individual—could never be simulated. In my own prenatal classes, our partners were asked to pinch our arms to "symbolize" contractions while we dutifully puffed and panted through the pain. It was ridiculous, of course. A labor contraction is about as much like a pinch in the arm as a baby is like a Barbie doll. Yet the experience was still infinitely worth having, if only for the repeated message that something extraordinary was going to happen, something for which one would need to muster all the support and all the strength she could find.

In the same way, I remember being told by a friend that contractions would feel like waves of very painful menstrual cramps. While many would argue that this is putting it extremely mildly, I found the analogy helpful. Of course, it did not adequately prepare me for the sheer force of labor. Nothing but the experience of childbirth itself will tell you exactly what to expect. Everything else is mere metaphor. But there's a lot to be said for mere metaphor. It's a fundamental way in which human beings make meaning, in which we advance stealthily on the unknown by means of the known.

I think of the metaphor of "wilderness," used by Phyllis Chesler (1981), to describe the early days of motherhood. What I am calling nurture shock, Chesler describes as a savage test of a woman's ability to survive the wilderness alone. She believes it is patriarchy that is to blame. Yet I am not so certain. I wonder now why I didn't simply call the midwife and ask for help, why I felt so strongly the need to "take it like a woman," alone and in silence.

Heaven knows we can't blame the patriarchy for the vagaries of infant sleep patterns, for the sheer biological helplessness of the newborn. Yet we do need to think about what our society contributes, or fails to contribute, in the way of preparing us to handle that helplessness. We can't change the wilderness, but do we really need to explore it solo, and under test conditions? And if we do not—and if this looming, amorphous enemy called "the patriarchy" is not to blame—then what exactly is stopping us?

If it is true, as Caplan suggests, that most women's sense of self-worth remains largely bound up with their identification as nurturers, the impact of nurture shock may prove profoundly unsettling, with after-effects ranging from a temporary loss of confidence and feelings of disorientation to depression or even full-blown psychosis.

Although we might prefer to think otherwise, I suspect that the self-esteem of today's young mothers is at least as vulnerable as that of our mothers. We are at least as afflicted by a peculiarly maternal performance anxiety (and probably more so, given the new pressures to achieve under which most of us labor). And, when all is said and done, we secretly believe as fervently as any previous generation that our children reflect to the world our own competence, "goodness" and "success" as people. The anxiety among mothers to get it right has never been higher. Ironically, the odds of doing so have probably never been lower.

This performance anxiety about mothering, which entails a straining for effect in order to mask the underlying insecurity, is what Harriet Goldhor Lerner calls "faking motherhood"—a form of social pretending she sees as endemic among today's young women. The less certain we are of what we're doing, and why we're doing it, Lerner suggests, the more liable we are to resort to bluff and bluster. In the end, we are afflicted with a kind of maternal machisma: we put on the mask of motherhood and make it all look so easy.

When writer and new mother Melissa West attempted to research the experience of motherhood behind the mask, she unearthed the same eerie silence. For,
although she located plenty of material on the joys of mothering, West could find
"none to tell me as well how truly difficult mothering can be. No one writing
about being awake in the middle of the night, in between visits to a sick child's
room, no sleep for days, crying from weariness and frustration and helplessness.
Nothing. Silence" (28).

But more revealing than West's first reaction on discovering so puny a literature was her second reaction: an almost reflexive guilt about her own maternal
shortcomings. "It can't be that I'm the only mother to have felt as if 'me' was
disappearing, suffocating under the giant midden of daily tasks. I can't be the
only one. Why is nothing written? Why? ... I KNOW WHY. Because I'm never
supposed to feel these feelings, ask these questions..." (28).

The machisma of the mask of motherhood conceals a multitude of expressions:
some of them indescribably joyous, other piercingly sad or thunderous with anger.
Yet of all the faces of motherhood unmasked, perhaps the commonest—and certainly the most crippling—is the face of maternal guilt. Without doubt, guilt lies
at the crux of the crisis of mothering affecting young women today. To an extent
unprecedented in previous generations, we suffer guilt over the things we do as
mothers and the things we leave undone. In the explosion of options available
to our generation, something has apparently been blown up. That something, I
would argue, is nothing less than a secure sense of our bearings as women: of the
unique and inalienable roles that belong to us, and—equally important—of the
awesome responsibilities that may be peculiarly ours to bear.

The gains for women in the past three decades or so of social change, since
we ourselves were mothered, have been enormous. Yet it is fitting—indeed it is
imperative—that we begin to reckon our losses as well. In relation to our motherhood, what we have lost is, in a sense, our innocence. For most of us, there is
no going back to a view of mothering as an instinctual, unproblematic, "natural"
sequence of events. Mothering is something we are no longer capable of pursuing mindlessly, in the sense of being unmindful of the import of our choices and
their potential consequences. Perhaps this helps in part to explain our malaise.
We are a bit like the centipede who managed to get along just fine until someone
pointed out how hard it must be to coordinate a hundred different limbs. He
never walked again.

Indeed, the more we learn about motherhood, the less able we are to mother,
it seems. And the more likely we are to fake it instead—adopting techniques and
strategies to fill the void of our depleted confidence, placing our trust in medical
and/or psychological experts, and spurning the wisdom of the experienced practitioners all around us ourselves, our mothers, our sisters, our friends. The great
sociologist of mothering, Ann Oakley (1992), points out that, in our society, "it
is not women ... who know about motherhood, but health professionals" (188).
The result, psychiatrist and mother of four Ann Dally argues, is a generation

of mothers whose diligence masks a tragic insecurity. Such women, she writes, "are frequent attenders of general practitioners, pediatricians, clinics and social workers. They buy baby books and magazines galore, thrive on the whole idea of techniques of baby and child care and are always searching for advice from outside rather than for their own feelings and intuition…" (245). Yet this "solution" only drives women still further into isolation and uncertainty, leading ultimately to an increased "anxiety about whether one is doing the right thing and to guilt when things go wrong" (Dally 122).

Dally and others contend that the present generation is locked into a vicious cycle in which our escalating expectations of performance as mothers leads inevitably to perceptions of inadequacy and guilt. Sociologist Jesse Bernard notes that "our way of institutionalizing motherhood breeds guilt into the very fabric of a woman's character. She blames herself for every deviation from the model … And the only way some can assuage their guilt is by constant dedication to the child" (79).

In such cases, as Terri Apter observed in *Why Women Don't Have Wives*, "the boredom of the mother infects the child, and makes the child ask for more and more of the mother's attention, because the child does not understand what is lacking" (154). The result, says Dally, is a "rigid permissiveness" that saps the vitality of the mother even as it thwarts the spirit of the child (245). Like the full-time working mother whose parenting style degenerates into a round of tricks and treats and cajolery (mirroring that of the full-time working father), we feel too damned guilty to say "no" and say it plainly.

Others, who attempt to find a way out of the motherhood morass by concentrating their energies on professional achievement, tend to fare little better. Their guilt is different in kind perhaps, but rarely in degree, from that of the professional mother at home whose strenuous efforts to stimulate her children leave everyone unfulfilled.

Nature endows women with the capacity to reproduce, but it is culture that has tended to confine women to that capacity … nature that has given woman a "golden touch"; culture that has rendered the blessing an infirmity. Yet even beyond the constraints of culture, females pay a price for their biological superiority. Sarah Hrdy has pointed out that sexual asymmetry in the form of male dominance is "nearly universal" among our closest relatives, the primates (7). The relationship between this social fact and the reproductive responsibilities of females is obvious and incontestable.

Yet what distinguishes the sexual politics of homo sapiens from those of our fellow primates is the meanings we have made of the distribution of reproductive power. The life of all creatures revolves around the work of conceiving, bearing, and rearing young. What is uniquely human is our choice either to celebrate that power or to fear it—and, out of fear, to deny, subvert, and distort it.

Above all, the mask of motherhood conceals the almost unbearable tension between our power as creators and the dependencies that this power engenders—in our children, in our men, and in ourselves. Yet it is crucial to understand that it is not the tension itself that is the result of "false consciousness," but the attempt to deny that the tension exists, or that it matters. The issues that swirl around motherhood appear problematic because they are problematic—and not because the patriarchy says so. On the contrary, the forces that constrain women today are the ones that minimize the difficulties we face, insisting that motherhood is no big deal after all. Assuring us that once we muddle through, "the real world" will be waiting to receive us on the other side.

Unmasking motherhood means facing the sobering fact that real life is not temporarily elsewhere (back at the office, say, or at the gym, or on the evening news) but right here (on the couch, in the kitchen, curled up in the crib). Unmasking motherhood means accepting that we are all of us making it up as we go along, and wishing we knew better. And when we get that far, we may be able to begin sharing what we really experience, and pooling what we really know, about life on the other side of the great divide of parenthood. We might even have a chance to produce a generation of daughters who will rise to the challenge of motherhood fearlessly, and without apology or pretence. The struggle to unmask motherhood is the first step in reconciling reproductive power with social rights and responsibilities—a peculiarly female challenge with repercussions for all humanity.

References

Adelaide, Debra, ed. *Mother Love*. Milsons Point, NSW: Random House Australia, 1996.

Apter, Terri. *Why Women Don't Have Wives: Professional Success and Motherhood*. London: Macmillan, 1985.

Barrett, Nina. *I Wish Someone Had Told Me*. New York: Simon and Schuster, 1990.

Bernard, Jesse. *The Future of Motherhood*. New York: Penguin, 1974.

Brown, Stephanie, Judith Lumley, Rhonda Small, and Jill Astbury. *Missing Voices: The Experience of Motherhood*. Melbourne: Oxford University Press, 1994.

Caplan, Paula J. *Don't Blame Mother: Mending the Mother-Daughter Relationship*. New York: Harper & Row, 1989.

"Celebrities' Lives Change Completely After They Give Birth." *The West Australian*. 17 May, 1996.

Chesler, Phyllis. *With Child: A Diary of Motherhood*. New York: Berkeley, 1981.

Chodorow, Nancy. *The Reproduction of Mothering: Psychoanalysis and the Sociology of Gender*. Berkeley and L.A.: University of California Press, 1978.

Dally, Ann. *Inventing Motherhood: The Consequences of an Ideal*. London: Burnett Books, 1982.

Dinnerstein, Dorothy. *The Rocking of the Cradle and the Ruling of the World*. 1976. London: The Women's Press, 1987.

Dowse, Sarah. "Connections around Childbirth." *Mother Love*. Ed. Debra Adelaide. Milsons Point, NSW: Random House Australia, 1996.

Firestone, Shulamith. *The Dialectic of Sex: The Case for Feminist Revolution*.

London: Paladin, 1972.

Friedan, Betty. *The Feminine Mystique*. New York: Dell Publishing Co., 1963.

Gibson, Margaret. *Becoming a Mother: A Book for Australian Women*. Sydney: Hale and Iremonger, 1986.

Hrdy, Sarah Blaffer. *The Woman that Never Evolved*. Cambridge: Harvard University Press, 1981.

Kitzinger, Sheila. *Ourselves as Mothers*. London: Transworld Publishers, 1992.

Knowles, Jane Price and Ellen Cole, eds. *Motherhood: A Feminist Perspective*. Binghampton, NY: Haworth Press, 1990.

Leach, Penelope. *Children First*. London: Penguin, 1994.

Lerner, Harriet. *The Dance of Deception: Pretending and Truth-Telling in Women's Lives*. New York: HarperCollins, 1993.

Oakley, Ann. *Becoming a Mother*. Oxford: Martin Robertson & Company, 1979.

Oakley, Ann. *Social Support and Motherhood*. Oxford and Cambridge: Blackwell, 1992.

O'Barr, Jean F., Deborah Pope, and Mary Wyer, eds. *Ties that Bind: Essays on Mothering and Patriarchy*. Chicago and London: The University of Chicago Press, 1990.

Place, Fiona. "Apocalypse Now." *Mother Love*. Ed. Debra Adelaide. Milsons Point, NSW: Random House Australia, 1996.

Rabuzzi, Kathryn Allen. *Motherself: A Mythic Analysis of Motherhood*. Bloomington: Indiana University Press, 1988.

Rich, Adrienne. *Of Woman Born*. London: Virago, 1977.

Rossiter, Amy. *From Private to Public: A Feminist Exploration of Early Mothering*. Toronto: The Women's Press, 1988.

West, Melissa Gayle. *If Only I were a Better Mother*. Walpole, NH: Stillpoint Publishing, 1992.

Chapter 28

Killing the Black Body
Race, Reproduction and the Meaning of Liberty

DOROTHY ROBERTS

The painful, patient, and silent toil of mothers to gain a fee simple title to the bodies of their daughters, the despairing fight, as of an entrapped tigress, to keep hallowed their own persons, would furnish material for epics.

— Anna Julia Cooper, 1893[1]

IN 1989, OFFICIALS in Charleston, South Carolina, initiated a policy of arresting pregnant women whose prenatal tests revealed they were smoking crack. In some cases, a team of police tracked down expectant mothers in the city's poorest neighborhoods. In others, officers invaded the maternity ward to haul away patients in handcuffs and leg irons, hours after giving birth. One woman spent the final weeks of pregnancy detained in a dingy cell in the Charleston County Jail. When she went into labor, she was transported in chains to the hospital, and remained shackled to the bed during the entire delivery. All but one of the four dozen women arrested for prenatal crimes in Charleston were Black.

We are in the midst of an explosion of rhetoric and policies that degrade Black women's reproductive decisions. Poor Black mothers are blamed for perpetuating social problems by transmitting defective genes, irreparable crack damage, and a deviant lifestyle to their children. A controversial editorial in the *Philadelphia Inquirer* suggested coerced contraception as a solution to the Black underclass. Noting that "[t]he main reason more black children are living in poverty is that the people having the most children are the ones least capable of supporting them," the editorial proposed reducing the number of children born to poor Black women by implanting them with the long-acting contraceptive Norplant. This thinking was supported by the best-selling book *The Bell Curve*, which claims that social disparities stem from the higher fertility rates of genetically less intelligent groups, including Blacks.

Along with this disparagement of Black motherhood, policymakers have initiated a new wave of reproductive regulation. The targeting of Black women who use drugs during pregnancy is only one example. State legislatures across the country are considering measures designed to keep women on welfare from having babies—a goal also advanced by Newt Gingrich's Contract with America and then incorporated in the newly enacted federal welfare law. The plans range from denying benefits to children born to welfare mothers to mandatory insertion of Norplant as a condition of receiving aid. Many family-planning clinics, with the support of Medicaid, are already encouraging young Black women to keep the risky device implanted in their arms. The emerging agenda is reminiscent of government-sponsored programs as late as the 1970s that coerced poor Black women by the thousands into being sterilized. Meanwhile, a fertility business devoted to helping white middle-class couples to have children is booming.

How can we possibly confront racial injustice in America without tackling this assault on Black women's procreative freedom? How can we possibly talk about reproductive health policy without addressing race, as well as gender? Yet books on racial justice tend to neglect the subject of reproductive rights; and books on reproductive freedom tend to neglect the influence of race. Few, if any, have addressed the many dimensions of governmental regulation of Black women's childbearing or the impact this repression has had on the way Americans think about reproductive liberty.

The story I tell about reproductive rights differs dramatically from the standard one. In contrast to the account of American women's increasing control over their reproductive decisions, centered on the right to an abortion, this book describes a long experience of dehumanizing attempts to control Black women's reproductive lives. The systematic, institutionalized denial of reproductive freedom has uniquely marked Black women's history in America. Considering this history—from slave masters' economic stake in bonded women's fertility to the racist strains of early birth control policy to sterilization abuse of Black women during the 1960s and 1970s to the current campaign to inject Norplant and Depo-Provera in the arms of Black teenagers and welfare mothers—paints a powerful picture of the link between race and reproductive freedom in America.

Several years ago I spoke at a forum in a neighborhood church entitled "Civil Rights Under Attack: Recent Supreme Court Decisions," sponsored by several civil rights organizations. I chose to focus on how the Supreme Court's decision in *Webster vs. Reproductive Health Services*, which weakened the holding in *Roe v. Wade* and denied women a right to abortion in publicly funded hospitals, hurt Black women. I linked the decision to a series of current attacks on Black women's reproductive autonomy, including the growing trend to prosecute poor Black mothers for smoking crack while pregnant. When it came time for questions, I was immediately assailed by a man in the audience for risking solidarity around racial issues by interjecting the controversial issue of reproduction. He thought it was dangerous to mention the word "abortion." He said that reproductive rights was a "white woman's issue," and he advised me to stick to traditional civil rights concerns, such as affirmative action, voting rights, and criminal justice.

While this man felt that the civil rights agenda should leave out reproductive health concerns, the mainstream reproductive rights agenda has neglected Black women's concerns. Public and scholarly debate about reproductive freedom has centered on abortion, often ignoring other important reproductive health policies that are most likely to affect Black women. Yet I came to grasp the importance of women's reproductive autonomy, not from the mainstream abortion rights movement, but from studying the lives of slave women, like those described by Anna Julia Cooper, who fought to retain control over their reproductive lives. The feminist focus on gender and identification of male domination as the source of reproductive repression often overlooks the importance of racism in shaping our understanding of reproductive liberty and the degree of "choice" that women really have.

I want *Killing the Black Body* to convince readers that reproduction is an important topic and that it is especially important to Black people. It is important not only because the policies I discuss keep Black women from having children but because these policies persuade people that racial inequality is perpetuated by Black people themselves. The belief that Black procreation is the problem remains a major barrier to radical change in America. It is my hope that by exposing its multiple reincarnations, this book will help to put this dangerous fallacy to rest. I also want this book to convince readers to think about reproduction in a new way. These policies affect not only Black Americans but also the very meaning of reproductive freedom.

My objective is to place these issues in their broader political context by exploring how the denial of Black reproductive autonomy serves the interests of white supremacy. I am also interested in the way in which the dominant understanding of reproductive rights has been shaped by racist assumptions about Black procreation. Three central themes, then, run through the chapters of this book. The first is that *regulating Black women's reproductive decisions has been a central aspect of racial oppression in America.* Not only do these policies injure individual Black women, but they also are a principal means of justifying the perpetuation of a racist social structure. Second, *the control of Black women's reproduction has shaped the meaning of reproductive liberty in America.* The traditional understanding of reproductive freedom has had to accommodate practices that blatantly deny Black women control over critical decisions about their bodies. Highlighting the racial dimensions of contemporary debates such as welfare reform, the safety of Norplant, public funding of abortion, and the morality of new reproductive technologies is like shaking up a kaleidoscope and taking another look.

Finally, in light of the first two themes, *we need to reconsider the meaning of reproductive liberty to take into account its relationship to racial oppression.* While Black women's stories are sometimes inserted as an aside in deliberations about reproductive issues, I place them at the center of this reconstructive project. How does Black women's experience change the current interpretation of reproductive freedom? The dominant notion of reproductive liberty is flawed in several ways. It is limited by the liberal ideals of individual autonomy and freedom from government interference; it is primarily concerned with the interests of white, middle-class women; and it is focused on the right to abortion. The full extent of many Americans' conception of reproductive freedom is the Constitution's protection against laws that ban abortion. I suggest an expanded and less individualistic conception of reproductive liberty that recognizes control of reproduction as a critical means of racial oppression and liberation in America. I do not deny the importance of autonomy over one's own reproductive life, but I also recognize that reproductive policy affects the status of entire groups. Reproductive liberty must encompass more than the protection of an individual woman's choice to end her pregnancy. It must encompass the full range of procreative activities, including the ability to bear a child, and it must acknowledge that we make reproductive decisions within a social context, including inequalities of wealth and power. *Reproductive freedom is a matter of social justice,* not individual choice.

Black women's earliest experience in America was one of brutal denial of autonomy over reproduction. In Chapter 1 of *Killing the Black Body* , I describe the exploitation of slave women's capacity to produce more slaves and the denial of their rights as mothers. After Emancipation, racism continued to corrupt notions of reproductive liberty, helping to direct the birth control movement which emerged early in this century. Chapter 2 explores the alliances between birth control advocates and eugenicists during the 1920s and 1930s, as well as the rampant sterilization abuse of Black women in later decades. It also considers the debate about family planning and genocide that took place within the Black community throughout this period. In Chapters 3 through 5, I demonstrate that a panoply of policies continue to degrade Black women's reproductive decisions. Plans to distribute Norplant in Black communities as a means of addressing their poverty, law enforcement practices that penalize Black women for bearing a child, and welfare reform measures that cut off assistance for children born to welfare mothers all proclaim the same message: The key to solving America's social problems is to curtail Black women's birth rates. In Chapter 6, I argue that race also determines the use and popularity of technologies designed to enable people to have children.

Finally, Chapter 7 presents a reconception of liberty that takes into account this relationship between race and reproduction. The book ends by proposing an approach to reproductive rights that acknowledges the complementary and overlapping qualities of the Constitution's guarantees of liberty and equality. This approach recognizes the connection between the dehumanization of the individual and the repression of the group. It provides a positive claim to state support for poor women's procreative decisions that counters proposals to cut funding both for children born to women on welfare and for abortion. It also adds a compelling dimension to the feminist claim that reproductive liberty is essential to women's political and social citizenship. Thus, I hope to show that, while racism has perverted dominant notions of reproductive freedom, the quest to secure Black women's reproductive autonomy can transform the meaning of liberty for everyone.

The greatest risk in writing a book about reproductive domination is that it will leave the false impression that Black women have been no more than passive puppets in a unidimensional plot to control their actions. I try to avoid that perception by showing throughout this book Black women's activism in the struggle to control their own bodies. The full story of Black women's resistance and its impact on the national movement for reproductive freedom is long overdue. As Anna Julia Cooper recognized a century ago, this "fight, as of an entrapped tigress … would furnish material for epics" (qtd. in Loewenberg and Bogin 329).

"Bearers of 'Incurable Immortality'"

Before turning to the history of reproductive regulation, it is important to recognize the images of Black women that form its backdrop. America has always viewed unregulated Black reproduction as dangerous. For three centuries, Black mothers have been thought to pass down to their offspring the traits that marked them as inferior to any white person. Along with this biological impairment, it is believed that Black mothers transfer a deviant lifestyle to their children that dooms each succeeding generation to a life of poverty, delinquency, and despair. A persistent objective of American social policy has been to monitor and restrain this corrupting tendency of Black motherhood.

Regulating Black women's fertility seems so imperative because of the powerful stereotypes that propel these policies. A popular mythology that portrays Black women as unfit to be mothers has left a lasting impression on the American psyche. Although these attitudes are not universally held, they influence the way many Americans think about reproduction. Myths are more than made-up stories. They are also firmly held beliefs that represent and attempt to explain what we perceive to be the truth. They can become more credible than reality, holding fast even in the face of airtight statistics and rational argument to the contrary. American culture is replete with derogatory icons of Black women—Jezebel, Mammy, Tragic Mulatto, Aunt Jemima, Sapphire, Matriarch, and Welfare Queen. Over the centuries these myths have made Black women seem like "nothing more than the bearers of 'incurable immorality'" (Gutman 541). In this introduction, I focus on those images that have justified the restrictions on Black women's childbearing explored in subsequent chapters.

Reproduction as Degeneracy

The degrading mythology about Black mothers is one aspect of a complex set of stereotypes that deny Black humanity in order to rationalize white supremacy (Frederickson; Jordan). The white founding fathers justified their exclusion of Blacks from the new republic by imbuing them with a set of attributes that made them unfit for citizenship. The men who crafted the nation's government, such as Thomas Jefferson, claimed that Blacks lacked the capacity for rational thought, independence, and self-control that was essential for self-governance (Takaki). Racist thinking dictates that Black bodies, intellect, character, and culture are all inherently vulgar (West 85-86). It reflects a pattern of oppositional categories in which whites are associated with positive characteristics (industrious, intelligent, responsible), while Blacks are associated with the opposite, negative qualities (lazy, ignorant, shiftless) (Crenshaw 1331, 1381). These disparaging stereotypes of Black people all proclaim a common message: it is the depraved, self-perpetuating character of Blacks themselves that leads to their inferior social status.

Scientific racism understands racial variation as a biological distinction that determines superiority and inferiority (Stepan; Gould; Fields 95). Only a theory rooted in nature could systematically account for the anomaly of slavery existing in a republic founded on a radical commitment to liberty, equality, and natural rights. Whites invented the hereditary trait of race and endowed it with the concept of racial superiority and inferiority to resolve the contradiction between slavery and liberty. Scientific racism explained domination by one group over another as the natural order of things: Blacks were biologically destined to be slaves, and whites were destined to be their masters. It also forged an indelible link between race and policies governing reproduction. Because race was defined as an inheritable trait, preserving racial distinctions required policing reproduction. *Reproductive politics in America inevitably involves racial politics.*

As both biological and social reproducers, it is only natural that Black mothers would be a key focus of this racist ideology. White childbearing is generally thought to be a beneficial activity: it brings personal joy and allows the nation to flourish. Black reproduction, on the other hand, is treated as a form of *degeneracy*. Black mothers are seen to corrupt the reproduction process at every stage. Black mothers, it is believed, transmit inferior physical traits to the product of conception through their genes. They damage their babies in the womb through their bad habits during pregnancy. Then they impart a deviant lifestyle to their children through their example. This damaging behavior on the part of Black mothers —not arrangements of power—explains the persistence of Black poverty and marginality. Thus it warrants strict measures to control Black women's childbearing rather than wasting resources on useless social programs.

George Frederickson's description of the rationale for Jim Crow laws parallels the welfare and crime reform rhetoric we hear today:

> If the blacks were a degenerating race with no future, the problem ceased to be one of how to prepare them for citizenship or even how to make them more productive and useful members of the community. The new prognosis pointed rather to the need to segregate or quarantine a race liable to be a source of contamination and social danger to the white community, as it sank ever deeper into the slough of disease, vice, and criminality. (255)

Blaming Black mothers, then, is a way of subjugating the Black race as a whole. At the same time, devaluing motherhood is particularly damaging to Black women. As Simone de Beauvoir wrote in *The Second Sex*, "It was as Mother that woman was fearsome; it is in maternity that she must be transfigured and enslaved" (171). Being a mother is considered a woman's major social role. Society defines all women as mothers or potential mothers. Motherhood is compulsory for women: most little girls expect to become mothers, and women who do not are considered deviant. Because women have been defined in terms of motherhood, devaluing this aspect of a woman's identity is especially devastating. It cuts to the heart of what it means to be valued as a woman.

Jezebel and the Immoral Black Mother

From the moment they set foot in this country as slaves, Black women have fallen outside the American ideal of womanhood (Davis 5-7; hooks; Guy-Sheftall 10; Morton). This contradiction became especially pronounced during the Victorian era. The nineteenth-century image of the True Woman was delicate, refined, and chaste. Although she was considered physically and intellectually inferior to men, she was morally superior to them. She was perfectly suited to the home, where she served as mother and wife. All of her attributes were precisely the opposite of those that characterized Black women. "Judged by the evolving nineteenth-century ideology of femininity," Black activist Angela Davis observed, "Black women were practically anomalies" (5).

Not only were Black women exiled from the norm of true womanhood, but their maternity was blamed for Black people's problems. Contrary to the ideal white mother, Black mothers had their own repertory of images that portrayed them as immoral, careless, domineering, and devious.

One of the most prevalent images of slave women was the character of Jezebel, named after the biblical wife of King Ahab. Jezebel was a purely lascivious creature: not only was she governed by her erotic desires, but her sexual prowess led men to wanton passion (White 28-29). As early as 1736, the South Carolina *Gazette* described "African Ladies" as women "of strong robust constitution' who were 'not easily jaded out' but able to serve their lovers 'by Night as well as Day.'" Jezebel was diametrically opposed to the prevailing vision of the True Woman, who was chaste, pure, and white. As an unidentified Southern white woman wrote in *The Independent* in 1904, "I cannot imagine such a creature as a virtuous black woman" (td. in Guy-Sheftall 46). This construct of the licentious temptress served to justify white men's sexual abuse of Black women. The stereotype of Black women as sexually promiscuous also defined them as bad mothers.

The myth of the lascivious Black woman was systematically perpetuated after slavery ended (Lerner 163-71; Giddings 85-89; hooks 55-60). While white women were placed on moral pedestals, "[e]very black woman was, by definition, a slut according to this racist mythology," writes historian Gerda Lerner. Lerner notes a number of practices that reinforced this view: "the laws against intermarriage; the denial of the title 'Miss' or 'Mrs.' to any black woman; the taboos against respectable social mixing of the races; the refusal to let black women customers try on clothing in stores before making a purchase; the assigning of a single toilet to both sexes of Blacks" (163-64).

Historian Philip A. Bruce's book *The Plantation Negro as a Freeman*, published in 1889, strengthened popular views of both Black male and Black female degeneracy. True to the "retrogressionist" ideology of the time, Bruce argued that, without the moral discipline imposed by slave masters, free Blacks were regressing to their naturally immoral state.[2] He devoted two chapters to an exposition of Black women's lascivious impulses, which he claimed had been loosened by Emancipation. Bruce explained Blacks' sexual promiscuity by the fact that "the procreative instinct being the most passionate that nature has implanted" was especially potent in Negroes. He traced the alleged propensity of the Black man to rape white women to "the sexual laxness of plantation women as a class" (84-85). According to Bruce, Black men lacked any understanding of sexual violation because their women were always eager to engage in sex.

Bruce explicitly tied Black women's sexual impurity to their dangerous mothering. He reasoned that Black women's promiscuity not only provoked Black men to rape white women but also led the entire Black family into depravity. Black women raised their children to follow their own licentious lifestyle: "Their mothers do not endeavor to teach them, systematically, those moral lessons that they peculiarly need as members of the female sex; they learn to sew in a rude way, to wash, to iron, and to cook, but no principle is steadily instilled that makes them solicitous and resolute to preserve their reputations untarnished" (qtd. in Guy-Sheftall 11-12). Because it was women who "really molded the institution of marriage among the plantation negroes," Bruce explained, "to them its present degradation is chiefly ascribable." Other authors of the period similarly blamed the immoral example set by Black mothers for Black criminality. For example, Howard Odum, a professor at the University of North Carolina, wrote a chapter, "The Home Life, Diseases and Morals of the Negro," in which he attributed Blacks' poor home life partly to the sexual and domestic laxity of Black mothers (165). Decadent Black mothers, then, were responsible for the menace that Blacks posed for American social order.

A corollary of the myth of Black promiscuity is the belief that Black women procreate with abandon. According to a prominent treatise on reproductive behavior published in 1958, most Blacks regarded "coitus ... as [an] inevitable, natural, and desirable activity to be enjoyed both in and out of marriage; contraception is little known and considered at best a nuisance and at worst dangerous or unnatural; and pregnancy is accepted as an inevitable part of life" (Gebhard 154).

The myth of Black people's innate hyperfertility has been given currency by J. Philippe Rushton, a psychology professor at the University of Western Ontario. In *Race, Evolution, and Behavior: A Life History Perspective*, recently reviewed with *The Bell Curve* in the *New York Times Book Review*, Rushton traces the evolutionary origins of physical differences between the races, including brain and genital size. Blacks adapted to Africa's unpredictable environment, he argues, by developing high fertility rates, bearing more children but nurturing each one less. Rushton claims that Black women ovulate more often and mature sexually faster than white women while "sperm competition" among sexually indiscriminate Black males "leads to enlarged penises and testes to make deeper and more voluminous ejaculations possible." Rushton denied he was a racist to *Rolling Stone* reporter Adam Miller, saying, "it's a trade-off; more brain or more penis. You can't have everything" (Miller 7). While Rushton's propositions may be extreme, the view of unrestrained Black childbearing is commonly held and bolsters efforts to impose family-planning regimes on Black communities. Lacking the inclination to control their own fertility, it is thought, Black women require government regulation.

Mammy and the Negligent Black Mother

If the "bad" Black Jezebel represented the opposite of the ideal mother, the asexual and maternal Mammy was the embodiment of the ideal Black woman. The image of Mammy was based on the Black female house servant who cared for her master's children. Pictured as rotund and handkerchiefed, Mammy was both the perfect mother and the perfect slave: whites saw her as a "passive nurturer, a mother figure who gave all without expectation of return, who not only acknowledged her inferiority to whites but who loved them" (hooks 85). It is important to recognize, however, that Mammy did not reflect any virtue in Black motherhood. The ideology of Mammy placed no value on Black women as the mothers of their own children. Rather, whites claimed Mammy's total devotion to the master's children, without regard to the fate of Mammy's own offspring. What's more, Mammy, while she cared for the master's children, remained under the constant supervision of her white mistress (Fox-Genovese 292; Ferguson 153, 171). She had no real authority over either the white children she raised or the Black children she bore.

During the Jim Crow era, Mammy became a cult figure. In a period of brutal racial repression her image served as a valuable symbol of a good Black woman. White citizens created a "Black Mammy Memorial Association" in Athens, Georgia, in 1910 to solicit support for a Black vocational school modeled after Booker T. Washington's Tuskegee Institute. The association's promotional pamphlet asked, "Did you not have an 'Old Black Mammy' who loved and cared for you?" The "Black Mammy Memorial Institute," named by the chancellor of the University of Georgia, was established to train the Negro "in the arts and industries that made the 'old Black Mammy' valuable and worthy ... where men and women learn to work, how to work and to love their work" (Patton 149, 153).

Mammy also appeared in great American novels, including works by Washington Irving, James Fenimore Cooper, William Faulkner, and Robert Penn Warren. She was embodied in Aunt Jemima for the Chicago Columbia Exposition in 1893 and appeared on pancake boxes for decades (Staples A22). Perhaps the best evidence of Mammy's rise to cult figure status was her prominence in American motion pictures, which usually portrayed her as inept, subservient, and comical (Mapp 42; Bogle; Morton 7-8). Hattie McDaniel won an Oscar for her memorable 1939 performance as Scarlett O'Hara's Mammy in *Gone with the Wind*.

While whites adored Mammy, who dutifully nurtured white children, they portrayed Black slave mothers as careless and unable to care for their *own* children.

Whites described Black women as bad mothers not only because of immorality but also because of incompetence. The scapegoating of Black mothers dates back to slavery days, when mothers were blamed for the devastating effects of bondage on their children. When a one-month-old slave girl named Harriet died in the Abbeville District of South Carolina on December 9, 1849, the census marshal reported the cause of death as "[s]mothered by carelessness of [her] mother" (Johnson, M. 493).[3] This report's attribution of a Black infant death to accidental suffocation by the mother was typical of the U.S. census mortality schedules in the South. Census marshal Charles M. Pelot explained: "I wish it to be distinctly understood that nearly all the accidents occur in the negro population, which goes clearly to prove their great carelessness & total inability to take care of themselves." It now appears that the true cause of these deaths was infant illness, due to the hard physical work, poor nutrition, and abuse that their mothers endured during pregnancy (Johnson, M. 496-508; Savitt 400).

Whites believed that Black mothers needed the moral guidance that slavery once afforded. Eleanor Tayleur, for example, argued that deprived of the intimate contact with their morally superior white mistresses, freed Black women displayed uncontrolled passion and ignorance. "The modern negro woman," Tayleur complained, "has no such object-lesson in morality or modesty, and she wants none." According to Tayleur, Black women exhibited a purely animal passion toward their children, which often led to horrible abuses:

> When they are little, she indulges them blindly when she is in good humor, and beats them cruelly when she is angry; and once past their childhood her affection for them appears to be exhausted. She exhibits none of the brooding mother-love and anxiety which the white woman sends after her children as long as they live. Infanticide is not regarded as a crime among negroes, but it is so appallingly common that if the statistics could be obtained on this subject they would send a shudder through the world. (qtd. in Guy-Sheftall 44)

The conception of Black women as unfit for motherhood was reinforced by their working lives. The virtuous mother depended on her husband for support, while women who worked for wages were confined to the home and opposed to wage labor never applied to Black women. While Victorian roles required white women to be nurturing mothers, dutiful housekeepers, and gentle companions to their husbands, slave women's roles required backbreaking work in the fields.

Even after Emancipation, political and economic conditions forced many Black mothers to earn a living outside the home (Jones). At the turn of the century nearly all Black women worked long days as sharecroppers, laundresses, or domestic servants in white people's homes. There was a dramatic racial disparity among married women who worked for wages at that time. In 1870, in the rural South, more than 40 percent of married Black women had jobs, mostly as field laborers, while over 98 percent of white wives were homemakers (Jones 63). In

Southern cities, Black married women worked outside the home five times more often than white married women.

The demands of work within white homes undermined Black women's own roles as mothers and homemakers (Jones 127-29). Black domestics returned home late at night (if not on weekends alone) and had to entrust their young children to the care of a neighbor, relative, or older sibling. Sometimes older children had to be left to wander the neighborhood. The great civil rights leader W. E. B. Du Bois, a passionate defender of Black women's honor, recognized the irony of Mammy's care for white children rather than her own. "Let the present-day mammies suckle their own children. Let them walk in the sunshine with their own toddling boys and girls and put their own sleepy little brothers and sisters to bed," he declared in a 1912 issue of his monthly paper, *The Crisis* (78). Americans have expected Black mothers to look like Aunt Jemima—dressed in an apron and headrag and working in a white family's kitchen. American culture reveres no Black madonna. It upholds no popular image of a Black mother tenderly nurturing her child.

The Matriarch and the Black Unwed Mother

White sociologists during the 1920s and 1930s elaborated on the theory of a Negro pathology stemming from sexual depravity by focusing on family structure. Sociological studies of Black family life claimed that Black women's independence promoted Black male jealousy and irresponsibility (Dollard; C. Johnson; Davis and Dollard). In *The Negro Family in the United Stated*, Black sociologist E. Franklin Frazier reiterated the thesis that dominant Black women, by perpetuating the slave legacy of unwed motherhood, were the cause of family instability. Frazier saw Black people's redemption in their adoption of white family patterns. These sociologists held Black families up against a white middle-class model and declared that they were defective.

This theory was reincarnated in the 1960s in the myth of the Black matriarch, the domineering female head of the Black family. White sociologists once again held Black mothers responsible for the disintegration of the Black family and the consequent failure of Black people to achieve success in America. This thinking held that Black matriarchs damaged their families in two ways: they demoralized Black men and they transmitted a pathological lifestyle to their children, perpetuating poverty and antisocial behavior from one generation to the next.

Daniel Patrick Moynihan popularized this thesis in his 1965 report, *The Negro Family: The Case for National Action.* Moynihan, then assistant secretary of labor and director of the Office of Policy Planning and Research under President Lyndon Johnson, argued that reforming the Black family was vital to President Johnson's War on Poverty. Playing on the theme of degeneracy, Moynihan described Black culture as a "tangle of pathology" that is "capable of perpetuating itself without assistance from the white world." The chief culprit, Moynihan asserted, was Blacks' matriarchal family structure. According to Moynihan:

At the heart of the deterioration of the fabric of the Negro society is the deterioration of the Negro family. It is the fundamental cause of the weakness of the Negro community .... In essence, The Negro community has been forced into a matriarchal structure, which, because it is so out of line with the rest of the American society, seriously retards the progress of the group as a whole.

Moynihan thus endowed poor Black women—the most subordinated members of society—with the power of a matriarch.

The last two decades have witnessed a revival of this castigation of Black single mothers. In a 1986 CBS special report, "The Vanishing Family: Crisis in Black America," host Bill Moyers lent liberal authority to Americans' fears about the moral depravity of Black childbearing (Gresham 116). The report featured scenes from a housing project in Newark, where young welfare mothers and the estranged fathers of their children epitomized the Black stereotypes of sexual promiscuity and laziness. Recent rhetoric casts single motherhood literally as the cause of all social problems. According to American Enterprise Institute fellow Charles Murray (1993), "Illegitimacy is the most important social problem of our time—more important than crime, drugs, poverty, illiteracy, welfare, or homelessness because it drives everything else" (A14). Former education secretary William Bennett called it "the single most destructive social pathology in modern American society."

While Blacks have the highest rate of unwed motherhood, the rate among whites has grown most dramatically, from 3 percent to 22 percent since 1965 (Smith 81). Today, there are more white babies than Black babies born to single mothers. Still, single motherhood is viewed as a Black cultural trait that is creeping into white homes. "White illegitimacy was generally not perceived as a 'cultural' or racial defect, or as a public expense, so the stigma suffered by the white unwed mother was individual and familial," Rickie Solinger observes in her history of single pregnancy between World War II and *Roe vs. Wade* (24-25). Black unwed motherhood, on the other hand, was seen as a major social problem: "Black women, illegitimately pregnant, were not shamed but simply blamed .... There was no redemption possible for these women, only the retribution of sterilization, harassment by welfare officials, and public policies that threatened to starve them." Charles Murray (1993) hammered in this point in his *Wall Street Journal* editorial, "The Coming White Underclass," which warns white Americans that their rising illegitimacy rate threatens to spread to white neighborhoods the same crime, drugs, and "drop out from the labor force" that now infects Black communities.

The Welfare Queen and the Devious Black Mother

The myths about immoral, neglectful, and domineering Black mothers have been supplemented by the contemporary image of the welfare queen—the lazy mother on public assistance who deliberately breeds children at the expense of taxpayers to fatten her monthly check. The picture of reckless Black fertility is made all the more frightening by a more devious notion of Black women's childbearing. Poor Black mothers do not simply procreate irresponsibly; they purposely have more and more children to manipulate taxpayers into giving them more money. A 1990 study found that 78 percent of white Americans thought that Blacks preferred to live on welfare (Smith 9). In a chapter of *Welfare Mothers Speak Out,* entitled "Welfare Mythology," the Milwaukee County Welfare Rights Organization depicts a common sentiment about welfare mothers:

> You give those lazy, shiftless good-for-nothings an inch and they'll take a mile. You have to make it tougher on them. They're getting away with murder now. You have to catch all those cheaters and put them to work or put them in jail. Get them off the welfare rolls. I'm tired of those niggers coming to our state to get on welfare. I'm tired of paying their bills just so they can sit around home having babies, watching their color televisions, and driving Cadillacs. (72)

Bob Grant, the popular New York radio talk show host, appealed to his listeners' stereotypes by imitating a welfare mother, using an exaggerated Black accent: "'I don't have no job, how'm I gonna feed my family?' I wonder if they've ever figured out how they multiply like that," Grant railed over the airwaves. "It's like maggots on a hot day. You look one minute and there are so many there, and you look again and, wow, they've tripled!" (Gourevitch 28, 30). Grant calls his welfare reform proposal the "Bob Grant Mandatory Sterilization Act."

Modern-day racist ideology, then, seems to have shed the assumption that Black people are entirely incapable of rational decision-making. Rather, Blacks are more likely to be blamed for the poor choices they make. Charles Murray, for example, argued in *Losing Ground* (1984) that Black Americans' deviant family structure stemmed from Black women's rational responses to welfare incentives. Black mothers are portrayed less as inept or reckless reproducers in need of moral supervision, and more as calculating parasites deserving of harsh discipline.

According to this view, far from helping children, welfare payments to Black single mothers merely encourage their transgenerational pathology. As Princeton English professor Wahneema Lubiano powerfully depicts this rhetoric, "She is the agent of destruction, the creator of the pathological, black, urban, poor family from which all ills flow; a monster creating crack dealers, addicts, muggers, and rapists—men who become those things because of being immersed in *her* culture of poverty" (323, 339). The media often connect the welfare debate to notorious cases of neglectful mothers, leaving the impression that all welfare mothers squander their benefits on their own bad habits rather than caring for their children. In February 1994, Chicago police conducting a raid found nineteen barely clothed Black children living in a filthy, rat- and roach-infested apartment with little more to nourish them than cans of corn and Kool-Aid. The mothers of these children were five sisters who were all unmarried and living on welfare.

"The Chicago 19" soon became the leading portrait of families supported by welfare (Williams 1159, 1164-66). As President Bill Clinton announced his proposals for welfare reform, for example, ABC's *World News Tonight* ran footage of the story as the backdrop. A reporter introduced the topic of welfare reform by stating, "Here's an example of the problem. When the police found nineteen children living in squalor in a Chicago apartment last winter, it was a shocking symbol of all that is wrong with the system. Their mothers received more than $5,000 a month in welfare." This bizarre family came to represent welfare mothers rather than the far more representative women who devote themselves to making ends meet for the sake of their children.

The New Bio-Underclass

Along with these disparaging images of Black mothers, the media increasingly portray Black children as incapable of contributing anything positive to society. Many Americans believe not only that Black mothers are likely to corrupt their children, but that Black children are predisposed to corruption. This trend is epitomized by the panic over "crack babies," Black infants irreparably damaged by their mothers' use of crack during pregnancy. It was erroneously reported that these children sustained neurological injuries that warped their emotional development, making them unresponsive as babies and uncontrollable as toddlers. Newspaper stories warned of a horde of Black children about to descend on inner-city kindergartens in need of high-cost special services (Cornell; Kleinfeld; Simmons). But the brain damage crack babies sustained was supposed to cut even deeper: lacking an innate social conscience, crack babies were destined to grow up to be criminals.

As I discuss in Chapter 4, there is no good evidence to support this caricature of the crack baby. Nevertheless, the frightening image spawned a cottage industry of angry letters to the editor calling for harsh measures to keep crack addicts from having babies. "Reducing her welfare payments will not stop this woman from having babies," wrote one commentator. "The only way to stop her is the dreaded 'S' word—involuntary sterilization, either surgically or with Norplant. The other alternative is to allocate our resources to caring for unlimited numbers of crack babies while other children continue to be without health care" (Weisenburger). The figures cited are so astronomical that it seems as if most Black children in America are crack babies impaired by a host of defects. "By the end of the 1990s the first 'crack babies' will be entering their teens," a Michigan prosecutor predicted. "It is estimated that by the year 2000 about 4, 000, 000 citizens of the United States will have experienced *in utero* exposure to controlled substances" (Tague 3).

The stories about hopelessly defective crack babies represent a new kind of bio-determinism. Instead of transmitting immutable deficiencies through their genes, these poor Black mothers inflict similar damage *in utero,* "callously dooming a new generation to 'a life of certain suffering, of probable deviance, of permanent inferiority'" (Greider 52, quoting columnist Charles Krauthammer). These negative predictions easily become self-fulfilling prophecies when adoptive parents are afraid to take home a crack baby, teachers expect the children to be incapable of learning, and legislators believe it is pointless to waste money on programs for children who cannot possibly achieve. The upshot of this version of Black biological inferiority is the same as its hereditary cousin, exemplified by *The Bell Curve*: since these children are unalterably defective, any attempt to improve their lives through social spending will be futile. Indeed, John Silber, the influential president of Boston University, "went so far as to lament the expenditure of so many health care dollars on 'crack babies who won't ever achieve the intellectual development to have consciousness of God'" (Greider 52).

The new biodeterminism presents drugs, poverty, and race as interchangeable marks that inevitably consign Black children to a worthless future. The stories about crack babies always depict Black children and they often assume they are on welfare. As one reporter wrote, "Call them 'welfare babies,' 'crack babies,' 'at-risk babies,' or 'deficit babies'—by whatever term, they constitute a new '*bio-underworld*' of infants who are disadvantaged almost from the moment of conception" (Gardner, emphasis added). In this author's mind, children exposed to crack, receiving welfare, or living a disadvantaged lifestyle are all the same and they are all biologically inferior—and they are all perceived to be Black. The primary concern of this sort of rhetoric is typically the huge cost these children impose on taxpayers, rather than the children's welfare. A letter on the editorial pages of the *Atlanta Journal,* for example, noted that, in addition to burdening society with the cost of hospital care, "[c]rack babies most often grow up in a culture of welfare dependency; there's the cost of adding their names to the welfare rolls" (Dickerson).

The powerful Western image of childhood innocence does not seem to benefit Black children. Black children are born guilty. The new bio-underclass constitutes nothing but a menace to society—criminals, crackheads, and welfare cheats waiting to happen. Blaming Black women for bringing up a next generation of degeneracy stigmatizes not only mothers but their children as well.

***

Black motherhood has borne the weight of centuries of disgrace manufactured in both popular culture and academic circles. A lurid mythology of Black mothers' unfitness, along with a science devoted to proving Black biological inferiority, cast Black childbearing as a dangerous activity. This view has justified the regulation of every aspect of Black women's fertility, policies I describe in *Killing the Black Body*. It has also induced a deep suspicion in the minds of many Black Americans that white-dominated family-planning programs are a form of racial genocide. But the objective of reproductive control has never been primarily to reduce the numbers of Black children born into the world. It perpetuates the view that racial inequality is caused by Black people themselves and not by an unjust social order.

Notes

[1]Quoted in Loewenberg and Bogin, 329. Free Black women purchased their

daughters and sisters from white slave masters to enable them to escape sexual abuse. A fee simple title gives the holder absolute ownership of property.

[2]On Bruce and regressionist ideology, see Gutman, 531-44.

[3]Johnson is quoting South Carolina Mortality Schedules, 1850, Abbeville District.

References

Bennett, William J. (written testimony) House Subcommittee on Human Resources. *Illegitimacy and Welfare: Hearings on H.R.* 4, 104th Cong., 1st sess., Jan. 20, 1995.

Bogle, Donald. *Toms, Coons, Mulattoes, Mammies, and Bucks: An Interpretive History of Blacks in American Films.* New York: Viking, 1973.

Bruce, Philip A. *The Plantation Negro as a Freeman.* Williamston: Corner House, 1889.

Cooper, Anna Julia. *A Voice from the South.* (1892) New York: Oxford University Press, 1988.

Cornell, Rich. "The Hidden Devestation of Crack." *Los Angeles Times.* 18 Dec., 1994. A1.

Crenshaw, Kimberle. "Race, Reform, and Retrenchment: Transformation and Legitimation in Antidiscrimination Law." *Harvard Law Review* 101 (1988): 1331-1381.

Davis, Allison, and John Dollard. *The Personality Development of Negro Youth in the Urban South.* 1940. Washington: American Youth Commission, 1962.

Davis, Angela Y. *Women, Race, and Class.* New York: Vintage, 1983.

de Beauvoir, Simone. *The Second Sex.* New York: Knopf, 1952.

Department of Labor, Office of Planning and Policy Research. *The Negro Family: The Case for National Action.* Washington, D.C., 1965.

Dickerson, Jeff. "Crack Babies Cost Us a Lot More Than $504 Million." *Atlanta Journal.* 20 Sept., 1991. A18.

Dollard, John. *Caste and Class in a Southern Town.* New York: Harper, 1937.

Du Bois, W. E. B. "The Black Mother." 1912. *W. E. B. Du Bois: A Reader.* Ed. David Levering Lewis. New York: Henry Holt and Company, 1995/ 294.

Ferguson, Ann. "On Conceiving Motherhood and Sexuality: A Feminist Materialist Approach." *Mothering. Essays in Feminist Theory.* Ed. Joyce Trebilcot. Totowa: Rowman, 1983. 153-182.

Fields, Barbara Jeanne. "Slavery, Race, and Ideology in the United States of America." *New Left Review* 181 (1990): 95-118.

Fox-Genovese, Elizabeth. *Within the Plantation Household: Black and White Women of the Old South.* Chapel Hill: University of North Carolina Press, 1988.

Frazier, E. Franklin. *The Negro Family in the United States.* Chicago: University of Chicago Press, 1939.

Frederickson, George. *The Black Image in the White Mind.* Middleton: Wesleyan University Press, 1971.

Gardner, Marilyn. "Crack Babies Disadvantaged from Day 1." *Houston Post.* 14 January 1990. F1.

Gebhard, Paul H., et al. *Pregnancy, Birth, and Abortion*. New York: Harper, 1958.

Giddings, Paula. *When and Where I Enter: The Impact of Black Women on Race and Sex in America*. New York: Bantam, 1984.

Gould, Stephen Jay. *The Mismeasure of Man*. New York: Norton, 1981.

Gourevitch, Philip. "Dial Hate." *New York Magazine*. 24 October, 1994. 28, 30.

Greider, Katherine. "Crackpot Ideas; Exaggerated Reports of Damage Done to Babies Born to Mothers Who Use Crack Cocaine." *Mother Jones* 20 (July 1995): 52-58.

Gresham, Jewell Hardy and Lerone Bennett Jr. "White Patriarchal Supremacy: The Politics of Family in America." *The Nation* (24-31 July 1989): 116-122.

Gutman, Herbert G. *The Black Family in Slavery and Freedom, 1750-1925*. New York: Pantheon, 1976.

Guy-Sheftall, Beverly. *Daughters of Sorrow: Attitudes Toward Black Women, 1880-1920*. Brooklyn: Carlson, 1990.

Herrnstein, Richard J. and Charles Murray. *The Bell Curve: Intelligence and Class Structure in American Life*. New York: Free Press, 1994.

hooks, bell. *Ain't I A Woman: Black Women and Feminism*. Boston: South End Press, 1981.

Johnson, Charles S. *Growing Up in the Black Belt: Negro Youth in the Rural South*. Washington: American Council on Education, 1941.

Johnson, Michael P. "Smothered Slave Infants: Were Slave Mothers at Fault?" *Journal of Southern History* 47 (4) (1981): 493-520.

Jones, Jacqueline. *Labor of Love, Labor of Sorrow: Black Women, Work, and the Family from Slavery to the Present*. New York: Vintage, 1986.

Kleinfeld, Judith. "Crack-Impaired Children Show Strange Behavior in School." *Anchorage Daily News*. 20 Feb., 1995. B8.

Lerner, Gerda, Ed. *Black Women in White America: A Documentary History*. New York: Vintage, 1973.

Loewenberg, Bert James, and Ruth Bogin, Eds. *Black Women in Nineteenth-Century American Life*. University Park: Pennsylvania State University Press, 1976.

Lubiano, Wahneema. "Black Ladies, Welfare Queens, and State Minstrels." *Race-ing Justice, En-Gendering Power: Essays on Anita Hill, Clarence Thomas, and the Construction of Social Reality*. Ed. Toni Morrison. New York: Pantheon, 1992. 323-363.

Mapp, Edward. "Black Women in Films." *Black Scholar* 4 (6/7) (1973): 42-46.

Miller, Adam. "Professors of Hate." *Rolling Stone* 20 October 1994: 106-112.

Milwaukee County Welfare Rights Organization. *Welfare Mothers Speak Out*. Eds. Thomas Howard Tarantino and Dismass Becker. New York: Norton, 1972.

Morton, Patricia. *Disfigured Images: The Historical Assault on Afro-American Women*. Westport: Greenwood, 1991.

Moynihan, Daniel Patrick. *The Negro Family: The Case for National Action*. Washington: United States Department of Labour, Office of Policy Planning and Research, 1965.

Murray, Charles. "The Coming White Underclass." *Wall Street Journal* 29 October 1993: A14.

Murray, Charles. *Losing Ground: American Social Policy, 1950-1980*. New York: Basic Books, 1984.

Odum, Howard. *Social and Mental Traits of the Negro: Research into the Condition of the Negro Race in Southern Towns*. New York: Macmillan Co., 1910.

Patton, June O. "Moonlight and Magnolias in Southern Education: The 'Black Mammy Memorial' Institute." *Journal of Negro History* 65 (2)(1980): 149-155.

Rushton, J. Philippe. *Race, Evolution, and Behavior: A Life History Perspective*. New Brunswick, NJ: Transaction, 1994.

Savitt, Todd L. "Smothering and Overlaying of Virginia Slave Children: A Suggested Explanation." *Bulletin of the History of Medicine* 49 (1975): 400=404.

Simmons, Sheila. "Greater Cleveland's First Crack Babies Are Now in School; How Are They Doing? And at What Cost to Society?" *Plain Dealer*. 11 Dec., 1994. 8.

Smith, Lee. "The New Wave of Illegitimacy." *Fortune* 129 (8) (18 April, 1994): 81-87.

Smith, Tom W. *Ethnic Images*. Chicago: National Opinion Research Center, University of Chicago, 1990.

Solinger, Rickie. *Wake Up Little Susie: Single Pregnancy and Race Before Roe v. Wade*. New York: Routledge, 1992.

Staples, Brent. "Aunt Jemima Gets a Makeover." *New York: Timed*. 19 October, 1994. A22.

Stepan, Nancy. *The Idea of Race in Science: Great Britain, 1800-1960*. Hamden: Archon, 1982.

Tague, Tony, Muskegon County Prosecutor. *Protection of Pregnant Addicts ad Drug-Affected Infants in Muskegon County, Michigan*. Muskegon: Muskegon County Prosecutor's Office, 1991.

Takaki, Ronald T. *Iron Cages: Race and Culture in Nineteenth-Century America*. New York: Knopf, 1979.

Weisenburger, Ted. "Who's Protecting Our Children?" *Arizona Republic* 18 September 1994: E1.

West, Cornel. *Race Matters*. Boston: Beacon Press, 1993.

White, Deborah Gray. *Ain't I a Woman? Female Slaves in the Plantation South*. New York: Norton, 1985.

Williams, Lucy A. "Race, Rat Bites, and Unfit Mothers: How Media Discourse Informs Welfare Legislation Debate." *Fordham Urban Law Journal* 22 (4) (1995): 1159-1196.

Winthrop, D. Jordan. *White over Black: American Attitudes Toward the Negro, 1550-1812*. Chapel Hill: University of North Carolina Press, 1969.

Chapter 29

The Baby and the Bath Water

Disabled Women and Motherhood in Social Context

CAROL THOMAS

IN HIGHLY INDUSTRIALISED societies today, childbearing is an option not an inevitability for most women. An increasing proportion of women in Britain do not give birth to children, and many are "child-free" through choice. However, the majority of women do have at least one child, and for most the experience of bearing and/or rearing children is something they would not want to forego. Of course, some women who do want to conceive experience the problems and distress associated with their own or their male partner's infertility. Others choose to parent singly, or to parent in same-sex relationships.

A proportion of women in all of the above categories have physical or sensory impairment and first hand experience of disability, but their experiences have been largely overlooked in sociological studies of pregnancy, childbirth and early motherhood. This paper reports on the analysis of data from 17 interviews with disabled women. These were conducted as part of a follow-up study associated with a much larger health authority commissioned research project on the *maternity preferences* of women of childbearing age resident in one city.[1] The disabled women who were interviewed were either contemplating childbearing, were pregnant, and/or had young children.

Whilst the voices of disabled women are almost totally absent in sociological work on reproduction and parenting, there is a small but growing literature on disabled women's motherhood experiences springing from the disability movement itself (Finger; Morris 1992; Marris). My interpretation of the interview data owes much to this literature, not least because I can relate to the issues at a personal level.[2] It is becoming clearer that disabled women's desires, decisions and experiences of childbearing and parenting are interlaced with additional concerns stemming from the disablism they encounter, their personal experience of living with impairment *per se*, and their knowledge about the possible effects of reproduction on their bodies.

Whilst the aim of this paper is to give an account of these women's experiences through a discussion of three of the themes which emerged in the analysis of the interview data, it can also be read as a contribution to the further development of a *sociology of disability* (in the Irving Zola tradition, perhaps? [Williams 1996a]) as distinct from the well established *sociology of chronic illness* (Bury 1991). In other words, the analysis presented here is informed much more by a disability than by a chronic illness paradigm. In relation to my usage of key terms this means that in common with those writing from a disability movement perspective, the meaning of the term *disability* is *not* the condition or functional consequence of being physically or mentally impaired. Rather, *dis-ability* refers to the disadvantaging affects—referred to by many as the "social barriers"—faced by people with impairments flowing from *disablism*, the ideological antipathy to what is considered to be undesirable physical, sensory or mentally-related difference or "abnormality" in western culture. Disability is a form of social exclusion and not a product of impairment *per se*. However, conceptualising disability as a social phenomenon is not unproblematic and Gareth Williams has recently referred to the "hotly contested terrain" of the meaning of disability (Williams 1996b: 194).

There are a number of dimensions to this contestation, but in conceptual terms debate revolves around the place and nature of "the social" in understanding disability. On the one hand, "disability theorists"[3] and medical sociologists are engaged in debate about the "divide" between the "social model" approach (a touchstone of those writing from a disability movement perspective) and mainstream sociological approaches (interactionist, phenomenological) which focus on the experience of living with chronic illness (for a review of this debate, see Barnes and Mercer). On the other hand, disability theorists and writers are engaged in a debate among themselves (a notably gendered debate) about the place in the social model of both the "personal experience of disability," and the "experience of impairment" (see Oliver; Morris 1996; Crow; French). At the heart of these debates are questions such as: is disability entirely socially constructed/created as suggested by the social model of disability (Oliver), or is this an over-socialised view (Bury 1996; Williams 1996a)? Can/should the social model of disability be developed to take on board the *experience* of disability, and/or the *experience* of impairment (Morris 1996; Crow; French), or would such a development be politically dangerous because it redirects attention back to the individual and away from the social barriers which really cause disablement (Oliver; Finkelstein; Campbell and Oliver)?

It is not my intention to explore these debates here, but against this backdrop it is necessary to outline my approach more closely. It is one which attempts to explore the *experiences* of these women in order better to understand the ways in which disablism manifests itself in the reproductive arena. Much of the research in the sociology of chronic illness tradition tends to concentrate on issues of identity and meaning associated with "living with" *particular* conditions (Bury 1991). My approach differs from this in that I am interested in looking at the common experiences of disability of women who may have a *range* of impairments and chronic illness. Furthermore, there are disability theorists who argue that personal experience (either of disability or impairment) has no place in social model analyses (or disability politics), because it deflects attention away from the "social barriers external to the individual." My starting point is that the study of personal experience can powerfully illuminate aspects of these "social barriers," and so point to areas for social change. This reaffirms the sociological position that the study of individual lives can very effectively illustrate the social (Evans; Plummer; Williams 1996a).

So, what can these women's experiences tell us about the ways in which disablism presents itself on the journey through conception, pregnancy, childbirth and early motherhood? The quotations and examples which are selected for use in this paper are those which best exemplify what I interpret to be manifestations of disability. Put in another way, they illustrate the problems and issues that the women faced, which were embedded in the social fabric of services and structures, and particularly in the social relationships in which they engaged. The manifestations of disability are considered in connection with the following themes which emerge through the data analysis: first, engagement with the "risk" discourse; second, the pressure felt by disabled women to demonstrate that they are, or could be, "good enough mothers"; and third, the experiences of receiving unhelpful "help" from health and social care workers. Whilst not the only themes yielded by the data, these are the ones reported here because of their particular sociological significance. They connect with much wider concerns within medical sociology: medical discourses and risk, the social construction of motherhood, and the social interaction between lay people and health professionals. Other themes reported elsewhere[4] related to issues of practical and environmental significance, for example, the design of maternity departments, the utility of equipment, and information needs. Evidence is presented which draws in particular on eleven of the 17 interviews, but exemplars relating to at least one of the themes could have been drawn from any of the interview transcripts. I make no pretence to be representing these women's experiences in their totality (and, of course, in many respects their maternity experiences are the same as those of non-disabled women documented extensively elsewhere). Following a discussion on methods the three themes are considered in turn.

Methods

The data from 17 interviews were the product of a study on maternity, motherhood and disability which was a follow-up of a much larger research project on (all) women's "maternity preferences." In the wake of *Changing Childbirth: Report of the Expert Maternity Group* (DoH), the main *Maternity Preferences* study was commissioned in 1994 by a health authority in the north of England to gather information on the forms and features of maternity provision which women of childbearing age favoured. It involved a postal questionnaire survey in 1995 with an achieved sample size of over 1,400 women of variable parity, aged between 16 and 44 years, resident in one city. The questionnaire contained items about experiences and intentions in connection with: preferences about the place of birth, features of ante-natal care, care during labour, and care and support in the immediate post-natal period. Through the medium of the questionnaire, women were invited to indicate if they would like to participate in a follow-up interview if they were disabled (that is, considered themselves to be disabled) and felt that this had affected or would affect their maternity care needs. Attempts were made to contact all of the women who responded to this invitation by telephone and/or letter (there were seventeen responses in total; some women sent in only a name and phone number, others an address and phone number). As a result, ten in-depth semi-structured follow-up interviews were conducted. A further three interviews with disabled women were organised through "networking" with a midwife and an occupational therapist. These two health professionals had worked with a number of disabled mothers and they agreed to contact a few women on our behalf to ask if they would be willing to be interviewed by a member of the research team. Another two interviews were arranged with women who were known to the researchers. Also included in the analysis were the data from interviews with two more disabled women which had been conducted in the pilot phase of the Maternity Preferences study, again using networking/reputational methods to obtain names. Thus, there are interview data from a total of 17 interviews. This "mixed method" of obtaining the sample of disabled women reflects, in part, the difficulties that there are in obtaining a sample when no pre-existing sampling frame is available. It was fortunate that a broad range of experience was represented in the sample associated with differences in: parity, age, the nature of the impairment(s), and the women's socio-economic status. However, it should be noted that all of the women were white.

The range of physical and/or sensory impairments represented in the sample is as follows, and included one woman with mental health problems[5]: deaf (Janet, Susan), hearing and visual impairment (Sheila), arthritis in spine (Helen); limb amputation above right knee (Fran), amputation below left elbow (Sarah); Chrohn's disease (Sally); systemic lupus erythematosus (SLE) (Mary); diabetes (Ann); epilepsy (Penny); back injury resulting in chronic back pain (Rachel); asthma (Lorna); mobility problems associated with cerebral palsy (Pat); Addison's disease (Angela); back pain and mobility problems associated with dislocated hip at birth (Sarah); bilateral dysplasia and osteoarthritis (Clair); high levels of anxiety, panic attacks and agoraphobia (Terry). The names used here are not real names, and care has been taken to avoid the inclusion of identifying details.

The in-depth semi-structured interviews were sensitively conducted in a conversational style. The author conducted the two "pilot" stage interviews and the rest were conducted by one interviewer recruited for the purpose, and overseen by the author.[6] With the women's permission, all interviews were tape recorded and transcribed. All covered issues to do with pre-conception plans and intentions, pregnancy, labour and delivery, the post-natal period, childcare and "being a mother"—building on the areas covered in the postal questionnaire. However, because of their variable childbearing histories, not all of these areas related to the actual, or past, experiences of all of the women:

•four were childless but were actively thinking about having a baby in

the next few years;
- two were pregnant—one with her first and the other with her second child;
- four had one child ranging in age from nine weeks to seven years;
- six had two children (children's ages ranging from one to twelve years); two of these mothers had been sterilised at the time of interview;
- one woman had six children, the youngest of whom was one year of age.

In relation to validity, I can claim, first, that the data generation methods were well matched to my research question: what can disabled women's experiences tell us about the ways in which disablism presents itself on the journey through conception, pregnancy, childbirth and early motherhood? Semi-structured interviews were an appropriate way to access experiences, allowing respondents to "tell their stories" and recount their experiences in ways which were meaningful to them with minimal researcher constraint. Second, I would defend the validity of my interpretation of the women's accounts in terms of disablism. Essentially, these accounts did three things: (a) outline the nature of their impairment(s), (b) tell their reproductive story, and (c) reflect upon how (a) affected (b) and vice versa. The analysis of the interview transcripts involved cross-sectional indexing of all of the data in the building up of 19 categories relating to aspects of experience and other social characteristics. It became apparent that these categories could be readily grouped into a number of substantive themes relating to the *social*, that is, to the problems and issues the women faced which were embedded in the social fabric of relationships, services and structures. Informed by a disability paradigm (as outlined above), it was possible to argue that these experiences/themes could be interpreted as manifestations of disability. Whilst the number of interviews was small and the findings are not empirically generalisable, the arguments are theoretically generalisable (Mason 1996) in the sense that the sample was not atypical of disabled women and the analysis has a much wider resonance.

Taking "Risks?"

The strongest theme to emerge from the data was that of "risk," an issue of growing interest to medical sociologists more generally (Gabe). Most of the women interviewed had faced issues to do with reproductive "risk" either to themselves or to their babies: would the health and/or survival of the foetus be put "at risk" because the condition was hereditary or because of drug treatments? Would their own health be placed "at risk?" The women could not avoid a close encounter with a medical discourse which has at its core the belief that if there is a risk of abnormality, or the risk of worsening an already abnormal bodily condition, then steps must be taken to avoid it; genetic counselling outlining the "risks," or the option/recommendation of a termination, should be given to those parents who are "at risk" of producing a baby with a serious impairment; women with impairments who are "at risk" of worsening their condition through pregnancy should be advised not to bear children. Of course, all women who come into contact with maternity services during pregnancy experience this medical risk discourse in some way (Lane), but for women whose bodies are already "abnormal," the encounter is a particularly sharp one, and there may be heavy personal costs to be borne. In what sense can this experiential encounter with the risk discourse relate to manifestations of disability? Before exploring this question, let us look at the nature of the women's encounters.

In general, the women interviewed did not question medically-defined reproductive risks, and tended to share in wider lay beliefs that "passing on" or "causing" impairment in a child was irresponsible and "unfair" to the child (see also Parsons and Atkinson). Sheila, for example, had retinitis pigmentosa (a hereditary visual impairment involving "tunnel vision" caused by progressive degeneration of the retina) and deafness in one ear (not hereditary) and spoke about the decision to be sterilised some years after the birth of her two sons in terms of risk. Sheila herself had had no signs of the visual impairment when her two sons were born. Now, she had marked impairment and her eldest son had signs of the condition, but it was too early to say whether her second son had this inheritance. She explained how the pattern of inheritance of retinitis pigmentosa cannot be predicted, it "skips" some offspring, and others become merely carriers. Her GP had suggested that she should be sterilised because of the hereditary nature of the condition. Sheila reported that her mother, to whom she was very close, had strongly supported the GP's view on the grounds that, "It's not fair, is it, on the children you bring through, 'cos you don't want them to suffer do you?" This had clearly been an emotionally painful course of action for Sheila. She and her new partner wanted a daughter: "otherwise I'd have kept going until I got a girl … I still pine a lot for a little girl but it weren't to be so … end of subject. You get over it." What is particularly interesting about this woman's account is that the decision to be sterilised was made reluctantly in the context of pressure from trusted figures of authority (her GP, her mother), and in the context of considerable uncertainty about the likelihood that any additional child would in fact "suffer" from the condition.

Another mother, Mary, with systemic lupus erthematosus (SLE, a chronic inflammatory disease of connective tissue affecting the skin and various internal organs requiring steroid and other drug treatment) had made the decision not to try for a second child because "it wasn't worth the risk" either to her own health or that of the baby. When she became pregnant with her first child, the medical team responsible for the treatment of her SLE had refused to believe her claim that she was pregnant, because they were convinced that her prescribed medication would prohibit conception. A scan had to be conducted to confirm her pregnancy for these specialists. The doctors advised her to continue with her medication at current levels throughout pregnancy, although following a move abroad during her pregnancy, she was later told by doctors in that country that "because of the tablets I'm on he could be slightly deformed—fingers and toes or something"

(Mary). She describes herself as having been "fit and healthy" throughout the pregnancy and her son was born, prematurely, with no apparent "deformities." On her return to the UK she was referred to a consultant rheumatologist who was the first doctor to give her detailed information about SLE, and in whom she had much confidence. Mary explained that she now knew that her steroid medication could and should have been reduced during pregnancy to reduce "the risks" to the baby. She talked about how her health had deteriorated in the years following the birth of her son. At one stage she had decided to try for another baby, and had been in contact with both her rheumatologist and the maternity hospital for advice about conception and pregnancy. She was given contradictory advice about "the risks" associated with her medication. The rheumatologist told her that one of her drugs was contra-indicated and that an abortion would be absolutely necessary if she became pregnant whilst on this drug, but the doctors at the maternity hospital asserted that the drug was "safe." She had stopped taking this drug but then had a "flare up" of her condition, "so I decided myself that it's not worth the risk ... there's no point in having another child if there's no mum there to look after them." She knew of cases where mothers had died of SLE following childbirth. This decision not to have another child had not been an easy one to make, and the health services had certainly indicated a willingness to assist her with conception and pregnancy if she had wanted to persist in her attempts to have another child:

> I said to my husband, I've got to go through the grieving process and he said why?, why?, why?, and I said because I've made a decision; I said that I can't risk having another one. I said the maternal instincts are still there so I sense, like, you've lost something, you've lost a part of you ... I've to go through the grieving process, I said you've got to give me time for that. ... I mean they told me [my son] was a miracle really, and at least I've got one. (Mary)

The issue of the risks to the woman of ceasing medication, or of reducing or increasing its levels, versus the risks to the foetus of continuing with pre-pregnancy levels of medication was also a key one for some other women, particularly those with either chronic back pain, epilepsy, diabetes, asthma, or mental health problems. Some of these women had experienced, or would expect, extra monitoring during pregnancy to ensure that the baby was developing "normally," and that their own health was not being compromised. The balance was sometimes a very fine one. For example, Penny (with epilepsy), said that because her medication meant there was a slim chance of foetal deformity, it was kept to a minimum. However, she did have one fit during pregnancy because her medication dosage was too low. This had distressed her because she had read that the oxygen supply to the baby can be dangerously reduced during a fit: "it can cause you to lose the baby." Penny believed that the doctors were at fault for not increasing her medication in proportion to her weight increase.

Rachel, who had chronic back pain following an accident, talked about having a baby in the future as a kind of "trade off": living with increased pain during pregnancy in return for having a "beautiful baby" at the end. She knew that her injections at the pain clinic would "have to stop" during pregnancy:

> I know I'm going to be in pain, it's my decision to have a baby and I've got to weigh it up … I can always think "well at the end of this I'm going to have a baby," you know, and then I can go back to the pain clinic and have some more treatment and so … I think that's the way I would have to look at it. (Rachel)

Terry, a respondent with mental health problems (anxiety and panic attacks, agoraphobia, depression), which had developed in the time since the births of her two children, agonised about the problem of medication and pregnancy. She experienced this as a real dilemma: she desperately wanted more children, especially with her new partner (she had two children by previous partners, both of whom had abused her emotionally and/or physically), but was terrified that she would not be able to "cope" without her drugs (especially Prozac):

> I've been told I can't 'ave a baby on medication so … I don't know if I've got the guts to actually start coming off them [the tablets]. I want to but the fear of being how I were without them is stopping me. I really, really want to come off 'em, I'm so scared I don't … I think if I were going to be like that I wouldn't even attempt to come off 'em, no matter how much I wanted a baby. (Terry)

Terry had not felt able to seek help from health professionals about this and clearly struggled alone with these tensions. In a life of considerable emotional hardship, she had gained tremendous satisfaction and self-belief through becoming a mother: "Satisfaction of thinking they're a little human being and … it depends on you for its care and you giving it and its thriving and you think, oh! you're doing something right."

Two mothers, Sarah and Pat, did give birth to children with impairments associated with hereditary conditions. Feelings of guilt after the birth of her first child were expressed by Sarah, a mother of six who was herself born with a dislocated hip—a hereditary condition which may or may not manifest itself in offspring:

> … when my first daughter was born, they thought that she had a dislocated hip as well and that was very sad. Well it was a very sad time for me because I felt that I'd done it to her you know … they told me when she was a day old when I think you are quite fragile anyway, and so that was a very bad time then for me because, you know, my beautiful new baby—and I'd made her not quite right, and then she had to have a harness when she was six months old and that particular consultant thought

she should wear it the whole time so we never took it off for a bath or anything for six months … there was a lot about our baby that didn't look normal and … it was a big iron thing round her legs. (Sarah)

Sarah's fourth child was also born with the condition but a different consultant suggested that a harness only need be worn at night. Sarah experienced this as much less problematic—it carried considerably reduced "guilt."

Pat's first child was diagnosed with a chronic condition as a baby. However, this child had cystic fibrosis which was completely unconnected to Pat's cerebral palsy. She and her husband were, unknowingly, carriers of the gene for cystic fibrosis. What is particularly interesting is her account of how some people made assumptions that her child's condition was a direct result of her own impairment (or at least, of its visible manifestations: some difficulty in walking, in maintaining balance, and a weakness in one hand) with the unspoken implication that she was irresponsible to have this child: "… I've just had a couple of people say is it related in any way to what you've got?', but that's, you know, their ignorance rather than anything else." Pat admitted to feeling "relieved" that her son's condition was not related to her cerebral palsy, and that his CF could not have been predicted. In fact, she had sensed some hostility from other people when she had been pregnant:

I do think that sometimes they thought that I shouldn't be pregnant. You know, nobody actually said anything but, and it wasn't anybody I knew or anything like that but … if I went on public transport and things like that. Not all the time, just once or twice … well they'd probably think that whatever I'd got the child has got a chance of being the same and they wouldn't know that what I'd got wasn't passed. (Pat)

Pat talked about her decision, made with her husband, to have a second child. She described this as "murderously difficult." They wanted another child, and thought their son should have a sibling, but they had to weigh this up against what they saw as other factors to take into consideration: the chances of a second child having CF or a different impairment, the effects that an early death of the first child would have on the second, her assessment of the impact of her own impairment on her ability to manage another child, especially one with CF, "'cos you get less capable of doing things as you get older." She did have a second child and it did not have CF. Six months after this birth, she decided to be sterilised: "… you can't have any more taking those risks can you? … I thought with all the odds against us" (Pat).

From the above we can see that considerations of "risk" were an important feature of the women's reproductive journeys, and we can also see that disabled women often share, albeit sometimes ambivalently, in the wider social and medical discourses about what constitute reproductive "risks." Having a child with an impairment is seen as something to be avoided, and if it occurs, is experienced with feelings of "guilt" which spring from the knowledge that their actions in having a child are widely seen as both irresponsible and "unfair" to the child. Such women often face very difficult decisions about whether to take the "risk" of childbearing if they have a hereditary condition which might be "passed on," or if they are on medication which may "damage" the foetus, or if their own condition may be worsened through reproduction. The women's accounts bear witness to the considerable "emotion work" involved in personal encounters with the risk discourse: worry, anxiety, guilt, lost hopes, unfulfilled dreams, spoilt identities.

But is this emotional burden simply an inevitable feature of the "personal tragedy" of living with impairment? Of course not. These individual experiences are shaped by encounters with wider discourses about personal responsibility, which accompany all women on the journey into motherhood, coupled with encounters with disablism. The key point is that the risk discourse is not a neutral one. What is and is not judged to be an acceptable risk hinges not just on life or death questions, or on purely biological criteria, but on social assumptions about the quality of life and intrinsic value of children and adults with impairments. As Freidson pointed out so well, medical knowledge about illness (or impairment) is social, and as such is "inevitably evaluational" (Freidson 208). Despite its apparently "scientific objectivity," medical knowledge inevitably draws on deep-rooted cultural antipathy for, and prejudices about, people with "abnormalities." Jenny Morris (1991) has argued that in our society, judgements are made about the quality of life of people with impairments which equate physical impairment (particularly severe impairment) with "lives not worth living," and that impairment is considered in abstraction from the social, economic, cultural and spatial circumstances which really do determine the quality of life. It is noteworthy that medical sociologists who have considered the reproductive risk discourse (for example, Parsons and Atkinson; Lane) have described lay encounters with it in connection with impairment and disability but have not commented upon or questioned its disablist character.

Drawing on Morris' work, and a wider literature springing from the disability movement, it is clear that a minority of disabled women have rejected the socio-medical discourse about risk and see it as part of an all-pervasive disablist ideology. They know that there are medically defined "risks," that is, probabilities of impairment effects for self or the baby, but they do not necessarily evaluate these risks negatively. Impairment *per se* is not equated with "the problem." Their perspective is clear: the problem is disability—the social barriers which socially exclude. Micheline Mason (1992), for example, has written about her great joy and sense of achievement in becoming a mother (a single parent) and about her decision to continue with an unplanned pregnancy though she knew that her child would inherit her own condition—"brittle bones" (osteogenesis imperfecta, giving her a tiny stature, deformed limbs and the need for assisted mobility):

Once I had made the decision to choose life, and whatever that may bring, the confirmation that the baby did indeed have brittle bones only seemed to make the initial decision more meaningful and special. (Mason 1992: 115)

Micheline Mason, who describes herself as a disabled activist, has been able to throw off disablist attitudes about the "tragedy" of having a child with an impairment, and, rather, to celebrate it and to demand that the disabling social barriers which are the real source of the disability experienced by disabled children and mothers, are removed.

To see the "risk discourse" as disablist (something of significance for all women) requires a change in consciousness which Morris (1991, 1996), Mason (1992), Anne Finger and others have made. The women in my study, like most disabled women, had not traveled that journey, or perhaps, had not had the opportunity to do so. This does not lessen, however, the power of their personal accounts to "tell of disablism." I would argue that in some very fundamental ways, their engagement with the medical risk discourse was an engagement with disablism, and that the considerable personal costs to be borne were one important aspect of the "manifestations of disability" they faced. To put this another way, that is, in "disability rights" terms, the powerful medical (and wider) discourse on reproductive risk acts as a social barrier in the sense that it plays an important part in "restricting activity"; in its light, decisions are made not to have a child/another child, or to be sterilised, or to terminate a pregnancy.

"Good Enough" Mothering?

A second theme which emerged strongly in the data analysis revolves around the fear of being judged inadequate as a mother, and of the consequences that this might bring. Again, all women who become mothers (and particularly those in pilloried groups such as "single mothers") experience this to a greater or lesser degree, especially in these times when public and professional discourses highlight concern for "children at risk," but this study suggests that disabled women are particularly vulnerable. A number of the women lived with this fear, believing that they might be seen by others—representing either the powers of the state (health visitors, community midwives, doctors, social workers and so on) or the power of the wider family—to fail to live up to being a "good mother." Two women had actually experienced the threatened or actual loss of their children, but perhaps surprisingly, not as a consequence of action by "officials" but as a consequence of family members taking unofficial action against their wishes. For example, Jane, who had lost her left arm below the elbow as the result of an accident, described the way in which her own mother wanted to "keep" her two-year-old daughter (born before the accident) because she believed that Jane would not be able to cope. Jane's mother had become involved in sharing the care of the child whilst Jane was in hospital having a series of operations over a number of months following the accident.

> I actually then had to ask solicitors to get involved because mum decided she wanted to keep [my daughter]—so mum went to the solicitors to try and ... there was an argument over access because I was quite happy for

mum to see her whenever. It was over coming home at night custody really ... I think looking at it from her point of view, now, she just decided that because I'd only got one arm I couldn't cope ... [that I] should be sat there in my rocking chair almost, you know, in a wheelchair and give up on everything ... I just said to mum, "you can see her whenever but I can cope," and I think that's what actually made us decide we'd like another child. Just to sort of prove that we could cope. (Jane)

The other respondent who had experienced a struggle over custody was Terry, who had mental health problems. Whilst she was going through a divorce with her first husband he took their child, without Terry's consent, to live with his own parents. Terry reports that these grandparents "tried to make me out to be mentally unstable," and only allowed her to visit her son for one hour per day over an eight month period until the custody case finally came to court. On one such visit she had been physically assaulted (requiring hospital treatment) by the grandmother when she tried to take her son out of the grandparents' house. She got legal assistance through the intervention of health care workers and was finally granted custody of her son by the court. Her fears about her children being removed from her care were ever present and certainly not helped by her own mother's refrain—"if you don't get better they'll take your children off you."

The fear of losing her children had begun to creep into Sarah's mind after the birth of her sixth child. She had begun to experience a lot of difficulties in walking and bending and had discomfort and pain (associated with residual impairment having been born with a dislocated hip):

It's very hard to think that I can't look after my own children, it's a very hard thing to come to terms with really. And I'm not quite at the point of saying "look, I can't really do this," but if I was I don't really know what would happen. I suppose the children get taken into care, don't they, when the parents say they can't cope?—but, you know, that's a very frightening prospect really so its easy just to think of treading along. (Sarah)

These fears had been heightened by a health visitor with whom Sarah had been discussing a future hospital admission for a hip replacement operation. Sarah was worried about child care arrangements because she would need some kind of help during the hospital stay and for some months afterwards whilst she was relatively immobile. The health visitor's reply was quite astonishing to Sarah:

... she said "well, the children won't all be able to go into care together you know," which wasn't what I was asking for because I wouldn't want my children to go into care you know, I mean, who would? What a response! (Sarah)

Living with the fear of losing the right to care for their children forces some mothers to go to great lengths to "present" themselves and their children as managing "normally"—often at significant personal cost in terms of comfort and emotional and physical well-being. One consequence is that assistance may not be requested when it is needed because the mother feels that her request may be interpreted to mean that she is not capable. Clair, a woman in the study with quite severe impairment (a wheelchair user from a very young age), spoke about her joys at giving birth to her son, but her anxieties that other people's prejudicial judgements might lead to her child being removed from her care, particularly as she was a single parent:

> I felt that it was going to happen very soon, that maybe the prejudice of someone who lived around me [a neighbour] would make them think that they'd got to ring up social services and that an investigation would start … it terrified me, it really did. I don't think I relaxed into motherhood until he was bout 18 months or two years old, I really don't think I did … I would love to have those months again cos I was so scared, tidying the house cos I knew somebody was coming who was from authority, you know, that when he was asleep … I was too busy doing jobs rather than enjoying him and relaxing. (Clair)

Jane also worried about professionals' judgements that she might not be able to manage. Despite having some practical difficulties in getting her new baby dressed and undressed several times a day for nappy changing whilst she was adapting to life without her left arm below the elbow, Jane struggled on with the dressing routine in the early weeks in order to "present" herself to others and to herself as a "fit" mother:

> I felt that she had to be dressed every day and I had to … otherwise people would think that I couldn't do it cos … certainly for the first six or eight weeks I felt that I … was letting her down because I couldn't get her back dressed properly, but after that I just got to the point where I thought, well, she's warm, she's healthy, as long as she's clean it doesn't matter. (Jane)

Jane noted that after the birth of her first child, before her accident, she had not worried at all about always having the baby dressed because she had "felt in control of things much more."

These accounts testify to the particular vulnerability that many women with impairments feel when they become mothers, or if they become impaired whilst fulfilling the socially defined obligations of motherhood. This feeling of vulnerability and insecurity is caused, in part, by their own concerns about managing some of the practical child care tasks because of the impairment, but in the main it is caused by disablism: the prejudicial attitudes of others and the failure to provide appropriate assistance to disabled women on their own terms. While the majority of non-disabled parents can take it for granted that the quality and character of their "parenting" is their own business—although this may be increasingly illusory (Abbott and Sapsford 1990)—disabled women really do feel under surveillance, and that feeling is usually well founded because disabled women are often assumed by professionals and lay people (often including close relatives) to be incapable unless they can prove otherwise: guilty until proven innocent.

Given the strength and widespread nature of disablist ideas which doubt the ability of women with impairments to be "good" mothers, to be able "to cope," it is not surprising that many disabled women—especially those with a recently acquired impairment—have to overcome doubt about their own capacity to become mothers, or may privately share in some of the social anxieties about the welfare of the children of disabled parents. Once again, the personal costs involved, including the actual loss of the right to parent, are in fact the consequences of the way that disability manifests itself rather than as something inherent in being impaired.

When "Help" is Not Helpful

The third but closely related theme concerns the women's experiences of receiving inappropriate or inadequate "help" from health professionals and social care workers. At issue here is the nature of the social interaction between professionals and disabled patients/clients in contexts where the professional maxim that "we know what is in the patient's best interests" finds full expression. Once again, a large literature on the medicalisation of childbirth suggests that many women experience a sense of loss of control over their bodies during pregnancy and childbirth as doctors and other health professionals "take over" (Roberts; Oakley; Garcia *et al.*). However, this experience of loss of control can be intensified when "disability" is an additional factor in the lay-professional encounter. Now, from a professional perspective, it is not just the "management" of the pregnant woman and new mother that is of concern, but the management of women with the additional problems that come with "being disabled." A number of women in the study gave accounts of individual health workers who, although well intentioned, had "taken over," had been unhelpful, or had lacked the information or skills they required. However, it is important to point out that all of the women said that some midwives, doctors (particularly some GPs), health visitors, "home helps" and others were "brilliant," "great" or "wonderful." Similarly, some friends and relatives were "great," "always there for me" (often this was their own "mum"), a "real safety net," but others were "hopeless," "fussing," "over-protective" or "taking over."

Jane's experiences illustrate this theme particularly well (she had lost her left arm below the elbow). She reported her well-meaning GP as saying: "… right, we'll get someone in, they can bath the baby and dress the baby, give the baby to you and you can sit there and nurse it and if you want we'll get someone in to help you bath." The first time the baby had needed a bath in hospital the midwives had said "we'll do this." Jane went on to explain that what she had really wanted was for someone to assist her with tasks like bathing the baby but not to do it for her. Her experience of professional assistance was a largely disempowering one. It had been a source of distress, and had undermined her self identity as a mother: "... when people wanted to take over I found I was getting really cross and I didn't want to get cross with the nurses. I'd take it out on [my husband] later—'they said they're going to bath that baby!'" "Taking over" also occurred in relation to breast feeding:

> I just really felt that I was being left out of the important decisions, you know, and as if, I did start feeding her myself and then felt it just wasn't . . . there was always someone fussing around me and, you know, "you can cope?" and "you'll have to put the head further into the crook of your arm" and it was always ... wanting to prod and poke and "are they all right?" I mean I only stuck with it about four or five days and then started feeding her with a bottle because I could to that myself. You know they used to bring the bottle with the teat on and I could do that. (Jane)

One midwife had said:

> "We'll come everyday and put the baby on the breast" ... they've got this vision of it all being so awful ... I must admit it didn't feel, being a mum didn't feel as natural with [my second], everything seemed much more difficult and I did get depressed.... (Jane)

Jane thought there should be "more emphasis on helping, not doing it; helping mum, not doing it for the baby." By the time the Health Visitor had started to call at home: "I'd already started saying 'right I can manage that' and she went the other way and said 'oh you can cope, you're managing really well and you can do this.'" In short, Jane's experience was largely one of inappropriate help or no help.

For other women, having taken the risk that they might be signaling their inadequacy as a mother by asking for "help," there were further personal costs to be borne. For example, Sarah, who had problems with walking and bending after the birth of her sixth child, had to endure being "re-assessed" by the Home Help Organiser in connection with a service she received which involved a Home Help transporting her older children to and from school:

> She [the organiser] turned up just before my daughter's first birthday party which was a bit difficult really and she only saw me sitting down and her line was "why are we only doing this for you two days a week?," you know, and I said I could manage the other days and she said "well,

perhaps we should stop then?." I found that very difficult really. I thought afterwards perhaps I should have got up and showed her how difficult it was for me to walk, but there's something really horrible about that. Well, that's something I've had to do for doctors all my life really and I found that quite demeaning, I didn't actually want to do that. (Sarah)

Sometimes, technological aids were required—and what women wanted was information about, and access to, appropriate aids. For example, the three hearing-impaired women in the study mentioned the use of aids such as "alarms" to indicate that the baby was crying, ante-natal information videos for hearing-impaired people, adapted telephones and doorbells and other equipment. In some instances, these women found out about aids by chance, or more often through meeting with other deaf mothers. This form of practical assistance was rarely offered by professionals in the health or social services; it was a case of repeatedly asking for and pursuing information. Another disabling barrier experienced by these hearing impaired women was associated with face-to-face communication with health professionals. Most professionals encountered did not know how to communicate effectively. For example, midwives rarely knew any basic sign language (and signing was not always wanted, anyway), and Susan reported having repeatedly to ask the midwives to "slow down" so that she could follow what they were saying by lip-reading. Janet was very angry when unwanted "help" was thrust upon her when she was in labour. The hospital midwives had arranged for an "interpreter" to be present at the birth to assist with communication. Janet felt that she did not want a stranger present at such a private time. In fact, she did not feel that an interpreter was needed at all, and that if anyone needed to interpret then it could be a close family member chosen by herself.

Pat, who had mobility and balance difficulties, would have appreciated help with some housework tasks both during her pregnancies and whilst her two children were small. She had also found bathing her babies difficult, although her husband helped with this. Additional assistance with housework and other tasks was not asked for, in part because she did not believe that services would be available, but in the main because she felt that asking for help makes "you feel a burden." This feeling was a common one among the women interviewed; you just had to "get on with it" and "do the best you can." As Sarah said, "I think its very, very difficult to ask for help." As noted previously, this is partly associated with the need to be seen "to cope" without additional help, to be a "good mother," but it is also because women feel they "should" be able to cope—that women always do have to cope. As in Pat's case, disabled women may also assume that there is no entitlement to assistance, or they may lack information about the services available.

What unites the accounts of inappropriate or inadequate assistance is that nobody appears first to have asked the women themselves what assistance, if any, they really wanted and how assistance could best be given. Professionals (and non-disabled lay people) assumed that they "knew best." It can be argued that this is a classic feature of disablism: the impaired person is constructed as "dependent," as reliant on the wisdom and help of expert others. Jenny Morris has written powerfully about this, that is, the disablism which constructs disabled women as the "cared for," ignoring and excluding them as "care givers" (1991, 1995). There is no recognition that dependency, which is a feature of everybody's life to some degree, is socially created. So pervasive is this view that non-disabled feminist writers have reproduced (and reinforced) it in their critique of community care policy in the UK (Morris 1991, 1995, 1996; Keith). In this critique, the characterisation of disabled women as cared for rather than as care givers is taken as given.

In fact, what is striking about the situation of the disabled women interviewed in this study is that their care-giving role was fundamental to the physical and emotional maintenance of others in the household, and that, even where a male partner was present, disabled women were, or continued to be, *the main* carers of children and other family members. The traditional sexual division of labour was very much intact whether or not the women needed any assistance over and above the help that women "normally" get within families. Furthermore, these women's self identities and aspirations were very firmly tied in with being a successful mother and running a home. Like many other disabled women, their personal fight in the face of disablism was fundamentally about the right to be mothers and home makers.

Nevertheless, it seems that the normative assumption that disabled people are dependent profoundly colours the way in which "help" is offered to women with impairments both by well-meaning professionals, and often by friends and relatives as well. Non-disabled people generally *assume* that disabled women will need particular forms of help and that they know best how to give it. In reproductive contexts, where maternity services already construct women as patients to be cared for by expert others, many disabled women receive a double dose of dependency creation. However, it is certainly not always the case that assistance is needed or wanted. Where it is, for example in the form of practical help with child-care tasks, the "help" which is offered is quite likely to be inappropriate, and/or conditional, or it may not be offered in any guise. Where "help" is unwanted but forced upon disabled mothers, or is inappropriate in its form, it can be experienced as a threat to the right to parent (as we saw in the previous section), and/or as intrusive and disempowering. These are some of the "manifestations of disability" faced. No help or the wrong help is the common lot of disabled women.

Conclusion

This paper has reported on the experiences of seventeen disabled women who were at different stages in their reproductive journeys at the time of interview. It has explored the ways in which disabled women's decisions about and experiences of childbearing and motherhood are interlaced with additional concerns which originate in the social fabric of services and structures, and particularly, in the social relationships between themselves and others. It has focused on three themes which emerged in the analysis of the interview transcripts: engagement with the medical "risk" discourse; the pressure felt by disabled women to demonstrate that they are, or could be, "good enough mothers"; and the experiences of receiving unhelpful "help" from health and social care workers. The interpretation of these personal experience narratives has taken place against the backdrop of current debates about the nature and meaning of disability, and the emphasis has been on what these women's accounts tell us about the manifestations of disability, or disablism, which women with impairments face when they think about having a child, become pregnant, come into contact with maternity and related services, and when they become mothers.

Disablism was evident in a number of ways: in the women's close encounters with the medical "risk" discourse, with its unspoken evaluative assumptions that, for example, to give birth to an impaired baby is to give birth to a life of lesser worth. This could entail living with the fear that one might be judged to be an inadequate mother, and that actions might follow involving the denial of the right to be a mother. Furthermore there might be disempowering encounters with (usually well-meaning) health and social care workers who frequently offered inappropriate help informed by a professional ethic that "we know best."

The paper has highlighted those features of the women's accounts which tell us something about the "differences" disability brings. It suggests that disabled women's reproductive journeys are strewn with social barriers of an attitudinal, ideological and material kind. I hope to have demonstrated that the exploration of these women's *experiences* can provide a deeper insight into the nature of these "social barriers." In doing so I also hope to have made a contribution to a sociology of disability which, whilst starting out from the experience of individuals, allows the examination of the social manifestations of disablism rather than pursuing ever deeper exploration of the "subjectivity of experience" (Williams 1996b: 202). The point of it all it is not, however, to generate knowledge for its own sake, but to inform those engaged in disability praxis.

I am grateful to the unnamed Health Authority which funded the follow-up study of disabled women in association with the Maternity Preferences study. I am also grateful to Hilary Graham for her helpful comments on an earlier version of this paper.

Notes

[1] The findings of the Maternity Preferences study are not yet fully in the public domain, and thus the identity of the Health Authority that funded the study is protected here.

[2] I was born without a left hand and now have a four-year-old child.

[3] "Disability theorists" is a term which has come to be used to identify those academics, most of whom are themselves impaired, who are researching/writing about disability from a "disability rights," or radical socio-political perspective (for example, see Swain *et al.*; Oliver; Barnes and Mercer).

[4]Please contact the author for information about the research report and papers in preparation.

[5]Whilst not an impairment as conventionally defined, mental health problems are, nevertheless, associated with disability because they carry the medical label of "mental illness" and, as such, gives rise to the experience of social exclusion.

[6]It is important to acknowledge the contribution of Sue Greig who carried out these interviews with considerable skill and sensitivity.

References

Abbott, P. and R. Sapsford. "Health Visiting: Policing the Family?" *The Sociology of The Caring Professions*. Eds. P. Abbott and C. Wallace. London: The Falmer Press, 1990. 120-152.

Barnes, C. and G. Mercer, G., eds. *Exploring the Divide: Illness and Disability*. Leeds: The Disability Press, 1996.

Bury, M. "Defining and researching disability: challenges and responses." *Exploring the Divide: Illness and Disability*. Eds. C. Barnes and G. Mercer. Leeds: The Disability Press, 1996. 17-38.

Bury, M. "The Sociology of Chronic Illness: A Review of Research and Prospects." *Sociology of Health and Illness* 13.4 (1991): 167-82.

Campbell, J. and M. Oliver. *Disability Politics: Understanding our Past, Changing our Future*. London: Routledge, 1996.

Crow, L. "Including All of Our Lives: Renewing the Social Model of Disability." *Exploring the Divide: Illness and Disability*. Eds. C. Barnes and G. Mercer. Leeds: The Disability Press, 1996. 55-73.

Department of Health. *Changing Childbirth: Report of the Expert Maternity Group*. London: HMSO, 1993.

Evans, M. "Reading Lives: How the Personal Might be Social." *Sociology* 27 (1) (1993): 5-13.

Finger, A. *Past Due: A Story of Disability, Pregnancy and Birth*. London: The Women's Press, 1990.

Finkelstein, V. "Outside, Inside Out." *Coalition* (April 1996): 30-36.

Freidson, E. *Profession of Medicine*. Chicago: University of Chicago Press, 1988.

French, S. *Disabling Barriers, Enabling Environments*. Eds. J. Swain, V. Finkelstein, S. French, and M. Oliver. London: Sage, 1993.

Gabe, J., Ed. *Medicine, Health and Risk: Sociological Approaches*. Oxford: Blackwell, 1995.

Garcia, J., R. Kilpatrick, and M. Richards, Eds. *The Politics of Maternity Care Services for Childbearing Women in Twentieth Century Britain*. Oxford: Clarendon Press, 1990.

Keith, L. "Who Cares Wins? Women, Caring and Disability." *Disability, Handicap and Society* 7 (2) (1992): 167-175.

Lane, K. "The Medical Model of the Body as a Site of Risk: A Case Study of Childbirth." *Medicine, Health and Risk: Sociological Approaches*. Ed. J. Gabe.

Oxford: Blackwell, 1995. 53-72.

Marris, V. *Lives Worth Living: Women's Experience of Chronic Illness.* London: Pandora, Harper Collins, 1996.

Mason, J. *Qualitative Researching.* London: Sage, 1996.

Mason, M. "A Nineteen-Parent Family." *Alone Together: Voices of Single Mothers.* Ed. J. Morris. London: The Women's Press, 1992. 112-125.

Morris, J. *Alone Together: Voices of Single Mothers.* London: The Women's Press, 1992.

Morris, J. "Creating a Space for Absent Voices: Disabled Women's Experience of Receiving Assistance with Daily Living Activities." *Feminist Review* 51 (Autumn 1995): 68-93.

Morris, J. *Pride Against Prejudice: Transforming Attitudes to Disability.* London: The Women's Press, 1991.

Morris, J., Ed. *Encounters With Strangers: Feminism and Disability.* London: The Women's Press, 1996.

Oakley, A. *From Here to Maternity: Becoming a Mother.* Harmondsworth: Penguin, 1981.

Oliver, M. *Understanding Disability.* London: Macmillan, 1996.

Parsons, E. and P. Atkinson. "Lay Constructions of Genetic Risk." *Sociology of Health and Illness* 14 (4) (1992): 437-455.

Plummer, K. *Telling Sexual Stories: Power, Change and Social Worlds.* London: Routledge, 1995.

Roberts, H., Ed. *Women, Health and Reproduction.* London: Routledge and Kegan Paul, 1981.

Swain, J., V. Finkelstein, S. French, and M. Oliver, eds. *Disabling Barriers, Enabling Environments.* London: Sage, 1993.

Williams, G. "Irving Zola, (1935-1994): An Appreciation." *Sociology of Health and Illness* 18 (1) (1996a): 107-125.

Williams, G. "Representing Disability: Some Questions of Phenomenology and Politics." *Exploring the Divide: Illness and Disability.* Eds. C. Barnes and G. Mercer. Leeds: The Disability Press, 1996b. 194-212.

Chapter 30

"Does the Word Lesbian Mean Anything to You?"
Lesbians Raising Daughters

KATHERINE ARNUP

JESSE AND I ARE walking down the street, chatting and catching up on the week's events. Two women approach us, holding hands, rainbow pins on their jackets. Jesse and I exchange knowing glances. "Does the word *lesbian* mean anything to you?" Jesse jokes, once they have passed, and we laugh at our shared "secret."

Few people watching that exchange would guess that we are a lesbian mother and her daughter. Indeed, many people could not even imagine that such a possibility exists. Yet, it has been suggested that ten percent of women are lesbians and that between 20 and 30 percent of lesbians are mothers (Herman 12). A recent study estimated that there are "between 3 and 8 million gay and lesbian parents in the United States, raising between 6 and 14 million children" (Martin 6). While no figures are available for Canada, we can assume that proportionately the number of lesbian mothers is equally high.[1]

It is, however, virtually impossible to estimate with any accuracy how many lesbian or gay parents there are. Unless they choose to come out, lesbian and gay parents are largely invisible to the world outside their homes. Many lesbian and gay parents conceal their sexual orientation for fear of losing custody of their children. Others, concerned that their children will suffer from discrimination and harassment, choose to hide their sexual identity. Furthermore, official record-generating agencies, including Statistics Canada, do not include sexual orientation in their census questionnaires. As a result, estimates are at best really educated guesses.

It is important to recognize that these estimates tell us nothing about the enormous diversity of the population of lesbian mothers. Lesbian mothers differ on many dimensions: how they became mothers; how they view their lesbianism; and, of course, how they parent. Many lesbians are mothers as a result of bearing children within heterosexual marriages or relationships; some through choice, some by accident. Other lesbians decide, as lesbians, to have children, sometimes with a partner, sometimes alone. Lesbian mothers may be women of colour or white; working class or middle class; able-bodied or disabled; young or old; immigrant or Canadian born; anglophone or francophone. Clearly, lesbian mothers reflect all the differences among women. In addition, the attitudes of the worlds in which lesbian mothers live can range from complete acceptance to total rejection. Ex-husbands, friends, children, work-mates, parents and siblings and daycare centres and schools respond to the revelation of a lesbian mother's sexual orientation in various more-or-less supportive ways, and these responses affect the ways lesbian mothers present themselves and their families. Some lesbian mothers remain "closeted" and live publicly like heterosexual single mothers. Others "come out" to family and friends, or at school and work. Most, perhaps, are "out" in some contexts and not in others. In our research, our writing and our political organizing, it is important to remember the diversity of these experiences.

Our Stories

A couple of years ago, my then six-year-old daughter Katie was playing with her doll. She had developed the habit of yanking up her shirt from her jeans and pushing her baby against her chest, an activity I had come to recognize as breast-feeding. As we sat in the study, Katie breast-feeding and me trying to work, she proclaimed: "You know, Mom, I'm a lesbian mother."

"Oh really," I responded, as casually as possible. "How do you figure that?"

"Well," she explained, "I'm a mother" (she pointed to her dolly), "and I love women" (she pointed to me), "so I'm a lesbian—and that makes me a lesbian mother," she concluded triumphantly.

I often think about that conversation, and imagine to myself a world that could be that straightforward, that simple. For Katie, born and raised the child of two lesbian mothers, that world, to a great extent, already exists. Homophobia and discrimination are distant forces in her life. Her world of Mom and Sue, sister Jesse and dog Sophie, is a safe place, a home with a family much like her friend Fatima across the street, the child of a mixed-race heterosexual couple, and of her friend Malia, next door, the adopted child of a single mother. As the picture books tell us, families come in many sizes and shapes, colours and genders, and no one family is the right one. Or at least that's how it is in Katie's world right now.

My daughter Jesse is six years older than Katie. Born in 1982, Jesse is one of the first children of the "lesbian baby boom" in Canada. When she was born I was not "out" to my parents, though I had already been with my partner for six and a half years. We trod the line between single parenthood and lesbian family carefully, inventing as we went, challenging when we could. Like Katie, Jesse found acceptance among friends and family; neighbours and schoolmates.

When she was about to enter Grade 6, however, we moved to Ottawa—a much less diverse city than Toronto, a place with far fewer lesbian families and many more Beaver Cleaver households. Jesse bolted back into the closet. She would not bring friends home, answer questions about her family or explain the presence of Sue in our household. Indeed, she pretended Sue did not exist.

She was just finishing Grade 7 when the book I was editing on lesbian parenting was about to be published. Jesse panicked. "Do you *have* to do that book?" she asked, hoping she could somehow talk me out of it. "All my friends will find out, and everyone will make fun of me." We talked about her fears and about the ways I could try to make things better—I agreed not to be interviewed by the local media, and, since many children from her class passed the women's bookstore on their way home from school, I promised to ask the bookstore not to display my book in the window. I suspect it was the first time an author had asked them not to display her book—but they understood, and were generous in accommodating my request.

We have lived in Ottawa for over four years now, and slowly Jesse has begun to bring her friends home. She still tends not to introduce Sue to them, as if somehow not mentioning her could make her disappear. And I often return to my study to find books turned around—lesbian titles of course—and the small rainbow flag that adorns my desk stuffed into a drawer.

What is my daughter afraid of? In essence, it is the fear of being different, and of being ridiculed because of that difference. For preteens and teenagers, both boys and girls, the desire to fit in is enormous. Their clothes, their makeup, their shoes, their backpacks, what they do on the weekend—one dares not deviate from some imagined (and not so imagined) standard of normal. Normal is broadcast into their homes each and every day on the TV shows they are addicted to, in the magazines they devour, on the ads they read in the subway. A certain height, a certain weight, a certain skin colour. A certain family formation.

It *is* hard for children to be different. But it is important to remember that children differ in many, many ways, and that the vast majority of children and their families do not, in fact, fit that model.

Does my being a lesbian make life difficult for my daughters? I doubt that there is a lesbian mother who does not sometimes worry about what effect her sexual orientation will have on her children. The fact of the matter is, however, that, apart from the fear of disclosure that my sexual orientation and, in particular, my work on lesbian parenting engenders, the hardest things about having me for a mother have nothing at all to do with my sexual orientation. They have to do with how I parent: that I won't let her stay alone in the house overnight, that I insist that she do her chores, that she only gets $12 a week allowance, and so on. While I suppose a case could be made that those are somehow connected to my sexual orientation, it's a pretty far stretch! As a twelve-year-old child living with her two mothers in Oakland, California, explained: "The hardest part of my life right now is that both of my moms are vegetarians" (Cade 53).

I do not mean to suggest, though, that there are no problems. I do think it is hard for our children when they stand out. But as the countless studies that have been conducted over the past decade and a half have confirmed, our children are learning valuable lessons about justice, about fairness, about discrimination and about diversity. Regardless of whether they end up being heterosexual or gay,[2] our children end up more tolerant and more accepting of a range of different behaviours and kinds of people than children brought up in non-lesbian-headed households.[3]

They end up that way because they are different—as the children of lesbians they have had to struggle with the notion that equates difference with bad. As

Audre Lorde argued so powerfully in a 1986 speech: " …if there is any lesson we must teach our children, it is that difference is a creative force for change, that survival and struggle for the future is not a theoretical issue. It is the very texture of our lives" (314).

Lorde's argument is echoed in this comment from Mandy, a twenty-four-year-old daughter of a lesbian mother:

> Mum's lesbianism and her strength of character have given me many choices in my life and so much freedom. My Mum brought me up so that I can take care of myself and so I'm confident enough to be myself. She taught me about being female in this society, about loving your body in a positive way, but being aware of the need to protect yourself from abuse by men. She made me aware of racism and other important issues at a very young age. (qtd. in Saffron 192)

On days that I worry the challenge is too great for our children, I take heart from the words of poet and essayist Adrienne Rich, whose work has inspired me for almost two decades. In the chapter on mothers and daughters in *Of Woman Born,* Rich writes:

> The quality of the mother's life—however embattled and unprotected—is her primary bequest to her daughter, because a woman who can believe in herself, who is a fighter, and who continues to struggle to create livable space around her, is demonstrating to her daughter that these possibilities exist. (250-51)

From our example as lesbian mothers, whether in partnership or as single parents, our daughters learn that choices do exist. Our lives, and the ways in which we organize them, challenge prescribed gender roles, something that is especially important for our daughters in a world that still teaches them that survival without a man is next to impossible. Our daughters see us as women being active agents in the world both outside and inside the home. Like single mothers, lesbian mothers, whether partnered or not, have to manage all the chores required to maintain a home and family, from changing the furnace filter to getting the car fixed, from cooking dinner to knowing whom to call when you can't do something yourself. Although lesbian couples can still fall into roles and patterns, the division of labour is not predetermined by gender stereotypes.[4] Furthermore, studies suggest that divisions of household labour tend to be more egalitarian in lesbian households than in heterosexual households.[5] For our daughters, that can provide an invaluable lesson about female resourcefulness, strength and self-reliance—lessons that can, perhaps, combat some of the messages our daughters receive from the outside world about female helplessness and unworthiness.

Regardless of how egalitarian and empowering our homes may be, we do not raise our children in a vacuum. On the contrary, like all women, lesbian mothers are profoundly affected by the political and legal climate within which we live and raise our children. In many places, lesbianism is still considered a "crime against nature," and a revelation of lesbianism can lead to criminal charges and imprisonment. Although the sexual activities in which lesbians might engage are not criminalized in Canada, provided they take place in the privacy of our own homes, nonetheless, lesbians' relationships with each other and with their nonbiological children remain largely "outside the law." Furthermore, in a number of American states, even "private acts" between same-sex partners remain criminalized. The ongoing parade of anti-gay initiatives in the United States and the opposition to sexual orientation protection witnessed in Canada indicates that the battles that the lesbian and gay movements have fought during the past twenty-five years are far from over. It is within this legal and political context, then, that we lesbian mothers are raising our daughters (and sons).[6]

These challenges are particularly great for lesbian mothers who gave birth to their children within the context of a heterosexual marriage—and who face a custodial challenge from their former husband. It is important for us to remember that the vast majority of lesbian mothers are still women who gave birth to children in heterosexual relationships, and the struggles of these women to retain custody of their children continue. Despite an apparent liberalizing in attitudes, despite "lesbian chic," despite *Ellen*,[7] lesbian mothers continue to lose custody of their children to ex-husbands, to child welfare agencies, to their own mothers—solely because of their sexual orientation.[8]

These decisions are rooted in the belief that living with a lesbian or gay parent runs contrary to the "best interests of the child." Where further explanation is provided, it is usually based on the rationale that a child will suffer the ill effects of peer pressure—teasing, derision and harassment—because of his or her parents' sexual orientation. There can be little doubt that peer pressure is a very real factor in our children's lives. But it is important to recognize that "[i]t is prejudice, rather than homosexuality itself, that represents the [real] source of difficulty for the children of lesbians and gay men" (Saffron 169).

As Lisa Saffron has recently noted:

> Fear of stigma is merely a defence of prejudice, ignorance and hatred, an implicit acceptance that society is, and should be, ruled by bigotry. It cannot be in the best interests of children to teach them to value conformity, to fear difference, to be ashamed and frightened of homosexuality and to live their lives according to the standards of people who hate. (167)

The Challenge

Here, then, is our challenge. We have to make the world a safe and accepting place for all our children, our sons and our daughters. We cannot afford to let the chance remarks slide, the "fag" this and "lezzie" that. One of the worst things you can call someone is still a "fag" and if you as a parent confront the remark, you're promptly told it's just a joke, that you are out of step, you just don't understand. The fact is that these are not harmless taunts. For the children of lesbians and gay men, and for the children who will grow up to be lesbian and gay, these remarks cut right to the bone. Our children are beaten up because of our sexual orientation. Gay and lesbian youth have staggering rates of suicide and suicide attempts.[9] Regardless of how rosy we may think things are, our children know that things are definitely NOT OK.

It is not just in the school yard that these remarks are made. We hear them in our workplaces, even in the classrooms where we teach and study.

It is not just the overt remarks that hurt our children. It is the absences. The failure to see representations of their families in the books, lessons and pictures in their classrooms. We all need to be there—me and my children, and you and your children—defending programs for lesbian and gay youth, defending the inclusion of diverse materials in the classrooms, fighting the bigots who seek to remove books like *Heather Has Two Mommies* from our libraries and our schools. Because together we can make a difference.

The Future

In the summer of 1996, our family, for the first time, attended the annual conference of the Gay and Lesbian Parents Coalition International.[10] For my partner and myself, it was a time of workshops and discussions, like many other conferences we have attended. But for Jesse, who attended the parallel conference for teenaged children of lesbian and gay parents,[11] it was an amazing experience. For the first time in her life, she was surrounded by her peers—other teenaged children of lesbian and gay parents—in a setting where our sexual orientation was simply not an issue. They were an amazing group of young people—dynamic, energetic, open, and challenging. Jesse was ecstatic. She rose at six a.m., raced off to breakfast with her new friends and returned to our rooms at the end of the day, long after we had fallen asleep. There were teenagers from all kinds of families, and I laughed to myself when Jesse explained to us on the way home in the car, "My situation is really pretty simple." It was certainly the first time she had ever felt like that!

A week after she came home from the conference, she "came out" to her best friend. "My Mom's gay," she explained.

"With Sue?" her friend asked.

"Yes" Jesse replied.

"Does this mean Sue will be moving in with you guys?"

"She already lives with us," Jesse had to admit, glancing quickly over the 21 years we've been together.

"If you ever need to talk about it," her friend offered, "just let me know."

How it will turn out for Katie is anyone's guess. She has Jesse as a pathbreaker, and lots and lots of other children of lesbian mothers to fight with her. In the years ahead, we hope she will have many other allies, challenging homophobia when they encounter it, not just for the benefit of my daughters, but for the benefit of all our children.

Research for this essay was supported in part by a grant from the Social Sciences and Humanities Research Council of Canada.

Notes

[1] In offering similar estimates, Charlotte Patterson (1992) explains: "Such estimates are based on extrapolations from what is known or believed to be known about base rates in the population. According to Kinsey, Pomeroy, and Martin (1948) and others ... approximately 10 percent of the 250 million people in the United States today can be considered gay or lesbian. According to large-scale survey studies ... about 10 percent of gay men and about 20 percent of lesbians are parents. Most have children from a heterosexual marriage that ended in divorce; many have more than one child. Calculations using these figures suggest that there are about 3-4 million gay or lesbian parents in the United States today. If, on average, each parent has two children, that would place the number of children of formerly married lesbians and gay men at about 6-8 million" (1026). In addition, experts suggest that an estimated five to ten thousand lesbians and gay men have become parents after coming out. I would suggest that such estimates vastly underestimate the number of "baby boom" parents.

[2] The studies also indicate that the vast majority of our children grow up to be heterosexual. Not surprisingly, this is an issue that has preoccupied the judicial and public minds in relation to lesbian and gay parents, and the statistic is frequently presented in custody cases involving lesbian mothers as evidence of the fact that lesbian mothers pose little danger to their children.

[3] In reviewing previous studies that compared lesbian families with heterosexual single-parent families, Maureen Sullivan reported that "there are no marked differences in parenting practices or effects on children's psychological development, except that children in lesbian households are often described as having more positive, tolerant attitudes towards unconventional lifestyles and social differences" (750). In a review of literature on lesbian families, Charlotte Patterson (1992) notes, "Children of lesbian mothers have described an increased tolerance for divergent viewpoints as a benefit of growing up in lesbian mother families (Rafkin), but systematic research in this area is still needed" (1038).

[4] The limited research on child-rearing practices of lesbian families suggests that "lesbian couples who have chosen to bear children are likely to share household and child care duties to a somewhat greater degree than do heterosexual couples." Two separate studies conducted by D. A. Osterweil and by S. I. Hand, cited in Patterson (1996: 284).

[5] Maureen Sullivan reports in her study of thirty-four lesbian couples that "[s]imilar to the egalitarian divisions of housework among lesbian couples without children

in other studies, the parenting practices combined with paid and unpaid domestic work of these lesbian coparents reflect explicit, self-conscious commitments to equity" (764).

[6]For a discussion of lesbian parents and the law, see Arnup (1997).

[7]In April 1997, sitcom star Ellen DeGeneres revealed the long-anticipated news that she is a lesbian on her widely syndicated television show, *Ellen*. While many television programs now include gay or lesbian characters, Ellen is the first actor in a leading role to come out.

[8]For a discussion of child custody cases involving lesbian mothers, see Arnup (1989).

[9]Gay teens are fourteen times more at risk of making a serious suicide attempt, according to a 1986 University of Calgary study. Earlier American studies corroborate these findings. See Gibson.

[10]Gay and Lesbian Parents Coalition International (GLPCI) can be reached at glpcinat@ix.netcom.com.

[11]The youth conference is organized by Children of Lesbians and Gays Everywhere (COLAGE). They can be reached at 2300 Market St., #165, San Francisco, CA 94114. Their e-mail address is colage@colage.org.

References

Arnup, Katherine. "Living in the Margins: Lesbian Families and the Law." *Lesbian Parenting: Living with Pride and Prejudice*. Ed. Katherine Arnup. Charlottetown: gynergy books, 1997. 378-398.

Arnup, Katherine. "'Mothers Just Like Others': Lesbians, Divorce, and Child Custody in Canada." *Canadian Journal of Women and the Law* 3 (1989): 18-32.

Cade, Carl E. "Two Moms, No Hamburgers!" *Different Mothers: Sons and Daughters of Lesbians Talk about Their Lives*. Ed. Louise Rafkin. San Francisco: Cleis Press, 1990. 50-53.

Gibson, Paul. "Gay Male and Lesbian Youth Suicide." *Preventions and Interventions in Youth Suicide*. Vol. 3 of *Report of the Secretary's Task Force on Youth Suicide*. Ed. M.R. Feinleib. United States Department of Health and Human Service, 1989. 110-142.

Herman, Ellen. "The Romance of Lesbian Motherhood." *Sojourner: The Women's Forum* (March 1988).

Lorde, Audre. "Turning the Beat Around: Lesbian Parenting 1986." *Politics of the Heart: A Lesbian Parenting Anthology*. Eds. Sandra Pollack and Jeanne Vaughn. Ithaca, NY: Firebrand, 1987. 310-315.

Martin, April. *The Lesbian and Gay Parenting Handbook: Creating and Raising Our Families*. New York: HarperCollins, 1993.

Patterson, Charlotte J. "Children of Lesbian and Gay Parents." *Child Development* 63 (5) (1992): 1025-1042.

Patterson, Charlotte J. "Lesbian and Gay Parents and their Children." *The Lives of Lesbians, Gays, and Bisexuals*. Eds. Ritch C. Savin-Williams and Kenneth M.

Cohen. Orlando: Harcourt, Brace and Company, 1996. 274-304.

Rafkin, Louise, Ed. *Different Mothers: Sons and Daughters of Lesbians Talk about Their Lives.* San Francisco: Cleis Press, 1990.

Rich, Adrienne. *Of Woman Born: Motherhood as Experience and Institution.* New York: Bantam Books, 1977.

Saffron, Lisa. *"What about the Children?" Sons and Daughters of Lesbian and Gay Parents Talk About Their Lives.* London: Cassell, 1996.

Sullivan, Maureen. "Rozzie and Harriet? Gender and Family Patterns of Lesbian Coparents." *Gender and Society* 10.6 (December 1996): 747-767.

Chapter 31

Emancipated Subjectivities and the Subjugation of Mothering Practices

MIELLE CHANDLER

Prologue

A DOG JUMPED and the three of them had to be scraped off the tarmac. This is what I think when the child tells me: "I want a motorcycle and a fast car." The child who cannot yet ride a two wheeler without training wheels wants a motorcycle and a fast car. The negotiation is starting early—I wasn't expecting this for another ten years or so.

A dog jumped and the three of them had to be scraped off the tarmac and I didn't go to the mourning. I got the news in bits and pieces on my answering machine. At first because I wasn't home when the phone rang and then, after that, because I wouldn't answer it.

A dog jumped and the three of them had to be scraped off the tarmac and I didn't go to the mourning because I didn't want my GPA to drop. It was in grave danger of doing so, you see, because I'd yelled at the elementary school principal and counsellor and the lady at the ministry and the after-school care person all on the same day about three weeks earlier. I'd burned those bridges right to the ground—no childcare, no childcare subsidy, no kindergarten class to send the child off to for a couple of hours a day—and then I had to call my professors and try to explain why it was I didn't think I could make it to class and could I please have an extension on that paper because I won't even be able to turn on my computer until about ten every night and by then I'm tired. Tired.

A dog jumped and the three of them had to be scraped off the tarmac and I didn't go to the mourning because I didn't want my GPA to drop. I needed every spare second to myself. I needed every spare second to myself to work on my papers. My papers. My papers which are about how we fundamentally are in-relation with. And here I was refusing to be in-relation with community because I was too in-relation with child to be able to be separate enough to struggle with Descartes, with Nietzsche, with Marx, with Mouffe, with Rawls in order to satisfy a GPA requirement which I needed in order to eventually become an individual with enough credibility to argue that we are not individuals but in-relation with.

I refused to be in-relation with others in grief in order to be in-relation with text in order to affirm that we are necessarily, rightly, importantly, crucially in-relation with.

A dog jumped and the three of them had to be scraped off the tarmac and I didn't go to the mourning because I didn't want my GPA to drop. What have I become?

To write a paper is to leave mothering, or, rather, it is to leave the type of sub-jectivity I engage in while mothering. A clean break is neither possible nor desir-able, mothering being my topic, and so integral to my identity. Indeed, to leave it would be to become someone completely different. As I write, a child asleep in the next room, part of me is still on duty, ready to battle dream monsters or change wet sheets, making a mental note to tell the babysitter (that is, the stand-in mother whose labour affords me, temporarily, a paper-writing subjectivity) that the child can't go swimming tomorrow (I'm worried the cold might turn into an ear infection), adding granola bars to the shopping list. The process is one of traveling between an individuated and separated subjectivity which allows me to write, and an actively in-relation subjectivity (if it can be called a subjectivity) which is born of mothering. It is an existence fraught with tension, for while each site demands my attention, the former requiring quiet sustained concentration, the latter the alertness of a catcher behind home plate, neither allows me to in-habit the other adequately.

A prejudice on which I build this text is that the conception of persons as separate autonomous beings has too long been predominant and privileged, that persons are also beings in-relation to and with. This idea exists in many discourses including ecological theories, economic theories, theories of socialization and consciousness, and linguistic theories. It is my position that although persons are not only autonomous, unitary, separated individuals but rather fundamentally, and at every level, encumbered; nonetheless, much modern western philosophy not only posits the self as separated, but esteems this separation as the basis of "freedom." Freedom, understood in this sense, is a fallacy—the esteeming of which constitutes one of the factors that enables and perpetuates the devalued status of the blatantly encumbered: mothers. In this chapter I deal specifically with an aspect of much feminist and lesbian feminist theory: a privileging of the emancipated subject, the free and autonomous, separated self.

In recent history, cultural feminism has tended to revalue mothering through celebrating it as a "feminine" trait, while radical feminism has tended toward a rejection of mothering, formulating it as a patriarchally defined and oppressive role of women.[1] Liberal feminism has simply argued for "fairness," claiming that men should do more housework. All three positions I find inadequate and problematic, the first for its sex and gender essentialism, the second for its antinatalism and the third because sharing devalued labour does nothing to revalue it, it simply spreads what is devalued more evenly between more persons within heterosexual nuclear families. Recent developments in feminist queer theory, however, provide a nonessentialist framework for a deconstructive analysis of both the esteeming of the unencumbered separated subject and the devalued status of mothering.

"Mother" as Practice

... *Mother* refers to the maternal function of women. (Rosi Braidotti, feminist academic). (Braidotti 77, emphasis in original)

... *Motherhood* is men's appropriation of women's bodies as a resource to reproduce patriarchy. (Jeffner Allen, radical lesbian feminist). (Allen 317, emphasis in original)

... A mother is the person who constitutes the fall-back position. A mother is the person who is there when nobody else is and when all other systems have failed.(Guy Allen, gay male mother). (qtd. in Dragu et al. 141)

Mothers must militantly make it clear that they are not expendable ... Mothers everywhere must caucus, organise unions, and put an end to their isolation through collective action. (Lucia Valeska, lesbian working-class mother.) (Valeska 75)

..."'Maternal' is a social category" (Sara Ruddick, white academic mother). (Ruddick 225)

"During counselling they said that I don't see myself as separate from my kids. They say my kids are me and I am me, but it's like one entity" (Martinique Somers, Black mother in Brooklyn). (qtd. in Dragu et al. 92)

It is my position that "mother" is best understood as a verb, as something one does, a practice which creates one's identity as intertwined, interconnected and in-relation. Mothering is not a singular practice, and mother is not best understood as a monolithic identity. Even among the low-income queer moms individuated by a panoptic welfare system in East Vancouver in the 1990s, the practices vary significantly. Who a mother is and what it means to be one is context-specific. I in no way wish to universalize my discussion of mother as practice. The examples I use and my understanding of practice is currently limited by the urban, western, nonaffluent, predominantly white, feminist sphere I inhabit.

Judith Butler (1990) speaks of gender as "a kind of becoming or activity," and claims that as such "gender ought not to be conceived as a noun or a substantial thing or a static cultural marker, but rather as an incessant and repeated action of some sort" (143). To be a woman is to consistently reenact femininity; it is an imitation, a theatrically produced effect. To be a lesbian, as far as I can tell, is to repetitively deviate from the heterosexual matrix in such a specifically regimented way as to be accepted by other lesbians as one. To be a mother is to enact mothering. It is a multifaceted and everchanging yet painfully repetitive performance which although, like "woman," involves the way one walks, talks, postures, dresses and paints one's face, orients these activities directly and instrumentally in-relation to and with the walking, talking, posturing, dressing, undressing, dressing, undressing, dressing, undressing and painting of face (or, rather, the washing of paint off of face) of another who, due to a relation of near-complete interdependence, is not separate.

The ongoing in-relation of wiping up vomit and taking temperatures, rocking to sleep, being interrupted, taking a shower only when the baby is asleep and then doing so very quickly lest it wake up, the act of being so in-relation to and with that one wakes up as one's milk begins to let down a minute before the baby wakes up to nurse, constructs one as something both more and less than an individual. To mother is to clean, to mop, to sweep, to keep out of reach, to keep safe, to keep warm, to feed, to take small objects out of mouths, to answer impossible questions, to…. It is ever-failing imitations of socially constructed ideals. It is a series of responses to the fundamental needs of another who is so interconnected with the self that there exists no definitive line of differentiation.[2] When one mothers one is not one's own person.

This is most acute when mothering an infant. Although one is not one's own person, one is not someone else's person either, for the infant is both and neither "other" than the mother and the same thing. It is widely acknowledged that infants and young children do not differentiate themselves from their mother (Chodorow 201; Hartsock 73). When mothering practice is such that the young child does not differentiate itself from the mother, the lines may also disintegrate for the mother. In cases where the practising mother has also carried and given birth to the child, lines of differentiation may never have formed (Young 407). In summation, "mother" is an identity formed through a repetition of practices which constitute one as so profoundly interconnected that one is not one, *but is simultaneously more and less than one.*

Practices of Subjectivity: "One" and "I"

There "is no reason," writes Butler (1990), "to divide up human bodies into male and female sexes except that such a division suits the economic needs of heterosexuality and lends a naturalistic gloss to the institution of heterosexuality" (143). I would like to suggest that there is no reason to divide up human bodies at all. Doing so suits the needs of western liberal capitalist democracies and lends a naturalistic gloss to the institution of individuality. Indeed, conceiving of the self as anything but divided, separated, individuated, problematizes the very foundations of our (if "we" are members of a western liberal democratic capitalist state) social, economic, political and judicial systems and disrupts the foundation of even the updated versions of the Social Contract.

Monique Wittig describes gender in language as stripping women of subjectivity, "the most precious thing for a human being" (80-81). In an effort to destroy gender Wittig goes further than simply dividing up bodies and individuating persons. She erases the possibility of a self defined in-relation. For Wittig, subjectivity in and of itself is an emancipatory goal exemplified in the linguistic use of "I":

Gender is ontologically a total impossibility. For when one becomes a locutor, when one says "I" and, in so doing, reappropriates language as a whole, proceeding from oneself alone, with the tremendous power to use all language, it is then and there, according to linguists and philosophers, that the supreme act of subjectivity, the advent of subjectivity into consciousness, occurs. It is when starting to speak that one becomes "I." This act—the becoming of the subject through the exercise of language and through locution—in order to be real, implies that the locutor be an absolute subject. For a relative subject is inconceivable, a relative subject could not speak at all. (80)

A relative subject, that is, a subject in-relation, then, is not a subject. Mothers, if understood as necessarily in-relation, are not subjects.[3] A similar sentiment can be found in Descartes statement that "dependence is manifestly a defect" (34). Indeed, Wittig's construction of subjectivity can be understood as Cartesian in a number of senses. Descartes constructs the world upon his own existence as a self-reflexive thinking subject. Wittig claims that with the speech act "I," which designates one as a self-reflexive thinking subject, "I reorganised the world from my point of view and through abstraction I lay claim to universality" (Wittig 81). Although Wittig's "I" differs at a basic level from the Cartesian "I" in that it is discursive, it is fundamentally Cartesian in its centrality, in its universality and in its singularity. It is upon his own existence as a thinking subject that Descartes constructs the rest of the world. It is the linguistic representation of the thinking subject through the use of "I" which acts, for Wittig, as a central axis for the reorganization of the world. It is this particular "I" that Wittig posits as emancipatory.

Wittig's lesbian is, materially, such an "I." Lesbians, as escapees from slavery, live as "I's." While women are relegated by heterosexuality to nonsubjectivity, lesbians claim subjectivity by separating from sociopolitical and economic relations of subordination to men.[4] This emancipation comes in the form of Cartesian selfhood; it comes in the form of an individual subject: ungendered, universal and whole (Wittig 80).

Although to abolish the two-gendered system altogether would effectively nullify both classes, slaves and masters, Wittig's approach is to create a world of masters, a world of "I's" and "one's." Slavery is to be abhorred, shunned and escaped from. The universalization of the universal subject, the master, the individual in the paradigm of the Social Contract, is what is to be aimed at. It is what lies beyond the two-gendered system of heterosexuality that enslaves the class "women." The challenge maternity poses to both the Cartesian self and Wittig's emancipated "I" is a self in-relation. It is a self symbiotically connected and within a bond of dependence. Perhaps as such the maternal self cannot be said to be a self. Perhaps this is an area where we must search for modes of being beyond subjectivity.

My concern is that in destroying the categories of sex and gender, what is created is a separated autonomous subjectivity as the only acceptable conception of selfhood. If the individual subject is understood as the only type that can lay claim to credibility by proclaiming itself "free" and "emancipated," the self as in-relation will become further marginalized, reviled and driven deeper into the closet. My concern is that a process of forced individuated freedom, while it may untie persons from specific gender identities, ties them instead to a specifically privileged type of subjectivity, a subjectivity the pronoun "one" is indicative of.

There is in French, as there is in English, a munificent pronoun that is called the indefinite, which means that it is not marked by gender, a pronoun that you are taught in school to systematically avoid. It is *on* in French—*one* in English … here is a subject pronoun which is very tractable and accommodating since it can be bent in several directions at the same time. First, as already mentioned, it is indefinite as far as gender is concerned. It can represent a certain number of people successively or all at once—everybody, we, they, I, you, people, a small or large number of persons—and still stay singular. (Wittig 83, emphases in original)

Mothers cannot properly be referred to with the pronoun "one." One (language becomes difficult here) is not singular when one mothers: one's identity is both plural (inclusive of the self and the children) and less than singular (one is not one's own self, but an extension of the children). If "woman" can be understood as a repetitive imitation of an illusive heterosexual original,[5] and "mother" as a set of practices in-relation with and to children, perhaps "one" can also be understood in action terms: as an enactment. Perhaps the pronoun "one," whether singular (designating one particular person), or plural (designating one of any number of people in general), is better understood as a verb-pronoun. "One," to again import Butler's structure, is perhaps an imitation for which there is no essential origin, a multiplicity of discursive constructions dating back at least as far as Descartes. Perhaps the individual subject is the naturalistic effect produced by centuries of repetition. As such it would be perpetually at risk, each site of repetition holding the potential (or posing the danger, depending how one looks at it) for coming undone, or at least for shifting. The individual subject, then, to further build on Butler's armature, is perhaps constituted as an effect of its expression, a constitution which gives the illusion of essence.[6]

Individuation and Emancipation

Michel Foucault is one of the theorists who takes seriously a rethinking of both emancipation and subjectivity. In "The Subject and Power," an essay concerning how human beings are made subjects, Foucault outlines three forms of struggle: struggles against domination, struggles against exploitation and struggles against prescriptions of individuation and identity. It is the latter I am most interested in, though I am dubious as to its divisibility from the first two. This third type of struggle is against a government of individuation that "separates the individual, breaks his links with others, splits up community life, forces the individual back on himself and ties him to his own identity in a constraining way" (Foucault 212). The idea I wish to put forth is that liberation itself constitutes a constraint to which the individual is tied. This kind of constraint can be seen in lesbian and feminist antinatalism which at one and the same time unties the identity "woman" from the identity "mother" and reties "woman" to an ideal of emancipated subjectivity. This untying and retying can be seen in the work of Simone de Beauvoir, which has been instrumental in shaping both the emancipatory project of, and conceptions of, maternity and motherhood in more contemporary feminist and lesbian feminist theory.

Instead of levying the allegation of antinatalism against de Beauvoir, I wish to agree that mothering does mean a loss of individual agency and autonomy for mothers. Indeed, in confining this loss of agency to the processes of pregnancy and birth, de Beauvoir does not go far enough. The loss of agency is most acute *after* the birth of a child, as I hope my characterization of mother as practice has illustrated. The problematic lies not in the equation of motherhood with non-subjectivity but in the privileging of an emancipated individuated subjectivity. The two are nicely played out in the following quote:

> Ensnared by nature, the pregnant woman is plant and animal, a stock-pile of celluloids, an incubator, an egg; she scares children proud of their young, straight bodies and makes young people titter contemptuously because she is a human being, *a conscious and free individual who has become life's passive instrument.* (de Beauvoir 495, emphasis added)

The anitnatalism of de Beauvoir can be read as an attempt to extricate the category "woman" from the prescriptivity of motherhood. As Linda Zerilli so aptly puts it, de Beauvoir's antinatalism "is a sophisticated and underappreciated feminist discursive strategy of defamiliarisation: a highly charged, always provocative, and at times enraging restaging of the traditional drama of maternity" (112). By retelling the maternal narrative as horrific, parasitic and alien, de Beauvoir allows women to see maternity as separate from their identities as women.

The problematic arises not with positing mother as nonsubject in this process of extrication, but rather with the *de-privileging* of mother nonsubjectivity, with representing mother nonsubjectivity in such a way as to elicit scorn, contempt, pity and the charge of self-enslavement. That maternity "robs" one of subjectivity is not at issue; that the subjectivity one is "robbed" of through maternity is equated with an unquestioningly privileged emancipation is the more accurate site of mother-subordination. The problematic lies in the honouring of a view of the individual subject, which lends itself to a specific submission of subjectivity, which ties one to a specific type of emancipatory self-hood, the "master" subject, the "one":

> No subject will readily volunteer to become the object, the inessential; it is not the Other who, in defining himself as the Other, establishes the One. The Other is posed as such by the One in defining himself as the One. But if the Other is not to regain the status of being the One,

he must be submissive enough to accept this alien point of view. (de Beauvoir xxiv)

Further, a "refusal to pose oneself as the Subject, unique and absolute, requires great self-denial" (de Beauvoir xxxi). While de Beauvoir does not tie *all* persons to an emancipated subjectivity, by denying legitimacy to any type of subjectivity, such as mothering, which does not partake of an emancipated master subjectivity, she ties the "liberated" woman to a prescriptive, individuated emancipation and the rest of us to submission and self-denial. "Woman" fails to "authentically assume a subjective attitude" because of sociopolitical and economic forced collusion with the (male) oppressors. Maternity constitutes such a collusion. The attainment of agency, of subjectivity, the claim of oneness, is the mark of liberation; it is what is to be fought for. While "woman," "a free and autonomous being like all human creatures" (de Beauvoir xxxv), can overcome her otherness, her relegation to nonsubjectivity, and, while it may be argued that in many respects, and to some extent "woman" has indeed achieved such autonomy (if such an attainment can be called "achievement"), such a possibility is not open to mothers, whose autonomy, in their capacity as mothers, remains fundamentally impaired.

I would like here to make a small deviation from my main argument in order to consider the meaning and significance of autonomy. In political liberal theory autonomy designates, firstly, a unitary independence, and, secondly, a self-government that precludes external restraints (Dworkin). The notion of autonomy is intimately linked to notions of freedom and liberty, the basic liberties (movement, speech, and so on) being based in a deontological notion of the self as autonomous. John Stuart Mill argues that one cannot autonomously choose to enslave oneself, for such an exercise of autonomy would preclude one's future autonomy. If motherhood is understood in slavery terms, such a precludement positions motherhood as, deontologically speaking, ethically wrong.

In one sense, de Beauvoir and others are not mistaken in characterizing motherhood as enslavement. For nonaffluent mothers, mothering is extremely restrictive. When I first became a mother, my freedom, along with my individuality, vanished. Freedom of speech? I could not even carry on a ten-minute conversation uninterrupted. Freedom of movement? It took all morning to get out of the house, and then they don't allow strollers on the buses and frown when you change diapers on the bus seats—but where else is there? Freedom of association? My friends were still meeting in pubs, where babies aren't allowed. I got kicked out of the gym because they said it was no place for a baby. Movies scared the baby, who then would cry, disrupting the audience, and evening meetings didn't work because they interrupted the baby's bedtime routine.[7] The mistake lies not so much in equating motherhood with a loss of freedom and autonomy, but rather in adopting autonomy as an ideal.

The feminist preoccupation with winning autonomy for women must face what has been lost in the battle, who has been subjugated by it and what the costs have been. When I assert that a revaluing of motherhood is in order, I speak as a mother forced to put her child into daycare at too early an age. The cries of the child, clinging, torn limb by limb from my body, still reverberate in my ears. I speak as a mother forced by emancipation to wrench my child from me, to, day after day, compartmentalize my child away, so that I could pretend for eight hours that I was an individual. That is the price, for many mothers, of autonomy, of freedom, of movement, of speech; that is the price of this text (and now that I have finished it, I'm going to go and pick up my child), and that is a price which is too high to pay.

On Refusal

The problematic arises when, in the name of liberation, untying "woman" from "mother" results in or leads to a delineation of liberation that precludes mothering. The question now becomes both how to liberate ourselves, mothers as mothers, from an all-pervasive nonmother liberation, and how to liberate the sign "lesbian" from designating a prescriptive emancipatory subjectivity. I have a small suggestion regarding the liberation of mother qua mother, regarding "lesbian"; however, I have, for now at least, reached an impasse.

Judith Butler (1990) speaks of the danger of being recolonized by the sign "lesbian," and asks: "If to become a lesbian is an *act,* a leave-taking of heterosexuality, a self-naming that contests the compulsory meanings of heterosexuality's *women* and *men,* what is to keep the name of lesbian from becoming an equally compulsory category?" (162, emphasis in original). In Foucauldian terms, what Butler is speaking of is the danger of "lesbian" becoming an identity one is tied to (or outside of, or in the margins of) in a prescriptive way.

For the type of individuation which binds the individual to specific and prescriptive identities in a constraining way, Foucault suggests the refusal of identity as a tactic of insubordination ("The Subject and Power"). It is this very tactic which Wittig employs in hailing "lesbian" as a refusal of heterosexual patriarchal enslavement, and which de Beauvoir engages in alienating "woman" from "mother." Butler problematizes this refusal by pointing out that "lesbian" as a refusal of heterosexuality reinscribes the very heterosexual matrix which it disavows, but, interestingly enough, adopts a highly sophisticated version of the Foucauldian refusal tactic in an attempt to rescue "lesbian" from its (already realized but disruptable) potential as a prescriptive and exclusionary sign. The strategy Butler (1990) suggests is: "a thoroughgoing appropriation and redeployment of the categories of identity themselves, not merely to contest 'sex,' but to articulate the convergence of multiple sexual discourses at the site of 'identity' in order to render that category, in whatever form, permanently problematic" (163).

Identity is a dangerous game not only because, as Foucault explains it, the government of individuation ties one to a specific identity in a prescriptive way, or, as Butler puts it, one faces being recolonized by the very sign that holds the promise of liberation; danger lies not only in being tied to a specific identity through individuating processes, but in being tied to a specific subjectivity through identificatory processes. Within lesbian discourses, "lesbian" ties one to an (ideally) emancipated, individuated and separated subjectivity. Butler's suggestion of rendering the category "lesbian" permanently problematic does not alter the status of the sign as signifying an emancipated subjectivity, but instead seeks to preserve the emancipatory potentiality of the sign in a way which its solidification would prohibit.

To refuse is not enough not only because to refuse would be to be defined by one's refusal, categorized by it, which, within a binary system of meaning, simply results in the reinforcement of the identity one refuses, but also because the refusal of an identity does little to alter the basic tenants of subjectivity. Further, refusal, while it may be an appropriate tactic for white male intellectuals, is impractical for mothers. To refuse the identity "mother" would necessitate a refusal of practices of mothering, which, although some mothers have resorted to this, is too much to ask of any mother. To refuse mothering would not only have very real consequences for the lives of children, not to mention the state, economy and future of "society" itself, but would also be a refusal of the kind of self a mothering self becomes through mothering. To suggest a refusal of mothering is to suggest one tear out what one is as a mother, that one split one's own identity in the most painful way imaginable. While practices of sex and gender lend themselves well to the refusal tactic, to interchangeability, self-reflexivity and, ultimately, to emancipation, practices of mothering do not.

Jean Baudrillard also suggests refusal, though of a slightly different sort:

> To a system whose argument is oppression and repression, the strategic resistance is the liberating claim of subjecthood. But this reflects rather the system's previous phase, and even if we are still confronted with it, it is no longer the strategic terrain: the system's current argument is the maximisation of the word and the maximal production of meaning. Thus the strategic resistance is that of *a refusal of meaning and a refusal of the word—or of the hyperconformist simulation of the very mechanisms of the system*, which is a form of refusal and of non-reception. (108, emphasis added)

As much as I respect and enjoy Baudrillard, I cannot help but think that mothering, to some limited extent, defies the production of meaning in late capitalist democracies, and thus defies both the possibility of a refusal of meaning and of hyper conformism. No matter how hard one tries to "hyperconform," to simulate the perfect mother, the baby will always disrupt the simulation. It will throw up all down your dress, refuse to nurse when it should, sleep through the night when it shouldn't, cry for hours when you've done everything right, and cause, out of shear frustration and fatigue, or from some love deeper than you knew could exist, a shattering of the simulation. Motherhood shatters simulations in much the same way I would imagine many larger catastrophes such as floods, earthquakes and wars do. One simply acts in panic and desperation.[8] Mothering, at least of infants, precludes a refusal of the word through obliterations of the word. The word is replaced by snorffles and milk and (lack of) sleep and smells and excretions. In making this claim I in no way wish to deny the discursive constructions of motherhood, nor do I wish to deny that mothering practices continue to serve western capitalist, patriarchal democracies well, but rather I wish to add that there is something about mothering practices that both underlie and go beyond the word, the construction, the institution and the image. This is not to say that mothering is anything other than practice, but rather that mothering practices at times preclude a refusal of meaning and make hyperconformism, at least sometimes, just plain impossible.

As a tactic, refusal is fraught with pragmatic and theoretical complications, and yet there is something very satisfying in the concept. *Hip Mama* is a zine put out and contributed to by mothers who are radical, poor, young, single, queer and angry (Gore). It embraces motherhood while subverting prevalent conceptions of the "good" mother. For example, while featuring an article by a mother recounting her homeless pregnancy, *Hip Mama* proclaimed teenage pregnancy "hip" thereby validating and giving voice to the extreme difficulties faced by homeless teen moms, while simultaneously fostering motherpride, allowing the embracement of teen pregnancies. *Hip Mama* features legitimating articles by socially illegitimated mothers: stripper moms, queer moms and poor moms. And it endows mothering practices with value without shying from the profoundly interconnected and prohibitive nature of nonaffluent western mothering.

If refusal is the only tactic at our disposal, then perhaps a useful refusal for mothers is a refusal to conform to emancipatory subjectivities that subjugate mother practices. Perhaps a useful refusal for mothers is to refuse to refuse: to embrace motherselfhoods and to demand social, economic and political respect for mothering practices. But even here we must tread carefully, for "a mistake concerning strategy is a serious matter" (Baudrillard 109), and identity is a dangerous game.

Mothers make my head turn. I want to kiss their tired eyes and lay them down not in ecstasy, for small hands are ceaselessly tugging, small tongues licking and mouths groping—but to sleep, alone, in puke-free warmth. I'll take the babies to the park. And perhaps some day, after the house is clean and there is enough money to cover the rent, we will uncork the small filigree bottle, if we can still find it, and discover what remains of our passions.

Notes

[1]More accurately, the rejection is not always total. There exists in much lesbian separatist literature from the 1970s and 1980s a glorification of raising daughters on woman-only land. Raising male children, however, is being a slave for the enemy. I have trouble with this genre of writing not only because of its sex and gender essentialism, but also, and especially, because it tends to posit solutions in self-righteous terms. I much prefer the Foucauldian practice of analyzing systems

and making small suggestions toward tactics of insubordination to the practice of thrusting totalizing theories onto peoples lives.

[2]This is a common complaint among new mothers.

[3]This is not to say that persons who happen to mother can never be subjects, it is simply to say that, within this particular framework, in order to be subjects, mothers must leave their "mother" subjectivity and inhabit an "I" subjectivity.

[4]Cheshire Calhoun, in her essay "Separating Lesbian Theory from Feminist Theory," points out that "contrary to Wittig's claim, the lesbian may as a rule have *less* control over her productive and reproductive labour than her married heterosexual sister. Although the lesbian escapes whatever control *individual* men may exercise over their wives within marriage, she does not thereby escape control of her productive and reproductive labor either in her personal life with another women or in her public life. To refuse to be heterosexual is simply to leap out of the frying pan of individual patriarchal control into the fire of institutionalised heterosexual control.... The lesbian may be free from an individual man in her personal life, but she is not free" (564-565, emphasis in original).

[5]Butler speaks of gender as drag, that is as a performance, an imitation for which there is no original, which, through a repetition of the performance, constitute naturalistic effects.

[6]This is the framework Judith Butler uses to discuss lesbianism in "Imitation and Gender Insubordination."

[7]All this suggests that it is not mothering practices that need changing but rather the adult-centric "public" sphere that could use comprehensive revamping.

[8]A friend of mine, and early childhood educator, aptly characterizes mothers with children under the age of six as living in a constant state of crisis.

References

Allen, Jennifer. "Motherhood: The Annihilation of Women in Mothering." *Mothering: Essays in Feminist Theory*. Ed. Joyce Trebilcot. Totowa: Rowman and Allenheld, 1984. 315-330.

Baudrillard, Jean. *In the Shadow of the Silent Majorities or, The End of the Social and Other Essays*. New York: Semiotext(e), 1983.

Braidotti, Rosi. *Nomadic Subjects: Embodiment and Sexual Difference in Contemporary Feminist Theory*. New York: Columbia University Press, 1994.

Butler, Judith. *Gender Trouble: Feminism and the Subversion of Identity*. 1990. London: Routledge, 1999.

Butler, Judith. "Imitation and Gender Insubordination." *The Lesbian and Gay Studies Reader*. Eds. Henry Abelove, Michele Aina Barale, and David Halperin. New York: Routledge, 1993. 307-320.

Calhoun, Cheshire. "Separating Lesbian Theory from Feminist Theory." *Ethics: Ann International Journal of Social, Political, and Legal Philosophy* 104 (3) (April 1994): 558-581.

Chodorow, Nancy. "Family Structure and Feminine Personality." *Feminism and*

Philosophy: Essential Readings in Theory, Reinterpretation, and Application. Eds. Nancy Tuana ad Rosemarie Tong. San Francisco: Westview Press, 1995. 199-216.

de Beauvoir, Simone. *The Second Sex.* New York: Vintage Books, 1989.

Descartes, René. "Discourse on the Method of Rightly Directing One's Reason and Seeking Truth in the Sciences." *Philosophical Writings: Descartes.* Eds. Elizabeth Anscombe and Peter T. Geach. New York: Macmillan Publishing Co., 1971.

Dragu, Margaret, Sarah Sheared, and Susan Swan, Eds. *Mothers Talk Back.* Toronto: Coach House Press, 1991.

Dworkin, Gerald. *The Theory and Practice of Autonomy.* New York: Cambridge University Press, 1988.

Foucault, Michel. "The Subject and Power." *Michel Foucault: Beyond Structuralism and Hermeneutics.* Eds. Hubert L. Dreyfus and Paul Rabinow. Brighton: Harvester Press, 1982. 208-226.

Gore, Ariel, ed. *Hip Mama: The Parenting Zine.* Oakland: Hip Mama, California, 1997.

Hartsock, Nancy. "The Feminist Standpoint: Developing the Ground for a Specifically Feminist Historical Materialism." *Feminism and Philosophy: Essential Readings in Theory, Reinterpretation, and Application.* Eds. Nancy Tuana ad Rosemarie Tong. San Francisco: Westview Press, 1995. 69-90.

Mill, John Stuart. *On Liberty.* London: Penguin Classics, 1985.

Ruddick, Sara. "Maternal Thinking." *Mothering: Essays in Feminist Theory.* Ed. Joyce Trebilcot. Totowa: Rowman and Allenheld, 1984. 213-230.

Valeska, Lucia. "If All Else Fails, I'm Still a Mother." *Mothering: Essays in Feminist Theory.* Ed. Joyce Trebilcot. Totowa: Rowman and Allenheld, 1984. 70-78.

Wittig, Monique. *The Straight Mind and Other Essays.* Boston: Beacon Press, 1992.

Young, Iris Marion. "Pregnant Embodiment: Subjectivity and Alienation." *Feminism and Philosophy: Essential Readings in Theory, Reinterpretation, and Application.* Eds. Nancy Tuana ad Rosemarie Tong. San Francisco: Westview Press, 1995. 407-419.

Zerilli, Linda. "A Process Without a Subject: Simone de Beauvoir and Julia Kristeva on Maternity." *Signs: A Journal of Women and Culture in Society* 18 (1) (1992): 111-135.

Chapter 32

Mothering and Feminism

Essential Mothering and the Dilemma of Difference

PATRICE DIQUINZIO

Mothering is frequently a subject of contention in American society and culture, and controversies about mothering usually have an urgent tone that suggests that fundamental issues and crucially important values are at stake. The resurgence of the women's movement in the second half of the twentieth century has intensified the contention surrounding mothering. The women's movement has made a wide variety of choices with respect to motherhood more available to and more socially acceptable for more women. But this outcome has also increased both the difficulty of women's decision making about motherhood and the public debate about the relative value of women's varied options concerning motherhood. Such conflicts and debates are evident in the significant number of real and fictional mothers and groups of mothers who have recently been the object of public scrutiny in the United States and beyond. Mary Beth Whitehead, Susan Smith, Deborah Eappen and Louise Woodward, Murphy Brown and Madonna; single mothers, teenage mothers, lesbian mothers, welfare mothers, and soccer moms have all been the focus of such scrutiny and debate. Teenage pregnancy, surrogate mothering, multiple births resulting from fertility treatments, mothering through IVF for women 50, 60, and older; extra-uterine gestation and cloning; abortion and day care; adoption and child custody law—all continue to generate controversy.

Much of this controversy surrounding mothering is a function of its social context. In Western, industrial capitalist societies like the United States, the nuclear family in which women have primary responsibility for child rearing—what Nancy Chodorow calls the male-dominated, father-absent family (181)—is a crucial component of social organization and individual development. The nuclear family and female child rearing sustain other structures of these societies, and persons" experiences of being mothered in this sort of family are pervasive and powerful. Thus, being a mother and being mothered are both imbued with tremendous social, cultural, political, economic, psychological, and personal significance. Everyone has a stake in the social organization of mothering, but these stakes can vary greatly. Although few persons share exactly the same position with respect to mothering, none has an unconflicted relationship to it.

Conflicts among women also play out in relationship to mothering. Some women do not want to be mothers and never do *so;* some women do not want to become mothers but nonetheless do; some women want to be mothers but are unable to do so for a variety of reasons; some women find great satisfaction and a sense of accomplishment in mothering; some women become mothers in circumstances that prevent their experiencing such satisfaction in mothering; and some women regret having become mothers. Many mothers report that mothering is a deeply ambivalent experience in which, at one time or another, they feel exaltation, despair, and many other emotions in between. In addition, the needs and interests of women who are mothers and women who are not, as well as the needs and interests of some mothers compared to others, can be at odds. The needs and interests of mothers who work for wages and those who do not, and of mothers who hire other women to care for their children, and of the women, often mothers themselves, whom they hire can come into conflict. Mothers who work for wages, mothers who are provided for by husbands or children's fathers, and mothers who receive public funds for their support can have opposing needs and interests.

Mothers can occupy many different positions with respect to the family; they can be married mothers, single mothers who are either divorced or never married, step-mothers, adoptive mothers, lesbian mothers with or without partners, foster mothers, surrogate mothers, other-mothers (Collins 119-122), or mothers who do not live with their children or do not have physical and/or legal custody of their children. Some of these positions are much more socially accepted and validated than others, and the needs and interests of mothers in more socially accepted relationships to the family can conflict with the needs and interests of mothers in delegitimated relationships to the family. At the same time, other kinds of social conflict—especially conflicts involving race, ethnicity, socio-economic class, and sexual orientation—can be particularly intense in relationship to mothering. For example, "welfare" mothers are often coded as African-American, family dysfunctions such as spousal or child abuse are often understood to involve mothers who are poor and/or members of minority groups, the enforcement of laws and social policies that criminalize pregnant women who drink alcohol or use drugs as child abusers often target mothers who are poor and/or members of minority groups, and lesbian mothers are often stigmatized as unfit, for instance, in legal proceedings regarding custody of their children.

Mothering is also a very contentious issue in American feminism, and many critics of feminism focus on what they believe feminism says or implies about mothering. Feminism in the United States, however, has never been characterized by a monolithic position on mothering. Some feminists have argued that mothering is the source of women's limitations or the cause of women's oppression, because it is the experience in which women most suffer under the tyranny of nature, biology, and/or male control. Others have argued that mothering is an important source of women's identity, a scene of women's most joyful accomplishments, a basis of women's value as members of society, and an impetus for women's political participation. Some feminist assessments of mothering agree that it can unite women in many shared experiences. But of such assessments, some emphasize women's deep and abiding love for their children and/or their pleasures and sense of accomplishment in child rearing, while others focus on the stifling confinement to home and family, the annoyances and frustrations of caring for children, the agonizing losses that mothering can entail, and the lack of control over the circumstances of their mothering that many women experience. Some feminist analyses of mothering emphasize that mothers of different racial and ethnic groups, religions, ages, socio-economic classes, and sexual orientations can have much in common in their day-to-day existence, their ongoing interests and concerns, and the shape and trajectory of their lives. But others focus on the specificity of different women's experiences of mothering, arguing that socially significant differences such as race, ethnicity, religion, age, socio-economic class, and sexual orientation so thoroughly shape women's situations and experiences of mothering as to preclude much commonality among mothers. Feminists have argued that mothering can unite women in political action, from local struggles for better schools and safer neighborhoods to global peace activism and anti-militarism. But they have also recognized that mothering can divide women, creating misunderstanding, suspicion, and hostility among women whose opportunities, choices, or experiences with respect to mothering are different. And feminists have seen that political activism conducted under the sign of mothering can alienate women who are not mothers, women who don't like being mothers, or women who don't want to be identified primarily in terms of their mothering.

Some of feminism's most pressing, but also most contradictory demands are issued in the name of mothering. For example, feminism demands that women have freedom, autonomy, and choice with respect to reproduction and child rearing. But feminism also demands that men participate at least equally in child rearing, which may limit mothers" autonomy. Feminism demands that social institutions, policies, and practices treat women as human individuals, with no reference to their actual or potential mothering, but also demands that social institutions, policies, and practices accommodate the needs and interests of mothers. Feminists have seen that when social institutions, policies, and practices treat women and men equally, without consideration of women's actual or potential mothering, this can benefit women who are not mothers (and all or most men) and disadvantage mothers (and men who do take significant responsibility for caring for children). But when social institutions, policies, and practices do take the needs and interests of mothers (and child rearing men) into account, this may benefit mothers and disadvantage women who are not mothers and men who have few or no child rearing responsibilities. In addition, feminists struggle among themselves over the meaning, significance, and control of medical interventions in reproduction, and of laws, social policies, and cultural practices that affect reproduction and mothering. Controversies among feminists about whether fertility treatments and surrogacy arrangements enhance women's freedom, autonomy, and choice with respect to mothering; reinforce the view that all women should be mothers; or enable some women to become mothers by exploiting other women are only a few instances of contention among feminists about mothering. Feminists also continue to struggle among themselves over the question of how best to reorganize social institutions, such as workplaces and schools, so that they will accommodate both mothering and women's freedom and equal opportunity.

Mothering and Feminist Theory

It is not surprising, then, that mothering is a very contentious issue in feminist theory. The central concepts of feminist theory, including sex, gender, embodiment, desire, consciousness, experience, representation, oppression, equality, freedom, and liberation are all relevant to understanding mothering and are regularly invoked in feminist analyses of mothering. But analyzing mothering also raises questions or problems about the meaning and implications of these concepts, problems that may only become apparent when these concepts are deployed in connection with mothering. Thus, mothering is both an important site at which the central concepts of feminist theory are elaborated, and a site at which these concepts are challenged and reworked. In addition, the issue of mothering often functions as a sort of lightning rod in feminist theory: other issues and disagreements in feminist theory are expressed in terms of mothering or get attached to the issue of mothering, and this brings all the intensity and contention associated with mothering to these disagreements. Furthermore, the various proposals for reorganizing mothering that feminism has articulated and attempted to put into practice have met with strenuous resistance in the United States, particularly compared to the reception and implementation of feminist proposals for change in other areas of social life. For example, feminism's demand for women's equal access to and participation in paid labor and public life has been much more widely accepted and put into practice than the corresponding demand that men take greater responsibility for child rearing and other domestic activities. This has left many mothers to face the "second shift," taking all or most responsibility for child rearing and domestic work while also meeting the demands of paid work (Hochschild). Feminism's demand for women's greater sexual freedom and for destigmatizing mothering outside of marriage, combined with men's failure to take greater responsibility for child rearing, has left many women struggling to raise children alone, with little or no support of any kind from the fathers of their children (Folbre). This uneven progress of feminism has especially complicated the lives of mothers, and has generated further feminist analyses of mothering, that are not necessarily consistent with each other.

But precisely for these reasons neither feminism nor feminist theory can afford to ignore the issue of mothering. To the extent that mothering, in all its diverse forms, remains an important aspect of many women's lives and that decisions about whether, when, and how to mother continue to face almost all women, feminism cannot claim to give an adequate account of women's lives and to represent women's needs and interests if it ignores the issue of mothering. And to the extent that mothering has been a primary site of women's oppression, it is likely that sexists and supporters of an antifeminist backlash will continue to insist that mothering be theorized and organized in their own terms. This will certainly have significant consequences, few of them consistent with feminist goals and values. The problematic outcomes of the uneven progress of feminism and the strong resistance to feminist ideas about reorganizing mothering also suggest that feminism and feminist theory need to explore further the issue of mothering, at least in order to determine the basis of this resistance to reorganizing mothering. Certainly it is possible to theorize women's situations and experiences, or to theorize gender, in ways that minimize the issue of mothering, or do not address it at all. But assumptions about women's mothering are so deeply embedded in U.S. society and culture and are so complexly intertwined with other fundamental beliefs and values that these assumptions are likely to be implicit in accounts of women's situations and experiences and in theories of gender that do not explicitly address mothering.

In this study of feminist thinking about mothering, I consider the difficulties of theorizing mothering and doing feminist theory in light of the relationship of feminism and individualism, the theory of subjectivity presupposed by the ideological formation that predominates in the United States. Feminism has to rely on individualism in order to articulate its claims that women are equal human subjects of social and political agency and entitlement. But, I argue, feminism has found it impossible to theorize mothering adequately in terms of an individualist theory of subjectivity. Thus, I ask, in what ways has feminism relied on individualism and in what ways has feminism challenged it? How has individualism facilitated feminism, and in what ways has it been an obstacle to feminism? In what ways have feminist theories of mothering participated in the complex relationship of feminism and individualism and in what ways have they reconfigured this relationship? What alternative theories of subjectivity has feminist theory looked to or devised in order to analyze mothering, and what have been the implications and effects of these alternatives for theorizing mothering, for analyzing other aspects of women's situations and experiences, for theorizing gender, and for representing women's needs and interests?

Briefly, my response to these questions takes the following form: I offer a theory of ideology in order to analyze the conflicted relationship of feminism and individualism. I understand individualism as the theory of subjectivity presupposed by the individualist ideological formation that is dominant in the modern United States. Thus, it is the theory of subjectivity that supports the material conditions and social relations sustained and justified by this ideological formation, and that mediates more or less successfully the contradictions that emerge in the attempt to maintain both liberal democratic political practices and capitalist economic arrangements. I show that, as a theory of subjectivity, individualism represents subjectivity in terms of identity, denies the effectivity of difference in subjectivity, and construes subjectivity in terms consistent with traditional Western conceptions of masculinity. Individualism relies on the metaphysics of substance, the modern, Western philosophical tradition that understands subjectivity in terms of mind/body dualism and includes an analysis of embodiment, social relations, and social contexts as instrumental to rather than constitutive of subjectivity.

Individualism is complexly related to what I call "essential motherhood". Essential motherhood is an ideological formation that specifies the essential attributes of motherhood and articulates femininity in terms of motherhood so understood. According to essential motherhood, mothering is a function of women's essentially female nature, women's biological reproductive capacities, and/or human evolutionary development. Essential motherhood construes women's motherhood as natural and inevitable. It requires women's exclusive and selfless attention to and care of children based on women's psychological and emotional capacities for empathy, awareness of the needs of others, and self-sacrifice. According to essential motherhood, because these psychological and emotional capacities are natural in women, women's desires are oriented to mothering and women's psychological development and emotional satisfaction require mothering. Essential motherhood also represents women's sexuality in terms of mothering; it holds that the primary goal of women's sexuality is motherhood and that women value sexual activity and pleasure primarily as a means to motherhood rather than as ends in themselves. Essential motherhood's account of women's sexuality thus requires women's heterosexuality, which it also construes as natural. Essential motherhood dictates that all women want to be and should be mothers and clearly implies that women who do not manifest the qualities required by mothering and/or refuse mothering are deviant or deficient as women. Essential motherhood is not only an account of mothering, but also an account of femininity.

So, while individualism is ostensibly gender neutral, insisting on the equal human subjectivity of men and women, essential motherhood posits a specifically feminine/maternal subjectivity and requires this subjectivity of all women. Essential motherhood represents mothering and femininity in terms that are at odds with subjectivity as individualism defines it, and so it has the effect of excluding mothers and women from individualist subjectivity. Individualism and essential motherhood together position women in a very basic double bind: essential motherhood requires mothering of women, but it represents motherhood in a way that denies mothers" and women's individualist subjectivity. Essential motherhood also masks the contradiction implicit in social formations that are based on an individualist theory of subjectivity but also deny women's individualist subjectivity. It does so by specifying mothering as women's proper function, and implying that women's mothering, rather than sexism or male dominance, explains women's exclusion from individualist subjectivity. Without questioning the individualist conception of subjectivity, essential motherhood's specification of femininity in terms of mothering implies that women fail to meet individualism's criteria for subjectivity. Thus, it also obscures the extent to which individualism defines subjectivity in terms that are derived from or based on situations and experiences more typical of men than of women.

Feminism in the United States has to rely on individualism to claim women's equal human subjectivity, because the intelligibility and political effectiveness of this claim are a function of its being expressed in terms consistent with the dominant ideology. If feminism cannot show that women are subjects as individualism defines subjectivity, then it cannot argue for women's equal political agency and entitlement. By relying on individualism to make this argument, feminism includes what I call an identity-based challenge to sexism and male dominance. But feminism also resists and challenges individualism—because of its relationship to essential motherhood, because it inadequately conceptualizes important aspects of women's situations and experiences, and ultimately because it inadequately conceptualizes subjectivity itself. Feminist theory argues that these effects of individualism are the result of its denial of the significance of difference for understanding subjectivity. Thus, feminism also includes what I call a difference-based challenge to individualism, or difference feminism, which reconceptualizes subjectivity in terms of difference. This reconceptualization of subjectivity recognizes the effects for subjectivity of socially significant differences among persons and of elements of difference operating within individual subjects. Ideological determination, however, is never total—there are always elements of contradiction within ideological formations, and among ideological formations, material conditions, and social relations. Thus, that which an ideological formation seeks to exclude or contain may nonetheless be effective within it, and thereby may be available for critique and rearticulation. The concepts of identity and difference are complexly interwoven and mutually dependent for their articulation in the individualist ideological formation. This means that the concept of difference persists-even in its disavowal-in feminism's identity-based challenge to sexism and male dominance, and the concept of identity persists—even as it is challenged-in feminism's difference-based challenge to individualism.

As a result of this interplay of identity and difference, feminism and feminist theory are characterized by "the dilemma of difference." This dilemma refers to the way in which feminism and feminist theory must deny or disavow women's difference, and differences among women, in order to argue for women's equality and to mobilize women as a group, but must also rely on the concept of difference to analyze the specificity of women's situations and experiences and to theorize differences among women. An important aspect of the dilemma of difference is that neither identity nor difference is without risks for feminist theory, so that whether it relies on or challenges individualism, feminist theory faces complex problems and often makes contradictory claims. I illustrate this aspect of the dilemma of difference by showing how this dilemma manifests itself in a number of paradoxes concerning embodiment, gender, and representation in feminist theory. I argue that in feminist theory the dilemma of difference and its resulting paradoxes are most salient and most difficult to resolve at the site of mothering. To show this, I focus on the ideological moments that occur in the accounts of mothering I consider. By "ideological moments" I mean those points in an account of mothering at which certain key concepts attempt to mediate, reconcile, and/or disguise the dilemma of difference and the paradoxes it produces for feminist theory. My analysis of feminist accounts of mothering shows that mothering is an important site at which the individualist ideological formation is elaborated and imposed, but it is also a site at which this ideological formation can be contested and reworked.

I proceed by way of close reading of a number of feminist analyses of mothering, and I juxtapose these analyses in ways that I believe generate productive discussion among them. My analysis of the theories of subjectivity at work in these accounts of mothering is the basis of my conclusion of the impossibility of motherhood. I argue that motherhood as essential motherhood specifies it cannot be adequately conceptualized in individualist terms; it is impossible to be a mother in the sense implied by the notion of motherhood, which suggests an essential identity or state of being. (For this reason I use the term "mothering" to refer to birthing and rearing children, and reserve the term "motherhood" to refer to the ideological construct of essential motherhood.) This impossibility of motherhood means that all attempts to theorize mothering inevitably encounter and must negotiate the dilemma of difference. But the risks of difference in theorizing mothering are formidable. These risks include the reconsolidation of all or most aspects of essential motherhood, including the social organization of mothering based on it, the social organization of mothering that oppresses women and that feminism intends to challenge and change. Theorizing mothering in terms of difference also risks capitulating to the double bind in which individualism and essential motherhood position women. By insisting on women's difference, for instance in analyzing women's situations and experience of mothering and their effects on women's consciousness and social relations, difference feminism jeopardizes feminism's claim to women's equal human subjectivity. On the other hand, the possible benefits for feminism and feminist theory of taking these risks of difference are also considerable. These benefits include the rearticulation of understandings of mothering that more adequately conceptualize mothering, more strenuously challenge individualism, and thus more strongly support the changes in the social organization of mothering that feminism advocates. The difficulty for feminist theory is that, in an individualist ideological context, the subversive and libera-tory possibilities of accounts of mothering that challenge individualism in terms of difference are never far removed from the risks of reconsolidating elements of essential motherhood that occur in the project of theorizing mothering. My read-ings of a number of feminist accounts of mothering show that the possible benefits of theorizing mothering in terms of difference nonetheless outweigh the risks it poses, and suggest how the project of theorizing mothering might best negotiate the dilemma of difference in feminism's current ideological context. I also argue that feminist theory must accept the inevitability of the dilemma of difference and its resulting paradoxes in theorizing mothering, and thus must embrace, or at least reconcile itself to, what I call a "paradoxical politics of mothering."

I begin with an analysis of the debate about the social reorganization of mothering between Charlotte Perkins Gilman and Ellen Key that took place in the United States at the beginning of the twentieth century to argue that the dilemma of difference and the prominence of this dilemma in connection with mothering have characterized feminism in the United States since its inception. I next consider the work of political philosopher Jean Bethke Elshtain, analyzing the account of mothering presupposed by the form of feminism for which she argues. I conclude that, not withstanding her explicit critique of individualism, Elshtain's account of mothering is so closely aligned with essential motherhood that it generates a very conservative form of feminist politics. Because the conservatism of Elshtain's version of feminism is partly a result of Elshtain's dematerializing account of mothering, I turn to Simone de Beauvoir's analysis of mothering in *The Second Sex* to see how a theorist explicitly concerned to theorize embodiment, especially female embodiment, deals with mothering. Here I argue that Beauvoir's existentialist theory of subjectivity relies on a version of mind/body dualism and an oppositional account of the self/other relation that are in many ways consistent with individualism. For this reason, her account of mothering is characterized by contradictions and reconsolidates crucial elements of the sexism and male dominance that she means to challenge. But I also argue that the figure of the pregnant woman as represented by Beauvoir suggests an alternative approach to theorizing subjectivity, and thus to theorizing mothering, than that on which Beauvoir relies. I read the figure of the pregnant woman in *The Second Sex* as suggesting an account of subjectivity according to which embodiment and subjectivity are reciprocally permeable and mutually over-determining, so that subjectivity is divided, partial, and fragmentary. My reading of the figure of the pregnant woman in *The Second Sex* raises the question of whether such an account of subjectivity can more adequately conceptualize mothering than individualism while also more adequately resisting the risks of difference.

With this possibility in mind I look to Sara Ruddick's work on mothering and to Julia Kristeva's representation of mothering in her essay "Stabat Mater." I argue that each of these accounts of mothering points in different ways to the need for a theory of subjectivity as partial, divided, and fragmented, and thus each extends the implications of my reading of Beauvoir's account of mothering. Ruddick's work on mothering and Kristeva's "Stabat Mater" also suggest how a theory of subjectivity such as the one I elicit from Beauvoir's account of mothering enables the reconceptualization of mothering in ways consistent with feminist practical and theoretical goals while also avoiding some of the most serious risks of difference. But neither Ruddick's nor Kristeva's account of mothering is entirely successful in negotiating the dilemma of difference. I explore the difficulties that Ruddick encounters in trying to theorize embodiment in terms that both support her practicalist account of mothering and adequately represent women's experiences of mothering, especially pregnancy and birth. Exploring these difficulties requires an analysis of Ruddick's use of feminist standpoint theory, including an analysis of what standpoint theory presupposes about experience. I also consider the difficulties presented by Kristeva's reliance on a Lacanian psychoanalytic framework for her account of mothering. The Lacanian framework of Kristeva's account of mothering generates her analysis of what I call the desire of/for the mother, which undermines Kristeva's goal of developing what she calls a "herethics', problematizes maternal subjectivity, and thus risks the recuperation of significant elements of essential motherhood.

To further consider the difficulties of theorizing mothering in psychoanalytic terms, I turn to Nancy Chodorow's *The Reproduction of Mothering: Psychoanalysis and the Sociology of Gender.* I argue that the object relations version of psychoanalysis that Chodorow deploys in order to explain the social reproduction of women's mothering allows a broader focus on, and thus a more complete analysis of, the determinants of the social contexts in which women's mothering is done than does Lacanian psychoanalysis. But I also show how the elements of Lacanian and Freudian versions of psychoanalysis to which Chodorow also appeals problematize her account of mothering. Chodorow's combination of object relations theory, Lacanian, and Freudian versions of psychoanalysis recuperates many elements of individualism that are more strenuously resisted by Kristeva's Lacanian psycho-analytic frame. But, while Lacanian psychoanalysis is a more promising basis on which to theorize mothering in resistance to individualism, its representations of the desire of/for the mother and maternal subjectivity are problematic. In addition, Chodorow's account of mothering, like Kristeva's, recuperates certain elements of essential motherhood, especially the requirement of maternal heterosexuality. For this reason, I bring Ruddick's critique of psychoanalysis to bear on these two psychoanalytically based accounts of mothering, and show that this critique has considerable validity in relationship to Kristeva's and Chodorow's accounts of mothering.

In light of Ruddick's critique of psychoanalytic approaches to mothering, I return to a consideration of the theoretical framework of Ruddick's analysis of maternal practice and birthgiving, including the difficulties she encounters in her attempt to theorize maternal embodiment and represent women's experience of mothering. I do so by considering two additional analyses of mothering in which the concept of experience plays a significant role: Adrienne Rich's account in *Of Woman Born: Motherhood as Experience and Institution,* and the account of black women's mothering presented by Patricia Hill Collins in *Black Feminist Thought: Knowledge, Consciousness and the Politics of Empowerment.* Here I argue that the concept of experience in these two accounts of mothering represents, not so much the reality of women's experience that is available for interpretation by feminist theory, as the expression of a desire for the kind of subjectivity promised but never provided by individualism. I particularly question the significance of the way that this concept of experience represents the desire for subjectivity as a desire for the mother, which resembles the desire of/for the mother that is also operative in psychoanalysis, especially Lacanian psychoanalysis. Just as I caution against the possible individualist elements of psychoanalysis and its tendency to recuperate aspects of essential motherhood, here I caution against the demand implicit in the appeal to women's experience and in psychoanalysis, that the mother represent a guarantee of the coherence and stability of subjectivity or that the mother console for the lack of any such guarantee. Feminist analyses of women's experiences must resist more strenuously the desire for the experience of subjectivity that individualism promises but docs not deliver than do Rich's and Collins's accounts of mothering.

On the basis of my readings of these feminist accounts of mothering, I conclude that feminist theory must reconcile itself to an ongoing engagement with the dilemma of difference, especially in connection with mothering. Feminist theory must recognize that, especially in connection with mothering, it will have "only paradoxes to offer" (Scott) as a result of its conflicted relationship to-its simultaneous reliance on and challenge to-individualism. But, while feminist analyses of mothering will inevitably encounter the dilemma of difference and thereby come to include paradoxical or contradictory conclusions, this does not mean that any particular account of mothering is just as useful and valuable as any other for feminist politics. Rather, feminism must determine which of its accounts of mothering or which aspects of its analyses of mothering to foreground in each of its multiple and contradictory struggles on behalf of women and/or mothers. Thus, I end with my views as to how feminism might decide the deployment of the paradoxical analyses of mothering that feminist theory generates.

Some of the feminist accounts of mothering on which I focus I chose because they have been much discussed by feminist thinkers, and their ideas and claims have been put to use in other feminist theoretical contexts; for example, Beauvoir's *The Second Sex* and Chodorow's *The Reproduction of Mothering*. Others I chose because I believe that they make important contributions to or illustrate important conflicts in feminist thinking about mothering, even though they have received somewhat less attention from and use by feminist theorists or are generally not thought of primarily in connection with mothering; for example, the work of Collins and Elshtain. For all of the thinkers whose work I examine, I focus on what they have written about mothering, even when the issue of mothering is one of many they addres3, as is the case with Beauvoir, Collins, Elshtain, Kristeva, and Rich. Thus, my readings of their analyses of mothering are by no means exhaustive or even representative of the entirety of their work in feminist theory. Most importantly, I have chosen to work with these thinkers and texts because when I consider them separately I find in them suggestive and illuminating tensions or conflicts, and when I consider them in relationship to each other I am able to bring them into productive discussion. This of course also means that I have left out of consideration many important works, such as Jessie Bernard's *The Future of Motherhood*; Elizabeth Badinter's *Mother Love: Myth and Reality;* Mary O'Brien's *The Politics of Reproduction;* Jane Lazarre's *The Mother Knot*; and Ann Ferguson's *Blood at the Root: Motherhood, Sexuality, and Male Dominance*; as well as thinkers such as Jane Gallop; Virginia Held; Luce Irigaray (1991, 1985a, 1985b); and Audre Lorde, whose work includes important analyses of mothering. This does not mean that this work is any less worthy of close reading and critical attention, but rather that I was not able to bring it into the discussion I hoped to stage here.

My goal in staging this discussion of feminist accounts of mothering is not to determine which of them is the best or most adequate account of mothering, although my conclusions as to which of them I find more or less problematic are fairly clear. Neither is it my goal to criticize these accounts of mothering in order to present my own account of mothering. Instead, I hope to contribute to feminist theory at one of its most conflicted sites by articulating some of the complexities and difficulties at stake in the issue of mothering. Feminist theory can only continue to theorize mothering, even though this necessitates feminist theory's continued engagement with the dilemma of difference and its resulting paradoxes. This is another way in which motherhood is impossible: it is impossible for feminist theory to avoid the issue of mothering and it is impossible for feminist theory to resolve it.

References

Badinter, Elizabeth. *Mother Love: Myth and Reality.* New York: Macmillan, 1980.

Beauvoir, Simone de. *The Second Sex.* 1952. New York: Vintage, 1989.

Bernard, Jessica. *The Future of Motherhood.* New York: Bantam Books, 1972.

Chodorow, Nancy. *The Reproduction of Mothering: Feminism, Psychoanalysis and the Sociology of Gender.* Berkeley: University of California Press, 1978.

Collins, Patricia Hill. *Black Feminist Thought: Knowledge, Consciousness, and the Politics of Empowerment.* New York: Routledge, 1991.

Elshtain, Jean Bethke. *Public Man, Private Woman.* Princeton, NJ: Princeton University Press, 1981.

Elshtain, Jean Bethke. "Antigone's Daughters." *Democracy* 2 (April) (1982a): 46-59.

Elshtain, Jean Bethke. "Feminism, Family and Community." *Dissent* 29 (Fall)(1982b): 442-49.

Elshtain, Jean Bethke. *Power Trips and Other Journeys: Essays. Feminism as Civic Discourse.* Madison: University of Wisconsin Press, 1990.

Elshtain, Jean Bethke. "Against Gay Marriage II: Accepting Limits." *Commonweal, November* 22 (1991): 685-86.

Elshtain, Jean Bethke. "Single Motherhood: Response to Iris Marion Young." *Dissent* (Winter) (1994): 267-69.

Ferguson, Ann. *Blood at the Root: Motherhood, Sexuality, and Male Dominance.* London: Pandora, 1989.

Folbre, Nancy. *Who Pays for the Kids? Gender and the Structures of Constraint.* New York: Routledge, 1994.

Freud, Sigmund. "The Infantile Genital Organization of the Libido." 1923. *The Standard Edition of the Complete Works of Sigmund Freud,* Volume 19. London: Hogarth, 1961.

Freud, Sigmund. "The Dissolution of the Oedipus Complex." 1924. *The Standard Edition of the Complete Works of Sigmund Freud,* Volume 19. London: Hogarth, 1961.

Freud, Sigmund. "Some Psychical Consequences of the Anatomical Distinction Between the Sexes." 1925. *The Standard Edition of the Complete Works of Sig-*

mund Freud, Volume 19. London: Hogarth, 1961.

Freud, Sigmund. "Female Sexuality." 1931. *The Standard Edition of the Complete Works of Sigmund Freud,* Volume 21. London: Hogarth, 1961.

Gallop, Jane. *Thinking Through the Body.* New York: Columbia University Press, 1988.

Gilman, Charlotte Perkins. *Women and Ecomomics.* 1898. Boston: Small, Maynard and Company, 1966.

Gilman, Charlotte Perkins. "Genius, Domestic and Maternal." *Forerunner* 1 (June) (1910a): 10-12 and (July): 5-7.

Gilman, Charlotte Perkins. "Comment and *Review.*" *Forerunner* 1 (December) (1910b): 25-26. [Review of Key, *The Century of the Child.*]

Gilman, Charlotte Perkins. "Comment and Review." *Forerunner* 2 (October) (1911): 280-82. [Review of Key, *Love and Marriage.]*

Gilman, Charlotte Perkins. "On Ellen Key and the Woman Movement." *Forerunner* 4 (February) (1913a): 35-38.

Gilman, Charlotte Perkins. "Education for Motherhood." *Forerunner* 4 (October) (1913b): 259-62.

Gilman, Charlotte Perkins. "Ellen Key's Attack on "Amaternal Feminism."" *Current Opinion* 54 (February) (1913c): 138-39.

Gilman, Charlotte Perkins. "Charlotte Perkins Gilman's Reply to Ellen Key." *Current Opinion* 54 (March) (1913d): 220-21.

Gilman, Charlotte Perkins. "The New Mothers of a New World." *Forerunner* 4 (June) (1913e): 145-49. 1913f. "Illegitimate Children." *Forerunner* 4 (November): 295-97.

Gilman, Charlotte Perkins. "As to "Feminism."" *Forerunner* 5 (February) (1914a): 45.

Gilman, Charlotte Perkins. "The Conflict Between Human and Female Feminism." *Current* Opinion 55 (April) (1914b): 291.

Gilman, Charlotte Perkins. "Feminism or Polygamy." *Forerunner* 5 (October) (1914c): 260-61.

Gilman, Charlotte Perkins. "Birth Control" *Forerunner* 6 (July) (1915a): 177-80.

Gilman, Charlotte Perkins. "Pensions for "Mothers" and "Widows."" *Forerunner* 5 (January) (1915b): 7-8.

Held, Virginia. *Feminist Morality: Transforming Culture, Society, and Politics.* Chicago: University of Chicago Press, 1993.

Hennessy, Rosemary. 1993. *Materialist Feminism and the Politics of Discourse.* New York: Routledge.

Hochschild, Arlie. *The Second Shift: Working Parents and the Revolution at Home.* New York: Viking Penguin, 1989.

Irigaray, Luce. *Speculum of the Other Woman.* Ithaca, NY: Cornell University Press, 1985a.

Irigaray, Luce. *The Sex Which Is Not One.* Ithaca, NY: Cornell University Press, 1985b.

Irigaray, Luce. *The Ethics of Sexual Difference.* Ithaca, NY: Cornell University

Press, 1991.

Key, Ellen. *The Century of the Child*. New York: G. P Putnam's Sons, 1909.

Key, Ellen. *Love and Marriage*. New York: G. P Putnam's Sons, 1911.

Key, Ellen. *The Woman Movement*. New York: G. P Putnam's Sons, 1912a.

Key, Ellen. "Motherliness." *Atlantic Monthly* 110 (October) (1912b): 562-70.

Key, Ellen. "Education for Motherhood." *Atlantic Monthly* 112 (July) (1913): 48-61 and (August) (1913): 191-97.

Key, Ellen. *The Renaissance of Motherhood*. New York: G. P Putnam's Sons, 1914.

Kristeva, Julia. "Stabat Mater." 1977. *The Kristeva Reader*. Ed. Toril Moi. New York: Columbia University Press, 1986.

Lacan, Jacques. *Ecrits: A Selection*. New York: Norton, 1977.

Lacan, Jacques. *Feminine Sexuality: Jacques Lacan and the Ecole Freudienne*. Eds. Mitchell and Rose. New York: Norton, 1985.

Lazarre, Jane. *The Mother Knot*. Boston: Beacon, 1985.

Lorde, Audre. *Sister Outsider*. Trumansburg, NY: Crossings Press, 1984.

O'Brien, Mary. *The Politics of Reproduction*. Boston: Routledge and Kegan Paul, 1981.

Rich, Adrienne. *Of Woman Born: Motherhood as Experience and Institution*. New York: Norton, 1976.

Ruddick, Sara. "Maternal Thinking." *Feminist Studies* 6 (Summer) (1980): 342-67.

Ruddick, Sara. "Pacifying the Forces: Drafting Women in the Interests of Peace." *Signs* 8 (Spring) (1983): 471-48.

Ruddick, Sara. "Preservative Love and Military Destruction: Reflections on Mothering and Peace." *Mothering: Essays in Feminist Theory*. Ed. J. Trebilcott. Totowa, NJ: Roman and Allanheld, 1984.

Ruddick, Sara. "Remarks on the Sexual Politics of Reason." *Women and Moral Theory*. Eds. Kittay and Myers. Totowa, NJ: Rowman and Littlefield, 1987.

Ruddick, Sara. *Maternal Thinking*. New York: Ballantine, 1989.

Ruddick, Sara. "Thinking About Fathers." *Conflicts in Feminism*. Eds. Hirsch and Fox Keller. New York: Routledge, 1990.

Ruddick, Sara. Thinking Mothers/Conceiving Birth." *Representations of Motherhood*. Eds. Bassin, Honey, and Mahrer Kaplan. Cambridge: Harvard University Press, 1994.

Scott, Joan Wallach. *Only Paradoxes to Offer: French Feminists and the Rights of Man*. Cambridge: Harvard University Press, 1996.

Chapter 33

Reimagining Adoption and Family Law

DRUCILLA CORNELL

I. Introduction

Why have feminists been reluctant participants in the politics of adoption? Today the law in most states pits two mothers against one another and the media dramatizes the purportedly hostile relationship between them. Think of the "heart-tugging" pictures of baby Jessica as she is removed from her adoptive parents to be given back to her birth mother and father. The press in general has never shown much sympathy for birth mothers. Nor has the feminist press, in which members of the various birth mothers' associations have tried to publish for years without success. These organizations have accused feminists of favoring adopting mothers, either because they are adopting mothers themselves or because, like the public in general, they have disdain for the birth mother who gave up her baby.

This reluctance may not spring from conscious attitudes about birth mothers. Custody battles between birth and adoptive mothers challenge one of our culture's deepest fantasies—that there can only be one mother and therefore we have to pick the "real" one. Picking one mother over another is a harsh judgment not easily reconciled with feminist solidarity. Feminist solidarity supposedly grew out of the shared experience of our oppression as women that Was uncovered when through consciousness-raising new meaning was given to what women have had to endure under male domination (MacKinnon). At first glance the so-called "birth mother" and the adopting mother do not recall a shared experience upon which solidarity can be based.

Adoption is fraught with issues of race, class, and imperialist domination that have persistently caused divisions in the second wave of feminism. The woman who is picked by law as the "real" mother is usually the one privileged by class and race. In international adoption the politics of imperialist domination and the struggle of postcolonial nations to constitute themselves as independent nations are inevitably implicated. Hence it is not surprising that one of the first steps in the constitution of nationhood is to end international adoptions in the courts (Schemo, see A).

Nor is it surprising to find that the language of adoption is the language of war.

In most states the "birth mother" "surrenders" her child to the state which then transfers the child to the adopting, predominantly white, middle-class, heterosexual parents. According to current law, what the "birth mother" surrenders is not just primary custodial responsibility of her child, but her entitlement to any kind of relationship with him or her in the future. She is denied even the most primitive kind of information as to the child's well-being. In states where records are closed, adopted children have to "show cause;' make some claim that they will be or have been physically or emotionally damaged if they are not allowed to get information about their heredity or the whereabouts of their "birth mother" and! or their biological father. Lorraine Dusky (1979) eloquently writes:

> They call me "biological mother:" I hate those words. They make me sound like a baby machine, a conduit, without emotions. They want me to forget and go out and make a new life. I had a baby and gave her away. But I am a mother.

We can see all the contradictions wrought by this demand for absolute surrender in recent lesbian co-parent adoptions. In such adoptions, the last thing the "birth" mother wants to give up is all access to her child. She wants to share joint custody with her lover. Yet it is still the exception to the rule that a lesbian can adopt her lover's "birth" child, ascending to the status of a legally recognized parent. There are almost no states in the United States that allow a gay or lesbian couple to openly adopt a baby as a couple. Single or coupled, gay men are almost entirely excluded from access to legally recognized parenthood. Due to the narrow heterosexist definition of the family embodied in our law as the norm, lesbian and gay couples are not given the right to adopt the children of their partners, a right that traditional heterosexual stepparents can take for granted and easily exercise. My own sketch of the fair conditions of family law reform expands the potential reach of para-parenting beyond traditional couple arrangements. It is only recently that single mothers are allowed to adopt because they, too, were not thought to meet the norm of the "normal heterosexual couple." The corrective I advocate to the unfair treatment of people who do not fit the heterosexist norm is not simply that gays and lesbians be given the right to parenthood if they can successfully show that they mimic the "normal" heterosexual couple. To adequately address the relationship of adopting mothers to birth mothers, and their children to both, we need to rethink our current conception of the legal family from the ground up.

For decades now, birth mothers' organizations have militantly protested against the surrender of their entitlement to the status of mother even if they chose or were forced by circumstances to forsake primary custodial responsibility of their child. Now adopted children are also in the process of challenging as unconstitutional their unequal treatment at the hands of the legal system. After all, non-adopted children have access to information about themselves and their genealogy. It seems obvious that adopted children are indeed being treated differently from other children. Could there be a compelling state interest that would legitimate such unequal treatment?

A feminist answer to that question has to be that there could be no compelling state interest that could legitimate the relinquishment of the birth mother's entitlement to access to her child or to the child's access to her. Why has adoption come to be understood as demanding the complete relinquishment of all access or even information about the child? We need a deeper analysis of why that relinquishment has historically been enforced and felt by many to be so necessary to the protection of "family values." Without this analysis we will continue to establish victors and vanquished in a war that is usually portrayed as being one between women.

Modern legal adoptions are only one form of adoption and are a recent historical event. Long before lesbian adoptions became possible to the limited degree they are now, informal "adoptions" in African American communities kept families together by extending them, rather than shutting out the birth mother. In these communities there are often two mothers, which avoids the demand to pick one as the "real" mother (see Klibanoff and Klibanoff, chap.16). What legal interests are at stake in the requirement that adoption demand total surrender both of the child and of all information about her? Why not identify adoption as only the signing away of primary custody?

Feminists have a strong political interest in insisting that the right to build families and to foster our own intimate lives be privileged over the state enforcement of any *ideal* of the good family. My own proposed guidelines for family law reform would change the very meaning of adoption as it is now legally and culturally understood.

II. Patriarchy and Its Legal Effects

For my purposes, the word patriarchy indicates the manner in which a woman's legal identity remains bound up with her duties to the state as wife and mother within the traditional heterosexual family. Our feminist demand must be for the full release of women from this legal identity which is wholly inconsistent with the recognition of each one of us as a free and equal person. Only on the basis of this recognition should we willingly subject ourselves to the law as an arm of the state.

We cannot demand release from a legal identity that defines and limits what it means to be a woman through state-imposed duties without challenging the legal institution of the monogamous heterosexual family. The duties that now define woman in her social identity, as in herself, rather than for herself, are inseparable from the conjugal institution of the heterosexual family. Therefore the redefinition of "woman" is inseparable from the demands of gays and lesbians to be free to create their own persons.

If we understand that women's legal identity in both family life and civil society remains bound up with an externally imposed set of duties we can at least make sense of why it is that the so-called birth mother is considered to have given up all entitlement to any kind of relationship with her child when she yields her duty to be the child's caretaker. Under the patriarchal scheme, a woman is entitled to protection by the state because she takes up her duties as caretaker of her family. If she forsakes those duties she is denied any of the protection given to mothers. Since she has no independent standing in civil society there is nothing left of her social life. Let me put it as clearly as possible: It is only in the context of a system of duties that remain bound up with women's legal identity in the heterosexual family that we can even begin to understand the unequal treatment of birth mothers and adopted children.

The relationship among legal identity in civil society, "social life" (Klibanoff and Klibanoff); and the system of duties in the heterosexual family can help us understand the driving anxiety about infertility which has haunted the history of modern adoptions. If a woman's social worth is inseparable from the fulfillment of her duty as a mother, then, if she cannot live up to that duty, she is confronted with the loss of her only social status. Of course, the obsession with genetic ties is also tied into unconscious fantasies about the meaning of masculinity and racial superiority (Roberts).[8]

To protect from public exposure the adopting mother's failure to be a woman because she has failed to meet the symbolic meaning of womanhood demands the erasure of the birth mother. It is not entitlement but rather the terror before the loss of identity that explains so much of the secrecy that surrounds adoption.

III. Donning a Citizen Identity

The scene of adoption is ensnared in imposed roles associated with women's legal identity within the heterosexual family. The first step in untangling ourselves from these imposed roles is to don our identity as citizens and to demand a full civil identity as persons. Simply put, as feminists we must insist that we are entitled to rights, not because we are mothers, but because we are citizens and persons.

The Argentinean movie *The Official Story* illustrates some of these points. An adoptive mother has blinded herself to the reality of her daughter's tragic circumstances of adoption. During the course of the film she discovers that her daughter is a child of one of the missing persons, probably murdered by the government. Gradually she comes to heed the call made to her by her daughter's grandmother. What relationship the two women will have to one another is left open, but it is clear that there can be no going back once the grandmother is accepted and embraced.

It is only by slowly freeing herself from the imprisonment of imposed familial duties that the adoptive mother can see her way to her responsibility as a citizen of Argentina. She sheds her exteriorized feminine identity, and in a profound sense becomes her own person, when she dons the identity of a citizen responsible for the fate of her country as well as for the destiny of her adopted daughter. Before, she left the world of politics to men. She dons her identity as citizen by taking her place in a demonstration beside the grandmother of her daughter. Her prior life in the conjugal institution of the heterosexual family does not survive her insistence on her political responsibility as citizen and her ethical responsibility to her daughter's grandmother. The woman's eventual embrace of the grandmother as someone entitled to a relationship to her daughter ended her life in the traditional family.

The Official Story presents in an extreme form the continuing presence of kidnapping disguised as an economic transaction in an adoption. *The Official Story* also graphically demonstrates the ability of the rich and powerful in many of the world's nations to steal children of the poor or the politically dispossessed. This phenomenon is well documented in heart-wrenching stories of the mothers of "the disappeared." The dictatorship in Argentina that allowed babies to be stolen for adoption is not an isolated event. Indeed, the open stealing of a person's children is part of the enactment of psychic as well as physical torture (Daniel). The message of *The Official Story* is clear: Disappeared persons do not have children because they are socially dead, and their social death is a preliminary obliteration foreshadowing their actual murder.

IV. Feminist Responsibility and International Adoptions

In my own case, as an adoptive mother, I also feel ethically compelled to recognize the rights of the other mother and of my own daughter's right to her person. In any adoption there are always two mothers as well as a biological sperm donor who may or may not deserve or wish to be designated as the father. When the two mothers, or mother and grandmother, are from different countries and linguistic traditions, the responsibility of the adopting mother to the birth mother does not go away. Indeed, it can be accentuated. We are inescapably confronted with a scene of adoption that is far from ideal given the unjust world we live in. The history of the child's adoption may not be as dramatically wrought with tragedy as that of the young girl in *The Official Story.* Still, at least in international adoptions, the adopting parents are confronted with the history of imperialism and economic devastation, which may be at least the partial explanation for why the child is being put up for adoption in the first place.

As I will argue shortly, we can certainly reimagine a different scene, one in which adoption does not carry with it the same burdens and responsibilities that are imposed by the reality that it is injustice that often makes one of the mothers give up her baby and all access to her. But given that we do live in an unjust world we have to confront the responsibilities that come with it. One way of trying to meet that responsibility is to demand the birth mother's right to access to the child she bore. In any world we can also demand that the child's freedom to know her mother be protected.

There is another responsibility to the adopted child, and one that cannot easily be imposed by law because it involves extensive affirmative duties. What are the responsibilities of an adopting mother who takes a child from a South American country, for example, and brings her to the United States? Is she simply to be assimilated to the adopting mother's or parents' country and culture? Assimilation comes at a cost to the child's freedom. The mother, mothers, or parents consciously or unconsciously cut the child from a past she will ultimately have to integrate as part of herself. If she is to be recognized as the ultimate source of her own representations of who she is, then certain decisions to keep her options open must be maintained by the parent.

If the child is from South America, for example, the meaning of her roots in Hispanic culture can only be kept alive for her if Spanish is maintained and/or taught and access to her country of origin is kept available.[1] A number of South American nations have now stopped international adoptions to the United States. Fierce opposition to the United States and bitter accusations against adopting parents have been made by many countries. This history should not be "whitewashed." Nor, of course, is the proper response guilt. But if the child's freedom is to be maintained, the adopting parents must face their responsibility for their daughter's or son's freedom. Obviously only a small part of that responsibility is met by demanding legal rights for birth mothers and adopted children, but doing so is at least a first step.

For many parents it may feel scary or even unnatural that their child has access to a language, a country, and a culture they cannot share. One of our most foundational and commonsense notions of a family is that its members belong to the same culture, language, and country. Given how deeply rooted this idea of the family is, it is hardly surprising that parents force their children to assimilate to their culture and forsake the country and language of the birth mother or parents. Yet forced assimilation takes away a child's freedom to design her personhood out of her unique personal circumstances, circumstances that the white adopting parent does not share.

Does the recognition of the child's freedom by, for example, maintaining her mother tongue interfere with the closeness of an adopted child to her adopting parents? Not at all. But it does demand that we think about parental relationships differently. In particular the mother-daughter relationship—known as the mother-child dyad—has been hindered by a story of too great closeness. The mother-child dyad purportedly arises because of the child's actual dependence on the maternal body for the intake of sustenance, that is, breast milk. In fantasy, both the mother and child blend together into one body, the breast no longer being part of the mother's person but a shared materiality that obliterates any division between the two.

Although this fantasy is held to be true for both male and female children, the traditional psychoanalytic story at least gives boys a way of identifying with the father's phallus so as to violently disrupt this fantasized unity with the mother. The mother and daughter, on the other hand, are never given a symbolic intermediary for their relationship that allows them to understand each other as separate persons and allows the mother to remain both intact and in the relationship to her daughter. But in reality, the fantasy mother-child dyad of traditional psychoanalysis is just that, a fantasy. The mother is simply a person with a breast-she cannot be reduced to The Breast. There is a relationship between two people from the beginning.[2]

In erotic poems that seem daring 2,700 years later, Sappho celebrates her daughter's "magnificence" and her joys in her daughter's stride, which expresses a freedom she has never known and which she mourns for as lost to herself. Sappho's erotic appreciation of her daughter is inseparable from the celebration of her daughter's physical freedom, her strength. Sappho sings of the distance between the two that makes a mother's poetic joy in her daughter's singularity possible. The daughter "whose skin of burnished gold pales the magnificence of the sun"[3] is uncapturable by the mother who cannot keep up with her daughter as she runs down the beach. This mother joys in the stride that takes her daughter into her own future, as she stays behind marvelling at the play of lights illuminating her daughter's beauty.

When we travel to Latin countries, and my daughter translates for her father and me because she is bilingual and we are not, I feel something akin to Sappho's joy in her daughter's strength. My daughter's beautiful Spanish leaves her mother, who stumbles around in the language, in awe. She has access to a culture that will never be mine. She can take me into worlds that I can never know from the inside out as she can. I joy and marvel at the richness of her universe. Like Sappho, that my daughter is worlds ahead of me, in this case when it comes to language, is not cause for sorrow. Rather, it is the source of joy in this being who is becoming her own unique person and can open my world by having her own.

V. The Imaginary Domain and the Right of Birth Mothers and Adopted Children

My argument so far has been that, even in 1999, the way in which women have been symbolically sexed is partly constituted by legal duties that have been imposed upon them. For us, our "selves" have been buried under these duties for far too long. As Luce Irigaray has written:

> Valorized by society as a mother, nurturer, and housewife (the community needs children to make up the future work-force, as defenders of the nation and as reproducers of society, aside from the fact that the family unit is the most profitable one for the State in that much of the work that is done within it goes unpaid, for example), woman is deprived of the possibility of interiorizing her female identity. (47)

Legal enforcement of monogamous heterosexuality has made the state and not the person the source of moral meaning of their sexuate being and how it should be lived with "all our kin.[4] Now, I want to argue, it is time we recognize that governmentally enforced sexual choices, let alone the outright denial of the right to parent to some persons because of their sexual lives, are inconsistent with the equal protection of what I call "the imaginary domain."

The imaginary domain is the moral and psychic space we need if we are to have meaningful sexual freedom. What do I mean by sexual freedom? Each one of us is formed sexually through a complex interaction with the sexual personas our culture imposes in the name of gender norms and roles that are still with us and that promote heterosexuality. By engaging with these personas in fantasy and in our actual lives, we are shaped into men and women. A human being cannot escape being formed through a web of identifications and relationships. These fundamental relationships and identifications are integral to who we are, and indeed become part of how we imagine ourselves. But what has been shaped can always be reshaped.

The imaginary domain is the moral and psychic space that allows us to become the ultimate source of how we evaluate and make sense of these identifications. Of course, we cannot simply step out of identifications the way we shed clothes. But we can engage personas so that they are remade even as they are assumed. In order to revise our sense of self and reimagine who we are as sexual creatures, we must be allowed to freely "act out" how we imagine ourselves and our relationships with others. If we have an imaginary domain provided as a matter of right we at least have the chance to individuate ourselves to become our own person.

Individuation does not imply anthropological individualism. Clearly, I do not believe it does since I have argued elsewhere that who we are as sexed beings is symbolic and formed by institutions. I use the word individuation to imply that the "who" of the person cannot be conflated with any sanctioned identity, including that of gender. The imaginary domain, then, is the psychic space a person has by right and which allows her or him to take on and evaluate his or her identifications, by representing who she is sexually and forming intimate relations as she sees fit.

Would the equal protection of the imaginary domain give rights to birth mothers and adopted children? First let us take the example of "birth mothers:" It is only too evident that the struggle of every woman to become who she is demands a confrontation with the connection between femininity and motherhood. For some women oppression imposed by race, class, national, and sexual identity has forced absolute separation from their children upon them. Carol Austin, who had to hide her own relationship to her lesbian lover in order for them to successfully complete an international adoption, describes the situation of the "birth mother" of their first adopted child as follows:

> A real joy for us was being able to spend a lot of time with Catherine's birth mother, Violetta, a twenty-two year old Quechua Indian who was also Julie's maid. When Violetta had become pregnant out of wedlock, she had been taken in by some distant members who struggled to care for their own five children. Living in a crowded, dirt floored home in a poverty-ridden neighborhood in Lima the family was not willing to care for another child. And if Violetta decided to keep her child, she

could not work. Violetta's and her child's survival depended upon her giving up this first born baby to adoption.

   Violetta did not have the economic option to take custodial responsibility for her child. Austin was only too well aware that Violetta's decision to give up her child was not a choice and Austin knew that no amount of emotional support from her could make up for Violetta's loss and sorrow that she could not keep her baby. Still, to whatever degree it might help Violetta, both Austin and her partner wanted her to get to know them-to know that her baby would be safe. They showed her pictures of where the baby was to live; they left their address with her so that she could check on her baby's well-being.

Certainly these measures, as reassuring as they may have been, could not make up for Violetta's terrible either/or, a forced sexual choice in the worst sense. Some adopting mothers have spoken of their feeling that their babies were destined for them. Austin was well aware that if this baby was destined for her and her lover, then Violetta was destined to be deprived of her child by economic circumstances. Measures could be taken to ameliorate Violetta's pain, but the poverty of her life circumstances remained. Austin's sensitivity to Violetta's horrible either/or, and the economic poverty and oppression that imposed it, came in part from her own struggles as an adopting lesbian parent.

Austin describes her pain at having to be disappeared in order to adopt a child for herself and her lover. Again, economics played a major role in the lovers' choice of who was to appear as a mother. Of course, Austin's circumstances were in no way comparable to Violetta's, but she did not have the same kind of professional job as her lover, who was put forward as most suitable for the role of (supposedly) single mother because of her professional and financial standing. But, in spite of her realization that this was the best way for the two of them to adopt a baby, Austin rebelled:

> I soon found myself emotionally stranded between anger and guilt. I felt angry and totally left out by my externally forced, yet self-imposed, invisibility. And right on the heels of my anger came guilt! It was after all, Jane who was putting in hours of meeting time, and it was her financial and personal history that was being dissected. I didn't envy her, yet I began to have an all or nothing reaction .... Finally immersion at any level, without recognition of my existence became impossible. How naive, I had been to assume, only a few months before, that my invisibility would not be a problem. The entire adoption situation had forced open some of my raw childhood wounds.

Austin's emotional pain at being forcibly rendered invisible sensitized her both to a birth mother's need to be seen and understood, and to the adopted child's need to be in touch with her national heritage.

Could a birth mother who chose or was forced to give up primary custody still know herself at the deepest recesses of her person to be a mother? Testimony from birth mothers have answered yes to that question. To rob her of her chance to struggle through what meaning being a mother still has for her is to make the state, and not the woman, the master over the construction of her sense of who she is. Birth mothers have rights, not as birth mothers, but as persons who, like all others, must be allowed the space to come to terms with their own life defining decisions about sexuality and family.

Lorraine Dusky (1979) is only one of many birth mothers who have described their anguish at the enforced separation from their child. In her case she also knew that there was crucial information that the adopted parents needed to have about her daughter. Dusky had taken birth control pills during the early stage of her pregnancy before she realized that she was pregnant. The pills were found to cause serious gynecological problems in the next generation. She tried to get the agency which had handled the adoption to pass the crucial information on to the adopting parents; she was desperate to know that her daughter received the proper medical attention. The agency told her that her daughter was fine. Tragically, the information was never passed along to her daughter's adopting parents. The adopting parents were, as it turned out, trying to locate Dusky because, although she did not suffer from gynecological problems, Dusky's daughter had suffered severe seizures, almost drowning twice: The adopting parents were desperate to communicate with Dusky about her medical history. Dusky finally found her daughter through the illegal adoption underground. The adopting mother recognized her as Jane's other mother, and Dusky has for many years now had a relationship with her daughter.

Dusky's story had a happy ending. But why did Dusky, white, middleclass, and on her way to becoming a successful journalist give her baby up in the first place? The story of her decision is inseparable from the sexual shame imposed upon women in the 1950s who did not get pregnant in the proper way; that is, within legal marriage. Abortion was illegal, and, like many women who hoped against hope that they were not pregnant, she put off an abortion. By the time she got access to an illegal abortion in Puerto Rico it was too late. Adoption was her only option. It had become her only option because abortion was illegal, and because of the blending of personal and political morality which made it close to impossible at that time for an unmarried white, middle-class woman to be a single mother. Dusky's decision exemplifies the enforced sexual choice that arises from denying women their equivalent chance to claim their person, and to represent their own sexuate being.

What should a "birth mother" relinquish when she relinquishes primary custody of her child? Only that, primary custody. The equal protection of the birth mother's imaginary domain out of which she can construct her personhood at least demands that she be allowed access to any information she desires to have about her child, and to have the chance to meet and explore with the child what kind of relationship they can develop.

Let me now turn to the rights of adopted children ensured by the imaginary domain. The child should have the same right to access information about his or her biological mother and father as the biological parents have to their child. Again, once we accept that even a primordial sense of self is not just given to us, but is a complicated lifelong process of imagining and projecting ourselves over time, we can see how important it is to have access to one's family history, if one feels the need for it. If the meaning of that history is inseparable from the struggle of postcolonial nations to achieve meaningful economic and political independence, then that history is political from the outset. Heritage is more than genetic. The break with the nation, culture, and language of one's birth, which is inevitably imposed by an international adoption, has to be available for symbolization. Under our current law an internationally adopted child is already subjected to second-class citizenship. Certain rights of citizenship, including the right to run for president of the United States, are denied. But even if we were to remove the taint of second-class citizenship, the child still needs to make sense of the break, to have the chance to recover herself and the meaning of keeping in touch with the linguistic and cultural traditions of her country of origin through her own imaginary domain.

Children should not have to show cause, let alone that they are emotionally disturbed because of their adoptive status. The demand to show cause is just one more way in which people who do not fit neatly into the purportedly natural heterosexual family are pathologized. Again, the imagined heterosexual adopting family is privileged as the one deserving of protection of the state, even against the child who is a member of it. My only serious disagreement with some of the literature written by birth mothers is the idealization of biological ties. There is an old Italian saying that blood seeks blood. But blood also robs, rapes, and murders blood. As Dorothy Roberts has also eloquently argued, the idealization of genetic ties is also intertwined with the most profoundly racist fantasies, including the desire for racial purity.

To conclude, adopted children and birth mothers should be allowed access to each other as part of the equal protection of their imaginary domain. We should have public records in which all adopted children and birth parents can register. A birth mother who was forced to give up her child obviously did not have her right to represent her own sexuate being protected. She had a decision thrust upon her either because of economic circumstances or, as in Dusky's case, because of the sexual hypocrisy that dominated this country in the 1950s. *Her right ought to be based on her personhood, not on the fact of her biological motherhood.* If, in spite of circumstances, she still represents herself as a mother who has given up primary custody but only that, she should be allowed to follow through in her efforts to reach her child. The fear of the hysterical birth mother is just that, a fear; the adoption resolves the issue of primary custody except in the few states where lesbian lovers are allowed joint custody. Dusky did not try to steal her daughter, Jane, from her adopting parents. She knew she could not undo what she had done. Jane has two mothers, and she has had to come to terms with that.

She calls Lorraine by her first name and not "mother"; perhaps to recognize the differential relationship between the two mothers. Yet everyone agrees that it is better "this way."

What of the woman who when she gives up primary custody also wishes to escape entirely from any imposition on her self of the role of mother? Such a woman should be allowed her refusal to register. If the past teaches us anything, many birth fathers will continue to wish to elude acknowledgment of their fatherhood by refusing to claim paternity or meet its responsibilities. But the law cannot make it illegal for the child to track down the "birth mother." In the end it is between them. This is an example of why I argue that we should not expect law to do more than provide us with the space to work through and personalize our complicated life histories.

Some "birth mothers" who have given up their babies for adoption have undergone a trauma. A legal system that makes the cut from her child absolute blocks any hope for recovery from this trauma, for the mother certainly, and maybe for the child. What the best law can do for adopted children and "birth mothers" who feel compelled to seek out one another is to provide them with the space to work through the traumatic event that has to some extent formed them. It cannot erase the past. It certainly cannot provide a magical "cure" to the emotional difficulties we all face in our intimate associations. Some adopted children will want to search for their birth parents and some will not. Some birth parents will want to be found; others will not.

Law cannot take the passion and complexity out of emotionally fraught situations. Still, the imaginary domain will give to the persons involved in an adoption the space to come to terms with their history and the meaning it has for them and the possibilities it yields for new ways of imagining themselves. It cannot heal trauma. It cannot protect a birth mother who is tracked by her child from the pain of confrontation with her child. Such a confrontation with her child could undoubtedly challenge her sense of who she has struggled to become. The protection of the imaginary domain demands that space be open to explore and establish relationships; it cannot provide the moral content of those relationships without delimiting the space that its justification demands be kept open.

VI. Family Law: Some Concluding Notes

If family law is to protect the imaginary domain, family law reform must be rooted in the transformation of women's civil identity and must be rid of all traces of patriarchy as well. What would be fair guidelines for a family law that protected the full civil identity of all who fell under its governance?

First and foremost the state could not impose any form of family as *the* good family, and so could not reenforce the heterosexual and monogamous nuclear family, even if such families continued to be one way in which people organized their sexual life and their relationships to children. Gays, lesbians, straights, and transvestites would all be able to organize their sexuality as it accorded with their own self-representation at the time.

But what about intergenerational relationships? Obviously children need care. And this means long-term commitment. How are we, as a society, to provide for the reproduction of the next generation given the need young children have for stable, lasting relationships? A considerable amount of time and devotion is needed to bring a child up. In our society the nuclear heterosexual family has been the institution assigned primary, if not the entire responsibility for the raising of children.

One popular justification for the heterosexual family is that it is in the best interests of the child to have two parents, a man and a woman, who live together. Statistically, we know that the divorce rate means that many children of heterosexual parents do not live in such families (Stacey). Is there any reason to think that living as a heterosexual makes one a better parent? There is absolutely no evidence other than that grounded in homophobia that this is the case.[5] Open gay and lesbian parenting is so new that there are few studies available. Those that exist show that gay and lesbian parents tend to have less conflict in the family, and that in itself may benefit children. They may also be, overall, economically more stable than their heterosexual counterparts. Moreover, their children are wanted. Both economic stability and the intense desire to parent have been noted as factors that have helped create healthy and happy children in these families (Stacey, chap. 5; see also Due.).[6] These preliminary studies should certainly assuage any legitimate fears that gays and lesbians will not be committed parents.

What would a non-heterosexist family law contribute to securing care for children? The interests of the state in securing care for children would have to be consistent with the equivalent evaluation of each one of us as a free and equal person, and children would be recognized as persons whose scope of rights would mature with time. I will suggest a reform structure consistent with the limit that must be placed on family law by the recognition of our full equality as persons, not specific legislative proposals. But I would argue that, to be legitimate, specific proposals would have to be guided by this structure.

First, regulation of the family should protect all lovers who choose to register in civil marriage, or some other form of domestic partnership. Many gays and lesbians have argued against the mimicry of heterosexuality inherent in the very idea of marriage (Kaplan, chap. 7). I am sympathetic to this line of reasoning. Still, it is consistent to demand as a right what you choose under your own construction of your own person never to exercise. The denial of this legal recognition is an illegitimate incorporation of moral or religious values into the basic institutions of a constitutional government. Moreover, because the government has no legitimate interest in monogamy it cannot enforce coupling. Simply put, if in the name of equality polygamy is to be allowed, so is polyandry, including multiple, civilly recognized sexual relationships amongst women.

Secondly, the government must provide a structure for custodial responsibility for children. If the government has no legitimate interest in a particular form of family life it should also have no legitimate interest in linking custodial responsibility only to those people who are in a sexual relationship. Two women friends who were not sexually involved could assume parental responsibility for a child; three gay men could also assume parental responsibility for a child; and finally, a traditional heterosexual couple could also assume parental responsibility for a child. The difference would be that custody would not be a given fact of their sexual unit. In other words, a man skittish about becoming a parent could choose to stay married to his partner and yet also choose not to share full custodial responsibility for his child, leaving his partner to take on custodial responsibility with another friend, or for that matter, a woman lover rather than himself.

To achieve the needed stability for children, the assumption of custodial responsibility would carry with it all that it does now-financial support, limits on movement, and so forth. Parents would be legally established at the time they assumed custodial responsibility; each child would have a legally recognized family. If there were others who, because of sexual affiliation with one of the custodial parents, wanted to assume legal status as a parent, it would be up to the initial group to decide whether or not they should be allowed to do so. The procedure would be similar to that of current stepparent adoptions. Custodial responsibility would remain for life; legal responsibility to custodial children would continue regardless of the sexual lives of the members of the custodial partnership or team. From my standpoint as a mother, I would prefer a "team;' but I understand that only to be my preference.

Those persons who have recently argued against divorce have done so because the stability of children is often profoundly undermined in divorce, let alone in an ugly custody battle. Divorce, or an end to a sexual liaison of one of the partners in the team, would not in any way affect custodial responsibility. The only reason for a partner or a team to legally sue to terminate someone else's custodial responsibility in the partnership, or team, would be what we now call the doctrine of extraordinary circumstances, for example, sexual or physical abuse. Children could also sue to separate themselves from one custodial partnership or team, but under the same doctrine. Under the age of majority the only requirement would be that they choose another custodian. Would adults owe financial support to other adults in this arrangement, if for example one member of the partnership or the team chose to stay home during the early years of the child's life? My answer would be only by contract.

Once signed on, you have signed on for life, which is why I believe that this conception of custodial responsibility meets the state's as well as the children's interest in stability. But could you add on? I have already advocated that you should be able to do so. For example, could you, as an adopting mother, embrace the birth mother in a relationship of shared custody? Could it be the other way around? It already is the other way around in lesbian couples, where the birth mother and her lover seek joint custody together.

The current often tortuous process of adoption has been eloquently observed by lesbian parents. The birth mother is a mother by birth. Her lover is denied parental status in most states. In states where she can achieve it, the birth mother frequently must give up her rights in order for her lover to adopt. This case forces us to confront how difficult it is for our society to conceive of two mothers raising a child together. We keep imposing a choice when it's the last thing the mothers want. It is only in a culture that imposes monogamous heterosexuality because it is only in that culture that the existence of two mothers is such a problem.[7] Patriarchy, as Irigaray eloquently describes, lets the man, not the woman, determine his line. Two mothers causes a problem only when a society is organized around patrilineal lineage. If both women are to be accorded civil status, then it follows that they are free as persons to assume custody together. This would end the pain associated with lesbian adoption.

Lesbian mothers are obviously in a relationship with one another. But so are adopting mothers who never meet the birth mother. The fear of the "return of the birth mother" haunts adoptions. But why? If she has signed away primary custody, she cannot take the child back. Why wouldn't this return be envisioned as a good thing, as it turned out in the case of Lorraine Dusky? As Dusky (1992) describes, "all of us long ago made peace with our places in Jane's life. She calls me Lorraine. "Mom" is her other mother."

There is a deep and profound sense that we do not own our children. All children can escape the confines of what we would make of them. That children are not property is recognized by their inclusion in the moral community of persons from birth. Obviously this idea of custodial responsibility and children's rights demands that we stretch our imaginations. It demands that we struggle to free ourselves from the picture of the family as "Mommy and Daddy and baby makes three." But if we are to truly take seriously what it means to treat each one of us as an equal person and thus not insist on a proper family or "normal" relations between the sexes, then we have to have the courage to do so. It is what is demanded of us by our civil duty.

I have little doubt that it is in the best interests of the children. Certainly it would meet the goal of ending the horrendous tragedy of a woman losing her children because she does not live up to some fantasy conception of what her duty as a mother *is*. If a woman was living up to her custodial responsibility it wouldn't matter whether she had one lover or many. It certainly wouldn't matter that she currently, or in the past, had another woman as lover. But rather than entitling women through the reciprocal right of mothers and children, I would do so through the reciprocal right of custodial partners and children. I would advocate this conception of parental entitlement because any state regulation based on normalized conceptions of femininity, including those of the mother as caretaker, is inconsistent with the equal protection of the imaginary domain.

The third legitimate state interest is the equitable distribution of the burdens of reproduction and the equal protection of the health of young children. Obviously we would have to have provisions for health care for children. I would also argue that we would have to have income maintenance for families. Mothering should no longer be a class privilege. In order to support oneself beyond the level of a guaranteed income, people have to work. Therefore, we would need to provide some kind of publicly funded child care as part of parental entitlement.

The structure of these reforms would provide stability to children and sexual freedom to adults. Since there would be no state-enforced normalized family, children who fall outside the norm would not be stigmatized. There wouldn't be any normal family, as if such a thing has ever existed. Part of the difficulty for adopted children is that they have fallen outside of the norm. By lifting the norm we lift the stigma.

VII. Brave New Families

Are these brave new families? In *Brave New World* Aldous Huxley fantasized about the totalitarian horror of the state outlawing families as dangerous sites of intimacy. In Huxley's tale, embryos were processed as so many duplicate prints to stamp out beings individuated enough to be persons. Love was outlawed, and indeed, the hero's great crime against the state is that, as a sign of individuality, he falls in love.

Like all totalitarian states, the brave new world fought valiantly to defeat the imaginary domain, the place of retreat, that kept the person, uncapturable, individuated from the regime. The regime's method of torture, similar to what Orwell imagined in 1984, articulates the centrality of defeating the imaginary domain in a totalitarian state. The state reaches into that sanctuary, breaking the divide between fantasy and reality by actualizing the victims' worst nightmares. The message is clear—there is no sanctuary from the state.

A family law that insists that this sanctuary is crucial to the protection of our inviolability clearly and firmly rejects the state control of persons of the brave new world. That state fears eros. In contrast, an equivalent law of persons that would allow us to initiate and set forth our own lives as lovers and parents celebrates eroticism.

Families are special because they offer a space for eroticism in which love and life can flourish.[8] Whether they are created through biology, technology, or adoption,[9] or some combination of each, the specialness of erotic connection will obviously make families different from other associations in civil society in and out of which people move freely. By erotic connection I do not just mean actual sexual attraction and relationships between adults. As I suggested in my reading of Sappho, mothers and daughters are erotically connected although this eroticism is rarely recognized. To recognize this connection is to get in touch with the possibility that one becomes a woman by loving another woman rather than by disavowing our love for her and more particularly our primordial longing for the mother's body. This disavowal is supposedly made necessary by the Oedipal complex which in turn assumes the child's normal progression to heterosexuality. What would the possibilities of love and attachment be once the enforcement of heterosexuality was no longer the law? Many of us are now at work in both dreaming up and trying to realize more varied forms of attachment and love within our own families.

I have argued strongly that adopted children and "birth mothers" should have access to each other if they seek it. The idea of the "birth mother" and an adopting mother living together as lovers is still obviously a brave new family to some. All that protecting the imaginary domain can do is to give us the space to try to dream up and live out love in our relationships to other adults and with our children. But this recognition would be a big step toward the dissolution of Hades, where those who have been denied their right to represent their own sexuate being have been banished.

Notes

[1] This demands the maintenance of dual citizenship, at least through childhood. Currently, the U.S. allows such dual Citizenship for adopted children until the age of twenty-one.

[2] One major contribution of feminist psychoanalytic theory has been to critically undermine the truth of the fantasy of psychoanalytic theory. See Benjamin.

[3] Excerpts from the poems of Sappho, translated by Emma Bianchi, unpublished manuscript on file with author.

[4] I borrow the phrase from Carol Stack's well-known book. Stack's ethnographic study of African American families showed that "kin" was a much broader concept than that which has dominated the white middle-class community. Stack's ethnographic work showed that biological ties did not define the parameters of the family.

[5] See testimony in *Baehr v. Miike*, WL 694235 (Hawaii Cir.Ct. 1996).

[6] Lesbian partners show the most *egalitarian* pattern in sharing household responsibilities. This example of integration of work and home life has seemed to be particularly beneficial to the self-esteem and general life outlook of girls raised by lesbians.

[7] Same-sex parenting seems incomprehensible only to a culture that imposes heterosexuality as the norm. Consider sociologist David Eggebeen's testimony in *Baehr v. Miike*, at 7, "[S]ame-sex marriages where children [are] involved is by definition a "step-parent relationship because there is one parent who is not the biological parent of the child."

[8] It is crucial to note that families have historically been sites of abuse and pain. See Gelles; Felder and Victor.

[9] For some, the realization of their desire to parent demands reliance on technology; lesbian couples frequently rely on sperm banks; many gay and straight men have turned to surrogates. Straight couples have also sought out reproductive technology. This kind of technology is extremely costly and obviously class limits who has access to it. Dusky worries that human beings born of this new technology are missing a piece, "like androids out of science fiction, they lack a full human parentage, that connection with our past that forms such a large part of our present. They fill the hole in their identity with rage."

But what is "full human parentage"? Isn't it better that we leave it to each of us to work through what it means to be lovers and parents, rather than have the state impose limits that will exclude some from representing their own sexuate being? Children born into love are the lucky ones. But I would at least hope that no one in 1999 would argue that natural sexual intercourse is necessarily loving. Can the act of artificial insemination be a loving act, as joyous to the lovers as any sex that transpires between heterosexual couples? The answer is, of course. It is not the body parts that make the love. I find nothing "out of kilter" about planning babies.

References

Austin, Carol. "Latent Tendencies and Covert Acts." *The Adoption Reader; Birth Mothers, Adoptive Mothers, and Adopted Daughters Tell Their Stories.* Ed. Susan Wadia-Ellis. Seattle; Seal Press, 1995.

Benjamin, Jessica. *Like Objects, Love Objects; Essays on Recognition and Sexual Difference.* New Haven, Conn.: Yale University Press, 1995.

Daniel, E. Valentine. *Charred Lullabies: Chapters in an Anthropology of Violence.* Princeton, N.J.: Princeton University Press, 1996.

Due, Linnea. *Joining the Tribe: Growing Up Gay and Lesbian in the 90s.* New York: Doubleday, 1996.

Dusky, Lorraine. *Birthmark.* New York: M. Evans, 1979.

Dusky, Lorraine. "The Daughter I Gave Away." *Newsweek* 30 March 1992.

Felder, Raoul and Barbara Victor. *Getting Away with Murder.* New York: Simon and Schuster, 1996.

Gelles, Richard J. *Family Violence.* Newbury Park, CA: Sage, 1987.

Irigaray, Luce. *I Love to You; Sketch of a Possible Felicity in History.* Trans. Alison Martin. New York: Routledge, 1996.

Kaplan, Morris. *Sexual Justice.* New York: Routledge, 1997.

Klibanoff, Susan and Elton Klibanoff. *Let's Talk About Adoption.* Boston: Little, Brown, 1973.

MacKinnon, Catharine A. *Toward a Feminist Theory of State.* Cambridge, Mass.: Harvard University Press, 1989.

Roberts, Dorothy. "The Genetic Tie." *University of Chicago Law Review* 62 (1) (Winter 1995).

Schemo, Diana Jean. "The Baby Trail: A Special Report; Adoptions in Paraguay: Mothers Cry Theft." *New York Times* 19 March 1996.

Stacey, Judith. *In the Name of the Family; Rethinking Family Values in the Postmodern Age.* Boston: Beacon Press, 1996.

Stack, Carol. *All Our Kin: Strategies for Survival in a Black Community.* New York; Harper and Row, 1974.

Chapter 34

The Omnipotent Mother
A Psychoanalytic Study of Fantasy and Reality

JESSICA BENJAMIN

Karen Horney began her classic essay on "The Dread of Woman" with Schiller's poem about "The Diver," whose search for the woman doomed him to the perils of the engulfing deep. In her remarks, Horney suggested that man's longing for woman is always coupled with "the dread that through her he might die and be undone." This fear may be concealed either by contempt or by adoration: while contempt for woman repairs the blow to masculine self-esteem, adoration covers dread with awe and mystery. Regarding the origin of these feelings, Horney declares, "If the grown man continues to regard woman as a great mystery, in whom is a secret he cannot divine, this feeling of his can only relate ultimately to one thing in her: the mystery of motherhood" (135). Modern disenchantment has no doubt worked to diminish the mystique surrounding procreation and motherhood. But of course, the fading of this immediate sense of mystery has hardly been enough to alleviate the dread of maternal power; it has only banished it to the darkness beyond the portals of enlightenment. There it remains alive, in the unconscious if you will, ready to serve diverse (divers) fantastic purposes.

Freud, in a more indirect way, addressed the same themes of mystery and motherhood when he quoted the Schiller poem in his remarks on "the oceanic feeling" in Civilization and Its Discontents: "I am moved to exclaim in the words of Schiller's diver: 'He may rejoice, who breathes in the roseate light'"(73). Freud allowed that the ego's earliest, primordial feelings are those of oneness with the world—"the oceanic feeling"—like that of the infant at the breast who does not yet distinguish the world from itself. But Freud rejected Romain Roland's contention that this feeling constitutes the foundation of religion, that is to say, of culture. Instead, Freud insisted that religious feeling centers on the need for rescue by the father from primary helplessness. Reading between the lines, we see that this helplessness is nothing other than dependency on the mother.

The notion that the child begins in helpless dependency upon a mother from whom he must separate has guided psychoanalytic thinking ever since Freud's formulations. The implications of this image of the mother and the child's relation to her are far-reaching. Simply put, this notion has repeatedly led to the proposition that men have to denigrate or dominate women because men are actually dependent on and envious of the mother who can give birth and nurture the young. Because it is necessary for men to separate from mother and give up their original identification with her, the pull to her is felt as a threat to their independent identity (for example, Marcuse; Stoller). This argument underlies the most common psychoanalytic explanations for male dominance; it has been elaborated by psychoanalysts sympathetic to feminism like Robert Stoller as well as the feminist theorist Dorothy Dinnerstein. In an important contribution, the French analyst Janine Chasseguet-Smirgel (1976) challenges Freud's notion that the vagina is unknown to children, suggesting that unconscious knowledge of this organ is actually a source of fear for the little boy. She points out that the boy's conscious image of the little girl as inferior and lacking an organ is the exact opposite of his unconscious image of the mother as omnipotent and overwhelming. The theory of phallic monism, which maintains that children know only about the penis, reflects the child's effort to repair a narcissistic wound, the sense of helplessness and dependency on the omnipotent mother. This primary helplessness later takes the form, in the boy's case, of the oedipal realization that he is too small to satisfy or complete mother. The original threat is not castration by the father but narcissistic injury in relation to the mother. Indeed, the admired and powerful phallic father actually saves the child from helplessness at the hands of the mother. The "natural scorn" for women that Freud often noted and the transfer of power to the father actually conceal and assuage terror of the omnipotent mother. Chasseguet-Smirgel, like many diverse psychoanalytic thinkers before her—Fromm and Lacan for example—accepts the transfer of power to the father as the only means by which the child can free himself or herself from the helpless subjection to the omnipotent mother and enter the realty of the wider world.

Dinnerstein, of course, sketches a similar relationship between early dependency on the omnipotent mother and paternal rescue as an escape from unfreedom. But she considers this constellation of mother and father to be not inevitable; rather, it is the source of all our cultural sickness. Inevitably, the infant projects omnipotence upon the first person who cares for her or him, and this projection is countered by conferring authority onto the father. Dinnerstein believes this process can be defused or modified only by setting up a different caretaking situation so that the child projects the earliest, undifferentiated feelings onto both parents. If men also nurtured children in infancy, if men also embodied the dangerous, enchanting thrall of early intimacy, we could no longer split off all the envy, greed, dread, and rage and apply it to women.[1] But, alas, the wish for omnipotence and the projection of it onto more powerful others are an inevitable result of dependency for which there is no antidote.

The difficulty with this analysis is that it provides only an external social solution to a psychological problem, the problem of omnipotence. It does not recognize any intrinsic psychic force that would oppose the tendency to project omnipotence onto the parental figure. Omnipotence can be distributed more equitably, but it cannot be countered or dissolved. Although Dinnerstein's vision exposes the fantasies about the mother more exhaustively than any other writer's, her argument assumes the omnipotence of the mother as a kind of psychic bedrock, whose consequences can at best be socially modified.

Chodorow (1978), despite her critique of Dinnerstein's assumptions, does wind up making a similar appeal to changing parenting arrangements. This makes more sense for Chodorow, since she sees the social basis as more determining than the psychological basis. She does not make the mother's psychic function into the prime motive of historical events, does not see maternal omnipotence and the reaction against it as a primary psychological fact underlying the social reality of gender domination. Together with Contratto, she criticizes Dinnerstein for assuming that the fantasy of maternal omnipotence springs from the real dependence on the mother, and also for her equating woman with mother. Women are much more than just mothers, and their active subjectivity encompasses more than fantasies about mothers (Chodorow 1979). Consistent with this position, Chodorow ascribes to the psyche an ability to recognize the mother's subjectivity, to see her as like subject and not just needed object. Hence there is a psychic force of differentiation that counterbalances omnipotence.

To postulate female mothering as an original universal cause of the human malaise as Dinnerstein does seems too omnipotent indeed. But Chodorow's suggestion that we counter that fantasy with so-called secondary-process knowledge of mothers as people (Chodorow and Contratto) inadequately describes how we really come to such recognition even as it too quickly forecloses an elaboration of the way omnipotence works. If psychic dread of the mother's power fuels and justifies men's social subjugation of women, it would be helpful to understand more deeply the fantasies that nourish it and the psychological force that might counteract it. I am not trying to postulate historical or psychic origins of that cycle, to invent an ultimate cause. But I do think that to intervene in or subvert that cycle now requires an understanding of the psychic forces that prevent or encourage such intervention.

If we assume that children do have the capacity to recognize the mother's subjectivity, to perceive her as human rather than as omnipotent, the question is, why don't they? This question has preoccupied me for some time. We cannot simply attribute the persistence of omnipotence fantasies to the child's early dependency upon the mother's care, to events in the preoedipal phase. That argument assumes, rather than explains, a paranoid reaction against dependency. Furthermore, we have had time enough to observe that dependency upon two parents eliminates neither the dread of woman nor the problem of omnipotence. Probably, as Chodorow (1979) and I (Benjamin 1988) have suggested, the decisive moment at which the mother becomes dreaded and 'repudiated is the oedipal phase, in which the male turns the table on the female and the reversal of power relations becomes enmeshed with male cultural hegemony. I intend to elaborate this insight and to suggest how the process of gender differentiation as we know it actually stalemates the potential recognition of subjectivity in the mother-child relationship. The deeply rooted cultural bifurcation of all experience under the poles of gender perpetuates the fantasy of omnipotence. By unpacking the relation between reality and fantasy in light of current theorizing about psychic development, we can clarify the association between omnipotence and gender.

I have been developing a point of view that encompasses the doubleness of psychic life (Benjamin 1990), both the fantasy of maternal omnipotence and the capacity to recognize the mother as another subject. For our purposes, we can align two contrasting moments of psychic life-a mode of intersubjective reality (by this I mean a relationship between two or more different subjects sharing certain feelings or perceptions) and a mode of fantasy as the unshared property of an isolated subject-with the capacity to recognize the mother as another subject and the fantasy of maternal omnipotence, respectively. Ideally these distinct tendencies of our psychic organization constitute a tension rather than a contradiction, an "either-or" as has often been supposed. In the best of circumstances, we do not get rid of dangerous fantasies; rather the fantasies exist in tension with reality. The fantasy world of the unconscious in which self and objects can be omnipotent is balanced by the relational world in which we recognize, empathize, and grasp the subjectivity of real others. This tension is roughly equivalent to that between the depressive and schizoid positions in Kleinian theory, which are no longer understood as successive but as dialectically alternating or complementary (Ogden). It is the *breakdown* of the tension between these two modes, and not the existence of fantasy (omnipotence) per se, that is detrimental to the recognition of other subjects.

This breakdown consists, in effect, of moving from the state in which I know my fantasy to be a result of my feeling-something even a child of three can at times realize-to a state in which I externalize, I project my feeling onto someone else. Here Horney's remarks on male dread of woman are once again prescient: "'It is not,' he says, 'that I dread her; it is that *she* herself *is* malignant, capable of any crime, a beast of prey, a vampire, a witch, insatiable in her desires. *She* is the very personification of what is sinister'" (135). The usage of "she is" is an important key to the whole matter. It signifies a collapse of reality and fantasy. All that is bad and dreaded is projectively placed on the other; all the anxiety is seen as the product of external attack rather than one's own subjective state. The issue, then, is not simply that male children disidentify with and then repudiate the mother. It is also that this repudiation involves the psyche in precisely those projective processes-"she is that thing I feel" -and these intensify the fear of the other's omnipotence and the need to retaliate with assertion of one's own omnipotence.

Before I go on to discuss the way this world historical power struggle gets anchored in the psyche, let me say a few words about the idea of a counterforce in the psyche that pushes for recognizing the mother and for intersubjective reality in general. This is a relatively new idea (see Chodorow 1979). For most of its history, psychoanalytic theory itself has reflected the imbalance between intersubjective reality and the intrapsychic. It has failed to conceptualize the mother as a separate subject outside the child. However, as I have discussed, elsewhere (Benjamin 1988, 1990), recent developments in psychoanalytic theory and infancy research are more consonant with a view of early development as a process that involves mutual recognition between mother and child.

Infancy theorists have argued that the metaphor of the mirror is not appropriate to represent early mothering (Beebe and Lachmann; Stern), that even at four months an attuned mother is not undifferentiated, does not create the illusion of perfect oneness and is not perfectly attuned. In her play she stimulates an incipient recognition of otherness, difference, discrepancy, and this pleases the infant, who likes the excitement that a brush with otherness brings. Later, at about nine months, the infant begins to be aware of the fact that, as Daniel Stern described it, separate minds can share similar states. Commonality, attunement, shared feeling can unite separate persons. At this point, the child is able to realize that another shares her or his excitement or intention and enjoys that fact. Likewise, the mother is aware of her child's capacity to share feeling and now takes pleasure in contacting her or his mind. Thus the infant's sense of the other develops incrementally through a tension between sameness and difference, union and disjunction.

We might say that the original psychoanalytic theory or ideal of a mother who offers a perfect oceanic symbiosis hardly captures the multiplicity and complexity of the infant's actual experience of life with mother. Yet this supposed state of oneness has been adduced to explain the fear of regression that is the basis of the dread of mother and of woman: the fear of being drawn back into the limitless ocean of maternal union. Of course, both women and men project the dangerous longing for a return to amniotic life onto mother, but how did this one partial image come to stand for the whole and so become the trope for the entire theory of infancy?

The new perspective on infant perception of the mother is, of course, not just a product of adhering to empirical observation; to assume that would be naive. Not surprisingly, scientific development can here be seen to reflect the changes in women's status and the ideology of motherhood as well as to help organize those changes. But this perspective on infancy suggests that the simple existence of dependency in infancy is, in itself, an insufficient explanation far man's infantile stance regarding his fantasy of the mother. Once our representation of the psyche includes the aspect of intersubjectivity, the capacity to differentiate and recognize other subjects—the "counterforce"—it is possible to see this working in counterpoint to omnipotence fantasies. How does an appreciation of a shared reality with the other person mitigate a fantasy that we, or they, are omnipotent? How does it open up a space in which fantasy can be expressed symbolically rather than concretely? And what impedes the evaluation of intersubjective space, of the ability to see the other's subjectivity and to take our fearful projections back into ourselves?

I have suggested that the fantasy of omnipotence is not an originary state but is a reaction to confronting the other.[2] It probably begins in the first crisis of recognizing the other, the first conscious encounter with the mother's independence, during the separation-individuatian phase. Margaret Mahler (Mahler, Pine and Bergman), whose observations of separation-individuatian have been so influential in current psychoanalytic thinking, called this crisis "rapprochement." In rapprochement a conflict emerges between the infant's grandiose aspirations and the perceived reality of her or his limitations and dependency. When the child begins to be aware that reality will not always bend to her or his will, that thought cannot always be translated into action, a pitched battle of wills can ensue, "a struggle to the death for recognition." Expressed in terms of intersubjectivity: the tension between asserting self and recognizing the other breaks down and is manifested as a conflict between self and other. The paradox of recognition is that we must recognize the other in return, else their recognition means little to us. In the very moment of realizing our own independence, we are dependent upon another to recognize it. At the very moment we came to understand the meaning of I, myself, we are forced to see the limitations of that self. At the moment when we understand that separate minds can share similar feelings, we begin to find out that these minds can also disagree. What if the other does not do as I wish, recognize my intent? There is a new sense of vulnerability: I can move away from mother-but mother can also move away from me.

It is no accident that the observational studies of this period focused on mother's leaving. For mother's departure (to work, to go out) confronts the child with mother's independent aims-a point usually ignored. This is therefore not just a matter of separation anxiety, as it is frequently portrayed, but of recognition: recognize my will, do as I want! Or rather, separation consists not so much of losing mother's presence as losing control of her coming and going. This conflict also confronts the mother with the problem of her own separate existence and so with conflict; she may experience the child's demands now as threatening, as tyrannical, irrational, willful. The child is different from *her* fantasy of the perfect child, who would want what she wants. In her mind, the child and she may switch places, the child now becoming the repository of omnipotent aspirations she once attributed to herself in the persona of the all-giving mother. The mother, as I shall discuss in a while, also has to be willing to relinquish her fantasy that she can be perfect and provide a perfect world far her child; she has to accept that injuring the child's sense of complete control over her is a step an the road to recognition.

This formulation of the process might make it seem that the mother bears sole responsibility for her own recognition by the child. I shall modify this notion of responsibility later on, but for now let us assume that at an individual level the mother often passes on her own solutions to the dilemma of omnipotence. If the mother is unable both to set a clear boundary for the child and to recognize the child's intentions and will, to insist on her own separateness and respect that of the child, the child does not really "get" that mother is also a person, a subject in her own right. Instead, the child continues to see her as all-powerful, either omnipotently controlling or engulfingly weak. Whether the child attributes the omnipotence to the mother or attributes it to herself or himself, the process of mutual recognition has not been furthered.

The paradox of recognition cannot be resolved. The "ideal" is for it to continue as a *constant tension* between recognizing the other and asserting the self. This crisis point poses a new and taxing demand to recognize outside reality, and so the tension between recognition and assertion breaks down and must be created anew at a more sophisticated level. In Mahler's theory, however, the rapprochement conflict appears to be resolved through internalization, what is called abject constancy. This means the child takes the mother in and is able to separate from her because her existence as an internal abject is not dependent on her being there an the outside and, more specifically, on her gratifying the child. In this picture, the child has only to accept mother's being disappointing; there is no need to shift her or his center of gravity to recognize that mother does this because she is a person in her own right.

How would we go about conceptualizing the way that a child begins to make this shift? What we are tracking here is how a person comes to have a sense of shared reality and appreciate the subjectivity of the other versus what reinforces the sense of omnipotence. The paint here is not to dismiss or denigrate fantasy, play, and the narcissism of Her or His Majesty the baby, but to acknowledge the necessity of a struggle between two important, but conflicting tendencies.

The British object relations theorist D. W. Winnicott, who was also a pediatrician, offered a way to think about the struggle that the child engages in to come to terms with the necessity of recognizing the other. Winnicott (1971) came up with the idea that in the course of development we do a rather paradoxical thing: we try to destroy the other person in order to discover that they survive. By destroying the other, he did not mean literally trying to annihilate them, but rather denying or negating their independent existence, refusing to recognize them. In fact, what he meant was to absolutely assert our right to have it our way and to make the other person subject to our fantasy, do our will. His idea was that by wiping out the person inside our mind (he calls it the sphere of our "omnipotence") we actually have the effect of placing the other outside our mind (outside "omnipotence"). Because, it is hoped, the other does not actually get destroyed, we discover the other to be outside our mental powers. By engaging in a fantasied act of maximum control, by negating the other's separate existence, we discover the outside reality.

Of course, this works only if the other actually does survive, which means that the person continues to be an effective, responsive, and nonthreatening presence. Winnicott (1964) specifically talks of how the baby has a terrible fit of rage and feels that he has destroyed everyone and everything around him, but as he calms down, he notices that everyone is just as before-still loving and still there. This allows the baby to distinguish between what he imagines and what is real, between inside and outside. When the destructiveness damages neither the parent nor the self, external reality comes into view as a sharp, distinct contrast to the inner fantasy world.

So in this model, fantasy and reality become differentiated, rather than one canceling out the other. And the way this happens is not that we suppress our omnipotence, deny our fantasy that the other can perfectly meet our wishes, but that we acknowledge them as fantasy and tolerate their distance from reality. The problem that so often occurs on this path to recognizing the other is that if the other retaliates, or caves in and withdraws, we don't really experience the other as outside us, but rather they seem to be just like our persecutory fantasy; they do not survive and become real. In this case, a power struggle is inaugurated, and the outcome is a reversible cycle of doer and done to. If the mother does not survive, a pattern is established in which there is no real other subject, no real feeling for the other. Let us imagine a mother who gives in to the child and never leaves. The child, feeling he or she has succeeded in controlling Mommy, now feels "Mommy is still my fantasy; Mommy is also afraid, and I can never leave Mommy without great anxiety either." Thus, even as the child loses contact with the real independent mother, the omnipotent fantasy mother, who is powerful in her need as well, fills the space. Now the child is no longer able to encompass the feeling "I am full of anxiety," but rather feels mother to be the source of the solution to anxiety. Alternatively, let us imagine that mother leaves and returns and they share a happy reunion. Now what the child feels is that the bad feeling about mother leaving and the projection of that anger onto mother, which would return as punishment or abandonment, is not true, was only a fantasy.

The flip side of Winnicott's analysis would be that when aggression is not worked through in this way, it continues to fuel fantasies of revenge and retaliation attributed to both self and other. The whole experience shifts from the domain of intersubjective reality into the unconscious domain of fantasy, from a feeling we can own to a projection onto the object. Where do we put the bad feeling? We keep it inside, projected onto the figure of a frightening, dreaded other. All real experience is also elaborated in fantasy, of course, but when the other does not survive and aggression is not dissipated, experience becomes almost exclusively fantastic. It is the loss of balance between omnipotence and recognition, between fantasy and reality, that is the problem (Benjamin 1990).

Ideally, a child's negotiation of conflict with the other (mother) allows the infant's original fascination with and love of what is outside her or his appreciation of what is different and challenging to continue under more complex conditions. This appreciation gives to separation an element of affection, rather than merely hostility: love of the world, not just leaving or distance from mother. To the extent that mother herself is placed outside, she can be loved: "I'll cut you in a hundred pieces!" says the little pirate waving a sword. At bedtime he snuggles up and reminisces fondly, "Remember I said I'm gonna cut you in a hundred pieces?" Now separation is truly the other side of connection to the other. This appreciation of the other completes the picture of separation and explains what lies beyond internalization-the establishment of shared reality.

Elsa First, a psychoanalyst who has worked with children, has provided some germane observations of how the toddler begins to establish shared reality, using fantasy and identification with mother to deal with mother's leaving in the third year of life. She observed the symbolic play in which mother's leaving for work was represented by the child. There was an evolution in the toddler play, first enacting an aggressive, retaliatory reaction and then moving into identification with the one who is leaving, putting the self in the place of the other based on understanding (once again) similarities of inner experience. The two-year-old's initial role-playing imitation of the departing mother is characterized by the spirit of pure retaliation and reversal: "I'll do to you what you do to me." But gradually the child begins to identify with the mother's subjective experience and realizes that "I could miss you as you miss me," and, therefore, that "I know that you could wish to have your own life as I wish to have mine." First shows how, by recognizing such shared experience, the child actually moves from a retaliatory world of control to a world of mutual understanding and shared feeling. Her analysis shows how the child comes to recognize that the leaving mother is not *bad* but *independent*, "a person like me."

We can sum up the problem of holding onto both shared reality and omnipotent fantasy. The initial response to the discovery of the difference between my will and your will is a breakdown of recognition between self and other: I insist on my way, I refuse to recognize you, I begin to try to coerce you; and therefore I experience your refusal as a reversal: you are coercing me. The capacity for mutual recognition must stretch to accommodate the tension of difference, to reach beyond coercion, and it does this through identification, expressed in communicative play that gives the pleasure of shared understanding. In this light, the early play at retaliatory reversal may be a kind of empowerment, where the child feels "I can do to you what you do to me." A necessary step, the ability to play with omnipotence fantasies, gives the child a certain freedom and it tests survival. But then the play expands to include the emotional identification with the other's position and becomes reflexive, so that, as First puts it, "I know you know what I feel." This advance in differentiation means, "We can share feelings without my fearing that my feelings are simply your feelings." There is now a space between the mother and child that allows differentiation of self and other, fantasy and reality.

The child who can imaginatively entertain his own and his mother's part—leaving and being left—has attained a space that symbolically contains negative feelings so that they need not be projected onto the object ("she is dreadful") or turned back upon the self ("I am destructive").[3] The mother has survived, has helped the child to contain and share these feelings, has provided a space in which they can be safely understood as fantasy. Now the child can use this space to begin to transcend the complementary form of the mother-child relationship. When the child is able to identify with the mother, the movement out of the world of complementary power relations into the world of mutual understanding means that power is not shifted back and forth like a hot potato but (momentarily, at least) dissolved.

The complementary structure dictates a reversible relationship, which allows one to switch roles but not to alter them or hold them simultaneously. One person soothes, the other is soothed; one person is recognized, the other negated; one subject, the other object. This complementarity does not dissolve power but keeps its positions, keeps it moving from one partner to the other; domination can be reversed but not undone. There are only two possible positions, with no space in between them to allow for difference. When the tension of mutual recognition breaks down-something that we see in the culture writ large-the absence of a real other creates a kind of void that has to be filled with fantasy, usually the kind of fantasy in which the other is threatening and must be subjugated. The cycle of destroying the reality of the other and replacing it with the fantasy of a feared and denigrated object, one who must be controlled for fear of retaliation, characterizes all relations of domination.

Ordinarily, I think, each child is exposed to both possible solutions to the problem of omnipotence-complementarity and mutuality. The paradox of recognition is not resolved once and for all in the second year of life but remains an organizing issue throughout life, becoming intense with each struggle for independence and each confrontation with difference. Ordinarily there is a necessary tension between complementarity and mutuality in the mother-infant relation. It is thus not my intention to suggest that maternal failure is responsible for the prevalence of omnipotence fantasies, of complementary structures, the persistence of domination. But how shall we even formulate the question of what keeps the complementary structures in place?

The question for psychoanalytic theory is how cycles of domination can be broken into rather than merely reversed. Obviously, the fantasy of maternal . omnipotence would be sustained even were male domination reversed in favor of women, a point often lost on anti psychoanalytic feminists. But by and large psychoanalytic theory has not even begun to conceptualize a way out of complementarity; it has tacitly accepted the existence of domination. Psychoanalytic theory has understood domination in terms of narcissism, the subjective position that underpins it: the inability to recognize the other and confront difference without surrendering to or controlling the other. The theory did not envision the overcoming of narcissism, the possibility of recognition and mutuality occurring within the dyad, which it conceived exclusively in the complementary metaphor of subject and object. In various ways, it insisted that only the intervention of a third figure, the father, could bring the child out of fantasy and into reality by giving up the mother. The assumption was that recognition of the other could not evolve within the relationship to the primary other, that two subjects alone could never confront each other without merging, one being subordinated and assimilated by the other.

One side of the coin was attribution of regressive traits to mother for holding the child back from civilization; the other side was the notion that only the father's intervention could break up the mother's omnipotence. Mother's failure, father's justification; mother's disparagement, father's idealization—these went together like a horse and carriage. The only alternatives were for the child to retain omnipotence for himself (I say "him" advisedly), remaining stuck in narcissism; or to displace the fantasied power on to the father.[4] The later oedipal solution, in which the father is "the third term" who creates space between mother and child, who creates symbolic capacity, is accepted in Lacanian feminist accounts as the only path to break up narcissism, "the Imaginary" (for example, Mitchell; Ragland-Sullivan).

So let us try a reversal here. In light of our present conception of the mother-child relationship, we can say that in the oedipal phase the boy is wrested away from the very possibility of establishing mutuality through identification. The boy displaces the mother's envied power onto father and then identifies with it rather than finding a way out of that power struggle. The oedipal theory inadvertently expresses the problem, but not its solution; the Oedipus complex does not dissolve narcissism; it displaces it. The seldom recognized effect of the oedipal phase is to shift the form of omnipotence. Whereas the child in the preoedipal phase is overinclusive (Fast) and wishes to be "everything"—that is, to polymorphously incorporate the organs and abilities of both sexes—the oedipal child repudiates all that is other and insists that what he (or she) has is "the only thing" (Benjamin, 1991-92). Thus the theory of phallic monism reflects the contempt for mother's organs and her value in general that is essential to the oedipal boy's move to deal with envy and difference: Everything I can't have is (worth) nothing. Traditional oedipal theorizing states that the boy realizes he cannot have mother, accepts the limit that father sets, and so gives up omnipotent control over the primary object. But at another level, omnipotence is restored through the repudiation of the mother, whereby that which he gives up is turned into nothing, and indeed, father now has "everything," the phallus.[5]

Thus, though the oedipal achievement of complementarity is supposed by the theory to represent mature acceptance of limits, being only the one or the other, it actually conceals the unconscious narcissistic omnipotence of being "the one and only." Having recognized the finesse in this maneuver, the point is still not to disavow or get rid of the oedipal structure, which is in any event no more possible than to get rid of the fantasy of omnipotence. The point might be to envision a next step, which partially dissolves this form of omnipotence and restores the balance of mutuality. Psychoanalytic theory, as Bassin has pointed out, has the potential to envision something beyond the oedipal organization of sexuality, a phase beyond the phallic have/have not that encompasses bisexuality, and this project will doubtless be part of the feminist revisioning of sexuality.

For the time being, however, the prevalent structure of male gender dominance can be understood as the oedipal complementarity writ large. The principal reaction to giving up identification with the opposite sex, or shall we say, to the discovery of exclusive difference in the oedipal phase is a reassertion of omnipotence in a new form. The new form, found in girls as well as boys, is chauvinism, based on repudiation: I must be the One, not the Other. I agree with Chodorow (1979) that men have been able to make their chauvinism hegemonic because of their position of power, not because only males are chauvinistic. We might argue that the disruption of identification brought about by the oedipal male repudiation of mother actually undoes mutuality and makes the complementary structure of doer and done-to the dominant residue of infancy. The model of complementary power relations has prevailed in the male orientation stance toward women, producing a formal fit between complementary subject-object relations and male-female relations. Dynamically, the omnipotent mother of this dyad becomes the basis for the dread and retaliation that subsequently inform men's exercise of power over women. The adult relation between men and women becomes the locus of the great reversal, turning the tables on the omnipotent mother of infancy.

This reversal works because the rigid complementarity and male repudiation of femininity produces a foreclosure of the intersubjective space of identification with the mother. This has several consequences: first, the mother is no longer recognized as a subject like the self, something I've said before; second, the omnipotence attributed to the mother cannot be defused by the identificatory fantasies and communicative interaction described earlier; third, the omnipotence of the overinclusive position cannot be integrated and so finds a more destructive expression in the chauvinism of being the one sex; fourth, the father is defensively idealized and becomes the final embodiment of this omnipotent oneness, which cannot be broken up in interaction with a real other subject; and finally, all the feelings of envy, guilt, and destructiveness cannot be symbolically contained as felt properties of the self but must be projected out as properties of the object: "She is dangerous, a goddess, a temptress."

It is not necessary that the fantasy of maternal omnipotence be dispelled, only that it be modified by the existence of another dimension-that of intersubjectivity. This dimension evolves, as we saw in the toddler's identification with the leaving mother, through the symbolic space of communicative interaction and fantasy play in the dyad. With the closing of this space, the projective power of the fantasy becomes more virulent: "she is that thing I feel." Segal, a psychoanalyst in the Kleinian school, called this a symbolic equation, a function prior to symbolization in which the symbol does not stand for something; it is that thing. In the symbolic equation (she is that thing) the verb to be forecloses the space in between (Ogden), a space opened by the verbs seem or feel, by the action of play and just-pretend. The attenuation of intersubjectivity can be conceptualized as an assimilation of the subject to the object (Horkheimer and Adorno), as the lack of the space in between subjects.

As the analyst Thomas Ogden has noted, the existence of potential space between mother and child allows the establishment of the distinction between the symbol and the symbolized. The subject who can begin to make this distinction now has access to a triangular field—symbol, symbolized, and the interpreting subject. The space between self and other can exist and facilitate the distinction, let us say, between the real mother and the fantasy mother (who is symbolized). This can happen in the early dyad without an intervening third person (Trevarthen), although in it the place of a third is generated.[6]

The dread of the mother, with which I began this inquiry, reflects the foreclosure of that intersubjective space between mother and child in which omnipotence is transformed through use of symbolic processes. Accordingly, the structural role of the oedipal father would then be not to create, as in genesis, a symbolic order out of an absence of symbolism. In reverse, it might be tempting to say that the father as symbol, or better yet, symbolic equation ("the paternal order") often substitutes an authority structure for the symbolic intersubjective process of the maternal dyad. This paternal symbolic structure is rooted in the intrapsychic situation of subject-object complementarity; it retroactively redefines the mutual intersubjectivity of mother and child as a threat to masculinity or a regressive flight from reality. But in fact, the imposition of a paternal order is no solution (or only an imaginary one) to the problem of recognizing the other subject; it is a theoretical fantasy. In reality, the structures of early intersubjectivity, "the maternal order," remain available to men as well as women and are no more the essential prerogative of mother than of father.

Indeed, any such opposing of a "maternal order" to theories of paternal order, even for the sake of argument, justifiably deserves to be considered a counter-idealization (Kristeva). Therefore, I wish to counter the preceding argument immediately with yet another reversal. I want to consider the difficulty that the fantasy of omnipotence poses for the mother herself. In seeking to define a space within the dyad, a symbolic potential that does not rely on a powerful idealized father of separation, feminist theorists have often been tempted to re-create a mirror image of the father—a perfect, ideal mother in whom the old wish for omnipotence is revived. In the current wave of feminism we have seen an outpouring of women's writing that seeks to restore a lost maternal or feminine order in writing, on the margins of culture, in the private spaces of play, creativity, and erotic life, in the nonverbal representations of mutuality—a different kind of symbolic space founded in intersubjectivity. In fact, to an astonishing degree the notion of finding one's own desire has been articulated through the image of woman as writer. Yet even as this search has appealed to the maternal image, it has had to contend with the constant companion of the maternal ideal, a deep fear of destroying one's mother or child by separating.

Given the centrality in current feminist thought of the figure of the woman writer (rather than, say, the woman politician-though this may be changing even as we speak), the conflict between woman's subjectivity and mothering responsibilities is formulated in terms of the desire for the inner, not the outer world. This effort to reclaim subjectivity presents the difficulty, or shall I say temptation, of the search for "the perfect mother" (Chodorow and Contratto). The perfect mother of fantasy is the one who is always there, ready to sacrifice herself—and the child is not conscious of how strongly such a fantasy mother makes him or her feel controlled, guilty, envious, or unable to go away. The child simply remains terrified of her leaving or of destroying her by becoming separate. In turn, the mother feels terrified of destroying her child with her own separation. Thus separation and guilt often emerge as the axis of conflict for contemporary women writers. When the dangers of separation that inspire guilt are seen as real rather than fantasized, space is foreclosed and the mother-child relationship becomes a zero-sum game: The mother's child "is" the obstacle to her self-expression and her self-expression "is" a threat to her child (again, the symbolic equation of the verb to *be*).

A kind of evolution of this problematic can be seen in the reflections of the feminist critic Susan Suleiman. Musing on the fear of separation, she offers for scrutiny her fantastic conviction, "With every word I write, with every act of genuine creation, I hurt my child" (1985). Subsequently, in a discussion of Mary Gordon's *Men and Angels*, Suleiman (1988) shows the outcome of this fantastic conviction to be a foreclosure of the space between reality and fantasy. She grapples with that foreclosure in Gordon's story, which reaffirms the zero-sum stakes of a mother's choice by depicting how a mother who chooses to pursue her own writing really does place her children at risk. Suleiman recognizes that this portrayal is inspired by the woman's unconscious clinging to an image of a perfect mother, and not merely by the social reality that mothers are almost exclusively responsible for their children. And Suleiman continues to inquire how to escape that equation in which the mother is to blame. At a still later point, Suleiman (1990 and chap. 16 below) proposes that there is a mother who can play with her child and thus be recognized "most fully as a subjectautonomous and free ... able to take the risk of 'infinite expansion' that goes with creativity," a mother who can open up the symbolic space of play.[7]

The difficult task this sets feminist consciousness is for a woman, as daughter or mother, to transform the space of inevitable separation and loss into a space of creation and play. Jane Lazarre, whose account of a stormy young motherhood, *The Mother Knot* (1976), conveyed the inability to conceive of separation without destruction, has sought to deconstruct the formula in which the mother must sacrifice her children or her self. Her new book, *Worlds beyond My Control* (1991 and chap. 2 above), takes its title from Sara Ruddick's *Maternal Thinking*: "To give birth is to create a life that cannot be kept safe, whose unfolding cannot be controlled, and whose eventual death is certain.... In a world beyond one's control to be humble is to have a profound sense of the limits of one's actions and of the predictability of the consequences of one's work" (72). Recognizing the illusion of the daughter who blames the mother and is determined to outdo her when she becomes a mother, Lazarre struggles to accept this condition.

Lazarre's character no longer constructs her children as obstacles to her writing, or her writing as obstacles to her mothering. She realizes, instead, that her obstacle is the dream of perfect symmetry, her own wish to be completely recognized, completely responded to, the fantasy of perfect self-expression in a perfect world. Her dilemma is, how can she continue to write, to love, to seek recognition, in the absence of the fantasy mother who would constitute that world? She comes to recognize that she cannot re-recreate that mother either in her writing or in her efforts to protect her children from the world. Rather, her character has to find a way to contain, through writing, the loss of an illusion that was common to both the "pristine beginning" of her writing and her "newborn's unscarred flesh": the illusion that she would achieve "the perfect reparation."

It seems to me that the early phase of feminist revival, the phase of rediscovering the mother, was characterized by this wish for perfect reparation. As is characteristic for such a wish, it reflected a needed effort to formulate what had been missing or lost, as well as a kind of manic denial of loss and a celebration of identity. The latter, a celebration of the sisterhood of all women, could be seen as a euphoric "return" to the earliest phase of mother-child mutuality: "You and I are feeling the same feeling."[8] No doubt, this excess lent credence to the critique of feminism, which contended that the banishing of the symbolic oedipal father invariably leads to such denial of difference. But this was an oversimplification of both the intentions and the aims of feminism. Further, as I have been proposing, that denial of difference simply adopts the preexisting positions of complementarity; it reflects a foreclosure of space for which the idealized father was the original model. The fantasy of the redeeming mother represented a kind of reversal, a substitution for the ideal father. Ultimately, though, whether it is a maternal or a paternal ideal, the fantasy of an omnipotent figure, in and with whom we are redeemed, condemns us to a life of denial of loss and to a world in which complementary power relations triumph over mutual understanding.

But the deconstruction of this fantasy should not be equated with the bitter disillusionment that turns us against ourselves, chastising ourselves as victims of false hope, of a childish longing for redemption. Nor does disillusionment alone constitute a real base for the knowledge of difference. By itself, it reflects only the disparagement of what was once loved, the countering of mania with depression, the refusal to grieve concealed by a repudiation of all longing. The real alternative to a defensive fantasy of omnipotence is the labor of mourning (Santner). And mourning gives rise to acts of reparation, which need not be perfect in order to restore the expressive space of connection to an understanding other. As I have suggested before, it is good enough for us to counterbalance fantasy with that real connection, which transforms in turn our relationship to fantasy, enabling us to own it as ours. This, in turn, allows the acceptance of loss to ameliorate the aggression that fuels omnipotence. Historically, the sedimenting of the omnipotence fantasy in our cultural life is too great to overcome except by adding this new layer of recognition and awareness of loss. So it is good enough—in fact it is better—not to disown all fantasy but simply to recognize that the other is not that thing I dread or that god I adore. Accepting that the other is outside our fantasy allows us to take our fantasy back into ourselves and begin to play. The intersubjective space of understanding can help contain the inevitable experience of leaving and losing the other, even of death. In the space of creativity and communication, the self can play, even with adoration and dread, can find consolation for the inevitable disappointment of not being, or having, everything.

Notes

[1]A questionable aspect of this argument is the assumption that there is no gender difference apart from parenting, which, however convenient, seems untenable because it leaves out cultural representation and the pervasiveness of gendering. [2]The fantasy of omnipotence is more than simply the original inability to differentiate thoughts from reality that is typical of infancy; it is a defensive reaction to

disappointment. The wish says, in effect, I wish I could control everything as I once did (thought I did) when mother did everything I wanted; or, if only mother would make everything perfect, which she could do if she wished. Once the cognitive capacity for distinguishing wish and reality begins to develop, mental omnipotence is a dynamic psychic matter, not a simply inability to differentiate.

[3]Of course, I am simplifying matters. Another way to describe this is that projection continues in the paranoid position, but the self occupies that position only at times; it is able much of the time to be in the position of taking back the projection and experiencing fantasy as such.

[4]Some examples of this way of formulating the father's role can be found among influential psychoanalytic writers such as Loewald and, of course, Chasseguet-Smirgel (1985). I realize that the Oedipus complex is not always interpreted in such a way as to stress the father-son relationship as one between subjects, and the mother-son relationship as an objectifying one. Certainly, it has sometimes been crudely understood as love of mother and hatred of father. But such hatred, as analysis consistently reveals, is a particular way of identifying with father. Even when oedipal theory stresses not the boy's identification with father but his rivalry or murderous impulses, we know that rivalry represents a kind of struggle to the death for recognition between subjects; indeed, in Hegel's description of the struggle it epitomizes it. And rivalry is a way in which to identify with someone while remaining opposed to him.

[5]Lacan, who emphasized the role of the phallus as the ultimate signifier, inadvertently gives a good example of the Oedipal move from loss of the object's love to devaluation of the object. He mistranslates the famous phrase uttered by Herr K. in the Dora case, "I get nothing from my wife" (an accurate rendering of the German), as "My wife is nothing to me."

[6]It may be that this symbolic function then becomes equated symbolically with the father as third person-as when the theory imagines that the father brings this function into being, rather than that under certain conditions the father as a symbol represents this function.

[7]Suleiman's second statement is part of a commentary on Gordon's Men and Angels that lucidly articulates the problem of splitting in the novel between a "good mother" and an "other mother," the alternate caretaker who takes on the badness (indifference, selfishness, even hostility) not acceptable in a good mother. And in her discussion of the mother playing she offers a vision of "boys (later to be men) who actually enjoy seeing their mother move instead of sitting motionless, a peaceful center around which the child weaves his play [Barthes]; of girls (later to be women) who learn that they do not have to grow up to be motionless mothers" (1990: 180).

[8]This phase was superseded by another reversal, one that denied sameness of feeling in favor of difference. In this simple negation, however, the principle of identity was preserved, this time sequestered in particular groups that opposed any universal feminine identity. Should we speculate that the historical dialectic will go according to plan, so that these might be followed by a phase of restoring

the tension between sameness and difference, particular and universal?

References

Bassin, D. "The True Genital Phase." Paper delivered at spring 1991 meetings of Division 39, Psychoanalytic Psychology, New York, 1991.

Beebe, B., and Lachmann, F. "Mother-Infant Mutual Influence and Precursors of Psychic Structure." In A. Goldberg Ed., *Frontiers of Self Psychology*. Hillsdale, NJ: Analytic Press, 1988. 3-25.

Benjamin, J. *The Bonds of Love: Psychoanalysis, Feminism and the Problem of Domination*. New York: Pantheon, 1988.

Benjamin, J. "An Outline of Intersubjectivity." *Psychoanalytic Psychology* 7 (Supp. 1990): 33-46.

Benjamin, J. "*Like* Subjects and Love Objects: Identificatory Love and Gender Development." Paper delivered at Psychoanalytic Association clinical workshop, New York and San Francisco, 1991-92. Forthcoming in *Like Subjects and Love Objects*. New Haven: Yale University Press, 1994.

Chasseguet-Smirgel, J. "Freud and Female Sexuality." *International Journal of Psychoanalysis*, 57 (1976): 275-87.

Chasseguet-Smirgel, J. 1985. *The Ego Ideal: A Psychoanalytic Essay on the Malady of the Ideal*. New York: Norton.

Chodorow, N. 1978. *The Reproduction of Mothering*. Berkeley: University of California Press.

Chodorow, N. "Gender, Relations and Difference in Psychoanalytic Perspective." 1979. *Feminism and Psychoanalytic Theory*. New Haven: Yale University Press, 1989.

Chodorow, N. and S. Contratto. "The Fantasy of the Perfect Mother." *Rethinking the Family: Some Feminist Questions*. Ed. B. Thome. New York: Longman, 1982.

Dinnerstein, D. *The Mermaid and the Minotaur: Sexual Arrangements and Human Malaise*. New York: Harper and Row, 1976.

First, E. "The Leaving Game: I'll Play You and You'll Play Me." *Modes of Meaning: Clinical and Developmental Approaches to Symbolic Play*. Eds. A. Slade and D. Wolfe. New York: Oxford University Press, 1988. 132-60.

Freud, S. "Civilization and its Discontents." 1930. *Standard Edition*. Vol. 23. London: Hogarth Press, 1953.

Horkheimer, M. and T. Adorno. *Dialectic of Enlightenment*. 1947. New York: Seabury Press, 1972.

Horney, K. "The Dread of Woman." 1932. *Feminine Psychology*. New York: Norton, 1973.

Kristeva, J. "Women's Time." *Signs* 7 (1981): 13-35.

Lacan, J. "Intervention in the Transference." 1966. *Feminine sexuality: Jacques Lacan and the École Freudienne*. Eds. J. Mitchell and J. Rose. New York: Norton, 1982.

Lazarre, J. *The Mother Knot*. 1976. Durham: Duke University Press, 1997.

Lazarre, J. *Worlds Beyond My Control*. New York: Viking, 1991.

Loewald, H. "Ego and Reality." 1980. *Papers on Psychoanalysis*. New Haven: Yale University Press, 1989.

Mahler, M., Pine, F., and A. Bergman. *The Psychological Birth of the Human Infant*. New York: Basic Books, 1975.

Marcuse, H. *Eros and Civilization*. New York: Vintage, 1962.

Mitchell, J. "Introduction." *Feminine Sexuality: Jacques Lacan and the École Freudienne*. Eds. J. Mitchell and J. Rose. New York: Norton, 1982.

Ogden, T. *The Matrix of the Mind: Object Relations and the Psychoanalytic Dialogues*. New York: Jason Aronson, 1986.

Ragland-Sullivan, E. *Jacques Lacan and the Philosophy of Psychoanalysis*. Urbana: University of Illinois Press, 1986.

Ruddick, S. *Maternal Thinking*. Boston: Beacon Press, 1989.

Santner, E. *Stranded Objects*. Ithaca, NY: Cornell University Press, 1990.

Segal, H. "Notes on Symbol Formation." *International Journal of Psychoanalysis* 38 (1957): 391-97.

Stern, D. *The Interpersonal World of the Infant*. New York: Basic Books, 1985.

Stoller, R. *Perversion: The Erotic Form of Hatred*. New York: Pantheon, 1975.

Suleiman, S. 'Writing and Motherhood." *The (M)Other Tongue*. Eds C. Kahane, S. Garner, and M. Sprengnether. Ithaca, NY: Cornell University Press, 1985. 352-77.

Suleiman, S. "On Maternal Splitting: A Propos of Mary Gordon's *Men and Angels*." *Signs* 14 (1988): 25-41.

Suleiman, S. 1990. "Feminist Intertextuality and the Laugh of the Mother." *Subversive Intent*. Cambridge, Mass.: Harvard University Press.

Trevarthen, C. "The Foundations of Intersubjectivity: Development of Interpersonal and Cooperative Understanding in Infants." *The Social Foundations of Language and Thought*. Ed. D. R. Olson. New York: Norton, 1980.

Winnicott, D. W. *The Child, the Family and the Outside World*. Harmondsworth, England: Penguin, 1964.

Winnicott, D. W. 1971. "The Use of an Object and Relating Through Identifications." *Playing and Reality*. London: Tavistock.

Chapter 35

Don't Blame Mother

Then and Now

PAULA J. CAPLAN

This chapter is about the practice of mother blame from the time leading up to my writing *Don't Blame Mother: Mending the Mother-Daughter Relationship,* [1] up to the present. First I shall explain what motivated me to write the book beginning in the mid-1980s, then I shall discuss how much of what was relevant then remains relevant today, and finally I shall describe the way I have attempted to put some themes about mother blame into theatrical form.

I became interested in mother blaming when I was working in a clinic where we were evaluating families, and I noticed that no matter what was wrong, no matter what the reason for the family's coming to the clinic, it turned out that the mother was always assumed to be responsible for the problem. And if, in the assessment interview, she sat right next to the child, my colleagues would say afterward, "Did you see how she sat right next to the child? She is smothering and over-controlling and too close and enmeshed and symbiotically fused with the child." But if she did not sit right next to the child, she was called cold and rejecting—and, if the child was a boy, castrating.

So my interest in mother blaming began because it seemed that there was nothing that a mother could do that was right, and it was particularly interesting and painful to me because I was a mother.

In 1986, when I received tenure and considered what I most wanted to teach, one of the two courses I created was about mothers. I wasn't aware at the time of any other course about mothers, so I started trying to design the course and talking to people about it. Often, both men and women would laugh and say, "What are you going to talk about for a whole semester?" or just, "Hah! A course about mothers?" You may remember that that was the reaction people had had ten years earlier to "Oh! You're going to have a course about women?"

Teaching that course to graduate students at the University of Toronto's Ontario Institute for Studies in Education led to my writing *Don't Blame Mother* (1989) in which I describe aspects of girls' and women's socialization that creates or exacerbates problems between mothers and daughters, as well as methods that mothers and daughters have found helpful in repairing rifts between them. (I did not believe and still do not believe that the mother-daughter relationship is more fraught with problems than the mother-son relationship or the relationships between fathers and their children of either sex; but as a feminist I was primarily concerned with the kinds of socially created—and, therefore, hopefully surmountable—barriers between women.) In addressing the question "To what extent is the content of *Don't Blame Mother* applicable today?" I find it depressing that most of the basic principles that concerned me as I wrote the book still apply today. I shall return to this point later.

After my experience in the clinical setting described earlier, I did some research with Ian Hall-McCorquodale (Caplan and Hall-McCorquodale 1985a, 1985b) looking at articles in clinical journals written by psychoanalysts, psychiatrists, social workers, psychologists, behavior therapists, and clinicians of all stripes. We found that mothers were blamed for virtually every kind of psychological or emotional problem that ever brought any patient to see a therapist. We were also disappointed to find that the sex of the person who was writing the paper did not determine the presence or absence of mother blaming, and, even more depressingly, that it didn't get better as the years passed after the resurgence of the women's movement during the 1970s. With respect to mother blame, so many therapists still seemed to be buried under their rocks.

When I began to bring up this subject of mother blame I pointed out that there are myths about mothers that allow us to take anything a mother might do and turn it into evidence of something "bad" about her. Important work that a mother does goes largely unnoticed, except when she doesn't do it, as when she is sick and can't make dinner. I would point out that nobody I knew of was likely to say to their mother, "That was a great week's work of dusting you did" or "That was a week of delicious and nourishing meals that you prepared." When I would say this, people would laugh-and still do, in fact.

So we have to ask: "Why does this make us laugh? Would you laugh if I said, 'Dad, the lawn looks great now that you have mown it'?" Nobody laughs at that. Why? Because we laugh at the unexpected. It is so unimaginable to us that anyone would express appreciation for, or a sense of valuing of, the work that mothers do as mothers and housekeepers and cooks and chauffeurs. So I used to talk about that.

As observed in a review of *The Time Bind: When Work Becomes Home and Home Becomes Work*, Arlie Hochschild points out that women increasingly spend time at paid work because they feel appreciated there. She says that even for relatively uninteresting work, such as factory work, women find work to be a greater source of self-esteem than home life. This was something that had concerned me years ago, because it seemed to me that, as in that story about no one thanking you for dusting, even if you work at a really boring, miserable job, every week or two somebody hands you a paycheck. The check might not be much, but it communicates the notion that somebody puts some value on the work that you do. And it's still no better in terms of mothering.

To come to the heart of *Don't Blame Mother,* there are mother myths I call the "Good Mother Myths" and mother myths I call the "Bad Mother Myths." The

Good Mother Myths set standards that no human being could ever match, such as that mothers are always, naturally, 100 percent nurturant. We have a double standard. We don't have that kind of expectation of fathers. So when, 1 percent of the time, mothers don't do what we wish they would do, we feel betrayed, because the myth is that they naturally are able to and in fact are desperate to be nurturant all the time. But when our fathers do anything nurturant, we feel that it is wonderful that Daddy did something like that. (Naturally, the answer is not to stop appreciating what fathers do but rather to be ready to give mothers equal credit when they are nurturant.)

The Bad Mother Myths allow us to take mothers' neutral or bad behavior-because mothers are human, so we do some bad things-or even mothers' good behavior, and transform it into further proof that mothers are bad. One example that disturbs me the most is the myth that mother-daughter closeness is sick, that it is a form of psychopathology. When *Don't Blame Mother* was first published and I was doing media interviews, every woman interviewer would confess, with the microphone turned off, that she talked to her mother every day. I would ask her, "How do you feel afterward?" and the woman would reply, "Oh, great. My mother has a great sense of humor, and we are great friends, and we give each other advice." I would then ask her, "Do you have a partner?" "Yes." "Do you talk to them every day?" "Yes." "Does that embarrass you?" "No." And I would ask, "Well, then, why did you confess that you talk to your mother every day?" These women would reply that they worried that the daily talks with their mothers were signs that they hadn't "individuated" or "achieved autonomy" from their mothers, and if they had been in therapy they would say, "I know it means we're enmeshed or symbiotically fused." My point here is that anything associated with mothers becomes devalued and pathologized.

If you look at the myths about mothers, you find that some of them are mutually exclusive (Caplan 1989). One of the Bad Mother Myths is that mothers are an endless drain on our energy. Just on the basis of strict physics principles, you cannot be constantly putting out force, as in giving nurturance, while constantly taking in force and energy as you are draining it from others. Another set of mutually exclusive myths involves the Good Mother Myth, according to which mothers naturally, perhaps for hormonal reasons, know everything they need to know about mothering, and the Bad Mother Myth, according to which mothers cannot raise emotionally healthy children without the advice of lots of experts.

I believe that these mutually exclusive myths continue to coexist because every society needs scapegoated groups if the people in power want to maintain their power. What happens if I'm in the powerful group and some member of the scapegoated group does something good? Somebody might get the idea that the scapegoated people are not as bad as I portray them to be, and if that's the case, maybe I don't deserve to have all of the power I have. So I have to make sure there is a myth for every occasion, so that no matter what the members of that scapegoated group might do, I can transform it into further proof that they are wrong, bad, or pathological and deserve to continue to have no power and be scapegoated (Caplan 1989). That is the powerful function that these myths serve, and that is why we need to keep questioning them.

This power hierarchy still exists, and the women's movement hasn't been able to change it yet. I think it hasn't changed partly because we often substitute the word *mother* for *woman*. For instance, people at a party may stop you when you tell a "joke" that is woman-hating, but if you change the word *woman* to *mother*, you can still get away with the comment. You are much less likely to have someone interrupt you to say, "I don't think that's funny, and I don't want you to go on like that."

What the women's movement can do is to make the repeated exposure of mother myths, the placing of them front and center, a priority. Anti-feminist backlash makes all feminist efforts more difficult, of course. But until we recognize the need for what we might call "the Norma Rae-ing of mothers' struggles," the need to reveal mothers' oppression and its systemic nature, few women of any ethnic or racialized group or class or sexual orientation (and certainly not women with disabilities or women who don't weigh the "right" amount) will be free. Why? Because we all had mothers, and so we're connected with what is done to, what is said about mothers. Because we have all been subjected as women to strong pressure to prove we are unlike our mothers. You'll often hear women say, "My greatest fear is that I will be like my mother." What I find that these women usually mean if you explore that statement is, "I don't want to be treated the way she has been treated. I don't want to be demeaned and undervalued the way she is." At the same time as we are taught not to want to be like our mothers, we are taught—sometimes subliminally—that we should want to be like our mothers, when they are passive, pliable, and ashamed of themselves. And no one is free until the truths about mothers are highlighted, because all women, and especially as we age (Siegel), are expected to be motherly, motherlike, as in being self-denying and serving others.

No, it's not getting any better—not socially and not in the research arena. A recent issue of the *American Journal of Orthopsychiatry* includes a longitudinal report on "Preschool Antecedents of Adolescent Assaultive Behavior" (Herrenkohl, Egolf and Herrenkohl). The researchers studied children from preschool through adolescence in an attempt to discern the determinants of adolescents' assaultive behavior. How did they look at the alleged determinants? Among other things, they observed what they call early in their article "parental interactions" with the young children. That really meant "mothers' interactions," even though 86 percent of the children in their study had both a male and a female parent in the home. When they looked at how mothers interact with children and then later on looked at which children become assaultive, it is not surprising that they concluded that it was the children's negative interactions with their mothers that led to their assaultive behavior. The methodology you choose can go far to determine the results that you get. I believe that there are at least two major methodological problems evident in this study. One is not looking at the fathers or the society in which the children live and what the determinants of their assaultive behavior might be. The second is a cause-effect problem. People who are assaultive when they are teenagers, for reasons that may have had nothing to do with their mothers, might have been difficult to handle as children, and thus their mothers' interactions with them would have been observed to be relatively "negative." For example, their mothers might have had to do more disciplining of them, more saying "no." That is just one example of the persistence of the practice of mother blame in "scholarly" journals.

Mother blame also persists on a grand scale in the arena of the diagnosis of mental illness. My book, *They Say You're Crazy: How the World's Most Powerful Psychiatrists Decide Who's Normal* (1995), is an expose of the *Diagnostic and Statistical Manual of Mental Disorders* (American Psychiatric Association) (also called the DSM). The DSM is the "Bible" of mental health professionals that lists 374 supposedly different mental disorders. It is marketed as "science," but the way it is put together is far from scientific, and pieces of relevant scientific research are often ignored or distorted. I became involved in learning about the DSM in 1985 because I was concerned about a new category the American Psychiatric Association was proposing to include in the DSM called "Self-Defeating Personality Disorder." This new category might be described as "the Good Wife or Good Mother Syndrome." It included criteria such as not putting other people's needs ahead of one's own, feeling unappreciated, and choosing less desirable options for their lives when clearly better ones are available. But this is what society still thinks we are supposed to do as a mother and as a "good" woman. Once involved, I was horrified when I learned about the way that the DSM's authors decide who is "normal." I ended up calling their process "Diagnosisgate" because of the similarities to Watergate in terms of lies, cover-ups, and distortions of what the research literature shows (Caplan 1995).

This "Self-Defeating Personality Disorder" is a real catch-22 for women. If women act in those ways, they supposedly have this mental disorder, but if they do not act in those ways, they are rejected and pathologized for not being real women, not being "good" women.[2] Because there was a virtual blackout of *They Say You're Crazy* by the major media, and I wanted people to know about the Diagnosisgate issues, I decided to write a play on the theme of who decides who is normal. The play is called *Call Me Crazy* (1996), and I shall include here a couple of excerpts from it. It is a comedy-drama with scenes alternating between relatively serious ones in a mental-hospital case-conference room and comedic-grotesque, "campy" ones like a quiz show called "What's My Diagnosis?" Almost all of the second act takes place in the conference room, and the psychology intern is making it possible for patients to tell their stories. I chose the stories for the two women and two men patients because they are typical of what happens in the traditional mental health system. For the two women's stories, this includes the therapists' disbelieving what women tell them and pathologizing women in general. Here is the story told by Patient 3:

PATIENT 3: I was a cheerleader in high school—and homecoming queen. During my second year in college, I married Eugene, my high school sweetheart. Then I got pregnant, and as soon as my tummy started to swell, he started getting drunk and beating up on me, calling me a fat pig, saying it made him sick to have sex with me. He left me the night our daughter Tammy was born. It was hard … being a single mother, working in a ribbon factory, trying to get my pre-pregnancy body shape back. At the factory, I met Sam. He's a truck driver, and he's gone a lot, but when he's home, he's wonderful—funny, gentle, a wonderful father to Tammy. I feel so lucky to have him, and I'm scared to death of losing him. He says he loves me, not how I look but who I am. I hope that's true, but I get so frightened of putting on weight. It's weird. Sometimes the only thing that makes me feel better when I get scared of getting fat and losing him … is eating … like a whole chocolate cake or a whole pot of macaroni and cheese at once. And as soon as I do that, 'course I get scared again right away … so … I make myself throw up. My stomach hurts, and my throat gets raw. I went to a psychologist, and she said I made myself throw up because I enjoyed that pain! I told her I didn't, but she didn't pay any attention. She said now that I didn't have Eugene around to hit me and call me names, I had to make the suffering myself! I told her I hate feeling bad, but thinking about losing Sam was even worse than throwing up to try to stay thin so he wouldn't go. She wouldn't listen. And I didn't know it then, but she wrote in my chart that I enjoyed suffering, that I had a mental illness called "Self-Defeating Personality Disorder." I found out because, when Tammy was four, Eugene suddenly showed up and went to court to take her from me. I'd stayed friends with his sister, so Eugene found out that I'd been seeing a psychologist. And they made her bring my chart to court. The judge sent Tammy to live with Eugene because I was mentally ill. I get to see her two hours every second Sunday.

This scenario is typical of what happens to women, often because of the kinds of women and mothers they are trying to be and because of the way that that gets constructed by the mental health system.

Here is one more excerpt from *Call Me Crazy*. No one has ever heard from Freud's mother, and I thought it was time. How many people even know her name? I went to the library, thinking that I wanted her to be a character in my play but that if I could find no interesting information about her, I would make something up. But as I began to read little fragments about her life in the biographies of her son, I found myself gasping, because it seemed pretty clear to me what she probably would have felt about the various things that happened to her. Notice how she wrestles with the question of what is good and normal mothering. In the play, she steps out of history to speak to the audience. The people who are in the case conference are behind her and have been talking about the DSM.

AMALIA: Thank you for coming. I'm Amalia Freud. Amalia Nathanson Freud. I lived to be ninety-five years old. For decades, I wanted people I met to know my son was the great psychoanalyst, winner of the Goethe Prize for literature. But behind their polite smiles I saw the thought, "This is the mother whose son discovered that all little boys want to have sex with their mothers." Discovered. Hah! Guessed. Claimed. Wrote a story.

A man says with aplomb, "This is what happens," and already it's a discovery. A woman says, "This is what happens," and she's exaggerating or manipulating.

And about girls and their mothers what did he "discover?" That our daughters resent us for not having had the courtesy to provide them a penis. That they look down on us because we don't have penises. I had five daughters. How do you think his words made me feel? I love my Sigmund, but this is too much....

Sigmund was a bright boy, brilliant probably. But maybe he had too much.

He told people he felt all his life like a conqueror because he was my "indisputable favorite." Hah! So he thought. The truth is I adored all of my children. How could I not? My husband, he valued me for my son. His first wife had two sons. Sigmund was my first-born, when I was twenty-one and his father was forty-one. I loved my daughters but kept having to have more—five in all—until Jacob got one more son ten years after Sigmund was born. Most of the time Sigmund was growing up, his father and all the other children and I shared three bedrooms, but he had his own. He needed to study. Often, he took his meals alone in there and received his friends there. He was the oldest child, so maybe it was right to give him his own room. He complained that his sister Anna's piano lessons were noisy when he was trying to study. We got rid of the piano. Anna and I were sad but not angry. We understood. Maybe he had too much. And he decided who was normal.

You know, he threw up his hands in despair and said, "What do women want?" He said women were a dark continent to him. (Shakes her head.) What's not to understand? Is it healthy to take a mother's love or a wife's love and make it seem so complicated?

(Shrugs her shoulders.) Normal, shmormal. Oh, I realize some people have to be put away-they can hurt themselves, or someone else. But it's a tough problem. You start putting people away, and somebody's going to decide who gets put away, somebody's going to choose the rules. Is what these guys (indicating the giant DSM) decide any better than what my son decided? Thinking about it makes my head hurt.

But I'll tell you what I have noticed. Who decides is who has the power.

And somehow, they seem to decide the people most like them are the normal ones, the good, the healthy, the deserving. It's the others who are derided, called dangerous … sent away. My five daughters—one went to New York, three were gassed in Auschwitz, and the last one starved to death in the camp at Theresienstadt.

Thank you for listening.

And then Amalia leaves the stage.

I want to close with what Patient 3, whom you heard from before, says about classifying people on the basis of the forms of their emotional anguish. What she says applies to seeing mothers and all women through the prism of the myths about mothers.

> PATIENT 3: When you look up at the night sky, there are lots of stars. There are no real constellations, but people decide how to divide up the stars into groups and give those groups names. And forever afterward they think they see the Big Dipper and Orion. It makes it hard to see, really see, one unique star as itself.

I hope that this sampling of the recent history of mother blame makes it clear that, despite some gains that feminists have made, there are still miles to go before we can relax in the knowledge that mother blame has been eradicated. For this reason, I suggest that we join together in declaring that women don't speak often enough and don't speak up often enough, certainly not in defense of mothers. Let us vow that at every possible opportunity we will protest, we will educate, even interrupt as we would a sexist or a racist "joke" when anyone in any setting utters or implies any of the dangerous myths about mothers.

This chapter is the slightly edited text of an address I gave on September 27, 1997, at York University, Toronto, for their International Conference on Mothers and Daughters.

Notes

[1] The new edition is scheduled for publication on Mother's Day 2000 by Routledge.

[2] For apparently political reasons, Self-Defeating Personality Disorder was removed from the most recent edition of the DSM, but that has not kept it from being used.

References

American Psychiatric Association. *Diagnostic and Statistical Manual of Mental Disorders IV*. Washington: American Psychiatric Association, 1994.

Caplan, Paula. *Don't Blame Mother: Mending the Mother-Daughter Relationship*. New York: HarperCollins, 1989.

Caplan, Paula. *They Say You're Crazy: How the World's Most Powerful Psychiatrists Decide Who's Normal.* Reading, Mass.: Addison-Wesley, 1995.

Caplan, Paula. *Call Me Crazy.* Script copyrighted by and available from author, 1996.

Caplan, Paula and Ian Hall-McCorquodale. "Mother-Blaming in Major Clinical Journals." *American Journal of Orthopsychiatry* 55 (1985a): 345-53.

Caplan, Paula and Ian Hall-McCorquodale. "The Scapegoating of Mothers: A Call for Change." *American Journal of Orthopsychiatry* 55 (1985b): 610-13.

Hochschild, Arlie ."A Review of Sex Role Research." *Changing Women in a Changing Society.* Ed. Joan Huber. Chicago: University of Chicago Press, 1973. 249-67.

Herrenkohl, Roy C., Brenda P. Egolf, and Ellen C. Herrenkohl. "Preschool Antecedents of Adolescent Assaultive Behavior: A Longitudinal Study." *American Journal of Orthopsychiatry* 67 (1997): 422-32.

Siegel, Rachel Josefowitz. "Old Women as Mother Figures." *Woman-Defined Motherhood.* Eds. Jane Price and Ellen Cole. New York: Harrington Park, 1990. 89-97.

Chapter 36

Where We Are Now

ANN CRITTENDEN

It is mothers who are picking up the slack, doing ... what has to be done, whether it makes sense or not, because no one else is available, able, or willing to do the job.

—Suzanne Bianchi, sociologist

One of the misleading impressions left in the wake of the women's movement is that it swept away women's traditional lives, like a sandstorm burying the artifacts of an ancient civilization. The media constantly remind us that women have become doctors, lawyers, merchants, chiefs, implying that no one is left to tend to the children.

The truth, as always, is far more complicated. Mothers have not abandoned home and hearth to go to "work." Mothers are working harder than ever, but their principal place of business is still the home. For all of the ink spilled about the high-tech economy, the majority of American mothers are still primarily engaged in the oldest economy in the world: the household.

Most people seriously underestimate how much of their lives contemporary American women spend on their children. There is even evidence that today's mothers are taking the tasks of reproduction more seriously than any previous generation. Recent research indicates, for example, that American mothers—whether they work outside the home or not—may be spending more time with their children than they did in the past (Sandberg and Hofferth; see also Bianchi). And married fathers are also putting in more time with the kids, although mothers as a group continue to devote far more hours to children than fathers do.[1]

These new data put the lie to conservative fears that once liberated women would liberate themselves from the responsibilities of child-rearing. They also raise questions about feminist hopes that men would become co-parents, sharing equally in the massive labor required to produce a well-prepared child. Neither the fears nor the hopes have come to pass. For whatever reasons—biology, social conditioning, institutional inertia, choice, or no other choice—children's lives are still overwhelmingly shaped by women, and children are still the focus of most women's lives.

Educator Johnnetta Cole once commented that for every child, someone has to be the mommy; the one who is responsible; the one who can be counted on day in and day out, on good days and bad. Whether she has a Ph.D. or an M.D., a B.A. or a G.E.D.; whether she is a conservative traditionalist or a Yuppie professional, for the most part, the mother is still the mommy.

Falling in Love

I first met Eleanor when she was an undergraduate at Yale in the mid-1970s. A tall, red-haired Irish-American girl from the working-class suburb of Winthrop, Massachusetts, she became one of the first women to graduate from that august institution. Blessed with boundless energy and enthusiasm, she proceeded to take on the world, confident that she would make her mark on it. She worked for various advocacy groups, served as a top aide to the lieutenant governor of Massachusetts, and even made a long-shot, unsuccessful run for Congress.

One late spring day a few years ago, we were having lunch in Boston's North End when Eleanor brought up the crucial life decision facing her. She had been trying for seven years to get pregnant, with no success. Now at age 37 she and her husband, Jack, were weighing two alternatives: either to adopt or to put their dreams of having a child aside for good.

A few months later, Eleanor called to say that she and Jack were leaning toward adoption. They had been introduced to a three-and-a-half-year-old child who was in a foster home after being removed from abusive parents. Jack and Eleanor had started seeing Veronica on weekends, and although they knew that she was troubled, they felt there was a good chance that they could bring some stability and happiness into her life.

I visited Eleanor and Jack a couple of times after Veronica began living with them. One night when I arrived for dinner, the house was filled with balloons, left over from Veronica's fourth birthday party. The little brown-eyed sprite was running around in her nightgown, obviously excited, and. eager to show me her new toys. She finally went to bed without too much trouble, and Eleanor and Jack discussed her progress. They were still letting Veronica spend some of her time with her last foster mother, to ease the adjustment into their home, and although she had "bad days," they believed. that the adoption would work. As hard as it was with her sometimes, they had decided that it was worth it.

Several months later, I received a call from Eleanor. She was having doubts. That was putting it mildly—she was in agony. Veronica would be fine for a few weeks and then would go to pieces, a hellion by day, screaming at night. Eleanor had calculated that she was putting in 58 hours during an average week just on childcare. Her husband and a baby-sitter were together spending an additional 20 hours a week on Veronica. Eleanor was not going to bed until one or two in the morning and getting up again at five or six.

It is such an enriching experience—that dimension is wonderful ....

But it's also emotionally exhausting. It's killing me. I don't know what to do.

Veronica had just been legally freed for adoption. Her mother was a drug addict, her father an alcoholic. It was hard to imagine two people more unfit for parenting. Eleanor knew what it would do to Veronica if she didn't go through with an adoption, but what would an adoption do to her?

She had just finished a year with Boston Edison, leading a team of about twenty people in designing an award-winning energy conservation program. For the first time in her life she was earning a six-figure salary, and her boss had approached her about the possibility of the two of them starting their own energy-efficiency consulting firm.

She was also working on a book and was president of Women of Vision, a network of prominent women interested in promoting institutional change on behalf of women. She thought that she might be able to do *one* of these projects and be a mother to Veronica, but that two, not to mention all three, would be impossible. She was willing to accept the trade-offs, but they were excruciating. "I love my work, and I've always derived a large part of my identity through my work," she told me. "I'm truly tortured. Men get a standing ovation if they miss a meeting because of parenting; women miss whole careers."

"Sometimes I think only a few people should choose motherhood as a vocation. But then I think, no—that's not fair either. Why do we have to choose like this?" Hers really was a choice; she was free to decide not to go through with the adoption. She was facing an exaggerated version of the American mother's dilemma.

Her friends had offered conflicting advice. One woman who had adopted a little girl had described it as "thirty-five years of misery." Another friend had urged her not to do anything that might make her less effective in her work. "Most women can be mothers," she had told her, "but only you can do what you can do for the world."

Eleanor finally made her decision after a particularly difficult night. Here is how she described the events in a letter to Veronica's foster mother: "I heard a piercing scream from Veronica's room, and I jumped up and flew to her bedside. She was standing on her bed, crying. I took her in my arms and brought her back to bed with me, holding her on top of me, stroking her back, saying, 'It's OK, Veronica. You're safe with us. We'll take care of you.' Meanwhile, she calmed down, and I brought her back to her room. Two hours later she knocked on my door, came over to my bed, threw her arms around me, and said, 'Will you be my mommy?' It was Mother's Day morning."

Eleanor later told me that she believes there are two main avenues to love. One is falling in love, a spontaneous, heartfelt response to a few enchanting people you may meet in life, The other avenue is choosing love, a rational commitment to another person to share your life with them, to care for and support them through good times and bad. Unlike falling in love, choosing love is a conscious decision with momentous, permanent consequences. Eleanor and Jack had already fallen in love with Veronica. And on Mother's Day, they also chose to love her, for life.

Jack has continued in his job with the city of Boston. But Eleanor has opted to work on a variety of independent projects that give her flexibility. She now spends more time on Veronica than on any other part of her busy life.

***

This is where we are. Most women, like Eleanor, are still embracing mother-hood, with all of its glorious, messy entanglements, assuming the awesome re-sponsibility of being a primary parent. This is why homemaking, the fundamental task associated with raising the young, is still the largest single occupation in the United States. As a group, working-age homemakers outnumber secretaries, stenographers, and typists; food preparation and service workers; schoolteachers; construction workers; mechanics and repairers; farmers, foresters, and fishermen; mathematical and computer scientists; and all of the writers, artists, entertainers, and athletes combined-not to mention lawyers, doctors, and other professionals. Even among women in their 30s, by far the most common occupation is full-time housekeeping and caregiving.[2]

Among married mothers with children under age eighteen, 28.4 percent of all those in the prime working years of 25 to 54 are not in the labor force, meaning that the only employment of these 6.9 million women is their home and children.[3]

The persistence of traditional family patterns cuts across economic, class, and racial lines. Uneducated married mothers are the: least likely to be employed, having the least to gain from a job. They calculate, quite correctly, that as long as there is one breadwinner in the family, their presence at home can create more value, and be more satisfying, than much of the (under)paid work they could find. But the United States also has one of the lowest labor force participation rates for college-educated women in the developed world; only in Turkey, Ireland, Switzerland, and the. Netherlands does a smaller proportion of female college graduates work for pay.[4]

The college-educated stay-at-home mother is a fixture: in American business and professional circles. With 60-plus-hour work-weeks the norm at the higher levels of the economy, a full-time "wife" is often the only thing that makes family life possible. A survey of chief financial officers in American corporations found that 80 percent were men with stay-at-home wives. Another survey of managerial employees revealed , that 64 percent of the male executives ,with children under age thirteen had nonworking spouses.[5] "The presence of a wife at home to care for family and personal matters is almost as much a requirement for success in business today as it was a generation ago," consultant Charles Rodgers ... told me, in an interview in his office in Cambridge, Massachusetts.

A second large group of wives and mothers-approximately 20 percent of mar-ried mothers with children under age eighteen-is officially classified as "working," but these women are employed part-time while their principal job is at home.[6] The government classifies a person as "working"—that is, in the labor force—if he or she is employed for as little as one hour a week, is merely looking for paid work, or works unpaid for at least five hours a week in a family business. Thus a "working mother" can be the wife who lends a hand one afternoon a week her husband's office; the mother who works a few evenings a week as a waitress after being home all day; or the consultant or editor who works out of a home-based office.[7] Even new mothers who are on maternity leave are "working mothers" because they remain employed.

Cheryl Evans, a Baltimore mother of four, was a licensed provider in her own home while her children were little, making her officially a working mother. And Deborah Fallows, a writer in Washington, D.C., who described herself as a "stay-at-home mom" for years, was a "working mother" because she earned a few hundred dollars a year from freelance writing. But in every real sense both of these women were mothers at home. Counting them as "working mothers" contributes to the false impression that most mothers are not available to their children during the day. On the contrary, a substantial majority of working mothers appear to be reducing their work hours during the child-rearing years. In 1996, for example, married working mothers on average put 1,197 hours into their paying jobs, a mere half of the 2,132 hours averaged by married fathers.[8]

Still, many mothers don't want or can't afford to put their jobs and careers on the back burner. Almost 18 million, roughly half of all women with children under 18, do work full-time; that is, at least 35 hours a week. And the tendency of mothers to work full-time is the long-term trend. Between 1994 and 1999 alone, nearly one million women a year moved from part-time to full-time employment, including a record number of mothers of even very young children (Uchitelle).

This historic movement of mothers into the workplace has aroused legitimate concern, particularly over the fate of infants who are placed in surrogate impersonal group care for long hours early in life. Yet there is no clear and consistent evidence that the change in family life has been harmful to children. Some of the most alarming assertions that working mothers are shortchanging their kids are based on "evidence" that upon close inspection melts away. One allegation—that American parents spend 40 percent less time with their children than they did in 1965—is simply false. After being repeated by countless officials and media pundits, and cited in congressional hearings, think tank reports, and books, the alarmist "40 percent decline" finally appeared in a correction, where it belonged.[9]

Another worrisome statistic appeared in a report issued in 1999 by the president's Council of Economic Advisers. This document contained a widely publicized warning that parents had 14 percent less time available for their children in 1999 than in 1969. But that does not mean fathers and mothers actually do spend less time with their kids. They could be sacrificing other activities. Fathers may be spending less time bowling, going fishing, or having a drink, after work with their colleagues, and mothers may be devoting fewer hours to shopping or playing bridge. In fact, this is exactly what is happening.

A closer look can assure us that the family is not undergoing a meltdown, that the essential function of the family—the care and upbringing of children-is not in crisis because mothers have gone to work. On the contrary, all the signs indicate that women today are taking on motherhood with a greater-than-ever awareness of its importance.

From Quantity to Quality

Back in the 1970s, Arleen Leibowitz, an economist at RAND, was one of the first researchers to discover that, all else being equal, as women become better educated, they tend to devote *more* time and attention to their children. Apparently, as women's horizons expand, and their opportunities multiply, their hopes and aspirations for their offspring increase as well. They delay child-bearing, have fewer children, and invent time and resources in each one. All over the world, across continents and cultures, as women advance they stop "having babies" and start "raising children," a process economist Ted Schultz described as a shift from "quantity to quality" in human reproduction.

Leibowitz speculated that as the average American woman gained better schooling and spent more of her life in the paid labor force, she would also probably spend more time with her children, not less (250). This prediction proved uncannily accurate. Sociologists, economists, demographers, and historians have all reported a profound shift from quantity to quality in child-rearing, not just in the United States but almost everywhere on the globe. Researchers have confirmed, for example, that the number of hours of primary care (that is, feeding, bathing, etc.) per child by white married mothers in the United States almost doubled between the 1920s and the1980s, a period in which the improvements in women's education and opportunities were nothing short of revolutionary (Bryant and Zick, especially 368; Council of Economic Advisors 11). Mothers in 1985 also spent more *overall* time on childcare than did mothers in the 1920s. When domestic economists W. Keith Bryant of Cornell University and Cathleen Zick of the University of Utah looked at the time diaries of American farm wives in the 1920s, they noticed that the women were so busy with a myriad of chores that they had little time for anyone member of their large broods.

Sociologists have also discovered that mothers today spend as much if not more time with their children as mothers did in the 1960s, despite the massive movement of mothers into the workplace during the intervening years (Bianchi 11). Sharon Hays, a sociologist at the University of Virginia, found for example, that despite their busy schedules, the professional women she interviewed used more intensive time-consuming child-rearing techniques than less educated women. They not only talked and read more to their children; they also favored giving their children choices. They engaged in negotiation rather than demanding strict obedience to firm rules, and put a high premium on developing independence and critical thinking, all of which take more time than simply laying down the law (86-94).[10] But Hays also observed that mothers at every socio-economic level now take it as a given that child-rearing is a very serious business, requiring a huge expenditure of time and effort. "I've had grandmothers tell me their daughters work far harder and spend more time with their children than they did," says Hays.

Sandra Espinoza, of Washington, D.C., a married mother of two, is a good example of this maternal determination. For six years, she worked as a full-time housekeeper for a family near her son's primary school, and for five more years she worked two jobs, as a housekeeper and a teacher of English as a second language. Every morning she had to get up at 6:30 A.M., fix breakfast for the family, and pack a lunch for her husband, a mechanic. She took a long bus ride across the city to her teaching job, began at 8:00 A.M, and ended at 2:30 P.M. Then another bus to her employer's home, where dirty dishes, unmade beds, piles of laundry, and all the rest awaited her. Four hours later, at 7 :00 P.M. she left for home, arriving back where she had started, just in time to fix dinner, help with homework, and on and on and on.

Through all these years, Mrs. Espinoza's overriding focus was her children. She and her husband never had dinners out alone, or vacations, or time enough to exercise. Their lives revolved around their church and kids.

At his mother's urging, Rafael, who was a friend of my son's, went to summer school for extra tutoring. Thanks to her efforts, he won scarce summer scholarships to city-run sports camps and attended a weeklong merchant marine program she discovered. She never missed a back-to-school night or a teacher conference, especially during the precarious early teen years. When her daughter, Rebecca, won a college scholarship for Hispanic girls, Sandra took one of her first trips ever out of the city to take her to school in Virginia.

I spoke to Mrs. Espinoza recently, and she told me she had finally decided to cut back to part-time work, quitting the domestic work. "I can't go on; I'm absolutely exhausted," she said. "I'm 43, the kids are in good shape, and I need some rest."

Sandra Espinoza's exhausting efforts help explain why the movement of mothers into the labor market appears to have had so little measurable impact on children's well-being, despite vigorous efforts by traditionalists to prove otherwise.[11] Working mothers just don't rest.

The Leisure Gap

Working mothers put in longer hours than almost anyone else in the economy. On average, they are estimated to work more than 80 hours a week.[12] Time-use surveys confirm that as women enter the workplace, they take on the equivalent of two full-time jobs, forcing them to cut back on everything in their lives *but* paid work and children. The first thing to go is housework. According to John P. Robinson, a sociologist at the University of Maryland, between 1965 and 1985, working mothers reduced the amount of housework they did from 27 hours a week to 20. In the mid-1960s; for example, the average dinner took two-and-a-half hours to prepare; today, it's ready in 15 minutes, according to a survey by grocery manufacturers (Walsh). But cookie-baking nostalgia aside, the shift to fast food has not destroyed the family or displaced that ritual marker of togetherness, the family dinner. In a 1998 survey two-thirds of all American families claimed that they managed to eat dinner together at least five nights a week, and an additional 23 percent said they ate together three or four times a week (Sagan).[13] So what if it is over pizza or at McDonald's?

The other incredibly shrinking thing in working mothers' lives is leisure. Women are protecting their children from a parental "time famine" by subjecting themselves to a "time crunch." Their grueling schedules explain why so many eventually decide to give up their paychecks, if they can afford to. It may be the only way they can get a good night's sleep.[14]

In intensive interviews, with 37 mothers who were working full-time in a California hospital, sociologist Anita Garey (1998) found that some were getting only three-and-a-half to four-and-a-half hours of sleep. "I'd say most were getting five or six hours a night," Garey told me in a telephone interview. "Sleep—not their children—is what they are giving up directly, along with couple's time…. The toll is tremendous."[15]

The root problem here is not the working mother, but the triumph of "turbo-capitalism," which has brought with it a steadily lengthening workday for white-collar employees and managers.[16] By the year 2000, Americans had the heaviest workload in the industrialized world, including Japan. There is no question that this speedup is putting unbearable pressure on conscientious parents, reflected in poll after poll, with both men and women calling for a shorter work week.[17]

The pressures are obviously greatest on single mothers. Almost 27 percent of American children are in families headed by a lone parent, usually a mother. A University of Michigan survey found that preteen children living with single mothers spent twelve to fourteen fewer hours week with parents than children living with married parents (Hofferth forthcoming; cited in Sandberg and Hofferth). When a 1995 *Washington Post* poll asked 702 randomly selected teenagers, "Do your parents spend too much time or too little time with you?" only 26 percent of those with married parents said too little time. Even more—30 percent—said their parents spent too much time with them. But half of the kids whose parents were divorced said they had too little time with their parents, and only 18 percent felt they spent too much time (*Washington Post*). Children report that the parent who is in truly short supply is the father, whether their parents are married or single, whether their mothers work or not. According to demographer Cheryl Russell, most children "say they spend enough time with their mothers. Most say their mothers 'almost never' miss events and activities important to them. In contrast, most children say their fathers 'frequently' or 'sometimes' miss important events. Many children say they would like to spend more time their fathers" (114). For teenagers, according to a study by the National Center on Addiction and Substance Abuse, "a bad relationship with fathers is so much more common than with mothers…. It's much rarer for moms to be absent or distant" (Walsh).[18]

Where Are the Fathers?

The mirror image of the myth that "mothers have flown the coop" is the myth that fathers are becoming equal parents. Many feminists want to believe this, because they want to think that traditional gender roles are being eliminated. Corporations want to believe it, because they want to assume that all their employees can be worked as if work were all there is to life. And men themselves are not averse to taking credit for turning over a new leaf. Thus the politically correct term for child-rearing is "parenting"—neatly disguising the fact that the mothers are doing most of the work. And a father's every paternal gesture is interpreted as a sign of the long-awaited new man. But wishing won't make it so, and for the most part, it isn't.

Almost everyone agrees that men. Are doing more housework and childcare than their own fathers did, particularly in households where the wife earns a hefty part of the family income. There is also good evidence that married fathers are spending almost as much time with their children on weekends as mothers do, taking them to sporting events and other outside activities (Yeung *et al.* 20-21).[19]

But the fact remains, as one recent study put it, "despite an overall increase in the relative involvement of fathers, household activities, caring for infants, studying and reading (with children) remain domains in which fathers have a very low relative contribution" (Yeung *et al.* 20). In the relatively rare households where the mother is the bigger breadwinner, mothers still spend more than thirteen hours a week more than fathers on childcare and household chores. This doesn't jibe with any theory about rational economic behavior. "The puzzling thing for an economist," says Richard Freeman, a Harvard economist, "is if her hourly earnings are higher than his, she should be the one who works more hours outside the home, and he should do more of the work in the home. And that isn't happening."[20]

Even when a wife earns more than half of the family income, the husband will typically contribute no more than 30 percent of the domestic services and childcare. And that estimate comes from surveys based on men's own statements about their family contributions, surveys that experts agree are biased on the upside. Even if a married man becomes unemployed, his proportion of housework and childcare almost never exceeds 30 percent. By contrast, when a married woman becomes unemployed, the percentage of domestic work she does averages 75 percent. "Our data shows that there is not a true gift exchange in marriage," economist George Akerlof told me. "Although there is a lot of variation, between most spouses there is not complete reciprocity."[21]

The care of babies and toddlers is still clearly a female monopoly. In families with preschool children, mothers appear to be putting in roughly three to four *times* as many hours as fathers. One study of 37 families of young children, representing various classes, races, and work patterns, found that the man rarely had primary responsibility for any *single* child-rearing duty. In *no* household did a father take responsibility for *all* child-rearing tasks (Hays 99-100).[22]

Before the arrival of the first child, couples tend to share the housework fairly equally. But something about a baby encourages the resurgence of gender roles. One woman who worked in advertising before she became a stay-at-home mother of two described the dynamic. "My husband used to shop, put something in the oven…. When you're both, out there all day, you're in it together. Once the children arrived, however, things changed. He works all week, and on the weekends he wants to relax. I'll have a list of five or six things I want him to do, but he wants to relax, watch sports on TV…. The baby will throw food on the floor, and even when he's sitting right there, I'll have to pick it up, put it away, take her away, put her to bed."

She remembers the moment when they started to play the "where" game:

> She: "Would you set the table?"
> He: "Where are the napkins?"
> She: "We've lived in the same house for twelve years and they're where they've always been."

Whether they work full-time, part-time, or not at all outside the home, mothers are much more willing to do what has to be done for children. Maryland psychotherapist Leah Steinberg told me, "In all my years of practice I've never had a man come into my office and say 'I need to cut back; I need to work part-time.' Women say this all the time." It is most often Mom who drops everything and runs if a child has an accident. Working mothers are more likely than working fathers to take time off to care for a sick child, resulting in far higher absentee rates. During an average week in 1989, full-time working mothers who were married and had a child under age six had more than double the average rate of absenteeism. Married fathers with preschoolers were well below the average (Meisenheimer II).

Mothers, working or not, go to more teacher conferences, attend more school meetings, and volunteer at school events more often than fathers. They even make up one-third of Little League softball coaches.[23] At a luncheon at my son's school for active parent volunteers, I counted three men in a roomful of roughly 50 women. At another parent meeting, it was a dozen mothers and three fathers—a typical ratio.

Mothers run the errands. Nationwide, working mothers of young children run more than twice as many errands on their way home from work as fathers do. A survey in Washington, D.C., found that women stopped at schools and daycare centers twice as often as men on the commute from work and were more likely to detour for errands. Men were twice as likely to go to a bar or restaurant ("Women's Commutes Often More Complicated").[24]

Despite the media's fondness for Mr. Mom, he remains an aberration. Of the 20.5 million American children under the age of five, only about 320,000 have fathers as their primary guardian-a minuscule 1.5 per cent (Casper; see also Nakamura). Recently, more *single* men have been living with children, often teenage sons. But single fathers are more likely than single mothers to have someone else in the household who helps with or actually provides the childcare. "Most are men living with women, such as their own mothers," says sociologist Andrew Cherlin, "and they're doing the real care for the children."

In 1994, 73 percent of men and women polled said taking care of the kids was the woman's primary responsibility, along with the cooking (80 percent), the grocery shopping (79 percent), the laundry (80 percent), the house-cleaning (76 percent), and the dishes (73 percent). Of all the household chores, men took primary responsibility for only one: deciding how the money would be spent (55 percent).[25]

***

Years ago, Gloria Steinem approvingly observed that, "we've become the men we wanted to marry." She meant that women no longer have to look to a man to fulfill their dreams of accomplishment or economic security; they can achieve these things themselves. This is true, but only if a woman decides not to have children. With the arrival of a child, a mother's definition of accomplishment becomes more complex, her workload goes up, and her income and independence go down. For all the changes of the last decades, one thing has stayed the same: it is still women who adjust their lives to accommodate the needs of children; who do what is necessary to make a home; who forgo status, income, advancement, and independence. Nowhere is this mote dramatically illustrated than in the experience of the nation's most educated women—ones who had the best shot at having it all.

Notes

[1]In no known human culture have males ever had the primary task of rearing small children. According to two preeminent scholars of children's history, one of the few things that can be said with certainty, amid the "extraordinary variety" in the historical "treatment of children," is that, "the vast majority of human infants have been and continue to be cared for primarily by females" (Hiner and Hawes 6). If this ever changed, writes Marion J. Levy, a sociologist at Princeton University, the implications would be more radical than the discovery of fire, the invention of agriculture, or the switch from animate to inanimate sources of power (xix, 20-23).

[2]Occupational data: was supplied by Steve Hipple of the Division of Labor Statistics, Bureau of Labor Statistics, March 6,2000.

[3]Unpublished data from the March 1999 Current Population Survey, provided by Steve Hipple.

[4]Female university graduates' labor force participation rates were provided by Agneta Stark, an economist at the University of Stockholm, during an interview in August 1997, in Stockholm.

[5]The 80 percent figure is in Trapp, Hermanson and Carcello. The 64 percent figure comes from Charles' Rodgers of Rodgers and Associates, Cambridge, Massachusetts, the consulting firm that conducted the survey. Still another recent survey found that only 39 percent of male M.B.A. graduates had full-time working wives. In contrast, 89 percent of female M.B.A.s have spouses who work full-time. See "Women and the MBA: Gateway to Opportunity."

[6]An even greater percentage of mothers of younger children are at home. In 1999, a little more than 40 percent of married women with children under age six were employed full-time, 20 percent worked part-time, and 38 percent were not employed at all. In only a little more than one-third (37.3 percent) of two-parent families with school-age children both parents are employed full-time, year-round. These statistics were provided by Steve Hipple of the Bureau of Labor Statistics.

[7]More than two million American women work in a home-based business. They average 23 hours of work (in the business) a week.

[8]Deborah Fallows made this comment during a panel discussion at the Harvard/Radcliffe twenty-fifth reunion in 1996, attended by the author (Council of Economic Advisers 4).

[9]The sensational statistic first appeared in an article by William R. Mattox, Jr., who was then at the Family Research Council, a right-wing group whose stated mission includes "promot[ing] and defend[ing] traditional family values in print." In the winter 1991 issue of *Policy Review*, a publication of the Heritage Foundation, Mattox warned that "the biggest problem facing American children today is lack of time with and attention from their parents." As his principal evidence he cited an alleged 40 percent decline between 1965 and 1985, based on a reading of data produced by John Robinson, a preeminent authority on how Americans use their time. Robinson later claimed that he had made a mistake, and that his 1985 numbers were in error, thus invalidating the 40 percent decline. For a discussion of this controversy see Whitman; Mattox (1996).

When I contacted Robinson in 1996, he was still furious over what he characterized as the "misuse of social science data by the family values groups. They take data out of context and use it to promote their narrow point of view." Robinson believes that exaggerated reports of a parental "time famine" are based on a willful misinterpretation of data by ideologues whose "agenda is to get women back into the home." When I contacted Mattox, he was still wondering whether Robinson's numbers had really been incorrect.

[10]Hays's observations have been corroborated by data from the 1997 National Study of the Changing Workforce, revealing that women with relatively high wages actually spend *more* time in childcare than women with relatively low wages. See Freeman (16).

[11]Married working mothers spend only about *three* fewer hours a week directly engaged with each child; that is, reading, playing, cooking, bathing, dressing, and so on (Hofferth).

[12]In one nationwide study of white married couples in the United States, the average workweek of the mother was 87 hours; in a different study, it ranged from 76 to 89 hours, depending on the age of the oldest child (Schor 20-21, 37).

A study at two high-tech companies in New England found that the average working mother had a total workweek of 84 hours, compared with 72 hours for working fathers and about 50 hours for married men and women with no children (Rodgers 1989: 125).

Studies in Canada have come up with an even greater leisure gap. The 1992 General Social Survey in Canada, which took into account both work in the home and paid work, found that married mothers worked on average *106.9 hours per week,* 21 hours more than fathers (Woolley 4).

[13]It is possible that this survey; of more than 1,000 families by National Family Opinion Research, overstated the family dining experience. Many parents might be reluctant to tell a strange interviewer that, "we don't have time to eat together more than once a week."

[14]In 1998, employed mothers reported having six hours a week less sleep than nonemployed mothers (55 hours compared with 61 hours) and significantly less free time (29 hours per week versus 41 hours) (Bianchi 16).

[15]Garey, an assistant professor of sociology at the University of New Hampshire, based her findings on interviews with women working in predominantly female positions, that is, nurses, nurses' aides, clerical workers, and administrative staff. The results are found in her book *Weaving Work and Motherhood* (1999).

[16]For all workers between the ,ages of 25 and 54, the average number of hours worked rose to 1,980 a year in 1995, from a post-World War II low of 1,840 hours in 1982. The number of people working extremely long hours—49 or more a week—has risen by as much as 37 percent since 1985.

[17]In a nationwide survey of 2,011 American adults, conducted in 1999 by Peter Hart and Robert Teeter for the *Wall Street Journal,* fully 83 percent said that" lack of involvement in their children's lives is a "very serious problem" facing society. In another survey, in 1997, by the Families and Work Institute, 70 percent of parents reported they didn't have enough time to spend with their children, period.

[18]In a *Newsweek* survey, 85 percent of teens said their mom cared "very much" about them; 58 percent said Dad cared "very much" (Kantrovitz and Winegert 39).

[19]These findings are based on 24-hour time diaries with a higher degree of accuracy than time-use data collected by other methods. The diaries were collected in two nationally representative surveys of the American population—the 1997 *Child Development Supplement* to the *Panel Study of Income Dynamics and The Time Use Longitudinal Panel Study, 1975-1981.* University of Michigan researchers analyzing these . data found that in 1997 married fathers' direct engagement with pre-teenage children on weekdays (one hour and thirteen minutes) was 67 percent that of mothers' and on weekends (3.3 hours) was 87 percent of mothers.'

Researchers have learned that men are also doing more at home· in Australia, Britain, the Netherlands, and all the Scandinavian countries. In Britain, the Netherlands, and Denmark, for example, men's share of housework, including childcare, increased from around one-quarter in the 1960s or early 1970s to 35 to 40 percent by the late 1980s, according to British economist Heather Joshi (see Bianchi 24). Nevertheless, in Australia, a 1992 survey found that men provided only 22 percent of the direct care of children (Ironmonger).

[20]Freeman's analysis is based on data derived from the 1997 National Study of the Changing Workforce.

[21]These findings will appear in George Akerlof and Rachel E.. Knorton, "Economics and Identity," *Quarterly Journal of Economics,* forthcoming. See also Gershuny,

Gordon, and Jones (185-86).

[22]The mothers in this study spent on average four times the hours the fathers did on childcare: 8.9 hours a day vs. 1.9 hours. Also see Ishii-Kuntz and Coltrane; Zick and Bryant (260).

[23]The 1996 National Household Education Survey found that 41 percent of mothers, and only 15 percent of fathers, volunteered at school. Survey findings reported by Rubenstein.

[24]The survey in Washington, D.C., was conducted by the Metropolitan Washington Council of Governments.

[25]This 1994 poll was conducted by *Yankelovitch Monitor*.

References

Akerlof, George. Personal communication. December 9, 1997.

Bianchi, Suzanne M. "Maternal Employment and Time with Children: Dramatic Change or Surprising Continuity?" 2000 Presidential address, Population Association of America, revised June 2000.

Leibowitz, Arleen. "Education and Home Production." *American Economic Association* 64 (2) (May 1974): 250.

Bryant, W. K. and C. D. Zick. "Are We Investing Less in the Next Generation? Historical Trends in Time Spent Caring for Children." *Journal of Family and Economic Issues* 17 (3/4) (Winter 1996): 365-91

See also Council of Economic Advisers, *Families and the Labor Market*, p. 13.

Casper, Lynne, Census Bureau. Personal communication. June 13, 1996.

Council of Economic Advisers. *Families and the Labor Market, 1969-1999: Analyzing the "Time Crunch."* Washington, DC, 1999.

Freeman, Richard B. "The Feminization of Work in the U.S.: A New Era for (Man)kind?" National Bureau of Economic Research, unpublished paper, 1999.

Garey, Anita. Telephone interview. December 11, 1998.

Garey, Anita. *Weaving Work and Motherhood*. Philadelphia: Temple University Press, 1999.

Gershuny, Jonathan, Michael Gordon, and Sally Jones. "The Domestic Labor Revolution: A Process of Lagged Adaptation?" *The Social and Political Economy of the Household*. New York: Oxford University Press, 1994.

Hays, Sharon. *The Cultural Contradictions of Motherhood*. New Haven: Yale University Press, 1996.

Hiner, N. Roy and Joseph M. Hawes. *Children in Historical and Comparative Perspective*. New York: Greenwood Press, 1991.

Hofferth, Sandra. Personal communication. June 2000.

Ironmonger, Duncan. "Counting Outputs, Capital Inputs, and Caring Labor: Estimating Gross Household Product." *Feminist Economics* 2 (3) (Fall 1996): 55-56.

Ishii-Kuntz, Masako and Scott Coltrane. "Predicting the Sharing of Household

Labor: Are Parenting and Housework Distinct?" *Sociological Perspectives* 35 (4) (1992): 629-47.

Kantrovitz, Barbara and Pat Winegert. "How Well Do You Know Your Kids?" *Newsweek* May 10, 1999.

Levy, Marion J. Jr. *Maternal Influence*. New Brunswick, NJ: Transaction Publishers, 1992.

Mattox, William R. Jr. "The Parent Trap." *Policy Review* 55 (Winter 1991): 6-14.

Mattox, William R. Jr. Letter. "It's Not a Myth." *Policy Review* (September-October 1996): 3.

Meisenheimer II, Joseph R. "Employee Absences in 1989: A New Look at Data from the CPS." *Monthly Labor Review* (August 1990): 28-33.

Nakamura, David. "Dads Who Rock the Cradle." *Washington Post* March 16, 1999.

Robinson, John P. "Who's Doing the Housework?" *American Demographics* (December 1988, reprint, 1993): 30-31.

Walsh, Sharon. "Hosts Around Nation Thankful for Takeout." *Washington Post* November 26,1998.

Rodgers, Charles. Personal communication. October 1994.

Rodgers, Fran Sussner. "Business and the Facts of Family Life." *Harvard Business Review* (November-December 1989).

Rubenstein, Carin. "Superdad Needs a Reality Check." *New York Times* April 16, 1998.

Russell, Cheryl. *The Master Trend*. New York: Plenum Press, 1993.

Sagan, Candy. "Dinner TIME." *Washington Post* March 3, 1999.

Sandberg, John F. and Sandra L. Hofferth. "Changes in Children's Time with Parents, U.S., 1981-1997." Unpublished paper, Population Studies Center, University of Michigan, April 2000.

Schor, Juliet B. *The Overworked American.* New York: Basic Books, 1992.

Trapp, Michael W., Roger H. Hermanson, and Joseph V. Carcello. "Characteristics of Chief Financial Officers." *Corporate Growth Report* 9 (1991): 17-20.

Uchitelle, Louis. "As Labor Supply Shrinks, a New Supply Is Tapped." *New York Times* December 20,1999.

Walsh, Edward. "Drug Use Tied to Father's Role." *Washington Post* August 31, 1999.

Washington Post December 14,1995.

Whitman, David. "The Myth of AWOL Parents." *U.S. News and World Report* July 1,1996: 54-56.

Woolley, Frances. *Research Notes: The Social Security Review and Its Implications for Women.* Canadian Advisory Council on the Status of Women, November 1994.

"Women's Commutes Often More Complicated." *Washington Post* March 3, 1999.

"Women and the MBA: Gateway to Opportunity." Report released by Catalyst, New York, May 2000.

Yeung, W. Jean, John F. Sandberg, Pamela E. Davis-Kean, and Sandra Hofferth. "Children's Time with Fathers in Intact Families." Unpublished paper, University of Michigan, March 1998 (revised September 1999). pp. 20-21.

Zick, Cathleen D. and W Keith Bryant. "A New Look at Parents' Time Spent in Childcare: Primary and Secondary Time Use." *Social Science Research* 25 (1996).

Chapter 37

The New Momism

SUSAN J. DOUGLAS AND MEREDITH W. MICHAELS

IT'S 5:22 P.M. You're in the grocery checkout line. Your three-year-old is writhing on the floor, screaming, because you have refused to buy her a Teletubby pinwheel. Your six-year-old is whining, repeatedly, in a voice that could saw through cement, "But mommy, puleeze, puleeze" because you have not bought him the latest "Lunchables," which features, as the four food groups, Cheetos, a Snickers, Cheez Whiz, and Twizzlers. Your teenager, who has not spoken a single word in the past four days except, "You've ruined my life," followed by "Everyone else has one," is out in the car, sulking, with the new rap-metal band Piss on the Parentals blasting through the headphones of a Discman.

To distract yourself, and to avoid the glares of other shoppers who have already deemed you the worst mother in America, you leaf through *People* (1998) magazine. Inside, Uma Thurman gushes "Motherhood Is Sexy." Moving on to *Good Housekeeping,* Vanna White says of her child, "When I hear his cry at six-thirty in the morning, I have a smile on my face, and I'm not an early riser." Another unexpected source of earth-mother wisdom, the newly maternal Pamela Lee, also confides to *People* (1996), "I just love getting up with him in the middle of the night to feed him or soothe him." Brought back to reality by stereophonic whining, you indeed feel as sexy as Rush Limbaugh in a thong.

You drag your sorry ass home. Now, if you were a "good" mom, you'd joyfully empty the shopping bags and transform the process of putting the groceries away into a fun game your kids love to play (upbeat Raffi songs would provide a lilting soundtrack). Then, while you steamed: he broccoli and poached the chicken breasts in Vouvray and Evian water, *you* and the kids would also be doing jigsaw puzzles in the shape of the United Arab Emirates so they learned some geography. Your cheerful teenager would say, "Gee, Mom, you gave me the best advice on that last homework assignment." When your husband arrives, he is so overcome with admiration for how well you do it all that he looks lovingly into your eyes, kisses you, and presents you with a diamond anniversary bracelet. He then announces that he has gone on flex time for the next two years so that he can split childcare duties with you fifty-fifty. The children, chattering away happily, help set the table, and then eat their broccoli. After dinner you all go out and stencil the driveway with autumn leaves.

But maybe this sounds slightly more familiar. "I won't unpack the groceries! You can't make me," bellows your child as he runs to his room, knocking down a lamp on the way. "Eewee-gross out!" he yells and you discover that the cat has barfed on his bed. You have fifteen minutes to make dinner because there's a school play in half an hour. While the children fight over whether to watch *Hot Couples* or people eating larvae on *Fear Factor*, you zap some Prego spaghetti sauce in the microwave and boil some pasta. *You* set the table. "Mommy, Mommy, Sam losted my hamster," your daughter wails. Your ex-husband calls to say he won't be taking the kids this weekend after all because his new wife, Buffy, twenty-three, has to go on a modeling shoot in Virgin Gorda for the *Sports Illustrated* swimsuit issue, and "she really needs me with her." You go to the TV room to discover the kids watching transvestites punching each other out on *Jerry Springer*. The pasta boils over and scalds the hamster, now lying prostrate on the floor with its legs twitching in the air. "Get your butts in here this instant or I'll murder you immediately," you shriek, by way of inviting your children to dinner. "I hate this pasta—I only like the kind shaped like wagon wheels!" "Mommy, you killded my hamster!"

If you're like us—mothers with an attitude problem—you may be getting increasingly irritable about this chasm between the ridiculous, honey-hued ideals of perfect motherhood in the mass media and the reality of mothers' everyday lives. And you may also be worn down by media images that suggest that however much you do for and love your kids, it is never enough. The love we feel for our kids, the joyful times we have with them, are repackaged into unattainable images of infinite patience and constant adoration so that we fear, as Kristin van Ogtrop put it movingly in *The Bitch in the House*, "I will love my children, but my love for them will always be imperfect" (169).

From the moment we get up until the moment we collapse in bed at night, the media are out there, calling to us, yelling, "Hey you! Yeah, you! Are you *really* raising your kids right?" Whether it's the cover of *Redbook* or *Parents* demanding "Are You a Sensitive Mother?" "Is Your Child Eating Enough?" "Is Your Baby Normal?" (and exhorting us to enter its pages and have great sex at 25, 35, or 85), the nightly news warning us about missing children, a movie trailer hyping a film about a cross-dressing dad who's way more fun than his stinky, careerist wife *(Mrs. Doubtfire)*, or Dr. Laura telling some poor mother who works four hours a week that she's neglectful, the siren song blending seduction and accusation is there all the time. Mothers are subjected to an onslaught of beatific imagery, romantic fantasies, self-righteous sermons, psychological warnings, terrifying movies about losing their children, even more terrifying news stories about abducted and abused children, and totally unrealistic advice about how to be the most perfect and revered mom in the neighborhood, maybe even in the whole country. (Even *Working Mother*—which should have known better—had a "Working Mother of the Year Contest." When Jill Kirschenbaum became the editor in 2001, one of the first things she did was dump this feature, noting that motherhood should not be a "competitive sport.") We are urged to be fun-loving, spontaneous, and relaxed, yet, at the same time, scared out of our minds that our kids could be killed at any moment. No wonder 81 percent of women in a recent poll said it's harder to be a mother now than it was twenty or thirty years ago, and 56 percent felt mothers were doing a worse job today than mothers back *then* ("Motherhood Today—A Tougher Job, Less Ably Done"). Even mothers who deliberately avoid TV and magazines, or who pride themselves on seeing through them, have trouble escaping the standards of perfection, and the sense of threat, that the media ceaselessly atomize into the air we breathe.

We are both mothers, and we adore our kids-for example, neither one of us has ever locked them up in dog crates in the basement (although we have, of course, been tempted). The smell of a new baby's head, tucking a child in at night, receiving homemade, hand-scrawled birthday cards, heart-to-hearts with a teenager after a date, seeing *them* become parents-these are joys parents treasure. But like increasing numbers of women, we are fed up with the myth-shamelessly hawked by the media-that motherhood is eternally fulfilling and rewarding, that it is *always* the best and most important thing you do, that there is only a narrowly prescribed way to do it right, and that if you don't love each and every second of it there's something really wrong with you. At the same time, the two of us still have been complete suckers, buying those black-and-white mobiles that allegedly turn your baby into Einstein Jr., feeling guilty for sending in store-bought cookies to the class bake sale instead of homemade like the "good" moms, staying up until 2:30 A.M. making our kids' Halloween costumes, driving to the Multiplex 18 at midnight to pick up teenagers so they won't miss the latest outing with their friends. We know that building a scale model of Versailles out of mashed potatoes may not be quite as crucial to good mothering as *Martha Stewart Living* suggests. Yet here we are, cowed by that most tyrannical of our cultural icons, Perfect Mom. So, like millions of women, we buy into these absurd ideals at the same time that we resent them and think they are utterly ridiculous and oppressive. After all, our parents—the group Tom Brokaw has labeled "the greatest generation"—had parents who whooped them on the behind, screamed stuff at them like "I'll tear you limb from limb," told them babies came from cabbage patches, never drove them four hours to a soccer match, and yet they seemed to have nonetheless saved the western world.

This book is about the rise in the media of what we are calling the "new momism": the insistence that no woman is truly complete or fulfilled unless she has kids, that women remain the best primary caretakers of children, and that to be a remotely decent mother, a woman has to devote her entire physical, psychological, emotional, and intellectual being, 24/7, to her children. The new momism is a highly romanticized and yet demanding view of motherhood in which the standards for success are impossible to meet. The term "momism" was initially coined by the journalist Philip Wylie in his highly influential 1942 bestseller *Generation of Vipers,* and it was a very derogatory term. Drawing from Freud (who else?), Wylie attacked the mothers of America as being so smothering, overprotective, and invested in their kids, especially their sons, that they turned them into dysfunctional, sniveling weaklings, maternal slaves chained to the apron strings, unable to fight for their country or even stand on their own two feet.[1] We seek to reclaim this term, rip it from its misogynistic origins, and apply it to an ideology that has snowballed since the 1980s and seeks to return women to the Stone Age.

The "new momism" is a set of ideals, norms, and practices, most frequently and powerfully represented in the media, that seem on the surface to celebrate motherhood, but which in reality promulgate standards of perfection that are beyond your reach. The new momism is the direct descendant and latest version of what Betty Friedan famously labeled the "feminine mystique" back in the 1960s. The new momism *seems* to be much more hip and progressive than the feminine mystique, because now, of course, mothers can and do work outside the home, have their own ambitions and money, raise kids on their own, or freely choose to stay at home with their kids rather than being forced to. And unlike the feminine mystique, the notion that women should be subservient to men is not an accepted tenet of the new momism. Central to the new momism, in fact, is the feminist insistence that woman have choices, that they are active agents in control of their own destiny, that they have autonomy. But here's where the distortion of feminism occurs. The only truly enlightened choice to make as a woman, the one that proves, first, that you are a "real" woman, and second, that you are a decent, worthy one, is to become a "mom" and to bring to child rearing a combination of selflessness and professionalism that would involve the cross cloning of Mother Teresa with Donna Shalala. Thus the new momism is deeply contradictory: It both draws from and repudiates feminism.

The fulcrum of the new momism is the rise of a really pernicious ideal in the late twentieth century that the sociologist Sharon Hays has perfectly labeled "intensive mothering" (4).[2] It is no longer okay, as it was even during the heyday of June Cleaver, to let (or make) your kids walk to school, tell them to stop bugging you and go outside and play, or, God forbid, serve them something like Tang, once the preferred beverage of the astronauts, for breakfast. Of course many of our mothers baked us cookies, served as Brownie troop leaders, and chaperoned class trips to Elf Land. But today, the standards of good motherhood are really over the top. And they've gone through the roof at the same time that there has been a real decline in leisure time for most Americans.[3] The yuppie work ethic of the 1980s, which insisted that even when you were off the job you should be working-on your abs, your connections, your portfolio, whatever-absolutely conquered motherhood. As the actress Patricia Heaton jokes in *Motherhood and Hollywood*, now mothers are supposed to "sneak echinacea" into the "freshly squeezed, organically grown orange juice" we've made for our kids and teach them to "download research for their kindergarten report on 'My Family Tree—The Early Roman Years'" (48-49).

Intensive mothering insists that mothers acquire professional-level skills such as those of a therapist, pediatrician ("Dr. Mom"), consumer products safety inspector, and teacher, and that they lavish every ounce of physical vitality they have, the monetary equivalent of the gross domestic product of Australia, and, most of all, every single bit of their emotional, mental, and psychic energy on their kids. We must learn to put on the masquerade of the doting, self-sacrificing mother and wear it at all times. With intensive mothering, everyone watches us, we watch ourselves and other mothers, and we watch ourselves watching ourselves. How many of you know someone who swatted her child on the behind in a supermarket because he was, say, opening a pack of razor blades in the toiletries aisle, only to be accosted by someone she never met who threatened to put her up on child-abuse charges? In 1997, one mother was arrested for child neglect because she left a ten-year-old and a four-year-old home for an hour-and-a-half while she went to the supermarket.[4] Motherhood has become a psychological police state.

Intensive mothering is the ultimate female Olympics: We are all in powerful competition with each other, in constant danger of being trumped by the mom down the street, or in the magazine we're reading. The competition isn't just over who's a good mother-it's over who's the best. We compete with each other; we compete with ourselves. The best mothers always put their kids' needs before their own, period. The best mothers are the main caregivers. For the best mothers, their kids are the center of the universe. The best mothers always smile. They always understand. They are never tired. They never lose their temper. They never say, "Go to the neighbor's house and play while Mommy has a beer." Their love for their children is boundless, unflagging, flawless, total. Mothers today cannot just respond to their kids' needs, they must predict them-and with the telepathic accuracy of Houdini. They must memorize verbatim the books of all the child-care experts and know which approaches are developmentally appropriate at different ages. They are supposed to treat their two-year-olds with "respect." If mothers screw up and fail to do this on any given day, they should apologize to their kids, because any misstep leads to permanent psychological and/or physical damage. Anyone who questions whether this is *the* best and *the* necessary way to raise kids is an insensitive, ignorant brute. This is just common sense, right (Hays 4-9)?

The new momism has become unavoidable, unless you raise your kids in a yurt on the tundra, for one basic reason: Motherhood became one of the biggest media obsessions of the last three decades, exploding especially in the mid-1980s and continuing unabated to the present. Women have been deluged by an ever-thickening mudslide of maternal media advice, programming, and marketing that powerfully shapes how we mothers feel about our relationships with our own kids and, indeed, how we feel about ourselves. These media representations have changed over time, cutting mothers some real slack in the 1970s, and then increasingly closing the vise in the late 1980s and after, despite important rebellions by Roseanne and others. People don't usually notice that motherhood has been such a major media fixation, revolted or hooked as they've been over the years by other media excesses like the O. J. Simpson trials, the Lewinsky-Clinton imbroglio, the Elian Gonzalez carnival, *Survivor,* or the 2002 Washington-area sniper killings in which "profilers" who knew as much as SpongeBob SquarePants nonetheless got on TV to tell us what the killer was thinking.

But make no mistake about it-mothers and motherhood came under unprec-edented media surveillance in the 1980s and beyond. And since the media traffic in extremes, in anomalies-the rich, the deviant, the exemplary, the criminal, the gorgeous-they emphasize fear and dread on the one hand and promote impos-sible ideals on the other. In the process, *Good Housekeeping, People, E!, Lifetime, Entertainment Tonight,* and *NBC Nightly News* built an interlocking, cumulative image of the dedicated, doting "mom" versus the delinquent, bad "mother." There have been, since the early 1980s, several overlapping media frameworks that have fueled the new momism. First, the media warned mothers about the external threats to their kids from abductors and the like. Then the "family values" crowd made it clear that supporting the family was not part of the government's responsibility. By the late 1980s, stories about welfare and crack mothers empha-sized the internal threats to children from mothers themselves. And finally, the media brouhaha over the "Mommy Track" reaffirmed that businesses could not or would not budge much to accommodate the care of children. Together, and over time, these frameworks produced a prevailing common sense that only you, the individual mother, are responsible for your child's welfare: The buck stops with you, period, and you'd better be a superstar.

Of course there has been a revolution in fatherhood over the past 30 years, and millions of men today tend to the details of child rearing in ways their own fathers rarely did. Feminism prompted women to insist that men change diapers and pack school lunches, but it also gave men permission to become more involved with their kids in ways they have found to be deeply satisfying. And between images of cuddly, New Age dads with babies asleep on their chests (think old Folger's ads), movies about hunky men and a baby (or clueless ones who shrink the kids), and sensational news stories about "deadbeat dads" and men who beat up their sons' hockey coaches, fathers too have been subject to a media "dad patrol." But it pales in comparison to the new momism. After all, a dad who knows the name of his kids' pediatrician and reads them stories at night is still regarded as a saint; a mother who doesn't is a sinner.

Once you identify it, you see the new momism everywhere. The recent spate of magazines for "parents" (i.e., mothers) bombard the anxiety-induced mothers of America with reassurances that they can (after a $100,000 raise and a personality transplant) produce bright, motivated, focused, fun-loving, sensitive, coopera-tive, confident, contented kids just like the clean, obedient ones on the cover. The frenzied hypernatalism of the women's magazines alone (and that includes *People, Us,* and *In Style),* with their endless parade of perfect, "sexy" celebrity moms who've had babies, adopted babies, been to sperm banks, frozen their eggs for future use, hatched the frozen eggs, had more babies, or adopted a small Tibetan village, all to satisfy their "baby lust," is enough to make you want to get your tubes tied. (These profiles always insist that celebs all love being "moms" much, much more than they do their work, let alone being rich and famous, and that they'd spend every second with their kids if they didn't have that pesky blockbuster movie to finish.) Women without children, wherever they look, are besieged by ridiculously romantic images that insist that having children is the most joyous, fulfilling experience in the galaxy, and if they don't have a small drooling creature who likes to stick forks in electrical outlets, they are leading bankrupt, empty lives. Images of ideal moms and their miracle babies are everywhere, like leeches in the Amazon, impossible to dislodge and sucking us dry.

There is also the ceaseless outpouring of books on toilet training, separating one sibling's fist from another sibling's eye socket, expressing breast milk while reading a legal brief, helping preschoolers to "own" their feelings, getting Joshua to do his homework, and raising teenage boys so they become Sensitive New Age Guys instead of rooftop snipers or Chippendale dancers. Over eight hundred books on motherhood were published between 1970 and 2000; only twenty-seven of these came out between 1970 and 1980, so the real avalanche happened in the past twenty years.[5] We've learned about the perils of "the hurried child" and "hyperparenting," in which we schedule our kids with so many enriching activities that they make the secretary of state look like a couch spud. But the unhurried child probably plays too much Nintendo and is out in the garage building pipe bombs, so you can't underschedule them either.

Then there's the Martha Stewartization of America, in which we are meant to sculpt the carrots we put in our kids' lunches into the shape of peonies and build funhouses for them in the backyard; this has raised the bar to even more ridiculous levels than during the June Cleaver era. Most women know that there was a massive public relations campaign during World War II to get women into the workforce, and then one right after the war to get them to go back to the kitchen. But we haven't fully focused on the fact that another, more subtle, sometimes unintentional, more long-term propaganda campaign began in the 1980s to redomesticate the women of America through motherhood.[6] Why aren't all the mothers of America leaning out their windows yelling "I'm mad as hell and I'm not going to take it anymore"?

So the real question is how did the new momism—especially in the wake of the women's movement—become part of our national common sense? Why have mothers-who have entered the workforce in droves at exactly the same time that intensive mothering conquered notions of parenting-bought into it? Are there millions of us who conform to the ideals of the new momism on the outside, while also harboring powerful desires for rebellion that simply can't be satisfied by a ten-minute aroma therapy soak in the bathtub?

There are several reasons why the new momism-talk about the wrong idea for the wrong time-triumphed when it did. Baby boom women who, in the 1970s, sought to enter schools and jobs previously reserved for men knew they couldn't be just as good as the guys-they had to be better, in part to dispel the myths that women were too stupid, irrational, hysterical, weak, flighty, or unpredictable during "that time of the month" to manage a business, report the news, wear a stethoscope, or sell real estate. Being an overachiever simply went with the terrain of breaking down barriers, so it wouldn't be surprising to find these women bring-ing that same determination to motherhood. And some of us did get smacked around as kids, or had parents who crushed our confidence, and we did want to do a better job than that. One brick in the wall of the new momism.

Many women, who had started working in the 1970s and postponed having children, decided in the 1980s to have kids. Thus, this was a totally excellent time for the federal government to insist that it was way too expensive to support any programs for families and children (like maternity leave or subsidized, high-quality day care or even decent public schools) because then the U.S. couldn't afford that $320 billion appropriation to the Pentagon, which included money for those $1600 coffee makers and $600 toilet seats the military needed so badly in 1984 (Lekachman 118-121). (Imagine where we'd be today if the government had launched the equivalent of the G.I. bill for mothers in the 1980s!) Parents of baby boomers had seen money flow into America's schools because of the Sputnik scare that the Russkies were way ahead of the U.S. in science and technology; thus the sudden need to reacquaint American kids with a slide rule. Parents in the 1980s saw public schools hemorrhaging money. So the very institutions our mothers had been able to count on now needed massive CPR, while the prospect of any new ones was, we were told, out of the question. Guess who had to take up the slack? Another brick in the wall of the new momism.

The right wing of the Republican party-which controlled the White House from 1980 to 1992, crucial years in the evolution of motherhood-hated the women's movement and believed all women, with the possible exception of Phyllis Schlafly, should remain in the kitchen on their knees polishing their husband's shoes and golf clubs while teaching their kids that Darwin was a very bad man. (Unless the mothers were poor and black-those moms had to get back to work ASAP, because by staying home they were wrecking the country. But more on that later.) We saw, in the 1980s and beyond, the rise of what the historian Ruth Feldstein has called "mother-blaming," attacks on mothers for failing to raise physically and psychologically fit future citizens.[7] See, no one, not even Ronald Reagan, said explicitly to us, "The future and the destiny of the nation are in your hands, oh mothers of America. And you are screwing up." But that's what he meant. Because not only are mothers supposed to reproduce the nation biologically, we're also supposed to regenerate it culturally and morally. Even after the women's movement, mothers were still expected to be the primary socializers of children (Peterson). Not only were our individual kids' well-being our responsibility, but also the entire fate of the nation supposedly rested on our padded and milk-splotched shoulders. So women's own desires to be good parents, their realization that they now had to make up for collapsing institutions, and all that guilt-tripping about "family values" added many more bricks to the wall.

But we are especially interested in the role that the mass media played, often inadvertently, and often, mind you, in the name of *helping* mothers—in making the new momism a taken-for-granted, natural standard of how women should imagine their lives, conceive of fulfillment, arrange their priorities, and raise their kids. After all, the media have been and are the major dispenser of the ideals and norms surrounding motherhood: Millions of us have gone to the media for nuts-

and-bolts childrearing advice. Many of us, in fact, preferred media advice to the advice our mothers gave us. We didn't want to be like our mothers and many of us didn't want to raise our kids the way they raised us (although it turns out they did a pretty good job in the end).

Thus, beginning in the mid-1970s, working mothers became the most important thing you can become in the United States: a market. And they became a market just as niche marketing was exploding-the rise of cable channels, magazines like *Working Mother, Family Life, Child,* and *Twins,* all supported by advertisements geared specifically to the new, modern mother. Increased emphasis on child safety, from car seats to bicycle helmets, increased concerns about Johnny not being able to read, the recognition that mothers bought cars, watched the news, and maybe didn't want to tune into one TV show after the next about male detectives with a cockatoo or some other dumbass mascot saving hapless women-all contributed to new shows, ad campaigns, magazines, and TV news stories geared to mothers, especially affluent, upscale ones. Because of this sheer increase in output and target marketing, mothers were bombarded as never before by media constructions of the good mother. The good mother bought all this stuff to stimulate, protect, educate, and indulge her kids. She had to assemble it, install it, use it with her child, and protect her child from some of its features. As all this media fare sought to advise mothers, flatter them, warn them and, above all, sell to them, they collaborated in constructing, magnifying, and reinforcing the new momism.

Here's the rub about the new momism. It began to conquer our psyches just as mothers entered the workforce in record numbers, so those of us who work (and those of us who don't) are pulled between two rather powerful and contradictory cultural riptides: Be more doting and self-sacrificing at home than Bambi's mother, yet more achievement-oriented at work than Madeleine Albright.[8] The other set of values that took hold beginning in the 1980s was "free-market ideology": the notion that competition in "the marketplace" (which supposedly had the foresight and wisdom of Buddha) provided the best solutions to all social, political, and economic problems. So on the job we were—and are—supposed to be highly efficient, calculating, tough, judgmental and skeptical, competitive, and willing to do what it takes to promote ourselves, our organization, and beat out the other guys. Many work environments in the 1980s and '90s emphasized increased productivity and piled on more work, kids or no kids, because that's what "the market" demanded. Television shows offered us role models of the kind of tough broads who succeeded in this environment, from the unsmiling, take-no-prisoners District Attorney Joyce Davenport on *Hill Street Blues* to Judge Judy and the no-nonsense police lieutenant Anita Van Buren on *Law and Order.* So the competitive go-getter at work had to walk through the door at the end of the day and, poof, turn into Carol Brady: selfless doormat at home. No wonder some of us feel like Sybil when we get home: We have to move between these riptides on a daily basis. And, in fact, many of us want to be both women: successful at work, successful as mothers.

Now, here's the real beauty of this contorting contradiction. Both working mothers *and* stay-at-home mothers get to be failures. The ethos of intensive mothering has lower status in our culture ("stay-at-home mothers are boring"), but occupies a higher moral ground ("working mothers are neglectful") (Hays 9). So, welcome to the latest media catfight: the supposed war between working mothers and stay-at-home mothers. Why analyze all the ways in which our country has failed to support families while inflating the work ethic to the size of the *Hindenburg* when you can, instead, project this paradox onto what the media have come to call, incessantly, "the mommy wars" (Hays 9). The "mommy wars" puts mothers into two, mutually exclusive categories—working mother versus stay-at-home mother, and never the twain shall meet. It goes without saying that they allegedly hate each other's guts. In real life, millions of mothers move between these two categories, have been one and then the other at various different times, creating a mosaic of work and child-rearing practices that bears no resemblance to the supposed ironclad roles suggested by the "mommy wars" (Hays 9, 18). Not only does this media catfight pit mother against mother, but it suggests that all women be reduced to their one role-mother-or get cut out of the picture entirely.

At the same time that the new momism conquered the media outlets of America, we also saw mothers who talked back. *Maude,* Ann Romano on' *One Day at a Time,* Erma Bombeck, Peg Bundy, *Roseanne,* Brett Butler, Marge Simpson, and the mothers in *Malcolm in the Middle* and *Everybody Loves Raymond* have all given the new momism a big Bronx cheer. They have represented rebellious mothering: the notion that you can still love your kids and be a good mother without teaching them Origami, explaining factor analysis to them during bath time, playing softball with them at 6:00 A.M., or making sure they have a funny, loving note in their lunch box each and every day. Since 1970, because of money and politics, the new momism has conquered much of the media, and thus our own self-esteem. But it has not done so uncontested. The same media that sell and profit from the new momism have also given us permission—even encouraged us—to resist it. However, it is important to note that much of this rebellion has occurred in TV sitcoms which, with a few exceptions, offer primarily short-term catharsis, a brief respite from the norms in dramatic programming, the news, and advice columns that bully us so effectively.

Okay, so men and kids—well, some kids, anyway—benefit from the new momism. But what do mothers get out of it besides eye bags, exhaustion, and guilt? Well, because of how women have been socialized, a lot of us think the competitive, everything-has-a-price mind set of the workaday world is crass, impersonal, and callous. Many of us, then, want our homes to embody a rejection of a world that celebrates money and screwing over other people, in part because we know all too well how that world has screwed over women and children. So, it's not surprising that many women are seduced by ads, catalogs, and TV shows that urge us to turn our homes into softly lit, plug-in scented, flower-filled havens in a heartless world. The new momism keeps us down by demanding so much of us, but keeps us morally superior because through it we defy a society so driven by greed and self-interest. Plus, many of us, having left a child home in the care of a man to return to find the kid eating Slim Jims and marshmallows for dinner, and the floor covered with spilled Coke, dirty socks, and guinea pig excrement, have concluded that men can't do it, so we shut them out and do it ourselves. We resent men for not helping us more, but also bask in the smugness that at least here, in this one role, we can claim superiority. So through the new momism women acquiesce to *and* resist good, old-fashioned sexist notions of how the world should work.

There are already bleacher loads of very good, even excellent books attacking the unattainable ideals surrounding motherhood, and we will rely on many of them here.[9] But while many of these books expose and rail against the cultural myths mothers have had to combat-putting your child in day care proves you are a selfish, careerist bitch, if you don't bond with your baby immediately after birth you'll have Ted Kaczynski on your hands, and so forth—they have not examined in detail, and over time, the enormous role the mass media have played in promulgating and exaggerating these myths.

We want to fill this gap, to examine how the images of motherhood in TV shows, movies, advertising, women's magazines, and the news have evolved since 1970, raising the bar, year by year, of the standards of good motherhood while singling out and condemning those we were supposed to see as dreadful mothers. We want to explore the struggle in the media between intensive mothering and rebellious mothering, and consider how it has helped make mothers today who we are. This imagery may have been fleeting, and it may have been banal, but it told common, interlocking stories that, over the years, evolved into a new "common sense" we were all supposed to share about motherhood, good and bad. This imagery has also provided us with a shared cultural history of becoming mothers in the United States, yet we may not appreciate the extent to which this common history has shaped our identities, our sense of success and failure as mothers, and the extent to which it ties us together through mutual collective memories. So instead of dismissing these media images as short-lived (and sometimes even stupid), let's review how they have laid down a thick, sedimented layer of guilt, fear, and anxiety as well as an increasingly powerful urge to talk back.

We've chosen to start roughly around 1970, for several reasons. This was when the women's movement burst onto the political scene as one of the biggest news stories of the year, and one of the central tenets of the movement was to critique how existing models of marriage and motherhood trapped millions of women in lives they found frustrating and in economic arrangements that were deeply unfair. At the same time, the soaring divorce rate was producing an unprecedented number of single-parent households, 90 percent of them headed by women. The "stagflation" of the 1970s—roaring inflation combined with rising unemployment (which Gerald Ford cleverly sought to combat by distributing "Whip Inflation Now" buttons to the citizenry)—also propelled millions of mothers into the workforce. In 1970, only 28.5 percent of children under age six had a mother working outside the home. By 1988, the figure had jumped to 51.5 percent. Nor was the idea of having children then as surrounded by the occluding, spun-sugar romance that encases it today. In a widely reported survey done by Ann Landers of 50,000 parents in the mid-1970s, a rather mammoth 70 percent said that if given the choice to do it again, they would not have children; it wasn't worth it (as reported in "Wondering If Children Are Necessary" 42).

In the 1970s and later, it was clear that the media would have to respond to this crisis in the 1950s common sense about motherhood. After all, some women (and men) welcomed these changes while others hated them. In fact, in the 1970s various TV shows, women's magazines, and movies incorporated the feminist challenge to motherhood in their wisecracking mothers and tales of self-discovery. Yet by the 1980s, the media began to backtrack. The result? An ever-expanding, thundering media avalanche of anxiety about the state of motherhood in America.

To give you an idea, let's look briefly at the news, which has played a much more central role in policing the boundaries of motherhood than you might think. Few books have reviewed the enormously influential role the nightly news played in shaping national norms about motherhood revisiting *Good Housekeeping* or *The Cosby Show* makes sense, but the news? Yet it is in the news that we can track especially well the trajectory of the new momism. Most people don't get (or want) to look at old news footage, but we looked at thirty years of stories relating to motherhood. In the 1970s, with the exception of various welfare reform proposals, there was almost nothing in the network news about motherhood, working mothers, or childcare. And when you go back and watch news footage from 1972, for example, all you see is John Chancellor at NBC in black and white reading the news with no illustrating graphics, or Walter Cronkite sitting in front of a map of the world that one of the Rugrats could have drawn—that's it.

But by the 1980s, the explosion in the number of working mothers, the desperate need for day care, sci-fi level reproductive technologies, the discovery of how widespread child abuse was-all this was newsworthy. At the same time, the network news shows were becoming more flashy and sensationalistic in their efforts to compete with tabloid TV offerings like *A Current Affair* and *America's Most Wanted* (Auletta 457-60). NBC, for example, introduced a story about day care centers in 1984 with a beat-up Raggedy Ann doll lying limp next to a chair with the huge words *Child Abuse* scrawled next to her in what appeared to be Charles Manson's handwriting. So stories that were titillating, that could be really tarted up, that were about children and sex, or children and violence-well, they just got more coverage than why Senator Rope-a-Dope refused to vote for decent day care. From the McMartin day-care scandal and missing children to Susan Smith and murdering nannies, the barrage of kids-in-jeopardy, "innocence corrupted" stories made mothers feel they had to guard their kids with the same intensity as the secret service guys watching POTUS.

Having discovered in the summer of 2001 that one missing Congressional intern and some shark attacks could fill the twenty-four-hour news hole, the cable channels the following year gave us the summer of abducted girls (rather than, say, in-depth probes of widespread corporate wrongdoing that robbed millions of people of millions of dollars). Even though FBI figures showed a *decline* in missing persons and child abductions, such stories were, as *Newsweek's* Jonathan Alter put it, "inexpensive" and got "boffo ratings" (see also Murr 38). It goes without saying that such crimes are horrific and, understandably, bereft parents wanted to use the media to help locate their kidnapped children. But the incessant coverage of the abductions of Samantha Runnion (whose mother, the media repeatedly reminded us, was at work), Elizabeth Smart, Tamara Brooks, Jacqueline Marris, and Danielle van Dam terrified parents across the country all out of proportion to the risks their children faced. (To put things in perspective, in a country of nearly three hundred million people, estimates were that only 115 children were taken by strangers in ways that were dangerous to the child [Alter].) Unlike mothers in the 1950s, then, we were never to let our children out of our sight at carnivals, shopping malls, or playgrounds, and it was up to us to protect them from failing schools, environmental pollution, molesters, drugs, priests, Alar, the Internet, amusement parks, air bags, jungle gyms, *South Park,* trampolines, rottweilers, gangs, and HBO specials about lap dancers and masturbation clubs. It's a wonder any women had children and, once they did, ever let them out of their sight.

Then there were the magazines. Beginning in the 1980s, and exploding with a vengeance in the '90s, celebrity journalism brought us a feature that spread like head lice through the women's magazines, as well as the more recent celebrity and "lifestyle" glossies: the celebrity mom profile. If any media form has played a central role in convincing young women without children that having a baby is akin to ascending to heaven and seeing God, it is the celebrity mom profile. "Happiness is having a baby," gushed Marie Osmond on a 1983 cover of *Good Housekeeping,* and Linda Evans, at the peak of her success in *Dynasty,* added in *Ladies Home Journal,* "All I want is a husband and baby." Barbara Mandrell proclaimed, "Now my children come first," Valerie Harper confessed, "I finally have a child to love," and Cybill Shepard announced, "I'll have a fourth baby or adopt!" (*Redbook* 1988a, 1988b). Assaulting us from every supermarket checkout line and doctor's and dentist's offices, celebrity moms like Kathie Lee Gifford, Joan Lunden, Jaclyn Smith, Kirstie Alley, and Christie Brinkley (to name just a few) beamed from the comfy serenity and perfection of their lives as they gave multiple interviews about their "miracle babies," how much they loved their kids, what an unadulterated joy motherhood was, and about all the things they did with their kids to ensure they would be perfectly normal Nobel laureates by the age of twelve. By the summer of 1999, one of *People's* biggest summer stories, featuring the huge cover headlines "BOY, OH BOY," was the birth of Cindy Crawford's baby. The following summer, under the headline "PREGNANT AT LAST!" we had the pleasure of reading about the sperm motility rate of Celine Dion's husband, information that some of us, at least, could have lived without. In 2003, Angelina Jolie claimed that her adopted baby "saved my life." The media message was that celebrity moms work on the set for twelve hours a day, yet somehow manage to do somersaults with their kids in the park, read to them every day, take them out for ice cream whenever they wanted, get up with them at 3:00 A.M., and, of course, buy them toys, animals, and furniture previously reserved for the offspring of the Shah of Iran. These were supposed to be our new role models.

In the women's magazines in the early 1970s, advertising focused on the mother and her alleged needs-whether for hand cream, hair dye, toilet cleaners, or tampons.[10] Anacin, for example, announced "Mother of 5 Active Children Tells How She Relieves Her Nervous Tension Headaches." (Ditch the kids with a sitter and head for Cozumel with Denzel Washington?) Rarely were mothers and children pictured together as some beatific unit. Ads showed mom spraying the kitchen with Lysol, or smiling in a field of daisies because she'd just used a fabulous Clairol product. When babies were pictured, they appeared alone.

But by 1990, images of children were everywhere, and there was a direct address from the ad to you, the mom, exhorting you to foresee your child's each and every need and desire. No doubt copywriters had read Dr. Spock's latest pronouncement that mothers had to "anticipate wishes which [the baby] can barely recognize let alone formulate" (cited in Hays 58). "Giving your kids a well-balanced meal when you're busy is no fun and games. Until now," proclaimed Banquet, a maker of frozen meals for kids. The gleeful face of a cherubic child beamed out from the ad, which informed us that this new "kid cuisine" featured a special "FunPak" with "puzzles and games that help kids learn about history, space exploration, and all kinds of interesting things" (*Redbook* 1990). Or you could "Help your children get free 'Learning Tools for Schools' with Scott Paper purchases." By saving the special apple seal from Scott paper products, you, Mom, could help your child's school get microscopes, audio/visual equipment, "and more" to "help your children prepare for the environmental and educational challenges of the future" (*Redbook* 1990). "Put a song in their hearts!" urged Disney as it hawked its sing-along videos, telling moms to "give your kids the magic of music" (*Redbook* 1990). Mothers learned that "your child will travel in style" with the new carrying case loaded with Legos, which "makes every trip a journey into imagination" (*Redbook* 1990).

The new momism, then, was also promoted through the toys and myriad other products sold to us and our kids. Coonskin caps and silly putty were just not going to cut it anymore. The good mother got her kids toys that were educational, that advanced gross and fine motor skills, that gave them the spatial sensibilities and design aptitude of Frank Lloyd Wright, and that taught Johnny how to read James Joyce at age three. God forbid that one second should pass where your child was idle and that you were not doing everything you could to promote his or her emotional, cognitive, imaginative, quantitative, or muscular development. And now mothers and children in ads were pictured in poses that made the Virgin Mary in the pieta seem neglectful. Dazzling, toothy smiles about to burst into full throaty laughter defined the new, characteristic pose of the truly engaged, empathetic mom as she hugged, held, nursed, and played with her kids, always with joyful spontaneity. The classic image was of a new, beaming mother, holding her baby straight up in the air and over her face, and smiling into its little elevated eyes, cheerfully unaware of the rather common infant behavior such an angle might produce: projectile vomiting.

All these media suggest, by their endless celebrating of certain kinds of mothers and maternal behavior and their ceaseless advice, that there are agreed upon norms "out there." So even if you think they're preposterous, you assume you'll be judged harshly by not abiding by them. In this way media portrayals can substitute for and override community norms (Milkie).[11] You know, when our kids say "all the other kids get to do it" we laugh in their faces. But when the magazines suggest, "All the other moms are doing this, are you?" we see ourselves being judged by the toughest critics out there: other mothers. Mothers who had thrown their TV sets out the window could still absorb all this through talks with friends, relatives, other mothers, and, most aggravating of all, their own kids.

At the heart of the new momism is the insistence that mothers inhabit what we in the academy would call the "subject positions" of our children as often as possible. (In the parlance of childcare experts, this means always climbing inside your child and seeing the world only and entirely through his or her eyes.) We like to think of ourselves as coherent and enduring selves, but we are just as much a composite of many, often contradictory identities or subject positions. The media, which bombard us with TV shows, movies, catalogs, ads, and magazines, serve as a kind of Home Depot of personas to draw from and put on, providing a rapid transit system among many identities (Thompson, chap. 7). "It's Sunday afternoon-shall I be Cindy Crawford or Joan Crawford?" (The kids pray for the former, and usually get the latter.) Surrounded by media morality tales in which we are meant to identify first with one type of woman and then another, women have gotten used to compartmentalizing ourselves into a host of subject positions, and this is especially true for mothers.

But to crawl inside our kids' own skin and heads, to anticipate and assume *their* subject positions, too, so we will know exactly how they will feel two hours from now and what they will need to make them feel loved, cherished, bolstered, stimulated-how did we get sucked into *this* one? And to do this we have to appreciate each and every more finely grained stage of child development so that we know exactly where in the kid's evolution to place ourselves. Yikes.

And have you noticed how we've all become "moms"? When we were kids, our mothers would say, "I have to call Christine's *mother,*" not "I have to call Christine's mom." Our mothers would identify themselves to teachers as so-and-so's *mother*. Today, thanks in part to Dr. Laura ("I am my kid's mom") and Republican pollsters (who coined the term "soccer mom" in 1996), we hear about "the moms" getting together and we have become so-and-so's mom. "Mom"—a term previously used only by children—doesn't have the authority of "mother," because it addresses us from a child's-eye view. It assumes a familiarity, an approachability, to mothers that is, frankly, patronizing; reminiscent, in fact, of the difference between woman and girl. At the same time, "mom" means you're good and nurturing while "mother" means you're not (note the media uses of "celebrity mom" versus "welfare mother" and "stay-at-home mom" versus "working mother"). "Mom" sounds very user-friendly, but the rise of it, too, keeps us in our place, reminding us that we are defined by our relationships to kids, not to adults.

Because the media always serve up heroes and villains, there had to be the terrible mothers, the anti-Madonnas, the hideous counterexamples good mothers were meant to revile. We regret to report that nearly all of these women were African American and were disproportionately featured as failed mothers in news stories about "crack babies," single, teen mothers, and welfare mothers. One of the worst things about the new momism is that it is like a club, where women without kids, or women deemed "bad" mothers, like poor women and welfare mothers, don't belong. It is—with a few exceptions, like Clair Huxtable on *The Cosby Show*—a segregated club.

At the very same time that we witnessed the explosion of white celebrity moms, and the outpouring of advice to and surveillance of middle-class mothers, the welfare mother, trapped in a "cycle of dependency," became ubiquitous in our media landscape, and she came to represent everything wrong with America. She appeared not in the glossy pages of the women's magazines but rather as the subject of news stories about the "crisis" in the American family and the newly declared "war" on welfare mothers. Whatever ailed America-drugs, crime, loss of productivity was supposedly her fault. She was portrayed as thumbing her nose at intensive mothering. Even worse, she was depicted as bringing her kids into the realm of market values, as putting a price on their heads, by allegedly calculating how much each additional child was worth and then getting pregnant to cash in on them. For middle-class white women in the media, by contrast, their kids were priceless (Hays 8). These media depictions reinforced the divisions between "us" (minivan moms) and "them" (welfare mothers, working-class mothers, teenage mothers), and did so especially along the lines of race.

For example, one of the most common sentences used to characterize the welfare mother was, "Tanya, who has children by different men" (you fill in the blanks). Like zoo animals, their lives were reduced to the numbers of successful impregnations by multiple partners. So it's interesting to note that someone like Christie Brinkley, who has exactly the same reproductive MO, was never described this way. Just imagine reading a comparable sentence in *Redbook*. "Christie B., who has three children by three different men." But she does, you know.

At the same time that middle- and upper-middle-class mothers were urged to pipe Mozart into their wombs when they're pregnant so their kids would come out perfectly tuned, the government told poor mothers to get the hell out of the house and get to work-no more children's aid for them. Mothers like us—with health care, laptops, and Cuisinarts—are supposed to replicate the immaculate bedrooms we see in Pottery Barn Kids catalogs, with their designer sheets and quilts, one toy and one stuffed animal atop a gleaming white dresser, and a white rug on the floor that has never been exposed to the shavings from hamster cages, Magic Markers accidentally dropped with their caps off, or Welch's grape juice. At the same time, we've been encouraged to turn our backs on other mothers who pick their kids' clothes out of other people's trash and sometimes can't buy a can of beans to feed them. How has it come to seem perfectly reasonable-even justified-that one class of mother is supposed to sew her baby's diapers out of Egyptian cotton from that portion of the Nile blessed by the god Osiris while another class of mother can't afford a single baby aspirin?

So who the hell are we, the authors, and what biases might we bring to this tour down motherhood's recent memory lane? Well, we are of a certain vintage-let's just say that if we were bottled in the *1960s,* we'd be about to go off right about now. So we have lived through the women's movement and its aftermath, and, between the two of us, have been raising kids from the *1970s* to the present. That does not mean we are authorities on child rearing (just ask our kids), but rather that we've seen very different takes on motherhood put forward and fought over, different fads and standards come and go. While neither of our lives comes close to those of Cindy Crawford or Kathie Lee Gifford (no nannies, no personal assistants, no cooks, no trainers, no clothing line named after either one of us, no factories in Paraguay), we are nonetheless privileged women. We live near excellent daycare centers and schools, we have health insurance, and we benefit from the advantages that come automatically with being white and heterosexual. So we have not stood in the shoes of mothers who don't have live-in partners, health insurance, or decent day care, who live in dangerous neighborhoods and substandard housing, who have to work two crappy jobs so they can feed their kids, or who have faced custody battles simply because they're lesbians. We can hardly speak for all, or even most mothers.

We can, however, replay the dominant media imagery that has surrounded most of us, despite our differences, imagery that serves to divide us by age and race and "lifestyle choices," and seeks to tame us all by reinforcing one narrow, homogenized, upper-middle-class, corporately defined image of motherhood. We speak as mothers who succumb to and defy the new momism. And our main point is this: Media imagery that seems so natural, that seems to embody some common sense, while blaming some mothers, or all mothers, for children and a nation gone wrong, needs to have its veneer of supposed truth ripped away by us, mothers. For example, while there have been "zany" sitcoms about families with "two dads" or a working mom living with her mother and a male housekeeper, the white, upper-middle-class, married-with-children nuclear family remains as dominant as a Humvee , barreling through the media and forcing images of other, different, and just as legitimate family arrangements off to the side. We want to ridicule this ideal—or any other household formation—as *the* norm that should bully those who don't conform. After all, as any mother will point out, the correct ratio of adult-to-kid in any household should be at least three-to-one, a standard the nuclear family fails to meet.

The new momism involves more than just impossible ideals about child rearing. It redefines all women, first and foremost, through their relationships to children. Thus, being a citizen, a worker, a governor, an actress, a First Lady, all are supposed to take a backseat to motherhood. (Remember how people questioned whether

Hillary Clinton was truly maternal because she had only one child?) By insisting that being a mother-and a perfect one at that-is the most important thing a woman can do, a prerequisite for being thought of as admirable and noble, the new momism insists that if you want to do anything else, you'd better prove first that you're a doting, totally involved mother before proceeding. This is not a requirement for men. The only recourse for women who want careers, or to do anything else besides stay home with the kids all day, is to prove that they can "do it all." As the feminist writer (and pioneer) Letty Cottin Pogrebin put it, "You can go be a CEO, and a good one, but if you're not making a themed birthday party, you're not a good mother," and, thus, you are a failure.

The new momism has evolved over the past few decades, becoming more hostile to mothers who work, and more insistent that all mothers become ever more closely tethered to their kids. The mythology of the new momism now insinuates that, when all is said and done, the enlightened mother chooses to stay home with the kids. Back in the 1950s, mothers stayed home because they had no choice, so the thinking goes (even though by 1955 more mothers were working than ever before). Today, having been to the office, having tried a career, women supposedly have seen the inside of the male working world and found it to be the inferior choice to staying home, especially when their kids' future is at stake. It's not that mothers can't hack it (1950s thinking). It's that progressive mothers refuse to hack it. Inexperienced women thought they knew what they wanted, but they got experience and learned they were wrong. Now mothers have seen the error of their ways, and supposedly seen that the June Cleaver model, if taken as a *choice,* as opposed to a requirement, is the truly modern, fulfilling, forward-thinking version of motherhood.

In the 1960s, women, and especially young women, were surrounded by mixed messages, one set telling them that there was a new day dawning, they were now equal to men and could change the world, the other telling them they were destined to be housewives, were subservient to men, and could never achieve equality. Electrified by the civil rights and antiwar movements and their demands for freedom and participatory democracy, women could no longer stand being pulled in opposite directions, and opted for equality. Of course, the contradictions in our lives did not vanish-in the wake of the women's movement we were supposed to be autonomous, independent, accomplished, yet poreless, slim, nurturing, and deferential to men (Douglas chap. 1). In the early twenty-first century, we see a mirror image of the 1960s, but without the proud ending: The same contradictions are there, but now the proposed resolution, like a mist in the culture, is for women to give up their autonomy and find peace and fulfillment in raising children.

In other words, ladies, the new momism seeks to contain and, where possible, eradicate, all of the social changes brought on by feminism. It is backlash in its most refined, pernicious form because it insinuates itself into women's psyches just where we have been rendered most vulnerable: in our love for our kids. The new momism, then, is deeply and powerfully political. The new momism is the result of the combustible intermixing of right-wing attacks on feminism and women, the media's increasingly finely tuned and incessant target marketing of mothers and children, the collapse of governmental institutions—public schools, child welfare programs—that served families in the past (imperfectly, to be sure), and mothers' own, very real desires to do the best job possible raising their kids in a culture that praises mothers in rhetoric and reviles them in public policy.

Plenty of mothers aren't buying this retro version of motherhood, although it works to make them feel very guilty and stressed. They want and need their own paychecks, they want and need adult interaction during the day, they want and need their own independence, and they believe—and rightly so—that women who work outside the home can be and are very good mothers to their kids. Other mothers don't want or need these things for the time being, or ever, and really would rather stay home. The question here is not which path women choose, or which one is "right." The question is why one reactionary, normative ideology, so out of sync with millions of women's lives, seems to be getting the upper hand.

The new momism has become the central, justifying ideology of what has come to be called "post-feminism." Ever since October 1982, when *The New York Times Magazine* featured an article titled "Voices from the Post-Feminist Generation," a term was coined, and the women of America have heard, ceaselessly, that we are, and will be forever more, in a postfeminist age.

What the hell is post-feminism, anyway?[12] You would think it would refer to a time when complete gender equality has been achieved (you know, like we'd already achieved a *feminist* state and now we're "post" that). That hasn't happened, of course, but we (and especially young women) are supposed to think it has. Post-feminism, as a term, suggests that women have made plenty of progress because of feminism, but that feminism is now irrelevant and even undesirable because it supposedly made millions of women unhappy, unfeminine, childless, hairy, lonely, bitter, and prompted them to fill their closets with combat boots and really bad India print skirts. Supposedly women have gotten all they could out of feminism, are now "equal," and so can, by choice, embrace things we used to see as sexist, like a TV show in which some self-satisfied lunk samples the wares of twenty-five women before rejecting twenty-four and keeping the one he likes best, or like the notion that mothers should have primary responsibility for raising the kids. Post-feminism means that you can now work outside the home even in jobs previously restricted to men, go to graduate school, pump iron, and pump your own gas, as long as you remain fashion conscious, slim, nurturing, deferential to men, and become a doting, selfless mother.

According to post-feminism, women now have a choice between feminism and antifeminism and they just naturally and happily choose the latter. And the most powerful way that post-feminism worked to try to re-domesticate women was through the new momism. Here's the progression. Feminism won; you can have it all; of course you want children; mothers are better at raising children than fathers; of course your children come first; of course you come last; today's children need constant attention, cultivation, and adoration, or they'll become failures and hate you forever; you don't want to fail at that; it's easier for mothers to abandon their work and their dreams than for fathers; you don't want it all anymore (which is good because you can't have it all); who cares about equality, you're too tired; and whoops—here we are in 1954.

Each of us, of course, has her own individual history as a mother, her own demons and satisfactions, her own failures and goals. But motherhood is, in our culture, emphasized as such an individual achievement, something you and you alone excel at or screw up. So it's easy to forget that motherhood *is* a collective experience. We want to erase the amnesia about motherhood—we *do* have a common history, it does tie us together, and it has made us simultaneously guilt-ridden and ready for an uprising. Let's turn the surveillance cameras away from ourselves and instead turn them on the media that shaped us and that manufactured more of our beliefs and practices than we may appreciate, or want to admit.

Especially troubling about all this media fare is the rise of even more impossible standards of motherhood today than those that tyrannized us in the past. For women in their 20s and 30s, the hypernatalism of the media promotes impossibly idealized expectations about motherhood (and fatherhood!) that may prove depressingly disappointing once junior arrives and starts throwing mashed beets on the wall. Peggy Orenstein reported in her 2000 book *Flux* that by the 1990s, "motherhood supplanted marriage as the source of romantic daydreams" for childless, unmarried women in their twenties and early to mid-thirties. To put it another way, "Motherhood has become increasingly central to women's conception of femininity, far more so than marriage." The women she talked to "believed children would answer basic existential questions of meaning" and would "provide a kind of unconditional love that relationships with men did not." They over-idealized motherhood and bought into the norm of "the Perfect Mother-the woman for whom childbearing supersedes all other identities and satisfactions" (Orenstein 105-106). A new generation of young women, for whom the feminine mystique is ancient history, and who haven't experienced what it took for women to fight their way out of the kitchen, may be especially seduced by media profiles suggesting that if Reese Witherspoon can marry young and become an A-list actress while raising a three-year-old and expecting another child, then you can "do it all" too. Just as Naomi Wolf, Susan Faludi, and Camryn Manheim sought to get women to say "excuuuse me" to the size-zero ideal, we would like women to just say no to the new momism.

Finally, *The Mommy Myth* is a call to arms. With so many smart, hardworking, dedicated, tenacious, fed-up women out there, can't we all do a better job of talking back to the media that hector us all the time? As we get assaulted by "15 Ways to Stress Proof Your Child," "Boost Your Kid's Brainpower in Just 25 Minutes," "Discipline Makeover: Better Behavior in 21 Days," and "What It Really Takes to Make Your Baby Smarter," not to mention "The Sex Life You Always Wanted—How to Have it *Now*" (answer: put the kids up for adoption), let's develop, together, some really good comebacks. And let's also take a second look at these "wars" we're supposed to be involved with: the "war" against welfare mothers, the "war" between working versus stay-at-home mothers. While these wars do often benefit one set of mothers over another, what they do best is stage *all* mothers' struggles, in the face of the most pathetic public policies for women and children in the western world, as a catfight. Then the politicians who've failed to give us decent day care or maternity leave can go off and sip their sherry while mothers point fingers at each other. Our collective dilemmas as mothers are always translated into individual issues that each of us has to confront by herself, alone, with zero help. These media frameworks that celebrate the rugged individualism of mothers, then, justify and reinforce public policies (or lack thereof) that make it harder to be a mother in the United States than in any other industrialized society.

As mothers, we appreciate all too well how much time and attention children need and deserve, and how deeply committed we become to our kids. We can be made to cry at the drop of a hat by a Hallmark commercial or a homemade Mother's Day card. We get roped into the new momism because we do feel that our society is not providing our kids with what they need. But the problem with the new momism is that it insists that there is one and only one way the children of America will get what they need: if mom provides it. If dad "pitches in," well, that's just an extra bonus. The government? Forget it.

We fear that, today, we have a new common sense about motherhood that may be as bad, or worse, as the one that chained mothers to their May tags in 1957. It wasn't always like this. There was a time in the now distant past when there was something called the Women's Liberation Movement. They are the folks who brought you "the personal is political." Enough lies have been told by Pat Robertson, Rush Limbaugh, and others about what feminists said about motherhood and children to fill a Brazilian landfill center. But when we exhume what feminists really hoped to change about motherhood, hopes buried under a slag heap of cultural amnesia and backlash, the rise of the new momism seems like the very last set of norms you would predict would conquer motherhood in America in the early twenty-first century. Let's go back to a time when many women felt free to tell the truth about motherhood—e.g., that at times they felt ambivalent about it because it was so hard and yet so undervalued—and when women sought to redefine how children were raised so that it wasn't only women who pushed strollers, played Uncle Wiggly, or quit their jobs once kids arrived. Of course these women loved their kids. But were they supposed to give up everything for them? Are we?

Anyhow, the next time you read about Sarah Jessica Parker's perfect marriage and motherhood, don't sigh and say, "Oh, I wish that was my life." Instead, say, "Give me a break." (Or, alternatively, "Give me a %$#$% break." Of course, most of you probably already say that.) Because, you know, if we all refuse to be whipsawed between these age-old madonna-whore poles of perfect and failed motherhood, designed to police us all, then we-all of us-get a break. And that, as you shall shortly see, was what feminists were asking for in the first place.

Notes

[1]See also Ruth Feldstein's excellent discussion of momism in *Motherhood in Black and White: Race and Sex in American Liberalism, 1930-1965* (especially chapter 2).

[2]Hays's book is must reading for all mothers, and we are indebted to her analysis of intensive mothering, from which this discussion draws.

[3]For an account of the decline in leisure time, see Schorr.

[4]See Katha Pollitt's terrific piece "Killer Moms, Working Nannies."

[5]Based on an On-line Computer Library Center, Inc., search under the word *motherhood,* from 1970-2000.

[6]Susan Faludi, in her instant classic *Backlash,* made this point, too, but the book focused on the various and multiple forms of backlash, and we will be focusing only on the use of motherhood here.

[7]For a superb analysis of the role of mother-blaming in American politics, see Feldstein (especially 7-9).

[8]This contradiction is central to Hays's argument.

[9]Most notable are Crittenden; Eyer; Chira; Maushart.

[10]This information based on a content analysis of the January, March, May, July, September, and November 1970 issues of *Ladies' Home Journal* and *McCall's,* and the January, March, and May issues of *Redbook.*

[11]We are grateful to Kris Harrison for pointing out this research.

[12]For an excellent discussion of post-feminism and the media see Press (38-49).

References

Alter, Jonathan. "Who's Taking the Kids?" *Newsweek* July 29, 2002; on-line edition.

Auletta, Ken. *Three Blind Mice: How the Networks Lost Their Way.* New York: Vintage, 1992.

Chira, Susan. *A Mother's Place: Choosing Work and Family Without Guilt or Shame.* New York: Perennial, 1999.

Crittenden, Ann. *The Price of Motherhood.* New York: Metropolitan Books, 2001.

Douglas, Susan J. *Where the Girls Are.* New York: Times Books, 1994.

Eyer, Diane. *Motherguilt.* New York: Times Books, 1996.

Faludi, Susan. *Backlash: The Undeclared War Against American Women.* New York: Crown, 1991.

Feldstein, Ruth. *Motherhood in Black and White: Race and Sex in American Liberalism, 1930-1965.* Ithaca: Cornell University Press, 2004.

Good Housekeeping January 1995.

Hays, Sharon. *The Cultural Contradictions of Motherhood.* New Haven: Yale University Press, 1996.

Heaton, Patricia. *Motherhood* and *Hollywood.* New York: Villard Books, 2002.

Lekachman, Robert. *Visions and Nightmares: America After Reagan*. New York: Collier Books, 1988.

Maushart, Susan. *The Mask of Motherhood*. New York: The New Press, 1999.

Milkie, Melissa. "Social Comparisons, Reflected, Appraisals, and Mass Media: The Impact of Pervasive Beauty Images on Black and White Girls' Self Concepts." *Social Psychology Quarterly* (June 1999): 190-210.

"Motherhood Today—A Tougher Job, Less Ably Done." The Pew Research Center for the People and the Press, March 1997.

Murr, Andrew. "When Kids Go Missing." *Newsweek* July 29, 2002; on-line edition.

Orenstein, Peggy. *Flux: Women on Sex, Work, Love, Kids and Life in a Half-Changed World*. New York: Doubleday, 2000.

People July 8, 1996.

People September 21,1998.

Peterson, V. Spike. "Gendered Nationalism: Reproducing 'Us' versus 'Them'." *The Women and War Reader*. Eds. Lois Ann Lorentzen and Jennifer Turpin. New York: New York University Press, 1998.

Pogrebin, Letty Cottin. Personal interview. February 2001.

Pollitt, Katha. "Killer Moms, Working Nannies." *The Nation* November 24, 1997: 9.

Press, Andrea. *Women Watching Television: Gender, Class and Generation in the American Television Experience*. Philadelphia: University of Pennsylvania Press, 1991.

Redbook April 1988a.

Redbook June 1988b.

Redbook September 1990.

Schorr, Juliet B. *The Overworked American*. New York: Basic Books, 1992.

Thompson, John. *Media and Modernity*. Stanford, CA: Stanford University Press, 1995.

van Ogtrop, Kristin. "Attila the Honey I'm Home." *The Bitch in the House*. New York: William Morrow, 2002.

"Wondering If Children Are Necessary." *Time* March 5,1979: 42.

Wylie, Philip. *Generation of Vipers*. New York: Holt, Rinehart and Winston, 1942.

Chapter 38

Right to Mothering

Motherhood as a Transborder Concern in the Age of Globalization

SHU-JU ADA CHENG

June was an illegal worker when I first met her at a church in Taipei, Taiwan, in 1999. After working illegally for more than four years, she decided to return home to the Philippines. People at the church were assisting her with the deportation process. By the time I interviewed her, she had been away from home for almost 15 years. She first worked in Saudi Arabia for eight years and returned home only twice during that time. She later worked in Hong Kong and decided to go to Taiwan for the higher wage. She had to leave her first Taiwanese employers because of the exploitative working conditions. They confiscated her passport, forced her to labor 15 hours a day, and prohibited her from going out regularly. They had her sleep in the attic and locked her from outside at night, afraid that she might run away or steal things. She pleaded with them not to do that since she would have no way of escape should a fire break out. When she asked her recruitment agent in Taiwan for help, her agent threatened her with deportation. She finally decided to escape for her own safety.

Becoming illegal gave her much needed freedom. She could share an apartment with other Filipinos, visit the church weekly, and maintain regular social contact. She could choose her own employers, set her own fees for the service, and arrange her own schedules. It also came with certain price though. There was no guarantee that employers could be easily secured. She had to be constantly on alert, looking out for the authority. While she longed for social contact, she could trust no one for fear of being reported. June finally cried when she talked about the price her family had to pay with her working abroad. Working overseas and not seeing her children grow up was the only way she, as a mother, could raise and support them. "If I could do it all over again, I would not have left the Philippines." She ended our conversation with this reflection on her long journey as a mother as well as an overseas contract worker.

June's story represents a unique tale of motherhood that merits particular attention in our contemporary era. We do not live in a globalized world connected solely through decentralized production processes, compressed informational networks, and unprecedented technological transformations. We also live in a close-knit global village connected through the labor, care, and emotions of Third

World women, who migrate to perform care labor for upper- and middle-class women in advanced economies in both the North and the South. We subsist in a global economy in which uneven developments compel less privileged women to cross borders to care for other families in the foreign land, in order to support their own families back home. We carry on transnational family affairs through which a generation of children cared for by other women at home as their maids, nannies, and substitute mothers. For the millions of migrant women like June, the issue of motherhood is not about male dominance, the public-private dichotomy, unequal gender division of labor, double shift, or struggle for individual autonomy. For them, they cannot mother their children the conventional way because economic deterioration and family survival compel them to seek overseas employment. They cannot fulfill the idealized image of motherhood, i.e., the full-time stay-home caretaker, because labor-receiving states establish control mechanisms to regulate their employment within the borders of nation-states. In short, their fundamental concern is the deprivation of their right to motherhood. And the deprivation of their right to mothering is firmly institutionalized in state policy, legitimated through state rhetoric, and materialized by practices of individual employers and employment agencies.

In this article, I locate the discussion of mothering, law, politics, and public policy from the broader perspective of the globalization of care, specifically the implications of state policy to the mothering experience of migrant women care workers, such as foreign domestics and nurses. Global restructuring of care has raised questions about the different mothering experience for migrant women, as suggested by such terms as "transnational mothering" (Hondagneu-Sotelo and Avila 548), "commodified motherhood" (Parrenas 2001: 73), and "fragmentation of motherhood" (Gamburd 186). These divergent forms of mothering extant in the transnational social field contest the grand narrative of a normative motherhood predicated upon the experience of privileged women in dominant groups, both locally and globally. Through centering the experience of migrant women, I argue that, in the era of globalization, the critical analysis on motherhood needs to transcend national boundaries and be broadened to include the ramifications derived from the global restructuring of care. More importantly, I contend that motherhood should be reconsidered as an important transborder concern that entails a critical transnational perspective and a cross-border strategic alliance of local and global feminist engagements in the politics of motherhood.

Empire of Care: Race and Motherhood in Transnational Era

June could not return to the Philippines for short visits while working in Taiwan because of her illegal status. She finally decided to surrender herself to the police because her youngest son was using drugs and was having trouble with the law. Away from her children for years, she has missed their birthdays, graduations, and important events in their lives. To compensate, she turns all her caring attention to her employers' children, who often regard her more as a maid than as a substitute mother. Channeling her love to other people's children mirrors what Sau-Ling Wong (69) terms as the diverted mothering, through which the care labor of women of color is diverted to the children and families of employing white women, away from the rightful recipients based on kinship or community ties. In the contemporary world, diverted mothering has its transnational implications, linking localized social reproduction globally. As Pierette Hondagneu-Sotelo (2000) discusses the ramifications of diverted mothering involved in the global commodification of social reproduction:

> The commodification of social reproduction is bound on a global scale with the international migration of women and their employment in domestic work. Immigrant women from Sri Lanka, Indonesia, the Philippines, and various Caribbean nations, like many Mexican and Central American women, migrate internationally for work in commodified social reproduction. Many of them leave their children and other family members behind in their country of origin, assigning the reproductive work of caring for these dependents to family members and paid care workers. (161)

The issue of paid domestic labor has re-surfaced as one of the major themes for interrogation for feminist scholarship in recent years. This recent scholarly interest extends yet also differs from the previous feminist scholarship, for the nature, characteristics, and power dynamics in paid domestic labor can no longer be examined simply through the social psychology of interpersonal relations or the structural analysis of gender, race, and class within the confines of nation-states. The personal is no longer simply the political; the personal is the global. Centering the story of Third World mothers is important in challenging the dominant feminist theorizing in motherhood, which is often predicated upon the experience of Western, white, middle-class women. As Patricia Hill Collins problematizes the assumed universal applicability of feminist theories in mothering:

> Feminist theories of motherhood are thus valid as partial perspectives, but cannot be seen as theories of motherhood generalizable to all women. The resulting patterns of partiality inherent in existing theories, such as, for example, the emphasis placed on all-powerful mothers as conduits for gender oppression, reflect feminist theorists' positions in structures of power.... Shifting the center to accommodate this diversity promises to recontextualize motherhood and point us toward feminist theorizing that embraces difference as an essential part of commonality. (62)

I borrow the title of Catherine Ceniza Choy's provocative book, *Empire of Care: Nursing and Migration in Filipino American History,* as the starting point for my reflections on the impact on Third World women's mothering experience of the globalization of care. Tracing the root of contemporary migration of

Filipino nursing professionals to the United States to American imperialism in Asia, Choy powerfully terms this global inequality exacerbated through nursing migration as "empire of care" (3). Continuing the historical legacy of colonialism and imperialism, this empire of care is a form of extraction of care resources between the First and the Third World. As she critiques the rational choice approach that reduces Filipino nursing migration to individual agency: "the desire of Filipino nurses to migrate abroad cannot be reduced to an economic logic, but rather reflects individual and collective desire for a unique form of social, cultural, and economic success obtainable only outside the national borders of the Philippines" (Choy 7).

Empire of care thus highlights the historical unequal relationship between states of labor sending and receiving nations in the global system. Grace Chang's (2000) study on immigrant domestics in the United States serves as a good example for us to examine the role of the state in sustaining the empire. She argues that the presence of immigrant women domestics in the United States results from the deliberate intervention of the state in the First World in order to continue the further exploitation of the Third World (3). This process of exploitation hinges upon the construction of immigrant women as welfare cheats and brood mares, thus resulting in the proposition and ratification of various anti-immigrants initiatives and the deprivation of their citizenship rights. As she maintains, "the goal of these laws and "reforms" is to extract the benefits of immigrants' labor while minimizing or eliminating any obligations or costs, whether social or fiscal, to the "host" U.S. society and state" (Chang 11).

Empire of care, be it based on the labor of nursing professionals or domestics, illustrates the continual exploitation of the South by the North, albeit through a different form, and reflects a contemporary global politics constitutive of a "new world domestic order" (Hondagneu-Sotelo 2001: 1). This world reordering of social reproduction, with Third World women occupying the center stage in the global system, signifies an international racial division of reproductive labor (Parrenas 2000: 560) and the racialization of national/transnational systems of care. Empire of care thus "creates not a white man's burden but, through a series of invisible links, a dark child's burden" (Hochschild 27). The global system of unequal distribution of care pulls migrant women away from "home" yet places them at "home" at the same time. It is exactly this paradox of their being home yet homeless that the divisive power of globalization, particularly in the intimate sphere, can be better understood. Further, the children of migrant women are in essence "motherless" amidst the latter's homelessness. It is this tension between mothering one's and other women's children that best describes the predicament of mothering facing migrant women in the age of globalization.

Motherhood, Nation, and the Global System of Female Labor: Comparative Cases

June's story, particularly the structural constraints placed upon her ability to mother from abroad, also raises the question of the nation in relation to the asymmetrical distribution of care labor in the global arena. The racialization of Canada's and Taiwan's immigration policies provides good examples for our understanding of the linkage between the project of nation building and the institution of domestic service. In the case of Canada, women from Europe constituted the major source of labor supply prior to the 1950s. White British women, "sought after for their future or potential roles as wives and mothers of the Canadian nation" (Arat-Koc 54), were recruited with the goal for their permanent integration within Canada "as nation-builders and civilizers" (Arat-Koc 54). The demographic composition among foreign domestics shifted during the 1970s when an increasing number of foreign domestics from the Caribbean and the Philippines started entering Canada. Immigration regulations were thus modified to accommodate this demographic shift as a result. Foreign domestics from the Third World were and continue to be constructed as undesirable others and unsuitable for inclusion as citizens of Canada. Canada's immigration policy thus creates a process of racial formation and racialization through which women of different national and racial identities experience discrepant integration within the Canadian society. This process of racial formation and racialization also structures their disparate access to citizenship rights. The uneven enjoyment of citizenship rights among these women workers thus contributes to hierarchies of citizenship, both nationally and globally. As Arat-Koc states:

> Immigration policies and practices have been key mechanisms in regulating the racial/ethnic composition of immigrant domestic workers and determining the status, conditions, and autonomy of those who have been allowed in. Through immigration policy, membership in the Canadian nation and state, and access to citizenship rights, have been regulated. Access to citizenship rights has been facilitated for domestics of the 'desirable' race/ethnicity, while made difficult or inaccessible for those of 'undesirable' racial/ethnic backgrounds. (56)

Similarly, the importation of foreign labor and foreign domestics also poses challenges to the formation of nationhood in Taiwan. Domestic service became a state-sanctioned legal occupation with the ratification of Employment Service Law in 1992. Since then, domestic service and foreign domestics became subject to Taiwan's immigration control and the regulation of its foreign labor policy. For the past decade, domestic service in Taiwan has become a racialized field, inundated with women from Southeast Asia. Foreign workers from Southeast Asia are generally seen as undesirably different, and their entry is deemed to unleash social ills, such as crime, disease, and prostitution. To prevent their permanent settlement, the state has adopted intrusive practices for stringent control, such as the prohibition of pregnancy and marriage, the proscription of family reunion, and the constricted freedom of association, residence, mobility, and employment. These practices, often in violation of migrants' human rights, institutionalize the exploitability of migrant workers, migrant women in particular. They also contribute to the formation of "racialized boundaries" (Anthias and Yuval-Davis 2) that constructs fictionalized borders between Taiwanese nationals and foreign workers. While Taiwan's foreign labor policy reflects foreign labor's relationship to the nation-state, the regulation over migrant women's reproductive and sexual decisions demonstrates the particular impact on migrant women of gendered and racialized nature of state policy. The state realizes its racial/nationalist project in shaping the composition of citizenry through controlling migrant women's sexuality, reproduction, and motherhood. As Anthias elaborates on the role of women in the reproduction of the nation:

> In all societies, women of different groups are encouraged to reproduce the nation differently and some are encouraged to 'grow and flourish' whereas others are seen as undesirable. For example, in many Western societies ethnic minority women's fertility may be seen as a threat to the nation, involving demographic and nationalist policing and ide-ologies (Anthias and Yuval Davis 1989) and the use of depo-provera and sterilization techniques against some (Anthias and Yuval Davis 1992). Indigenous mothers who give birth to many children (termed polytechna mothers in Cyprus) may be rewarded whereas migrants and their descendents in this situation may be subjected to policies and discourses of inferiorization. Although women are members of collectivities they are subjected to different rules and experience them differently. (32-33)

The above comparative descriptions of Taiwan and Canada illustrate the similarity shared by two different sociopolitical contexts in the nexus of nation building and national/global restructuring of care. They highlight migrant women's precarious position in terms of their human rights and citizenship entitlements, both locally and globally. Therefore, the linkage among racial formation, gendered practices, nation building, and global restructuring of care cannot be ignored.

Motherhood, Citizenship, and Transborder Concern

The institutionalization of migrant women's ultra-exploitability raises funda-mental questions about their lack of citizenship rights and entitlements. First, it illustrates that violence facing these women is not simply the result of individual acts of abusive employers; instead, it derives from state control and regulations. It is exactly the differential citizenship statuses, i.e., citizen vs. non-citizen, between native employers and foreign domestics that legitimate employer-employee power asymmetry. Migrant women's status as non-citizens calls attention to the state's realization of nationalist/racial projects through the regulation of their sexuality, reproduction, and motherhood. In other words, they face structural as well as intimate violence.

Second, the regulation of migrant women's sexuality, reproduction, and motherhood points to their disparate meanings for women differentially positioned along national and global hierarchies. Empire of care speaks to the reality that migrant women from the Third World are deprived of their right to determine their sexual activities, reproductive choices, and motherhood concerns because of the intimate surveillance in both private and public spheres. This reality calls attention to the necessity to expand the definitions of citizenship rights and entitlements to include the particular experience of migrant women in the aspect of sexuality, reproduction, and motherhood. In other words, migrant women's individual and collective rights to these central facets of human existence complicate sexual, reproductive, and family politics in national and global terrains.

Third, the experience of migrant women also problematizes linear and evolutionary conceptions of citizenship development. Upper- and middle-class women in labor receiving nations, as a result of the advancement of political and socio-economic rights, are able to enter the workplace and gain visibility in the public sphere. However, their entry depends neither upon the redistribution of household labor within the private sphere nor upon the recognition of care as socially valuable work in the public sphere. The global unequal distribution of care has enabled female employers to resolve their individual needs for childcare without making demands on the state. Their participation in the public sphere hinges upon the stunted enjoyment of civil, political, and socio-economic rights of women from less developed regions and nations. As Abigail Bakan and Daiva Stasiulis state:

> For the Third World non-citizen in search of First World citizenship, gaining access to social rights—particularly "the right to a modicum of economic welfare and security" (Marshall 1950, 78)—commonly supersedes entry to civil and political rights. Thus, to gain certain social rights such as access to adequate health and educational services, citizens of the Philippines or Jamaica exit their home countries and, in so doing, forfeit a range of regionally and nationally defined civil, political, social, and cultural rights. These forfeited rights may include the rights of land ownership, associated with citizenship and residence in less developed countries. They also give up certain social rights, such as the right to live with one's children and other family members, the right to freedom of choice of domicile, and access to networks of support in the provision of health care, child care, food, and so on. (45-46)

In other words, the stunted enjoyment of citizenship and human rights by contemporary migrant women has coincided with the gradual expansion of rights for citizens of marginalized groups within receiving nation-states. This paradox illustrates the necessity to reconsider motherhood, from the standpoint of migrant women, not only as an issue of choice but also as that of right.

Conclusion: From the Choice of Motherhood to the Right to Mothering

The reemergence of paid domestic labor as an important issue for feminist scholarship speaks to the missing revolutions in feminism in materializing equal distribution of care both within and across national borders. Indeed, the privatization of care provision illustrates the state's appropriation of women's care labor, migrant women in particular, and the gendered/racialized nature of national/transnational systems of care. Rather than challenging the devaluation of women's work and that of care as a whole, the availability of migrant women's care labor enables labor receiving states to deepen the privatization of childcare and evade the commitment to the collective responsibility for social reproduction. Migrant women's care labor serves as a cheap solution for the inadequacy of public provision of care in labor receiving nations. Their mothering experience speaks to the simultaneous de-nationalization and re-nationalization of motherhood as well as the maintenance of empire of care in the age of globalization.

Empire of care heightens the nexus between the local and the global. It speaks to the necessity for building alliances within and across national borders and for the joint pursuit of local and global justice for multiple forms of equality. It also points to the urgency of collaborative local and global feminist interventions in the pursuit of motherhood as a transborder concern. From the perspective of migrant women, it is not the choice of motherhood but the right to motherhood/mothering that is in jeopardy in the transnational era.

References

Anthias, Floya. "Metaphors of Home: Gendering New Migrations to Southern Europe." In *Gender and Migration in Southern Europe: Women on the Move*, edited by Floya Anthias and Gabriella Lazaridis. Oxford: Berg, 2000. 15-47.

Anthias, Floya, and Nira Yuval-Davis. 1992. *Racialized Boundaries: Race, Nation, Gender, Colour and Class and the Anti-Racist Struggle.* London: Routledge.

Arat-Koc, Sedef. "From 'Mothers of the Nation' to Migrant Workers." In *Not One of the Family: Foreign Domestics Workers in Canada*. Abigail B. Bakan and Daiva Stasiulis, eds. Toronto: University of Toronto Press, 1997. 53-79.

Bakan, Abigail B., and Daiva Stasiulis. "Foreign Domestic Worker Policy in Canada and the Social Boundaries of Modern Citizenship." *Not One of the Family: Foreign Domestic Workers in Canada*. Abigail B. Bakan and Daiva Stasiulis, eds. Toronto: University of Toronto Press, 1997. 29-52.

Chang, Grace. *Disposable Domestics: Immigrant Women Workers in the Global Economy*. Cambridge, Mass.: South End Press, 2000.

Choy, Catherine Ceniza. *Empire of Care: Nursing and Migration in Filipino American History*. Durham: Duke University Press, 2003.

Collins, Patricia Hill. "Shifting the Center: Race, Class, and Feminist Theorizing about Motherhood." *Mothering: Ideology, Experience, and Agency.* Evelyn

Nakano Glenn, Grace Chang, and Linda Rennie Forcey, eds. New York: Routledge, 1994. 45-65.

Gamburd, Michele Ruth. "Nurture for Sale: Sri Lankan Housemaids and the Work of Mothering." *Home and Hegemony: Domestic Service and Identity Politics in South and Southeast Asia.* Kathleen M. Adams and Sara Dickey, eds. Ann Arbor: University of Michigan Press, 2000. 179-205.

Hochschild, Arlie Russell. "Love and Gold." *Global Woman: Nannies, Maids, and Sex Workers in the New Economy.* Barbara Ehrenreich and Arlie Russell Hochschild, eds. New York: Henry Holt and Company, 2002. 15-30.

Hondagneu-Sotelo, Pierrette. *Doméstica: Immigrant Workers Cleaning and Caring in the Shadows of Affluence.* Berkeley, CA: University of California Press, 2001.

Hondagneu-Sotelo, Pierrette. "The International Division of Caring and Cleaning Work: Transnational Connections or Apartheid Exclusions?" *Care Work: Gender Labor and the Welfare State.* Madonna Harrington Meyer, eds. New York: Routledge, 2000. 149-162.

Hondagneu-Sotelo, Pierrette, and Ernestine Avila. "'I am Here, But I am There': The Meanings of Latina Transnational Motherhood." *Gender and Society* 11 (1997): 548-71.

Parrenas, Rhacel Salazar. *Servants of Globalization: Women, Migration, and Domestic Work.* Stanford, CA: Stanford University Press, 2001.

Parrenas, Rhacel Salazar. "Migrant Filipina Domestic Workers and the International Division of Reproductive Labor." *Gender and Society* 14 (2000): 560-80.

Wong, Sau-Ling C. "Diverted Mothering: Representations of Caregivers of Color in the Age of 'Multiculturalism.'" *Mothering: Ideology, Experience, and Agency.* Evelyn Nakano Glenn, Grace Chang, and Linda Rennie Forcey, eds. New York: Routledge, 1994. 67-91.

Chapter 39

The Globalization of Love

Transnational Adoption and Engagement with the Globalized World

EMILY J. NOONAN

I am walking and my two-year old daughter is toddling through a small "Third World" arts and crafts store located in a Western North Carolina community. The store is filled nearly to capacity with visitors from the local Christian retreat center and tourists who are passing through as they view the fall foliage. We are all searching for gifts to give for holidays, weddings, housewarmings, and birthdays. During our twenty minutes in the cramped shop, four women asked me about my child. This is not an uncommon experience. Though we have some common features—black hair, dark eyes—our skin tones do not match. I am a white woman born in Kentucky, and my daughter is a brown-skinned child born in Guatemala. "Is she adopted?" "Where is she from?" "Where did you get her?" "Was it hard to adopt?" "How long have you had her?" After their questions are answered, the conversation continues. Several women seem to want to connect with me; they tell me of their nieces, cousins, and friends who have adopted children born outside of the U.S. They fuss over my child, smiling, cooing, and speaking to her in Spanish.

Boston Globe columnist Ellen Goodman wrote of her newly adopted granddaughter for her July 4th column:

> Together, we have all learned about the globalization of love. America is continually made and remade by newcomers. But this daughter from China has reminded us how small our world is and how vast: a village you can traverse in a day and a place of stunning disconnects and differences, have and have-nots. Ours was already a global family, brought together with luck of the draw and pluck of the ancestors who came from places as far away as Italy and England, Russia and Germany. On this Fourth of July, we add another continent to our heritage and another child to our list of supreme good fortune. Welcome, Cloe, to America. (A13)

The above anecdotes reflect the attention and interest directed toward the practice of transnational adoption. In these stories (just a few of the many I could tell), shoppers, strangers, and journalists have tales to tell or comments to make about the role adoption has played in their own lives. And these stories tell us that transnational adoption, the families it creates, and the implications it holds for families in far-away countries are of concern and interest to the public. The above commentators are participating in discourse about transnational adoption that highlights anxieties about the formation of families, race, ethnicity, culture, distance and travel, as well as inequalities of wealth and power. Adoptive parents similarly negotiate these problems and questions through adoption-related media, community discussion, and their narratives of the adoption experience.

My own position in the so-called "adoption triad"—birth parent, adoptive parent, and child—is unusual, ill-defined, and reflective of changing configurations of family in contemporary America. I began dating my now-partner while she was in the process of adopting a baby girl from Guatemala. Seven months into our relationship, she traveled to Guatemala to take custody of a six-month-old baby, Maria. Both academics, my partner and I live in different cities about 200 miles apart. I commute weekly, spending four days with my family in small-town North Carolina and three days in my rented room in suburban Atlanta. My parental role defies simple definition. I'm partial to "long-distance co-parent," while Maria (now a two-year-old) has inexplicably christened me "Giggy." My relationship to the transnational adoption process is similarly unsettled, as I am not the legal adoptive parent and have not had some of the same experiences as most adoptive parents. Although I became a parent in a much different way than do most adoptive parents, my decision to be part of an adoptive family was just as deliberate, and I have been emotionally and physically invested in this family since before Maria's arrival.

I must be clear that I am attempting to neither romanticize nor demonize transnational adoption. My partner and I struggle with the contradiction between the joy our daughter has brought us and the knowledge that the system through which she came to us has the capacity to exploit impoverished and oppressed people for the benefit of relatively wealthy ones. Writing about the adoption of Native American children by white families, Pauline Turner Strong states, "[a]doption across political and cultural borders may simultaneously be an act of violence and an act of love, an excruciating rupture and a generous incorporation, an appropriation of valued resources and a constitution of personal ties" (471). Like Strong, I hope that my work will highlight the complications and contradiction of transnational adoption. By illustrating the ways in which adoption-related discourse both reproduces and challenges racist and neo-colonial relations, I hope to challenge such narratives and encourage adoptive parents to reconsider how they approach the process.

Transnational adoption began in the years following World War II and the Korean War. Since the early 1990s, however, the practice has become "unprecedented in magnitude and visibility" (Volkman 1). Transnational adoption has become an increasingly common practice worldwide, with an estimated 30,000 children migrating between over one hundred countries a year (Selman 206). The United States adopts more children from outside its borders than do citizens of all other countries combined (Scrivo), with the number of such adoptions increasing rapidly over the past few years, from 11,316 in 1996 (U.S. Immigration and Naturalization Service) to 21,100 in fiscal year 2002 (U.S. Department of Homeland Security). It is estimated that each day, twenty American couples adopt a child from a foreign country (Zeppa). The majority of transnationally adopted children come from four nations: China, with 6,062 adoptions in FY 2002; Russia with 4,904; Guatemala with 2,361; and South Korea with 1,713 (U.S. Department of Homeland Security).

The overwhelming majority of children adopted by U.S. citizens come from non-Western and "Third World" countries of the global south. Not surprisingly, transnational adoption has frequently been criticized as a neo-colonial, imperialist practice (Altstein and Simon 2; Hoelgaard 203; Masson 148; Pilotti 32; Tizzard 746) or described as a "manifestation of exploitation of poorer nations by more affluent ones" (Freundlich 88). Or as Barbara Katz Rothman said of the class dynamics of adoption, both domestic and transnational: "Thirty-two-year-old attorneys living in wealthy suburbs do not give up their children to nineteen-year-old factory workers living in small towns" (130).

With an average cost of $20,000 per adoption, U.S. citizens spend over $300 million annually on transnational adoption (Varnis 39). Thus it is frequently described and criticized as an industry (Graff,), a system of trade (Triseliotis 48), and as a market (D'Amato 669; Triseliotis 49) that can "fluctuate on demand" (Elton). The process of transnational adoption is also characterized as a system of "supply and demand" (Hoelgaard 207; Jacot 37), with "Third World" countries as "suppliers" with a "surplus of healthy children" (Altstein and Simon 2). Transnational adoption of children born in Guatemala has been described critically as "one of the most successfully nontradtionalist exports…It brings in more money than snow peas and broccoli" (Riley).

In addition to issues of neo-colonial exploitation, it is also crucial to keep in mind the particular ways the process of international adoption is gendered. Most children adopted by U.S. citizens are girls. Girls account for sixty-five percent of internationally adopted children in FY 2002 (U.S. Department of Homeland Security). This figure is largely attributed to adoptions of Chinese children, nearly all of which are girls.

Given the acceleration in the number of transnational adoptions in the United States, as well as the paucity of research in disciplines other than social work and psychology (Volkman 4), the practice of transnational adoption needs to be analyzed for the ways it is embedded in the globalization of capital, people, cultures, and ideologies. In their introduction to an edited volume on reproduction in a globalized world, Faye Ginsburg and Rayna Rapp argue, "[p]eople everywhere actively use their local cultural logics and social relations to incorporate, revise, or resist the influence of seemingly distant political and economic forces" (1). How do adoptive parents from the United States "incorporate, revise, or resist" discourses of globalization through the process of forming families through transnational adoption, and how do these discourses depend upon various narratives about race and gender?

Texts produced by American adoptive parents and international adoption agencies such as web pages, print publications, and adoption story testimonials reveal the ways international adoption can be examined as a practice that is embedded in global capitalist flows of capital, ideas, and cultures. Using Arjun Appadurai's idea of ethnoscapes, I will analyze discourse about international adoption that negotiates differences in American, white, and First World cultures and ethnicities of the adoptive parents and the non-Western, non-white, and Third World cultures and ethnicities of the adopted children. These negotiations occur within a context of immense economic disparity between the First and Third Worlds, as well as a history of colonialism, racism, and exploitation. Adoption texts expose these negotiations of ethnicity and culture between the First and Third World actors involved in the international adoption process. Also, as the majority of adoptees are girls, this negotiation occurs using images (both print and visual) of female children. Discourses of cultural and ethnic difference and similarity in international adoption commonly occur with girl children as the object of negotiation.

Although actors in the process of international adoption can be birth parents, children, adoptive parents, social workers, lawyers, and adoption agency staff, only the adoptive parents and adoption agents have widespread access to media production equipment, especially the Internet. While future research plans include analyses of narratives produced by people of birth countries, in this paper, I will examine how adoptive parents and adoption agents negotiate differences among First and Third World cultures and ethnicities within the context of global capitalism. Adoptive parents and adoption agents negotiate anxieties about cultural and ethnic difference in a variety of ways. I will examine how textual discourse of international adoption uses images of romanticized globalization, minimize the cultural and ethnic difference of internationally adopted children, exaggerate the American-ness of the children, and fetishize stereotypical characteristics of adopted children in order to make cultural and ethnic difference safe and uncomplicated for First World adoptive parents.

It's a Small World After All:
Globalization, International Adoption and Invisible Borders

As I am conceiving transnational adoption as a process tied to globalization, a brief review of globalization theory as it is related to transnational adoption is useful here. Globalization is commonly described as the exchange of labour, capital, and ideologies in the amplifying system of capitalism. However, the complexity of the process makes it difficult to develop theories or even definitions of globalization. According to Fredric Jameson, cited in John Beynon and David Dunkerly's *Globalization: A Reader*, globalization is: "the intellectual property of no particular field, yet seems to concern politics and economics in immediate ways, but just as immediately culture and sociology, not to speak of information and the media, or ecology, or consumerism and daily life" (4). In other words, globalization is not merely a system of economic exchange, and an all-encompassing definition should attempt to take non-economic factors into account. Anthony Giddens's definition of globalization includes social as well as economic forces. He describes globalization as "the intensification of world-wide social relationships which link distant places in such a way that local happenings are shaped by events occurring many miles away and vice-versa" (qtd. in Beynon and Dunkerly 4).

For the purposes of this project, I am concerned with a few key ideas related to globalization. The first concerns how people perceive global spatial relationships. In his definition of globalization, Roland Robertson emphasizes "the scope and depth of consciousness of the world as a single place (qtd. in Beynon and Dunkerly 47). Mike Featherstone describes globalization as "the emergence of the sense that the world is a single place" (171). Due to changes in configurations of power and challenges to hegemonic world histories, globalization supports ideas that "the world is one place, that the globe has been compressed into a locality, that others are neighbours with which we must necessarily interact, relate and listen" (172). Similarly, transnational adoption can be seen as an interaction that renders distance and borders between nations, ethnicities, and cultures indistinguishable, or at least surmountable.

Texts produced by adoption agencies emphasize globalization. The names of agencies show that international adoption unites all cultures as one, minimizing differences in language, culture, and ethnicity. For example, the Small World Adoption Foundation of Missouri clearly describes itself in relation to international adoption, a practice that de-emphasizes borders and differences in culture. It operates in, and creates, a "Small World." Other agencies, such as Los Niños International Adoption Center, minimize national borders and cultural difference through their logos. The Los Niños logo is made up of a blue globe covered by fluffy white clouds and a bright yellow sun. This circular arrangement is foregrounded by the agency's title and an airplane filled with small children of different colors, with one child sitting on the plane's nose. The tail of the plane shows a barely visible U.S. flag. The slogan for Los Niños is "We're Wrapping the World in Family Ties™." Also significant is the use of the Spanish language by adoption agencies. Los Niños International Adoption Center takes its name for the Spanish phrase for "children." Their logo goes so far as to translate the phrase. "Los Niños (Children's) International Adoption Center," it says. Despite differences in culture, languages, and ethnicity between adoptive parents and adopted children, international adoption (as facilitated by Los Niños) can be a unifying, conflict-free process. The Los Niños logo situates international adoption as a multiculturist, humanitarian, and harmonious enterprise. In other words, the use of romanticized images of international travel and exchange that occurs in international adoption renders cross-cultural difference and questions of neo-colonialism unproblematic for American adoptive parents. In other words, images associated with the process of international adoption add to and appeal to Featherstone's idea that "the world is becoming one place."

EMILY J. NOONAN

The Ethnoscapes of International Adoption

The second theory I am concerned with has to do with the movement of people from one area of the globe to another, resulting in negotiation of cultural meanings by those confronted with traveling people. Arjun Appadurai uses the term "ethnoscape" to describe the "landscape of persons who constitute the shifting world in which we live" (33). He uses examples of "tourists, immigrants, refugees, exiles, guest workers" (33) to describe transnational movements of people from various nations, regions, and of different ethnicities. Those participating in transnational adoption can be seen as prime examples of players in the global movement of persons that comprise Appadurai's ethnoscapes.

Appadurai also highlights the instability apparent in ethnoscapes, arguing that they are "deeply disjunctive and profoundly unpredictable because each of these landscapes is subject to its own constraints and incentives…at the same time as each acts as a constraint and a parameter for movements in others" (35). The ethnoscapes of traveling and migrating people are inherently unstable, as they occur within the context of post-colonialism and racism. Westerners involved with transnational adoption must negotiate the meanings of cultures and ethnicities of the children adopted from non-Western countries and attempt to make sense of the political and social implications inherent in such global interactions. Adoptive parents and adoption agents must also define their own identities in relation to the asymmetrical power relations that exist in transnational adoption process. These negotiations occur in a variety of ways. Parents and agents often minimize the cultural and ethnic differences between themselves and the children involved in the interaction in order to make international adoption. This minimization can be done by emphasizing the American-ness of the children, by minimizing the degree of difference, by describing their own familiarity (or lack thereof) with the child's birth culture, and through imagery reflecting the multicultural location of the child, rendering cultural difference unimportant. Parents and agents also attempt to deal with cultural difference by marking and fetishizing adoptee children as representations of an entire culture or heritage. This type of discourse is most likely to draw on the child's gender, as well as race and ethnicity, in the negotiation of cultural difference between adopter and adoptee.

Minimizing Difference

The most common type of international adoption narrative involves the de-emphasis of the child's birth culture and an emphasis on the adoptive culture, usually through verbal and visual invocations of American nationalism. Adoption agency websites frequently feature pictures of adopted children situated with an image of the American flag. Several pictures depicted the U.S. flag draped behind the child (1ˢᵗ Steps Adoption International) or the child wearing flag-patterned clothing (Great Wall China Adoption). Linda Donovan, a director of an adoption agency, says of internationally adopted children: "The bottom line is they are American" (qtd. in Deam). This variety of discourse prioritizes American citizenship above all else.

Other adoption texts make use of nationalist symbols, but do not explicitly privilege American-ness. Though they have since changed their website design, a previous version of the Great Wall China Adoption website played on the notion of dual nationalities or heritages in the artwork and designs within the site. The link buttons leading site visitors to other pages were comprised of the Chinese and U.S. flags. Another site, AdoptShoppe, sells clothing, books, jewelry, and other items to adoptive families. One popular item is the "Crossed Flags Tees and Sweatshirts." These pieces of clothing are "Personally designed for your family and children with their heritage in mind" and are embroidered with the American flag crossed with the flag of the child's birth country. Through these images, the differences between American-ness and foreign-ness are erased and are assimilated into American-ness. Of course, as in the images of adopted children with a U.S. flag, American-ness is implicitly privileged, as the United States is the country of citizenship and residency for both the adoptive parents and their newly adopted Chinese children. By locating American-ness as central to the international adoption process, these texts contribute to discourse that de-emphasizes the cultural difference of internationally adopted children.

Another common way of minimizing cultural differences between the children and Western adults involved in international adoption is accomplished when adoptive parents use their knowledge of the child's birth culture in explaining their adoption of a foreign-born child. Several adoptive mothers cited language preparation and their engagement with Spanish culture as reasons they chose to adopt from Guatemala. Adoptive mother Tina Davis: "Given my fluency in Spanish and my interest in the Latin American culture, Guatemala seemed like the perfect choice for us." In a similar vein, Karen Scott states, "Even the interest I had in high school many years ago for the Spanish language was even then preparing me for this future." In these cases, cultural difference is bridged through high school Spanish classes and an "interest" in Guatemalan culture. Other parents declare their lack of familiarity with a given country, but dismiss the importance of such knowledge. Sue Mertens, who adopted a baby boy from Guatemala begins the telling of her adoption story: "Guatemala … I knew it was a Spanish-speaking country, located somewhere south of Mexico, and vaguely recalled that there had been a civil war there years ago, but I have to admit that I knew very little else about the country."

Cultural difference is minimized in other ways as well. In an essay for *American Demographics*, New York City resident Tama Janowitz dismisses concerns that her adopted China-born daughter will attract attention and questions from strangers by describing other examples of difference in her life. Her husband, an Englishman, orders ham sandwiches with butter. Their dogs are hairless Chinese Cresteds (48). She claims she is used to comments and questions from strangers. Janowitz goes on to describe her multicultural neighborhood, made up of "an amazing mix of people." "Is there anyone left who does fit in?" Janowitz asks

(49). Using the image of a metropolitan family, Janowitz dismisses the ethnic difference of her child.

These examples show some of the ways in which adoptive parents and adoption agencies attempt to minimize the differences between the child's birth and adoptive cultures. Each of these textual examples contributes to discourse attempting to make international adoption unproblematic, and to erase vestiges of colonialism and racism in the international adoption process.

The Emphasis and Fetishization of Difference

Adoptive parents and agencies also negotiate the ethnoscape of international adoption through the fetishization of adopted children. Adopted children can be marked, or fetishized in several ways. The status of the child as adopted, or foreign, can be emphasized. For example, one publication in a popular finance magazine said "The Americans like their little Chinese acquisitions" ("Give me your squalling masses," 1996). This statement fetishizes adopted children as cultural commodities. Though it is not explicit, this statement commodifies girl children as a cultural import from China, as nearly all of the children adopted from China are female. An article in *The Advocate* on the adoption of Chinese girls by lesbians blithely stated, "By now lesbians may have more Chinese daughters than Mazda Miatas" (Rich). This statement not only equates children with a consumer purchase such as a car, but also equates an ethnicity or nationality (Chinese) with consumerism. The ethnic difference of "Chinese daughters" is highlighted in order to describe the location of American lesbians in international adoption.

Alternately, texts emphasize and fetishize the ethnicity or cultural difference of an adopted child. In these cases, adopted children are seen as representations of whole cultures, their bodies embodying stereotypical characteristics of the non-Western culture. This sort of fetishizing often occurs in relation to girl children. An adoptive parent described his newly adopted Russian daughter: "she has the coordination of a Russian gymnast or ice skater." The use of fetishizing language, whether about children as commodities or as embodiments of stereotypical characteristics again renders ethnic differences harmless. If a child is comparable to car, or the characteristics of an ethnically different child can be distilled down to stereotypes, then issues related to race and ethnicity can be rendered unimportant.

Conclusion

The exchange of capital, as well as the language of economics marks the practice of international adoption as a process intricately tied to global capitalism. The process is also part of changing public ideologies that reinforce the feeling that the globe is shrinking and people from different nations are more tightly connected. International adoption can also be seen as contributing to and creating ethnoscapes, whereby the individuals involved with adoption attempt to ascribe and negotiate meanings of differences in culture and ethnicity that appear to exist between parents and their adoptive children. The disparate ways in which parents and adoption agents negotiate cultural differences using both the ethnicity and gender of their children reveals how international adoption discourse can be seen in relation to established narratives of capitalism, postcolonialism, and multiculturalism. The overarching discourse of international adoption, as created by American parents and adoption agents renders cultural and ethnic difference unimportant, invisible, and non-threatening.

Analyzing the changes in global circulations of people, goods, capital, and ideas is central to understanding how individuals and groups related to one another. Transnational adoption provides a framework through which we can see some of the ways globalized capitalism operates. Practices of globalization and related processes have a profound effect on how individuals think about and interact with peoples, places, and cultures. These interactions and ideologies make real differences in the lives of others—particularly when they reproduce racist, sexist, and neo-colonial systems. My hope is that analyzing the texts of potentially racist and sexist systems can ultimately help alter these systems in ways that truly benefit impoverished children and families.

References

1ˢᵗ Steps Adoption International, Inc. February 25, 2004. Online: http://www. kids4us.org.

AdoptShoppe. February 25, 2004. "Crossed Flags Tees and Sweatshirts." Online: http://www.adoptshoppe.com.

Altstein, Howard, and Rita J. Simon, eds. *Intercountry Adoption: A Multinational Perspective*. New York: Paeger, 1991.

Appadurai, Arjun. 1996. *Modernity at Large: Cultural Dimensions of Globalization*. Minneapolis: University of Minnesota Press.

Beynon, John, and David Dunkerly, eds. *Globalization: A Reader*. New York: Routledge, 2000.

D'Amato, Anthony. "Globalizing Adoption." *Christian Century* 30 June-7 July 1999: 668-669.

Davis, Tina. "The Davis Family." *Christian World Adoption*. Accessed February 25, 2004. Online: http://www.cwa.org/davis.html.

Deam, Jenny. "Why Not Take All of Me?" *The Denver Post*. September 1, 2002. Online. LexisNexis. 8 October 2002.

Elton, Catherine. "Adoption Vs. Trafficking in Guatemala." *Christian Science Monitor* 17 October 2000: 1. Online. Academic Search Premier. 14 October 2002.

Featherstone, Mike. "Global and Local Cultures." *Mapping the Futures: Local Cultures, Global Change*. Eds. Jon Bird, Barry Curtis, Tim Putnam, George Robertson, and Lisa Tickner. New York: Routledge, 1993. 169-187.

Freundlich, Madelyn. "Families Without Borders—I." *UN Chronicle* 36 (2)

(1999): 88-89.

Ginsburg, Faye D., and Rayna Rapp, eds. *Conceiving the New World Order: The Global Politics of Reproduction.* Los Angeles: University of California Press, 1995.

"Give me your squalling masses." *Economist* 3 February1996: 22-24. Online. Academic Search Premier. 14 October 2002.

Goodman, Ellen. "Cloe's First Fourth." *Boston Globe* July 3, 2003: A13.

Graff, Nicole Bartner. "Intercountry Adoption and the Convention on the Rights of the Child: Can the Free Market in Children be Controlled?" *Syracuse Journal of International Law and Commerce* Summer 2000. Online. Lexis Nexus. 22 October 2002.

Great Wall China Adoption. February 25, 2004. Online: http://gwcadopt.org

Hoelgaard, Suzanne. "Cultural Determinants of Adoption Policy: A Columbian Case Study." *International Journal of Law, Policy and the Family* 12 (1998): 202-241.

Jacot, Martine. "Adoption: For Love or Money." *The UNESCO Courier* February 1(1999): 37-39.

Janowitz, Tama. "Diaper Diplomacy." *American Demographics* 21 (5) (1999): 48-49.

Los Niños International Adoption Center. Accessed February 25, 2004. Online: http://www.losninos.org.

Masson, Judith. "Intercountry Adoption: A Global Problem or a Global Solution?" *Journal of International Affairs* 55 (1) (2001): 141-166.

Mertens, Sue. "Family Stories." *Cradle of Hope Family Stories.* Accessed February 25, 2004. Online: http://www.cradlehope.org.CHAC_families/mertens.html.

Pilotti, Francisco J. "Intercountry Adoption: A View from Latin America." *Child Welfare* 64 (1) (1985): 25-35.

Rich, B. Ruby. "Frames of Mind: Ming has Two Mommies." *The Advocate* 18 July 2000. Online. ProQuest. 23 October 2002.

Riley, Michael. "Families without borders: International adoption surges as would-be parents weigh risk, reward." *Denver Post* August 18, 2003.

Rothman, Barbara Katz. 1989. *Recreating Motherhood: Ideology and Technology in a Patriarchal Society.* New York: W.W. Norton & Company.

Scott, Karen. "The Scott Family." *Christian World Adoption.* Accessed 25 February 2004. Online. Available http://www.cwa.org/scott.html.

Scrivo, Karen Lee. "The Parent Trap." *National Journal* March 4, 2000. Online. Academic Search Premier. 13 October 2002.

Selman, Peter. "Intercountry Adoption in the New Millennium; The 'Quiet Migration' Revisited." *Population Research and Policy Review* 21 (2002): 205-225.

Small World Adoption Foundation of Missouri. Accessed February 25, 2004. Online. Available http://www.swaf.com.

Strong, Pauline Turner. "To Forget Their Tongue, Their Name, and Their Whole Relation." *Relative Values: Reconfiguring Kinship Studies.* Eds. Sarah Franklin and Susan McKinnon. Durham, NC: Duke University Press, 2001. 468-493.

Tizzard, Barbara. "Intercountry Adoption: A Review of the Evidence." *Journal of Child Psychology and Psychiatry* 32 (5) (1991): 743-756.

Triseliotis, John. "Intercountry Adoption: Global Trade or Global Gift?" *Adoption & Fostering* 24 (2) (2000): 45-54.

U.S. Department of Homeland Security. "Table 12. Immigrant-Orphans Adopted by U.S. Citizens by Gender, Age, and Region and Country of Birth Fiscal Year 2002." *Yearbook of Immigration Statistics, 2002*. Washington, D.C.: U.S. Government Printing Office, 2003. 46-47.

U.S. Immigration and Naturalization Service. "Table 15. Immigrant-Orphans Adopted by U.S. Citizens Gender, Age, and Region and Country of Birth Fiscal Year 1996." *Statistical Yearbook of the Immigration and Naturalization Service, 1996*. Washington, D.C.: U.S. Government Printing Office, 1997. 59.

Varnis, Steven L. "Regulating the Global Adoption of Children." *Society* January/February 2001: 39-46.

Volkman, Toby Alice. 2003. "Introduction: Transnational Adoption." *Social Text* 21 (74): 1-5.

Zeppa, Stephanie. "'Let Me In, Immigration Man': An Overview of Intercountry Adoption and the Role of the Immigration and Nationality Act." *Hastings International and Comparative Law Review* (Fall 1998). Online. LexisNexis. 22 October 2002.

Chapter 40

Mother-Worship/Mother-Blame

Politics and Welfare in an Uncertain Age

MOLLY LADD-TAYLOR

"Bad" mothers are all around us: in the news, on sitcoms, and in jail. Judith Scruggs, whose son committed suicide, was convicted of a criminal offense for failing to provide him with proper care (Scarponi, 2003). Andrea Yates, who killed her five children to protect them from the devil's grasp, was found guilty of murder when a jury rejected the claim that she was mentally ill ("In-Depth Special: The Case of Andrea Yates"). "Bad" mothers also abound on television comedies; the intrusive Marie on "Everybody Loves Raymond" and "Malcolm in the Middle's" hysterical mom are always good for a laugh. But where are the "good" mothers in contemporary culture? Except for Lorelei Gilmore, the very un-motherly mother on television's "Gilmore Girls," they are very hard to find.

In many ways, the disappearance of the "good" mother is a welcome develop-ment. You can't have a "good mother"—at least the way the dominant culture defines her, as selfless, nurturing, and true—without a bad mother to compare her to. I used to think the opposite was also true: the bad mother was only bad when compared to a mother who was good. But now I'm not so sure.

I was curious about what had happened to the good mothers, so I did an informal survey at my kids' school. My question—who is a "good" mother (and why)?—provoked a great deal of disagreement. For example, some people said Jane was a good mother because she is so attentive to her children, but others said that is what makes her a bad mother; her children have no space! The only agreement was among my children. When asked who's a good mother, they all agreed, "Not you, Mom."

Unable to find any good mothers in the schoolyard, I decided to try a Google search. The internet is full of "bad" mothers: unmarried mothers, teen mothers, mothers on drugs, mothers on welfare. Fortunately, it's full of their defenders too. But good mothers (or even, as the psychiatrist D. W. Winnicott would say, "good-enough" mothers) are a lot more obscure. The "good mothers" I found through Google were almost all tied to Mothers' Day—or God. "How are mothers and Jesus alike?" one web-published sermon asked. Both are willing to make the ultimate sacrifice and lay down their lives for their children. The only difference is that when a mother dies, she stays dead, and Jesus came back to life (Christ our Savior Church).

The invisibility of "good" mothers in mainstream politics today is a significant historical change. One hundred fifty years ago, the good mother was an icon of North American political culture. Men did the nasty work of business and war, according to nineteenth-century gender ideology, while mothers stayed home in "woman's sphere," bearing and nurturing children and protecting their families from the heartless world outside (Evans; Prentice *et al.*).

The maudlin mother-worship of Victorian times reached its peak in 1908, when Mothers' Day was established in the United States by Anna Jarvis, an unmarried non-mother who apparently found in lobbying for Mother's Day a way to achieve the public visibility and career her late mother had opposed (Jones). Women's groups initially objected to Mothers' Day as too sappy, but Christian Sunday Schools, politicians, and the flower industry recognized it as a great opportunity. The holiday came into its own during the First World War, when good mothers were defined as those who made the ultimate sacrifice of sending their sons to war. American Mothers' Day literature claimed to be honouring all mothers, since war was a national project and (as one clergyman explained), "Rich and poor can meet on the common ground of love, reverence and appreciation for the mother" (Jones 188). In reality, however, the patriotic, Christian, white, middle-class orientation of Mother's Day excluded a lot of mothers.

That exclusion is precisely the point: mother-worship is always bound up with mother-blame. This was especially true in the years around the First World War, when industrialization, immigration, changing gender roles, and the twin projects of nation-building and (in the U.S.) empire-building heightened elite concerns about population "quality." Physicians, clergy, and politicians praised racially fit (white middle-class) mothers who had large families, but worried aloud about the uneducated masses who did the same (Valverde; Ladd-Taylor). U.S. President Theodore Roosevelt even coined the term "race suicide" to goad educated white protestants into having more children. Honouring the white mother of a large family as "sacred," he heaped scorn on her childless counterpart, who "shirks her duty, as wife and mother, [and] earns the right to our contempt" (174). The eugenics movement exemplifies the interdependence of mother-worship and mother-blame. Eugenicists used propaganda to convince "superior" women to have lots of children, but used the law to prevent the reproduction—and immigration—of the so-called unfit (McLaren; Paul).

This is the context in which women activists forged powerful "mothers" movements in the United States, Western Europe, and throughout the British Commonwealth. Maternalism, or maternal feminism as it is often called in Canada, was especially influential in shaping public policy in the United States, where working-class organizations were weak and efforts to enact class-based welfare legislation, such as health insurance, had failed (Kealey; Michel and Koven). Women who did not have the right to vote claimed political authority as mothers. "Woman's Place is Home," one suffragist declared, "But Home is not contained within the four walls of an individual house. Home is the community. The city full of people is the Family.... And badly do the Home and Family need their mother" (Dorr 327). They hoped the message was clear: women could not fulfill their maternal obligations unless they had political power.

Activists from a variety of political perspectives drew on the image of the good mother to press their demands for higher education, better treatment of wage-earning women, and the vote. The American reformer Jane Addams, Canada's Nellie McClung, and numerous colleagues in women's clubs and social settlements used the metaphor of the selfless mother, who like a soldier literally risked her life bearing children for the nation, to convince male politician-voters that publicly-funded kindergartens, health clinics, playgrounds, day nurseries, and welfare services would not undermine a mother's love for her child. After all, they said, nothing could weaken that essential mother-child bond. Birth controller Margaret Sanger and anarchist Emma Goldman tied their radical demands for birth control and female emancipation to the needs of working-class mothers. Even never-married women, such as Addams, cast themselves as "social mothers" so their femininity was never in doubt (Berg; Ladd-Taylor).

In the United States, mothers' movements were generally middle class and racially segregated, but they were not only white. African-American activists often described themselves as the "civic mothers" of the race and established health and educational services within their communities. They also used "good mother" rhetoric to get white women to face their own racism and privilege. At an 1899 meeting of the National Congress of Mothers, Mary Church Terrell urged white women to "put yourselves for one minute" in the place of a black mother—"(you could not endure the strain any longer) and imagine if you can, how you would feel if situated similarly.... [I]nstead of thrilling with the joy which you feel as you clasp your little ones to your breast, [you would tremble] with apprehension and despair" (Terrell 407).

As Terrell's eloquence and a number of recent scholars have shown, the white middle-class mothers' movement left many women behind. Maternalists never questioned women's "natural" responsibility for homemaking, they took for granted the superiority of English protestant middle-class culture, and they truly believed that every child needed two heterosexual parents and a mother who stayed home full-time. As a result, they supported programs, like mothers' pensions, which provided a small amount of support for single mothers and children in so-called "suitable" homes (e.g., where single mothers didn't have sex or work long hours outside the home), rather than childcare or better-paying jobs. In the United States, mothers' pensions evolved into Aid to Dependent Children, or welfare; in Canada, they formed the basis of the 1944 *Family Allowance Act*, a universal child benefit. Both programs were discontinued in the 1990s, but maternalist thinking about children's need for a suitable, stay-at-home mother still reverberates in American and—to a lesser extent—Canadian welfare politics (Christie; Mink; Strong-Boag).

The most progressive reformers, like Jane Addams, defended disadvantaged mothers on the grounds that if they were bad mothers, it was because of conditions, like poverty or poor housing, that were beyond their control. But others were not so forgiving. Maternal feminists had always cast a suspicious eye at low-income mothers, but the presumption that motherhood united women across the boundaries of class, race, and nation was also inclusive. As a result, when maternal feminism disappeared from the political landscape in the 1920s, mother-blaming grew more vicious. It also reached into the middle class. Childrearing advice, which had once idealized mother-love, now characterized it as a "dangerous instrument" and "stumbling block" to child development. Mothers' pensions, which at least had acknowledged mothers' contribution to society, became Aid to Dependent Children or (in Canada) family allowances. Although women continued to be influential in the child welfare field, they considered themselves professionals first. Claiming political authority on the basis of motherhood was no longer a winning strategy (Ladd-Taylor; Ladd-Taylor and Umansky).

In the 1920s and 1930s, politicians rarely talked about the need to dignify motherhood or protect maternal welfare. They did, however, talk a great deal about protecting society from "bad" mothers and their imperfect children. The "bad mother" discourse of the interwar years reached its peak—and did its greatest damage—in the campaign for eugenic sterilization. The U.S. Supreme Court upheld the constitutionality of compulsory sterilization in 1927, and eventually 33 states and two Canadian provinces enacted sterilization laws. More than 60,000 North Americans, mostly women, were forcibly sterilized (McLaren; Reilly).

Public support for eugenics waned in the 1930s and 1940s, but political mother-blaming thrived. In striking contrast to the First World War, when good-mother imagery was pervasive, pundits of the World War II era were obsessed by the evils of "America's traditional sweet, doting, self-sacrificing Mom" ("'Moms' denounced as peril to nation" 11). The positive image of the virtuous mother who made the supreme sacrifice by sending her sons off to war was displaced by the domineering "Mom," who kept them tied to her apron strings and—according to the U.S. Army psychiatrist Edward Strecker—caused the alarming instance of psychoneurosis in servicemen (cited in Terry,). In their popular but bizarre diatribe on *Modern Woman: The Lost Sex*, Ferdinand Lundberg and Marynia Farnham (1947) catalogued the unspeakable harm that rejecting, over-solicitous, dominating, and over-affectionate mothers did to their children—and society. In their view, most mothers needed psychotherapy to learn to accept their passive feminine role and yield to male authority in the family.

Although the 1950s are often associated with the archetypal good mother June Cleaver and (if you believe conservatives) the golden age of the family, Cold War anxieties accelerated the mother-bashing frenzy. Smothering stay-at-home moms were accused of turning their sons into homosexuals or communists, working mothers of neglecting their kids and producing juvenile delinquents, and black "matriarchs" of causing black men's unemployment and poverty (Feldstein; Ladd-Taylor and Umansky).

Today, we live in another uncertain age, when war, terrorism, and an economic downturn are leading people back to the perceived security of the home. Yet with the majority of mothers in the workforce, the home no longer seems as safe as it once did. Smothering or neglectful "bad" mothers are still blamed for youth violence, drug abuse, and dangerous sexual practices. In contrast to the past, however, the "good" mother is nowhere to be found.

Hoping to restore the "good mother" to American political culture, the Motherhood Project of the Institute for American Values recently launched a pro-family campaign based on the "maternal feminist" values of Jane Addams. Led by prominent neo-liberals like Sylvia Ann Hewlett and Jean Bethke Elshtain, the project promotes the Victorian concept of the home as a safe and "separate" sphere. It draws a distinction between the "values of the motherworld," such as "sacrifice, humility, and forbearance," and the grasping values of the moneyworld (Institute for American Values). It preaches the universality of mothering and mother-values, where class, race, and cultural background become irrelevant in the face of a common motherhood. And, like its early twentieth-century counterpart, the Motherhood Project emphasizes children's need for a two-parent, heterosexual married family. The Institute for American Values advocates a number of "family-friendly" policies, including tax reform, paid parental leave, flextime in the workplace, restrictions on advertisements, marriage education for welfare recipients, and legislation making it more difficult to obtain a divorce. Like its early-twentieth century counterpart, the new "maternal feminism" effectively encourages reproduction among the elite, but discourages it among the young, unmarried, and poor. For example, Hewlett's highly publicized *Creating a Life: Professional Women and the Quest for Children* laments what she sees as the tragic childlessness of high-achieving women, while *The War Against Parents: What Can We Do For America's Beleaguered Moms and Dads,* which she co-authored with Cornel West, proposes restructuring welfare benefits to privilege married two-parent families, and reconfiguring the legal system to make it easier to adopt a child. As feminist historian Rickie Solinger shows, the simplification of adoption procedures would serve mainly to facilitate the transfer of babies from poor and unmarried "bad" mothers to more affluent (and therefore "better") ones.

A major problem with the Motherhood Project's implicit opposition of "good" and "bad" mother is that, especially in the United States, the "bad" mother has so much greater symbolic power. Since the 1980s, the "bad" mother (who in recent years is almost always black and a crack addict or "welfare queen") has become a central icon of U.S. political culture. According to Solinger, such shrill "bad" mother rhetoric, along with 20 years of attacks on welfare, abortion rights, and women's health services, is making motherhood a "class privilege" in the United States. She suggests that this is partly because U.S. feminists employed the rhetoric of choice, rather than rights, in asserting the right to legal abortion. If the decision to have (or not have) a baby is seen as a choice, not a right, women who are young, poor, disabled, or on welfare but still "choose" motherhood can be criticized for making a bad choice.

Political mother-blaming exists in Canada, of course, but it is nowhere near as vindictive and mean-spirited as it is in the United States, and it has not set such deep roots in welfare policy and the courts. A brief comparison of two highly publicized "bad mother" cases in the mid-1990s is illustrative. In 1995, Tabitha Pollock's three-year old daughter was found beaten to death at her home in Illinois, and Tabitha's live-in boyfriend admitted to the beating. Forensics found evidence of considerable abuse, but Tabitha denied any knowledge that her children were mistreated. The other adults in the household—her boyfriend's parents and his brother's girlfriend—claimed ignorance too (*People v. Pollock*).

Tabitha Pollock, but not her boyfriend's parents, was charged with first-degree murder. Although not present when the crime was committed, she was a parent who had failed to protect her child from an abuser, and the law of accountability applied. Witnesses for the prosecution criticized Tabitha's mothering and testified to her prior bad acts: she once let the little girl climb on a bookcase, which almost fell on top of her, and she failed to keep her children or their clothes sufficiently clean. The Department of Children and Family Services had been called in to investigate, but found no evidence of abuse. Nevertheless, a jury concluded that Tabitha Pollock was not merely a "bad" mother, but a murderer as well. She was convicted of first-degree murder and sentenced to 36 years in jail. She served seven years before her conviction was overturned by the Illinois Supreme Court (*People v. Pollock*; Liptak,).

Renee Heikamp was 19 years old and homeless when her first child Jordan was born in Toronto in 1997. As a young mother at risk, she was put under the care of the Catholic Children's Aid Society, which placed her in a women's shelter. There, surrounded by lots of people, her baby starved to death when only five weeks old. Heikamp admitted to feeding her baby water, instead of formula, but blamed social workers and her lack of education. The social workers said Renee had deliberately misled them. Although Renee and her social worker were both charged with criminal negligence causing death, in a controversial ruling after several months of testimony, a judge threw out the charges. In 2001 a coroner's jury ruled baby Jordan's death a homicide—a finding that had no legal bearing on the mother—and issued 44 recommendations focused mainly on improving services for mothers on the streets ("Jury rules baby's starvation a homicide").

Both cases involved a tragic and preventable death, a malfunctioning child protection system, bad mothering, criminal charges, and intense media attention. But while Pollock spent several years in jail, the judicial proceedings surrounding the Heikamp case focused more on the appalling failure of the child protection system than on the mother's crime (Blatchford).

Why the difference? It is not, as some would like to think, that Canadians are more caring. It is because Canada established a welfare state in the decades after World War II, and a welfare state offers considerable protection from mother-blaming. It is much easier to be a not-bad mother when one has health insurance, paid parental leave, the possibility of affordable childcare, a reasonably safe environment—and lives in a society where "welfare" is not (not yet?) a dirty word.

Singing the praises of a welfare state is not a policy prescription, and right now it seems far more likely that Canada will lose its welfare state than that the United

States will acquire one. Still, the divergent histories of the U.S. and Canadian welfare systems, considered alongside the mother-blaming culture both countries share, should lead us to approach any attempt to revive maternal feminism with caution. Early twentieth-century maternalists tried to build support for child welfare programs by appealing to mother-love and mother-values, but their policies did not empower all mothers and children, and they did not lead to a fair, comprehensive welfare system. Instead, they led to programs that assisted some "good" mothers, but demeaned mothers considered bad. We should leave mother-worship back in the twentieth century and set our sights in the twenty-first century on expanding mothers' rights and eliminating mother-blame.

References

Berg, Allison. *Mothering the Race. Women's Narratives of Reproduction, 1890-1930.* Urbana: University of Illinois Press, 2002.

Blatchford, Christie. "Only in death did he begin to matter." *National Post.* April 5, 2001. Online: http://www.fathers.ca/renee_heikamp1.htm

Christ Our Savior Church. "The Good Shepherd and Good Mothers." Sermon No. 622. May 14, 2000. Online: www.cosrock.org/Sermon-2000-05-14.htm.

Christie, Nancy. 2000. *Engendering the State: Family, Work, and Welfare in Canada.* Toronto: University of Toronto Press.

Dorr, Rheta Childe. *What Eight Million Women Want.* 1919. New York: Kraus Reprint, 1971.

Evans, Sara. *Born for Liberty: A History of Women in America.* New York: Free Press, 1989.

Feldstein, Ruth. *Motherhood in Black and White: Race and Sex in American Liberalism, 1930-1965.* Ithaca: Cornell University Press, 2000.

Hewlett, Sylvia Ann. *Creating a Life: Professional Women and the Quest for Children.* New York: Talk Miramax Books, 2002.

Hewlett, Sylvia Ann and Cornell West. *The War Against Parents: What We Can Do for America's Beleaguered Moms and Dads.* New York: Houghton Mifflin, 1998.

"In-Depth Special: The Case of Andrea Yates." CNN.com. 2001. Online: http://www.cnn.com/SPECIALS/2001/yates/

Institute for American Values. "Watch Out for Children: A Mothers' Statement to Advertisers." 2000. Online: http://www.watchoutforchildren.org/

Jones, Kathleen. 1980. "Mother's Day: the Creation, Promotion and Meaning of a New Holiday in the Progressive Era." *Texas Studies in Literature and Language* 22: 175-196.

"Jury rules baby's starvation death a homicide." CBC News. *National Magazine.* April 12, 2001. Online: http://www.cbc.ca/national/news/heikamp/

Kealey, Linda, ed. 1979. *A Not Unreasonable Claim: Women and Reform in Canada, 1880s-1920s.* Toronto: Women's Press.

Ladd-Taylor, Molly. *Mother-Work: Women, Child Welfare and the State.* Urbana,

IL: University of Illinois Press, 1994.

Ladd-Taylor, Molly, and Lauri Umansky, eds. *"Bad" Mothers: The Politics of Blame in Twentieth-Century America.* New York: New York University Press, 1998.

Liptak, Adam. "Judging a mother for someone else's crime." *New York Times,* November 27: A 17, 2002.

Lundberg, Ferdinand, and Marynia Farnham. *Modern Woman: The Lost Sex.* New York: Grosset and Dunlap, 1947.

McLaren, Angus. *Our Own Master Race: Eugenics in Canada, 1885-1945.* Toronto: McClelland and Stewart, 1990.

Michel, Sonya and Seth Koven, eds. *Mothers of a New World: Maternalist Politics and the Origins of Welfare States.* New York: Routledge, 1993.

Mink, Gwendolyn. *The Wages of Motherhood: Inequality in the Welfare State, 1917-1942.* Ithaca: Cornell University Press, 1995.

"'Moms' denounced as peril to nation." *New York Times* April 28, 1945: 11.

Paul, Diane. *Controlling Human Heredity: 1865 to the Present.* New Jersey: Humanities Press, 1995.

People of the State of Illinois v. Tabitha Pollock. No. 3-96-1077. Third District Court. 10 December 1999. Online: www.state.il.us/court/Opinions/AppellateCourt/1999/3rdDistrict.

Prentice, Alison *et al. Canadian Women: A History.* Toronto: Harcourt Brace Jovanovich, 1988.

Reilly, Philip R. *The Surgical Solution: A History of Involuntary Sterilization in the United States.* Baltimore: John Hopkins University Press, 1991.

Roosevelt, Theodore. "Address to Congress on the Welfare of Children," *National Congress of Mothers' Magazine* 2 (1908): 174

Scarponi, Diane. "Connecticut woman convicted of contributing to son's suicide." *Herald Online* October 6, 2003. Online: http://www.heraldonline.com/24hour/nation/story/1020455p-7162856c.html

Solinger, Rickie. *Beggars and Choosers: How the Politics of Choice Shapes Adoption, Abortion, and Welfare in the United States.* New York: Hill and Wang, 2001.

Strong-Boag, Veronica. "'Wages for Housework': Mothers' Allowances and the Beginning of Social Security in Canada." *Journal of Canadian Studies* 14 (1979): 24-34.

Terrell, Mary Church. "Mary Church Terrell Greets the National Congress of Mothers." 1899. *Root of Bitterness: Documents of the Social History of American Women.* Ed. Nancy Cott et al. Boston: Northeastern University Press, 1996. 406-8.

Terry, Jennifer. "'Momism' and the Making of Treasonous Homosexuals. *"Bad" Mothers.* Eds. M. Ladd-Taylor and L. Umansky. New York: New York University Press, 1998. 169-190.

Valverde, Mariana. The Age of Light, Soap and Water. Toronto: McClelland and Stewart, 1993.

Winnicott, D. W. "Transitional Objects and Transitional Phenomena." *International Journal of Psychoanalysis* 26 (1953): 137-143.

Chapter 41

The "Problem" of Maternal Desire
Essential Mothering and the Dilemma of Difference

DAPHNE DE MARNEFFE

IT WOULD SEEM that everything it is possible to say about motherhood in America has already been said. Beckoning us from every magazine rack, beaming out from every channel, is a solution or a revelation or a confession about mothering. Yet in the midst of all the media chatter about staying on track, staying in shape, time crunches, time-savers, and time-outs, there is something unvoiced about the experience of motherhood itself. It sways our choices and haunts our dreams, yet we shy away from examining it with our full attention. Treated both as an illusion and as a foregone conclusion, it is at once obvious and invisible: our desire to mother.

The desire to mother is not only the desire to have children, but also the desire to care for them. It is not the duty to mother, or the compulsion to mother, or the concession to mothering when other options are not available. It is not the acquiescence to prescribed roles or the result of brainwashing. It is the longing felt by a mother to nurture her children; the wish to participate in their mutual relationship; and the choice, insofar as it is possible, to put her desire into practice.

Maternal desire is at once obvious and invisible partly because it is so easily confused with other things. Those fighting for women's progress too often misconstrue it as a throwback or excuse, a self-curtailment of potential. Those who champion women's maternal role too often define it text of service—to one's child, husband, view eclipses is the authentic desire to me herself—a desire not derived from a child's need, though responsive to it; a desire not created by a social role, though potentially supported by it; rather, a desire anchored in her experience of herself as an agent, an autonomous individual, person.

As common wisdom would have it, "mother" and "desire" do not belong in the same phrase. Desire, we've been told, is about sex. Motherhood, we've been told, is about practically everything but sex. A century ago, sexuality was repressed: blooming young women in Freud's day contracted odd symptoms-paralyzed arms, lost voices—as a way to adapt to social mores that inhibited women's awareness or expression of their sexual desires (Breuer and Freud).[1] Today, sexuality is everywhere, and the desire to mother is more prone to obfuscation. Partly owing to five decades of feminist writing, women's sexual desire no longer comes as much of a surprise. Maternal desire, by contrast, has become increasingly problematic. It is almost as if women's desire for sex and their desire to mother have switched places in terms of taboo.

The taboo against wanting to mother operates as a strange new source of inhibition for women. Some try not to think about motherhood while they pursue more immediate professional goals. Others deny the extent of their maternal wishes, which become clear only after hard-won insight in psychotherapy. Still others try to minimize their desire to nurture their child, setting up their lives to return to n is born, never fully cognizant that there n return to. For one woman, wanting to stay at home with her child is an embarrassing reversal of previous priorities. Another can't decide whether caring for children is a choice or a trap. Another feels she needs to maintain earning power and professional status if she wants to safeguard her self-esteem. For Freud's patients, sexual desire was frustrated by a restrictive model of decent womanhood, which emerged from complex social and economic forces. Today, maternal desire is constrained by a contemporary model of self that has developed in response to more recent economic and social realities.

Fifty years ago, women who wished to realize professional ambitions dealt with gender inequality by refusing or relinquishing motherhood. Twenty years ago, mothers evaded gender inequality by keeping up their professional pace and not letting motherhood interfere with their work. Women continue to recognize the impediments to earning power and professional accomplishments that caring for children presents. But the problem remains that for many women, these approaches to attaining equality don't deal with the central issue, namely that caring for their children *matters* deeply to them.

What if we were to take this mattering seriously, to put it at the core of our exploration? Even to pose the question is to invite almost instant misconstrual. It's as if this would recommend to women to live through others, forsake equality, or relax in the joys of subsidized homemaking. But that reflexive misinterpretation is itself evidence of how difficult it is to think about maternal desire as a positive aspect of self. The problem is on view in the ways we talk about motherhood and work. Defenders of mothers' employment often begin by enumerating its benefits to children, families, and above all mothers themselves. Then they abruptly switch to the claim that mothers can't afford *not* to work, so we may as well spare ourselves the unnecessary pain and guilt of even examining its potentially troubling aspects. This rhetorical on-two punch appears designed to fend off a candid consideration of the whole complicated arena of mothers' competing desires, and especially the desire to care for their children. It is not the stay-at-home mother whom this evasion hurts most, but the working mother who longs to spend more time with her children. For her, the need for a frank, legitimizing public discussion of maternal desire is particularly acute.

I juxtapose "maternal" and "desire" to emphasize what we feel oddly uncomfortable focusing on: that wanting to care for children is a major feature of many women's lives. We often resist thinking through its implications because we fear becoming mired in clichés about woman's nature, which will then be used to restrict women's rights and freedoms. But if we resist thinking about maternal desire, or treat it as a marginal detail, we lose an opportunity to understand ourselves and the broader situation of women. To take maternal desire as a valid focus of personal exploration is not a step backward but a step forward, toward greater awareness and a truer model of the self.

*

There are many historical reasons why the desire to mother has rarely surfaced as a point of inquiry. For most of human history, women exercised relatively little choice about becoming mothers. "A woman can hardly ever choose," the novelist George Eliot, nee Mary Ann Evans, wrote in 1866. "She must take meaner things, because only meaner things are within her reach" (cited in Felix, chap. 27). In the nineteenth century, industrialization and urbanization irrevocably changed patterns of work and family. The work of production moved outside the home, and child rearing became mothers' dominant focus. This shift in maternal activity, prompted by economics, soon shaped standard ideology as well: raising her children was a good mother's sacred calling. If she wanted something different or something more, then something was surely wrong with her.

In the twentieth century, gender roles were transformed. Betty Friedan's 1963 call for women to become whole persons, actualizing themselves in public and private realms, catalyzed the expansion of opportunity that had begun earlier and spearheaded the feminist political movement that would begin dismantling gender discrimination. Although "glass ceilings" and insidious gender biases persist, educated women are omnipresent in the once male precincts of medicine, journalism, and law. Women at all class levels are out working, as sales reps, firefighters, and civil servants. Mothers work outside the home in record numbers.

Many would agree that the problems of access Friedan and others decried—of admissions to schools, colleges, and corporations—have largely been redressed. Yet all the access in the world doesn't solve the difficulties that arise when women become mothers; for if a mother wants to spend time caring for her children, her relationship to work necessarily changes. In the 1960s and 1970s, spending time with children was viewed as a roadblock to pursuing personal aspirations. Today, women's successful integration into careers creates a roadblock to spending time with children. Regardless of the decade, it seems, "there is never a 'good' time to have a baby" (Luker 170).

In a 1999 *New York Times* piece, the feminist writer Naomi Wolf lamented the lack of political will among very bright college women. One Yale student was quoted as saying, "Women my age just have to accept that we can't have it all" (154). Wolf discerned in this young woman's attitude an apathy toward social change and an indifference to the history of women's hard-won struggles. Yet I suspect that if we delve more deeply into what young women like this one are saying, we will find a rather realistic appraisal of the ways that women's integration into the workplace has not managed to adequately address a fundamental concern. That concern is less whether one can squeeze procreation into one's life than how to be the *kind* of mother one wants to be.

The conservative critique of feminism has offered one perspective on the conflicts contemporary mothers face, questioning the benefits to mothers of egalitarian marriage, universal day care, and feminist-inspired ideals of self-actualization (see, for instance, Crittenden, D.). Too often, though, any useful observations they make are undercut by an urge to lay at feminism's door just about every problem women encounter. The French critic Roland Barthes decided to analyze contemporary mythologies because he "resented seeing Nature and History confused at every turn," prompting him to dissect the "ideological abuse" hidden behind the "decorative display of *what-goes-without-saying*" (11). Feminism's critics frequently settle for the "decorative display," the attractive but unfounded claim that nature is nature and always will be. They ignore the fact that feminism has inspired constructive changes in women's lives in areas that just a generation ago appeared as intractable "nature." Feminism, more than any other social force, has helped us question the view that our history *is* our nature.

At the same time, feminists concerned with the rights and opportunities of women can fail to appreciate the positive motivation—the authentic expression of self—that many women bring to the task of caring for their children. Some voice frustration at women's repeated "retreats" to the world of child rearing, seeing them as a personal or political regression. Others blame baby care experts who advocate spending time with children for trying to impose self-sacrifice on mothers.[2] These critics seem unwilling to apply their critical acumen to their own assumption that mothers *experience* caring for their children as self-sacrificing.

The view that caring for one's children amounts to self-sacrifice is a very tricky psychological point for women, and a confounding point for theory. It is confusing partly because the term "self-sacrifice" is potentially applicable to two different aspects of experience, the economic and the emotional. When it comes to their economic well-being, it is all too true that women sacrifice themselves when they become mothers. Time taken out of the workforce to nurture children, lost years accruing Social Security benefits, and a host of other economic factors result in unequivocal economic disadvantages to mothers. At the same time, from the point of view of emotional well-being, a mother often sees her desire to nurture her children as an intrinsically valuable impulse, and as an expression of what she subjectively experiences as her authentic self. This inconsistency presents contemporary women with one of the core paradoxes of their lives as mothers.

Considering for a moment the issue of self-sacrifice strictly from a psychological point of view, what is trickiest for women is the fact that some of what they find meaningful about mothering can be construed, from some vantage points, as self-abnegating. There are moments in the day-to-day life of every mother when the deferral of her own gratifications or aims is experienced as oppressive. But a narrow focus on such moments and the belief that they adequately capture, or stand for, the whole experience of mothering fail to appreciate the overall context in which those deferrals take place. When she relinquishes control over her time, forgoes the satisfaction of an impulse, or surrenders to playful engagement with her child even as she feels driven to "accomplish something," the surface quality of capitulation in these decisions belies their role in satisfying her deeper motives and goals. These deeper goals have to do, ultimately, with the creation of meaning. In the seemingly mundane give-and-take of parenting—playing, sharing, connecting, relaxing, enduring boredom, getting mad, cajoling, compromising, and sacrificing—a mother communicates with her child about something no less momentous than what is valuable in life, and about the possibilities and limits of intimate relationships.

This process can be one of extraordinary pleasure. There is the sensual, physical pleasure of caring for small children; the satisfaction of spending most of our waking hours (and some of our sleeping hours) with the people we love the most, taking care of their needs; the delight in being able to make our child happy and in being made happy by our child. There is the pleasure of being "alone together," of doing things near one another, feeling comforted by the presence of the other while attending to our own activities. There are also the enormous gratifications of watching children develop, grow, and change, and of being involved in the people they become.

Devoting time to caring for children is not, of course, all about pleasure and good feeling. It is also grounded in a sense of meaning, morality, even aesthetics. The choice to do so can express, for example, a value about time, having to do with the desire to create an atmosphere where time is not a scarce commodity and children's sense of time has a place. It can express an ideal about service, to one's immediate community and to a range of broader ethical and political goods associated with raising children well.

It can express a value about relationships. Managing one's rage, quelling one's desire to walk out the door on squalling children and dirty dishes, and feeling one is going to faint of boredom at the sheer repetitiveness of it all and yet continuing anyway are some of the real emotional and moral quandaries that caring for children routinely presents. Many mothers believe, for all their daily struggles with irritation and fatigue, that there is something intrinsically meaningful about managing and overcoming those states in the process of caring for one's children.

When the activities of mothering me interpreted as self-limiting, they tend to be treated dismissively. In Susan Faludi's book *Backlash,* the value of mothers spending time raising their children is articulated either by right-wing ideologues who are trying to suppress women's freedom and equality or by disaffected feminists lapsing into a defeated sentimentality.[3] Author Myriam Miedzian comments that life at home with children amounts to "shining floors and wiping noses" (qtd. in Shalit 4).[4] Time with children is often framed in feminist analyses as a form of drudgery unfairly allotted to women, remediable through shared parenting or better day care. It is as if the day-to-day practice of mothering places unreasonable or unjust demands on mothers and is part of the oppression of women's gender-based role. Yet in an era of unparalleled choice for women, spending time caring for children cannot be glibly interpreted as a deficiency or inhibition.

One of the goals of feminism in the last twenty-five years has been to dismantle the ideal of the all-giving, self-sacrificing mother, an ideal with which previous generations of mothers did battle. But we can better understand the situation of mothers today if we don't view this image of the mother as an eternal ideal, because, in fact, for the current generation of mothers, the ideal has shifted. More recently, the ideal of the supermom has been by far the more vivid and immediate. This cultural ideal pressures mothers to perform excellently on all fronts, in a job, with their children, with their partner, at the gym, and in the kitchen, making those fifteen-minute meals.

The supermom ideal plays into people's fantasies that if they work hard enough to get everything "right," they will not lose anything, that nothing will have to be sacrificed. What we had in the previous ideal was a woman who lost herself to her children and her mothering. What we have in the supermom ideal is a woman who loses nothing. But in fact, the problem with trying to do everything is that it changes radically your perception of the time you have. Anyone who has tried to "fit everything in" can attest to how excruciating the five-minute wait at the supermarket checkout line becomes, let alone a child's slow-motion attempt to tie her own shoes when you're running late getting her to preschool.

Most women today are not struggling to break out of the ideal that instructed them to sacrifice everything for their children. They are more likely beset with the quandary of how to break out of the "do everything" model so that they will have more relaxed time for their relationships. Whereas the past ideal may have hindered women's search for autonomy and self-determination in the wider world, the current ideal makes it harder to express their desire to care for their children.

It may be the supermom ideal that Naomi Wolf's seemingly apolitical college women are rejecting when they say they can't "have it all." These young women may intuit, well before their mothering years, that life may require them to make a conscious and planned departure from the "do everything" model that preoccupied the generation of women that preceded them.

***

Huge shifts in women's lives—brought on by the availability of birth control, educational and economic access, and the possibility of diverse life choices- have finally created the potential for mothering to be a chosen activity in ways unimaginable for the vast majority of women throughout history and still in many parts of the world today. At the same time, the proliferation of choices presents new challenges, as it creates expanded arenas for conflict, indecision, and doubt.

In trying to understand our conflicting goals and desires from the inside, we might begin with that science of desire, psychoanalysis. The psychoanalytic method is a powerful means for understanding the desires women bring to mothering. It is, after all, a method designed to elucidate what we feel and what we hide from ourselves. It reveals to us that our desires, motives, and beliefs never have a single fixed meaning, and that they are not always what they announce themselves to be. Listening to patients in the clinical consulting room discloses the obvious fact that every woman brings to mothering her own personal history, temperament, and sense of herself. For any given woman, the desire to mother can be a heartfelt longing, a fantasy, an excuse, something to be denied—or all of the above, at different times. One woman extols the value of being an extremely attentive mother. She worries that if she doesn't make her kids' sandwiches every day and watch all their sports games, she's a bad mom. Meanwhile, her own work as a graphic designer languishes. At this time in her life, her notion of being a good mother keeps her from expressing other important aspects of herself. Another woman has little time to attend to her children's daily routines and takes pride in raising children who are as self-reliant as she is. For her, finding the time to help her children constitutes a healing liberation from her own exacting standard of self-sufficiency. Each of these mothers seeks a greater sense of vitality and meaning, but they differ in where they started and where they are going.

The personal meanings of mothering are endlessly complex, and the particular conflicts vary from person to person. Yet it seems that today, a mother's desire to care for her children is the side of the conflict that gets the most simplistic public airing, even by its partisans, and the side that mainstream feminism has done the least to support. Consequently, it is not uncommon for mothers to have a hard time seeing how their desire to care for their children is playing a role in their dilemmas.

For example, a 35-year-old professional woman who was employed full-time dwelled on the potential inadequacy of her child care arrangement, worrying that her ten-month-old was unhappy, even though she could not think of any specific reason for concern. She attained greater clarity when she realized that the real issue was that she was *missing* her baby, and her sense of anxiety over child care then gave way to a more intelligible sense of yearning. It was hard to become aware of missing her baby, because she had operated with the assumption that if the baby was all right while she was away, she would—or should—feel all right about being away too.[5]

For this person, it took psychotherapy to make her aware that she was missing her child; but her quandary points to a more general cultural phenomenon. In the current milieu, women rarely perceive their desire to care for their children as intellectually respectable, and that makes it less emotionally intelligible as well. On a broader social level, mothers' need and desire to work and its importance to their self-sufficiency and self-expression get a strong public hearing, but mothers' needs and desires with respect to nurturing their children receive comparatively little serious discussion. Maternal desire tends to be treated as background noise or unspoken assumption rather than as something explicit, valuable, and important to include as an issue relevant to women's lives.

Our national discussion of child care, for example, understandably focuses on the reality that most parents need to work. Because the discussion appears to deal with an immutable fact of life, it is sometimes viewed as impractical, even elitist, to raise questions concerning the *feelings* of the parents and children involved. But progressive calls for universal affordable day care ignore a jumble of inconvenient emotions, including parents' desire to take care of their own children. Many mothers feel torn up inside being apart from their babies and children many hours a day, yet they feel realistic or mature when they are able to suppress those feelings. The terms of the discussion don't admit the possibility that pleasure is a reliable guide, or that desire tells us anything about truth.

Developmental psychology is one domain that studies the impact of pleasure on human growth. In the past two decades, it has undertaken an increasingly nuanced investigation of mother-child interaction, revealing the central role of shared emotional states and shared pleasure in healthy human development (i.e., Stern; Beebe and Lachmann). The research on mother-infant interaction teaches us about the making of mutual meaning, and about the roots of emotional complexity and richness. Yet, for the most part, these findings remain marginal to our public debates about day care. Their perceived irrelevance hints at our difficulty in making the *mutual* parent-child relationship a focal point in our reflections on child care.

The importance of the mutual parent-child relationship and a mother's desire to participate in that relationship are masked by the rhetoric of children's "needs." When exasperated callers to talk-radio shows insist on children's "need" to be taken care of by their parents, they are making a statement not primarily about facts, but, rather, about values. Children are not all alike; one two-year-old may happily trot into day care while another desperately protests. Children survive, and some even thrive, in a range of circumstances, including circumstances they wouldn't choose for themselves if given a say in the matter. The emphasis on children's "needs" represents an attempt to create a socially sanctioned arena for children's "wants" and what we want for them. In a sense, "needs" are a post-Freudian way to talk about values, a way to demarcate and honor those things we consider of greatest importance to human well-being.

The oft-heard question about day care—"Does day care hurt children?"—turns children into the repository of our *mutual* desire for human connection. If the studies show that children do fine in day care, we independent adults are supposed to go about our business without remorse. On this view, mothers' feelings simply aren't relevant; the only issue is day care's effects on children. But what is good for parents and what is good for children are equally relevant in a moral evaluation of day care. And adults' desire to nurture their children is much more passionate and complex than the opposition of dependent child and independent adult would have us believe.

***

Motherhood calls for a transformed individuality, an integration of a new relationship and a new role into one's sense of self. This is a practical *and* a psychological transformation. It is screamingly evident that as a society we are grudging and cramped about the practical adjustments required by motherhood, continually treating them as incidental and inconvenient. Like an irritated bus passenger who is asked to move over and make room, we appear affronted by the sheer existence of mothers' needs. The disheartening, thorough analyses of this problem by feminist economists cannot be improved upon and are there for all to read.[6]

But these practical difficulties, not to mention the views that underlie them, also have far-reaching *psychological* implications. They affect how we appraise and experience the whole issue of inner maternal transformation, the "space" we will allow motherhood to occupy in our psyches. If everything around us seems designed to obstruct our integrating the full force of our maternal devotion into a life responsive to our prior commitments, our outlook and values about what we should "do" with our maternal desire can come to be subtly shaped.

This conflict is not lost on young women. Naomi Wolf's Yale student's "we can't have it all" response reflects one resolution among many to a question that confronts virtually every young woman at some point or another: namely, how she will integrate her maternal potential into her mature identity. The first stirrings of this question accompany a girl's sexual development in adolescence, for that is when she not only becomes capable of sexual and maternal expression but also meets up with cultural norms and ideals of successful adulthood. Cultural ideals about control, in particular, resonate with girls' psychological need for self-control at this stage, with both constructive and problematic effects. On the one hand, educated and upwardly mobile girls in contemporary society face a decade, perhaps two or even three, between their sexual maturation and childbearing, a span that gives them enormous opportunity for self-development and self-definition. Contemporary female adolescence is a time when a girl can optimally find a balanced perspective on the issue of self-control, one that will help her arrive at an integrated sense of herself as an individual woman and potential mother.

On the other hand, in our culture the very idea of control is laden with gender implications. Control, conceived as an aspect of adult autonomy, is at odds with our image of motherhood. The whole arena of pregnancy, childbirth, and the daily activities of mothering involve decreased personal control, and loss of control is among the cultural and personal anxieties that maternal desire raises. For some young women struggling toward a sense of identity, it is not surprising that motherhood comes to symbolize everything antithetical to the independent life they want to pursue. And the pressure on women to aspire to a certain model of control as a signature of adulthood is one of the social factors that can riddle maternal wishes with conflict.

It is true that the satisfying, somewhat predictable march of "progress" in one's life without children is replaced, when children arrive, by a messier, more ambiguous process of "becoming." In this sense, motherhood can seem an agitating distraction, even a threatening derailment. Yet the sense that motherhood robs us of individuality derives part of its power from a cultural definition of individuality that pits the "serving the species" script of procreation against the notion of giving birth to oneself. This definition asserts itself in adolescence, when girls observe the difficulty in integrating the desire to mother with the idea of a work life. It rears its head at the end of college, when it can be an embarrassment to admit that one would like children sooner rather than later. When women move into the workforce, they observe the correlation of motherhood with a loss of power, pay, and prestige. External conditions resonate with internal anxieties, making it difficult for many women to evaluate their own desires with respect to mothering.

The prevailing notion that motherhood and individuality are in pitched conflict may also play into what some women writers have described as their obliviousness to mothers and babies before they began considering motherhood themselves.[7] In the old days, women lived out their years in dense webs of female relationships, presiding together over birth, nurture, and death; women couldn't avoid children even if they tried.[8] But today, smaller families and freedom in charting our own course mean that women can choose to live in relative isolation from children. There are plenty of women, of course, who simply aren't interested in children, for a host of reasons. A friend spent her youth raising her siblings; she'd seen all the "becoming" she could take and was liberated by the prospect of living her own life. Yet, I detect in the obliviousness described in these writings neither a simple response to changed social realities nor a lack of interest in motherhood, but rather a motivated sense that preserving one's selfhood depends on shutting out an interest in children. That outlook can foster a kind of self-development, but it can also contribute to a deferral of childbearing that later, if it contributes to infertility, can be tinged with almost unbearable regret.

The incompatibility between motherhood and individuality has perhaps nowhere been more reflexively presumed than in the Pro-choice rhetoric surrounding the issue of abortion. There, it has been perceived as dangerous to emphasize either the moral ambiguity of abortion or women's desire to mother, for fear of fueling a politically regressive view of women's place. The resulting approach has been to frame the issue almost solely in terms of a woman's right to govern her own body. But for many women, including many proponents of reproductive choice, the wrenching ambiguity of abortion has to do with how difficult it is to place in clear opposition one's interests as an individual and as a potential mother, or one's interests and a potential child's interests. Their intuition is closer to that which Gwendolyn Brooks captured in her poem about abortion, "the mother": "oh, what shall I say, how is the truth to be said?/You were born, you had body, you died./It is just that you never giggled or planned or cried./Believe me, I loved you all./Believe me, I knew you, though faintly, and I loved, I loved you /All."[9]

The tension between motherhood and individuality also surfaces in the seeming split screen between our cultural fascination with babies and the less articulated desire to care for them. Just as there are thousands of falling-in-love stories but many fewer tales of slogging to make a marriage work, there are countless media images of the miracle of pregnancy or the adorableness of babies but little that represents the day-to-day care of children. Perhaps it was ever thus. History provides a wealth of examples, from Cleopatra onward, of women who birthed babies, delegated caregiving, and emerged with their freedom of movement intact. And certainly from a psychological point of view, the desire to have a child and the desire to care for that child may coexist in the same person, but they are not the same thing. One woman captured the difference when she said, "My mother thinks I should try to spend more time with the children I already have, but I can't get the idea of having another one out of my mind."

Still, it is striking how the desire to have a child is today the object of such intense focus and, increasingly, extraordinary measures, whereas the desire to care for children is Singularly unriveting, even a bit déclassé. A woman may believe that caring for children will express, rather than compromise, her individuality or her valued goals, but she regularly meets up with social and economic incentives that pull her in a different direction. In the course of educated young women's lives, for instance, it is usual to acquire training and jobs before children. A couple marries, both members work, and without giving it much thought, they develop a lifestyle predicated on two salaries. When they have a child, the mother may find that as her maternity leave draws to a close, she isn't itching to get back to work. Instead, she yearns to be with her child. Her change of heart presents the couple with the need to rethink their relationship and their decisions about lifestyle and money. They may conclude that it is going "backward" to give up one salary; and anyway, decisions made on the basis of two salaries, like buying a house, cannot be easily reversed. Rueful acceptance overrides her yearning: spending time caring for their children is a "luxury" they can't afford. Suddenly, like so many things in American life—health care, good schools, fresh air—motherhood has turned into something of a luxury. You have time for it only if you are very lucky.

Margaret, a lawyer, left a rewarding job at 40 to stay home with her second son. She had worked fifty hours per week during her first son's infancy. Wisecracking by nature, she is uncharacteristically solemn when discussing her decisions:

I'll never get over the regret I feel at missing my first child's babyhood. What amazes me still—you'd think I'd get over it—is how completely taken *off* guard I was by wanting to be with him. Before you have kids, you have the almost swaggering attitude that you won't fall into the mommy trap. You don't believe that once you're there, you'll genuinely *want* to be with your kids. Now whenever I'm in a position to counsel younger associates, I tell them, "Set up your marriage, finances and domestic life so that they don't depend on your continued wage earning, because hard as it is to imagine, once you have kids, you may not want to do what you're doing anymore.

Today's young women face a different social landscape from that of women a generation ago, and thanks to the struggle of the women who preceded them, they can take for granted access to work and public attention on work-family balance. The softening of rigid trade-offs has given younger women more latitude in assessing for themselves the relative satisfactions of work and family. To some older women, this can look like a regression to nonfeminist values. For others, it can lead to reflection on the choices they made and the social climate in which they made them. Elisa, a therapist with a college-age child, recounted that when she was a young mother, she left her child to go back to work with great sadness and trepidation, but she felt sure that it was the progressive thing to do. She and her friends "were looking at our own mothers as frustrated and depressed, and we had a clear sense of the importance of learning from their situation and making a life for ourselves. Now I look back with an incredible sense of longing; but I can't say I would do it differently, because that is who I was." Intergenerational discussions, potentially difficult as they are, can offer a rich opportunity for reflection to women at all stages of life.

***

I have been arguing that we do not know how to think about the desire to mother. We have trouble understanding it within ourselves, in terms of our psychological and feminist theories, and in the public debates and institutions that structure our lives. The critical issue that has eluded theory and social debate is that caring for young children is something mothers often view as extraordinarily important both for their children *and* for themselves.

Reframing the mothering role in this way calls into question a number of views that hang in the cultural air, We are all familiar with these views: mothering is a sacrifice of the mother for the sake of the child; mothering will not be valued until it is paid work; careers enhance personal growth, while caring for children breeds stagnation; children disrupt, rather than foster, the realization of individual goals. Such views contribute to the emphasis some mothers place on "returning to normal" after children are born. They may also help to explain the surprise some women feel when they realize how much they want to spend time caring for their children.

In the popular American mind-set, there's always a second chance. So it comes as a shock to realize how fast children grow up, and how quickly they no longer crave your company or respond to your influence in the ways they once did. The time-limited nature of mothering small children, the very uniqueness of it, itself seems almost like an affront to women's opportunity, demanding as it does that mothers respond at a distinct, unrepeatable moment with decisions, often radical ones, about how to spend their time. Unfair as it may seem, the fleetingness is real. In that light, the fact that childbearing absorbs but a small portion of women's adult life span—often seen as a reason to "stay on track"—should point us toward prizing this brief period of our lives, and not just on a personal or individual level; as a culture, we need to express our recognition of its value through our laws, our policies concerning work and family, and our theories of psychological development.

Caring for one's children at home is sometimes dismissed as a choice open only to privileged women. But in fact, mothers at all socioeconomic levels face difficult decisions regarding the time they spend with their children. Moreover, the devaluation of mothering operates at various levels of social and economic reality and in many intersecting ways. If we open our eyes to the commonalities in mothers' experience, we might begin to develop some political consciousness, even solidarity, about the larger-scale problems that the devaluation of mothering inflicts upon everyone. It should not be acceptable to any of us, for instance, when politicians maintain both that middle-class children need their mothers at home and that welfare mothers should be joining the workforce when their children are four months old.

Economic necessity is always a fact of life, and economic privation affects those who suffer from it in every sphere of their lives. The mothers least likely to find fulfillment in their low-wage jobs are also those least likely to have time to enjoy being with their children. This group of mothers and children suffer a disproportionate negative burden. But for those people with some choice, an emphasis on economic necessity can itself be used to obscure the realm of feelings on which wise and satisfying choices draw. No one can banish economic need; but being aware of how we feel about time apart from our children, and being attuned to our children's feelings about it, are central to clarifying our priorities.

Why is this a book about mothers? Because caring for small children is compellingly central to many women's sense of themselves to a degree still not experienced by many men. If current research is correct, this may be changing, as more men place value on family time. From custody rights to employer policies, fathers are increasingly questioning the givens that have framed men's life courses in the past.[10] But for the moment, the care of children remains a predominantly female occupation. Some argue that this is a problem in need of correction—that true equality of the sexes cannot be achieved until child rearing and work responsibilities are equally shared. But whatever position one takes on this matter, and whatever one's social ideal for the division of labor, the idea that equality between men and women—or fairness between any two partners—can come about *only* through similar life courses and a parallel allocation of labor may constitute an abstraction by which few people actually want to live.

We need to speak accurately about the character of maternal desire, resisting its caricature either as sentimental false consciousness or woman's nature. Teasing apart the psychological and ideological strands of maternal desire can help individual women consider its role in their lives and make choices based on a conscious awareness of their own conflicts and wishes.[11] Maternal desire is not, for any woman, all there is. But for many of us, it is an important part of who we are. And among such women, it is time to start a conversation.

Notes

[1]For a deft, definitive guide to Freud's writings on women, see Young-Bruehl. In *The History of Sexuality,* the philosopher Michel Foucault brilliantly demonstrated how incessant, seemingly "free" social discussion of sex served to regulate and define sexual expression. Similarly, though it may seem that people "can't stop talking about motherhood," their very volubility may serve to obscure, and even discount, important aspects of maternal experience.

[2]"Regression": see, for instance, Sandra Scan quoted in Chira 13. "Baby care manuals": see, for instance, Chira (chap. 3); Eyer.

[3]See especially chaps. 4 and 11.

[4]Not unusually, Miedzian's offhandedly dismissive comment about caring for children and home is followed, in the body of the book, by a critique of "our national lack of interest in and lack of respect for childrearing" (71).

[5]Because my argument concerns the ways mothers are subtly and not so subtly encouraged to downplay their desire to care for their children, my examples and

vignettes tend to illustrate that side of the dilemma. This emphasis should not be taken to mean that there are not equally valid and painful dilemmas from the other side; that, for instance, a mother may feel duty-bound to care for her children and inhibited in expressing her other desires or needs.

[6]Among the most trenchant recent accounts for the general reader, see Burggraf, *Feminine Economy and Economic Man;* Folbre, *Invisible Heart;* and Ann Crittenden, *Price of Motherhood.* For a liberal political perspective on similar issues, see Harrington, *Care and Equality.*

[7]Examples include Cusk, *Life's Work;* Alden, *Crossing the Moon;* Ann Crittenden, *Price of Motherhood;* and Maushart, *Mask of Motherhood.*

[8]For more historical context, see Ehrenreich and English's classic work *For Her Own Good;* and Dally, *Inventing Motherhood.*

[9]This poem appears by special consent of the Brooks Permissions, with the understanding that Gwendolyn Brooks did not want this work to promote the causes or arguments made by those on either side of abortion rights issues.

[10]On changing attitudes toward family time, see, for instance, Radcliffe Public Policy Center. On fathers with primary custody, see, for instance, Goldberg. On child support, see, for instance, Harden.

[11]In making an argument in an arena as sensitive as motherhood, one runs the risk of seeming either to take an overly personal viewpoint that leaves out other equally valid perspectives or, conversely, to try to speak for everyone, thereby blurring the crucial differences between mothers of diverse personalities, tastes, classes, and cultural identifications. My aspiration here is perhaps best understood as a response to the need for "clear, accessible, stimulating general hypotheses" identified by the philosopher Susan Bordo in *Unbearable Weight* (223).

References

Barthes, Roland. *Mythologies.* New York: Hill and Wang, 1972.

Beebe, Beatrice and Frank M. Lachmann. *Infant Research and Adult Treatment: Co-constructing Interactions.* Hillsdale, NJ: The Analytic Press Inc., 2002.

Bordo, Susan. *Unbearable Weight.*

Breuer, Josef and Sigmund Freud. *Studies on Hysteria.* New York: Basic Books, 1957.

Brooks, Gwendolyn. "The Mother." *Blacks.* Chicago: Third World Press, 1994.

Chira, Susan. *A Mother's Place.* New York: HarperCollins Publishers, 1988.

Crittenden, Danielle. *What Our Mothers Didn't Tell Us.* New York: Simon and Schuster, 2000.

Dally, Ann. *Inventing Motherhood.* New York: Schocken, 1987.

Ehrenreich, Barbara and English, Deirdre. *For Her Own Good.* Norwell: Anchor Press, 2005.

Eyer, Diane. *Motherguilt.* New York: Random House Value Publishing, 1997.

Faludi, Susan, *Backlash.* New York: Crown Publishers Group, 1991.

Eliot, George. *Felix Holt, the Radical.* New York: John B. Alden, 1883.

Foucault, Michel. *The History of Sexuality.* Vol 1. New York: Vintage, 1980.

Friedan, Betty. *The Feminine Mystique.* New York: Dell, 1963.

Goldberg, Carey. "Single Dads Wage Revolution: One Bedtime Story at a Time." *The New York Times* June 17, 2001.

Harden, Blaine. "Dead Broke Dads' Child-Support Struggle." *The New York Times* January 29, 2002.

Luker, Kristin. *Dubious Conceptions, 170.* Boston: Harvard University Press, 1997.

Radcliffe Public Policy Center. "Life's Work Project." President and Fellows of Harvard College, 2000.

Shalit, Wendy. *Return to Modesty.* New York: Free Press, 2000.

Stern, Daniel. *Interpersonal World of the Infant.* New York: Basic Books, 2000.

Wolf, Naomi. "Future Is Ours to Lose." *New York Times* May 16, 1999.

Young-Bruehl, Elisabeth. *Freud on Women: A Reader.* New York: W. W. Norton and Co. 1990

Chapter 42

"We Will No Longer Be Silent or Invisible"
Latinas Organizing for Reproductive Justice

ELENA R. GUTIÉRREZ

It is commonly believed that issues of reproductive health and sexuality are not of concern to Latinas or their communities. As Latinas are predominantly Catholic, it is assumed that they are all against abortion, do not use birth control and are not active participants in political struggles for reproductive freedom. These ideas persist not only among the general public but in the pro-choice movement and feminist scholarship as well.[1]

The continual marginalization of women of color in organizing wholly erases the significant roles that Latinas have played in the development of both mainstream reproductive rights efforts and community-based reproductive health and sexuality agendas. In fact, as activist-historian Elizabeth Martinez points out, "Latinas' views on reproductive rights are often more radical than Anglo women's views and not 'conservative' as some people say, because their definition of choice requires mo re profound social change than just abortion rights or preventing pregnancy" (188). Grounded in the realities of their communities, Latinas insist that broader issues, such as racism and classism, influence their reproductive lives, and that true reproductive freedom necessitates an end to all forms of social inequality. As this and the following two chapters demonstrate, Latinas are organizing for their reproductive and sexual health rights and have developed innovative organizing strategies, principles, and practices grounded in the needs and cultures of their communities.

A challenge in documenting the activism of Latinas, however, is the diversity of communities and individuals that are placed within the category.[2] With national origins from countries in Central and South America and the Caribbean, Latinas have a wide variety of racial, ethnic, religious, and linguistic traditions. Latino communities are geographically dispersed throughout the U.S., and their cultures are regionally distinct and complex. Totaling more than 40 million, Latinas and Latinos are members of communities and families with various citizenship statuses, great inter generational differences in acculturation, identity formation, and socioeconomic status. With the 2000 Census, Latinos became the largest minority group in the U.S., at 12.5 percent of the population (U.S. Census Bureau 1), and are expected to comprise 25 percent of the U.S. population by 2050.

As some of the first scholarship attempting to document Latina organizing for reproductive justice, this analysis focuses primarily on the two largest Latino groups in the nation, Puerto Ricans (9.6 percent) and Mexicans (58 percent), about whom the most written material is available (U.S. Census Bureau 2).

Myths and Misconceptions

Images of Latinas circulating in popular media and academic research promote the idea of a "generic Latina," ignoring the complex social, historical, and cultural contexts within which Latinas·live.[3] In place of nuanced and multidimensional representations of Latinas are a handful of highly exaggerated and conflicting stereotypes upon which many people base their understanding of Latinas in the U.S. Generally, the images are of passive, childlike females who are subservient to their husbands in particular and men in general. Latinas are represented as traditional women-heavily influenced by Catholicism-and therefore sexually repressed (Silverman). Or, when depicted as sexual beings, their sexuality is explicitly linked to their being Latina-meaning that they are characterized as tropically "exotic" and hypersexual. When depicted as sexually liberated, their liberation is written off as acculturation into the white mainstream society, reinforcing the idea that white women's sexuality is the norm and all others are aberrations (Juarez and Kerl). Always heterosexual, Latinas are defined by a strict virgin/whore dichotomy of sexuality and reproductive behavior. In both cases, a Latina is believed incapable of using birth control (King). These stereotypes serve to justify state, medical, and social intervention in their reproduction.

These core images shift and assume different meanings when applied to particular communities in different historical moments and social contexts. For example, Puerto Rican women have historically been cast in a variety of hypersexualized images that classify them as sexually deviant (Briggs 4). Extending beyond the island to Puerto Rican women living on the U.S. mainland, various social and political representations present them as exotically sexual beings who carelessly bear many children who will ultimately become welfare dependents and drain social resources.[4]

Mexican-origin women are also ideologically associated with their fertility, but in contrast to the hypersexuality of Puerto Rican women, a strict Catholic traditionalism and over-identification as mothers is emphasized (Andrade). The childbearing of Mexican immigrant women is increasingly suspect and often criminalized. For example, Proposition 187[5] in California targeted poor, pregnant Mexican immigrant women, blaming them for the state's and the nation's problems. Mexican women were depicted as purposely crossing the border to give birth in publicly financed county hospitals to gain citizenship status and thus eligibility for public assistance.[6] These representations provide the ideological justification for punitive policies that shape Latinas' reproductive experiences (Mullings). They also influence how health care professionals treat Latinas (Scrimshaw, Zambrana and DunkelSchetter).

The Reproductive and Sexual Health Status of Latinos

Although research on Latinas and their health is sparse, studies report that, overall, they experience poor health,[7] with disproportionately high rates of cervical cancer, sexually transmitted diseases, HIV/AIDS, teenage pregnancy, obesity, diabetes, domestic violence, and unintentional injuries compared to other women (Amaro and de la Torre). These circumstances are exacerbated by the extremely low rates of health care delivery to Latinas caused by financial, institutional, and cultural barriers. Low levels of education and income contribute to high poverty rates in Latino communities and, concomitantly, poor health status. Almost one-third of Latinos report no health insurance coverage and Latinas are the least likely of any group to have access to regular health care or health insurance coverage.[8] Since many Latinas communicate in Spanish, the predominantly English-speaking health care system presents significant challenges to health care delivery (Derose and Baker). Recent anti-immigrant sentiment has also increasingly discouraged many Latinos from seeking health care. As many providers have limited knowledge and understanding of Latina cultures, when immigrant and U.S.-born Latinos do receive medical attention, many report high dissatisfaction with the health care they receive. Few feel that their health care providers genuinely care about their wellbeing (Amaro; Giachello).

Latinas are more likely to have children at younger ages.[9] Almost 17 percent of births to Latinas are to adolescents under the age of 20, with Puerto Ricans having the highest percentage of teen births (21.9 percent) of all racial or ethnic groups (Ventura et al.). Latinas have historically received low rates of prenatal care. In the past ten years, their use of prenatal services during the first trimester has increased significantly (Ventura *et al.*).[10] When they do receive prenatal care, however, Latinas experience a low level of satisfaction, and complain of a poor quality of care and a lack of culturally sensitive treatment (Handler *et al.*).

Latinas also experience a high incidence of and mortality due to cervical cancer (Napoles-Springer and Pérez-Stable). The high rates may be tied to a host of environmental factors. Due to their concentration in service and agriculture industries, Latinas have high exposure to toxins. They are at high risk from the effects of teratogenic chemicals (known to cause malformation in a fetus) in the workplace and home because they are over-represented in three of the major labor market categories in which exposure is high: clerical (radiation), service (cleaning chemicals), and operatives and laborers (pesticides, herbicides, and chemicals). Agricultural laborers are also at high risk for exposure, and many communities experience high rates of infertility, stillbirths, fetal abnormalities, and cancers (Riddell; see also, San Martin).

Latinas face additional sexual health risks; perhaps the cause for most concern is that Latinas currently represent 20.2 percent of the total AIDS cases among women (Center for Disease Control and Prevention cited in Giachello 119). AIDS is the third leading cause of death for Latinas between the ages of 15 and 24. Latinas also have among the highest rates of chlamydia, gonorrhea, and human papilloma virus (HPV) (Center for Disease Control and Prevention cited in Giachello 121). Lack of basic knowledge about sexually transmitted diseases (STDs), lack of health insurance, and cultural and linguistic barriers to the health care system prevent Latinas from being able to prevent and/or treat STDs.

Research consistently shows that Latinas are pro-choice. Furthermore, they have abortions at a rate proportionately higher than any other group,[11] with 20.1 percent of all abortions being obtained by Latinas (Physicians for Reproductive Choice and Health and the Alan Guttmacher Institute; see, also, Erickson and Caplan). They are 2.5 times as likely to have an abortion as white women (Alan Guttmacher Institute). While Latinas are actively seeking abortion services, they are among that group of poor women most likely to suffer from lack of access to safe abortions. When they do have abortions, Latinas disproportionately suffer from medical complications. Rosie Jimenez, an important symbol in the reproductive rights movement, is a clear reminder to Latinas that abortion is about more than choice (see Frankfort and Kissling).

History of Reproductive Oppression

Puerto Rican Women: Legacies of Colonialism

But the first and most important site of Puertorriquena struggle is the female body. The body represents the unique and culturally revered capacity to procreate, symbolizes the taboo realm of sexuality, and carries with it the honor or shame of the family. The body is at once a valued (often exploited) instrument for social survival and an object for enforcing social control. .. Sexuality, reproduction, motherhood, and family need to be redefined in light of the experiences of colonization, inter-lingualism, and the development of capitalism in Puerto Rico. (Flores *et al.* 221)

While the population control policies that have been implemented in Puerto Rico by the U.S. government have gained some attention, issues of reproduction and sexuality were in fact at the center of Puerto Rican politics even before North American involvement (Briggs). Control of women's sexuality and reproduction was central to the colonial relationship the island's residents first experienced with the Spanish, beginning in 1508, and continues to be a key factor in the neocolonial status it maintains with the U.S.[12] Activist-historian Aurora Levins Morales contends that "from the first treaty with Ponce de Leon to the present, successive invaders of our country have tried to control our people by controlling our wombs." Over the centuries and through today, colonialism, neocolonialism, and capitalism have shaped the sexual and reproductive politics of Puerto Rican women (Azize-Vargas and Avilés; Lopez; Briggs). Beginning with Spanish colonization, legislation was enacted to contain the reproductive and sexual behaviors of women. According to Levins Morales, "From the earliest days an astonishing proportion of the laws, decrees, and government correspondence coming out of Spain concern women's sexuality and reproduction, and their movements from one place to another," all in an effort to prevent interracial sex and reproduction in the colony. Spanish women were encouraged to migrate to the island, and in 1526 a brothel was established to deter Spanish soldiers from having sex with women from the island. When African slaves were brought to the island, it also became a capital crime for Spanish men to have sex with African women (Morales 7).

Although more research is needed on the control of women's sexuality since Spanish colonization, it has been well documented that for the last 100 years the land and population of Puerto Rico has been used as a base upon which to conduct social and scientific experiments. In 1898, following the Spanish-American War, the U.S. claimed Puerto Rico as its territory. Since then, reproductive and other social experiments on the island were fundamental to the relationship between the U.S. and Puerto Rico. Essentially, Puerto Rico and its people have served as a laboratory for American contraceptive policies and products. For example, the contraceptive foam, the intrauterine device (IUD), and many varieties of the pill were all tested the on the bodies of Puerto Rican women before ever making their way to the mainland U.S. market (Mass 73). When laws against birth control prevented medical trials of the contraceptive pill on the mainland U.S. during the 1950s, pharmaceutical companies conducted field trials in Puerto Rico. There were several experimental studies testing various birth control pills that often led to dangerous consequences. In one experimental study of the birth control pill on 838 Puerto Rican women, five women died. The incident was not reported to the Food and Drug Administration (FDA), and the drug was declared safe (Mass 26).

The United States government has also sponsored population control in Puerto Rico. Designed to remedy unemployment, a dragging economy, and "overpopulation," the program centrally promoted sterilization of women (Briggs). Although federal funding of other contraceptives was not widely available in Puerto Rico until 1968, and abortion was illegal until 1973, tubal ligation—the most popularly performed method of sterilization-had been available, for little or no cost, to most women since 1937. Because sterilization was available in Puerto Rico and not in the United States, Puerto Rican women provided an opportunity for surgeons to practice and refine the technology before it was marketed in the U.S. Although these policies were generally accepted by Puerto Rico's ruling class, the support of United States funders and policy-makers catapulted their development. In the mid1940s, Clarence Gamble, a leader in the U.S. eugenics movement, with political connections and a financial empire, implemented a full program of sterilization in Puerto Rico. Within a few years tubal ligation was so common that sterilizing Puerto Rican women after childbirth was almost routine, with consent often obtained either during labor or right after childbirth. Legally, women were to be "well-advised" of the medical justifications for sterilization, but in reality they seldom were and many of the women didn't understand the procedure was irreversible.

Campaigns to sterilize women were often tied to development. During the 1950s, Operation Bootstrap efforts to boost the Puerto Rican economy encouraged women to enter the workforce to increase manufacturer productivity. As the procedure became common for most Puerto Rican women, "Puerto Rican women became predisposed to sterilization because of its widespread availability and convenience, social acceptance, and overall lack of [other] viable options" (Lopez 242-243). Some women agreed to sterilizations only after doctors told them that the procedure could be reversed and that they could have children later. Others were simply uninformed, not knowing of or being told about other birth control options. Still others were economically coerced. Such practices continued without much public reaction until Puerto Rican Nationalists and Catholics joined together to expose the genocidal campaign of sterilization. By 1965 about 35 percent of the women in Puerto Rico had been sterilized, two-thirds of them in their 20s (Lopez 240-241).

Although there are important distinctions between the realities of Puerto Ricans living on the island and those who settle in the continental U.S., statistics show that the reproductive experiences of both groups are similar. Like Puerto Rican women living on the island, those in the New York area have rates of sterilization much higher than the level for all women in the U.S. (Salvo, Powers, and Cooney). It is suspected that, for Puerto Rican women, sterilization has replaced other methods of birth control, as many Puerto Rican women wish to be sterilized whether living in the U.S. or Puerto Rico. Anthropologist Iris Lopez argues that the continued high rates of sterilization for Puerto Rican women living on the island and in the continental U.S. are a direct effect of population control policies of the U.S. government in Puerto Rico (Lopez 240-241).

Mexican American Women in the Southwest

While sexual and reproductive abuse of Native women began during the Spanish colonization of Mexico, Mexican-origin women's reproduction has been an issue of public concern in the United States since at least the turn of the twentieth century. During the 1920s, national debates raged about increased immigration to the U.S. and its impact upon the "racial stock" of the nation. Fears grew among whites about the effects immigration might have upon the cultural and social fabric of the country. During the heyday of eugenics, racist ideas about the cultural inferiorities of Mexicans and their excessive fertility became part of the political discourse in the Southwest. Questioning whether newly arrived Mexican immigrants would shed their native (and presumably inferior) cultures to adopt mainstream Anglo-Saxon values, habits, and customs, Americanists (who believed that immigrants could succeed in the United States only if they gave up their own cultural habits and adopted "Anglo" practices) and public health officials designed programs to promote the assimilation process. Programs specifically targeted Mexican immigrant women and their children, identifying them as the primary agents for cultural change (Sanchez Jr.). Mexican American families were inculcated with American ideals of family planning and family size in hopes that this would ultimately convince women to have fewer children. While perhaps intended to facilitate their integration into the country, the underlying message of these programs to alter Mexican women's reproductive and child rearing practices was that, without direction, Mexican women would not be proper mothers or citizens.

Like Puerto Rican women, Mexican-origin women were also used as guinea pigs for contraceptive trials. In 1971, Dr. Joseph Goldzheir, of the Southwest Foundation for Research and Education, conducted a study designed to test whether symptoms associated with the pill (nervousness, depression, and headache) were direct effects of the pill or psychological. The trial, sponsored by Syntex Labs and the Agency for International Development, included a total of 398 women, all of whom were poor and 80 percent of whom were Mexican American. Half the women were given one of three actual prescription birth control pills, and the other half a placebo. The women were told that the pills might not be 100 percent effective and that they should also apply vaginal cream. Though the women were never fully informed that they were involved in a medical experiment, Goldzheir argued that the experiment was entirely ethical. When asked why clinic clients were not fully informed, Goldzheir replied, "If you think you can explain a placebo test to women like these, you've never met Mrs. Gomez from the west side." All of the women involved already had two or more children, had gone to the clinic for the specific purpose of obtaining contraceptives to avoid another pregnancy, and had never before used an oral contraceptive. Of the 74 who were prescribed the placebo, 10 became pregnant. As residents of Texas, where abortion was illegal, all were forced to bear children they had specifically visited the clinic to prevent.[13]

Also like Puerto Rican women, throughout the Southwest, Mexican-origin women were targeted for sterilization. Hundreds of women were sterilized without their knowledge between the years of 1969 and 1973 at the University of Southern California-Los Angeles County Medical Center (Velez-Ibañez; Espino; Gutiérrez). Many of the women were coerced into signing permission forms during labor, after doctors had threatened to withhold pain medication unless they agreed to sterilization, or were never asked for their consent. They described being approached during labor by primarily English-speaking personnel who coerced and harassed them to "consent" to a tubal ligation. If a patient would not consent, some doctors performed the procedure anyway, without telling the woman. Sometimes doctors would lie, telling a woman that she would die if she were not sterilized, or that the state of California only allowed three children born by cesarean section before sterilization was necessary.

As other chapters in this book document, poor women of color bore the brunt of the abuse, and many have argued that sterilization abuse of poor women and women of color in the 1970s was a direct outgrowth of eugenics (Del Castillo). In addition to Puerto Rican and Mexican-origin women, other Latinas, poor women, and women of color were sterilized in teaching hospitals across the nation.[14]

As individuals and in collective organizing, Latina activists have resisted these abuses and promoted reproductive freedom. In past decades, Latinas throughout the nation have planted the seeds of organizing to improve the reproductive and sexual health experiences of their communities.

Latina Organizing for Reproductive Freedom

Latinas' resistance to reproductive oppression occurs as part of broader community resistance to the social, economic, and political exploitation that Latinos face in the U.S. Alongside other activists, Latinas have actively struggled and organized around labor and education issues, sexism within their own communities, and environmental and social discrimination. And although the historical record may not highlight their achievements, Latinas have also fought for reproductive freedoms.[15]

The widespread exposure of the reproductive abuse of Latinas catalyzed concerted efforts that coalesced as part of the social justice movements of the 1960s and '70s. In that period, Latina activism occurred within and outside of Latino Nationalist and mainstream women's rights organizations, both of which tended to marginalize the issues of Women of color. Beginning locally and within grassroots organizations, these efforts provided the basis for the development of a distinctive Latina reproductive rights platform that emerged in the more formal, national-level organizations during the 1980s and '90s.

Organizing During the 1960s and '70s

Throughout the second half of the twentieth century Latinas fought for their right to bear children in addition to struggling around a host of other issues such as labor organizing, welfare rights, education, and childcare.[16] At times, Latina efforts to organize around issues of birth control or sexuality from a liberatory framework challenged Nationalist agendas that so often proscribed that women's role in community advancement was to produce lots of children. These pronatalist agendas stemmed from historic and contemporary birth control experimentation and sterilization abuses. Believing that their communities were literally at risk of being demolished by state efforts, Nationalists considered these abuses tantamount to genocide.

However, while Chicano and Puerto Rican Nationalists denounced the abuses that occurred, they ultimately adopted differing stances toward abortion. For example, shortly after the New York State abortion law legalizing pregnancy termination up to 24 weeks went into effect on July 1, 1970, Carmen Rodriguez became the first woman to die from a legal abortion. Leaders of the Young Lords Party (YLP), a Nationalist organization, argued that, within a racist medical system that already mistreated Puerto Ricans, the new abortion law promised to be yet another form of genocide. Upon Rodriguez's death, Gloria Cruz, the YLP health captain, warned,

A new plan for the limitation of our population was passed-the abortion law. Under this new method we are now supposed to be able to go to any of the city butcher shops (the municipal hospitals) and receive an abortion. These are the same hospitals that have been killing our people for years. (cited in Nelson 114)

In response to these concerns, the Young Lords opened community-run clinics that offered a broad range of birth control options, including abortion. Similar community-based clinics were opened in Los Angeles, some created by the Brown Berets, a Chicano Nationalist organization like the Young Lords. However, while the Young Lords believed that abortion was an important component of comprehensive health care, the Brown Berets were adamantly anti-abortion and pushed a more traditional pronatalist Nationalist agenda. They argued that all forms of birth control were tools of genocide, and any attempt to end a pregnancy that might result in future revolutionaries was decried.[17]

The divergent stances on abortion taken by two Latino grassroots organizations indicate that there is no singular Latino stance on abortion or reproductive politics. It also demonstrates the difficult situation Latinas and others face in reproductive politics. As expressed in the Young Lords' statement on women:

Third World sisters are caught up in a complex situation. On the one hand, we feel that genocide is being committed against our people.... On the other hand, we believe that abortions should be legal if they are community controlled, if they are safe, if our people are educated about the risks, and if doctors do not sterilize our sisters while performing abortions.[18]

While Puerto Rican women were able to successfully integrate the struggle for reproductive freedom into the Young Lords Party platform, Chicanas more often developed their own complementary organizations. However, they did not retreat into a separate entity but continued to demand that so-called "women's" issues be acknowledged in the struggle for Chicano equality. Despite efforts to stifle women's issues in the Chicano movement, the first National Chicana Conference was held in May 1971 in Houston, Texas. At this meeting, discussions of abortion, birth control, marriage, and other feminist issues were central.

In her recollections of the proceedings at the conference, Francisca Flores regards issues of family size as fundamentally an issue of bodily self-determination:[19]

The issue of birth control, abortions, information on sex, and the pill are considered "white" women's lib issues and should be rejected by Chicanas according to the Chicano philosophy which believes that the Chicana women's place is in the home and that her role is that of a mother with a large family. Women who do not accept this philosophy are charged with betrayal of our culture and heritage—OUR CULTURE HELL!

On another level, part of Chicana efforts to fight for their reproductive autonomy was to counter the Nationalist narrative, which prescribed that their role in the revolution was to produce lots of brown babies. Chicana writers such as Sylvia Delgado questioned the Nationalist prerogative of procreation.

> We accuse genocide. La Raza's cry. So we turn to increasing the popula-tion. But what kind of padres are we, if we are going to see our sons raised in slavery, with cut-rate education, poverty, and to watch our children die? I say no to fools who say women are tools for copulation and birth. Unwanted babies are not loved in the mother nor by those who must toil for them. Don't people think that 15- and 16-year-olds are listening to their ban on birth control? While parents and peers taboo sex, they know what they are feeling in sexual terms. Are we going to go down as saying intercourse is to make babies while in our heads we are glad that in the past lays we had, there was no pregnancy. (3)

Breaking the silence about Chicana sexuality and the right to make their own reproductive decisions, activists ignited a discussion that has helped to envision different roles for women from those traditionally defined by the Nationalist movement. The development of a Chicana feminist consciousness led to the es-tablishment of many new grassroots organizations focused upon the issues women found central to gaining equality. Latinas became involved in all areas of women's organizing-in domestic violence and sexual assault movements, educational and social policy efforts, and the fight for welfare rights.

Opposing Sterilization Abuse

Latinas across ethnicities in Los Angeles, San Francisco, and New York came together to organize legal, grassroots, and legislative measures against the steriliza-tion abuse of Latinas and other women of color. While individual efforts took place on both the East and West Coasts, ultimately Latinas began communicating and working together. In New York, many Puerto Rican anti-sterilization abuse activists were previously involved in similar organizing in Puerto Rico. Others had come to be involved in reproductive rights issues as an outgrowth of their work within the Puerto Rican Socialist Party. Similar to the women within the Chicano movement, many women struggled to bring women's issues to the forefront of a decidedly Nationalist agenda. With reproductive rights at the center of their women's platform, women like Maria Sanchez, Martina Santiago, Elsa Rios, and Eugenia Acuna organized and attended demonstrations and mobilized against sterilization abuse and the lack of informed consent procedures.

The Committee to End Sterilization Abuse (CESA) was founded in 1974, spearheaded by Dr. Helen Rodriguez-Trias, Dr. Raymond Rakow, and Maritza Arrastia, editor of *Claridad*. Although CESA was a multi-ethnic coalition, La-tinas were crucial to the group's efforts. Comprised of a coalition of individuals and groups, including the Puerto Rican Independence Movement, the Puerto Rican Socialist Party, the Center for Constitutional Rights, the Marxist Edu-cation Collective, and the Committee for the Decolonization of Puerto Rico, the group was formed on the basis of rumors of sterilization abuse and recent statistics showing that sterilizations in public hospitals in primarily Puerto Rican neighborhoods had increased 180 percent. CESA initially organized to collect information about sterilization to document abuse and educate others about the issue, developing fact sheets and statistics. Largely due to CESA's mobilization and the community outcry against sterilization abuse, sterilization guidelines for the state of New York were developed, with CESA's influence strongly represented on the advisory committee. These laws and regulations ultimately became a model for many other state regulations and the federal regulations that were later established.

In 1979, CESA united with the Committee for Abortion Rights and Against Sterilization Abuse (CARASA) and several other organizations, such as the Mexican American Women's National Association, the Center for Constitutional Rights, and the Chicana Nurses Association in a coalition to monitor the compliance of New York City hospitals with new city laws. This New York coalition became part of the Reproductive Rights National Network (R2N2) in 1981 (Gordon 434-435).

Meanwhile, much of the activism in California revolved around a particular case of abuse at Los Angeles County Medical Center and the lawsuits that followed. In 1975, eleven Mexican-origin women filed a civil suit against the Los Angeles County Medical Center, claiming that each of them had been involuntarily sterilized between 1971 and 1974. The women asked the court to require the U.S. Department of Health, Education, and Welfare to mandate that hospitals receiving federal funds provide sterilization counseling and consent forms in Spanish. The court ruled against the women, attributing the non-consensual sterilization to a "communication breakdown" between the women and their doctors. The appeal of the court's decision was also denied. In large part, this legal effort, and the connected attempts to bring attention to the issue and raise money for the case, resulted from an already established network of Chicana grassroots organizations fighting for issues of childcare, health care, and educational opportunities for their children.[20]

The Mexican American Legal Defense and Education Fund (MALDEF) Chicana Rights Project worked with this network to file a petition with the State of California Department of Health for the adoption of more strenuous regulation of consent procedures for sterilization operations. Organizers in San Francisco and around the state turned to CESA in New York for advice and assistance. Although Latina organizing against sterilization abuse occurred on both coasts, this was perhaps the first prolonged national communication between Latinas concerned about reproductive and sexual rights.

In addition to legislative battles, Latina activists staged protests, held rallies, circulated petitions, and gave speeches in order to educate the public and the women's movement about sterilization abuse in their communities. They also broadened the meaning of reproductive rights and identified the value of women organizing along racialethnic lines. As Dagmaris Cabezas wrote in 1977:

This is a struggle where Puerto Rican women have to lead the way, because only the Puerto Rican woman can best understand her own reality. I don't think anyone has the right to tell her what position she must take. There are women who opt for sterilization or abortion because their economic reality pushes them in that direction. Therefore, one can't separate that struggle from the struggle for better day care centers, for equal pay for equal work, for a better education, and for all rights that a woman must have to make a free choice in this society. (19)

Although not solely Latina, CESA was perhaps the most significant reproductive rights development on the East Coast, and a significant step in the development of a national Latina reproductive rights agenda because it was founded and largely run by Latinas. According to Eugenia Acuña, who was a member of a CESA chapter in Connecticut, CESA was important because for the first time she was able to connect issues of national liberation and women and work with other Latinas.

We did research on sterilization rates in New Haven. We organized women in the community and got at least one community clinic to look at what it was doing. The thing about CESA that was so important was that here were some Latinas who were also feminist, and cared about reproductive rights but from a Latina point of view. That was like coming home.

For others like Acuña, coming together with other Latinas to struggle against reproductive abuse was a significant event. Until that point, many Latina health workers and activists had experienced isolation. With new connections and experience working together, CESA led to the founding of the first Latina-specific reproductive rights organizations in the U.S. and to coalition work among various organizations.

Organizing from the 1985 to the Present

Before discussing the evolution of a number of Latina reproductive health entities over the past 30 years, it is important to emphasize that, even before Latinas came together to work in collaboration, many were already individually doing the hard work of health education or providing health services in their communities, often in addition to activism against reproductive abuse. Usually working in isolation, and with very limited resources or support, during the 1980s and '90s a cadre of Latina health professionals grew across the nation. Those who were drawn to women's health education and services were usually the first to develop a reproductive and sexual health curriculum for Latinas and the only ones in their clinics or organizations voicing those concerns.

Many of these health educators worked in both Latino communities and mainstream reproductive rights networks. For example, Eugenia Acuña, a Chilean who migrated to the U.S. and received a masters in public health from the University of Puerto Rico, worked in a wide variety of positions in New York City, some at the same time: health department, bureau of maternity services, community centers, coordinator of Hunter College reproductive rights education project, health education, and the International Reproductive Rights and Health Action Group. Many other Latinas followed similar paths in their own communities, providing health care information at different forums, developing curricula, and training other educators. As these practitioners developed their expertise and became acquainted with one another, many realized the need to begin organizing formally together to share information, combine agendas, and provide mutual support.

The Latina Roundtable on Health and Reproductive Rights (LRHRR) was founded in October 1989 by a number of women—mostly Puerto Rican and Dominican—including Jenny Rivera, Diana Correa, Celina Romany, and Elsa Rios (Montanez). These community leaders were concerned about the health crisis among Latinas and felt the need to organize a Latina response to escalating attacks against their reproductive rights. Being the only Latina reproductive rights organization in New York, LRHRR quickly emerged as a major community education and health policy group, addressing Latina health and reproductive rights issues on a local, state, and national level. At the time, LRHRR was the only visible women of color organization in the state exclusively devoted to advocating for increased access to a full range of quality and affordable health services and reproductive options for Latinas. Its first executive director was Wilma Montanez, a longtime reproductive rights advocate who started her career as a community health worker and family planning counselor working with youth and immigrant communities. Her involvement with issues of HIV/AIDS and women, along with her commitment to include community-based input in public policy, positioned the organization as a critical player in the reproductive rights movement, locally and nationally. Composed of Latina health providers, attorneys, community activists, educators, and policy analysts, the LRHRR was instrumental in providing a Latina analysis and action plan on the most restrictive reproductive rights policies of the late 1980s and '90s, which included waiting periods for abortion, parental involvement in abortion decisions, welfare reform, mandatory HIV /AIDS testing, and treatment of pregnant women. Although many social service agencies within the New York City Latino community were concerned with some of these issues, there was reluctance to adding a gender lens to issues such as HIV/AIDS; reproductive rights continued to be considered a white woman's issue that did have a place on the long list of other community concerns.

The LRHRR's coalition-building and networking efforts provided a safe place for Latinas to meet and collaboratively develop advocacy strategies to be used to influence public policy. LRHRR meetings provided much-needed support to activists who felt that their desires to include and strengthen the voice of women within their own organizations were not always welcomed. One of LRHRR's most memorable activities was organizing clinic defense efforts in the South Bronx in response to Operation Rescue in July 1992. This event marked the first time a group of Latinos took a public position defending abortion services in the community. When Montanez left LRHRR in 1996 to become the reproductive rights program officer at the Jessie Smith Noyes Foundation, Luz Rodriguez took the helm. Under her leadership, LRHRR received a grant from the Ford Foundation that helped initiate the Sister Song Collective, which has since gained national recognition as a force for women of color working for reproductive justice. Consistent with other nonprofit organizations with fragile infrastructures, LRHRR closed its doors in 1998. During its short stint, LRHRR succeeded in proving that Latinas on a local level could have an impact on national policies and, most importantly, that Latinas are involved in the reproductive rights movement (Montanez).

In the 1990s, Amigas Latinas en Accion, a Latina feminist collective in Boston, advanced its Latina perspective on reproductive health through Mujeres en Acción Pro Salud Reproductiva: Northeast Project on Latina Women and Reproductive Health.[67] They used data collected from women to advocate for policy changes. They promoted Latina leadership and distributed bilingual, bicultural informational materials on reproductive health and sexuality. Ultimately, these programs developed into a support group in which women discussed issues of sexuality and the body. Many participants said it was the first time that they had ever talked about such topics, and its developers considered it lithe first step in empowering women to articulate their unique identities and to reclaim their rights as Puerto Rican women" (Flores *et al.*).

National Latina Institute for Reproductive Health

The National Latina Institute for Reproductive Health (NLIRH) established itself in 1994 as the first independent national organization for Latinas on reproductive rights issues. Initiated by the Hispanic Outreach Project of Catholics for a Free Choice in 1991, its primary objectives were to provide information and technical assistance to national Latina/o organizations that wished to work on issues of reproductive health, and to promote the involvement of Latina/o organizations in pro-choice efforts. Starting with a four-member advisory committee, the group rapidly grew.[22] Developing audiovisual and written materials that encompassed the cultural attitudes, values, perspectives, and languages of Latinas with regard to issues of choice, the project was also centrally involved in the mainstream pro-choice movement. The NLIRH newsletter, *Instantes,* featured educational articles about reproductive health and rights from a Latina viewpoint and included legislative analysis. The group's first director, Aracely Panameño, developed the organization to more broadly define its mission to include a broad array of health issues that spoke to the diversity of Latina/o communities in the U.S.

From 1996 through 1999, the NLIRH held a series of forums across the nation to bring Latinas interested in working on reproductive and general health issues together and to promote regional and national collaboration in the development of a Latina reproductive politics platform. The NLIRH agenda was driven by the needs and voices of Latinas at the grassroots rather than being directed from the top down. The goal was to encourage the formation of state coalitions, networking circles, and statewide reproductive rights agendas. The delegates invited to each forum included health care providers and policy-makers, teachers, clinic staff, activists, and others concerned with Latina reproductive rights. They presented a summary of the health status of Latinas in their region and strategized about how to implement policy changes based upon their findings. Regional health leaders also addressed the delegates and spoke of the reproductive health concerns experienced in the region. For example, Olga Sanchez from the Mexican American Legal Defense and Education Fund discussed the ties between welfare reform and anti-immigrant legislation in California. Other speakers showed how access to dental care and environmental degradation are related to reproductive health. Skill-building for those who provide health services to Latino populations was also part of the agenda.

The forums brought Latina reproductive health practitioners together for the first time ever and planted seeds for activist collaboration in advocating for Latina reproductive health rights in their own communities. However, maintaining collaborations proved difficult, as scheduling, distance, and lack of financial and other resources prevented groups from developing. Many regions struggled to continue this work beyond the forums. In 1998, the NLIRH expanded its efforts to strengthen and institutionalize state coalitions. By providing funding and technical assistance, it hoped to empower state coalitions to undertake outreach and educational projects and to participate in local and state health policy discussions. This effort was deliberately aimed to "grow" the movement: "Recognizing the high rate of burn-out experienced by many of us involved in activist work, NLIRH's intent in working with coalitions was to create permanent, staffed, and funded entities designed around a common overall goal-to improve Latinas' health."[23] Unfortunately, NLIRH's quick expansion, together with its ever-broadening scope, ultimately spread the still-young organization too thin. Although the NLIRH was forced to close its doors for a few years, it reopened in 2003, and recently moved into the forefront of organizing for Latina reproductive and sexual freedom as one of the co-sponsors of the 2004 March for Women's Lives. Moreover, the NLIRH has spawned other organizations, one of them being the Colorado Organization for Latina Opportunity and Reproductive Rights (COLOR).

The two case studies which follow demonstrate that Latina efforts have successfully reframed reproductive issues to reflect their cultural and political realities and developed innovative organizing strategies and principles. Perhaps more importantly, as Dr. Helen Rodriguez-Trias pointed out, "The ingenuity of women in grassroots community organizations was the main factor enabling the continuation of reproductive health services to women." The next chapter discusses the oldest organization working on behalf of Latinas and their reproductive rights-the National Latina Health Organization.

This essay is written *en memoria* de Helen Rodriguez-Trias, who was dedicated to improving the health conditions and life circumstances of U.S. Latinas. In the 1970s, Rodriguez-Trias spoke out tirelessly against sterilization abuse of Puerto Ricans. A founder of the Committee to End Sterilization Abuse, her efforts were crucial in establishing informed consent guidelines for sterilization that protect all women. Throughout her career she was active in the Women's Health Movement, serving on the boards of the National Women's Health Network and the Boston Women's Health Book Collective. An expert in maternal and child health, she was the first female director of pediatrics at Lincoln Hospital in the Bronx, New York in 1970, the first Latina medical director of the New York State Department of Health AIDS Institute in the 1980s, and the first Latina president of the American Public Health Association in 1992. In 1996, she helped found and co-direct the Pacific Institute of Women's Health, a non-profit dedicated to improving women's health and well-being. She was awarded a presidential Citizen's Medal of Honor for her work on behalf of women and children, AIDS patients, and the poor. An inspiration to many, this history is written so that her work, and the efforts of so many others who strive to better the life circumstances of their communities will not go unknown.

Notes

[1] For example, Angela Pattatucci-Aragon asserts that: "While reproductive autonomy has been top priority among non-Hispanic feminists, it has been of secondary importance to Latina feminists. They have concentrated upon basic survival issues such as adequate childcare, and public safety. Thus, Latinas have often been the subjects, but not the participants, in discussions focusing on reproductive rights."

[2] The terms Latino and Hispanic were created by the U.S. government to categorize people of Latin American descent living in the U.S. However, as markers they erase differences in national origin and racial/ethnic status, citizenship status, etc., and promote the representation of Latinos as a monolithic group. Moreover, while they may be defined as such through this definition, individuals who officially fall into this group mayor may not personally identify as Latina/o, though research shows that Latinos are increasingly self-identifying as Latina/o: see Flores-Gonzalez; Oboler._

[3] The term, "generic Latina" is borrowed from a play with the same title by Chicago's Teatro Luna, an all-Latina troupe. Their play demonstrates that media images often treat Latinas as caricatures and stereotypes, flattening the deep diversity within Latina cultures. Cofer also writes of the homogenization of Latinas in "The Myth of the Latin Woman: I Just Met a Girl Named Maria."

[4] For an extended discussion, see Briggs.

[5] Passed in 1994, but later overturned, Proposition 187 was a statewide referendum that barred undocumented immigrants from public services such as non-emergency health care, welfare and public schools.

[6] The so-called "Save Our State" initiative constructed the high fertility of Mexican women as emblematic of the myriad problems caused by increasing immigration from Mexico.

[7] While I will highlight some of the major trends in the reproductive health status of Latinas here, a thorough analysis is beyond the scope of this chapter. For a more complete assessment of the status of Latina reproductive health, see Giachello.

[8]Although Latinos have very high labor force participation, they are in great part members of the working poor and are concentrated in low wage jobs that do not offer health insurance. In 1995, 21 percent of Latinos ages 15-44 reported no health insurance coverage, compared with 7.5 percent of whites and 9.3 percent of African Americans of that age group (Abma et al. 19). See also de la Torre et al.

[9]This may partially be explained by the fact that most Latino births are to Mexican American women, who represent roughly 70 percent of Latinas of childbearing age. They also have the highest fertility rate of any racial/ethnic group. Birthrates (the number of births per 1,000 population) of Latino origin were as follows, 26.4 for Mexican Americans, 19.0 for Puerto Ricans, 10.0 for Cubans, and 23.2 for Central and South American women in the United States (Ventura et al.).

[10]There are significant intra-group differences; however, "in 1998, about 6.3 percent of all Latino mothers had late or no prenatal care at all, compared to 2.4 percent and 7 percent of white and African American mothers, respectively. Within the Latino population, Mexican American mothers (6.8 percent), those from Central and South America (4.9 percent), and Puerto Ricans (5.1 percent) were most likely to delay or not receive prenatal care at all. The percentage for Cuban mothers was the lowest of any other racial and ethnic group (1.2 percent)." Mexican mothers reported the lowest use of early prenatal care (72.8 percent).

[11]See Pesquera and Segura for an overview of recent studies on Latina attitudes towards abortion. See, also, National Latina Institute for Reproductive Health.

[12]For a discussion of the neocolonial status of Puerto Rico, see Cabán; Meléndez and Meléndez.

[13]Goldzheir, who was considered a pioneer in testing oral contraceptives and was a consultant to several drug companies, refused to accept any responsibility for the impact of the experiment on these women's lives, attributing their pregnancies to their carelessness in using the cream. He announced his findings at the American Fertility Society meetings in New Orleans in April 1971, "Placebo Stirs Pill 'Side Effects'."

[14]For example, Dominican women were also sterilized at Gouvenor Hospital and Beth Israel Hospital on the Lower East Side of New York City ("Sterilization: Dominican Women in NYC").

[15]Although this history focuses on public organizing, we must begin to acknowledge the other ways in which women have actively participated in the struggle for reproductive rights. As suggested by Mary Pardo, women's activism not only occurs at the organizational level but also often takes place in individual interaction. Latinas are politically active not only in public spheres-for example, in mobilizing a grassroots effort to stop the building of an incinerator in their neighborhood-but also in their everyday lives (see Pardo). For example, keeping the control of reproductive and sexual health in their own hands has been a priority for many Latinas. The birthing of children by *parteras,* or midwives, occurs in many Latino communities. Moreover, as Latinos are increasingly dependent upon Western medicine, women's friendship and communication networks provide another primary means of obtaining and sharing information about health care options

and negotiation of the health care system. These "informal" communications also serve an important purpose of allowing women to exchange important information with others .. such as whether experiences at particular health clinics have been positive or negative, or in which hospitals Latinos have been treated poorly.

[16]For a more elaborate discussion of Chicana feminist organizing see Ruiz; Segura and Pesquera.

[17]The roles of women in the Young Lords Party and within Chicano Nationalist groups such as the Brown Berets varied; differences arose in part, but not completely; due to the groups' differing perspectives on women's roles in revolution. Young Lords had a very outwardly pro-mujer position—see their position paper on women. For more on the Young Lord's position on reproductive politics, see Nelson. For more on Chicano Nationalist positions see, Gutierrez (forthcoming).

[18]The Young Lords Party position is cited in Gladden's book, *Mujer en Pie de Lucha* (53-54).

[19]For more extensive coverage of the events at the Conferencia de Mujeres Por La Raza, see Anonymous (16); Olivarez.

[20]For more thorough discussions of these events, see Espino; Gutiérrez (2003).

[21]This project was based out of the Hispanic Health Council in Hartford, Connecticut.

[22]The committee was originally comprised of Sally Martinez (vice president of the Women's Division of the League of United Latin American Citizens), Bambi Cárdenas Ramirez (member of the U.S. Commission on Civil Rights), Alice Cardona (assistant director of the New York State Division of Women) and Aida Giachello (Professor of sociology at the Jane Addams School of Social Work at the University of Illinois, Chicago).

[23]COLOR, letter to forum participants, April 1998.

References

Abma, J. *et al.* "Fertility, Family Planning and Women's Health: New Data from the 1995 National Survey of Family Growth." *Vital and Health Statistics* 23 (19) (1997).

Acuña, Eugenia. Personal interview by Elena R. Gutierrez, September, 4, 2002.

Alan Guttmacher Institute. *Facts in Brief: Induced Abortion.* Online: http://www. agi- usa.org/pubs/fb _ induced_ a bortion.html.

Amaro, Hortensia. "Psychological Determinants of Abortion Attitudes Among Mexican American Women." Ph.D. dissertation, University of California Los Angeles, 1982.

Amaro, Hortensia and Adela de la Torre. "Public Health Needs and Scientific Opportunities in Research on Latinas." *American Journal of Public Health* 92 (4) (2002): 526.

Andrade, Sally J. "Social Science Stereotypes of Mexican American Women: Policy Implications for Research." *Hispanic Journal of Behavioral Sciences* 4 (2) (1982): 223-244.

Anonymous. "Chicanas of Today Say What They Want." *El Grito Del Norte* October 2, 1971: 16.

Azize-Vargas, Yamila and Luis A. Avilés. "Abortion in Puerto Rico: The Limits of a Colonial Legality." *Puerto Rico Health Sciences Journal* 17 (1998): 27-36.

Briggs, Laura. *Reproducing Empire: Race, Sex, and U.S. Imperialism in Puerto Rico.* Berkeley: University of California Press, 2002.

Cabán, Pedro A. *Constructing a Colonial People: Puerto Rico and the U.S., 1898-1932.* Boulder: Westview Press, 1999.

Cabezas, Dagmaris. "Mal'iana is Not Good Enough." *Nuestro* 1 (4) (1997): 19.

Chavez-Silverman, Susana. "Tropicolada: Inside the U.S. Latino/a Gender B(l)ender." *Tropicalizations: Transcultural Representations of Latinidad (Re-Encounters with Colonialism).* Eds. Frances R. Aparicio and Susana Chavez-Silverman. Hanover, NH: University Press of New England for Dartmouth College, 1997.

Cofer, Judith Ortiz. "The Myth of the Latin Woman: I Just Met a Girl Named Maria." *One World, Many Cultures.* Eds. Stuart Hirschberg and Terry Hirschberg. Boston: Allyn and Bacon, 1998. 167-175.

de la Torre, Adela *et al.* "The Health Insurance Status of U.S. Latino Women: A Profile from the 1982-1984 Hispanic HHANES." *American Journal of Public Health 86* 4 (1996): 534-537.

Del Castillo, Adelaida. "Sterilization: An Overview." *Mexican Women in the United States: Struggles Past and Present.* Eds. Magdalena Mora and Adelaida Del Castillo. Los Angeles: UCLA Chicano Studies Research Center Publications, 1980. 65-69.

Delgado, Sylvia. "Chicana: The Forgotten Woman." *Regeneración* 2 (1) (1971): 2-4.

Derose, Kathryn P. and David W. Baker. "Limited English Proficiency and Latinos' Use of Physician Services." *Medical Care Research and Review* 57 (1) (2000): 76-91.

Erickson, Pamela and Celia Patricia Kaplan. "Latinos and Abortion." *The New Civil War: The Psychology, Culture, and Politics of Abortion.* Eds. L. J. Beckman and S. M. Harvey. Washington, DC: American Psychological Association, 1998.

Espino, Virginia. "Women Sterilized as You Give Birth: Forced Sterilization and Chicana Resistance in the 1970s." *Las Obreras: Chicana Politics of Work and Family.* Ed. Vicki Ruiz. Los Angeles: UCLA Chicano Studies Research Center Publications, 2000.

Flores, Francisca. "Conference of Mexican Women: *Un Remolino.*" *Regeneración* 1 (1971): 1-5.

Flores, Candida *et al.* "La Mujer Puertorriqueña, Su Cuerpo, y Su Lucha por la Vida: Experiences With Empowerment in Hartford, Connecticut." *From Abortion to Reproductive Freedom.* Ed. Marlene Gerber Fried. Boston: South End Press, 1990.

Flores-Gonzalez, Nilda. "The Racialization of Latinos: The Meaning of Latino Identity for the Second Generation." *Latino Studies Journal* 10 (3) (1999): 3-31.

Frankfort, Ellen with Frances Kissling. *Rosie: The Investigation of a Wrongful Death.* New York: Dial Press, 1979.

Francisca Flores, "Conference of Mexican Women: *Un Remolino,*" *Regeneración* 1 (1971): 1-5.

Giachello, Aida L. "The Reproductive Years: The Health of Latinas." *Latina Health in the United States: A Public Health Reader.* Eds. Carlos W. Molina and Marilyn Aquirre-Molina. San Francisco: Jossey-Bass, 2003. 77-131.

Gladden, Dorinda Moreno. *Mujer en Pie de Lucha.* Mexico City: Espina del Norte Publications, 1973.

Goldzheir, Joseph. "Placebo Stirs Pill 'Side Effects'." *Medical World News* (1971): 19.

Gordon, Linda. *Woman's Body, Woman's Right: A Social History of Birth Control in America.* Rev. ed. New York: Penguin Books, 1990.

Gutierrez, Elena R. *Fertile Matters: The Racial Politics of Mexican Origin Women: s Reproduction.* Austin: University of Texas Press, forthcoming.

Gutiérrez, Elena R. "Policing 'Pregnant Pilgrims': Situating the Sterilization Abuse of Mexican-Origin Women in Los Angeles County." *Women, Health, and Nation: Canada and the* U.S. *Since 1945.* Ed. Georgina Feldberg *et al.* Montreal: McGili-Queen's University Press, 2003. 379-403.

Handler, A. *et al.* "Women's Satisfaction with Prenatal Care Settings: A Focus Group Study." *Birth* 23 (1) (1996): 31-37.

Juarez, Ana Maria and Stella Beatriz Kerl. "What Is the Right (White) Way to Sexual? Reconceptualizing Latina Sexuality." *Aztlan* 28 (1) (2003): 7-37.

King, Lourdes Miranda. "Puertorriqueñas in the U.S." *Civil Rights Digest* 6 (3) (1974): 20-27.

Lopez, Iris. "An Ethnography of the Medicalization of Puerto Rican Women's Reproduction." *Pragmatic Women and Body Politics.* Eds. Margaret Lock and Patricia A. Kaufert. New York: Cambridge Studies in Medical Anthropology, 1997. 240-259.

Martinez, Elizabeth Sutherland. "Listen Up, Anglo Sisters." *De Colores Means All of Us: Latina Views for a Multi-Colored Century.* Cambridge, MA: South End Press, 1998.

Mass, Bonnie. "Puerto Rico: A Case Study of Population Control." *Latin American Perspectives* 4 (4) (1977): 66-81.

Meléndez, Edwin and Edgardo Meléndez. *Colonial Dilemma: Critical Perspectives on Contemporary Puerto Rico.* Boston: South End Press, 1993.

Montanez, Wilma. Personal interview. July 30, 2002.

Morales, Aurora Levins. "Piecing a History Together: the Women of Boriken." *Women's Review of Books* 9 (10-11) (1992): 8-9.

Mullings, Leith. "Images, Ideology, and Women of Color." *Women of Color in* U.S. *Society.* Eds. Maxine Baca Zinn and Bonnie Thornton Dill. Philadelphia: Temple University Press, 1994. 265-289.

Oboler, Suzanne. *Ethnic Labels, Latino Lives: Identity and the Politics of Representation in the* U.S. Minneapolis: University of Minnesota Press, 1995.

Pesquera, Beatriz and Denise Segura. "'It's Her Body, It's Definitely Her Right': Chicanas/Latinas and Abortion." *Voces: A Journal of Latina Studies* 2 (1): 103-127.

Napoles-Springer, A. and E. Pérez-Stable. "Risk Factors for Invasive Cervical Cancer in Latino Women." *Journal of Medical Systems* 20 (5) (1996): 277-294.

National Latina Institute for Reproductive Health. *Latinas and Abortion*. Washington, DC: NLIRH, 1999.

Nelson, Jennifer A. "Abortions Under Community Control: Feminism, Nationalism, and the Politics of Reproduction Among New York City's Young Lords." *Journal of Women's History* 13 (1) (2001): 157-180.

Olivarez, Elizabeth. "Women's Rights and the Mexican American Woman." *Regeneracion* 2 (4) (1974): 40-42.

Pardo, Mary. "Creating Community: Mexican American Women in Eastside Los Angeles." *Community Activism and Feminist Politics: Organizing Across Race, Class, and Gender*. Ed. Nancy A. Naples. New York: Routledge, 1998. 266-300.

Pattatucci-Aragon, Angela. "Hispanic/Latina Women and Reproductive Rights" in the *Historical and Multicultural Encyclopedia of Women's Reproductive Rights in the U.S.,* ed. Judith Baer (Westport, CT: Greenwood Press, 2002), 103-106,

Physicians for Reproductive Choice and Health and the Alan Guttmacher Institute. *Overview of Abortion in the* U.S. 2003. Online: http://www.prch.org.

Riddell, Adaljiza Sosa. "The Bioethics of Reproductive Technologies: Impacts and Implications for Latinas." *Chicana Critical Issues*. Ed. Norma Alarcon. Berkeley: Third Woman Press, 1993.

Rios, Elsa. Personal interview. September 4, 2002.

Rodriguez-Trias, Helen. "Women Are Organizing: Environmental and Population Policies Will Never Be the Same." *American Journal of Public Health* 84 (9) (1994): 1379-1382.

Ruiz, Vicki L. "La Nueva Chicana: Women and the Movement." *From Out of the Shadows: Mexican Women in Twentieth-Century America*. Ed. Vicki L. Ruiz. New York: Oxford University Press, 1998. 99-126.

Salvo, Joseph J., Mary G. Powers, and Rosemary Santana Cooney. "Contraceptive Use and Sterilization Among Puerto Rican Women." *Family Planning Perspectives* 24 (5) (1992): 219-223.

Sanchez Jr., George J. "'Go After the Women': Americanization and the Mexican Immigrant Woman, 1915-1929." *Unequal Sisters: A Multicultural Reader in U.S. Women's History*. Eds. Ellen Carol Dubois and Vicki L. Ruiz. New York: Routledge, 1990. 250-263.

San Martin, Nancy. "Children of the Fields; Birth Defects Occur at an Alarming Rate Among Guatemalan Migrant Workers." South Florida *Sun-Sentinel* July 14, 1996.

Scrimshaw, Susan C. M., Ruth E. Zambrana and Christine Dunkel-Schetter. "Issues in Latino Women's Health: Myths and Challenges." *Women's Health: Complexities and Differences*. Eds. Sheryl Burt Ruzek *et al.*Columbus: Ohio State University Press, 1997. 329-347.

Segura, Denise A. and Beatriz M. Pesquera. "Beyond Indifference and Antipathy: The Chicana Movement and Chicana Feminist Discourse." *The Chicano Studies Reader: An Anthology of Aztlrm, 1970-2000.*Eds. Chon A. Noriega *et al.* Los Angeles: UCLA Chicano Studies Research Center Publications, 2001. 389-410.

"Sterilization: Dominican Women in NYC." *Triple Jeopardy* (December 1973).

U.S. Census Bureau. *The Hispanic Population: Census 2000 Brief.* Washington, DC: Bureau of the Census, May 2001.

Velez-Ibañez, Carlos G. "Se Me Acabó La Canción: An Ethnography of Non-Consenting Sterilizations Among Mexican Women in Los Angeles." *Mexican Women in the U.S.: Struggles Past and Present.* Eds. Magdalena Mora and Adelaida Del Castillo. Los Angeles: Chicano Studies Research Center, UCLA, 1980. 71-91.

Ventura, Stephanie J. *et al.n*"Births: Final Data for 1998." *National Vital Statistics Reports* 48 (3) (2000). Online: http://www.cdc.gov/nchs/data/nvsr/nvsr48/nvs48_03.pdf.

Chapter 43

The Motherhood Religion

JUDITH WARNER

I wonder how these kids will grow up feeling about their parents. How much resentment and how many theories will come out about the negative aspects of this overzealous involvement? It just does not look healthy or normal to me, especially with the mothers typically on the edge and stressed all the time. How much of this stress will be reflected on the kids? My mom was upset and stressed all the time and I know how profoundly this has impacted my whole attitude toward life.

—39-year-old working mother in Virginia

THERE'S A STORY we mothers tell ourselves these days, in books and in magazines and in movies and on TV, and even in conversations with our friends.

And that story—which is usually told over the head of a toddler, or accompanied by the visual image of a mom making dinner for six while she does homework for four—is that we now live our lives in the totalizing, ultra-child-centered way we do because we have realized that liberated motherhood wasn't all it was cracked up to be.

It wasn't good for children and it wasn't good for mothers. And so now we are using all our freedom and choice to set the situation right. We are giving our children what they "really" need. We are giving ourselves what we "really" need—a degree of intense child-bonding that both feminism *and* Spock denied to previous generations.

All of which is good. And right. And, on a very basic level, the way things were always meant to be. The only problem is that this story—the Gospel According to Which We Mother—has no actual basis in fact.

There's no proof that children suffered in the past because their mothers put them in playpens. There's no proof that children suffer today because their mothers work. None of the studies conducted on the children of working mothers—in the 1950s, 1960s, 1970s, 1980s, and 1990s—have ever shown that a mother's work outside of home *per se* has any impact upon her child's well-being.[1] (The quality of care a child receives while the mother's away, on the other hand, has a *major* impact on that child's well-being, but that's a whole other story.[2])

Studies have never shown that total immersion in motherhood makes mothers happy or does their children any good. On the contrary, studies *have* shown that mothers who are able to make a life for themselves tend to be happy and to make their children happy. The self-fulfillment they get from a well-rounded life actually makes them more emotionally available for their children—in part because they're less needy (Chira).

All of this research has been around for decades. But somehow, we've managed to miss it. Just as we manage, each day, not to notice the fact that the pained-faced Mommy getting down on her knees at kindergarten drop-off time and draping herself over her son's tiny shoulders isn't a very happy person. We manage *not* to acknowledge, despite endless clues from our children's doctors and teachers, that our preferred parenting style is *not* terribly conducive to promoting future happiness. We persist in doing things that are contrary to our best interests—and our children's best interests. And we continue, against all logic, to subscribe to a way of thinking about motherhood that leaves us guilt-ridden, anxious, and exhausted.

Why do we do this? I think it's because, as far as motherhood is concerned, our beliefs don't come from experience or observation. Real life, science, or even common sense has little to do with these beliefs. They're articles of faith. Matters of religion—the American Motherhood Religion. And as such they have a life and an inner logic all their own.

***

When I talk about the Motherhood Religion, what I mean is all the ways that motherhood in America has been unmoored from reality and turned into theology. Or how, time and again, motherhood has been made into an overdetermined thing, invested with quasi-ecclesiastical notions of Good and Evil. And while the definitions of Good and Evil have sometimes changed, one thing has always remained the same: in times of trouble, making a religion of motherhood has provided people with a kind of refuge. It has offered a psychological fix, a collective salve for people weary of a soul-bruising world. The Motherhood Religion soothes anxiety. Over and over again.

It did so in the late eighteenth century, when the ideal of mother as sacred teacher and moral guide came to American shores. It came from England and it had sprung there from some new and very potent sources of anxiety: middle-class life was changing. The nature of work was changing, pulling fathers out of their homes and into a separate world of moneymaking labor. This meant that family life was undergoing a major revolution. Whereas in the past, child care had been woven into a whole tapestry of work done in and around the home by mothers and fathers and servants together, now children were more and more alone with their mothers. Fewer middle-class households could afford to have servants. And what servants they did have now were much lower class than in the past. These servants were deemed untrustworthy, coarse, and uncultured. Potentially, even, corrupting for children (Block 16). And so, to a much greater degree than ever before, it fell to mothers to make sure their children came out all right. Particularly as regarded moral and spiritual guidance.

Out of this situation, from the sermons and the parenting books that made their way from England to American shores, the Motherhood Religion was born. Ministers and authors taught English and American mothers that their hands-on duties were not just essential but sacred. If they did everything right, their children would be saved. If not ... well, it was better not to contemplate the consequences of bad motherhood. For they were nothing less than Evil.

In the nineteenth century, the Industrial Revolution pushed even more fathers out of the home. It relieved mothers of many of their non-child-centered duties, as they could now buy many of the household goods they'd once made themselves. The new era also raised a lot of new fears: What would happen to a world taken over by the ever-encroaching demands of business? Where would spiritual life reside? What would be left of the human? And what would become of comfort and care in a world of rapacious competition?

The Victorian cult of motherhood answered all these anxieties. The exclusive domesticity of the "Angel in the House" provided a refuge from the world of commerce. The idea of mothers' sweet tenderness offered an antidote to the callousness of the world of industry. And the notion of motherhood as woman's *one and true calling* compensated nicely for the fact that, in truth, middle-class married women simply didn't have much else to do anymore (see Block; Margolis).

In the early twentieth century in America, the birth rate was falling. The first wave of feminist activists were demanding the vote, education for women, self-determination, and independence. Many Americans reacted with horror. And their fears helped sustain the new maternal ideal that rose at the turn of the century: Mother as a doting angel with vital responsibility for every aspect of her child's spiritual and physical existence (Margolis 49).

Another period of acute anxiety came in the years immediately following World War Two. During the war, many mothers had gone to work, filling essential jobs left empty by the men who had gone to war. This was considered a good and patriotic and socially necessary thing. And the stamp of approval bestowed upon mothers' work even extended to daycare, which the government subsidized for some women working in the war industries. Women working for the industrialist Henry J. Kaiser, for example, had access to day-care centers staffed by certified teachers, doctors, psychologists, and nutritionists. There were infirmaries and, for additional fees beyond the one-dollar-a-day cost of child care, there were extra services on offer, like dinners to go, mending, grocery shopping, and child immunizations. Topping it all off, by availing themselves of these services, women were told they were doing the Right Thing. As a Kaiser brochure put it, if a mother's load was lightened, "the better able she would be to give love and affection to a young child" (qtd. in *Glamour*, October 1994: 114).

After the war, the GIs came home needing jobs and wondering what had happened to their families while they'd been away. Had their wives been faithful? Did their children remember them? What roles would they play now that women had been running the show? And, more generally, how would a sense of comfort and normality be returned to life after the horrors of the battlefield?

Most women went home from their jobs, comforted and encouraged, beatified by the Feminine Mystique. This dogma of domestic sanctity guaranteed that there was still such a thing as a man's world in America. And a woman's world, for that matter. And something that could be called home. All of which was anchored in place by Mother's loving care. As one contemporary domestic guide put it, "She it is who will create the world after the war" (qtd, in Margolis 77).

But real life didn't live up to the Mystique. It kept changing. Increased wealth, in the decades after the war, created a hunger for former luxuries—things like cars, vacations, and college educations that now felt like middle-class necessities (Coontz 26). A wife's salary was often what a family needed to make these things affordable. Then, in the mid-1960s, came inflation. Now women's salaries were needed not just for luxuries bur for *real* necessities (Beels 28). And so more and more women—mothers included—left home to earn the money needed to buy them.

It's commonly believed that the women's movement came along and then, in its wake, women dropped their aprons and headed off to work, seeking self-fulfillment and personal liberation.[3] But that's really not the way things happened. Women left home first. They started going to work in big numbers in the 1950s. Because of an unusual confluence of demographics (the small size of the Eisenhower generation, and the huge size of the postwar baby boom), there was a great demand for labor—and for female labor in particular. By the mid-1950s there was a national shortage of teachers, nurses, and clerical workers. Manpower Inc. was so desperate for woman workers that it was offering them incentive gifts for sending in their neighbors and friends.[4] To persuade women to take on more jobs and work more days, the temp agency offered prizes for productivity and pointers on household efficiency.

The kinds of jobs women took were not necessarily fulfilling. They were *jobs*, after all, not careers, and *women's* jobs at that. But they paid the bills. And as the 1950s advanced, women's workforce participation skyrocketed. By 1956, at perhaps the height of the period we think of as the at-home-mom Feminine Mystique years, one third of the workforce was female. About two-thirds of those working women were married, and more than half of those married women had children of preschool or school age (see Walker 88).

Over the course of the 1950s, the number of working mothers *alone* grew by 400 percent (Coontz 26). By the late 1960s, almost 40 percent of mothers with children between the ages of six and seventeen were employed (Ryan 196). And after that, as the cost of living kept rising, the numbers just kept going up. In 1971, almost half of all American women with school-age children had jobs, as did almost one-third of women who had children under age six.[5] By 1972, for the first time, more mothers of school-age children were employed than not (Margolis 65). By the mid-1970s fully half of all mothers were working, including 39 percent of mothers of preschool children, and after that the rate increased—particularly for mothers with young children—with each passing year.[6]

This was a massive change, and it happened very fast. Faster than people could get their minds around it. Faster than our institutions could change to accommodate it. And, of course, it left a massive amount of anxiety in its wake. How could a family without a mom at home work? What were women going to do? What were children going to do? You could hear this anxiety in the outraged tone with which the psychological establishment reacted in the 1950s to the first set of statistics showing the steady stream of mothers into the workplace. It showed up in the early writings on attachment theory and, notably, in the horrified protests of psychologists like Rene Spitz. And then came the trickle-down effects: the catastrophizing over the lives of "latchkey" kids and "insecurely attached" day-care babies. The warnings from politicos and pundits that mothers' work might very well condemn whole generations to grow up as sociopaths.

This catastrophizing was no doubt a symptom of extreme cultural anxiety—like that, writ large, of a person with an anxiety disorder whose autonomic nervous system can't distinguish between a crowded subway car and an attack by a grizzly bear. And that cultural anxiety lasted so long and fused itself so totally to the issue of working motherhood that, as the decades passed, it became all but impossible to separate it out from the reality of working motherhood. The result was that by the 1990s, when 73 percent of mothers with children over age one were working (as were 59 percent of those with infants)[7], certain beliefs—that mothers' work was bad, that separation was agony, and that children needed full-time mother care—no longer sounded like mere worries or opinions. They were articles of faith.

***

Looking back now at the 1990s, the anxiety is clear—as is the way that motherhood was called upon to quell it. The early part of the decade was marked by a recession. College-educated white men (the infamous "angry white males") were particularly hard-hit, both by unemployment and, if they were employed, by the increasing pressures of a hypercompetitive marketplace (Faludi). What was their future? they worried. What was their purpose? Would they ever again be able to coast self-confidently through life? Would there ever again be enough jobs to go around?

There was plenty of anxiety on hand for women, too. For they also were hard hit by the recession. In the job-poor years of 1990 and 1991, for the first time since the end of World War Two, their influx into the world of work actually *stopped* (Hayghe 41). (It picked up again when the economy revived.) Many women lost jobs. Many others (of the baby-boom generation) who kept their jobs discovered that just as they were getting to the point when they might have risen to the top, their work lives were becoming unmanageable. There was no guaranteed family leave—only 40 percent of women in the workforce then had the right to take maternity leave and to have a job waiting for them when they returned. Only 10 percent of employers were providing their employees with child-care assistance—and most of the time this took the form of little more than counseling or referral services (cited in Kaminer 143). Only 5 percent of business and government employees offered day care or helped their employees pay for it. It was an impossible situation. After two decades of advancement, women were maxing out in their careers. They couldn't even think of breaking through the glass ceiling if they wanted to spend any time with their kids; in fact, in many professions, if they wanted to devote time to their families, they could barely hold down a job at all. The optimism of the 1970s had run aground with experience and left them in a rut.

Women worried: What was their future? What were they to do about the unforeseen and now seemingly unresolvable conflicts in their lives? How could they make sense of the fact that they couldn't live up to the full scope of their ambitions if they wanted to have kids? How could they get their minds around the fact that—despite all the boosterism of the you-can-do-it-all 1980s—they *couldn't* do it all?

All this anxiety set the stage for the reemergence of the sacred stay-at-home mother. With her holistically healing message about returning to the hearth. The new stay-at-home dogma offered salve for bruised professional egos. It helped men remember that they *were* still men, and helped women see that if they didn't succeed as they'd planned they weren't failures, they simply had redefined their "priorities" and had joined in the trend toward "new traditionalism." (What was true for mothers, however, wasn't true for fathers. When men went home and took care of their kids—as increasing numbers did in the early 1990s—there was no talk about the dads' having found new "priorities." They were just unemployed. So that, in 1993, when the job market improved, and the proportion of dads staying home fell back down to 16 percent, from a high of 20 percent in 1991 (Adler 58), it came without fanfare, in contrast to the enormous hype generated in 2001 when the percentage of mothers with infants in the workforce dropped—also 4 points—from 59 to 55 percent.[8])

Then came the New Economy. With a new set of realities, which made mothers' work—indeed, *all* work—all the more difficult to reconcile with the needs of families. There was, first and foremost, the fact that good, affordable child care was getting harder and harder to find. The full-employment economy meant that the caliber of people entering the child-care profession as nannies or day-care workers was getting lower and lower.[9] The quality of day care available to *most* families was abysmal. Day-care work was considered the province of the extremely unskilled—like women transitioning from welfare (Hays). Nannies had to earn a living wage, and in cities where the cost of living had skyrocketed, the cost of at-home care for children was pushed out of the reach of all but the best-off families.

After two decades of political leadership intent on shrinking our government, there was virtually no political will to make things better. When the Clinton administration proposed a series of measures to improve the quality and availability of child care, they were met by a chorus of commentators who said people didn't want them. (*Do you want the government raising your children?*) Addressing the most glaring problem in American child care—the lack of national standards—was simply considered a hopeless cause.[10]

Some (in fact, relatively few) women could now choose to stay home. Many more women were effectively put in the situation of *having* to stay home—either because their now sixty-hour workweek was incompatible with family life or because their husbands' seventy-hour workweek meant that if they didn't stop working there would literally be *no one* at home with the kids.

All this led to a *lot* of anxiety. And to a new cult of domesticity, which, like the cult of domesticity that coincided with the Industrial Revolution, helped soothe the stresses of living life in an increasingly rapacious age. There was the stress of raising superchildren to compete in a fiercely competitive world. There was the stress of raising a family with virtually no social safety net. The stress of keeping up with the newly rich neighbors. There was the need, once again, for an oasis from the world of money and work, because with cell phones and e-mail and a 24/7 economy, oases of tranquility were hard to find.

The new cult of motherhood offered peace. A sense of greater safety. The promise of *getting out*.

With the old promise of the 1970s and early 1980s—that women could proudly and happily lead multifunctioning lives—giving way to a grinding sense of impossibility, and with the notion of the "balanced life" teetering into oblivion, the idea that it was, after all, better for a women to be home with her children emerged as the "truth" of the day. The fact that families were being buffeted by economic forces beyond their control was replaced by a story of how women were taking control and "choosing" to go home and dedicate themselves to full-time motherhood, or "choosing" lower-paid dead-end jobs without benefits because they offered "flexibility." A response to economic conditions was reencoded as a new social ethic.

And this remained true when, in the next turn of the screw, a *lack of jobs*, post 9-11, was once again redefined by the terms of the Motherhood Religion. To capture this, I think of Belen Aranda-Alvarado, a member of Harvard Business School's class of 2002, who told the *Los Angeles Times* how the mind game of turning necessity into morality worked. Explaining how her male peers (and erstwhile competitors) cheered her decision to stay home and work as an "entrepreneur," she said, "They kind of see me as having the perfect solution [to the recession] that is socially acceptable" (quoted in Marsh, Part 5, 1).

The new cult of domesticity of the boom years—and the sad years that followed—created its own set of anxieties for mothers. How could they fit the self-sacrificing demands of total-reality motherhood into their prior self-conception as self-determining women? How could they make their worship of success jibe with their new devotion to the idea of family life?

The Mommy Mystique helped make it all come out okay. The revived ideal of raising kids as a woman's "life's work" comforted those uncomfortable with their decision (by choice or by default) to stay home with their children or to downgrade their workplace ambitions once they'd seen that ambitious work was incompatible with ambitious motherhood.

The Mommy Mystique soothed the anxieties caused by lifestyle changes—caused by economic changes—that had not been (indeed, have yet to be) entirely acknowledged and digested. This is different from the recent past, when the Motherhood Religion helped people deal with their anxiety over women's changing roles. People have largely accepted the idea of those changes now. What they haven't accepted (or even really conceptualized) is what we have to do to make those changes *work*.

Think about it: women might have responded to their anxieties differently at the end of the twentieth century. Instead of losing themselves in planning perfect birthday parties, they might have demanded more of their employers or of their government. They might have asked more of their husbands. But doing that—even *thinking* about that—would have exposed them to an even greater degree of anxiety. Because it would have meant tackling the sources of their problems. Because it would have meant trying to *do something* about their lives. Which would have meant destabilizing their marriages (and being confronted with the fact that, most probably, their husbands wouldn't change), or knocking their heads against the wall in seeking new government policies for social change. Women have known, I think, deep in their guts, that neither route would reap rewards. So they shut that sort of thinking down.

And having shut down their willingness to confront real-life motherhood, with its real-life problems and anxieties, they took refuge instead in the morality play version of modern motherhood that we see performed—and debated and discussed and dissected and critiqued all around us every day.

That was an unfortunate decision. Because the moralizing, the pontificating, the hypocrisy, and the pressure that keep the Motherhood Religion alive in our time aren't doing mothers any good. In fact, they are doing many mothers a lot of harm.

***

Andrea Yates, of course, is a very extreme example of how things can go haywire when motherhood is made into a religion and its every act is invested with the moral weight of Good and Evil. But lesser examples proliferate: in the endless self-flagellation, the guilt, and the utter idiocy of so much of The Mess:

> *For my daughter's fourth birthday I didn't make a cake from scratch and write "Happy Birthday, Emma" on it. I had to work. I made the cake from a mix and put on whipped cream and Emma said, "Where's Emma?" and I felt just terrible.*

> *If I have a day where I have someone who comes to the house to take care of my daughter, I feel very guilty if I'm doing something other than doing the groceries or going to the dry cleaner.*

> *My guilt comes from a school environment where you can never do enough, and there are always people who are doing more than you.*

I feel guilty that I don't know how to enjoy my children!

The maddening chant of our Motherhood Religion haunts working mothers and stay-at-home moms alike. Working moms have to run from a chorus detailing their evils. If their children seem fine, they must constantly question their just-fineness. If their financial situation isn't dire, they must constantly justify themselves to others, to make their working acceptable. Because they are told that it is unnatural for them to be working, because they are told it is selfish for them to work unless there is a dire financial necessity for it, many are plagued not only by guilt but also by a pervasive feeling that there is something *wrong* with them if they don't feel guilty about working.

Stay-at-home mothers are made, by our religion of productivity, to feel they have no worth if they are not earning money. The religion of feminism makes them feel that they are letting down the Girls' Team. The cult of total-reality motherhood tells them that they are saints—which would be flattering except that they don't generally *feel* like saints (they often feel bored and impatient and frustrated and tired)—which leaves them wondering what is wrong with *them* for feeling that way.

All this moralizing we routinely do is a ridiculous waste of time and energy. And it also rests upon assumptions that have no basis in reality. Chief among them: that mothers do what they do most of the time out of choice.

***

"Choice" is the fetish word of our generation, perhaps the most sacred of all our articles of faith. It runs through all discussions of motherhood, and inspires most of the quasi-moral fables we read so frequently in the press. It was the buzzword that recurred endlessly in the coverage of Sylvia Ann Hewlett's 2002 book, *Creating A Life: Professional Women and the Quest for Children*, which depicted the stark "choices" made by childless top female professionals and advised younger women to be "intentional" about marrying young and having children as soon as possible. It comes up again and again in the stories of how college women are taking the long view in planning their lives—choosing easily Mommy Trackable careers, for example, which will allow them to stop, have children, then start up work all over again (Kirk; *Business Week*, Nov. 2002). And it's the founding principle of the so-called Mommy Wars—which wouldn't exist without the notion that there are two warring camps of moms who've made diametrically opposed life choices, one camp having chosen the "selfish," modern track of ambition and the other having taken the "selfless," natural track of stay-at-home motherhood.

People repeat these ideas about our "choices" all the time. Even working mothers buy into them. And yet, *they just aren't true.*

I have by now talked to hundreds of women. And what I see is that working and stay-at-home moms do what they do not so much by choice—by choosing from a series of options arrayed before them like cereals on a supermarket shelf—but out of a very immediate and pressing sense of personal necessity. There are many aspects to that sense of necessity—money, status, ambition, the needs of the children and of the family as a whole—all of which play themselves out, in various ways, in individual women's lives. And all of those aspects of personal necessity are part and parcel of the condition of motherhood not external to it, not accessory to it, not a "selfish" deviation from it. They grow naturally out of what women have done—and who they have been—throughout their lives. So their paths as mothers are not so much "chosen" as *devolved* from who they are, who they've been, and what the material conditions of their families require.

Penelope Green once put this succinctly, with remarkable honesty, in an essay called "Family Value" that ran in *Vogue* in 2001. In response to a friend, who had remarked on Green's having had to "shelve her career" for her baby, she wrote that her nonjob of writing 30 hours a week had "never been a question of 'choice' or 'sacrifice.'" "I work the way I work," she said,

> because it gives my parenting life the only shape that feels right to me .... Maybe you could even say it is not so much the fact of my child as it is a lack in me—of talent or love or maybe a little of both—that keeps me out of circulation. Hell, maybe I just went as far as I was able, career-wise. Maybe I got bored; certainly I got lazy. Probably my daughter is a convenient excuse. (Green 170)

We all know the reasons why working mothers work (since they must constantly justify themselves): money, above all, but secondarily, satisfaction, adult companionship, intellectual stimulation, a sense of security and independence and status—the ability, in short, to provide for their families and remain true to themselves. But from talking to women, I've found that the reasons that stay-at-home moms stay home are not all that different, in that, at base, they spring both from a psychological need for self-fulfillment and an effort to meet the material needs of their families. (And *not*, as many commentators would have us think, from a moralistic idea of what was the "right thing to do.")

Very often, the material condition that makes them stay home is a husband's nonstop work schedule. But there are other concrete reasons as well: Child-care costs that amount to more than a mother's take-home pay. Or working hours or a lack of job flexibility that simply makes being a working mother impossible. ("When my daughter had chicken pox it was not an excusable absence," one stay-at-home mom who formerly worked at a large telecommunications company told me. "When I was pregnant, with partial paralysis, it was not an excusable absence—even though I couldn't drive.") Some stay-at-home moms I met had had a bad experience with child care: "I went through nine nannies in two years," said a Washington professional on an open-ended leave. "I think the sequence of changes had a really high cost. I can't quantify how it was for my children, but for me it was really hard." Some quite simply had had joyless, low-paying jobs that weren't worth keeping—particularly when balanced against the cost and low quality of day care.

"I didn't have any kind of life before that I enjoyed," admitted one stay-at-home military wife with two children. "If I were not going to stay at home, it would have to be for something really meaningful."

The psychological reasons for staying home were varied and complex. Women whose mothers had worked out of dire financial necessity and hadn't been able to afford to have nannies simply associated working motherhood with stress and deprivation and anxiety. "My mom had five kids and often worked two jobs," recalled a 28-year-old former clerical worker for a government agency turned stay-at-home mom. "Often she'd go through jobs because they'd want to fire her for taking a couple of hours off to come with us to the doctor's office. I watched, and I didn't want it to happen to me. I didn't want my only contact with my kids to be in the morning rushing out. My mom was always rushed, worried about getting it all done. There's no joy in that." Some women, who'd had working mothers in communities where most mothers stayed home, remembered feeling uncomfortably different. Those whose mothers had not been able to afford babysitters—at a time when there were no after-school programs—remembered feeling very much alone. "At the other kids' houses it was warm and there was food cooking. Their moms were there after school and could go on field trips. I would lose my key on purpose in elementary school so I could go home with one of my friends," recalled a 35-year-old Washington, D.C., stay-at-home mom who went home with her brothers and sisters after school to an empty house after her parents' divorce sent her mother back to work. "I wanted to be Doris Day when I grew up."

Others just couldn't deal with being physically separate from their children. "Before I started staying home, I was the breadwinner," says a Washington, D.C., mother who recently, after years at home, began part-time work again.

> I was making three or four times what my husband was making, easily. And then, after my twins were born, I said, 'I'm not going back.' We could not afford it. We had just bought a new house. We had a lien on our bank account from the IRS. We could not pay our taxes. We went into counseling. It was awful. But it was a nonnegotiable for me. Because I couldn't live with that kind of feeling.

There were status reasons, too—often unstated but clear—like wanting to be a homemaker because of early shame at being the *one* child in the neighborhood with a working mom. There were women for whom stay-at-home motherhood was a mark of success, of having *arrived* solidly in the middle class. "I grew up around people who had to work. I didn't know anybody who stayed at home unless they were on welfare," said a stay-at-home Washington mom with three kids. For these women, whether they came from middle-class, lower-middle-class, or poor backgrounds, stay-at-home motherhood was the culmination of a lifelong ambition, one that had been nurtured, and worked at, consciously or not, the whole of their adult lives, necessitating the choice of the right kind of husband with the right kind of earning potential to make a stay-at-home future possible.

I found that when women were able to act in line with their natural inclinations and ambitions—whether to work or stay at home—they were generally happy, and generally felt that their children were happy, too. Whereas those whose natural inclinations and ambitions had been thwarted—*whether they were working or stay-at-home moms*—were sure that they and their kids would be better off if they changed course, and either went to work or went home. The morality of the situation—whether they felt it was good or bad for their children—derived, not from some external sense of the morality of their "choices," but from the amount of happiness generated by any given arrangement. And that general sense of happiness or well-being began when a mother's sense of personal necessity was satisfied.

***

There's a really interesting way to illustrate what I mean about personal necessity and motherhood and the idea that you can't separate personal necessity *from* motherhood. It means taking a look, not just at mothers today or at our foremothers in past decades or centuries, but also at our relatives, the primates, as I learned from reading Sarah Blaffer Hrdy's fascinating 1999 book, *Mother Nature.*

Hrdy, an anthropologist trained in sociobiology, became personally interested in the mess of motherhood when, early on in her career, she stumbled between the twin pulls of her work and her young daughter and wondered why it was so hard to make everything fit together. She had read Bowlby and believed in his ideas about bonding and didn't want to do anything that would disrupt her connection to her daughter. But at the same time, the desire to work was so strong within her and felt so natural.... Could it really be so out of line, she wondered, with motherhood?

Thinking about contemporary human society didn't offer Hrdy much by way of answers. But thinking about out primate relatives did.

While studying other primates, Hrdy was struck by the fact that, unlike human mothers today, other primate mothers have always managed to pull together what we consider to be opposite and mutually exclusive goals: providing for children and nurturing them with loving, hands-on care. Moving into the human realm, she noted that in the Pleistocene era women carried their babies as they foraged or gathered firewood. What was it, she wondered, that made their multitasking lives come together so naturally? There had to be, she thought, an "ancient female motivation" that explained how they Did It All.

That ancient motivation, she came to see, sprang from certain material realities of primate life: High-status female primates ate. Low-status female primates were eaten. Or were chased away from food. Or saw their babies eaten by other females. And so primate mothers, in order to keep their children alive, had to be ambitious. They had to secure "status" for themselves and their offspring so that they'd have access to fought-over resources like food and shelter. Hrdy writes:

> Establishing an advantageous niche for herself was how Flo, the chimpanzee female that Jane Goodall studied for so many years, stayed fed,

guaranteed access to food for her offspring, and kept them safe from interference by other mothers. Eventually, Flo's high status made it possible for her daughter Fifi to be among the few females who would remain in her natal place to breed—in Fifi's case, inheriting her mother's territory. Even more impressive data documenting the connection between female status and all sorts of reproductive parameters ... have been compiled for Old World cercopithecine monkeys like macaques and baboons. These data strongly suggest that generalized striving for local clout was genetically programmed into the psyches of female primates during a distant past when status and motherhood were totally convergent. (110-111)

Primate mothers' "striving for status," Hrdy saw, was every bit as natural and necessary a part of their mothering as was the care and feeding of their young. Their ambition helped their children to survive and, as a result, was *the* ultimate form of mother care.

We've dropped this "striving for status" function from our contemporary definition of motherhood. But Hrdy is convinced that we are more tightly linked to our ancestors than we think. For one thing, we are still struggling for limited resources. And for another, the sense of the necessity of providing for our children—securing them the status and resources that will allow them to "survive or prosper," as Hrdy puts it—is still hard-wired into our brains. Which means that "natural" motherhood today should know no conflict between providing for our children (i.e., "working") and nurturing them (i.e., "being a mom"). *Both* are part of our evolutionary heritage; both are equally "child-centered" imperatives.

What's "unnatural" about motherhood today, if you follow Hrdy's line of thinking, is not that mothers work but rather that their "striving for status" and their "maternal emotions" have been compartmentalized (Hrdy xiii). By putting the two in conflict—by insisting on the incompatibility of work and motherhood—our culture does violence to mothers, splitting them, unnaturally, within themselves. And the nature of work today makes this split worse. The demands of the contemporary workplace, which often require long working hours and long commutes, force mothers to separate from their children for excessive periods of time. Lack of flexibility completes a picture in which women really *are* forced to choose between providing for and nurturing their children. This means that mothers' instinctual drives to "seek status" are put in conflict with their children's instinctual needs for succor. "The conflict ... is not between maternity and ambition," Hrdy writes, "but between the needs of infants and the way a woman's ambition plays out in modern workplaces" (112).

No wonder motherhood in America today feels so messed up. No wonder so many mothers feel incomplete, like something's always lacking from their otherwise chockablock-full lives. No wonder so many suffer from anxiety—a kind of existential anxiety, a feeling of powerlessness, as though disaster lurked around every corner.

For me, Hrdy's findings, whether or not they're applied literally to understanding the lives of modern mothers, provide a very apt metaphor for understanding the mess that plagues us today. For they show that the so-called "choices" most of us face in America—between more-than-full-time work or 24/7 on-duty motherhood—are, quite simply, *unnatural*.. They amount to a kind of psychological castration: excessive work severs a mother from her need to be physically present in caring for her child, and excessive "full-time" motherhood of the total-reality variety severs a mother not only from her ability to financially provide for her family but also from her adult *sense of agency*, as it sucks her so deeply down into the infantile realm of her children.

In saying this, I am not necessarily making an automatic argument for working motherhood, for in some marriages, I believe, the nature of the husband's work is such that the wife has to stay home in order to provide for and protect her children. And staying home clearly is the fulfillment of some women's strivings for status. I am just making the argument that if a woman loses her sense of agency—of her potential ability to provide for her child—she will, very slowly, crack apart. As did so many postwar moms, urged back home in the days of the Feminine Mystique. As do so many stay-at-home moms today. And if a mother is deprived of her ability to nurture and care for her child—as are women today who must work excessive hours or consign their children to inadequate care—she too will suffer deep within her core.

***

Both working mothers and stay-at-home moms are ambitious. Both are status-seekers. These facts are obvious to anyone with the eyes to see them. (Life on the soccer field is rapacious. The world of play dates can be inhuman. Running volunteers for the school auction can be an exercise in cruelty.) So why can't we acknowledge that what we do is value-neutral? Why do we continue to invest goodness in stay-at-home motherhood and evil in work? *Why must we take refuge in theology instead of dealing with real life?*

Imagine how productive it would be if we stopped obsessing on the morality of staying at home versus working and focused instead on the material conditions that stress all mothers to the point where they founder and drown in The Mess. First of all, we would find that working mothers and stay-at-home moms' interests, ambitions, goals, and needs were strongly aligned. And then, by focusing on the facts of their lives, we would be able to start to define some national priorities for policy that would actually help ease families' lives.

For the moment, all this is little more than a pipe dream. Because it's impossible, in a culture that's constantly making a religion of everything, to stop and look at the facts. It's almost impossible to *get* at the facts, because they're constantly being couched in the terms of our favorite theologies. This is true of the way we talk to one another, of the way journalists write about motherhood—even, says Shari Thurer, a psychologist who reviewed decades of thinking and writing about motherhood for her 1994 book, *The Myths of Motherhood*, of social science:

The psychological research to date continually looks for bad outcomes from maternal employment and other-than-mother care instead of looking for bad outcomes from the lack of societal supports to mothers. In other words, the way psychologists have been framing their research questions reflects the culture's idealized myth of motherhood. So while research has failed to demonstrate the deleterious effects of day care, it has also failed to demonstrate the deleterious effects of no day care—because it did not set out to find them. The unfortunate result is that our psychological research has inadvertently contributed to the maintenance of the status quo, instead of stimulating questions about social change and help for mothers. (291)

This is precisely what happened with Jay Belsky's day-care research in the late 1980s. It happened at the time of the publication of Stanley Greenspan and T. Berry Brazelton's 2000 book, *The Irreducible Needs of Children*, in which the authors made an argument for better day care, and challenged society to come up with more ways to help families. (*USA Today* headlined its coverage "Stay Home with the Kids If You Can.")

It is what happened in 2002, when newspapers across the country ran with the news that mothers' work made their children unable to learn—despite the fact that the study that occasioned this news, conducted by researchers at Columbia University, had found that mothers' work, per se, didn't do *anything*. It was poor-quality care that was keeping kids back. (Three-year-olds with working mothers who were emotionally available to them and could afford to pay for "the best child care possible" scored just the same, researchers found, as the kids of stay-at-home moms (Gutner).) It happened again in the summer of 2003, when the largest long-term study of child care in the United States was summed up by journalists to say that day care was making kids aggressive. This even though the study had concluded that what was really going wrong for aggressive kids in day care was, once again, the poor quality of the care (Gilbert).

Both the 2002 and the 2003 studies concluded that what really mattered for children wasn't whether or not their mothers worked but whether or not their families could afford to provide them with top-quality care. But, as has happened over and over again, these results pointing to the effects of class and of inadequate child care in America were recast to denounce working motherhood. ("Here's Another Thing to Feel Guilty About," was the subject line of the group e-mail sent my way.) The net result was that talk radio was swamped with the usual crusading callers; politicians were spared the need to come up with solutions, and mothers were left with no greater option than to throw up their hands and take their nightly Ambien. Because there was nothing else they could do in the face of such an impossible situation.

Except, of course, to refuse to accept that the situation was impossible.

"Instead of saying, 'I feel terrible. I feel guilty,' maybe [women] can take these results and advocate for [national] family-leave policies that create more options for mothers of babies," said researcher Jeanne Brooks-Gunn, the lead author of the 2002 day-care study, as she expressed her frustration with all the hand-wringing and guilt expressed in the study's wake by working mothers. "Every other industrialized nation has done it. Why can't we?" (qtd. in Banks).

Mother Image Problems

The way we mother today isn't entirely new.

Back in the 1920s, the converts to "scientific motherhood" were already practicing a (more emotionally ascetic) form of total-reality motherhood. It meant constant vigilance, a perfect monitoring of food intake and activities, chauffeuring children to and from music and dancing lessons, and total immersion in the advice books of the new child-care experts. As one upper-middle-class mother in Middletown, Connecticut, proudly put it, in 1929, "I accommodate my whole life to my little girl" (quoted in Ryan 202).

Teach-your-kids-to-read books have been around since the early 1960s. R. Fitzhugh Dodson's 1970 best seller *How to Parent* boasted a reading list of guides to help parents intellectually stimulate their children and encouraged mothers to apply their teachings to lay the groundwork for later intellectual growth and professional success. But new levels of wealth and our own post boomer generational peculiarities have brought the demands of being a "special kind of mother" to a new fever pitch. Our Spockian mothers may have been told to make us their life's work, but they appear, mostly, to have taken expert advice with a grain of salt. Many now express horror with our way of taking what the experts say literally. They see us singing and rolling on the floor in our sweatpants, getting glitter glue and soy milk everywhere, and they think we're crazy. Our children have no "boundaries," they say. They're spoiled rotten. They think it wouldn't be a bad thing if we were to go out for an evening with our husbands. Do something with our hair, at least. *Get a life.*

So much for progress.

It would be easy to categorize the shift toward self-sacrificial motherhood that began in the late 1980s as part of the widespread cultural reaction against women's advancement detailed in 1991 by Susan Faludi's *Backlash*. It's true that the broadening of messages advocating self-sacrifice and a devotional form of stay-at-home motherhood corresponded to the coming into its own of the Christian Right as a force in mainstream American politics. But I don't think that's a sufficient explanation. Cultural messages don't just come from outside and above. If they don't take root in fertile minds, they can't stick.

And these new messages about motherhood stuck with us despite the fact that many of our own mothers turned up their noses at our excessive mothering techniques, despite the fact that many pediatricians were highly vocal in warning us not to fall into the most popular forms of hysteria du jour, despite the fact that there were always some experts appearing in the media, writing books and issuing appeals for rationality and calm. Despite the fact that, in our heart of hearts, we knew that self-sacrificial motherhood wasn't really a very good thing.

After all, plenty of us, in the 1960s and 1970s, had had over-involved mothers—the kind that experts warned about back then. Mothers who too closely monitored our homework, got over-busy at our schools, or generally bordered on living our lives for us. Those of us who did came out of it with no illusions about the virtue of practicing such a "selfless" form of motherhood. "My dad didn't stand a chance against us." … "The bulk of our life was and is spent with [my mother] mad at us for one reason or another, since to her we never appreciated her and did not love her," women told me as they remembered the double bind of being on the receiving end of another person's total ambition.

Many women I spoke with recalled their mothers' immersion in the minutiae of their lives as a way of exerting some control within families where they really had no power. And they said that they did not want to repeat that pattern in their own families now. "One golden rule for me, based on observing my mom, is: to always be a little bit selfish and take care of myself, otherwise I will resent my child and she will bear the brunt of my dissatisfaction and stress," said one working mother in Virginia. "I want to take care of myself better in order to be able to give her more love and affection, and not torment her by making her feel guilty for all that I have given up for her willingly or as a result of having her."

But these sentiments, so common and so commonsensical, don't generally get much airtime today.

For some reason, our cultural receptors are tuned differently. In our abuse-wary, separation-averse time, we hear the cries of abandonment and loss and pain that we believe issue forth from our children and not the words of warning against over-involvement that experience, expert opinion, and common sense provide. Trying to be perfect, we mother in ways that we know *full well* aren't healthy.

It is as though, as one woman I interviewed put it, we all suffer from "mother-image problems." And these "mother-image problems," like the body-image problems rampant in our society, where average models are 5'11" and weigh 117 pounds and average women are 5'4" and weigh 140 pounds, have a kind of funhouse-mirror effect on our self-images as mothers. They push us to strive for impossible goals that diminish and undermine us—*and aren't even good for our children.*

Something about the ideal of motherhood we carry in our heads is so compelling that even though we can't fulfill it and know that we probably shouldn't even try, we berate ourselves for falling short of succeeding. It is in service to that "something" that we continue to pursue the goals of total-reality motherhood. It is not, I believe, because we really, truly believe in our heart of hearts that a good mother is deeply self-sacrificing. No—I would argue instead that, like a woman obsessively trying to weigh 117 pounds, what we are trying to do, in religiously following the rites and rituals of ideal motherhood, is assuage some kind of deeper longing inside us.

For some women, I think, it is a longing for the world of their childhoods, when someone was there to take care of things. For other women, who did not feel sufficiently cared for by their mothers, it's a desire to give their children the kind of comforting childhood they didn't have—and to "reparent" themselves in the process. Overall, I think, it's a longing to *get things under control*.

For it is the sense of control that underlies the appeal of Donna Reed, with her world of "routine and order and organization and competence," as Lonnae O'Neal Parker put it. It is the sense that *somebody* has things under control and is able to achieve with graceful ease all the things that we find so painfully challenging.

And this, I think, is the real reason why we mother the way we do. It gives us a feeling of control that is very comforting (and very familiar). It suits us psychologically. It allows us to assuage our anxiety. And it fits where we are as a society.

Notes

[1]Social science studies conducted over the past four decades have consistently shown that whether or not a mother is home full-time with her child or not is not, in and of itself, a determinative factor in her child's development. Studies of the effect of a mother's work—the usual vector that confers self-definition, self-sufficiency, and independence—from the mid-1950s onward have always had the same result: that there is no evidence that work *per se* impacts on children one way or another. (This conclusion occurs throughout the sources I have cited.)

In 1955, in response to widespread public outrage over the news that one-third of mothers of school-age children were employed, F. Ivan Nye and Lois Wladis Hoffman began to compare the levels of happiness and quality of relationships of children of working and nonworking mothers. After eight years of study, they found no significant differences in school performance, psychosomatic symptoms, or closeness to their mothers between the two groups. In 1964, the sociologist Alice Rossi, reviewing the literature that then existed on working motherhood, concluded, "There is a wide-spread belief in our society that children suffer when they are not cared for, full-time, by their own mothers. Social science does not support this belief. The essential finding of all the studies on children ... is that the children of working mothers are not different, in any significant way, from [those of] mothers who stay at home" (11).

In the mid-1970s, Jerome Kagan of Harvard interpreted a series of studies of the effects of nonmother care on young children, controlling out some sources of problems in children by not including families where there was obvious chaos or strain, making sure the day care was of the highest quality, and controlling for class and ethnicity. He then found that there were no significant differences in intelligence, language, social skills, or attachment among children who were taken care of by their mothers, babysitters, or day-care workers—even if they were as young as three months old when they began in nonmother care (see Beels 28).

In 1988, Ellen Galinsky and Judy David in *The Preschool Years* reviewed the research on the effects of a mother's employment outside of the home and concluded that, all things being equal, a mother's work had no particular effect at all on her children. "Children are not necessarily helped or harmed by the fact that their mothers are employed and they are cared for by others," they wrote. "The impact of a mother's employment depends; it depends upon the children's experiences in their families and in their child-care situations" (365-66).

In 1996, a far-reaching study of 1,300 families followed since 1991 found that there were no differences in degrees of attachment to their mothers among infants taken care of by their mothers or in day care (see Chira).

Summing up all these studies, *Redbook* has noted, "Research has consistently shown that the key factor in children's well-being is the mother's happiness with what she's doing—whether that's staying home or working outside it" (Connor and Lusardi 50). *Parenting* magazine—like *Redbook*, hardly a hard-line champion of working motherhood—said in 2001, "Research conducted over the past five decades shows that a mother's decision to work or stay home isn't a good predictor of how her children will turn out, for better or worse (unless their care is substandard)" (Holcomb 84).

[2]See studies just mentioned. Also those mentioned at the end of this chapter.

[3]"The women's movement shifted public opinion" on working motherhood is how the *New York Times* put it, reflecting a typical view of this, in a recent article on changes in mothering practices through time (Cohen 2003).

[4]See "The Married Woman Goes Back to Work," *Woman Home Companion* (October 1956): 42. Reprinted in Walker 87-95.

[5]See "A Woman's Place Is on the Job," *Newsweek*, 26 July, 1971.

[6]And it kept on going: by 1978, the first time that the U.S. Census Bureau counted mothers of infants under age one who were at work, 30 percent of mothers of infants were working at least part-time and 41 percent of mothers with a child under two were employed (Weiner 377). By 1984, 60 percent of women with children under eighteen were employed (Margolis 65). By 1998 (the last year for which government data is available), 73 percent of mothers with children over the age of one were employed and 59 percent of mothers of infants—a record high—worked at least part-time.

[7]See "Record Share of New Mothers in Labor Force, Census Bureau Reports," United States Department of Commerce press release, October 24, 2000.

[8]This was a trend detected by the U.S. Census Bureau and detailed in its "Fertility of American Women" report released in October 2001. Based on a survey of 30,000 women, the Census Bureau found that between June 1998 and June 2000 the percentage of women in the workplace with infant children declined from 59 percent to 55 percent. See, among many other places, Warner (64); Marsh.

[9]Author interview with Harvard University economist Ken Rogoff.

[10]Author interview with former Clinton administration staffers.

References

"A Woman's Place Is on the Job." *Newsweek.* Jul. 26, 1971.

Adler, Jerry. "Building a Better Dad." *Newsweek* 127 (25) (June 17, 1996): 58-64.

Banks, Sandy. "Shoveling Guilt onto the Working Mom's Pile." *Los Angeles Times*. Jul. 20, 2002.

Beels, Christian. "The Case of the Vanishing Mommy." *New York Times Magazine*. Jul. 4, 1976. 26-28.

Block, Ruth H. "American Feminine Ideals in Transition: The Rise of the Moral Mother, 1785-1815." *History of Women in the United States: Domestic Ideology and Domestic Work, Part I*. Ed. Nancy F. Cott. Munich: K.G. Saur, 1992. 3-28.

Bowlby, John. *Attachment and Loss*. New York: Basic Books, 1969.

Brazelton, T. Berry, and Stanley I. Greenspan. *The Irreducible Needs of Children: What Every Child Must Have to Grow, Learn, and Flourish*. Cambridge: Perseus Books, 2000.

Chira, Susan. "Study Says Babies in Child Care Keep Secure Bonds to Mothers." *New York Times*. Apr. 21, 1996. A1.

Cohen, Patricia. "Visions and Revisions of Child-Raising Experts." *New York Times*. Apr. 5, 2003. D7.

Conlin, Michelle. "Mommy is Really Home from Work." *Business Week* (3809) (Nov. 25, 2002): 101.

Connor, Lee, and A. Lusardi. "Can You Afford to Stop Working?" *Redbook* 188 (November 1996): 50-53.

Coontz, Stephanie. "Nostalgia as Ideology." *The American Prospect* 13 (7) (Apr. 8, 2002): 26-27.

Dodson, Fitzhugh. *How to Parent*. Los Angeles: Nash Publishing, 1970.

Faludi, Susan. *Backlash: The Undeclared War Against American Women*. New York: Crown, 1991.

Faludi, Susan. *Stiffed: The Betrayal of the American Man*. New York: William Morrow, 1999.

"Fertility of American Women." U.S. Census Bureau report. Released October, 2001.

Galinsky, Ellen, and Judy David. *The Preschool Years: Family Strategies That Work*. New York: Times Books, 1981.

Gilbert, Susan. "Two Studies Link Child Care to Behavior Problems." *New York Times*. Jul. 16, 2003. A12.

Green, Penelope. "Family Value." *Vogue* (March 2001).

Gutner, Todd. "Working Moms: Don't Feel So Guilty." *Business Week* (3800) (Sept. 23, 2002): 127.

Hayghe, Howard V. "Developments in Women's Labor Force Participation." *Monthly Labor Review* 120 (9) (September 1997): 41-46.

Hays, Sharon. *Flat Broke with Children: Women in the Age of Welfare Reform*. New York: Oxford University Press, 2003.

Hewlett, Sylvia Ann. *Creating a Life: Professional Women and the Quest for Children*. New York: Talk Miramax Books, 2002.

Holcomb, Betty. "Should You Quit Work?" *Parenting* 15 (5) (June/July 2001): 84-89.

Hrdy, Sarah Blaffer. *Mother Nature*. New York: Pantheon, 1999.

Kaminer, Wendy. *A Fearful Freedom: Women's Flight from Equality*. Reading: Addison-Wesley, 1990.

Kirk, Laura Meade. "Mom's Juggling Act." *Providence Journal-Bulletin*. May 12, 2002: L09.

"Let's Stop Lying About Day Care." *Glamour*. (October 1994): 114.

Margolis, Maxine I. *Mothers and Such: Views of American Women and Why They Changed*. Berkeley and Los Angeles: University of California Press, 1984.

Marsh, Ann. "Mommy, Me and an Advanced Degree." *Los Angeles Times*. Jan. 6, 2002.

Nye, F. Ivan and Lois Wladis Hoffman. *The Employed Mother in America*. Chicago: Rand McNally, 1963.

"Record Share of New Mothers in Labor Force, Census Bureau Reports." United States Department of Commerce press release. Oct. 24, 2000.

Rossi, Alice. "Women Re-entering the Work Force." *Society* 35 (2) (January/February 1998): 11-16.

Ryan, Mary P. *Womanhood in America*. New York: New Viewpoints, 1979.

Spitz, René. *The First Year of Life*. New York: International Universities Press, 1965.

Thurer, Shari L. *The Myths of Motherhood: How Culture Reinvents the Good Mother*. Boston and New York: Houghton Mifflin, 1994.

Walker, Nancy A. *Women's Magazines, 1940-1960: Gender Roles and the Popular Press*. Boston and New York: Bedford/St. Martin's Press, 1998.

Warner, Judith. "Why We Work." *Working Mother* 24 (8) (September 2001): 64.

Weiner, Lynn Y. "Reconstructing Motherhood: The La Leche League in Postwar America." *Mothers and Motherhood: Readings in American History*. Eds. Rima D. Apple and Janet Golden. Columbus: Ohio State University Press, 2000. 362-388.

Chapter 44

Domestic Intellectuals

Freedom and the Single Mom

JANE JUFFER

THE YEAR IS 1992. On the campaign trail, Vice President Dan Quayle blames single mothers for the dissolution of family values. He derides Candace Bergen's character Murphy Brown, a successful television anchorwoman, for flaunting fatherhood and making the decision to become a single mother "just another lifestyle choice." Quayle's denunciation is echoed in policy-making circles by conservative guru Charles Murray and others, who characterize single mothers as lazy, promiscuous, and nearly unredeemable.

A decade later. The Family Friendly Programming Forum, a consortium of advertisers that funnels seed money to promising shows, subsidizes for the fourth straight season WB's *The Gilmore Girls,* which features a never-married mother and her teenage daughter who are integral members of a tight-knit community. Jennifer Aniston's girl-next-door character on *Friends,* Rachel, gets pregnant and decides to keep the baby but not marry Ross, the father. *Sex and the City's* Miranda also decides to become a single mom. The winner of the 2004 American Idol contest is Fantasia Barrino, a nineteen-year-old single mom from High Point, North Carolina, who one night brings her one-year-old daughter Zion up on stage and urges all single moms to believe that they can do whatever they want. The runner-up is sixteen-year-old Diana DeGarma, daughter of a single mom from Snellville, Georgia. Wal-Mart, site of family values, runs a commercial showing a woman trailed by her children, saying: "I'm a single mom, and I depend on Wal-Mart to get by."

Wal-Mart also appears as a champion of single mothers in the film *Where the Heart Is,* in which Natalie Portman plays a penniless pregnant teenager named Novalee Nation. Abandoned by her boyfriend in Sequoia, Oklahoma, Novalee chooses the local Wal-Mart as her temporary home, sneaking into the store to sleep at night. She gives birth amid the racks of clothing and promptly becomes a national media celebrity, mother of the "Wal-Mart baby." The president of Wal-Mart sends her $500 and promises a job at any store in the country. Paying homage to the nation that embraces rather than judges her, Novalee names the baby "Americus" and proves that she can indeed embody the entrepreneurial spirit of her daughter's birthplace, becoming a prize-winning photographer and building her own home. Americus is no bastard child. She redefines the nation that Wal-Mart once stood for—the nation of nuclear families buying American. Now, any family that can "buy American" merits respect.

Dan Quayle seemed especially irked that Candace Bergen's character was treating mothering as a "lifestyle choice." Now, the very notion of single mothering as a lifestyle choice has been used to validate the practice, to lift it out of the realm of dependency and shame into the realm of freedom and full citizenship.

Such is the claim made by Single Mothers by Choice (SMC), the nation's largest support network for single mothers. They define a "single mother by choice" as "a woman who decides to have or adopt a child, knowing she will be her child's sole parent, at least at the outset. Typically, we are career women in our thirties and forties. The ticking of our biological clocks has made us face the fact that we could no longer wait for marriage before starting our families." The group was started in 1981 by Jane Mattes, a "single mother by choice," and now claims several thousand single women around the world as its members. They share resources and information through the Internet and local chapters, advising women about assisted reproductive technologies, sperm donors, adoption, and how to raise a child without a father. The group distances itself from any form of dependency. Says Mattes, we are "single women who chose to become mothers, single mothers who are mature and responsible and who feel empowered rather than victimized," "we are at least as able, if not more able, to support a child and ourselves as is the average man," "without recourse to public funds" (10).

Low-income single mothers as activists demonstrate a more ambivalent relationship to the discourse of self-reliance. At the Rebecca Project in Washington, D.C., a group of mainly single mothers goes through addiction treatment programs and then, upon recovery, may become grassroots organizers on Capitol Hill and elsewhere, lobbying for more just welfare policies that include monies and time for addiction treatment. In 2003, they succeeded in persuading senators to propose welfare legislation that allows six months of treatment time to be considered as work under the welfare-to-work requirements, a small but significant victory. Rosetta Kelly, an addict for 37 years and single mother of three, describes how her life changed through the intersection of personal responsibility and public policy:

When I was using, I never had food in the house or clean clothes for the kids. Now, putting policy into my life, I'm more responsible. The cabinets, refrigerator, the freezer are full of food.... To go to the staffers and tell them my story and for them to see it really wasn't what they thought it was and to hear someone tell their stories who's actually lived it—that is fulfilling to me. Now I have a belief system—I get on the pulpit and I preach—those are the things I do now. My life is full. I have a son now who turned anger towards me into love, and I've learned how to love him. Those are the things I do now. I'm just trying to be a responsible member of society.

For Kelly, demonstrating that she is a responsible mother and citizen is not antithetical to a project of community building that locates each individual within a support network.

There is no typical single mom. Yet at the same time, single mothers in the United States at the turn of the century all live with the imperative to demonstrate self-sufficiency. With that demonstration comes an erasure of the stigma that has historically marked single mothers in this country and even the recognition that single mothers don't always have to be self-sacrificing in order to qualify as good mothers. Borrowing a term from the Italian antifascist activist and theorist Antonio Gramsci, I argue that single mothers are the new "organic intellectuals." As he postulated, "Every social group, coming into existence on the original terrain of an essential function in the world of economic production, creates together with itself, organically, one or more strata of intellectuals which give it homogeneity and an awareness of its own function not only in the economic but also in the social and political fields" (Gramsci 301). I am also redefining the term to encompass the work of mothering, as Gramsci didn't attend to the domestic sphere. Single mothers are "domestic intellectuals," operating within the usually denigrated realms of child care and housework to rearticulate these realms as ones of political, economic, and social possibility. Fantasia Barrino, the women of the Rebecca project, and the members of Single Mothers by Choice are all domestic intellectuals; they have emerged at a particular point in history, at specific locations, and have begun to articulate a sometimes homogeneous but often contradictory identity category. Single mothers are the exemplars of the shifting American family, showing that women can raise children in nonpatriarchal households. They are also the representatives of the neoliberal dream of self-sufficiency, identified by President George Bush as no longer outsiders to the nation: "I believe Americans in need are not problems; they are our neighbors. They're not strangers; they are citizens of our country," he said, while campaigning for welfare reform in 2002 (Meckler A1). Single mothers "do heroic work" in raising their children alone, Bush added, even as he proposed still stricter welfare-to-work requirements than were passed in the 1996 *Personal Responsibility Act.*

Single moms put together everyday life at a complex conjuncture of social, economic, political, and cultural forces. And there are more of us every day. The 2000 U.S. Census and other demographic studies show a remarkable growth in single-parent families due to both divorce and new births; by some estimates, one-third of all babies are now born to single moms, and less than 25 percent of all families conform to the nuclear configuration. New possibilities for mothering without men are due to the feminist and gay movement's challenge to patriarchal notions of family, the liberalization of divorce laws, an increase in numbers of financially independent women, and developments in new reproductive technologies. Single mothers emerge as a respected identity group in the context of the neoliberal production of the self-regulating citizen-consumer-subject. This conjuncture of forces can be seen in the remarkable explosion of positive media representations of single moms over the last decade; from *Austin Powers* to *The Cat in the Hat,* single mothers are the new darlings of popular culture.

At the same time, the project of neoliberalism and its insistence on cutting social programs and expanding private enterprise has been making life increasingly difficult for many single mothers. Governmental support for low-income mothers has been steadily declining for years, signified most dramatically in the 1996 Personal Responsibility Act (PRA) that turned welfare administration over to the states in the form of Temporary Assistance to Needy Families, which limits aid to five years and institutes strict work requirements during that time. The poverty rate in women-headed households is higher than it is for any other demographic group.

The Bush administration proposes marriage as a solution; the PRA included numerous provisions to "promote marriage, reduce out-of-wedlock births, and 'encourage the formation and maintenance of two-parent families'" (Mink 73). Access to child care for all single mothers is woefully inadequate. There continues to be discrimination against mothers, especially lesbians, in custody cases, where they are held to higher standards of "good parenting" than men. In many locations, single women are not treated as equals to married women when they seek to become mothers through assisted reproductive technologies and adoption. Despite the enormous potential for technologies and adoption to sever the links between biology and the family, opening the door for different kinds of kinship, the sheer cost of both assisted reproduction and adoption make them accessible to a fairly select group. Furthermore, the medical establishment and the legal system still assume heterosexual couples make the best parents.

In these complicated times, all single mothers are asked to prove their ability to govern themselves as subjects of freedom—freedom from any kind of dependency—in order to qualify as "normal." We can usefully ask the same set of questions about the acceptance of single mothers as Nikolas Rose (1999) asks about the governance of all subjects under neoliberalism: "How have we come to define ourselves in terms of a certain notion of freedom? How has freedom provided the rationale for all manner of coercive interventions into the lives of those seen as unfree or threats to freedom: the poor, the homeless, the mad, the risky, or those at risk?" (16). I would add to his list of questions: What spaces of freedom are produced for single mothers who want to maintain alternative family formations? Is it possible to operate outside the state regulation of maternal bodies in a manner that is not purely self-serving?

This book takes on these questions in all their complexity, never dismissive of the practical, everyday realities of single mothers and never sanguine about the effects of an acceptance based on autonomy. At this point in history, the valorization of self-reliant single mothering dominates, and thus the single-mother family presents a fairly limited challenge to the nuclear family even though the possibilities are vast and the stories of single mothers inspiring. Autonomy grants single mothers a kind of respect; however, the respect is most quickly earned if single mothers operate as if they were a nuclear family, temporarily minus the live-in dad. This principle guides both policy—with its sometimes explicit endorsement of marriage—and media representations, which give little attention to alternative forms of family. As such, the endorsement of single mothers usually ignores possibilities for alternative family formations—such as extended families and community child care—that have been common at different historical moments for some ethnic and indigenous populations.

Still, there *are* other possibilities, generated in a space somewhere between the state and the individual. Self-reliance does not always mean solitude; it can encompass community groups, churches, support networks, extended families, and friends. Sometimes this sounds suspiciously like the solutions proposed by neoliberalism. At other times, however, it's a more organic, grassroots response, as offered by the women of the Rebecca Project, who have combined personal responsibility with solidarity and mainstream legislative lobbying. Community support for single mothers may also emerge from a history of well-founded suspicion of state regulation. In Chicago's Humboldt Park neighborhood, the Puerto Rican Cultural Center's program for single mothers is part of the struggle for collective self-determination, based on the fact that Puerto Rico is a colony of the United States. In the Rio Grande Valley of Texas, undocumented single moms help form neighborhood associations premised on the belief that undocumented people are entitled to basic human rights that the state denies them because they don't have legal papers. Across spaces, I found what feminist political theorist Wendy Brown calls the struggle for "collective self-legislation," the "desire to participate in shaping the conditions and terms of life," which "remain a vital element-if also an evidently ambivalent and anxious one—of much agitation under the sign of progressive politics" (4).

The critical question is this: Can the conditions under which certain single mothers are accepted be turned, reimagined, reconceived, and transformed so that all single mothers—indeed all mothers—are supported in caring for themselves and their children, thus leading to the growth of family structures that represent true alternatives to the traditional nuclear family and its predictable gendered and sexual roles?

In part, this book is an attempt to make sense of my own experience as a single mom in academia, where the pressure to demonstrate self-sufficiency has been intense. Seeking alternatives, I've returned to some of the activist communities where I lived and worked before becoming a mother, to the Puerto Rican Cultural Center in Chicago and to Proyecto Libertad, an immigrant rights' group on the Texas-Mexican border. I have sought out other groups, including the Rebecca Project. I have studied corporate America's attention to mothers' issues—including the corporate university—and examined television and film for their representations. I have probed policy realms—welfare, immigration, medical, and legal—to understand what rules govern our lives and what agency might be wrested from within those structures. In short, I have tried to capture the complexity of single mothers' lives, both represented and real, without claiming that this picture is in any way exhaustive.

This book blends the personal, the practical, and the political as it addresses readers inside and outside of academia. It is shaped partially by frustration with my primary academic field—cultural studies—due to both its institutional disregard of child-care issues and its theoretical dismissal of mothering, something

I'll address again later in this chapter. Yet cultural studies has also been very useful in helping me formulate a methodology for analyzing the current conditions that shape single mothering. Perhaps most importantly, this work is guided by cultural studies' desire to participate in social change, a desire that means one never knows ahead of time the answers to the questions one is asking. To intervene in the present conditions is to see how power is articulated across sites, how it insinuates itself into everyday life, and how people make do in conditions not of their own making.

The three major sections of the book derive from some of the most important governing concepts in cultural studies: everyday life, spaces, and ethics. Within each of these sections, other "keywords" play an important role: care of the self, community, mobility, organizing, choice, and bodies. I'm drawing loosely on Raymond Williams's influential *Keywords in Cultural Studies* (1976). Williams's book historicized and contextualized terms that were shaping cultural studies in Britain in the 1960s, and his book continues to help define the field. Similarly, each of my keywords represents issues critical to cultural studies; however, my discussion of these issues also shows how cultural studies has failed to treat mothering as an issue worthy of research and writing. Our lack of attention to mothering perpetuates the division between private and public, a division visible in the still vaunted category of the "public intellectual," a role Williams occupied and which still informs the academic left's attempt to define its spokespeople. This tradition can be traced (although this isn't the only source) to Gramsci's notion of the organic intellectual.

The dominant class has its intellectuals, its naturalized leaders, says Gramsci, who emerge from generation to generation as part of the process through which hegemony is maintained. The business entrepreneur, for example, is an organic intellectual, an "organizer of the masses of men" (301), who works to maintain capitalism. Hegemony is sustained primarily through two interlocking systems: the class division between manual and mental labor and the schools, which reproduce the class division, allowing only certain people access to the status of intellectual. There is nothing intrinsic that defines an intellectual; rather, the role is the product of particular social and historical relations, which reproduce themselves until and unless marginalized groups can develop their own intellectuals, thus interrupting the class division. For Gramsci, all men have the potential to become intellectuals: "All men are intellectuals, one could therefore say, but not all men have in society the function of intellectuals" (304).

Gramsci suggests that one must rise above physical labor to become an intellectual, which virtually ensures that mothers, as mothers, will never become organic intellectuals. The domestic sphere is not perceived to be a site of intellectual activity. The organic-as-public intellectual is completely divorced from domestic work, which is implicitly posited as the most manual, the least stimulating of labor. It's not that women can't become intellectuals but rather that they won't in their capacity as mothers. Yet many of the skills Gramsci describes are skills that mothers practice daily, most importantly the skill of organizing. What we organize, however, seems not to circulate with value in public. Child care, cooking, laundry, lawn mowing, and bottle cleaning are not part of civil society, the educational system, or obvious realms of governance.

Gramsci's model still seems operative in many left intellectual circles. Yet in mainstream society, perhaps times have changed. In the United States at the turn of the twenty-first century, single mothers have emerged as entrepreneurs and exemplars of how to succeed, writing self-help books and starring in films and television shows. This emergence qualifies them to speak on behalf of other single mothers, showing them how to distance themselves from state aid and other forms of dependency. Yet this is not the kind of domestic intellectual who will define a strong alternative to hegemonic forms of family, for her rhetoric risks mimicking the rhetoric of choice and self-sufficiency that governs liberal capitalism and liberal feminism. What will enable us to articulate an oppositional position, where single mothers are supported in sustaining truly different family formations, where boys and girls can be raised to challenge gendered and sexual norms and where marriage does not become the most expedient solution to exhaustion?

The answer lies in organizing outside one's immediate interests, in the social project of the Rebecca Project, for example. Although the group does not escape the rhetoric of personal responsibility, their insistence on reciprocity and commitment represents more of a possibility that they will articulate an oppositional politics than Single Mothers by. Choice, whose focus on the individual can be easily absorbed into mainstream conceptions of family. To be a domestic intellectual is not to transcend the domestic, defined as a realm of giving and bodily interdependence, but to connect that realm to other sites. Domestic intellectuals give value to the work of mothering—to the pure organicity of birth, diaper changing, nursing; they are organic intellectuals who do not rank intellectual over bodily labor but rather live out their convergence.

There are many kinds of domestic intellectuals, and I am definitely not excluding some single mothers, such as those in SMC, because they seem less explicitly oppositional than those in the Rebecca Project. Precisely because organic intellectuals do not rise above their class but remain part of it and the larger social spheres that define it, contradictions are to be expected. There is, as I shall argue throughout this book, the practical matter of everyday survival that sometimes makes appeals to choice and autonomy a necessity. Yet I will also look throughout this book for domestic intellectuals who carve out positions of collaboration that make "choice" a less autonomous endeavor. Ideally, the domestic intellectual does not seek an individual position of esteem that lifts her above other single mothers; rather, organizing produces a collective position of resistance to the pressures of assimilation to the nuclear family. The domestic intellectual does not act as a mediator authorized to speak on behalf of single mothers who remain behind, "mired" in the work of raising children. Rather, the domestic intellectual moves from home to school to library to park to Congress to the streets, mapping paths, expanding single mothers' access to one another and to other sources of assistance.

The domestic intellectual is not a luminary. She may or may not attract media attention. She operates within the mundane and everyday routines of domestic life. She is an organizer and as such she provides insights into how to valorize organizing in other realms, such as the academy (where organizing is routinely devalued in comparison to publishing and other individual acts). To use Foucault's terms, the domestic intellectual is a specific intellectual, one who has "gotten used to working, not in the modality of the 'universal,' 'exemplary,' the 'just-and-true-for-all,' but within specific sectors, at the precise points where their own conditions of life or work situate them" (1972: 126). It's interesting that Foucault positions specific intellectuals at different points, not just the academy, where it is perhaps too easy to adopt the mode of the "universal" intellectual. Domestic intellectuals act as an antidote to universal claims, connecting rather than transcending places of life and work.

The domestic intellectual speaks frankly out of personal experience—another realm often demeaned in cultural studies. Drawing here on feminist practice, I write out of a personal desire to express some of the difficulties and joys of single mothering, to share my own experiences and those of women I've interviewed, and in the process to present something useful to single moms. My keywords also represent some of the most operative terms in the contemporary organization of the lives of single mothers in the United States. They serve as a vocabulary for thinking about the agency of single mothers, insofar as they define both how single mothers are viewed and governed and how we might think about ourselves and the possibilities for reshaping our lives. I hope the nonacademic reader finds that the theory woven throughout the chapters derives as often from the interviews and situations as it does from academia.

"Academia" can't be homogenized, and I'm sure there will be various academic readers who object to my impure methodological approach. In this respect, this is truly a cultural studies project, for the field does not respect disciplinary boundaries as it pursues the best tools for the project at hand: "The choice of research practices depends upon the questions that are asked, and the questions depend on their context" (Grossberg, Nelson, and Treichler 2). I am reluctant to identify the disciplines represented here because I have in fact drawn on whatever resources seem most useful for understanding the history and current state of single mothering in the United States. In doing so, I am abdicating any claims to be an "expert" in any discipline, for such disciplinary policing actually works against a full understanding of the many forces shaping single mothering today.

Freedom from Marriage?

Single mothering emerges as a state of possible freedom: freedom from marriage, freedom from the stigma of "out of wedlock" births, freedom to have different sexual partners, freedom to raise children in alternative fashion. Yet the question remains: How free are most single mothers to pursue these possibilities? Some of that freedom is impeded by the privileges that marriage continues to confer.

Marriage in the United States has been based on the same political and moral values that shaped the country, as Nancy Cott argues in her history of the institution: "Political and legal authorities endorsed and aimed to perpetuate nationally a *particular* marriage model: lifelong, faithful monogamy, formed by the mutual consent of a man and a Woman, bearing the impress of the Christian religion and the English common law in its expectations for the husband to be the family head and economic provider, his wife the dependent partner" (3). These are public as well as private roles, and Cott describes the many ways the legal system shapes citizenship in relation to gender, sexuality, and race. Although marriage ostensibly represented the freedom to choose a partner in a ceremony validated through a social contract, it was, like other forms of contract, not as free for some as for others. The legal doctrine of coverture basically "turned the married pair legally into one person," says Cott, "enlarging" the husband while the wife gave up her legal rights: "He became the one full citizen in the household, his authority over and responsibility for his dependents contributing to his citizenship capacity" (12). As Carole Pateman argues, marriage was constitutive of liberal society, dispersing patriarchy across public and private, two separate but complementary realms. A sexual contract was the basis for the social contract guaranteeing fathers' rights: "The original pact is a sexual as well as a social contract: it is sexual in the sense of patriarchal—that is, the contract establishes men's political right over women—and also sexual in the sense of establishing orderly access by men to women's bodies" (2). Marriage became the means for controlling the products of sexual desire—babies—making those products the property of men.

Marriage also determined citizenship by excluding racial categories of people deemed "unworthy" of belonging to the nation: slaves had no access to legal marriage, and it wasn't until 1967, in the case of *Loving v. Virginia,* that the U.S. Supreme Court struck down race-based state laws restricting marital freedom (sixteen states still considered marriage across race lines a crime; Cott 4). Immigration quotas and policies have also been used to regulate which "outsiders" may gain citizenship through marriage, a practice that continues to the present. And of course the current debates about gay marriage testify to the ongoing exclusionary powers of the law based on the desire to determine what constitutes a proper family.

Throughout much of U.S. history, bearing children outside marriage has carried heavy penalties for women and their children. Because marriage was the basis for citizenship, the "bastard" had no "recognized legal relations with his or her parents, particularly not those of inheritance, maintenance, and custody. Nor did the illicit couple have any rights or duties toward their spurious issue" (Grossberg 197). Illegitimate children were used to enforce proper sexual conduct, and mothers have suffered the consequences of violating this conduct. Hence Nathaniel Hawthorne's rendering of Hester Prynne and the real stories of single moms that have been told throughout the twentieth century. Said one unmarried mother living in Pittsburgh in the post-World War II years: "I fear no hell after death, for I've had mine here on earth. Let no man or girl deceive herself—hell hath no punishment like the treatment people give a 'fallen woman.'

The heartache, tortured thoughts, recriminations, fear, loneliness could not be put on paper. Neither can the scorn, insult, and actual hate of self-righteous and ignorant people" (qtd. in Solinger 33)._

Until the 1930s, all single mothers, regardless of race, were considered "ruined" due to a biological defect, says Rickie Solinger: "Illegitimacy occurred at the intersection of negative sociological and biological conditions and was an expression of an inhering, unchanging, and unchangeable 'physical' defect" (16). After World War II, it became possible for women who got pregnant outside marriage to redeem themselves—but only if they gave the baby up for adoption. The explanatory emphasis in terms of white single pregnancy shifted from biological defect to psychological neuroses, in part, says Solinger, because the number of single mothers was increasing—it simply became unrealistic to claim they were all ruined women.[1] Because the problem was psychological rather than biological, single mothers could be cured of their illness. By admitting they were sick and agreeing to give up their babies, white unwed mothers could be made marriageable again and assume their proper roles as mothers (Solinger 86). By contrast, black unwed mothers in the postwar years continued to be portrayed as biologically unfit, "unrestrained, wanton breeders, on the one hand, or as calculating breeders for profit on the other" (9). It was a Catch-22: their sexuality was seemingly uncontrollable, intrinsic, not a choice—yet their decision to keep their babies indicated too much choice, a savvy cunning deployed to subvert the state. They were not considered eligible for psychological treatment, nor were they pressured to put up their babies for adoption. The "white public" resented money going to black welfare mothers. "In the mother-blaming mode of the postwar decades, many analysts identified the black single mother's alleged hypersexuality and immorality, her resulting children, and the public expense as traceable to the source: the Negro woman who gave birth, as it were, to black America, with all its 'defects'" (Solinger 49).

In the mid-1960s, the nuclear family assumed normative force through the writings of social scientists including Daniel Moynihan, Nathan Glazer, and Oscar Lewis, all of whom, in varying ways, blamed black and Latino families for inherent psychological and moral deficiencies that trapped them in a cycle of dependency. Most to blame, especially in Moynihan's report, "The Negro Family: A Case for National Action," were "dominating" black women, who, by working for wages *and* rearing families on their own, had emasculated black men, causing their lack of motivation and turn to criminal activities. Black and Latina single mothers were both disempowered and terribly powerful, and the very traits of hard work and family loyalty that should have received praise were demonized (Feldstein 143). Oscar Lewis's book *La Vida* on Puerto Ricans was more sympathetic in that he identified the structural conditions of migration and capitalism as reasons for poverty, but he also tended to blame Puerto Ricans generally for failure to assimilate, and especially husbands and fathers for abandoning their families (Pérez 58).

This brief history of marriage serves as a reminder that the nuclear family is a socially constructed norm that often precludes one from thinking about other kinds of families and other ways of taking care of kin, both biological and non-biological. The nuclear family/children as property model is an Anglo norm that should not be used to gauge the validity of "family." It wasn't always so and it needn't continue to be so, even though policy decisions continue to be based, in many ways, on the traditional family. One has only to look at Native American and African American communities to find alternatives. Patricia Hill Collins describes the practice of "othermothers"—"women who assist bloodmothers by sharing mothering responsibilities," which she traces historically: "The central-ity of women in African-American extended families reflects a continuation of both West African cultural values and functional adaptations to race and gender oppression" (219). The importance of women does not necessarily indicate the absence of husbands and fathers, as they may play significant roles in family life without living in the home, or while living in the home without being as powerful as the women. Nevertheless, the absence of men is due in part, as Collins sug-gests, to racism and poverty—hence her nod to "functional adaptations." Shared child-raising practices contribute to a people's self-reliance, says Collins: "Black women's relationships with children and other vulnerable community members is not intended to dominate or control. Rather, its purpose is to bring people along, to—in the words of late nineteenth century Black feminists—'uplift the race'—so that vulnerable members of the community will be able to attain the self-reliance and independence essential for resistance" (233).

In other ways, marriage as the only acceptable way to have and raise children began to lose its normative hold in the 1960s. Beginning around 1965, the rate of formal marriage began dropping while the divorce rate rose. The number of unmarried-couple households recorded by the Census Bureau multiplied almost ten times from 1960 to 1998 (Cott 203). The women's liberation and gay rights' movements challenged sexual norms, leading for perhaps a relatively brief period in the 1960s and early 1970s to an increasing acceptance of sexual experimentation even within marriage. *Roe v. Wade* was a landmark decision in the feminist battle for women to control their reproductive fates. No-fault divorce was first adopted in California in 1969; by 1985, every state had some version of it. The 1964 *Civil Rights Act* included "sex" as an unwarranted basis for discrimination and helped feminists dismantle sex distinctions in employment and education. Although women continue to be paid less than men for comparable labor, increasing financial independence for some women allowed them to choose single mothering more readily. There was less pressure for women who got pregnant "out of wedlock" to give up their babies for adoption. Groups such as the National Welfare Rights Organization and the Sisterhood of Black Single Mothers organized on behalf of single mothers. Solinger identifies the mid-1970s as the period in which the term "single mother" gained currency, replacing "unwed mother" and indicating a newfound respect and acceptance for mothers of different income levels. This acceptance was reflected in Supreme Court decisions, the creation of educational support programs for young mothers, and sympathetic mainstream media coverage.[2]

It was a relatively brief moment of acceptance, however; at the same time, there was growing resentment about the expansion of social programs. With Ronald Reagan's rise to power came a renewed demonization of the single mother as the source of social problems.[3] The very category of "choice" that had been deployed to liberate women from the articulation of marriage and morality was turned against single mothers who couldn't show their financial independence. I'll elaborate more on the demonization of dependency later in this introduction.

Nevertheless, by the mid-1970s, the denunciation of single mothers was by no means automatic, and, increasingly, people lived in families that did not fit the Ozzie and Harriet ideal. The proportion of adults who declined to marry at all rose between 1972 and 1998 from 15 percent to 23 percent. By the end of the century, people living alone comprised one-quarter of all households. Half of all marriages now end in divorce. More than one-third of all babies are now born to unmarried mothers, compared to 5 percent in 1960. Rates of single mothering have increased most rapidly among non-teenage white women: "White women's rate of unmarried childbearing more than doubled after 1980. Black women's rate moved up only 2 percent during the same years, so that where their rate had been 4 or 5 times that of whites in 1960, in the late 1990s it was only about twice as high. As a result of both non-marriage and divorce among women with children, one fifth of family-based households of whites were female-headed in the 1990s, as were almost three fifths of black families and almost one third of Hispanic families" (Cott 204).

For many mothers, marriage is no longer a prerequisite of good citizenship, not even when there are children involved. Single moms aren't immediate objects of shame and exclusion. The sexual contract is not intrinsically necessary for liberal society to function, notes Wendy Brown: "As women are no longer required to enter a sexual contract-subordination in marriage-for survival or societal recognition (although these both continue to be enhanced by heterosexual marriage), liberal political orders no longer need refer to an imaginary social contract for their legitimacy" (137). Capitalism doesn't need the nuclear family or marriage in order to thrive.

Perhaps because of the growing acceptance of single-parent families, however, there is an ongoing conservative push to restore the "sanctity" of marriage. In 1996, Congress passed and President Bill Clinton signed the Defense of Marriage Act, which defined marriage as the legal union between a man and a woman. Much of the congressional debate on the bill revealed a bipartisan consensus on the proper way to raise children. As Senator Robert Byrd, Democrat of West Virginia, said, "If same-sex marriage is accepted, America will have said that children do not need a mother and a father, two mothers or two fathers will be just as good. This would be a catastrophe." Eight years later, after the state of Massachusetts legalized gay marriage, President Bush called for a constitutional amendment defining marriage as the union between a man and a woman, hoping to keep other potentially renegade states in line. "Ages of experience have taught humanity that the commitment of a husband and wife to love and to serve one another promotes the welfare of children and the stability of society," Bush said in a February 2004 press conference.

Furthermore, marriage continues to carry with it considerable material benefits: "A 1996 report from the U.S. General Accounting Office found more than *one thousand* places in the corpus of federal law where legal marriage conferred a distinctive status, right, or benefit" (Cott 2). In *The Trouble with Normal*, Michael Warner cites some of the entitlements marriage confers, including a variety of state income tax advantages, rights relating to inheritance, award of child custody in divorce proceedings, the right to spousal support, the right to post-divorce property division, and more (117-118). Not surprisingly, then, while one in two marriages end in divorce, the national rate of remarriage is high. These continued rights suggest that the legacy of gender subordination that historically defined marriage as an institution *does* still matter in terms of a liberal discourse that organizes jurisprudence, public policy, and public consciousness. In other words, you can be a single mom with no particular stigma attached, but the legal system and economic and public policy will still work against you, making marriage seem like the most attractive option for ensuring the long-term well-being of yourself and your children.

Given this conflicted and generally exclusionary history, it is not surprising that some academic theorists, especially in queer studies, express considerable reservation about relying on marriage as a venue for inclusion. Inclusion in what? Heteronormative privilege? As Michael Warner argues, "as long as people marry, the state will continue to regulate the sexual lives of those who do not marry. It will continue to refuse to recognize our intimate relations—including cohabiting partnerships—as having the same rights or validity as a married couple" (96). As Judith Butler rightly asks, why should marriage be seen as the only way of securing kinship? Both Warner and Butler take issue with gay and lesbian activists who argue for the right to marriage, arguing that to subject oneself to the state's regulation will produce new exclusionary effects. For Warner, an appeal to marriage flies in the face of a queer politics that resists normalization: "Marriage, in short, would make for good gays-the kind who would not challenge the norms of straight culture, who would not flaunt sexuality, and who would not insist on living differently from ordinary folk" (113). As Butler puts it,

> In the case of gay marriage or of affiliative legal alliances, we see how various sexual practices and relationships that fall outside the purview of the sanctifying law become illegible or, worse, untenable, and how new hierarchies emerge within public discourse. These hierarchies not only enforce the distinction between legitimate and illegitimate queer lives, but they produce tacit distinctions among forms of illegitimacy. The stable pair who would marry if only they could are cast as currently illegitimate, but eligible for a future legitimacy, whereas the sexual agents who function outside the purview of the marriage bond and its recognized,

if illegitimate, alternative form now constitute sexual possibilities that will never be eligible for a translation into legitimacy. (3)

In the same fashion, single mothers who make it clear that they want some day to remarry are "eligible for future legitimacy" and thus granted temporary respect and even admiration. By contrast, single mothers who work to construct alternative and long-standing family formations and who construct a political and social identity around single mothering as a preferred status represent a less legitimate, although perhaps not completely illegitimate, position. Again, this legitimacy rests on their ability to demonstrate lack of need.

Cultural Studies and Domesticity

Could it be, then, that single mothers are queer? If so, why do academic theorists, such as Warner and Berlant, who are so eager to embrace the margins, offer so little in the way of material support or even intellectual acknowledgment of single moms? In Warner's chapter on marriage, for example, considerable attention is paid to alternative forms of intimacy that queer culture embraces outside heterosexual culture, but there is no sense that children are part of this queer counterpublic. He says, "Between tricks and lovers and exes and friends and fuckbuddies and bar friends and bar friends' tricks and tricks' bar friends and gal pals and companions 'in the life,' queers have an astonishing range of intimacies" (116). There are clearly no children among this "welter of intimacies" that are constructed outside of traditional frameworks of social obligations.

In general, cultural studies has failed to take seriously the politics of domesticity, family, parenting, and children, perhaps because domesticity seem so irrevocably bourgeois, so linked to property, containment, and essentialized identities—so unable to be rearticulated to something more in line with the perceived politics of cultural studies. Often, this disregard is implicit. Occasionally, it becomes explicit. Responding to a proposal by the American Association of University Professors that professors with newborn babies should be granted more time to achieve tenure, cultural studies scholar Cary Nelson told the *Chronicle of Higher Education* that the proposal "has an odd echo of Republican family values, that nothing matters more than the raising of your family. I'm not amongst those who idealize children" (Wilson 2001). The *Chronicle* also sponsored an online forum on the AAUP proposal, and although some people were supportive, many more wrote in to say how tired they were of "children and breeders getting all the consideration all the time."

By not theorizing issues of home spaces and their bodies, cultural studies misses the opportunity to rearticulate conservative invocations of family and to build discursive support for alternative families, including single mothers, gay and lesbian parents, and parents of children with disabilities, as well as for heterosexual couples who want to raise their children in a less nuclear fashion. Indeed, our silence on issues of domesticity threatens to cede the territory of the family to the right, as conservative politicians and intellectuals capture the media limelight on matters of marriage, children, and families.

An important exception to this tendency is Lawrence Grossberg's new book, *Caught in the Crossfire: Kids, Politics, and America's Future*, which appeared just as *Single Mother* was entering production. One of Grossberg's objectives in describing the current conditions structuring the lives of youth in the United States is to "take seriously the particular set of alliances and interests that I call the New Right, to treat it with respect and to begin to understand its thoughts and appeals for significant portions of the American public" (xiii).[4]

Some important work has been done in relation to the home, especially in media studies by scholars such as Janice Radway, Lynn Spigel, David Morley, Roger Silverstone, and Ellen Seiter. Cultural studies has been fascinated with youth culture, yet "youth" seems to begin at adolescence, when youth *leave* the home. It seems fair to say that the majority of articles and books produced on space deal with spaces other than the home. The 1990s was characterized by a publishing explosion on globalization, diaspora, migration, citizenship, geography, cities, public policy, citizenship, civil society, sex in public, public intellectuals, and so on. Since 1990, *Cultural Studies* and *Public Culture* [5] have published only a handful of articles on domesticity, and articles specifically focused on mothering and children are even fewer.[6] Work on various public spheres is often articulated to/through theories of citizenship, to a politics of civil society and public policy, again to the exclusion of the home as a site where citizenship is also formed. Domesticity did not figure, for example, in the debates on policy studies in cultural studies in the early and mid-1990s, mainly instigated by Australian cultural studies scholars such as Tony Bennett, Stuart Cunningham, Ian Hunter, Tom O'Regan, and John Frow.

The turn to spatial analysis in cultural studies thus happens almost always in relation to public formations—museums, cities, nations, hospitals, and schools—via theorists such as LeFebvre, Foucault, and Deleuze and critical geographers such as Mike Davis, David Harvey, Edward Soja, and Doreen Massey. Also important in this context is the work on globalization, migration, and diaspora by scholars such as Arjun Appadurai, Paul Gilroy, George Yudice, Alberto Moreiras, Saskia Sassen, Michael Hardt and Antonio Negri,[7] and many others. In most of this work, home in the domestic and familial sense rarely enters into the discussion, especially in the context of parenting and child-care issues. Rather, the focus is on mobility across and between nations; as David Morley comments, "In recent years much has been made of the idea of postmodernity. Images abound of our supposedly de-territorialised culture of 'homelessness': images of exile, diaspora, time-space compression, migrancy, and 'nomadology.' The concept of home often remains as the un interrogated anchor or alter ego of all this hyper-mobility" (3). As an example of the focus on mobility, Morley cites the founding statement of the journal *Public Culture*, in which editors Appadurai and Carol Breckenridge describe the late twentieth century as "an increasingly cosmopolitan world" (qtd. in Morley 9).

The tendency to devalue the domestic can also be seen in cultural studies' critique of neoliberalism as a form of privatization, which implicitly positions the home, again, as a site of bourgeois privilege to be counteracted with a revitalized politics of the public sphere. Henry Giroux, for example, argues that "within the increasing corporatization of everyday life, market values replace social values, and people appear more and more willing to retreat into the safe, privatized enclaves of the family, religion, and consumption" (xi). It's interesting here to note the conflation of family, religion, and consumption, all of which are articulated to an interiorized notion of home, which is seemingly impervious to public debate and progressive change. Similarly, Michael Warner and Lauren Berlant argue that "ideologies and institutions of intimacy" are offered as "the only (fantasy) zone in which a future might be thought and willed, the only (imaginary) place where good citizens might be produced away from the confusing and unsettling distractions and contradictions of capitalism and politics. Indeed, one of the unforeseen paradoxes of national capitalist privatization has been that citizens have been led through heterosexual culture to identify both themselves *and their politics* with privacy" (193).

This is tricky territory. Although it is certainly important to critique the privatization of public services and sites, I would argue that it is not necessary in the process to either ignore or demean the home (an "institution of intimacy") and to suggest that it is only in "public" where progressive politics occur. It is important, as feminists have argued, to challenge the assumption that "home" is private, to show its material connections to other spaces. The above critiques of neoliberalism seem to cede the home to the right because they offer no alternative conceptions and exhibit no desire to rearticulate the home. How, for example, might queer politics open up the home to diverse practices? What might those diverse practices be? How would mothering and child care change? What are the mundane details of everyday life that would remain largely domestic, in the material space of the home, and how would those practices redefine public discourses of caring? How are citizens shaped in home spaces in ways that might not collude with neoliberalism?

Similarly, an emphasis on policy in the rapidly developing field of disabilities studies has too often elided the home, say Rayna Rapp and Faye Ginsberg. They argue that disabilities studies has not acknowledged the "intimate arena of kinship as a site where contemporary social dramas around changing understandings and practices of reproduction and disability are often first played out" (535). One of their main points is that caretaking of disabled children requires extended support networks and thus reveals the limits of the "gendered nuclear family model" (540). In the same special issue of *Public Culture,* Veena Das and Renu Addlakha show that the strategies used by Indian families in Punjab and Delhi to cope with relatives with various disabilities had a powerful impact on their public identities, and that one should not assume that citizenship is constituted at public sites that act unidirectionally on the home. Das and Addlakha argue for "(1) displacing citizenship from its conventional association with publics defined through civility and (2) displacing domesticity from its conventional place in particularistic loyalties" (530).

Cultural studies has always cited as one of its defining features a concern for its own conditions of practice. Incessantly self-reflexive, cultural studies has produced many articles and talks on the question of how to define itself in relation to existing disciplines, how to fully acknowledge the institution without becoming too embedded in it. Several prominent scholars in the field have written extensively about the need to support graduate student unionization. Yet despite all this talk about institutional conditions, little attention had been paid to childcare issues—to providing child care at conferences, working for better maternal-leave policies and more child-care centers on campuses, and incorporating children in social events. As a field and a practice, cultural studies has not provided material support for alternative forms of family and parenting within the academy, thus implicitly endorsing the nuclear family as the most viable and practical form for raising children.

Despite the fact that much recent cultural studies theory has led away from analyzing the home, there is nothing intrinsic to the theories that precludes such analysis. In fact, I hope to show in much of this book that the theories of space, migration, and mobility can be very useful in illuminating the conditions shaping single mothering. In turn, single mothers offer cultural studies critical insights into and thus possibilities for redefining the neoliberal agenda.

Liberalism/Neoliberalism

Neoliberalism insofar as it suggests a new political and economic phase of government may be a misnomer. As some critics note, neoliberalism is more accurately seen as an intensification of liberalism, with its foundations in free-market economics, rational individualism, and property accumulation. There have been brief periods in the United States of a limited welfare state, extending from the New Deal of the 1930s to the Great Society of the 1960s, but since then, there has been a steady and growing consensus about the need to dismantle even that commitment to social programs. Democrats and Republicans alike agree, notes Lisa Duggan, on the "neoliberal agenda of shrinking public institutions, expanding private profit-making prerogatives, and undercutting democratic practices and noncommercial cultures" (xv). Through the practices of deregulation, flexible labor, and privatization, the gap between rich and poor has widened around the world, obviously to the benefit of Western creditors and corporations. As the state withdraws, neoliberals exhort "civil society (the 'voluntary' sector) and 'the family' to take up significant roles in the provision of social safety nets" (Duggan 10). These intertwined impulses of neoliberalism—the demonization of dependency and the insistence on autonomy—are powerful forces determining the subject positions available to single mothers.

It wasn't always so. Early forms of assistance to single mothers who couldn't support their children were actually meant to encourage them to stay home—although only if they had not chosen to be single mothers—widows, for example, or women abandoned by their husbands. These women were considered worthy recipients of the various forms of public assistance that began in the early 1900s-assistance that positioned the state as the replacement for the absent father. The Mothers' Pension Program, for example, was instituted in 1921, based on the belief that mothers' most important service was mothering, not semiskilled labor. Only certain mothers qualified, notes welfare scholar Mimi Abramovitz: "Only women with permanently absent husbands due to death, long-term imprisonment, and incurable insanity were routinely eligible in all states. Such eligibility rules distinguished among women according to their marital status and denied aid to other husbandless women viewed as departing from prescribed wife and mother roles" (201). Although standards were gradually broadened to include some divorced mothers by 1931, widows still headed over 80 percent of the more than 60,000 families receiving aid nationwide.

Making aid contingent on morality continued in the implementation of the Aid to Dependent Children (ADC) program that was part of the landmark 1935 Social Security Act. Says Abramovitz: "The ADC program perpetuated the mother's pension philosophy that maternal employment negatively effected child development and that 'deserving' women belonged in the home. Like its forerunner, ADC subsidized mothers to reproduce the labor force and maintain the non-working members of the population, but made receipt of a grant highly conditional upon compliance with the family ethic" (318). Although the act didn't contain any specific "suitable home" provisions in the manner of the Mothers' Pension program, "the preliminary legislative debates, the congressional committee reports, and an early version of the bill implicitly granted states permission to evaluate ADC applicants' moral character" (318). Supervision of the "morals" of recipients included questions about sexuality, home visits, and requirements for proof of paternity before aid could be received. Suitable home rules were often used to deny aid to black women, especially in the South, where state officials wanted to ensure a low-wage labor pool (Arnott 288).

State supervision was most intense for those mothers who seemingly *chose* to have their babies, or, once pregnant, chose to keep their babies rather than give them up for adoption. The choice rendered them suspect. Public aid was given reluctantly, only with surveillance and stipulations. When single mothers were very young, or very poor, or in other conditions when "choice" seemed like an unlikely possibility, the dependency of the single mother-her need, in other words, for some kind of state support-was explained by shaming her sexuality rather than by examining the conditions that caused some women to become pregnant, such as lack of access to birth control and sexual education. This burden fell particularly heavily on women of color.

We arrive at the 1960s and the birth of the culture of poverty theory, which appealed to many people across the political spectrum. The 1960s saw a renewed commitment to social welfare, but this very commitment produced public resentment against its recipients. The culture of poverty theory "appealed because it suggested that black unwed mothers achieved or deserved their fate. As a consequence, it suggested American culture was absolved of any responsibility for both black illegitimacy and the problems it caused black girls and women in the community in general" (Solinger 83). Through the push toward "welfare reform" in the 1990s, the unregulated sexuality of single mothers on welfare was cited as reason for their failure to make the "right choice" and then targeted as the cause of poverty.

Since sexuality represents the irrational choice that leads to dependency, single mothers are told to pursue the seemingly rational alternative of paid labor that will lead to self-sufficiency and thus remove them from the realm of scrutiny and shame. At least if you work, goes the reasoning, you are not asking the state/ taxpayers to be responsible for your bad choices. The 1996 *Personal Responsibility Act* was hailed and criticized as the bill that "ended welfare as we know it," but Congress has been passing welfare-to-work laws since the 1960s. In 1967, Congress established the Work Incentive Program, which "disqualified adults and older out-of-school children from AFDC payments if they refused to accept employment or participate in training programs" (Trattner 330). Richard Nixon further pushed the welfare-to-work agenda, proposing a plan that "was coupled with an elaborate system of penalties and incentives designed to force recipients to work. "In the final analysis," he said, "we cannot talk our way out of poverty; we cannot legislate our way out of poverty, but this nation can work its way out of poverty. What America needs now is not more welfare but more workfare" (qtd. in Trattner 339). Several decades passed before Congress passed another significant poverty bill-the Family Support Act (FSA) of 1988. According to feminist legal critic Martha Fineman, "The FSA's primary objective was to link poverty with the lack of a work ethic, thereby attaching welfare recipients to a new workfare scheme. This was accomplished in two ways: first, by mandating that the single mother work (or train for work); and second, by establishing a system for substituting support from fathers for state support ... thus transforming a child's primary source of support from public to private hands" (110).

In the last two decades, the cheap labor pool created through denial of benefits to black women has increasingly included immigrant women, both undocumented and documented, as Grace Chang says in *Disposable Domestics*. Welfare reform is linked to immigration policy in an insidious manner, leaving the most vulnerable of women-single immigrant mothers, many of whom are undocumented, without recourse to public assistance for their children: almost half of the projected $54 billion savings in welfare cuts from the 1996 act was achieved by restrictions on immigrants. The assumption underlying welfare and immigration policy is that poor women of color are less valuable as mothers to their own children than as domestic, factory, and field workers.

The alternative to work, built into both welfare and immigration policy, has been marriage, which acts as both a moralizing and a privatizing force. As welfare scholar Gwendolyn Mink argues, by making it so difficult to survive on reduced payments and by instituting new requirements for establishing the paternity of the father and collecting payments from him, the Temporary Assistance to Needy Families program introduces a new level of assault on the "intimate associational rights" of poor women. She summarizes the TANF provisions:

Under the paternity establishment provision, a mother must disclose the identity of her child's biological father or must permit the government to examine her sex life so that it can discover the DNA paternal match for her child. Under the child support enforcement provision, a mother must help government locate her child's biological father so that the government can collect reimbursement from him for the mother's TANF benefit. A mandatory minimum sanction against families in which mothers do not cooperate in establishing paternity or collecting child support enforces government's determination that a biological reproductive nexus constitutes a social family. (69)

Other elements of TANF encourage marriage: states get a "performance bonus" if the percentage of children living in married families increases, and they can use TANF funds to encourage marriage classes and counseling. States receive a bonus if the "illegitimacy" rate drops without an increase in abortion rates. Abstinence is also encouraged; a provision of the 1996 PRA pays states to "teach groups which are most likely to bear children out-of-wedlock" that "sexual activity outside the context of marriage is likely to have harmful psychological and physical effects" and that one should "attain self-sufficiency before engaging in sexual activity" (qtd. in Mink 70).

Given the troubling history of welfare's intervention in the lives of poor women, we might ask: At what cost do we turn to the state for assistance? Wendy Brown argues that the right's attack on "big government" since the mid-1970s has led the left to uncritically defend the welfare state: "As the Right attacked the state for sustained welfare chiselers and being larded with bureaucratic fat, liberals and leftists jettisoned two decades of 'Marxist theories of the state' for a defense of the state as that which affords individuals 'protection against the worst abuses of the market' and other structures of social inequality" (15). Brown cites the work of several prominent progressives, specifically a book called *The Mean Season: The Attack on the Welfare State,* authored by "democratic socialists" Fred Block, Richard Cloward, Barbara Ehrenreich, and Frances Fox Piven. The back cover says 'our boldest social thinkers argue for (the welfare state's) real, hard-won accomplishments. More than a defense of the welfare states, economic efficiency and fairness, *The Mean Season* is a reaffirmation of those decent, humane values so much under attack in Reagan's America'" (qtd. in Brown 15). Clearly skeptical about the complicity of liberal humanism with liberal policies, Brown asks rhetorically:

"What kind of attachments to unfreedom can be discerned in contemporary political formations ostensibly concerned with emancipation? What kinds of injuries enacted by late modern democracies are recapitulated in the very oppositional projects of its subjects?" (xii).

A good question. However, Brown runs the risk here of dismissing the everyday lives of single mothers for whom welfare assistance can provide the means for leaving an abusive partner, for feeding one's children, and for eventually freeing oneself from the state. As the organizers of the Rebecca Project demonstrate, single mothers emerge *from within* the prevailing economic and social conditions; one cannot transcend or reject them.

The Self-Regulating Mom

The neoliberal alternative to dependency is personal responsibility, which has indeed been used to remove the stigma from single mothers who can demonstrate self-sufficiency. It would seem that the self-supporting single mom, through no singular power of her own even though it is represented as such, puts more pressure on the low-income single mother to distance herself from dependency in order to gain respect. In fact, ethnographers of poor women say that their interviewees' main goal is to become self-reliant: "In the long run, the goal of most mothers was to earn enough to eliminate the need for any government welfare program and to minimize their dependence on family, friends, boyfriends, side-jobs, and agencies" (Edin and Lein 64).

I would like to avoid creating a binary of middle-class versus welfare moms along the lines of self-sufficient versus dependent. In reality, single mothers' lives are much more complicated than this, and the desire for self-reliance emerges in different contexts not completely determined by governmental imperatives. Yet even when self-reliance seems to be a purely individual endeavor, I argue that we should not dismiss it, as academics are wont to do in relation to anything that hints of an "autonomous self." Nikolas Rose (1996) writes about the poststructuralistic critique of the enlightened, reasoned individual:

At the very moment when this image of the human being is pronounced passé by social theorists, regulatory practices seek to govern individuals in a way more tied to their "selfhood" than ever before, and the ideas of identity and its cognates have acquired an increased salience in so many of the practices in which human beings engage. In political life, in work, in conjugal and domestic arrangements, in consumption, marketing, and advertising, in television and cinema, in the legal complex and the practices of the police, and in the apparatuses of medicine and health, human beings are addressed, represented and acted upon as if they were selves of a particular type: suffused with an individualized subjectivity, motivated by anxieties and aspirations concerning their self-fulfillment, committed to finding their true identities and maximizing their authentic expression in their life-styles. (169-170)

Herein lies the dilemma. The appeals to an "individualized subjectivity" are disseminated at so many sites of governance that it comes to seem like the only option. President Bush, for example, exhorts single mothers to work in order to be free, and this coincides with the self-help tendency to focus on internal motivation, as if that were distinct from social conditions. It seems especially dangerous to extol the powers of the self at a time when social support is steadily dwindling, replaced by the neoliberal version of the self-regulating subject.

Yet I'm reluctant to dismiss this popular discourse. In part, my reluctance stems from the recognition that there is simply no outside—although one can criticize the reliance on the self, one cannot dismiss the fact that millions of people believe in it. Hence, in order to change that belief, one must first engage with it—go through it rather than around it. As well, I'm aware of the fact that appeals to the self will have different effects in different situations. When it comes to mothering, an appeal to the self actually counters the conservative tendencies to essentialize the selfless mother. I want to laugh when I read the following bit of advice from Andrea Engber and Leah Klungness in their popular guide, *The Complete Single Mother: Reassuring Answers to Your Most Challenging Concerns* (129), but I also understand where the advice comes from and, in some ways, I draw some comfort from it. Don't worry about what anyone else thinks about single mothers, they say: "The only expectations that you should strive to meet are the ones that you create for yourself ... when you allow other people's views to alter your opinion of yourself, you risk losing the ability to care for yourself" (130). The authors prescribe a series of feel-good exercises: pat yourself on the back, tape affirming notes to the refrigerator, walk around the house reciting nice things about yourself (130). The same language of self-affirmation appears in a March 13,2005, *New York Times* article on the phenomenon of "parent coaches," the new class of entrepreneurs who give advice to stressed-out parents on how to handle their unruly kids. One such coach, Mary Scribner, advises Marcia, a single mother of a troubled seventeen-year-old daughter, to "take time for self-care," and when this seems to work in helping Marcia stay calm during an argument with her daughter, Scribner says, "Give yourself a pat on the back, Mom" (Belluck A23).

Although the advice seems rather pathetic, it is also an implicit critique of the lack of material and emotional support for mothering: if no one else will encourage you, then you must do it for yourself. The more systemic solution would be to address the policies and structures that make single mothers feel like they have to compliment themselves, but I also think we cannot dismiss the simple but important question: What is to be done in the meantime? The conditions of single mothering—indeed of all mothering—require a different lens through which to view various aspects of self-help. How are single mothers to survive in a world that grants them respect only if they are autonomous beings? How does the appeal to a singular self constitute a subject able to speak, act, and care for oneself? What can be accomplished if you believe yourself to be empowered and "normal"? How is the self assembled across a number of discourses (economic, cultural, political) that prompt single mothers to this belief? Does the appeal to individual freedom and choice necessarily preclude support and community? Or, given the general lack of support for parenting outside the nuclear family, is the appeal to self a necessary component for single mothers to begin building a support community that extends beyond the home?

Choice becomes the word a single mother uses to convince herself and perhaps others that she is in control of her life, when there are so many things that feel out of control. The endless details of everyday life can be managed but rarely set aside completely, as my journal entry illustrates:

September 19, 2001
Constant striving against chaos. The obsession with details, multiple events coalescing in one's mind-pick up the glass, carry it to the sink, use that napkin to wipe up some dog hair on the kitchen floor, write my undergrad class assignment on one computer while Alex is doing homework on the other computer, switching back and forth between my assignment and the internet site from which he needs information. Take the dog for a walk, first meet Alex in the garage where he's getting his scooter, but remember the cardboard box that the pizza came in for the garbage can so the kitchen doesn't stink like leftover pepperoni. Wash dishes while I'm talking on the phone, grade papers while I'm sitting at the stoplight, read an article while I'm walking to pick up Alex at school. It's all part of maintaining, organizing.

A single mother knows she would benefit from a support network, extended family, or community, and she may look about for something that resembles any of those formations. They are hard to find. In the meantime, the life you are trying to manage is making you extremely tired, and the self is dissolving into a series of harried fragments.

What's encouraging, then, is to see these harried lives and concerns increasingly represented by the mainstream media. On television and Internet sites, in film, self-help books, and romance novels, through media coverage of celebrities and in advertising, single mothers are encouraged to see themselves as autonomous agents but also as people deserving of certain rewards and desires. In Part I of this book, "Everyday Life," I analyze these media texts as a set of guidelines for both single moms and others who are curious about this newly valorized identity group. Yet there is still a gap between the representation and the reality. To illustrate this gap and to situate the analysis within the space of a particular home, I also describe in "Everyday Life" how television shapes some of my own experiences as a single mom of a young boy.

Spaces of Community

The increasing pressure on single moms to reject dependency and prove autonomy illustrates the paucity of options available within the terms of liberalism. As Nancy Fraser and Linda Gordon argue, what is missing in the "dominant understanding of civil citizenship," which opposes the individual enterprise of contract law to the stigmatized dependency of charity, is "a public language capable of expressing ideas that escape those dichotomous oppositions, especially the ideas of solidarity, non-contractual reciprocity, and interdependence that are central to any humane social citizenship" (125-126). Yet some communities *have* developed such a language of reciprocity and solidarity, devising hybrid ways of living that combine independence and solidarity.

We can't assume that self-reliance and community are antithetical terms. In the second part of this book, "Spaces," I show how self-reliance can be articulated through group identity and community formation and thus represent an alternative to isolated notions of the self *and* to the demonization of dependency. This is not to say these efforts escape the terms of liberal governance but rather that activists are savvy pragmatists, able to create both practical solutions and long-term hope. Who has the luxury of purism? In the different spaces to which I turn, single mothers work as organizers, cobbling together whatever strategies work for raising their children.

What extends across all the sites studied in this book, from media texts to corporate America to community projects, is the desire for personal agency, what academic critics might dismiss as complicity with liberalism's emphasis on the individual. Yet empowerment becomes complicated by the formation of a community that exceeds the individual. And while the appeal to governmental policy realms may seem like an uncritical concession to the powers of the state, this move also becomes more complicated when seen in the context of everyday life. In Part II, I analyze this complex mixture of strategies and conditions as they play out in the three spaces-the corporate university, the Puerto Rican Cultural Center, and the Rio Grande Valley in Texas, all spaces I occupy and have occupied as an academic, activist, and single mother.

I want to be clear that I'm not nostalgic for community as a response to government or capitalism. And I'm trying hard not to romanticize community, although admittedly at times that is difficult to resist. My longing is due to the conditions of the space in which I work, given the highly individuated and isolating work practices of academia, where few colleagues or administrators have recognized child raising as worthy work. It thus comes as little surprise that single mothers don't really feel part of the academic community. Community formation depends on a shared recognition that mothering is indeed work, something that exists for the both the Puerto Ricans and the mothers of the Rebecca Project.

Undocumented legal status complicates the creation of community, as single mothers avoid making their presence more visible and often live alone or perhaps with a few close relatives or friends. Along the U.S.-Mexican border, Proyecto Libertad has had some success in organizing neighborhood associations, but in my interviews with undocumented women, one sentence, in slight variation, recurred: "I have to do this on my own." Some women come to this position after failed marriages with abusive husbands—husbands they often have married to gain legal status, as immigration policy makes marriage the most expedient route to legality and thus to safe and sustainable work. Other women simply decide that they would rather live on their own than risk partnership with men who may exploit their undocumented status, even if that means piecing together odd jobs at less-than-minimum wage: selling Mary Kay cosmetics, cleaning hotel bathrooms, and waiting tables at strip clubs. They become entrepreneurs, savvy about how to negotiate the potential of the "American dream" even as they see its unfairness.

Working across these spaces, it becomes clear that the category "single mother" is highly diverse. Indeed, in certain spaces, such as the Rio Grande Valley, single mothers might not even claim that identity with any kind of recognition that it signifies in a wider, political sense. Yet it also becomes clear that some single mothers are operating as domestic intellectuals, and that political power may be garnered through forming alliances across a fluid and heterogeneous identity category. Because we must work through policy realms, via activist strategies, the category "single mother," deployed strategically, can do important work toward increasing the agency of all single mothers, perhaps even all mothers.

Identity Politics?

Who counts as a single mom? Some cases are clear, others not so clear. The 40-something woman who decides she wants a child and gets inseminated with donor sperm is obviously a single mom. What about the divorced mom who shares physical custody with her ex-husband? The 20-something woman who lives with her father's baby but doesn't get married? And what's to be gained and lost by drawing lines? How, indeed, politically efficacious a category is "single mom"?

How one becomes a single mom shapes life as a single mom. In the last part of the book, "Ethics," I examine three ways in which moms become single—divorce, assisted reproductive technologies, and adoption—analyzing the legal, medical, and social scientific discourses that shape these options. What are the ethics of these practices? Foucault asks, "What is ethics, if not the practice of freedom, the conscious practice of freedom?" (1997: 284). It's true that all these options represent choices of single moms to free themselves from reliance on a husband and father for their children. It's also true that the freedom to choose removes mothering, to some degree, from the realm of essentialism that has kept women and their children defined by predictable gendered and sexual roles. New reproductive technologies hold considerable potential for reformulating the family, for disarticulating kinship from biology. The parent is joined by others in the act of reproduction-perhaps a surrogate mother, a sperm donor, the doctor doing the insemination. As anthropologist Marilyn Strathern notes, "making visible the detachment of the procreative act from the way the family produces a child adds new possibilities to the conceptualization of intimacy in relationships. However minimal the role of those involved, dispersed conception may provide a model for relations that can take on a kinship character even where they cannot take on a family one" (353). The problem for many single mothers who conceive via assisted reproduction, however, is that no network remains after the act of conception.

Pure choice is an illusion, always shaped by structures and institutions. Single mothers by divorce are often held to the contradictory expectations of the judicial system, expected, for example, to both support their children financially and to spend many hours at home providing a stable environment. Much sociological and popular literature on divorce sounds a warning about the effects on children; there is particular concern about sons' ability to develop "normally" when single mothers raise them—a topic I explore in chapter 5 of *Single Mother*, "Mothers and Sons." Furthermore, choice is limited by the fact that many single mothers cannot afford new reproductive technologies or adoption. Insurance policies in many states discriminate against single mothers, assuming that only couples suffer from infertility. Infertility clinics prefer couples, and many adoption agencies still discriminate against single moms, especially lesbians. Increasingly, single women are pursuing transnational adoptions, which further complicates the category of choice: the mothers who are forced to give up their babies due to poverty and war can hardly be said to have made that choice.

Because of these differences in privilege, it is critical, as many feminists have written in respect to the category "woman," to keep in mind the heterogeneity of the category "single mom." It should be a capacious and flexible category that nevertheless coheres around mutual issues. Problems arise when the category becomes exclusive, as in the rhetoric of Single Mothers by Choice, whose set of criteria for who counts as a single mom is designed to set them off from the stigma of welfare. They engage in a politics of exclusion and moralism, creating categories of "others" in a manner that plays into the politics of worthy and unworthy subjects.

The task of both theorizing and living the identity of "single mom" is a difficult one. On the one hand, as I demonstrate throughout this book, marriage is still the norm in many instances and locations. Even when there is no stigma attached to single mothering, material privilege accrues to the married couple. Hence, resistance to this category is necessary. We need to present clear alternatives in the interest of revealing the norm and how it works to discriminate, to make life harder for those who choose, to whatever degree, to live on the margins. Resistance can produce pride, solidarity, cohesiveness, as we have seen over and over again in the various articulations of identity politics. These feelings are especially important when life continues to be difficult; identity groups provide inspiration, ideas, resources, and companionship.

Yet identity politics often ventures into the territory of resentment that Wendy Brown identifies in *States of Injury*. Identity remains indebted to the very structures it critiques, such that some perverse kind of thrill, some martyrdom is gained through the retention of the problematic category: "Politicized identity, premised on exclusion and fueled by the humiliation and suffering imposed by its historically structured impotence in the context of a discourse of sovereign individuals, is as likely to seek generalized political paralysis, to feast on generalized political impotence, as it is to seek its own or collective liberation through empowerment" (70-71). The danger lies in positing single mothers as victims of patriarchy in order to make claims for social change. In this line of arguing, it is only by virtue of being a victim that a subject can claim agency. The victim needs her oppressor in order to consolidate her identity, in order to continually make claims on the very institution that has defined her identity in the first place. We see this tendency in the work of Martha Fineman, who has written extensively on how legal policy shapes mothering: "Single motherhood as a social phenomenon should be viewed by feminists as a practice resistive to patriarchal ideology .... As such, the existence of single motherhood as an ever-expanding practice threatens the logic and hold of the dominant ideology" (125). The single mother then is faced with the difficult prospect of retaining her status as victim in order to represent a political position of always potential but never quite realized transgression.

However, being a transgressor may be, in terms of everyday life, very difficult. A celebration of transgression may well transcend the details of everyday life-and thus offer no effective alternative to the conservative idealization of mothers. That position, like many associated with aggressive identity politics, turns potential allies into oppressors, and it relies on the retention of the oppressor/oppressed binary for the formation of identity. It thus offers limited possibilities for effecting material change. Identity should be a category you pass through on your way to a less restrictive life, one more defined by the freedom to raise children in a loving, shared environment. This desire for something more expansive than "single mom" as an identity is better for single moms in the long run, who must address the question: What will be my identity after my child grows up?

An alternative politics would make everyday life in all its mundane details visible and show how both governmental and feminist rhetoric often ignore everyday complexities. We need to recognize single mothers in their positivity, their singularity, apart from any relation to an Other (everyone who's not a single mom should pity us). This entails recognizing the specific conditions of single mothering, not to set her apart from everyone else but to show that there is nothing essentially true about mothering-it's constituted through the cumulative practices of everyday life, in which anyone can share.

Notes

[1]Solinger says that in 1957, for the first time, the official number of illegitimate births in the United States broke 200,000, but that is considered a serious undercount.

[2]In *Ordway v. Hargraves* (1971), the U.S. Supreme Court made it illegal for schools to expel unwed pregnant girls. In 1975, with the passage of Title IX, Congress denied federal funding for schools that did not comply with Ordway (Solinger 96).

[3]As governor of California, Reagan proposed that "the third child and subsequent illegitimate children of an unwed mother 'should be statutorily removed for adoption'" (Solinger 132).

[4]*Caught in the Crossfire* is an important analysis of economic, political, and cultural conditions that have made it seem like America's youth are to blame for a host of social problems. It does not deal much, however, with mothering and everyday domestic issues.

[5]I realize that I am raising but not directly confronting the difficult question of what constitutes work in cultural studies. By focusing on these two journals, major publications, and major figures, I do not mean to preclude other work but rather

to point to exemplary sites where cultural studies has developed.

[6]I should acknowledge that *Cultural Studies* published my article on mothering, "Dirty Diapers and the New Organic Intellectual," 17 (2) (2003): 168-192.

[7]Hardt and Negri did include a short section on maternal work as a kind of "biopolitical production," but this section was cut, later appearing in a special issue of *Cultural Studies* along with other omitted sections.

References

Abramovitz, Mimi. *Regulating the Lives of Women: Social Welfare Policy from Colonial Times to the Present.* Boston: South End Press, 1988.

Amott, Teresa L. "Black Women and the AFDC: Making Entitlement out of Necessity." *Women, the State, and Welfare.* Ed. Linda Gordon. Madison: University of Wisconsin Press, 1990.

Belluck, Pam. "With Mayhem at Home, They Call a Parent Coach." *New York Times.* March 13, 2005. A1, 23.

Bennet, Tony. "Putting Policy Into Cultural Studies." *Cultural Studies.* Eds. Lawrence Grossberg, Cary Nelson, and Paula Treichler. New York: Routledge, 1992. 23-37.

Block, Fred, et al. *The Mean Season: The Attack on the Welfare State.* New York: Pantheon Books, 1987.

Brown, Wendy. *States of Injury: Power and Freedom in Late Modernity.* Princeton: Princeton University Press, 1995.

Butler, Judith. "Is Kinship Always Already Heterosexual?" *differences: A Journal of Feminist Cultural Studies* 13 (1) (2002): 14-44.

Chang, Grace. *Disposable Domestics: Immigrant Women Workers in the Global Economy.* Cambridge: South End Press, 2000.

Cott, Nancy F. *Public Vows: A History of Marriage and the Nation.* Cambridge: Harvard University Press, 2000.

Cunningham, Stuart. *Framing Culture: Criticism and Policy in Australia.* North Sidney, NSW: Allen and Unwin, 1992.

Das, Veena, and Renu Addlakha. "Disability and Domestic Citizenship: Voice, Gender, and the Making of the Subject." *Public Culture* 13 (3) (2001): 511-531.

Duggan, Lisa. *The Twilight of Equality? Neoliberalism, Cultural Politics, and the Attack on Democracy.* Boston: Beacon Press, 2003.

Edwin, Kathryn, and Laura Lein. *Making End Meet: How Single Mothers Survive Welfare and Low-Wage Work.* New York: Russell Sage Foundation, 1997.

Engber, Andrea, and Leah Klungness. *The Complete Single Mother: Reassuring Answers to Your Most Challenging Concerns.* Holbrook: Adams Publishing, 1995.

Fieldstein, Ruth. *Motherhood in Black and White: Race and Sex in American Liberalism, 1930-1965.* Ithaca: Cornell University Press, 2000.

Fineman, Martha Albertson. *The Neutered Mother, the Sexual Family and Other Twentieth-Century Tragedies.* New York: Routledge, 1995.

Foucault, Michel. *Michel Foucault: Ethics, Subjectivity, and Truth*. Ed. Paul Rabinow. Trans. Robert Hurley. New York: New Press, 1997.

Foucault, Michel. "Truth and Power." *Power/Knowledge: Selected Interviews and Other Writings, 1972-1977*. Ed. Colin Gordon. New York: The New Press, 1980. 109-133.

Fraser, Nancy, and Linda Gordon. "Contract versus Charity: What Is There No Social Citizenship in the United States?" *The Citizenship Debates*. Ed. Will Kymlicka. Minneapolis: University of Minnesota Press, 1998.

Frow, John, and Meaghan Morris, Eds. *Australian Cultural Studies: A Reader*. Urbana: University of Illinois Press, 1993.

Giroux, Henri. *Public Spaces, Private Lives: Beyond the Culture of Cynicism*. Lanham: Rowman and Littlefield, 2001.

Glazer, Nathan, and Daniel Moynihan. *Beyond the Melting Pot: the Negroes, Puerto Ricans, Jews, Italians, and Irish of New York City*. Cambridge: MIT Press, 1963.

Gramsci, Antonio. *An Antonio Gramsci Reader: Selected Writings, 1916-1935*. Ed. David Forgacs. New York: Schocken Books, 1988.

Grossberg, Lawrence. *Caught in the Crossfire: Kids, Politics, and America's Future*. Boulder: Paradigm Publishers, 2005.

Grossberg, Lawrence, Cary Nelson, and Paula Treichler. Introduction. *Cultural Studies*. Eds. Grossberg, Nelson, and Treichler. New York: Routledge, 1992. 1-22.

Grossberg, Michael. *Governing the Hearth: Law and the Family in Nineteenth-Century America*. Chapel Hill: University of North Carolina Press, 1985.

Hill Collins, Patricia. "Black Women and Motherhood." *Rethinking the Family: Some Feminist Questions*. Eds. Barrie Thorne and Marilyn Yalom. Boston: Northeastern University Press, 1992. 215-245.

Juffer, Jane. "Dirty Diapers and the New Organic Intellectual." *Cultural Studies* 17 (2) (2003): 168-192.

Lewis, Oscar. *La Vida*. New York: Random House, 1966.

Massey, Doreen. *Space, Place, and Gender*. Minneapolis: University of Minnesota Press, 1994.

Mattes, Jane. *Single Mothers by Choice: A Guidebook for Single Women Who Are Considering or Have Chosen Motherhood*. New York: Random House, 1994.

Meckler, Laura. "President Proposes Welfare Overhaul." *Centre Daily Times*. Feb. 27, 2002. A1, A3.

Mink, Gwendolyn. "From Welfare to Wedlock: Marriage Promotion and Poor Mothers' Inequality." *Good Society* 11 (3) (2002): 68-73.

Morley, David. *Home Territories: Media, Mobility, and Identity*. London and New York: Routledge, 2000.

Moynihan, Daniel. "The Negro Family: A Case for National Action." Report of the Office of Policy Planning and Research, United States Department of Labor. March, 1965.

Negri, Antonio, and Michael Hardt. "'Subterranean Passages of Thought':

Empire's Inserts." Compiled by Nicholas Brown and Imre Szeman. *Cultural Studies* 16(2) (2002): 193-212.

Pateman, Carol. *The Sexual Contract*. Cambridge: Polity Press, 1988.

Pérez, Gina. "An Upbeat Westside Story: Puerto Ricans and Postwar Racial Politics in Chicago." *Centro Journal* 13 (2) (Fall 2001): 47-68.

Radway, Janice. *Reading the Romance: Women, Patriarchy, and Popular Literature*. Chapel Hill: University of North Carolina Press, 1984.

Rapp, Rayne, and Faye Ginsburg. "Enabling Disability: Rewriting Kinship, Reimagining Citizenship." *Public Culture* 13 (3) (2001): 533-556.

Rose, Nikolas. *Inventing Our Selves: Psychology, Power, and Personhood*. New York: Cambridge Studies in the History of Psychology, 1996.

Rose, Nikolas. *Powers of Freedom: Reframing Political Thought*. Cambridge: Cambridge University Press, 1999.

Seiter, Ellen. *Sold Separately: Children and Parents in Consumer Culture*. New Brunswick: Rutgers University Press, 1993.

Silverstone, Roger. *Television and Everyday Life*. London: Routledge, 1994.

Single Mothers by Choice Website. <http://mattes.home.pipeline.com/index.html>

Solinger, Rickie. *Beggars and Choosers: How the Politics of Choice Shapes Adoption, Abortion, and Welfare in the United States*. New York: Hill and Wang, 2001.

Spigel, Lynn. *Make Room for TV: Television and the Family Ideal in Postwar America*. Chicago: University of Chicago Press, 1992.

Strathern, Marilyn. "Displacing Knowledge: Technology and the Consequences for Kinship." *Conceiving the New World Order: The Global Politics of Reproduction*. Eds. Faye D. Ginsburg and Rayna Rapp. Berkeley: University of California Press, 1995. 346-364.

Trattner, Walter. *From Poor Law to Welfare State: A History of Social Welfare in America*. New York: Free Press, 1999.

Warner, Michael. *The Trouble With Normal: Sex, Politics, and the Ethics of Queer Life*. New York: Free Press, 1999.

Warner, Michael, and Lauren Berlant. "Sex in Public." In Michael Warner, *Publics and Counterpublics*. New York: Zone Books, 2002. 187-208.

Williams, Raymond. *Keywords: A Vocabulary of Culture and Society*. New York: Oxford University Press, 1976.

Wilson, Robin. "A Push to Help New Parents Prepare for Tenure Reviews." *Chronicle of Higher Education*. Nov. 9, 2001. A10.

Chapter 45

High Risk

Who a Mother Should Be

ARIEL GORE

When I was pregnant with my first child, my OB called it "high risk." At age 18, I was too young.

I'm pregnant with my second child now and I'm on that "high risk" list again. This time, at age 36, they say I'm too old.

In between my two "risky" pregnancies, I've struggled with all the maternal rules and expectations that get heaped on all of us; the boundaries I always seem to be on the wrong side of; the simple life choices I make for happiness and necessity and learn, usually too late, land me once again on someone's "high risk" list. Because being too young was just the beginning.

Maybe I can paint you a picture of those early days: Before *Hip Mama* and *Mothers Who Think* and *Alternadad*, before you could google up "alternative mothering" on the internet, before Lauryn Hill and Gwyneth Paltrow and Angelina Jolie made motherhood cool, I pushed a second-hand stroller down Haight Street in San Francisco.

"Breeder!" some punk yelled at us from across the street.

I looked down at my plain cotton spit-up covered clothes from the Goodwill.

"It's yuppie scum like you who are fucking this city up!" the guy railed on, his face twisting into a strange mask.

But the "yuppie scum" at my daughter's new daycare didn't seem to want anything to do with me, either. They looked down their nose-job noses at me with a mixture of pity and concern.

Maia started to fuss in her stroller, so I pulled her out, sat down on the curb, and lifted my shirt to let her nurse. A bike messenger almost got hit by a Muni bus craning his neck to stare at us.

How could it be that the simple acts of getting knocked up and having a baby had alienated me from every single subculture I had ever heard of?

Maia fell asleep sweetly in my arms there on the curb, and I lifted her back into her stroller, careful not to wake her. I pushed on through the light summer drizzle, made my way up to the Anarchist Bookstore, a little closet of a shop. I pawed through the zines—*EcoPussy* and *Wizard Man* or some such. I sighed. My pussy wasn't feeling very ecological these days and I was pretty sure I couldn't get into wizardry. I started to turn away, but suddenly the punk from across the street was standing right in front of us. "Why do you go to Barnes and Noble, breeder?"

I turned back toward the zine shelf so as not to let him see the tears well up in my eyes. And just as I turned, from the bottom of the rows of anarchist, hippie, feminist, and punk publications, a little Xeroxed something glowed up at me with a quote from Emma Goldman: "We, who pay dearly for every breath of pure, fresh air must guard against the tendency to fetter the future." Japanese electronica seemed to burst from speakers unseen and cartoon stars floated from the homemade zine and filled the tiny store.

I grabbed issue #1 of *The Future Generation* "for subculture parents, kids, friends and others," quickly convinced the guy behind the old-fashioned register to let me pay the $2 in food stamps, and then I locked eyes with the mean unpunk punk and snarled: "fuck off."

It's a powerful thing, to find a little Xeroxed island home in a sea of alienation.

As those early years of motherhood crawled by, I didn't find another issue of *The Future Generation*, but I longed for a place where I could tell the truth about my experience without being expected to apologize for the fact that I was a "breeder," apologize for my age or anything else.

Back then, I didn't know very many other women with children--but I didn't make any real attempt to reach out. I understood all the cultural messages I was getting--from the voices on the nightly news to the whispered gossip in my neighborhood: The people without kids didn't want to know me and when it came to the "breeders" I was different, too. I was different from the one's who weren't so "high risk," different from the ones who had husband (or at least stories of death and divorce to explain their lack thereof). I was different from the ones who had middle-class jobs and two-storey houses, different from the ones who could offer their children "real love" in the form of security, different from the ones who weren't considered pariahs.

I didn't find that place where I could tell my truth, so I started my own zine, *Hip Mama*. A little publication in the sea of alienation—maybe that's what I needed. When I put out the first issue I didn't know if anyone would read it. How many of us were we? These *other* mothers like me. These outsiders. *High risk*. I unconsciously imagined a readership that looked a lot like I looked at the time: young, single, urban, struggling to finish college. I sent my zine out into the world like a message in a bottle: *Is anybody else out there?* Miraculously, my message was read.

At first I heard from women very much like myself—the college moms and the young moms, the urban moms and the poor moms, the queer moms and the artist moms. Some even showed up in person. We met for coffee in my the living room of my apartment while the kids made construction-paper collages and finger-paint messes. But pretty soon, *knock, knock,* women who didn't look so much like me arrived.

"We're high-risk, too," they whispered.

I didn't believe them. Were they trying to infiltrate my new-found clan? Were they, in fact, government informants? That's how isolated I'd been--I could hardly fathom the isolation of anyone else. *You're married*, I thought. *The world loves you. What do you want with us?* Or, *you've got a job that pays ten dollars an hour, what do you know about hunger?* But it turns out that the world does not love very many of us. An independent woman thinking for herself--married as she may be—has always been "high risk" when it comes to the patriarchy. Mothers who work outside the home for wages high or low have always been accused of abandoning their children. Stay-at-home moms are called financially neglectful, maternally smothering, or personally anti-feminist. Whether we listen to Tupac Shakur, The Ramones, or the Dixie Chicks, mother-haters will take the opportunity to rage at us from their bikes.

And the world tells us all—in a thousand ways—that we are not enough for our children. The world tells us we are too young, too old, too poor, too extravagant, too permissive, too controlling, too urban, too rural, too eccentric, too square and everything in between.

Show me a mother who has never been fed the guilt of inadequacy and I'll show you a mother who isn't pregnant yet.

Serious debates in Congress centered on "How to punish the parents without hurting the children." Punish us for what? For being human, usually. As mothers, especially as new mothers, short on sleep and the tenuous confidence that comes with experience, it's easy to slip into believing those voices.

I've been publishing *Hip Mama* for thirteen years now and I've accepted a thousand thank-yous from moms who say mine was the only voice of support they heard in a choir of discouragement. "It's so hard to be told over and over that I am unworthy," one mom told me after a talk I gave.

"I know," I told her. But she didn't believe me.

She thought, as we all sometimes do, that she was alone. She thought that someone like me—someone who has spent the better part of her life as a mom fighting those voices of discouragement—would be immune to the power of "shoulds." But how could I be?

Have I ever ignored my daughter because I was too busy writing about effective parenting? Have I ever done what might be considered an eccentric proportion of my grocery shopping at 7-Eleven? Have I ever uttered a hurtful word? Morphed into an overprotective Big-foot mama? Served empty calories for dinner? I have. Of course I have. And my daughter, as a teenager, has often joined that choir to remind me of my every shortcoming.

When she was a baby I had to write one of those "Who am I?" essays college freshman are forever being asked to produce. In it I wrote about my new motherhood:

> *I am caught between the tides, between moons new and old ... caught somewhere between who I am, who I have been, and who I think a mother*

should be … I feel too young, feel that I should be more together if I'm going to be a mother, that I should be able to offer something more, that I am not enough, and yet wanting to be honest.…

I was embarrassed when I got to class and heard the other essays—the ones by upbeat, childless eighteen-year-olds that said, "I am an environmentalist," or "I love to swim," or "I am an Italian American." But even then I knew this feeling of being caught between the tides, between who I was and who the world tells us a mother should be, was significant. Back then I felt I "should" be more together, and over the years I have been able to fill in the blank with dozens of other things I have felt, or heard, I "should" be.

I have felt, and been told, that I should have blown it as a mother a thousand times by having Maia too young, not having enough money, having too much money, spoiling her, depriving her, sending her to public school, sending her to private school, living in the city, being single, having lovers, not getting the film from her fifth birthday developed until she was six, and more.

Pregnant with my second now, the voices have already begun. "*How* did you get pregnant?" people ask, incredulous, because my partner is a woman.

"Don't tell your grandmother," my mother warns me. "It will kill her."

I don't ask my mother why she thinks this, but I do wonder what ever happened to "congratulations" and I guess, as a teen mom, I always wrote people's rude intolerance off to the fact that I was young. But I am grown now, am I not? I'll be 37 when this kid is born. Was I so naïve to imagine folks would just *trust me* on this one?

When I went to apply for state medical insurance, I was referred to a "Pregnancy Resource Center" for documentation that I was, indeed, pregnant--not just sporting a serious beer gut. There, in a pink wallpapered room, a woman wearing a pink blouse and elastic-waist jeans sat me down and demanded to know, "Are you for or against abortion?"

"I'm just here for a pregnancy test," I told her. "Adult and Family Services sent me."

"For or against abortion?" she insisted.

"I'm pro-choice."

"FOR ABORTION," she scrawled across my intake form. "I see here you're single," she continued, and launched into a lecture on "the kind of relationship God wants you to have." The she showed me pictures of developing fetuses and assured me that God wanted me to have the baby. "And remember, it's never too late to consider adoption—there are plenty of couples out there who'll be able to give your baby the kind of security and stability a child needs."

I just nodded, speechless.

Two months later I walked into a sushi bar and a fellow customer gasped: "Don't you know pregnant women aren't supposed to eat sushi!?"

As a matter of fact, I do know. And I know we are not supposed to drink or smoke, eat soft cheese or tuna fish, drink coffee or green tea, take too much vitamin

C or too little iron, think negative thoughts or tell our fellow sushi customers to fuck off. I also know that even if we consume only organic seaweed and feed our children brown rice and goat's milk, they will, first chance they get, sneak off to McDonald's and buy themselves a Happy Meal. I am not ill-informed. But so many of these health and safety announcements aimed at regulating mothers smack to me of a government *pretending* to care about children when in fact, beyond guilt-tripping and sometimes even criminalizing the parents, it has every intention of leaving children behind.

So, yeah, I've heard the choir of discouragement. I've heard all the criticisms that come from relatives, friends, acquaintances and the world at large—and I have, at times, joined that choir. As one mother wrote in *Hip Mama* when describing all the "shoulds" she had heard since she bore her children, "When an outside critic wasn't on the case, I did the job myself.

We have to stop that. Even when we cannot quiet our outside detractors, we have to resist the urge to join them.

One mom I know recently confessed that at three o'clock in the morning, after having tried to get her one-year-old to sleep for hours, she "lost it." She screamed, loud and fierce, "I am going to die," and then leapt out of bed, ran to the front door of their studio apartment, and started kicking it. "I think I really frightened her," my friend kept telling me, as if her baby would be scarred for life. "I'll never forgive myself."

"Under the circumstances," I suggested, "'I am going to die' seems like a pretty reasonable thing to scream. And the door, well, a pretty reasonable thing to kick."

The world tells us all—in a thousand ways— that there is no margin for error in mothering. But I am here to tell you that there is a margin, and it is wide. Just as the occasional piece of chocolate cake can't make you fat, just as a few days off won't make you a lousy employee, blowing it as a mother every once in a while doesn't spell disaster for your kids' psyches. It simply doesn't.

We are human beings, after all, and sometimes we have to roar. We may feel caught between the tides, caught between who we are and who we think we ought to be, but we can also be honest. We can offer our children the whole of who we are, high-risk 3:00 am roaring and all.

Portions of this essay have appeared, in different forms, in The Mother Trip *(Seal Press, 2000) and* The Future Generation *(Atomic Books, 2007).*

References

Gore, Ariel and Bee Lavender. *Breeder: Real-Life Stories from the New Generation of Mothers*. Seattle: Seal Press: 2001.

Chapter 46

Giving Life to the People

An Indigenous Ideology of Motherhood

KIM ANDERSON

OVER THE LAST 30 years, feminist scholars have been exploring the inherent oppression of motherhood in twentieth-century western society. Adrienne Rich first
wrote about the "institution of motherhood" in 1976, differentiating between the
"experience" of mothering and the "institution" of motherhood as prescribed by
western patriarchy. In so doing, Rich inspired a search for agency and empowered mothering that is ongoing (see, for example, O'Reilly). Much of this work,
however, has been about the experiences or ideologies of white, middle-class
motherhood in western society. Women of colour have been the subject of some
scholarly work, but relatively little has been written about Native women.[1] Whereas
Native women have definitely been caught up in the "history and ideology"[2] of
patriarchal western motherhood, they have also maintained and revived their own
distinct ideologies of motherhood. This paper explores the collectivist, spiritual
and sovereign elements of what might be referred to as an Indigenous[3] ideology
of motherhood.

Writing about an "Indigenous ideology of motherhood" is, of course, an exercise
in making generalizations about peoples who are extremely diverse. Even within
our nations, the life experiences and perspectives of one individual may be radically different from another. This being said, Indigenous peoples on the whole
do share many common values, epistemologies and worldviews as outlined by
various Indigenous scholars (see Ermine; Little). Paula Gunn Allen's observations
that in "traditional"[3] tribal lifestyles, "the welfare of the young is paramount, the
complementary nature of all life forms is stressed, and the centrality of powerful women to social well-being is unquestioned" (2, 3) are particularly relevant
to understanding the value afforded to mothers in an Indigenous ideology of
motherhood.

In addition to having common values, epistemologies and worldviews, Indigenous peoples also share a history of interference. As I was pondering on a way
to succinctly write about Native motherhood, I was reminded of a formula that
a late "othermother/auntie"[4] friend of mine provided me when I was a young
woman first endeavouring to understand the struggles related to the history of our
people. "It all comes back to the three deadly c's," she said, waving her cigarette

and looking at me over the glasses perched on her nose. "Capitalism, Christianity, and colonialism!" Thinking about my friend's "triple c" formula, tongue-in-cheek though it was, helped me to devise the categories that I have used to explore an Indigenous ideology of motherhood. Through collectivism, spirituality and the application of sovereignty, Native mothers have shaped empowered mothering experiences in spite of the capitalist, Christian and colonial frameworks that have worked together to support patriarchal western motherhood in Native communities. I will thus look at what has happened to our mothering as a result of the incursion of "the three c's," and examine how contemporary Native women and communities are crafting experiences and ideologies of mothering as strategies of resistance, reclamation and recovery.

Collectivism

Historians of the western family have documented the introduction of public and private spheres that accompanied the industrial revolution.[5] This shift from family centered working environments, to one in which men worked away from the home and women were left to care for the household and children was accompanied by middle-class ideals of motherhood which posited the mother as the "angel of the home." In spite of the fact that few working-class mothers could afford to devote themselves exclusively to mothering (see, for example, Bradbury), these ideals were upheld and have underpinned North American ideologies of motherhood for the last two hundred years (see Pierson, Levesque and Arnup; Apple and Golden). Capitalism has not been kind to these angels, however. Frederick Engels located female subjugation in the rise of private property and the modern family, and Marxist feminist sociologists have since written about how mothers have been exploited for their reproductive and domestic labour (Fox; Luxton). Mothers today, according to Sharon Hays, continue to be oppressed by "the logic of individualistic, competitive, and impersonal relations" (18). Whether working outside the home or not, mothers are now subject to the demands of "intensive mothering," a selfless nurturing to countervail "the ethos of rationalized market societies" (Hays 18).

Native women, however, have had less direct and more recent encounters with capitalism and as a result, less experience with the ideologies of patriarchal western motherhood. At the time Engels was writing, Native peoples had long been involved in trade, but were still largely working within traditional economies tied to the land and built around kinship systems. These economies involved gendered roles in which men were responsible for hunting, fishing and trapping, and women were responsible for refining the products of men's labour (i.e., preparing meats and tanning hides), for harvesting, farming and hunting or trapping smaller animals. The "separate spheres" of traditional Native economies could not have been characterized by the public/private dichotomy, nor were they hierarchical or inherently oppressive to one gender. They were understood to be interdependent, equally valuable, and flexible (see Anderson 2000a). In land based economies, women were recognized for their productive as well as their reproductive labour, as described by Cree/Métis Elder Maria Campbell:

> In olden times you were taught skills that you would need as a woman and you were valued for those skills because they meant "life" for your people. You were valued for how well you could skin and cut up a buffalo or a moose and preserve it. How well you could tan a hide, sew clothing, and make baskets. Later it was also how well you could garden and preserve the food. You were also valued for your dignity, kindness, generosity and courage. Sometimes you were valued as a hunter and protector. All of these skills and characteristics were needed to nurture and protect life. (qtd. in Anderson 2003: 177)

Because these economies were upheld through kinship systems, mothers lived and worked in extended family units, precluding the possibility of an isolated and subordinate mother as family servant. In matrilineal societies, such as the Haudenosaunee (Iroquois), women were considered "owners" of the land and soil, as they farmed the land collectively (Noel 81).[6] With mothers engaged in duties related to production, infant care would have been undertaken by the collective, with assistance provided to mothers by older children and the elderly. The "angel in the home" was more likely tilling fields or trapping small animals while "other-mothers" helped with the care of her biological children. Grandparents had a particularly strong role as teachers and caregivers of the young in Native societies across North America (Schweitzer). The welfare of women and children was thus linked to interdependencies between families, and between networks of women.

After herding Native peoples onto reserves in the late nineteenth century, the state (both in Canada and the U.S.) set about the task of dealing with "the Indian problem" by trying to fashion Native men, women and families in the image of Euro-western people. This entailed moving men towards farming or the wage economy, and training women for their exclusively domestic roles. Residential schools took on the job of providing a gendered education that would foster a male breadwinner family model. Boys were trained in trades and farming techniques and girls were schooled in "domestic science," indicating, as J. R. Miller points out, "that [girls] were confined in their vocational training almost exclusively to skills suitable for a future as wives, mothers and homemakers" (220). Yet because the policies of the very same state(s) thwarted Native success in the capitalist system,[7] the gendered transition to public and private spheres never fully took root. Today, a different version of the traditional collectivist interdependencies remains, as scarcity and cultural oppression have precluded the full flowering of Western liberalism and individual autonomy in Native communities (see Udel). This is true of Indigenous societies elsewhere in the world. Brenda F. McGadney-Douglass *et al.* have documented "a compelling common denominator of collectivism" in mothering practices among colonized Indigenous peoples in Canada, the United States, Africa and Australia (106). They note the significance of the work provided by grandmothers and other kin in colonized environments where women must work together to ensure the survival of their children (McGadney-Douglass *et al.*106).

In North America, there are many examples of how the male breadwinner model has been forestalled in Native communities. Patricia Albers has demonstrated that the marginalization of Sioux men from the capitalist economy meant that` production continues to be organized around "kinship and the creation of use-value" (subsistence) (222), which leaves Sioux women with a degree of autonomy and influence in their communities. Jo-Anne Fiske (1992) has documented how Carrier women's involvement in the fisheries—in part because men were pushed out of the business—allowed them to gain some economic status through net fishing. Fiske writes of "a shift towards female-centered households dependent on female earnings" in which men are reliant on their female kin. Because of economic necessity, "extended families of three to four generations under the direction of the eldest woman are the most stable economic unit" (205). John Lutz has studied the "ebb and flow" of Lekwammen women's economic power, stating, "Long-standing, seasonal, gender, and family based modes of organizing labour adapted and became integrated into colonial and industrial patterns and so persisted among the Lekwammen into the 1950s" (1992: 241). Regarding contemporary Native family economies, Memee Lavell-Harvard and Jeannetten Corbiere Lavell have stated "For most members of the Aboriginal community, everyday survival is still dependent on extensive networks of family and friends who support and reinforce each other" (189).

Many Native mothers thus continue to live and work within extended kin networks that distinguish them from the nuclear family mother who depends on her husband's income. Native grandmothers and sometimes grandfathers continue to play a significant role in raising children, often as the primary caregivers.[8] This is not to say that the collectivist model of child care is all encompassing, or that all Native mothers are adequately supported to carry out empowered mothering. According to a Canadian statistical report produced in 1996, the proportion of single mothers among registered Status Indians is increasing. One in three of the mothers in this population were single mothers, a figure twice as high a proportion of single mothers among other Canadians. In urban areas, thirty-eight percent of Registered Indian families with children 0-15 were single mother families. The average annual income of these single mother families was less than $16,000, and one third of these mothers were raising three or more children (Hull). The dire conditions in which many Native women are mothering are very clear.

Native mothers may be at greater risk in urban environments, where they have less kin support (McGadney-Douglas *et al.* 110-111). Yet in the urban environments with which I am familiar, Aboriginal organizations have stepped up to address the need by developing social services and support for Native mothers which operate as "families of the heart" or alternative kinship systems. Kin names evoke the collectivist/kinship model some of these organizations are trying to re-create. For example, Native Child and Family Services of Toronto (a child welfare agency) has a "Ninoshe" or "auntie" program in which older women work with young mothers in their homes, offering support in the manner of a female family member. Métis writer Joanne Arnott has written about the transformative experiences that resulted from her participation in "traditional parenting skills programs" in Vancouver. Joanne Arnott describes the facilitators of these programs in kinship terms; the first program she attended was facilitated by "Grandmother Harris" and Ellen Antoine, who she describes as "Auntie, mother, elder sister" (97-98). Family support workers (primarily women) can thus fulfill an "othermother" or auntie role for women who are seeking the wisdom, nurturing and guidance of older kin. This is especially important for those who have no extended family support system upon moving to the city.

Although varying in degree, ongoing collectivist strategies have positioned Native mothers differently from Eurowestern mothers, and they have affected the value Native mothers place on motherhood and family. Lisa Udel contrasts Native family ideologies with feminist interpretations that frame the family as "the locus of gender conflict," noting that the latter models are based on white, middle class nuclear families, and focused on "the economic dependence of women and the inequitable division of labour" (51). Citing Evelyn Glenn, Udel noted that, "women of colour often experience their families as a 'source of resistance to oppression from outside institutions" (51; see also Glenn 101). For Native mothers, family can be the site of resistance and renewal as well as a necessary financial support. As Mc-Gadney-Douglass *et al.* have stated in their article on international Indigenous mothering trends, "Traditions that emphasize cooperation and collaboration, as well as pragmatism and good decision-making for common goals, have time tested value" (119).

Spirituality

Family may be "the locus of gender conflict" in much of the theoretical work on motherhood, but the female body has also been the subject of much feminist angst. In an article on "women-centered societies" Maria-Barbara Watson-Franke notes that, "Western feminism, just like western patriarchy, has been, clearly, uncomfortable with the body, and, especially the maternal body" (76). Native women have not been so conflicted about the body, however. This is because within Indigenous ideologies of motherhood, the maternal body is a metaphor for power.

Indigenous ideologies of motherhood are grounded in Native spirituality, as metaphors of the powerful maternal body are based in pre-Christian cosmologies that speak to the authority of women's ability as life-givers. The female body was synonymous with the power of creation and the ability to sustain that creation. Birth, mothering and the power of the feminine were central in creation stories of most Native peoples of the Americas. As Native American scholars M. Annette Jaimes and Theresa Halsey have stated, "...virtually all indigenous religions on this continent exhibit an abundant presence of feminine elements within their cosmologies" (319). They note:

> When contrasted with the hegemonic masculinity of the deities embraced by such "world religions" as Judaism, Christianity and Islam—and the corresponding male supremacism marking those societies that adhere to them—the real significance of concepts like Mother Earth (universal), Spider Woman (Hopi and Diné), White Buffalo Calf Woman (Lakota), Grandmother Turtle (Iroquois), Sky Woman (Iroquois), Hard Beings Woman and Sand Altar Woman (Hopi), First Woman (Abenaki), Thought Woman (Laguna), Corn Woman (Cherokee), and Changing Woman (Diné) becomes rather obvious. (Jaimes and Halsey 319)

Paula Gunn Allen has written about the symbolism of woman-as-mother in Keres Pueblo, Hopi, Navajo, Lakota and Abenaki spiritual traditions. Allen argues that, "A strong attitude integrally connects the power of Original Thinking or Creation Thinking to the power of mothering." Mother is the one who has the power "to make, to create, to transform" (Allen 29), according to this ideology.

"Mother" is a concept thus connected both to the original creation of the world, and to the work that is ongoing to sustain it. Jordan Paper has traced the historical presence of female deities and Earth as mother in Indigenous cultures across North and South America. Drawing on evidence from missionaries, anthropological literature and petroglyphs, Paper shows how various Indigenous peoples understood the earth to be "the life giving female cosmic creator" and "the mother of all life." He points out that contemporary Native peoples continue to see the earth in this manner, stating, "The symbolic anthropomorphization of the earth extends to all its parts. Streams and rivers are understood as the veins and arteries of Earth: water is her life-giving fluid. Sacred herbs, such as sweetgrass are understood as the hair of Earth; hence, sweetgrass is braided in the northern Native American hair style" (Paper 14).

Women's power was thus understood to come from their capacity to create and nurture. This was not understood to be a selfless act of infinite giving, however. Native principles of reciprocity prevented an endless taking from our first mother, the Earth. If mother was to continue to provide, so the logic went, she must be nurtured in return. Anishnaabe Elder Edna Manitowabi relates a story she heard from a Cree elder about how the "old world" (Europe) was used up to the point where she could not give life anymore. Manitowabi makes the distinction between selfless giving and nurturing, stating, "In our original teachings, men celebrated "mother life." They honoured and respected women, acting reciprocally as oshkabeweis, helpers" (qtd. in Anderson 2000a: 188).

Life was understood to be sustained through cyclical processes of rebirth and renewal, in which men and women played distinct roles. Women had the power of menstruation, for within that ceremony they cleansed themselves and began a process of renewal respecting "the blood of the people" (Anderson 2000a: 74-

75). Giving birth was understood to be the "sacred work" of women,[9] and this work allowed them to act as intermediary between heaven and earth via their bodies (see Anderson 2000a: 73). Because they had the ability to cleanse, birth and renew, Native women did not always participate in some of the ceremonies that simulated the regenerative cycles. The dome shaped sweat lodge, for example is equated with the womb of mother earth, where one goes to purify and seek out rebirth and renewal (see Bedard 70). Although many Native women "sweat" today, this was not always the case because of the understanding that the monthly periods were the women's way of purifying.[10] The Sun Dance was (and is) another prevalent ceremony, in which the dancers laboured for days, eventually piercing the flesh. This was a measure of sacrifice that resembled the sacrifice that women make in birthing children (see Anderson 2000a: 164-65). It was done to ensure the health, renewal and future of the people and, as such, women did not dance or tear in this ceremony historically as they had done so in giving birth.

Traditional Native spiritualities and ceremonies have survived and have been undergoing a process of renewal since the 1960s, but the de-centering of women that took place through Christian imperialism can not be underestimated. Choctaw scholar Devon Mihesuah has documented the disempowerment that Native women experienced in the colonial process, and has commented:

> Among those who preferred to try and "civilize the savages" were Euro-American missionaries, who pressured Natives to convert to Christianity, which, among other things, included them accepting the concept of the male god and thus reinforcing the superiority of males. (48)

"When "God the father" took over from "mother the creator," sin was introduced to Indigenous women's bodies. Menstruation became the curse, and "illegitimate" birth had the potential to be a source of shame (see Andersom 2000: 85-94). Ceremonies that legitimated women's lifegiving powers went underground, female spirits were considered evil (Paper 16-17) and women were no longer recognized as spiritual leaders (Anderson 2000a: 71-78).

Native women are now reclaiming the sacred vitality of their bodies by re-introducing Native spiritual concepts of womanhood and motherhood into their life practices. Puberty rites and ceremonies such as berry fasting are making a comeback because they offer an opportunity to instill a sense of their power in pubescent girls. The purpose is not to simply prepare young women to be biological mothers, but to equip them with the attitudes they will need to make sacrifices, to understand what it means to take responsibility, and to care for themselves and for "the people." These practices are built on spiritual traditions that validate girls and women, and may include the telling of female-centered creation stories.[11]

Aboriginal midwives are also making a comeback, and are calling for women to reclaim "the ceremony of birth" (Couchie and Nabigon). Young Native mothers are choosing to validate their bodies as sites of empowerment, and are calling on

Native practices (i.e., plant medicines) and spiritual traditions to assist them in this process. This was not available to many Native mothers of previous (colonized) generations, as described by Cree/Métis artist Jaime Koebel:

> Pregnant at 17, my own mother did not feel the joy and wholesomeness of carrying a child. Instead, she was forced by family and society to feel shame and guilt for being pregnant.... I decided that I would have to be my own role model on how to live in a symbiotic relationship with my body and unborn child.... I spoke to a trusted Elder about the importance of being pregnant and on being proud of my pregnancy. (i)

Koebel sought out Elders who could teach her spiritual traditions related to birth. Her births included welcoming ceremonies that demonstrate a resistance to colonized motherhood and the renewal of an Indigenous ideology motherhood in her experience.

The recall and application of Native practices and spiritual traditions is not universally available, as many Native mothers continue to feel isolated and alienated by their birth experiences (Whitty-Robers, Etowa and Evans). Yet many Native women at least have avenues to pursue empowerment through Native ideologies of motherhood that are based in Native spiritual practices. Native women look to traditional and sacred stories, ceremonies and practices to empower themselves as individuals, but also to advance broader goals of Indigenous revival and sovereignty.

Sovereignty

One definition of sovereignty is "freedom from external control," and sovereignty in this sense characterizes many of the practices found within an Indigenous ideology of motherhood. In an article about the distinct nature of mothering among Native women and women of colour, Patricia Hill Collins has identified "two problematic assumptions" of centering motherhood theories on white, middle-class women. She states:

> The first [assumption] is that a relative degree of economic security exists for mothers and their children. The second is that all women enjoy the racial privilege that allows them to see themselves primarily as individuals in search of personal autonomy, instead of members of a racial ethnic group struggling for power. (1994: 48)

The section on collectivism has explored how economic insecurity and marginality can prevent Native from adopting a mothering that is grounded in western liberal notions of the autonomous self. This section explores how Native women engage in mothering by seeking a freedom for self that is inherently connected to resistance and recovery efforts for the family, community and nation. Indigenous ideologies of motherhood involve establishing freedom from external control in the wake of a colonial history.

It is important to first examine what "freedom from external control" meant in traditional Native mothering practices and ideologies. Collins has identified "the struggle to control their own bodies and to preserve choice over whether to become mothers at all" as a key component in racial ethnic women's struggle for "maternal empowerment" (1994: 53). Native women can refer to a history in which they had autonomy in this area, as there is evidence that they had the means and allowance to practice birth control and to manage family size and population growth (see Anderson 2003: 178-181). Their sexual practices varied from nation to nation, but Native women generally had much more sexual freedom than their white contemporaries because it was understood that sex was a natural part of women's lives (Anderson 2000a: 85-94). Control over their bodies and mothering practices was also enhanced by extended family and kin structures which protected women from abuse from their male partners. Native mothers were not obliged to stay with the fathers of their children, as divorce was relatively easy (Anderson 82-84). In the case of separation, children typically stayed with the mother, as they were considered to belong to her (Anderson 2000a: 82-84; Noel 81).

The fact that "the welfare of the young [was] paramount" (Allen 3) in traditional societies worked to the advantage of mothers, who were honoured as their first teachers. Mothers held autonomy and authority within the family and community because there was tremendous value placed on how they could influence the upcoming generations. Okanagan writer Jeannette Armstrong relates how mothering was connected to overall governance of the people:

> The role of Aboriginal women in the health of family systems from one generation to the next was one of immense power.... In traditional Aboriginal society, it was woman who shaped the thinking of all its members in a loving, nurturing atmosphere within the base family unit. In such societies, the earliest instruments of governance and law to ensure social order came from quality mothering of children. (viii)

Mothering was also validated as a source of wisdom and power through political systems. Tom Porter has explained how this worked in traditional Mohawk society.

> My grandma and the old leaders at home used to say, "It is the mother who knows her children better than anybody else does." So if you want to get a reference on someone, you go and find that person's mother and ask her what the person is like, because she knows.... So when it comes time to make leaders, they ask the woman, "Who amongst all your sons or nephews is of good quality? Who amongst all of your relatives has the natural goodness to be a chief? The mother will be the one to know, and

that is why in our nation the woman was chosen for this duty. (19)

Porter goes on to explain how women were not only responsible for choosing the chiefs, which they did through discussions of their own councils, but also for removing (dehorning) them if they were not acting in the best interests of the people (17). Among the Carrier, "reproductive roles were central to women's claims to social prominence," and Jo-Anne Fiske notes that women who had mothered well rose to become "influential as family spokespersons" (202). The leadership role and authority of grandmothers was unquestioned in many Native societies. (Anderson 2000a: 119-120).

Colonization involved the denigration of Native womanhood and the implementation of a series of external controls on Native motherhood. One of the first projects was to cast Native women as "bad mothers." As Native mothers came into contact with white "civilization," they were constructed as lax in discipline, dirty, and in need of training (Carter 1997: 161-162; Rutherdale 106). The proposed solution to their inadequate parenting was to contain them within a monogamous, patriarchal, nuclear family unit, in which the husband would be the breadwinner and the Native wife could take up her duties as mother and homemaker.

As discussed previously, residential schools instilled gendered ideals, an experiment which included encouraging residential school graduates to marry each other and get on with the project of raising "civilized" children (Miller). Joan Sangster has written about how Native girls who were considered neglected or "delinquent" were institutionalized in training schools where they learned about western motherhood, housekeeping and wage labour; attitudes and skills that were thought to be lacking in their own families (2005: 186). Other Canadian historians have written about regulation of sexuality among Native girls and women throughout the late nineteenth and twentieth centuries (Brownlie; Barman 2005, 2006; Sangster 2006), the goal of which was to create what Joan Sangster has called "heteronorms characterized by marriage and monogamy, male breadwinning/female domesticity and premarital sexual purity" (2005: 179). "Field matrons" were sent out to instruct Native American women in the ways of the western housewife and mother (Emmerich) and missionaries took on a primary role in instilling practices of conjugality and domesticity (Perry). Myra Rutherdale's work on women missionaries in northern Canada demonstrates a paternalistic maternalism in their work. These missionaries assumed the superiority of "white" motherhood, infantilized Native peoples, and "mothered" the Native women and girls they encountered by trying to reshape them as the guardians of Christian morality.

For all the training they received in white motherhood, Native women were still prohibited from mothering (and grandmothering) their own children. The residential school system in Canada operated between 1879 and 1996, expanding greatly after 1910 to the point where by 1930 almost 75 percent of Native children were in residential schools (Foumier and Crey 61). This system greatly disrupted traditional parenting techniques, breaking the intergenerational ties of parenting and education between parents, grandparents and children (Ing). Native girls (and boys) who went to residential school later found themselves at a loss for parenting skills, having had no time with role models in their own families and communities. Following on the heels of the residential school system, the child welfare system began to remove Native children from their families and communities in staggering numbers in what has come to be known (in Canada) as the [1960s] "Sixties Scoop."[12] Within a few decades, "one in four status Indian children could be expected to be separated from his or her parents for all or part of childhood," a figure that rises to one in three if non-status and Métis children are included (Fournier and Crey 88). Even though Native children represented less than four percent of the population, by the early 1980s they made up 50, 60, and 70 per cent of the child welfare caseloads in the provinces of Alberta, Manitoba and Saskatchewan respectively (Bennett and Blackstock 23). The child welfare system continues to exert tremendous control over Native mothers, with one in ten status Indian children in care in three sample provinces in Canada (First Nations and Family Caring Society 7).

Through the 1876 *Indian Act*, the Canadian state played a further role in severing women from community connections that were key to mothering. The *Act* decreed that women who married non-Native men lost their Indian status and the rights that went along with it. This included losing the right to live on their home communities. By cutting the ties to their home communities, the Act made Native women dependent on their spouses and "without recourse in the event of domestic violence, divorce or widowhood" (Lavell-Harvard and Lavell 187). Native women who married status Indian men also lost rights to live in their home communities, an edict which prevented them from the nurturing and protection of their own kin. Jeannette Corbiere Lavell explains:

> They separated us from our communities and also made it difficult, if not impossible, for us to raise our own children in our communities where they would have the benefit of close contact with our parents and extended family, and our traditional culture. (Lavell-Harvard and Lavell 189)

Because the *Indian Act* also granted Indian status to white women who married Native men, it supplanted Native women with white women who could then assume their roles as "mothers of the nations." Mi'kmaw film-maker Cathy Martin frames this as a deliberate colonial act that was an attack on the authority and roles held by Native mothers. She states:

> In order to break down and destroy a culture, you have to get to the root of it. The heart of Aboriginal cultures is the women, as givers of life. So it makes sense to start making policies that would banish the women, the givers of language, culture and life. They are the ones who

bring Native children into this world and teach them their way. It made sense to make a policy so that white women could come in and take over that role and start teaching the white ways. This was a form of cultural genocide. (qtd. in Anderson 2000a: 70)

After disrupting traditional parenting systems and removing children, the state had another solution to breaking down and controlling motherhood: eliminate it altogether. Various studies have shown that between twenty-five and fifty percent of Native American women were involuntarily sterilized while they were in the hospital to have children between the years of 1970 and 1976 (Torpy; Lawrence; Smith). This work was done under the auspices of Indian Health Services in the United States. To my knowledge, this travesty has not yet been documented in Canada, although I am personally aware of a number of Native women who underwent involuntary sterilization in Canada during this period. More work is also needed to determine the impact of the early twentieth century eugenics movement on Native motherhood.[13]

This history of "external controls" on Indigenous motherhood has framed the sovereigntist agenda within Indigenous ideologies of motherhood. At the most fundamental level, birthing children can be seen as an act of sovereignty in and of itself. Writing about Native women's "motherwork," Lisa Udel has argued:

> Given the history of the IHS campaign to curtail Native women's repro-ductive capacity and thus Native populations, Native women emphasize women's ability, sometimes "privilege," to bear children. Within this paradigm, they argue, Native women's procreative capability becomes a powerful tool to combat Western genocide. Motherhood recovered, along with the tribal responsibility to nurture their children in a tradi-tional manner without non-Indigenous interference, assumes a powerful political meaning when viewed in this way. (47)

For some Native mothers, giving birth has set in motion the beginning of an intergenerational process of reclamation and recovery. This process often begins with a reclaiming of the "Indigenous self" by seeking out culture-based knowledge and practices. Margo Greenwood and Sarah de Leeuw have written about the success of parenting programs that "foster Indigeneity" in Native mothers (179). They argue that culture-based programs such as Aboriginal Head Start may be one of the best avenues for diminishing state incursions (like child welfare) into the lives of Native mothers (Arnott 97-98). Joanne Arnott's description of the "traditional parenting" program activities she participated in demonstrate how indigeneity is central to the recovery of empowered motherhood:

> We spoke of our lives. We learned to drum. We studied the medicine wheel, and we learned to sing. We heard traditional stories, and we learned how to dance them. We visited the museums, at the university,

to examine our people's clothes, and we learned how to sew. (97-98)

Arnott describes a collectivist project of building networks of women who are then "driven toward action, toward helping one another by sharing our knowledge and experience, toward becoming a helping force in our own lives, families and communities" (98).

Anishnaabe scholar Leanne Simpson has written about how re-introducing Native traditions of pregnancy, birth and mothering can lead Native children to "rise up and rebel against colonialism in all its forms, to dream independence, to dance to nationhood" (32). Simpson refers to Mohawk midwife Katsi Cook's assertion, "that the production and reproduction of human beings is integral to sovereignty and that this sovereignty falls in the domain of the female universe" (29). She writes:

> When I became pregnant with my first child, my dreams of liberation, of freedom, of self-determination and of nationhood, became stronger and more urgent. My pregnancies and the subsequent births of my children were opportunities to put the politics of liberation into practice by challenging the contemporary western medicalization of pregnancy and birth and by grounding my process in the knowledge of Anishinaabegweg (Anishinaabe women). Pregnancy became a way of linking self-determination with the self-determination in the Anishinaabeg Nation and the responsibilities of women in re-building Indigenous nations. As I began to understand the power of the physical process of birth and re-birthing, it became clear to me that the responsibilities of Indigenous women as life-givers, as transformers, and as vitalizers are responsibilities Anishinaabewekeg have to our nation whether or not we physically give birth. (27)

Simpson makes the connection between biological mothering and the way in which mothering figures as a metaphor for women's roles and responsibilities in the community at large. The larger sense of mothering translates to a sense of authority that all women have for the people, by virtue of being "life-givers."

The application of lifegiver status and responsibilities does not have anything to do with whether women give birth or not. As Anishinaabe scholar Renée Elizabeth Mzinegiizhigo-Kwe Bédard has stated, "Being a mother is about family, spirituality, relationships" (74). I have interviewed many non-biological mothers who understand their activism and leadership roles within this ideology of motherhood, who see women's responsibility to "all of the people" stemming from their lifegiving capacity. One such woman told me, "I've approached my work as somebody who really wants to see the community heal and recover.... I haven't had any children, by choice, really. I sort of feel like I had a big family to look after" (see Nahwegahbow qtd. in Anderson 2000a: 173). Leadership and vision, thus, come from this ideological positioning of women as mothers.

According to Cree Judge Mary Ellen Turpel, "It is women who give birth both in the physical and in the spiritual sense to the social, political and cultural life of the community."

Contemporary leaders and community members alike are known to equate motherhood with women's leadership. In her work on women chiefs, Cora Voyageur has reported that female chiefs are expected to be "more motherly, gentler and more humanitarian in their policies and decision-making" (241). In my own study of twelve women chiefs across Canada, half of them talked about women's leadership styles in terms of motherhood.[14] Joanne Fiske (1992) has also written extensively about the application of an ideology of mothering in formal and informal politics. In her work on the Carrier, Fiske notes that public leadership emerges from domestic authority, as senior women in the community take responsibility for the resources and well-being of the younger generations through kinship networks, voluntary associations and community service work (211). She demonstrates how Carrier women "look to the past for guiding ideals and role models" including matrilineal society where there are biological mothers, clan mothers and community mothers "who teach us to look after our people" (Fiske 1992: 210). Traditional Carrier cosmology, involving "the old woman" is also central to this model of women's leadership (213).

While Fiske shows that the ideology of motherhood can be effective at the local level, her work demonstrates that this ideology is often less effective at the tribal or national level. Fiske reports that Carrier Sekani Tribal Council discussions related to Bill-C31 and citizenship did not include discussions of "the future of womanhood" or the "ideological formulation of motherhood" (Fiske 1993: 27). In her studies of the national political application of traditional motherhood, Fiske notes the shift between "rights" and (traditional) "responsibilities" discourses. She points out that the Native women's movement began as a "legal rights discourse" entitled "Indian Rights for Indian Women (Fiske 1993: 24). The primary goal of this movement was to re-instate Indian women, yet as tensions grew with the male dominated political organizations, the "rights" discourse shifted to a "moral/cultural discourse that embraced notions of traditional motherhood" (Fiske 1993: 24). Fiske argues that this shift was intended to distance Native women's political activism from western individualism and feminism; to frame their activism, rather, as a collectivist strategy in the interests of the nation (1996: 71). When the Native Women's Association of Canada (NWAC) was shut out of the 1992 constitutional talks, however, they took their case to court, arguing that their individual and collective rights had been violated. Fiske sees the return to a legal rights discourse as the failure of the traditional motherhood discourse, arguing that "[women's] leadership imagines a neo-traditional community for which essentialist womanhood stands as a metaphor, [while] male leadership's goals emulate the masculinist state" (1996: 72).

Fiske's work demonstrates that the Indigenous motherhood discourse does not carry the same political weight it once had. Nonetheless, Native women continue to call on this discourse to support their activism. The Native Women's Association of Canada today promotes themselves as the "grandmother's lodge," and still calls on roles of motherhood to define their purpose. In formal and informal organizations, Native women ground themselves in Indigenous ideologies of motherhood to signify their authority as leaders of change. They posit that this discourse does not distance them from men or community, from past or future, from spirit or material worlds because it is the about being connected to "all our relations" and the responsibilities we have to them.

Conclusion

Indigenous ideologies of motherhood are distinct from patriarchal western models of motherhood, and this means that strategies for empowered mothering are also distinct. Rather than seeking to break gendered patterns of family dynamics, Native women may seek to re-introduce gendered roles and responsibilities that come from a time when Native motherhood signified authority. Native mothers do not necessarily seek their status as autonomous individuals, and Native youth may not feel the need to individuate by separating from the maternal authority of their mothers, aunties, and grandmas.[15] Native mothers can seek out the benefits of fulfilling their roles in interdependent communities that value care-giving and the wisdom that comes with it.

Perhaps the most important part of the Indigenous ideology of motherhood equation, and the most neglected (even in this paper), is the interdependent nature of mothering. Patricia Hill Collins has cautioned against what can happen to Black mothers who are expected to carry their communities, stating:

> …[mother]work often extracts a high cost for large numbers of women. There is loss of individual autonomy and there is submersion of individual growth for the benefit of the group. While this dimension of motherwork remains essential, the question of women doing more than their fair share of such work for individual and community development merits open debate. (1994: 50)

Taken uncritically, ideologies of Native mothering run the risk of heaping more responsibility on already overburdened mothers. With so many Native mothers struggling to raise their children in poverty or in situations of abuse or neglect, we must question the logic of asking mothers to "carry the nations."

Indigenous ideologies of mothering might rightly be accused of creating "intensive mothering," Indian-style, if we are not careful to remember some of the fundamental principles involved. Reciprocity and "the complementary nature of all life forms"[16] are key. We must ask ourselves: Where are the men? Where are the communities? Where is nation and where is the state? And—not to forget—where are the children? What are all of these parties providing for mothers and mothering women as they work through their onerous duties? As noted earlier, Indigenous philosophies about Mother Earth warn against an endless taking from her; this is simply not sustainable. Perhaps the next step in exploring Indigenous ideologies of motherhood could be mapping out the "roles and responsibilities" of the relations that surround Native mothers as we cycle into the next stage of renewal.

Notes

[1] There are many terms used to describe the Indigenous peoples of North America, including Native, Native American, Indian, Indigenous, Aboriginal, First Nations, Métis and Inuit, and so on. I will use "Native" here as it is a term widely used at the grass roots level and something which can be applied to Indigenous peoples in Canada and the United States.

[2] As employed by Rich (34).

[3] I have used Indigenous in this instance to refer to first peoples in a broader international context, as the collectivist, spiritual and sovereign elements of motherhood are evident among Indigenous peoples outside of North America as well. See Brenda F. McGadney-Douglass, Nana Araba Apt and Richard L. Douglass, "Back to Basics: Mothering and Grandmothering in the Context of Urban Ghana," in D. Memee Lavell and Jeannette Corbiere Lavell, Eds., *Until Our Hearts Are On the Ground: Aboriginal Mothering, Oppression, Resistance and Rebirth*, (Toronto: Demeter Press, 2006), pp. 105-124.

[3] I use "traditional" in this paper to refer to culture-based values, worldviews and practices that are have their roots in pre-contact life ways of Indigenous peoples.

[4] Native women often use the term "auntie" to describe what Black women refer to as "othermothers." That is to say, women who assist in raising those who are younger than them by nurturing and teaching (see Collins 1991: 119; James 45; and Jenkins 206).

[5] For a good Canadian historiography of family that considers the family dynamic in relation to capitalism, see Comacchio. For a concise overview of the changing historical constructions of childrearing and motherhood, see Hays (19-50).

[6] For a thorough look at the roles and authorities of Iroquois women, see Mann.

[7] For an overview of how the Canadian state foiled Native farming economies, see Carter (1990).

[8] I am currently involved with a committee at Statistics Canada that has developed a national Aboriginal Children's Survey, in which we explore relationships and child care arrangements, including the role of extended family. The forthcoming data will give us abundant information about Aboriginal parenting practices (see also Schweitzer).

[9] McGadney-Douglass *et al.* discuss the impact of urbanization and dislocation, the scattering of kin, commoditization of labour, and breakdown of community sanctions as part of the colonization of Aboriginal motherhood worldwide (110-111).

[10] See the much quoted teachings of Anishnaabe Elder Art Solomon in *Songs for the People: Teachings on the Natural Way* (34-35).

[11] See the teachings of Dakota Sioux Elder Eva McKay in *In the Words of Elders: Aboriginal Cultures in Transition* (Kulchyski, McCaskill and Newhouse 296).

[12]For an example of this, see Anderson (2000b).

[12]A term originally used by Patrick Johnson in *Native Children and the Child Welfare System.*

[13]Angus McLaren offers an excellent reality check to the myth that Canada was "spared the virulent racism and class consciousness" of the United States and Britain (9), but there is little attention to how Native mothers were targeted in the eugenics movement, which surely they were.

[14]Forthcoming in an anthology entitled, *First Nations Women's Contributions to Culture and Community* (Stout and Valaskakis).

[15]For some of the major theoretical work on the western need to break from maternal authority and simulate the autonomous male, see Ruddick; Chodorow.

[16]As quoted from Paula Gunn Allen at the beginning of this paper.

References

Albers, Patricia C. "Sioux Women in Transition: A Study of Their Changing Status in Domestic and Capitalist Sectors of Production." *The Hidden Half: Studies in Plains Indian Women.* Eds. Patricia Albers and Beatrice Medicine. Lanham, MD: University Press of America, Inc. 175-234.

Allen, Paula Gunn. *The Sacred Hoop: Recovering the Feminine in American Indian Tradition.* Boston: Beacon Press, 1986.

Anderson, Kim. *A Recognition of Being: Reconstructing Native Womanhood.* Toronto: Sumach Press, 2000.

Anderson, Kim. "Honouring the Blood of the People: Berry Fasting in the Twenty-First Century." *Expressions in Canadian Native Studies.* Eds. Ron F. Laliberte *et. al.* Saskatoon, SK: University of Saksatchewan Extension Press, 2000. 374-394.

Anderson, Kim. "Vital Signs: Reading Colonialism in Contemporary Adolescent Family Planning." *Strong Women Stories: Native Vision and Community Survival.* Eds. Kim Anderson and Bonita Lawrence. Toronto: Sumach Press, 2003: 173-190.

Apple, Rima D. and Janet Golden, eds. *Mothers and Motherhood: Readings in American History.* Columbus: Ohio State University Press, 1997.

Armstrong, Jeannette. "Invocation: The Real Power of Aboriginal Women." *Women of the First Nations: Power, Wisdom, Strength.* Eds. Christine Miller and Patricia Chuchryk. Winnipeg: The University of Manitoba Press, 1996. viiii-xii.

Arnott, Joanne. "Dances With Cougar: Learning from Traditional Parenting Skills Programs." *Until Our Hearts Are On the Ground": Aboriginal Mothering, Oppression, Resistance and Rebirth.* Eds. D. Memee Lavell-Harvard and Jeannette Corbiere Lavell. Toronto: Demeter Press, 2006. 94-104.

Barman, Jean. "Aboriginal Women on the Streets of Victoria: Rethinking Transgressive Sexuality During the Colonial Encounter." *Contact Zones: Aboriginal and Settler Women in Canada's Colonial Past.* Eds. Katie Pickles and Myra Rutherdale. Vancouver: University of British Columbia Press, 2005. 205-227.

Barman, Jean. "Taming Aboriginal Sexuality: Gender, Power and Race in British Columbia, 1850-1900." *In the Days of Our Grandmothers: A Reader in Aboriginal Women's History in Canada.* Eds. Mary-Ellen Kelm and Lorna Townsend. Toronto: University of Toronto Press, 2006.

Bedard, Renée Elizabeth Mzinegiizhigo-Kwe, "An Anishinaabe-kwe Ideology on Mothering and Motherhood." *"Until Our Hearts Are On the Ground": Aboriginal Mothering, Oppression, Resistance and Rebirth.* Eds. D. Memee Lavell-Harvard and Jeannette Corbiere Lavell. Toronto: Demeter Press, 2006. 65-75.

Bennett, Marlyn and Cindy Blackstock. *A Literature Review and Annotated Bibliography Focusing on Aspects of Aboriginal Child Welfare in Canada.* Winnipeg: First Nations Child and Family Caring Society, 1992.

Bradbury, Bettina. *Working Families: Age, Gender and Daily Survival in Industrializing Montreal.* Toronto: McClelland and Stewart, 1993.

Brownlie, Robin Jarvis. "Intimate Surveillance: Indian Affairs, Colonization, and the Regulation of Aboriginal Women's Sexuality." In Katie Pickles and Myra Rutherdale, Eds., *Contact Zones: Aboriginal and Settler Women in Canada's Colonial Past.* Vancouver: University of British Columbia Press, 2005. 160-178.

Carter, Sarah. *Lost Harvests: Prairie Indian Reserve Farmers and Government Policy.* Montreal and Kingston: McGill-Queen's University Press, 1990.

Carter, Sarah. *Capturing Women: The Manipulation of Cultural Imagery in Canada's Prairie West.* Montreal: McGill-Queen's University Press, 1997.

Chodorow, Nancy. *The Reproduction of Mothering: Psychoanalysis and the Sociology of Gender.* Berkeley: University of California Press, 1978.

Collins, Patricia Hill. *Black Feminist Thought: Knowledge, Consciousness, and the Politics of Empowerment.* New York: Routledge, 1991.

Collins, Patricia Hill. "Shifting the Center: Race, Class, and Feminist Theorizing About Motherhood." *Mothering: Ideology, Experience, and Agency.* Eds. Evelyn Nakano Glenn, Grace Chang and Linda Rennie Forcey. New York: Routledge, 1994. 45-65.

Comacchio, Cynthia. "'Beneath the 'Sentimental Veil': Families and Family History in Canada." *Labour/Le Travail* 33 (Spring 1994): 279-302.

Couchie, Carole and Herbert Nabigon. "A Path Towards Reclaiming Nishnawbe Birth Culture: Can the Midwifery Exemption Clause for Aboriginal Midwives Make a Difference?" *The New Midwifery: Reflections on Renaissance and Regulation.* Ed. Farah M. Shroff. Toronto: Women's Press, 1997: 41-50.

Emmerich, Lisa. "Right in the Midst of My Own People: Native American Women and the Field Matron Program." *American Indian Quarterly,* 15 (2) (1991): 201-216.

Engels, Frederick. *The Origin of the Family, Private Property and the State.* 1884. Intro. Eleanor Burke Leacock. New York: International Publishers, 1972.

Ermine, Willie. "Aboriginal Epistemology." *First Nations Education in Canada: The Circle Unfolds.* Eds. Marie Battiste and Jean Barman. Vancouver: University of British Columbia Press, 1995. 101-112.

First Nations Child and Family Caring Society. *Wen:de – The Journey Continues:*

The National Policy Review of First Nations Child and Family Services Research Projects: Phase Three. Winnipeg: Author, 2005.

Fiske, Jo-Anne. "Carrier Women and the Politics of Mothering." *British Columbia Reconsidered: Essays on Women.* Eds. Gillian Creese and Veronica Strong-Boag. Vancouver: Press Gang Publishers, 1992. 198-216.

Fiske, Jo-Anne. "Child of the State, Mother of the Nation: Aboriginal Women and the Ideology of Motherhood." *Culture* 13 (1) (1993): 17-35.

Fiske, Jo-Anne. "The Womb is to the Nation as the Heart is to the Body: Ethnopolitical Discourses of the Canadian Indigenous Women's Movement." *Studies in Political Economy* 51 (Fall 1996): 65-95.

Fournier, Suzanne and Ernie Crey. *Stolen From Our Embrace: The Abduction of First Nations Children and the Restoration of Aboriginal Communities.* Vancouver: Douglas and McIntyre, 1997.

Fox, Bonnie. *Hidden in the Household: Women's Domestic Labour Under Capitalism.* Toronto: The Women's Press, 1980.

Glenn, Evelyn Nakano. "Racial Ethnic Women's Labour: The Intersection of Race, Gender and Class Oppression." *Review of Radical Political Economics*, 17 (3) (1985): 86-108.

Greenwood, Margo and Sarah DeLeeuw. "Fostering Indigeneity: The Role of Aboriginal Mothers and Aboriginal Early Child Care in Responses to Colonial Foster-Care Interventions." *"Until Our Hearts Are On the Ground": Aboriginal Mothering, Oppression, Resistance and Rebirth.* Eds. D. Memee Lavell-Harvard and Jeannette Corbiere Lavell. Toronto: Demeter Press, 2006: 173-183.

Hays, Sharon. *The Cultural Contradictions of Motherhood.* New Haven: Yale University Press, 1996.

Hull, J. *Aboriginal Single Mothers in Canada, 1996: A Statistical Profile*, Ottawa: Minister of Public Works and Government Services Canada, 2001.

Ing, Rosalyn. "Canada's Indian Residential Schools and Their Impacts on Mothering." *"Until Our Hearts Are On the Ground": Aboriginal Mothering, Oppression, Resistance and Rebirth.* Eds. D. Memee Lavell-Harvard and Jeannette Corbiere Lavell. Toronto: Demeter Press, 2006. 157-172.

Jaimes, M. Annette and Theresa Halsey. "American Indian Women at the Centre of Indigenous Resistance in Contemporary North America." *The State of Native America: Genocide, Colonization and Resistance.* Ed. M. Annette Jaimes. Boston: South End Press, 1992. 311-344.

James, Stanlie M. "Mothering: A Possible Black Feminist Link to Social Transformation." *Theorizing Black Feminism: The Visionary Pragmatism of Black Women.* Eds. Stanlie M. James and A. P. Busia. New York: Routledge, 1999. 44-54.

Jenkins, Nina. "Black Women and the Meaning of Motherhood." *Redefining Motherhood: Changing Identities and Patterns.* Eds. Andrea O'Reilly and Sharon Abbey. Toronto: Second Story Press, 1998. 201-213.

Johnson, Patrick. *Native Children and the Child Welfare System.* Ottawa: Canadian Council on Social Development, 1983.

Koebel, Jaime. "Explanation of Artwork." *Atlantis: A Women's Studies Journal/Revue d'etudes sure les femmes* 29 (2) (Spring 2005): i.

Kulchyski, Peter, Don McCaskill and David Newhouse, eds. *In the Words of Elders: Aboriginal Cultures in Transition.* Toronto: University of Toronto Press, 1999.

"Until Our Hearts Are On the Ground": Aboriginal Mothering, Oppression, Resistance and Rebirth. Eds. D. Memee Lavell-Harvard and Jeannette Corbiere Lavell. Toronto: Demeter Press, 2006.

Lawrence, Jane E. "The Indian Health Service and the Sterilization of Native American Women." *American Indian Quarterly* 24 (3): 2000: 400-419.

Little Bear, Leroy. "Jagged Worldviews Colliding." *Reclaiming Indigenous Voice and Vision.* Ed. Marie Battiste. Vancouver: University of British Columbia Press, 2000. 77-85.

Lutz, John. "Gender and Work in Lekwammen Families, 1843-1970." *In the Days of Our Grandmothers: A Reader in Aboriginal Women's History in Canada.* Eds. Mary-Ellen Kelm and Lorna Townsend. Toronto: University of Toronto Press, 2006: 216-250.

Luxton, Meg. *More Than a Labour of Love: Three Generations of Women's Work in the Home.* Toronto: The Women's Press, 1980.

Mann, Barbara Alice. *Iroquoian Women: The Gantowisas.* New York: Peter Lang, 2000.

McGadney-Douglass, Brenda F., Nana Araba Apt, and Richard L. Douglass. "Back to Basics: Mothering and Grandmothering in the Context of Urban Ghana." *"Until Our Hearts Are On the Ground": Aboriginal Mothering, Oppression, Resistance and Rebirth.* Eds. D. Memee Lavell-Harvard and Jeannette Corbiere Lavell. Toronto: Demeter Press, 2006: 105-124.

McLaren, Angus. *Our Own Master Race: Eugenics in Canada, 1885-1945.* Toronto: McLelland and Stewart, 1990.

Miller, J.R. *Shingwauk's Vision: A History of Native Residential Schools.* (Toronto: University of Toronto Press, 1996).

O'Reilley, Andrea, ed. *From Motherhood to Mothering: The Legacy of Adrienne Rich's Of Woman Born.* Albany: State University of New York Press, 2004.

Paper, Jordan. "Through the Earth Darkly: The Female Spirit in Native American Religions." *Religion in Native North America.* Ed. Christopher Vecsey. Moscow, ID: University of Idaho Press, 1990: 3-19.

Perry, Adele. "Metropolitan Knowledge, Colonial Practice, and Indigenous Womanhood: Missions in Nineteenth-Century British Columbia." *Contact Zones: Aboriginal and Settler Women in Canada's Colonial Past.* Eds. Katie Pickles and Myra Rutherdale. Vancouver: University of British Columbia Press, 2005. 109-130.

Porter, Tom. "Traditions of the Constitution of the Six Nations." *Pathways to Self-Determination: Canadian Indians and the Canadian State.* Eds. Leroy Little Bear, Menno Boldt and J. Anthony Long. Toronto: University of Toronto Press, 1984. 14-21.

Rich Adrienne. *Of Woman Born: Motherhood as Experience and Institution.* New York: W. W. Norton and Company, Inc., 1986.

Roach Pierson, Ruth, Andrée Lévesque, and Katherine Arnup, eds. *Delivering Motherhood: Maternal Ideologies and Practices in the 19th and 20th Centuries.* New York: Routledge, 1990.

Ruddick, Sara. *Maternal Thinking: Toward a Politics of Peace.* Boston: Beacon Press, 1989.

Rutherdale, Myra. *Women and the White Man's God: Gender and Race in the Canadian Mission Field.* Vancouver: University of British Columbia Press, 2002.

Sangster, Joan. "Native Women, Sexuality and the Law." *In the Days of Our Grandmothers: A Reader in Aboriginal Women's History in Canada.* Eds. Mary-Ellen Kelm and Lorna Townsend. Toronto: University of Toronto Press, 2006. 301-335.

Sangster, Joan. "Domesticating Girls: The Sexual Regulation of Aboriginal and Working-Class Girls in Twentieth-Century Canada." *Contact Zones: Aboriginal and Settler Women in Canada's Colonial Past.* Eds. Katie Pickles and Myra Rutherdale. Vancouver: University of British Columbia Press, 2006. 179-201.

Schweitzer, Marjorie Marjorie M. Schweitzer, ed. *American Indian Grandmothers: Traditions and Transitions.* Albuquerque: University of New Mexico Press, 1999.

Simpson, Leanne. "Birthing and Indigenous Resurgence: Decolonizing Our Pregnancy and Birthing Ceremonies." *"Until Our Hearts Are On the Ground": Aboriginal Mothering, Oppression, Resistance and Rebirth.* Toronto: Eds. D. Memee Lavell-Harvard and Jeannette Corbiere Lavell. Demeter Press, 2006: 25-33.

Smith, Andrea. *Conquest: Sexual Violence and American Indian Genocide.* Cambridge: South End Press, 2005.

Solomon, Arthur. *Songs for the People: Teachings on the Natural Way.* Toronto: New Canadian Publications, 1990.

Torpy, Sally J. "Native American Women and Coerced Sterilization: On the Trail of Tears in the 1970s." *American Indian Culture and Research Journal* 24 (2) (2000): 1-22.

Turpel, Mary-Ellen. "Patriarchy and Paternalism: The Legacy of the Canadian State for First Nations Women." *Canadian Journal of Women and the Law* 6: 174-192.

Udel, Lisa J. "Revision and Resistance: The Politics of Native Women's Motherwork." *Frontiers* 22 (2) (2001): 43-62.

Voyageur, Cora J. "The Community Owns You: Experiences of Female Chiefs in Canada." *Out of the Ivory Tower: Feminist Research for Social Change.* Eds. Andrea Martinez and Meryn Elisabeth Stuart. Toronto: Sumach Press, 2003. 228-247.

Watson-Franke, Maria-Barbara. "'We Have Mama but No Papa': Motherhood in Women-Centered Societies." *From Motherhood to Mothering: The Legacy of Adrienne Rich's* Of Woman Born. Ed. Andrea O'Reilly. Albany: State University of New York Press, 2004. 75-87.

Whitty-Rogers Joanne, Josephine Etowa, and Joan Evans. "Becoming and Aboriginal Mother: Childbirth Experiences of Women from one Mi'kmaq Community in Nova Scotia." *"Until Our Hearts Are On the Ground": Aboriginal Mothering, Oppression, Resistance and Rebirth.* Eds. D. Memee Lavell-Harvard and Jeannette

Chapter 47

Resisting, But Not Too Much

Interrogating the Paradox of Natural Mothering

CHRIS BOBEL

RECENTLY, I INVITED a local breastfeeding advocate and La Leche League leader named Mary Beth[1] to my "Gender and the Body" class. She framed her talk around "the many obstacles to making breastfeeding work in contemporary western society." Mary Beth promoted constant mother-baby togetherness and the rejection of the shiny new gadgets that new parents are expected to acquire whether they can afford them or not, and made a compelling feminist argument for keeping baby close. Women can and should trust their bodies to nourish their babies, she said. Say no to the male dominated medical establishment. Say no to patriarchal constructions of the sexualized breast. Take it back. And she was effective. As Mary Beth presented her argument, I watched my students process the information. One student caught my attention, angst evident on her face. During the lively Q an A she finally burst out with the following:

> I'm really struggling with this…. On the one hand, I am trying to fight oppression and claim my place in society, get recognized in the work force, you know get liberated. But now you are telling me that to be really free, I should go back home and take care of babies, breastfeeding them all the time. And it does sound really great. But I feel stuck. I don't know what I am supposed to do!

As she spoke, I nodded knowingly. This dilemma haunts many feminists as they struggle to define and shape their lives and is the knot at the center of feminist mothering scholarship. Mothering scholar and sociologist Evelyn Nakano Glenn pointed to the conflict between feminists who regard maternally-derived gender differences as oppressive and those who reclaim motherhood as a source of power and status when she wrote:

> We are reluctant to give up the idea that motherhood is special. Pregnancy, birth, and breast-feeding are such powerful bodily experiences, and the emotional attachment to the infant so intense, that it is difficult for women who have gone through these experiences and emotions to

think that they do not constitute unique female experiences that create an unbridgeable gap between men and women (22-23).

My aim in this chapter is to respond to this dilemma by looking closely at the kind of attached mothering practice that Mary Beth advocates as an expression of feminism.

Mary Beth is part of an emerging social movement of women I call "natural mothers." The natural mothers give birth to their babies at home; they homeschool; they grow much of their family's produce, and sew many of their clothes. The natural mothers seem, at first glance, an anachronism, recalling a time when some women derived their identities from raising families and excelling at the domestic arts. While their contemporaries negotiate daycare, babysitters, and bottle-feeding, the natural mothers reject almost everything that facilitates mother-child separation. They believe that consumerism, technology, and detachment from nature are social ills that mothers can and should oppose.

The natural mothers constitute a counterculture that enacts a particular form of activism, a kind of "everyday activism," to use Baumgardner and Richards' term or what New Social Movements scholars increasingly find in contemporary social movements—a focus on the day to day content of personal lives, linked with issues of identity rather than economic grievances characteristic of, for example, working class movements (see Johnston, Larana, and Gusfield). Natural mothers, working at the level of the individual and the familiar, seek to change culture one family at a time. But what is natural mothering's promise for social change? Does this particular kind of mothering trap or liberate women?

Getting to Know Natural Mothering

In the mid 1990s, I grew to know several small intersecting communities of natural mothers. I spent over two years in the field—participating in playgroups with my toddler and attending La Leche League meetings (the international breastfeeding support organization). I joined a food coop and "Creating Stronger Families (CSF)," an association of those who chose home-schooling, homebirth, and other parenting alternatives. CSF met for monthly potlucks and "working bees" in which members assisted the host family with a house project, and held an annual weekend conference that drew families throughout the Midwest. Later, I interviewed 32 natural mothers I met during the course of my fieldwork. Through these observations and interviews, I learned that Natural Mothering merges two lifestyle practices—Voluntary Simplicity and Attachment Parenting—while taking inspiration from Cultural Feminism.

Consciously anti-materialist and anti-consumerist, Voluntary Simplicity promotes a life freed from, as one of my informants put it, "biggering and bettering."

Voluntary Simplicity, also called Simple Living, dictates a lifestyle that derives meaning from relative austerity, minimized consumption and the belief that individual well being is entangled with the well being of society at large (Longacre). Proponents of this lifestyle reject material preoccupations and opt for recycling, and in some cases, bartering and trading in place of traditional market exchange. They seek meaning in "doing it oneself," freed from the constraints of institutions and experts.

The practice of Attachment Parenting (AP), which is related to Voluntary Simplicity, addresses the concerns of parents who seek to depart from what they believe is the norm in a changing, alienating, and child-decentered culture. Family practice physician William Sears, together with his wife Martha Sears, R.N., popularized AP in their 30 books on pregnancy, birth, infancy, toddlerhood, discipline and nighttime parenting, beginning with *The Baby Book* in 1993. Now, the Sears are joined by their two oldest sons (also pediatricians) who characterize AP as "just doing what comes naturally" (http://www.askdrsears.com/faq/ap2.asp). AP, the Sears argue, is the best way to create and maintain a bond with your children. AP facilitates healthy physical, spiritual, emotional and moral child development by placing a premium on extensive mother-child physical contact: "This style is a way of caring that brings out best in parents and their babies (1993: 2), they say. The Sears acknowledge that AP is not new, but simply "common sense parenting we all would do if left to our own healthy resources" (2).[2] Notably, while the practice is called Attachment *Parenting* and not mothering, this terminology is misleading. On the popular website AskDrSears.com, it is stated that "for the first year or two, a child is primarily bonded to his mother" and AP practices inscribe and support this bond. Mothers are attached to children and fathers and other potential caregivers operate merely in supporting roles.

Finally, as a movement that celebrates, rather than denigrates gendered qualities of nurturance and care, Natural Mothering is inspired by cultural feminism's unapologetic reclamation of domesticity and maternity. Cultural feminism, derived from Radical Feminist Theory, is also known as feminine feminism, domestic feminism, and difference feminism. It differs from more popular liberal feminist theory which regards essentialism as the source of women's subordination. Cultural feminist theory, on the contrary, names the devaluing of women's essential differences (whether biologically derived or culturally constructed) as problematic and at the root of sexism. Cultural feminists believe that women have developed their unique social orientation in the context of the domestic sphere, especially through the practice of mothering, as Nancy Chodorow famously argued. Creating a climate that celebrates rather than denigrates difference is the aim of cultural feminists. Natural mothering is seen as a concrete expression of this conceptualization. Nearly 50 percent of the natural mothers I studied explicitly identified as feminists; others expressed ideas compatible with feminist politics but did not call themselves feminists. Many of the mothers expressed frustration with a particular kind of feminism (typically seen as *the* feminism) which they saw as dictating that working outside the home was a measure of a woman's worth; they preferred a feminism that foregrounded their identity as women and resisted male standards. For example, as natural mother Grace Burton stated:

> I feel that the women's movement of the 1960s robbed me of something.
> It did get me more pay in the workplace, and I don't mind that, but they
> also made me be in the workplace, and I mind that immensely.

In short, natural mothering is cultural feminist theory in practice.

So how does Natural Mothering, the product of these practices and ideologies, make sense of itself? In short, I argue that Natural Mothering is ultimately paradoxical. While it resists both technology and capitalism, it stops short of resisting patriarchy. Natural mothers accept the category 'woman' as it is socially constructed and fail to acknowledge the privilege necessary to enact their lifestyle. Thus, natural mothering's promise as a project of recreating motherhood, and by extension, society at large, is compromised (Bobel). Because it lacks a comprehensive and honest self-critique, its criticism of the institutions it resists is evaporated and its message is left open to co-optation.

Interrogating the Paradox

This paradox demands a closer look. I found it expressed in the form of two key contradictions that each create a distinctive theoretical tension. The first contradiction centers on *choice*. The natural mothers spoke of a conscious and intentional decision to mother naturally, consistent with their identities as feminists and everyday activists for social change. One informant, whom I call Michelle Grant-Jones, is a mother of three with a B.A. in Women's Studies. Early in our interview, she admitted that "[she] might not look like much of feminist trooping around with [her] kids with no goal really before [her]" but was careful to draw a stark distinction between "stay-at-home mothers" of an earlier generation and herself. Her life, she asserted, was freely chosen and consistent with her feminism which recognizes the essential experience of womanhood, and by extension, motherhood. The distortion of this particularly raced and classed history of women's labor aside, her generational comment is interesting. Embedded in this discourse of choice lays a contradiction. Note, for example, the following exchange I had with Teresa Reyes, a biologist turned natural mother of four who shared how her plans shifted after the birth of her first baby. She originally planned to return to work and leave the baby with her husband, but something changed:

> I just felt I had no choice…. I suppose I was a little surprised, because
> after she was born it was not an option for me to leave her.

Still other mothers responded to my query, why natural mother? with the response: "I just knew." I heard repeatedly how, when the mothers were faced with a decision, they simply followed their instincts and intuition. When I pushed them to provide a rationale for their choices, they paused and looked away wistfully, 'I don't know. It just felt right to homebirth, to extend breastfeed, to keep baby in bed with us' they told me in various iterations. Their mothering practice

CHRIS BOBEL

relied on a particular embodied knowledge. But, of course, this begs a question: if knowledge is derived from the body, from a body regarded as natural and unmediated by culture, and if behavior is actually driven by instinctual impulse rather than reasoned response, is this choice? The natural mothers told me in no uncertain terms that they could NOT mother in any other way. Hence, the last rational choice they made was the choice to embrace an ideology of "nature knows best," an ideology shaped by biologically determinist and historically and culturally gendered understandings of women, mothers, and families. Simply put, natural mothering was the "choice" that chose them.

The second contradiction revealed in the discourse of natural mothering centers on *control*. The natural mothers believe they have wrested control of their personal lives from institutions and experts claiming to "know best." For example, natural mothers push birthing practices, patently resisting the obstetrical medical establishment. Natural mothers were shopping local food coops, buying in bulk, and buying shares in Community Supported Agriculture before major "natural foods" chain stores brought such natural, local and whole foods into the trendy, overpriced current in the mainstream. This suggests that natural mothers *do* (or at least *did*) exist on the margins, trailblazing, pushing institutions, and as a result, raising awareness. Natural mothering is radical in the very real ways it questions features of family life in an advanced capitalist society.

But if mainstream culture is rejected, does something else fill that void? The mothers spoke passionately of the importance of "taking mothering back" from institutions and "experts," and simultaneously waxed, with a blend of awe and resignation, on the futility of resisting *nature*. Over and over again, I heard stories of the mothers' abiding faith in nature, which served as a model and resource to them. Stacey Thurer McReardon, aspiring writer and mother of four, shared that when she learned to stop, in her words, "tweaking things," she adopted a philosophy of letting nature run its course and she was much happier for it. Ingrid Kitzinger, a mother of three, referred to childbirth as something you don't really control, something "that just happens to you." Clearly, this is a narrative of respecting omnipotent nature. But when the mothers spoke of nature, they spoke of a monolithic and static concept, predating humankind, which remains pure and unadulterated. To them, nature is the perfect model for human behavior because it is separate from and unpolluted by human manipulation. This view, of course, is problematic; it denies the many ways in which nature is indeed culturally constructed and thus dynamic. But to these mothers, the "fact" of nature's separation from culture is what renders it so appealing and powerful. Furthermore, the mothers told me, listening to nature led them to tune into the powerful mother-child bond. This relationship, they maintain, fuses mothers and children virtually into a single entity, extending the relationship developed during pregnancy. In this view, maternal self-sacrifice is not at the root of contemporary mothers' difficulties; rather, a culture that casts mothers and children in opposition in direct affront to "nature," is the root of personal and social dysfunction.

Among the serious repercussions of the merged mother-child identity at the heart of natural mothering is the way it marginalizes fathers. When I pressed the mothers to say why they, as women, were the designated stay at home care-giver, practicing what Sharon Hays calls "intensive motherhood," explanations based on biological difference surfaced. Primarily due to the importance placed on breastfeeding, mothers seldom shared infant feeding with fathers or other potential caregivers. Over time, these feeding norms established caring patterns that persisted throughout mothers' *and* fathers' parenting careers. When the mother is positioned as the singular food source and furthermore, when nursing becomes the primary means of comfort for baby, mothers are quickly constructed as irreplaceable.[3] Based on a deeper understanding of the paradoxes of natural mothering, I turn to a brief discussion of this particular style of parenting's po-tential for social change.

Can Natural Mothering Fulfill Its Promise?

Most of the natural mothers viewed their lives as strategic missions to effect so-cial change. For example, Grace Burton claimed passionately: "I've decided that absolutely everything I do is political." But the expression of this politicization varies among the mothers. While some natural mothers participate in public ac-tions, such as "nurse ins"[4] most strive to effect social change through their daily practice of mothering outside the mainstream. But, I ask, can natural mothering reform society, one family at a time, or is it simply a form of narcissistic retreat devoid of impact beyond the empire of the individual family?

Sociologist and mothering theorist Barbara Katz Rothman conceptualizes American motherhood as "resting on three deeply rooted ideologies—capitalism, technology and patriarchy (26)." Katz Rothman argues that the effect of the three ideologies has been to split motherhood apart, forcing it into a series of dysfunc-tional dualisms such as mind and body, public and private, personal and political, work and home, production and reproduction and masculine and feminine, and I add to this list: nature and culture. Natural mothering, I argue, ably resists two of these three institutions: capitalism and technology, challenging the bifurcations that these institutions forge. But at the same time, its discourses of choice and con-trol, deeply paradoxical at their core, fail to resist the third institution: patriarchy. The mothers' surrender of agency to so-called instinct and a romanticized view of nature reifies an essentialist construction of womanhood. Theirs is a politics of accommodation. Like maternalists of earlier eras who used their femininity to pressure men to take them seriously as moral role models and to exercise some authority, at least in the domestic sphere (see Cott; Epstein; Ryan), the natural mothers push boundaries of their role while embracing specific features of it; they "bargain with patriarchy" (Kandiyoti). Deniz Kandiyoti uses this term to convey the complex set of "rules and scripts regulating gender relations to which both genders accommodate and acquiesce, yet which may nonetheless be contested, redefined, and renegotiated" (286). That is, women, given their context-bound existence, strategize within their particular constraints, enabling them to resist where and when possible. Natural mothering, a lifestyle that is simultaneously rebellious and obedient, represents precisely the kind of negotiation within male-dominated and -defined circumstances that Kandiyoti theorizes.

Because natural mothering accommodates patriarchy, its potential for social change is compromised. But this is not the only reason, I venture, that the movement is limited. The privilege necessary to enact this particular lifestyle constructs natural mothering as the domain of the few, especially because natural mothers themselves seem blind to this privilege. Consider, for example, my conversation with natural mother Jeanette Zientarski who spoke of mothering as "changing the world." She argued for an instinctual basis for her natural mothering much like the intuitively derived practice beyond the scope of rational choice I discussed earlier. When asked, "why isn't this kind of mothering instinctual for everyone?" she met the question with silence. Recall that the natural mothers "just know" what is in the best interest of their children—mothering this way is driven by feeling, by gut level awareness. Thus, intellectualizing their "choices" is impossible, they told me, implying that my question was the wrong one, that I just didn't get it. But how can it be that some mothers operate on instinct while others do not? There must be a deeper explanation, and so, I turn to the characteristics of the natural mothers themselves.

All the informants were white and all appeared to be heterosexual; 88 percent were married; 87 percent owned homes; 75 percent of the husbands were white-collar professionals. 81 percent of the mothers had attended college and 69 percent had completed a degree (many of them advanced degrees). Fifty-three percent had significant and often extended travel experience, including living abroad, Peace Corps and missionary work. Obviously, this demographic does not reflect the general American population. These privileged women have access to resources as wives and homemakers, enjoying the prestige that accompanies their class, race, and sexuality. Since beginning my research on natural mothers, I've learned that the population is a bit more diverse than I first encountered. "Hip Mamas" (typically women in their 20s and early 30s with a political and or Punk edge who identify with icon of "the next generation of mothers" mother-writer Ariel Gore, lesbian mothers, and working class mothers also number among the women. But, on the whole, the natural mothers still enjoy what Pierre Bourdieu calls "cultural capital."

Because most natural mothers are white and college educated, they are less likely to come under attack for their alternative "choices." Imagine a poor woman of color spotted publicly breastfeeding an older child—she is vulnerable in a way a woman of more social privilege is not. A mother receiving state aid does not have the option of waiving vaccinations while an economically secure mother with private insurance does. An immigrant woman known to use herbal remedies to treat illness may be scolded by her child's pediatrician. At the same time, a more privileged mother may meet similar resistance, but her decision will not be seen as a consequence of her assumed ignorance or her" backward" culture. In sum, natural mothering is a parenting lifestyle not possible for everyone.

But it is not only the necessity of some measure of privilege that undermines the force of the movement to effect social change. The absence of an analysis advanced by the movement itself is noted, including the relative blindness the mothers have to their own cultural capital. This blind eye became apparent to me when I asked the mothers to describe the "typical natural mother." Their answers ranged from "people suspicious of popular culture," "Moms attuned to the sense of the natural," and people with "a strong sense of self." No one cited race, class, or sexuality characteristics as meaningful. This silence was profound and raises serious questions about the viability of a movement that does not fully see itself.

As I've shown, while the natural mothers resist technology and capitalism, they fail to challenge patriarchy. Natural mothers work to extract meaning and power from the maternal role, marshalling tremendous creativity and resourcefulness, and framing their choices with pride and a hope for social change. As homeschoolers, homebirthers, and natural health care consumers, they turn their backs on the mainstream. In so doing, they ask important questions about our parenting holy grails. But at the same time that the natural mothers live on the margins and swim upstream, they capitulate to definitions of womanhood and motherhood written in the service of patriarchy. Theirs is not a project of rebelling against the expectation that mothers foreground their children's needs. Theirs is not a project of challenging fathers to roll up their sleeves and provide more instrumental care (as both Nancy Chodorow and Sara Ruddick prescribed). Furthermore, because natural mothering fails to see the fundamental place of privilege in enactment of the lifestyle, it is vulnerable to coopation. Natural Mothering resists, but not too much.

Notes

[1]This is a pseudonym as are the names of the informants I will discuss later in the paper.

[2]Of course, AP is not contained in the affluent "first world." Meredith Small for example, takes great care to point out the historical and global practice of AP, demonstrating the anomaly that is Western-style parenting with its premium on independence and mother-baby separation

[3]This, of course, is neither a new observation nor an original argument. Over 30 years ago, Michelle Rosaldo pointed to women's childbearing and lactation as impairing their mobility and thus, dooming them to domesticity and subordination.

[4]An activist tactic through which mothers publicly breastfeed their children in protest of policies which ban or otherwise undermine breastfeeding (see Harmon).

References

Baumgardner, Jennifer and Amy Richards. *Manifesta: Young Women, Feminism and the Future*. New York: Farrar, Straus, and Giroux, 2000.

Bobel, Chris. *The Paradox of Natural Mothering.* Philadelphia: Temple University Press, 2002.

Bourdieu, Pierre. "The Forms of Capital." *Handbook for Theory and Research for the Sociology of Education.* Ed. J. G. Richardson. New York: Greenwood Press, 1986. 241-258.

Brasile, Monica. "Exotics in Labor: The Primitive Body in U.S. Childbirth Discourse." National Women's Studies Association Annual Conference. Milwaukee, WI, 2004.

Buskens, Petra. "The Impossibility of "Natural Parenting" for Modern Mothers." In Andrea O'Reilly, ed. *Mother Matters: Motherhood as Discourse and Practice.* Toronto, Canada: Association for Research on Mothering, 2004.

Chodorow, Nancy. *The Reproduction of Mothering: Psychoanalysis and the Sociology of Gender.* Berkeley: University of California Press, 1978. 98-110.

Cook, Daniel. "The Mother as Consumer: Insights from the Children's Wear Industry." 1917-1929. *Sociological Quarterly* 36 (3) (1995): 505-522.

Cott, Nancy. *The Bonds of Womanhood: "Woman's Sphere" in New England, 1780-1835.* New Haven, CT: Yale University Press, 1977.

Davidson, J. *The Joy of Simple Living: Over 1, 500 Simple Ways to Make Your Life Easy and Content—At Home and At Work.* Emmaus, PA: Rodale Books, 1999.

Elgin, Duane. *Voluntary Simplicity: Toward a Way of Life That is Outwardly Simple and Inwardly Rich.* 2nd Ed. New York: William Morrow, 1993.

Epstein, Barbara. *The Politics of Domesticity: Women, Evangelism, and Temperance in Nineteenth-Century America.* Middletown, CT: Wesleyan University Press, 1981.

Glenn, Evelyn Nakano. Introduction. "Social Constructions of Mothering: A Thematic Overview." *Mothering: Ideology, Experience and Agency.* Eds. E. N. Glenn, G. Chang and L. R. Forcey. New York: Routledge, 1994. 1-29.

Gore, Ariel. *The Hip Mama Survival Guide: Advice from the Trenches on Pregnancy, Childbirth, Cool Names, Clueless Doctors, Potty Training and Toddler Avengers.* New York: Hyperion, 1998

Gore, Ariel. *The Mother Trip: Hip Mamas Guide to Staying Sane in the Chaos of Motherhood.* Boston: Seal Press, 2000.

Gore, Ariel and Bee Lavender, eds. *Breeder: Real-life Stories from the New Generation of Mothers.* Boston: Seal Press, 2001.

Harmon, Amy. "Lactivists' Taking Their Cause, and Their Babies to the Streets." *The New York Times.* 7 June 2005. Online: http://www.nytimes.com/2005/06/07/nyregion/07nurse.html?ei=5088anden=0c55cf357d95bd30andex=1275796800andpartner=rssnytandemc=rssandpagewanted=print.

Hays, Sharon. *The Cultural Contradictions of Motherhood.* New Haven: Yale University Press, 1996.

Johnston, Hank, Enrique Larana, and Joseph Gusfield, eds. *The New Social Movements.* Philadelphia: Temple University Press, 1994.

Kandiyoti, Deniz. "Bargaining with Patriarchy." *Gender and Society* 2 (1988): 274-290.

Katz Rothman, Barbara. *Recreating Motherhood: Ideology and Technology in a Patriarchal Society.* New York: W. W. Norton, 1989.

Levering, Frank and Wanda Ubranska. *Simple Living: One Couple's Search for a Better Life.* Winston-Salem, N.C.: John F. Blair Publishers, 2003.

Lockwood, Georgene. *Complete Idiot's Guide to Simple Living.* New York: Alpha Books, 2000

Longacre, Doris. *Living More With Less.* Scottdale, PA: Herald Press, 1981.

Luhrs, Janet. *The Simple Living Guide.* New York: Broadway Books, 1997.

Pierce, Linda Breen. *Simplicity Lessons: A 12-Step Guide to Living Simply.* Carmel, CA: Gallagher Books, 2003.

Rosaldo, Michelle Zimbalest and Louise Lamphere, eds. *Woman, Culture, and Society.* Stanford: Stanford University Press, 1974.

Ryan, Mary. *The Cradle of the Middle Class: The Family in Oneida County, NY, 1790-1865.* Cambridge: Cambridge University Press, 1981.

Small, Meredith F. *Our Babies, Ourselves: How Biology and Culture Shape the Way We Parent.* New York: Anchor Books, 1998.

St. James, Elaine. *Living the Simple Life: A Guide to Scaling Down and Enjoying More.* New York: Hyperion , 1998

Stoller, Debbie. *Stitch-n-Bitch: The Knitter's Guide.* New York: Workman Publishing Company, 2004

Chapter 48

Feminist Mothering

ANDREA O'REILLY

"We were conspirators, outlaws from the institution of motherhood; I
felt enormously in charge of my life"
—Adrienne Rich, *Of Woman Born*, 194-195

THIS CHAPTER, drawing from my writings on motherhood over the last several
years, will reflect upon what it means to be a feminist mother and practice feminist
mothering. Initially, when I began working on this chapter for the Reader on
maternal theory, I planned to simply reproduce one of my articles on feminist
mothering or, at the very most, write a new chapter based on a particular concern
or theme of feminist mothering. However, as I was reading through my work on
feminist mothering—both published and unpublished—I became increasingly
overwhelmed by the task at hand. If I wrote the chapter solely on the challenge of
defining feminist mothering and developing a theory of such, I would be unable
to analyze feminist mothering as a specific—and transgressive—mode of children
rearing. But if the latter becomes the focus I would have to disregard what I
consider to be the primary aim of feminist mothering, namely the empowerment
of mothers. After several false starts, I realized that to do justice to the complex,
compelling, and often conflicting themes of feminist mothering, both its risks
and rewards, I would have to structure this chapter in the form of introductory
Reader to the larger topic of feminist mothering.

This chapter, developed from my published works on feminist mothering as well
as from my recent reflections on the subject matter, is to be read as an overview of
the central issues, questions, and concerns of feminist mothering. In so doing, it
looks at feminist mothering from the perspective of both mothers and children.
The chapter is divided into three parts. The first section looks at the problematic
of defining feminist mothering and develops a possible theory of such. The second
section examines the meaning of feminist mothering for children. In particular, this
section considers how feminist mothering may be beneficial to children, likewise
it explores whether feminist mothering undermines the aims of maternal practice.
As section two champions anti-sexist childrearing and maternal activism on behalf

of children as an essential and important dimension of feminist mothering, section three calls for a more mother-centred emphasis in theories and practices of feminist mothering. It does for two reasons: to afford women more power in mothering and so challenge oppressive patriarchal discourses of motherhood—particularly that of intensive mothering—that deny women this power.

The chapter, as it considers various themes of feminist mothering, takes as its central argument that feminist mothering must first and primarily be concerned with the empowerment of mothers. While a challenge to traditional gender socialization is, of course, integral to any theory and practice of feminist mothering, the empowerment of mothers, in my view, must be the primary aim of feminist mothering if it is to function as a truly transformative theory and practice. Moreover, anti-sexist childrearing only becomes possible with this empowerment of mothers. Mothers cannot effect changes in childrearing in an institution in which they have no power as in the case with patriarchal motherhood. Anti-sexist childrearing depends upon motherhood itself being changed. In other words, only when mothering becomes a site, role, and identity of power for women is feminist childrearing made possible. In dismantling patriarchal motherhood you invest mothers with the needed agency and authority to affect the desired feminist childrearing. Only then does anti-sexist childrearing become possible.

Feminist Mothering: From the Problematic of Definitions to the Possibility of Theory

Mothering and Motherhood

In *Of Woman Born*, Adrienne Rich, when discussing a vacation without her husband one summer, describes herself and her sons as "conspirators, outlaws from the institution of motherhood" (195). She writes:

> I remember one summer, living in a friend's house in Vermont. My husband was working abroad for several weeks and my three sons—nine, seven, and five years old—and I dwelt for most of that time by ourselves. Without a male adult in the house, without any reason for schedules, naps, regular mealtimes, or early bedtimes so the two parents could talk, we fell into what I felt to be a delicious and sinful rhythm.... [W]e lived like castaways on some island of mothers and children. At night they fell asleep without murmur and I stayed up reading and writing as I had when a student, till the early morning hours. I remember thinking: This is what living with children could be—without school hours, fixed routines, naps, the conflict of being both mother and wife with no room for being simply, myself. Driving home once after midnight from a late drive-in movie ... with three sleeping children in the back of the car, I felt wide awake, elated; we had broken together all the rules of bedtime, the night rules, rules I myself thought I had to observe in the city or become a "bad mother." We were conspirators, outlaws from the institution of

motherhood; I felt enormously in charge of my life. (194-195)

However, upon Rich's return to the city, the institution, in her words, "closed down on us again, and my own mistrust of myself as a 'good mother' returned, along with my resentment of the archetype" (195).

Rich's reflections on being an outlaw from the institution of motherhood and the references she makes to being a "good" and "bad" mother are drawn from the distinction she develops at the beginning of *Of Woman Born* between mother-hood and mothering. Central to *Of Woman Born* and developed by subsequent motherhood scholars is the key distinction Rich makes between two meanings of motherhood, one superimposed on the other: "the *potential* relationship of any woman to her powers of reproduction and to children"; and "the *institution*—which aims at ensuring that that potential—and all women—shall remain under male control" (13, emphasis in original). The term motherhood refers to the patriarchal institution of motherhood which is male-defined and controlled and is deeply oppressive to women, while the word mothering refers to women's experiences of mothering which are female-defined and centred and potentially empowering to women. The reality of patriarchal motherhood thus must be distinguished from the possibility or potentiality of feminist mothering. To critique the insti-tution of motherhood therefore "is not an attack on the family or on mothering *except as defined and restricted under patriarchy*" (Rich 14). In other words, while motherhood, as an institution, is a male-defined site of oppression, women's own experiences of mothering can nonetheless be a source of power.

It has long been recognized among scholars of motherhood that Rich's distinc-tion between mothering and motherhood was what enabled feminists to recognize that motherhood is not naturally, necessarily, or inevitably oppressive, a view held by some Second Wave feminists. Rather, mothering, freed from motherhood, could be experienced as a site of empowerment, a location of social change if, to use Rich's words, women became "outlaws from the institution of motherhood." However, as *Of Woman Born* interrupted the patriarchal narrative of motherhood and cleared a space for the development of counter narratives of mothering, it did not generate a discourse on feminist mothering. While much has been published on patriarchal motherhood since Rich's inaugural text—documenting why and how patriarchal motherhood is harmful, indeed unnatural, to mothers and chil-dren alike—little has been written on the possibility or potentiality of feminist mothering. "Still largely missing from the increasing dialogue and publication around motherhood," as Fiona Green writes, "is a discussion of Rich's monumental contention that even when restrained by patriarchy, motherhood can be a site of empowerment and political activism." (2004: 31).

The introduction to my edited volume *Feminist Mothering* begins with a review of recent publications on motherhood in the mainstream media. These books would suggest that the selfless and doting mother of yesteryear has, like the eighteen-hour bra, fallen out of fashion. These authors, particularly those that write in the self-help genre, call for a new style of mothering, one that advocates balance and admonishes guilt. Bria Simpson for example, asserts in *The Balanced Mom: Raising Your Kids Without Losing Your Self,* "We need to continue, rather than deny, the development of ourselves to be fulfilled" (2). She goes on to write: "As you try so fervently to help your children develop into their best selves, I encourage you to refocus some of that energy into living *your* best life" (3, emphasis in original). Likewise, Amy Tiemann, in her recent book *Mojo Mom: Nurturing Your Self While Raising a Family*, claims that "all women need to continue to grow as individuals, not just as Moms" (xvi). Overcoming the guilt of motherhood is the focus of many recent books, as with the best-selling book, appropriately entitled *Mommy Guilt: Learn to Worry Less, Focus on What Matters Most, and Raise Happier Kids* (Bort, Pflock, Renner). Other writers challenge the excessive child-centredness of contemporary parenting practices and call for a more "children should be seen and not heard" philosophy of childrearing. Christie Mellor in *The Three-Martini Playdate: A Practical Guide to Happy Parenting* for example, asserts:

> You were here first. You are sharing your house with them, your food, your time, your books. Somewhere, in fairly recent memory, we have lost sight of that fact. Somehow a pint-sized velvet revolution was waged under own noses, and the grown-ups quietly handed over the reins. We have made concession after concession, until it appears that well-educated, otherwise intelligent adults have abdicated their rightful place in the world, and the littlest inmates have taken over the asylum. (12)

She goes on to say that "it is time to exert a little autonomy and encourage some in your child" (13). Other writers advocate shared parenting. In *How to Avoid the Mommy Trap: A Roadmap for Sharing Parenting and Making it Work* (2002), Julie Shields argues that *"the best alternative to parenting by mother is parenting by father"* (17, emphasis in original). She goes on to explain, "Since fathers can parent, too, we should not start from the assumption that mothers, and mothers alone, must choose whether to work, cut back, or hire a replacement caregiver. Instead, we can change our approach to seeking ways to provide babies the best start in life, at the same time, giving mothers *and* fathers the best opportunity for happiness, individually and together" (19).

Whether the emphasis be maternal autonomy or shared parenting, less guilt and more balance, these writers challenge traditional or, in academic parlance, patriarchal, motherhood practices. Similar to Betty Friedan, who exposed "the problem that has no name" more than 40 years ago, these writers insist that women must achieve and sustain a selfhood outside of and beyond motherhood. And similar to Adrienne Rich who attributed mothers' exhaustion and guilt to the isolation of patriarchal motherhood and its impossible standards of perfection, these writers likewise recognize that mothers require more support and less judgement if they are to obtain satisfaction in motherhood.

However, while these authors certainly challenge patriarchal motherhood, they do not use the word feminist in this critique, nor do they call their new mother-positive mode of mothering a feminist practice. Given this, can these new models of mothering be called feminist mothering? Does the mother have to identify as a feminist for her mothering to qualify as a feminist practice? Or more pointedly, can we have a practice of feminist mothering without a politic of feminism? And who decides and determines this?

I opened *Feminist Mothering* with such questions to illustrate the difficulty of defining a feminist practice and theory of mothering. While a challenge to patriarchal motherhood has been a central concern of feminist scholarship since at least Rich's classic book *Of Woman Born* in 1976, there has been very little academic discourse on the subject of feminist mothering. This dearth of feminist research on motherhood is indeed perplexing and troubling. A review of feminist scholarship on motherhood reveals that only three books look specifically at the topic of feminist mothering: *Mother Journeys: Feminists Write About Mothering* (1994), Tuula Gordon's book, *Feminist Mothers*, and Rose L. Glickman's *Daughters of Feminists*, books now ten-plus years old.[1] More recently, the journals *off our backs* (2006) and *Journal of the Association for Research on Mothering* (2006) include articles on feminist mothering in their issues on "Mothering and Feminism." Likewise, two of my recent edited volumes *Mother Outlaws: Theories and Practices of Empowered Mothering* (2004b) and *From Motherhood to Mothering: The Legacy of Adrienne Rich's Of Woman Born* (2004a) incorporate sections on feminist mothering. More recently I edited a volume specifically on the subject on feminist mothering; as well my book *Rocking the Cradle: Thoughts on Motherhood, Feminism, and the Possibility of Empowered Mothering* (2006) examines the topic of feminist mothering.

In my writing I use the term feminist mothering to refer to an oppositional discourse of motherhood, one that is constructed as a *negation* of patriarchal motherhood. A feminist practice/theory of mothering, therefore, functions as a counter narrative of motherhood: it seeks to interrupt the master narrative of motherhood to imagine and implement a view of mothering that is *empowering* to women. Feminist mothering is thus determined more by what it is not (i.e., patriarchal motherhood) rather than by what it is. Feminist mothering may refer to any practice of mothering that seeks to challenge and change various aspects of patriarchal motherhood that cause mothering to be limiting or oppressive to women. Rich uses the word courageous to define a non-patriarchal practice of mothering, while Baba Copper calls such a practice radical mothering. Susan Douglas and Meredith Michaels, more recently in *The Mommy Myth,* use the word rebellious to describe outlaw mothering. "Hip" is Ariel Gore's (see Gore and Lavender) term for transgressive mothering. For this chapter, the term feminist is used—though with a proviso as explained below—to signify maternal practices that resist and refuse patriarchal motherhood to create a mode of mothering that is empowering to women. Or, to use Rich's terminology, a feminist maternal practice marks a movement from motherhood to mothering, and makes possible a mothering against motherhood.

What is in a Name? Defining Feminist Mothering

Feminist mothering, as noted above, functions as a counter narrative or oppositional discourse: its meaning is constructed as a *negation* of patriarchal motherhood. In other words, our understanding of feminist mothering is determined more by what it is not (i.e., patriarchal motherhood) rather than by what it is. However, as we recognize that feminist mothering, in its origins and function, is a counter narrative, I believe we need to define more directly, more specifically, this mode of mothering, in both theory and practice. In her book *Feminist Mothers*, the first and still only book length study of the subject matter, Tuula Gordon in her concluding chapter "What is a Feminist Mother?" observes, "[I]t seems impossible to conclude by explaining what a feminist mother is, or to answer the underlying question of how people conduct their lives according to alternative ideologies, in this case feminism" (148). However, Gordon does say that her study of feminist mothers reveals some 'particular factors"; they are:

> The way in which [mothers] challenge and criticise myths of motherhood; the way in which they consider it their right to work: the anti-sexist (and anti-racist) way in which they try to bring up their children; the way in which they expect the fathers of the children to participate in joint everyday lives; and the way in which many of them are politically active. (149)

Gordon goes on to conclude:

> Feminism emphasizes that women are strong, that women have rights as women, and they can support each other as women. Thus "feminist mothers" have been able to develop critical orientations towards societal structures and cultures, stereotypical expectations and myths of motherhood. They do that in the context of exploring how the personal is political, and with the support of the networks of women which place them beyond "collective isolation." (150)

Rose L. Glickman in her book *Daughters of Feminists* likewise emphasizes that feminist mothering must be understood as lived resistance to the normative—stereotypical—expectations of both motherhood and womanhood. She writes:

> "[For these feminist mothers] there is no 'apart from their feminism' and no matter how ordinary their lives seem from the outside to the casual observer, *their feminism was a profound defiance of convention*…Flying in the face of tradition, feminist mothers expected their daughters to do the same" (22, emphasis added). "The mothers' struggle," Glickman continues, "to shake off the dust of tradition was the basic dynamic of the daughters' formative years" (21).

Whether it manifested itself in combining motherhood with paid employment, insisting that fathers be involved in childcare, engaging in activism, creating a life outside of motherhood, these studies reveal that feminist mothering developed in response to the mother's dissatisfaction with, dislike of traditional mother-hood. Commenting upon Gordon's study, Erika Horwitz in her thesis "Mothers' Resistance to the Western Dominant Discourse on Mothering" observes: "Her findings suggest that mothers can hold beliefs that are not in agreement with those promoted by the dominant discourses on motherhood. Gordon alerts us to the possibility that *the process of resistance entails making different choices about how one wants to practice mothering*" (58, emphasis added). Both Gordon and Glickman look specifically at mothers who identify as feminists while Horwitz in the above thesis and her later chapter "Resistance as a Site of Empowerment: The Journey Away from Maternal Sacrifice" is interested in "the experiences of women who believe they were resisting the dominant discourse of mothering...[but] who may or may not see themselves as feminist" (2004: 44, 45). Empowered mothering thus signifies a general resistance to patriarchal motherhood while feminist mothering refers to a particular style of empowered mothering in which this resistance is developed from and expressed through a feminist identification or consciousness. While the two seem similar, there are significant differences that warrant further elaboration. To this discussion I now turn.

In her chapter, "Resistance as Empowerment" (noted above), Erika Horwitz argues that while resistant, empowered mothering is characterized by many themes, they all centre upon a challenge to patriarchal motherhood. These themes include: The importance of mothers meeting their own needs; Being a Mother does not fulfill all of women's needs; Involving others in their children's upbringing; Actively questioning the expectations that are placed on mothers by society; Challenging mainstream parenting practices; Not believing that mothers are solely responsible for how children turn out; and, Challenging the idea that the only emotion moth-ers ever feel toward their children is love. In an earlier collection *Mother Outlaws* (2004b) I explored how empowered mothering begins with the recognition that both mothers and children benefit when the mother lives her life and practices mothering from a position of agency, authority, authenticity and autonomy. As well, this perspective, in emphasizing maternal authority and ascribing agency to mothers and value to motherwork, defines motherhood as a political site wherein mothers can affect social change through the socialization of children and the world at large through political-social activism. Empowered mothering thus calls into question the dictates of patriarchal motherhood. Empowered mothers do not regard childcare as the sole responsibility of the biological mother nor do they regard 24/7 mothering as necessary for children. They look to friends, family and their partners to assist with childcare and often raise their children with an involved community of what may termed co-mothers or othermothers. As well, in most instances, these mothers combine mothering with paid employment and/ or activism, and so, the full-time intensive mothering demanded in patriarchal motherhood is not practiced by these mothers. Further, many of these mothers call into question the belief that mothering requires excessive time, money and energy, and thus they practice a mode of mothering that is more compatible with paid employment. They see the development of a mother's selfhood as beneficial to mothering and not antithetical to it as is assumed in patriarchal motherhood. Consequently, empowered mothers do not always put their children's needs before their own nor do they only look to motherhood to define and realize their identity. Rather, their selfhood is fulfilled and expressed in various ways: work, activism, friendships, relationships, hobbies and motherhood. These mothers insist upon their own authority as mothers and refuse the relinquishment of their power as mandated in the patriarchal institution of motherhood. Finally, as noted above, empowered mothers regard motherhood as a site of power wherein mothers can affect social change, both in the home through feminist childrearing and outside the home through maternal activism. Motherhood, in the dominant patriarchal ideology, is seen simply as a private, and more specifically an apolitical enterprise. In contrast, mothering for these mothers is understood to have cultural significance and political purpose. Building upon the work of Sara Ruddick, these mothers redefine motherwork as a socially engaged enterprise that seeks to effect cultural change through new feminist modes of gender socialization and interactions with daughters and sons.

Feminist mothering differs from empowered mothering in so far as the mother identifies as a feminist and practices mothering from a feminist perspective or consciousness. A feminist mother, in other words, is a woman whose mothering, in theory and practice, is shaped and influenced by feminism. Thus, while there is much overlap between empowered and feminist mothering, the latter is informed by a particular philosophy and politic, namely Feminism. The women's demands that their husbands be more involved or that they need time off from motherhood in the Horwitz study did not derive from a larger challenge to gender inequity. For example, one woman in the study remarked that "If I was going to love that baby, have any quality of time with that baby, I had to get away from that baby. I had to meet my own needs" (2004: 48); and another mother "chose to paint her nails while her baby cried in her crib because 'she has needs and wants'" (2004: 47). These women resisted patriarchal motherhood, in one woman's words "to have a higher quality of life," or in the words of another "to make me a better mother for my children" (2004: 52). The reasons for their resistance are more personal than political and as a consequence are not developed from an awareness of how motherhood functions as cultural/ideological institution to oppress women in patriarchal society. These mothers resist patriarchal motherhood simply to make the experience of mothering more rewarding for themselves and their children. In so far as this aim challenges the patriarchal mandate of maternal selflessness, sacrifice and martyrdom, these mothers are resistant in their insistence upon more time for themselves and support from others. However, these demands do not originate from a feminist desire to dismantle a patriarchal institution. In contrast, feminist mothers resist because they recognize that gender inequity, in particular male privilege and power, is produced, maintained and perpetuated (i.e., though sexist childrearing) in patriarchal motherhood. As feminists, feminist mothers reject an institution founded upon gender inequity, and as mothers, they refuse to raise children in such a sexist environment. Thus, while in practice the two seem similar—i.e., demanding more involvement from fathers, insisting upon a life outside of motherhood—only with feminist mothering does this involve a larger awareness of, and challenge to, the gender (among other) inequities of patriarchal culture.

While the above discussion helps to distinguish between empowered and feminist mothering, it begs the larger question of how to define Feminism itself. Feminism, as scholars of Women's Studies are well aware, is composed of many "perspectives and positions": Socialist, Liberal, Radical, Womanist, Third Wave to name but a few. For the purpose of this collection, I rely upon a very open-ended definition of feminism: the recognition that most (all?) cultures are patriarchal and that such cultures give prominence, power and privilege to men and the masculine and depend upon the oppression, if not disparagement, of women and the feminine. Feminists are committed to challenging and transforming this gender inequity in all of its manifestations: cultural, economic, political, philosophical, social, ideological, sexual and so forth. As well, most feminisms (including my own) seek to dismantle other hierarchical binary systems such as race (racism), sexuality (heterosexism), economics (classism) and ability (abilism). A feminist mother, therefore, in the context of this definition of feminism, challenges male privilege and power in her own life and that of her children. In her own life, this would mean the mother insisting upon gender equality in the home and a life and identity outside of motherhood. As well, it would mean that the important work of mothering would be culturally valued and supported and that mothers, likewise, would perform this motherwork from a place of agency and authority. In the context of children, feminist mothering means dismantling traditional gender socialization practices that privilege boys as preferable and superior to girls and in which boys are socialized to be masculine and girls feminine. Feminist mothering thus seeks to transform both the patriarchal role of motherhood and that of childrearing.

However, the word Feminism remains troubled. In her book on feminist daughters Glickman wrote:

> I ruled out daughters whose mothers' lives can surely be described as feminist, but who reject the label. Once, in my search for Latina daughters, I spoke with the head of a Latino women's health collective. She said she couldn't help me because "although we have the consciousness, in our culture we don't use the word." The consciousness without the word is not what I'm looking for. (xv-xvi)

However, in insisting upon the word feminist, you will inevitably, as the above incidence demonstrates, exclude the mothering experiences of women of colour. The term Feminism, as African American scholars Patricia Hill Collins and bell hooks among others have argued, is understood to be a white term for many black women. As one daughter, a woman of colour, in Glickman's study commented: '[Feminism] has overwhelmingly, statistically, benefited white women disproportionately to women of colour" (168). And another daughter remarked "Here you are reading all these feminist writers who are telling you to bust out of the kitchen and get into the work force. What does that have to do with the majority of women of colour who have always been in the kitchen *and* the work force at the same time?" (169, emphasis in original). Indeed, as the mothers of colour in Gordon's study emphasized, "black women are critical of feminism dominated by white women for ideological, political and strategic reasons" (140). The question thus remains: How do you develop a specific study of feminist mothering without excluding the many women—women of colour and working class women—who eschew or disavow the word Feminism? While, I do not believe there are easy answers to such questions, I see a broader understanding of feminism, to include womanist, anti-racist, global feminist perspectives, as a way to begin talking about women of colour and their specific theory and practice of feminist mothering.

A Theory of Feminist Mothering: Maternal Agency, Autonomy, Authority and Authenticity

Feminist mothering functions as a counter practice that seeks to challenge and change the many ways that patriarchal motherhood is oppressive to women. Numerous feminist scholars have detailed the various ways that patriarchal motherhood constrains, regulates and dominates women and their mothering. In an earlier volume, *Mother Outlaws* (2004b), I organized these themes under eight inter-related 'rules' of 'good' motherhood as dictated by contemporary patriarchal ideology. They are: 1) children can only be properly cared for by the biological mother; 2) this mothering must be provided 24/7; 3) the mother must always put children's needs before her own; 4) mothers must turn to the experts for instruction; 5) the mother must be fully satisfied, fulfilled, completed and composed in motherhood; 6) mothers must lavish excessive amounts of time, energy and money in the rearing of their children; 7) the mother has full responsibility but no power from which to mother; 8) motherwork, and childrearing more specifically, are regarded as personal, private undertakings with no political import. The patriarchal ideology of motherhood makes mothering deeply oppressive to women because it requires the repression or denial of the mother's own selfhood; as well it assigns mothers all the responsibility for mothering but gives them no real power from which to mother. Such "powerless responsibility," to use Rich's term, denies a mother the authority and agency to determine her own experiences of mothering. Moreover, in defining mothering as private and non-political work, patriarchal motherhood restricts the way mothers can and do affect social change through feminist child rearing and maternal activism.

The dominant ideology also reserves the definition of good motherhood to a select group of women. I open my Women's Studies course on "Mothering-Motherhood" asking students to define a 'good' mother in contemporary culture: What does a good mother look like; who is she? Students commented that good mothers, as portrayed in the media or popular culture more generally, are white, heterosexual, middle-class, able-bodied, married, thirty-something, in a nuclear family with usually one to two children, and are ideally full time mothers. Words such as altruistic, patient, loving, selfless, devoted, nurturing, cheerful were frequently mentioned to describe the personality of this ideal patriarchal mother. Mothers who, by choice or circumstance, do not fulfill the profile of the good mother —i.e., they are too young or old; or are poor or lesbian—are deemed 'bad' mothers. Likewise, women who do not follow the script of good mothering —i.e. they work outside the home or engage in maternal activism—are seen as 'fallen' mothers in need of societal regulation and correction.

Feminist mothering refuses this patriarchal profile and script of "good" mothers and "good" mothering. And in so doing, it challenges and changes the various ways patriarchal motherhood becomes oppressive to women, as noted in the eight themes above. Thus, while feminist mothering functions as an oppositional discourse and thus defies definition, it is characterized by several themes that coalesce to form a specific theory of feminist mothering. In *Of Woman Born* Rich writes: "We do not think of the power stolen from us and the power withheld from us in the name of the institution of motherhood" (275). "The idea of maternal power has been domesticated," Rich continues, "in transfiguring and enslaving woman, the womb—the ultimate source of the power—has historically been turned against us and itself made into a source of powerlessness" (68). The central aim of feminist mothering is to reclaim that power for mother. It seeks to imagine and implement a theory and practice of mothering that is empowering to mothers.

Feminist mothering refers to a particular style of empowered mothering in which resistance is developed from and expressed through a feminist identification or consciousness. A feminist mother, as discussed above, seeks the eradication of motherhood as she recognizes that such is a patriarchal institution in which gender inequality, or more specifically the oppression of women, is enforced, maintained and perpetuated. Feminist mothering is thus primarily concerned with the empowerment of mothers. Thus a theory of feminist mothering *begins with recognition that mothers must live her life and practice mothering from a position of agency, authority, authenticity and autonomy.* A feminist standpoint on mothering affords a womam a life, a purpose and identity outside and beyond motherhood; as well it does not limit childrearing to the biological mother. Likewise, from this standpoint, a woman's race, age, sexuality or marital status does not determine her capicity to mother. A feminist theory on motherhood also foregrounds maternal power and confers value to mothering. Mothering, thus from a feminist perspective and practice, redefines motherwork as a social and political act. In contrast to patriarchal motherhood that limits mothering to privatized care undertaken in the domestic sphere, feminist mothering, more so than empowered mothering, regards such as explicitly and profoundly political and social.

Feminist mothering, thus, is equally concerned with feminist practices of gender socialization and models of mother–child relations so as to raise a new generation of empowered daughters and empathetic sons. However, a theory of feminist mothering insists that the latter—anti-sexist childrearing—depends on the former—the eradication of patriarchal motherhood. A review of feminist thought on motherhood, however, reveals that a critique of the institution of motherhood and a concern with new modes of childrearing have developed independently of each other, and that feminists committed to the abolition of motherhood and the achievement of mothering have seldom considered what this means for the mother *herself*, apart from the issue of childrearing.

Fiona Green, in her research on feminist mothering, interviews feminist mothers who, in Green's words, "live Rich's emancipatory vision of motherhood" (2004: 130). Driven by their feminist consciousness, their intense love for their children and the need to be true to themselves, their families, and their parenting, [these] feminist mothers," Green writes, "choose to parent in a way that challenge the status quo" (2004: 130). They do so, according to Green, by way of two different approaches: "overt strategies of resistance" and "subversive strategies of resistance" (2004: 130). To illustrate the first strategy Green gives the example of a lesbian lone parent who births and raises a child without any connection to man. "No man ever called the shots in my home," the woman explains, "nor did a man ever support me in any way. So that is really breaking the rules in the patriarchy" (2004: 131). According to Green, this is "a deliberate act of resistance to dominant conceptions and practices of mothering" (2004: 131).

The second strategy is less overt; with this approach, mothers "under the cover of the institution of motherhood effectively challenge patriarchy, and their subversive activity often goes unnoticed" (2004: 132). Green provides examples of two heterosexual married mothers to illustrate this strategy: one who raises a son to make him consciously aware of social injustices, while the second mother "actively encourages the nurturing and non-competitive tendencies of her son, while supporting her daughter in her pursuits of maths and science" (2004:133). The second subversive strategy thus seems to focus on childrearing undertaken by women in the institution of motherhood while the former, the overt strategy, involves a challenge to the institution itself and is concerned with the empowerment of the mother. In the example of overt resistance, when discussing the mother's choice to rear her daughter with an othermother during a difficult time in her daughter's adolescence, Green comments that this mother "enjoy[ed] a level of freedom and strength that she would not have experienced had she conformed to patriarchal [motherhood]" (2004: 132).

I refer to Green's research here because it illustrates well the way the two demands of feminist mothering both interface and underpin one another. Feminist mothering seeks to dismantle motherhood *for mothers themselves*, so that they may achieve empowerment in mothering. That is reason enough to abolish motherhood. However, in so doing, we also invest mothers with the needed agency, authenticity, and authority to affect the feminist childrearing they desire. Feminist mothers recognize that the changes we pursue in childrearing are made possible only through changes in mothering

The various features of feminist mothering noted above may be organized by way of four inter-related themes that I have termed: Motherhood, Family, Childrearing and Activism. Central to each theme is a redefinition of motherhood from a feminist-maternal perspective. "Good" mothers in patriarchal motherhood, for example, are defined as white, middle-class, married, stay-at-home moms; while "good" mothers from the feminist perspective are drawn from all maternal identities and include lesbian, non-custodial, poor, single, older and "working" mothers. Likewise, while patriarchal motherhood limits family to a patriarchal nuclear structure wherein the parents are married and are the biological parents of the children and the mother is the nurturer and the father is the provider, the formation of feminist families are many and varied to embrace single, blended, step, matrifocal, same-sex, and so forth. And as patriarchal motherhood characterizes childrearing as a private, non-political undertaking, feminist mothers foreground the political-social dimension of motherwork. More specifically, they challenge traditional practices of gender socialization and perform anti-sexist childrearing practices so as to raise empowered daughters and empathetic sons. Finally, for many feminist mothers, their commitment to both feminism and to children becomes expressed as maternal activism. Mothers, by way of maternal activism, use their position as mothers to lobby for social and political change. Whether it is in the home or in the world at large, expressed as anti-sexist childrearing and maternal activism, motherwork, for feminist mothers, is redefined as a social and political act through which social change is made possible.

Whether it is expressed as maternal activism or as a challenge to patriarchal family norms, feminist mothering centres upon maternal agency, authority, autonomy and authenticity. Amy Middleton, however, in a recent article, "Mothering Under Duress: Examining the Inclusiveness of Feminist Mothering Theory" argues that such a definition is problematic because it limits feminist mothering to, in her words, "educated, middle to upper class women with access to financial and human resources." She writes: "These criteria and the way in which they are realized in these women's lives are extremely difficult, and in some cases impossible, for women who do not have access to recourse such as substantial finances and good childcare and/or women who are in other situations of duress such as being in an abusive relationship, having a mental illness or being addicted to drugs or alcohol." This criticism suggests that I have been less than clear in my use of these terms. The terms agency, authority, autonomy, authenticity, are not to be read as restricted to economic and educational resources. Rather, these terms are to be read in the context of a resistance to patriarchal motherhood. The concept of authenticity, for example, refers to the refusal to wear, what Susan Maushart terms, the "mask of motherhood." The mask of motherhood, Maushart explains, is an "assemblage of fronts –mostly brave, serene, and all knowing—that we use to disguise the chaos and complexity of our lived experience" (2). To be masked, Maushart continues is "to deny and repress what we experience, to misrepresent it, even to ourselves" (1-2). "The mask of motherhood," Maushart continues, "keeps women from speaking clearly what they know and from hearing truths too threatening to face" (7). "Authentic"mothering, in contrast, seeks to unmask motherhood and refuse to partake in, what Mary Kay Blakely has termed, "the national game of Let's Pretend—the fantasy in which we are all supposed to pass for perfect mothers, living in perfect families" (12). To be authentic is to be truthful and true to oneself in motherhood.

Similarly, authority refers to confidence and conviction in oneself as a mother. Authority means, in this instance, the refusal to, in Sara Ruddick words, "relinquish authority and repudiate one's own perceptions and values" (112). As well, agency means not power but, in Rich's words "to refuse to be a victim and then go on from there" (246). From this perspective, agency, authority, authenticity and autonomy are as available to 'marginalized' women as they are to women of privilege. In fact, I would argue that such agency, authority, autonomy and authenticity of empowered mothering are *more* evident in the maternal practices/theories of mothers who are poor, lesbian, young or women of colour as evidenced in the collection *Breeder: Real-Life Stories from the New Generation of Mothers* (Gore and Lavender). Privileged women, I would suggest, with more resources and status in motherhood, are often less able or likely to perceive and oppose their oppression. Furthermore, when I speak of agency and the like I do not mean to say that mothers necessarily have these things but rather that empowered mothers understand that they *should* have them and seek to attain them. 'Patriarchal' mothers, in contrast, do not believe that mothers need or want agency, authority, autonomy, or authenticity. Or put another way: patriarchal motherhood depends on the very denial of maternal agency, authority, authenticity and autonomy. When I use such terms I mean to signify struggle not necessarily success. Again to quote from Rich: "The quality of the mother's life—however, embattled and unprotected—is her primary bequest to her daughter, because a woman who can believe in herself, who is a fighter, and who continues to struggle to create liveable space around her, is demonstrating to her daughter that these possibilities exist" (247). This is what a mothering of agency, authority, autonomy, and authenticity seeks to demonstrate and achieve and, as such, it is certainly not restricted to women of privilege.

Feminist Mothering and Children

Feminist Mothers are Better Mothers

The central argument of my research is that feminist mothering, in affirming maternal agency, authority, autonomy and authenticity, makes motherhood more rewarding, fulfilling and satisfying for women. Such mothering allows woman selfhood outside of motherhood and affords her power within motherhood. As well, the practice of othermothering or co-mothering, the ability to combine motherhood with work (paid employment and/or activism), and limiting the time, energy, money spent on children relieves women of much of the isolation, dependency, boredom, and exhaustion experienced in patriarchal motherhood. It is evident that feminist mothering is better for mothers. Such mothering is also better for children. We understand that mothers content with and fulfilled by their lives make better mothers. Likewise, we recognize that children raised by depressed mothers are at risk. I want to suggest as well that feminist mothers are more effective mothers. Anyone who has been in a plane knows the routine if oxygen masks are required: put on your mask and then assist children with theirs. This instruction initially seems to defy common sense; children should be helped first. However, the instruction recognizes that parents must be masked first, because only then are they able to provide real and continued assistance to the child: unmasked they run they risk of becoming disoriented, ill or unconscious due to lack of oxygen and then of course would be of no use to the child. I see this instruction as a suitable metaphor for feminist mothering; mothers, empowered, are able to better care for and protect their children.

In her recent book *A Potent Spell: Mother Love and the Power of Fear,* Janna Malamud Smith references the myth of Demeter and Persephone to illustrate this theme; children are better served by empowered mothers. Demeter, Smith argues "is able to save her daughter because she is a powerful goddess who can make winter permanent and destroy humankind" (59). "Demeter," she continues, "possesses the very qualities that Mothers so often have lacked—adequate resources and strength to protect their children, particularly daughters" (59). Therefore, and contrary to patriarchal, or more generally accepted, wisdom, what a child needs most in the world, Smith argues, "is a *free and happy* mother" (167, emphasis added). Smith explains:

> [W]hat a child needs most is a free mother, one who feels that she is in fact living *her* life, and has adequate food, sleep, wages, education, safety, opportunity, institutional support, health care, child care, and loving relationships. "Adequate" means enough to allow her to participate in the world—and in mothering—….A child needs a mother who has resources to enable her to make real choices, but also to create a feeling of adequate control—a state of mind that encourages a sense of agency, thus a good basis of maternal well-being, and a good foundation on which to stand while raising a child. Surely, child care prospers in this soil as well as, if not better than in any other. What is more, such a mother can imagine a life of possibility and hope, and can so offer this perspective to a child. [Finally] a child needs a mother who lives and works within a context that respects her labour, and that realistically supports it without rationalizing oppression in the name of safety, or substituting idealization or sentimentality for resources. (158)

Ann Crittenden, who is cited by Smith, elaborates further: "Studies conducted on five continents have found that children are distinctly better off when the mother possesses enough income and authority in the family to make investing in children a priority" (120). The emergence of women as independent economic actors, Crittenden continues, is not depriving children of vital support; it is giving them more powerful defenders. Depriving mothers of an income and influence of their own is harmful to children and a recipe for economic backwardness" (130). To return to the story of Demeter: "It is only because Demeter has autonomy and independent resources," as Smith explains, "that she can protect Persephone" (241). Conversely, "when a culture devalues and enslaves the mother, she can [not] be like Demeter and protect her daughter" (244). Therefore, and as Smith concludes: "If we are really interested in improving the lot of children, our best method would be laws and policy that supports mothers and mothering" (187). It is indeed remarkable, as Smith notes, that "[n]o society has ever voluntarily turned its laws and riches toward liberating mothers" (168).

The free mother valued by Smith and recognized as essential for the well-being of children however will be not found in the patriarchal institution of mother-hood or in the practice of intensive mothering. Patriarchal motherhood robs women of their selfhood and power, and intensive mothering, in its emphasis on excessive time, attention and energy, makes it difficult, nay impossible, for mothers to be autonomous and independent. Feminist, or to use Smith's term free, mothering thus only becomes possible in and through the destruction of patriarchal motherhood. Such mothers can better protect and defend their children as Smith observes. As well, and as noted above, feminist mothers can make real and lasting changes in society through social-political activism and in the way they raise their children. More specifically feminist mothers chal-lenge and change—in the home and in the world at large—the gender roles that straightjacket our children, and the harm of sexism, racism, classism and heterosexism more generally. I believe that patriarchy resists feminist mother-ing precisely because it understands its real power to bring about a true and enduring cultural revolution.

The Paradox of Feminist Mothering and the Promise of a Feminist Maternal Practice

As the above section looks at the benefits of feminist mothering for children, this section considers its risks. More specifically it considers whether feminist mother-ing fosters or undermines the aims of maternal practice. My writing on feminist mothering frequently draws upon my experience of raising three children—a son and two daughters—in a feminist household. Of interest to me in my reflections is how my children came to be feminists in a patriarchal culture. All three of my children—my son Jesse, 22 years old and my two daughters Erin, 20 and Casey, 17—identify as feminists. How did this happen? What made this possible? With my son, I explore my challenge to traditional practices of male socialization that mandates both mother-son disconnection and `macho' masculinity in boys. With my daughters I examine both anti-sexist parenting practices and the need for mothers to model a feminist life in order to mentor the same for their girl children. In particular, I argue that my daughters could not have grown to be feminist women in patriarchal motherhood. If I had mothered in this institution, I certainly could not have lived and modelled a feminist life; nor would I have had the agency and authority to impart feminist childrearing to my daughters. The emphasis of my writing thus has been on how my children came to be feminists with little attention paid to the effect of such in their own lives. While I discuss at some length how my children were frequently ridiculed, bullied and ostracized for their feminist practices and beliefs, I did not theorize upon how this related to the larger requirements of motherwork, namely the preservation, nurturance, and socialization of children.

Over the last several years, as my children became teenagers and the assaults upon them became more frequent and hateful, I began to reflect upon how my feminist mothering seemed to be in conflict with my maternal practice. More specifically, I struggled with how I could reconcile the demands my motherwork—keeping my children safe and ensuring that they have a sense of belonging in their culture—with the desires of my feminism, which means raising my children to challenge that very same culture and put themselves at risk in doing so. Preoccupied with and perplexed by this inherent and perhaps irresolvable paradox of feminist mothering, I returned to the writing of Sara Ruddick to consider whether feminist mothering could be understood as a form of maternal practice

In *Maternal Thinking: Toward a Politics of Peace*, Sara Ruddick argues that the work of mothering, that mother-work, is characterized by three demands: preservation, growth, and social acceptance. "To be a mother," continues Ruddick, "is to be committed to meeting these demands by works of preservative love, nurturance, and training" (17). The first duty of mothers is to protect and preserve their children: "to keep safe whatever is vulnerable and valuable in a child" (80). "Preserving the lives of children," Ruddick writes, "is the central constitutive, invariant aim of maternal practice: the commitment to achieving that aim is the constitutive maternal act" (19). "To be committed to meeting children's demand for preservation," Ruddick continues, "does not require enthusiasm or even love; it simply means to see vulnerability and to respond to it with care rather than abuse, indifference, or flight" (19). "The demand to preserve a child's life is quickly supplemented," Ruddick continues, "by the second demand, to nurture its emotional and intellectual growth" (19). Ruddick explains:

> To foster growth ... is to sponsor or nurture a child's unfolding, expanding material spirit. Children demand this nurturance because their development is complex, gradual, and subject to distinctive kinds of distortion or inhibition.... Children's emotional, cognitive, sexual, and social development is sufficiently complex to demand nurturance; this demand is an aspect of maternal work ... and it structures maternal thinking. (83)

The third demand of maternal practice is training and social acceptability of children. This third demand, Ruddick writes:

> is made not by children's needs but by the social groups of which a mother
> is a member. Social groups require that mothers shape their children's
> growth in "acceptable" ways. What counts as acceptable varies enormously
> within and among groups and cultures. The demand for acceptability,
> however, does not vary, nor does there seem to be much dissent from
> the belief that children cannot "naturally" develop in socially correct
> ways but must be "trained." I use the neutral, though somewhat harsh,
> term "training" to underline a mother's active aims to make her children
> "acceptable." Her training strategies may be persuasive, manipulative,
> educative, abusive, seductive, or respectful and are typically a mix of
> most of these. (21)

"In any mother's day," Ruddick concludes, "the demands of preservation, growth and acceptability are intertwined. Yet a reflective mother can separately identify each demand, partly because they are often in conflict" (23).

A feminist mother, as a mother, is committed to the safety, well-being and social acceptability of her children and yet as a feminist, that same mother knowingly and deliberately raises her child to be critical of the dominant culture and to cause, as a result, possible harm—physical and psychological—to her children. Rich has argued that as feminist mothers we worry that we may turn our sons "into misfits and outsiders" (205). I would argue that as feminist mothers, we *do* make our children—both sons and daughters—misfits and outsiders and that this is in direct conflict with our responsibility as mothers to ensure safety and social acceptability for our children. As a feminist and as mother I recognize daily this contest of allegiance; when my teenage daughter challenges a sexist remark in her classroom I applaud her as a feminist and, yet, as a mother, I worry that this will only heighten her social isolation in high school. And that she will spend another Saturday night sad and alone, shunned by her peer group for "being such a freak."

Writing on this paradox of feminist mothering I am reminded of the work of black mothers of sons who speak of a similar paradox. Marita Golden, in her book *Saving Our Sons: Raising Black Children in a Turbulent World,* says this of her son: "The unscathed openness of Michael's demeanour was proof that he had been a protected, loved child. But this same quality was also suddenly a liability, one that he had to mask" (95). Nurturing black sons to be confident and proud, mothers recognize that these same traits, because they may be misconstrued as insolence, obstinacy, and arrogance by other black youth, police or whites generally, put their sons at risk. Golden realizes that this paradox of mothering black sons necessitates a new mode of mothering. This mode of mothering is perhaps best expressed by Audre Lord, who writes: "Black children must be raised as warriors. For survival they must also be raised to recognize the enemy's many faces." She goes on to say:

> The strongest lesson I can teach my son is the same lesson I teach my
> daughter; how to be who he wishes to be for himself. And the best way
> I can do this is to be who I am and hope that he will learn from this not
> how to be me, which is not possible, but how to be himself. And this
> means to move to that voice from within himself, rather than to those
> raucous, persuasive, or threatening voices from outside, pressuring him
> to be what the world wants him to be. (77)

A feminist mother must likewise develop a new mode of mothering and teach
her children to be true to themselves by modelling such in her own life. This, as
Rich has noted, "means that the mother herself is trying to expand the limits of
her life. To *refuse to be a victim*: and then to go on from there. (246, emphasis
in original)

Two years ago I interviewed my teen daughters on their experience of being
raised by a feminist mother for an article I was writing. From their commentary
it became evident that my daughters perceived and experienced their upbringing
as anti-sexist childrearing and that my daughters understood their childhood in
this way. They both mentioned several times that we didn't 'girl' them in their
upbringing (Casey spoke of how fishing, playing with frogs, and getting dirty in
the mud was a normal part of her childhood.) As well they commented on how
they did not experience the 'normal' sexist feminization of daughters; they didn't
play with Barbies, wear make up or listen to the Spice Girls. As well, both of them
emphasized the importance of being offered alternative—empowered—examples
and images of womanhood (feminist books/music, Goddess figures etc). But
equally my daughters spoke about how they learned feminism directly from the
way I lived my life. This came up far more than I had anticipated. What they
remember about me is "working, standing up to traditional gender roles and
always talking about issues." They saw me living a life outside of motherhood. As
Erin remarked: "You had a long relationship with dad, work, friends, partying.
You did everything: you never had a shitty non-life." My daughters, in watching me live my life, learned that feminism was possible, do-able, and normal.
And, as importantly, they learned that motherhood does not, should not, shut
down other dimensions of a woman's life: work, sexuality, friendship, activism,
leisure and so forth. Listening over and over again to my daughters' voices as I
transcribed the interview, I finally "got" Rich's insight at a deeply personal level.
To paraphrase Rich: The quality of my life—however, embattled and unprotected it may have been—was my primary bequest to my daughters, because in
believing in myself, in fighting, in struggling to create liveable space around me
I demonstrated to Erin and Casey that these possibilities exist. Feminist mothering of girls is not about choosing blue over pink, or trucks over dolls but about
living, to use the title of Marilyn Waring's work, *as if women counted*. And more
specifically, in the context of motherhood, feminist mothering demonstrates
to our daughters that women have a selfhood outside of motherhood and have
power within motherhood.

Having spent over twenty years committed to both maternal practice and feminist mothering I have yet to resolve the paradox of feminist mothering. However, what I have come to understand from interviewing my daughters, rereading Ruddick's theory of maternal practice and remembering Lorde and Rich's words on staying true to ourselves, is that feminist mothering may be seen as an expression of maternal practice. While feminist mothering does, in the first instance, run counter to the safety and social acceptability requirements of maternal practice, it does, in allowing our children to grow outside and beyond the gender straightjackets of patriarchal culture, foster the nurturance of children, the second demand of maternal practice, thus enabling our children to become happy and healthy adults. Moreover, what I have learned as a feminist mother is that we must teach our children not only to resist patriarchy but more importantly how to keep safe and sane in so doing. We need to model to our children our own lived resistance and to share with them our stories of success and sorrow. And most importantly we must create a feminist community and work towards a feminist world so that our children will have that sense of belonging that is essential for well-being and makes possible resistance.

As a mother of grown children I can speak about feminist mothering with a good measure of composure and confidence. My kids have turned out just fine and are, more or less, content with their lives and doing the same things that 'normal' kids do. They have not sprouted two heads or morphed into anti-social loners as a result of being raised by a feminist mother. This is not to say that feminist mothering has been easy; on the contrary there were many days, and even more nights, that I wondered and worried whether I was doing right by my children by raising them to be such strong feminists. And, of course, my children likewise suffered as a result of being raised in a feminist household, particularly as they grew up in a rural and very conservative community. But ultimately I believe that feminist mothering has made me a better mother and my children, better people. Speaking of her experience of coming to feminism Erin said: "I was always a freak. I couldn't avoid it because it was so saturated. I didn't realize that I was doing feminist things, it was just the way I acted. I was a loud girl. If I had something to say I said it. Feminism did make it harder for me growing up because it made me different but it was so worth it in the end. I came out the other side of all that. I am my own person. The girls I grew up with are still playing all those games. Still trapped in that world ... still don't say what they think." Casey commented: "I feel the same way. Worth it in the end though going through it was hard particularly in elementary school. I was always a freak. I couldn't be pretty. I just failed. I didn't know how to dress 'normally'. As you grow older you come to appreciate it more. I live in this world without being swallowed up."

Like my daughters, I too believe that feminist mothering is ultimately more about rewards than risks, that it is indeed "worth it in the end." And in this, feminist mothering may be seen as full and complete expression of maternal practice.

ANDREA O'REILLY

Feminist Mothering and Mothers

Towards a Mother-Centred Theory of Feminist Mothering: Realizing the Promise of the Demeter Archetype

Feminist literature on motherhood has allowed for new progressive styles of childrearing and generated maternal activism. Despite this, I believe that it has not gone far enough in its attempts to transform motherhood *for the mother herself,* to realize fully the maternal power and fury promised in the Demeter archetype. Current thinking on feminist mothering, in its emphasis upon child-rearing and in its strategy of rationalization, fails to develop a revolutionary model of mothering that takes as its aim and focus the empowerment of *mothers.* I believe that we need to develop a more radical and militant politic that is, in the style of the Demeter archetype, more discordant, direct, and defiant in our critique of patriarchal motherhood.

Adrienne Rich in *Of Woman* Born interprets the Demeter/Persephone myth, particularly as it was enacted in the Eleusinian mysteries, as representing every daughter's longing for "a mother whose love for her and whose power were so great as to undo rape and bring her back from death" (240). As well, the myth, Rich continues, bespeaks *"every mother's [longing] for the power of Demeter [and] the efficacy of her anger..."* (240, emphasis added). In patriarchal culture where there are so few examples, in either life or literature, of empowered mothering, Demeter's triumphant resistance serves as a model for the possibility of mothering first imagined by Rich in *Of Woman Born.* The central aim of feminist mothering, as discussed above, is to, likewise, envision and achieve a model of mothering that is, in both theory and practice, empowering. However, as I prepared this chapter for this Mother Reader, I reflected upon the triumphs and tribulations that I and other scholars have experienced in our attempts to imagine and implement a truly feminist theory/practice of mothering. In particular, I began to question whether my research and that of feminist scholarship on motherhood more generally, has truly and fully actualized the potential of the Demeter archetype, and more specifically "her power and the efficacy of her anger." I want to suggest that while the new feminist literature on motherhood has allowed for new progressive styles of childrearing and generated maternal activism, it has not gone far enough in its attempts to transform motherhood *for the mother herself,* to realize fully the maternal power and fury promised in the Demeter archetype.

In her book *Mother Without Child: Contemporary Fiction and the Crisis of Motherhood,* Elaine Tuttle Hansen argues that "the story of feminists thinking about motherhood since the early 1960s is told as a drama in three acts: repudiation, recuperation, and, in the latest and most difficult stage to conceptualize, an emerging critique of recuperation that coexists with ongoing efforts to deploy recuperative strategies" (5). I want to argue, using Hansen's metaphor, that as feminist theory moves from a repudiation of patriarchal motherhood to a recuperation of motherhood (i.e. the formation of feminist mothering) we must not lose sight of what must be the primary and central aim of our challenge to patriarchal mother-hood, namely the empowerment of mothers. In other words, as repudiation and recuperation define the first two acts of the feminist resistance to motherhood, the final act must be expressed more specifically as a revolution of motherhood for mothers themselves. As of late, we have lost this focus and our tone has become tame and timid and our manner cautious and circuitous. Instead of demanding change for mothers, we are now requesting them for children.

Feminist mothering, whether it is termed resistant, courageous, hip or rebel-lious, operates as counter narrative of motherhood. It seeks to interrupt the master narrative of motherhood to imagine and implement a view of mothering that is *empowering* to women. Two central themes of feminist mothering literature, as discussed above, are anti-sexist childrearing and maternal activism. Both per-spectives emphasize maternal power and ascribe agency to mothers and value to motherwork. As a consequence, mothering in feminist theory and practice becomes reconfigured as a social act. While patriarchal motherhood defines motherwork as solely privatized care undertaken in the domestic sphere, feminist mothering regards such as explicitly and profoundly political and public.

This political-social dimension of mothering is manifested in two ways. The first occurs in the home wherein these mothers bring about social change through the anti-sexist childrearing of children.[2] Termed "A Politics of the Heart" as I do, or "Home is where the Revolution is" as Cecelie Berry does, this perspec-tive regards the motherwork undertaken in the private sphere as having social consequence and political significance. The second way that mothering, in feminist practice, becomes a public act is through maternal activism. For many feminist mothers, their commitment to both feminism and to children becomes expressed as maternal activism. Mothers, through maternal activism, use their position as mothers to lobby for social and political change, usually for and on behalf of children. Central to the feminist challenge to patriarchal motherhood is this redefinition of motherwork as a political act, undertaken at home and in the world at large.

Anti-sexist childrearing and maternal activism are significant and essential tasks of feminist mothering. However, maternal activism on behalf of children and feminist childrearing for children, does not in any real manner address the needs of mothers. More specifically, I would argue that in defining feminist mothering in this manner, we have, consciously or otherwise, discounted and disregarded what must be the first and primary aim of feminist mothering; namely the empowerment of mothers. Feminist scholarship has documented well how and why patriarchal motherhood is oppressive to mothers; however, when this same scholarship seeks to imagine a feminist mode of mothering, the focus inexplicably shifts from the mother to children (anti-sexist childrearing) and/or to a world apart from the mother (maternal activism). In its first stage, a repudiation of patriarchal moth-erhood, the mother, and her discontent, was our foremost concern; however in the second stage, recuperation, as we seek to re-conceive and reclaim mothering, the mother, while still crucial, frequently becomes instrumental to larger, and seemingly more important, objectives of social change. In other words, mothers are accorded agency to affect social change through childrearing or activism but little attention is paid to what this agency does or means for the mother herself in the context of *her own life*.

Equally troubling is the way much of this literature justifies and rationalizes the reasons for feminist mothering. Too often, the demand to empower mothers is recast as a strategy for more effective parenting. Erika Horwitz, as discussed above, argues that empowered mothering is characterized by women insisting on "the importance of mothers meeting their own needs" and the realization that "being a mother does not fulfill all of women's needs." However, in most instances, the mothers' demands for agency and autonomy are repositioned as requirements of the children. As one mother explained, she resisted patriarchal motherhood, "to make me a better mother for my children" (52). Janna Malamud Smith, as well, draws upon the myth of Demeter and Persephone but does so to argue that children are best served by empowered mothers. Rereading my own work, I recognize that I too have been complicit in this questionable tactic of rationalization and justification. In both theory and practice, my demands for empowered mothering are defined and defended as necessary and essential *for children*. Like much of feminist scholarship on motherhood, my campaign for feminist mothering centred upon how this would benefit children most notably by way of the argument that empowered mothers are more effective mothers.

While I do believe that feminist mothers are more effective mothers and that anti-sexist childrearing and maternal activism are worthwhile aims and are made possible by dismantling patriarchal motherhood, I still wonder and worry why the rhetoric of rationalization has become the strategy of choice among feminist activists and scholars today and why our campaigns for social change centre on children, and not ourselves as mothers. Why can we not simply demand that motherhood be made better for mothers themselves? Why are our demands for maternity leaves, flex-time, greater involvement of partners in the home etc. always couched and explained as being for and about the children? Why are mothers' demands for more time, money, support and validation only responded to when they are seen as benefiting children? I realize that this rhetoric is often employed strategically by feminists to make gains for mothers that otherwise would not be possible in a patriarchal culture. Patriarchal culture will accord mothers resources if they use them on behalf of children; the mother can take time for herself if this makes her a better mother for her children. While I appreciate the utility of this tactic, it still deeply troubles me. Such a strategy will certainly backfire. Moreover, and most importantly, real change for mothers can not be achieved if such is always defined as for and about children. While I am not suggesting that we do away with a strategy that has proven effective, I do believe that we must, likewise, lobby for and on behalf of mothers; to secure and guard a place for mothers between the proverbial baby and the bathwater. Only as an empowered and enraged Demeter, can we, I believe, achieve a truly transformative and transgressive feminist theory and practice of mothering.

Feminist Mothering as Resistance to Intensive Mothering and the "New Momism"

A central theme of contemporary feminist writing on motherhood has been a critique of intensive mothering. Beginning with Sharon Hays' *The Cultural Contradictions of Motherhood*, feminists have identified the many ways that the discourse of intensive mothering operates as regulatory discourse to oppress women (see Valerie Walkerdine and Helen Lucey; Sharon Hays; Chris Bobel; Judith Warner; and Susan Douglas and Meredith Michaels in this *Reader*; Petra Bueskens; Andrea O'Reilly (2004a); and Bonnie Fox. However, this critique of intensive mothering has not, with the exception of Susan Douglas and Meredith Michaels' discussion of rebellious mothering, developed an alternative model of mothering that would counter the "anti-mother" principles of intensive mothering and thus allow for a more mother-centred, and hence empowering, mode of mothering. Feminist mothering is such a model of mothering for not only does it provide an alternative to intensive mothering, it enables, nay empowers, mothers to challenge and change the various ways that the discourse of intensive mothering regulates and tyrannizes women.

Intensive mothering is characterized by three inter-connected themes. The first defines mothering as *natural* to women and essential to their being, conveyed in the belief, as Pamela Courtenay Hall notes, that "women are *naturally* mothers, they are born with a built-in set of capacities, dispositions, and desires to nurture children [... and that this] engagement of love and instinct is utterly distant from the world of paid work..." (337). Secondly, the mother is to be central caregiver of her biological children; and third, children require full-time mothering, or in the instance where the mother must work outside the home, the children must always come before the job. This model of mothering, as Sharon Hays explains in *The Cultural Contradictions of Motherhood*, "tells us that children are innocent and priceless, that their rearing should be carried out primarily by individual mothers and that it should be centered on children's needs, with methods that are informed by experts, labor intensive, and costly" (21). She emphasizes that intensive mothering is "a historically constructed *cultural model* for appropriate child care" (21, emphasis in original). "Conceptions of appropriate child rearing," she continues,

> Are not simply a random conglomeration of disconnected ideas; they form a fully elaborated, logically cohesive framework for thinking about and acting toward children.... [W]e are told that [intensive mothering] is the best model, largely because it is what children need and deserve. This model was not developed overnight, however, nor is intensive mothering the only model available to mothers. (21)

Sharon Hays argues that intensive mothering emerged in the post-war period. I contend, in contrast, that while the origins of intensive mothering may be traced back to this time, intensive mothering, in its fully developed form, came about in

the early 1990s. Hays argues, as noted above, that intensive mothering is characterized by three themes: "first, the mother is the central caregiver;" "mothering
is regarded as more important than paid employment;" and that such mothering
requires "lavishing copious amounts of time, energy, and material resources on
the child" (8). I would suggest that while the first two characterize mothering
from post-war to present day, only mothering of the last fifteen years can be
characterized by the third theme: namely children require copious amounts of
time, energy and material resources.

The post-war discourse of good motherhood demanded that mothers be at
home full time with their children; however, such did not necessitate the intensive
mothering expected of mothers today. Today, the ideology of good motherhood
demands more than mere physical proximity of mother-child: contemporary mothers are expected to spend, to use the discourse of the experts, "quality time" with
their children. Mothers are told to play with their children, read to them and take
classes with them. As the children in the '50s and '60s would jump rope or play
hide-and-seek with the neighbourhood children or their siblings, today's children
dance, swim and 'cut and paste' with their mothers in one of many 'moms and
tots' programs. And today, children, as young as one month old, are enrolled in a
multitude of classes from water-play for infants, French immersion for toddlers,
karate for pre-schoolers, and competitive skiing, skating or sailing for elementary
school children. (An article I read recently also recommended reading and singing to your child in utero). Today, although they have fewer children and more
labour saving devices—from microwaves to take out food—mothers spend more
time, energy (and I may add money) on their children than their mothers did in
the 1960s. And the majority of mothers today, unlike forty years ago, practice
intensive mothering while engaged in full-time employment. Mothering today, as
in the post-war era, is "expert driven." However, mothering today is also, under
the ideology of intensive mothering, more child-centred than the "children should
be seen but not heard" style of mothering that characterized the post-war period.
Indeed, as Susan Douglas and Meredith Michaels observe in *The Mommy Myth*,
"Intensive mothering [has become] the ultimate female Olympics" (6).

Douglas and Michaels term this contemporary discourse of motherhood "the
new momism":

> The insistence that no woman is truly complete or fulfilled unless she
> has kids, that women remain the best primary caretakers of children,
> and that to be a remotely decent mother, a woman has to devote her
> entire physical, psychological, emotional, intellectual being, 24/7, to her
> children. The new momism is a highly romanticized view of motherhood
> in which the standards for success are impossible to meet. (4).

However, as Douglas and Michaels go on to explain, "The new momism involves
more than just impossible ideals about women childrearing, it redefines all women,
first and foremost, through their relationships to children. Thus, being a citizen, a

worker, a governor [and so forth] are suppose to take a backseat to motherhood" (22). "The new momism," Douglas and Michaels continue, "insists that if you want to do anything else, you'd better first prove that you're a doting, totally involved mother before proceeding. The only recourse for women who want careers, or to do anything else besides stay at home with the kids all day, is to prove they can 'do it all'" (22). A crucial dimension of the "new momism," which has particular relevance to the motherhood memoir, is the concept of choice.

> Central to the new momism is the feminist insistence that women have choices, that they are active agents in control of their own destiny, that they have autonomy. But here's where the distortion of feminism occurs. The only truly enlightened choice to make as a woman, the one that proves, first, that you are a "real" woman, and second, that you are a decent, worthy one, is to become a "mom" and to bring to child rearing a combination of selflessness and professionalism…. Thus the new momism is deeply contradictory: it both draws from and repudiates feminism. (Douglas and Michaels 5)

Moreover, in its assertions of female agency and autonomy, the "new momism" denies and distorts the fact that most mothers have little or no choice in the making of their lives. The concept of choice, as feminist theory has shown us, is a Liberal fiction that serves to disguise and justify social inequities, particularly those of gender.

For me the most worrisome part of the new momism is that being a stay-at-home mother is constructed as the mother's choice. Again to return to Douglas and Michael's discussion of choice, they write:

> The mythology of the new momism now insinuates that, when all is said and done, the enlightened mother chooses to stay at home with the kids. Back in the 1950s mothers stayed home because they had no choice. Today having been to the office, having tried a career, women supposedly have seen the inside of the male working world and found it be the inferior choice to staying home, especially when her kids' future is at stake. It's not that mothers can't hack it (1950s thinking). It's that progressive mothers refuse to hack it…. The June Cleaver model, if taken as a *choice*, as opposed to a requirement, is the truly modern fulfilling forward-thinking version of motherhood. (23)

While many of the advocates of intensive mothering expose the concept of choice for what it is—a fiction and a fallacy—they, nonetheless, see their full-time mothering as inevitable and necessary. Others, though, do deflect and disguise the very real structural and familial inequities mothers face by way of a narrative of choice. A writer in the collection *Breeder,* who practices attachment parenting as a college student, for example, explains that she decided to quit school when pregnant with her second child because "I was tired every day, tired all over, and the prospect of spending the next several months so impossibly tired was too much for me" (83). So, as she goes on to explain, "Feeling that I faced a *choice* between my future and my present, I withdrew from my classes" (emphasis added, 84). Later she writes, "My education has not been put on hold; on the contrary, I am a full-time student in an accelerated toddler studies program. My three-year old is experimenting with wet-on-wet watercolours, and the baby will be walking soon. Now that's what I call progress" (85). As someone who gave birth to three children in five years while an undergrad and later a grad student, I can certainly understand being "impossibly tired," but the reasons for this such tiredness are as much the result of her adherence to the new momism discourse which requires her to be the main caretaker of the children 24/7 via attachment parenting. Had she used some childcare, insisted upon shared parenting (her partner is not even mentioned in the story), and renounced "natural" and intensive mothering, she would have had, in all likelihood, the time and energy to combine motherhood with her studies. (This is not to negate the need for structural change in workplaces.) But because of her adherence to the new momism philosophy of mothering, she simply cannot see these as possibilities and thus must accept societal and familial gender inequities as both inevitable and natural. More troublesome is that all of this is narrated and justified in the language of feminism.

A theory and practice of feminist mothering provides mothers with the very power that intensive mothering denies. In its challenge to the basic tenants of intensive mothering—mothering must be provided 24/7, may only be done by the mother, and motherhood is the most important and essential dimension of womanhood—feminist mothering does not restrict or reduce a woman's identity and purpose solely to motherhood. Moreover, in its insistence upon real shared parenting, (partner, daycare, othermothering, etc.) and critique of the excessive child-centeredness of intensive mothering, feminist mothering allows women the time and energy to develop a selfhood beyond motherhood. The young woman discussed above, had she practiced *real* feminist mothering, would not have had to choose between her children and herself. And feminist mothering, in its attention to maternal activism—particularly as it calls for better social and work polices for mothers (mothers centres, maternity leave, childcare, family leave, flex time, etc.)—helps to bring about larger social changes to make mothers' lives better. Finally, feminist mothering, particularly in its most mother-centred emphasis as discussed above, makes mothers' needs and wants central and does so without rationalization and justification. In each of the above themes, feminist mothering not only affords mothers agency, authority, autonomy, and authenticity but, in so doing, enables mothers to challenge and change the very patriarchal discourse of intensive mothering that causes motherhood to be oppressive to women.

Conclusion

In her recent article "Developing a Feminist Motherline: Reflections on a Decade of Feminist Parenting," Fiona Joy Green, reflecting upon the experiences shared by the feminist mothers she interviewed, observes, "I am struck by the need to continue sharing and recording feminist motherline stories to ensure that the difficult, yet rewarding work of feminist mothering remains a communal and political endeavour" (2006: 18). She goes on to say:

> A feminist motherline provides the space and a place for feminist mothers to record and pass on their own life-cycle perspectives of feminist mothering and to connect with those of other feminist mothers. Additionally, a motherline ensures that feminist mothers have a connection with a worldview that is centred and draws upon feminist's crucial gender based analysis of the world—including parenting. It also promises a legacy of feminist mothering and motherwork for others (2006: 18).

With Green, I believe that "motherline stories contain invaluable lessons and memories of feminist mothering, as well as support for mothers" (18). Looking back at two-plus decades of feminist mothering, I realize that it has been precisely these stories, shared across telephone lines, kitchen tables and more recently keyboards, that have sustained me as a feminist mother. I remember a few years back when my eldest daughter was going through a particularly difficult time, I emailed Fiona in despair, convinced that it was my feminist mothering that had caused my daughter's life to become such a mess. A few hours later when the depression had all but settled in, I checked my emails to find in bright caps on the computer screen the subject heading: YOU ARE A GOOD MOTHER AN-DREA! Fiona's words of understanding, encouragement, and reassurance helped to restore my confidence and conviction as a feminist mother and enabled me to continue anew the difficult but necessary work of feminist mothering. Building upon my work of cultural bearing in African American Culture,[3] Green argues that mothers, in sharing their stories of feminist mothering, are similarly cultural bearers of feminism. I would like to conclude this chapter on feminist mothering with Green's words because for me they best represent the promise of feminist mothering as explored in this chapter:

> "Through developing a feminist motherline, with feminist mothers being the cultural bearers of feminism in their daily lives, empowerment for mothers and children is surely to follow."

Notes

[1]Several books have examined the relationship between feminism and motherhood but very little has been published on feminist mothering. For two important works on the former topic, see Umansky; Chase and Rogers.

[2]In my scholarship on African American motherhood I argue how, in the instance of African American mothers, the political-social dimension of motherwork as-

sumes as its central aim the empowerment of black children. Please see my book *Toni Morrison and Motherhood: A Politics of the Heart* (2004c).
[3]Please see my book on Toni Morrison (2004c), noted above.

References

Abbey, Sharon and Andrea O'Reilly. *Redefining Motherhood: Changing Identities and Patterns.* Toronto: Second Story Press, 1998.

Association for Research on Mothering. Online: www.yorku.ca/arm.

Berry, Cecelie. *Rise Up Singing: Black Women Writers on Motherhood*, New York: Random House, 2005.

Blakely, Mary Kay. *American Mom.* Chapel Hill: Algonquin Books, 1994.

Bort, Julie, *et al. Mommy Guilt: Learn to Worry Less, Focus on What Matters Most, and Raise Happier Kids.* New York: American Management Association, 2005.

Bueskens, Petra. "From Perfect Housewife to Fishnet Stockings and Not Quite Back Again: One Mother's Story of Leaving Home." *Mother Outlaws: Theories and Practices of Empowered Mothering.* Ed. A. O'Reilly. Toronto: Women's Press, 2004. 105-119.

Canadian Oxford Dictionary. Toronto: Oxford University Press, 1998.

Chase, Susan E. and Mary F. Rogers. *Mothers And Children: Feminist Analyses and Personal Narratives.* New Brunswick, NJ: Rutgers University Press, 2001.

Copper, Baba. "The Radical Potnetial in Lesbian Mothering of Daughters." *Politics of the Heart: A Lesbian Parenting Anthology.* Eds. Sandra Pollack and Jeanne Vaughn. Ann Arbor: Firebrand Press, 1987.

Davey, Moyra. *Mother Reader: Essential Writings on Motherhood.* New York: Seven Stories Press, 2001.

Douglas, Susan and Meredith Michaels. *The Mommy Myth.* New York: Free Press, 2005.

Fox, Bonnie. "Motherhood as a Class Act." *Social Reproduction.* Eds. K. Bezanson and M. Luxton. Montreal: McGill-Queens, 2006. 231-262.

Gore, Ariel and Bee Lavender. *Breeder: Real-Life Stories from the New Generation of Mothers.* Seattle: Seal Press: 2001.

Glickman, Rose L. *Daughters of Feminists.* New York: St. Martin's Press, 1993.

Golden, Marita. *Saving Our Sons: Raising Black Children in a Turbulent World.* New York: Doubleday, 1995.

Gordon, Tuula. *Feminist Mothers.* Houndsmills: Macmillan, 1990.

Green, Fiona Joy. "Developing a Feminist Motherline: Reflections on a Decade of Feminist Parenting." *Journal of the Association for Research on Mothering* 8 (1/2) (Summer/Winter 2006): 7-20.

Green, Fiona. "Feminist Mothers: Successfully Negotiating the Tension Between Motherhood as 'Institution' and 'Inexperience.'" *From* Motherhood to Mothering: The Legacy of Adrienne Rich's Of Woman Born. Ed. Andrea O'Reilly. Albany: SUNY Press, 2004. 125-136.

Hall, Pamela Courtenay. "Mothering Mythology in the Late 20th Century: Science, Gender Lore and Celebratory Narrative." *Canadian Woman Studies: An Introductory Reader*. 1st ed. Eds. Nuzhat Amin *et al*. Toronto: Inanna Publications and Education Inc., 2006. 337-345.

Hays, Sharon. *The Cultural Contradictions of Motherhood*. New Haven: Yale University Press, 1996.

Horwitz, Erika. "Resistance as a Site of Empowerment: The Journey Away From Maternal Sacrifice." *Mother Outlaws: Theories and Practices of Empowered Mothering*. Ed. Andrea O'Reilly. Toronto: Women's Press, 2004.

Horwitz, Erika. "Mothers' Resistance to the Western Dominant Discourse on Mothering." Unpublished dissertation, Simon Fraser University, 2003.

Kinser, Amber. *Mothering in the Third Wave*. Demeter Press, 2007.

Maushart, Susan. *The Mask of Motherhood*. New York: New Press, 1999.

Mellor, Christie. *The Three-Martini Playdate: A Practical Guide to Happy Parenting*. San Francisco: Chronicle Books, 2004.

O'Reilly, Andrea. *From Motherhood to Mothering: The Legacy of Adrienne Rich's Of Woman Born*. Albany: SUNY Press, 2004a.

O'Reilly, Andrea, ed. *Mother Outlaws: Theories and Practices of Empowered Mothering*. New York: SUNY Press, 2004b.

O'Reilly, Andrea. *Toni Morrison and Motherhood: A Politics of the Heart*. New York: SUNY Press, 2004c.

O'Reilly, Andrea. *Rocking the Cradle: Thoughts on Motherhood, Feminism, and the Possibility of Empowered Mothering*. Toronto: Demeter Press, 2006.

O'Reilly, Andrea, ed. *Feminist Mothering*. Albany: SUNY Press. Forthcoming 2008.

Rich, Adrienne. *Of Woman Born: Motherhood as Experience and Institution*. New York: W. W. Norton, 1986.

Ruddick, Sara. *Maternal Thinking: Toward a Politics of Peace*. Boston: Beacon Press, 1989.

Simpson, Bria. *The Balanced Mom: Raising Your Kids Without Losing Your Self*. Oakland: New Harbinger Publications, 2006.

Shields, Julie. *How to Avoid the Mommy Trap: A Roadmap for Sharing Parenting and Making it Work*. Sterling: Capital Books, 2002.

Smith, Janna Malamud. *A Potent Spell: Mother Love and the Power of Fear*. Boston: Houghton Mifflin, 2003.

Tiemann, Amy. *Mojo Mom: Nurturing Your Self While Raising a Family*. Spark Press, 2006.

Trebilcot, Joyce, ed. *Mothering: Essays in Feminist Theory*. Totowa: Rowman and Allanheld, 1983.

Tuttle Hansen, Elaine. *Mother Without Child: Contemporary Fiction and the Crisis of Motherhood*. Berkeley: University of California Press, 1997.

Umansky, Laura. *Motherhood Reconceived: Feminism and the Legacy of the Sixties*. New York: New York University Press, 1996.

Waring, Marilyn. *As If Women Counted: A New Feminist Economics*. 1988. San Francisco: HarperSanFrancisco, 1990.

Chapter 49

Con el Palote en Una Mano
y el Libro en la Otra

LARISSA MERCADO-LÓPEZ

ON A RECENT evening in April of 2006, my daughters and I stood, holding hands, in front of the university's "Border Crossing" statue, created by the late Luis Jiménez. The university's conservative student organization was petitioning to have the statue removed because, according to them, it allegedly depicted "illegal activity," and the Chicana/o graduate student group I belonged to was having a peace vigil in honor of the immigrants the statue represented. As we stood, I could not help but feel that my history was being effaced and that my family and I were being personally attacked, and I knew that my failure to act would render me complicitous in that attack. I gazed at the woman huddled on top of her husband's shoulders, her child's hands wildly reaching out of the hand-made *rebozo* she clutched around her shoulders, and I empathized with that woman—a crosser of borders, a protector of children, a vehicle of tradition, a survivor who goes against the current and stays above the water. As the conservative student group whispered their opposition to our vigil, I looked over and noticed some of my own *raza* in that crowd. I wondered how many of them were carried by their mothers across those very same literal and figurative waters. Clutching my daughters' hands, I resolved that my decision to include my children in la lucha was not one of simple choice, but of necessity: if we don't involve our children in our own movimientos, they will surely become a part of someone else's.

Atravesando y Llorando

I like to think that I am *una traviesa*, one who traverses the boundaries of destiny and tradition, what Gloria Holguín Cuádraz would refer to as an "adulteress to our class and culture" (217). I have followed the Chicana's traditional path in an untraditional way, becoming the expected wife and mother while maintaining a space in the academy. I've made tortillas while reading Anzaldúa; nursed babies with my left hand while typing with the right; carried a diaper bag on one shoulder and a backpack on the other; tickled baby feet while typing out footnotes. A pejorative term, "*traviesa*" has become who I am, an identity that allows me to find strength in the contradictions that I embody as a Chicana mother-scholar.

However, from combating demoralizing feelings of guilt and inadequacy as a mother to feeling out of place and illegitimate as a scholar, my journey as a Chicana mother/activist in graduate school has not been one without struggle. Criticized for her decision to pursue fulfillment *outside* of the home, the Chicana mother in academia at times suffers from the "Llorona complex," a stigma that shrouds Chicanas who choose not to have children in order to pursue their career or who 'sacrifice' their children to pursue other personal passions (Castillo 186). But the wail of the academic Chicana mother/Llorona is not for the children she leaves at home, but for those others who complicate her existence, who refuse to allow her to occupy that space where she can negotiate her identity as a mother, a scholar, an artist, and an activist. Before I began to embrace my maternity as an intersectional, politicized identity, I struggled to negotiate my spheres of scholarly, artistic, and maternal identities, problematically attempting to perform these identities one at a time. However, I have come to realize that the only way to avoid becoming una Llorona is to perform my motherhood as a function of my politics and my politics as a function of my motherhood.

In her essay "The Mother-Bond Principle," Ana Castillo questions and challenges constructions of motherhood, examining the structural, cultural, and religious underpinnings that have reduced women to mere wombs in the nationalist project. Castillo advocates for Chicanas to appropriate a Xicanista consciousness to examine their perceptions of motherhood as performed by their mothers as they begin to form their *own* identities as mothers. She states, "We are daughters of women who have been subject to a social system—compounded doubly by Mexican traditions and U.S. WASP dominance that prohibited them from opportunities that may have challenged their creative and intellectual potential in more ways than being wife, mother, and assembly line worker" (188). This systematic refusal to recognize a "creative and intellectual potential" is one that has confined the Chicana mother to her home, to her children, to her position in the labor market. Whether by the demands of capitalism or the guilt from Catholicism, the Chicana mother has learned to quell her yearning to create in ways other than producing the goods of capitalism or birthing children. While it can be argued that Chicana mothers have been held responsible for the reproduction of significant cultural traditions, such traditions are typically those which are able to be performed within the parameters of the mother's domestic sphere and that support or emphasize the qualities, practices and expectations of the traditional mother, such as cooking, caring for children and nurturing their religious identities; motherhood, in these cases, defines the parameters of the Chicana's participation in cultural reproduction. Likewise, aesthetic reproduction often has been confined to what can be performed in the home and within the mother's role. As a result, our own Chicana mothers, traditionally, have channeled their creative energies not through the paintbrush or the plume or the instrument (at least not in public), but through the intensive care of their gardens, the beautiful hand-knitted *estrellitas* in their tapestries, and the perfect symmetry of their tortillas. I've witnessed this act of creation in my own *abuela*, whose incessant rose gardening, knitting, and stitching baffled me as a teenager. Small stacks of tablecloths and pillowcases always lay strewn about; the table cloths that actually made it to the table were covered in plastic. She knitted in the day and late at night, in the dining room, guided only by a distant kitchen light and the glow from the television I watched in her living room. And as I fell asleep I was almost always sure to hear the creaking of the floorboards as her soft steps approached me to cover me with one of her many holey, knitted *colchas,* blankets that offered no protection from the cold but always warmed me inside.

Nationalism has co-opted the rhetoric of motherhood to keep Chicana mothers from searching for fulfillment outside the home, demanding that the woman remain all-sacrificing for the good of the nation and cultura. Virgin/whore or Tonantzin-Guadalupe/Malinche-Llorona, the Chicana mother constantly finds herself navigating between these binaries, searching for that space where motherhood can be performed in ways that are meaningful and fulfilling.

Chicanas Working in M/other(ly) Ways

The first "official" attempt to reconstruct Chicana motherhood occurred in 1971, when 600 Chicanas gathered in solidarity in Houston, Texas for the first national Chicana conference (Vidal 21). It was the first time that Chicana leaders of the Chicana/o Movement had gathered in a safe, non-sanctioned space to discuss the issues not being discussed by their male counterparts, particularly those concerning their needs as women and mothers. The Chicana leaders resolved, "Chicana motherhood should not preclude educational, political, social, and economic advancement," challenging the socially and culturally constructed definitions and limitations of "motherhood" (21). This articulation marked the beginning of the Chicana's efforts to liberate Chicana mothers from their nonnegotiable confinement to their homes, husbands, and children. Ideally, the Chicana mother was now "free" to pursue personal, intellectual, and artistic development, and to seek the fulfillment and happiness that motherhood alone could not always satisfy.

The Chicanas of the Chicana/o Movement expanded the definitions of "woman," "wife," and "mother" through their work in the public sphere as political organizers and scholars. Taking to the streets and the classrooms, these Chicanas involved themselves in shaping the policies that affected their households and their ways of living. As the personal became more political, the parameters that defined their domestic sphere grew past their tiny yards and past their streets, surpassing school districts, cities, even counties. Their political work was inextricable from their personal work, and almost always one and the same.

It is now more than thirty-five years later. Binaries of Chicana motherhood still exist, so I am forced to articulate my own conceptualization of Chicana motherhood, which I have come to call third-space Chicana maternal praxis. Theory informs my mothering, but my mothering/maternity has the potential to challenge theory. As a Chicana mother-scholar I am an embodiment of discursive and cultural contradiction; nothing is stable. I continue to carve out ways to be the feminist that I am by confronting these contradictions, by acknowledging my maternal, brown body not as an organ for patriarchal movements but as a body of knowledge(s). I am constantly reminded of my body's materiality when I return home between semesters to my tiny town of 2,400 in South Texas. When asked how my degree is coming along, I cannot help but imagine that when I state, "I'm a full-time student," my *tia* or *tio* really hears, "I'm a part-time mom." I find it frustrating that the work I do as an academic is not considered intrinsic to my work as a mother, because my desire to expend my energy in Chicana feminism, theory and literature is kindled by my love for my daughters and my concern for (and fear of) the world they are living in. Whether I am articulating Chicana third-space maternal pedagogies in the writing classroom or questioning the absence of Chicana representation in university committees, the work I do in the university is to ensure the inclusion and *validation* of my children and all other Chicanitas from the first day they set foot on a college campus. As an instructor of Freshman Composition, I am already shaping and training the social actors who will, or have already begun to, interact with future Chicana university students. My influence, my work, my *mothering* begins now and here.

My decision to continue with graduate school and enter a Ph.D. program after having children was fueled by a very different reason from my decision to go to graduate school prior to my children's births: then it was about what I wanted to do; now it is about what I *must* do. As women, under the law we have the choice to become mothers; as mothers, however, *we have no choice* when it comes to doing the *work that matters*. And this is where my frustration lies. I cannot comprehend why my work as an academic and an activist is not considered work that matters to the well-being of my family, when my family—biological, cultural, and global—is the reason I do this work. I do not understand why a mother's work must always be restricted to that which is necessary to maintain the environment of the home, when the climate of the home is so contingent on the work that is done in the external social/political/ecological environment. When I vote as a mother, I am influencing policies that determine whether or not I will receive assistance with food and medical care, or maintain protection of my reproductive rights. I may not resolve the immigration debates or end domestic violence by voting or marching in the streets, but I am part of the solution, and my children will gain the sense of understanding that they, too, can work to improve their world.

Perhaps what is needed is not only an extension of "work" but also an extension of "home;" maybe then the work (artistic, political, and domestic), the skills, the strategies of living that mothers have so finely honed and developed to ensure the survival of the home and family will be applied to maintain the survival of the cultural community, the city, the world.

Dolores Huerta, one of the great Chicana civil rights activists and mother of eleven children, has advocated throughout her life for the involvement of the mother and children in politics and the movimiento. "Lower your homemaking standards," her official website states; "I always like to say that for every unmade bed, some farm workers got a $1 an hour or more" (par. 6). As a graduate student and activist I have come to the realization that I will never "get ahead" in my housework, much less keep up with it. But the work I am doing is not like the laundry that can be done late at night before I go to bed: the urgency of the society we live in is much too great to be ignored or postponed. Chicana mothers must be involved because they are most in tune with the needs of the family. If they are not involved, the Chicana/o family runs the risk of being under- or misrepresented, which often leads to being underserved.

Towards a Libratory Paradigm of Chicana Motherhood

I call for a reconfiguration of Chicana motherhood, a motherhood in which the academic/political work that I am doing now—and that I will continue to do in the future—is considered just as important to the health and development of my children as the food I am putting on the table. It will be a motherhood that is as much about nurturing the body, spirit, and mind of the mother as nurturing those of the children, a motherhood that extends beyond the socially constructed parameters of the home and flows across city, county, state, and national borderlines. Whereas the resolution on Chicana motherhood once read, "Chicana motherhood should not preclude educational, political, social, and economic advancement" (Vidal 21), it is vital that it now read "Chicana motherhood *must include* educational, political, social, and economic advancement."

Chicana mothers today are situated on the cusp of tradition, a location of potential empowerment where they can negotiate the traditions handed down to them as well as the possibilities of creating new ones. Chicana motherhood is a site of conflict, where values of the past come into contact with those of the present; it is a site of contradiction, where brown, maternal bodies must negotiate their identities within public spaces. But rather than dwell over her fragmentation, the Chicana mother can approach her position as an opportunity to create new models of motherhood, and to help others achieve transcendence into a motherhood that allows for personal and political development.

Chicana mothers today are slowly becoming aware of this space of empowerment, and are turning to public service and the arts to affect social and cultural change. Organizations such as Latina Mami in Austin, Texas and Chicana Mama in Phoenix, Arizona were begun to fill the void for support and resources for Latina and Chicana mothers. From maternity clothes to ESL classes to culturally enriching playdates, these organizations are committed to the care and physical and intellectual/cultural growth of both mother and child. In addition, testimonios, such as Nina Marie Duran's *Elijah on My Mind*, are opening up possibilities for dialogue and consciousness-formation. Duran's short testimonio on young motherhood is one of few accounts of Chicana motherhood to forge its way into the exploding scene of "Mommy Lit." While Duran's book does not specifically address the complexities of *Chicana* motherhood, it is the absence of the recognition of these complexities that demands the writings of Chicana mothers. Cherríe Moraga's *Waiting in the Wings: Portrait of a Queer Motherhood*, a memoir about

Chicana lesbian motherhood, and Ana Castillo's essay "The Mother-Bond Principle" are two of the only works to specifically address Chicana motherhood, and while they are seminal contributions to mother of color scholarship, more work is needed to attend to the multiplicitous identities within the maternal Chicana community. My sister and I recently had a conversation about the lack of literature on motherhood that features *Chicana* mothers on and between the covers, besides the occasional, government-issued "how-to" manual on infant nutrition and development. While the physical experience of pregnancy and childbirth is, for the most part, transcultural, the ways (myths, religious beliefs, etc.) in which we *interpret* and make meaning of the childbearing and child-rearing experience vary greatly across cultures. Third-wave efforts to free women from essentialist identities have yet to fully attend to the *semiotics* of the pregnant body, especially that of the brown Chicana. The absence of Chicana mothers from this scene obscures the cultural and social differences between Chicana motherhood and the dominant perception of (Anglo) motherhood, necessitating that Chicana mothers take up the pen to write their way back into literature, into the social fabric, into motherhood.

Chicana motherhood is not simply a vocation but a call to action; it is an opportunity to pass on important traditions, as well as an opportunity to discard those that do not benefit the family and to create new traditions that do. As I continue in my graduate studies I will approach everything I do as a responsibility of motherhood, and along the way I will share my story with the hope that others will share theirs. I will write, I will create, I will protest: I will mother. The work I will do for my global and cultural families will be inextricable from that which I do for my biological family, for the work I do as a mother-scholar is a labor of love, and anything one does for love is truly the work that matters.

References

Anzaldúa, Gloria. *Borderlands/La Frontera: The New Mestiza*. San Francisco: Aunt Lute Books, 1999.

Castillo, Ana. *Massacre of the Dreamers: Essays on Xicanisma*. New York: Plume, 1994.

Cuádraz, Gloria Holguín. "Diary of a Llorona Ph.D." *Telling to Live: Latina Feminist Testimonios*. Ed. The Latina Feminist Group. Durham: Duke UP, 2001.

Durán, Nina Marie. *Elijah on My Mind: A Little Boy Who Loves Me More Than Any Man Ever Could*. Deadwood: Wyatt-MacKenzie, 2006.

Huerta, Dolores. "Parenting Guidelines." 14 March 2006. Online: http://www. doloreshuerta.org/Parent%20Guidelines.htm.

Moraga, Cherríe. *Waiting in the Wings: Portrait of a Queer Motherhood*. Ithaca: Firebrand Books, 1997.

Vidal, Mirta. *Chicanas Speak Out*. New York: Pathfinder, 1971.

Chapter 50

Territorializing Motherhood

Motherhood and Reproductive Rights in Nationalist Sentiment and Practice

PATRIZIA ALBANESE

In 1985, CANADIAN author, Margaret Atwood, published the *Handmaid's Tale*. The book is a dystopian futuristic novel about the rise to power of a totalitarian theocracy, where after a "revolution" all women's bank accounts were frozen, they were barred from engaging in paid work and were expected to live as dependents on their husbands. A specially selected group of highly trained women were expected to reproduce babies for the barren elite, and live a life as walking wombs—reproducers of the nation.

While this may sound virtually impossible, Atwood herself admitted that her novel was based on facts and events that appeared in newspaper articles that she clipped from around the world. In fact, was this not one of the reasons given by (imperialist) Western governments for their military involvement in Afghanistan —to liberate Afghan women from the profoundly patriarchal and fundamentalist Taliban regime?[1] This chapter will briefly present a central debate within traditional theories of nationalism, which I argue is easily resolved by assessing how nations and nationalists idealize and prescriptively construct images of women, as mothers, in/of their nations. Following that, I analyze and present examples from a select number of nationalist regimes in twentieth-century Europe to show how motherhood is manipulated and used in the promotion of a monolithic view of the nation. I will here outline what nationalist regimes attempted to do to "their" women through an analysis of nationalist policies and speeches. I have chosen examples from twentieth-century Europe to demonstrate that one need not look long and hard, nor look into "the deep past," nor point fingers at (or invade) this or that "fundamentalist regime" to find examples of the archaizing and re-patriarchalizing tendencies found within nationalism. This chapter will conclude with a brief discussion of transnational motherhood, often a product of economic and social unrest and displacement that results from ethnic conflict, nationalism and war.

Theories of Nationalism

Traditional theories of nationalism have been embroiled in a debate about whether nationalism is a product of modernity or a conservative response to it. Proponents of the first thesis, that nationalism ushers in modernity or is part and parcel of modernity, point to its modernizing elements such as its power to liberate "the people" from autocratic rule (Gellner), its rational cosmopolitan currents (Kohn), its ability to transform outcasts into modern soldiers, "brothers in harmony" (McNeill 51) or "bearers of sovereignty" in a "collective solidarity" (Greenfeld 7). In contrast, others argue that nationalism is an anti-modern response to the "predicament of modern man," where nationalism provides a remedy for human alienation, and "looks inwardly, away from and beyond the imperfect world" (Kedourie 82). Allen Buchanan noted that nationalism promotes illiberal tenets, as nationalist ideology grants the nation a unique moral status above all others. I argue that the answer to whether nationalism is liberalizing, modernizing and democratizing, or its opposite lies in assessing a nation's treatment of women—which most traditional theories of nationalism have failed to do (Albanese 2004).

Over the past two decades, we have seen a growing literature on the gendering of nationalism. For example, a number of thinkers have noted that women were a particular concern of nationalist regimes because of their prescribed roles within the family (Yuval-Davis and Anthias,; Kristeva; Calhoun; Dua). For example, according to Julia Kristeva, when it comes to nations and nationalism, "women have the luck and the responsibility of being boundary-subjects" (35). Similarly, Nira Yuval Davis and Floya Anthias noted that, among other things, with the rise of nationalism, women come to be seen as biological reproducers of ethnic collectivities. Craig Calhoun noted that nationalism is a distinctly gender-biased ideology wherein family becomes the source of a nation's continuity in time and where men are seen as martyrs and women as mothers (231). Chandra Mohanty explained that imperialism, militarization and globalization all traffic in women's bodies, women's labor, and ideologies of masculinity/femininity, heteronormativity, racism and nationalism to consolidate and reproduce power and domination (9). Similarly, Na Young Lee noted that "in normative national narratives, only those women who are considered modest and chaste can be a symbol of national collective identity or the bearers of the collectivity's honor (461).

Why is it so? First off, nationalism, by its very nature, sanctions exclusion. It postulates the nation as a biological, self-perpetuating category of people which hinges upon the biological and ideological similarity of its members—after all the root of the word "nation" is the Latin verb *nasci*, meaning "to be born" (Albanese 1996: 187) and the use of the terms "motherland" and "fatherland" are intentional classificatory categories of kinship, and imply relational descent (Grosby 43). This similarity is often believed to be maintained by preserving its biological "purity," uncontaminated by foreignness—the Other. The nation and nationalists preserve their raison d'être by maintaining real or imaginary blood ties that are believed to solidify into concrete national boundaries (Albanese 1996: 187). As Robert Kaiser noted, "homelands do not come ready-made, but rather are the outcomes of the 'national construction of social space'" (231). In other words, nationalism has a tendency to homogenize whoever/whatever is contained within these boundaries, superficially obscuring diversities that exist within (for example, social class differences and other inequities; also historically, religious and racial diversity have been used to divide or "overlooked" to unite masses into nations), while at the same time creating and/or magnifying differences across boundaries, nationalities and cultures. Where necessary, divided histories are mended, and divided memories, experiences and identities forgotten or denied. Singular, similar and simple become the norm, if not the law.

Imagery has "played an important part in the creation of national consciousness" (Smith 2004: 82). Anthony Smith noted that for nationalists, "the distinctiveness of their nation lies quintessentially in their cultural heritage, above all, in their unique fund of myths, memories and traditions" (2002: 18). Therefore, nationalists place great importance on symbols, with an over-emphasis on traditions, which Eric Hobsbawm argued created the powerful illusion of primordiality and continuity. Hobsbawn noted that inventing traditions "is essentially a process of formalization and ritualization, characterized by reference to the past, if only by imposing repetition (4). In reality, and contrary to nationalist ideology, "tradition is dynamic, contested, is claimed by different groups at different moments and is continually *reinvented* in the present" (Edensor 526). Nationalists at once (re)invent tradition and deny they are doing so.

The image of the prolific, chaste, and virtuous "national mother" is a strikingly common symbol across nations. Nationalists need women as mothers, as both symbols of the nation and actual cultural and biological reproducers of it. Traditional, patriarchal (highly gendered) images of women as mothers are central to the nationalist project of myth-making (the idea of the nation) and its actual biological continuity into the future (the "practice" of nation-making). Pure and virtuous mothers are believed—and expected—to reproduce the nation in body (blood/children/future nationals) and mind (preservation of past traditions, food and ritual, and "mother tongue," to name a few). Heterosexual women/mothers symbolize and are expected to preserve the nation's past, present and future.

In this, the differential treatment of men and women "of the nation" is justified, and believed to be necessary to ensure/secure the group's survival. The nation's future is believed to hinge upon the chastity of "its" women—jealously guarded or protected from the ravaging hands of the "Other," while at once generously presented for the sexual indulgence of the virile and masculine ethnic "Self" (Albanese 1996: 188). As such, the weight of national reproduction is placed squarely upon "its" women's wombs, and images of the essential woman and mother are reified and enforced. To challenge, question or stray is deemed treasonous—as many feminists questioning their nationalist leaders have found out.

Nationalism reifies patriarchy, reinforcing archetypes of the masculine warrior/hero and feminine, virtuous, innocent, pure, clean women/mother. Double standards and self-sacrifice, for the greater good of the nation become the expected norm, with criminalization or vilification of dissent or difference, part of its practice. These ideas are engendered through symbols, in everyday public space and discourse, especially in times of conflict. Greg Gow for example, noted that both nationalist and anti-colonial nationalist, their opponents, used images of motherhood in the Oromo liberation struggles within Ethiopia. The same was found to be true by a number of feminists who found themselves on different sides of the Yugoslav conflicts throughout the 1990s (Drakulic; Ivekovic; B.a.B.e.; Morokvasic; Ugresic; Einhorn and Sever).

My work builds upon existing research with an aim to identify, outline and assess the effectiveness of policies and practices that are constructed around the ideas that women physically reproduce nations through childbearing, and are also culturally significant, as women more than men, are viewed as primary social-izers of children, and keepers of the symbolic hearth. My research indicates that contrary to contemporary theories of nationalism that suggest that nationalism is a modernizing force, beneficial to *all* group members, the entry of "the people" into politics and military life did not initially include women. "National frater-nity" and "brothers in harmony" accurately denotes the absence of women from the early benefits of nationalism because until recently women were excluded from national formal education, universal high culture, literacy, politics and the promise of legal equality as citizens.

The political man is constructed as rational, objective and devoid of emotion in peace time (Ala) and defenders of the nation in war (Albanese 2001). In con-trast, women are pictured as virtuous reproducers of the nation (Albanese 2006), stereotypically innocent victims, needing protection from men (Ala; Albanese 2004). In nationalist rhetoric, this is believed to be far too important to be left in the hands of individual women. Within this nationalist rhetoric, it is then the role of the nationalist state to see to it that it is done "correctly" and that women be wholly committed to the task.

Four European Cases

The map of Europe was significantly altered at various points the twentieth century. National borders in Europe were redrawn after the partitioning of the Habsburg (Austro-Hungarian) and Ottoman (Turkish) empires following the First World War and again after the collapse of communism in the Soviet Union and other parts of Eastern Europe. At both historical points, one of the instruments used in the carving was nationalism (Albanese 2006: 9). Both periods provided an abundance of cases to study the position and use of women in nationalist ideology. I settled on four: Germany, Italy, Russia and Yugoslavia, because Germany and Italy, were highly nationalistic in the first (interwar) period and less nationalistic in the second (post-1989). Revolutionary Russia and the Kingdom of Yugoslavia were multi-national (non-nationalistic) constructs at the end of the First World War, but were highly nationalistic in the conflict- ridden, post-1989 period.

With nationalists in power (first in Nazi German and Fascist Italy, and later in post-1989 Russia and parts of the former Yugoslavia), and because of the ethno-centric and xenophobic nature of nationalism, these nations' women gained special attention from their nationalist leaders, as actual or potential walking wombs. Women became the focus of nationalist attention because they were expected to be "mothers of the nation," reproducers of the ethnic self and cultural carriers. Women as mothers symbolized the nation's vulnerable existence at the hands of their ethnic nemesis, but were also expected to secure its future glory.

In all four cases, Nazi-Germany, fascist Italy, post-soviet Russia and post-Yugoslav Croatia, looking at leaders' speeches, writings and proposed policies, we see attempts at re-patriarchalization of women's roles. We can trace a time, before the nationalist rise to power, when women had some (relative) autonomy in their respective societies, even early in the century. With the rise to power of nationalists this was threatened, and attempts were made to return women "to their natural place," in the home, subordinating their autonomy and at times their health and well-being for the "greater good of the nation."

In Weimar Republic, for example, before Hitler's rise to power, women rose from six percent of all university students, just after the First World War, to 35 percent. They made up about one-third of the labour force, and women in Germany at the time, were the most unionized in Europe. In passing the 1927 *Maternity Protection Act,* Germany became one of the first nations to endorse the International Labour Organization's rulings on the rights of women workers. This is short lived.

With Hitler's rise to power, he ordered women to relinquish their jobs and dedicate themselves to "feminine virtues" (until they were needed for the war effort, of course!). In June 1933 legislation mandated the immediate dismissal of all women whose husbands were employed by government. Women doctors were only allowed to practice if they merged their practice with their physician husbands (if they had one). Quotas and caps of ten percent were placed on women candidates for higher education—to prevent women from entering the professions.

"Kinder, Kirche und Kuche," part of the back to the home movement were promoted as the ideal for women. In speeches and decrees Hitler stated that women ("pure blooded/Aryan" German women) were the guardians of the family and that each mother, in giving children to German was worthy of being called a hero "and being waited on hand and foot by the nation" (Thomas cited in Albanese 2006: 32). Hitler promoted pronuptialist policies and early marriages by providing marriage loans and promotions for men who were engaged. The marriage loans, for example, were interest-free loans that were reduced by 25 percent with the birth of each child. In other words, loan repayment was cancelled after the birth of a fourth child. Racially pure (Aryan) and prolific women were given medals of honour for their service to the nation on August 12, the birthday of Hitler's own mother (gold for mothers of eight, silver for mothers of six, and bronze for mothers of four children).

Hitler also overturned liberal abortions laws that were put in place in 1926, before Hitler's rise to power. That is, in 1926 the German government liberalized abortion laws, by reducing the severity of sentences for women having abortions and abortion providers (abortion became a misdemeanor rather than a crime).

Only one year later, in 1927, the German Supreme Court ruled that abortion for medical reasons was legal if it posed a danger to the mother, effectively allowing for a wider interpretation of the abortion law, and the creation of birth control and abortion clinics across the country (Albanese 2004). Hitler not only declared "German boy, do not forget you are a German, and little girl, remember that you are to become a German mother" (12), he actually passed laws to ensure this, by introducing the most severe legislation against abortion and birth control in all of Europe in 1933, making abortion a "crime against the race" (Albanese 2004).

Very similar patterns were evident and measures were put in place in Mussolini's Italy. In Mussolini's May 26, 1927, Ascension Day Speech, he talked about Italy's "demographic problem." He imposed a bachelor or celibacy tax on unmarried men, to fund some of his pronatalist programs. He had marriage loans as well, and fertility prizes (one medal is featured on the cover of my book). The laws that had previously decriminalized abortion (in 1889) were overturned, now banning abortion. The sale of contraceptive devises and sex education in general were also banned (Albanese 2004).

In one of his speeches, Mussolini declared:

> the birth rate is not simply an index of the progressive power of the nation; it is not simply as Spengler suggests, "Italy's only weapon"; it is also that which distinguishes the Fascist people from the other peoples of Europe as an index of vitality and the will to pass on this vitality over the centuries. If we do not succeed in reversing this trend, all that the Fascist revolution has accomplished and will accomplish in the future will be perfectly useless, as at a certain point in time fields, schools, barracks, ships and workshops will be empty. (1964a: 216)

Mussolini was actually obsessed with the physical fitness of Italians, but clearly not of women's individual reproductive health. Believing women were ill-prepared for the sacred and difficult mission of maternity, Mussolini set out to control their bodies, choices and reproductive practices—again, for the future good of the nation.

In more recent years, with the revival of nationalist sentiment in the Soviet Union and Yugoslavia, we see attempts at initiatives which although seemingly not as harsh, echoed or resembled Nazi Germany's and Fascist Italy's initiatives. Russia newspapers had headlines like "Is Russia dying?" (Sargeant cited in Albanese 2006: 103). Even Mikhail Gorbachev, in his book *Perestroika*, wrote:

> Over the years of our difficult and heroic history, we failed to pay attention to women's specific rights and needs arising from their role as mother and home-maker, and their indispensable educational function in regards children. Engaged in scientific research, working on construction sites, in production and services and involved in creative activities, women no longer have enough time to perform their duties

at home—housework, the upbringing of children and the creation of
good family atmosphere. (117)

Yeltzin's wife Naina, was presented as the ideal wife. She was quoted as saying:
"I choose his ties, I take care of his shirts and suits ... there is an unbreakable rule
in our family: I must never ask my husband about anything relating to his work."
Newspaper and magazine articles expressed views like the most successful "type"
of woman is one who "reasons delicately and realistically. She lets a man feel the
necessity of his leadership in life, lets him take charge in the family but always
under her hidden control" (Kay cited in Albanese 2006: 101).

A president's degree entitled "On Measures of Social Support for Families with
many Children" promised that local authorities should give plots of land, banks
should give interest free loans, and pharmacies should give free prescription medication to large families. None of this came to pass. Following the recommendations
of a vocal and largely male anti-abortion movement—who actually wanted an
outright ban—abortions went from being free, to costing up to half of a woman's
monthly income. This happened at a time that the wage gap was actually widen-
ing and calls for women's withdrawal from the labour force was voiced by many,
including the famous Russian writer, Aleksandr Solzhenitsyn.

According to data published in the *Bulletin of the World Health Organization*
(Gurina *et al.*), there have been sharp declines of direct obstetric deaths, most
often caused by sepsis and hemorrhage, over a twelve year period (1992-2003).
Death rates were especially high in 1992-1994 in St. Petersburg due to higher
mortality from illegal abortions (Gurina, Vangen, Forsen and Sundby). Natalia
Gurina *et al.* noted that over half the hemorrhage and sepsis deaths were due to
(illegal) abortions caused by strict abortion laws (until 1991) and lack of access
to appropriate health services (in 1991-1994). Maternal mortality rates in St.
Petersburg declined over the course of the study, most likely due to "liberalized
abortion legislation, improved management of abortion by development of family planning services and better access to medical units with high quality care"
(288). The Russian government's concern with the demographic "situation" was
a centerpiece in Putin's annual "State of the Union Address in 2006 ("Vladimir
Putin on Raising Russia's Birth Rate" 385).

It was widely noted that immediately following the break-up of Yugoslavia,
the status of women was declining and there was a rise in traditional attitudes
about gender (Kunovich and Deitelbaum). A study of gender attitudes in Croatia
revealed that between 1985 and 1989 there was an increase in the proportion of
men and women who supported more traditional roles for women (Kunovich
and Deitelbaum). They found that out-group polarization in particular (i.e.,
distrust of "others") had the most powerful effect on gendered family role and
policy attitudes. Clearly, these views were fueled by the government in power and
its supporters. For example, in Croatia, feminist authors, journalists and activists
(especially non-nationalist) were vilified and harassed (Urgesic; Morokvasic; Albanese 1996; B.a.B.e.; Ivekovic; Tax; Drakulic). For example, one Catholic priest

and nationalist leader Don Bakovic asked his followers: "which is more important to us, Croatia's future or 13 existing women's organizations which have not given birth to 13 children all together?" (B.aB.e. cited in Albanese 2006:120).

Their then leader, Franjo Tudjman, gave a state of the nation address, which received a standing ovation when he said:

> Esteemed deputies of both chambers of the Croatian Assembly, from this position, I dare say, the gravest and most devastating consequence of the subjugation of the Croatian people, the unnatural communist system and the anti-Croatian Yugoslav state is the most worrying demo- graphic situation in Croatia. It is such that the Croatian people would face extinction if we were not to take resolute steps. (FBIS 67)

One of the steps he proposed was that "Mothers of four or more children should be given the average salary earned by her social equals, so that she is able to devote herself to bringing up children and be financially provided for, for life. Families with more children should be given concessions when it comes to housing issues. Single people should pay higher taxes" (FBIS 68).

Strategies were developed, on paper (because the money simply did not exist in the national budget), to "boost an ethnically clean birth rate in Croatia" and make abortion much harder to obtain. Posters on some streetcars read "each unborn baby is an unborn Croat" and one political meeting was closed with the greeting "go home and make a new Croat" (Morokvasic cited in Albanese 2006: 118).

In sum, it was clear from leaders' speeches, writings and proposed policy shifts that women's autonomy and health are expected to be "sacrificed" or become secondary to the supposed needs of their "threatened" and "vulnerable" nations. The nation's health and longevity came first, in almost all matters, clearly at the expense of women's choices, rights and reproductive health.

We see in these cases that the nationalist discourse on/about women is simple: women are expected to be reproducers of nations or walking wombs. They are expected to give up/sacrifice their bodies and shut down their minds, desires, needs, etc. to be and do "motherhood," for the sake of the invisible, seemingly homogenized collective—the nation. If nationalist leaders could not (and they often did not) simply convince women to willingly do this, they did so through appeals, decrees, laws, bans, punishment, promises, propaganda, tokens and rewards.

Pronatalist family policies, with their potentially negative impact on women's rights and health, are an integral part of the mythology of nationalism. National- ism depends upon the propagation of political myths to give it credence with the public. Nationalism often embraces a "palingenetic vision" or doctrine of genetic rebirths (the nation's biological continuity through time) which becomes an in- dispensable instrument of dictatorial power (Quine 36). In other words, to help capture the consciousness of "the people," nationalist regimes construct an image of the nation as the embodiment of "a momentous national resurrection" which is particularly appealing at a time of economic hardship and instability.

In modern times, on top of reproducing the nation, the repatriarchalizing of family roles in nationalist rhetoric and practise seems to be expected to work in other ways as well. For example, a man's powerlessness in a politically and economically changing society was expected to be offset by his renewed power in the home, and a woman's pride was expected to be restored as she became a heroic child bearer, filling the most "sublime" profession in the nation. If her return to the home as housewife and mother was complete, the nation not only secured its future, but solved other immediate problems as well—she liberated jobs that were expected to be filled by men. Therefore the strength of nationalism lies in its ability to revive its real or mythical glorious past, correct its unjust present, and secure a vibrant, fecund and economically prosperous future glory.

Transnational Motherhood

Nationalism, ethnic conflict, political repression and war actually result in economic and social unrest, which in turn displace entire segments of a population. Secessionist wars in Yugoslavia, for example, resulted in the realization of nationalist dreams of the establishment of independent "homelands" but also cleansed and displaced a large number of people from across the republics. The break-up of the Soviet Union similarly resulted in economic unrest ("de-development, de-modernization, or reprimitivization" [Ishkanian 388]) flinging individuals and families either temporarily or permanently, across national borders and even continents, in search of social and economic stability. Often, women and mothers found themselves apart from their children, partners and extended families, in search of economic opportunities.

A body of literature has emerged on global diasporas and transnational migrations. Some of this literature has focus on the experiences of migrant women, as "mobile mothers" (Ishkanian 383; Hondagneu-Sotelo and Avila 254) or transnational prostitutes (Lee 456; Kempadoo and Doezema), again, symbolically demarcating and maintaining boundaries of nation, gender and sexuality. Living apart from their families, transnational women and mothers are then operating in a framework that differs from the ideal, normative image of motherhood (Nicholson 14; also see Zimmerman, Litt and Bose), both in their nation's construction of the notion and in the "host" society's. As economic conditions necessitate the sharing of child-rearing responsibilities, often across borders, these mothers are "othered" at home and abroad.

According to Martha Fineman "mother" is a universally possessed symbol, and a "pivotal factor in defining our understanding of our own familial, sexual and social circumstance" and is significant in our construction of universal meanings (72). Fineman also noted that "mother" is neither fixed nor containable. Nationalist ideology relies upon state prescribed notions of motherhood, which aim to biologically and ideologically reproduce a particular, (exclusive) image of the nation. Having said this, we should also be cautious of nationalist discourse that depicts "western sexuality" as liberation and "non-western piety" as oppressive. As I alluded to in the introduction, this type of discourse has also been used as a nationalist and imperialist justification for war (against Iraq and Afghanistan, Cohler; also see Eichler for a gendered analysis of the Chechen Wars). Both possibilities, when state imposed, serve to essentialize "their" women, vilify diversity and silence opposition within national boundaries, "other" their foes, and rally masses into a nationalized frenzy. Both forms of prescriptive and normative motherhood and sexuality serve nationalist agendas and are detrimental to women's autonomy.

Notes

[1]See Cohlerfor a critical discussion on U.S. involvement in Iraq and Afghanistan.

References

Ala, Jacqui. "Enriching the Critical Discourse of Feminist Studies in International Relations: New Discussions of the Role of Women in Conflict, Peace Making and Government." *Politikon* 33 (2006): 239-249.

Albanese, Patrizia. *Mothers of the Nation: Women, Families and Nationalism in 20ᵗʰ Century Europe.* Toronto: University of Toronto Press, 2006.

Albanese, Patrizia. "Abortion and Reproductive Rights Under Nationalist Regimes in Twentieth Century Europe." *Journal of Urban Life and Women's Health* 3 (2004): 8-33.

Albanese, Patrizia. "Nationalism, War and Archaization of Gender Relations in the Balkans." *Violence Against Women* (International Journal) 7 (2001): 999-1023.

Albanese, Patrizia. "Leaders and Breeders: The Archaization of Gender Relations in Croatia." *Women in Post-Communism: Research on Russia and Eastern Europe.* Eds. B. Wejnert, M Spencer, with S. Drakulic. Greenwich: JAI Press. 1996. 185-200.

Atwood, Margaret. *The Handmaid's Tale.* Toronto: McClelland and Stewart, 1985.

B.a.B.e. (Be Active, Be Emancipated). Status of Women in Croatia. Zagreb, 1995.

Buchanan, Allen. *Secession: The Morality of Political Divorce from Fort Sumter to Lithuania and Quebec.* Boulder, Co: Westview, 1991.

Calhoun, Craig. *Nationalism.* Minneapolis: University of Minnesota Press, 1997.

Cohler, Deborah. "Keeping the Home Front Burning: Renegotiation Gender and Sexuality in US Mass Media after September 11." *Feminist Media Studies* 6 (2006): 245-261.

Drakulic, Slavenka. "Women and the New Democracy in the Former Yugoslavia." *Gender Politics and Post-Communism.* Ed. Nanette Funk and Magda Mueller. New York: Routledge. 1993. 123-30.

Dua, Enakshi. "Beyond Diversity: Exploring the Ways in Which the Discourse of

Race Has Shaped the Institution of the Nuclear Family." *Scratching the Surface: Canadian Anti-Racist Feminist Thought,* Ed. E. Dua. Toronto: Women's Press, 1999, 237-60.

Edensor, Tim. "Reconsidering National Temporalities: Institutional Times, Everyday Routines, Serial Spaces and Synchronicities." *European Journal of Social Theory* 9 (2006): 525-545.

Eichler, Maya. "Russia's Post-Communist Transformation: A Gendered Analysis of the Chechen Wars." *International Feminist Journal of Politics* 8 (2006): 486-511.

Einhorn, Barbara and Charlotte Sever. "Gender and Civil Society in Central and Eastern Europe." *International Feminist Journal of Politics* 5 (2003): 163-190.

Fineman, Martha. *The Neutered Mother, the Sexual Family and Other Twentieth Century Tragedies.* New York: Routledge, 1995.

Foreign Broadcast Information Service (FBIS). "President Tudjman's State of the Nation Address." *Daily Reports* 27 December 1994: 52-72. FBIS-EEU-94-248

Gellner, Ernest. *Nations and Nationalism.* Ithaca, NY: Cornell University Press, 1983.

Gorbachev, Mikhail. *Perestroika.* New York: Harper and Row, 1987.

Gow, Greg. "Viewing 'Mother Oromia'" *Communal/Plural* 9 (2001): 203-222.

Greenfeld, Liah. *Nationalism: Five Roads to Modernity.* Cambridge: Harvard University Press, 1992.

Grosby, Steven. *Nationalism: A Very Short Introduction.* Oxford: Oxford University Press, 2005.

Gurina, Natalia A., Siri Vangen, Lisa Frosen, and Johanne Sundby. "Maternal Mortality in St. Petersburg, Russian Federation" *Bulletin of the World Health Organization* 84 (4) (2006): 283-290.

Hitler, Adolf. *Mein Kampf.* 1925. Boston: Houghton Mufflin, 1943.

Hobsbawm, Eric. "Introduction: Inventing Traditions" *The Invention of Tradition.* Eds. Eric Hobsbawm and Terrence Ranger. Cambridge: Cambridge University Press. 1983. 1-14.

Hondagneu-Sotelo, Pierrette and Ernestine Avila. "'I'm Here, But I'm There': The Meanings of Latina Transnational Motherhood." *Global Dimensions of Gender and Carework.* Ed. Mary K. Zimmerman, Jacquelyn S. Litt and Christine Bose. Stanford: Stanford University Press. 2006, 254-263.

Ishkanian, Armine. "Mobile Motherhood: Armenian Women's Labor Migration in the Post-Soviet Period." *Diaspora* 11 (2002): 383-415.

Ivekovic, Rada. "Women, Democracy and Nationalism After 1989: The Yugoslav Case." *Canadian Woman Studies/les cahiers de la femme* 16 (1995): 10-13.

Kaiser, Robert. "Homeland Making and the Territorialization of National Identity." Ethnonationalism in the Contemporary World. Ed. Daniele Conversi. London: Routledge. 2004, 229-247.

Kedourie, Elie. *Nationalism.* 1963. 4th ed. Malden, MA: Blackwell, 1993.

Kempadoo, Kamala and Jo Doezema, eds. *Global Sex Workers: Rights, Resistance and Redefinition.* New York: Routledge, 1998.

Kohn, Hans. *The Age of Nationalism.* New York: Harper and Row, 1962.

Kristeva, Julia. *Nations without Nationalism.* New York: Columbia University Press, 1993.

Kunovich, Robert and Catherine Deitelbaum. "Ethnic Conflict, Group Polarization and Gender Attitudes in Croatia" *Journal of Marriage and Family* 66 (2004): 1089-1107.

Lee, Na Young. "Gendered Nationalism and Otherization: Transnational Prostitutes in South Korea." *Inter-Asia Cultural Studies* 7 (2006): 456-471.

McNeill, William. *Polyethnicity and National Unity in World History.* Toronto: University of Toronto Press, 1985.

Mohanty, Chandra Talpade. "US Empire and the Project of Women's Studies: Stories of Citizenship, Complicity and Dissent." *Gender, Place and Culture* 13 (2006): 7-20.

Morokvasic, Miriana. "Nationalism, Sexism and Yugoslav War" *Gender, Ethnicity and Political Ideologies.* Ed. N. Charles and Helen Hintjens. London: Routledge. 1998. 65-90.

Mussolini, Benito. "Discorso dell'Ascensione" (Ascension Day Speech) *Opera Omnia di Benito Mussolini.* Vol. 22. Florence: La Fenice, 1964a. 360-90.

Mussolini, Benito. "Il Numero Come Forza" (Strength in Numbers). *Opera Omnia di Benito Mussolini.* Vol. 23. Florence: La Fenice, 1964b. 209-17.

Nicholson, Melanie. "Without their Children: Rethinking Motherhood Among Transnational Migrant Women." *Social Text 88.* 24 (2006): 13-33.

Quine, Maria. *Population Politics in Twentieth Century Europe.* London: Routledge. 1996

Smith, Anthony. *The Antiquity of Nations.* Cambridge: Polity Press, 2004.

Smith, Anthony. "When is a Nation?" *Geopolitics* 7 (2002): 5-32.

Solzhenitsyn, Aleksandr. *Rebuilding Russia: Reflections and Tentative Proposals.* New York: Ferrar, Strauss and Giroux, 1991.

Tax, Meredith. "The Five Croatian Witched: A casebook on 'Trial by Public Opinion' as a From of Censorship and Intimidation" Paper prepared for the International PEN Women Writers' Committee, 1993.

Ugresic, Dubravka. *The Culture of Lies.* London: Phoenix House, 1998.

"Vladimir Putin on Raising Russia's Birth Rate (Documents)." *Population and Development Review* 32 (2006): 385-389.

Yuval-Davis, Nira and Floya Anthias, eds. *Women-Nation-State.* New York: St. Martin's Press, 1989.

Zimmerman, Mary K., Jacquelyn S. Litt, and Christine E. Bose, eds. *Global Dimensions of Gender and Carework.* Stanford: Stanford Social Sciences, 2006.

Copyright Acknowledgements

"Leaving Home: The Young Man's Rite of Passage" by Olga Silverstein and Beth Rashbaum was originally published in *The Courage to Raise Good Men*, by Olga Silverstein and Beth Rashbaum. New York: Viking. © 1994 by Olga Silverstein and Beth Rashbaum. Canadian Rights reserved. Reprinted by permission of Sanford J. Greenburger Associates and International Creative Management.

"Negotiating Lesbian Motherhood: The Dialectics of Resistance and Accommodation" by Ellen Lewin was originally published in *Mothering: Ideology, Experience and Agency*, edited by Evelyn Nakano Glenn, Grace Chang and Linda Rennie Forcey. New York: Routledge. © 1994 Routledge. All Rights reserved. Reprinted by permission of Taylor and Francis Books.

"Beyond Mothers and Fathers: Ideology in a Patriarchal Society" by Barbara Katz Rothman was originally published in *Mothering: Ideology, Experience and Agency*, edited by Evelyn Nakano Glenn, Grace Chang and Linda Rennie Forcey. New York: Routledge. © 1994 Routledge. All Rights reserved. Reprinted by permission of Taylor and Francis Books.

"Why Can't a Mother Be More Like a Businessman" by Sharon Hays was originally published in *The Cultural Contradictions of Motherhood*, by Sharon Hays. New Haven: Yale University Press. © 1998 Yale University Press. All Rights reserved. Reprinted by permission.

"A Sketch in Progress: Introducing the Mother Without Child" by Elaine Tuttle Hansen was originally published in *Mother Without Child: Contemporary Fiction and the Crisis of Motherhood*, by Elaine Tuttle Hansen. Berkeley: University of California Press. © 1997 University of California Press. All Rights reserved. Reprinted by permission.

"Faking Motherhood: The Mask Revealed" by Susan Maushart was originally published in *The Mask of Motherhood: How Becoming a Mother Changes Our Lives and Why We Never Talk About It*, by Susan Maushart. New York: New Press. © 1997 New Press. All Rights reserved. Reprinted by permission.

"Introduction" by Dorothy Roberts was originally published in *Killing the Black Body: Race, Reproduction, and the Meaning of Liberty*, by Dorothy Roberts. New York: Vintage. © 1998 Vintage. All Rights reserved. Reprinted by permission of Random House, Inc.

"The Baby and the Bath Water: Disabled Women and Motherhood in Social Context" by Carol Thomas was originally published by *Sociology of Health and Illness*, Vol. 19.5 (1997). Oxford: Blackwell Publishing. © 1998 Blackwell Publishing. All Rights reserved. Reprinted by permission.

"Right to Mothering: Motherhood as a Transborder Concern in the Age of Globalization" by Shu-Ju Ada Cheng was originally published in *The Journal of the Association for Research on Mothering*. Vol. 6.1 (Spring/Summer 2004). Reprinted by permission of the author and publisher.

"The Globalization of Love: Transnational Adoption and Engagement with the Globalized World" by Emily J. Noonan was originally published in *The Journal of the Association for Research on Mothering*. Vol.6.1 (Spring/Summer 2004). Reprinted by permission of the author and publisher.

"Mother-Worship/Mother-Blame: Politics and Welfare in an Uncertain Age" by Molly Ladd-Taylor was originally published in *The Journal of the Association for Research on Mothering*. Vol. 6.1 (Spring/Summer 2004). Reprinted by permission of the author and publisher.

"The 'Problem' of Maternal Desire" by Daphne de Marneffe was originally published in *Maternal Desire: On Children, Love, and the Inner Life*, by Daphne Marneffe. New York: Little Brown and Company. © 2004 Little Brown and Company. All Rights reserved. Reprinted by permission.

"We Will No Longer Be Silent or Invisible: Latinas Organising for Reproductive Justice" by Elena R. Gutiérrez was originally published in *Undivided Rights: Women of Color Organize for Reproductive Justice*, edited by Jael Silliman, Marlene Gerber Fried, Loretta Ross and Elena Gutiérrez. Cambridge: South End Press. © 2004 South End Press. All Rights reserved. Reprinted by permission.

"The Motherhood Religion" by Judith Warner was originally published in *Perfect Madness: Motherhood in the Age of Anxiety*, by Judith Warner. New York: Riverhead Books. © 2005 by Judith Warner. All Rights reserved. Reprinted by permission of Riverhead Books, an imprint of the Penguin Group (USA) Inc.

"Introduction: Domestic Intellectuals: Freedom and the Single Mom" by Jane Juffer was originally published in *The Single Mother: The Emergence of the Domestic Intellectual* by Jane Juffer. New York: New York University Press. © 2006 New York University Press. All Rights reserved. Reprinted by permission.